THE OXFORD HANDBOOK OF

EARLY MODERN THEATRE

The was no single 'Elizabethan stage'. Early modern actors exploited various opp tunities for patronage and profit between the 1570s and 1642, whether touring, performing at inns, in country houses, in purpose-built theatres, at court, at the iversities or at the inns of court. This authoritative and comprehensive coll ion of new essays explores the social, political, and economic pressures und which the playing companies of Shakespeare and his contemporaries operatec t shows how they evolved over time to meet new challenges such as the opp ition of City of London authorities, the possibility of permanent location in Lon n, the re-emergence of boy companies *c.* 1600, and the great increase in court perf mance which began under James I. Essays also explore the practical everyday busi ss of playing: acquiring scripts and playhouses, dramatic authorship, the cont bution of financiers and entrepreneurs, rehearsing, lighting, music, props, style of acting, boy actors, and the role of women in an 'all-male' world. A number of c tributors address the methodologies of theatre history itself, questioning its phi sophical premises and evaluating the nature of the evidence we have, such as that om stage directions in play-books or from the visual records. The collection as hole offers a challenging account of the world of the players in Tudor-Stuart En d, revising old assumptions and so inviting us to explore anew the plays wh were written for them and which are their greatest living legacy.

Ri ard Dutton is Humanities Distinguished Professor at Ohio State University. He is best known for his work on early modern censorship, including *Mastering the R els: the Regulation and Censorship of English Renaissance Drama* (1991). *Ben J n, 'Volpone' and the Gunpowder Plot* (2008) is his third monograph on Jonson. holarly editing includes Jonson's *Epicene* (2003) for the Revels Plays (of which a general editor), and *Volpone* for the Cambridge Ben Jonson. He is working he revisions of Shakespeare's plays for court performance.

THE OXFORD HANDBOOK OF

EARLY MODERN THEATRE

Edited by

RICHARD DUTTON

OXFORD
UNIVERSITY PRESS

Great Clarendon Street, Oxford OX2 6DP

Oxford University Press is a department of the University of Oxford.
It furthers the University's objective of excellence in research, scholarship,
and education by publishing worldwide in

Oxford New York

Auckland Cape Town Dar es Salaam Hong Kong Karachi
Kuala Lumpur Madrid Melbourne Mexico City Nairobi
New Delhi Shanghai Taipei Toronto

With offices in

Argentina Austria Brazil Chile Czech Republic France Greece
Guatemala Hungary Italy Japan Poland Portugal Singapore
South Korea Switzerland Thailand Turkey Ukraine Vietnam

Oxford is a registered trade mark of Oxford University Press
in the UK and in certain other countries

Published in the United States
by Oxford University Press Inc., New York

First published 2009

First published in paperback 2011

British Library Cataloguing in Publication Data
Data available

Library of Congress Cataloging in Publication Data

Library of Congress Control Number: 2009921243

Typeset by SPI Publisher Services, Pondicherry, India
Printed in Great Britain
on acid-free paper by
CPI Antony Rowe, Chippenham, Wiltshire

ISBN 978–0–19–928724–6 (Hbk.)
978–0–19–969786–1 (Pbk.)

2 4 6 8 10 9 7 5 3 1

In Memoriam

Herbert Berry
and
Scott McMillin

Preface

This collection grew out of my conviction that it would be helpful to bring together in a single volume something of the remarkable work currently being done in early modern theatre history and its associated fields. Scholars of early modern literature and drama have famously made a 'return to history' since the 1980s. Theatre historians never had to 'return' to history, but they have had to rethink the nature of the history in which they are engaged, the kinds of evidence with which they can work, and what they should make of it. At stake is a fuller, truer, and more nuanced sense of 'the place of the stage' (in Steven Mullaney's resonant phrase) in the early modern world.

The recent work on this is so disparate—on the acting companies, theatres (including the court, universities, the Inns of Court, households, and the streets), the conditions of acting (lighting, music, sound, rehearsals, properties, licensing), dramatic authorship, repertory, stage directions, patronage, the court and the city, entrepreneurs and finance, the roles of women and of boys, theatre historiography itself—that it is difficult to keep track of it all and to appreciate the points of interconnection between all of these fields. The days have long since gone when we loosely spoke of a single (Shakespeare- and London-centred) 'Elizabethan Stage'. The most comprehensive theatrical research undertaking of our time, the Records of Early English Drama project, based in Toronto, has done more than anything else to broaden our horizons, and its fruits are apparent in many of the essays here. But we are still coming to terms with the multiplicity of early modern stages—and their corresponding multiple cultural contexts—which have taken its place. I hope this volume will forward that process and offer a variety of points of engagement with current scholarship.

I did not ask contributors to offer a student overview of their fields. I invited them rather to concentrate on issues of particular interest or concern, to engage with the research frontiers. Their essays are thus contributions to the ongoing debates with which they engage, not merely surveys of the literature. Beyond that brief I did not wish to impose any rigid agenda on their work, though inevitably my own choice of subject areas and of contributors will have made a foundational mark. The decision to start with a series of essays on the acting companies, dividing the period *c.*1570–1642 into six blocks of ten to fifteen years, with separate essays on the earlier and later boy companies, arises from the conviction that the conditions of playing changed rapidly throughout the era—and that keeping track of this is a prerequisite to understanding so much else. Old patterns of touring adapted (or not!) to the opportunities afforded by the fixed playhouses in and around London, as the needs of the court and patrons and the concerns of the city and local authorities changed, as modes of dramatic authorship evolved, as plague intervened, and as boy companies waxed and waned. Individual companies either rose to new challenges or languished; some found niches within an increasingly sophisticated market. The styles of the drama they produced inevitably changed in tandem with these circumstances. That is a base reality from which everything else follows (though a complex and contested 'reality'), as I hope is reflected through these essays.

It would have been wonderful to be able to include more essays on individual companies—Roslyn Knutson's work on the repertory of the Chamberlain's/King's Men (1991), Scott McMillin and Sally-Beth MacLean's work on the Queen's Men (1999), Andrew Gurr's on 'The Shakespeare Company' (2004), and Lucy Munro's on the Children of the Queen's Revels (2005), for example, have proved how valuable such work can be. I would also have liked to have had more essays on the playhouses they used. But constraints of space, even in a volume of this size, meant that I had to settle for illustrative samples rather than comprehensive representation. The same is even more true of subjects as diverse as the role of women in that playhouse world, or boy apprentices, or the practices of authorship which the needs of the actors generated. I hope, nevertheless, that the volume is more than the sum of its parts, and that it reflects something of the sheer energy, interconnected resourcefulness, and ingenuity both of early modern theatre itself and of the current scholarship devoted to it.

That is one reason why I decided to create a single composite Bibliography for the volume. It was inspired by the bibliography in John D. Cox and David Scott Kastan's seminal collection *A New History of Early English Drama* (1997), where familiar and unfamiliar items from disparate fields rub shoulders in the most thought-provoking fashion. It offers the serendipity of the most inspiring libraries and can in itself be a useful tool for navigating the whole field covered by this volume. Contributors have been free to cite play-texts from wherever they choose, a freedom which, however, threatened to clog and clutter the Bibliography. I have therefore adopted the following practice: original and other early texts are cited in the composite Bibliography in the normal way, under 'Primary Sources: Printed Texts'; so too are complete modern editions, like the Herford and Simpson *Jonson* and the Wells and Taylor *Oxford Shakespeare* (listed under author, not editor). Where, however, plays are cited from individual modern editions these are normally only indicated in a footnote within the relevant essay.

The titles of lost plays (i.e. ones for which the title has survived but no version of the text) appear as roman in quotation marks. The titles of plays that survive in manuscript but have since been published are italicized.

The Bibliography—indeed, the whole volume—would never have been completed without the heroic efforts of two research assistants, who worked on it at different times, and I want to express my heartfelt gratitude to Dr Marisa Rose Cull (now Assistant Professor of English at Randolph-Macon College in Virginia) and to Erin Kelly for their labours. I also owe particular thanks to David Kathman, who stepped in at a late stage to write the essay on inn-yard playhouses, in addition to the one on apprentices, which he was already commissioned to write. This was made necessary by the death of Herbert Berry, who died after agreeing to contribute that chapter. Scott McMillin was similarly commissioned to write on manuscript play-texts, but sadly did not live to get round to it. The dedication to Herb and Scott is a mark of respect for their immense contributions to early modern theatre history. They were sometime members of the long-standing theatre history seminar at the annual meeting of the Shakespeare Association of America, as are many of those whose essays do appear here. Long may it contrive, phoenix-like, to resurrect itself each year. I want also to thank another of its members, Bill Ingram, who offered me helpful advice and encouragement from the conception of this project. I am happy to be able to salute in print his enormous generosity. Thanks finally to Rachel Clark for her invaluable assistance on the index.

Richard Dutton

Ohio State University
June 2008

Contents

PART II LONDON PLAYHOUSES

PART III OTHER PLAYING SPACES

PART IV SOCIAL PRACTICES

PART V EVIDENCE OF THEATRICAL PRACTICES

Figures

Maps

Contributors

Ian W. Archer is Fellow and Tutor in History at Keble College, Oxford. He is author of *The Pursuit of Stability: Social Relations in Elizabethan London* (Cambridge University Press, 1991, 2003), and numerous articles on various aspects of the social and political history of early modern London. He is Literary Director of the Royal Historical Society, and general editor of its online Bibliography of British History. He is currently working on a general book on early modern London.

John H. Astington is Professor of English and Drama at the University of Toronto. His research and publications have been largely concentrated on the drama and theatre history of England in the sixteenth and seventeenth centuries, although he has also been editor of the journal *Modern Drama*, and reviewer of contemporary Canadian drama for the *University of Toronto Quarterly*. He has published widely in journals dealing with the early modern period, and is the author of *English Court Theatre 1558–1642* (Cambridge University Press, 1999) and contributor to *Thomas Middleton and Early Modern Textual Culture* (2007), the companion volume to *The Oxford Middleton*. He is currently working on a study of actors and acting, *The Art of Stage Playing*.

Mark Bayer is Assistant Professor of English at the University of Texas at San Antonio. He is the author of *Theatre, Community, and Civic Engagement in Shakespeare's London* (forthcoming, University of Iowa Press) and numerous articles on Shakespeare and early modern literature and culture.

Mary Bly is an Associate Professor of English Literature, and Director of Graduate Studies, at Fordham University. Her first book, *Queer Virgins and Virgin Queans on the Early Modern Stage* (2000), was published by Oxford University Press; she is currently finishing *The Geography of Puns*, a project addressing the geographical, linguistic economies of early modern London, with particular attention to the liberties.

Martin Butler is Professor of English Renaissance Drama at the University of Leeds. His books include *Theatre and Crisis 1632–1642* (Cambridge University Press, 1984) and *The Stuart Court Masque and Political Culture* (Cambridge University Press, 2008). He has edited *Cymbeline* for the New Cambridge Shakespeare (2005) and *The Tempest* for Penguin (2007), and (with David Bevington and Ian Donaldson) is general editor of *The Cambridge Edition of the Works of Ben Jonson* (2008).

S. P. Cerasano is the Edgar W. B. Fairchild Professor of Literature at Colgate University in Hamilton, NY. The author of numerous books and essays on Renaissance drama and various aspects of theatre history, she is currently writing a book on Henslowe's diary and is editing Edward Alleyn's diary for Oxford University Press. Currently, she is the editor of the annual journal *Medieval and Renaissance Drama in England.*

Ralph Alan Cohen is the Founding Executive Director and Director of Mission at the American Shakespeare Center in Staunton, Virginia. He was the project director for the building of the Blackfriars Playhouse there. He is also the Gonder Professor of Shakespeare and Renaissance Literature in Performance in the Master of Letters and Fine Arts program at Mary Baldwin College. He has directed twenty professional productions of plays by Shakespeare and his contemporaries. In 1990 he directed a student production of Thomas Middleton's *Your Five Gallants,* which he also co-edited for Oxford University Press's *Collected Works of Thomas Middleton.*

Alan C. Dessen, Peter G. Phialas Professor (Emeritus) at the University of North Carolina, Chapel Hill, is the author of eight books, four of them with Cambridge University Press: *Elizabethan Stage Conventions and Modern Interpreters* (1984); *Recovering Shakespeare's Theatrical Vocabulary* (1995); *Rescripting Shakespeare* (2002); and, co-authored with Leslie Thomson, *A Dictionary of Stage Directions in English Drama, 1580–1642.* In 2005 he gave the annual British Academy Shakespeare lecture. Between 1994 and 2001 he was the director of ACTER (A Center for Teaching, Education, and Research). Since 1994 he has been editor or co-editor of the Shakespeare Performed section of *Shakespeare Quarterly.*

Richard Dutton has been Humanities Distinguished Professor at Ohio State University since 2003. Previously he was at Lancaster University for thirty years. He is best known for his work on early modern censorship, including *Mastering the Revels: The Regulation and Censorship of English Renaissance Drama* (Macmillan, 1991) and *Licensing, Censorship and Authorship in Early Modern England: Buggeswords* (Palgrave, 2000). *Ben Jonson, 'Volpone' and the Gunpowder Plot* (Cambridge, 2008) is his third monograph on Jonson. His scholarly editing includes Jonson's *Epicene* (2003) for the Revels Plays (of which he is a general editor), and *Volpone* for the Cambridge Ben Jonson. He is working on the revisions of Shakespeare's plays for court performance.

Gabriel Egan is Reader in Shakespeare Studies at Loughborough University. In 2002 he edited *The Witches of Lancashire* for Nick Hern Books, in 2004 Oxford University Press published his book *Shakespeare and Marx,* and in 2006 Routledge published his book *Green Shakespeare. Shakespeare and Marx* was translated into Turkish and published by Hil Yayin of Istanbul in 2006. His most recent book was the *Edinburgh Critical Guide to Shakespeare* (Edinburgh University Press, 2007). He is currently writing a history of the twentieth-century theory and practice of editing Shakespeare called *Reading Shakespeare's Mind*, which Cambridge University Press will publish in 2010.

R. B. Graves is Dean of the College of Fine and Applied Arts and Professor of Theater at the University of Illinois at Urbana-Champaign. His publications include articles on ancient Greek drama, and early modern and Irish theatre, and books on contemporary Asian drama and Shakespearean stagecraft. His *Lighting the Shakespearean Stage* (Southern Illinois University Press, 1999) won the 2001 Sohmer-Hall Prize of the International Shakespeare Globe Centre in London. He was co-editor and translator of *The Metacultural Theater of Oh T'ae-sŏk* (University of Hawai'i Press, 1999), an anthology of avant-garde Korean plays that won the 2002 Korean Literature Translation Award.

Peter Greenfield is Professor of English at the University of Puget Sound. He is the editor (with Audrey Douglas) of *Cumberland, Westmorland, and Gloucestershire* for the *Records of Early English Drama* series and editor of the annual journal *Research Opportunities in Medieval and Renaissance Drama.* He has written extensively on travelling players and on dramatic activity outside London. He is currently editing the dramatic records of Hampshire, Hertfordshire, and Bedfordshire.

Eva Griffith is AHRC Research Associate at the University of Durham, working on the Oxford University Press full-scale edition of the works of James Shirley. Her publications include work on the Jacobean stage with the *Oxford Dictionary of National Biography* entries on Susan Baskervile, Anne Bedingfeild, and 'Banks, the exhibitor of Morocco the performing horse'. She is currently completing a monograph on the Red Bull playhouse.

Andrew Gurr is Professor Emeritus at the University of Reading, and until recently Director of Globe Research at the International Shakespeare Globe Centre, London. His books include *The Shakespearean Stage 1574–1642* (3rd edn, 1992), *Playgoing in Shakespeare's London* (3rd edn, 2004), and *The Shakespeare Company 1594–1642* (2004), all for Cambridge University Press, and *The Shakespearian Playing Companies* (Clarendon Press, 1996). He has edited several Renaissance plays, including *Richard II* and *Henry V*, and the Quarto *Henry V.*

Heather Hirschfeld is an Associate Professor of English at the University of Tennessee, Knoxville. The author of *Joint Enterprises: Collaborative Drama and the Institutionalization of the English Renaissance Theater* (University of Massachusetts Press, 2004), she is currently working on a project on revenge tragedy and the Reformation. She has published articles in journals such as *ELH*, *Shakespeare Quarterly*, *Shakespeare Studies*, *Renaissance Drama*, and *PMLA*.

William Ingram teaches at the University of Michigan in Ann Arbor. His essays on theatre history have appeared in journals and collections, and his books include

English Professional Theatre, 1530–1660 (Cambridge University Press, 2000; in collaboration with Glynne Wickham and Herbert Berry), a documentary source book; *The Business of Playing* (Cornell University Press, 1992), a study of the growth of playing companies and playhouses in the 1570s and 1580s; and a biography of Francis Langley, builder of the Swan playhouse. He has also published essays on the use of computers in literary study, one fruit of which was a concordance to Milton's English poetry, one of the earliest computer-generated concordances, published in 1972.

David Kathman is an independent scholar in Chicago, Illinois. His archival research on boy actors, theatrical biography, and London livery companies has resulted in articles in *Shakespeare Quarterly, Shakespeare Survey, Early Theatre, Research Opportunities in Medieval & Renaissance Drama*, and *Notes and Queries*, as well as various reviews and book chapters. His current research focuses on inns, taverns, and halls where plays were performed in sixteenth-century London. He has a Ph.D. in linguistics from the University of Chicago and works as a mutual fund analyst for Morningstar.

Roslyn L. Knutson, Professor of English at the University of Arkansas at Little Rock, is the author of *Playing Companies and Commerce in Shakespeare's Time* (Cambridge University Press, 2001) and *The Repertory of Shakespeare's Company, 1594–1613* (University of Arkansas Press, 1991). She has published in numerous journals, annuals, and essay collections. Her long-term projects include a search for the narratives behind lost plays of the Admiral's Men in Henslowe's diary and a study of Marlowe's plays in repertory, 1587–93.

Natasha Korda is Associate Professor of English at Wesleyan University, Middletown, Connecticut. Her publications include *Shakespeare's Domestic Economies: Gender and Property in Early Modern England* (University of Pennsylvania Press, 2002) and *Staged Properties in Early Modern English Drama* (Cambridge University Press, 2003), which she co-edited with Jonathan Gil Harris. She is currently working on a book entitled *Labors Lost: Women's Work and the Early Modern English Stage.*

Anne Lancashire, Professor of English at the University of Toronto, has edited plays by Lyly and by Middleton, and is most recently the author of *London Civic Theatre: City Drama and Pageantry from Roman Times to 1558* (Cambridge University Press, 2002), and of 'The Mayors and Sheriffs of London 1190–1558' in C. Barron (ed.), *London in the Later Middle Ages* (Oxford University Press, 2004). She has written extensively on medieval and early modern drama and theatre history, and is the editor of the forthcoming *Records of Early English Drama* volumes of the City of London and company records of early drama, pageantry, and music, 1275–1558.

Sally-Beth MacLean is Professor of English at the University of Toronto and Executive Editor/Associate Director of the *Records of Early English Drama* (REED). She is also directing the development of the REED Patrons and Performances web site and other electronic publishing initiatives for the series. She co-authored *The Queen's Men and their Plays* with Scott McMillin (Cambridge University Press, 1998), a book that won the 1999 Sohmer-Hall Prize from the Globe Theatre. Her research interests have focused recently on provincial performance venues in fifteen counties and cities in England for the REED web site, and on a study of Lord Strange's Men in collaboration with Lawrence Manley.

Kathleen E. McLuskie is Director of the Shakespeare Institute in Stratford upon Avon. She has written numerous articles on the plays of Shakespeare and his contemporary playwrights and is author of *Feminist Readings of Renaissance Dramatists* and *Dekker and Heywood: Professional Dramatists.* She has edited Webster's *The Duchess of Malfi*, a collection entitled *Plays on Women*, and a collection of essays entitled *Shakespeare and the Modern Theatre.* She has taught at the universities of Kent and Southampton (where she was also deputy vice-chancellor responsible for education and widening access) as well as spending time as a visiting professor in the universities of the West Indies, Colorado, and Massachusetts. She is currently working on an AHRC-funded project, Interrogating Cultural Value in the Twenty-First Century: The Case of Shakespeare.

James J. Marino is Assistant Professor of English at Cleveland State University. His current book project is *Owning William Shakespeare: Early Modern Drama as Intellectual Property.*

Lucy Munro is a lecturer in English at Keele University. Her publications include *Children of the Queen's Revels: A Jacobean Theatre Repertory* (Cambridge University Press, 2005) and editions of *Pericles* for *William Shakespeare: Complete Works*, edited by Jonathan Bate and Eric Rasmussen (Palgrave Macmillan, 2007), and Edward Sharpham's *The Fleer* for Globe Quartos (Nick Hern Books, 2006). She has also written essays on subjects including female pirates, 1630s tragicomedy, the reception of early modern comedy in print, and children in film versions of *Richard III.* She is a contributing editor to forthcoming editions of the plays of James Shirley and Richard Brome, and is writing a book-length study of archaism in early modern literary culture.

Alan H. Nelson is Professor Emeritus in the Department of English at the University of California, Berkeley. His specializations are palaeography, bibliography, and the reconstruction of the literary life and times of medieval and Renaissance England from documentary sources. His most recent solo publication is *Monstrous Adversary: The Life of Edward de Vere, Seventeenth Earl of Oxford* (Liverpool University Press, 2003). He was editor of *Cambridge* and is one of four editors of the recently published *Oxford* (2 vols), both in the *Records of Early English Drama* series (Toronto: University of

Toronto Press, 1989, 2004). He is currently at work on *London: Inns of Court*, also for *Records of Early English Drama*. His monograph *The Library of Humphrey Dyson* is forthcoming from the Oxford Bibliographical Society.

Thomas Postlewait teaches in the School of Drama, University of Washington. Since 1991 he has served as editor of the award-winning series Studies in Theatre History and Culture at the University of Iowa Press. Over forty volumes have been published. His publications include *Prophet of the New Drama: William Archer and the Ibsen Campaign* (Greenwood Press, 1986) and *The Cambridge Introduction to Theatre Historiography* (2008). He edited *William Archer on Ibsen: The Major Essays, 1889–1919* (Greenwood Press, 1984), and co-edited *Victorian Science and Victorian Values* (New York Academy of Sciences, 1981), *Interpreting the Theatrical Past: Essays in the Historiography of Performance* (University of Iowa Press, 1989), *Theatricality* (Cambridge University Press, 2003), and *Representing the Past* (forthcoming, 2009). He has taught at Cornell University, MIT, the University of Georgia, Indiana University, and Ohio State University, and has served as President of the American Society for Theatre Research (1994–7) and Vice-President for Research in the Association for Theatre in Higher Education (1998–2000). He is editor of the forthcoming letters of Bernard Shaw and William Archer (University of Toronto Press), and is preparing a study on historical research methods and problems for English Renaissance theatre.

Jacalyn Royce teaches at the University of Puget Sound in Tacoma, Washington, where she is chair of the Theatre Arts Department. She teaches history, classical acting, and playwrighting. Jac received her Ph.D. from Stanford University and her BA from the University of California at Santa Cruz. A professional theatre director and member of the Dramatists Guild of America, Jac is currently Artistic Director of the Northwest Playwrights Alliance.

Tom Rutter is Senior Lecturer in Renaissance Literature at Sheffield Hallam University. He has published several articles on early modern drama, and his book *Work and Play on the Shakespearean Stage* is forthcoming in 2008. He is currently working on a book about the repertory of the Admiral's Men.

Michael Shapiro is Professor Emeritus of English at the University of Illinois, where he began teaching in 1967. He has also taught at Cornell, Reading, and Tamkang universities. He is the author of *Children of the Revels* (Columbia University Press, 1977) and *Gender in Play* (University of Michigan Press, 1994), as well as articles, notes, and reviews in early modern English drama. He currently works on revisions, adaptations, and appropriations of *The Merchant of Venice.*

Andrew Sofer is Associate Professor of English at Boston College. He is the author of *The Stage Life of Props* (University of Michigan, 2003), runner-up for the Barnard Hewitt Award for Outstanding Research in Theatre History. He has published numerous essays on Shakespeare, Renaissance drama, and modern drama, and has directed many new and classic plays. He is currently working on *Dark Matter*, a study of theatre and invisibility.

Alan Somerset is Professor Emeritus of English at the University of Western Ontario, retired after forty-one years, specializing in Shakespeare and the theatre of his time. He is the editor of *Shropshire* for *Records of Early English Drama* (2 vols, Toronto: University of Toronto Press, 1994), and author of *The Stratford Festival Story: A Catalogue-Index to the Stratford, Ontario Festival 1953–1990* (Westport, CT: Greenwood Press, 1991), as well as numerous articles, papers, and reviews. He is currently completing his edition of *Staffordshire* and *Warwickshire* for REED, and is engaged in creating, with Dr Sally-Beth MacLean, the Patrons, Performances, and Playing Places web site.

Tiffany Stern is the Beaverbrook and Bouverie Fellow and Tutor in English Literature at University College, Oxford. Her monographs are *Rehearsal from Shakespeare to Sheridan* (Clarendon Press, 2000), and *Making Shakespeare* (Routledge, 2004); with Simon Palfrey she co-authored *Shakespeare in Parts* (Oxford University Press, 2007). She has edited the anonymous *King Leir* (Nick Hern with Globe Education, 2002) and Sheridan's *The Rivals* (A. & C. Black, 2004), and is editing George Farquhar's *Recruiting Officer*, Brome's *Jovial Crew*, and Shakespeare's *Merry Wives*. She is a general editor of the New Mermaids play series, and is on the editorial board of the journals *Shakespeare*, *Shakespeare Bulletin*, *Shakespeare Yearbook*, and *Review of English Studies*. Her current project is to complete a monograph, *The Fragmented Playtext in Shakespearean England.*

W. R. Streitberger, Professor of English at the University of Washington, is co-editor of an anthology, *Drama: Classical to Contemporary* (Prentice Hall, 1998, 2001), and author of a number of books and articles on English literature and drama from the late fifteenth to the middle seventeenth century. He is editor of *Jacobean and Caroline Revels Accounts, 1603–1642*, Malone Society Collections, 13 (1986), and *Edmond Tyllney, Topographical Descriptions, Regiments, and Policies of England, Wales, Scotland, and Ireland* (Garland, 1991). He is also author of *Court Revels, 1485–1559* (University of Toronto Press, 1994) and of articles on the biographies of two of the Masters of the Revels, Sir Thomas Benger (d. 1572) and Edmond Tyllney (d. 1610), published in *Review of English Studies* (1978, 2004). He is currently writing a book on the revels at Elizabeth I's court and London commercial theatre.

Frances Teague is Josiah Meigs Distinguished Teaching Professor of English at the University of Georgia. Teague has written or edited half a dozen books, most recently *Shakespeare and the American Popular Stage* (Cambridge University Press, 2006). She also does research on early modern women writers and serves on the advisory board of the Women's Studies Institute.

Suzanne Westfall, Chair of the Department of English and Theater at Lafayette College, holds a Ph.D. from the Drama Centre at the University of Toronto. Since arriving at Lafayette in 1981, she has directed over thirty productions for the College Theatre and written widely about theatre and performance, ranging from ancient Greek tragedy to the performance art of Ping Chong. She is the author of *Patrons and Performance: Early Tudor Household Revels* (Clarendon Press, 1990) and the co-editor, with Paul W. White, of *Shakespeare and Theatrical Patronage in Early Modern England* (Cambridge University Press, 2002).

INTRODUCTION: EARLY MODERN THEATER HISTORY: WHERE WE ARE NOW, HOW WE GOT HERE, WHERE WE GO NEXT

WILLIAM INGRAM

I

> Most working historians tend to be impatient of anything which looks like methodological discussion.
>
> Keith Thomas, 'An Anthropology of Religion and Magic, II'

My epigraph says less about methodology than about Keith Thomas's own sense of his discipline's aversion to it, at least before 1975, when these words were published. His generalization, which was probably not true even then, is surely not true now, thirty years on, when 'methodological discussion'—the discussion of both procedural and theoretical questions—is a staple of the discipline of history. A few years later, in 1979, the editorial board of *Past and Present* stated that it 'has long been conscious of the need to initiate discussion of general points of historical inquiry, theory and method', and declared its intent to publish essays on such topics at regular intervals, beginning with an essay by Lawrence Stone on the revival of narrative in the writing of history (Stone 1979). But this was catch-up rather than innovative; the editorial board's move may have been prompted by the success of another journal, *History and Theory*, founded two decades earlier and devoted entirely to the issues whose importance *Past and Present* was belatedly acknowledging.

Since that time, judging from recent books by historians with titles like *Practicing History*, or *The Methodology of History*, or *History and Tropology*, or *Historical Representation*, or *Language and Historical Representation*, or *The Writing of History*, or *New Methodologies in History Writing*, most historians nowadays are quite ready to see 'What is history?' as a complex question, meriting serious conversation rather than what Keith Thomas took to be impatient tolerance. The absence of books with similar titles or themes in the field of theater history[1] may be evidence of a perceived absence of interest by theater historians in such issues, or perhaps just evidence of the continuing smallness of our field relative to history in general. Perhaps a critical mass has to be reached before theoretical questions become pressing. Whatever the reason, the void suggests that we lag behind our historian colleagues in finding such questions important. In that sense, we theater historians have until recently given the impression of being more impatient of these matters than Thomas declared historians themselves to be.

So I begin with two questions intended to measure the impatience levels of the readers of this volume. My first question: Is theater history a form of social or cultural history, and if so, do those disciplines have theoretical underpinnings (however contested) that should be of interest to theater historians? My second question is more impertinent: Where is the boundary between theater history and fiction? This latter question is not frivolous, though it has, like all questions we ask, an agenda already embedded in it (Martindale 1993: 15). Nor is this latter question even original with me; it's merely my version of a larger question about history in general, a question that has engaged historians at various times, such as James West Davidson, who asked in 1984 if there was a boundary between history and fiction, while acknowledging that the question was not original with him either. Some years earlier it had engaged Nancy Partner, who wondered if the question had 'not been much explored' because it—falsely—seemed so self-evident, and who, two decades later, concluded that in order to write history at all one needed 'to call on the fiction-making capacity of the mind' to such an extent that the real question is how history 'can separate itself out from fiction at all' (J. Davidson 1984: 332; Partner 1977: 195; 1995: 33).

Thucydides would have understood such arguments, as he would have understood E. L. Doctorow's generalization that 'There's no fiction or nonfiction now, there's only narrative' (J. Davidson 1984: 332). Certainly the dominant mode in the writing of theater history nowadays—indeed, of history in general, despite the *Annales*

[1] The rare exceptions are noted below.

school—is narrative, and much writing in theater history today is not unlike the final chapters of a good mystery novel, where the seemingly insoluble problems to which the reader was introduced at the beginning prove in the end to be susceptible to solution after all.

Problems and solutions are the stuff of narrative, whether fictional or historical. Whether this is because we have a 'culturally conditioned need' to represent the past 'in some kind of narrative logic', or whether fictional strategies are our own consciously preferred choices for structuring historical narratives, or whether the boundaries between the humanities and the social sciences in general are more porous and problematized than we acknowledge, the fact remains, as Hayden White has told us, that historical writings, like fictional writings, are constructed 'around particular narrative and rhetorical strategies' even when they are 'most rigorously bound to the rules of evidence and scientific methodology' (Spiegel 2005: 23; Otter 2005; Eley 1996: 207).

Plus ça change, one might be tempted to think as one reflects upon the history of our own discipline as well as upon that of the historians. A principal impetus for the revolution in historical thinking in the nineteenth century was a desire to discredit the then current belief that history was a branch of literature—or of rhetoric, as Lawrence Stone would have it (Stone 1979: 3)—and that 'mere history' could have little utility until linked with some more noble or virtuous discipline. Macaulay and Carlyle, perhaps the last of their breed in a line stretching from Clarendon or even from Camden, wrote their works in the face of new movements and ideologies that by the middle of the nineteenth century had rejected the notion that the sensibilities of the cultivated mind, linked with a persuasive prose style, were a sufficient guarantor of historical value, and had replaced that notion with a new paradigm, less committed to a search for the 'moral lessons' history might afford than to an emphasis upon its own internal coherence and to a new focus upon primary research among documents (Otter 2005: 109).

These attitudes, revolutionary in their day, are the background noise of our own thinking, and the entailment is that we see history today almost reflexively as a scholarly discipline devoted without question to archival research and documentation. But this notion, now almost two centuries old, has been under attack by historians for some time. Leopold von Ranke's dictum (Ranke 1824, p. vii) that the task of the historian was not to produce universal truths but simply to show how things actually were—'Er will blos zeigen wie es eigentlich gewesen', a claim generally understood to have initiated the 'documentary turn' that followed—has now been disassembled, the recovery of 'how things actually were' being one of the casualties of the recent turn by historians to theory and methodology.

The activity we call theater history, which was born of a literary impulse in the midst of this nineteenth-century historiographic transition, was for a long time uncertain of its own status. For most of its early practitioners, despite the new energizing of historical studies at large, theater history seemed inescapably a branch of literature, more about theater than about history, fathered by a devotion to the plays of Shakespeare, and centered upon—or at least sheltered within—an activity whose closest affinity was with poetry rather than with social or cultural or political affairs. It was sometimes viewed by those outside the discipline as a regrettable distraction from the proper study of dramatic poesy.

There was, of course, no question about the attractiveness of the plays themselves (that is, of Shakespeare's plays); their popularity from the eighteenth century onward was one of the enabling forces in the shifting of literary studies in general from a narrow foundation in philology at its earlier extreme to a later interest in reflecting upon aesthetic, moral, and spiritual concerns. This attack upon philology was a kindred manifestation of the Romantic spirit at work among the historians; as history was to be untethered from literature, so literary study was to be untethered from philology.

But now we're back where we started, with literature and history once more converging, undoing their divorce and rediscovering old commonalities, including a new awareness of the importance of language, with historians discussing 'practice theory' and 'the linguistic turn', finding new interest in the work of Saussure and Derrida and Foucault, or in such nearer narrativist contemporaries as Hayden White, Dominick LaCapra, Frank Ankersmit, Hans Kellner, Nancy Partner, or Allan Megill. Joining the chorus, Stephen Orgel has usefully reminded us that theater history 'is no different from any other kind of history', which ideally would mean (though it doesn't yet seem to) that theater historians engage in the same kinds of methodological debates as do other historians (Orgel 2004: 1).

This turn of events would have alarmed our predecessors, early twentieth-century theater historians such as E. K. Chambers or W. W. Greg, scholars whose labors still anchor much of our own work, if only subliminally. Greg did indeed urge the importance of 'the development of method' (Greg 1904–8, vol. ii, p. ix), but what he meant by that is best embodied in Chambers's own great works, especially the four-volume *Elizabethan Stage*, where 'method'—or a 'linguistic turn', could he have known the phrase—meant getting as far away from the literary as possible. Anyone who has read Chambers knows that he succeeded.

Even by the middle of the twentieth century this gap was still apparent, as was the clear distinction between *dramatic* history, a subset of literary history, and *theater* history, still a kind of handmaid or orphan. One pursued dramatic history at mid-century (as I did in graduate school) by reading widely outside the Shakespearean box, urged on by the critical essays of T. S. Eliot, and by the exhortations of F. R. Leavis that the verbal was a gateway to the moral. But we didn't read theater history, nor did our professors lecture on it; for them, theater history had only a little more value than it had had a century earlier; it still lacked a foothold and a rationale.

My graduate school professors would have been as perplexed as Greg and Chambers could they have seen where current thinking now stands. They would wonder not merely at the increasing centrality of theater history, but even more at historians concerning themselves with 'linguistic turn historiography', or at serious scholars like White or LaCapra or Ankersmit or Spiegel analysing narrativist strategies and asserting that 'no historical account is possible without some form of troping or emplotment' (Spiegel 2005: 23). They would wonder even more at Hans Kellner's redefining of history as 'a discourse that is fundamentally rhetorical', or his claim that representing the past requires 'the creation of powerful, persuasive images' best understood as 'metaphors or proposals about reality' (Kellner 1995: 2). This would have seemed to them a serious confusion of history with literature, that is, with fiction.

But those are the issues historians are wrestling with today. And yet, despite Doctorow's insight, the traditional distinction between the genres of literature and history continues to govern our assumptions about the difference between fiction and fact. Fictional narratives do not form the basis of our factual research in theater history because fictional accounts do not serve us as evidence. Yet it is becoming increasingly difficult to assume that the texts we label as 'historical' have any greater value as evidence. What theater historians lack, according to Peter Holland, is any 'assumed and shared methodology based on an acceptance of what constitutes evidence', nor have they manifested any agreement on 'how that evidence generates the potential for meaning'. He also reminds us, almost as an aside, that engaging in the practice of theater history 'is not the same as understanding or theorizing' it (Holland 2004*a*, pp. xiii, xii).

Nancy Partner concurs, reminding us that everything regarded as 'evidence' is of course *evident* simply by virtue of its existence, but it is not thereby 'evidence'. Only when we transform it into a meaningful piece of a past whole—however we may conceive that 'whole'—does it become 'evidence'. In this sense, she says, 'all of historical evidence is a major trope, a figure of speech and thought'. Since no collocation of pieces of 'evidence', however large, can reproduce the whole of the past, she argues that 'the trope of metonymy, which extrapolates a whole thing from its contiguous part, is the organizing concept and argument of even the dryest and most cautious historical construct'. Partner, like Hans Kellner, is as much a rhetorician as a historian, and insights like theirs are beginning to be shared by theater historians as well, for example by Peter Holland, who voices concern about the 'remarkably little investigation of the methodological bases' upon which so much of our previous and even current scholarship is based, or on 'the theoretical bases' on which theater history 'has been or might be constructed' (Partner 1986: 105–6; Holland 2004*a*, p. xii).

If our preferred practice is positivist or essentialist, our only defense against such uncongenial assertions about our failure to be theoretical will probably be to go back into the archives and find more documents; in other words, to add to our discipline's 'traditionally positivist accumulation of data', in Holland's words. Ronald Vince echoes Holland in describing the largely unexamined 'documentary imperative' that 'continues to characterize most theatre history'; and Joseph Donohue finds the 'gathering and labeling of evidence' without a consideration of the assumptions and values underlying such activity to be 'an excessively narrow' notion of the discipline (Holland 2003, p. xvi; Vince 1989: 7; Donohue 1989: 177).

On the other hand, Virginia Scott hopes 'to see more of us in the archives, because unknown treasures live there', though she concurrently hopes we will 'seek wisdom' about our enterprise 'from other historians and historiographers and not always from anthropologists, sociologists, and philosophers' (Scott 2004: 191–2). She's right about archives; for some of us, archives are magnets, and documents unquestionably comforting, a tangible physical substantiation of a past reality. But they are not without their problems. Christopher Hill learned many years ago that 'Their apparent objectivity is frequently spurious' (Hill 1977: 17). Two things, and only two, can be said unambiguously about surviving documents: one, that they have somehow survived where other similar documents often have not (for conspiracy theorists this alone may be grounds for suspicion), and two, that they contain particularized information set down by a particular writer, with greater or lesser coherence depending upon the writer's command of syntax. One cannot go further than this; one cannot demonstrate a concord between the contents of a documentary account and the actual circumstances it purports to record. Nor can one presume, even subliminally, that the documents that have not survived would, if found, strengthen the narratives we perceive to be implicit in the ones we already have. It has been traditional practice to give surviving documents the benefit of the doubt, to presume that the information they give us forms the proper backbone of whatever narrative we may wish to construct. Perhaps we have no choice but to begin this way with any document. But we must never forget that this is a choice we make, not a requirement of our discourse. So we should practice skepticism whenever we can. Indeed, Christopher Hill has warned us emphatically that a historian must be skeptical of '*all* his sources' (Hill 1977: 18).

I would extend that skepticism to include whatever narrative construct those sources seduce us into preferring. Like our children, our sources often achieve unearned perfection in our eyes simply because they are ours, and we tend to resist when our preferred narratives for them are upset by new data. But we should expect such upsets and should welcome them, and skepticism of our existing sources is the first step. We might begin by being skeptical of second-party documents, that is, documents written by someone other than the provider of the information. One example would be the depositions of witnesses in a court case, where a person summoned by the court would respond orally to a set of prepared questions while the court transcriber wrote down what he believed or understood the deponent to be saying. Depositions in theatrical cases are a major source of data for theater historians, yet such depositions present problems of their own, probably insoluble ones. Not simply that two deponents may disagree over the same matter, but the deeper question of whether the depositions as written represent unambiguously what the deponents actually said or meant to say.

Another familiar form of second-party document is the will, sometimes written with care and deliberation by a scrivener in consultation with a testator in good health, but more usually written by the parish clerk at the bedside of a terminally ill testator surrounded by potential beneficiaries. Our assumption that the final written and signed document reflected the testator's actual desires is often an act of faith. While some stage players remembered their fellow players in their wills, others did not; we devise our own explanations for these inclusions or omissions, which often reflect no more than our desire to write the kind of narrative we want to write. Nor did a testator's signature upon a will necessarily reflect authenticity; Alan Nelson has recently discovered, among the State Papers, a lawsuit contesting the 1625 will of one John Busby, in which the complainant argued, with seemingly strong evidence, that Busby's signature on his will was written by his mother, Busby himself being too weak to write his name and (so the complainant averred) too insensibly near death even to understand what he was signing (or not signing).

We should keep the Busby case in mind as we do our research. We cannot with assurance presume that the contents of second-party documents like parish vestry minutes, livery company records, privy council minutes, and the like—or even of first-party documents like letters—furnish us with 'evidence' reflecting the truth about the circumstances they purport to describe. They reflect, as do our own letters and diaries and notes, one way of seeing the world, and not the only way. Though we try to find our sources meaningful, they may nonetheless be in some degree fictional. Indeed, 'the central fictionality of history', according to Partner, is 'its unrelenting meaningfulness'; the one thing that reliably separates history from novels is that 'histories are relentlessly overplotted'. While a good novelist will withhold information, a historian (she says) must tell all, withhold nothing, offer any explanation that will allow the source, the information, to acquire significance (Partner 1986: 102).

Robert Stein carries the point further; for him, nothing is inherently a source. A piece of information becomes a source 'only as it enters into a transaction with a historian to serve the historian's purposes, when it is used, in other words, as "a document"'. Historians, he notes, regularly use sources 'for purposes other than those for which they were intended'—our own use of Shakespeare's will is probably the best-known instance of this—because history is an activity in the present. Stein posits a triangular relation among 'a present entity' (a surviving text), a present reader of that text, and a present 'disciplinary structure (in this case, history) that supplies the reader with an interpretive context, a purpose for reading and a protocol for interpretation'. So, for Stein, the mere presentation of data, however accurate, is not yet history, not without the 'disciplinary structure' and the 'protocol' that are the key mediating factors between the historian and the document (Stein 2005: 69).

But do we have those keys? Until very recently, many theater historians would have had difficulty describing the disciplinary structure and protocols governing their own work. As an escape from such a requirement, some of us might have been tempted to say, 'Of course there's a theoretical basis for my work, but I don't need to explicate it because it's implicit in what I do'; but that's imprecise, evasive, and in some cases perhaps not entirely honest. Andrew Gurr tells us that the appeal of anecdotalism—itself a specialized form of fiction—to New Historicists and others is 'precisely because it is so imprecise'. However, he believes we theater historians have little better to show, because 'Our knowledge and our use of the texts and contexts of early modern drama are as imprecise as any anecdote' (Gurr 2004*a*: 71). For Gurr, protocol and disciplinary structure are not yet in evidence, though fiction may be.

II

> Geschichte beginnt mit Chronik und endigt mit Essay.
>
> Leopold von Ranke

> Although I don't believe causal arguments are useless, I would certainly maintain that the attribution of causes is a construction, one manner of being historical, and it ought not to be privileged over functional historical narratives.
>
> Albert H. Tricomi, *Reading Tudor–Stuart Texts through Cultural Historicism*

Theater history certainly began with chronicle, as Ranke said it would. Early theater history practitioners such as F. J. Furnivall and F. G. Fleay provided us with the beginnings of our discipline in chronicle form, and chronicle remained a powerful influence upon E. K. Chambers and G. E. Bentley. Even in the late 1970s Lawrence Stone declared the narrative mode in history unambiguously to be 'the organization of material in a chronologically sequential order' (Stone 1979: 3). And despite Ranke's prediction that it would transmute into something else, chronicle seems to be with us still, like Osric, forever leaving but never gone. Ranke's end point, which I understand to be the reflective essay—as opposed to the demonstrative essay, which often has chronicle at its heart—has only recently found practitioners in our discipline. Mostly, when we write, we describe events or happenings and aim for explanations of their causes. Albert Tricomi thinks causes are overrated (my second epigraph), and events as well, finding fault with 'positivist proponents of event-based analyses', or indeed with anyone—this presumably would include Stone, just cited—who claims 'categorically that event-based arguments of the sequential sort are *the* way to write history' (Tricomi 1996: 12–13).

The 'event' has been for some time a vexed category in historical thinking. Almost two decades ago William Sewell said, 'most historians take the effectivity of events so much for granted that their accounts of events tend to lack a theoretical edge'. Marshall Sahlins, an anthropologist rather than a historian, had earlier observed that most historians 'live in the narrative element' and as a result lacked any sense of the event as a theoretical category. Sewell, considering these remarks, found them a fair description of his own earlier practice, and concluded that only after exploring the methodologies of other disciplines did he 'recognize events as a category in need of theoretical work' (Sewell 1996: 264; Sahlins 1991: 15).

Peter Holland has observed, in his assessment of the ongoing REED project, that London-centric theater historians have not 'theorized the position within the central strategies of theatre history of almost any form of event that is non-metropolitan and/ or non-professional' (Holland 2004*b*: 53–4). But this doesn't go nearly far enough. Sahlins and Sewell would no doubt tell us that 'within the central strategies of theatre history' (whatever those may be) we have not theorized the notion of events at all, of events as a category, whether or not professional, whether metropolitan or rural.

Jaques, a metropolitan turned rural, was untroubled by such concerns. His Seven Ages speech in *As You Like It*—a 'strange eventful history' in his view—exemplifies the notion that life is apprehended not as a continuum but as a series of stations, each emblematizing a pivotal moment in an uncertain progress. Later in the play, Touchstone parodies this step-by-step view of life's progress with his disquisition on the seven stages of a quarrel. Perhaps Ganymede does so as well in her anatomy of Oliver and Aliena, who 'no sooner met but they looked; no sooner looked but they loved', and so on, passing swiftly from one marker to the next, 'and in these degrees have they made a pair of stairs to marriage'.

We theater historians have until recently tended reflexively to make the same assumptions. We would be likely to note the first appearance of a text, or playing company, or playhouse, or critical stance, or the first major modification of any of these, as an event, while the subsequent continuing existence of the same entity would be not an event, but rather some other kind of phenomenon. Though we all publicly agree that the subsequent continuity is as important as the first appearance, in practice we have tended to scant it in our narratives, finding change more interesting than continuity. Early researchers in the archives like Malone or Halliwell would emerge from their documentary rummagings with evidence for some event or occasion, much like Little Jack Horner with his plum, and the assembling of such evidence, often in books called *Historical Account of the Rise and Progress of the English Stage* or *Chronicle History of the London Stage* or *Biographical Chronicle of the English Drama*, solidified the 'eventful history' approach. (W. W. Greg praised the 'careful chronicling' of the last two of these works, both by F. G. Fleay, saying they had 'revolutionized the methods of theatrical history'; Greg 1904–8, vol. ii, p. ix.) We are the heirs of this tradition, and we have built our own stairs to marriage out of the same materials. The older among us were taught that the seven ages of the theater began in 1576 and ended in 1642, and a survey of current texts on theater history will show this to be a still current trope, along with surprising agreement about what the most important intervening eventful dates were as well. Like Jaques, modern practitioners of the discipline have been charmed by Touchstone's methodology; event by event we develop and develop, and thereby we hang our tale. It's only a short step to believing that motley is the only wear.

But even our dependence upon 'events' does not make them equivalent to (or reducible to) what surviving documents tell us about them. Monika Otter finds 'the truly important referents' of historical narrative nowadays to be 'not things, people, or places but "events"; and "events" are arguably already an abstraction from reality—someone's attempt to order and emplot raw data into a before/after, cause/effect' arrangement. Such an arrangement is inescapably narrative, as Nancy Partner has noted: even 'The most rigorously eventless, characterless, "non-narrative" history has to tell something, has to begin somewhere and proceed and conclude' (Otter 2005: 125–6; Partner 1986: 93). Frank Ankersmit has explored narrative as one way a historian might 'attempt to give an acceptable account of part of the past'; but John Zammito found problems even in this formulation, asking 'what makes something an "account?" What makes it "acceptable?"' Shannon Jackson raises similar queries: 'What counts as an argument? What kind of work must be done to support it? What is rigor? What is research?' (Ankersmit 1983: 207; Zammito 2005: 156; Jackson 2004: 242).

These are new kinds of questions, and healthy ones. Otter reminds us that the traditional event-centered narrative had for centuries been spared such interrogation; she instances Isidore of Seville's 'historia est narratio rei gestae, per quam ea quae in praeterito facta sunt dinoscuntur' ('history is a narration of events, through which that which occurred in the past is known'). This formulation generally prevailed through the twentieth century—witness Stone—despite its being assaulted (though not killed) in France by the *Annales* school, which rejected it for being overly concerned with such trivial and insignificant issues as individual events; it was dismissed as 'l'histoire événementielle', inferior to their own preferred narrative mode, 'l'histoire de la longue durée' (Otter 2005: 113; Stone 1979: 3).

Gareth Stedman Jones offered a further twist, telling us we must get beyond the Isidorean (and Rankean) identification of history with pre-given past events. History, in his view, is 'an entirely intellectual operation which takes place in the present and in the head. The fact that the "past" in some sense "happened" is not of primary significance since the past is in no sense synonymous with history.' He reasserted what is by now a mainstream position in historical study, namely that the historian doesn't reconstruct the past, but rather constructs something else from the residues of the past which have survived into the present. Louis Montrose has echoed this view, claiming that we have no access to the past unmediated by 'surviving textual traces'. Frank Ankersmit noted that the texts we ourselves produce add a further layer of mediation, and he faulted those who believe 'that nothing of any interest happens' on the trajectory from the initial evidence to the text we ourselves write. Geoff Eley, sounding the same note, saw history as not 'the archival reconstruction of what happened' but rather 'the continuous contest over how the past is approached or invoked'. All saw as dangerous the assumption that the structure of a historical narrative reflects some presumed structure inherent in the past itself, and all agreed that procedural protocols are needed. 'The distinction', wrote Stedman Jones, 'is not that between theory and non-theory, but between the adequacy or inadequacy of the theory brought to bear' (Stedman Jones 1976: 296; Ankersmit 2001: 51; Montrose 1996: 6; Eley 1996: 214).

But what theories are commonly brought to bear in theater history, and how might we determine their adequacy or inadequacy?

III

> History, it has been well said, offers a series of answers to which we do not know the questions. The historian's difficult job is to reconstruct the questions from the recorded answers.
>
> Christopher Hill, *History and Culture*

> History is perhaps the most thoroughly hermeneutic creation of all culture: from the 'inside' because historians begin by creating a text, the Past,

> through the interpretive creation of and with evidence; and from the 'outside' because they then proceed to explain it.
>
> Nancy Partner, 'Making Up Lost Time'

One can hardly imagine two more divergent views of the historian's work than those of my two epigraphs, by an older and a younger member of the profession, the perhaps unconscious positivism of the former deftly encircled by the linguistic turn of the latter. In the spirit of such circling, and with my second epigraph as an exemplar, let me now return to the first of my opening questions: Is theater history a form of social or cultural history, and if so, do those disciplines have theoretical underpinnings (however contested) that ought to be of interest to theater historians? For Ronald Vince, theater is without question 'a sociocultural phenomenon', and its study 'in some major aspects a branch of social history' (Vince 1989: 14). And social historians, in turn, are major players in the ongoing debate over the place of theory in historical writing, according to Gabrielle Spiegel, because 'the deepest challenge posed by the "linguistic turn" was to the practice of social history'. Spiegel sees 'the rise of cultural history (and its socio-cultural cognates in anthropology and sociology)' as having been governed by 'discontents arising from the then dominant practice of social history, Marxist and non-Marxist alike' (Spiegel 2005: 4). If this is the case, then we may have a fairly straightforward answer to the first part of the question: those social historians and cultural historians who were trained as historians are quite likely as caught up in the questions I've already addressed, as are any other group of historians; perhaps more so. And if Vince is right about theater history being a kind of social history, then the answer to the second part of my question is yes.

But persons who come to the study of society and culture from some other point of origin than graduate study in history—for example, from graduate study in literature (as I do)—may find themselves less well trained and therefore less engaged with these issues, or less alert to their importance. And, until recently, despite Vince (whose background is also in literature), theater historians have tended to fall into this latter category.

There are exceptions, of course. *Interpreting the Theatrical Past*, a ground-breaking collection of essays published in 1989, raised a number of cogent questions about the theoretical underpinnings of our discipline, questions that remain healthily unresolved, and continue to be discussed in ever widening circles, as evidenced by the publication in 2003 of another collection of essays, entitled *Theorizing Practice: Redefining Theatre History*, with a largely different set of contributors. Fifteen years after co-editing the earlier volume, Thomas Postlewait asked—and not for the first time—if we can 'specify a vital academic rationale' for theater history, 'distinct from the definitions and rationales that shape each of the other disciplines in the arts' such as humanities and social sciences. He wondered if 'we, like musicology, have distinct features as an academic field' (Postlewait 2004: 184). The implication of his query was that we do not, and that we should. Ronald Vince had earlier proposed the 'axiom' that the boundaries of the discipline of theater history 'tend to expand in direct ratio to the intensity of the efforts to define and confine it', and predicted that any effort to restrict the definition of theater history 'as a precondition of study' would prove 'both arbitrary and self-defeating'. For Vince, a home for theater history that encompassed both literary study and theater practice was the desideratum. Postlewait, perhaps reflecting on these assumptions, offered a quiet disagreement, confessing his own belief—like Virginia Scott's—in the prior centrality of 'historical study, historical training, and historical understanding'. But then, in a moment of introspection, he asked, 'But am I merely announcing my preference for what I happen to do? If so, I am part of the problem—one more person with a special interest that substitutes for a disciplinary program, one more earnest teacher who proclaims an academic mission on the basis of what I see in the mirror' (Postlewait 2004: 184–5; Vince 1989: 13–14).

This is bravely stated, and is a central conundrum. Is theater history a distinct and definable field, with a set of commonly agreed—or at least energetically debated—methodological premises, or is it merely the uncritical sum of what practicing theater historians happen to be doing at any given time? If the latter, then does its definition change whenever people change what they're doing? Where on the continuum between a free-floating, methodologically empty cluster of individual researchers and a circumscribed, overdetermined, ideologically rigid group project does our discipline now stand?

One answer might be that it stands everywhere along that continuum, and thus has no center. Among the common charges levied against theater historians by those who are not their friends are the following: that they are anti-theoretical; that they are overawed by 'facts'; that they believe documentary evidence always trumps imaginative hypotheses; that their discourse remains linear while the discourse of those around them grows richer and more complex; that they are more interested in the questions for which they have answers than in those 'other' questions, and that they are often scornful of colleagues who, lacking data, nonetheless tackle the other questions; that there is an unconscious Bardic teleology in their premises, shown by their valuation of the origins of Shakespearean associations—the Globe, the Blackfriars, the King's players, Stratford—above those phenomena that led elsewhere, e.g. to the Red Bull or to the children's companies or to the provinces; and that the books and essays they themselves write easily support the above charges. Until recently, there would have been some truth in each of these observations. But increasingly such opinions may be viewed as assessments of who we were rather than who we are. The work we're doing now, as reflected in the essays in this volume, furnish ample material for a response to these charges.

But it's also true that, for scholars of the early modern period, it's harder to write proper theater history today than it has ever been before. In part this is true because there exists no general agreement among theater historians about what 'proper' theater history looks like. Setting aside those studies of social or cultural history that appear to be 'theater history' because they are dressed up with references to play-acting and playgoing, one is still left with a broad range of perspectives among practitioners of the discipline. One scholar will argue that the proper center of interest for theater historians is the play-text in performance upon the stage; another will insist it is research in the archives; still another will claim it embraces anything performative, wherever and however performed; yet another will say theater must be set in its social and political context; still another will see economics as the key to all mysteries; and so on. But these differing opinions haven't yet become starting points for a debate. Theater history has, for a very long time now, resembled golf more than tennis.

But even when done right—and there's scant consensus on what that phrase might mean—the writing of theater history is difficult. Theater history is, properly, the writing of theater history. The accumulation of data, while commendable, requires intervention before it can become history. Our predecessors, having had far fewer documents to work with than we do, and knowing far less about the early theater than we do, had an easier time of it, because they were freer to construct narratives to fit their meager data. We have more data now, but more data means more contradictions, more inconsistencies, more evidence that is incommensurate with other evidence, and a greater awareness of what kinds of data are still missing. As a result we are forced into more confusions than our predecessors could have imagined. It's no longer easy—in addition to being no longer fashionable—to write the master narrative that commands general assent; there are too many opportunities for other narratives, other points of view.

And so to the first procedural dilemma for a theater historian. Are ambiguities and contradictions in our data problems to be solved, requiring a selective narrative supporting one preferred interpretation against others and offering that as 'what really happened'? Or are they a condition inherent in the data and in the nature of our own scholarship, requiring a fuller and more accommodating narrative with room for ambiguity and contradiction and alternative versions? All questions do indeed have agendas already written into them, and by now mine must be clear.

Clifford Geertz maintained that the anthropologist's task was principally interpretive, and for Frank Ankersmit the same was true of the historian, but Ankersmit complicated the issue by noting that interpretations are 'under-determined', because 'only an infinite number of interpretations could account for all the known data'. The entailment of this position is that anyone interested in accounting for the data must be hospitable, even welcoming, to more than simply his or her own interpretation. Or in his words, 'a maximum of clarity can only be obtained [by] a *proliferation* of historical interpretations and not by attempting to *reduce* their number'. This proliferation is one way to avoid what Hans Kellner describes as our tendency 'to eliminate rather than to entertain possibilities'. Geertz, were he still alive, might have termed Ankersmit's protocol 'thick interpretation' (Ankersmit 1994: 33, 72; Kellner 1989: 45).

Allan Megill's essay on grand narratives in history focuses more on theory than on interpretation, and concludes with a section entitled 'The Theory Postulate: Always Theorize'. But how do we theater historians make sense of such a requisite? Megill's premise is that we live in 'a world that no longer believes in a single History', but this is not so clear in the world of theater history, where fresh instances of the grand, all-explaining narrative are still to be found. Megill does envisage 'a greater attentiveness of historians to theory', yet acknowledges that 'there are different theories and different ways of being attentive to them'. Echoing Ankersmit, he suggests we approach our work 'having a greater humility and reflexiveness concerning its own assumptions and conclusions'. In the same vein, Shannon Jackson urges us to 'resist singularity', by which she means 'learning to value varieties of thinking that you do not share and (even more to the point) varieties of practice in which you do not excel'. Geertz would likely have recognized this as another way of saying 'thick' (Megill 1995: 172; Jackson 2004: 241).

We may call these arguments theorizing if we wish, or we may simply understand them as proposals for ways of proceeding. The terminology is irrelevant. But self-awareness seems to be part of the mix, much as it was for the economist J. M. Keynes when he remarked of his fellow economists (as Terry Eagleton has reminded us) that those who disliked theory, or claimed to get along better without it, were simply in the grip of an older theory.

IV

> Even in the most austere scholarly report from the archives, the inventive faculty—selecting, pruning, editing, commenting, interpreting, delivering judgements—is in full play. [Thus] claims for historical knowledge must always be fatally circumscribed by the character and prejudices of its narrator.
>
> Simon Schama, *Dead Certainties*

A year after Schama's remarks were published, David Perkins proposed that narrative history could not make use of the techniques and strategies of modernist and postmodernist fiction, because such techniques had been consciously developed 'in opposition to traditional, linear narrative and closure'. In Perkins's view they 'problematize such narratives, expose them as mere artifice, deny their claim to be explanatory. And they do this on the basis of an interpretation of life that emphasizes the truth of incoherence and inexplicability.' Perkins found it typical of postmodernist cultural criticism to emphasize 'that historical reality is an array of particulars, heterogeneous and unstructurable' (Perkins 1992: 48, 59).

But what Perkins found inappropriate for historical narrative, Hans Kellner found desirable, approvingly calling such strategies 'crooked readings', that is, readings that 'unfocus the texts they examine in order to put into the foreground the constructed, rhetorical nature of the past, and to bring out the purposes, often hidden and unrecognized, in our retrospective creations' (Kellner 1989: 7). Kellner described with disparaging amusement the common if mistaken belief—perhaps Perkins's belief—that the 'first duty of the historian' is to follow the 'influential tradition of scholarship, which presumes (*a*) that there *is* a "story" out there waiting to be told, and (*b*) that this story can be told straight by an honest, industrious historian using the right methods' (Kellner 1989, p. vii).

But the master narrative is no longer in fashion, as Kellner well knows; it has been called in question with increasing vigor in recent years by scholars in a variety of fields. The classical scholar Charles Martindale tells us, 'there is nothing outside the discourses of history by which accounts of the past can be tested or checked. There is no independent access to historical "reality" outside the discourses which constitute it' (Martindale 1993: 19–20). W. W. Greg was beginning to think along these lines a hundred years ago, when he told us there was 'no such thing as a clearly defined historical field', that 'facts are linked to other facts in all directions, and investigation merely leads to further and yet further questions' (Greg 1904–8, vol. ii, p. ix). The 'further questions', and our welcoming of them, still remain the key. The physicist Niels Bohr, rejecting essentialism, famously remarked in 1927 that physics was not about things but about the results of experiments. Perhaps theater history too will one day be less focused upon things and more upon the various ways of dealing with those things; not 'Here's my narrative' but 'What various narratives are potential here, and how can I do them all justice, even if I find some of them uncongenial?'

We will never know all we wish to know, we will never fill all the gaps in our information, and we will always have more questions. But those questions are a sign of health in our discipline, not a sign of inadequacy. Questions are always more important than answers; as Socrates well knew, anyone can come up with an answer. Coming up with the right question is far more valuable, for the right question keeps reminding us that there are other answers in play that may be as useful as the one we favor. 'All historians know'—Nancy Partner risks a generalization here, but it's a good one to conclude with—'all historians know that history is no longer the discipline busily fulfilling its positivistic promise to tell it all as it really happened. And, in fact, that cultural moment, of naïve assertions about splicing together an entire, indubitable, objectively once-existing Past, was a very brief digression in history's longer, more richly compromised life' (Partner 1986: 117).

We have survived that digression, and are now experiencing what Herbert Blau calls 'the swift accrual of history affecting theatre history' (Blau 2004: 253). If this 'accrual' brings with it a heightened interest in methodological issues of the kind historians themselves see as important, then we should be pleased that we're at such an interesting juncture in the development of our own discipline.

PART I

THEATRE COMPANIES

CHAPTER 1

ADULT PLAYING COMPANIES TO 1583

W. R. STREITBERGER

In March 1583 Elizabeth I's Principal Secretary, Sir Francis Walsingham, asked Edmond Tilney, then Master of the Revels, to choose a new company of players to serve under the Queen's patronage. Tilney drafted players from several sophisticated companies to create the largest and most talented playing company of the era, one that dominated in the Queen's Revels throughout the 1580s and continued to play in the provinces until the end of her reign. It is generally agreed that this development was one of the important milestones in the history of Elizabethan theater because it linked the subsequent fortunes of commercial theater to the interests and regulation of the Crown. It is less well understood how this development came about. Professional playing in England was several centuries old in 1583 and the first royal company had been created nearly a hundred years before that date.

I

Professional theater in England dates from as early as the fourteenth century, when groups of players who earned their livelihood from their performances traveled the countryside in search of audiences. These early professional players can be distinguished from amateurs who performed folk plays in towns and villages throughout the country, from guild members who performed civic-sponsored cycle plays in wealthy towns, and from student players who performed for school and university audiences. But distinctions of this sort cannot be pushed too far, for professional players used a variety of material and performed all over the countryside, in university towns, in the great houses of the nobility, and at court. Early on, neither the social status nor the business of professional players was clearly defined. The term 'play' could cover a variety of activities including singing, dancing, tumbling, juggling, rope-dancing, fencing, minstrelsy, and improvisational performances, as well as performing roles in drama, and, to a certain extent, this virtuosity was characteristic of companies throughout the period (Streitberger 1994: 233–5). Their idea of genre was flexible and inclusive; ours is the reverse—definitive and exclusive.

Some early playing companies were independent, known by the names of their leading players, but by the late fifteenth century others were under community sponsorship, such as the players of High Wycombe, Coventry, Kingston, and St Albans. Still others were patronized by the nobility and known by the names of the noblemen they served. The Duke of Gloucester and the Earls of Oxford, Essex, Derby, Northumberland, Buckingham, Shrewsbury, and Arundel all had companies of players in the fifteenth century. Patronage accomplished several goals. It ensured entertaining revels given by the nobles in their great houses on the traditional feasts, developed their reputations as patrons of the arts, and extended their influence among the boroughs and towns in which their companies performed. Patronage created a favorable climate for players as well, for it afforded them protection from local magistrates as they traveled, and it served as a recommendation to mayors of the towns and villages in which they sought to perform (Blackstone 1988: 120).

By the end of the fifteenth century the royal family began to patronize players. Prince Arthur's company first performed in 1495, and his younger brother Henry (later Henry VIII), whose Lord Warden's company began performing at the same time, took over patronage of the Prince's company after Arthur's death in 1502 (I. Lancashire 1984: 374, 389). Patronage of playing companies by members of the royal family continued through Henry VIII's reign and was resurrected again in James I's reign. By the opening of the sixteenth century professional playing companies were already widespread phenomena, appreciated at all levels of society. Their development across the sixteenth century is not simply the story of the growth of a commercial enterprise, for the fortunes of players continually intersected with the interests of the nobility and of the court. Their growth, indeed their survival, is in great measure attributable to the fact that the nobility and the monarch became patrons.

When Henry VII created a company of players in 1494, he set a precedent for the patronage of a royal company that would continue almost unbroken until 1642. The King's players dominated in the revels on state occasions and during the season from Christmas to Shrove Tuesday by their lavish productions furnished with expensive costumes and properties and by the fact that they were scheduled to perform more frequently than any other players. Like the Gentlemen Players of the Chapel Royal, who performed at court from 1505 to 1512 and later at Edward VI's and Mary's coronations, the original King's players were essentially a household, rather than a touring company. Initially there were four of them: Richard Gibson, John English, Edward Maye, and John Hammond, who was replaced in 1504 by John Scott and William Rutter, increasing their number to five. They were paid an annual fee of £6 13*s.* 4*d.* and livery, in addition to rewards for specific performances. None of them, so far as we know, were full-time players. English appears to have been a joiner who was employed to purchase silks for Henry VII's coronation, and helped to produce pageants and disguisings at court. Gibson was Yeoman Tailor and Porter of the Great Wardrobe who became Sergeant of the Tents, and as deputy to the Master of the Revels he helped to produced virtually all of the revels and tournaments at court from 1510 to his death in 1534 (Streitberger 1994: 48–50).

In 1515 Henry VIII restructured the King's players into two groups, one consisting of the original players and the other of the new King's players (Streitberger 1992). The original players continued to perform at court each year until their retirement, sometime between 1521 and 1528. The new King's players were created as a touring company, and much evidence of their performances survives from the provinces, but they were also invited to perform at court every year. The creation of this company is one of the milestones in the development of English theater, for it permanently linked the royal company to professional playing. In part this may have been a quasi-political decision because sending his players to towns and villages throughout the country enhanced Henry's reputation as a patron of a genuinely popular medium. But it must also have been designed to put the new King's players more directly in touch with the living sources of that popularity. It would enable his players to acquire the polish that only constant practice in performing could develop and it would acquaint them with the variety of entertainments then popular on tour. The royal players not only enhanced the King's image in the provinces but by their travels brought to court the kind of contemporary, popular drama being played throughout the countryside, contributing variety and vitality to the revels. And the royal company continued to be used for these purposes. Called the Queen's players under Mary and Elizabeth I, they performed at court at least until the end of Mary's reign, and they continued as a touring company until the early 1570s (Chambers 1923: ii. 77–85).

Evidence of the size, composition, and organization of early professional companies derives from surviving play-texts and cast lists. Several play-texts suitable for acting by professionals survive from Henry VII's and Henry VIII's reigns. *Mundus et Infans* (*c.*1522) has only five parts, which could be divided between two actors. Henry Medwall's *Fulgens and Lucrece* (1497) and John Bale's *1 and 2 King John* (1538) could be acted by five players. We know that the early King's company had only from four to five players, and during the reigns of Edward VI and Mary many surviving texts could be performed by from four to six players. The anonymous *Jack Juggler* (1555), for example, could be played by five. The conclusion from this evidence is that many late fifteenth- and early sixteenth-century companies were comprised of from two to six members.

Two hybrid moralities (transitional plays that combine the vice character from the morality tradition with the developing plot conventions of the history play), Thomas

Preston's *Cambyses* (*c.*1561) and John Pickering's *Horestes* (*c.*1567), reveal significant developments in professional companies by the middle of the sixteenth century. They document an increase in the number of roles for characters, and consequently an increase in the number of players needed to perform them. *Cambyses* has thirty-eight parts for from six to eight men and from two to four boys. *Horestes* contains twenty-seven roles for from six to eight players. Surviving texts of popular plays show a steady increase in length over the course of the sixteenth century, the corollary to which was a steady increase in the size of the companies performing them (Bradley 1992: 230–5). Popular plays before Elizabeth I's reign average less than a thousand lines, a figure consistent with an average of between two and six players needed to perform them. Cast lists for longer plays dating from the 1560s and 1570s suggest that the average size of companies had increased to as many as from seven to eight players, and with the development of commercial theater in London this number increased still further.

Another corollary to the increase in length of plays during the 1560s was that doubling of roles had to be expanded. By the first decade of Elizabeth I's reign as many as three to four minor roles might be performed by a single player. Doubling was a century-old practice of the professional companies that continued to be used even after the establishment of commercial theater in London. Some plays written for professional companies, like Bale's fellows (*c.*1538?–*c.*1562?), evidence a fairly equal division of roles, suggesting some equality among members of the company (Bradley 1992; Bevington 1962: 265–73). But in other professional companies a hierarchy developed. Many early touring companies were composed of a leading player and one or more subordinate players. In early popular moralities, like *Mankind*, the leading player performed the role of the vice while his fellows performed less demanding roles. The secularizing tendencies in later sixteenth-century drama offered opportunities for other important roles. In *Cambyses* and *Horestes* the lead player performed the role of the principal human character rather than the vice, whose part fell to a subordinate but still important player. The rest of the cast in both these plays have small roles easily divided among supporting players. *Cambyses* and *Horestes* register the transition between the spectacular and entertaining plays built around the vice characters of the early Tudor drama and the great human figures of the late Elizabethan period, such as Hieronimo, Tamburlaine, and Hamlet.

The tendency in the composition of professional companies over the course of the century was in the direction of larger companies capable of handling longer and more complicated plays which increased the need for more players. Not all players had backgrounds as entertainers; some left their trades for an opportunity to join companies. Among the new King's company in Henry VIII's reign, for example, John Young was a mercer, George Birch a courier, and George Mayler was a merchant tailor or glazier (Chambers 1923: ii. 81). Membership in a guild does not necessarily indicate that an individual actually practiced a trade. Ben Jonson, for example, kept up his dues with the bricklayers long after he ceased to work in the trade, and it may be that several of Shakespeare's colleagues who were members of London guilds—Robert Armin and John Lowin were goldsmiths; John Hemmings was a grocer; and

John Shank a weaver—similarly kept their memberships without working in those trades. Evidence from the 1570s and after indicates that playing companies became guild-like in their organization. The growing distinction between leading and supporting players underlies the late-century distinction between master players and hired actors. Master players, usually 'sharers' (who shared the costs of productions and the receipts for each performance), were named in patents as legally responsible members of the company. Sharers regulated the affairs of the company, approved new plays, and usually performed the principal roles in them. They also hired stage-keepers, prompters, wardrobe keepers, musicians, and minor players. By the late sixteenth century some playing companies with bases in London were quite large.

While some women later became active in the business side of the companies through marriage or inheritance, there is no evidence that women ever performed on stage with English companies until the late seventeenth century. There is also no evidence from a pre-Elizabethan play that offers positive evidence that boys performed the roles of women characters in professional companies (Bevington 1962: 76; Bradley 1992: 230). Female and juvenile parts were avoided if possible. Those that were included were played by men. Evidence suggests that employing boys in professional adult companies dates from early in Elizabeth I's reign. *Horestes* requires a boy to play both male and female roles. In *Cambyses* adult males play female roles, and the roles of a leading and a younger boy performer are segregated. By late century boy players had become commonplace in professional companies.

Few texts survive from the period, and our understanding of the repertories performed by early professional companies is based on a small amount of evidence. Possibly the material used by early companies was improvisational, based on set plots, ballads, or news, but evidence suggests that by the 1560s and 1570s some professional companies kept a variety of plays in their repertory. The manuscript play the *Book of Sir Thomas More* (*c.*1590–3) contains a play within a play acted by the fictional Lord Cardinal's players. Their repertory was supposed to have included *The Cradle of Security, Hit the Nail o' the Head, Dives and Lazarus, The Four P, Impatient Poverty, Lusty Juventus*, and *The Marriage of Wit and Wisdom*. The latter four of these plays survive, and we have an eyewitness account by R. Willis of the performance of the first in Gloucester in about 1570. Willis was a boy at the time, and he fondly remembered the sweet songs, the colorful costumes, the moral import, and the entertaining action (Douglas and Greenfield 1986: 363; Bevington 1962: 13–14, 18–19). The titles in the repertory of the fictional Lord Cardinal's players, ranging from biblical and morality to humanist debate plays, fit in well enough with the known venues of early professional companies: the great houses of the nobility, municipal buildings in towns, greens in villages, churches or churchyards, and inn-yards. Companies carried enough scripts to entertain whatever audience they were scheduled to play.

There were scores of companies on the road all throughout this period, and the demand for play-texts was intense. Scripts owned by companies were important assets. In the early part of the century they were difficult to obtain, as an anonymous letter among Sir Thomas More's papers shows. They were also expensive. In October

1538 Lady Lisle wanted her agent in London, John Husee, to acquire a play on an ecclesiastical subject. Husee reported that they were 'hard to com by' and they were expensive: 'they askethe aboue' 40*s*. for an 'Enterlude' (Brewer et al. 1965, *Addenda*/2, no. 1362; W. Nelson 1956, p. xxix; Westfall 1990: 113). And so, in addition to more actors, the developing theater industry also required more playwrights. Anonymous popular playwrights contributed most of the plays that have survived, but humanists like John Heywood and John Skelton, propagandists like John Bale, and in the 1560s university-educated men like Thomas Preston and John Pickering wrote plays for professional companies.

II

Because of its density of population London offered companies the possibility of large audiences. That, coupled with a developing professional infrastructure, made the environs of the city an attractive site for the development of a commercial theater industry. Evidence of playing spaces in and around the city survives from as early as the 1520s, when John Rastell built a stage at Finsbury Fields. The Almshouse at Rounceval had been used as a 'playhouse' in 1531. In 1557 a play was suppressed at the Boar's Head near Aldgate. John Brayne, James Burbage's brother-in-law, built a playhouse called the Red Lion about a mile east of the city in 1567 (Reed 1926: 230–3). Technical support, costumes, and properties were also readily available. From at least as early as the beginning of Henry VII's reign, master artists and artisans along with their journeymen and apprentices had been building pageants, painting cloths, and making properties for court revels every year. Costumes were available as well. John Rastell sued his associate Henry Walton for hiring out his costumes to players, among them to George Mayler, one of the King's players. Throughout the century London mercers like William Buttry, Christopher Milliner, and Thomas Gylles ran a business in part by supplying properties and material needed for costumes at court and at the London houses of the nobility (Feuillerat 1908: 409; Ingram 1992: 69–72). Over the dozen or so years between 1572 and 1583 several specific political and economic developments conspired to encourage the development of a commercial theater industry in and around London: playing spaces, some capable of accommodating large audiences, were opened or built, some playing companies were granted legal status, and opportunities surfaced for some of them to perform in the revels at court.

Between 1575 and 1578 nine commercial theater spaces were opened in the city and its environs. Herbert Berry has remarked that this was 'an astonishing event. Nothing of the kind had happened anywhere or would happen again in London for centuries' (Berry 2002: 148). The Victorian explanation for this phenomenon singles out the building of the Theatre as the culminating moment in a causally related series of events. The 1572 request by Leicester's players to be taken in to his household was connected to the patent issued to them in 1574 and to the restrictive measures taken against players by London authorities. These events are imagined to have led James Burbage to build the Theatre out of the jurisdiction of the city authorities in 1576. Versions of this explanation can be found repeated today, but many theater historians working on the subject find it as implausible as William Ingram does (Ingram 1992: 22; Bradbrook 1962: 55–6). The story has an appealing romantic plot in which the forces of imagination, protected and encouraged by Leicester and the court, resist philistine repression by the city fathers, but there is no documentary evidence to connect the supposed chain of events.

There are other explanations. One advanced in recent years argues that these same developments were used by the court to limit rather than to encourage the growth of the theater industry (McMillin and MacLean 1998: 1–36). The argument has principally to do with the career of the Queen's company and with events during the 1580s. While those subjects are beyond the scope of this essay, the argument is connected to events between 1572 and 1583. It is argued that Leicester's company dominated court revels during the 1570s and that the patent issued to them in 1574 giving them the right to perform in London and elsewhere as long as their plays were approved by the Master of the Revels gave them an opportunity to do what the later Queen's company were to do. They were to dominate the theater industry by forming an all-star troupe to perform plays with a moderate Protestant message on a large and lucrative touring schedule. All this came to an end in 1576 when James Burbage, who was too independent to be controlled for these purposes, built the Theatre in Shoreditch, but the project was revived in 1583 when Sir Francis Walsingham, backed by Leicester, created the new Queen's company.

This political explanation has advantages over the romantic story. It suggests a motive for the Council's manipulation of playing conditions in and around London, and it suggests that the 1574 patent to Leicester's players was connected to an attempt to center control of plays at court. But as with the romantic story, the main problem is the lack of documentary evidence. Leicester's company was no more of an all-star troupe than Lincoln's, Sussex's, or Warwick's. They all had celebrity players, and they all made fairly regular appearances in the revels between 1572 and 1583. There is no evidence to demonstrate that an attempt was made to control Burbage in his plan to build the Theatre in 1576 and none to show that the new Queen's company was created by Walsingham with Leicester's backing.[1] These notions depend on resurrecting Conyers Read's 1913 notion of faction, in which Leicester and Walsingham are imagined to be the dominant members of an aggressively Protestant party in the

[1] Tilney's note in the 1582–3 Revels account justifying reimbursement for horse hire when he attended at court to choose the new Queen's company of players (Feuillerat 1908: 359) has been variously interpreted. McMillin and MacLean have argued that Walsingham acted in concert with Leicester in forming this company, but there is no documentary evidence to support the idea (McMillin and MacLean 1998: 27; MacLean 2003: 261–2). The notion that Walsingham acted alone is traceable to Chambers 1923: ii. 104–5: 'the business was in the hands of Sir Francis Walsingham. Lord Chamberlain Sussex, to whom it would naturally have fallen, was ill. Walsingham's agency in the matter is confirmed in

Privy Council who behave as modern party politicians do (Read 1913). The concept of faction has been subjected to intense scrutiny by contemporary historians over the past twenty-five years. Read's notion of a Privy Council split by rivalry over foreign policy and religion in the 1570s and 1580s has been undermined by a number of leading historians. So has Sir John Neale's equation of faction with clientage networks advanced in the 1950s, which oversimplifies and trivializes political disputes. True factions of the kind found in the late Henrician or Edwardian courts scarcely existed until the 1590s, and every major historian now writing on the Tudor court agrees.[2]

There is an explanation for the opening of so many commercial theatrical venues in the mid-1570s, one that adopts a current understanding of faction at Elizabeth I's court and that fits the documentary evidence we have. The Council did regulate the theater industry to benefit the court, but in the process it created the conditions for a viable commercial theater in London. Plays had been performed in court revels from the beginning of Henry VII's reign, and from 1494 the royal playing company was used to emphasize the King's status as patron. The King's (and later the Queen's) players continued to be used in this way until Mary's reign, but they were not being maintained at full strength. In the 1540s there were eight royal players, but after 1552, when Henry Harryot disappears, and then in 1556, when John Birch, Richard Cooke, and Thomas Sowthey disappear, no new appointments were made to their ranks (Blackstone 2002: 206). Elizabeth reappointed the remaining four members of the company to their posts 'during pleasure'. The New Year's reward they were paid in the Chamber accounts for 1558–60 suggests that they may have performed, but the evidence is ambiguous (Chambers 1923: ii. 83–4). In any event the Queen's players

the account of the formation of the company inserted by Edmund Howes in the 1615 and 1631 editions of Stowe's Annales.' There are two important points to be made about this. First, Howes does not identify his source, and so his report cannot 'confirm' anything. Secondly, Howes does not say that Walsingham created the company; he says 'at the request of Sir Francis Walsingham, they were sworn the Queen's servants and were allowed wages and livery as grooms of the chamber'. Their appointments as players to this new company together with their wages and allowances would have to be drawn up—usually by the Principal Secretary—for the Council's approval before being sent to the Queen for signature. As Principal Secretary and hence chief coordinator of Council business, it is no more peculiar that Walsingham should send a letter to Tilney than it was for Richard Leys to petition Burghley, *c.*1570, still Principal Secretary, to have the Revels Office investigated (Feuillerat 1908: 407). Evidence documents Walsingham's involvement in helping Burghley and Sussex to solve Revels Office problems from as early as 1574. The only conclusion warranted by this document is that Walsingham was acting for a Council that had been working in concert for over a decade to reform the Queen's Revels.

[2] Conyers Read's notion of a Privy Council split by rivalry over foreign policy in the 1570s and 1580s has been undermined by Wernham (1980: 8–13), MacCaffrey (1981: 17–20, 444), S. Adams (1995: 20–45), and Hammer (1995: 66–8). Loades (1992: 163), Collinson (1994: 41), and P. Williams (1996: 242) agree. S. Adams (2002), the principal historian working on the Earl of Leicester's papers, argues that faction at Elizabeth's court has been overstressed and oversimplified. Theater historians have paid too much attention to infighting as the main principle of politics and too little to practical cooperation among leading members of government. Doran (1996: 216), for example, who is concerned to emphasize that personal antagonisms, political rivalries, and policy differences were as much a feature of Elizabeth's court as consensus between 1558 and 1581, nevertheless agrees that Adams is 'certainly correct in emphasizing that... In the field of policy making, Cecil, Leicester, and Walsingham frequently cooperated.'

never appeared at court again but continued to perform in the provinces until the early 1570s. When they died—John Brown and William Reading in 1563, Edmund Strodewicke in 1568, and John Smith in 1580—their vacancies were not filled. We can only speculate on the reasons that Elizabeth allowed the royal company to wither away, but whatever the reason, for the first time since 1494 it left the monarch without a playing company to emphasize her status and patronage in her revels (Chambers 1923: ii. 77–85).

Sir Thomas Benger, Elizabeth's Master of the Revels from 1560 to 1572, responded to this situation by dominating his revels with spectacular, visually oriented productions consisting of a number of masques and other entertainments and an average of about four plays each year between Christmas and Shrovetide (Streitberger 2004: 674–81). Thirty-four of these plays were performed by boy companies. Only eleven were performed by adult companies—four by Lord Rich's company, three by Sir Robert Dudley's, two by the Earl of Warwick's, and two by Sir Robert Lane's. After Benger's unexpected death in 1572 a remarkable change occurred. Adult companies, virtually ignored by Benger when they performed an average of less than once a year, now appeared an average of about six times a year until 1583. Such a radical change in the revels could not have occurred without the Queen's approval. Her personality dominated every aspect of her court, and to belabor a well-known point, she particularly enjoyed plays. By a wide margin she had more plays produced at her court that had any of her predecessors, and she was an apt interpreter of them, occasionally helping befuddled ambassadors with glosses and explanations (Hume 1892–8: i. 633; Guzmán de Silva to Philip II of Spain, April 1567). Part of the explanation for the new interest in adult companies may well be the broad appeal of their material. *Cambyses* is built on the model of a popular morality, but it contains historical characters, classical elements, and political advice. It was played in the countryside, in London, and at court probably by Sir Robert Dudley's company in 1560–1. *Horestes*, usually identified with the *Orestes* performed at court probably by Lord Rich's company in 1567–8, is also aimed at a broad audience, combining comic and classical material while making a political point.

Professional entertainers were also developing reputations for their innovations. In a letter of 1579, Gabriel Harvey compares Spenser's praise for his work to the commercial London theater:

> you haue preiudished my good name for ever in thrusting me thus on the stage to make tryall of my extemporall faculty, and to play Wylsons or Tarletons parte. I suppose thou wilt go nighe hande shortelye to send my lorde of Lycesters or my lorde of Warwickes, Vawsis, or my lord Ritches players, or sum other freshe startupp comedianies unto me for sum newe devised interlude, or sum malt-conceivid comedye fitt for the Theatre, or sum other painted stage whereat thou and thy lively copesmates in London maye lawghe ther mouthes and bellyes full for a pence or twoepence appeece. (Harvey 1884: 67; Chambers 1923: ii. 4–5)

While three of the four companies Harvey mentions had performed at court between 1560 and 1572, he had in mind mainly the companies that had reformed themselves in the 1570s around celebrity performers, such as Robert Wilson of Leicester's company and Richard Tarlton of Sussex's. Harvey singles out not only the inventive quality of plays but also the fame of such celebrities and the genuinely entertaining quality of their performances. There is yet more evidence to suggest that skill in performance was one of the attractions of the professional companies in the 1570s. The duties of the Revels officers included 'perusing' a number of plays each year in an effort to find suitable material for the Queen's Revels, and the evidence we have indicates that between 1567 and 1572 Sir Thomas Benger produced three plays by one of the companies Harvey mentions—Lord Rich's players—and two plays by an earlier version of Warwick's company—Sir Robert Lane's players (Feuillerat 1908: 145).

From Chamber account payments we know the name of three of Lane's players: Laurence Dutton, John Greaves, and Thomas Goughe. Laurence Dutton was one of the more famous players of the age. In the following year he appeared at court again, this time as a member of the Earl of Lincoln's company (Edward Fiennes, Lord Clinton, Lord Admiral, Earl of Lincoln from May 1572). Probably, as Chambers suggested, the entire company may have left Lane's to serve under Lincoln as a result of the statute of 1572 (Chambers 1923: ii. 97, iv. 269–71). Laurence appeared again at court in 1573–4, this time as a member of Lord Clinton's company. Probably, as Chambers also suggested, the company is identical to Lincoln's, transferred to his son after the Lord Admiral was created Earl of Lincoln. But it is certain that Laurence Dutton along with his brother John, another of the celebrity players of the age, joined the Earl of Warwick's company. After a decade of absence from the Queen's Revels, Warwick's players were now invited to perform at court on 14 February 1575 and again every year until 1 January 1580. The disappearance of Warwick's company from the revels after that is traceable to yet another move by the Dutton brothers, this time to the Earl of Oxford's company, for which they were ridiculed (Chambers 1923: ii. 98–9). The evidence indicates that sophistication in performance, represented here by the movement of two famous players, is one of the keys to invitations to perform at court. And this is borne out by evidence from the entire period in question. Leicester's players, who had not been invited to perform at court since 1563, gave seventeen performances in the revels between 1572 and 1583. During this period his company had at least three celebrity players—Robert Wilson, John Laneham, and William Johnson—all of whom were all drafted by Tilney into the new Queen's players in 1583. Sussex's company gave thirteen performances in the revels between 1572 and 1583. The company gave up John Adams, and the greatest celebrity player of the age, Richard Tarlton, 'the wonder of his time', to the new Queen's company in 1583. Lane's, Lincoln's, Clinton's, and Warwick's companies together gave a total of eighteen performances between 1572 and 1583, when they had among their members one or more of the Dutton brothers. Tilney drafted John into the new Queen's company and Laurence joined later (McMillin and MacLean 1998: 194–7). Virtually all of the companies performing at court between 1572 and 1583 were led by celebrity players.

Our only indication of the repertories of these companies comes from play titles in the Revels accounts. Titles cannot tell much of the story, but from them it appears that Leicester's company performed romances and moral plays, supplemented by pastorals and plots based on biblical subjects and folk characters. Sussex's and Warwick's companies appear to have performed classical subjects and romances supplemented with more common plots. Some scholars believe that politically charged plays formed much of the repertory of Leicester's company, based on the fact that he had presented such entertainments before the Queen on several occasions: the 1561 Inner Temple entertainments at court, the 1575 entertainments at Kenilworth Castle, and the 1578 Lady of May entertainment at Wansted (MacLean 2003: 266–71). While these were occasional entertainments, one of Leicester's players, Robert Wilson, is credited with writing at least three politically pointed plays. Then, too, it is speculated that the company may have performed plays by William Wager, as well as the moral interlude *New Custom*, which reflected Leicester's position on church vestments (Dutton 1991: 66–72; P. White 1993: 64–6, 180; 1994: 38–52). But politically pointed plays were not unique to Leicester's company. *Horestes*, a politically topical play in 1567–8, was probably performed by Lord Rich's players, and it is a fair guess that other companies performed such plays as well (Axton 1982: 29–33).

Of all the plays performed at court by adult companies between 1560 and 1583 only three texts survive, along with one Revels account detailed enough to guess at production values in another. As a result, our knowledge of the dramaturgy and of the production values in plays of this period is limited. We do know that leading players from Sussex's, Leicester's, and Warwick's companies were drafted into the new Queen's company in 1583, and based on a study of extant plays believed to have been part of their repertory, Scott McMillin and Sally-Beth MacLean have illuminated some aspects of their dramaturgy. The Queen's company's episodic plays were structured on an interplay between the stately and the comic, and their productions were characterized by certain distinctive features that contrasted markedly with the predominately blank-verse plays by Marlowe, Kyd, and Shakespeare that would replace them in the 1590s. Chief among these characteristics was a visual literalism in which important effects were organized around visual emblems, and by a tendency to make the same point several times over. The acting style was impersonation by stereotype, including the generous use of pantomime and pageantry together with improvised battle scenes without dialogue. And they employed a medley of verse styles, none of which were capable of expressing the pressure of realistic psychological experience (McMillin and MacLean 1998: 121–69).

Some of these same qualities are found in our two examples from the 1560s. *Cambyses* and *Horestes* use a variety of verse styles: rhyme royal, short-line couplets, sixteeners, and, for the higher-class characters, fourteeners which are capable of replicating in two lines the meter of a ballad stanza. While the verse and dialogue of *Cambyses* was thought ludicrous enough by the 1590s for Shakespeare to parody it both in *A Midsummer Night's Dream* and in *1 Henry IV*, in the 1560s its style was a refreshing departure from the earlier moralities. Elizabethans were satisfied not only to hear plays in fourteeners, but also to read serious poetry in the meter, including versified psalms. The subtitle of *Cambyses*, 'A lamentable tragedy, mixed full of pleasant mirth, containing the life of Cambyses, King of Persia... his one good deed of execution, after that many wicked deeds and tyrannous murders... [and]

his odious death by God's justice', illustrates the power of the dramatic forms that were being pioneered in the professional theater at this time. The mixture of comedy and tragedy, the inner development suggested in the main character, his villainy, and its containment by providential justice anticipate some of the greatest Elizabethan plays of the late century. As in *Horestes*, the conventions of the early Tudor morality are thoroughly mixed with those of the developing Elizabethan history play. Historical characters interact with personified abstractions and with malevolent and amusing vices. The historical scenes vie for time with the comic ones where the vices interact with common soldiers and clownish country folk. In *Cambyses* classical characters like Venus and Cupid also make an appearance. The assumption behind this inspired lunacy is that plays are capable of representing reality in complex ways. The anachronisms insist on the synchronicity and contemporaneity of history (Fraser and Rabkin 1976: 59–60). And history's relevance to contemporary life, strongly implied in *Horestes*, is made explicit in the epilogue to *Cambyses*, where it is hoped that Elizabeth I and her Council will 'practice justice', 'maintain God's word', and correct abuses. A number of the titles of the plays performed at court during the 1570s begin with the phrase 'The History of...', which suggests that the dramaturgy of these lost plays may have been similar in some respects to that of *Cambyses* and *Horestes* and to the plays of the new Queen's company. But, as Roslyn L. Knutson points out, since most of the play titles and even more of the texts owned by the companies have not survived, it is 'difficult to identify early modern English playing companies by their dramaturgy' (Knutson 2002: 180). We simply do not have enough evidence to answer interesting questions: How did the Dutton brothers bring to life a play like 'The Irish Knight' (1577)? What qualities led the Clerk of the Revels to describe Wilson's, Johnson's, and Laneham's work in 'A Greek Maid' (1579) as 'a Pastoral or History'? How did the Queen and her court respond to the great Richard Tarlton's performance in 'The History of Murderous Michael' (1579)?

The information we have about two other plays provides some insight into production values. *The Rare Triumphs of Love and Fortune* performed before Elizabeth I in 1582 by Derby's company exhibits the influence of Roman comedy rather than the morality. There is no vice character, but there is a parasite, and the verse forms, a mixture of iambic pentameter and fourteeners in blank verse and rhymed couplets, are much more controlled and sophisticated than those of *Cambyses* and *Horestes*.

Spectacle is important as well. The Revels Office built two 'houses' (timber-framed structures covered with canvas and painted) of a city and a battlement for the scenery of this production, which presumably complemented its dual plotting. The play delivers on the promise of its title page to provide 'manye fine Conceites with great delight'. There are a number of masque-like shows that produce speaking pictures of historical and mythological characters: Troilus and Cressida, Alexander, Dido, Pompey and Caesar, and Hero and Leander. Music accompanies Venus' triumph at the end of the third act, and 'Trumpets, Drummes. Cornets and Gunnes' accompany Fortune's triumph at the end of the fourth. The spectacle required in *The Knight of the Burning Rock*, performed by Warwick's company in 1579, was much more elaborate. The Revels accounts make clear that the main scenic property was a gigantic wooden-framed device covered with canvas and painted to resemble a rock. It contained room enough inside for stage hands to operate an elevating system that could rise through a trap door in the rock and also to produce the flames and smoke that belched from its crevices. The story had to do with enchantment, and the rock was a hellish prison. Eventually the forces in control of it were defeated by the powers of good who employed siege ladders to scale it. Since the rock was so large and the plot required so many extras for the siege, the action must have been performed on the hall floor rather than on a stage. It is clear from the evidence that staging at court could employ large scenic properties, and on occasion spectacular sets. But it is difficult to generalize the evidence to other performances because this play was produced when the Duke of Anjou's agent, Jean de Simier, was at court to propose a marriage alliance with Elizabeth. The Queen was anxious to impress her French guests, and spent more money for entertainment in this year than she had since 1575. Nevertheless, the productions of these two plays raise important questions: were scenic 'houses' and grand spectacles also used in the commercial theater? While we cannot be sure, it seems unlikely given the fact that playing companies had to transport their properties while touring the countryside. But, as John Astington has pointed out, there are likely to have been degrees of variation in both court and commercial productions (Astington 1999*a*: 102–3).

III

While the Queen's taste, the developing sophistication of plays, and the reputations of celebrity performers may all have been contributing factors, the radical change in the Queen's Revels beginning in 1572 was triggered by external events: by a change in key personnel in her government and by a crisis in the Revels Office. William, Lord Howard of Effingham, Lord Chamberlain since Mary's reign, was not exercising his duties in the spring of 1572 and he died the following January. William Paulet, Marquess of Winchester, the Lord Treasurer, who had been royal counselor to four monarchs, had died in March 1572. Sir William Cecil was created Lord Burghley and made Lord Treasurer, and Thomas Radcliffe, third Earl of Sussex, was made Lord Chamberlain. With these two key appointments the personality of the Queen's government changed. In contrast to their predecessors, Sussex and Burghley were both aggressive managers. They were busy men, involved in virtually every issue facing the government during their tenures of office. Nevertheless, documentary evidence clearly demonstrates that they were personally involved in an effort that stretched over a period of about a dozen years to remodel the Revels Office. There is no evidence that they worked from an approved plan. Rather, they took a hands-on approach, doing research and experimenting with promising ideas before settling on a course by about 1578–9, but reforms continued to be made afterwards. They were aided in this project by the regulatory actions of the Privy Council, of which they were principal members.

Government regulation dates from the early Tudor period, when players were not considered to be part of a profession. Their activities were regulated by their patrons, and this system continued to be a means of controlling their behavior and of restricting their numbers throughout the period. But certain political events of the early to mid-sixteenth century encouraged the Crown to take special precautions against seditious matter in plays and elsewhere. These events included the dissemination of Lutheran tracts during the 1520s, Henry VIII's divorce, his encouragement of the Reformation in the late 1530s, his reversal of policy by discouraging it in the early 1540s, and the accession of the Protestant Edward VI in 1547, followed by his Catholic sister Mary in 1553, and then by her Protestant sister Elizabeth I in 1558. The regulations the Crown imposed on the drama and the injunctions it issued against players were linked to censorship of the press and had roots in ecclesiastical laws against teaching heretical doctrine and in civil laws against treason. Since they spoke in public, players fell under the laws and regulations governing censorship, and since they moved about the countryside they fell under the statutes concerning vagabonds and beggars. Enforcement fell short of intention, and abuses by players continued to be of concern to all the Tudor monarchs. As a measure of his contempt for them, Henry VIII considered using common players as galley slaves in his 1542–4 French campaign (Brewer et al. 1965: xx/1, no. 812; Streitberger 1994: 156). Edward VI and Mary insisted on their own signatures on play licenses.

Elizabeth I's government attempted to address the problems caused by players principally through the patronage system. The Proclamation of 16 May 1559 distinguished between common players performing interludes in English on the one hand and players within patronized companies on the other (Chambers 1923: iv. 263–4). Performances by common players were to be licensed by mayors or justices, and any violation of decorum was to be punished by local peace officers. The behavior of household companies, on the other hand, was to be supervised by their patrons. As a result, household companies were driven closer to their patrons and to become dependent on their licenses to travel and perform while common players were marginalized, driven into the category of borderline criminals. Patrons and magistrates were also directed in the proclamation to suppress any play that treated subjects relating to religion or government. However, an exception was made for what might be shown before 'grave and discrete persons' (Chambers 1923: iv. 267). This was an important clause, for, as Richard Dutton points out, the implication that these matters might be put on stage in privileged contexts, such as in the houses of the nobility or at court, ultimately had the effect of generalizing the standard (Dutton 2000: 6).

Elizabeth's use of patronage to control players was furthered by the Proclamation of 3 January 1572 ordering the enforcement of the statute against unlawful retainers, the latest of many similar proclamations dating back to Henry VI's reign which, among other things, restricted patronage of playing companies to those at the rank of baron and above. Then, on 29 June 1572, a parliamentary Act against rogues, vagabonds, and sturdy beggars was passed, which included 'Common players in interludes' among these undesirable groups (Chambers 1923: iv. 269–71). By 1572 Elizabeth's government had established several key positions regarding players. Companies needed a license to travel and permission to perform, and there was a policy prohibiting the discussion of religion and government on stage. However, the exceptions made for plays performed before sophisticated audiences made the policy largely ineffective. The Privy Council's intention in 1574 to use the Master of the Revels to monitor the content of plays was formalized in 1581, in the second part of a commission issued to Edmond Tilney, preferred to his 1579 patent as Master by one of his cousins, Charles, Lord Howard of Effingham, later Lord Chamberlain, Lord Admiral, and Earl of Nottingham (Streitberger 1978: 20; Feuillerat 1908: 51–2). Tilney was charged to examine all plays offered for performance. His exercise of this commission developed by degrees into a full-blown system of government censorship (Dutton 2000). The Council was not only concerned to assert control over the content of plays, it was also interested in regulating the conditions of playing in London to benefit the Queen's revels. It suppressed plays on five occasions between 1574 and 1581, principally because of public health concerns (Chambers 1923: iv. 261–4; Wickham 1959–81: ii/1. 327–9). During this same period it also insisted on allowing certain playing companies to perform in order to develop material and polish performance skills for the revels. Such government regulation in the climate of nascent capitalism was part of the price of doing business. Then, too, service to the monarch could be thought of in philosophical or religious terms. When the anonymous writer of a *c.*1573 memorandum on the Revels Office explained how to produce revels successfully, he presented the need for cooperating artists to suppress their individual egos as something close to a spiritual exercise, for in the process 'every man may learn somewhat the more what service meaneth'. Burghley thought of it specifically in religious terms (Feuillerat 1908: 11–2; Hammer 1999: 333). For those less spiritually oriented, the first part of the 1581 commission issued to Tilney gave him the power to imprison for indefinite periods anyone who refused to cooperate in producing the Queen's Revels (Feuillerat 1908: 52).

When Sir Thomas Benger died unexpectedly by early July 1572, there were several good reasons not to appoint a new Master of the Revels. Significant complaints had been lodged with the Council about Benger's mismanagement of the Revels Office, and costs had risen (Feuillerat 1908: 407, 409). The Queen paid a bill of over £1,500 for the 1571–2 season, and when she was asked to pay an almost identical sum for the 1572–3 she refused. The bill remained unpaid for over two years while her counselors attempted to find a solution (Feuillerat 1908: 412, 474). Further, the Revels Office had been designed by Henry VIII for a household structured very differently from Elizabeth's. The dysfunctional nature of the Office was apparent from early in Mary's reign, which Elizabeth had unsuccessfully attempted to fix in 1560. As early as 1572 Burghley began soliciting memorandums from knowledgeable individuals, which provided the basis for many of the changes later introduced into the Revels

Office (Feuillerat 1908: 5–17). Burghley personally overlooked finances and Sussex personally took charge of the Revels Office, appointing the Clerk of the Revels and Tents, Thomas Blagrave, 'acting Master' under his own letter of authority (Feuillerat 1908: 191, 225). Sussex was the first Lord Chamberlain ever to exercise this kind of supervision in the Revels Office, and there is much evidence of his personal attention to details between 1573 and 1578 (Feuillerat 1908: 191–312). Everything that Blagrave did—the companies he invited to court, the changes he made to their plays, his designs for productions—was scrutinized and approved by Sussex. This arrangement for producing revels is identical to that at Henry VIII's court between 1510 and 1542, when the Master of the Revels was a high-ranking courtier on personal terms with the sovereign who also held a position on the Privy Council (Streitberger 1994: 70–4). Sussex was in fact functioning as Master of the Revels, and Blagrave, no matter what informal title Sussex gave him, was his assistant. Sussex was often in ill health and had help from time to time in discharging his duties. His cousin Charles, Lord Howard of Effingham, certainly helped to produce revels in 1574–5, very probably in 1576–7 and 1577–8 when his playing company performed at court, and possibly on other occasions. Their cousin Henry Carey, Lord Hundson, Lord Chamberlain in 1585, also helped with the revels in 1582, when his playing company performed at court (Chambers 1907: 31–9).

The idea that the Lord Chamberlain ordinarily supervised the Revels Office derives from E. K. Chambers, who thought of the royal household as a 'tripartite' organization superintended by three principal officers. The collection of offices and duties that constituted the Chamber, for example, was imagined to be a hierarchical 'department' headed by the Lord Chamberlain. All offices of the household, even those not physically located inside the palace and which were separately funded, were required to conform to this scheme. To make it work Chambers borrowed an idea from the writer of the *Liber Niger* (1478), who describes the Great Wardrobe as an office 'outward of the Chamber', and by analogy Chambers brings other offices—the Revels, the Tents, the Works, the Toils—under the authority of the Lord Chamberlain (Chambers 1923: i. 84–5). All subsequent studies in theater history have adopted as fundamental assumptions the notion of a royal household organized along modern bureaucratic lines with a clear chain of command, but no historian writing on the household over the past twenty-five years comes to these conclusions.[3]

The system of government by Privy Chamber that developed in the early Tudor period made the King's Gentlemen of the Privy Chamber among the most powerful and influential individuals at court. Sir Thomas Cawarden, appointed first Master of the Revels by patent in 1545, was one of these Gentlemen. He was not a 'deputy' of the Lord Chamberlain. That office, which went unfilled between 1541 and

[3] Chambers's (1923: i. 27–105) description of the institutions of the royal household stood as the standard work on that subject until the 1980s, when revisionist studies on the structure of the earlier Tudor household were published by D. Starkey, J. A. Murphey, and, most importantly for our purposes, on Elizabeth I's Privy Chamber, by P. Wright (1987). Based on this work, Loades (1992) undertook a new description of the royal household specifically because Chambers does not provide students, particularly those interested in politics, with a manageable guide.

1543, was politically useless in 1545, and there was even talk of dropping it altogether. But Mary's accession brought crashing down the whole Privy Chamber edifice that had dominated the court for forty years. The interesting story of the Chamber from 1553 throughout the rest of the century is still to be written, but one of its main subjects would be the Chamberlain's attempt, along with other officers such as the Principal Secretary, to reacquire their old authorities and responsibilities lost to the Gentlemen of the Privy Chamber. Sussex and Burghley were most aggressive in steadily trying to reclaim these authorities, but the Chamber over which Sussex presided was not an 'office' or 'department' in the modern bureaucratic sense. It was a patchwork affair that had neither a clear organization nor a chain of command. There is no evidence that the Lord Chamberlain exercised any control in the day-to-day running of the Privy Chamber, or that he had any control over its staff (P. Wright 1987; Loades 1992: 42, 44–59). Neither did he exercise authority over the Master of the Revels until Sussex appointed Blagrave to work as his assistant. During the 1570s Sussex and Burghley, backed by the Council, altered the structure and function of the Revels Office. Tilney's appointment in 1579 was a compromise between the old idea of a Master on personal terms with the sovereign who devised all entertainments for the court, and the new idea of a Master developed under the leadership of Sussex and Burghley between 1572 and 1578. This new idea of a Master was to be the Crown's agent in regulating the commercial theater, and from this source he was to supply most of the shows for the Queen's revels. Such 'outsourcing' of important work was not unique. The Council approved a contract, or 'bargain', in 1579, renewed in 1584, with John Hawkins for the routine maintenance of the Queen's warships, and some of the same individuals involved in remodeling the Revels Office—Lincoln, Howard, and Burghley—were key figures in this arrangement. The outsourcing of maintenance to Hawkins saved the Crown approximately £2,000 a year, and continued until 1587, when Hawkins resigned the contract because he could no longer profit from it (Hammer 2003: 96). The outsourcing of creative and production work in the Revels Office also produced a significant savings for the Crown. The revels between 1576 and 1589 averaged between £1,000 and £1,250 a year less than they had between 1571 and 1573.

The fact that part of Tilney's income derived from his licensing activities must have been an incentive to do a thorough job in regulating the commercial theater. But the complicated new arrangement required close consultation and cooperation with the Council. In 1581 Tilney went to court to 'satisfy' Burghley, Sussex, and the Queen about his plans for the Office, and then in 1583 Walsingham asked Tilney to choose the players for the new Queen's company. Tilney was one of the Queen's cousins, a member of one of the oldest families in the country with very powerful connections in upper levels of government and society. He cooperated, of course, but he was not a 'functionary' in the Lord Chamberlain's office, nor was he a 'deputy'. These terms are not only too crude and too modern to do justice to the dynamic of the relationships here, but they fail to account for the documentary evidence about his independence. Sometime during the 1590s Tilney, who was at odds with one of the lord chamberlains about an uncertain contentious issue, characterized the letters he had received from him as arrogant.[4]

No doubt the sudden increase in the number of performances at court by adult companies in 1572–3 was driven initially by expedience. There was no Master of the Revels to devise new entertainments, and five members of the Council were patrons of playing companies. All three adult companies chosen to perform in the revels in this year were patronized by the counselors Sussex, Leicester, and Lincoln. Costs of productions continued to be a problem, but by 1576–7, the same year in which Burghley instituted yet another economy campaign, production costs in the revels were radically reduced (S. Adams 2002: 26; Loades 1992: 211–12). One reason for the change was a reduction in the number of masques produced each year, from six in 1571–2 to one beginning from 1576–7. This produced a change in the revels by 1579 so remarkable that Chambers wondered 'whether the invention of Court poets had failed, or whether for some other reason Elizabeth had become discontent with masks' (Chambers 1923: i. 167). The evidence suggests that the Council had adopted one of the key recommendations of the *c.*1573 memorandums, namely that the Queen distinguish between ordinary and extraordinary entertainments in her revels. In effect, the idea was to schedule expensive masques only when needed for diplomatic or other purposes and to schedule less expensive entertainments such as plays on ordinary occasions.

It would not take financial brilliance to realize that masques, with their elaborate custom-made costumes, properties, and scenery, were more expensive to produce than plays, but it would take some ingenuity to imagine that if production costs could be transferred to playing companies invited to court the entire structure and function of the Revels Office might change (Streitberger 1978: 23). And that is exactly what happened. Evidence for this is found in the accounts of the Treasurer of the Chamber, who paid rewards to companies who performed at court. The ordinary reward for a performance at court was 10 marks (£6 13*s.* 4*d.*), but by 1575–6 £10 became the standard reward. In the interim the Treasurer records reasons for the increase, which were associated with the costs of transporting themselves and their 'furniture' to court (Cook and Wilson 1961: 7–11). The reduction in the cost of revels was achieved by producing fewer masques and by transferring material and labor costs of play productions to the companies. In 1573–4 all of the plays and masques produced by the Revels Office were 'furnished', but in the 1578–9 account a careful distinction is made among productions furnished with 'many' things and some with 'sundry' things (Feuillerat 1908: 193, 286). Some entertainments were still mounted on a spectacular scale, like *The Knight in the Burning Rock* in 1579, but the trend toward transferring production costs continued, and eventually, between 1589 and 1593, the Revels Office was placed on a set budget for ordinary charges so small that it

[4] See Streitberger (1976) for a facsimile and transcription of Tilney's 25 January (n.d.) letter to Sir William More, and, on dating the letter, see Streitberger (2008). The Lord Chamberlain Tilney refers to is probably Sir William Brooke, Lord Cobham, but there is no documentary evidence to show that the contentious issue was Shakespeare's *1 Henry IV.* See also P. White (2002).

could not have borne production costs (Chambers 1923: i. 93, 224–5). This shift had far-reaching consequences for the development of the drama, for practices in the commercial theater where elaborate scenery and spectacular visual effects were more difficult to mount must have increasingly influenced productions at court (Astington 1999*a*: 102–3). Properties and scenic houses continued to be used in court productions, but after 1578–9 gone from the Revels accounts are the long lists of frames, canvas, and material to construct the elaborate scenic structures that had characterized Benger's productions, along with the material and labor to fabricate all of the costumes.

While there is no documentary evidence to connect reforms in the Revels Office directly to the opening of commercial theaters, the circumstantial evidence is overwhelming. The opening of so many venues for public performance between 1575 and 1578 by men who were routinely involved in the revels at just the time Sussex and Burghley were reforming the Revels Office is too striking to be coincidental. Sebastian Westcott, Master of the Children Choristers of Paul's, which performed eleven plays in the revels between 1572 and 1583, opened a commercial venue in the cathedral almonry in London in 1575. Richard Farrant, Deputy Master of the Children of the Chapel and Master of the Children of Windsor Chapel, which performed thirteen plays in the revels during this same period, opened a commercial venue in Blackfriars by 1577. James Burbage, a member of Leicester's company, which performed seventeen plays in the revels during this period, opened the most famous of the commercial theaters in Shoreditch in 1576. Jerome Savage, a member of Warwick's company, which performed thirteen plays in the revels during this period, opened a commercial theater in Newington by 1577. It has long been suspected that Sussex's company, which performed thirteen plays in the revels during this period, used the Curtain in Shoreditch as a commercial venue after 1577 (Chambers 1923: ii. 402). Four inns located within the city itself: the Bel Savage (1575), the Bull (1577), the Bell (1577), and the Cross Keys (1578), also hosted companies performing in the Queen's revels. The appearance of so many commercial venues was exactly what was needed to further the changes initiated by Sussex and continued by Tilney. It created a lively commercial environment in which celebrity entertainers and their companies could develop appropriately sophisticated material; it provided a means of generating income for the companies to offset costs associated with their productions; and it benefited the court, for the most fashionable entertainments in the revels were now the least expensive.

Between 1572 and 1583 there were at least thirty-five companies with known patrons, but the adult companies that offered all fifty-six plays in the revels during this period were patronized by only ten of them, all members of the Queen's family or close personal friends. Sussex, Howard, Hunsdon, and Derby (Strange) were the Queen's cousins—grandchildren or great-grandchildren of Thomas, second Duke of Norfolk, by his two wives, Elizabeth and her cousin Agnes Tilney. Lincoln (Clinton) was stepfather to Elizabeth's half-brother Henry Fitzroy (d. 1536). Leicester was the Queen's favorite, and his brother Warwick was a lifelong personal friend. Furthermore, six of the ten patrons were members of the Privy Council: Lincoln (from 1558),

Leicester (from 1562), Sussex (from 1570), Warwick (from 1573), Hunsdon (from 1577), and Howard (from 1584). Their signatures on Council letters to local authorities indicate that they were in concert in regulating playing conditions to favor their companies so that they could entertain the Queen. There is no evidence that they competed with one another for a larger share of performances at court. In fact the evidence indicates that they were principally interested in quality (Feuillerat 1908: 238; Haigh 1998: 71–2, 85–6; S. Adams 2002: 30).

The creation of the new Queen's company in 1583 was an outgrowth of developments in the revels over the course of more than a decade of reforms initiated by Sussex and Burghley, assisted by Howard and Hunsdon, and furthered by Tilney. The key aesthetic ingredient sought in the revels between 1572 and 1583 was the talent of celebrity players, but these players were disbursed among several leading companies. Combining them into one company patronized by the Queen promised to make Tilney's and the Council's job of regulating the commercial theater industry a bit easier. For the Council would continue to do just that to ensure that this new company could prepare for their appearances at court, where Tilney used them to dominate his revels schedule throughout the decade. Not only would this outsourcing arrangement continue to stabilize costs in the Revels Office; it would lead to the development of a system of government censorship in the commercial theater industry.

CHAPTER 2

ADULT PLAYING COMPANIES 1583–1593

SALLY-BETH MACLEAN

Two pivotal events bookend the decade 1583–93 in Elizabethan theater history. In March 1582/3 the careers of several leading acting companies were disrupted by the formation of a large new company with a formidable list of principal players. No actor would have resisted the casting call by Edmond Tilney, Master of the Revels, acting under the direction of Sir Francis Walsingham, Principal Secretary to Queen Elizabeth. And none of the patrons of these acting companies would have questioned the departure of their players to join the new Queen's Men, a company that was to dominate the court's annual festive revels as well as the provincial performance calendar across the country for most of the following decade. Never until this point had an acting company of this size and depth of talent been assembled.

We know the origins of some but not all of the twelve actors, and those we do know something about were undoubtedly chosen for their star power. Robert Wilson, John Laneham, and William Johnson were plucked from Leicester's Men; John Adams and Richard Tarlton, 'the wonder of his time' according to a contemporary annal, from Sussex's; and John Dutton from Oxford's (Stow 1615: 697). The rest—John Bentley, Lionel Cooke, John Garland, Tobias Mils, John Singer, and John Towne—were culled from the same or other companies whose patrons we can only guess at. Evidence of their individual fame endured beyond their heyday, as Thomas Heywood's tribute in 1612 suggests:

to do some right to our English Actors, as Knell, Bentley, Mils, Wilson, Crosse, Lanam, and others: these, since I neuer saw them, as being before my time, I cannot (as an eye-witnesse of their desert) giue them that applause, which no doubt, they worthily merit, yet by the report of many iuditial auditors, their performance of many parts haue been so absolute, that it were a kinde of sinne to drowne their worths in Lethe . . . Heere I must needs remember Tarleton, in his time gratious with the Queene his soueraigne, and in the peoples generall applause. (Heywood 1612, E2^{v})

Ten years later there were other large companies in serious competition with the Queen's Men, but their participation in the burgeoning commercial theater in London suffered a major disruption when a serious epidemic of the bubonic plague in the city led to the extended closure of playhouses. On 23 June 1592 the Privy Council had banned playing in and about London until 29 September because of apprentice riots in Southwark, but the spread of disease later in the same year necessitated further restrictions. Orders were issued by the Privy Council on 28 January 1592/3 to ban performances in the city and suburbs through the rest of the year, with the exception of a brief period between 29 December 1592 and 1 February 1592/3 (Dasent et al. 1890–1964: xxii. 549–50, xxiv. 31–2). The resulting upheaval in evolving performance practices for the most successful companies led to notable changes in 1594 that will be the subject of the chapter following.

Business Practices

Available evidence suggests that 1583–93 was a period of transition in company practices. The previous decade had been marked by several strategic steps taken by central authorities, including the first crown patent to an acting company, Leicester's Men, which received a license in 1574 to perform throughout the kingdom, and the 1581 special commission granted to Tilney, as Master of the Revels, to license all plays and playing places, with the power to send the uncooperative to prison (Dutton 1991: 47–9). The regulation of theater in the period will be treated elsewhere but the growing role of government censorship cannot have been far from the minds of those in the business.

Our sources of information for Elizabethan professional acting companies are varied and imperfect. Before 1592 we must rely primarily on royal household records such as treasurer of the Chamber and Revels accounts for performances at court; London and provincial civic orders regulating performance; civil and ecclesiastical court records documenting the sometimes turbulent relations of players with local authorities; and accounts of performance payments by towns and private households across the country. Provincial records being systematically surveyed for the Records of Early English Drama series have identified at least thirty-eight royal, noble, and gentry patrons with acting companies between 1573 and 1583. How many of these played in the inns or new purpose-built theaters in London cannot be easily traced, but Revels accounts reveal that only ten of these companies were privileged to perform at court. Predictably, as has been pointed out above, their patrons were all members of the Queen's extended family or close personal network, and the majority belonged to the Privy Council.

After the formation of the Queen's Men, a very different system of selection for performances at court was instituted and the number of acting companies invited declined markedly. Between 1583 and 1591 the Queen's Men dominated the court calendar, although boys' companies continued to find royal favor until 1590 (Astington 1999*a*: 231–3). The Admiral's Men was the only other adult acting company to appear more than once, perhaps partly because their rising star, Edward Alleyn, distinguished them from the rest. Tilney's hijacking of star actors from the leading companies of the day seems to have had an impact beyond the court. Leicester's Men, one of the most active troupes at court and in the country before 1583, disappears from the records until 1585, when a second troupe was likely re-formed in time to accompany their patron, as part of a lavish entourage, to the Low Countries, where he had been appointed governor-general (MacLean 2002: 262–5). Sussex's troupe, which lost its pre-eminent clown, Tarlton, also lost its patron, when the ailing Thomas Radcliffe, Lord Chamberlain of the household, died in June the same year. The Earl of Derby seems to have lost his appetite for patronizing players altogether at this time, giving us grounds to speculate that his company too had furnished actors for the Queen's Men. Certainly Tilney would have had ample opportunity to observe the skills of Derby's Men during several court appearances between 1578 and 1583. All in all, we can count fewer than twenty active adult troupes in the provincial records in 1583–4, although the number does increase subsequently as new companies formed.

The Queen's Men, initially disruptive to the competition and dominant for almost a decade, can furnish a relatively well-documented example of successful company practices in the 1580s. Deliberately assembled to entertain their patron at Christmas and Shrovetide, and licensed to tour the kingdom wearing the royal livery, the twelve principals consistently enjoyed the highest level of reward in recognition of the Queen's authority as well as, perhaps, their own talents. Following a long-established tradition, they made annual touring in the provinces a regular part of their performance calendar (see Map 2.1), not only to find new audiences and fill the company purse, but also, as some have argued, to perform plays informed by moderate Protestant ideology in the service of the Crown's interests during an unstable political era (McMillin and MacLean 1998: 18–36). The extent of provincial records uncovered in recent years has laid to rest old prejudices about actors being driven reluctantly onto dusty country roads to face uncouth and ill-paying audiences in open marketplaces and crowded inn-yards. Yet for companies like the Queen's Men, the city inns and suburban playhouses were important venues as well, even though they seem not to have had a fixed address in London—individual playhouse affiliations may only have developed in the 1590s. In the fall of 1583 the company followed a practice set by other leading troupes in the 1570s, moving into the city in the late autumn to 'exercise their playing' at two local inns before performances at court (McMillin and MacLean 1998: 45–6). The special license to the Queen's Men exclusively for these performances

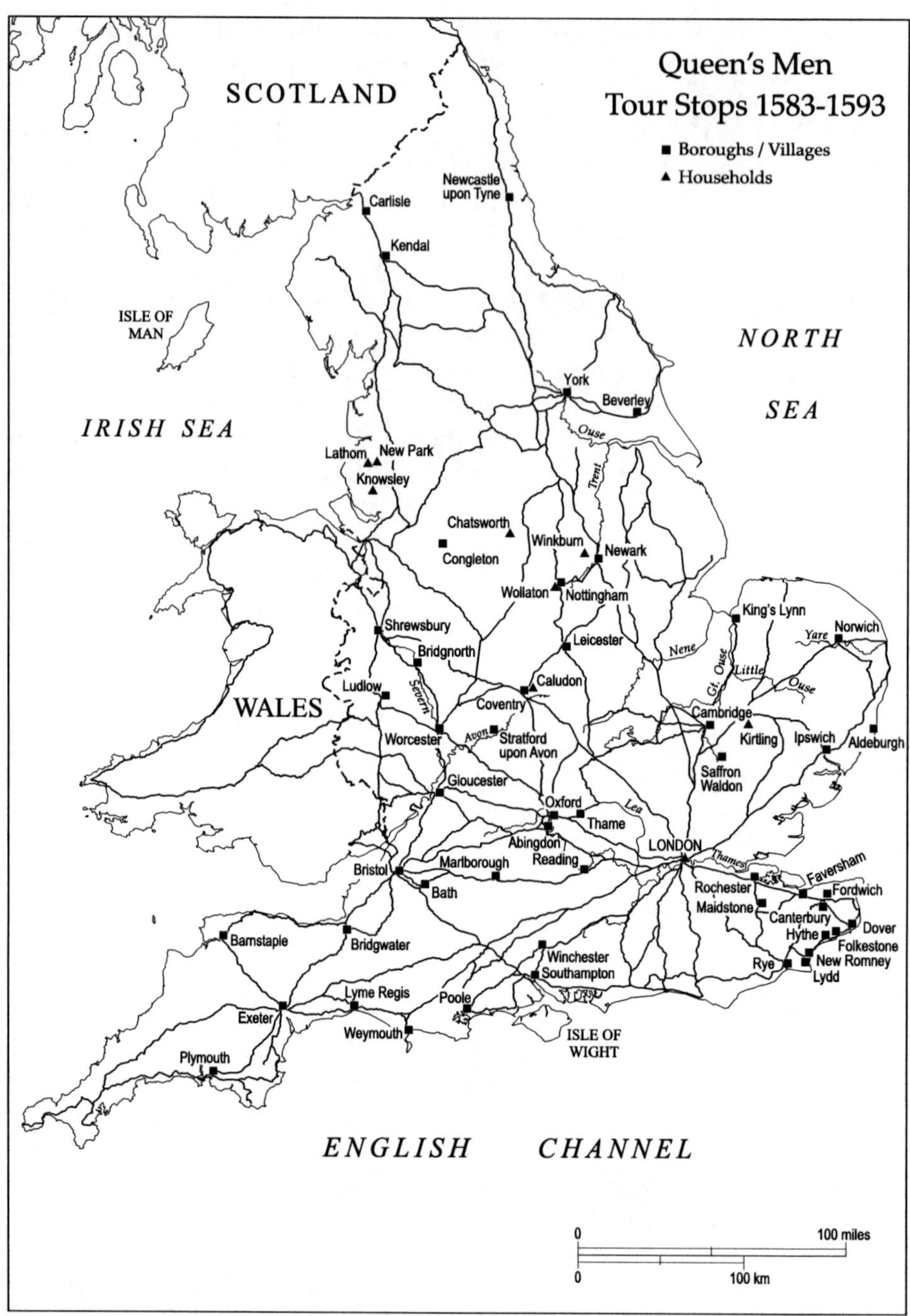

Map 2.1 Queen's Men tour stops 1583–1593.

was granted by the city under pressure from the Privy Council, an indication not only of their privileged status but also of the attempt to reduce the activities of other companies. We can be amused by an exasperated complaint from the Corporation of London, facing a petition for renewal of the license the next year, recalling that 'all the places of playeing were filled with men calling themselues the Quenes players' (Chambers and Greg 1908: 172). Actors are a resourceful, creative lot, not easily controlled by authorities.

Profits, therefore, came from a variety of sources and we are probably safe to assume that, as partners, players would have shared such profits and most, if not all, of their costs. For a leading company such as the Queen's Men, there was: the standard reward to be had for a headlining performance at court, typically £10; the regulated reward allocated by civic authorities for the requisite performance before the mayor and council in provincial towns, sometimes augmented by a 'gathering' at the door of the town hall; the often more generous payments, including free bed and board, from noble and gentry hosts in private residences across the country; and the gate taken from performances at city inns and playhouses, provincial inns, and other venues such as church houses, though rental fees or some share of the proceeds must have been required at many if not all such locations, even if the paper trail has been lost. In addition, there was the possibility of bonus payments from the more engaged patrons or their friends, gifts such as those made by the Earl of Leicester to Tarlton and the Queen's Men during their early years and recorded in his surviving household accounts for 1584–6 (MacLean 2002: 262).

We might consider the Queen's Men as exemplifying the peak of a business model that would be eclipsed, though no one in 1583 would have guessed quite how soon. Their market was broader than most because of their license to tour countrywide and the special consideration of their interests in London and at court by the Privy Council and the Master of the Revels which gave them opportunities to perform for larger audiences. Theirs was a mobile existence with twin motives: to promote their patron's name and influence and to raise profit shares. Part of the enterprise depended on star power. Tarlton in particular must have been a draw for audiences. Famous for his 'wondrous plentifull pleasant extemporall wit', he could sing, improvise, jig, wield a weapon with skill—he was elected a Master of Fence in 1587—and even wrote a popular comedy, *The Seven Deadly Sins*, for the company (Stow 1615: 697). He would have been a tough act to follow when he died in September 1588, probably while other members of the company were on the road. Perhaps it was not a coincidence that during this same year the Queen's Men added a different type of headline attraction to their performances. Touring records across the country show that by August, if not before, an acrobatic act had been incorporated that drew special notice. And this was no minor group of tumblers but the troupe led by a recognized talent in his own right, featured at court year after year: John Symons, formerly of Lord Strange's Men and then briefly under the patronage of the Earl of Oxford (Cook and Wilson 1961: 21–4). By 1588 Symons was a Queen's man too, touring with his tumblers in partnership with the players. The next year a similar strategy was employed, this time with a Turkish rope-dancer, another type of sensational act that seems to have had wide appeal (McMillin and MacLean 1998: 63, 178–80).

Companies of the period did combine from time to time with each other in the late sixteenth century, perhaps in order to mount plays that required larger casts or specialized talent, such as musicians or Symons's acrobats. In 1591, for example, the Children of the Chapel toured with one branch of the Queen's Men in the south and midlands, while another branch led by John Laneham combined with Sussex's Men (McMillin and MacLean 1998: 62, 181–2). There seems to have been more permeability in the membership of these acting troupes than is often recognized.

One of the more multi-talented Queen's Men, the playwright and 'quicke delicate refined extemporall witte' Robert Wilson, rejoined Leicester's Men for their innovative tour of the Low Countries in 1585–6, as did Robert Browne, a member of Worcester's troupe (Stow 1615: 697; MacLean 2002: 264). More famously, Edward Alleyn, keeping his identity as an Admiral's man, joined forces with Strange's Men in the early 1590s, writing letters home (some extant) from several performance stops, to help us glimpse the partnership in progress. Some of these decisions to collaborate must have been made to create buzz in the marketplace, implying entrepreneurship that was gradually letting go of older patronage priorities.

The flip side of the coin, in business terms, was of course the cost of maintaining a company perpetually on the move. There is no Burbage's diary or collection of Tarlton letters to tell us about playhouse management or touring and domestic arrangements made by actors while they were on the road in the 1580s. G. E. Bentley has outlined some of the basic expenses that we might envisage, primarily for London and court performances in the 1590s: costumes, wages for hired men and other functionaries (e.g. musicians, gatherers, bookkeepers), new plays, licensing fees, and traveling costs (Bentley 1984: 29). William Ingram provides a more detailed analysis of touring expenses, adding horse hire, feed and stabling, food, and lodging (except at private residences) to the list (Ingram 1993). To this can be added informal profit-sharing arrangements at privately owned venues in local towns and occasional rental of venues like the Sherborne church house in Dorset (Hays et al. 1999: 271–3).

An important source of information about acting company membership costs comes from the 1592 will of Simon Jewell. The terms of the will lay out some useful details concerning business arrangements made by lead actors in a company of the period. There were clearly six sharers in Jewell's troupe, which must have toured, given the mention of £37 associated with the joint purchase of 'horses waggen and apparrell newe boughte'. Jewell assumes in his calculation of personal assets that his share in the company stock had individual value. Part of the money owing to him from his fellow actors is 30*s.* for plates, sugar, and banqueting stuff (i.e. basic props); £13 6*s.* 8*d.* (from a not inconsiderable total value of £80) for the common stock of apparel; and a further £6 3*s.* 8*d.* for his share in purchasing the horses, wagon, and new apparel. His personal debts included 30*s.* for a pair of velvet hose and 44*s.* 5*d.* still owing for the new apparel bought for the company. This amount, to be paid to a 'Mr Johnson', suggested to Scott McMillin that Jewell was a member of one touring branch of the 1590s Queen's Men, along with William Johnson and four others (McMillin 1976: 176). Jewell's gifts are also indicative of his life as a player, especially that of 'all my playenge thinges in a box and my veluet shewes' to Robert Nicolls, likely another member of the company

(Edmond 1974: 129–30). The anticipation of Jewell's share in money to come from Lady Pembroke implies either that the company may have been commissioned to perform at one of her family residences or that they had earned her special approval—Mary Edmond and others would interpret this as evidence of her husband's patronage. Mention of wagons is sparse in the records but we are probably safe to assume that most companies would have shared similar purchases of a common stock of apparel and basic props, possible if not easy to transport on foot or horseback.

Although the principal players in a company apparently shared profits and costs, we can deduce from payments made at court and occasionally in provincial records that one or two may have taken the lead in managing company affairs. John Dutton is mentioned as a payee in the Chamber accounts for the Queen's Men between 1589 and 1591, around the same time that a 'Mr Dutton' is specifically named as payee for the company in provincial accounts. It is likely that he and his brother Laurence were leaders of one branch of the Queen's Men in this period while John Laneham, another 1583 recruit mentioned by name in court and provincial accounts, acted as an informal manager for the other (McMillin and MacLean 1998: 62–3, 179–83). This was not a new development. Laurence Dutton, like his brother somewhat infamous for his changing allegiances, had taken the lead for payments at court in the 1570s, as a member first of Sir Robert Lane's troupe, then Lincoln's, Clinton's, and finally Warwick's Men (Cook and Wilson 1961: 5–10).

The variety of records available for the Queen's Men therefore shed some light on the business practices of a commercially and artistically successful acting company of the 1580s. By 1591, however, they had lost their favored status at court and we cannot ignore the emerging presence of fresher companies with new talent and different goals. While the Queen's Men continued to tour the countryside, they were maintaining an older tradition, representing the central authority but no longer full participants in the commercial theater of the 1590s. We must look instead to the Admiral's Men with their star, Edward Alleyn, and as an example here, to Ferdinando Stanley, Lord Strange's Men, for a newer model, briefly redirected during the plague years but resilient when the theaters reopened in 1594.

Strange's Men is an intriguing company, not only because some of its members eventually formed the core of the new Chamberlain's Men in 1594, the troupe that has had an exceptional influence on theater history narratives because Shakespeare was a member. Provincial touring records in the 1570s indicate that the teenage Ferdinando was an early adopter of the patronage tradition, with a surprisingly well-paid troupe of 'vaulters', despite the youth and relatively minor political influence of their patron. Within a mere four years, Lord Strange's tumblers had achieved the highest recognition: a performance before the Queen at Whitehall (Cook and Wilson 1961: 16). Court festivities for two of the next three years continued to feature their 'feats of activity' led by John Symons. Strange's troupe continues to surface in the provincial accounts until 1584–5. The court records for Christmas 1584/5 may help to explain the subsequent gap in Lord Strange's theatrical patronage: Symons and his fellows performed their popular feats of activity but for the first time under the patronage of Oxford (Cook and Wilson 1961: 22). For the next two years, Symons and company maintained their court appearances, but without a patron named, probably because the Queen herself had assumed that role.

A few provincial records help us track the rise of a second innovative performance troupe under Strange's patronage, this time an acting company which flourished between 1589 and 1593. The formation of this second troupe coincides with the brief period covered by the only extant Stanley household book, which shows that the family preference was for the professional theater offered by playing companies operating at the national level: Leicester's and Queen's (once in company with Essex's). The other 'players' named without patron or town of origin who performed for the assembled Stanley family at some point during Christmas and Shrovetide between 1587 and 1589/90 was arguably the new home troupe, Lord Strange's Men (MacLean 2003: 217–18, 225 n. 51).

Leicester's Men, who played twice in July 1587 at Lathom, the Earl of Derby's principal residence, were forced by their patron's death in September 1588 to seek another patron. Several of their most talented members found a willing alternative in Lord Strange: Leicester's comic star, the clown Will Kempe, as well as at least two others, George Bryan and Thomas Pope, probably migrated to Strange's patronage soon after Leicester's death. All three had been venturesome participants in Leicester's Continental tour in 1585–6, even travelling beyond the Low Countries to the Danish court at Elsinore and, in Pope and Bryan's case, to the Elector of Saxony's court at Dresden. Such independent activity suggests a spirit of entrepreneurship that may have carried forward into their next acting partnership.

Quite strikingly, the new Strange's Men do not show up in provincial accounts on a regular basis between 1589, when they are known to have been performing in London at the Cross Keys, and late June 1592, when they left the Rose theater to tour the south and south-west (see Map 2.2). Other companies, including the Admiral's Men, continued to maintain a provincial presence during these years so the absence of Strange's is exceptional. The evidence suggests that the company had a different goal, setting their sights on achieving commercial success in London and at court, a feat they accomplished quite remarkably. It is generally accepted that Strange's was the largest company of its era, likely modelled on the Queen's Men, but able to mount more ambitious and daring theater than the royal troupe could compete with by the end of their first decade. Shakespeare was one of several brilliant young playwrights writing in a new style for Strange's Men in the early 1590s. Strange's repertory, known from the title pages of a handful of extant published plays, and from the detailed accounts in Philip Henslowe's diary itemizing their performances at the Rose, also included plays by Thomas Kyd and Christopher Marlowe, the hit-makers of their day. Versification and performance styles had changed, and key members of the older generation of stars had passed away to be replaced in the public and royal eye by Edward Alleyn, the Admiral's man who joined forces with Strange's company in the early 1590s.

By 1592 they were dominant at court during the Christmas and Shrovetide seasons, with the Rose theater as a base for extended performances in repertory recorded in Henslowe's diary from 19 February 1591/2 to 22 June 1592 and 29 December 1592 to 1 February 1592/3 (Foakes 2002: 16–20). What seems to have forced this troupe on the

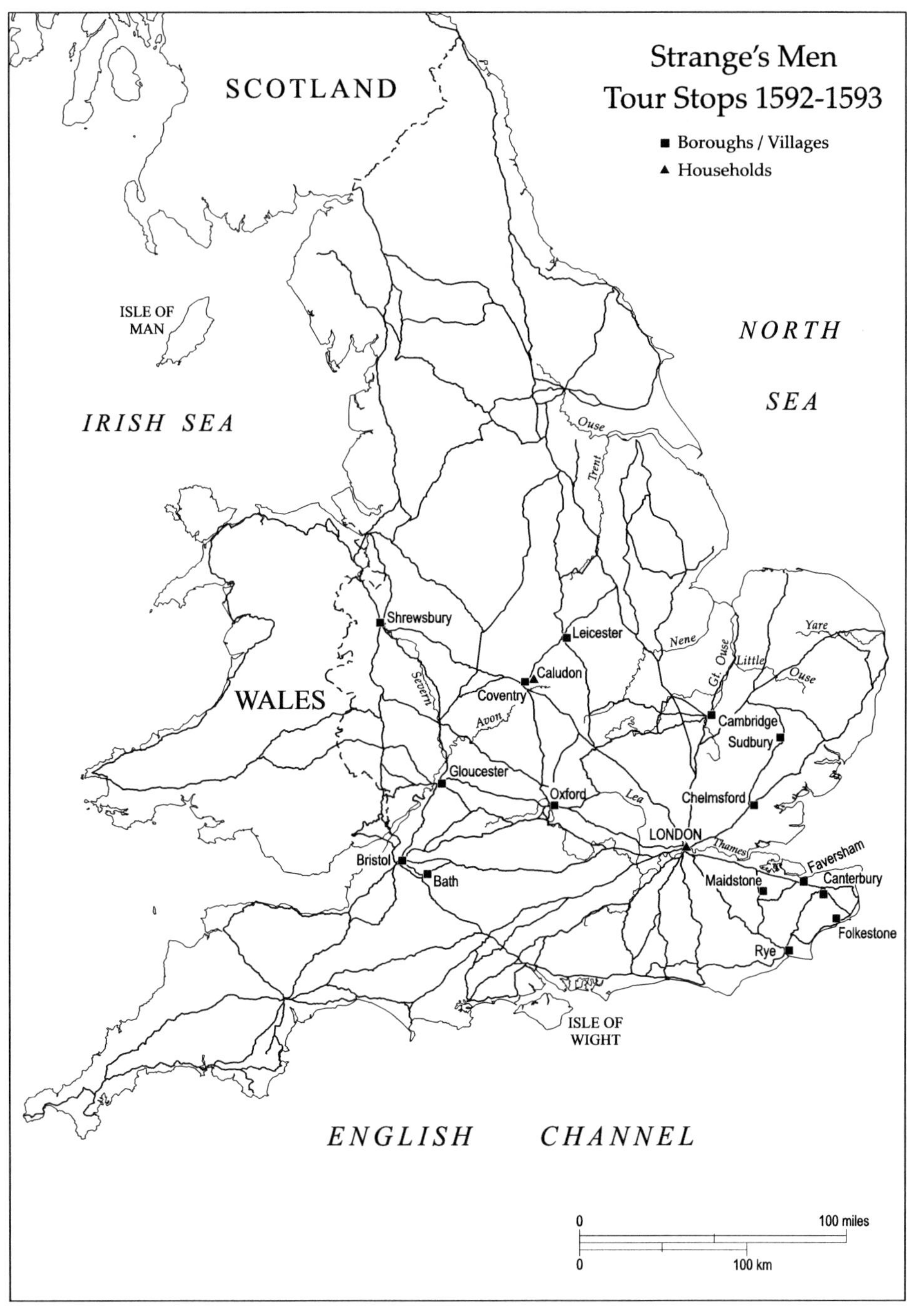

Map 2.2 Strange's Men tour stops 1592–1593.

provincial roads was theater closures in the London area resulting from inhibitions against playing during 1592–3. They raised some stout resistance to the inevitable retreat to the provinces to make their living for the duration. An undated petition to the Privy Council by Strange's Men, most likely from 1592, survives among the Henslowe papers at Dulwich College to present their arguments and give witness to their priorities:

fforasmuche (righte honorable) oure Companie is greate, and thearbie o[r] chardge intolerable, in travellinge the Countrie, and the Contynuaunce thereof, wilbe a meane to bringe vs to division and seperacon, whearbie wee shall not onlie be vndone, but alsoe vnreadie to serve her ma[tie], when it shall please her highenes to commaund vs, And for that vse of o[r] plaiehowse on the Banckside, by reason [by reason] of the passage to and frome the same by water, is a great relief to the poore watermen theare, And o[r] dismission thence. Nowe in this longe vacation, is to those poore men. A greate hindraunce, and in manner an vndoeinge, as they genrallie complaine. (Foakes 2002: 283–4)

In the past this petition has been over-interpreted to represent a generally negative attitude towards playing outside London that the provincial records do not support. Rather, it should be read as specific to Strange's Men, who were clearly lobbying as persuasively as they could to maintain their preferred status quo in London and at court. When they did relocate to the provinces during 1592–3, they apparently did not divide and were not broken for lack of audiences and income. But they did not feel impelled, as tradition might have encouraged, to promote their patron's name about the countryside. Their business was flourishing in the metropolis and, by invoking the likely impact of their departure on the Thames watermen, they recognized their role in the larger urban economy. Unlike acting companies of the 1580s, they had an established base at the Rose on Bankside, where they could mount their large-cast plays with sensational special effects and the support of extra hired theater personnel six days a week (Manley 2001). Although their patron did not have great political clout in the south, the company had rapidly built a dynamic operation there on the basis of acting and playwriting talent. The celebrity of Edward Alleyn, their artistic collaborator, helped to guarantee returning audiences and steady income as well as the choicest dates on the court calendar (Cerasano 2006). When the theaters reopened in 1594, Strange's Men were looking for a new patron after Ferdinando Stanley's fall from grace and subsequent mysterious death, but the business model that they helped to pioneer would flourish anew.

Patronage

Two of the most successful acting companies have furnished examples of evolving business strategies in the period, though the gaps in the record inevitably limit the scope of the analysis. The documentary evidence for tracing relationships between patrons and their companies is similarly elliptical. Even the hope that we might know more if personal account books, journals, and private correspondence survived in greater numbers is speculative. What is clearly apparent, however, is the continuation of a basic requirement for professional acting companies, who still had to operate under the 1572 Act against rogues, vagabonds, and sturdy beggars, legislation which essentially required aristocratic patronage for performers who wanted to stay on the right side of the authorities. Patronage remained officially restricted to those at the rank of baron and above, although the list of companies on the road between 1583 and 1593 reveals that not all members of the gentry were obedient to the statute against unlawful retainers, despite its periodic iterations from the fifteenth century on—Sir Peter Legh's players and Sir Thomas Lucy's players are just two examples in our period.

As mentioned above, the formation of the Queen's Men had a direct impact on some of the leading companies in 1583. For a measurement of professional success, we must still look to the companies singled out to perform at court. Two of the patrons whose actors performed during Christmas and Shrovetide 1582/3 did not maintain their companies. Only Henry Carey, Lord Hunsdon, seems to have continued as a patron in this decade, though his players were not among the more active in the provinces. In fact, this is a troupe we wish we knew more about, as the few clues are tantalizing. All we know at this time is that an acting company had been formed by Hunsdon by 1581, when they showed up in York in the north and Norwich in East Anglia, touring on a wide circuit until 1588, when they made their final known appearance in Saffron Walden with Leicester's Men.[1] The company was good enough to be invited to court twice in this period, the first time in December 1582 and the second on Twelfth Night 1585/6, jointly with the Admiral's Men and recently renamed the Lord Chamberlain's Men in recognition of their patron's new office. They seem likely to have played London as well, probably at the Theatre, where the owner, James Burbage, formerly under Leicester's patronage, called himself 'my Lord of Hunsdon's man' while stoutly resisting an order to pull down his playhouse in 1584 (see below).

When the Queen's monopoly on adult company performances at court begins to ease, the patrons have mostly new faces, apart from the durable Earl of Leicester, whose recast company appeared once, during Christmas 1586. Edward de Vere, the seventeenth Earl of Oxford, also sponsored acting troupes from 1580 to 1587, but distinguishing the activities of his adult company from his boys' company or his brief patronage of Symons's tumbling act in the mid-1580s is no easy task. Charles Howard, Lord Admiral, more consistently patronized one of the most important adult companies, which appeared at court twice during the 1585/6 Christmas season and then from 1588 onwards, as well as in London and in the countryside, with or without their star player, Alleyn. Strange's Men dominated the court calendar between 1591 and 1593, although three other troupes, all patronized by the higher nobility, surface then for the first time. The first Earl of Hertford, a sporadic patron between 1590 and 1607, had entertained the Queen at Elvetham during her summer progress in 1591, so his players may have been invited to court the same year in return

[1] Saffron Walden Town Hall, Chamberlains' Accounts, p. 129.

(Gurr 1996*b*: 311). Thomas Radcliffe, third Earl of Sussex and Lord Chamberlain until 1583, had been an active patron with a successful company in the 1570s. His brother Henry, the fourth Earl, would follow the family tradition, his troupe becoming very active from 1585 onward; their one appearance at court during Christmas 1591 follows on a joint tour with one branch of the Queen's Men during the previous spring (McMillin and MacLean 1998: 62–3, 181). The third company, which performed twice at court in 1592, was newly patronized by an older member of the nobility who came late to that role: Henry Herbert, second Earl of Pembroke and Lord President of the Marches of Wales. His motives for patronage remain subject for debate, but the troupe, which did not manage its provincial tour successfully the following year, has aroused more commentary than others comparable because it had some plays by Shakespeare in its repertoire.

Apart from the Lord Admiral and Leicester, and perhaps mindful of the special role of the Queen's Men, privy counselors between 1583 and 1593 did not patronize acting companies, although they did take action to protect the interests of players when London officials attempted to curtail their activities. The other active companies were relatively few in number and their careers are mostly traceable in the provinces. Prominent among them were Worcester's Men, the players of Edward Somerset, the fourth Earl, who pursued a vigorous touring circuit from the year after their patron's accession to the title until Queen Anne took them into her favor. Somerset's father had also had one of the more active touring companies, notable for counting a teenage Edward Alleyn among its members. Predictably, Leicester's stepson and protégé Robert Devereux, second Earl of Essex, must also have seen the promotional advantages of an acting company. Essex's Men toured annually across the country, perhaps bolstering their patron's national ambitions and local connections in the process, but there is no trace of them yet in London or at court during these years. One other member of the higher nobility patronized a company mentioned as one of those playing at a London suburban theater, probably the Curtain, in June 1584, when the Lord Mayor made his move to pull down the Shoreditch playhouses after turbulent incidents in that area (Chambers and Greg 1908: 166). Philip Howard, thirteenth Earl of Arundel, was following a long-standing family tradition of patronage with a company mostly active in 1584–5, in East Anglia, where the patron held lands. Whether they would have gone on to greatness is moot. Howard, a recusant, was imprisoned in April 1585 and attainted in 1589, so his players must have rapidly looked elsewhere for their livery.

The other acting companies with any claim to continuous activity between 1583 and 1593 were all patronized by lesser members of the nobility, none of them holding more than regional offices: Henry, Lord Berkeley; Giles Brydges, Lord Chandos; John, Lord Darcy; Edward Parker, Lord Morley; Edward Seymour, Lord Beauchamp; and Edward, Lord Stafford. Lord Berkeley's patronage, for example, has been characterized by Peter Greenfield as sporadic, perhaps because of his legal troubles during the 1570s. He enjoyed some useful family connections with Tilney and Carey that may have encouraged him to form a second company in 1578, when advancement at court might have seemed feasible. A 1581 court record about an affray featuring an assault on Berkeley's Men by disorderly gentlemen from the Inns of Court shows that they did perform in London, albeit irreverently on the sabbath, but we cannot track them beyond that one incident in the city (Chambers 1923: iv. 282). However, the company was steadily active in the south and midlands until the mid-1580s, most typically at Coventry near the patron's residence at Caludon and in the south-west, where the principal Berkeley lands had been held for generations. Berkeley's financial difficulties mushroomed after a costly legal settlement against him in 1584, so it is no surprise that his patronage did not continue for long thereafter (Greenfield 2001). The membership of most of these companies is obscure, but Chandos's Men have a decided claim to fame in their clown, Robert Armin, who would later play leading roles with Shakespeare's company. Perhaps Armin was already an attraction in the 1580s when Chandos's troupe toured in the south, where their patron held his lands and offices. Annual tours by this company are on record until Brydges' death in 1594.

In summary, there was some resilience in patronage of acting companies after the initial shock to the system in 1583. What we might consider a conservative approach probably continued to exist among many of the provincially based patrons, who gave their liveries and agreed to the licensing of players who may have performed on an occasional basis at their households during Christmas and Shrovetide according to a centuries-old custom, but who augmented their income by touring, either in the regions where their patron held lands and local offices, or where friendly relationships existed. Without sufficient documentation surviving from the patrons' households in this period, or, for that matter, consistency in provincial touring accounts, it is impossible to speculate further.

There are, however, some reliable clues to the degree of clout that patrons had to offer the companies touring under their names. For example, in November 1580 the Gloucester Common Council moved to put some restraints on the number of performances in the city, concerned that 'great sums of money' were being spent by many people and that servants, apprentices, and journeymen were being lured from their work by visiting players. The regulations specify that the Queen's players be allowed to perform three plays within three days or less; the players of barons and higher nobility be granted two plays within two days or fewer; and that others of lower degree licensed to perform be allowed one play on one day. Beyond such advantages granted on the basis of social hierarchy was the ranked system of rewards made by civic officials for performances required before the mayor and council in provincial towns. Still in Gloucester during the 1580s, we find the following allocations for adult acting companies in the account year 1584–5, in order of generosity: Leicester's 20*s.*; Essex's 13*s.* 4*d.*; Sussex's 13*s.* 4*d.*; Berkeley's 10*s.*; and Stafford's 6*s.* 8*d.* When the Queen's Men came two years later, they got the highest level, 30*s.*, but the powerful Leicester's name clearly carried more weight than other members of the higher nobility. Berkeley and Stafford, as barons of the realm, might be seen as sharing a place at the low end of the scale, but Berkeley had regional influence that might account for his players' somewhat higher reward (Douglas and Greenfield 1986: 306–7, 309). Another example from a smaller town on the other side of the country almost a decade later, when the Queen's Men were no longer ascendant, shows the same hierarchical system in operation. In 1592–3, at Faversham in Kent, the rewards ranged as follows: Queen's still at the highest level, with 20*s.*, but Strange's Men also at 20*s.*, presumably a testimonial to their recognized artistic quality and popularity; Admiral's (without Alleyn) 10*s.*; Hertford's 10*s.*; and Beauchamp's at the lower end of 6*s.* 8*d.* (Gibson 2002: ii. 561). Similar financial evidence is on record across the country, though the size of the town purse for such rewards varies according to the local economy.

Whether royal, earl, or baron, the patron's license allowed an acting company to tour, to play first for the mayor and possibly elsewhere in a town, and to expand their performance opportunities by visiting the private residences of nobility and gentry (at least sometimes thanks to their patron's friendly or family connections). When they got into trouble with local authorities, as they certainly sometimes did, they could call upon their patron for assistance. In their very first summer, some of the Queen's Men got into a lethal scuffle during a performance at the Red Lion inn in Norwich, leaping from the stage, rapiers in hand, to pursue an audience member who resisted paying at the gate. In the process an innocent bystander was killed, but only Henry Browne, a local man who joined the affray, ended up in jail for any length of time. John Singer's confidence in his status as a Queen's man is evident in his comment to Browne over the corpse: 'be of good Chere for yf all this matter bee layed on the thowe shalt haue what ffrendshipe we can procure thee'. Singer and Bentley, the chief offenders, escaped with little more than fines, and although it is unlikely that the Queen herself was called upon, there must have been members of the Privy Council helpful on her behalf who eased their passage back onto the tour (McMillin and MacLean 1998: 42–3). Another instance, in London during the June 1584 troubles in Shoreditch, featured the irascible Burbage, whose resistance to civic authority also hints at direct connections between patron and liveried retainer. When confronted with a letter to suppress his playhouse from the City Recorder, William Fleetwood, Burbage invoked the protection of his patron:

> he sent me word that he was my Lo of hunsdons man and that he wold not come at me, but he wold in the mornyng ride to my lord/then I sent the vndershereff for hym and he browght hym to me/and at his commyng he stowtted me owt very hastie/ ... And then I mynding to send hym to prison he made sute that he might be bound to appere at the Oier & determiner, the wh^ch^ is to morrowe/where he said that he was suer the Court would not bynd hym being a Counselers man ... (Chambers and Greg 1908: 163–8)

Burbage's confidence in his patron was evidently well placed: the order to pull down the Shoreditch playhouses was not carried out. The most powerful patrons could also create opportunities at court, as Leicester must have done for his companies, before and after 1583. The arrival of the Admiral's Men on the court calendar during the late 1580s may have been linked initially with their patron's prominence and familial links with Carey, the Lord Chamberlain, as much as with their growing artistic success.

It is equally apparent that when patrons ran into trouble, financial or political, their acting companies might either be cut loose or choose to seek elsewhere. Berkeley's company is an example of the former and Arundel's, the latter. Even

Strange's Men, so confident in their success in the city and at court before they set out on tour in 1593, never returned as expected to play for the Queen at Christmas. Their patron, who had one of the better claims to the throne through his mother's line, fell under suspicion of treasonous activities shortly after his accession as the fifth Earl of Derby; months before his death in April 1594, his company had ceased to appear anywhere as Derby's Men, though whether they or their embattled patron severed the relationship is not known.

In return for these benefits to the players, a patron could appreciate the promotion of his (or her) name in the provinces and, for the most successful, at court. The cost of swelling the ranks of liveried retainers in this way seems to have been relatively minor, especially in this period, when some of the better acting companies were developing as commercial enterprises. Without personal accounts to scrutinize, we must hesitate to generalize. Leicester, whose accounts do survive for a brief time in the 1580s, is probably not typical. The degree of his interaction with his own players and those of the Queen has been mentioned above, but his heightened awareness of political advantages to be had from lavish display, imposing entourages, and a touring company which made contact with urban and individual clientele across the kingdom should not be interpreted as characteristic of the lesser nobility, the Sheffields and Morleys of the realm (MacLean 2002). In fact, there was probably considerable variation both in the motives for patronage and in individual relationships throughout the period.

Repertories

There are several primary sources to consider in piecing together information about company repertories. The first is the Revels accounts of performances by acting companies at court. In the period between 1583 and 1593 accounts survive for 1582–3, 1584–5, and 1587–8. The play titles linked with specific adult companies from 1 January 1582/3 onwards are as follows: in 1582/3, 'A History of Ferrar' (Chamberlain's) and 'A History of Telomo' (Leicester's), both preceding the formation of Queen's Men in March 1583 and both play-texts lost; in 1584/5, 'Pastoral of Phyllida and Choryn', 'History of Felix and Philiomena', and two described as 'inventions', 'Five Plays in One' and 'Three Plays in One', all presented by the Queen's Men and none of which survive. The titles of plays performed are not given in the 1587–8 accounts (Chambers 1923: iv. 136, 159–62).

Aside from recognizing a court appetite for pastorals during the festive season, we can deduce little more about repertory in the 1580s, even for the most prominent companies. Throughout our period provincial accounts are silent on the subject of plays performed on tour—the interest of their recorders was typically in the name of the company and the amount paid. Even the rare eyewitness account from Shrewsbury in 1590 focuses on the marvels of the tumbling and rope-dancing act rather than on any play performed by Queen's Men (Somerset 1994*a*: i. 247). The plays published were few and far between. Robert Wilson's *Three Ladies of London* as 'publiquely played' at London appeared in 1584, probably from Leicester's Men, though Wilson may have brought it with him into Queen's Men (Greg 1970: i. 164). Only one other directly associated with an adult company, *The Rare Triumphs of Love and Fortune* by an anonymous playwright, appeared in print in 1589. Derby's Men had performed a play of this title at court in 1582.

Scott McMillin has characterized the 1580s as a period of 'actors' theatre' when publication did not have an important place. The attitude towards the release of playbooks for printing seems to have started shifting in 1590, when Marlowe's two-part *Tamburlaine the Great* (from Admiral's) and Wilson's *Three Lords and Three Ladies of London* (from Queen's) were published. The Queen's *Troublesome Reign of King John* was issued the next year, catching the trend of publishing in two parts, followed by three more in 1592: Kyd's *Spanish Tragedy* (from Strange's) and the unattributed *Arden of Faversham* and *Soliman and Perseda* (McMillin and MacLean 1998: 84–96; Greg 1970: i. 170–92). Subsequent developments will be discussed in detail in Chapter 3, but it is worth noting here a slowly developing trend towards publication, perhaps, as Peter Blayney has suggested, for promotional purposes (Blayney 1997: 385–6). Certainly Marlowe's *Tamburlaine* succeeded in print as it had and would continue to do on stage. If reprinting is any indication of success, then *Tamburlaine*, reprinted in 1593 and several times thereafter, made an impact that Wilson's Protestant morality apparently did not. McMillin has conservatively identified nine plays that can be confidently counted as part of the repertory of the Queen's Men, either through title page attribution in 1590s publications, or through knowledge of company membership, in Wilson's case. Studying the company through its repertory, predominantly English histories or comedies with English settings, has revealed certain characteristics that may help explain its eclipse at court and in London during the second decade of its career, though the history play that the Queen's Men probably launched, perhaps with the *Famous Victories of Henry V*, was to flourish when Shakespeare revisioned the genre. The dramaturgy of Queen's Men plays featured a medley style, with scope for physical comedy, visual excitement, and a literalism, sometimes overbearingly repetitive, that emphasizes 'truth and plainness' over the alluring poetic images coming under attack by puritan critics when the company was formed. The versification could also be described as medley, ranging from fourteener to rhyme royal, blank verse, and prose. Therein lay a major contrast with plays being written by Marlowe and others for companies catching the public taste with their new poetics in blank verse (McMillin and MacLean 1998).

The repertory of one new-wave company in the early 1590s is known to us through the lucky survival of a remarkably detailed source, the diary of theatrical accounts kept by Philip Henslowe, owner of the Rose theater, where Strange's Men were based from 19 February to 22 June 1592 and, for a shorter span, from 29 December 1592 to 1 February 1592/3. The diary's details permit, for the first time, an understanding of how a professional company at the top of its game kept the audience coming back, day after day, during a long period in residence. Lawrence Manley, in his ongoing study of Strange's repertory, has counted 105 performances of twenty-four different plays (some of Henslowe's variant titles can be baffling) during the first period and twenty-nine further performances of an additional three or four new plays over the turn of the year (Manley 2001: 115). Plays changed daily and the first performance of any new play drew a larger house, with consequent profits (Knutson 1984*b*: 2–5). Roslyn Knutson has noted that the known repertories of companies from 1588 to 1594 suggest 'the availability of generically diverse, theatrically innovative, and poetically exciting material'. Her helpful summary of Strange's exemplary repertory at the Rose, 1592–3, runs as follows, omitting a few plays not easy to identify:

> The company performed 27 plays, three of which appear to have been tragedies, nine to have been history plays, and the remaining some form of comedy. Two of the tragedies were revenge plays: *The Spanish Tragedy* and *The Jew of Malta*; the third, *Machiavel*, might have been. The history plays represented material as diverse as the English chronicles (*Harry of Cornwall*, *Henry VI*), the Mediterranean world (*Titus and Vespasian*, *Muly Mollocco*), empire in the Far East (*Tamar Cham*, parts one and two), and European religio-political turmoil (*Massacre at Paris*). The comedies were equally diverse, including a magician play (*Friar Bacon*), a romance (*Orlando Furioso*), a moral history (*A Knack to Know a Knave*), a biblical moral (*A Looking Glass for London and England*), a pastoral (*Cloris and Ergasto*), a craft play (*The Tanner of Denmark*), and a 'wonders' narrative (*Sir John Mandeville*). In addition to illustrating a range of popular formulas, the repertory of Strange's Men contained multi-part plays. *Four Plays in One* was possibly a set of related playlets like 2 *Seven Deadly Sins*. *The Comedy of Don Horatio* was a prequel to *The Spanish Tragedy*. *Tamar Cham* was a two-part serial. *Friar Bacon*, if it was *John of Bordeaux*, was a sequel of sorts to *Friar Bacon and Friar Bungay* in the repertory of another company, Queen's Men. *Machiavel* was perhaps a spin-off of *The Jew of Malta*, which Strange's Men were themselves playing. (Knutson 2002: 185)

Of these, the survival count of texts is typically limited: ten out of twenty-seven. One of these lost plays, *Harry of Cornwall*, we know was taken on the 1593 provincial tour because Edward Alleyn mentions it specifically in a letter home to his wife from the south-west, where the subject matter presumably would have found an appreciative local audience (Foakes 2002: 276).

One likely advantage for a company on tour was a less demanding repertory—fewer plays were needed because no performance stop would have lasted longer than a few days at most. How many of the plays in Strange's repertory would have been taken on tour? It is impossible to document provincial repertories of acting companies, though perhaps the time has come to ask whether those requiring more elaborate props and staging would have been chosen, given the realities of transportation in the period. And were plays produced for featured performances at court necessarily taken on the road? Were some plays chosen for a particular purpose, such as the political agenda that seems to have driven the Queen's Men's touring or for their topical interest for a region (e.g. *Harry of Cornwall*) or a landed patron (e.g. another play attributed to Strange's Men on the title page, *Faire Em the Miller's Daughter of Manchester*, possibly for the Stanleys, who had a featured local Lancashire family in their affinity)? We simply don't know, but we can begin to ask such questions.

CHAPTER 3

ADULT PLAYING COMPANIES, 1593–1603

ROSLYN L. KNUTSON

By any measure, 1593 was a very bad year for the playhouse business. The late summer outbreak of plague in 1592 continued in the suburbs of London. In the parish of St Botolph without Bishopsgate, which bordered the parishes of Norton Folgate, where Christopher Marlowe lived, and St Leonard, Shoreditch, where the Theatre and Curtain playhouses stood (and the James Burbage family lived), burial entries for 172 people were recorded in the parish register in July 1593, compared to seven in July 1592 and ten in July of 1594; 259 burials were entered in August 1593, compared to twenty-two in 1592 and fourteen in 1594 (Hallen 1889: i/3. 302–16). Companies took to the road, visiting towns as widespread as Newcastle upon Tyne (Sussex's Men), Lyme Regis in Dorset (Admiral's Men), and Norwich (Queen's Men).[1] Yet there was plague in the countryside too, and town fathers were chary of any travelers who might bring the pestilence with them. Even so, Strange's Men were able to mount a tour in the summer of 1593 along a route apparently plague-safe and financially rewarding. The company of Pembroke's Men was not so lucky. As Philip Henslowe, entrepreneur of the Rose playhouse in London, recorded in a letter dated 28 September 1593 to his son-in-law Edward Alleyn, Pembroke's Men did not make enough money on the road to cover their expenses, and they had to sell off their theatrical gear to cover debts (Foakes 2002: 280). Also, companies were geographically estranged from their playwrights, who for the most part stayed in London. One in particular, William Shakespeare,

[1] Records of Early English Drama (REED) Patrons and Performances web site.

apparently considered a change of focus for his skills from drama to poetry. No one therefore could have predicted that the business of playing would enjoy unprecedented commercial success and expansion in the next decade. Theater historians construct differing narratives about this decade in the theatrical marketplace, but they generally agree that the salient issues are the companies' business models; patrons and political critics; playing venues; the repertory; the book trade; and audiences.

Business Models

By 1593 adult playing companies in England had operated with uneven results under variations of two business models. One drew its strength from the affiliation of patron with player organization. Companies secured a license to play from the authority of their lord, but for the most part, as a business, they relied upon themselves as a partnership of sharers who covered expenses and divided profits. The typical pre-1593 company of this sort, whether it performed in London or toured primarily in its patron's provincial areas of influence, lived financially from one cluster of performances to the next, receiving perhaps no more material reward from their lord than a suit of livery and a letter of introduction. The Queen's Men in 1583 perfected this business model (McMillin and MacLean 1998). They had the authority of the Queen herself and key politicians; but when the player dimension of the organization faltered, through both a loss of personnel and repertorial competition, the company was unable to sustain its business at the peak level of the mid-1580s. The Queen's Men continued to have a substantial presence in the countryside through the 1590s, and they played for a time in London (see below), but by 1593 they had slipped from the first rank of commercially successful companies.

The second business model added an entrepreneurial level to the affiliation of patron and player. At their best, these entrepreneurs coupled business acumen with playhouse building, thus providing playing companies with a venue at their disposal as well as a partisan whose own business interests coincided with those of the company sharers. The quintessential exemplar of this model is James Burbage, who was instrumental in the construction of the Theatre in Shoreditch in 1576. Burbage had been a player with Leicester's Men in 1572, and he might have had some role in his brother-in-law's venture into the construction of playhouses, namely the Red Lion at Mile End in 1567 (Ingram 1992: 112). Whatever their relationship previously, Burbage and John Brayne (the brother-in-law) were partners in 1576, and the alliance that brought Brayne's capital together with Burbage's connections with companies proved immediately successful.[2] By 1585 it had duplicated itself at the nearby Curtain,

[2] I imply here that Burbage at the very least facilitated the lease of the Theatre (and Curtain) to companies with which he was associated, as well as with the Queen's Men, and that arrangement makes sense, but it is not established by extant documents.

with Henry Laneman replacing John Brayne as moneyman and James Burbage as theatrical entrepreneur (Ingram 1992: 219–38).[3] Versions of this model were replicated at the Rose, where Philip Henslowe by 1592 was teamed with Edward Alleyn, whose company of players, the Admiral's Men, would play at the Rose from 1594 to 1600; at the Swan, where Francis Langley had a far more troubled relationship with companies of players, specifically Pembroke's Men in 1597 (Ingram 1978); and at the Boar's Head, where Oliver Woodliffe and Richard Samwell were partnered with Robert Browne, chief player of Derby's Men (Berry 1986). The model survived into the 1630s primarily in the person of Christopher Beeston, whose playhouse ventures included both the Red Bull (1605) and the Phoenix (aka Cockpit, 1617).

The one significant variation to the alliance of entrepreneur and adult playing company in the 1590s occurred when the Globe playhouse was constructed in 1599 and players who were sharers became investors in the playhouse (and thus 'housekeepers'). In the Globe venture, the Burbage family was represented by Richard and Cuthbert, sons of James, who had died in 1596; the Burbage brothers enlarged the number of investors in the playhouse itself by selling shares to five players: William Shakespeare, Augustine Phillips, Thomas Pope, John Heminges, and Will Kempe. An indication of the success of this consortium is its replication in the company's second and indoor playhouse, Blackfriars, in 1608, in which Shakespeare and Heminges bought shares, along with fellow players Henry Condell and William Sly.[4] In contrast, Edward Alleyn and Philip Henslowe kept the partnership to themselves when they built the Fortune playhouse; they also did not copy the Burbages' addition of a private house to their theatrical investments, as Christopher Beeston was to do with the Phoenix/Cockpit.

All this stability of companies with playhouses, however, was in the future. As 1593 became 1594, a pressing concern for the players was to find a place with the fragments of troupes that had survived the business climate of 1593. Two documents illustrate the flux of organizations in the spring of 1594. One is the title page of the 1594 Quarto of *Titus Andronicus*, which claims that the play was performed 'by the Right Honourable the Earle of *Darbie*, Earle of *Pembrooke*, and Earle of *Sussex* their Seruants' (Greg 1970: i, no. 117). Scott McMillin expresses the venerable opinion on this claim, which is that 'the play passed among these three companies, probably in the order specified' (McMillin 1991: 216). The appearance of the play in the repertory of the last-listed company, Sussex's Men, appears to confirm serial ownership. But this explanation raises issues of accuracy and chronology, both with the company names and with the play. Strange's Men became Derby's Men in September 1593, when their patron succeeded his father as earl; however, by September 1593 Pembroke's Men had already broken up. Therefore, if Strange's/Derby's Men owned *Titus Andronicus*

[3] Warwick's Men, led by Jerome Savage, might have been similar entrepreneurs in their connection to the Newington playhouse, a mile south of London Bridge (Ingram 1992: 170, 243–5).

[4] Scholars have assumed that 'Thomas' Evans, the seventh-named sharer in the lease, is a clerical error for 'Henry' Evans, who had recently been running a boys' company at Blackfriars (Andrew Gurr is an exception; 1996*b*: 295). Three player–investors from the Globe syndicate were gone in 1608: Kempe left the company shortly after 1599; Pope (1603) and Phillips (1605) were dead.

before it passed into the repertory of Pembroke's Men, the title page of the Quarto should designate Strange's Men, not Derby's. Yet the opinion of serial ownership relies on the accuracy of the title page. Also, if *Titus Andronicus* was an old play in January 1594 (as serial ownership requires), Henslowe's designation of it as 'ne' means that the play was not genuinely new but merely new to Sussex's Men (or newly licensed).[5] Paul E. Bennett offers an Occam's-razor-like explanation: that *Titus Andronicus* 'was first performed by a mixed company of actors, mostly Sussex's, as Henslowe notes, but also with a few of Derby's and Pembroke's' (1955: 462). By this explanation, *Titus Andronicus* might indeed have been new in January 1594.

A second document attesting to the reorganization of companies in 1594 is the book of accounts, or 'diary', kept by Philip Henslowe of theatrical business at the Rose, 1592–1603. Henslowe recorded four waves of playing in the spring of 1594: Sussex's Men, from 27 December 1593 to 6 February 1593/4; Sussex's Men 'to geather' with the Queen's Men, for Easter Week, 1–8 April 1594; the Admiral's Men, 14–16 May; and the Admiral's Men and Chamberlain's Men, 3–13 June, at the Newington playhouse (Foakes 2002: 21). Theater historians see two patterns in this sequence. Sussex's Men and Sussex's with Queen's appear to be temporary and expedient gatherings of players whose previous affiliations had broken down. The Queen's Men appear still to be reorganizing in May 1594 and June 1595, when Philip Henslowe lent his nephew Francis cash to buy shares (Foakes 2002: 7, 9). In contrast, the Admiral's Men and the Chamberlain's Men appear to be the initial formation of companies that would soon solidify into the juggernauts of the playhouse world for the next decade. The personnel of both companies were to remain relatively stable, with a few exceptions: in 1597 the Admiral's Men acquired players from Pembroke's Men (owing to Francis Langley's souring business at the Swan), and they lost Edward Alleyn, who retired in 1597 but returned in 1600 for the opening of the Fortune; and some time between 1599 and 1602 the Chamberlain's Men lost three players to Worcester's Men (Will Kempe, John Duke, and Christopher Beeston).

Patrons and Political Critics

Andrew Gurr designates the Admiral's Men and the Chamberlain's Men in 1594 a 'duopoly', and he attributes the hegemony implicit in the term to decisions by the companies' respective patrons:

[5] There are fewer provable errors in Henslowe's use of 'ne' for new plays than are often supposed. Unless *Titus Andronicus* is a fifth, Henslowe used 'ne' for plays known to be old only four times: for the two parts of 'Tamar Cham' in the Admiral's 1595–6 repertory and for 'Joronymo', presumably *The Spanish Tragedy*, in January 1597 (Strange's Men had played all three, in spring 1592); and for 'Alexander and Lodowick' in January 1597, when the first two performances are annotated 'ne'.

Shakespeare and his plays were gathered up in May 1594 to form an essential component of a new company set up by Henry Carey, the Lord Chamberlain.... In... alliance with his son-in-law Charles Howard, the Lord Admiral, he set up two new companies to serve his official purpose.... London's two leading actors, Edward Alleyn and Richard Burbage, were each allocated a company of fellow-players and a playhouse belonging to someone in their family, and each company was given a set of already famous plays. One secured Marlowe's, the other Shakespeare's. (Gurr 2004*c*, p. xiii)

Of the several controversial claims here, the statement that Carey, in league with Howard, set up the Chamberlain's Men and the Admiral's Men in 1594 specifically interrogates the role of patrons in the formation and commercial success of the adult playing companies. By asserting Carey and Howard's active participation, Gurr appropriates the business model illustrated by the Queen's Men, that is, commercial theatrical organizations conceived by powerful noblemen for some political agenda of their own. Gurr appropriates also two motives attributed to the patrons of the Queen's Men, specifically, to provide a ready supply of entertainers for the Queen and to find 'a means to limit the competition among companies' (1993*b*: 160, 164). The first of these motives is undisputed; lord chamberlains were responsible for the Queen's entertainment, as illustrated by the formation of Sussex's Men, who in 1572 enjoyed the patronage of Thomas Radcliffe, Earl of Sussex and also Lord Chamberlain. Henry Carey is in fact a tardy example, given that he became Lord Chamberlain in 1585 but brought a company under his patronage to court only once before 1594. The second motive is more inference than fact. Out of a general sense that theatrical activity was viewed as politically subversive and conducive to public disorder, many theater historians have interpreted various governmental orders to restrict playing and shut down theatrical venues as attempts to control the industry. McMillin and MacLean attribute a motive of industry-wide control to Walsingham in the formation of the Queen's Men, but they do not have documents to substantiate that intent (1998: 12–14). Gurr cites a Privy Council minute in 1598 that orders two companies licensed and one suppressed as proof of Carey and Howard's intent in 1594. However, for other theater historians, that four-year stretch of time without restrictions except plague closures and orders to jail the players of lewd plays undermines the argument that the government generally and Howard and Carey specifically desired to contain the burgeoning theatrical industry.[6]

There is no disagreement, however, that the lord mayors wanted restraints on playing. They petitioned the Privy Council in November 1594 to suppress the Swan playhouse as well as 'all such places built for that kind of exercise' (Chambers 1923: iv. 316); on 13 September 1595 and 28 July 1597 they asked for a 'finall suppressing', specifying 'the Theator & Bankside' on the former date and adding the Curtain playhouse on the latter. On that very July date, the Privy Council ordered that houses built exclusively for playing be 'plucked downe' (Chambers 1923: iv. 323). The 19 February 1598 Privy Council order to license the Admiral's Men and Chamberlain's Men and suppress a third company might

[6] Because records from the Privy Council for August 1593–October 1595 are lost, neither the scholars for nor those against the argument for the privileging of two companies in 1594 have documentary support.

more plausibly be read in the context of these repeated calls for total suppression than in that of the formation of the companies in 1594. On 22 June 1600 the Privy Council, reiterating its support for the Admiral's Men and Chamberlain's Men, updated its authorization to reflect their new playhouses, the Fortune and the Globe. Further, the Counselors forbade playing on Sundays and during Lent, and limited playing to two days a week. This order illustrates why some theater historians question the force of attempts to control playing in the 1590s, if not also Privy Counselors' motives. On the one hand, two companies obviously were being singled out in 1598 and 1600 for a privileged status. Yet, as evidence of activities from the Rose, Swan, and Boar's Head playhouses proves, more than two commercially successful companies were playing in London post-1594. Also, while the Privy Counselors clearly meant to reduce the frequency of performances in 1600, no theater historian believes that the adult companies followed such orders to the letter. As the repetition for the umpteenth time of an injunction against Sunday and Lenten playing illustrates, documents may express an official position, but they do not necessarily reflect reality for the socks and buskins on the ground.

The Master of the Revels was one government official who did have regular contact with the adult playing companies, specifically those who gave performances at court. According to Richard Dutton, the royal patent granted to Leicester's Men in 1574 'is the first document to associate the Master of the Revels with "seeing and allowing" plays as a prior condition to their public performance' (1991: 28). Edmond Tilney, who was master throughout this decade, exercised his authority on the play *Sir Thomas More*, and thus provided the template by which scholars have interpreted his effect as official censor on the commercial playhouse world. In his order *c*.1593 to the company owners to leave out the insurrection altogether, Tilney was responding not to the principle of staging riots but 'to matters of immediate moment, to the over-specific shadowing of particular people and current events, rather than to considerations of doctrine' (Dutton 1991: 85). In the decade following 1593, Tilney licensed a number of plays that caused trouble for many people but not, apparently, for him. Examples include *Richard II*, which is generally considered the play commissioned for performance at the Globe by the Essex faction on the afternoon before the Earl's failed rebellion; an unnamed play performed at the Curtain in May 1601, in which one or more characters too closely impersonated 'some gentlemen of good desert and quallity' (Chambers 1923: iv. 332); and *Poetaster*, which Ben Jonson claimed had been restrained by some authority but apparently not the Revels Office. The case of the lost 'Isle of Dogs' (Swan, summer of 1597) shows the variety of official scrutiny that any given play might provoke. Tilney could censor it, or not. The Lord Mayor and aldermen could ask that all the playhouses be shut down, then watch as nothing happened. Privy Counselors could order playhouses plucked down, but, if they so chose, not enforce the order; they could order the arrest of players and dramatists; they could send inquisitors to the prisoners; and, when it suited them, they could order the prisoners released.[7] This political environment notwithstanding, the business of playing thrived.

7 For the details of the relevance of 'The Isle of Dogs' to this network of pressures, see Ingram (1978: 167–96) and Wickham et al. (2000: 438–9).

Playing Venues

When playing resumed in and around London in 1594, the companies had four playhouses available and at least four inns. By claiming that the Lord Admiral and Lord Chamberlain 'allocated . . . a playhouse' to their new companies (2004*c*, p. xiii), Andrew Gurr implies that the playhouses were not commercially autonomous. Yet James Burbage and Philip Henslowe apparently had no difficulty leasing their playhouses prior to 1594. The Curtain, too, was a profitable establishment well past 1603; two players, Thomas Pope with the Chamberlain's Men (d. 1603) and John Underwood with the King's Men (d. 1624), specified their shares in the Curtain as assets in their wills, and in 1611 a third player, Thomas Greene with Queen Anne's Men, 'held, or had lately held, the whole playhouse' (Wickham et al. 2000: 405). In contrast, the playhouse adjacent to Newington Butts, though available to the Admiral's Men and Chamberlain's Men in June 1594, was torn down a year later, in part because its owners had other uses for the property (Ingram 1992: 176–7).

The Rose was home to the Admiral's Men from 15 June 1594 into the summer of 1600. When that company moved to its new playhouse, the Fortune, in the fall of 1600, other companies moved into the Rose. Pembroke's Men were there in October 1600 (Foakes 2002: 164), and Worcester's Men spent the year of 1602–3 there (Foakes 2002: 213ff.). In an entry dated 25 June 1603, Henslowe recounts his failed attempt to renew the lease on the property and grouses that he 'wold *R*ather pulledowne the play*e*howse' than meet the owner's new requirements for the lease (Foakes 2002: 213). Whatever Henslowe's actions, the life of the Rose as a playhouse was over. Two opinions on the Admiral's Men's building of the Fortune are current: one is that the company couldn't take the competition from their new neighbors, the Chamberlain's Men, who built the Globe catty-corner across Maid Lane in the summer of 1599 (Gurr 1996*b*: 243–4); another is that disrepair at the Rose led Henslowe and Alleyn to construct the new facility (Cerasano 1994*b*: 19). Alleyn, who had retired in 1597, returned to the Fortune for several years and reprised many of his famous roles, not the least of which were in plays by Christopher Marlowe such as *The Jew of Malta* (May 1601) and *Dr Faustus* (November 1602).

The Chamberlain's Men moved to the Theatre after the run at Newington, perhaps both before and after a stint of touring. They might have continued at the Theatre for years had not Giles Allen, who owned the land on which the playhouse stood, added conditions to a renewal of the lease in the spring of 1596 that the Burbages would not accept. Allen wanted cash, an easier time getting his rent, and in the near future a conversion of the property to some other use (Wickham et al. 2000: 331–2). Confronted thus with a stubborn landlord, the Burbages scrambled for a playing place. James Burbage, who had anticipated the difficulty of bargaining with Allen, bought property in Blackfriars in February 1596. He invested substantially in renovations of the upper rooms for use as a playhouse, but his investment was put on hold when neighbors in the Blackfriars district objected (including George Carey, who had become the company's patron on his father's death in July 1596). James Burbage died in February 1597; Allen continued to resist the Burbages' version of a lease, and the Chamberlain's Men moved next door to the Curtain for a year. By the spring of 1599 the Burbage brothers were building a new playhouse, the Globe, from the timber and wood from the Theatre, which they had had dismantled at Christmastime 1598 and carted across the Thames to newly leased property in Maid Lane. The Chamberlain's Men operated at the Globe starting in late summer 1599 until a fire destroyed the building in 1612; a new Globe was built in its place, which housed the company until the parliamentary government outlawed playing in 1642.

Two new playhouses were built in the 1590s, the Swan and the Boar's Head. The hypothesis of a duopoly makes no room for these enterprises, yet both had periods in which they were genuinely competitive. Moreover, their periods of failure appear to have more to do with the temperament of their entrepreneurs and the health of their players than with any real or titular privileging of the Admiral's Men and Chamberlain's Men at their playhouses. The Swan was built in 1595 by Francis Langley on the south bank of the Thames and west of the Rose. William Ingram muses that Langley 'would have seen great numbers of Londoners' coming by the river and crossing his property in Paris Garden to arrive at the Rose for an afternoon of playgoing; this was commercial traffic he might 'intercept' with another playhouse (1978: 106). Ingram posits a company led by George Attewell, possibly including Francis Henslowe and thus possibly a version of the Queen's Men, as occupants of the Swan in the autumn of 1595 (1978: 114–20). However, the best-known occupancy of the playhouse is a run by Pembroke's Men that began in February 1597. In August the company played the notorious 'Isle of Dogs', and some of the players plus Ben Jonson (co-author of the play) landed in jail. Subsequently, three players left Langley, the Swan, and Pembroke's Men to join the Admiral's Men at the Rose; five more soon followed, later arguing that they had tried to resume playing at the Swan but found Langley impossible as a landlord. Allegedly he sued these five and they counter-sued (Ingram 1978: 186–91). As a result, another group, maybe the remainder of Pembroke's players with new fellows, leased the Swan, but after the summer of 1598 playing there ceased until 1610 (Wickham et al. 2000: 439). Former Pembroke's players who became Admiral's Men in 1597 were buying back their clothing from Langley as late as October 1598 (Foakes 2002: 68, 98, 99).

The Boar's Head playhouse was built in 1598. Oliver Woodliffe had leased the inn in 1594 that would be converted to the playhouse, and he left his partner, Richard Samwell, in charge.[8] When the 1598 building phase was remodeled and enlarged in 1599, Samwell brought in Robert Browne, leader of the Earl of Derby's Men, who could provide both money and players. The company was authorized in the summer of 1599 by the Privy Council (Wickham et al. 2000: 105, no. 57). Woodliffe sold out to Francis Langley, fresh from the debacle at the Swan. Browne's company played successfully at the Boar's Head for several years with a repertory including Thomas

[8] Unless otherwise noted, the information on the Boar's Head here is in Berry's headnote to the playhouse documents in Wickham et al. (2000: 532–5).

Heywood's two-part *Edward IV* (Berry 1986: 126), but soon Browne was also sucked into the legal maelstrom. Worcester's Men, now with Heywood writing for *them*, played at the Boar's Head in 1601–2 before moving to the Rose, and they would return to the Boar's Head as Queen Anne's Men in 1603 until they moved to the Red Bull, *c.*1606 (Berry 1986: 124). Worcester's Men, enlarged by players from Oxford's Men, were granted a license to play in March 1602, after their patron, Edward Somerset, and the Earl of Oxford petitioned the Privy Council (Wickham et al. 2000: 109, no. 59).[9] Browne's company returned to the Boar's Head at the exit of Worcester's Men to the Rose in the fall of 1602. Edward Alleyn inquired after Browne during the hiatus of London playing in 1603, and his wife, Joan, answered on 21 October 'that Browne of the Boares head is dead & dyed very pore' (Foakes 2002: 297).

When the Boar's Head inn was remodeled into a playhouse, it ceased being an inn (Wickham et al. 2000: 452). In 1593, however, there were four inns—the Bull, the Bell, the Bel Savage, and the Cross Keys—that hosted playing companies yet continued to provide bed and board to Londoners and travelers. Because no documents identify company *x* at *y* inn in the 1590s, this venue has not figured prominently in narratives about the expansion of the theatrical marketplace after 1593. Recently, however, three scholars have quickened interest in inns as playing places for adult companies in this decade. Andrew Gurr hypothesizes from a letter dated 8 October 1594 and written to the Lord Mayor by Henry Carey, Lord Chamberlain and patron of the Chamberlain's Men, that the Chamberlain's Men played regularly indoors at the Cross Keys in the winter months (Gurr 2005). Paul Menzer offers the title-page phrasing 'in the Cittie' of *Hamlet*, Q1, as supporting evidence of the company's inn-playing. Joining this discussion, Lawrence Manley assembles documentary evidence on the space available at inns for playing and the appeal of inns especially in winter; further, he considers the implications for company revenues of inns as venues (Menzer 2006*b*; Manley, forthcoming).

The Gurr, Menzer, and Manley arguments challenge the truest of truisms about playhouse venues in this decade, namely, that the Admiral's and Chamberlain's Men dominated the London theatrical marketplace precisely *because* they had beautiful and commodious outdoor playhouses at their disposal year round. If the Chamberlain's Men (for example) were spending two or three months through the winter at an inn, numerous aspects of this truism require interrogation. Concerning politics: was there a ban on inn-playing post-1594, and if so, did it have any force? Could the request of the company's patron override such a ban? Concerning repertories: would the players suspend performances for the winter of offerings with loud and smoky stage business, as Andrew Gurr suggests they did later in the move to Blackfriars (1994: 58)? Would they have played daily? If not, what would they have cut from the repertory for truncated weeks of performance? Concerning profits: what revenue might the company have received from a winter venue with the same prices as the Theatre or Globe (Wickham et al. 2000: 295) but possibly fewer performances per week in smaller spaces, particularly indoor spaces (if indeed inns had rooms for

[9] Thus the Privy Council, as it had for Derby's Men in 1599, further undermined its own limitation in 1598 and 1600 of two licensed companies.

playing)? And what of the Burbages? Would they have been happy to leave the Theatre dark while the Chamberlain's Men shared the gallery receipts with the owner of the Cross Keys instead of them?

If players wanted indoor playing spaces, they could find them on tour. Until the documentary evidence on provincial playing was published in volumes under the auspices of Records of Early English Drama (REED), the research consortium based in Toronto, theater historians had worked from a number of wrong-headed deductions about touring, including venues, audiences, economics, reasons for touring, and reception by provincial civic authorities. In brief, the REED evidence makes clear that the most common provincial site was an indoor hall, the audiences were often a mix of townspeople and VIPs, the companies' rewards made touring economically satisfactory, the repertories reflected companies' London offerings (neither dumbed down nor necessarily shortened), companies toured out of habit and commerce more than plague or financial exigency, and the players were particularly welcome when their shows offered political advantage to the local VIPs such as looking good to the companies' patrons. The subject of this essay, 'Adult Playing Companies, 1593–1603', expands exponentially when companies in the provinces are added to companies in London. The REED Patrons and Players web site documents the presence of at least twenty-five companies of adult players who performed exclusively in the provinces in the decade from 1593 to 1603.[10] Some appear in currently published REED records for just a few performances in this decade: for example, the players of the Earl of Bedford (1), Lord Eure (5), Lord Sandys (3), and Lord Sudder (1). But others have frequent performances sustained over several years and located in more than one town or county: for example, the players of Lord Dudley, six performances from 1600–3 in Coventry, Herefordshire, and Cheshire; Lord Huntingdon's players, fourteen performances from 1596 to 1603–4 in Coventry, Norwich, Bristol, Newcastle upon Tyne, and Herefordshire; Lord Monteagle's players, fourteen performances from 1593 to 1603 in Somerset, Dorset, Newcastle upon Tyne, Coventry, Norwich, Westmorland, and Yorkshire; Lord Morley's players, eleven performances from 1593 to 1603 in Gloucestershire, Newcastle upon Tyne, Norwich, Coventry, Bristol, and Cumberland; Lord Ogle's players, thirteen performances from 1593 to 1602 in Gloucestershire, Newcastle upon Tyne, Coventry, Dorset, and Somerset; and Lord Stafford's Men, eight performances from 1594 to 1603 in Dorset, Somerset, Gloucestershire, Dorset, Bristol, Herefordshire, Newcastle upon Tyne, and Yorkshire. The playing places most frequently cited in conjunction with these performances are civic halls variously designated 'booth', 'common', 'guild', 'town', and 'moot'.

Joining these provincial companies on the road were the adult companies that also played sporadically or extensively in London. For one, there is the company of the Queen's Men, who toured throughout the decade, giving more performances and being paid better than any other company. Derby's Men toured every year except perhaps from 1598 to 1600, dates coincident with the start of the Boar's Head.

[10] Additional REED data is posted to the web site regularly; readers are advised to run searches of their own and not rely on the unavoidable obsolescence of statistics here.

Worcester's Men also gave provincial performances, even in 1601–2 and 1602–3, when they were staging runs at the Boar's Head and Rose (respectively). A company of Pembroke's Men, considered defunct late in 1593, was reconstituted and on the road in 1596–7, prior to their lease of the Swan, and in 1598–1600, following the breakup that accompanied Langley's mismanagement in August 1597. The Chamberlain's Men, fresh from performances with the Admiral's Men at Newington in June 1594, may have gone straight to the Theatre as the Admiral's Men did to the Rose, and as a company staking out its territory in a duopoly might, but they are in Marlborough around September (Chambers 1923: ii. 193). The Admiral's Men also toured; a coordination of REED records with Henslowe's lists of performances for 1594–7 gives shape and timing to their routes.

In addition, companies performed at court, at the Inns of Court, and at private houses in and outside of London. The Chamberlain's Men are a good example of the three venues, in that during this decade they performed at court every Christmas, at Gray's Inn on 28 December 1594 and Middle Temple on 2 February 1602, and at houses in the country (e.g. Exton Hall, Rutland, January 1596) and in London (George Carey's house, March 1600). A view of these performances from the perspective of the court has the Chamberlain's Men clearly favored, 1594–5 to 1598–9, with nearly twice as many dates (twenty-one) as the Admiral's Men (eleven). In 1599–1600 other companies began to appear, including Derby's Men with three performances (1599–1601), the Children of Paul's with two (1600–1 and 1602–3), the Children of the Chapel with five (1600–2), Worcester's Men with one (1601–2), and Hertford's Men with one (1602–3). As Barbara Palmer definitively illustrates, a substantial number and variety of adult companies performed at two residences of Bess of Hardwick (Palmer 2005: 294–7). At Chatsworth in 1593 there are performances by the Queen's Men (28 June) and Lord Ogle's players (11–17 November).[11] At Hardwick there are performances by Lord Ogle's players, 15–21 December 1594; Lord Chandos's Men, 28 September–4 October 1595; Lord Essex's Men, 10 November 1595; the Queen's Men, 5–11 September 1596; Lord Ogle's players, 26 December–1 January 1596/7; Lord Essex's Men, 4–11 September 1597; Lord Huntingdon's players and a set of players unnamed (both in December 1599); the Queen's Men, September 1600; and Lord Thomas Howard's players, 11 October 1600.

Repertory

Philip Henslowe's diary is the place to start a discussion of repertory issues. From 19 February 1592 to 5 November 1597 Henslowe recorded the titles of plays performed at

[11] As a rule, the spread of dates such as 11–17 November indicates that items before or after the record of playing were dated precisely but not the record itself.

the Rose (plus the ten-day stretch at Newington in June 1594), along with dates of performances and his take for each performance. In October 1597 he began systematically to enter payments for playbooks and apparel, a practice he maintained into March 1603 for the Admiral's Men; he did likewise for Worcester's Men, August 1602 into May 1603. Consequently, it is possible to construct approximate repertory lists for companies at the Rose, 1592–1603,[12] and from these lists to identify repertorial principles on size, proportion of new plays to old, rhythm of stage runs, and diversity of subject matter and dramatic formula (Knutson 1991: 20–39). In many cases, even though most of the plays are lost, it is possible to identify the subject matter from the title, for example, 'Long Meg of Westminster' (1594–5) or 'Pythagoras' (1595–6). W. W. Greg went a step further by suggesting narrative sources for specific plays, including chapbooks, ballads, chronicles, and earlier plays on the same subjects. Still, the narratives behind lost plays such as 'Crack Me This Nut' (1595–6) and 'The Blind Eats Many a Fly' (1602–3) are anybody's guess. The generic formula of the lost plays is sometimes evident in the title, as in 'The French Comedy'. For others such as 'Warlamchester' (1594–5) both subject and genre are also lost.

But is Henslowe's diary a template for the repertorial strategies of other companies in its time? Fifty years ago, most theater historians would have said no. However, in 1961 R. A. Foakes and R. T. Rickert brought out an edition of the diary, in the introduction of which they challenged the low opinion of Henslowe and his business methods formulated by John Payne Collier in 1845 and repeated less scornfully by subsequent scholars. In 1962 Bernard Beckerman extended Henslowe's rehabilitation to a study of the repertory of the Chamberlain's/King's Men at the Globe; he argued that 'the practices of Shakespeare's fellows were in harmony with those of other companies' (1962: 14). Gradually Beckerman's has become the definitive position (Knutson 1991: 19–20). The corollary, though, is that there were many more dramatists writing for companies at the Theatre, Curtain, Swan, Boar's Head, and Globe than we now can identify. Henslowe's payments, 1597–1603, name seven dramatists, plus two unnamed, that would otherwise have vanished from theater records: William Boyle, William Haughton, R. Lee, a 'Pett', William Rankins, a 'Robinson', Antony Wadeson, an 'other Jentellman', and 'th*e* oth*er* poet*e*' (Foakes 2002: 124, 220). Henslowe also names several player–poets: William Bird, Charles Massey, Samuel Rowley, and Robert Shaa. Perhaps some of these men wrote for the Chamberlain's Men, along with others better known such as Thomas Dekker and Ben Jonson. There are also plays for which there is no authorial ascription, as in the following from the repertory of the Chamberlain's Men, 1594–1603: *Mucedorus*, *A Warning for Fair Women*, *A Larum for London*, and 'Cloth Breeches and Velvet Hose'. Obviously, if the companies in London matched the Admiral's Men in repertorial size, the names of a lot of dramatists are missing.

[12] An accurate list is impossible because Henslowe uses variant titles for some plays in the records for 1592–7, and those for 1597–1603 contain payments for plays left unfinished as well as omit revivals for which no additional expenses were incurred. There are, of course, other kinds of mistakes, as in repetitive dating; nevertheless, the diary remains the most illuminating document available on company repertories.

Accepting that the adult companies had similar repertorial habits, theater historians have come to recognize varieties of duplication by which companies promoted their offerings (Knutson 1991: 48–55). In addition to acquiring multi-part plays, the Admiral's Men often marketed these serials by scheduling them in tandem (e.g. the two-part 'Hercules', 7 May 1594–18 December 1595). If the Chamberlain's Men (as one example) followed suit, the Shakespearean tetralogy on the Wars of the Roses might have been played on consecutive afternoons in the late summer and fall of 1594. In addition, the Admiral's Men acquired plays with serial episodes from chronological historical time but not serialized by title, for example 'Valteger' (1596–7), 'Uther Pendragon' (1597), and 'King Arthur' (1598).[13] Moreover, they alternated plays on similar subjects; for example, the two-part 'Tamar Cham' was scheduled on the heels of Christopher Marlowe's two-part *Tamburlaine*, as though it were a two-part prequel. But the Admiral's Men also promoted plays on similar subjects by scheduling them in proximity. Marlowe's *Dr Faustus*, for example, was sometimes paired with either the lost 'Wise Man of West Chester' or the also lost 'French Doctor' (e.g. 23 and 24 January 1595, 7 and 8 February 1595). In some cases, the similarity was a theatrical hoax but advertising success, as in Ben Jonson's *Every Man In his Humor* and *Every Man Out of His Humor* for the Chamberlain's Men. A similar marketing ploy may lie behind the choice of title for *A Knack to Know an Honest Man* (Admiral's Men, 1594), which obviously invites playgoers to remember *A Knack to Know a Knave*, played by Strange's Men in 1592–3.

The case of the two 'Knack' plays raises the issue of competition across company lines. By privileging Shakespeare's and Marlowe's plays in his birth narrative of the Admiral's and Chamberlain's companies, Gurr implies that a model of competition would be Shakespeare's plays versus Marlowe's. However, widening the repertorial lens demonstrates additionally the value of lost plays and plays without company assignment, as well as the companies and playing venues marginalized by the concept of a duopoly. Two examples here must suffice. By the time Shakespeare had written *The First Part of the Contention Betwixt the Two Houses of York and Lancaster* (*The Contention*) and *The True Tragedy of Richard, Duke of York* (*The True Tragedy*), the Queen's Men probably had already been playing *The True Tragedy of Richard the Third*, which was printed in 1594; by January 1594 at least, Sussex's Men were playing 'Buckingham' (presumably, the title character was Richard Crookback's Duke of Buckingham). Shakespeare soon contributed *Richard III* to the mix. A similar competition might have been repeated with some of the same plays plus new ones in 1599–1600. This much is certain: the Admiral's Men had two plays belonging loosely to the period of the Wars of the Roses, 'Owen Tudor' and a play designated as '2 Henry Richmond'. Whatever the narrative of the lost 'Owen Tudor', certain historical connections would have been known to audiences at the Rose: that Owen Tudor had married Katherine, the widow of Henry V; that he had grandfathered Henry Richmond (Henry VII); that he had fought in the battle of Mortimer

[13] Vortigern (i.e. 'Valteger'), a fifth-century Celtic warlord, tricked Uther (then a toddler) out of his father's kingdom. When grown, Uther took revenge.

Cross on the side of Henry VI (his stepson); and that he was executed on the order of the soon-to-be-king, Edward of York (Edward IV). The opening scenes of '2 Henry Richmond' included characters familiar to Richard III's reign of terror: Richard himself, Elizabeth (either Woodville or York), Catesby, and Lovell (Foakes 2002: 287–8). How might these plays compete with offerings of other companies? The first three editions of the Chamberlain's Men's *Richard III* were printed in 1597, 1598, and 1602; *The Contention* and *The True Tragedy* were reprinted in 1600. Such life in a bookstall suggests that any part or parts of this Shakespearean serial might have been revived in these years. But perhaps the Chamberlain's Men did not participate. Derby's Men certainly did. They had a two-part *Edward IV*, which was entered in the Stationers' Register on 28 August 1599, 'when the company was just settling into the Boar's Head', and printed in 1599 and 1600 (Berry 1986: 126). Over the two parts, Heywood dramatizes the progress of Matthew and Jane Shore from happily married couple to estrangement to semi-reconciliation in death. Worcester's Men also joined in with 'A playe wherin shores wife is written' by Henry Chettle and John Day in 1603 (Foakes 2002: 226). The Queen's Men's old *True Tragedy of Richard III* was not reprinted after 1594, but that fact does not rule out the memory for long-time playgoers—and dramatists—of Jane Shore's beggary.

A second example includes at least eight plays on stage between 1591 and 1598, both new and in revival: Peele's *Edward I*, company unknown, Q1593; the anonymous *Jack Straw*, company unknown, Q1593; Marlowe's *Edward II*, Pembroke's Men (1592–3), Q1594; the anonymous 'Longshanks', Admiral's Men, 1595–6, lost; the anonymous *Edward III*, company unknown, Q1596; the anonymous *Woodstock*, company unknown, undated manuscript; Shakespeare's *Richard II*, Chamberlain's Men, Q1597; and the anonymous 'Alls Perce' (or 'Alice Perrers'), Admiral's Men, 1597–8, lost.[14] The obvious connection is the sequential reigns of four Plantagenet monarchs: Edward I to Richard II. But from a marketing point of view, there are additional points of contact, rich in irony. For example, in *Edward I* (which may or may not be the 'Longshanks' in Henslowe's play list) the King, in a merry mood, shaves himself onstage to show Queen Eleanor the folly of ordering that Englishmen remove their beards; the christening of Prince Edward follows, celebrated with patriotic chest-thumping and an elaborate show. In *Edward II* that patriotic fervor is turned against the King, and he too is shaved onstage, in puddle water, in the lead-up to his murder. The newly crowned boy king, Edward III, rules the stage at the end of *Edward II*; in *Edward III*, in a scene widely believed to have been written by Shakespeare, he flirts with the Countess of Salisbury. If the lost 'Alls Perce' told Bandello's version of the story (Bandello 1890: iv/2, no. 4), that Countess of Salisbury was Alice Perrers, who (unlike Jane Shore) protected her virtue with the threat of suicide until the King proposed, then married her. The referentiality of *Edward II*, the one play by Marlowe that the Admiral's Men did *not* acquire, and *Richard II* are well known; what is not

[14] W. W. Greg called this play 'Alice Pierce', and said nothing was known of it (1904–8: ii. 189). Bill Lloyd suggested to me that it might instead be 'Alice Perrers', mistress of Edward III. Greg's other supposition, which seems reasonable, is that the play was initially owned by the company of Pembroke's Men at the Swan in 1597 (1904–8: ii. 187).

remarked as frequently is that Shakespeare avoids Jack Straw's rebellion, though many have noticed the similarity between that rebel and Shakespeare's Jack Cade (2 *Henry VI*, possibly in revival, 1594–6). The anonymous *Woodstock* also skips the Peasants' Revolt, but it does bitterly evoke the battlefield success at the end of *Edward III* by having first the ghosts of the Black Prince and then Edward III powerless to warn Woodstock of his imminent death.

Book Trade

In the old scholarship, stationers are perceived as adversaries of the playhouse world, pirating texts and publishing unauthorized 'bad' quartos. Now scholars are more interested in the commercial value of playbooks for stationers and the possible partnerships between stationers and playwrights. Peter Blayney lays to rest the issue of stationers as pirates, partly by demonstrating (as do others such as Gerald Johnson) that the professional practices of numerous stationers were moral, legal, and unexceptional. Blayney argues further that playbooks were insufficiently popular to justify piracy. Alan Farmer and Zachary Lesser counter the argument on unpopularity with statistics that suggest an increasing demand for playbooks around 1600, evident in the volume of first and 'second-plus' editions (2005: 10). Another feature of the relationship between the stage and print media in the decade of 1593–1603 is the eagerness of some dramatists such as John Marston and Ben Jonson to get their plays into stationers' hands.

There are two periods in the decade of 1593–1603 in which the companies themselves appear eager to get their plays into print. Blayney ties the first of these phenomena, December 1593–December 1595, to a desire on the part of companies to advertise the resumption of playing in London after the long hiatus due to plague (1997: 386). For theater historians, it is worth noting that there is little consistency in the advertising material. Several plays such as *Jack Straw*, *Locrine*, and *The Contention* have title pages with generously descriptive subtitles but no mention of company ownership, author, or venue. The title pages of others such as *Edward II* and *A Knack to Know a Knave* offer outdated company information. Another, *The Battle of Alcazar*, provides apparently accurate information about ownership by the Admiral's Men on the title page, but that information cannot be verified because the play does not appear by that title in Henslowe's diary. Only for *The Massacre at Paris* is the title page information ideal: narrative action provided in the subtitle, company ownership (Admiral's Men) verifiable by Henslowe's diary, and author (Christopher Marlowe); ironically, the text printed with the exemplary title page is as bad as 'bad' quartos get.

Blayney is not as certain about motives in the second period, May 1599–October 1601 (1997: 386), but possible contributing factors are a campaign advertising the patrons of the companies, the expansion of their own business into new playhouses, and the renewal of competition with the children's companies (Knutson 2001: 68–73).

In significant difference with the cluster of printings in 1593–5, the typical 1600–1 publication is a recent repertory item with a 'good' text and accurate title page information (none, however, mentions its playhouse venue). The consistent quality of the 1600–1 quartos reinforces the argument that the companies themselves made the scripts available to stationers. An exemplar is *2 Henry IV* (Q1600), which was probably new in 1597–8; its title page describes the action, advertises the company owners, and names the author. Furthermore, its copy is 'good'. Others in the 1600–1 batch miss one or more critical details: the two-part *Edward IV* advertises Derby's Men but not the author; *Look About You* claims to be an Admiral's play but does not use a title verifiable by Henslowe's records; and *Two Lamentable Tragedies* provides neither company nor author on the title page of its quarto.

Audiences

The debate about audiences concerns the class of playgoers, their taste relative to class, their gender, and their loyalty to one venue or another. The old scholarship tends to segregate audiences according to class as well as venue. Typical is R. B. Sharpe, who assigns the Admiral's Men audiences of '*older*, less sophisticated, more middle-class types' (1935: 19), which by implication gives the Chamberlain's Men younger, more sophisticated, and higher-class playgoers. Though Sharpe admits that 'audiences cannot have been mutually exclusive' (1935: 21), he nonetheless seeks to prove that the repertory of each company was fine-tuned 'to distinct tastes in their audiences' (1935: 21). Sharpe's assessment is based on both preference for Shakespeare's plays and a disdain for repertory offerings in categories of popular culture. Though Sharpe does not say so, his contrast between audiences of the Admiral's and Chamberlain's Men is essentially the argument made for the clientele at private playhouses with children's companies, adjusted to fit two outdoor playhouses. Ann Jennalie Cook (1981) and Andrew Gurr (1987) do much to dispel these biases, even though they disagree on the relative percentage of members of the leisured class at the outdoor playhouses. It is simplistic but perhaps illustrative to consider the playgoing habits of one Edmund Pudsey, a Derbyshire gentleman who lived in London *c.*1600. Pudsey kept a commonplace book in which he entered scraps of plays. From these scraps, it appears that he either saw or read plays that had been performed at the following playhouses: the Rose, the Fortune, the Globe, the Boar's Head, Paul's, and Blackfriars (Knutson 2001: 144–5). The question is whether he was a typical playgoer in his appetite for different theatrical venues.

Perhaps as scholars pursue the inter-repertorial competition among companies, they will accumulate evidence that speaks to the issue of the loyalty or promiscuity of playhouse audiences in 1593–1603 and thus shed further light on the class, taste, and gender of Elizabethan playgoers.

CHAPTER 4

ADULT PLAYING COMPANIES 1603–1613

TOM RUTTER

For two obvious and related reasons, 1603 seems a highly appropriate date at which to begin a new chapter in the history of early modern theatre companies. First, it marks the end of one reign and the beginning of another: Elizabeth died on 24 March, and James was crowned on 25 July. More specifically, as far as the playing companies were concerned, it brought a wholesale change in theatrical patronage. In *The Time Triumphant* (1604), his panegyric on the new king's arrival in England and progress through the City of London, Gilbert Dugdale follows a description of James's munificence in 'creating Knights of gentlemen, Lordes of Knights and Earles of Lords' with the observation that he also

> to the meane gaue grace, as taking to him the late Lord chamberlaines seruants now the Kings acters: the Queene taking to her the Earle of Worsters seruants that are now her acters, the Prince their sonne Henry Prince of Wales full of hope, tooke to him the Earle of Nottingham his seruants who are now his acters, so that of Lords seruants they are now the seruants of the King Queene and Prince. (Dugdale 1604, B1^{v})

The letters patent appointing the erstwhile Lord Chamberlain's servants the King's Men are dated 19 May 1603, making this one of the earliest acts of James's reign; the servants of the Earl of Worcester and of the Lord Admiral (who became Earl of Nottingham in 1597) had respectively become Queen Anne's Men and Prince Henry's Men by February 1604 (Chambers 1923: ii. 208, 229, 186 n. 1).

As the first section of this chapter will attempt to show, these changes of patronage had significant repercussions for the adult companies over the decade that followed.

The next section, however, will consider patronage in relation to other factors that affected the companies' business structures and commercial fortunes between 1603 and 1613, notably the security that two of the companies enjoyed at their playhouses from the turn of the century, the revival of the children's companies around the same time, and the prevalence of plague throughout much of the decade. The final section will focus on the companies' core product, the plays in their repertories, identifying two further and conflicting influences on dramatic production: the need for playing companies to be competitive, and the evolution of distinctive company styles.

PATRONAGE

In the passage quoted above, Dugdale presents the elevation of the adult companies from servants of nobility to servants of royalty as an example of James's regal grace, placing it within the context of the liberal ennoblements for which the new king's progress south towards London is notorious. However, historians of the theatre such as E. K. Chambers, Glynne Wickham, and Richard Dutton have tended to see it not just as an honour but as the culmination of a tendency towards centralized control of the theatre that was already prevalent during the reign of Elizabeth. 'Legislation had progressively limited the privilege of patronizing a troupe of actors: in 1572 knights and gentry lost it; in 1598 justices of the peace lost the power to authorize performers in their own right' (Dutton 1997*b*: 297). When the Elizabethan Statute for the Punishment of Rogues and Vagabonds and Sturdy Beggars was revised in July 1604, barons and other nobles also lost the right of dramatic patronage, effectively restricting it to members of the royal family (Wickham et al. 2000: 131). Furthermore, in 1598 the right to perform regularly in London and its environs had been restricted to the Chamberlain's and the Admiral's Men, and in 1600 it was stipulated that these companies were to perform only at the Globe and the Fortune respectively (Dutton 1997*b*: 296; Wickham 1959–81: ii/1. 104–5). Not only was the change of patronage a symptom of state interference in the drama as well as royal approbation; rather than being a straightforwardly Jacobean phenomenon, it was a 'further advance on... lines already laid down' (Chambers 1923: i. 302).

This narrative has been disputed, however, by J. Leeds Barroll, who questions the degree of royal interest in the drama that it appears to assume. In fact, he argues, it is more likely to have been the players themselves who took the initiative in obtaining royal patronage: the Chamberlain's Men, whose patron, George Carey, was mortally ill at the time of the succession, may have used an influential ally such as the Earl of Pembroke to obtain James's favour, encouraging the other companies to follow suit (Barroll 1991: 31–49). While Barroll's argument is speculative, it is at least a salutary reminder that royal patronage had significant attractions for those companies lucky enough to obtain it. In a society that was very much concerned with status, where one major playwright took pains to obtain a coat of arms for his father and another boasted to William Drummond that his grandfather 'served King Henry 8 & was a Gentleman' (Jonson 1925–52: i. 139), the right to call oneself the servant of royalty was presumably an appealing one. However, the change of patronage also offered the companies more tangible benefits, one of which became obvious during the long closure of the theatres that began at Elizabeth's death and appears to have continued, as a result of the plague, up to 9 April 1604. During the winter the King's Men received a grant of £30 from the Treasurer of the Chamber, a practice that was repeated when plague struck in 1608–9 and 1609–10 (Chambers 1923: i. 218); presumably it was felt that, as the King's servants, the company needed to be maintained during periods of financial hardship.

If actors were servants of royalty, it also meant they could generally expect a higher level of reward from the provincial authorities when they toured. The Chamberlains' and Wardens' account book of Coventry records that when the King's Men came to that city in 1603 they received 40*s*., as compared with payments of 20*s*. each to Worcester's and Nottingham's; the Queen's Men had received 40*s*. in 1593 and 1594 (Ingram 1981: 362, 338, 341). The year 1603 seems to have been one of unusual munificence: on the four previous occasions when Worcester's Men had come to Coventry since 1599, they had never received more than 10*s*. As Queen Anne's Men, however, they were given 20*s*. in 1607 and 1608, and 40*s*. in 1606, 1609, and 1613 (Ingram 1981: 353–60, 370–6, 386). The same city rewarded Lady Elizabeth's Men with the generous sum of £4 in 1612 and 1613, perhaps remembering the Princess's visit to Coventry in 1604 (Ingram 1981: 383, 386, 364–5). A similar pattern occurs in York, where Worcester's Men received 30*s*. in April 1599, less than the Queen's (40*s*.) but more than Lincoln's and Monteagle's (20*s*. each); as Queen Anne's Men, however, they received £4 in 1606 (Johnston and Rogerson 1979: i. 488, 521). When the same company visited Norwich in October 1609, they were paid 30*s*., in comparison to the 20*s*. that had typically been given to nobleman's servants since 1603, although less than the Duke of York's Men were given in May *not* to play—a phenomenon I shall discuss in more detail later on (Galloway 1984: 121–34). Royally patronized companies were not always better rewarded than others, but it happened frequently enough to be described as a significant advantage of their new status.

A final way in which the companies profited from James's accession was through the marked increase in the number of court performances that it brought. While the largest number of plays performed at court during a year of Elizabeth's reign was thirteen, between 1 September 1600 and 31 August 1601, from 1603–4 to 1613–14 the average was twenty-four (including performances by children's companies), reaching a peak of forty-four in 1611–12 (Barroll 1975: 50–1). This growth may be ascribed partly to the King's own hospitality—he brought forward the beginning of the season to early November, and occasionally had plays in Lent—but more obviously to the fact that, unlike Elizabeth, James had a family. Dudley Carleton wrote to John Chamberlain in January 1604 that while James had seemed to take 'no extraordinary pleasure' in plays over the Christmas season, 'The queen and prince were more the players' friends, for on other nights they had them privately' (Carleton 1972: 53); in view of this, it must be remembered that just because a company performed at court does not mean that it performed before the King. According to Andrew Gurr, Prince Henry's Men played at court forty-four times between 1603 and 1613; however, of these performances at least sixteen were before the Prince, not King James (Gurr 1996*b*: 255–6).

While the interest that Queen Anne, in particular, took in the production of masques at court is well known, beginning with *The Vision of the Twelve Goddesses* in 1604, the effect of royal patronage on the output of the professional companies is less clear—though their personnel did, in fact, take speaking roles in court masques, an experience that may lie behind the incorporation of masque elements in plays such as *The Tempest* (Orgel 1975: 39, 45–8). Anne is supposed to have attended plays, presumably at court, 'in order to enjoy the laugh against her husband', according to the French ambassador, Beaumont (Chambers 1923: i. 325), but this is very different from saying that she instigated any such satire. Indeed, as far as performances at court are concerned, the arrival of a new royal family seems to have been not so much a creative stimulus as an opportunity to restage old material. Of eleven performances the King's Men gave at court between 1 November 1604 and 12 February 1605, at least eight were of old plays, namely *Every Man in His Humour, Every Man Out of His Humour, The Merry Wives of Windsor, The Comedy of Errors, Henry V, Love's Labour's Lost*, and *The Merchant of Venice* (twice); the other plays were *Measure for Measure, Othello*, and the otherwise unknown 'The Spanish Maze' (Chambers 1923: ii. 211). In the public theatres, however, there are indications that from early on in James's reign plays were staged by the adult companies that sought to reflect the interests of their patrons. In 1604 the King's Men apparently produced a play, now lost, on the Gowrie conspiracy of 1600, when an attempt was made on James's life by John Ruthven, Earl of Gowrie, and his brother Alexander; according to John Chamberlain, writing in December 1604, 'whether the matter or the manner be not well handled, or that it be thought unfit that Princes should be played on the stage in their lifetime, I hear that some great councellors are much displeased with it, and so 'tis thought shall be forbidden' (Chambers 1923: i. 328). It seems unlikely that the King's Men would have deliberately set out to stage a play in which their new patron was unfavourably represented; rather, it may have been an ill-conceived attempt to tell the story of his providential deliverance from treason. *King Lear* (1605–6) and *Macbeth* (1606) are two more fortunate instances where the King's Men dealt with matters about which James is known to have been concerned, namely the union of the British kingdoms and witchcraft; the title page of the former, published in quarto in 1608, advertised it as having been 'played before the Kings Maiestie at Whitehall vpon S. *Stephans* night in Christmas Hollidayes' (Shakespeare 1608).[1]

A less familiar instance where a connection can be made between a company's output and the identity of its patron is Samuel Rowley's play *When You See Me, You*

[1] Except where indicated, dates of performance are taken from Harbage (1964). Quotations from Shakespeare—other than from early copies, which are cited in the Bibliography—or from supporting editorial material refer to Shakespeare (1974, 1994). Quotations from Jonson are from Jonson (1925–52).

Know Me, staged by Prince Henry's Men in or before 1605. The play depicts the reign of Henry VIII, from the death of Jane Seymour onwards, with an idiosyncratic approach to chronology and incident that is quite understandable given the potential of the subject matter to cause offence; Andrew Gurr presents it as an example of the Elect Nation plays, 'stimulated by the surge of nostalgia for Tudor glories that followed Elizabeth's death', in which Prince Henry's and Queen Anne's Men specialized (Gurr 1996*b*: 244). However, the company's choice of subject matter may derive from causes beyond the tastes of its public audience. The full title given in the 1605 Quarto is *When You See Me, You Know Me, or, The Famous Chronicle Historie of King Henry the Eight, with the Birth and Vertuous Life of Edward Prince of Wales*, 'As it was playd by the high and mightie Prince of Wales his seruants. By SAMVELL ROVVLY, seruant to the Prince' (Rowley 1605). A link between the Prince of Wales depicted in the play and the Prince of Wales whose servants wrote and performed it is thus emphasized from the beginning, and is reiterated through Henry's words to Jane as she goes into labour:

> Now I*ane* God bring me but a chopping boy,
> Be but the Mother to a Prince of Wales
> Ad a ninth Henrie to the English Crowne,
> And thou mak'st full my hopes.
>
> (Rowley 1605, B1^{r})

In the event the child is named Edward, because he is born on St Edward's day; but the King's wish for a ninth Henry has a prophetic resonance, in that the son of James I was expected eventually to assume this title. '[T]he hope that *England* hath, is now in him,' King Henry will later say of his son, and elsewhere, 'he is all our hopes, | That what our age shall leaue vnfinished, | In his faire raigne shall be accomplished' (Rowley 1605, H2^{r}, F1^{v}). In 1605 the 11-year-old Henry, whose devout protestantism is paralleled by Prince Edward's in the play, must have seemed like just such an image of youthful promise ('Henry Prince of Wales full of hope', to repeat Dugdale's formulation); for the modern reader the irony of Edward's early death, of which Jacobean playgoers were aware, is compounded by the knowledge that Henry himself was not to live past 18.

When You See Me, You Know Me is one instance where a play's Tudor setting and Protestant sympathies seem to owe as much to the identity of its company's patron as to a desire to appeal 'to the city and citizens' (Gurr 1996*b*: 244). It should be emphasized, however, that Prince Henry's was not the only company to stage plays in this idiom: *Sir Thomas Wyatt* (1602–7) and the two parts of *If You Know Not Me You Know Nobody* (1603–5) were both performed by the servants of Queen Anne, and in these instances the link between a play and the religious sympathies of its patron is rather harder to draw. This question of the repertories, and the diverse forces by which they were shaped, is one to which I shall return later; first, however, it will be necessary to give a brief sketch of the evolving commercial context in which those repertories developed.

Business Structures

Because Henslowe's records of play receipts end at July 1600, and his records of expenditure on playing companies' behalf at March 1603/4, there is no body of information about the day-to-day activities of any one playing company between 1603 and 1613 as there is for the previous decade (Henslowe 2002, p. xxviii). However, it can be cautiously asserted that, for the adult actors at least, this was a period of relative stability. All three of the London companies taken into royal patronage in 1603–4 were still in existence in 1613, although Prince Henry's Men had become the servants of the King's son-in-law Frederick V, the Elector Palatine ('the Palsgrave') following Henry's death, thus proving more durable than their patron. Furthermore, two other companies, the servants of Prince Charles and of Lady Elizabeth, had gained patents to play in London in March 1610 and March 1611 respectively (Chambers 1923: ii. 242, 246). This situation contrasts noticeably with that of the 1590s, which saw a wholesale reorganization of the London playing companies in 1594 and the demise in the capital of the Earl of Pembroke's Men following the 'Isle of Dogs' affair of 1597. It also contrasts with the situation of the children's companies between 1603 and 1613. When in 1608 the Children of the Queen's Revels caused offence by staging plays on James's Scottish mines and on the conspiracy of Byron, the King ordered their dissolution and the closure of the playhouses; in combination with the closure of the theatres due to plague between summer 1608 and early 1610 (see below), this 'led to the disintegration of the Children of the [Queen's] Revels and the Children of the King's Revels... the Children of Paul's having folded around 1606', although a reconstituted Queen's Revels company went on to perform at Whitefriars from 1610 (Munro 2005: 21–5; Dutton 2002).

Some other pieces of evidence support the argument that during this decade the condition of the adult professional theatre in London was comparatively stable. The wills of several actors indicate that they died possessed of substantial sums: for example, in a will dated 22 July 1603 and proved 13 February 1604 the King's man Thomas Pope disposes of over £200 in ready money plus several properties, jewellery, and shares in the Globe and Curtain playhouses. The King's man Augustine Phillips, in a will dated 4 May and proved 13 May 1605, makes individual bequests totalling over £100, for which he assumes the third part of his estate will be sufficient. Finally, the Prince Henry's man Thomas Towne, in a will dated 4 July and proved 1 August 1612, bequeaths over £30 in addition to the lands and goods he leaves to his wife (Honigmann and Brock 1993: 68–75, 88–90). Obviously, the fact that bequests were made does not automatically mean that sums were available to cover them, but in these instances the testators evidently felt themselves to be men of substantial assets. Furthermore, it apparently became possible in this period to retire on the proceeds of a career in the theatre, as Shakespeare did—although it must be remembered that Shakespeare, like Pope and Phillips, was in the unusual situation of owning shares in the playhouse where he acted, and thus received a greater portion of the profits from performance than was usual for players. It is noticeable, incidentally, that in their wills Pope, Phillips, and Towne all refer to themselves as gentlemen, and in *An Apology for Actors* (1612) Thomas Heywood reinforces the impression that some players, at least, were achieving a degree of respectability: 'Many amongst vs, I know, to be of substance, of gouernment, of sober liues, and temperate carriages, house-keepers, and contributary to all duties enioyned them, equally with them that are rank't with the most bountifull' (Heywood 1612, E3^r^).

As far as the companies themselves are concerned, the fortunes of the King's Men appear to suggest that during the first decade of James's reign it was possible for an adult playing company not just to survive, but to flourish. The most obvious indication of this is the fact that, from 1608 onwards, the company was uniquely in a position to perform at two theatres, the Globe and the Blackfriars. It had effectively owned the Globe since its construction in 1599, insofar as money to buy the lease and to erect the playhouse had come from the company members Richard Burbage, John Hemmings, William Kempe, Augustine Phillips, Thomas Pope, and William Shakespeare, along with Burbage's brother Cuthbert. By 1608 the shareholders were the Burbages, Hemmings, Pope, Shakespeare, Henry Condell, and William Sly (Wickham et al. 2000: 493–4). In the same year, however, the problems of the child actors gave the company the opportunity to expand into the playhouse at Blackfriars. The Burbages had inherited the property from their father, James, who bought it in 1596 and built a theatre there but was prevented from making it the home of the Chamberlain's Men when local residents objected. Since 1600 the playhouse had been leased to Henry Evans, and performances had been given there by the Children of the Queen's Revels. On the departure of the children, the lease was bought back and equally divided between the Burbages, Condell, Hemmings, Shakespeare, Sly, and one Thomas Evans, with the result that the Burbages owned the land and received both the rent and—with the other shareholders—a portion of the takings at plays (Wickham et al. 2000: 501–3, 507–8, 515–17). The decision to use two theatres was one in which the company persisted after the Globe burned down on 29 June 1613, spending twice as much on the building of the new Globe as their lease obliged them to and continuing to alternate between it and the Blackfriars (Wickham et al. 2000: 607). Gurr calls this 'much more an investment in nostalgia than an investment for profit, since their income would have remained much the same from playing at the Blackfriars all the year round as it would from the two playhouses used seasonally' (Gurr 1996*b*: 118); however, it can also be seen less sentimentally as an investment in the Jacobean status economy. One might compare the £1,400 spent on rebuilding the Globe with the £1,300 spent the same year by the Grocers' company on the staging of Thomas Middleton's *The Triumphs of Truth*—'the most expensive mayoral pageant of the Renaissance' (Bergeron 1971: 179). Like the pageant, commissioned to celebrate the election of the playwright's namesake Thomas Middleton as Mayor, the costly rebuilding of the Globe was a piece of conspicuous expenditure that served to emphasize one company's disposable wealth and pre-eminent status. No other playing company was in a position to alternate between two theatres, leaving one empty while it played in the other.

Why were the years 1603–13 such good ones for adult professional companies in comparison to the previous decade? No doubt the bringing of the companies into royal patronage was an important factor. It provided a resolution of sorts to the struggle between the Privy Council and the Mayor and Corporation for control over the London theatre that had been ongoing during the 1580s and 1590s: the 1603 patent of the King's Men licensed them to perform, plague permitting, 'as well within their now usual house called the Globe within our County of Surrey, as also within any Town Halls or Moothalls or other convenient places within the liberties and freedom of any other city, university, town, or borough whatsoever within our said realms and dominions', and similar wording was to be used when Prince Henry's and Queen Anne's Men finally received formal patents in 1606 and 1609 respectively (Wickham et al. 2000: 123; Chambers 1923: ii. 188, 231). Attempts by the Mayor and Corporation to restrict playing in London during this period seem to have been more limited and temporary in their aims than they were in the previous decade: whereas a letter of 28 July 1597 had called for the 'fynall suppressinge of... Stage playes', arguing that 'neither in politie nor in religion they are to be suffered in a Christian Commonwealth', on 12 April 1607 the Mayor requested of the Lord Chamberlain only the 'restrayninge' of stage plays during the present time of plague (Chambers 1923: iv. 321, 339). It is noticeable that when the former liberty of the Blackfriars came under the jurisdiction of the city in September 1608, the Mayor and Corporation of London do not appear to have made any attempt to stop the King's Men from performing there, although they did try to do so after receiving petitions from citizens of the parish in late 1618 and early 1619 (Chambers 1923: ii. 480, 511; Wickham et al. 2000: 522). In fact, the focus of conflict between players and municipal authorities seems to have shifted somewhat from London to the provinces. A minute dated 23 September 1607 in the house books of York city council runs as follows:

> And now the Quenes Ma*ies*ties Players have made suite to this Court that they might be pe*rm*itted to plaie in this Cittie and have showed a licence from her Ma*ies*tie that they maie be pe*rm*itted to plaie in all Cittye and Townes Corporate It is agreed by thes pr*esent*es that they shalbe pe*rm*itted to playe [suche] in this Citties so as they do not plaie on the Sabaoth daies & on the night*es*. (Johnston and Rogerson 1979: i. 522)

This is testimony to the invaluable usefulness of royal patents as far as the companies were concerned, since the York authorities were beginning to prevent companies without them from playing, albeit with some recompense from the municipal coffers: in March 1607, 30*s*. were given to 'my L*or*d Dudley players w*hi*ch plaid not', and 40*s*. were given to Lord Eure's in September 1608 according to the same formula (Johnston and Rogerson 1979: i. 524, 528). That this attitude stemmed from a distrust of itinerant actors rather than a zealous interpretation of the 1604 Statute for the Punishment of Rogues and Vagabonds and Sturdy Beggars, or a disapproval of playing in general, is suggested by the Corporation's temporary granting of a petition from Richard Middleton and others requesting that they be permitted to build a theatre for locals to perform in, 'w*hi*ch might be A meanes to restrayne the frequent Co*m*minge thervnto of other Stage plaiers, and they would yeild x li. p*er* annu*m* vnto this Corporac*i*on', though they reversed this decision a few months later (Johnston and Rogerson 1979: i. 530–1). The phenomenon of non-royal companies being paid not to play had also arisen in Norwich, where in October 1609 Queen Anne's Men were paid 30*s*. and presumably, as in March 1611, given leave 'to play for one weeke so that they play neither on the saboth day nor in the night nor more then one play on a day'; in 1610–11, however, Lord Bartlett (Berkeley?)'s, Lord Chandos's, Lord Eure's, and Lord Monteagle's were all paid not to play—as, indeed, were the Duke of York's ('Lo*r*d Abonye his men') (Galloway 1984: 134–6). The instances provided above suggest that questions that had been largely resolved in London—the relative authority of civic bodies, nobles, and Crown, the permissibility of plays on the sabbath, the frequency of playing, and who should be allowed to profit from it—were still contentious elsewhere in the country.

A second reason for the comparative stability of the years 1603–13 may have been that the principal companies were now reasonably settled in their respective playhouses. The King's Men controlled the Globe through the group of sharers who jointly owned it, and their lease on the land where it was built was due to last until Christmas 1629, making any quarrels such as the one between the Burbages and Giles Allen over the Theatre much less likely. They were on even surer ground at the Blackfriars, where the Burbages owned the land as well as shares in the playhouse. The Fortune was jointly owned by Philip Henslowe, who had been the landlord of the Admiral's Men at the Rose, and Edward Alleyn, the company's former lead actor; Prince Henry's/the Palsgrave's Men continued to play there, and in the playhouse which replaced it when it was burned down in 1621, until the end of their existence (Wickham et al. 2000: 493, 611, 638–9). The disadvantages of not having a permanent home are indicated by the problems that Lady Elizabeth's Men experienced following their amalgamation with the Children of the Whitefriars in 1613. As they complained two years later, they had agreed with Henslowe 'that they should enter bond to play with him for three years at such house and houses as he shall appoint', but he failed to honour his agreement to enter bond 'to find them a convenient house and houses, and to lay out such moneys as four of the sharers should think fit for their use in apparel'. The company ended up having to share the Hope theatre with the bear-baitings also staged there by Henslowe, who furthermore failed to pay them 50*s*. as promised 'in consideration of the company's lying still one day in fourteen for his baiting' (Wickham et al. 2000: 219). The King's and Prince Henry's Men were by now insulated from such problems.

A third factor that may have contributed to the adult companies' stability is one that initially may rather have seemed a threat. In the 1603 Quarto of *Hamlet* Gilderstone informs the Prince that the actors are travelling because 'the principall publike audience that | Came to them, are turned to priuate playes, | And to the humour of children' (Shakespeare 1603, E3^{r}), and this may be an indication that the adult companies had lost some business owing to the revival of children's companies at St Paul's in 1599 and at the Blackfriars in 1600 (see A. Cook 1981: 128–9; Gurr 2004*b*: 82). However, the genuine degree of the threat posed to the business of the adult actors is debatable. The children did not perform daily, perhaps only 'once a weeke' as the Epilogue to *Eastward Ho* (1605) implies (Jonson 1925–52: iv. 619), and Richard Burbage owned the land on which the Blackfriars theatre was built, thereby indirectly profiting from the company that performed there (Knutson 2001: 38). It can further be argued, however, that the existence of the children's companies benefited the adults by diverting potentially offensive or risky materials away from the public theatres. In the wake of the 'Isle of Dogs' affair of 1597 the Privy Council ordered the demolition of the theatres in Shoreditch and Bankside (although this order was never executed), while *Sejanus* (1603) led to Ben Jonson (though not the King's Men) being accused of 'popperie and treason' and examined by the Privy Council (Wickham et al. 2000: 100–1; Jonson 1925–52: i. 141). With the aforementioned exception of the Gowrie play, however, the other offensive plays of 1603–13 seem to have been written for the Children of the Queen's Revels: *Philotas* (1604), *Eastward Ho*, *The Isle of Gulls* (1606), *Byron* (1608), and the 1608 Scottish mines play (Dutton 2002: 335). By contrast, the adults seem by now to have tended to avoid dangerous subjects: in *An Apology for Actors* Heywood condemns plays that inveigh 'against the State, the Court, the Law, the Citty, and their gouernements', and the 'liberty which some arrogate to themselues, committing their bitternesse, and liberall inuectiues against all estates, to the mouthes of Children' (Heywood 1612, G3^{v}). It was the children at Blackfriars, not any of the adult companies, who performed the plays that led to the theatres being closed in 1608.

That the King's Men, Queen Anne's Men, and Prince Henry's/the Palgrave's Men survived the years 1603–13 intact is the more remarkable given the extent to which the London theatres were affected by plague during that decade: as Barroll emphasizes, 'Between 1603 and 1611, the playhouses in London were closed off and on for a period of at least sixty-eight months' (Barroll 1991: 19), including one particularly lengthy period between July 1608 and January 1610 when they were not open at all. Evidently, one way in which the companies coped was by touring the provinces: during the long period of closure between May 1603 and April 1604, for example, the King's Men played in Coventry, Booth Hall in Shrewsbury, Bath, and Bridgnorth, while during the 1608–10 closure they are recorded as having played at Coventry, Dunwich, Ipswich, Hythe, New Romney, Oxford, and Dover (Gurr 2004*c*: 59–60). A more contentious issue is whether the London companies still 'expected to tour as a normal requirement of their occupation, not as an act of desperation' (Greenfield 1997: 252). The partial nature of the record, and its frequent lack of precision over dates, makes this difficult to determine. However, it can be said that at least one of the three main London companies, Queen Anne's, regularly played in the provinces when there was no plague in the capital, for instance in Shrewsbury between Michaelmas 1611 and 1612 (J. Somerset 1994*a*: i. 301), in Barnstaple between Michaelmas 1612 and 1613 (Wasson 1986: 49), in Bridgwater in 1612 (Stokes and Alexander 1996: i. 59), and in Coventry in 1613 (Ingram 1981: 386). On 14 March and 23 September 1612 they visited Londesborough, one of the Yorkshire residences of the Clifford family—a salutary reminder of the importance to touring companies of provincial 'great houses' as well as urban centres (Palmer 2005: 298). Conversely, it would be understandable if the King's Men and Prince Henry's Men, now settled at the Globe and the Fortune, toured primarily during times of plague; the aforementioned royal subsidies, like that of £40 in January 1609 'by way of his ma*jes*t*ies* rewarde for their private practise in the time of infecc*i*on that thereby they mighte be inhabled to performe their service before his Ma*jes*tie in Christmas hollidaies 1609' (Chambers 1923: iv. 175) may have made even this exigency less urgent.

Repertories

It may seem odd that in the foregoing discussion of the adult companies' commercial fortunes between 1603 and 1613 no attention has been paid to the core product on which they depended for their income, namely the plays they performed. If, for example, the King's Men were indeed pre-eminent during the period, was this not in large part because William Shakespeare was their principal dramatist? The importance of the creative talents on which companies were able to draw is obvious; however, the plays of Shakespeare, along with those of other well-known King's Men dramatists such as Jonson and Fletcher, need to be considered in the context of the repertory in which they appeared. No company could have survived on the plays of Shakespeare alone, however outstanding; as Bernard Beckerman argued in 1962, Shakespeare's company must have used business methods similar to those that can be extrapolated from Henslowe's diary for the Admiral's and Worcester's Men, offering 'about seventeen new plays a year, grouping them in two seasons so that a new play was presented every fourteen to fifteen days' (Beckerman 1962: 13). More recently, Roslyn Knutson has written of a 'battery of plays offered to the public on a daily basis', in which duplications of other companies' successes, revivals of and sequels to popular plays, and (in a word) 'fillers' were of prime importance (Knutson 1991: 4, 48, 37, 50, 13–14). Thus, the success of all the adult companies depended on their being able to stage a large and evolving repertoire of plays which capitalised both on their own and on other companies' successes. Shakespeare's plays, as Knutson shows, relied upon this repertory system as well as participating skilfully in it: 'Shakespeare supplied the kinds of plays that audiences liked, with stories that they liked, in dramatic formulas that they liked' (Knutson 1991: 165). This model assumes a degree of similarity between the adult companies' repertories, and in fact there seems to be a degree of critical agreement that, at least during the 1590s, the Chamberlain's Men and the Admiral's Men offered repertories that were 'strikingly similar and surprisingly narrow' in their range (Gurr 2004*b*: 176). A more contentious issue, however, is whether the repertories began to diverge in the period covered by this chapter. Andrew Gurr has suggested that when the children's companies were revived at the end of the 1590s, their dramatists made a conscious attempt to appeal to an audience of gallants and law students, and that this precipitated a split between the Chamberlain's Men and the rest: while the 'return of the boy players at Paul's and the

Blackfriars in 1599 may have sharpened the sense of loyalty to citizen values in the Henslowe writers', the Chamberlain's took the path of 'competing with the boys and their new fashions' (Gurr 2004*b*: 181–2). This echoes the view of Brian Gibbons that, unlike those of the other adult companies, 'after 1600 many of the plays performed by the King's Men at the Globe shared the satiric and intellectually questioning mood' of the children's plays (Gibbons 1980: 14). Furthermore, John Astington has recently suggested that the revival by the Admiral's Men of old plays such as *The Spanish Tragedy* and *Dr Faustus* when the Fortune opened in 1600 'established something of a speciality of the northern playhouses and their performers', setting 'a fashion for retro, and the deliberate retention, perhaps, of an older barnstorming style' associated with Edward Alleyn (Astington 2006: 130–1). By contrast, Knutson suggests that the adult companies continued to stage plays in similar genres and on similar subjects into the Jacobean period, while Alexander Leggatt sees the more important distinction as being that between the public playhouses of the adult companies and the private ones of the children (Leggatt 1992: 1). This final section will try to isolate the extent to which the years 1603–13 did indeed see a divergence between the adult repertories.

First, it needs to be stressed that the notion of an absolute distinction in audience composition between the adult and children's companies, still less between different adult companies, is chimerical. Notwithstanding the attempts of dramatists such as John Marston to present the private theatres as elite spaces in which 'A man shall not be choakte | With the stench of Garlicke, nor be pasted | To the barmy Iacket of a Beer-brewer' (Marston 1601, H3^{v}), the privileged evidently continued to attend the public amphitheatres (Gurr 2004*b*: 82–3; Knutson 2001: 18; Leggatt 1992: 28). Their theatregoing habits seem to have extended beyond the Globe: Marta Straznicky argues that the 'design and typography' of Red Bull plays in print, as well as their presence in the libraries of the gentry, indicates that the socially privileged 'were among the patrons of this repertory', at least on the page and presumably on the stage (Straznicky 2006: 144, 150). Secondly, the kinds of play that Gurr argues Queen Anne's and Prince Henry's Men began to specialize in during this period were also performed by the King's. Wentworth Smith's lost play 'The Freeman's Honour' (*c*.1600–3) seems on the basis of its dedicatory epistle to have been intended to celebrate the Merchant Taylors' company (Knutson 1991: 88), making it comparable to plays on illustrious citizens such as the second part of Heywood's *If You Know Not Me You Know Nobody* (Queen Anne's Men), which celebrates Thomas Gresham's building of the Royal Exchange. The King's Men play *The London Prodigal* (1603–5) not only shares the genre of prodigal play with the second part of *The Honest Whore* (written by Thomas Dekker for Prince Henry's Men, *c*.1604–5) and *The Wise Woman of Hogsdon* (Thomas Heywood for Queen Anne's Men, *c*.1604); its stress on the disastrous effects of idleness and unthriftiness, and on the dignity of honest labour, is much closer to the social attitudes articulated in plays by the other adult companies than to those to be found in city comedy. Conversely, the King's Men were not the only company to stage satirical urban drama in the style of the children's companies—a phenomenon encouraged by the mobility of some dramatists between companies. After writing two plays in the city comic vein for the Children of Paul's with John Webster in 1604 and 1605 (*Westward Ho* and *Northward Ho*), Thomas Dekker went on to write the two-part play *The Honest Whore* for Prince Henry's Men (the first part in collaboration with Thomas Middleton, who himself had written several plays for Paul's). The play contains a number of city comic elements, in particular its staging of class conflict between gallants and a citizen (who in Part II is entrapped into being arrested for handling stolen goods in a typically city comic intrigue), its thematic interest in prostitution and depiction of urban low life, and its location of scenes in Bedlam (Part I) and Bridewell (Part II), despite its ostensibly Italian setting.

From a different perspective, however, *The Honest Whore* could instead be used to highlight the differences between the adult repertories. The linen-draper Candido, though eccentric in his refusal to be vexed by the various attempts of his wife and the gallants to rouse his anger, is a more sympathetic portrayal of a citizen than is normal for city comedy: obvious contrasts are with the villainous draper Quomodo from Middleton's *Michaelmas Term* (Paul's, *c*.1605) or the gullible tobacconist Drugger from *The Alchemist* (King's Men, 1610). Furthermore, the moral trajectory of the two plays, tending towards the regeneration of Bellafront (in Part I) and Hippolyto (in Part II), is a world away from the cynicism of (for example) *Volpone* (King's Men, 1605–6), whose knaves and fools are still knaves and fools at the end of the play; indeed, the convention of individual reformation is mercilessly parodied by Jonson, Chapman, and Marston in the person of Quicksilver in *Eastward Ho* (Queen's Revels, 1605). Gibbons's comment that the *Ho* plays in which Dekker was involved are city comedies only superficially is, perhaps, just as applicable to *The Honest Whore*: 'The conventional playwright tends to *flavour* his plot with the genre's style of dialogue, references, and settings; these he regards as the plainest distinctive elements of the genre' (Gibbons 1980: 106–7). However, from the point of view of company history the question of whether *Westward Ho* and *The Honest Whore* are really city comedies or not is beside the point: the important thing is that their authors were *trying* to write plays that looked like city comedies in the interests of reproducing a successful formula. *The Honest Whore* can thus be seen as competing for the attentions of playgoers with *The Phoenix* (Paul's, 1602–4), *The Dutch Courtesan* (Queen's Revels, 1603–4), and *Volpone*, not as the product of an entirely discrete tradition; at the same time, its celebration of a worthy though humorous citizen aligns it with plays from its own repertory such as *The Shoemaker's Holiday* (1600).

The Honest Whore seems to indicate that while, as Knutson argues, commercial imperatives encouraged a degree of similarity between the companies' dramatic offerings, the various repertories did have distinctive identities. In order to illustrate this notion more fully, the final part of this chapter will concentrate on Thomas Heywood's play *The Rape of Lucrece*, printed in 1608 as having been performed 'by her Majesties Seruants at the Red-Bull' (Heywood 1608, A1^{r}) and published again in 1609, 1614, 1630, and 1638. One important influence on the play is Shakespeare's poem of the same name (1594), which was reprinted in 1607, although whether the publication of the poem stimulated the production of the play or the popularity of the play (implied by the three quartos in seven years) lay behind the reprinting of the poem is hard to determine. More significantly for this chapter, the play shows the influence of two King's Men plays in particular, namely *Sejanus* and *Macbeth.* Although the action of *Lucrece* takes place some five centuries before that of *Sejanus*, Heywood's Rome is comparable to Jonson's, being a dictatorship characterized by an atmosphere of violence and paranoia. How to live under such conditions preoccupies the characters in both plays; Lepidus' resolution to 'liue at home, | With my owne thoughts, and innocence about me, | Not tempting the wolves iawes' (IV. 296–8) (Jonson 1925–52: iv. 428) is paralleled by Lucretius' belief that 'home breedes safety, | Dangers begot in Court' (Heywood 1608, C1[r]). The influence of *Macbeth* is most evident in Heywood's villainess Tullia, wife of Tarquin Superbus, who like Lady Macbeth finds her ambitions frustrated by her sex and resolves to fulfil them through her husband:

> I am no wife of *Tarquin:* if not King:
> Oh had God made me man, I would haue mounted
> Aboue the base tribunals of the earth,
> Vp to the clowdes, for pompeous soueraintie,
> Thou art a man, oh beare my royall minde,
> Mount heauen and see if *Tullia* lag behinde.
>
> (Heywood 1608, A3[v])

The scene where Tullia rides her chariot over the corpse of her father, the deposed Servius ('For mounted like a Queene, twould doe me good | To wash my Coach-nailes in my fathers blood'; Heywood 1608, B2[v]), makes startlingly literal the parricidal implications of Lady Macbeth's 'Had he not resembled | My father as he slept, I had done't' (II. ii. 12–13: Shakespeare 1974: 1319).

Not only does this Queen Anne's Men play show the influence of two plays of the King's Men, however; if one follows the usual dating of *Coriolanus* to 1608–9 (Shakespeare 1994: 2–7), the relationship seems to have been reciprocal. Unlike *Sejanus*, *Coriolanus* shares with *Lucrece* its setting in Rome as the city became a republic; we are told at II. ii. 95 that the young Martius fought against Tarquin 'And struck him on his knee' (Shakespeare 1974: 1410). The graphic depictions of battle in scenes iv–x of *Coriolanus* echo the spectacular final scenes of *Lucrece*, which offer battles, a collapsing bridge, Mutius Scevola burning his hand, and a climactic 'fierce fight with sword and target' between Brutus and Sextus Tarquin; Brutus, like Martius, enters 'all bloody' (Heywood 1608, K1[r], I3[v]). Shakespeare may also have taken from Heywood (1608, D2[r]) the unconventional image of a powerful woman kneeling before her son, as Volumnia does to Martius in Act V, scene iii, of *Coriolanus.* Finally, Virgilia's refusal to go 'over the threshold till my lord return from the wars' (I. iii. 74–5) (Shakespeare 1974: 1401), despite Valeria's entreaties, echoes the moment where Lucrece declines a dinner invitation in Collatinus' absence: 'wiues should not stray, | Out of their dores their husba*n*ds being away' (Heywood 1612, F1[v]). While some critics of *Coriolanus* have emphasized the influence of the satirical drama performed by the children's companies and developed in King's Men plays such as *Sejanus* and *The Revenger's Tragedy* (1606–7) (Foakes 1971: 4, 81, 92; Dollimore 2004: 29–30, 218–30), the play can also be seen, therefore, as responding to a popular success by another adult company. The King's Men, incidentally, went on in January 1612 to perform *Lucrece* at court in collaboration with Queen Anne's (Chambers 1923: iv. 126), suggesting an essential compatibility of the two companies' theatrical styles.

However, just as the contrasts between *The Honest Whore* and other city comedies are as important as the similarities, so Heywood's *Lucrece* shows significant differences of emphasis to *Sejanus* and *Coriolanus*. First, in Heywood's play 'Lucrece is made a model of the good housewife' (M. Johnson 1974: 127), developing a theme mentioned only briefly in the Argument to Shakespeare's poem. She lives frugally, rises early, and goes to bed late; the scene where she disciplines her servants for 'casting amorous glances, wanton lookes, | And pretty beckes, fauouring incontinence' at one another (Heywood 1608, D4^{r}) recalls Cleaver and Dod's admonition to a wife 'in her husbands absence, to see good orders obserued, as he hath appointed: to watch ouer the manners and behaviour of such as bee in her house, and to helpe her husband in spying out euils that are breeding' (Cleaver and Dod 1598: 60). While Lucrece's fellow Romans applaud her behaviour, however, the same is not true of Shakespeare's Virgilia. Valeria sees her as wanting to be 'another Penelope: yet they say, all the yarn she spun in Ulysses' absence did but fill Ithaca full of moths' (I. iii. 82–4: Shakespeare 1974: 1401). Conversely, Heywood presents Lucrece in a way paralleled in other Queen Anne's plays. Although she is something of a Protestant housewife *avant la lettre*, her husband's absence also gives Sextus Tarquin his opportunity to rape her; this motif of women's work making them sexually vulnerable to men is one also to be found in *The Wise Woman of Hogsdon* (Heywood, *c.*1604) and *Match Me in London* (Dekker, *c.*1611–13).

As well as having affinities with other works in the Queen Anne's repertory, *Lucrece* reflects its company auspices in the way narrative and characterization are shaped according to the available acting talent. While the play resembles *Sejanus* in examining the merits of retirement as a response to tyranny, the character Valerius, we are told, 'has vsurpt a stranger garbe of humour', being now 'all musicall' and expressing his discontent through song:

> When *Tarquin* first in Court began,
> And was approued King:
> Some men for sodden ioy gan weepe,
> And I for sorrow sing.
>
> . . . . .
>
> Let humor change and spare not,
> Since *Tarquins* proud I care not:
> His faire words so bewitch my delight,
> That I dote on his sight.
> Now all is gone new desires embraceing,
> And my deserts disgracing.
>
> (Heywood 1608, C1^{r-v})

The sheer incongruity of the songs in *Lucrece* is striking, most disturbingly so in the bawdy catch describing Lucrece's rape, 'an astonishing example of crudeness and bad taste' (Baines 1984: 111). One way of making sense of them might be as an attempt to reproduce the jarring mood of the Porter scene in *Macbeth*; another might be as a capitulation to the supposedly 'uneducated audiences' at the Red Bull (Baines 1984: 139). However, a different explanation is offered by the 1609 edition of *Lucrece*, which includes some 'few songs, which were added by the stranger that lately acted Valerius his part' (Heywood 1609, K2^r). Given that the 1608 edition refers to Valerius' 'stranger garbe of humour', it appears that the part was written specifically with this unnamed entertainer in mind; thus, one of *Lucrece*'s most distinctive features seems to derive in part from a temporary addition to its company's personnel.

Conclusion

The fact that Heywood's development of the role of Valerius appears to have been shaped by the presence of the 'stranger', much as Shakespeare's writing of clown parts for the Chamberlain's/King's Men has been said to reflect the replacement of the actor Will Kempe by Robert Armin in 1599 (Wiles 1987), illustrates one of the underlying assumptions of this chapter: that many of the most important forces affecting early modern dramatic production related not so much to individual dramatists as to playing companies. Focusing on the years 1603–13, I have singled out royal patronage, relationships between players and playhouse owners, plague, and competition, although other factors such as the availability of acting talent could easily have been discussed in more detail. Furthermore, the factors I do identify frequently pulled the companies in different directions. Most obviously, while playing companies had royal patrons, their day-to-day survival depended on their competing successfully for socially diverse audiences; more specifically to this period, while the need to be competitive encouraged a degree of similarity between the repertories, differences of emphasis are visible between them, whether because of the playwrights companies chose to employ or because (as Gurr suggests) they reacted in different ways to the return of the child actors in 1599–1600. It is precisely because the acting companies were sites of tension between such diverse influences—where the creativity of dramatic writers came into contact with the demands of the market, the influence of patrons, the restricting and enabling shape of a troupe of actors, and the spur and the burden of an existing repertory—that they are so potentially rewarding as objects of critical and historical study.

CHAPTER 5

ADULT PLAYING COMPANIES 1613–1625

JAMES J. MARINO

On 29 June 1613, at the first performance of William Shakespeare and John Fletcher's *All Is True*, the Globe playhouse burned to the ground (Chambers 1923: ii. 419–20; Wickham et al. 2000: 499–500). The destruction of this iconic theater, at the premiere of Shakespeare's final play, might be imagined a conveniently catastrophic mark for the end of an era. But the conflagration led to nothing more than a piece of colorful London news and a substantial expense for the actors who owned the Globe; none of the audience was hurt, and nothing fundamental about the Jacobean theater changed. The Globe was promptly rebuilt, and improved, while the King's Men continued performing in their Blackfriars venue. Shakespeare had begun to be replaced even before the Globe had, and was already collaborating with the man who would replace him as his company's in-house playwright. If the Age of Shakespeare had ended, no one much noticed. If the Era of Fletcher had begun, it was far too politic to call undue attention to itself.

The replacement of the lost Globe with a replica of itself is emblematic of London theater practice, and especially of the King's Men's practices, during this period, emphasizing continuity and identity over interruption and change. When the Lord Chamberlain's Men had built the first Globe from the timbers of their previous playhouse, the Theatre, they had given the partially recycled building a new identity; two decades later, forced to build an entirely new structure, they insisted that it was no different from its predecessor. But the actors who opened the original Globe had been men in their twenties and thirties who had been together as the Lord Chamberlain's Men for just five years. The company that built the second Globe had endured for nearly two decades and achieved a position of unrivaled pre-eminence on the London stage. The primary challenge for the King's Men between 1613 and 1625 was to ensure the company's survival beyond the working lifetime of its founders, all of whom had left the stage for good by the end of 1619.

The King's Men had not simply replaced their playhouse, but were in the process of replacing themselves. They had no desire to draw attention to the differences between their old Globe and their new, because they needed their audiences to experience transitions from old to new as one seamless succession, and to perceive a changing cast of performers in the context of a persistent governing identity. The building was new, but it was 'still' the Globe; the faces on stage were new, but they were 'still' the King's Men. The company's approach to generational transition avoided conflict, preserved the company hierarchy, and persistently cast the new in terms of the old.

The leading company's consolidation of its dominance limited the prospects for the other companies, and oddly diminished the general level of competition between the London playhouses (although individual players and entrepreneurs were as personally competitive as they had ever been). Other companies founded in the late Elizabethan period, such as Queen Anne's Men or the Palatine's Men, could stay in business for the rest of James I's reign by performing their repertories of old favorites to perennially loyal audiences. The reliable market value of the successful plays, the commercially canonical products of the previous two decades, was enough to sustain a company even when it lost much of its patronage at court (although obviously the traditional combination of market revenue and patronage was more lucrative). There was now livable space in the shadow of the King's Men. While none of the existing companies had the resources to compete with the leading troupe, neither did they need to do so. A company might fall to a relatively distant second or third in the London pecking order and yet remain economically secure.

The challenges were greatest for younger actors, who struggled in a theatrical economy that was far better developed and far better capitalized than that of the previous generation, with far narrower opportunities for newcomers. The entrepreneurial theater business of the 1580s and 1590s, which had presented investors with outsized risks and opportunities, had been replaced with a relatively stable competitive environment dominated by reliable sources of income. A world of venture capitalism, of risky investments redeemed through enormous competitive energy, had given way to a world of secure investments, of proven blue chips with safe returns. The rebuilt Globe was more expensive than its predecessor, but far less risky; the revenue it would generate was predictable, a full return on the investment assured. A new venture, such as a new playing company with young players and new plays, was at an enormous disadvantage.

Young actors needed to combine with members of the older generation, either by joining one of the established companies or by entering a dependent relationship with an individual financier. (The maturation and consolidation of the theatrical economy had only strengthened the leading theatrical capitalists, including Philip Henslowe, Edward Alleyn, John Heminges, and the Burbage brothers.) But it had become almost impossible for a group of newcomers to form a stable, independent playing company. Without economic independence, artistic independence was impossible; no young company managed to present a sustained alternative to the previous generation's dramaturgy. Sooner or later, and usually much sooner, the leading young talents in London were under their elders' management.

Repertories

The increasing stability of the London theater, and all that such stability entailed (the dominance of the leading troupe, the difficulties of young actors, and the emphasis on continuity), was founded upon one basic cultural and economic fact: the durability of the playhouse repertories. The English professional stage had developed a body of plays which remained marketable for decades after their first performance. This had not been the case when the first London playhouses had been built in the 1560s and 1570s, nor had it been the case for the post-Armada generation of Edward Alleyn and Richard Burbage, Shakespeare and Marlowe. Plays from the 1570s seldom appear in performance records from the 1590s and later; they seem to have become dramaturgically obsolete, at least for actors who needed a paying crowd. Even plays from the earlier 1580s did not remain commercially viable for long. But beginning in the late 1580s, the London playhouses began to create successful dramas that could be revived indefinitely. Not every play succeeded, and most of those that did required occasional revision to freshen them up. But each season added to the number of durable hits that age could not wither nor custom stale, and many of their commercial lifespans seemed indefinite. It was a basic reality of both art and business that audiences would never stop paying to see Kyd's *Spanish Tragedy. Hamlet* lasted long enough for the 'little eyases' about whom Rosencrantz complains to grow up and play Rosencrantz (or Hamlet) themselves. It was in this theatrical generation, for the first time, that *Dr Faustus* itself might be older than the actor playing Dr Faustus.

The company repertories constituted a canon, in the most practical sense, although it was not quite the canon as prescribed by such critics as Philip Sidney or Francis Meres, and still less the canon endorsed by twenty-first-century universities. There was a reliable appetite for plays which had long since fallen out of fashion with the upper end of the theatrical market. A Florentine diplomat in London reports an embarrassing story about the Venetian ambassador, Antonio Foscarini, who allegedly enjoyed slumming in the downmarket playhouses. One day, according to the Florentine correspondent, Foscarini had gone to the now ancient Curtain, 'a place as dubious as they come, where you would never see the face of a gentleman, let alone a nobleman'. Foscarini apparently got in trouble when the actor speaking the epilogue invited the audience 'to come back the next day and to pick a play', suggesting a specific choice by name.

But the crowd wanted another and began to shout '*Friars, Friars*' because they wanted one that usually took its name from the friars, meaning frati. Whereupon our blockhead turned to his interpreter [who] explained that this was the name of a comedy about friars. So loosening his cloak, he began to clap his hands just as the mob did and to shout, 'frati, frati'. (Wickham et al. 2000: 415–16)

Foscarini, standing in the middle of the groundlings, was immediately mistaken for a Spaniard by the intensely nationalistic crowd, who hooted and jeered at him. The play which brought on this diplomatic discomfiture is most likely Robert Greene's *Friar Bacon and Friar Bungay*, which was already between 20 and 25 years old and would continue in repertory until at least 1630, when a newly printed edition advertised recent performances by the Palatine's Men.[1] The spectators at the Curtain were not only willing to pay money to see this theatrical warhorse yet again, but insisted on seeing it, insisted on paying. No matter how many times the members of the audience had already seen the 'Friars' (and the demand implies prior acquaintance), they were actually impatient for the next performance and refused to watch something else first. This is the most literal form of popular demand: a crowd of customers shouting to see a decades-old play again *tomorrow*.

Jonson mocks this consistency of taste in his Induction to *Bartholomew Fair* in 1614: 'Hee that will sweare, *Ieronimo* [i.e. *The Spanish Tragedy*], or *Andronicus* are the best playes yet, shall pass vnexcepted at, heere, as a man whose Iudgement shewes it is constant, and hath stood still, these five and twentie, or thirtie yeeres.... such a one, the *Author* knowes where to finde him' (Jonson 1925–52: vi. 14). Jonson's frustration here is palpable and understandable. He knew where to find 'such a one' quite easily; there were more than enough spectators whose judgement had remained constant for twenty-five years. Jeers at the Curtain, Fortune, and Red Bull playhouses' retrograde offerings became commonplace, an easy and reliable way to establish the jeerer's comparative sophistication, and one of the reasons this bit of rhetorical snobbery stayed reliable is that the repertories being mocked stayed the same.[2]

It will not do to take these barbs and their class agenda at face value, writing about the hoary and antiquated repertories of the 'citizen theaters', while taking William Shakespeare's popularity as a sign of his dramatic achievement. Stuart playgoers' enthusiasm for Shakespeare is typically taken as evidence of his artistic superiority, while the playgoers' enthusiasm for other plays is typically taken as evidence of their deficient taste. But Shakespeare's durability and the durability of his fellow playwrights must be viewed as part of a single phenomenon. (Indeed, Jonson makes an explicit link between Shakespeare and the outmoded repertory, while Beaumont's *Knight of the Burning Pestle* mocks *1 Henry IV* as a chestnut; as far as the younger playwrights are concerned, Shakespeare and Kyd are in it together.) If Shakespeare's longevity on the Jacobean stage was a triumph, it was a triumph shared by Thomas

[1] Greene's play dates from the end of the 1580s or the very beginning of the 1590s, and Greene himself was dead by 1592; Foscarini was ambassador to England between 1611 and 1615.

[2] For example, the first satire in George Wither's *Abuses Stript and Whipt* (London, 1613) describes a fool whose 'poetry is such as he can cull | From plays he heard at Curtain or at Bull' (Wickham et al. 2000: 570). Act IV of Beaumont's *Knight of the Burning Pestle* mocks the Red Bull by name: ''Tis stale; it has been before at the Red Bull' (Francis Beaumont, *Knight of the Burning Pestle*, New Mermaid Edition, ed. Michael Hattaway, 2nd edn (London: A. & C. Black, 2002), lines 31–2).

Kyd and Robert Greene and Thomas Dekker and the anonymous author of *Mucedorus*. If the continuing popularity of old plays was a symptom (of poor taste, of stubborn backwardness, of embarrassingly proletarian leanings) then Shakespeare must be reckoned part of the disease.

Neither should contemporary attacks on the class and tastes of particular audiences be accepted uncritically as proof of any stable, easily legible difference. (If nothing else, it should be remembered that the musty 'drum and trumpet' repertories of the northern suburbs included the works of Marlowe.) The appetite for old plays was not confined to any particular social class, and revivals were a staple of the theatrical diet in the private playhouses and at court.

Records of Christmas performances are not always as complete or as specific as historians would like, but the records for the seasons of 1612–13 and of 1624–5 happen to be unusually full.[3] In the winter of 1612 and 1613, the King's Men gave twenty court performances of eighteen plays; as Roslyn Knutson has pointed out, only four were new (Knutson 1991: 143).[4] Of the two plays which enjoyed a second performance, one (*Philaster*) was fairly recent, but the other (*Much Ado About Nothing*) had been in print since 1600. Several of the eighteen King's Men plays from the 1612–13 season would return to court repeatedly (visibly recurring even in the sometimes spotty records), throughout the rest of the era. King James and his courtiers were evidently happy to watch *The Merry Devil of Edmonton* more than a decade after its first performance, willing to see *The Winter's Tale* every five or six seasons, pleased to watch Jonson's *Alchemist* as if their judgements had stood constant over the intervening years.

The less established companies, with smaller dramatic inventories, still mixed revivals with new works. Prince Charles's servants gave a play in two parts identified only as '*Knaves*', either a work now lost or else, perhaps, the already positively ancient 'Knack' plays (*A Knack to Know a Knave* and *A Knack to Know an Honest Man*) from the first half of the 1590s.[5] The Lady Elizabeth's servants performed something called *Raymond, Duke of Lyons* but also gave revived Marston's *Dutch Courtesan* (which got a repeat performance). The so-called Children of the Queen's Revels, the last vestige of the old Blackfriars boys, had fairly new Fletcher plays to give, performing *The Coxcomb* and acting *Cupid's Revenge* (which they had also given the previous season) twice, but also played Chapman's significantly older play *The Widow's Tears*.

By Christmas of 1624 almost the entire court season consists of old work. On 26 December the court watched Fletcher's new play (*Rule a Wife and Have a Wife*), followed on successive days by Jonson's *Volpone* (from 1605) and *Cupid's Revenge* by Fletcher (originally written for the Children of the Queen's Revels, between 1609 and 1611). On New Year's day, as if to confirm Jonson's old joke about judgements

[3] Chambers abstracts the relevant passages of the Chamber accounts and Revels accounts for the earlier season (Chambers 1923: iv. 177–81). Bentley divides the same records by company for the seasons after 1616 (Bentley 1941–68: i. 94–6, 194).

[4] Knutson argues out that many of the plays from 1612 to 1613 echoed or otherwise recalled earlier plays; by 1624–5 the repeats would no longer be echoes or derivatives but the old plays themselves.

[5] Henslowe first records *A Knack to Know a Knave*, marked as 'ne', on 10 June 1592. His first record of *A Knack to Know a Knave*, also marked 'ne', is 22 October 1594 (Henslowe 2002: 19, 25).

unchanged after twenty-five or thirty years, the court saw a Falstaff play, recorded simply as *Falstaff*. The Christmas season concluded on Twelfth Night with *Greenes Tu Quoque*, which was the second-newest play on offer that year; the titular Greene had died in 1612.

Not only were four of the five plays revivals, but three of the titles appear in the court records for the season of either 1611–12 or 1612–13, or both. *Greenes Tu Quoque* had been presented twice over the winter of 1611 and 1612, '*Falstaff*', if both notations refer to the same play, during the subsequent winter, and *Cupid's Revenge* in both years. It is almost as if the season itself, rather than the individual dramas, were the repeat offering, as if the Master of the Revels had simply ordered the players to repeat a 10-year-old selection of entertainments. The number of performances is drastically shorter in 1624 than in 1612, but it is worth noting that as the absolute number of plays shrinks, the percentage of old plays rises. The old works were not the second-best option, and were not used simply to fill out a season built around newer offerings. The old plays were the reliable winners, the mainstays, and new plays were the trial offerings, valuable chiefly for their potential to become part of the repertory. A shorter schedule seems to have meant less of the untested material, rather than less of the old material.

The audience's voracious demand for novelty in the 1590s (when Philip Henslowe often records a new play in his so-called diary every two weeks or so) had given way over time to a demand for familiarity. That appetite for the familiar stretched from Whitehall to the groundlings' pit, across the public and private theaters alike, and through every segment of the audience. The London companies continued to commission new plays throughout the reign of James I, but the established companies were now primarily in the business of marketing the plays that they had once been in the business of creating. They bought new works to embellish their existing repertories, not to replace or rebuild them. This naturally meant less overall demand for new plays, but also less demand for innovation. Playwrights were no longer building a body of English drama from the ground up; neither was there the opportunity, as there had been for Marlowe and Kyd, of rendering one's predecessors commercially obsolete. The plays of the previous generation would not die, the audiences would not let them die, and most of the people buying new plays had a vested interest in keeping them alive and profitable. The basic idiom of Stuart drama had been set.

The consolidation of playhouse repertories into a standard canon was not simply an artistic development, but a material change that governed how theater was made. Successful plays were valuable financial assets for the companies who owned them, investments which had long since repaid their principal and now generated more or less dependable profits with almost no risk. The companies founded during Elizabeth's reign could now invest less of their revenue in new plays and put more of their profits elsewhere. Scripts had always been a highly speculative, hit-or-miss investment; although companies spent more on costumes than on any individual script, the real cost of a successful play can only be reckoned by factoring in the cost of the less successful scripts. Now the company sharers (or their financial backers) reaped greater profits, some of which could be reinvested in costumes, theater buildings, and wages for hired men, and some of which could be saved as capital for future exigencies. A group like the King's Men had spent two decades building up their material resources and consolidating their business. The freedom to invest less, relatively speaking, in new material could only accelerate their financial growth. A group of young men beginning a new playing company was at a nearly insurmountable disadvantage, but the other companies from the Elizabethan era could hang on despite almost any number of reverses. The income from performing old plays was enough to ensure even a slipping troupe's survival.

The Citizens of the Suburbs

In 1613 two of the three oldest companies in London were regrouping after the death of a key figure. Queen Anne's Men, who had begun as Worcester's Men during Elizabeth's reign, had lost their leader, the famous clown Thomas Greene. Prince Henry's Men, who had originally been the Lord Admiral's Men, had lost their patron, Henry, the Prince of Wales.

The death of a declining company's patron raises thorny questions about the causal relationship between the decline and the loss of patronage, questions that can not be conclusively answered except with reference to the questioner's starting assumptions. It cannot be clear, at this remove, how much the loss of court favor was a sign of the company's fading quality and how much of that loss of favor was a root cause of difficulties. While the Admiral's Men had been the Lord Chamberlain's Men's peers, and likely their betters, in 1594, by the death of Prince Henry in late 1612 they clearly enjoyed less favor than the King's Men, as measured by frequency of court performance; later they also fell behind Queen Anne's Men.

After Henry died, his old company was placed under the patronage of James I's new son-in-law the Elector Palatine, Frederick V, and for the rest of its collective existence the group was identified by one of Frederick's titles (as the Count Palatine's Men, the Palsgrave's Men, or the King of Bohemia's Men). This meant that the players now had the patron least connected to the English throne, the most marginally connected to James himself: a royal in-law. The new heir to the throne, Prince Charles, kept his own recently formed troupe (although that troupe was often unstable and seldom thriving). The princes' sister the Lady Elizabeth held on to her own fledgling company. And the late Prince Henry's actors did not perform throughout the theatrically crowded celebrations of Christmas and the Lady Elizabeth's wedding. Although the court saw dozens of plays, the dead prince's troupe gave none of them, and did not perform before the Elector who would become their patron.

One might simply read these events as signs of the company's already diminished quality, and take the choices made by various court figures as transparent indicators of artistic merit. In this simple narrative, Prince Henry's Men were not taken up by another royal sibling because the company's quality had fallen off and they were no longer desirable clients. But what if the royal patrons were agents in the company's decline, rather than purely passive (and reliable) witnesses? What if their decision not to encourage the company was a cause (if not the sole cause) of its weakening? One key member of Prince Henry's servants, the clown John Shank, would defect for the King's Men sometime after Prince Henry's Men were reassigned to Frederick. (Shank's name is on the initial patent for the Elector Palatine's Men, but begins appearing on King's Men's patents by 1619; Chambers and Greg 1909: i/3. 276, 280–2.) Since Shank went on to serve as the principal clown of the most successful company in London until 1635, his departure must have been a loss for the company, just as his continued membership in 1613 belies the notion that the company was no longer talented enough to perform at court. Shank only leaves after Prince Henry's Men have been frozen out of a full Christmas season and then relegated to a disengaged and mostly nominal patron. In the case of Shank (an important and very concrete case), the loss of on-stage talent follows, rather than precedes, the loss of courtly connections.

It is difficult to imagine that a company belonging to a living Prince Henry would have been excluded from the Christmas revels, and doubtful the Jacobean court ever saw the royal acting companies in purely aesthetic terms, uncolored by their patrons' influence and prestige. It is more likely that Prince Henry's Men were kept from court performances out of deference to their late patron's memory than because the quality of their acting was lagging; a performance by the dead prince's comedians might have provided an unseemly reminder of the recent and untimely death in the royal family. And if the Lady Elizabeth and Prince Charles preferred their own companies, the very fact that the companies belonged to them, that they had publicly invested their personal favor in them, might suffice to explain the preference.

The Elector's company did not perform at court until April 1613 (their one court performance that year), a full three months after being given to their new patron. They were paid for three plays in 1615; there is no record of any further court performances. However, the Elector Palatine's Men did not need court favor, nor even the payments from Whitehall performances. Their company was two decades old, and fully capitalized, with a well-established playhouse, a stock of costumes, and a repertory of well-known plays. They could not hope to compete with the King's Men any more, either financially or artistically, but they could survive comfortably on old standbys. All they required from the court was the fiction of royal patronage and its attendant permission to perform; if the German-speaking Frederick was a patron chiefly in name, that was enough. The Palatine's Men became probably the first solely commercial theater company in London's history, only earning patronage income (in the form of municipal rewards) when traveling.

Meanwhile, the third long-established company in London, Queen Anne's servants, were also taking on a new commercial focus. The entrepreneurial Christopher Beeston (whose career Eva Griffith illuminates in detail elsewhere in this volume) succeeded to the company's leadership late in 1612, after Thomas Greene's death. Beeston would become one of the chief impresarios in London, a financier like Philip Henslowe, John Heminges, or Cuthbert Burbage. His ambitious planning led to the construction of the Cockpit in 1617, and even after the setback of the original Cockpit's destruction that March, Beeston managed to become landlord to two companies (the older Queen Anne's Men and the new Prince Charles company) at two playhouses. His investments were ultimately made possible by the overall resources of Queen Anne's Men, which provided Beeston the revenue stream and the reliable expectation of profits that such capital investment required. (The economic difference between the older companies and the newer ones during this period can be illustrated with one basic fact: between 1613 and 1625 all three of the established companies rebuilt playhouses, and one of them also built a new one. None of the younger groups ever had the capital to build a playhouse at all.) Beeston's finances could be chaotic, and the complicated web of debts owed to him and by him demonstrates just how badly English banking still needed to evolve. But Beeston's single-handed savings and loan operation was only possible because his companies were established enough to ensure him steady revenue. Companies such as Queen Anne's Men had become a reliable bet.

Exeunt the Clowns

The fact that both Queen Anne's Men and the Elector Palatine's Men had lost their most visible clowns provides a convenient metaphor for the changing significance of clowning itself on the Jacobean stage. The adult companies had always made clowns and jigs a significant part of their dramaturgy, and while the boys' companies had not, the distinction between adult actors with clowning and child actors without had presumably seemed a straightforward convention to theatergoers, as apparently natural as the later division between musical and non-musical theater. But the final demise of the children's companies had ended any such neat split. While the boys' theater had ceased to exist as an institution, its plays, its playwrights, its playgoers, and many of its players were now circulating through the whole of theatrical London. One of the central questions for the Jacobean stage was the extent to which the adult companies would adopt the distinctive elements which had evolved in the boys' troupes.

When the children's companies had existed as an alternative venue, these questions could have been avoided. Perversely, the extinction of the boys' theatrical world may have accelerated the spread of their idiosyncratic traditions into the adult companies. Before 1609 a playgoer who had developed a preference for the boys' aesthetic, with perhaps more music but certainly no clowns or jigs, could simply go to the Blackfriars. After 1613, and the demise of the Whitefriars company, there was nothing that could be remotely described as a boys' theater to visit, and all of the playgoers' theatrical tastes had to be satisfied in one of the adult companies' playhouses. The question of how to integrate the two performance traditions was one for each company to solve on its own.

The leaders of the established companies had to perceive both temptation and danger in the Blackfriars and Paul's approach to theater. Certainly, the boy's theaters had produced a number of successful (and often quite sophisticated) plays, and developed a following with a fashionable audience. Both the boys' scripts and their spectators were valuable acquisitions. But the boys' distinctive and eventually notorious emphasis on satire required caution. Although the children had been accorded significantly more license than their elders had been, they had nonetheless pushed beyond their allowed limits, and eventually incurred the authorities' wrath.[6] However attractive the properties, the talents, and the modish reputations developed in the boys' theater must have seemed to the leaders of the adult companies, the prospect of provoking the court (and still worse, the King) could not have been tempting in the least.

The Palatine's and Queen Anne's Men, in the northern suburbs, evidently chose to forgo both the opportunities and the risks presented by the new approaches, retaining instead the familiar jigs at the end of their familiar plays. To some extent, this created some market specialization for these companies, who if not catering exclusively to a single audience did exclude certain kinds of fare from their menus; some kinds of theatrical experience could only be sought elsewhere. But such a drift toward specialization underlines the stability of the overall market; one can only stop changing with the evolving fashions when confident that one will never go out of fashion completely. The King's Men strove for a compromise or synthesis between the older styles and those which had evolved among the boys. Although they lured Shank away from the Fortune, he was evidently forced to give up his closing jigs at the Blackfriars and Globe; the King's Men would not do without a clown, but now circumscribed his traditional role. Shank was only permitted to clown within the scripted drama. The contemporary epigraph that said he was 'counted but a gull' since 'he did leave to sing his rhymes' points, in a punning way, to the plight of the theatrical fool shorn of his traditional prerogatives, a mere gull (Chambers 1923: ii. 339; Bentley 1941–68: ii. 563). (In time Shank seems to have regained some of his perquisites, since William Heminges writes of his talent for jigs; Bentley 1941–68: ii. 563.) The King's Men's overall strategy was a middle way, taking up the Blackfriars's literary sophistication and its polished Fletcherian tragicomedies but avoiding its dangerous penchant for satire. To the extent that the boys' satiric tradition was upheld by anyone, it was left to the superannuated boys themselves.

Beleaguered Youth

Among the most valuable legacies of the defunct boys' companies were their talented alumni, the so-called 'little eyases' of the Folio *Hamlet* text. The oldest of these 'boys'

[6] The Blackfriars children provoked the King so thoroughly in 1608, according to Sir Thomas Lake, that he 'vowed they should never play more, but should first beg their bread' (Wickham et al. 2000: 126; Lemon and Green 1857: 73–4; Chambers 1923: ii. 53–4). The Whitefriars boys survived, however, to incur the wrath of Arbella Stuart over Jonson's *Epicene* in February 1610 (Jonson 1925–52: vi. 144–7).

were now men in their twenties. There were also a number of young London actors who had begun as apprentices in the adult playing companies, and had now grown to the age of freedom, as well as newer actors, such as Joseph Taylor, who had not had theatrical childhoods. But the former leaders of the so-called Blackfriars boys, the Children of the Chapel, were a unique case.[7] They were already well known, and had been performing in front of upscale audiences since they were 12 or 13. They had spent their teen years playing the chief roles in sophisticated dramas by Jonson, Beaumont, Fletcher, George Chapman, and similarly ambitious playwrights. And they were most adept at the fashionable tragicomedies that Fletcher was making successful; after all, he had begun his writing career with them, and they had grown up acting his works.

They also, perhaps, faced disadvantages that other young actors did not. It is not clear what resources or what other options the Blackfriars alumni possessed. They had not necessarily been given an education which fit them for other professions. The Blackfriars enterprise had not been attached to a school, as the Children of Paul's had been, and had been governed by a combination of fractious businessmen rather than by a schoolmaster. Although Jonson claimed at various points that Nathan Field and the deceased Salomon Pavy had been his 'scholars', and purported to have read Horace and Martial to Field, surely such ad hoc pedagogy implies some lack of more regular instruction (Riggs 1989: 92). At least some of the boys, including Field, had originally been impressed into the company's service, and a surviving lawsuit from an anxious father in 1601 argues that the boys were being educated for nothing except acting.[8] At the same time, the Blackfriars inmates probably lacked the privileges that came with serving a formal apprenticeship as the boys in the adult companies did (privileges that David Kathman's contribution to this volume explains in depth). William Ostler and John Underwood and Nathan Field did not gain their freedom in the City of London, and did not have access to capital through their guild brethren, because they had no guild. If the former Blackfriars boys were not quite gentlemen or scholars, they were just as certainly not drapers or goldsmiths.

The simplest career path, of course, was to join one of the adult companies, and two key Blackfriars alumni, Ostler and Underwood, had done so almost immediately after the dissolution of the Children of the Chapel.[9] The King's Men had acquired the boys' old theater, had acquired several of their old plays, particularly Beaumont and Fletcher's plays, and were in the process of acquiring Fletcher. It made sense to acquire the services of some of the principal 'boys' as well. The charismatic Ostler quickly rose to be a part-owner of both the Blackfriars and the Globe; Underwood waited longer to buy shares in the playhouses, but was eventually allowed to do so. Ostler also married the daughter of an important member of the King's Men, John Heminges. It would be tempting to think that Ostler rose quickly in the company because he was a senior partner's son-in-law, but the converse seems to be true. When Ostler died unexpectedly, Heminges kept his daughter from properly inheriting the

[7] The alumni of the Paul's boys are harder to trace, and no adult Jacobean actor can be decisively linked to that company.

[8] The National Archives (TNA), STAC 5 C46/39; I. Smith (1964: 176); Wickham et al. (2000: 510–11).

[9] Ostler and Underwood begin appearing in King's Men cast lists in 1610, in Jonson's *Alchemist*.

shares in the playhouses, and the young widow was forced to sue her father. (The final disposition of the suit is lost, but Thomasine Ostler had been legally declared executrix of her husband's estate, and her father had no conceivable legal right to distrain her inheritance. Nonetheless, Heminges managed to hold on to the playhouse shares; Wallace 1909*a*; Chambers 1930: ii. 58–64.)[10] Ostler had not been allowed to buy the real estate, not because he was Heminges's son-in-law, but because he was valuable to the older partners. Both the marriage and the shares in the theater buildings had been meant to bind him to the company as tightly as possible.

Nathan Field, meanwhile, tried to hold together some semblance of the Blackfriars group, as the Queen's Revels company at Whitefriars. Even so, by 1613 Field and his colleagues of that moment were amalgamated with the Lady Elizabeth's Men, a company that also included Joseph Taylor and several other talented young actors. Their brief career together shows both the artistic promise a new company could hold and the difficulties in keeping that promise. Two of the plays written for the company during 1613 and 1614, Jonson's *Bartholomew Fair* and Thomas Middleton's *Chaste Maid in Cheapside*, are in their different ways important and ground-breaking comedies, distinct from anything that had come before. (Jonson's complaint about Hieronimo and Andronicus comes in the context of this innovative play for a young cast.) A troupe that continued producing such innovative work might have presented an artistic challenge to the established repertories, an alternative to the old staples and reassuring tragicomedies at the Blackfriars and the Globe. But if the Lady Elizabeth's Men wanted to overthrow the older generation, they would need the older generation to finance the revolution.

A new company needed plays, but also needed a playhouse and costumes. The playhouses had to be rented, which meant splitting the take with a landlord, and the choices were generally shabby; *A Chaste Maid in Cheapside* was performed at the antiquated Swan, *Bartholomew Fair* at the Hope, which doubled as a bear-baiting arena and smelled accordingly. The costumes, always a far greater expense than new plays, were only to be had by buying surplus from the existing companies, at the seller's price, which meant hundreds of pounds of debt. The first document attesting to the formation of the Lady Elizabeth's Men is a bond of £500 due to Philip Henslowe (Henslowe 1907: 18, 11; Chambers 1923: ii. 247; Bentley 1941–68: i. 176). (For comparison, the original Globe had cost £700, and its 1613 reconstruction £1,400.[11]) In 1615 the company composed its 'Articles of Oppression Against Mr. Henslowe', complaining that he contrived to keep them in debt 'else [Henslowe] will have no rule'.[12] One of the players' charges is that Henslowe held their hired men's contracts in his own name, although the Lady Elizabeth's sharers paid the wages, and that Henslowe would withdraw the hired men in order to 'break' the company (forcing the sharers to default on their bonds and to refinance).

[10] Thomasine Heminges's lawsuit is recorded in TNA, KB 27/1454, m. 692.

[11] TNA, REQ 2/706 (bottom); Wickham et al. (2000: 493, 612–13); Berry (1987: 230).

[12] Dulwich College Library, Henslowe Papers, MS I, art. 106; Henslowe (1907: 86–90); Wickham et al. (2000: 218–20).

This seems excessive, but debt was the basic condition of young actors. Nathan Field frequently borrowed from Henslowe individually in order to avoid arrests for debt (Chambers 1923: ii. 317; Henslowe 1907: 66–7). When Taylor joined the Lady Elizabeth's, John Heminges had him arrested over a debt Taylor's previous company owed Heminges for second-hand costumes, arguing that Taylor was the debtor 'most able to pay' (which is to say, the most successful) (Chambers 1923: ii. 243–4). Heminges knew perfectly well that Taylor could not pay him, but he must have forced Taylor to compound with him for his freedom (and interrupted the newer company's performances while Taylor was jailed). Heminges, like Henslowe, used his power as a creditor to disrupt the younger company as an enterprise and to keep specific valuable individuals in his debt. Heminges's two goals complement one another neatly. As long as the company remained unstable as a business, the player could not free himself from debt to Heminges, and remained entangled with him; every time Heminges lured a key player away from the company, the company was destabilized. The newer companies remained sources of fresh talent for the old without ever growing secure enough for the talent to grow independent.

The King's Men recruited Field, probably with several playbooks, away from the Lady Elizabeth's Men in 1615, presumably to replace the dead Ostler; the Lady Elizabeth's Men split, and Taylor returned to Prince Charles's men. In 1619 the King's Men recruited Taylor, presumably after the death of Richard Burbage.[13] The King's Men could remain on top of London's theatrical hierarchy by trumping mortality with money. They could afford to replace their star, their chief playwright, their playhouse, in almost every case with a newer and more fashionable model.

Forced to Tour

Unable to succeed without an outside financier, Prince Charles's men entered Beeston's orbit as his second company. They continued as such until the death of Queen Anne, when her company became the patronless 'Revels company' and was relegated to the Red Bull while Prince Charles's Men took over the Cockpit. As in the earlier case of Prince Henry's Men, Queen Anne's Men may have become less prestigious over the period of time before their patron's death, or the loss of the patron itself might have caused their fall in status. But in this case the ageing company had few resources of its own; Beeston could transfer plays between his companies just as he transferred the companies between his theaters.

The Lady Elizabeth's Men, meanwhile, took more or less permanently to the provinces for several years, under the leadership of Joseph Moore. Although they

[13] Bentley makes the strongest documentary case for Taylor as Burbage's direct replacement (Bentley 1941–86: ii. 591).

had been unable to prosper long in London, even with Taylor and Field acting and Jonson writing, the Lady Elizabeth's Men flourished in the country, and laid the foundation for later success. The most important factor in their provincial success was a quasi-monopoly on touring granted to them by the authorities. Moore had been given a letter authorizing him to prevent any other companies from traveling with duplicates, or 'exemplifications', of the company's patent while the main company remained in London (Galloway 1984: 151–2; Chambers 1923: iv. 343–4; Wickham et al. 2000: 143–4). Moore carried this reformist message from the authorities in the process of touring at the head of his own troupe. Essentially, Moore was deputized to prevent the London companies from sending specialized touring units into the country, and rewarded for enforcing the law by the semi-monopoly that its enforcement gave his company. The other companies were of course permitted to tour, but only at the expense of vacating London. The Lady Elizabeth's Men, who had no easy foothold in the capital, were left the lion's share of England as compensation.

Some theater historians have accepted the practice of traveling with a duplicated patent as both novel (although the Queen's Men had adopted a similar technique in the 1580s; Gurr 1996*b*: 204) and abusive. Essentially, this is to accept Joseph Moore's narrative of events wholesale. But it is by no means clear that the practice Moore policed (for his own direct benefit) was detrimental. Indeed, the short-sighted prohibition that Moore was licensed to enforce probably undermined the court's ability to project its cultural values throughout provincial England, and both Peter H. Greenfield and Siobhan Keenan rightly argue that the tightened restrictions hastened the 'decline of touring' in the late Jacobean era (Greenfield 1997: 265–7; Keenan 2002: 165–85).

The practice of touring with a duplicated patent is a natural corollary of James's restriction of playing companies to royal patrons (Greenfield 1997: 265; Keenan 2002: 173). Although slow to take real effect, the restriction eventually shrank the number of playing companies in England, and gave priority to the royally approved groups in London. Requiring this handful of successful companies to leave their safely profitable playhouses idle whenever they wished to tour had the predictable effect of diminishing touring, but by sending a second unit into the country the royal companies brought London's drama and London's values to a wider national audience. Forcing the King's, Queen Anne's, and Palatine's Men to choose between the country and the capital led them, unsurprisingly, to neglect the country. Keenan justly points out that any permanent split between the metropolitan and touring incarnations of one company would also work to divorce the metropolis from the provinces, but the proscription on splitting companies made the cultural split more complete (Keenan 2002: 183–4). With duplicated patents, provincial audiences would never have seen the London companies' stars, but would have seen those companies' plays. The prohibition enforced by the Lady Elizabeth's Men kept the most important London companies out of the countryside for long stretches and limited the exportation of drama from the capital.

Conclusions

Six years in the country was enough to repair the Lady Elizabeth's Men's fortunes, and Moore returned to London in 1622. (A touring unit of the Lady Elizabeth's Men remained in the country; the prohibition had served its purpose and Moore could be trusted not to enforce it on his own fellows; Gurr 1996*b*: 406–7.) The returned company became Beeston's tenants at the Cockpit, but had now grown stronger than Prince Charles's Men, who had stayed at home. The Lady Elizabeth's took over occupancy of the Cockpit, Beeston's better venue, and over the last few years of James's reign staged a number of innovative and well-crafted plays.

By the late teens and early twenties, the Palatine's and Queen Anne's positions had finally begun to slip below those of the younger companies. The death of Queen Anne doubtlessly accelerated her former company's decline, Beeston could reassign most of their repertory to younger actors, and when the Lady Elizabeth's Men returned it was the former Queen Anne's Men who left London for the provinces. The Palatine's Men suffered their most grievous setback in 1621, with the burning of the Fortune playhouse.[14] Like their more prosperous rivals the King's Men, the Palatine's company rebuilt their house, but they could not overcome the financial blow as quickly. They seem to have lost their playbooks and costumes in the fire, and hence their specialized capital (Gurr 1996*b*: 249–51). Perhaps as importantly, they did not have an alternative venue as the King's Men did; the fire made them renters once more, until the rebuilding was done.

Andrew Gurr notes the flurry of more than a dozen new plays that the Palatine's Men offered for licensing in 1623 and 1624, an influx Gurr interprets as an attempt to replace a lost inventory of playbooks. It might also represent an attempt, finally, to catch up with more fashionable inventories; perhaps the Palatine's Men needed better-heeled customers, or the chance at a court performance, to help replace lost income. In any case, the sudden quantity of new material signals an end to the basic strategy of relying upon revivals of old plays, and it indicates substantial investments in new material by a company that already had other financial difficulties. The company became more reliant than ever upon their financier, Edward Alleyn, and the outside investors to whom he sold shares of the rebuilt Fortune.[15]

The rebuilding left only three actors from the Palatine's Men as householders in the Fortune, but in this the company at least superficially resembled the King's Men, between two to four of whose householders, at various moments, still acted. (In 1623 the King's actor–householders were Henry Condell, John Underwood, and Richard Robinson, who had married Richard Burbage's widow.) The King's Men had become a more hierarchical organization than it had been in 1594 or 1599, with fewer actors participating in the company's full profits and more reliance on financiers such as Cuthbert Burbage and John Heminges. It grew harder to cut new members into the

[14] TNA, SP 14/124, fo. 92^{v}; Wickham et al. (2000: 546).

[15] Dulwich College Library, Dulwich, Mun. 58; Henslowe (1907: 28–30); Wickham et al. (2000: 640).

ownership of the company's playhouses and the accruing profits, because several shares had passed to partners' widows or heirs, and because Heminges had bought up several himself. The structural problems that would boil over in the 'Sharers' Papers' dispute of 1635, which hinged on the distribution of playhouse shares after Heminges's death, were already building. And by the end of 1624 the overall leadership of the company was distinct from the onstage leadership. When the company needed to apologize to Sir Henry Herbert, the Master of the Revels, in December 1624 (for staging *The Spanish Viceroy* without his license), neither of the householders' names are included in the apology (J. Q. Adams 1917*a*: 21; Bentley 1941–68: i. 14). Heminges and Condell were leaders of the company, and listed on royal patents, but the actual artistic management now belonged to a younger generation; it was the leading actors, not the leading businessmen, who had offended and who had to apologize to Herbert.

Nonetheless, the King's Men thrived by combining the old and new without acknowledging any important differences between them. Younger actors took up old and familiar roles. Fletcher, as company playwright, tailored his new plays and occasionally stitched up the old ones to maximize the impression of continuity. A season at the Globe or Blackfriars presented old plays and new as if they shared a single dramatic perspective. The newer works did not replace or revise the standards alongside which they appeared, but reframed them, inviting the audience to imagine the older works through the idiom of the new.

The great exception, and perhaps the last resurgence of the old satiric Blackfriars tradition, was the notorious *Game at Chess* incident in August of 1624. The actors staged Middleton's topical play for nine consecutive playing days, after which arrest warrants were issued, the play was banned, and the players were forbidden the stage for ten days (Chambers and Greg 1911: 380–1; Gurr 2004*c*: 261). But this colorful incident only serves to confirm how safe the King's Men's position had become, how far they stood above their professional rivals, and how secure they were in continued favor. They could quite deliberately provoke the court's displeasure (their decision to play the same drama every day, exploiting the brief window before its inevitable banning, demonstrates their premeditation), and have the consequences blow over after a mere week and a half. (Compare the official wrath over 'The Isle of Dogs' in 1597.) They were now too much part of the establishment to be punished for terribly long. Nor do they seem to have been much concerned about maintaining their primacy under the next king. Between the destruction of the original Globe and James I's death in 1625, the company had made itself into an institution, no longer the individual servants of an individual monarch but a quasi-national establishment belonging to the throne itself.

In 1625 both John Fletcher and King James died. The King's Men already had a new playwright and a new patron in line.

CHAPTER 6

ADULT AND BOY PLAYING COMPANIES 1625–1642

MARTIN BUTLER

DESPITE the fact that the London theatre companies were suspended from playing by order of Parliament in September 1642, an inhibition that lasted (with minor infractions) down to 1660, the seventeen years of Caroline theatrical activity were a time of comparative prosperity and stability. Only in the final months of this period, as London's social and economic life was thrown into disarray by the constitutional crisis at Westminster—which by spring 1642 had seen assemblies of riotous crowds, an increasingly acute confrontation between King and Parliament, and Charles's eventual withdrawal from the city—were the activities of the playhouses seriously disrupted by political events. In his prologue for *The Sisters*, staged at the Blackfriars in April 1642, James Shirley reflected nervously on how thin playhouse attendance had become:

> Our poet fears the whole town is not well,
> Has took some physic lately, and for fear
> Of catching cold dare not salute this air.
>
> (Shirley 1833: v. 356)

This situation he ascribes to Charles's move to the north, followed by much of the court, for 'I hear say | London is gone to York.' Other indications from this year, such as the paucity of new plays presented to Sir Henry Herbert for licensing, suggest a theatrical world experiencing a sudden and catastrophic downturn. But in other respects, before 1642 the playhouses seem to have been performing vigorously and with little sense that their activities were likely to be curtailed for political reasons. The old idea that the closure of the playing companies came as the culmination of a long-term and progressively terminal decline is not supported by the evidence of rude health that marks the immediately preceding years. While the Caroline stage did from time to time exhibit signs of political strain, economically the playhouses were thriving as much as ever.

As we shall see, the stability of Caroline playing was in some respects more apparent than real, since before the onset of the political crisis there were various factors that troubled theatrical activity (plague, competition between companies, conflicts between companies and managers, complaints from local residents). Nonetheless, around 1630 the total theatrical economy had achieved what we might think of as a steady state. When in that year the Salisbury Court playhouse in Whitefriars was opened as a new venture, the number of theatres and playing companies operating was at its peak and would remain stable for the next decade. During this period, five companies were active, performing at six venues. The dominant company was the King's Men, who alternated between two playhouses. Their winter operation was located at the small, roofed Blackfriars theatre, which attracted an expensive and fashionable clientele, and in summer they moved their activities to the large arena-style amphitheatre, the Globe, which played to more heterogeneous audiences with ordinary citizens prominent among them. Next in status came the Queen's Men, who performed from 1625 to 1636 at the Cockpit (or Phoenix) in Drury Lane, a fashionable roofed theatre owned and operated by the former player Christopher Beeston. The Salisbury Court, home in 1630 to the Children of the Revels (or the Company of His Majesty's Revels), was also set up as an elite enterprise, being initially a company of youths, as its name indicated. It was led by the managerial team of Richard Gunnell and William Blagrave, then by Richard Heton after Gunnell's death in 1634 (Blagrave probably died in 1636). Both the Queen's Men and the Company of the Revels collapsed in the long plague closure of 1636–7, and during these months Beeston took the opportunity of forming his own adolescent troupe at the Cockpit, called the King and Queen's Young Company. The Queen's Men were then reconstituted at the Salisbury Court by Heton, but although the name was the same, to all intents and purposes this was a new company. There was, then, significant disruption to life at the Cockpit and Salisbury Court; notwithstanding, the number of troupes playing at these houses remained constant across the decade.

The other two playhouses were amphitheatres of long standing: the Fortune in Golding Lane and the Red Bull in Clerkenwell. Both of these playhouses attracted socially diverse audiences whose tastes in drama were correspondingly backward-looking and robust. Their companies were known for a broader style of playing than that enjoyed in the hall theatres: they specialized in low comedy, outsize adventure, spectacle, and acting sometimes exaggerated to the point of rant—what Andrew Gurr calls 'drum-and-trumpet plays with wide-mouthed and loud-voiced players'

(Gurr 1996*b*: 439). During the seventeen-year period, two companies were associated with the Red Bull and Fortune: the Red Bull company (which developed out of the old Jacobean Prince's Men), and a company at the Fortune known as the King and Queen of Bohemia's Men (which was put together from the Jacobean Lady Elizabeth's and Palsgrave's Men), and which became the basis of the company reorganized in 1631 into a new Prince's Men. However, this picture is complicated because at several points during the reign these two companies traded playhouses; so, for example, during the years 1634–40 the Red Bull company were in fact playing at the Fortune. Even so, it will readily be seen that, whatever the vagaries of companies changing in composition or moving between theatres, the total mass of theatrical activity in any year between 1630 and 1642 remained the same, and that—with three hall playhouses and three amphitheatres—the spectrum was divided equally between the so-called elite and popular traditions.

This last point is important, since it is easy to forget about the existence of the Caroline amphitheatre companies, whose repertoires were composed of revivals or of plays that rarely made it into print. Virtually all surviving new plays in the period come from the hall playhouses, and this has sometimes led to the tradition of popular theatre being ignored or dismissed as of no account. Yet the fact that the King's Men chose to hold on to their amphitheatre playhouse as a venue for summer performances indicates that they too saw the citizen market as by no means insignificant or unprofitable. Andrew Gurr has highlighted the anomaly created by the company continuing to divide its operation in this way, and keeping two playhouses going where only would have done: he calls it 'a proud, exclusive, and uneconomical choice' (Gurr 1996*b*: 297; cf. Gurr 2004*c*: 118). Still, during the summer months many of the fashionable playgoers who would have frequented the halls left London for their country estates, so the two-pronged commercial strategy must have made sense, even though the company had to tweak their repertoire to meet tastes at the Globe. The strategy had its own inbuilt principle of economy: it allowed the King's Men to tap into the popular market during the times when the other hall companies would have been experiencing reduced attendances.

On the basis of this picture, in which the outlines of theatrical activity are stable even if from time to time some internal details changed, it is tempting to conclude that playing in Caroline London had reached a point of economic balance. The totality of Caroline theatre had both expanded and diversified so that it filled the space available, making for what looks like a perfect fit between supply and demand. There is, of course, some evidence of new initiatives that were being developed in the period in response to potential gaps in the market. The Salisbury Court was a brand new enterprise in 1630, which, after a shaky start, managed to carve out for itself a permanent, if not impregnable, place in the theatrical economy. Christopher Beeston's activities at the Cockpit, as we shall see, were similarly responsive to changes in taste and new opportunities. Perhaps the most striking new initiative was the attempt by William Davenant in 1639 to open an amphitheatre in Fleet Street, barely a stone's throw from the Salisbury Court. Davenant's amphitheatre would have been a radical enterprise cutting across the traditional generic divisions. He was granted a licence to stage not just plays but visual and musical spectacles—'action, musical presentments, scenes, dancing, and the like'—all of which sounds like a precursor of the semi-operatic shows that he eventually began to produce in 1656 (Bentley 1941–68: vi. 305–6). Davenant's plans never came to anything, though he gained general building permission and might conceivably have erected a playhouse had he been able to procure the necessary capital. In the event, he satisfied his ambition another way: in 1640 he was helicoptered into management of the Cockpit company when they fell into hot water following an unlicensed performance, probably of Richard Brome's politically sensitive comedy *The Court Beggar.* It was not only cheaper for Davenant to take over an existing company but safer too, given the uncertainty over what the market could bear. It allowed him to appropriate an enterprise that had already proved its worth rather than embark on a new scheme that could have either flourished or failed. Since his amphitheatre remained unbuilt, the question remains moot as to whether Caroline London could realistically have supported as many as seven acting companies.

It seems evident that in absolute terms most of these companies were flourishing. The King's Men had much the most prosperous operation. Their financial success was guaranteed by the depth and quality of the repertoire that they had built up, by their two-pronged commercial strategy, of dividing their activities between the elite market in the winter and the popular market in summer, and by their privileged status as the premier troupe, who boasted the King's patronage and performed most frequently at court, for which they could expect regular and generous payments of £20 a performance. The level of company earnings is suggested by the payments from benefit performances which Sir Henry Herbert recorded in 1628–33, which show that the average receipts for such afternoons were £15 15*s.* in the winter and £6 13*s.* in the summer (Bentley 1941–68: i. 24). These are figures for the second days of old revived plays; new plays were likely to have done even better. The so-called 'Sharers' Papers'—documents from a dispute of 1635 between three of the King's Men players and the sharers in the Globe and Blackfriars playhouses, arbitrated by the Lord Chamberlain—also give substantial estimates for the company income: the house-keepers claim that the three actors were each earning around £180 annually even though they had no shares in the playhouse (Wickham et al. 2000: 224–5, 227). This figure was probably exaggerated, but it does indicate the expectations that the players had (for comparison, a clergyman might earn £20 a year). This was at the top end of the theatrical tree, but even less well-established operations were making good returns. In the years 1637–40 Sir Henry Herbert earned on average £97 a year from the one-ninth share that he held in the Salisbury Court playhouse, indicating a total annual profit to the housekeepers of £873 (Bawcutt 1996: 208). The fact that the Prince's Men and Red Bull company held together during the long plague closure of 1636–7, when the Queen's Men and the Company of the Revels collapsed (both more prestigious troupes), suggests that, although the amphitheatre companies had lesser literary pretensions, their finances, too, were sound. A share in the Prince's Men in the 1630s cost as much as £100 (Bentley 1977–8: 222).

The Caroline period, then, saw the establishment of the theatre companies as permanent institutional presences within the London landscape, on an apparently solid economic footing, and with a measure of financial security. The stabilization of the companies at five for over a decade corresponds with the tentative economic recovery that London was beginning to experience in the 1630s, as the benefits of the Caroline peace were gradually being felt and the city consolidated its position as a powerhouse of urbanization. Nationally, the economic picture was extremely depressed, and would remain so for some time, as the 1620s had brought poor harvests, overseas warfare, plague, a disastrous slump in the cloth industry, and record inflation. But for the metropolis, Charles's realization in 1630 that he had to keep peace with his neighbours, and his attitude of detachment from a Europe that everywhere else was ravaged by the effects of war, helped to restore international trade links and bring on the surplus revenue, cosmopolitan ethos, and habits of luxury living that inevitably followed. The 1630s saw hints of an urban boom, particularly in the crystallization of a fashionable beau monde that was keen on coming to London for the sake of its pleasures and leisure activities, rather than for the business, legal, or political reasons that had traditionally powered the drift towards the city. This development was further facilitated by the relative novelty of coaches as a means to bring up one's whole family, and by the emergence of new and distinctively urban social forms: the term 'ball', meaning a social assembly for dancing or general enjoyment, dates from the 1630s, and is first used in this sense in Shirley's Cockpit comedy *The Ball* (1632). Many of those coming to town did so because of their connections to the court, or because they belonged to the vast community of attendants and service personnel that Whitehall drew around itself: 'the court is now filled with the families of every mean courtier', George Garrard complained in 1637 (Strafford 1739: ii. 129). But while the court's needs drove some of these changes, the beginnings of a London season and the arrival of a critical mass of social elites residing seasonally in town ensured that high society became focused on spaces and pleasure-seeking in the city as well as Whitehall. The new world of fashion had one foot inside the court and one without, its complex identity deriving from the double impetus of courtiership and urbanization. One did not have to be a courtier to enjoy the city: Simonds D'Ewes complained that Hyde Park and the bowling greens were even more densely populated when Parliament was in session (see Butler 2004: 443).

These developments created a social topography in which the playhouses were crucial, for they offered the urban beau monde neutral meeting-grounds and places of pleasure, and began to function as environments towards which the world of fashion gravitated to constitute itself, in order for its members both to see and be seen. The King's Men played to audiences at the Blackfriars in which gentlemen and aristocrats were prominent, and very occasionally royalty: Henrietta Maria took her nephew Prince Charles Louis there in 1636 to see Lodowick Carlell's romantic drama *Arviragus and Philicia* (Bentley 1941–68: i. 48). A series of quarrels sparked off at the Blackfriars, between Sir John Suckling and Sir John Digby, Lord George Digby and William Crofts, the Duke of Lennox and the Earl of Pembroke, and Peter Legh and

Valentine Browne, out of which several duels came or threatened to come (Bentley 1941–68: i. 42, 47–8; Butler 1984*b*). Such encounters are suggestive of the processes of internal self-definition experienced among a community of social elites during a period when they were attempting to establish their own territory and mark out the internal hierarchies and boundaries that went along with it. The King's Men were so closely identified with these elites that they became the company of choice for the many gentlemen playwrights who at this time tried their hands at amateur playwriting. Some of this drama trickled into the Cockpit too (which staged plays by Thomas Killigrew, a royal page), and at the end of the decade the Salisbury Court also made a bid to attract amateur playwrights (Butler 2006: 117–20). However, neither of these companies could compete with the coup arranged by Suckling in 1638 when he presented the King's Men with gorgeous costumes for his tragicomedy *Aglaura*—'eight or ten suits of new clothes', said Garrard, 'an unheard of prodigality' (Strafford 1739: i. 150).

At the same time, the hall repertoires became socially formative because of the way that they reflected and helped to define the manners and mores of the spectators that frequented them. As the hall companies increasingly addressed themselves to the tastes of their elite audiences, so their drama provided images of life in fashionable circles, against which the spectators could measure their own behaviour and breeding. In plays of contemporary urban life, such as Richard Brome's *The Weeding of the Covent Garden* (Blackfriars, 1633?) and *The Sparagus Garden* (Salisbury Court, 1635), or Thomas Nabbes's *Covent Garden* (Cockpit, 1633), the favourite watering holes of a newly urbanized metropolitan class were put on stage, and their habits, etiquette, and speaking tones were held up for admiration, imitation, and critique. The depiction of fashionable life in Shirley's *The Ball* (Cockpit, 1632) seemed so dangerously up-to-the-minute that Sir Henry Herbert commanded Beeston to leave out some passages which he took for satirical portraits of real lords and courtiers. And no less symptomatic of a cultural climate shifting away from a narrowly partisan nationalism and towards an urbane civility and more outward-looking cosmopolitanism was the arrival in London of several companies of French players, such as the troupes that played at the Blackfriars and Red Bull in 1629 and at the Cockpit in 1635.

All of these shifts had the effect of naturalizing the theatres and binding them to London's metropolitan development. At a time when London was expanding exponentially and continuing to draw huge numbers of incomers at all social levels, the theatres too became crucial to the burgeoning processes of urbanization. They helped to facilitate what Lawrence Manley calls sedentarism—'ways of perceiving the self and society that encouraged settlement and civility, allayed anxieties, and encouraged innovation' (Manley 1995: 16)—making them increasingly intrinsic to London's identity. Inevitably, the companies continued to be complained against by residents whose localities were disrupted by their activities. This was especially so in the Blackfriars precinct, where the residents never reconciled themselves to the disturbance caused by the playhouse in their midst and the thronging of coaches. The playhouse's neighbours petitioned the Bishop of London in 1631 and the Privy Council in 1633, with little success beyond an order to coachmen that they should not hang around outside the playhouse during the performances; in 1640 the return of Parliament gave them another avenue of complaint, and a petition against the disruption to trade duly followed. But in other respects, these years are notable for the absence of complaints either from or to the Mayor, aldermen, and other civic bodies. Perhaps the city fathers thought that theatregoing was so entrenched that there was no longer any point in objecting to the playhouses, or perhaps they had implicitly started to accept their sedentarist function, their part in the metropolitan scene. Certainly Caroline playgoing was more embedded in ordinary urban life and carried less social stigma than had ever been the case in the past.

The other side to this question of urbanization is the changing institutional relationship between the theatre companies and the court, and the gradual distancing of direct personal controls by the monarchy into a system that was more functional and utilitarian. Andrew Gurr has valuably observed that the accession of Charles I brought a shift in regulation and a new attitude towards company licensing (Gurr 1994*b*: 137, 417–18). Under James, all companies had been given a direct patronage relationship to members of the royal family, so that each was technically bound to the service of the prince in whose name they were licensed—even if, as in the case of the Palsgrave's Men and the Lady Elizabeth's Men, that royal figure was resident overseas (or, as with Queen Anne's Men after 1619, if the company managed to outlive its patron). In the Caroline period, the number of companies operating was in excess of the royal patrons available to sponsor them, and the Jacobean system was tacitly dropped. Instead, the companies received their licences directly from the Master of the Revels, acting as the King's representative, so the expectation of a direct and personal tie between the companies and individual royalty was diluted. Of course, the King's Men and Queen's Men continued to bear the name of their patrons, and livery allowances were made for them, by which they technically became members of the royal households. So too, after Prince Charles was born in 1630, the Prince's Men were created for him out of existing troupes and sworn as royal servants; they even once accompanied the court on progress.

But in Jacobean terms there are some anomalies here. Although the King's Men received a royal patent in June 1625, no such document was ever drawn up for the other companies, and when further royal children were born during the decade no attempts were made to invent theatre troupes for them. At the same time, when the new Prince's Men were licensed, the old title of King and Queen of Bohemia's Men was allowed to lapse. This rather cruelly reflects Charles's inattentiveness to his exiled sister and brother-in-law and the fact that Prince Charles's birth meant that the Palatines were displaced from the line of succession, but it also attests to the withering away of the old principle that each royal family member should have his or her own players. Even more strikingly, the two companies of youths—who were licensed not in their own right but through their managers, Blagrave (who was deputy to the Master of the Revels), Heton, and Beeston (who were also royal servants)—carried names which indicated only in generic terms their service to the court, and the Red Bull company was never awarded any royal title at all. Instead, the companies' authorization was underwritten by the licences for travel which Sir Henry Herbert issued to them annually. Significantly, during a crisis among the reconstituted Queen's Men in 1639 Heton drew up a long draft for a royal patent in which he hoped to be named the company's 'governor', but there is no sign that it ever got anywhere (Bawcutt 1997).

In many areas of the English economy, Charles's reign was notable for its administrative centralization and for a drive to make the King's authority effective at all levels of national life (K. Sharpe 1992: 209–74). What this meant for the theatre companies was a standardization of regulatory practices, combined with a dilution of the intensely personalized patronage relationships that had previously been in place. Sir Henry Herbert effectively became the bureaucrat through whom all theatrical regulation was switched, with occasional reference upwards to the Lord Chamberlain, who, as head of the King's household, was his line-manager. The changed relationships were spelled out by the Earl of Pembroke in 1640 when, putting Davenant into William Beeston's place at the Cockpit, he described the company as 'authorised by me (as Lord Chamberlain to His Majesty)' (Bentley 1941–68: i. 334). Of course, the monarchy did sometimes interest itself directly in the practical needs of its theatre companies. Charles gave the King's Men 100 marks to tide them over the plague closure of 1625–6, and Henrietta Maria gave Beeston £30 and Heton £50 during the 1636–7 plague (Butler 2006: 112–13). It should have potentially helped the Salisbury Court players that Sir Henry Herbert was a sharer in the playhouse, and that their landlord was the Earl of Dorset, who as Chamberlain to the Queen was in a position to do them good. However, when Heton, in his draft of his patent, attempted to prevail upon Dorset to forge a direct relationship between the company and the Queen's household, there is little evidence that the response went any further than the Earl's interests as a landlord required (see Butler 2006: 113). It is, then, symptomatic of the comparatively laissez-faire approach that now prevailed that, in the plague closure of 1636–7, during which both the Queen's Men and Company of the Revels were liquidated, Heton is found complaining that the Queen had very nearly fallen victim to market forces: 'when her Majesty's servants were at the Cockpit, being all at liberty, they dispersed themselves to several companies, so that had not my Lord of Dorset taken care to make up a new company for the Queen, she had not had any at all' (Bawcutt 1997: 186). In future, companies would be increasingly identified in relation to the theatre at which they played rather than the royal patronage of which they boasted, a shift which acknowledged the commercial realities of a burgeoning theatrical marketplace. So, for example, the Company of the Revels are sometimes referred to in official documents as 'the company of the Salisbury Court', and the Red Bull company as 'the players of the Fortune'. We even find the King and Queen's Young Company being named simply as 'the players of the Cockpit in Drury Lane' (Bentley 1941–68: i. 285, 277, 332). The lines of political authority had become more focused and clearly defined, but so too had the companies' loyalties to the market.

In this new economic and regulatory environment, the people who stood to gain the most were those with investments in bricks and mortar, and who were in a position to capitalize on their friendships at the Revels Office. One leading theme of

Caroline theatre is the power of the playhouse managers, personalities like Beeston, Gunnell, and Heton, whose enterprising, entrepreneurial approach generated some of the period's most original developments. Beeston was already happily ensconced at the Cockpit well before 1625, and for the next ten years he continued to run a prosperous operation with the new Queen's Men. While the Cockpit never quite became the aristocratic theatre of choice, it increasingly challenged the King's Men for a share of the fashionable market. Shirley was Beeston's house dramatist, whose plays were so admired by Sir Henry Herbert that he set *The Young Admiral* down in his office-book as 'a pattern to other poets, not only for the bettering of manners and language, but for the improvement of the quality' (Bawcutt 1996: 180). Other playwrights courted by Beeston included John Ford and Ben Jonson, and there was a big success in 1634 with Thomas Heywood's *Love's Mistress*, which was taken up at court and restaged with scenes by Inigo Jones, as a birthday gift to Charles from Henrietta Maria. The lurking rivalry between the King's and Queen's Men bubbled to the surface in 1630, when Davenant's *The Just Italian* flopped at Blackfriars and Thomas Carew printed verses defending the play and attacking spectators who flocked to the Cockpit, 'that adulterate stage, where not a tongue | Of th'untuned kennel can a line repeat of serious sense' (Carew 1949: 96). In response to this, Shirley's *The Grateful Servant* was rushed into print with a sheaf of poetic replies from friends of the Cockpit, including Philip Massinger—now house dramatist at Blackfriars, but formerly a Cockpit playwright (see Gurr 1988; Beal 1980). By 1636 the Queen's company had built up a repertoire scarcely less impressive than the King's Men's, and were performing at Whitehall almost as frequently as their rivals.

Beeston's firm managerial hand showed itself after May 1636, when the long plague closure gave him the opportunity of radically reorganizing the Cockpit operation. During these months the Queen's Men were broken up, despite their profitable history, and several of their leading players were cut adrift. When the playhouse reopened in October 1637, it had a completely new troupe composed of youths, with some adult actors but otherwise harking back to the old Jacobean boys' company model. It seems probable that the impetus for this sea change came from Beeston himself, for he had the new troupe well in hand from early in the plague closure. He trialled the boys at court in February 1637 and ran briefly into trouble in May when they performed publicly at the Cockpit despite the continuing inhibition. Beeston's reply to censure was that he had been 'commanded to erect and prepare a company of young actors for their Majesties' service' (Bentley 1941–68: i. 327), though in fact the warrant to swear him as governor of the new company post-dates the court performances and so was less likely to have been its cause than consequence. The inference is either that the Lord Chamberlain had done the commanding, or that he had ratified *ex post facto* an initiative on which Beeston was already embarked. Either way, Beeston and Pembroke were working hand in glove to create the new company. Subsequently, Pembroke intervened personally in the company's affairs on several occasions: he issued the edict of August 1639 which protected their repertoire, stopped *The Court Beggar* being performed in 1640 and put Davenant in as the new governor, and (John Orrell argues) commissioned designs from Inigo Jones for early experiments with scenery at Drury Lane (Orrell 1985: 60–4). It seems clear that Beeston and Pembroke had a close relationship, and that this greatly advantaged Cockpit operations. Now running a company of youths and not just as leader but as 'governor', enjoying the Lord Chamberlain's direct support, and retaining all the old Queen's Men's rich repertoire (even though a new Queen's Men had been reconstituted at Salisbury Court), Beeston's position was strong indeed. In a petition to the House of Lords *c.*1640 complaining of the damage done by Beeston to the old Queen's Men, Richard Blagrave's widow claimed that he had deliberately 'taken occasion to quarrel with the company to the end he might have a company that would take what he would be willing to give them' (Bawcutt 1996: 216). This confirms the impression that, even if the authority to rearrange the Cockpit came from the Lord Chamberlain, the managerial style was quintessentially Beeston.

In setting up a troupe of youths, Beeston had further solidified his position by stealing a march on the Salisbury Court, which was the first Caroline theatre to revive a boys' company on the Jacobean model. In 1630 both the Salisbury Court playhouse and the Children of the Revels were innovative enterprises, the house being the first new London theatre since the Drury Lane Cockpit, and the troupe being the first boys' company since the demise of the Whitefriars boys *c.*1613—a remarkable new departure in a theatrical scene from which traditions of juvenile playing had apparently faded away. The company consisted of fourteen youths, and Gunnell hired Thomas Randolph, perhaps as house dramatist, to provide plays suited to their talents: Randolph's *The Muses' Looking-Glass* and *Amyntas* were wittily satirical but inoffensive dramas tailored to the boys' abilities, that emphasized music, impersonation, and female roles, and promoted an overriding company style rather than relying on star turns by individual performers. Other plays were supplied by Shirley, Brome, and (probably) the young Thomas Jordan, who was one of the boy players (Butler 2006: 103–5). Unfortunately the company quickly ran into difficulties and did not survive long in this form. The theatre was prevented from opening by plague, destroying its cash flow, and Gunnell and Blagrave found themselves mired in lawsuits with their business partner, Christopher Babham, over their respective financial obligations. Then in 1631, following the birth of a new crown prince, the Prince's Men were constituted at the Salisbury Court and the Children of the Revels were displaced to the Fortune—a venue which one would have thought uncongenial to the boy company's style. Perhaps unsurprisingly, when the troupe returned to the Salisbury Court *c.*1633–4, its composition had altered significantly, for it now had a core of nine mature adults, and so was much closer to the typical Caroline norm: thereafter it was known simply as the Company of His Majesty's Revels. Once the 1636–7 plague closure finally ended its life, a revived Queen's Men, on the standard adult model, was cobbled together at Salisbury Court from the remnants of the Revels company plus fugitives from the old Queen's Men who had been stranded by Beeston's revolution at the Cockpit. This effectively confirmed the demise of the original company profile, allowing Beeston's King and Queen's Young Company to seize the initiative which in 1630 had been his rivals' distinctive selling point.

At the Salisbury Court, Gunnell and Heton attempted to run an operation like Beeston's, in which the managers called the shots. The original expectation was that both troupe and theatre business would always be driven by the managers, working with the close support of the Revels Office. The Revels Office had its hands deep in the enterprise, for as well as Dorset's presence as landlord, Sir Henry Herbert had a one-ninth share in the playhouse, and Blagrave was his deputy. Aside from the advantage of institutional backing, Blagrave had the unique privilege of being able to license some of the plays which his own playhouse went on to perform (as he did with Henry Glapthorne's *The Lady Mother*). Further, Gunnell was one of the sharers in the Fortune, and as a former actor he had a personal connection with the Palsgrave's Men, one of the companies from which the King and Queen of Bohemia's Men was created, and out of which, in turn, came the Prince's Men. Heton was later to state that Dorset was responsible for procuring Prince Charles's patronage for this company in 1631 (Bawcutt 1997: 186), in which case it seems as if the complicated shuffling of companies between the Salisbury Court and Fortune at this point may reflect the consortium's response to the financial failure of their original enterprise. The boys were shunted sideways after only a few months at the playhouse, and a new adult company was brought in by Gunnell. This demonstrated a changed idea of how the Salisbury Court would be positioned. From having been a showcase for an innovative playing company, the playhouse became the venue for an adult troupe on the old model, supported by a prestigious royal title.

However, despite their royal patronage, the Prince's Men never achieved any reputation for refined and sophisticated drama such as was associated with the other hall theatres, and the plan in turn seems to have fallen apart around 1633–4, when the Prince's Men switched theatres to the Red Bull, and the Revels company came back from the Fortune, with their place at the Fortune being taken by the Red Bull company. This three-way switch, moving companies between and around separate houses at which the owners of the hall theatre had some influence, could be taken as an example of managerial power in action. This is the explanation interestingly argued by Gurr, who speculates that the rearrangement was a consequence of Gunnell's death in 1634 (Gurr 1996*b*: 428). But other options are possible too: perhaps the Prince's Men did not flourish at the expensive hall playhouse any more than the boys had, or perhaps the regrouping was linked to the expiry of the original lease on the Red Bull in 1634 (see Wickham et al. 2000: 564). Moreover, in a lawsuit of 1640, the playwright Richard Brome makes it clear that the Prince's Men had in fact left for the Bull while Gunnell was still alive (Haaker 1968: 301), and in a separate lawsuit of 1635 one of the company, William Bankes, states that their departure from the Salisbury Court came about when the leaders of the Prince's Men, Ellis Worth and Andrew Kane, 'quarrelled with the housekeepers of the said house at Salisbury Court and did break off from the said company and settled themselves at the playhouse called the Red Bull' (Bentley 1977–8: 236). Heton confirms this account, saying that the Prince's Men, 'being left at liberty, took their opportunity of another house, and left the house in Salisbury Court destitute of both a service and a company' (Bawcutt 1997: 186). It is difficult to avoid the conclusion that while Gunnell could readily impose his will on a boys' company, this was a harder thing to achieve with an adult troupe. Managerial control could not be guaranteed so long as the playing companies had a measure of autonomy deriving from their licences and shareholding arrangements, and so long as they resisted adhering to a specific playhouse. There was an enduring tension between the interests of theatre managers and those of the playing companies, which continued to be a source of instability despite the apparent consolidation of power in the hands of the owners.

Revealingly—and surprisingly, given the troupe's long-term stability and success—we can see this same tension at work in the affairs of the King's Men, in the dispute enshrined in the 'Sharers' Papers'. The King's Men differed from Gunnell's and Beeston's companies in two ways: they ran themselves as a self-governing collective, as was still the case with the Prince's Men and the Red Bull company, and the core members of the company had shares both in the troupe and in the two playhouses at which they performed. This unique situation helps to account for the success of the company's operation over time, as well as for their freedom to move at will between two theatres. Such an arrangement, in which one theatre or the other always stood empty, was only possible because the interests of the sharers and the householders had always been structurally integrated, so that there was no resulting conflict of financial interest over the absence of income from both houses at once. But even the King's Men started to experience disagreements between company and householders in the 1630s, because over time the profiles of the two groups gradually diverged. As members of the consortium aged and died off, so shares passed to people who were only indirectly connected with the company, while the company recruited new players who were not part of the original consortium and so could not participate in the profits. At the same time, an internal imbalance developed, as the income from the housekeepers' shares (so the players complained) increased to nearly three times that of the player–sharers (Gurr 2004*c*: 117). The Lord Chamberlain resolved the dispute by ordering that the complainants should be permitted to buy shares in the theatres, but the mere fact of the disagreement is a straw in the wind. It shows how far the structure of Caroline theatre as a whole was affected by the imbalances that grew up between companies and theatre owners during a time of exceptionally settled playing.

At the Cockpit, Beeston (and, after 1638, his son William) responded to this problem by concentrating control of the company and ownership of the playhouse, including its all-important assets of costumes and playbooks, in his own hands. Hence, when Pembroke issued his 1639 order protecting the Cockpit repertoire against performance by any other company—presumably meaning the Queen's Men, for these were the plays that had originally been staged by the old Queen's Men when they were resident at Drury Lane—he stated that they 'do all and every of them properly and of right belong to the said house, and consequently that they are all in his [William Beeston's] property' (Bentley 1941–68: i. 331). Such an order was a landmark change, since for the first time it asserted that the repertoire was owned by the theatre rather than by the company (as had hitherto been the form of words when plays were licensed). It vastly strengthened Beeston's hand, for it meant that the boys were tied to the theatre and could not legally have taken their repertoire to any other playhouse even had they wanted to. But at the Salisbury Court, the worry of Gunnell's successor, Heton, was precisely that over his relations with the company, that the manager find himself with an empty theatre, as had happened to Gunnell around 1633–4. In the notes that he drew up in 1639 with his proposed patent, Heton attempted to impose the principle that the company should be articled to stay with the playhouse for seven years, and that the title of the Queen's Men should be associated with the playhouse rather than the troupe. He wanted the patent to name him as personally responsible for 'electing her Majesty's company of comedians', and that any players who left the Salisbury Court to act elsewhere should immediately 'cease to be her Majesty's servants, and only the company remaining there to have that honour and title'. The reason for this, he argued, was that 'if they should continue at liberty as they now are, and have power to take her Majesty's service along with them, they would make use of our house but until they could provide another upon better terms and then leave us, as in one year and half of their being here, they have many times threatened' (Bawcutt 1997: 185–6). This draconian design has been read as revealing Heton's ambition to become an autocratic playhouse manager on the Beeston model: he wanted to be named the company's 'governor', which was the same title that Beeston and Davenant had with the boys at the Cockpit. But the difference is that Heton's aspirations were driven as much by paranoia as opportunism, for they rested on a fear about the insecurity of the playhouse manager's position. His business plan was premissed on the supposition that the players' continuing freedom of self-determination would inevitably conflict with the interests of theatre owners.

Heton's remarks suggest that his management was much weaker than Gunnell's had been. With Blagrave's death some of the old ties connecting the Salisbury Court to the Revels Office were severed, and the new partners, John Robinson and Nathaniel Speed, had no links of this kind (Haaker 1968: 297). But whatever Heton's local difficulties, the affair is revealing of the economic and institutional climate affecting Caroline theatre more widely, since behind it we can sense two sets of factors working to transform the larger context. One is that Heton was reacting to a state of intensified commercial competition between the playhouses towards the end of the decade. For all that the playhouses had long competed with one another, there were usually economic ties cutting across their rivalry. So, for example, Blagrave at the Salisbury Court had a share in the Queen's Men at the Cockpit, and Beeston had a share in the Salisbury Court boy actor Stephen Hammerton (Bawcutt 1996: 216, 176–7). Beeston was also happy to allow his house playwright, Shirley, to help build up the Children of the Revels' repertoire. But after the reorganizations of 1636–7, the battle for the audience share seems to have become more heated and antagonistic. Davenant was one major irritant, whose plans for a new venture had clearly caused panic in the dovecote. Heton complains that one of the Queen's Men's 'chief fellows' was involved in the Fleet Street project, 'which no man can judge that a fellow of our company, and a well-wisher to those that own the house, would ever be an actor in';

on top of this, other players had 'treated upon conditions for the Cockpit' or attempted to 'beg our house from the King' (Bawcutt 1997: 186). Heton writes as if relations between the house and the company were radically dysfunctional, but he could not have been the only manager anxious about the precedent set by the upheavals of 1636–7 and looking warily towards Fleet Street. Much the most immediate threat, though, came from Beeston, who, having outmanoeuvred him in 1636–7, continued to snap painfully at his heels. Here the bone of contention was the playwright Richard Brome. Brome had been house dramatist at the Salisbury Court—'inveigled' from the Prince's Men by Gunnell, according to Brome himself (Haaker 1968: 301), and signed to a three-year contract in 1635—but during the plague closure he fell out with the company (who were unable to keep up his salary) and sold several plays to Beeston, who could afford to pay him. After playing resumed, Brome started to make up the backlog on the plays he owed Heton, and was offered a new seven-year contract in 1638, but playwright and company were unable to agree terms for the plays still to be provided, while (Brome claimed) those he did produce were 'cavilled at and rejected'. Whatever the truth of this, Brome avoided signing the contract and jumped ship to the Cockpit, where he hoped 'to enjoy the fruits of his labours more beneficially and peaceably' (Haaker 1968: 304). Shortly afterwards, Heton and the Queen's Men commenced a suit for breach of contract against him in the Court of Requests.

Possibly these disputes were matters of personality, and attest simply to the bad blood between Brome and his former employers. But they are also symptomatic of underlying large-scale shifts, as the companies sought to reposition themselves in 1637–40 and compete for the core market. Brome had provided a strong repertoire for the Salisbury Court: *The Sparagus Garden*, he claimed, earned the company £1,000 profit, and Heton and Beeston clashed over ownership of *The Antipodes*, which was staged at Salisbury Court in 1638 but printed by Brome in 1640 with a note that it should have gone to 'my most deserving friend Mr. William Beeston, unto whom it properly appertained' (Brome 1640, sig. L4^{v}). Heton had anticipated that Brome would provide him with twenty-one plays during the period 1638–45; instead, he found himself without a house dramatist and with all the previous Queen's Men's plays denied to his company by Pembroke's 1639 order. Subsequently, the Salisbury Court revived Thomas Goffe's *The Careless Shepherdess* with a customized 'Praeludium' firing barbs at Brome, and Brome replied with an epilogue to *The Court Beggar* defending the Cockpit's reputation, and put jokes in the dialogue complaining about players going to law with their poets, the context for which must have been the lawsuit. The Salisbury Court Praeludium further adjusted the company profile by making a strong defence of gentlemen playwrights. This was another hit at Brome, who was notorious for his hostility to the amateurs, but it also predicted the future at the playhouse, for Heton's later commissions were increasingly drawn from this pool of talent—a risky choice indeed, as it put the Salisbury Court into direct competition with the Blackfriars, where such plays were part of the staple fare (Butler 2006: 120). Perhaps Heton felt that, without the service of an experienced house playwright, he could not compete with Beeston on his own ground and had to find a strategy that would give his operation a more distinct identity. If so, this suggests that at the end of the decade managers had started to become acutely self-aware about their audience share and the need to differentiate their brand from their competitors'. It is a sign of the theatres settling down to a market economy the opportunities of which were rich but finite, and in which they needed to compete for the same spectators.

The other general—and entirely unpredictable—factor working to unsettle the Caroline theatrical world was the plague. The owners and companies were unlucky that after a period of twelve years in which plague deaths had consistently kept below the level at which playing was automatically suspended, the accession of Charles in 1625 coincided with the onset of the most virulent epidemic since the Black Death, and further severe visitations followed in 1630, 1636–7, 1640, and 1641. All of these epidemics interrupted playing in London, sometimes for months on end, and often with calamitous results for the companies. Notably, during the sixteen-month closure of 1636–7 the Queen's Men and the Company of the Revels fell apart, and the King's Men were reduced to petitioning the Privy Council for permission to play, pleading they had 'spent what they got in many years before' (Bentley 1941–68: ii. 664). So too in the closure of 1630, the Children of the Revels were driven to the breadline before they had begun playing, which may have forced the exchange of theatres in 1631, and perhaps the 1640 closure had the same impact on the Prince's Men and Red Bull, who swapped theatres at that point for no visible reason. If we are looking for the factor that was most detrimental to theatrical continuity in this period, then plague is the obvious candidate. It is striking that (with the exception of the 1634 reshuffle considered in detail above) the watersheds of company reorganization, when troupes either collapsed, cast off personnel, or shifted between playhouses, all corresponded with periods when the theatres were dark, or had recently been so. Indeed, in August 1642, as playing was stopped for reasons of public order, the number of plague deaths had just again hit the nominal ceiling of forty, so the theatres would probably have closed at that moment even without parliamentary intervention (Bentley 1941–68: ii. 671). When the parliamentary order asserted that 'public sports do not well agree with public calamities, nor public stage-plays with the seasons of humiliation' (Firth and Rait 1911: i. 26), it was referring to the Irish rebellion and the imminent onset of civil war at home, but it used language familiar to all for whom acts of public contrition were the customary response to providential punishments. All those involved in the theatre industry must have felt that if any recurrent problem was inimical to the survival of their profession, it was plague rather than puritanism.

The hiatus created by the parliamentary inhibition makes it difficult to assess the affairs of the Caroline playing companies because it prevents us from evaluating what would have come next had the theatres continued to perform. While the end of the drama was swift, this is not an outcome that one would have predicted from a solely economic analysis of the preceding years. On the contrary, the companies had in many ways fallen into settled practices which showed every sign of continuing beyond 1642, and which gave golden opportunities to enterprising businessmen like Beeston and Davenant, or to a man like Heton, accustomed to thinking in seven-year cycles. What did complicate theatrical affairs was the diverging interests of players and owners, the quickening of economic competition, and the repeated disruptions caused by periods of enforced closure. The onset of war in 1642 and the loss of the fashionable urban culture that had flourished before this date made it inevitable that the companies would suffer, but the roots of that crisis lay elsewhere. It reflected not the drama's internal economic decline but Charles's failure to maintain a valid social consensus.

CHAPTER 7

EARLY (PRE-1590) BOY COMPANIES AND THEIR ACTING VENUES

MICHAEL SHAPIRO

ACTING by boys in early modern England originated in grammar schools and religious institutions. Schoolmasters who followed the new humanist curriculum used theatrical performance to familiarize their students with colloquial Latin and to cultivate 'good behavior and audacity', i.e. eloquence and poise in public speaking (M. Shapiro 1977: 2–5; Richard Mulcaster, quoted in DeMolen 1991: 166). Choirmasters of private chapels, cathedrals, and even some parish churches sometimes trained their boy choristers to perform plays, usually at Christmas, in addition to singing at worship services.[1] At some point in Elizabeth's reign, some of these groups performed with sufficient regularity and perhaps also with sufficient skill to be called companies. Groups of adult actors, by contrast, started out as small itinerant bands, sometimes loosely patronized by aristocrats. After the most successful adult troupes began to find more or less permanent homes in London in inns and taverns and after 1576 in specially built large, open-roofed playhouses, the major boy companies performed in halls in their own institutions and briefly in a small indoor playhouse in Blackfriars. In 1590, however, playing by boy companies ceased and did not resume until 1599.

[1] The standard sources for the history of the boy companies are Chambers (1923: ii. 1–76) and Hillebrand (1964). Also helpful are M. Shapiro (1977); Gair (1982); and Gurr (1996*b*: 218–29). Parts of this essay appeared in M. Shapiro (2002, 2006).

To explain the history and evolution of the boy companies, some scholars have constructed a teleological narrative which marks the steps that led to their emergence as profit-oriented enterprises before 1590. Chief among them is Alfred Harbage, who argued in *Shakespeare and the Rival Traditions* (1952) that the boy companies were pawns of mercenary masters and profiteering managers. He pointed out that the boys charged higher prices and played before elite audiences in halls or small indoor 'private' playhouses, while adults charged lower admission fees and played before socially mixed audiences in large, open-roofed 'public' theaters.

In *Children of the Revels* (1977), I countered that the profit motive, though an obvious aspect of the boy companies after their revival 1599, was less prominent before 1590. I argued that the boy companies were essentially court entertainers during the first half of Elizabeth's reign and that their productions in their own small and therefore somewhat exclusive playing spaces were rehearsals for and perhaps revivals of the plays they performed at court. Their reputation, including its possible commercial value, was based on their role as providers of theatrical entertainment to the court. Unlike adult companies, who brought commercial entertainment to court, the children, especially in the years before 1590, brought court theater to wider audiences.

This is not to rule out any pecuniary concern on the part of the masters of boy companies, but rather to place their theatrical activities within a broader framework of court entertainment, a framework in which profit and patronage, commodification and court ritual, were often inseparably intertwined. Choirmasters and schoolmasters received monetary rewards for bringing their companies to perform plays at court, but it is far from clear whether the money went to defray production costs for items not provided by the Revels Office, to the coffers of the sponsoring institution, to the masters themselves, or to some combination of the above. To Harbage, such rewards were 'the *vera causa* of juvenile professionalism' (Harbage 1952: 33), payments in a commodified system of exchange, rather than, at least in part, symbols of reciprocal bonds within a ritualized system of gift-exchange.

The Ritual of Court Performance

Court performance was the crucial factor in the development of the early boy companies, if not their *raison d'être*, and can best be understood as part of an elaborate structure of ceremonial activity centered around the sovereign. John Astington describes this activity as 'a kind of theatre, in which the serious business of civil order, prosperity, national interest, and state power is symbolized by rituals involving the enthroned monarch' (1999*a*: 2). Plays, masques, and other entertainments thus addressed domestic and diplomatic concerns but usually did so through the veil of allegory, while the entertainments in and of themselves and the rewards given to those who presented them signified reciprocal relationships based on service and obligation (M. Shapiro 2002: 272–6). Unlike the temporary and limited obligations stipulated in contract and trade, symbolic gift-exchange insures endless reciprocity to the mutual benefit of both parties.

Gift and commodity systems of exchange not only coexisted in early modern England but constantly interpenetrated one another, essentially because the distinction between making money and offering service was far from clear-cut. As Elizabethan courtiers knew only too well, it was costly to perform service, and hence some mechanisms to recoup costs needed to be devised so that loyal subjects might serve their sovereign and receive her bounty without depleting their own resources. Monopolies, patents, reversions, wardships, and a host of other lucrative privileges and offices granted by the Queen would repay such loyalty and engage the recipients in a series of reciprocal gestures of obligation and reward. In short, the sovereign could bestow lucrative favors upon those who had pleased her with gifts and service, so that they could afford to continue to please her with more gifts and service (MacCaffrey 1961: 41–4).

Early modern English theater illustrates the blurring of distinctions between commerce and patronage. Maintaining or hiring small acting troupes was, for the nobility and some members of the gentry, an integral part of the elaborate ethos of hospitality or housekeeping, and such practices continued long after the theater became part of London's commercialized entertainment industry (Westfall 1990: 122–51; Heal 1990: 1–191). The official patrons of such troupes, as well as the other aristocrats in whose halls such troupes performed, regarded the plays they paid for as gift offerings to them, or from them to their guests, or from them to the Queen if the plays of their 'servants' were accepted for court performance. For the actors, performing under the name of an aristocratic patron shielded them from the vagrancy laws when they traveled about the countryside, performing plays for money in marketplaces, town halls, and the banqueting halls of other aristocrats. If theater in the early modern period was a rich mixture of ceremonial and commodified systems of exchange, the boy actors represent a particularly vivid example.

Sapientia Solomonis: The Play as Ritual

A close look at a single play performed by boys before Elizabeth can help us understand what it meant to entertain the sovereign. It was performed on 17 January 1566, by the pupils of the Westminster grammar school before Queen Elizabeth, her guest Princess Cecilia of Sweden, and members of her Privy Council. Although *Sapientia Solomonis* is listed in many reference works as a court play, strictly speaking it is not: it was not performed at one of the royal residences in or near London but on the grounds of Westminster Abbey, probably in the College Hall, or the Dean's Hall (Birck 1938: 39–45). It nevertheless illustrates how a play by a boy company could easily accommodate itself to the ceremonial nature of royal entertainment through its allegorized content as well as in its symbolic role as gift-offering.

This production apparently fulfilled the statutory requirement dating from about 1560 that the Westminster grammar school students produce a Latin play and an English play each year between Christmas and Twelfth Night. The date of this performance, eleven days later than the statutes stipulated, coincided with the celebration of the seventh anniversary of Elizabeth's coronation on 15 January. The previous year, the Queen may have attended a performance of a Roman comedy at the school, probably Plautus' *Miles Gloriosus* and perhaps also Terence's *Heauton Timorumenus*, but on this occasion, she was not offered a work by 'a comic poet', as the Prologue puts it, but 'a serious history, drawn from the sacred fount of truth', i.e. the Bible (Birck 1938: 27, 53). The text chosen for the occasion was an adaptation of a Latin work about King Solomon, written by Sixt Birck, a German humanist schoolmaster, and published in 1555 (Birck 1938: 27, 10–14). Like Birck's text, the Westminster version dramatized incidents from the life of King Solomon: his prayer for and the granting of wisdom, his judgement in the case of the two women who claimed maternity of the same child, his negotiations with Hiram of Tyre, and the visit of the Queen of Sheba.

To make the play suit the occasion, the adaptor wrote a Prologue and Epilogue (Birck 1938: 14–33). The Prologue resembles those written for plays performed at court. It opens with the familiar courtier's trope of confessing the company's inadequacy in the face of its illustrious spectators, whose pardon must be sought in advance. One spectator possessing particularly keen judgement is the Queen, who in fact had become the school's patron when she restored her father's endowment upon her accession and whose continued favor and patronage is therefore requested: 'May Your Majesty, we beg, look favorably upon this play now to be performed by a boys' company which has been fostered, indeed, by your generosity, O gracious Queen, always august and powerful' (Birck 1938: 53). The Epilogue makes the allegorical connection of Elizabeth with Solomon explicit. They are both just, merciful, and wise. Solomon's wisdom is analogized to Elizabeth's restoring Protestant worship when she came to the throne, and his visitor from Sheba is compared to Elizabeth's guest, 'the illustrious Princess Cecilia' (Birck 1938: 129).

Such allegorical parallels had implications for religious policy and foreign relations. Associating Elizabeth's restoration of protestantism with the wisdom of Solomon was a deft compliment to her skill in returning England, after Edwardian puritanism and Marian catholicism, to her father's Anglican heritage. The Epilogue's assertion of confidence in that middle way, articulated on the grounds of Westminster, implied the abbey's support for the still-controversial Elizabethan Settlement. Linking Sheba to Cecilia had implications for international diplomacy. Cecilia was the sister of King Eric of Sweden, and the wife of the Margrave of Baden, a small German principality. Eric's goodwill was valued for economic and political reasons: England was attempting to break into the lucrative Baltic shipping trade and was seeking alliances with Protestant rulers of Europe to counterbalance the powers of Catholic France and Spain (Wernham 1966: 284; Neale 1934: 72, 76). Like many court plays, *Sapientia Solomonis* was at once both part of a ceremonial exchange of gifts and a vehicle for political statement.

While the Epilogue articulates what shrewd observers of the play and its occasion might have concluded on their own, few court plays offer such explicit interpretation, but rather leave the decoding of allegory, or 'application', to the audience itself. As court plays were performed before a restricted audience entangled in issues of royal favoritism and court policy, they were frequently scrutinized for allegorical meanings of topical significance. The prevalence of the practice is suggested by such disclaimers as the one in the Prologue to Richard Edwards's *Damon and Pithias*, performed at court during the Christmas of 1564–5: 'We talk of *Dionysius's* court, we mean no court but that' (Edwards 1980: 20; M. Shapiro 1977: 46–8).

In addition to its political allegory, *Sapientia Solomonis* seems to have been intended as a gesture of homage to Elizabeth as patron of both the school and the company. Whereas most plays performed before Elizabeth by children's companies were given at court and were therefore financed by the Revels Office, *Sapientia Solomonis* seems to have been paid for by Westminster itself, according to a bill found in the abbey's archives for 'expenses for the furniture and setting for A play entytled, SAPIENTIA SOLOMONIS'. The list of expenses records a payment by the school to the officers of the Revels of 13*s.* 8*d.* for their time and labor, and stipulates a charge of 21*d.* for boat hire 'for the conveyance of the apparel from the Revels unto Westminster, & from thence unto the Revels again' (Birck 1938, between 40 and 41). Moreover, there is no record of expenses either in the Chamber accounts or the Revels accounts for *Sapientia Solomonis*, although there was a payment to the Children of Paul's for performing a play before Elizabeth and Cecilia at the latter's lodgings in the Savoy. For *Sapientia Solomonis*, the bill for expenses of 52*s.* 10*d.*, which included costs usually paid for out of the Revels accounts, was to be paid as reimbursement to 'Master Brown', probably Thomas Browne, then headmaster of the school. There is no other recorded payment to Browne himself either in the abbey or in the Revels accounts for his work in adapting or staging the production. Finally, the play's own status as a gift-offering was symbolically embodied in the specially prepared presentation volumes, ornate manuscripts of the text, similar to the copies of *Miles Gloriosus* presented the previous Christmas to the Queen and four of the nobility (Chambers 1923: ii. 72). The Westminster accounts describe the royal presentation copy of *Sapientia Solomonis*, which was written in red and black ink and bound 'in vellum with the Queen's majesty her arms & silk ribbon strings' (Birck 1938, between 40 and 41) Like plays performed at court, *Sapientia Solomonis* addressed its royal and aristocratic spectators, not at court but in the company's own space, but did so through its allegorized content and its status as a gift-offering.

THE BOY COMPANIES AT COURT

In addition to inviting schoolboys and choristers to perform before them, the early Tudor sovereigns had their own resident group of boys: the Children of the Chapel Royal, a handful of boy choristers maintained primarily to supplement the adult members of the Chapel Royal in providing music at worship services, but who also appeared in pageants and other court entertainments. In 1526 Henry VIII raised the number of boys in the Chapel Royal to twelve, where it remained fixed, as compared with ten at the Windsor Chapel (Chambers 1923: ii. 25, 61–2). Masters of the Chapel Royal held the right to 'take up', or impress, boys as needed to fill the ranks, although they were not permitted to conscript boys from major choirs like those at St Paul's, Windsor, or Westminster (Hillebrand 1964: 42). William Cornish, who served as Master of the Chapel Royal from 1509 to his death in 1523, had performed plays with some of the adult choristers early in the reign of Henry VIII. At some point he fashioned the Children of the Chapel Royal into an acting company of their own. Although the Chapel's boy choristers had appeared in pageants, the children's company gave its first recorded play at court in 1515, performing a lost interlude of *Troilus and Pandor* (Hillebrand 1964: 53–4). Under Cornish's direction the troupe received rewards for performing eight times before the King between 1517 and 1521 (Streitberger 1994: 90, 95; Hillebrand 1964: 48–59). Under Cornish's successor, William Crane, who served as Master of the Chapel Royal from 1523 to 1545, the Chapel children performed plays before the King 'in every Christmas season for which documentary evidence exists' (Streitberger 1994: 138). Similarly, Crane's successor, Richard Bower, who held the mastership of the Chapel from 1545 to 1561, had his choristers present plays at Edward's first two Christmases after his father's death (Streitberger 1994: 183–5).

Grammar school troupes such as the Westminster pupils also performed plays at the early Tudor court. As we have seen, while performing Latin plays was an important element in the humanist scheme of education throughout western Europe, some schoolmasters also saw value in having their pupils perform English plays. The headmaster of Eton, William Malim, writing in 1560, allows that 'at times the Master may also present plays in the English language, provided they are written with wit and humour' (Gair 1982: 3). Malim also advocates selecting the best and most accomplished plays for the students to perform publicly ('with spectators looking on') during the month of December.

Accordingly, masters of London grammar school troupes entertained the court with Roman comedies, neo-Latin plays, and original English plays of various types. On 10 November 1527 Henry VIII and his guests, who included an embassy from France, were entertained by a Latin anti-Protestant play performed by the students of John Rightwise, Master of St Paul's grammar school, the same boy company which also performed Terence's *Phormio* on 7 January 1528 before Cardinal Wolsey and the resident ambassadors (A. Lancashire 1992: 29–30). The Westminster schoolboys, as we have seen, entertained Elizabeth with a neo-Latin play, *Sapientia Solomonis*. Nicholas Udall, who brought his grammar school students from Eton to play before Cromwell in 1538, and his pupils from Westminster grammar school to play before Mary in 1554, wrote *Ralph Roister Doister*, an English play heavily indebted to Roman comedy, for one such occasion (Streitberger 1994: 381 n. 8). Unlike the chorister troupes, which were limited to ten or twelve boys, the grammar schools probably had a larger pool of actors to draw upon for their theatrical productions.[2]

[2] Bevington (1962: 8–47) argues that, until the latter part of the sixteenth century, most adult troupes, which made their living by touring, were limited in size to four, six, or possibly eight actors, and perhaps

Elizabeth's fondness for boy companies preceded her accession to the throne in 1558. On 12 February 1552, as an 18-year-old princess living at Hatfield House, she was entertained by the Children of Paul's, under the direction of Sebastian Westcott, a key figure in the development of the boy companies during the first two decades of Elizabeth's reign (Lennam 1975: 19–33; Hillebrand 1964: 117–24). On that particular occasion, he received a disproportionately large sum of £4 19*s*. for 'the charge of the children with the carriage of the players garments' (Hillebrand 1964: 116). Unfortunately, there is no way to know how much, if anything, was left for the cathedral or for Westcott himself after the children's expenses and the transportation of costumes, let alone how much of that remainder went to cover other production costs.

After she became queen in 1558, Elizabeth instituted the practice of celebrating Christmas and Shrovetide with extended periods of revelry highlighted by masques and by plays performed by troupes of actors—adult and boy companies—who were active in the London area. The court official responsible for arranging and overseeing these productions was the Master of the Revels, a position created by Henry VIII and held under Elizabeth by Thomas Cawarden (the incumbent at the time of her accession), by Thomas Benger from 1560 to 1572, by Thomas Blagrave on an interim basis until 1578, and by Edmund Tilney from 1578 until 1610.

The Master of the Revels was responsible for the plays to be performed at court. His first task was to 'peruse' them, i.e. audition them in space belonging to the Revels Office. From the Westminster accounts, we learn that the abbey's grammar school students rehearsed one or both of their Latin comedies of 1564–5 before Benger (Chambers 1923: ii. 72). Even if a play was 'preferred', the Master of the Revels could, if he deemed it necessary, 'reform it' by insisting on the alteration or excision of material he deemed inappropriate. As some entries in the Revels accounts indicate, he and his staff were also responsible for outfitting the halls to be used, for supplying candles and rigging the lighting, for furnishing costumes, 'howses', and other scenic elements, and for transporting them to the site of performance and back again to the Revels storehouses.[3]

The Master of the Revels and his staff worked closely with the boy companies in the first half of Elizabeth's reign, when these troupes appeared at court nearly twice as often as adult companies did. Among these boy companies were the Children of the Queen's own Chapel Royal, but more frequent entertainers were boy choristers of other institutions—St Paul's Cathedral, St George's Chapel, Windsor, and Westminster Abbey, as well as grammar school students from Westminster and the Merchant

one or two boys to play women and children. By contrast, the plays of the boy companies, who usually performed in and around London, could have as many as ten or a dozen actors onstage at once. When the auspices of an extant play are uncertain, Bevington uses the size of the troupe to determine whether the play was performed by boys or adults.

[3] 'Howses', or 'mansions' or 'domi', were probably booth-like affairs made of lath and canvas, but may also have included large central structures representing castles, rocks, and city walls and battlements (Chambers 1923: i. 71–105; Craik 1958: 11–15). For imaginative reconstructions of performances under such conditions, see Bevington and Hunter (1991: 181–90) and Bevington (1996: 49–59).

Taylors' School. The Chamber accounts record rewards on such occasions given to the masters of these troupes. The usual reward of £6 13*s.* 4*d.* per play was later increased by the inclusion of a gratuity of £10, but then remained fixed well past 1590. Although presented as a gift-offering to a loyal subject, it may also have been intended to defray production costs.

The Chapel children entertained Elizabeth at her second Christmas Revels, probably on New Year 1559, under the direction of Richard Bowers, at whose death in 1561 Richard Edwards became Master of the Children of the Chapel Royal. Edwards was much celebrated in the period for his lyric poetry as well as for his plays, all lost but for *Damon and Pithias*, performed by the Chapel children before Elizabeth probably at Christmas 1564 and possibly revived when they appeared at Lincoln's Inn a month or so later at Shrovetide (Hillebrand 1964: 74–85).

Richard Mulcaster's students from the Merchant Taylors' School entertained Elizabeth at court several times between 1572 and 1576, and one last time in 1586, the year Mulcaster left the school's employ (DeMolen 1991: 12). No texts of plays performed by the Merchant Taylors' troupe survive, but one might infer from the titles of lost plays, such as *Timoclea at the Siege of Thebes*, that Mulcaster, like other masters of boy companies at this time, were inclined toward plays featuring captive maidens and other types of pathetic heroines (M. Shapiro 1977: 154–71).

Westcott's choristers from St Paul's were Elizabeth's particular favorites. They may have been the troupe which appeared at court as early as August 1559 or Christmas 1560–1, but their first unambiguous recorded appearance after Elizabeth became queen was during Christmas 1561–2. For the next two decades, they were the most popular troupe of adults or children to entertain the Queen, appearing on about two dozen subsequent occasions. For these productions, Westcott was usually the official recipient of the standard reward. Although we cannot tell how much money, if any, he personally made from such appearances, his will indicates that he had acquired some wealth and property, although, as almoner and choirmaster of St Paul's, Westcott had other sources of income beyond the fixed sum he received as a reward for bringing plays to court (Hillebrand 1964: 327–30).

Westcott was almoner and choirmaster at the cathedral from 1547 to his death in 1582. He seems to have continued the theatrical tradition established by the previous almoner and choirmaster, John Redford, under whom he had served for a year or so as a vicar-choral, though there is no trace of a court performance during Redford's tenure. Both men were officially granted ten boy choristers for the cathedral choir, but might have augmented that number for theatrical productions with other, unknown personnel (Chambers 1923: ii. 10). Redford's one extant play, *Wit and Science*, is an educational morality play evidently performed by the Paul's choirboy troupe. Westcott's single extant play, *The Marriage of Wit of Science*, is a radical revision of Redford's interlude. The titles of lost plays performed under Westcott's leadership, such as 'Scipio Africanus' and 'Iphigenia', suggest that his troupe, like Mulcaster's, were attracted to military heroes and pathetic heroines (M. Shapiro 1977: 154–71; Lennam 1975: 48; Pincombe 1996: 17).

In addition to the rewards for plays at court, another sign of royal patronage was the protection Westcott received against those who objected to his religious views and practices. In the 1560s, despite the government's vigorous attempts to establish Anglican practice throughout England, Westcott was often in trouble with ecclesiastical and municipal authorities for alleged Catholic sympathies, if not outright recusancy. He was threatened with excommunication and hence dismissal, and at one point was briefly imprisoned in the Marshalsea. He nevertheless retained his post at St Paul's, and while there is no direct evidence of royal protection, he was at one point defended by Robert Dudley, Earl of Leicester, himself a royal favorite. As Dudley was generally regarded as sympathetic to the institutionalizing of the Protestant reformation, his protecting of Westcott may have been requested by his own patron, Elizabeth (Lennam 1975: 21). Westcott was also given extraordinary powers to draft talented boy choristers from any other choir in England, and on one occasion the Privy Council interceded when someone else tried to impress one of his choristers (Lennam 1975: 37; Hillebrand 1964: 123–4). Such privileges and protection given to Westcott might well be an illustration of the kinds of obligation which he earned by his service as court entertainer and which were symbolized by the ritual exchange of gifts.

Westcott's choristers, along with other boy companies, were the pre-eminent court entertainers during the first half of Elizabeth's reign. Between 1558 and 1576 boy companies appeared at court forty-six times, as against thirty-two appearances for the adult troupes. From 1576 to 1583, however, adult companies performed at court thirty-nine times to seventeen performances by boy companies (Chambers 1923: ii. 4). After 1576 some boy companies stopped performing at court entirely.

The Children of the Windsor Chapel, for example, who had played regularly at court, did not appear after 1576, the year Richard Farrant, their Master since 1564, took over from the ailing William Hunnis as Master of the Chapel Royal. Farrant seems to have amalgamated the two companies, for both are listed as having performed the lost 'Mutius Scevola' before Elizabeth on Twelfth Night 1577. He also seems to have been involved with the Earl of Oxford's boys, which was most likely a combination of his own choristers from the Chapel Royal (and possibly those from Windsor Chapel) with the choirboys from St Paul's. This combined troupe played at court in 1583–4 and 1584–5 under Oxford's patronage, but the Chapel children also appeared under their own name in 1583–4, for the last time until 1600–1.

Oxford was also the titular patron of an adult troupe which had at one time styled itself as Worcester's Men and which also performed at court during Christmas 1583–4 under his name, as did a troupe of acrobats the following season. As a patron of entertainers, he was following the lead of members of the Privy Council like Leicester, Howard, and Sussex, whose adult companies performed at court during the late 1570s. In this farrago of theatrical patronage, Oxford was striking the classic pose of courtier—asserting his magnanimity and deploying his servants to entertain his sovereign. Having returned to royal favor after a sordid affair with one the Queen's ladies-in-waiting, he was evidently hoping to maintain his relationship with Elizabeth and thereby to receive gifts or privileges which might remedy his chronic financial problems (A. Nelson 2003: 231, 266–73, 290).

If Oxford's boys was an amalgamation of pre-existing chorister troupes, it may represent a desire on the part of the Revels Office, and perhaps higher authorities, to tighten control over the activities of the London boy companies by reducing their number. Perhaps the same desire to consolidate the number of adult companies working in the London area had led to the granting of a crown patent to Leicester's Men in 1574 which gave them preferred status among adult troupes. Similar motives may underlie the formation by the Master of the Revels in 1583 of the Queen's Men, an 'all-star' company of adult actors, who for the next decade performed at court several times each year, far more often than any rival adult troupe (McMillin and MacLean 1998: 12–17).

Like the Queen's Men among the adult troupes, the Paul's boys emerged as the dominant boy company in court performance after the mid-1580s. They alone played at court every Christmas from 1586–7 to 1589–90. Sometime after Twelfth Night 1590, the troupe fell abruptly from favor and did not appear again before Elizabeth until 1600–1. The loss of court patronage seems to be explained in the Address of the Printer to the Reader in the 1591 Quarto of Lyly's *Endymion*, which reports that 'the Plays in Paul's were dissolved' (Bevington 1996: 74), evidently because of their involvement in the Martin Marprelate controversy, even though they apparently took the anti-Martinist side favored by Elizabeth and most of the high-ranking aristocracy in this dispute over the Anglican episcopy. There is no evidence as to what precisely in their productions was deemed offensive (Hillebrand 1964: 143–50; Gair 1982: 110–12; Dutton 1991: 74–7).

In short, whereas the boy companies had been the principal entertainers at court festivities before 1576, they gradually ceded that role to adult troupes and by 1591 had abandoned it altogether. The reasons for this apparent shift in court taste may have had little to do with aesthetic preferences, for the Master of the Revels, whose job it was to choose which troupes entertained Elizabeth, could shape its taste as well as reflect it. The gradual decline of the boy companies as court entertainers may indeed be a function of the government's efforts to consolidate the number of troupes in the London area. This decline might also be the result of diminished support for court production by the Revels Office, which might also account for performances in their own playing spaces.

The Boy Companies and their Own Playhouses

The usual explanation, then as now, for the boy companies' use of their own playhouses is the need to rehearse the plays they might try out before the Master of the Revels and perhaps eventually bring to court. Such was the argument used by the

Privy Council in a letter dated 4 December 1578 to the Lord Mayor instructing him to permit the Chapel children, the Children of Paul's, and four adult troupes 'to exercise playing within the City' as they have been 'appointed to play this time of Christmas before her Majesty' (Chambers 1923: iv. 278). For adult troupes, the need to rehearse before a court performance was more of a legal fiction than it was for the boy companies. The adults gave 'rehearsals' wherever they could gather a paying audience, in their London venues or on the road, and by so doing earned their daily bread. Boy companies were made up of grammar school students and choristers, had other duties besides the preparing and performing of plays, and were therefore tied, to some extent, to their home institutions. The records show appearances by boy companies at Inns of Court, residences of aristocrats, and in the provinces, but these scattered and isolated incidents are a far cry from the regular performances given by adult troupes outside of their court appearances.[4] For the boy companies, performances in their own halls, later to become known as private theaters, could more accurately be understood as rehearsals for auditions before the Master of the Revels and perhaps for subsequent court performance (Dutton 1991: 26–8).

While some scholars see performances in such spaces as evidence of early commercialization of the boy companies, these occasions might instead be construed as responses to economy measures taken within the Revels Office. After 1572, with Lord Burghley, a new economy-minded Lord Treasurer, and Blagrave, an acting Master of the Revels without official appointment, the overall expenditures of the Revels Office fell from £1,500 a year in 1571–3 to £670 in 1573–4 to £580 in 1574–5 (Chambers 1923: i. 90). Assuming that such a reduction affected its various activities more or less evenly, the Revels Office would have had less money at its disposal for furnishing apparel and scenic elements for court masques, fewer of which were produced during this period, and even for court plays.

At about the same time adult troupes were responding to increased competition by raising their own standards of production. To this end, they evidently spent more of their own money on costumes and other physical requirements and may therefore have required less assistance from the Revels Office (Astington 1999*a*: 21). Moreover, as adult troupes were accustomed to touring, they could readily transport their costumes and portable scenic elements to court when needed for performance. By contrast, boy companies depended more heavily on the Revels Office for assistance with productions at court or, as in the case of *Sapientia Solomonis*, on the resources of their own institutions to finance productions intended for a limited number of performances in their own playing spaces. But with the Revels Office on a shorter financial leash, plays by adult troupes probably seemed more economical to produce at court than those by boy companies. In response, the masters of boy companies may have wished to generate funds to supplement or replace those allocated by their own institutions or available from the Revels Office in order to meet the competition of their adult counterparts for slots in the court's calendar of entertainment.

[4] Gurr (1996*b*: 226) suggests that sporadic records of provincial appearances by both children's troupes during the 1590s indicate commercialism. But these half-dozen or so recorded provincial appearances seem too few and far between to represent serious commercial intentions.

There were precedents for such use of private spaces even before the draconian cuts in the Revels budget. As we have seen, the Westminster schoolboys performed *Sapientia Solomonis* on the abbey grounds in 1566, although there is no evidence that they charged admission to defray production costs. Other boy companies did perform before paying spectators in the spaces of their institutions during the late 1560s and 1570s, but very little is known about such spaces, which were most likely halls at the masters' disposal, converted temporarily into playhouses, but ultimately under the control of the sponsoring institution.

The earliest recorded instance of a boy company giving such rehearsals before paying spectators involves the Merchant Taylors' boys, who at some point in the 1560s or early 1570s began to charge a fee for admission to their performances in the guildhall. In March 1574, however, the masters of the guild forbade the use of their hall for plays, on the grounds that 'every lewd person thinketh himself (for his penny) worthy of the chief and most commodious place without respect of any other either for age or estimation in the commonweal' (Chambers 1923: ii. 75). Kathleen McLuskie sees this incident as evidence that such rehearsals were an independent enterprise rather than a part of the life of the guild (1991: 127), a step toward commercialization perhaps, though not necessarily what Gurr calls 'Mulcaster's commercial exploitation of his boys' (1996*b*: 220; cf. DeMolen 1991: 166). Mulcaster's students may have performed in the guildhall to rehearse for their appearances at court at Shrovetide 1573 and 1574 or in preparation for an audition before the Master of the Revels. The troupe continued to perform at court even after the order forbidding it to use the guildhall, appearing before Elizabeth on 15 February 1575 and 6 March 1576, but not again thereafter until their last appearance on 12 February 1583. What is not known is whether the ban remained in force or was rescinded, what effect if any it had on court appearances, and whether or not the troupe found other space for rehearsals.

Like Mulcaster, Westcott had his choristers of Paul's rehearse before paying spectators in some sort of theater on the cathedral grounds during the 1570s, if not earlier. The existence of such a playhouse is suggested by Westcott's will, which records bequests 'to Shepard that keepeth the door at plays' and to 'Pole the keeper of the gate', presumably one of the gates of the churchyard (Hillebrand 1964: 330). In 1575 the Repertory of the Court of Common Council recorded a complaint to the cathedral authorities that 'one Sebastian . . . keep[s] the plays and resort of the people to great gain', a complaint which suggests that some kind of playing space was used by choristers for the master's personal profit (Hillebrand 1964: 123). Whether maintained solely for his own personal profit or out of a desire to generate additional funds for the production of plays that might be accepted for court performance, or some combination of both motives, Westcott established and maintained a fee-charging playhouse somewhere on the grounds of St Paul's Cathedral.[5]

Unlike Mulcaster's and Westcott's troupes, some boy companies apparently responded to the diminished support from the Revels Office by simply ceasing to

[5] Gair (1982: 44–56) claimed to have located the theater, but his conclusions have not been widely accepted. See E. Jensen (1984–5: 82–4); Hollindale (1985: 80–1); M. Shapiro (1982: 3–5); Berry (1978: 77–82).

perform at court. The grammar schools at Paul's and Westminster had long stopped performing at court, and Eton made a final appearance in 1572–3. Richard Farrant, however, responded to this challenge by outdoing Mulcaster and Westcott: in 1576 he rented space expressly for the Children of the Chapel Royal (perhaps including Windsor choristers) to use for rehearsals. This space was in the precinct known as Blackfriars, a former Dominican priory located in a 'liberty', which, like the grounds of St Paul's Cathedral, was an area exempt from the jurisdiction of the municipal authorities, who strove to curtail if not eliminate theatrical activity in London throughout the early modern period.

While not much is known about the configuration of the first Blackfriars theater, it is the only indoor playhouse used by a boy company about which we know anything at all. Farrant pulled down one or more partitions to create a large rectangular hall, similar in size and shape to a typical Tudor banqueting hall. According to one detailed analysis of the surviving documents, approximately one-third of the hall served as the playing area and the rest as an auditorium capable of seating 120–30 spectators (I. Smith 1964: 130–53). The texts of the three plays known to have been performed at this theater—Peele's *The Arraignment of Paris* and Lyly's *Campaspe* and *Sappho and Phao*—call for a trap (and therefore for a raised stage), two doors, and a discovery space, the standard features of many theaters during this period. A raised stage could have been installed in any banqueting hall used for court performance but in its absence performers could have adapted their text accordingly, as they must often have had to do when playing away from their customary venues.

These three first Blackfriars plays all bear the hallmarks of court entertainment. Peele's *The Arraignment of Paris*, which presents its version of the mythological story of Paris having to choose the fairest of three goddesses, is resolved when he hands the apple to Elizabeth, who must therefore have been in the audience. Implicit allusion to Elizabeth occurs in the two plays by John Lyly, which were advertised on their title pages as having been 'played before the Queen's Majesty' (Bevington and Hunter 1991: 1, 141). Like Farrant's single extant play, *The Wars of Cyrus*, which may also have been performed at the first Blackfriars playhouse, these works dramatize monarchs who conquer or resist sexual temptation and remain celibate, thereby flattering Elizabeth in her persona as Virgin Queen.

After Farrant's death in 1580, Hunnis acquired the lease to the Blackfriars playhouse. His intent, according to the Earl of Leicester, was 'to practise the Queen's Children of the Chapel, being now in his charge, in like sort as his predecessor did for the better training them to do her Majesty service' (Hillebrand 1964: 91). But Hunnis transferred the lease to Henry Evans, a former associate of Westcott's, who in turn sold the lease to the Earl of Oxford, who gave it to Lyly. Under its various leaseholders, the playhouse was used for the next four years by a combination of Chapel and Paul's choristers under Oxford's sponsorship. It is hard to know precisely how Oxford, Lyly, and Evans divided the task of managing the troupe that performed under the Earl's name. Lyly wrote plays and evidently had a hand staging them, according to a disparaging remark by Gabriel Harvey (Hunter 1962: 75). Like his patron, Lyly saw his involvement in court entertainment as the way to royal favor, and continued to write plays for court even after he had severed his connection with Oxford, although he received little more than a veiled hint from Elizabeth around 1588 that he might someday receive the reversion to the mastership of the Revels and a honorific title of 'Esquire of the Body' (Hunter 1962: 77). Evans probably handled the troupe's business affairs and may have brought the Paul's choristers into the combined company after Westcott's death in 1582 (Hillebrand 1964: 135). In 1584, however, the owner of the Blackfriars property evicted the children's troupe.

Perhaps it was Evans's past association with Paul's that permitted the troupe, or perhaps just the Paul's contingent, to shift its operations back to the playhouse on the cathedral grounds, which had passed under the control of the new choirmaster, Thomas Giles. Because Evans was to become a key figure in the directorate of the Chapel children after their revival in 1599, he is thought by some scholars to have been the principal agent of the commercialization of the pre-1590 boy companies, although the evidence suggests that his role in their theatrical activities was minimal under Westcott and limited to a year or two thereafter with Oxford's boys.

Throughout the 1580s, Lyly's plays were performed by the amalgamated or separate children's companies both at court and in the private theaters at Blackfriars and Paul's, and the early printed texts often include different prologues and epilogues for the different venues. Whatever the venue, these extra-dramatic addresses strike the same courtly posture, gracefully sounding the tropes of *sprezzatura*, the self-deprecating ploy advocated by Castiglione for use when a courtier is entertaining his patron, which suggests that a similar ambience prevailed at court, Blackfriars, and the theater at St Paul's (M. Shapiro 1977: 38–51; cf. Dutton 1991: 61–5; Pincombe 1996: 18–19).

As separate troupes or as an amalgamated company, the boy company at Blackfriars went downhill after the loss of the lease. Perhaps the Chapel children did not appear at court after 2 February 1584 because they no longer had a playhouse in which to rehearse or generate funds for court performance. Oxford's boys, whatever its actual composition, appeared at court for the last time during the following Christmas of 1584–5. That the Children of Paul's continued to play at court throughout the later 1580s suggests that their own playhouse on the cathedral grounds remained a viable alternative to the Blackfriars until it too closed around 1590. Once back in their own playhouse, the company could use it for auditions and for rehearsals for court performances, and perhaps generate the revenues, necessary now that the Revels Office had scaled back its own production activities, which made such performances possible.

The Importance of the Early Boy Companies

The legacy of the pre-1590 boy companies is twofold: their work influenced subsequent playhouses and subsequent playwrights. These companies were the first to establish the small indoor playhouse as the standard venue for theatrical entertainment in England, and some of the artistic strategies they discovered by working in such spaces made a lasting impression on English dramatists.

Adult troupes performed in such indoor venues as guildhalls, town halls, and private banqueting halls when they toured the provinces, and in inns and taverns before they became fixtures in their own open-roofed theaters. But after 1576 the primary venues for adult troupes were those same large, open-roofed playhouses. By contrast, boy companies performed only in halls, whether in their home institutions, on tour, or at court. When Mulcaster, Westcott, and Farrant established what were in effect the earliest private theaters in England, they were most likely replicating conditions of banqueting halls and indoor playhouses familiar to all acting companies of the period.

These playhouses set the pattern for the future development of English theaters. Evidently noting the success of the first Blackfriars theater, James Burbage in 1596 leased a different but larger space in the same former priory. He bequeathed it to his son Richard, who was prevented by the opposition of the neighbors from opening a theater for the Lord Chamberlain's Men. Instead, in 1600 he sub-leased the space to Henry Evans, who established a theater to be used by the Children of the Chapel Royal, the so-called second Blackfriars theater. This theater was so successful, from both the aesthetic and the commercial standpoints, that Burbage reclaimed the theater in 1608 when the sub-lease expired. Within a year or two, the King's Men began to perform there as well as at the Globe, and did so until 1642 (I. Smith 1964: 247).

Gradually, other London-based acting companies began to favor small indoor playhouses such as Blackfriars over the larger, open-roofed theaters like the Globe. By 1630 the indoor venues were clearly the wave of the future. Herbert Berry summarizes the situation:

> The London stage that had consisted largely (and during the 1590s entirely) of public playhouses came to consist of three public playhouses (the Fortune, Red Bull and Globe) and three private [Blackfriars, the Phoenix, and Salisbury Court]. Public playhouses, even the Globe, were associated with crude spectators, fustian, and stage battles. In private playhouses, the best writers and players offered refinement of language and plot to elite spectators who paid more money to see plays indoors by candlelight. (Berry 2002: 160)

When the theaters reopened after the Restoration, indoor playhouses soon became the only venue, and open-roofed amphitheaters were a thing of the past.

Lyly may have been referring to just this quality of refinement in his Blackfriars Prologue to *Sappho and Phao*, when he promised that the play would evoke 'inward delight, not outward lightness... [and] soft smiling, not loud laughing' (Bevington and Hunter 1991: 201). Smaller playing areas meant less reliance on fencing and acrobatics, staple features of plays by adult troupes. Better acoustics allowed dramatists to call for subtler and more varied musical effects, a distinct advantage for choirboy companies, trained in singing and the playing of instruments. Sophisticated musical effects became part of the appeal of plays produced by the King's Men when they took over the second Blackfriars theater. The intimacy of a hall playhouse or a banqueting hall at court also encouraged dramatists to write for socially cohesive audiences capable of appreciating subtle allusions to specific individuals, issues, and situations and to shared concerns about events outside the world of the play.

Writing for the boy companies encouraged playwrights like Edwards and Lyly to exploit differences in size and age by using smaller, younger boys in comic subplots of servants to parody or comment on the actions of their social superiors who populated the main plots, a technique widely practiced by later dramatists. Lyly in particular developed a type of play organized thematically, that is, around multiple and contrasting perspectives on a common problem or idea, a structure quite different from the more episodic dramaturgy of adults' plays at this time. These small indoor venues also seemed to encourage a refined and nuanced style of writing, which in the hands of a writer like Lyly developed into an instrument for articulating antithetical thoughts and feelings, and for reinforcing those antitheses by means of rhetoric, rhythm, and sound. In his plays about love, for example, Lyly provided later dramatists with a rough model for exploring the nature of romance and sex by means of contrasting 'backstairs' subplots and of witty, delicate repartee between lovers who are both victims and observers of their feelings. The coarse but often wise perspectives of servants and the elegant banter of amorous couples fed directly into Shakespeare's romantic comedies and through Shakespeare to writers like Congreve and Sheridan, Wilde and Shaw, in short, into the mainstream of world drama.

CHAPTER 8

THE BOY COMPANIES 1599–1613

MARY BLY

THE years 1599–1613 were the heyday of boy theater companies: the decade in which they occasionally triumphed over adult companies, occasionally snubbed the government, and frequently performed some of the best plays available in London.[1] When *Hamlet*'s Rosencrantz remarks that fashionable 'little eyases' are 'tyrannically clapped', he refers to these companies, who reigned like tyrants over the London theatrical scene, stealing audiences and applause.[2] Until the last fifteen years, scholarship sharply differentiated between the repertories of adult and boy companies;

[1] References to plays and other early texts are to the following editions: *The Puritan, or, The Puritan Widow*, ed. Donna B. Hamilton, in Middleton (2007: 509–42); id., *The Works of Thomas Middleton*, ed. A. H. Bullen, 8 vols (Boston: Houghton, Mifflin, 1885–6); William Shakespeare, *Hamlet, Prince of Denmark*, ed. Philip Edwards, New Cambridge Shakespeare, rev. edn (Cambridge: Cambridge University Press, 2003); George Chapman, *Plays and Poems*, ed. Jonathan Hudston, texts prepared by Richard Rowland (London: Penguin, 1998); John Day, *The Isle of Gulls* (repr. Thomas White, 1831); Dekker (1884–6; 1953–61: ii); Ben Jonson, *Epicene, or, The Silent Woman*, ed. Richard Dutton (Manchester: Manchester University Press, 2003); Thomas Heywood, *An Apology for Actors* (London: Shakespeare Society, 1841); John Marston, *Antonio and Mellida*, ed. G. K. Hunter (Lincoln: University of Nebraska Press, 1965); id., *The Dutch Courtesan*, ed. David Crane (London: A. & C. Black, 1997); id., *The Fawn*, ed. Gerald A. Smith (Lincoln: University of Nebraska Press, 1965); id. et al., *The Insatiate Countess*, ed. Giorgio Melchiori (Manchester: Manchester University Press, 1984).

[2] William Shakespeare, *Hamlet*. The entire passage, II. ii. 354–60, appears in different versions in Q1, Q2, and F, where it is much expanded. Knutson's persuasive look at the 'little eyases' passage (found only in the Folio) argues that this version of the comment dates from a 1606–8 revival and speaks directly to the Queen's Revels repertory. I disagree with Knutson's reading of 'tyrannically clapped' as prophesying rigorous imprisonment. I prefer Philip Edwards's 2003 New Cambridge note of 'inordinately,

Rosencrantz's comment fueled an argument that the companies were bitterly competitive, sponsoring 'rival traditions', according to Alfred Harbage's 1952 book of that title.

More recently, as scholars turned to looking closely at specific companies—the players, authors, managers, audiences, and locations—their research overturned the theory of rival traditions. Roslyn Knutson concludes that 'the war between the men's and boys' companies [was] largely myth' (1995: 4).[3] Rather than considering boys' plays as an undifferentiated unit, scholars are now examining each company's repertory as the product of local influences, investigating, for example, the ages of the boys in a given theater, or the influence of location on performance.[4] Crucially, responsibility for a given repertory is now apportioned to more than its dramatists. Lucy Munro writes of the Queen's Revels company, for example, that '[their] plays were created not only by the dramatists, but also through the ideas and desires of the company's shareholders, licenser, patrons, actors, and audience' (2005: 165).[5] Another emerging focus of study, collaborative writing, also points toward a wider, more complicated understanding of the genesis of a given repertory (Bly 2000; Cathcart 2000; Masten 1997; Munro 2005). Thus, while scholars recognize the uniqueness of boys' plays, they are investigating the tyrannical clapping of their audiences by looking at the uniqueness of boy companies.

This essay will try to strike a balance between pointing toward new investigations into local repertory differences, while providing an overview of those aspects that unite boys' plays. For even if the repertories were not designed in opposition to those of adult companies, they did offer a particular type of pleasure. Their plays would have been recognizable not only owing to the age of their actors, but owing to similar preoccupations, delights, and jokes. Audiences packed these theaters looking for a distinct type of drama, and the theaters' commercial success reflects the appeal of their offerings. Five key characteristics recur in many boys' plays of this period.[6] They

outrageously clapped' (see also Ann Thompson and Neil Taylor's 2006 Arden). The boys were certainly reprimanded in 1606–8, but I think Knutson weakens her own argument for the King's Men's purported warning by indicating that the adult company considered such punishment 'tyrannical' or outrageous (Knutson 1995: 23).

[3] Harbage's view of a repertory shaped by competition persists in spite of evidence, as in Gurr's *Shakespearian Playing Companies*, which argues that 'adults reacted by going in conspicuously different directions' (Gurr 1996*b*: 115); see Foakes (1970); McCarthy (2006). A more fruitful response is shown by G. K. Hunter's investigation of ways by which adult companies adapted to the closing of the boys' theaters by trying to adopt some of their successful techniques (Hunter 1997).

[4] For full-length studies of children's companies, see M. Shapiro (1977); Gair (1982); Bly (2000); Munro (2005).

[5] Much of what we know about the organization of boys' companies comes from litigation generated by partnerships and bankruptcies. Irwin Smith has pointed out that the Queen's Revels management in the Blackfriars spawned nine intra-partnership litigations and six other involving outsiders (I. Smith 1964: 189). In a similar vein, William Ingram's painstaking research into the King's Revels has pieced together numerous lawsuits, allowing a glimpse of the management, playwrights, and actors (Ingram 1985).

[6] I want to thank the members of my graduate seminar in the spring of 2007: we read through every extant boys' play, and our discussions contributed not only to my summary of these five qualities, but greatly to my understanding of bawdy humor. Thank you to Gregory Blume, Julie Fifelski, Kirk Quinsland, and Stephanie Pietros.

exhibit a wild, often humorous, fascination with erotic matters, body parts, and cuckoldry; they emphasize the beauty of the boy actor, toying with homoerotic desire; they engage in dangerous satire of the court and government; they often challenge the audience's suspension of disbelief; and they make abundant use of song and learned languages, reflecting the boys' skills as students and musicians. I will first sketch the history of the boy companies operating in 1599–1613, and then turn to discussion of these unifying qualities.

The Companies and their Playhouses

The boy company that played in the Blackfriars theater between 1600 and 1608 was known variously as the Children of the Queen's Chapel Royal, then as the Children of the Queen's Revels, the Children of the Revels, and finally, the Children of the Whitefriars.[7] The Queen's Revels, as this troupe is generally labeled, was initiated by Henry Evans, who leased the Blackfriars playhouse from Richard Burbage. Joined by Nathaniel Giles and James Robinson, he used a warrant allowing him to 'press' boys into the royal choirs and virtually kidnapped some youths, leading to lawsuits and recriminations.[8] The company quickly developed a reputation for comical satire, for plays that were innovative in form and perilously contentious in their political views. Rosencrantz may well be speaking of the Queen's Revels when he says that boys make men 'afraid of Goose-quils'; Chapman's *The Conspiracy and Tragedy of Charles, Duke of Biron*, for example, infuriated the French ambassador owing to its depiction of the French queen slapping the King's mistress. In 1608 a note from Sir Thomas Lake to Lord Salisbury signaled out the King's displeasure with the 'lewd words' of 'the Children of the Blackfriars', indicating that 'his Grace had vowed they should never play more, but should first beg their bread, and he would have his vow performed' (Wickham et al. 2000: 126). Yet most theater historians believe that the Queen's Revels did not disband, but moved to a different theater. Shakespeare's adult company, the King's Men, took over the Blackfriars while the disgraced boy company moved to the Whitefriars theater sometime in 1609, playing there until 1613, when they merged with an adult company.

Before the Queen's Revels moved to the Whitefriars theater, the playhouse housed a boy company known as the King's Revels. This small troupe performed for around a year, between 1607 and 1608. The structure of the company is unique in theatrical

[7] See Hillebrand (1964). The final manifestation as 'Children of the Blackfriars' may be an entirely new enterprise, absorbing parts of the disassembled Queen's Revels. See below and Dutton (2002).

[8] The four partners in the Blackfriars enterprise sued each other with vigor, resulting in fifteen lawsuits in all. See I. Smith (1964: 189). For Nathaniel Giles's commission to impress children and a bill of complaint from Henry Clifton protesting the kidnapping of his son, see Wickham et al. (2000: 263–67, 510–11).

history, in that the financial partners who gathered together to start the company also turned their hand to writing plays. Other companies were run by financiers, or by actor–partners; this is the only company owned and operated by a group of apparently 'frustrated playwrights', to use William Ingram's phrase (1985: 217; see Cathcart 2005). This circumstance allows scholars to posit the kind of intimate knowledge of the company and audience that we can only surmise when it comes to the dramatist Middleton, for example, who wrote for several companies. We can compare the King's Revels playwright–owners to John Marston, who, as a shareholder in the Queen's Revels, wrote plays explicitly for his company and its audience. Unfortunately, the King's Revels was quickly driven into bankruptcy by plague closures, leaving the theater free for the arrival of the Queen's Revels company in 1609.

The third boys' theater was located in the grounds of St Paul's Cathedral. The Paul's boys, who were drawn from cathedral choristers, performed from 1599 to 1606. The company began when a new choir director, Edward Peers, set the boys to acting as well as singing. Like the Queen's Revels, the Paul's boys performed comical satires, although they apparently limited their satire to a more local, community level. In 1603 the boys performed a Chapman play that depicted, under 'colourable and feigned names', according to the law case that ensued, the life of a local heiress who promised herself in marriage to three men, finally marrying a fourth (Wickham et al. 2000: 314–15). We know from a 1608 sermon by William Crashaw that the company repeatedly brought 'religion and holy things upon the stage', mocking the Puritans who lived just outside the cathedral (Crashaw 1608: 171). The troupe ceased playing in 1606, and from 1608 to 1610 two theatrical rivals bribed Peers with £20 a year to keep the theater dark, a sign of the strength of their audience.[9]

By the end of the sixteenth century, the Queen and her Privy Council exercised firm control over theatrical activities, from the licensing of plays by the Master of the Revels, to the licensing of playhouses. Purpose-built playhouses were forbidden within the City of London, leading to the establishment of all three boys' theaters in liberties within the city. These several-block-wide areas were exempted from royal and mayoral jurisdiction, a circumstance that allowed them to house criminals, prostitutes, and private theaters. The liberties were free from jurisdiction owing to their having originally housed monasteries and retaining the right to sanctuary; by 1599 (more than sixty years after Henry VIII dissolved those monasteries) each of these urban spaces had gained its own reputation. That reputation influenced, to some extent, the theater's reputation, its repertory, and the makeup of the audience. Playwrights always knew the company, and thus the audience, for which they were writing, and that distinction is reflected in specific repertories. When dramatists were shareholders in a given company, the connection between location and content grows even tighter. Thus, the particular nature of a given liberty is a critical vector in understanding its repertory.

[9] See Corrigan (2001) for a lively conspiracy theory suggesting that the Blackfriars syndicate deliberately brought down Paul's from within.

While it is difficult to encapsulate the fluid nature of such neighborhoods, quick distinctions can point the way to future research. The Blackfriars was home to noblemen and wealthy gentlemen. The King's Men (Shakespeare's company) first leased the theater in 1596, but noblemen living in the liberty blocked performances by the adult company through a petition to the Privy Council, citing traffic problems and noise. Those noblemen did allow the Queen's Revels to perform, and apparently they delighted in satirical weapons plied against well-known men, some of whom may have been in the audience. St Paul's Cathedral was, as I noted above, surrounded by Puritans, who found themselves under fire from the boys in at least one play. The anonymous play *The Puritan* not only stages thieving, foolish Puritans, but it contains a bowdlerization of the Nicene Creed, the profession of faith that would have been spoken daily within the cathedral itself. The play seems to indicate that the players have made a practice of snubbing their neighbors, noting that a preacher was brought 'drunk upo'th'stage once, as he will be horribly drunk' (I. iv. 182–3). Another aspect that might have infuriated churchgoers was that Paul's plays are among the most erotically explicit performed on the early modern stage; Richard Flecknoe's 1664 *Short Discourse of the English Stage* attributes the closing of this theater to 'people growing more precise, and Playes more licentious' (Chambers 1923: iv. 369). And the third liberty, the Whitefriars, was a notable red-light district. One of the shareholders in the King's Revels, Lording Barry, wrote his only play for the company: entitled *Ram Alley, or, Merry-Tricks* (i.e. meretrix: prostitute), it offers a coarse, pun-filled look at one of the district's most famous streets. The fact that the King's Revels repertory has been described as going 'beyond all other companies in the obscenity of its plays' should offer little surprise (J. Q. Adams 1913).

One fruitful way of understanding the importance of location is to examine how playwrights nimbly change their product when writing for one theater as opposed to another. Ben Jonson's *Epicene*, written for the Queen's Revels after they moved to the Whitefriars, is a wild, sarcastic tale of sexual misadventure, perfect for an audience in the brothel-laden Whitefriars. It is nothing like the cheerful city comedy he wrote the previous year for the Queen's Revels when they were housed in the Blackfriars (Bly 2007; see also Yiu 2007; Howard 2007: 212–13).[10]

I want to offer a final look at this situation through the lens of some of the newest work in the field. Paul Yachnin persuasively argues that 'Over time, the companies' self-descriptions narrowed, stabilized, and thereafter tended to determine what kinds of plays the companies performed and how those plays were received' (2003: 764). I have suggested that part of the stabilization process results from the reputation of the liberty in which a theater was located, and that playwrights deftly addressed these changes in location by altering their offerings. Thus, when the Queen's Revels troupe moved to the Whitefriars, playwrights took notice of the reputation of that theater and (crucially) its audience, and changed their texts to suit. But Richard Dutton

[10] I don't want to imply that plays were limited to the theater audience for which they were written: Middleton's *A Trick to Catch the Old One* appeared at Paul's and then at the Blackfriars; Marston's *Parasitaster* made a reverse journey, from the Blackfriars to Paul's.

offers a second, fascinating way of examining the history of the Whitefriars theater. He has suggested that the Queen's Revels never moved to the Whitefriars, but that the 'Children of the Whitefriars' who appeared there in 1609 were actually a new entity, engineered as such by the Revels Office (2002: 339). The new company would have used the defunct King's Revels patent, but would have a new artistic policy. These two theories are not incompatible—but they point to the fact that much of the theatrical history of boy companies is still being considered, argued over, and revisited.

Erotic Material

Boys' plays are drenched in sexual jokes. A fascination with body parts, body processes (farting is a recurrent theme), and references to sexual acts pervades almost every play, and is found in the repertories of all three companies. Puns on private parts are ubiquitous. Marston's *The Insatiate Countess*'s first line offers a succinct example: 'What should we do in this Countess's dark hole' (I. i. 1). What indeed? Scholars such as Michael Shapiro have suggested that the preponderance of bawdy material is directly relevant to the actors' ages: 'bawdry and erotic material is used to remind the audience of the obvious disparity between child actors and adult characters' (1977: 108). In other words, the pleasure of the dirty joke is less in itself than in the shock of hearing a child lisping the words.

This theory should be viewed with caution, given recent scholarly attention to the ages of the boys. The median age of the troupes appear to vary not only company to company, but within the life-cycle of a given company.[11] In 1600, for example, Queen's Revels actors seem to have been between 10 and 14, but Nathan Field was 19 by 1606, and still performing for them. The troupe included a 21-year-old by 1613 (Munro 2005; Kathman 2005*b*).[12] A similar pattern can be glimpsed as the Children of Paul's morph into the Youths of Paul's when playing before the King in 1606. Ann Blake finds a number of actors who were youths, rather than children, joining the boys' troupes at age 13 or older (Blake 1987). Discussion of erotic material in a specific play, then, must be linked to close attention to the composition of the cast at the time of first performance.

[11] Paul's is generally considered to have performed with younger boys than the other two companies, yet even that company changed to the 'youths' of Paul's over time. David Kathman's study of all documentary evidence related to boy actors (in adult companies as well as boy companies) leads him to conclude that female roles were played by adolescent boys 'no younger than twelve and no older than twenty-one or twenty-two, with a median of around sixteen or seventeen' (Kathman 2005*b*: 220).

[12] It is often assumed that the boys must be young owing to choirs requiring pre-adolescent voices. Interestingly, at least one choirboy, the future composer Thomas Morley, appears in a 1574 list of boy singers for Paul's—although he was 17 years old. It may be that these choirs encompassed a larger span of ages than we assume (Ball 1962: 9).

Part of the problem is that 'boy' now connotes childlike qualities. But the boy actor Nathan Field wrote *The Woman Is a Weathercock* for the Queen's Revels, performing it both at court and in the Whitefriars theater. He was 25 by 1612, and still acting for the 'Children of the Whitefriars'. Similarly, William Barksted was 17 when the King's Revels troupe opened for the first time. He collaborated on the rewriting of *The Insatiate Countess* while performing in the Whitefriars theater; from his arrest in a brothel and his publication of *Myrrha* in 1607, we can deduce that he was not childlike, within our understanding of the word.

Yet the prevalence of bawdy humor clearly does stem, in some fashion, from youthful actors; many of the puns have the shining brilliance of pre-pubescent humor. A threat in Marston's *Dutch Courtesan* that a vintner will be made to 'fart crackers' is a good example (IV. v. 124). Phallic jokes are everywhere, many of them involving priapism or insufficiency. Mistress Honeysuckle's complaint in *Westward Ho* that her husband's 'old' pen is 'stark naught, and wil cast no inck' is typical (Dekker 1953–61: ii; II. i. 121–3). Phallic celebration is also popular: *Westward Ho*'s invitation to a maiden to 'Hang thy virginity upon the pole of carnality' resonates with this kind of intense interest in the penis and its attributes (IV. v. 57).

Cuckoldry is another prevalent strain, less easy to explain by reference to adolescent humor. It is rare for a boys' play not to include at least one joking reference to nightcaps and horns; many of the plays are structured around what can be summed up as male terror. One way of explaining this strain is to note that while the plays exhibit fear of cuckoldry, they also offer a kind of voyeuristic pleasure in watching a wife be seduced. Both aspects emphasize the uncontainable nature of female desire. A standard line comes from Chapman's *All Fooles*, a play that ends with a lengthy discourse on the 'Horned Age': '*Gazetta*, you sayd, is unchaste, disloyall, and I wot not what; Alas, is it her fault? is shee not a woman? did she not suck it (as others of her sex doe) from her mothers brest?' (III. i. 180–2).

This emphasis on women's sexuality occasionally slips into truly virulent misogyny, as in Marston's *Parasitaster, or, The Fawn*: 'this is the lady made of cutwork, and all her body like a sand box, full of holes, and contains nothing but dust' (III. i. 99–101). Yet the flip side of an emphasis on women's desire is the depiction of women's desire for freedom. Heroines in boys' plays routinely demand what we might call equal rights. The Widow in *The Puritan*, for example, mourns her husband by boasting that her purse and her carriage were openly hers; Tysefew's proposal to Crispinella in *The Dutch Courtesan* includes a promise that 'If you will be mine, you shall be your own. My purse, my body, my heart is yours' (IV. i. 79–80).

While erotic material is found in adult company plays, I would argue that boy company plays not only rely more heavily on bawdy language, but in tandem, the plays are more physically adventuresome. Kissing happens rarely in the adult theater, a fact that has been attributed to the male–boy cast. But boys frequently kiss each other on their own stages: Marston's *Antonio and Mellida*, for example, features a scene in which the lead characters are directed to kiss at the end of every line. This attribute has led to twentieth-century assessments of boy theaters as 'houses of erotic display', curiously echoing early modern warnings of the dangers of boy actors, as in

John Rainolde's 1599 assertion that '*beautiful boyes by kissing doe sting and powre secretly in a kinde of poison*' (Barbour 1995: 1006; Rainolds et al. 1974: 18).

Another aspect of this erotic carnival is that boys' plays veer close to a level of sexual explicitness rarely if ever seen in the adult theater. In *Blurt, Master Constable*, for example, the concubine Imperia brings a handsome Frenchman to the floor with her, inviting him by repeating 'down' and 'here'. The implication is that the two entwine in a horizontal position on the stage. Boys' plays sometimes point to sexual acts supposedly taking place on the balcony, or in the recessed area of the stage, as when Hercules in Marston's *Parasitaster* blesses the marriage bed of his son, on the balcony above: 'You genital, | You fruitful, well-mix'd heats, O, bless the sheets | Of yonder chamber' (v. i. 5–7).

The fact that private stages were much smaller than public stages likely increased the sense of erotic intimacy between the actors and audience, in terms of both bawdy puns and ground-breakingly explicit scenes. Peter Womack writes of Jonson's work that his eroticism brings together 'the sexual, the theatrical, and the illicit' (1986: 120). I would extend his observation to boy repertories: in these plays, illicit kisses and erotic references become the backbone of theatrical display.

Homoerotic Material

The erotic attraction of the boy actors themselves has been extensively studied in the last twenty years. Clearly, boy actors, whether cross-dressed in adult theaters, or acting in breeches in boy theaters, were used to 'mobilize desire', as Richmond Barbour puts it (1995: 1007). We know from contemporary comments that the boys were seen as both beautiful and, to some extent, available. Thomas Dekker's *Gull's Hornbook* notes that paying for a stool on the stage of a private theater will 'purchase the deere acquaintance of the boyes'; Middleton's *Father Hubbards Tale* advises that one should go to the Blackfriars to find 'a nest of boys able to ravish a man'.[13]

Homoerotic material in boys' plays often emphasizes an effeminate type of beauty, one that nears femininity. One example from the Queen's Revels repertory occurs in Marston's *Dutch Courtesan* when Cocledemoy encounters a young boy: 'my delicate boy... To what bawdy house doth your master belong?' The implication of beauty for sale is enhanced when Cocledemoy tells him to put his hat back on: 'kill thy itch and heal thy scabs' (signs of venereal disease) (II. i. 167, 169–70, 173–4). This type of homoerotic interest often focuses around pages likely enacted by the youngest members of the cast. A typical example is when Herod in *Parasitaster* encounters a little page and calls him a 'most sweet youth', remarking that 'He would yield tart juice and he were squeez'd' (I. ii. 25, 12–13).

[13] Dekker (1884–6: ii. 249); *The Works of Thomas Middleton*, viii. 77.

A crucial focal point for homoerotic innuendo is the position of a boy actor dressed as a girl, then disguised as a boy. Double cross-dressing allows for seductive dialogue between a man and a boy, though the boy character is 'really' a girl. Studies of the homoerotics of cross-dressed boys have pointed, in Bruce Smith's words, to a 'jokey but interested awareness of the boy's body beneath the woman's weeds' (1994: 137). The issue of homoerotic desire is no small matter for boy companies; I have argued that the focus of desire in the King's Revels repertory is almost entirely on the male body (Bly 2000; see DiGangi 1997). The King's Revels version of the erotic performativity I described in the last section of this essay is found in John Mason's *The Turke*, in which the lead clown character takes an early modern form of Viagra and then prances around the stage boasting of having raised a 'standing' spirit. These plays invoke desire for the male body in a sensually celebratory manner.

Current work on homoerotic material has large consequences for our understanding of seventeenth-century sexuality. Early queer theorists maintained that there was no category for 'homosexual', and that the very idea was inconceivable at the time (Bray 1982; Orgel 1996). My work on the King's Revels repertory is akin to Theodore Leinwand's study of *Michaelmas Term* (performed by the Paul's boys), which argues that the play stands in sharp opposition to claims that a sodomitical subject was inconceivable in early modern England. In *Michaelmas Term*, when Shortyard is asked to seduce Easy, he is told to 'Give him a sweet taste of sensuality... Drink drunk with him, creep into bed to him, | Kiss him and undo him, my sweet spirit' (I. i. 122, 127–8). As Leinwand notes, the play is 'interlaced with *doubles entendres* which, when activated, seem to replot the play sodomitically' (1994: 2). This depiction of homoerotic pleasure is not presented in the threatening light some queer theorists have discerned in early modern attitudes toward sodomy: the depiction of acceptable erotic pleasure is a cheerfully wide one. The clear inference is that the depiction and celebration of male homoerotic pleasure was commercially viable in this period, particularly to audiences of boy companies.

Music and Literacy

Boys' plays frequently pause for a song, in the manner of a contemporary musical. In 1600, for example, the Queen's Revels was advertised as presenting for Queen Elizabeth a 'showe with musycke and speciall songes' (M. Eccles 1958: 100). Between 1600 and 1613 the Queen's Revels used song in 72 percent of their plays (M. Shapiro 1977: 236). Dutton goes so far as to suggest that the Paul's boys went out of business in 1606 partly because they never established the reputation for music that was a selling point of their rivals (2002: 343). Plays also offered an opportunity for a sort of vaudeville effect, when the boys would break into dancing. *Jack Drums*

Entertainment, for example, is named after a rustic country dance, and seems to have contained many mini-entertainments.

Clearly, audiences looked to these plays for musical intervals, although it's important to note that adult companies also frequently included music. Jonson wrote more elaborate, polyphonic songs for the trained boy actors than he did for adult actors; his polyphonic songs point to the basis for theater licensing in the period: while adult companies were allowed to play before audiences so they could gain sufficient practice to play before the monarch, boy companies were drawn out of royal choirs (Chan 1980). As Roger Bowers points out, boy companies' primary job of work was to sing from the chancel choir stalls the three liturgical services stipulated by the Elizabethan Book of Common Prayer, although there are definite grounds for thinking that separate acting and singing groups may have formed (2000: 70, 82 n. 1).

In contrast to the 'day job' of the boy actors, the few boy company songs that have survived are generally racy vocal solos, such as 'Love for such a cheery lip', from *Blurt, Master Constable*, which was published with a setting for single voice by Edward Pearce, and 'The dark is my delight', sung by the courtesan Francischina in *The Dutch Courtesan* (Sabol 1958). Music seems to have emphasized the boy companies' innovative use of erotic expression on stage, rather than foregrounding their choral abilities. One has to sympathize with Henry's Clifton's outraged complaint, after his son Thomas was impressed into the Queen's Revels through a royal patent to gather singers for the Chapel Royal, that the stolen children were 'no way able or fit for singing, nor by any the said confederates endeavoured to be taught to sing, but... abusively employed, as aforesaid, only in plays and interludes' (Wickham et al. 2000: 265).

Satire

In 1609 Thomas Heywood described boy companies as taking liberties by making fun of great men's faults, 'supposing their juniority to be a priviledge for any rayling, be it never so violent' (Dutton 1991: 128). The Queen's Revels company, in particular, inclined toward ruthless portrayals of important noblemen. After *Eastward Ho*, Chapman, Jonson, and Marston almost had their ears and noses cut for writing, in Jonson's words, 'something against the Scots'.[14] Day's *Isle of Gulls* was another play that flirted with disaster when some of the men's parts were acted with Scottish accents. That play depicted a king falling in love with a man disguised as a woman; given James's well-known penchant for male favorites, its mockery was recklessly

[14] See Ben Jonson, George Chapman, and John Marston, *Eastward Ho!*, ed. C. G. Petter (London: BBC, 1973), app. 3.

perilous (Dutton 1991: 165–93). The lost play 'The Silver Mine' apparently depicted the King as drunk at least once a day (Munro 2005: 29).

A key point about this particular company is that, for an unknown reason, as of 1604 their plays were approved for performance by their own licenser, the playwright Samuel Daniel, rather than by Tilney, the Master of the Revels. Daniel appears to have been profoundly inept in this role; within a few weeks of the patent being issued, he was brought before the Privy Council to answer charges that his own *Tragedy of Philotas* offered a positive depiction of the Essex rebellion. As Richard Dutton has noted, there are many uncertainties to do with the licensing of early modern boys' plays, including the issue of Daniel's role (Dutton 1991; Clare 1999).

The question of who enjoyed—and paid to attend—these plays is fascinating, and still a matter for lively debate. Alfred Harbage (1952) made a distinction between privileged, elite audiences of private theaters versus working-class audiences of public theaters. His view has been disputed by Ann Jennalie Cook (1981), whose study of audience composition proved that aristocrats and gentry were attending public theaters (see also Armstrong 1959). Steven Mullaney's *Place of the Stage* (1995) makes a more sophisticated argument, suggesting that plays running at private theaters relied on the existing social order, whereas public theater performances threatened the ideology of the ruling class. His argument thus circles back to Harbage. More recently, Paul Yachnin has argued that playgoers such as John Donne enjoyed seeing their own alienation (and yet fascination with) the court played out (Dawson and Yachnin 2001: 41–5).[15] This idea invokes a love–hate relationship with aristocratic power, seized on and commercialized by private theaters.

We know that the boy company audiences included aristocrats, gentry, and law students. Homoerotic playfulness does not imply an all-male audience; as Richmond Barbour notes of the page in *Epicene*, boys can be an object of desire to men and women (Barbour 1995: 1016–17; see Orgel 1996). Jonson's Prologue to *Epicene* seems to signal a wide economic span in the Whitefriars audience, since he promises to please lords, knights, squires, waiting wenches, city wives, and, finally, the 'men, and daughters of *white-Friars*'; 'daughters of Whitefriars' is generally taken as a synonym for 'prostitutes' (Prologue, 22–4). The Prologue suggests that the composition of boy company audiences may be more closely tied to location than we generally assume when lumping all private theater audiences together. Certainly I would argue that we should be very careful about labeling boy audiences 'elite', as when Barbour recently wrote of 'elite Whitefriars playgoers' (1995: 1016).

One aspect that is often neglected in discussing audience is the fact that the boy companies also played at court. According to a 1604 letter from the French ambassador, Anna of Denmark enjoyed Queen's Revels performances, since the ambassador talks of comedians bringing the King publicly onto the stage, and his wife attending 'these representations in order to enjoy the laugh against her husband' (Munro 2005: 33).

[15] Yachnin notes that populux entertainment, as he describes it, also figures importantly at large amphitheaters but applies most readily to the Blackfriars and Paul's.

This anecdote brings enjoyment of comical satire to the very highest social level. The fact that the Queen's Revels continued to flout authority, even after threats against their authors and some Bridewell imprisonments, suggests that there was considerable cultural capital to be had in mocking the court. The further question of why, for example, the King's Revels did not engage in this kind of satire, even given its clear profitability, seems to turn again to the question of audience. In short, repertories suggest that satire of the court was financially successful in a Blackfriars milieu, and less so before the 'daughters of Whitefriars'; Jonson risked having his nose cut when writing for a Blackfriars audience, but engages in a very different kind of sexual, cultural satire when writing *Epicene* for a Whitefriars audience.

META-THEATRICALITY

Boys' plays persistently challenge the audience by referencing the artificiality of stage practice. This characteristic can be seen in the earliest plays of the period, which sometimes open with inductions featuring actors in partial undress, or discussing their parts or ages. While these moments invite the audience to enjoy the fabricated nature of dramatic presentation, others strain the audience's credulity. For example, almost all boy company plays include a 'disguised' character who, after the point he dons his disguise, is unrecognized by all, including his nearest and dearest. *Parasitaster* involves a father leaving his court, returning, and being unrecognized by his son. *The Dutch Courtesan*'s Cocklemedoy plagues the same innkeeper over and over again in various disguises, some as slight as a change in accent. Lovers in disguise are regularly ignored by their beloveds, even when it seems the disguise was little more than a cloak. One of the best explanations of this phenomenon I've read comes from a 1975 article by Ejner Jensen, who writes that the disguise convention is a tactic 'to be exploited, transformed and re-ordered into ever more arresting designs. At times it seems the very emblem of a disoriented and opaque moral world' (1975: 7).

Part of the pleasure of these plays lies in the exuberant acceptance of theatrical convention. Some scholars have reasoned from that artificiality to the proposition that the plays were acted as outright parodies, 'vehicles for child-actors consciously ranting in oversize parts' (Foakes 1962; see Caputi 1976). The question of how these plays were acted is one that is not readily solved. Maurice Charney begins with the assumption that boys' 'performances must surely have been quite different in tone, mood, quality and overtone from those of the adult companies' (1975: 19). Gair posits an 'anti-mimetic' mode, arguing, for example, that Paul's boys did not use false beards because he finds fake hair on a 14-year-old 'obviously comic' (1982: 143–4). However, Will Fisher has pointed out that several plays performed by Paul's boys did assign beards to various characters. Fisher also notes, more importantly, that the parodic assumption suggests that femininity can be produced by the boys without laughter, while adult masculinity cannot. He persuasively argues that the importance of beards in the period as a signifier of masculinity suggests that young boys were 'in drag' while playing men as well as women (2006: 89). The key question is whether dramatic illusion was maintained by boy actors in drag—for if it wasn't, as Ejner Jensen points out, 'the audience at these plays participated in an experience fundamentally different from that of any theater audience before or since' (1968: 101).

Given the preponderance of sexual material in these plays, the question of parody is particularly acute at those moments. Jackson Cope argues that the boys' limitations are explicitly turned to comedy during suggestive scenes in Marlowe's *Dido*: eroticism is 'mocked by the parody of boys playing it absurdly' (1974: 320). Similarly, Michael Shapiro argues that bawdry pointed to 'sexual immaturity of the actors' (1977: 106). Both of these assumptions grow from an idea of boyish innocence; if one thinks that the 'fundamental attraction of the boy actors for the Jacobean public was the whimsical charm of a masquerade', as did Harold Hillebrand, then sexual material must be conceived as jarring (1964: 271). From that viewpoint, courtship scenes—and kisses—become opportunities for snickers rather than titillation.

However, the corollary that playwrights would have had to write manuscripts explicitly to be acted in burlesque is a major point against the theory of non-mimetic acting. Marston's play *The Malcontent* moved between the Queen's Revels and the King's Men; Marston and Dekker's *Satiromastix* moved from Paul's to the King's Men (Knutson 1991: 44–5).[16] Paul Yachnin's study of the Paul's play *The Puritan* together with Shakespeare's *Twelfth Night* notes that the plays 'would have seemed more alike to their first audiences and readers than they seem to us', so that while we may now see the plays as extravagantly different, that was not the case in the period (2003: 762). I would argue that Yachnin's observation about these two plays extends to the repertories of adult versus child companies. The various tortured means by which scholars have explained how boys act are unnecessary if the difference was never really there. Acting these plays with total disregard for dramatic illusion means that the best parts of excellent plays would be thrown away—and moreover, that playwrights wrote them knowing their work would be played merely for laughs. It's an extremely unlikely proposition.

The lush desire of Franchescina in *The Dutch Courtesan* cannot be played for laughs without ruining the play; similarly, the measured solemnity of Bussy in *Bussy D'Ambois* requires an actor with a formidable memory and the ability to command the stage, whether expressing rage or grief. At least some boy actors were tremendously skillful, and could play their parts as men, women, and boys, as required by the text. Evidencing their skill, several boys moved to adult companies: Nathan Field, William Barksted, John Underwood, and William Ostler all went on to

[16] As Ann Blake's study of Marston (who was writing for a company in which he held financial shares) points out, the likelihood that an author would write plays meant to be performed as parodies is unlikely and arguments utilizing Marston's work are based on misrepresentations of the plays in question (Blake 1987). Another relevant point is that William Percy offered five of his plays to the master of the St Paul's boys. Three of the plays contain notes offering variations 'if for Paul's' versus 'for [adult] actors'. See Wickham et al. (2000: 317 n. 1).

long careers. Shen Lin suggests that playwrights could either highlight the youth of the players or rely on older actors for mature realism: the attractive principle at work here is acceptance of a playwright's practical assessment of a given company in a specific year (1991).

One characteristic of boy plays that points not to burlesque but to serious acting is the presence of passages in Italian, French, or Latin. *Antonio and Mellida*, for example, includes a love scene conducted entirely in Italian. It could be that this material is concealed in a foreign language owing to its erotic nature ('Dammi un bacio da quella bocca beata': 'Give me a kiss from your blessed mouth'), but snippets of foreign language appear everywhere (IV. i. 203). These moments have also been explained by reference to a learned audience. But, on another level, the moments of foreign language speak to the position of the boy actor, who is, supposedly at least, a schoolboy. It seems to me that boy plays constantly toy with the audience's awareness of the actor beneath the character, flirting with the boundaries of dramatic illusion—just as they do with erotic boundaries.

Thus, positing the boys as excellent actors doesn't mean that their plays didn't constantly challenge themselves—and the audience—to maintain suspension of disbelief. As Ann Blake argues, those moments which disrupt a character, indicating the boy actor underneath, 'force the audience to contemplate the reality behind the theatrical illusion and then, the next moment, to set that aside and accept the illusion with, as it were, a strengthened trust' (1987: 481). Leslie Thomson's analysis of Beaumont's *Knight of the Burning Pestle* similarly finds that the play heightens audience consciousness of dramatic convention at the most important moments, such as the play's conclusion (2006: 68–70). The question of dramatic illusion seems to me to sum up the manifest difficulties—and innovations—of a boys' play. The plays subvert and disbalance the normal relation between the audience and the actor. At their best, they seduce the watcher by promising intimacies: the backstage of the theater, the dear acquaintance of the boys, the inside jokes about dramatic practice and theatrical illusion.

Conclusion

Many of the points I've raised in this essay coalesce to give the impression of plays that present staccato pleasures: dirty jokes, homoerotic allusions, ridiculous disguises, pointed contemporary satire, a song, or a dance. But it would incorrect to think that these various attributes overwhelm the plays or the plots. Boy companies offered some of the most experimental and wildly original plays of the period; modern performances have proved that many of them are still hilarious in performance.

In the Induction to Day's *Isle of Gulls*, three gentlemen sitting on the stage bicker about what they'd like to see in the upcoming performance. One wants a play that will anatomize vice, and character a great man's life; the second demands 'baudry' and a 'good cuckolding'; the third requests a 'stately pend historie' (Induction, 14–15). It is possible to view the boy company repertories as growing from market pressure, as dramatists served up plays that offered bitter observation and illicit erotic playfulness to eager audiences. Obviously the plays were remarkably sensitive to the market. In many cases, playwrights wrote their first plays for a boy company; it may be that, having no reputation and no set voice, these writers were more responsive to audience demand. The more interesting question, perhaps, is why certain qualities became so popular.

The subject of boy companies and their plays is one of the richest areas for future scholarly endeavor. Scholars attempting large cultural studies of early modern England often fall into inaccuracies because of neglect of these plays; from these texts are coming much of the evidence that overturns arguments about early modern culture and theater, confidently posed by critics not familiar with these repertories. Questions of collaborative authorship, erotic desire, and theatrical audience are only a few of the areas still open to exploration. Study of boy plays offers a rich look at the fabric of early modern culture, specifically at the marketability of laughter, whether it's wielded against the Crown or in depiction of bedtime intimacies.

PART II

LONDON PLAYHOUSES

CHAPTER 9

INN-YARD PLAYHOUSES

DAVID KATHMAN

Of all the places in and around London where plays were regularly performed between 1576 and 1642, by far the least known and least studied are the four inns within the City limits that hosted plays between the mid-1570s and the mid-1590s.[1] These include the Bell Savage on Ludgate Hill, the Bull in Bishopsgate Street, the Cross Keys on Gracechurch Street, and the Bell on Gracechurch Street, just north of the Cross Keys. Until recently, virtually no information was available about any of these inns, and all four have generally been ignored or glossed over in histories of the Elizabethan stage. This is unfortunate because, as Herbert Berry has noted, they contradict so much of what we think we know about Elizabethan playhouses (Berry 2006: 121). They hosted plays for at least twenty years within the jurisdiction of the City of London authorities, three of them (the Bull, Bell, and Cross Keys) well within the City walls, all while continuing to operate as inns. This defies the common narrative which has the players decamping to the suburbs around 1576 to escape the hostility of disapproving London authorities.

In recent years, many new archival records relating to the four inns have emerged, allowing us to reconstruct their histories in considerable detail.[2] These discoveries include the identities of numerous people, previously unknown to theater historians,

[1] In this chapter, the word 'City' with a capital C refers to the area of London under the control of the Lord Mayor, the Aldermen, and the Common Council, roughly but not exactly corresponding to the area bound by the medieval city wall.

[2] These new records were found by the late Herbert Berry and myself, working independently but sharing leads and new discoveries with each other. Herb and I were planning to collaborate on a book about the London inn-playhouses, and his research will form an important part of my forthcoming book on inns, taverns, and similar playing places in sixteenth-century London.

who owned or leased the inns during the times they were hosting plays. Although these people did not have to put up as much capital as the entrepreneurs who built playhouses from scratch, such as Philip Henslowe or Francis Langley, at the very least they tolerated the regular use of their establishments by players, and had to deal with various authorities who regulated playing. In addition, we can infer quite a bit about the physical characteristics of these inns and the playing conditions there. The following pages will outline some of what we now know about these neglected but important Elizabethan playing places, and the second half of the chapter will consider the Bull as a more in-depth case study.

Early London Inn-Playing

The practice of playing in London inns did not become established until the middle of the sixteenth century, only a couple of decades before the first custom-built playhouses. There was certainly plenty of dramatic activity in the city during the medieval and early Tudor periods, admirably documented by Anne Lancashire (2002), but this was mostly either civic in nature, such as the Lord Mayor's Show and the Midsummer Watch, or religious, such as the Clerkenwell Play in the fourteenth and early fifteenth centuries. Only in the 1540s do we start to see good evidence of professional playing in private establishments in London. Initially these seem mostly to have been taverns, where playing was presumably indoors, but there is also evidence of outdoor playing in yards, similar to what we find later in inn-yards. For example, on 1 April 1543 the Court of Common Council made Ambrosius Chapman, citizen and draper, sign a bond saying that he would no longer stage any disguisings or plays 'to allure & gather any multytude of people in a c*er*tayn yard or voyd growne called the Carpent*ers* yard in the p*ar*ishe of saint Botolf in london', late in the tenure of one Gray, carpenter, deceased.[3] The following day, the Court of Aldermen made three other citizens (William Blytheman, George Tadlowe, and Thomas Hancock) promise not to allow plays in their 'dwelling houses' without a license from the Lord Mayor (Chambers 1931: 290). Blytheman's 'dwelling house' was specified as 'the Erle of Northumb*er*londes place', which was actually a large inn-like structure with a yard, though there is no evidence that it was being used as an inn around this time (Kingsford 1917: 56–9).[4]

[3] London Metropolitan Archives (LMA), Corporation of London MSS, Journal 15, COL/CC/01/01/015, fo. 23^{v}. This record is mentioned by Anne Lancashire (2002: 268 n. 82), and will be fully transcribed by her in the forthcoming Records of Early English Drama volume on Civic London.

[4] The 'dwelling houses' of Tadlowe and Hancock are not named, but my research has revealed that they must have been the White Horse and Bishop's Head taverns, across Lombard Street from each other in the parish of St Mary Woolnoth. I presented many details about all three establishments in an unpublished paper presented at the 2006 Shakespeare Association of America meeting in Philadelphia, all of which will be incorporated into my upcoming book.

In the 1550s and 1560s explicit references to inns sometimes start to appear in such City records, alongside references to taverns and other drinking houses. For example, on 2 March 1553 the Common Council declared that no man should sing a song called Three Men's Song 'in or at any Taverne Inne Alehouse wedings ffeasts or eny man*er* of such songe or songs excepte the same be songe in A co*m*en playe or enterlude'. On 29 November 1565 the Lord Mayor ordered the Alderman of Cheap ward 'that no manner of co*m*en playe or enterlude be from hencefourth permitted or suffered' in any 'taverns Innes victualinge houses or in enny oth*er* place or places' where admission was charged. A Lord Mayor's precept of 3 January 1569 forbids any interludes or plays 'in anny house Inne or Brewhouse' after five o'clock in the afternoon until the following Shrovetide (Chambers 1931: 294, 300–1, 303).

We can identify two London-area inns where plays were performed during this period, though both were outside the official jurisdiction of the City of London. On 5 September 1557 the Privy Council ordered the Lord Mayor to send his officers to the Boar's Head without Aldgate, north-east of the city, where 'a Lewde playe called a Sacke full of Newes shalbe plaied this daye' (Berry 1986: 16). The Boar's Head was an inn located on Whitechapel High Street about 250 yards outside Aldgate, just outside the 'bars' that marked the boundary of the City's jurisdiction. Much later, in 1599, the inn was converted into a full-time playhouse, and from various documents we can get a good idea of what it was like before the conversion. The yard where plays were performed in 1599, and presumably also in the 1550s, was a little more than 120 feet long north–south at its longest point, about 30 feet wide at the north and south ends, but with a wider squarish area roughly 55 by 55 feet in the middle. A two-storey gallery ran along the eastern edge of the yard, and would have allowed people to view a play in the wide middle part of the yard from anywhere along its 100-foot length.[5]

On 12 December 1557, three months after the arrest of the players at the Boar's Head, another crackdown took place at the Saracen's Head in Islington, about a mile and a half north-west of the City. According to the account in John Foxe's *Acts and Monuments* (independently confirmed in its outlines by Henry Machyn's diary), a Scottish religious dissenter named John Rough was preaching to a secret gathering of fellow Protestants at the Saracen's Head in Islington, under the pretense of attending a play scheduled to be performed there. An informer had tipped off the authorities, and the vice-chamberlain of the royal household arrived during the service to arrest Rough, who was indicted and eventually executed. Even though this particular play was apparently a pretext, the Saracen's Head must have been known as a place where plays were performed. We cannot reconstruct its physical layout as we can with the Boar's Head, but the inn was probably located near the conjunction of Goswell Street (the northern continuation of Aldersgate Street) and St John's Street. Thomas Jordan's 1641 comedy *The Walks of Islington and Hogsdon* is partly set in the Saracen's Head; the text of the play suggests that the inn was a popular place of entertainment

[5] Berry (1986: 139–55) includes plans and sketches by C. Walter Hodges depicting the Boar's Head yard both before and after the construction of the playhouse. The construction of 1598–9 involved building new galleries to wall off the squarish middle area from the rest of the yard, and expanding the gallery on the eastern side to increase its capacity.

for city gallants, with a public room large enough for musicians and dancers (Brownstein 1971*a*).

After two decades of repeated attempts to regulate playing in City venues (including inns), the authorities took a step that was to have significant effects. An Act of Common Council dated 6 December 1574 specified, at great length, that before any innkeeper or tavern keeper could have a play or interlude performed on his premises, he must have the playscript and playing place approved by the relevant authorities, post a bond with the Chamberlain of London, and pay a fee earmarked for the City hospitals (Chambers 1923: iv. 273–6). Although this Act has often been seen by theater historians as an attempt to suppress playing within the City, the Common Council went out of its way not to suppress such playing entirely, but merely to regulate it more strictly.[6] While the Act undoubtedly did have something to do with the rise of the suburban playhouses shortly afterward, the greater cost of land within the City must also have been a significant factor. The new regulations did not prevent the Bull, the Bell Savage, the Cross Keys, and the Bell from hosting plays regularly for the next twenty years; all four were well-established businesses that continued as inns throughout their lives as playhouses. The history of London inn-playing in the last quarter of the sixteenth century is essentially the history of those four inns, to which we now turn.

London Inn-Playing in the Late Sixteenth Century

The earliest reference to playing at any of the four inns comes in the Prologue to George Gascoigne's *Glasse of Governement* (1575), which refers to the Bell Savage as a place where a man may 'hear a worthy jest' or 'feed his eye with vain delight', since 'an interlude may make you laugh your fill'. The following year, William Lambarde's *Perambulation of Kent* also mentions playing at the Bell Savage. Lambarde describes a shrine where pilgrims formerly had to make three separate payments before they could be assured of any benefit: 'no more than such as go to Paris Garden, the Bel Savage, or some other such common place to behold bear-baiting, interludes, or fence play can account of any pleasant spectacle unless they first pay one penny at the gate, another at the entry of the scaffold, and the third for a quiet standing' (Berry 2000*a*: 297). This is essentially identical to the system we find later at playhouses such as the Globe.

[6] Ingram (1992: 119–49) discusses the 1574 Act in considerable detail, arguing that it was mainly intended as a way of funding the cash-poor City hospitals, and that the movement of many players to the suburbs was an unintended consequence.

Over the next few years, we find other references to playing at all four inns, indicating that they were becoming well known as playing venues (Berry 2000*a*: 297–9). At Shrovetide 1577 the Revels Office paid 10*d.* for 'the carriage of the parts of the well counterfeit from the Bell in Gracious Street to St. John's to be performed for the play of Cutwell'. (Here 'St. John's' is the Revels Office in the dissolved Priory of St John in Clerkenwell.) The first page of John Florio's Italian–English phrase book *First Fruites* (1578) contains the dialogue 'Where shall we go? To a play at the Bull, or some other place.' Stephen Gosson's *School of Abuse* (1579*b*) rails against most plays and players, but Gosson notes his approval of 'the two prose books played at the Bel Savage' and '*the Jew* and *Ptolemy* shown at the Bull', as well as two other plays usually performed at the Theatre. Even James Burbage and John Brayne, the owners of the Theatre, used the inns for City playing. On 1 January 1578 Burbage and Brayne's company was scheduled to play at the Bell in Gracechurch Street, and on 23 June 1579 Burbage was arrested 'as he came down Gracious Street towards the Cross Keys there to a play' (Mateer 2006: 343; Berry 2000*a*: 298).

During this same period, references in the minutes of the Court of Governors of Bridewell Hospital, which was mainly concerned with sexual crimes, give us some interesting snapshots of a few of the people who went to plays at all four inns (Salkeld 2004; Capp 2003). On 27 May 1576 a woman named Godlyffe White, wife of John White, testified before the court 'that wallys wife and she the said whites wyffe and one harry Androes a taillor went to a play at the bell in Gratious street', and that after the play 'they went all to one Sybernes in Newgate m*ar*kett And ther the said harry had the carnall vse of the said wallys wyffe in the kitchen'.[7] Other testimony shows that Godlyffe White was a prostitute, and her husband was her pimp, so Wallis's wife was presumably another prostitute, and Androes the tailor her customer. On 29 December 1577 Mark Osborne testified that 'a yere and more sens' (thus, sometime in 1576), a barber named Roger Barrett met with 'Reignoldes wiffe the Joyner' at the house of Osborne's master, John Smith, on a Sunday when Smith was out of town. After drinking together, 'they went to a play at the Bell savedge', after which they came back to Smith's house and 'the said Barbo*r* had thuse of the bodye of the said Reignoldes wiffe that night'.[8]

On 11 February 1579 a player named John Gibbes testified that Amy Mason alias Foster, 'beinge at the crosse keyes wher he plaied wth his fellowes then she desired one Thomas Rowe his fellowe to bringe her acquainted wth him', and that 'Thomas did soe at anothe metinge on sondaie after at ther plaie'. After being assured that Mason

[7] Bethlem Royal Hospital Archives and Museum, Beckenham, Kent, GL MS 33011/3 (microfilm of original), fo. 10^{v}. Salkeld gives White's first name as 'Godlysse', but it appears to be 'Godlyffe' in the manuscript.

[8] GL MS 33011/3, fos 267^{v}–268. Salkeld quotes part of this testimony, somewhat inaccurately, and goes on to discuss Barrett's claim 'that he had a boxe on the eare for a womans sake in a play'. Capp paraphrases the testimony, but he misinterprets the reference to the Bell Savage, asserting that the party went to a play at the Bell along with an otherwise unknown man named Savedge. The fact that the house was in the Little Old Bailey, very close to the Bell Savage, makes it fairly clear that the Bell Savage is meant.

was a single woman with money who 'bore him good will', Gibbes visited her house several times, spending the night at least once.[9] Two weeks later, on 28 February, a married woman named Elizabeth Everys described a sordid affair she had with one Benjamin Gunston, whom she met at a play at the Bull in Bishopsgate. After leaving her husband and descending into the seedier side of London, Everys was driven to become a prostitute after Gunston abandoned her.[10] The only other reference in the Bridewell minutes to a specific playing place is a description of an outing on Whitsunday (7 June) 1579, when a motley crew of individuals, who turned out to be the operators of a bawdy-house and their clients, went to a play at the Curtain.[11] The Bridewell minutes contain no references to the Theatre, or to the playhouses at Newington Butts, St Paul's, or the Blackfriars, all of which were active in the late 1570s. The impression one gets from these stories is that the inn-playhouses within the City were the preferred entertainment venues for habitués of London's sexual underworld, though of course this is a small sample size, and may not be representative.

Such evidence largely ceases in the early 1580s owing to a wave of anti-theatricalism by City authorities, but enough survives to show that the four inns continued to be popular venues when playing was allowed. On 28 November 1583 the London Court of Aldermen issued a license permitting the newly formed Queen's Men to play at the Bull and the Bell and nowhere else in the City until the following Shrovetide (3 March 1584), on holidays, Wednesdays, and Saturdays only, not on Sundays or during times of divine service (Berry 2000*a*: 300; Chambers 1931: 314–15). Among the dozen players named in the license is the famous clown Richard Tarlton, and the posthumous *Tarlton's Jests* includes several anecdotes of his playing activities at the four inns. We are told that 'at the Bull in Bishopsgate Street, where the Queen's Men oftentimes played, Tarlton coming on the stage, one from the gallery threw a pippin at him', and later that Tarlton, in 'a play of Henry the Fifth' being performed at the Bull, played a judge in addition to his regular clown's part when one of the actors was absent. Another anecdote in the book relates how Tarlton, after having played at the Bell, came into the adjacent Cross Keys and encountered Banks and his famous trained horse Morocco performing. After Tarlton's death in 1588, a ballad was entered on the Stationers' Register entitled 'Tarlton's recantation upon this theme given him by a gentleman at the Bel Savage without Ludgate, "now or else never", being the last theme he sang' (Berry 2000*a*: 301–2).

The license to the Queen's Men covered only the period from late November to early March, illustrating the fact that inn-playing in London was largely, though not exclusively, a winter phenomenon. The restrictions we saw earlier from the 1550s and

[9] GL MS 33011/3, fo. 367 (Gibbs's quoted testimony), fo. 364^{r-v} (earlier testimony from Gibbs and from Mason's servant on 5 February).

[10] GL MS 33011/3, fo. 373^{r-v}. The manuscript actually says that Everys met Gunston during a play at the 'bell at Bysshopsgate', so it is possible that the meeting was at the Bell. However, it seems much more likely that the scribe mistakenly wrote 'bell' for 'bull' than that he mistakenly wrote 'Bishopsgate' for 'Gracious Street'.

[11] GL MS 33011/3, fos 397^{v}–399. This case is described in more detail by Capp (2003: 162).

1560s tended to cover a similar time-frame, and specific instances of inn-playing tend to occur in the winter, such as the raid on the Saracen's Head in December 1557. On 8 October 1594 Lord Hunsdon, patron of the Lord Chamberlain's Men, wrote to the Lord Mayor seeking permission for his company of players 'to play this winter time within the City at the Cross Keys in Gracious Street', as they had been accustomed to do (Berry 2000*a*: 304). Some scholars, such as Wickham (1959–81: ii/1. 188) and Gurr (2005: 54), have assumed that this winter bias must be because playing at inns took place indoors. While there is evidence for some nighttime winter playing within the City (Menzer 2006*b*: 176–7), all the evidence specifically relating to the four City inn-playhouses points to outdoor playing, even in the middle of winter. It appears that the main reason players preferred to play in inns in winter was not because they provided shelter from the cold, but because they were more convenient for the London audience than the suburban playhouses during the months when darkness fell early, curfews were in effect, and weather conditions were treacherous. Among the extensive evidence for such a restriction, the most explicit is the Corporation of London's 1584 ruling 'that no playeing be in the dark, nor continue any such time but as any of the auditorie may returne to their dwellings in London before sonne set, or at least before it be dark' (Chambers 1923: iv. 302).[12]

Numerous references from the first half of the 1590s show that the four inns were still popular playing venues then. In 1592 the introduction to the translation by 'H.O.' of Vasco Figueiro's *The Spaniards Monarchie* includes an allusion to the Bull as a place where one could see over-the-top debauchery. In May 1594 Lady Anne Bacon, mother of Francis and Anthony, wrote to Anthony Bacon at his new house in Bishopsgate Street that a clergyman, Mr Henshew, had warned her that 'the Bull inn there, with continual interludes, had even infected the inhabitants with corrupt and lewd dispositions'. She worried to Anthony that 'to have so near a place haunted with such pernicious and obscene plays and [a] theatre able to poison the very Godly, and do what you can, your servants shall be enticed and spoiled' (Berry 2000*a*: 303–4; 1988). A few months later, as we just saw above, Lord Hunsdon wrote to the Lord Mayor asking permission for his players to play that winter at the Cross Keys, as they 'have been accustomed for the better exercise of their quality'. Hunsdon's claim is supported by the fact that five years earlier, on 6 November 1589, Strange's Men, many of whose members went on to form the nucleus of the Chamberlain's Men, had defied a different Lord Mayor's order to play at the Cross Keys (Berry 2000*a*: 302–4).

Within a few years, however, playing at the four inns within the City had permanently ceased. No contemporary record explicitly documents the suppression, though pressure had been building for some time from such theatrical foes as Sir John Spencer, Lord Mayor in 1594–5 (Whitney 2001). Richard Flecknoe later wrote in 'A Short Discourse of the English Stage' (1664) that actors set up theaters, 'first in the City (as in the inn-yards of the Cross Keys and Bull in Grace and Bishopsgate Street at this day is to be seen), till that fanatic spirit which then began with the stage and after ended with the throne banished them thence into the suburbs' (Berry 2000*a*: 305).

[12] Much of this evidence is discussed by Manley (forthcoming). See also Menzer (2006*b*, esp. 172–5).

Some evidence seems to suggest that playing in the four inns had ceased by 1596, when two foreign visitors to London noted the existence of four playhouses—presumably the Theatre, Curtain, Rose, and Swan—but ignored the inns. In November of that same year, a petition against a proposed Blackfriars playhouse says that 'now all players being banished by the Lord Mayor from playing within the City... they now think to plant themselves in liberties' (Berry 2000*a*: 440–1, 508). However, any suppression may have been temporary, and Menzer (2006*b*) argues quite plausibly that playing continued within the City of London at least until 1600. Regardless of the exact date, by the end of Elizabeth's reign the Bull, Bell, Cross Keys, and Bell Savage had ceased being regular playhouses, though occasional playing in suburban inns continued into the seventeenth century. Two inns outside the City limits were converted into full-time playhouses—the Boar's Head in 1598–9 and the Red Bull by 1607—but they ceased being inns when they became playhouses (Berry 2000*a*: 452–92, 564–94).

The Bull: Physical Characteristics

The evidence we have seen demonstrates that these four inns within the City limits were popular playing places in the last quarter of the sixteenth century, but some key questions remain. For example, what were these inns like physically, and what was it like to see a play there? To illustrate the answers to these questions, we can consider the Bull as a detailed case study. The Bull is the only one of the four London inn-playhouses of the late sixteenth century that survived the fire of 1666, so post-fire maps depict the original building rather than a reconstruction, and can thus be treated with a bit less skepticism. The earliest such map to provide significant detail was Ogilby and Morgan's *Large and Accurate Map of the City of London*, published in 1676.[13] This map depicts individual buildings as well as parish and ward boundaries, allowing us to place the Bull and determine its dimensions with a fair amount of accuracy.

The Bull was on the west side of Bishopsgate Street, a major north–south thoroughfare in the north-east part of the City. It was in the south-west corner of the parish of St Ethelburga the Virgin within Bishopsgate, with the parish boundary extending along the south and west walls of the inn. Immediately north of the Bull was another inn, the Green Dragon, and immediately north of that was yet another inn, the Four Swans. As depicted by Ogilby and Morgan, the Bull was quite a bit bigger than either of these neighboring inns. It extended about 250 feet west from its

[13] This map is reproduced at original size in Hyde et al. (1992). All my references to Ogilby and Morgan are to this edition, and all measurements are based on the scale of 100 feet per inch, or 4 feet per millimeter.

frontage on Bishopsgate Street, and the western part of the inn (starting about 140 feet west of the street) extended north behind the Green Dragon; thus, the Bull had a sort of L shape, surrounding the Green Dragon on two sides. That western part was about 140 feet wide, and its north edge abutted on the southern edge of the westernmost part of the Four Swans; the part closer to Bishopsgate Street abutted to the north on the Green Dragon, and was between 50 and 95 feet wide at various points.[14]

Ogilby and Morgan depict three separate yards in the Bull. To get to the first yard from Bishopsgate Street, one went through a long, 85-foot covered passageway that was presumably big enough for coaches to pass through. This yard was about 60 feet long east to west, about 25 feet wide (north–south) at its widest point, and about 18 feet wide in its narrower western part. From there, one went west through a 20-foot covered passage to get to the second yard, which was only 20 feet wide but about 70 feet long. From this second yard, two more covered passageways extended north. The first passageway led to the inn's third yard, which Ogilby and Morgan depict as irregularly shaped, about 45 feet by 35 feet at its widest and longest points. The other passageway led to a long L-shaped yard or passageway, about 20 feet wide at its widest point, which eventually opened onto Broad Street to the west, in the parish of St Peter-le-Poer. This yard or passageway does not appear to have been part of the Bull, though it did allow access to the Bull from Broad Street.

The presence of three yards in the Bull would presumably have made the logistics of hosting plays there easier; some of the yards could still be used for inn business such as the loading and unloading of coaches, while plays were performed in another yard. The Bull's northernmost yard would seem to be ideal for such purposes, since the other two yards were part of the passageway from Bishopsgate Street to Broad Street, and thus would have seen much more traffic.[15] The dimensions of this northern yard, roughly 45 feet by 35 feet, would have made it comparable in size to the original yard of the Rose playhouse, which was about 45 feet across before the playhouse's 1592 expansion (Berry 2000*a*: 422). In having multiple yards, the Bull was similar to the Bell Savage, which is depicted by Ogilby and Morgan as having two separate yards and multiple passages big enough for a coach, but unlike the Bell and the Cross Keys, each of which appears to have had a single yard with one main entrance.[16]

Another way that the Bull was similar to the Bell Savage, but unlike the Bell and the Cross Keys, is in its use for prizes played under the auspices of the Masters of Defence, the official organization for teachers of fencing in and around London. Such prizes were public demonstrations in which fencing students qualified for

[14] These measurements are necessarily approximate; it is not always clear from Ogilby and Morgan's map where one property ends and another begins, and the property lines may not have been the same in 1676 as they were a century earlier.

[15] M. Wood (2003: 125) includes a map of Bishopsgate Street, based on Ogilby and Morgan, and suggests that plays were performed in this north yard of the Bull.

[16] Berry (2006) discusses the Bell Savage and its yards. In my upcoming book I will discuss what we can glean about the physical structure of the Bell and the Cross Keys.

various levels of proficiency; they attracted audiences similar to those who went to plays, and were advertised with bills posted around the city, just as plays were. At least thirty-nine such prizes took place at playhouses between 1573 and 1590, and twenty-one of these were at the Bull, making it by far the most popular venue for fencing prizes during this time. Another five prizes were at the Bell Savage, seven were at the Curtain, and six were at the Theatre (Berry 1991: 32–3). From the fact that these four venues were used interchangeably for fencing prizes, presumably the playing–fencing areas were similar.

In the middle of this period, on 1 July 1582, the Earl of Warwick wrote to the Lord Mayor and Aldermen asking them to permit his servant John David 'to playe his prouest prices in his science and profession of defence at the Bull in Bishopsgatestrete or some other conuenient place... within the liberties of London'. Three weeks later, the Lord Mayor replied that he had prohibited David from playing his prize at an inn, 'wch was somewhat to close for infection', and had 'appointed him to playe in an open place of the leaden hall more fre from danger and more for his Comoditie'. Two weeks later, an increase of plague forced the authorities to restrict all public gatherings within the City, but the Lord Mayor gave permission for David to play his prize 'if he may obteine lawefully to playe at the Theater or other open place out of the Citie' (Berry 1991: 2; Chambers and Greg 1907: 55–8). Here the Bull is contrasted with 'open places' such as the Leadenhall market and the Theatre. It might be possible to argue from this that the Bull's playing space was enclosed, even indoors, but the Lord Mayor's wording—that the Bull was 'somewhat to close for infection'—suggests that it was outdoors but smaller than those of the other places, requiring people to crowd closer together. Support for this interpretation comes from the fact that, as depicted by Ogilby and Morgan, each of the three open markets at Leadenhall was larger than all three of the Bull's yards put together, and would have been a much more open space than the Bull could offer. The exact size of the Theatre's yard is uncertain, but its main attraction in this context was that it was outside the City in a much less congested area than the Bull.

This evidence for outdoor playing at the Bull and the Bell Savage supplements some of the evidence we saw earlier. Recall the passage from Lambarde's *A Perambulation of Kent* that mentions those who 'go to Paris Garden, the Bel Savage, or some other such common place to behold bear-baiting, interludes, or fence play', where they must 'first pay one penny at the gate, another at the entry of the scaffold, and the third for a quiet standing' (Berry 2000*a*: 297). Bear-baiting was certainly an outdoor activity, and the presence of scaffolding also implies an outdoor venue. We also saw the story of Tarlton going on stage at the Bull, where 'one from the gallery threw a pippin at him' (Berry 2000*a*: 301); galleries were an outdoor feature of inns, from which people could see the yard.

An anecdote from Robert Greene's pamphlet *The Third and Last Part of Conny-Catching* (1592) confirms the existence of outdoor playing at the Bull, even in winter, and provides some further evidence about playing conditions there (Greene 1923: 37–9). Greene describes how a young cutpurse 'In the Christmas holydaies last came to see a play at the Bull within Bishops gate, there to take his benefit as time and place would permit him'. The cutpurse quickly nipped a purse and 'stepped into the stable to take out the mony', but was disappointed to find nothing but white counters, a thimble, and a broken threepence. The young man then 'spied a lustie youth entring at the doore' whom he recognized as 'one of the finest Nippers about the towne', whereupon he followed the lusty youth and his girlfriend as they moved to ply their trade 'where both they might best beholde the play'. When the lusty youth stole a purse and tried to pass it surreptitiously to his female accomplice, 'she being somewhat mindfull of the play, because a merriment was then on the stage, gaue no regard'. The young cutpurse filched the stolen purse and passed the purse with the worthless white counters to the girlfriend before quietly slipping away.

Though the story about the cutpurses is most likely fictional, the background details about the Bull are presumably accurate. Many of Greene's plays were performed by the Queen's Men, so he was undoubtedly familiar with one of their main London venues, and would expect many of his readers to be familiar with it as well. The events in the anecdote apparently take place in an enclosed outdoor space with a single entrance; the young cutpurse steps into a stable immediately after filching a purse, then looks up to see the lusty youth 'entring at the doore'. There is also a stage, and the audience is able to walk around freely to get a better view. All this is consistent with plays being performed on a stage set up in the Bull's third yard, with some of the audience in galleries surrounding the yard, and the rest standing in the yard itself.

In contrast to the Bull and the Bell Savage, evidence for outdoor playing at the Bell and the Cross Keys is scant; their physical configurations, plus the fact that they never hosted fencing prizes or similar activities, suggest that playing at those inns may have been indoors in a hall. This is especially true of the Bell; it had a single long, narrow yard unconducive to a stage or large crowds, and it definitely had a hall on the upper floor near Gracechurch Street.[17] Some evidence suggests possible outdoor playing at the Cross Keys, but it is relatively weak. The building had a single yard large enough for a stage, but a play there would have required shutting down the inn's regular activities, unlike at the Bull. As we saw above, Richard Flecknoe did write in 1664 that the players set up theaters in the City 'in the inn-yards of the Cross Keys and Bull in Grace and Bishopsgate Street', but he was writing nearly a century after the fact. The anecdote we saw about Tarlton confronting Banks and his trained horse Morocco at the Cross Keys must have occurred outdoors, presumably in the inn-yard, but this was not necessarily the same place where plays were performed.[18]

[17] I discuss some of the evidence for this hall in Kathman (forthcoming).

[18] The pamphlet *Maroccus Extaticus* (1595) describes another performance by Banks and Morocco in the yard of the Bell Savage, and an accompanying woodcut depicts spectators standing on a scaffold about 3 feet above the ground, leaning on a railing (Berry 2006: 133).

The Bull: Owners and Operators

While the physical layout and size of London's inn-playhouses are important for reconstructing the playing conditions there, information about the people who owned and operated them can help illuminate the social context in which these inns existed. Much has been written about the entrepreneurs who built the earliest custom-built playhouses such as the Theatre and the Rose, but as recently as 2000, Herbert Berry was able to write of the inns that 'virtually nothing is known for certain about either the ownership of these places or what was done to make them playhouses' (Berry 2000*a*: 295). The situation has now improved considerably, so that it is possible to trace the owners and leaseholders of all four inns during their time as playhouses. As a concrete illustration, we once again turn to the Bull.

For many years, the Bull in Bishopsgate Street was owned by St Helen's Priory, located across the street in what is now the church of St Helen, Bishopsgate, and the surrounding buildings. In 1539 the priory's property, including the Bull, was seized by Henry VIII as part of the dissolution of the monasteries.[19] From then until the Restoration, the Bull was technically owned by the Crown, but was controlled by tenants who paid a nominal rent and held the property in free and common burgage, a type of feudal tenure that usually involved a long, narrow building fronting on a street. We can consider such tenants owners for all intents and purposes, since they collected rent and could freely sell and bequeath the property.

By the early 1570s, the owner of the Bull (in the above sense) was William Mease, citizen and grocer of London.[20] Mease had been freed as a grocer on 25 October 1547 after serving an apprenticeship with Edward Oxborough, and had married Julian Gorley at St Peter Cornhill on 6 October 1549.[21] On 28 August 1573 William Mease made his will.[22] One-third of his estate went to 'Iulian my welbeloued wieff', and another third was to be equally divided between 'my twoe children George Mese and Isabell Mese vnadvanced by me in my lieff tyme'. Mease's other two children, Elizabeth Wilson and Susan Billingsley, had already received their marriage portions, and thus had already been 'advanced and promoted'. The third part of William Mease's estate was reserved for other bequests, mostly to various relatives. The

[19] The priory's last tenant in the Bull was Richard Berde, citizen and girdler, who on 10 June 1533 took over an earlier twenty-one-year lease granted in 1526 to Thomas Larke, citizen and merchant tailor, at a yearly rent of £9 14*s*. On 1 January 1535 Berde became the receiver and collector for all the priory's properties, and as late as 1556 he was still receiving an annuity of 40*s*. as a former officer of the priory (Cox 1876: 13, 15, 27).

[20] Somewhat confusingly, Mease owned another property in Bishopsgate Street called the Bell, which he bought from Thomas Malyn in 1565 and then leased back to Malyn (LMA, Hustings Roll 255, CLA/023/DW/01/254, nos 141, 142). However, this Bell was to the south in St Peter Cornhill parish, and a later lawsuit (The National Archives (TNA), REQ 2/40/3) shows that Malyn still occupied it in 1581.

[21] Guildhall Library, City of London, MS 11571/5, fo. 299^{v}; Gower (1877: 222).

[22] TNA, PROB 11/55/218. Actually, two different wills for William Mease survive, both with the same date, though only the second one was probated. In the first will (TNA, PROB 11/55/217^{v}), Mease bequeathed most of his property to his son George, except a messuage in Bishopsgate Street (not the Bull) which he left to his daughter Isabel.

executors were his wife, Julian, and son George, and the overseers were 'my faithfull and trustie ffrends Mathew harison and Will*iam* Dale'. Mease was buried in St Peter Cornhill on 24 September 1573, and the will was proved on 30 September (Gower 1877: 122).

William Mease's will does not mention the Bull or any other properties by name, but other documents provide some details about his estate. An inquisition post mortem taken on 16 June 1574 reveals that Mease had owned two messuages in the parish of St Ethelburga within Bishopsgate worth £14 per annum in rent (one of which would have been the Bull), two in St Botolph, Bishopsgate, worth £3 per annum, and four parts of five messuages in St Peter Cornhill worth £6 per annum (Madge 1901: 186–7). A quitclaim dated 19 December 1581 provides more details. By this time Isabel was apparently out of the picture, perhaps because she had sold her share of the estate, and Julian had remarried, to Henry Bellingham, gentleman of Chichester, Sussex. In the quitclaim, Julian and Henry confirm that they have released to George Mease, son and heir of William Mease, deceased citizen and grocer of London, all their interest in various properties. These include various messuages in St Botolph, Bishopsgate, with nine tenants named; one messuage called the Bull located in St Ethelburga within Bishopsgate, now in the tenure of Mathew Harrison, citizen and cordwainer; and various messuages in St Peter Cornhill, in the tenures of William Dale, leatherseller, and five other tenants.[23] Here we find that William Mease's 'faithfull and trustie ffrends' Mathew Harrison and William Dale, whom he made overseers of his will, were also his tenants, and that Harrison was the leaseholder of the Bull in 1581.

Other evidence shows that Mathew Harrison had occupied the Bull for at least a dozen years before 1581, and thus that he was in charge when it began hosting plays and fencing prizes in the mid-1570s. This evidence is contained in the St Ethelburga churchwardens' accounts,[24] which list the amounts collected quarterly from each householder of the parish to pay the wages of the parish clerk. The collectors wrote the names in the same order each year, starting on the west side of Bishopsgate Street at the parish's southern boundary, where the Bull was located; thus, the first name on the list is always the person who occupied the Bull.[25] Mathew Harrison occupies this initial position from the earliest surviving list in 1569–70 to the winter of 1583–4, when the Bull served as one of the winter homes of the Queen's Men. Harrison also appears first for St Ethelburga in the Crown's lay subsidy list of 1577, when he was assessed on £50 of goods, the second most in the parish. The fifth and sixth names on that list are 'Edward Walker of the grene dragon' and 'Mathew Buck of the thre Swans', the hosts of the two inns just to the north of the Bull, who were assessed on £5 and £15 of goods respectively.[26]

[23] LMA, Hustings Roll 265, CLA/023/DW/01/264, no. 65.

[24] Guildhall Library, MS 4241/1.

[25] The correlation is not perfect; in some years, the residents of Peahen Alley, the Wrestlers, Clark's Alley, and Pigott's rents were broken out separately after the main listing, and eventually the clerk began a separate list of 'Arrearages' for people who had not paid.

[26] TNA, E179/145/252w/153–4, as transcribed by Alan Nelson and published on his web site, <http://socrates.berkeley.edu/~ahnelson/SUBSIDY/subs.html>.

Mathew Harrison had apparently been unmarried when he started leasing the Bull, but on 29 November 1572 he married Johanna Sowle, widow, in St Sepulchre parish outside Newgate (Foster 1887: 635). She was the widow of John Sowle, citizen and farrier, whose will[27] had only been proved a few months before, on 7 June 1572. After a dozen years of marriage, Mathew Harrison died in 1584, whereupon Johanna took over the management of the Bull.[28] Starting in 1584–5 the parish subsidy list shows 'Mrs Harrison' in the initial spot, and she continued to occupy the Bull for the next five years as the inn continued to host plays and fencing prizes, making her one of a small handful of women to own or lease a playhouse in pre-Restoration London. The most prominent of the others was Susan Baskervile, who, interestingly enough, owned significant interests in two playhouses (the Boar's Head and the Red Bull) that had once been inns (Sisson 1954; Griffith 2004).

Johanna Harrison made her detailed will[29] on 13 May 1588, describing herself as 'Joane Harrison of the parishe of St Ethilboroughe in Bishopsgatestrete', widow, but asking to be buried in St Sepulchre near her late husband John Sowle. She included bequests both to the Cordwainers' Company, of which she was free as the widow of Mathew Harrison, and to the master and wardens of the Farriers, John Sowle's company. There are many minor bequests to relatives (including a son, John Love, presumably from an earlier marriage) and to former servants. Most of the estate, however, was equally divided between William Webb the elder, citizen and farrier, and Thomas Wrightson, citizen and scrivener, who were also named executors. William Webb was John Sowle's former servant, named in Sowle's will sixteen years earlier, but he had now risen to be 'farri*or* to the queenes maiestie'. Webb and Wrightson proved the will on 21 October 1589, presumably not long after Johanna Harrison died. Exactly when she was buried remains unknown, because the burial registers for St Sepulchre do not survive before 1662.

This will makes no mention of the Bull, or indeed of any other real estate, but presumably the lease went to Webb and Wrightson along with the rest of the estate not specifically listed. They apparently had no interest in leasing an inn, for within a few months the lease had passed to Thomas Parris, citizen and innholder. In the 1589–90 St Ethelburga parish subsidy list, 'Mr Parryshe for 3/4 of a yere' replaced 'Mrs Harrison' at the head of the list.[30] Since the parish fiscal year began and ended at Michaelmas (29 September), the fact that Parris paid a subsidy only for three-quarters of a year means that he had moved to the parish around Christmas 1589, or roughly two months after Johanna Harrison's will was proved. Thereafter Parris headed the parish subsidy list every year, serving as a churchwarden in 1594–5, until the lists stop in 1615. He made his will as 'Thomas Parris Cittizen and Inholder of

[27] TNA, PROB 11/54/140.

[28] The parish subsidy list for 1583–4 shows Mathew Harrison paying for a whole year, but elsewhere the accounts for the same year show a receipt of 6*s*. 8*d*. for 'the buriall of Mathewe Harrison in the churche', so perhaps he died near the end of the fiscal year, around Michaelmas 1584.

[29] TNA, PROB 11/74/199.

[30] Guildhall Library, MS 4241/1, p. 109.

London' on 19 October 1615, and it was proved on 2 May 1617.[31] No mention is made of the Bull, but there is a bequest to the poor of St Ethelburga, suggesting that Parris was still living there.

George Mease had continued to own the Bull and collect the rent from the Harrisons, and then Thomas Parris, throughout its life as a playhouse. At some point, probably around 1600, he sold it to Edward Walker, owner of the adjacent Green Dragon, who continued to lease it to Parris. Walker made his will on 20 April 1602, describing himself as Edward Walker of the parish of Ethelburga within Bishopsgate, citizen and saddler.[32] Among many other bequests, Walker bequeathed to his son Thomas 'all that Messuage Tennement or Inne comonlie called the Bull with all yardes stables backsides edificies and buildings therevnto belonginge which I latelie purchased of Georg Mease nowe in the teanure or occupation of Thom*as* Parris Inholder scituate and being in the parrishe of St. Ethelburge in Byshopsgatestreate in london'. To his other son, George, Walker bequeathed 'all that my Messuage or tenem*en*t or Inne wherein I now dwell comonlie called the name of the Grene Dragon scituate in the Parrishe of Sainte Ethelburge aforesaid'.

When Edward Walker mentioned the Bull in his will, playing there had already ceased, as we saw earlier. Memories of the Bull's past as a playhouse eventually faded; in the seventeenth century it was best known as the London stopping place of Thomas Hobson, the famous Cambridge carrier, at whose death in 1631 Milton wrote two humorous elegies. It survived the fire of 1666, as noted earlier, and continued in use as an inn for another two centuries after that. No photographs of the Bull from before its demolition in 1866 are known, but there are some photographs of the adjacent Green Dragon, Edward Walker's other inn, taken before it, too, was demolished in the late nineteenth century.[33] No doubt there had been many changes in the building over the course of three centuries, but these photographs provide a tangible link to a time, almost forgotten now, when crowds had thronged to London inns to see the antics of Tarlton and the plays of Shakespeare.

[31] TNA, PROB 11/129/369. [32] TNA, PROB 11/99/269.

[33] One of these photographs is reproduced in M. Wood (2003: 128).

CHAPTER 10

THE THEATRE IN SHOREDITCH, 1576–1599

GABRIEL EGAN

The Evidence

For thirty-seven years the wood and plaster structure of the first permanent playhouse built in England since the Romans left in the fifth century CE stood for all to see, to celebrate, or to argue over. Then, as suddenly and surprisingly as it came, the building disappeared. This is a perpetual hazard of theatre history: a picture is identified by a scholar as showing a subject of interest, say a venue, a person, or a play being performed, and is pored over by other scholars hoping to wring every drop of information from it, and then it is snatched away by a fresh identification of its subject as something or someone less interesting than was previously thought. Thus is it with the engraving variously known as *The View of the Cittye of London from the North towards the Sowth* (the title written on it) or the Utrecht engraving (from the university library in which it was found in the 1950s) or the Abram Booth picture (from the name of the man who owned it).

In 1964 Sidney Fisher identified the playhouse in the engraving as the Theatre in Shoreditch, thereby overturning the identification of the playhouse as the Curtain that was made by the modern finder of the picture ten years earlier, Leslie Hotson (S. Fisher 1964: 2–6; Hotson 1954). Fisher's identification of the Theatre stood for thirty-seven years until itself overturned by Herbert Berry's proof that Leslie Hotson was right—it really is the Curtain (Berry 2000*a*). By the sort of coincidence that theatre historians learn to treat as nothing more than a rhetorical opportunity in the shaping of their narratives, the physical playhouse frame itself also stood for thirty-seven years, being erected in the summer of 1576 and named the Theatre, then dismantled and reassembled on a new site in 1598–9 and renamed the Globe, and finally consumed by fire during a performance in the summer of 1613.

As things currently stand, then, there is no extant picture of the Theatre and all that we know must be derived from writings. In this respect we are lucky, for none of the playhouses discussed in this Handbook left as copious a documentary record as the Theatre because it was the subject of a series of legal battles from the 1570s to the early 1600s, for which were prepared dozens of witness statements that recall its construction, ownership, financing, daily operations, and occupancy. First discovered in the mid-nineteenth century, the documents from the lawsuits were systematically transcribed and interpreted in the early twentieth century (Stopes 1913; Wallace 1913) but they will here be cited, where possible, from the most recent documentary collection, which has the merit of correcting errors in the earlier books and of modernizing the spelling (Wickham et al. 2000).

These records can be supplemented by biographical researches (including such things as records of birth, apprenticeship, marriage, and death) of the central figures involved in the Theatre project, and the best finding aid to locate those researches is David Kathman's *Biographical Index to the Elizabethan Theater.*[1] With Kathman's help, I can report that for James Burbage (who, together with his brother-in-law John Brayne, initiated the project) the essential references are Stopes (1913), Chambers (1923), Nungezer (1929), Ingram (1988), M. Eccles (1991*a*), Honigmann and Brock (1993), Edmond (1996), and Ingram (1992). For John Brayne the essential references are Loengard (1983), Ingram (1992), Honigmann and Brock (1993), and Edmond (1996). For Peter Street (who took down the Theatre and re-erected it as the Globe) the essential references are Ingram (1992) and Edmond (1993). These are the sources on which the present narrative is based, supplemented by pre-publication access to the results of archaeological researches on the site of the Theatre kindly supplied by Julian M. C. Bowsher, Senior Archaeologist at the Museum of London Archaeology Service.

ORIGINS

One of the two partners in the Theatre, the grocer John Brayne, built a kind of prototype playhouse in 1576 called the Red Lion. Only one fact was known about the Red Lion project until the 1980s: that the Carpenters' Company books record Brayne's dissatisfaction with 'such scaffolds' made by a William Sylvester 'at the house called the Red Lyon' and that the company had reached a settlement in the

[1] <http://shakespeareauthorship.com/bd>.

case. Once the company inspectors had perused the work and ordered such improvements as they saw fit, and Sylvester had completed them, thereby enabling 'the play which is called *The Story of Samson*' to be given a performance there, Brayne would pay Sylvester for the work (Wickham et al. 2000: 291). E. K. Chambers guessed that this Red Lion was an inn, and recorded it alongside the records for the other inns at which playing took place: the Bull, the Bell, the Bel Savage, and the Cross Keys (Chambers 1923: ii. 379–80). Chambers noticed that Brayne was later involved in the Theatre with his wife's sister's husband, James Burbage, but—presumably allowing the paucity of evidence about the Red Lion to condition his estimation of the relative values of the projects—he called the Theatre a 'far more important enterprise'.

As it turns out, the Theatre was the more important building, but this could not properly be established until a legal historian, Janet S. Loengard, came across previously unnoticed records of the Court of King's Bench showing that the dispute went further than the Carpenters' Company court and that another carpenter, John Reynolds, was also involved in the project (Loengard 1983). Most extraordinarily of all, the documents uncovered by Loengard revealed that the Red Lion was not an inn but a farm, that the playhouse was built in its courtyard, that it comprised a stage 5 feet off the ground and 40 feet by 30 feet in span and a 'certain space or void part of the same stage left unboarded' (for a trap?), with an attached turret rising to 30 feet (from the ground, presumably), and galleries for spectators (Wickham et al. 2000: 292). On this evidence, and in the absence of any indication that the structures were only temporary, Loengard claimed that the Red Lion deserves to supplant the Theatre as the first purpose-built playhouse of the modern era.

Loengard's transcription showed that 7 feet from the top of the turret there was to be an interior floor, and that at its top should be 'some suffycyent compasse brases', which seemed to be referred to later as 'four [leus?] braces' (Loengard 1983: 309–10). Loengard confessed herself unable to explain what 'leus' braces might be—the term seems absent from architectural handbooks—but theatre historians were quick to provide answers. John Orrell noted that a '"lewis"... is an X-shaped cramp used in hoisting machinery' and speculated that the curved compass braces were made to cross like a lewis for 'structural rigidity as well as good looks' (Orrell 1988: 25). John Astington wondered whether there was an etymological connection with the word 'lee' (also spelt 'lew') meaning sheltered from the wind, and hence that the 'leus' braces enabled the projection of a 'cantilevered extension' of the floor 7 feet from the top of the turret that sheltered the stage below it 'in order to allow flying machinery to be worked from that position' (Astington 1985: 457). Thus the Red Lion's design anticipated the 'jutty forwards' of the upper two levels of the Fortune playhouse and the cantilevering of the roof of the Hope.

Stuart E. Baker also thought that the explanation was to do with flying, and noted that a 'lewis' was 'in essence an expandable metal tenon designed to fit into a dovetail mortise which was cut into a large stone'—lifting gear in other words—and that the brace was the substantial wooden structure needed to allow a 'lewis' to be adapted to theatrical flying (Baker 1995: 145). Orrell and Astington relied on Loengard's transcription of the document—the only one available at the time—but Baker ought to have used Berry's fresh transcription that eliminated the need for speculation: the phrase was 'the same four braces' (in Latin, 'eisdem quatuor lez brases') and Loengard's 'leus' was really law French 'lez' meaning 'the' (Berry 1989: 148). This tale of theatre historians chasing ignis fatuus is worth relating not only as a warning regarding the accuracy of sources, but also because it illustrates the desire to find evolutionary patterns of development in theatre design. Since later theatres had complex flying machines, the thinking goes, must not the early theatre have had primitive ones adapted from other technologies? And since there was subtle projection and cantilever carpentry at the Fortune and the Hope, why not simpler versions of the same at the Red Lion?

As should be clear from this Handbook's treatment of the particular venues, theatre historians no longer think that there was a generic design-model of 'Elizabethan theatre' upon which the individual buildings played minor variations. Yet there is still a strong desire to think in evolutionary terms, and although it can trick us into finding antecedents that do not rightly exist, the impulse is not entirely to be resisted. The Red Lion must stand as some kind of prototype to the Theatre, not least because an intelligent man like John Brayne can hardly be assumed to have learnt nothing from his project of 1567 when he embarked on the much more substantial building of 1576. Loengard was wrong to claim that the Red Lion was more than just a prototype for the Theatre, because, although there is no mention of dismantling the playhouse (as she observed), the structure was inherently impermanent. As Berry noted, it cost about £20 (less than 3 per cent of the cost of the Theatre), the contracts do not call for foundations to be made, only that the structures rest on 'plates' on the ground, and there is no mention of a roof or walls (Berry 1989: 145). Unlike the Theatre, it was an ephemeral affair in which no great amount of capital was invested.

In 1576 Brayne and James Burbage joined forces to build something much more substantial, and even by the originally estimated cost of around £200 (eventually far exceeded) it was to be ten times more impressive than the Red Lion. Because we know rather more of its design than we know of its predecessor's (a matter treated more fully in the next section), we can speculate within certain limits about why the Theatre turned out the way it did. Before there were permanent, purpose-built theatres, the players must have noticed that any large inn at which coaches unloaded had an enclosed yard within which a temporary stage might easily be mounted, and the elevated galleries which provided access to the rooms around the yard would have provided further accommodation for spectators with the additional benefit of protection from the elements. Less capacious, but more comfortable and dependable, would be a room inside the inn, and the final deciding factor might well have been the weather.

The innovation of placing of a temporary stage within an inn-yard must be counted among the origins of the late sixteenth-century theatre, but the virtually circular structures of the Theatre, the Curtain, the Rose, the Swan, and later the Globe cannot be explained as mere alterations of the inn-yard layout. Foreign visitors in London who saw the wooden amphitheatres commented on their likeness to the stone amphitheatres of Roman times, and indeed, in naming their 1576 playhouse the Theatre, Brayne and Burbage appear to have been deliberately invoking this antecedent. A possible additional inspiration was the animal-baiting arenas which had developed from simple circular wooden fences (animals within, spectators without) to become multi-storey structures containing many hundreds of spectators on staggered degrees, such as the one in Paris Garden that fatally collapsed upon its patrons in January 1583.

Superficially, a temporary stage erected within an animal ring might seem much like an open-air amphitheatre, but Oscar Brownstein pointed out that the heavy fencing needed to keep the agonized animals from attacking the spectators would have made it difficult for spectators to see the stage (Brownstein 1979). This argument has convinced most theatre historians that the animal rings were entirely irrelevant to the design of the theatres, but recently Iain Mackintosh and Jon Greenfield reopened the question by arguing that the surface of the yard at the Rose and the Fortune theatres was substantially lower than the ground outside the theatre. Such a sunken yard overcomes Brownstein's objection that a stout fence, inimical to drama, was needed to keep the audience safe (Mackintosh et al. 2006). This would also explain why the Fortune contract called for the yard wall to be topped with iron spikes: to keep the animals in.

It must be admitted, then, that we do not know where the peculiar design for the Theatre came from. Richard Hosley and John Orrell saw an antecedent in a banqueting house erected in Calais for Henry VIII's meeting with the emperor Charles V immediately after the conclusion of the Field of the Cloth of Gold in 1520 (Hosley 1979: 60–74; Orrell 1988: 30–8). This building was circular with three stacked galleries, each of which had a raked floor so those at the back could see over the heads of those in front. The timber frame reminded contemporaries of the Roman playhouses and they used the terms 'theatre' and 'amphitheatre' to describe it. Like the Theatre, this building could be dismantled and removed. However, although there was a similar building at Ardre, near Calais, these were uncommon structures and it is hard to imagine a route by which their design could influence a grocer and a joiner in London fifty years later. On the present evidence, it is best to think of the Theatre as arising *ex nihilo* because we have nothing earlier to serve as a model.

Without a picture of the Theatre, and no convincingly antecedent design, theatre historians look elsewhere. From the later lawsuits, we know something of the business relations that gave rise to the Theatre, and these are especially useful for contextualizing the location where the playhouse stood. The site chosen by Brayne and Burbage already had buildings on it, the most important of which was the Great Barn occupied by a butcher named Robert Stoughton, who used his space as a slaughterhouse, and by an innkeeper, whose use of the space is unknown, named Hugh Richards, who lived in the same small London parish as Burbage and hence might have been the one who drew the availability of the site to Burbage's attention (Ingram 1992: 185). Although the owner of the land, Giles Allen, denied it, the Great Barn was later said by witnesses to be in poor condition, and even Allen admitted that the other buildings on the site—a mill-house with a tenement building attached, plus two other tenements—were in bad shape.

The lease on the site was signed by Burbage alone on 13 April 1576 but began on 25 March 1576. Owning the lease meant that Burbage received the rents from the properties on the site, so whatever else we think about Burbage, he was a slum landlord. Under the terms of the lease, Burbage paid about £14 a year (according to Allen's later recollection) and had to make £200 worth of repairs to the properties on the site in the first ten years, which done, Allen had to offer Burbage another twenty-one-year lease. We do not know when work began on the construction of the Theatre, nor who built it, although a likely candidate as chief builder is James Burbage's brother Robert, who was a carpenter. James Burbage himself was a joiner, so he would have worked on furniture and fittings rather than whole buildings—although it is not impossible that he superintended the work. Among the improvements made immediately was the propping up of the dilapidated Great Barn with shores against the much sturdier playhouse next to it.

Deponents in the subsequent lawsuits agreed that the playhouse was in use even before its construction was fully completed, and on 1 August 1577 the Privy Council mentioned it when banning playing because of the threat of plague (Wickham et al. 2000: 336). It is worthwhile to note, in passing, that although cynics have suggested otherwise—'Enemies of the theatre often used the plague threat as a reason to have them closed' (Dollimore 1985: 77)—the prevention of public gatherings seems not to have been opportunistic, was the right thing to do in times of plague (modern countries with limited antibiotics do the same now), and probably saved lives (Barroll 1991: 70–116).

The Structure

In the absence of pictorial evidence, our knowledge of the features of the Theatre comes from two main sources: the lawsuits that mention expenditure on the structure and parts of the building, and the plays that were performed there. In respect of the evidence from plays, we are hampered by the fact that, with a couple of isolated exceptions, we cannot determine which players, and hence which plays, appeared at the Theatre prior to the settlement of 1594 (described below) that confined Shakespeare's company there. The provision in the lease for the removal of whatever Burbage put up, and the fact that the Theatre was indeed taken down and removed from the site, indicate that, although it was sturdy, the building was designed to enable dismantling. There is no mention of stonemasons in connection with its erection, repairing, or taking down, and hence it was essentially a wooden structure with brick foundations. By the same logic, the absence of any mention of thatchers in the copious records about the construction implies that the roof was tiled.

When Giles Allen and Cuthbert Burbage tried to negotiate a new lease in the 1590s, they discussed the possibility of turning the Theatre into tenement flats (Wallace 1913: 216). This tells us that, although there were (we assume) degrees of raked seating in the galleries, the rakers that supported the seats were added after flat floors had been put in rather than being integrated into the structure and used to help brace it. This indicates a floor-on-floor method of construction in which one wall (presumably the outer) rose in a single plane while the other had jetties so that each storey overhung the one below. The advantage of completing each floor before continuing to the next is lost if there is no jetty and both inner and outer main posts must rise to the full height of the building. Only the floor-on-floor method of construction is compatible with later conversion to tenements, and it also minimizes the need for overnight propping, reduces the number of joints which must be mated at one time, and provides a convenient working surface (the unnailed floorboards) which can take the place of scaffolding (McCurdy 1993: 9–12).

Just how the timbers were joined is a matter of scholarly dispute. Because it was possible to dismantle the Theatre in a few days around Christmas 1598, and because there was £40 worth of ironmongery in the building, Berry wondered if the timbers were held together by metalwork rather than with fitted joints, mortises, tenons, and dowels as was usual (Berry 1979: 35; Wallace 1913: 137). Orrell, on the other hand, thought it a marvelous feat of conventional carpentry, prefabricated off-site and delivered as a kit of parts (Orrell 1988: 41–5). Lack of standardization in sizes meant that parts were not exchangeable: the whole structure would be test-fitted together at the 'framing place' to make sure it worked, and then shipped to the final destination. For such a complex building the order of sequence of assembly was crucial since the workmen needed room to fit the tenons into their mortises, and because this was uniquely a polygonal building the complications were multiplied by the shoulders of the tenons not being the usual right angles.

In 1585 James Burbage and Allen tried (unsuccessfully) to negotiate a new lease, the text of which unsigned draft survives because it is quoted in one of the later lawsuits. This lease gives Allen and his wife and family the right to

> enter or come into the p*re*misses & their in some one of the vpper romes to have such convenient place to sett or stande to se such playes as shalbe ther played freely w^th^out any thinge therefore payeinge soe that the sayde Gyles hys wyfe and familie doe come & take ther places before they shalbe taken vpp by any others. (Wallace 1913: 177–8)

This indicates that at least part of the spectating gallery space was subdivided into 'rooms', as we know was the case at the Swan, the Fortune, and the Hope because these are called for in the construction contracts.

This draft lease also indicates that spectators could sit or stand in the galleries. Although she mistakenly read this lease as pertaining to the Curtain rather than the Theatre, Tiffany Stern rightly noted that a gallery is now, and was then, a place in which one expects to stand and walk rather than to sit, and she pointed out that the label 'porticus' attached to the topmost gallery in Johannes de Witt's drawing of the Swan is the Latin word for a covered walkway (Stern 2000*b*). William Lambarde described the penny-by-penny system of collecting the take at public arenas: 'first pay one penny at the gate, another at the entry of the scaffold, and the third for a quiet standing' (Wickham et al. 2000: 297). (In an uncharacteristic slip, Wickham, Berry, and Ingram slightly misquote Lambarde, omit his direct assertion that this system applied at the Theatre (Lambarde 1576, Q2^{r}), and point the reader to the wrong edition and with a page reference that applies to no edition, so the record is still best represented in Chambers 1923: ii. 359). To make this agree with his conviction that spectators sat in the galleries, Andrew Gurr asserted that '"to get a standing" meant to find a viewing-place, whether standing or sitting' (Gurr 1992*b*: 122), which is not a sense recorded in the *OED*. Perhaps, in the light of the draft lease for the Theatre, we should instead take Lambarde as literally referring to standing spaces.

We know that the Theatre had a 'Theatre yard' and an 'Attyring housse or place where the players make them readye' because the actor John Alleyn, Edward Alleyn's brother, referred to them in his evidence for one of the lawsuits (Wallace 1913: 126, 127). As for the physical fabric of the place, the foregoing is almost all we know from the legal documents; one snippet remains. A witness described how he, together with Margaret Brayne (John Brayne's widow) and her supporter Robert Miles, went to the Theatre 'vp*p*on A playe daye to stand at the do^{r} that goeth vppe to the gallaries of the said Theater to take & Receyve for the vse of the said Margarett half the money that shuld be gyven to come vppe into the said Gallaries at that do^{r}' (Wallace 1913: 114).

This is puzzling, for it seems to say that just one door led to the galleries, which suggests that, if there were stairs to the upper galleries, there was only one staircase. Lambarde's penny-by-penny system, on the other hand, implies that access to the upper galleries was had after entrance to the yard, for which one paid the first penny. Other evidence for other venues suggests a traditional arrangement whereby the owner of a venue normally kept half the income from the galleries, giving the other half of the galleries' income and the whole of the yard income to the players. But the Theatre was unusual because when James Burbage's company of actors, the Earl of Leicester's Men, were playing there, he effectively handed over a proportion of the income that he collected as owner of the venue to himself as leader of the players. John Alleyn claimed that even in this he cheated (Wallace 1913: 101).

Why then would Margaret Brayne feel entitled to all of the gallery income? Even if, as one might argue from the complex legal arrangements patched up between Brayne and Burbage, she thought herself entitled to all the venue-owner income for a time, surely the most she could claim would be the usual owner's half of the gallery take? Perhaps this is what the witness was implying: she and her supporter took up the collection of income at a single door because (as everyone knew) there were two such doors and by this means she hoped to collect all her rightful half. As Richard Hosley pointed out, the witness referred to one door but was answering a question about collections taken at 'the doares of the said Theatre' (Wallace 1913: 112; Hosley 1979: 49). However, Hosley was writing when the Utrecht engraving was still thought to show the Theatre, and with the loss of that picture we now cannot assert, as he did, that the building had two diametrically opposed external staircases (Hosley 1979: 54).

To say more about the design and facilities of the Theatre, we must turn now to the evidence from plays. The only systematic work on what the drama implies about this venue is Wickham (1979), which argued that no theatre had a stage cover before the Rose got its in 1592, and that later venues (the Swan, the Globe, the Hope) copied this innovation and also copied the Rose's installation of a 'throne' in the heavens (for supernatural descents onto the stage) in 1595. Wickham pointed out that theatre historians have long assumed the existence of a heavens with all its appurtenances (such as stage posts and a concealed winch) at every playhouse, but that this is not supported by the evidence. The desire, it seems, has been to imagine a singular, generic Elizabethan playhouse design. But if the Theatre had a heavens with a descent machine in 1576, why would Philip Henslowe not have built one at the Rose in 1587, and instead had to retro-fit these features in 1592 and 1595?

De Witt refers to four amphitheatres in London in 1596 and claims that the two south of the river (the Rose and the Swan) are 'more remarkable' (Wickham et al. 2000: 441) than the two north of the river (the Theatre and the Curtain), and this, according to Wickham, supports the idea that the stage cover was an innovation of the 1590s Bankside theatres. Not one of the many legal documents about the Theatre transcribed by Wallace mentions a stage cover or pillars, nor do any extant plays written and performed between 1576 and 1591, either in dialogue or in stage directions. Perhaps surprisingly, no play by Christopher Marlowe needs a floor-level trap, or stage pillars, or stage cover/heavens, or flying machine.

Wickham admits that the 1592 edition of Thomas Kyd's *The Spanish Tragedy* (*c.*1587–90) has a scene that might use a stage post as a stake for tying a prisoner to, but since the order given—and thankfully soon rescinded—is to burn him at the stake it would surely make better sense to use a property stake; after all, who would believe that the soldiers would set light to one of the theatre's stage posts? Similarly, Robert Wilson's *The Three Lords and Three Ladies of London* (*c.*1587–90) has dialogue and a stage direction in the final scene that refer to a 'post' and to 'the contrary post' and this certainly suggests use of the two stage posts. But then again this play probably belonged to the Queen's Men and 'two posts had to be forthcoming wherever they presented it—at court or on provincial tours as well as in a London playhouse: so the ambiguity cannot be removed entirely' (Wickham 1979: 8).

Concerning the playhouse 'heavens', no surviving play first performed between 1576 and 1595 calls for the appearance of deities other than by 'Enter' and 'Exit', except John Lyly's *The Woman in the Moon* (*c.*1590–5), which was 'written for boys and court performance' and hence does not tell us about open-air amphitheatre conditions, and Robert Greene's *The Comical History of Alphonsus, King of Aragon* (*c.*1587–8), which is more problematic (Wickham 1979: 9–12). This last play's opening stage direction reads 'Let Venus be let down from the top of the stage', and at the end there is 'Exit Venus. Or if you can conveniently, let a chair come downe from the top of the stage, and draw her up.' Other deities in the play make pedestrian entrances and exits, and Greene clearly allows for the possibility that his ideal of flight might not be realized. When printed in 1599 this play belonged to the Henslowe–Alleyn company at the Rose.

There is an ambiguous stage direction in the 1599 edition of Greene's *A Looking Glass for London and England* that refers to a 'throne' which appears to be 'set downe over the Stage', but Wickham argued—not entirely convincingly—that 'set downe over' here merely means 'placed upon' (Wickham 1979: 12). Thus, all the plays that in any way suggest pillars or heavens or flying date from after the building of the Rose, and we ought not to assume on playscript evidence that earlier venues such as the Theatre had these facilities. Perhaps, Wickham wondered, part of the attraction of moving the Theatre to make the Globe was that the Burbages did not want to invest in upgrading the Theatre to the standard of the Rose and the Swan with the uncertainty of the lease hanging over them, so instead they moved to Bankside, where they could build a new, better playhouse than those of Henslowe and Langley.

If Wickham is right—and on the present evidence his seems the most reasonable supposition—should we then say there is no reason to suppose that there was any kind of 'turret' or 'house' built within the yard of the Theatre? After all, why make such a thing if not to project from it a stage cover, supported by stage posts, and 'fly' characters onto the stage from within it? We are caught here in a recurrent dilemma of historical studies: should we take an absence of evidence (the absence of dramatic uses that Wickham detected) as evidence of an absence? In this case, there is ample evidence that some kind of 'turret' or 'house' was present at other venues built before and after the Theatre: as we have seen, the Red Lion (built in 1576 by one of two men who built the Theatre, John Brayne) had its 'tower', De Witt's interior drawing of the Swan shows a 'mimorum aedes' (players' house) in the playhouse yard, and exterior pictures of the Rose, the Globe, and the Hope seem to show the roof of some kind of 'turret' rising in their playhouse yards. The Utrecht engraving shows the top of a 'turret' at the playhouse, and, even reassigned to the Curtain, this evidence has a bearing on the Theatre, since if it lacked a 'turret' the Theatre was unusual. The only parallel might be the first phase of the Rose playhouse (1587–92), which seems on archaeological evidence to have had no stage posts, stage cover, or 'turret' (Bowsher 2007).

THE OCCUPANTS, THEIR PLAYS, AND THEIR AUDIENCES

From the theatre historian's point of view, Burbage and Brayne's choice of the name the Theatre for their playhouse was unhelpful because it is often difficult to know whether a documentary allusion to something going on in 'the theatre' means their house specifically or the whole collection of playhouses generally. (In the same way, we today might enquire what is on at 'the cinema' without meaning any place in particular.) In the following collation of the evidence I exclude doubtful cases.

For most of the history of the Theatre we have little direct evidence of which companies played there, and little reason to trust inferences from indirect evidence. The unreliability of inferences arises because until 1594 there was little in the way of what Andrew Gurr called 'settled practices' regarding the various companies' use of London playhouses (Gurr 1996*b*: 19–35, 78–104). As described by Gurr, a Privy Council order of 1594 gave a two-part monopoly (a duopoly) of London playing to Richard Burbage's newly formed troupe called the Chamberlain's Men (including the promising new writer–performer William Shakespeare) and Edward Alleyn's troupe called the Admiral's Men, confining each to one playhouse, the Theatre and the Rose respectively. From this point on, we can confidently say that a new play written for the Chamberlain's Men would have been first performed at the Theatre, and that the dramatist writing it would most likely know that.

It may be that Gurr's notion of a duopoly overstates the case somewhat, since if the Theatre and the Rose had the London market to themselves it is difficult to understand why two new playhouses sprang up. A year after the Privy Council order, Francis Langley built the Swan playhouse in a site apparently chosen so that patrons who crossed the river southwards by boat and alighted at Paris Garden stairs would pass Langley's new playhouse before reaching the Rose (Ingram 1978: 106). In 1598 Oliver Woodliffe adapted the Boar's Head inn into a playhouse, and the continued demand for new places (in addition to the officially authorized venues of the Theatre and the Rose) is attested by Langley's joining this project after the Swan was closed by the Privy Council order of 28 July 1597 (Berry 1986: 29–63). Whatever the official position, London seems to have remained an openly competitive market for playing.

Nonetheless, the Privy Council duopoly of 1594 seems to have kept the two main companies, Burbage's and Alleyn's, more or less permanently installed in their respective venues, so we need not consider further the Theatre's occupancy for the period 1594 to 1598. For the earlier years, we have only scraps of evidence. James Burbage was leader of Leicester's Men when the Theatre was constructed, so it is not unlikely that this company played there when it was first opened. It is clear from the legal documents that the Theatre was in use before the construction work was 'fully finished' (Wallace 1913: 135). Evidence of the first certain date for use of the Theatre is the Privy Council order of 1 August 1577 ordering it closed for prevention of plague (Wickham et al. 2000: 336).

Although he speaks of a plurality of theatres, the sermon by Thomas White delivered at Paul's Cross on 3 November 1577 can only refer to the Theatre, its neighbour the Curtain, and/or perhaps the playhouse at Newington Butts: 'beholde the sumptuous Theatre houses, a continuall monument of Lo*n*don's prodigalitie and folly'. White took comfort in the present ban on playing because of plague, for he saw another connection—aside from the danger of congregation, which one can scarcely complain of in a public sermon—between drama and the sickness: 'the cause of plagues is sinne, if you looke to it well: and the cause of sinne are playes: therefore the cause of plagues are playes' (White 1578, C8^{r}).

On 24 August 1578—Bartholomew day, sacred to rabid anti-Catholics since the Paris massacre of 1572—the sermonizer John Stockwood enquired:

What should I speake of beastlye Playes...haue we not houses of purpose built with great charges for the maintena*n*ce of them... [?] I know not how I might with the godly learned especially more discommende the gorgeous Playing place erected in the fieldes, than to terme it, as they please to haue it called, a Theatre, that is, euen after the maner of the olde heathenish Theatre at Rome. (Stockwood 1578, J7[v])

Significantly, for Stockwood the drama is objectionable not only for its thematic content but also because the venues are opulent and therefore decadent. Even taking into account their theological objections to the whole enterprise, the evidence of White and Stockwood indicates that the Theatre was, as its £700 cost suggests, an impressive, even beautiful, building.

Mid-twentieth-century visual impressions of open-air amphitheatres such as the film of *Henry V* (Olivier 1944) and Irwin Smith's scale model of the Globe based on John Cranford Adams's book (J. C. Adams 1942) incorporated into a public display at the Folger Library in Washington, reflected theatre historians' emphasis upon the Tudor vernacular elements in the architecture and decoration, the use of wood and plaster. These impressions tend to understate the European classical influence that prompted the owners to paint the wood to look like marble and the plaster to look like stone. The evidence for this in relation to the Globe is cited in Chapter 11 of this Handbook, and, in respect of the Swan, Richard Southern and C. Walter Hodges were the first to make full use of the evidence of Johannes de Witt (Southern and Hodges 1952). More recently the evidence that may be drawn from non-dramatic public buildings of the period has been collated and interpreted (Ronayne 1997; Keenan and Davidson 1997).

The myth of Tudor theatrical plainness is perpetuated by the set of the recent film *Shakespeare in Love*, which is nonetheless accurate in other matters (Madden 1998). Theatre historians now emphasize the tendency of Elizabethans to paint lavishly every part of their public buildings that they could get a brush to. If John Ronayne is right that there was a building tradition of plain outsides and gorgeous insides, it is likely that the exterior decoration of playhouses was subdued compared to the interior (Ronayne 1987: 26) and hence White and Stockwood either took the risk of venturing inside the Theatre in order to be revolted at its 'sumptuous' and 'gorgeous' appearance, or the decadence within was even worse than they knew.

Plays were not the only entertainment at the Theatre: sword-fighting was displayed on 25 August 1578 (Wickham et al. 2000: 340) and periodically thereafter. The following year Stephen Gosson, in acknowledging that among the harmful plays and players were a few exceptions, identified 'The *Black Smiths daughter*, & *Catilins* conspiracies usually brought in at the Theater' (Gosson 1579*b*: C6[v]–C7[r]). The qualifier 'usually' corroborates other evidence that, before the 'settled practices' of the 1590s, the troupes travelled between playhouses around London as well as touring the country. In a letter of 14 June 1584, William Fleetwood wrote to Lord Burghley that with a couple of exceptions the Privy Council had agreed to 'the suppressing and pulling down of the Theatre and Curtain' and that 'the Queen's players and my Lord of Arundel his players' agreed to stop playing (Wickham et al. 2000: 346). Assuming the normal way of pairing items thus listed, this tells us that the Queen's Men were in residence at the Theatre at the time.

The following year James Burbage made a profit-sharing deal with Henry Lanman, the owner of Curtain, the purpose of which is uncertain (Wickham et al. 2000: 348–9) and of which William Ingram has made the best sense; his interpretation is followed here (Ingram 1992: 227–35). The deal with Lanman was that profits of the Theatre and the Curtain would be pooled and split fifty-fifty for a period of seven years. In order to avoid giving Brayne's widow, Margaret, her share, Burbage later claimed that under the deal he and Brayne gave Lanman a half-share in the Theatre, but this was not true: it was purely a profit-sharing arrangement.

The deal was said to have arisen in order to make the Curtain 'an Esore' to the Theatre, or possibly (the syntax is ambiguous) because the Curtain was already 'as Esore' to the Theatre. It is impossible to say which is meant, because no one has a satisfactory explanation of the term 'Esore' and the whole thing is mysterious. It has been argued that 'easer' (something to relieve a strain) is what is meant, and that the Queen's Men were so numerous in the mid-1580s that they could not fit in the Theatre and chose to split into two groups to occupy two venues. As Ingram pointed out, this would not require the playhouse owners to enter into a deal, and he rejected the idea.

Most likely, Ingram argued, Lanman did not live near the Curtain and in 1585 he needed someone to run the place for him because his previous manager, Richard Hickes of the Newington Butts playhouse, died. The deal was for seven years, rather than perpetual, because its real purpose was to get the Curtain off Lanman's hands by selling it to Burbage and Brayne over time. Presumably, by insisting that the profits of the two playhouses were shared, Burbage and Brayne were given an incentive to run both venues well rather than letting the Curtain languish until they took full possession in 1592.

It is well known that there was at least one play (maybe more) about a Prince Hamlet long before Shakespeare's version was first published in 1603, although it is impossible to say who wrote it (or them).[2] In *Wits Misery*, Thomas Nashe described the son of Beelzebub and his wife, Jealousy, as walking 'for the most part in black vnder colour of grauity, & looks as pale as the Uisard of ye ghost which cried so miserally at ye Theator like an oisterwife, *Hamlet, reuenge*' (Lodge 1596, H4^{v}). Since Shakespeare's company, the Chamberlain's Men, were in residence at the Theatre for the preceding two years, this is presumably an allusion to their version, and perhaps it was Shakespeare's work since it shows the familiar concern for the wearing of black clothes to make a grave impression.

Now that we have reached the 1590s, we can simply tabulate the surviving plays written for the Chamberlain's Men between 1594, when the Privy Council confined them to the Theatre, and mid-1598, when they left it. Assuming that the dates and ascriptions are correct, these were likely to be plays written for, and first performed at, the Theatre. Below I give the span of years within which the first performance took

[2] William Shakespeare, *Hamlet*, ed. Ann Thompson and Neil Taylor, The Arden Shakespeare (London: Thompson Learning, 2006), 44–9.

place, determined from Harbage (1964) or, in the case of Shakespeare, from Wells et al. (1987), and where the span falls partly outside 1594–8 it should be understood that the play is less reliably associated with the Theatre than is the case for those plays whose spans fall wholly within these limits.

1591–5	Anonymous	*1 Richard II*
1594	William Shakespeare	*The Comedy of Errors*
1594–5		*Love's Labour's Lost*
1595		*A Midsummer Night's Dream*
		Richard II
		Romeo and Juliet
1596		*King John*
1596–7		*The Merchant of Venice*
		1 Henry IV
1597–8		*2 Henry IV*
		The Merry Wives of Windsor
1598		*Much Ado About Nothing*
	Ben Jonson	*Every Man in His Humour*
1598–9	William Shakespeare	*Henry V*
	Anonymous	*A Warning for Fair Women*
1598–1600	Anonymous	*A Larum for London*

Plays first performed in 1598 might in fact have premiered at the Curtain rather than the Theatre, because the Chamberlain's Men appear to have decamped there during the summer. To see why they did, we must consider the disassembly of the Theatre and its reassembly as the Globe.

Deconstruction

The term 'deconstruction' was coined by the philosopher Jacques Derrida for his book *Of Grammatology* (Derrida 1976) and it has passed into common usage as a synonym for taking apart something, usually an artistic work. This is unfortunate, as Derrida meant something more complex and interesting, which was the taking apart of a social construct (say, patriarchy, or our categories of mental health, or an assumption of Western cultural superiority) precisely in order to show that it is a social construct, not a simple 'given' of existence like our need to breathe air, and having taken it apart to reconstruct the elements in a new and better configuration. That is, deconstruction is at least as much about construction as destruction. To help out a Japanese translator of his work, Derrida referred to one sense as 'To disassemble the parts of a whole. To deconstruct a machine to transport it elsewhere' (Derrida 1999: 283).

When Burbage and Brayne built their playhouse, the most familiar use of the word 'theatre' was not as a playing place but as a book wherein was offered 'a "view" or "conspectus" of some subject' (*OED* 'theatre', *n.* †7), as in the title of John Speed's *The Theatre of the Empire of Great Britaine* (Speed 1611 [1612]) and earlier similar titles. (By another of the coincidences that abound in this case, it was within a specimen of Speed's book that a second copy of the formerly believed to be unique Utrecht engraving was found in 1996—it had been 'tipped in', in bookmaker's parlance—and this new copy helped Herbert Berry establish that the represented playhouse was not the Theatre; Berry 2000*c*: 200.) The name Burbage and Brayne gave their building was, then, bookish and contemporary as well as spectacular and classical, and the structure combined these intellectual and artistic impulses as much as it combined Tudor vernacular and classical architecture.

The Theatre was, moreover, a machine for presenting plays; it was the hardware for running the dramatic software (playscripts), as Andrew Gurr put it (Gurr 1989: 1). In 1598 the Burbages deconstructed the Theatre in the proper Derridean sense: they disassembled their machine, transported it elsewhere, and rebuilt it. This daringly demonstrated that the seemingly immovable (a given) was in fact a human construct that can be remade afresh if so desired, and it also enacted a transference from object to subject that the word 'theatre' had undergone in acquiring the sense of 'A thing displayed to view' (*OED* 'theatre', *n.* †8) as well as the means by which the thing was displayed. Fittingly, then, the Theatre, a means for viewing the world, became the Globe, the world to be viewed.

After an abortive attempt to relocate to an indoor playhouse in the elite Blackfriars district (I. Smith 1964: 172–3), a story told in Chapters 11 and 12 in this Handbook, James Burbage died in February 1597. The lease on the site of the Theatre was set to expire on 25 March 1597, so Burbage's son Cuthbert took up fresh negotiations with Giles Allen for its extension or renewal. In a subsequent court case Cuthbert Burbage claimed that while they argued about a new lease, Allen let the players 'contynue in possession of the p*re*misses for diverse yeares' and took the agreed rent (Wallace 1913: 184).

The Theatre was described as 'vnfrequented' and in 'darke silence' (Guilpin 1598, D6^{r}) by Edward Guilpin in his collection *Skialetheia*, entered in the Stationers' Register on 15 September 1598, so by this date the Chamberlain's Men must have moved elsewhere. The obvious place to go was the Curtain since, as we have seen, James Burbage had a deal with its owner Henry Lanham, and by now the Burbages, perhaps in partnership with members of the playing company (several later passed on shares in the Curtain in their wills; Ingram 1992: 235), probably owned the Curtain.

We can be sure that the Chamberlain's Men did not leave the Theatre before the summer of 1598 because Allen, in his answer to Cuthbert Burbage, agreed that he allowed the company 'to enioye the premiss*es* after the first lease expired for the space of a yeare or two' and paying 'onelie the ould rent' (Wallace 1913: 196). The Theatre was disassembled by the Burbages and removed from Allen's land to a newly leased site on Bankside, probably in a few days beginning 28 December 1598 (Berry 1987: 4–7).

Leaving Shoreditch one way or another (to Blackfriars or Bankside) must have been in Shakespeare's mind around this time, and the solution to the disagreement with Allen about the terms of a new lease was to invoke a clause in the old one which allowed Burbage and Brayne to 'take downe and Carrie awaie . . . all such buildings . . . as should be builded . . . for a Theatre' (Wallace 1913: 191). Thus, the players' property could be readily extricated from the landlord's, and, although the Theatre's timbers were removed while he was out of town (Berry 1987: 6–7), Allen could hardly claim that this was wrong in principle under the old lease; the dispute hinged on whether his taking the rent constituted a tacit extension of the lease that allowed the removal.

Nearing the expiration of the lease on site of the Theatre and as the problems of relocation loomed, Shakespeare wrote *The Merchant of Venice*, which got its first performance in 1596 or 1597. In the play, the court concludes that Shylock's contractual arrangement with Antonio gives him possession of the pound of flesh ('The court awards it, and the law doth give it' and 'The law allows it, and the court awards it'; IV. i. 297, 300) but catches him with the insoluble problem of extracting it without harming the rest of the body, which still belongs to Antonio. A part of Allen's subsequent claim against the Burbages was for damage done to his property, £2 worth of grass, during the removal of the Theatre (Wallace 1913: 164) but a truly substantive issue about which witness after witness was questioned was the condition of other buildings on the same site that Brayne and Burbage were supposed to keep in good order.

In particular, there was the decrepit Great Barn close to the Theatre, which Allen claimed Burbage had neglected, while the Burbages insisted that this barn was improved by being propped against the much sturdier playhouse (Wallace 1913: 223–43, question 10, and the answers of Richard Hudson, Thomas Bromfield, Thomas Osborne, William Furnis, William Smythe, Randulphe Maye, and Oliver Tylte). Answers to questions about the Great Barn tell us that only the 'twoe or three Shores' running to it from the Theatre kept it standing, and that when the playhouse was removed these had to be sunk into the ground instead. The foundations for the Theatre were of course left behind, and recent archaeological work on the site seems to have uncovered these foundations, located by their proximity to the Great Barn foundations. The likelihood is that the Theatre's exposed foundations provided the new location for the shores once the Theatre was gone (Bowsher 2006). By this time, the Great Barn was apparently no longer used by Stoughton the slaughterman and Richards the innkeeper (see above), but rather was converted into residential tenements (Wallace 1913: 201–2).

The players in the Theatre had cause to consider the loss of livelihood that follows the loss of one's place of business, and the tenants of the Great Barn had cause to consider the loss of their homes if the Theatre that literally supported them were gone. A creative mind might see the players' and the tenants' cases as two sides of the same coin, or, as Shylock puts it:

> You take my house when you do take the prop
> That doth sustain my house; you take my life
> When you do take the means whereby I live.
>
> (*The Merchant of Venice*, IV. i. 372–4)

Shylock's metaphor (and Allen's intentions in framing the lease) had real correlates in the props that linked the buildings and thereby linked their interests. The play represents as an impossibility the extricating of linked properties, and was written around the time the players were addressing precisely the same problem.

The Significance of the Theatre

The Theatre was the first of a kind of venue—the open-air amphitheatres—that lasted until the general closure of playhouses by Parliament in 1642. Although the players always wanted to move into indoor playhouses within the City of London, where they could play to richer, smaller audiences, the tradition of demotic outdoor playing that the Theatre established survived. In describing this tradition it is easy to overstate the importance of the southern bank of the river Thames, where the Rose, the Swan, the Globe, and the Hope were located, and it is worth remembering that the northern and eastern suburbs were just as important as homes to the Theatre, the Curtain, the Boar's Head, the Fortune, and the Red Bull.

As well as establishing the tradition, the Theatre might even be said to have spawned the design in virtually a genetic sense. If Herbert Berry is wrong and Irwin Smith, John Orrell, and Peter McCurdy are right that custom-made wooden joints and not metalwork held the main timbers of the Theatre together (Berry 1979: 35; I. Smith 1952; Orrell 1988: 41–5; McCurdy 2007), then the new building made from these timbers, the Globe, was exactly the same size and shape as the Theatre. (The third alternative is that the tenons were cut off to take the Theatre apart and fresh joints were made when the timbers were reassembled, but such wanton vandalism would make the new building considerably smaller than the old one and is belied by the involvement of Peter Street in the disassembly and by the several days he took to complete the work.) Thus, the structure erected in 1576 effectively lasted on two sites until destroyed by fire in 1613. A second Globe playhouse was immediately constructed on the site of the first.

In February 1635 the two men charged by the Commissioners for Buildings for reporting on buildings in the liberty of the Clink, the churchwarden John Hancock and the constable George Archer, made an entry in the final, fair-copy report for St Saviour's parish, noting, 'The Globe Playhouse nere Maidlane built by the Company of Players wth timber aboute 20 yeares past vppon an old foundacon...' (Hancock and Archer 1635). Since this second Globe was built on the foundations of the first (which naturally survived the fire), it must have been exactly the same size and shape. Thus, Brayne and Burbage's design of 1576 survived the full span of early modern theatre covered from its inception to its suppression. As is described in Chapter 11 in this Handbook, we have pictorial evidence for the two Globe playhouses and can be fairly sure that they were twenty-sided (or thereabouts) polygons of 100 feet diameter. If the 'genetic' ancestry sketched here is right, so was the Theatre.

CHAPTER 11

WHY THE GLOBE IS FAMOUS

ANDREW GURR

THE Globe was Shakespeare's workplace for the ten years when he wrote his greatest plays. From *As You Like It* in 1599, through *Hamlet* in 1600 and the other great tragedies, with the later Roman plays to *Cymbeline* and *The Winter's Tale* in 1609, it was the playhouse for which he designed all his plays up to *The Tempest*, the first and only play he wrote for the company's indoor theatre, the Blackfriars. He was also a part owner of the Globe. In 1599 he paid £100 to help get it built out of the skeletal remains of James Burbage's old Theatre, the first of the London playhouses in regular use from 1576. As the workplace where his greatest plays were first staged, the Globe has come to stand as the frame inside which Shakespeare painted his greatest works.

In reality, except for ten short years, it never deserved that unique status. From its foundation in 1594 the Shakespeare company which built the Globe regarded outdoor playhouses as their location only for summertime. They always preferred indoor places to play at through the winter. Once the Privy Council assigned them to the Globe's predecessor in the northern suburbs, the Theatre, in May 1594, that October they persuaded their Privy Counsellor patron, the Lord Chamberlain, to ask the Lord Mayor of London for permission to play through the winter at the Cross Keys inn, an inner-London tavern whose main room had often been used for staging plays. The plea was evidently unsuccessful, because in the following winter their financier, owner of the Theatre, and father of their leading player, Richard Burbage, built a new indoor playhouse for the company. He chose to locate it in a great hall in the precinct of the Blackfriars, where the Lord Mayor's authority did not run. In the event, a petition of residents of the Blackfriars, who did not want common players in their neighbourhood, stopped them from using it. Father James Burbage died soon after, and, when the lease of the Theatre's land expired and the landlord expelled the players, the company found itself without any playhouse.

The plan Burbage's two sons subsequently devised was an act of desperation, but it proved remarkably successful. Since the cost of building the Blackfriars had wiped out old Burbage's resources, his two sons, one inheriting the lost Theatre and the other the empty Blackfriars, somehow had to find enough money for a new playhouse. At first they rented the Theatre's neighbour, the Curtain, while Cuthbert, the new owner of the Theatre, kept trying to persuade its landlord to renew the lease. His brother Richard kept the company playing while searching for some alternative use for his inheritance, the Blackfriars. After eighteen months in the rented playhouse, the brothers reached an agreement with five of the company's sharers to finance a replacement for the Theatre. Their own contribution was the Theatre's framing timbers, huge baulks of oak up to 30 feet in length, while the five players, one of them Shakespeare, each put up £100 to cover the costs of rebuilding it in a new location, on Bankside.

The plan was a desperately bold new venture. The new playhouse, soon licensed by the Privy Council as one of the only two authorized playing places in London, was relabelled the Globe. It was located barely 50 yards from the other originally licensed playhouse, the Rose, and not much further from the chief bear-baiting house. The arrival of the other company so close to their own ageing playhouse made the Rose company shift northwards to a site not far from the old Theatre, where they built the Fortune. With easy access over London Bridge or by ferry, the Bankside in Surrey was an ideal site for recreationing Londoners.

The financing of the Globe was a venture with one real novelty which secured the company's future for more than forty years, until Parliament stopped all playing in 1642. The five, later four, playing sharers who helped pay for the construction became what is known as 'housekeepers', renting the playhouse to the company. As both company sharers and housekeepers, they controlled the company's policy and all its activities. Its interests were maintained by the five players who held all but one of the shares in the playhouse and a majority of the eight, later ten, shares in the company. This sharing created a thoroughly cooperative system of management and financial control.

Judging from the Lord Chamberlain's letter to the Lord Mayor in October 1594, the Shakespeare company always wanted a roofed playhouse for the winter to accompany its summertime use of the open-air venue. The fruit of that ambition was Richard Burbage's inheritance, the Blackfriars, given him by his father's will in February 1597, shortly after the Privy Council upheld the residents' petition that prevented the company from using it. Two years later, while the Globe was being built, he rented it to a company of boy players. They used it once a week without any outcry from the local residents. One of the many ironies in *Hamlet*, first staged in 1600, is the information the prince receives about the boys forcing the adult players to go on their travels, since, as everyone knew, Richard Burbage playing the prince was in reality the boys' landlord.

Once the Blackfriars became available, in 1609 the company could for the first time run a two-season programme, relegating use of the Globe to the summer only. When after four seasons of use it burned down, the company affirmed its loyalty to the dual-playhouse system by paying to have it rebuilt. The Blackfriars, with its much smaller audience capacity but much higher prices, was already proving more profitable than the Globe. It was the venue for the rich and socially ambitious, whereas the Globe was designed for the masses. Whether the company's motives came from simple loyalty to the two-venue system or continuing devotion to the apprentices and artisans who crowded round the stage at the Globe in contrast with the gallants sitting on stools on the stage itself at Blackfriars, the company's house-keepers chose to dig deep and raise the money to build a second Globe. The result Ben Jonson called 'the Glory of the *Banke*', and John Chamberlain wrote was reckoned to be 'the fayrest that ever was in England' (Jonson 1925–52: viii. 208; McClure 1939: i. 544).

The Story 1594–1608

The story of the Globe begins in 1594, five years before it was built. In May of that year, a compromise was reached between the Privy Counsellor responsible for playing, Henry Carey, the Lord Chamberlain, and the Lord Mayor of London over playing in London. The Council upheld professional playing whereas successive lord mayors opposed it. A deal was made to set up a 'duopoly', comprising two new playing companies, one under Carey's name and the other under that of his son-in-law Charles Howard, the Lord Admiral. Each was allocated to a licensed playhouse outside the city, Carey's in a northern suburb, the Theatre in Middlesex, and Howard's at the Rose on the south bank, in Surrey. Playing inside London itself was forbidden, the two companies at their suburban playhouses the only ones allowed to play anywhere near London. Setting up the duopoly satisfied the Chamberlain's duty to provide plays for the Queen every Christmas, and softened the mayoral grievance over the troubles that came from the huge crowds that gathered at plays.[1]

The loss in 1597 of the licensed Theatre was a handicap in financial rather than political terms. Once the company built and occupied the Globe, it was named as the Theatre's replacement by an order of the Privy Council signed on 22 June 1600. The same order licensed the other company's new playhouse, the Fortune, built by Peter Streete, the man who erected the Globe. How far the urge to build the Globe as a

[1] This term for the two licensed companies was first applied by Richard Dutton (1991: 111). For a detailed examination of the long-running quarrel over plays between Guildhall and the Council, see Gurr (2005).

replacement for the lost Theatre was impelled by the Privy Council's plan to license just two playhouses in the suburbs we cannot be sure. To the two younger Burbages the need to pay the Curtain's owners rent must have been an equally good reason for constructing their own playhouse. For all the loss the Burbages suffered when their plan for a winter playhouse to match their open-air venue went wrong, the first three years of the duopoly must have shown them the value of a regular playing place carrying the security of a Privy Council licence. If one adds the income from the company's rent, the motive for them building their own replacement for the Curtain is clear.

What could not have been clear was how they might afford it. Eventually, they contracted a master carpenter, Peter Streete, to demolish the old Theatre and rescue from it all the framing oak timbers and as much more of the decorative carvings and other materials from the skeleton as he could, and reuse them for the frame and finishing of a new playhouse in a new location. The Bankside was next to the other duopoly company's playhouse, so should conform to the Privy Council's plan. They took out a lease of the new site for thirty-one years, ten years longer than the Theatre's. They made Streete go into his demolition work on 12 December 1598, just before the Christmas break, no doubt in the hope that Giles Allen, owner of the Theatre's land and arguably of the building on it, would not notice until it was too late. They were right in that, although the disappearance of the building did not stop Allen from suing them for everything from trespass to the theft of the building materials. As inheritor of the Theatre, Cuthbert Burbage had to fight Allen in the law courts for the next three years, until Allen and Cuthbert had exhausted their eagerness and their money in the fruitless struggle. Like so many lawsuits of the time, it sank into the legal quicksands and disappeared from sight.

The materials rescued from the Theatre gave Peter Streete much of what he needed to build the new playhouse, but not nearly enough to pay him and his workmen their wages for the six months or more that it took to complete the structure, let alone the additional materials—bricks and mortar for the new foundations, new timbers, and boards—plus wages for the plasterers, woodcarvers, thatchers, and painters who had to do all the specialized work. That led the Burbages to set up the unique agreement with their playing company's senior sharers that in the event kept the company at the forefront of the playing companies for the next forty-three years.

The labour of building and financing the Globe was in its way and its time heroic, and aptly enough was adjudged a Herculean effort by its supporters. Some such thought must have been in the minds of the players when they named it the Globe and chose as its emblem the figure of Hercules upholding it: Hercules and his load too, as Hamlet called it in 1600.[2]

In a heavily authoritarian age, the agreement between the two Burbages and five of the Chamberlain's Men's sharers, John Heminges, Will Kempe, Augustine Phillips, Thomas Pope, and Will Shakespeare, was an exceptionally cooperative act. It arose

[2] Edmond Malone first reported the idea of the emblem and its likely motto, 'Totus mundus agit histrionem', a supposition widely debated, but affirmed on good evidence by Dutton (1989).

Figure 11.1 The first engraving of the Globe, by John Norden.

Norden was a Londoner, a man of many parts, one of whose interests was in creating a bird's-eye view of London from the tower of St Saviour's, now Southwark Cathedral. His first depiction appeared in 1593, in *Speculum Britanniae* (see Foakes 1985: 6–7). He revised it for a 1600 reissue, under the title Civitas Londini. The revision depicted three amphitheatres, the Bear Garden, the Rose, and the Globe, in a conventional form with flags flying over all three (see Foakes 1985: 10–11). A crudely drawn inset showed them again, named 'Bearegard', 'The stare', and 'The globe' (Foakes 1985: 12–13; Figure 11.3).

from the professional players' custom as touring companies of 'sharing' the profit and loss of their enterprises. Sharing in a playhouse extended the tradition of sharing the company's main assets, their playbooks and costumes, into a more material form. The Privy Council's policy of issuing exclusive licences to the playhouses of the duopoly companies made it desirable and practicable. A majority of the company sharers became 'housekeepers' and ruled company policy. Even when the clown Will Kempe sold his share, the five playing sharers and the brother of the leading sharer were enough in number to outvote the rest of the consortium. The players had control of their playhouse, and the senior playing sharers who were 'housekeepers' had rent from their new property to augment their share of the company's profits. That was the best guarantee of a durable tenure.[3]

The Privy Council soon endorsed the company's plan by licensing the Globe in place of the Theatre for the finest decade of Shakespeare's plays, from *Henry V*, *Julius Caesar*, and *As You Like It* in 1599 until *Cymbeline* and *The Winter's Tale* in 1609. The new management system thrived. Within a month of King James arriving in London in April 1603, he acknowledged their leading place among the playing companies by making himself their patron. From then on they dominated the London playhouse scene. They were ordered to perform at court nearly twice as often as all the other

[3] For a more detailed study of the new management system instituted with the Globe's finances, see Gurr (2004*c*, ch. 1).

groups put together. Moreover, thanks largely to their new status as the King's Men and courtiers, in August 1608 Richard Burbage finally retrieved his Blackfriars playhouse. For once the residents were silent about the takeover. The company could at last institute the scheme they first dreamed of in October 1594, when their original patron asked the Lord Mayor if they could use a city inn for the winter. From then on the company played at the Globe through the summer, and at the Blackfriars through each winter. To compensate his fellows for the consequent halving of their income from the Globe, Richard gave each of them an equivalent share in the Blackfriars and its rents.

Once the two playhouses were in operation, the Globe turned out to bring in less rent than the Blackfriars. On occasions in later years the housekeepers rented it out in winter to acrobats for outdoor shows. Otherwise each of the two playhouses had a fallow season, when repairs and repainting could be done. Loyalty to the idea of a winter and a summer season remained with the company for all its long life. When the Globe burned down in 1613 the housekeepers clubbed together and paid the giant cost of building a replacement. Not all of them were prepared to undertake the huge expense, however. William Shakespeare, now resident in Stratford but a recent purchaser of a property in the nearby Blackfriars gatehouse, must have chosen to opt out as a housekeeper rather than pay for another Globe. In his will of 1616 he bequeathed his gatehouse property to his elder daughter, but made no mention of any continuing interest in the Globe or Blackfriars.

The Theatre in 1599

The concept that gave rise to the Globe first appeared as early as 1567, when James Burbage allied himself with his brother-in-law to build a ring of galleries around a stage in Stepney. The point was to make audiences pay their money before they came within view of the stage. It made sense to use the surrounding walls not just as a barrier but as an elevation of encircling galleries with benches, to augment the numbers facing the stage. A roof was added to these encircling galleries for shelter against bad weather. The obvious models for such auditoriums were the circular arenas in which animals were baited, and probably also some travellers' inns with square yards built to accommodate coaches, with galleries around them and a stage built in the yard for use by travelling players. The point of building such arenas was baldly commercial. Companies travelling the country to play in marketplaces had to get their money by walking through the crowd with a hat, taking whatever it pleased the bystanders to give. Walled arenas required the folk who stood around the stage in the new theatres to pay for their entertainment in advance. The alleged ability of the 1576 Theatre to accommodate 3,000 people seems to show that Londoners were ready to flock to the suburbs in sufficient numbers to justify huge outlays on such structures.

By then the popularity of plays performed for money was evidently massive. In 1575 and 1576 London acquired three open-air amphitheatres while the city gained two indoor theatres.[4] That may in fact have been optimistic, because in the following twenty years only one new playhouse, the Rose, was built before Marlowe and Shakespeare renewed playgoers' enthusiasm and a new series of playhouses started appearing in 1595, with the Swan. The first flowering of specially built playhouses in 1575 and 1576 did not last long. In 1587 the Surrey playhouse was superseded by the Rose on Bankside, and both of the indoor playhouses had closed by 1590. In part this may have been because, despite mayoral objections keeping the amphitheatres in the suburbs until 1594, the professional companies still used inns in the city, whether they had open yards or large interior rooms for entertainment.

James Burbage's experience with the Red Lion in 1567 must have been what led him on to build the Theatre in 1576. Twenty-three years later that structure was to provide the Globe's framing timbers. As a consequence, apart from the refinements suggested by using it, the Globe's design really dates from 1576. Consequently, like all the playhouses built between 1567 and 1629, it gave priority to the ear over the eye, and grouped its audiences so that they surrounded the stage on all sides.[5] The smaller numbers at what we think of as the rear of the stage made up for it by being priced higher and having a higher social quality than the yard where people stood around the stage. The tradition of playing in marketplaces from which the designers emerged made them include this standing room, because it was routine with the removable booth stages of the travelling companies. This was a unique feature of the open-air amphitheatres, and gave an obvious priority to the most visible members of the audience, those who could stand at the edges of the stage with their chins on the rim of the stage itself. The height of the stage at the Red Lion, the only one for which we have an exact measurement, was 5 feet. That elevation was high enough to prevent audience members from readily climbing onto it, perhaps a necessary protection for the players.

Such close proximity to the stage, matched only by the visitors who sat in the lords' rooms or the adjacent gentlemen's rooms, gave best position both to the privileged audience members who paid most and to those who paid least. Most of the gallery seating was behind the yard's 'understanders', as they were sarcastically known. That was a feature unique to the Globe and its amphitheatre peers. At the indoor theatres, where everyone had a seat, the price of places was much more like modern pricing, where the more you pay the closer you can get to the stage. A box on the stage flanks or a place in the degrees on the stage balcony were the most costly at 2*s.* or more, followed by a seat in the pit, and after that a bench in the

[4] The Theatre and the Curtain in Shoreditch in Middlesex were matched by a playhouse a mile south of the Thames in Surrey at Newington Butts. Two playhouses for boy companies, at St Paul's and the Blackfriars, in city precincts that were free from the Lord Mayor's control, were also opened in these two years.

[5] Evidence for the complete circle of audience at both outdoor and indoor playhouses is given below, in the section 'Unsettled Questions'.

galleries. The cheapest places were at the rear of the topmost gallery, equivalent to the balcony 'gods' in an operatic theatre. That was where Jonson said a shop's foreman could judge for his sixpence. The close proximity to the stage of the Globe's understanders inevitably made the amphitheatres much more populist as venues than the roofed theatres where the cheapest seats were six times the Globe's price for the yard.

The Skeleton and its Decoration

The Theatre's twenty-sided skeleton of framing timbers gave the Globe a frame that might have been as much as 99 feet in outside diameter. Calculations from the few fragments of the underground remains that the Museum of London archaeologists uncovered in 1989 suggested a shape of a size matching up quite well with the dimensions in a drawing that Wenceslaus Hollar made in the 1630s of the second Globe (Figure 11.4).[6] Since the second Globe was said in a legal document of 1634 to have been built on the foundations of the first Globe, a close agreement between the interpretation of the remains and Hollar's careful drawing is fairly persuasive. Nonetheless, since the size of the Rose, the only early playhouse of which more than half has been excavated, makes its dimensions at 73 feet markedly smaller—in fact small enough to fit inside the yard of a 99-feet diameter Globe—this interpretation of the Globe's original size has been questioned. It is possible that the new Globe in Southwark, with its design based on an interpretation of the evidence that indicates twenty sides with a 100-feet diameter, is larger than the original Globe. In the absence of a more complete excavation of the original remains, the actual size of the original Globe must be seen as still conjectural.

However weighty those doubts, the shape is generally clear. A twenty-sided polygon built of an oak timber frame, each beam a foot square and up to 30 feet in height, was erected on a brick foundation rising a foot or more above the surface level of Southwark's marshy ground. Twenty gallery bays, each measuring roughly 12 feet 6 inches long centre to centre and 9 feet wide between the outer and the inner walls, created the main seating space.[7] The walls within the oak structure were infilled by crisscrossing oak laths and plugging the façade inside and out with lime plaster. The exterior walls were probably limewashed, as were the interior walls facing the yard. The yard itself was surfaced in rough Elizabethan concrete, probably the mix of cinders, ash, and hazelnut shells sold as a by-product of Southwark's soap factories (Orrell 1992). The gallery roofing was thatched, and the whole interior decorated

[6] Analysis of the archaeology of the Globe appears in Mulryne and Shewring (1997: 41). The findings are described more fully in the section 'The Archaeology and Dimensions'.

[7] From the evidence of the Rose excavation and the Fortune contract, it seems the size of the bays at the Rose, the Globe, and the Fortune was almost identical. See Orrell (1997*a*: 59, 64).

Figure 11.2 The Theatre, from an engraving by Abram Booth, *The View of the Cittye of London from the North towards the South*, 1600.

The engraving shows a tall structure with what have been identified as two stair turrets on its flanks. If it shows the Theatre, as most scholars believe it does, it was drawn by 1597, a year or so before the playhouse was pulled down to provide timbers and decoration for the Globe. A less distinct building to the right also has a flag flying over it, and has been taken to be the Theatre's near neighbour the Curtain. According to Herbert Berry (2000c), however, who has studied a recently discovered second version, the drawing was done in or after 1600 and the engraving in 1610 or later, and must show not the by then demolished Theatre but the Curtain, with another but unidentifiable flag-flying building to its right. Berry describes the engraving in detail, noting its many omissions and liberties taken with positioning and with design, and claims that some of its details depend on Norden's *Civitas Londini* of 1600.

with carved wooden statuary, probably Muses and grotesques or satyrs, as the Fortune contract specifies: 'carved proporcions called Satiers to be placed & sett on the top of every the same postes' (Chambers 1923: ii. 437). All the woodwork was painted in bright colours.

The stage, if its size and shape matched that specified in the Fortune contract, was constructed so that it projected as a rectangle of roughly 27 feet by 40 from the three south-westerly bays into the middle of the yard. It therefore had its back to the summer sun, as Hollar depicted the second Globe. Its cover, upheld by two pillars painted to seem marble like the pair in De Witt's drawing of the Swan (Figure 11.8), must have extended over the whole stage, justifying one of its names, the 'shadow', in order to protect the players and their expensive costumes from sun and rain.

The stage front, or *frons scenae*, had two doors on each side of a curtained central opening, known as the 'discovery space'. A balcony over the central opening served as '*above*' in stage directions.

The best evidence for the design of the stage and its entry doors in the *frons scenae* is the stage directions in the plays written to be staged at the Globe and its partner the Fortune.[8] Both stages appear to have had a central trapdoor, matched above in the 'shadow', or 'heavens', by another for lowering a chair seating a boy playing a god, and perhaps for flinging down fireworks to simulate bolts of lightning. The roof over the stage probably also had an opening for the trumpeter, as at the Swan, and for firing 'chambers', or cannon, of the sort that produced the wadding which burned the Globe down by setting light to the gallery thatch during a performance of *Henry VIII* on 29 June 1613. The two entry doors in the *frons scenae* were set well apart on each side of the central opening. Each entrance was usually closed by a large door, probably with a grille in it allowing the offstage players to hear their cues to enter. Both doors were used every time one player greeted another at the start of a scene, or two left separately, as Kent and the gentleman do when they are searching for the mad king in the storm in *King Lear*, and Kent says 'your pain | That way, I'll this' (*Tragedy of King Lear*, III. i. 32–3[9]).

The central opening must have been wide enough to admit a throne or a bed, as in *Othello* and *Romeo and Juliet*, and, at the Rose, Tamburlaine riding in his chariot drawn by four kings. It was usually closed off with a tapestry cloth, the 'arras' through which Hamlet slays Polonius. 'Scenes' set behind it were 'discovered', as Nerissa does the three caskets in *The Merchant of Venice*, and Volpone gloating over his gold at the opening of his play. The two flanking doors were used for oppositional entries such as the Montague and Capulet servants at the beginning of *Romeo and Juliet*, while the central opening was chiefly used for the entry of authority, such as the Duke who separates the quarrelling servants, and for the final exits in the comedies when the opposed parties are at last united. Like the auditorium, all the stage features were adorned with carvings and painted in rich colours, the posts simulating the marble of Roman theatres. Once inside the structure's plain lime-washed exterior walls, the effect on audiences must have been like opening a magic box full of colours (Ronayne 1997).

The Social Range and Places

The social range in the audiences at the Globe ran from earls to beggars. In the decade when the Globe was built, the satirist John Davies wrote that the crowd emerging

[8] A detailed analysis of this evidence can be found in Gurr (1996*c*).

[9] References to Shakespeare's plays are to Shakespeare (1986).

from an open-air playhouse after the concluding jig would consist of 'a thousand townsemen, gentlemen, and whores, | Porters and serving-men': citizens, gentry (with their ladies), and unskilled workmen, plus the women who worked with their bodies (Epigram 17, 'In Cosmum', 7–8: Davies 1876). That was the conventional listing of the time for London's typical playgoers. Plays attracted all types. In a letter to his brother of 1602 Philip Gawdy reported gleefully that the Lord Mayor, called on to press more men into service for the war, had overreached himself by first sending his officers into the public playhouses. As a result, he noted,

> uppon the Tuesday following their was a proclamation in London that no gentleman, or serving man should any more be impressed, for the weake before they did not only presse gentlemen, and sarvingmen, but Lawyers, Clarkes, country men that had lawe causes, aye the Quenes men, knightes, and as it was credibly reported one Earle... All the playe howses wer beset in one daye and very many pressed from thence. (Gawdy 1906: 120–1)

At the opposite end of the social range from this earl were beggars in the yard. As John Taylor the Water Poet reported, the Globe was on occasions prepared to admit a whole family of beggars to the yard: 'Yet have I seene a beggar with his Many | Come in at a Play-house, all in for one penny' (J. Taylor 1621, $C3^r$).

Women other than whores are less well attested, but the presence of respectable ladies and citizen wives was often noted. They were unlikely to form a majority in any audience, since women of good repute had to be accompanied by a man or a youth—ladies by their pages, citizen wives by an apprentice of their husband's. Husbands and wives commonly went together. Unmarried women would normally be escorted by male family members. The doctor and charlatan Simon Forman, who reported on four plays he saw at the Globe in 1611, went twice to the Curtain in April 1599 chiefly to meet a woman he hoped to marry. Her uncle escorted her.[10]

Distribution of the social types around the Globe's auditorium went by wealth. Earls and other members of the nobility would sit in the lords' rooms over the stage, costing them sixpence; that was half an old shilling, roughly what a skilled artisan could expect to earn in a long day's labour. Other gentry and their ladies would pay threepence for the 'gentlemen's rooms', on cushioned benches in the bays closest to the stage. In the galleries sat the citizenry, those people who preferred not to stand or to rub shoulders with the groundlings, and could afford the extra penny it cost over the minimal payment, the yard's single penny. This distribution did not prevent those paying least from taking the most prominent places around the stage. Indeed, the withdrawn position of the richer members of the audience, their removal into the more elevated seating areas confronting the crowd in the yard, may have served as a form of detachment. Since the gallery-sitters could see and hear the crowd as readily as they could see and hear the players on the stage, their more marginal position may have left them feeling more like judges than members of the crowd. There is no doubt that the groundlings were the main participants in the show. Jonson, however,

[10] For a more detailed comment on the routine social composition of playgoers at the Globe, see Gurr (2004*b*, ch. 3).

regularly called his more discerning audience judges.[11] While that was probably a hopeful description, it did suit those on the benches better than the understanders around the stage.

In the absence of clear evidence for access to the galleries, it seems likely that the lowest level of gallery was socially less elevated than the two upper levels. De Witt's drawing of the Swan shows at least two *ingressi*, or stairways, up from the yard into the lowest gallery. They make sense as forms of access, since they made it easy for the people in the yard to pay an extra penny for a roof over their heads if it started raining heavily in the course of a performance. The *ingressi* might even have been the standard form of access for the lowest gallery, leaving the external stair turrets for access only to the two upper levels. Such a divide would have a social impact, keeping the upper galleries literally superior to the lowest level. If so, the lowest gallery level was closest in position as well as social composition to the yard.[12]

Differences in behaviour between the yard and those seated are not easy to calculate. There is one reference to a group of gallants playing cards while sitting "over the stage", which suggests that inattention was not unusual in the superior seating areas. Certainly the crowd in the yard must have dominated the expression of audience feeling. The range of emotions the standers felt about what they were paying for was the most audible and visible feature of their behaviour, and the yard's reactions to the play would most easily infect the rest of the audience.

The Archaeology and Dimensions

For two centuries now the original Globe has been the subject of intense scrutiny, and a miasma of theories has swirled around its likely shape. For the first 150 years, until 1948, it was thought to be a tall octagon, as depicted in Cornelius Visscher's 1616 engraving, made in Amsterdam. This concept was best represented in designs made by John Cranford Adams in the 1930s for an octagon with inner and outer stages. In 1948, however, I. A. Shapiro wrote an analysis of the various engravings of the Bankside and its playhouses. He showed that Visscher was thoroughly unreliable, and that most of the other pictures were copies of his fanciful design. Only Wenceslaus Hollar's engraving of 1644, Shapiro claimed, had any degree of accuracy. Following this discrediting of Visscher's octagon, a fresh and positive approach to the Globe's likely design appeared in a book by C. Walter Hodges in 1953.[13] The news,

[11] See, for instance, *Every Man Out of His Humour*, Induction 160, commendatory verses to Fletcher, *The Faithful Shepherdess*, and *The Alchemist*, Prologue 3.

[12] One study of this possibility is Gurr (1996*a*).

[13] There is no hard evidence that Visscher ever came to London. He seems to have based his engraving on an old Agas map of 1572, and copied from hearsay what he was told had been built subsequently at different locations, including the Bankside. John Cranford Adams turned his octagon into an elaborate design, in a book, *The Globe Playhouse* (1942). The basis for his octagonal design, however, was

Figure 11.3 Norden's inset of 1600 in *Civitas Londini*, showing the Rose and the Globe.

An inset supplement to the revised panorama originally issued in 1593, this 1600 drawing seems more reliable than the view in the 1600 engraving, which depicts the Globe as a shadowed version of the Rose. Apart from the fact that it evidently seemed circular, or at least many-sided, and had a thatched roof, the detailing is regrettably minimal.

however, was not good. Hollar's engraving showed the second Globe, not the first, and the only well-validated illustration left after Shapiro's cull was a tiny illustration by the Londoner John Norden, showing the Beargarden, the Rose, and the Globe as tiny circles with hatched lines to mark their thatched roofs (Figure 11.3).

Some years after the disappointment Shapiro's demolition work evoked, under the impetus of Sam Wanamaker's plan to create a reconstruction of the Globe on Bankside, John Orrell produced a remarkable study, *The Quest for Shakespeare's Globe*. It examined in detail the drawing Hollar composed in the 1630s. It began by showing that Hollar must have used a perspective glass from the tower of Southwark Cathedral, 400 yards from the Globe, to make the careful tracing in pencil, from which came his famous 1644 engraving, the *Long View* of London (Figure 11.5). Orrell used an Ordnance Survey map of London to prove that the buildings in Hollar's drawing that survive today are positioned with an accuracy of between 1 and 2

discredited only six years later by I. A. Shapiro (1948). C. Walter Hodges set a new ball rolling in 1953, with his elegant and wonderfully illustrated *The Globe Restored* (Hodges 1953), especially its second edition, revised in 1968. The principal subsequent studies are by Orrell (1983, 1997*a*).

Figure 11.4 Hollar's drawing of the second Globe, made from the tower of St Saviour's, now Southwark Cathedral, in the 1630s.

John Orrell took this drawing of the second Globe, which Hollar prepared in the 1630s as part of his general panorama viewed from the tower of Southwark Cathedral as the best evidence about the first Globe, before the archaeological discoveries of 1989, for the outline shape of the Globe, since the second Globe was built on the foundations of the first. Its double-hutted roof over the stage Orrell thought was most likely an improvement added when it was rebuilt in 1613–14. The original is at the Mellon Foundation, Yale.

degrees of arc, a remarkably exact record. Registering this remarkable precision gave Orrell a justification for using the drawing to ascertain the dimensions of the second Globe's polygon. Legal documents had already been found stating that it had been erected on the foundations of the first, so Orrell concluded that its shape provided at least a basis from which to create a reconstruction of the first Globe.

At the heart of Orrell's meticulous study of Hollar's work in *The Quest for Shakespeare's Globe* sits his proof of the general accuracy of Hollar's drawing of the Globe and its environs. He established this by locating his landmark buildings on a modern Ordnance Survey map. Checking the positions of the major buildings that survive in London from Hollar's time, he found Hollar drawing them within 1 and 2 degrees of arc of their places on the Ordnance Survey map. This was such a remarkable level of accuracy for Hollar that Orrell concluded he must have traced his images on the kind of panoramic glass that Hollar's predecessor John Norden shows himself using for his own earlier panorama. This proved a decisive argument, and gave a sound basis for his own subsequent designs for the original Globe. Most of these locations were on the north side of the river, and it has been suggested that the buildings closer to him, such as the Globe and the Bear Garden, were drawn in more freely than the more remote buildings. The evidence for his drawing of the Globe itself does show some late inked-in revisions. But in the absence of more positive evidence, Orrell's conclusion about his accuracy must stand.

Figure 11.5 The drawing for Wenceslaus Hollar's *Long View* of the second Globe.

The full *Long View* engraving (Figure 34.5) made from this section of Hollar's drawing showing the second Globe and the Hope, or Bear Garden, reversed the names of the two playhouses.

New evidence from other sources, however, is always likely to upset even the most meticulous work of this kind. Orrell's arguments appeared in an updated form in *Rebuilding Shakespeare's Globe*, to which he contributed one chapter on the Globe and another on the Inigo Jones theatre. These two chapters were intended to provide the key information about the principles on which Sam Wanamaker's project to build a replica of the open-air Globe was based, along with its sibling, a version of the Shakespeare's company's indoor theatre, the Blackfriars. Sadly, the book was launched in April 1989, just two months after the remains of the Rose had been located under the newly demolished Southbridge House in Park Street, Southwark, and at the height of the uproar about the developers' plan to destroy the remains.[14]

The necessarily limited and tentative analysis of the Rose's remains in 1989 supplied information about many details, most valuably the composition of the yard's surface and drainage, the composition of the foundations on which the groundsills holding the frame of oak timbers were set, and the material used for the walls and the thatch (lime plaster with split oak laths, and water reeds, also known as Norfolk reed). The uncovering of a section of the original Globe in October of the same year was even more significant.

[14] The debate was strenuous, and only in small part a victory for the preservationists. It has been broadly summarized by C. Eccles (1990). A subsequent legal ruling by Justice Schiemann in 1990 declared that 'interest' in the Rose and Globe sites can be interpreted only as direct financial interest, disqualifying any scholar's, historian's, or theatregoer's involvement as irrelevant. See Gurr (1992*a*).

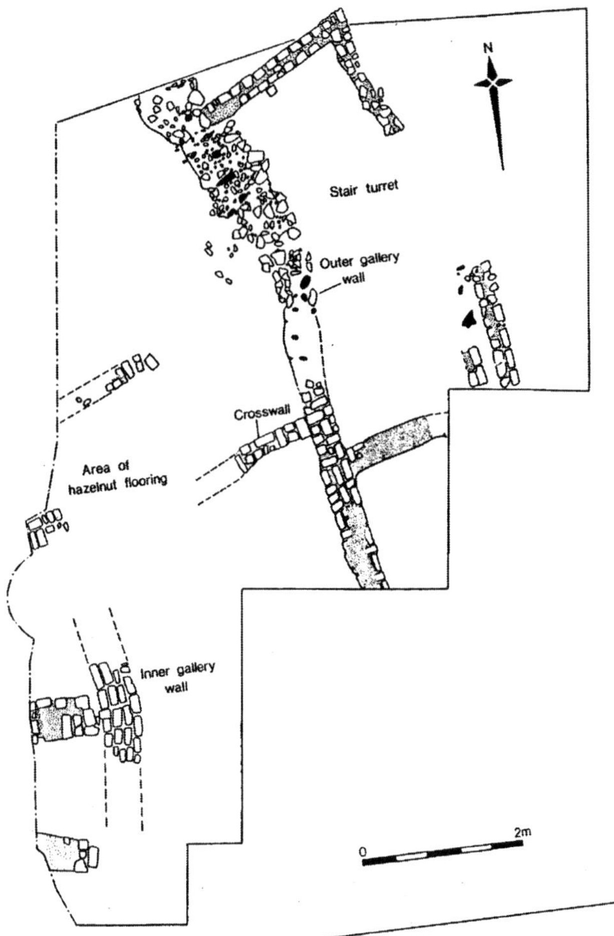

Figure 11.6 A section of the Globe's remains, all that could be excavated in 1989.

This reproduction is from a drawing of the 1989 excavation published by the Museum of London Archaeology Service. It appears to show sections of the outer and inner gallery wall foundations in an aggregate of stones and bricks, with the basis for an angled lobby or outhouse around a pillar base in the outer wall, and parts of two brick-wide corridor walls leading through the galleries into the yard. Small stones to provide a good footing in the mud were found outside this lobby, and some hazelnut shells inside the yard.

The key feature of the 10 per cent of the Globe remains excavated was the pair of angles, one in the inner and the other in the outer gallery foundations, since they gave a means of measuring the auditorium diameter. Lines bisecting the two angles should meet in the centre of the polygon, providing a way to calculate its radius and an indication of the likely number of sides for the polygon. The conclusion Orrell and others reached from this was that the full diameter must have been pretty close to

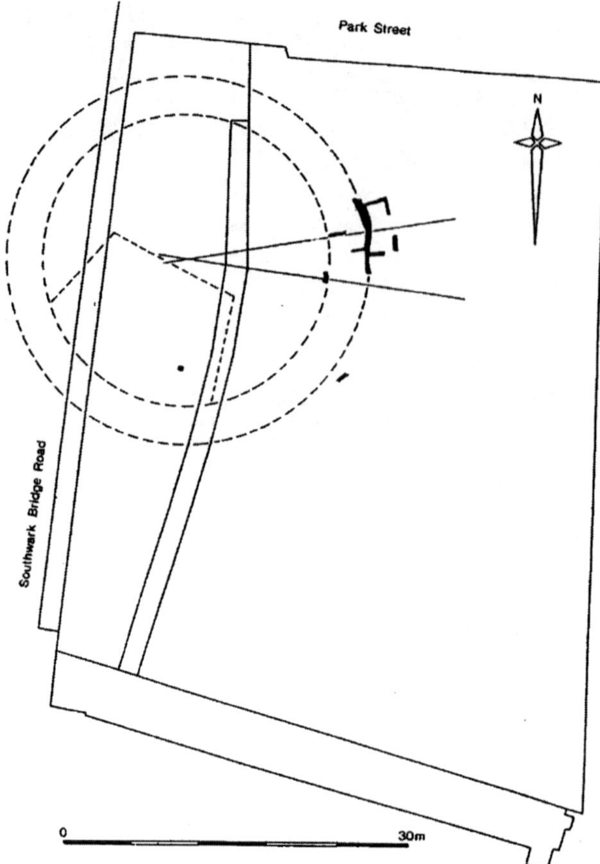

Figure 11.7 An extrapolation from the Globe's remains.

A diagram based on Figure 11.6, showing the remains and their likely extensions. By using Euclidean geometry John Orrell bisected the outer and inner gallery angles, and extended their lines and those of the few straight wall structures to identify twenty sides and the most likely radius of the polygon.

what Hollar drew in the 1630s in his picture of the second Globe, a matter of almost 100 feet, but that the number of sides was twenty, rather than the twenty-four presumed in previous calculations.

Franklin Hildy challenged this extrapolation from the archaeological evidence at a Globe seminar in 1992. He argued that the two angles and the geometrical extrapolations taken from them were an insufficient basis for calculation of the theatre's size, and that in any case Orrell's measurements, based on a photocopy of the original graph paper on which the archaeologists recorded their findings, were themselves an inadequate basis for calculation, since photocopying even from graph paper can create distortions of as much as 2 per cent. He argued for a likely dimension of not more than 90 feet, and a possible shape for the polygon of perhaps only eighteen sides (Hildy 1993). His argument was cogent, and any firm conclusions from the few remains so far uncovered by the archaeology will have to stay as tentative as they are, so long as English Heritage, which is responsible for the remains of the Globe, maintains its current policy of keeping them covered up and unstudied.

Unsettled Questions

Orrell's work, while still not substantially challenged, leaves many aspects of the original Globe's design unclear. For all the studies by the combination of scholars, historians of construction, engineers, and archaeologists who helped to design Wanamaker's new Globe, many questions remain unsettled. Among the more contentious issues, as this study of the archaeological evidence suggests, are its overall size, or rather that of its frame, the Theatre, built in 1576. Of the many other unsettled questions the chief ones include everything the archaeological finds do not touch: the shape and role of the cover over the stage with its supporting pillars, and the general shape of the stage, its balcony, and its entrance doors. There are also doubts about the auditorium entrances and the access provided by the stair turrets, not to mention the question of what the playhouse looked like inside, its interior decoration. Also we need to know more about the impact its distinctive shape had on the early audiences.

The Globe's exterior dimensions may well be the most fragile of these issues. John Orrell made a good match between the outside diameter shown in Hollar's drawing of the second Globe and the evidence that he deduced from the foundations dug up in 1989, which claim a good correspondence between the drawing and the archaeological evidence.[15] His conclusions about the archaeological evidence have been challenged, as we have noted, on the grounds that he worked from a photocopy of the original grid paper on which the archaeologists marked their findings, and photocopies can create distortions. When the original grid plan is used to bisect the angles in the foundation brickwork, the resultant shape might shrink to as little as 90 feet in diameter. This counter-claim has been supported by the archaeologists, who had measured the adjacent Rose as no more than 72 feet in outside diameter, and could not credit the Globe with being so much larger than the playhouse on Bankside that it superseded. Pending further excavation of the Globe site, which English Heritage has announced will not be made possible in the foreseeable future, the matter rests in a state of uncertainty.

Similar doubts overlie the systems of access to the auditorium. Comments on the burning of the first Globe in 1613 noted that there were only 'two narrow doors' to

[15] Orrell's conclusions are available in Orrell (1997*a*), especially the diagrams on pages 41 and 92, reproduced here as Figures 11.6 and 11.7. The fragments of the Globe's foundations locate one of the stair turrets at a rather different angle from Hollar's drawing, but the chief doubt is over the precise geometry of the angles that show the outside shape in conformity with Hollar.

Figure 11.8 Van Buchell's drawing of the Swan, made in 1596.

Johannes De Witt, who visited London from Amsterdam in 1596, drew the original of this picture on his visit to the recently built Swan playhouse on Bankside. His depiction, generally thought to be unreliable in a number of features, and certainly not a very skilful drawing, shows audience sitting on the stage balcony. It survives in a copy by his friend Arendt van Buchell, now in the Rijksuniversiteit Library in Utrecht.

escape by. This suggests that access was through the two stair turrets shown in Hollar's drawing, where incoming audiences would split, going either upstairs to the upper galleries or through into the yard and the lowest gallery. That would require, in addition to the two stair turrets, at least two forms of the *ingressus* inside the yard, as shown in De Witt's drawing of the Swan (Figure 11.8). Such a form of access would create a social division between the lowest level of the galleries, which the standers in the yard might pay to occupy when it rained, and the upper levels, which the wealthier clients chose from the outset. In turn that might identify the nature of the audiences who occupied what became known as the 'twopenny galleries' at the middle level. Such a division in the lobby of one of the stair turrets would separate the one-penny payers going into the yard from those who paid to go up the stairs to either of the upper galleries. It would fit Thomas Platter's account of the penny-by-penny payments made, ultimately to reach a cushioned seat in a gentleman's room (Wickham et al. 2000: 413). It certainly seems to suit the peculiar shape of the lobby foundation found to be part of the Globe remains, and strengthen the likelihood that the 2-ton upright the lobby was wrapped around might have provided a newel post for the turret's staircase to pivot round, as it does in so many of the great houses surviving from the time. That, however, gives only faint support to the conjectural nature of any deductions from the fragmentary archaeological evidence.

What remains least clear is perhaps the priority given in Shakespeare's time to what we call the 'backstage' locations. The great were grouped in seats or benches closest to the stage, on the balcony which we think of as 'behind' the stage, and in the adjacent 'gentlemen's rooms' in the galleries. Their presence must have been seen from the yard as creating a halo of the bright colours worn by the great, since they surrounded the stage above and on each side, while the drably coloured apprentices and artisans stood below in the yard, forming the other half of the circuit of faces and clothing. It may be, of course, that this social division of the Globe's audiences did not merely mark the differences in status, clearly identifiable vertically, from the lowly in the yard upwards through the galleries, where the superior were seated literally on high, but also registered visually its own subdivisions of one gallery level from another. If the idea suggested above, that the lowest of the three tiers of gallery was associated by its *ingressi* with the lowly in the yard, whereas the upper levels welcomed the gentry and richer citizens with their cushions, the vertical divide of the Globe's customers was there clearly and constantly, along with the opposed locations of the great behind the stage, comfortably seated as they were at the rear, facing the lowly on the three sides of the yard confronting the players on the stage.

It may be that over the years the position of the great above and behind the stage began to affect audience attitudes. All the early playhouses gave priority to hearing over seeing, but it may well be that the immediacy of sight gradually overruled the priority of hearing that the playhouses were designed for, as the staging of plays at the Globe settled into the patterns that were used for staging Shakespeare through the next forty-eight years. As time went on, the newly fixed design of the stage with its three planar entrances in the *frons scenae* may have begun to affect the basic patterns of staging, diminishing the priority of the ear that went with playing in marketplaces and inn-yards in favour of what the standers in the yard could see. The two flanking stage doors, with their obvious use for a play's opposing sides to enter by, and the central opening and its association with the locus of authority, must have invited a rather more two-dimensional staging than the old booths and their focus on stage movement to hold the attention of the masses grouped around the stage.[16]

From the time of the first commercial playhouses built in 1567 and the last in 1629, all the early playhouses were designed for hearing rather than for seeing. Seeing is best in a two-dimensional layout, with the audience, or rather the spectators, grouped facing the stage. Hearing improves the closer you are to the speaker, so a

[16] Among the many studies of what Shakespeare wrote into his plays for their staging at the Globe that came in the wake of Bernard Beckerman's classic study *Shakespeare at the Globe, 1599–1609* (Beckerman 1962), the consequences of the three entry doors in the Globe's planar *frons* are looked at in Gurr (1999).

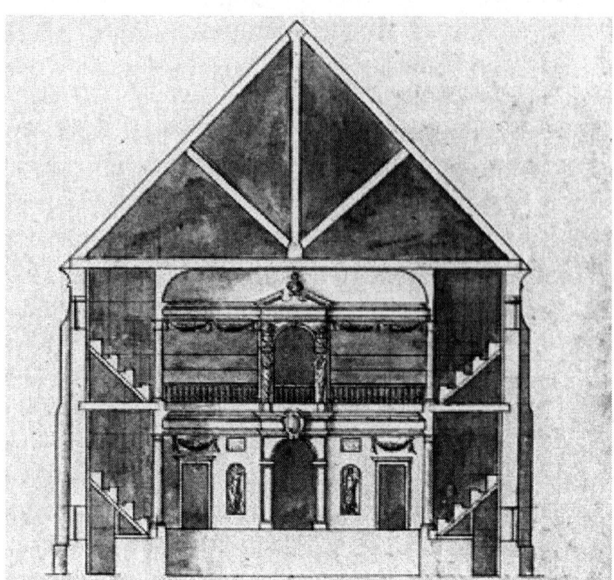

Figure 11.9 The Inigo Jones plans for a Jacobean playhouse.

The stage and *frons scenae* from a design preserved at Worcester College, Oxford, donated to the college by and possibly a copy made by Inigo Jones's assistant John Webb. It shows boxes on each flank of the stage, and the lines drawn beside and behind the central Music Room on the stage balcony represent the 'degrees', or benches, for other sections of the wealthy in the audience.

circle or three-dimensional shape provides the best facility for listeners, or audiences. Consequently, the design of the Globe and all its equivalents was basically circular, with an auditorium that completely encircled the stage. The two surviving drawings depicting the interior of an early playhouse both show a complete circuit of players. In De Witt's drawing of the open-air Swan in 1596 he drew figures watching the play from the stage balcony (see Fig. 11.8).

In the Inigo Jones drawing of a Jacobean indoor playhouse he drew two levels of boxes on each side of the stage, and two tiers of 'degrees', or benches, at the rear of the stage, on either side of the central Music Room. His allocation of seating allowed nearly 200 people on the sides and what we think to be the back of the stage. Both the Swan's balcony and the boxes and rearward 'degrees' were the most expensive places in both kinds of playhouse. High social quality made up for the lack of quantity at the sides and rear of these and all the other stages of the time, including the Globe. The physical structure of all the Elizabethan and early Stuart playhouses catered for hearing rather than for seeing. Only the royal court under James and Charles saw masques and plays designed primarily for the eye.

Audience attitudes at the Globe are not easy to calculate, but one of the less than perfectly settled questions has, for all its obscurity, some surprisingly clear answers. The fourth-wall stage realism to which European theatre had become accustomed

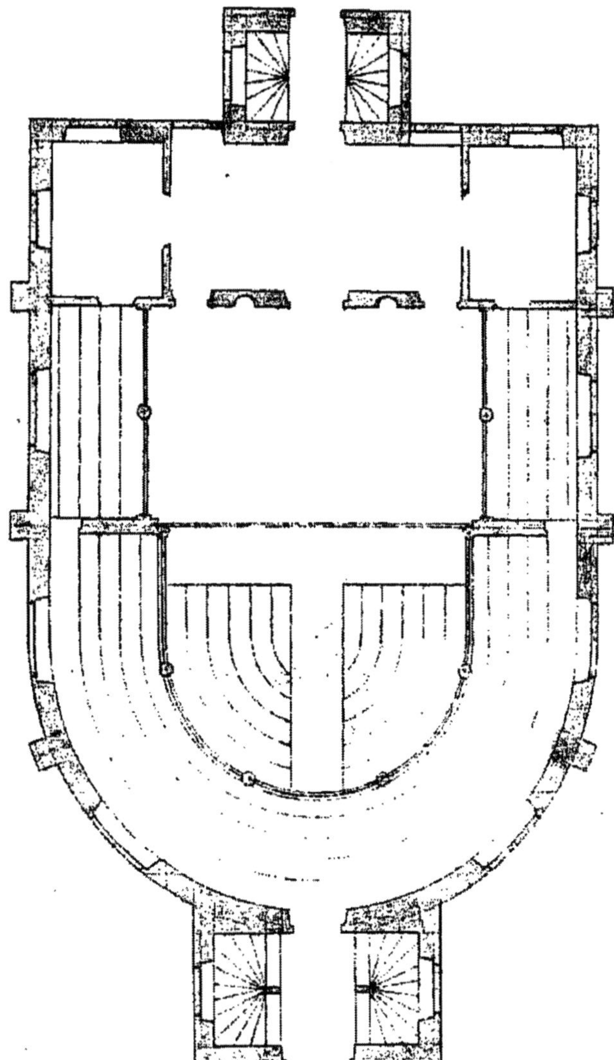

Figure 11.10 The Inigo Jones plans for a Jacobean playhouse.

Oddly to modern eyes, Jones's design sets out the pit seating in a half-circle, instead of facing the stage. Its centre is the front edge of the stage, reflecting the assumption that all the audience must sit concentrically round the main speaker's position. The usual explanation for such a curvature, that it retained the circular shape of the original cockfighting arena, is invalid if the design was not made in 1616 for the Cockpit in Drury Lane. Gordon Higgot maintains that it was drawn by Webb in 1660. If so, it must be a copy of a Jacobean design, since it was clearly designed for an audience that would surround the stage, not sit in front as in playhouses with a proscenium arch (Higgot 2006).

over the centuries up to *Waiting for Godot* was not a feature of the Shakespeare company's staging. A stage bare except for the colourfully dressed players and occasional tables or beds could never have been entirely dependent on passively receptive audiences and passive emotions. Audiences, being in full daylight and fully visible to the players, had to be addressed directly. Soliloquies were never just private musings, but confidences spoken like asides directly to the visible hearers. Crammed closely together, and as visible to one another as to the players, audiences behaved not as individuals but as a crowd. The collective emotions of crowds in public events are felt and heard inescapably. Inside the Globe the feelings of players and their audiences were an interactive process. The key difference of playing then from now derives from the distinctive shape of the Globe, a place where visible crowds could openly register their feelings about the stories they witnessed.

CHAPTER 12

THE MOST CONVENIENT PLACE: THE SECOND BLACKFRIARS THEATER AND ITS APPEAL

RALPH ALAN COHEN

A consideration of the relative fame of the Globe and the Blackfriars is instructive. The Globe is an icon of English dramatic and literary history and one of the most famous buildings in the world. The Blackfriars playhouse, the first purpose-built (or refitted) indoor theater in the English-speaking world and the most profitable early modern theater during England's biggest boom in playmaking, is neither an icon nor—beyond specialists who would read this chapter—at all well known. The reason for this disproportion in public awareness is partly the romance of the open-air theaters, partly the greater number of Shakespeare's plays first staged at the Globe, and partly the relative number of images we have of each of the theaters. Of Globe-like theaters we have illustrations of exteriors ranging from Ralph Agas's map (*c.*1590) to John Norden's (1600) to J. C. Visscher's (1616) to Wencelas Hollar's careful rendering in his 1647 panorama, and of the interior of an open-air theater we have the Swan drawing (*c.*1596).[1] We have no image at all of the exterior of the Blackfriars, and the only images we have of the interior of an early modern indoor theater are the plans for the Phoenix, the 1632 vignette of *Messalina*, and the *Roxana* drawing of 1662 illustrating what is presumed to be one of the Tennis Court theaters. This disproportionate visual representation of the two theaters has led to the conflation of our understanding of the two buildings, a conflation that has privileged the extraordinary experience of seeing a play at an outdoor theater and left the impression that going to a play at the second Blackfriars was a sort of miniature of the Globe experience. The evidence, however, from the plays themselves and from eyewitness accounts suggests a greater degree of difference between the two experiences, and gives rise to the possibility that, in terms of the way we conceive of theatrical enterprise, the combination of place, performance, and audience at the second Blackfriars was in some ways a distinct phenomenon. Accordingly, this essay will look at the place, at performance in the place, and at the audience with an eye to what may be theatrically remarkable about that mix at the second Blackfriars.[2]

The Blackfriars is the name by which a precinct in the south-west corner of the City of London came to be known because 5 acres of it were home to a Dominican monastery established there in 1275, and Dominican friars wore black robes. In 1538 the friars resigned their deed to the property and its buildings to Henry VIII, and among those buildings was a two-storey structure whose large upstairs hall had been the frater, or dining room, for the friars and which had served as a parliament chamber and the very hall in which Henry held his divorce proceedings against Catherine. In December 1576 Sir William More, who had come into sole possession of the property in 1560 (Chambers 1923: ii. 480), leased parts of the building, then subdivided by partitions, to Richard Farrant (I. Smith 1964: 135). Farrant, who had been organist to the Queen at St George's Chapel in Windsor and later Master of

[1] In a crossover from academic images to popular, we also have the beautifully illustrated work of C. Walter Hodges (1953), whose imagined Globe(s) populate a vast number of schoolbooks.

[2] On Friday 21 September 2001 the American Shakespeare Center opened a re-creation of the second Blackfriars playhouse in Staunton, Virginia. The shell of the building is a twenty-first-century brick structure that includes a modern lobby on the ground floor and on the floor above, modern dressing rooms and a rehearsal space in the basement, and a good number of restrooms on all three floors. The theater inside this shell is a timber-framed room whose dimensions—length, width, and conjectured height—match those of the second Blackfriars, and whose overall design and decor are an attempt to replicate what the second Blackfriars might have looked like. The architect for the project was Tom McLaughlin, and among the people he consulted in his design were Frank Hildy, theater historian; Andrew Gurr, then head of research at Shakespeare's Globe in London; and Peter McCurdy, the builder of Shakespeare's Globe. The Staunton Blackfriars was the project of a touring company—then Shenandoah Shakespeare (of which I am the founding executive director)—begun thirteen years earlier, and the building was a natural outgrowth of the company's mission of applying original practices to its productions. At the heart of the construction of this third Blackfriars was and is a desire to explore how the plays and how performance might have worked in the second Blackfriars, and some of the company's results provide a useful context for looking back at the second Blackfriars.

the Children of Windsor, was Deputy Master of the Children of the Chapel Royal. He leased from More the old frater that had served as a parliament chamber and two of the lower rooms, got permission to remove the partition in the two lower rooms, and, apparently without permission, tore down other partitions presumably in order to reclaim the space as a hall where the children could put on plays for the public (Chambers 1923: ii. 496). Whether he put the playing space in part of the frater or used two of the lower chambers mentioned in his lease, the makeshift theater Farrant constructed in More's building became the first Blackfriars theater.

The second Blackfriars theater, and the subject of this essay, was more certainly the frater or large upper chamber in the same building *after* James Burbage purchased the property for £600 on 4 February 1596 (Chambers 1923: ii. 503). We do not know in what condition Burbage found the room. In a suit ten years earlier, More had complained of the state in which Farrant had left the property and twice mentioned Farrant's having 'pulled down partitions' in order 'to make that place apt... as a continual house for plays' (I. Smith 1964: 46). Burbage may or may not have found that the walls had been put back up over the decade. The deed specifies 'all those seven great upper rooms as they are now divided, being all upon one floor and sometime being one great and entire room'. The fact that the document describes 'the upper rooms as they are now divided' and the use of the word 'sometime' in reference to the room as 'one' certainly suggest that the Burbage first had to do the kind of demolition that Farrant once before had done in creating the first Blackfriars, probably downstairs. But Burbage, and presumably his two sons, had something grander in mind: the renovation of the space as a purpose-built galleried theater. This they did, but before they could move their operations into the second Blackfriars, in November of 1596 the residents of the district successfully petitioned the Privy Council to ban the Lord Chamberlain's Men from performing in their new space. James Burbage died three months later, and Richard and Cuthbert had to turn for help to the actors in the company, because Giles Allen, the landlord of the property on which stood their outdoor playhouse, the Theatre, was refusing to renew the lease on their only usable theater. Together with five of the Lord Chamberlain actors, the Burbage brothers formed a syndicate for shared interest in a new theater, dismantled that three-galleried theater, took the timber across the Thames, and built a new outdoor playhouse they called the Globe. In 1600 Richard leased the Blackfriars space to Henry Evans, who was allowed, with his Children of the Chapel, the little 'eyases' Hamlet complains of, to perform a play once a week. On 19 May 1603, shortly after James came to the throne, the Lord Chamberlain's Men came under his patronage, and five years later, in 1608, the King's Men were finally able to take possession of James Burbage's masterpiece of entrepreneurship, the first purpose-designed indoor theater.[3]

[3] The most thorough account of the fortunes of the Burbage family is Andrew Gurr (2004*c*). Gurr includes many of the documents relating to the Blackfriars.

The Appearance of the Second Blackfriars

Consider for a moment the differences in background and in the needs of Richard Farrant and James Burbage, who, twenty years apart from one another, thought that it would be a good idea to use the Blackfriars building as a theater. Richard Farrant was a musician who had attached himself to the court through his skill at church music, first as master of the choristers of the choir of St George's Chapel, Windsor Castle, and, later, as master of the choristers at the Chapel Royal. In short, he had a day job, and, beyond his need for a convenient location to present plays to the court and to make something extra by charging for attendance, his interest in the Blackfriars was the acquisition of a place to house his choristers (Bowers 2004). As to his patrons, they expected the kind of show that they could see at the nearby almonry of St Paul's Cathedral, where the Children of Paul's, under the direction of Sebastian Westcott, charged admission to small audiences to see plays prepared for presentation at court. Part of the appeal of Farrant's enterprise may have been its quasi-clandestine nature, and thus not only the small size but also the unfixed nature of the venue amounted almost to a benefit. For him the idea of 'theater' as activity rather than as a locale was paramount, and for that a hall would serve.

By contrast, James Burbage, by profession a joiner, became an entrepreneur who had virtually invented the purpose-built outdoor playhouse, and he made his living by daily attracting people—in the thousands, if possible—to that building. He would not, like Farrant, be leasing the building in Blackfriars; he would be investing the earnings of twenty years in order to buy it, and moving indoors, whatever its advantages might be, meant that Burbage was going to lower by as much as 80 per cent the number of people to whom he could sell tickets. So he not only needed to acquire the largest space possible, he also needed it to accommodate as many people as possible, and he needed it to be an attraction in itself. For Burbage the place and the nature of the 'theater' as a building were paramount, and he needed something more than a hall.

The Galleries

To have a theater, not a hall, the first thing the company required was galleries. G. E. Bentley and Irwin Smith both calculate that the dimensions of Burbage's hall were 66 feet long by 46 feet wide, a total floor area of the space of 3,036 square feet (Bentley 1941–68: vi. 6; I. Smith 1964: 165). If the dimensions of the Theatre in Shoreditch were similar to those of the Globe built from its timbers, then the Lord Chamberlain's Men were leaving a space that by John Orrell's calculation was over 7,000 square feet at its ground level and moving into a space less than half that large. This drop in capacity made the addition of a galleried space and maximum occupancy a financial imperative. References to 'galleries' in the plural confirm their presence, so the question is whether there were two or three. The reference to 'my worshipful friends in the middle region' in Act V, scene iii, of John Marston's *The Dutch Courtesan* appears to support the case for three, but the word could obviously have been a lateral as opposed to a vertical description (Chambers 1923: ii. 514). Finally, the size of the investment the Burbages claimed to have made in the renovation (Chambers 1923: ii. 512) indicates that the work done on the interior was extensive enough to include a third tier and suggests the importance to the Burbages of a project that in every way possible would replicate the theater building that had sustained them for twenty years.

The Size of the Stage

We can only estimate the size of the stage. Because we have evidence of boxes on either side, we can assume the width of the stage was not as much as the 46-foot width of the building.[4] If the boxes on either side were in line with the front of the side galleries, and if those galleries were deep enough for three rows of benches with legroom, then the minimum depth of the boxes would be roughly 8 feet on stage left (east) and stage right (west), leaving a possible stage width of 30 feet across.[5] Again, the presumption here is that the Lord Chamberlain's Men would have been intent on maximizing the size of their audience, while still preserving enough space for actors and the gallants on the stage. As to the depth of the stage, the frequency with which plays require a fairly large ensemble to dance—for example, in the sheep-shearing scene in *The Winter's Tale*, where, with its 'dance of twelve Satyrs' (IV. iv. 328. 1),[6] no fewer than twenty-two performers needed to be on stage—argues for a stage no less than 15 feet in depth.[7] The requirements of the large population of certain scenes played at the second Blackfriars, the stage business such as dance and combat the company would have needed to perform, and the added clutter of the gallants on their stools, would have competed with the need to maximize audience capacity. That competition

[4] The case of Lord Thurles of Ireland brought in Star Chamber makes clear not only that there were boxes on either side but also that those boxes were probably at stage floor level: 'his Captaine attending and accompanying my Lady of Essex in a box in the playhouse at the blackfryers, the said lord coming upon the stage, stood before them and hindred their sight. Captain Essex told his l[ordshi]p, they had payd for their places as well as hee, and therefore intreated him not to depriue them of the benefit of it. Wherevpon the lord stood vp higher and hindred more their sight. Then Capt. Essex with his hand putt him a little by. The lord then drewe his sword and ran full butt at him, thoufh hee missed, and might have slaine the Countesse as well as him' (Bentley 1941–68: vi. 6).

[5] Irwin Smith, assuming, I think wrongly, that there were no boxes at the side of the stage but instead two rows of gallant stools tucked neatly to the sides, says, 'A width of 34 feet would seem to be the irreducible minimum' (1964: 309).

[6] References to Shakespeare are from Shakespeare (1997*c*). Those to *The Knight of the Burning Pestle* and *The Alchemist* are from Bevington (2002). Those to *The Devil Is an Ass* are to the Revels Plays edition, ed. Peter Happé (Manchester: Manchester University Press, 1994). Those to Fletcher's (or Fletcher and Massinger's) *The Custom of the Country* are from the Globe Quartos edition by Nick de Somogyi (London: Nick Hern Books, 1999), with line numbering supplied.

[7] Smith, citing the battles, armies, masques, and pageants of plays like *Cymbeline, The Roman Actor*, and *The Maid's Tragedy*, estimates that the stage would have needed to be 22 feet in depth, which would leave '44 feet for the north–south depth of the auditorium' (I. Smith 1964: 306–8).

makes likely a stage that took up as much as but no more than one-fifth of the square footage of the hall, and thus a stage as large as 25 × 25 feet seems possible.

Anything larger would be at odds with the many reports of gallants on stage, and we should not underestimate the crowding on stage created by the gallants sitting on their stools. Ben Jonson's Prologue to *The Devil Is an Ass* describes a situation in which actors seem to have had to act *around* the stage sitters.

> *The Devil is an Ass*: That is, to day,
> The name of what you are met for, a new play.
> Yet, grandees, would you were not come to grace
> Our matter, with allowing us no place.
> Though you presume Satan a subtle thing,
> And may have heard he's worn in a thumb-ring,
> Do not on these presumptions force us act
> In compass of a cheese-trencher. This tract
> Will ne'er admit our vice, because of yours.
> Anon, who worse than you the fault endures
> That your selves make? When you will thrust and spurn,
> And knock us o' the elbows; and bid, turn;
> As if, when we had spoke, we must be gone,
> Or, till we speak, must all run in to one
> Like the young adders at the old ones mouth? (lines 1–15)

The passage makes clear that the gallants did not sit decorously to the side during the show; instead, they encroached on the actors' playing space, seemed to resent when actors blocked their view, and took up so much room that actors not speaking their lines had but one place to stand while they waited to speak.

The *Frons Scenae*

As to the height and the architecture of the *frons scenae*, again our best evidence comes from the plays, but all we can say for certain is that it had two doors, a discovery space, and a balcony where actors and musicians could play. The unveiling of Hermione's 'statue' in *The Winter's Tale* and the discovery in *The Tempest* of Ferdinand and Miranda playing chess are by themselves sufficient evidence for a discovery space. Some evidence exists for thinking that the balcony was partitioned, especially the scene from *The Devil Is an Ass* where Wittipol courts Mistress Fitzdottrel at what are supposed to be adjoining windows. Irwin Smith takes the word 'window' literally and posits actual windows at both a second-level and a third-level balcony. However much appeal actual windows in the balcony might have had as a piece of realistic decor, professional players whose repertory rotated daily would be unlikely to have traded in flexibility for occasional verisimilitude. Beyond that, Smith seems not to have considered the possibility that audience members might sit above, where the windows would have been both a visual and an aural obstruction. For him, the '"boxes and lords' rooms" were two names for the same thing, and both were names for small compartments in the lowest of the three tiers of the galleries running along the three sides of the auditorium' (I. Smith 1964: 295). The 1640 vignette of *Messalina*, however, and the 1662 frontispiece to *The Wits, or, Sport upon Sport* show—at least to the beginning of the Restoration—that the use of the term 'lords' room' to refer to a space above the stage for prosperous audience members applied as well to indoor theaters.

Decoration

As with so much else, the nature of the second Blackfriars' specific decorative features and the general level of richness are uncertain, but doubtless the Lord Chamberlain's Men did all they could by way of paint and carved decoration to create a sense of visual opulence.[8] If Burbage and company felt this ornamental imperative for the public playhouse, we may fairly imagine that they made an even greater effort at decorative opulence at the Blackfriars where their audience was on average much more affluent and would have been in closer proximity to decorative features on the stage. The plays make references to what must have been painted features of the Blackfriars. In *Cymbeline*, for example, before Jupiter 'descends in thunder and lightning, sitting upon an eagle', the apparition of Posthumus' father appeals to the god to 'peep through thy marble mansion' (v. v. 186. 1–2; 181). In all probability, the actor was referring to the 'heavens' above the Blackfriars stage and to a painted marble sky. We may then imagine that this kind of embellishment adhered in the case of the major visual components of the space and especially, of course, of the *frons scenae*.

In addition to the lavishness of painted wood, evidence suggests that painted cloths or tapestries might have provided a more narrative sort of visual excitement as well as a different texture to the feel of the space (Ill 2007: 26). Beyond the certainty that the arras boasted pictorial qualities is the possibility that hangings may have decorated the auditorium itself. Henslowe's inventory suggests that painted cloths were within the budgets of an acting company, and, again, if the Burbages were intent on creating a theatrical destination, the precedent of manorial halls and their decorations might well have been part of their plan to attract a clientele able to pay seven times as much to go to a play.

Lighting

A visualization of the playhouse in the second Blackfriars theater must above all consider the lighting.[9] The frater of the Blackfriars was a medieval hall that in all

[8] See John Ronayne, and Keenan and Davidson, both in Mulryne and Shewring (1997).

[9] The best account of lighting in this period and the one on which I have most relied is the extraordinary work of R. B. Graves (1999). Martin White, who has experimented with candlelight in his Wickham theater, a reconstruction of an indoor playhouse based on the 1616 drawings by Inigo Jones or John Webb, provides some more insight in White (1998).

likelihood would have had the kinds of stone-framed windows we associate with large ecclesiastical buildings, and the use of the building as a parliament suggests that it must have provided a fairly well-lit room in the daytime. And it was in the daytime that the King's Men performed their plays for paying customers at the second Blackfriars. In theatrical terms they played in a kind of twilight, in its original sense of 'between light', and used candlelight in a room that probably had available sunlight. The proportions of each of these light sources no doubt varied, and those variations were the result of the time of day, the time of year, and perhaps the kind of play. Performances started no later than three in the afternoon and ended no later than six, which means that in the winter months, during the last two acts of the play, the proportion of candlelight grew, perhaps until it provided all of the room's illumination (Gurr 1992*b*: 96). In late spring and early autumn, however, the sunlight from the windows would have more than equaled the illumination from the candlelight, and at those times the artificial lighting would have been more decorative than functional. According to R. B. Graves, 'A plausible interpretation of the facts is that summertime performances dispensed with much or even all artificial light and that wintertime performances relied on a mixture of natural and artificial light' (1999: 130). Such a varying circumstance may or may not have appealed to the King's Men. On the one hand, natural light was convenient, economical, and brighter; on the other hand, candlelight was privileged, partly controllable, and more dramatic. A reference by Dekker in *The Seven Deadly Sinnes of London* suggests that indoor playing companies found a way to match the light in the room to the matter of their play when he compares a dreary cityscape to 'a private Play-house, when the windowes are clapt downe, as if some Nocturnal, or dismall Tragedy was presently to be acted' (I. Smith 1964: 302).

In short, the King's Men, had they so wished, might have been able to darken the room for effect. Part of that effect may have been to give its audience a sense of privilege by reminding them of what the artificial light was like in a court performance, and it may have been, as Dekker's quotation suggests, a tonal choice for tragedies. Sarah Ann Ill, in an April 2007 presentation of her master's work at Mary Baldwin College's graduate program in Shakespeare and Renaissance Drama in Performance demonstrated the remarkable impression the company could have achieved by the strategic deployment of black hangings. She identifies John Fletcher's *The Custom of the Country* (1619) as the one extant Blackfriars play that calls for black hangings to appear *during* the performance. A wedding feast is in preparation when the title custom of the play, that the Governor gets to have a bride's maidenhead, inspires the stage direction at the entrance of her father: '*Enter CHARINO* and Servants in blacks, covering the place with blacks'. Charino says:

Hang those blacks there,
The emblems of her honour lost. All joy,
That leads a virgin to receive her lover,
Keep from this place... (p. 18; I. ii. 3–6)

Ill suggests that in Act III, when a happy reversal of fortune helps Charino's daughter avoid deflowering at the hands of the Governor, an embedded stage direction in the speech of Zabulon, the head servant, has 'the stage reflect the play's newfound optimism':

> Be quick, be quick! Out with the banquet there!
> These scents are dull; cast richer on, and fuller...
> ...Give fair attendance.
> In the best trim and state make ready all.
>
> (pp. 46–7; III. ii. 1–2, 5–6)

Ill concludes that 'in the same hurried spirit that Charino's servants originally hung the blacks, Zabulon's whisk them away, restoring the playhouse to its familiar appearance'.

In her presentation, Ill had actors play the moment and attendants in the balcony dropped the black hangings while two attendants on the stage removed them. The entire process took less than five seconds, and the effect of having brightened the entire room was remarkable (Ill 2007: 46–8).

The visual impact of such moments owes much to the largely fixed nature of the stage and the *frons scenae*. Against that background even small changes can significantly influence the appearance of the room, and this kind of change applies as well to the use of such signifiers as torches, candles, and lanterns. Martin White describes the kind of effect that he discovered in producing plays in his Wickham theater:

> In experiments in our reconstruction at Bristol we found that even a slight reduction in the (admittedly quite dim) light effected a substantial change in the stage atmosphere, and that this change could be swiftly achieved by snuffing the wall-mounted candles on the side boxes and on the rear façade. The removal of the 'wax lights' at the end of 3.6 [of *'Tis Pity She's a Whore*] will make the stage darken further, especially as the candles have been the focus point of the audience's eyes, while the change in scene may allow time for more candles to be extinguished in further preparation for the following scene which needs to replicate a street at night. (White 1998: 171)

What might perhaps be hardest to imagine for modern readers accustomed to artificial illumination as bright as daylight is the quality of the light in an indoor hall and how little of it was necessary. To estimate the amount of candlelight companies might have used, Graves, using the evidence for the cost of the candles recorded in an article of agreement between the housekeepers and the actors at Salisbury Court in 1639, computes that the 'total number works out to about two to four dozen candles for each performance', and he adds that the actual illumination would not have been more than 'the power of one sixty-watt bulb' (1999: 129–30).[10] In short, a side-effect of the glut of light available to moderns has been to blunt the sensitivity of our eyes to the nuances of low light that would have pleased early modern audiences.

[10] At the third Blackfriars theater in Staunton, we have seven eight-light chandeliers and thirty-six sconces, all with adjustable electric lights, and our experience since we opened the playhouse in 2001 is that audiences have adjusted to and enjoyed lower levels of light than we provided when we opened. The

The Audience

The beginning of Laurence Olivier's film adaptation of *Henry V* puts the viewer into a reimagined Globe, where orange-women sell their wares, groundlings crowd around the stage, and a prompter who looks a lot like William Shakespeare sits with the book next to the door stage right. Also left and right on the Globe stage sit a number of well-dressed gallants. Though a prompter might have sat on the stage of the Globe, gallants did not. If the Blackfriars has a special place in the history of early modern drama and perhaps in the history of theater generally, the patrons around and on the stage are perhaps its most important legacy—and the one that distinguishes it most from the Globe.

The audience itself made up a large component of what one would see at the Globe. Tiffany Stern makes this point about the audience:

> Attempts are often made to find out what the hangings and carvings of the Blackfriars and Globe might have looked like. What is less often thought about is the background to plays that can actually be determined—their living decoration.

That 'living decoration' was more prominent at the Blackfriars because it was on stage, and Stern reminds us as well to think about what the patrons in their dress did to the visual impact of the performance they surrounded:

> The closed audience, as visible as the actors on the stage during performance, were more prominent than wall paintings. And the Blackfriars audience around and on the stage will have been strikingly different from the one around the Globe... In the enclosed space of the Blackfriars, shut out from the realities of daily life, everyone was warm enough to show their best wardrobe to full advantage...

Thus,

> Blackfriars plays can be assumed to have been set against a rich backdrop of colored silks, satins, and feathers.

level of light we use now, however, is several times brighter than the 60 watts that Graves suggests would have come from the twenty-four to forty-eight candles at the Salisbury Court. But two experiments we have conducted in which we used candlelight provided by twenty candles in candelabra tempt us toward reducing the light for our public shows. In the first of these two experimental sessions, presided over by Frank Hildy and me, our aim was to see how long it took the eye to adjust to low levels of light, and in the second session, presided over by Jenny Tiramani, who was the Globe's 'master of dress', to see how various materials and jewelry showed up on stage when lit by candlelight. We learned in the first experiment that, after three to five minutes, the eye in the stalls, looking at a stage lit by just three candles, can distinguish an actor's mouth moving when that actor is up to 12 feet from the light source. In the second experiment, what we saw was that satin and reflective metals within 6 feet of a five-branched candelabra seemed to pulsate in the candlelight. As an indication of the degree to which we are unused to processing information in the low light early moderns were accustomed to, both these sessions required that we drape cloth over the exit lights in the theater, because that light, not normally noticeable in the light levels we use for our shows, even from a distance overwhelmed our ability to gauge the illumination of the candles.

Stern adds to this visual image the remarkable quality of light mentioned above and paints a convincing picture of an extraordinary scene:

> The magnificent audience on entrance into the theater was bathed in strong artificial light, the quantity as well as quality of which was overwhelming.... The rich yellow flames brought out the shimmer from the jewels and metallic threads embedded in the sumptuous clothes of actor and audience alike.... lights... contributed to the unreality of the Blackfriars and everything that happened in it. (Stern 2006: 42–4)

Beyond the question of illumination, Stern has us consider the way that the fashion for feathers—particularly in the Blackfriars district, which was famous for its feather makers and merchants—might have added a surreal element to the scene as the actors in the midst of a plumed audience performed on a stage 'framed by feathers' (2006: 42–3).

This audience also affected the scene in another way—by the force and energy of their mass in the chamber. Estimates of the size of the audience at the second Blackfriars range from 558 (Wallace 1912) to 955 (Harbage 1941), and a consideration of what those numbers would have meant in terms of the feeling in the room is worthwhile. The Royal Shakespeare Company's Swan theater, for example, is larger by 10 feet in every direction than the second Blackfriars. Using Smith's estimate of the height of the room as 38 to 40 feet (I. Smith 1964: 292), the second Blackfriars had 115,368 cubic feet compared to the current Swan's 204,288. The seating capacity of the current Swan theater (now under renovation in the RSC's remodeling of its theaters) is 450, and a full house there certainly has a great deal of human energy. By comparison, the second Blackfriars would have had as many as twice the number of people in half the volume. In thinking about the second Blackfriars, about its attraction, its productions, and its general level of excitement, one should imagine the visual effect on the energy of so many people in that contained space. In this respect, the second Blackfriars was news. The addition of the tiers to the old Blackfriars hall in 1596 gave it a feature that no other indoor playing space to that time would have offered. Since none of the successive Jacobean and Caroline theaters held as many people, the kinetics of this number of people in multi-level indoor space would remain a feature unique to the second Blackfriars.[11]

[11] The actors' experience at the Blackfriars playhouse in Staunton speaks to the influence that the 'pressure' of human mass has on the shows in a tiered timber room. This third Blackfriars presently has but two tiers, and yet a full house palpably changes the feeling in the room. Standees in the back of both tiers create the impression of a wall of faces, and audience members sitting on the front rows of the second tier, who inevitably lean on the railings and look down at the stage, together with patrons in the Lords' Room above, who are looking down on the action, serve as a directional focus for the entire house. The numbers themselves (we have 310 marked spaces on our benches, but with standees, we have had as many 360 in the house, and on several occasions for school matinees where we can squeeze students onto benches, we have had over 400) create a bodily excitement off which our actors (who are sharing the same light as the actors) feed. What is more, we have found—somewhat counter-intuitively—that the larger the numbers in the space, the greater is the overall sense of attentiveness in the room.

The Experience of the Second Blackfriars

Patrons at the second Blackfriars, then, may have gone there in part because the theater held unusual visual appeal for audiences, an appeal that in some ways separated it from the attraction of the Globe and other outdoor venues. While they were there, they found other ways in which the experience of a play at the second Blackfriars theater may have been different. Certainly one attraction of the indoor theaters, as I suggest above, was the sense of social status implicit even in the term 'private playhouse'. Audiences at the first and second Blackfriars went there in part because its cost and its patronage made it a status symbol; there they would be the 'in crowd' in both senses of the word. The evidence of the plays and of references to attendance at the second Blackfriars is that going to a play provided an event for audiences that was more varied, more social, and more self-aware than plays at the Globe and other outdoor theaters had been, or, in some important respects, could ever be.

Interludes: 'Play Music'

Plays at the second Blackfriars had intervals between acts, in part to allow time to trim the candles. These breaks in the action would obviously have interrupted and thus shifted the attention of the audience from the play. During the interlude, music and dancing not necessarily connected to the matter of the play meant not only that audiences would have a break from the dramatic narrative at hand but also that the shift in their attention was sanctioned by the authority of the producing company. On one level, these brief entertainments, in diverting the attention of the audience away from the business of the play, were merely providing time for the trimming of the candles, but on another level they signaled that an audience could and should look elsewhere for engagement while they were at the Blackfriars. Of course, one place they were to look was above at the musicians' gallery, where an ever more popular orchestra was making the second Blackfriars celebrated for its music. G. E. Bentley quotes as evidence for the prominence of music at the second Blackfriars the memoirs of Bulstrode Whitelocke, in which he describes how an air he had written was played 'by the Blackfryars Musicke, who were then esteemed the best of common musitians in London' (Bentley 1941–68: vi. 32–3).[12] As Bentley points out, the tradition associating the Blackfriars with good music began with the boys who played

[12] Bentley also quotes the remark of Richard Ligon in *A True and Exact History of the Island of Barbados* that they wished 'to send for the Musick, that were wont to play at the *Black Fryars*, and to allow them a competent salary, to make them live as happily there, as they had done in *England*' (1941–68: vi. 33).

there before the King's Men reclaimed the space. In whatever ways they preserved that tradition, the King's Men may have also been claiming for their new theater some of the privilege associated with the royal choristers and the audiences who had patronized them. One way that the plays proper seem to have asserted a connection with the court was in the incorporation of more dance- and masque-like spectacle, a development clear in Shakespeare's *Winter's Tale*, *Tempest*, and *Henry VIII*.

This diffusion of attention added up to an event that was necessarily more about the audience than an uninterrupted play would have been. Such a shift would have increased the audience's self-awareness in a number of ways. To begin with, the break with the dramatic narrative provided a moment for critical response, a moment when those spectators who were not already letting others know how they felt about the play might 'officially' do so, even in a word or a look. The contrast, too, between the entertainment that was—the play—and the entertainment that interrupted it—the interlude—would inevitably invite comparison, however subconsciously. Thus, the intervals would stimulate in audience members the critical reaction that Ben Jonson among others complained of so bitterly and take them mentally out of the play proper while heightening their consciousness of themselves. This heightened audience awareness of its own presence and importance at the play is the main feature of the Blackfriars experience, and the company took advantage of this distinction to an extraordinary degree.

Meta-theatrics

The King's Men capitalized on this emerging audience gestalt by occasionally producing plays that reminded the audience that they were at the Blackfriars, and Shakespeare wrote two plays that traded on the history of the building. Consider the reverberations of the divorce proceedings of Catherine of Aragon in *The Winter's Tale* and later, of course, in *Henry VIII*. In the earlier play, Leontes puts on trial 'a great king's daughter' who is forced to 'talk for life and honor fore | Who please to come and hear' (III. ii. 37–40). Perhaps no one made a connection between Perdita and Elizabeth nor saw in the Oracle any rebuke of a Henry whose successive marriages seemed doomed and who left behind a sickly son, but surely there was some frisson, some awareness that 'it happened here in this very room', when the Officer in Act III, scene ii, announced:

> It is his highness' pleasure
> That the Queen appear in person here in court. Silence! (lines 8–9)

But if the King's Men were only glancing at the history of their indoor theater with their production of *The Winter's Tale* and its trial of a good queen, they were quite baldly doing so in Act II, scene iv, of *Henry VIII*, which re-creates the divorce proceedings against Catherine that took place in the chambers that had become the second Blackfriars theater. This, of course, is the play whose presentation on 29 June 1613 ended in the fire that burned down the Globe. Whether the company had previously staged the play at the Blackfriars is doubtful; the play 'had beene acted not passinge 2 or 3 times before'[13] and the company would likely have moved to its summer quarters at the Globe before they premiered the show. What seems certain is that the company planned to stage *Henry VIII* (*All Is True*) at the Blackfriars and take advantage of the historical connections to the events in the play. King Henry himself provides what amounts to a promotion for the company's theater:

The most convenient place that I can think of
For such receipt of learning is Blackfriars;
There ye shall meet about this weighty business. (II. ii. 137–9)

The inevitable result of such a reminder to the audience is to see themselves at a historical event, to imagine themselves in the place of the court, and to have their awareness of being in a specific place among a particular crowd take equal precedence with fictive narrative before them.

This kind of meta-theatrics works in a different way in *The Alchemist*, which Ben Jonson sets in the district of the Blackfriars and makes the contemporary setting crucial to the business of the play:

T he sickness hot, a master quit, for fear,
H is house in town, and left one servant there;
E ase him corrupted, and gave means to know
A cheater, and his punk; who, now brought low,
L eaving their narrow practice, were become
C ozeners at large; and, only wanting some
H ouse to set up, with him they here contract,
E ach for a share, and all begin to act.
M uch company they draw, and much abuse,
I n casting figures, telling fortunes, news,
S elling of flies, flat bawdry with the stone,
T ill it, and they, and all in fume are gone.

(The Argument, 1–12)

The Blackfriars, a liberty of the City and safe from a variety of City ordinances, was in fact a hotbed of the kind of activity that the play depicts, and the play's three explicit reminders that the audience is close to the action would certainly have occasioned some enjoyable self-awareness. In the first act, during their argument, Subtle, in answer to Face's rhetorical question 'Who am I?' says,

you were once (time's not long past) the good,
Honest, plain, livery-three-pound-thrum; that kept
Your master's worship's house here in the Friars (I. i. 15–18)

and 110 lines later Doll, referring to the feather trade in the district, tells Face his is

a whoreson, upstart, apocryphal, captain
Whom not a Puritan in Blackfriers will trust
So much, as for a feather!

[13] Henry Bluett, in M. J. Cole (1981: 352).

Andrew Gurr has suggested that the play's self-reference is more specific than its setting in that general locale. He posits the possibility that the usurpation of Lovewit's house by Face, Subtle, and Doll glances at the occupation of the theater from the time that Henry Evans leased it for the Children of the Chapel in September of 1600 until the lease returned in 1608 to Burbage and the King's Men (Gurr 2004*c*: 116–17).

The Blackfriars children themselves had already brought this tradition of theatrical self-reference at the second Blackfriars to its zenith in Francis Beaumont's *The Knight of the Burning Pestle* (1607). The premise of the play is the interruption of a production of 'The London Merchant' at the second Blackfriars by two citizen playgoers, George and Nell, who spend the entire show bullying the boy actors, criticizing the work of the author, and commenting to the audience. At its foundation is the idea that the playgoing enterprise is inextricably connected to its audience, that the theatrical event itself is contingent on their pleasure, and that their pleasure or their displeasure will be constantly on display. But *Pestle* also suggests the extent to which the Blackfriars might have shifted the nature of the theatrical event from the primarily presentational mode that obtained in the outdoor theaters toward the partially social. Nell's comments to the gentlemen in the audience ('Now I pray, gentlemen, what good does this stinking tobacco do you? Nothing I warrant'; I. ii. 137–8), as well as the Boy's apologies for the disruption ('It is not our fault, gentlemen'; IV. i. 53–4), are separated from the audience by fewer degrees than those of the Chorus in *Henry V*. In the former, the collective experience of being part of an audience at the play ('On your imaginary forces work'; Prologue, 18) at times takes precedence over the generalized subject matter in the play; in the latter, the Chorus, like so many prologues, acknowledges the audience in a way that subordinates them to the business of the play. This shift seems almost certainly the consequence of a literal mingling of actor and audience on the Blackfriars stage.

The narrowed demographic, moreover, of the audience at the Blackfriars made possible a more direct mirroring of the audience.[14] While an audience at the Rose was able, if it wished, to see itself in plays like *The Shoemaker's Holiday*, an audience at the Blackfriars seeing *The Devil Is an Ass* had no choice but to see itself when Fitzdottrel boasts he is going to the Blackfriars to see a play called 'The Devil Is an Ass'. And Middleton similarly constrains his audience to look in the mirror when he calls his play *Your Five Gallants*. Indeed, the King's Men's move to the Blackfriars may help explain why Jonson revised *Every Man in His Humour*, written for the Curtain, from its generalized Florentine setting to a carefully imagined London. The characters who people that play, ranging primarily from would-be gentry to gentry, would certainly have found their counterparts in the audience with them at the second Blackfriars.

Taken together the distinguishing characteristics of the second Blackfriars—its historic and royal associations, its tiered and crowded volume, its mixture of real light and candlelight, its interludes with their alternative entertainments, its

[14] Andrew Gurr (2004*b*) and Ann Jennalie Cook (1981) discuss the shift in audience that followed when the King's Men took possession of the Blackfriars.

intermingling on stage of actors and audience, its narrowed demographic—made for an unprecedented interpenetration of the fictive and the social worlds. This emerging aesthetic of plays bound inextricably to their audiences would persist through the Restoration, where the diary entries of the inveterate playgoer Samuel Pepys reveal a gaze at least as attached to the audience as to the play.[15] In the eighteenth century Hogarth's illustrations of *The Beggar's Opera* show that the tradition established at the first and second Blackfriars continued. Audience members crowd the scene on stage left and right in a way that makes it difficult to tell who is in the play and who is at the play. This physical intrusion by the audience into the world of the play and the mingling of patron with performer is the legacy of the second Blackfriars, where privileged society, perhaps in mimicry of the interaction at court masques, competed for the stage.

But while the court masque may have helped to inspire expectations of a mingled social and theatrical experience at the Blackfriars and in later English theaters, the work of Inigo Jones and the other scenic innovators in designing lavish *mise-en-scènes* for the masque had also engendered a competing aesthetic, one in which technological advances would privilege the capacity of theater to create the illusion of different and separate worlds, and in that aesthetic the visual presence of the audience would become a hindrance. By the end of the nineteenth century, the curtained proscenium arch and the darkened theater audience had all but extinguished the idea of theatrical events like those that took place at the Blackfriars that mingled performance and social presence. The idea, however, of such events survived in a romanticized image of the Globe, and other of the early modern London amphitheaters, where the transaction between audience and performance, though present, was but a prelude to the theatrical world of the second Blackfriars.

[15] Pepys's entry on Saturday 27 December 1662 is typical: 'after dinner with my wife to the Duke's Theatre, and saw the second part of "Rhodes", done with the new Roxalana; which do it rather better in all respects for person, voice, and judgment, then the first Roxalana. Home with great content with my wife, not so well pleased with the company at the house to-day, which was full of citizens, there hardly being a gentleman or woman in the house; a couple of pretty ladies by us that made sport in it, being jostled and crowded by prentices' (Pepys 1662).

CHAPTER 13

THE RED BULL PLAYHOUSE

MARK BAYER

PERHAPS the most well-known event ever to occur at the Red Bull, and the incident that has most forged that playhouse in the dramatic history of the period, was not a play at all, and did not even occur at that theater. In 1617 the Servants of Queen Anne, the resident theatrical troupe who had enjoyed over a decade playing at the Red Bull, a large amphitheater-style theater erected in what had previously been an inn in the north-west suburb of Clerkenwell, moved to the Cockpit, a significantly more intimate and highbrow private theater in Drury Lane. Many in the community, including many whom we can reasonably assume were frequent playgoers, reacted violently and vociferously. A letter of 5 March from the Privy Council to the Lord Mayor and Aldermen reports that the previous day, Shrove Tuesday, 'a Rowte of lewde and loose p[er]sons Apprentices, and others' committed 'tumultuous outrages... in attempting to pull down a Playhowse belonging to the Queenes Ma[ts] Servants'. Their attempts were not unsuccessful, as a letter of 8 March confirms: 'Though the fellows defended themselves as well as they could, and slew three of them with shot, and hurt divers, yet they entered the house and defaced it, cutting the players' apparel into pieces, and all their furniture, and burnt their play-books, and did what other mischief they could' (Bentley 1941–68: i. 161–2).

Apparently the rioters gathered at the Fortune, another theater in nearby Finsbury, and moved to the Cockpit with a clear design to cause damage to the newly occupied playhouse. The group was large, homogeneous, organized, and intent on achieving their goals. The next day, a contemporary writes:

> the prentizes... to the nomber of 3. or 4000 comitted extreame insolencies... a Justice of the Peace coming to appease them, while he was reading a Proclamation, had his head broken

with a brick batt. Th'other part, making for Drury Lane, where lately a newe playhouse is erected, they besett the house round, broke in, wounded divers of the players, broke open their trunckes & what apparrell, bookes, and other things they found, they burnt & cutt in peeces. (Bentley 1941–68: vi. 54)

The sheer number of apprentices involved in this altercation proved a force too large for either the players or the municipal authorities to deter, and the fact that plays were not presented at the Cockpit for several months suggests that the attack sufficiently registered their grievances. Indeed, the crowd was so animated by the prospect of the removal of dramatic entertainment from the Red Bull that a year later rioters planned a similar demonstration, seeking this time to target both the Red Bull and the Cockpit. In the end history did not repeat itself, and further damage was prevented when authorities received word of their intentions (Bentley 1941–68: ii. 220).[1]

What can this highly violent altercation tell us about the Red Bull playhouse, the plays performed there, and its place within the broader London theatrical industry? Based on this evidence, the repertory of the theater, and random comments from contemporaries, historians have, quite naturally, concluded that the theater was a 'citizen' playhouse, specializing in bombastic drama that appealed to a certain type of playgoer who sought action, heroic spectacle, and a broad style of acting rather than intellectually sophisticated entertainment and satire (Butler 1984*a*: 181–4; Bentley 1941–68: vi. 238–47; Gurr 1987: 189–96). As the actions of the rioters suggest, Red Bull audiences were remarkably loyal, making that theater one of the most popular and most notorious playhouses in early modern London until their closure in 1642 and even beyond into the Restoration. While I don't wish to challenge many of these long-standing assumptions concerning this playhouse, I do want to cast them in a slightly different light. Is it wholly correct to attribute the playhouse's success solely to its repertory or to the company of players that performed there? What, in other words, were Red Bull audiences loyal to? Although in 1612 William Turner draws a rather sharp distinction between 'the players of the bankside... [who] will teach... idle tricks of love' and the Red Bull where they 'play the man', the repertory wasn't really as 'masculine' as this quotation might lead us to believe; many plays performed there highlight the exploits of women, even showing how women's agency offers a form of resistance to the exploitation of tradesmen by their social superiors in Dekker's *Match Me in London* (*c.*1611). And while it is certainly true that a disproportionate number of the plays performed there depict the heroic actions of larger than life figures punctuated by innovative special effects, the Red Bull also staged numerous comedies and even such subtle tragedies as Heywood's *Rape of Lucrece* (1607). Finally, unlike the Globe and Blackfriars, where the same relatively stable

[1] Accounts of this event, its motivations, and its aftermath range from issues of cost and distance (Gurr 1987: 175–82), a breach of the moral economy of the community (Bayer 2001), as well as the suggestion that the altercation had little to do with playing at all, but that 'rather than regular patrons, [the apprentices] behaved like outcasts, raging against expensive pleasures denied to them' (A. Cook 1981: 252–3).

company of actors was resident for over forty years, the Red Bull experienced a much higher turnover in personnel, suggesting that it would be difficult for audiences to remain loyal to actors or troupes who frequently moved back and forth between various other venues (Gurr 1996*b*: 438).

In order to assess the popularity and longevity of this playhouse, and to delineate its place in the early Stuart theatrical market, I want to try to move beyond the generalizations that have too often been the source of its reputation. I wish to suggest here that the Red Bull's popularity probably had as much to do with the social niche that the playhouse occupied for many Londoners for whom the theater was more than a venue to witness staged drama, but a source of mutual conviviality and shared meaning, a comfortable and familiar public forum to interact with fellow citizens. In trying to understand the drama staged there within the broader patterns of London social life and the recreational habits of the capital's artisans and apprentices, it is my hope that we can attempt to understand the playhouse from the perspective of those who attended it, not simply generically as a 'citizen' playhouse that staged popular yet largely forgettable drama, but as an important part of the social life of London and its northern suburbs, especially for artisans and apprentices whose entertainment options were limited by issues of cost and mobility.

The rioters are a good place to begin this discussion because their chief motivation was not the eradication of theatrical entertainment generally, but the loss of the Red Bull specifically as a regular venue for staged drama. Playgoers, after all, had several other options readily available when the Red Bull closed. The Fortune, only a few hundred yards distant, continued to perform plays, including many that were remarkably similar in form and content to those staged at the Red Bull. Audiences particularly enamored with productions staged at the Red Bull could even witness the same company performing many of the same plays at the Cockpit, even though the distance, higher price, and markedly different social setting would have been a significant deterrent to most of those who had previously attended the Red Bull. Neither was this riot, like some others in Jacobean England, simply the release of youthful aggression or an expression of displeasure with playgoing in general (Manning 1988: 202–3). Although they gathered at the Fortune, the rioters did not attempt to damage that theater, nor was there any evidence of violence directed at any persons other than those belonging to Queen Anne's Men, suggesting that for one reason or another the Cockpit and the Red Bull were of special interest. Finally, this group was not an anonymous or irrational mob: it was composed mainly of law-abiding apprentices rather than criminal 'masterless men'. The actions of the rioters, then, seem to have been motivated by their more specific dissatisfaction with the Queen's Men, who they thought to be abandoning the Red Bull, and, in a real sense, a betrayal of trust for the playgoers who relied on it for recreation and social bonding.

Several well-known contemporary references to the Red Bull, many of them disparaging, tend to confirm that the playhouse did attract a disproportionately large number of tradesmen and apprentices, and specialized in the bombastic spectacle and ridiculous farce that this group of playgoers probably tended to prefer. Allusions to the 'terrible teare throats' who acted there (by Edmund Gayton in 1654) and the 'musty phrases' and 'lame blank verse' that they so ardently recited (by Leonard Digges in 1623 and Peter Heylyn in 1621, respectively) are so frequently repeated in more recent discussions of the period that they have become normative for our understanding of the theater (quoted in Gurr 1987: 234–5, 251). Satire, too, was frequently directed at that theater. The clown in Thomas Tomkis's *Albumazar* (*c.*1614) mocks apprentices who, apparently, attempt to impress women 'with complements drawne from the plaies I see at the Fortune and the Red Bull, where I learne all the words I speake and understand not' (C4^{v}–D1^{r}). Such derogatory comments extend from what was happening onstage to those who witnessed the action. Thomas Carew alludes to 'the men in crowded heapes that throng | To that adulterate stage' (quoted in Gurr 1987: 238), while James Wright, looking back at the period 'before the wars', lists 'The Red Bull at the upper end of St. John Street', along with the Fortune, as theaters 'mostly frequented by citizens, and the meaner sort of people' (Wright 1699, B3^{r}). These comments certainly tell us something about the demographic of the Red Bull and its repertory, but more than this, they illustrate how the dramatic history of this playhouse has predominantly been written from 'above', by those of a decidedly higher social status who were predisposed to look upon the venue and the audiences who frequented it with mocking derision, if not downright contempt.[2] The dearth of evidence that plagues historians of the early modern theater generally is compounded in this instance by the fact that the preponderance of commentary about the reputation of the Red Bull is written with a distinct class bias. These remarks, however, when read together with the actions of the apprentices on Shrove Tuesday, suggest that the Red Bull was not an anonymous site of dramatic entertainment for a deracinated and heterogeneous audience, but an important *social* institution for a certain type of playgoer, and that its theatrical practice might be usefully interpreted in this light. It is the vociferous acclamation of a largely plebeian audience, so widely ridiculed by some, that remained a constant at the theater, even when its management and repertory was in turmoil, and while the general character of the theatrical market in London underwent rapid change.

How the Red Bull became such a popular venue with audiences remains something of a mystery. Its origins, like most theatrical projects in early modern London, have more to do with fiscal expediency, the desires of investors, and the permission of various municipal authorities than with the social concerns that motivated audiences. The original impetus for the playhouse came from Martin Slater, an itinerant actor who sought to form a company of players under the patronage of the Duke of

[2] These five individuals represent something of a cross-section of the Stuart intellectual and cultural elite. Edmund Gayton was a physician, writer, soldier, and fellow of St John's College, Oxford; the son of the noted mathematician and parliamentarian, Leonard Digges was a versatile poet and translator who wrote a dedicatory epigram for the First Folio; Peter Heylyn was a theologian and historian, the biographer of Archbishop William Laud with close ties to the monarchy; the poet Thomas Carew, another graduate of Oxford, was an accomplished poet, soldier, and courtier; and James Wright was a barrister of the Middle Temple who could name Sir William Bromley, Speaker of the House of Commons and Secretary of State, among his closest friends. Tomkis's *Albumazar*, staged before the King at Cambridge University by the 'gentleman of Trinity College', is about as far removed from the public playhouses as plays got.

Holstein, the brother of Anne, King James's queen consort (Wickham et al. 2000: 564). Slater, who in 1605 identified himself as 'one of her Ma^{tes} servauntes', sought to find a permanent home for the company now patronized by the Queen but intended for Holstein. Along with Aaron Holland, Slater took out a lease from one Anne Beddingfield on an inn-yard that he sought to convert into a full-time playhouse at the upper end of St John Street in the parish of St James's, Clerkenwell, belonging to the estate of one Henry Seckford, a 'Tudor arriviste' and the Master of Requests during Elizabeth's reign (Tames 1999: 28; on his connection to the Red Bull, see Griffith 2001: 6–11).[3] Slater petitioned the Privy Council to lift the standing prohibition against renovations and new building in Clerkenwell, claiming that he had 'altered some stables and other rooms . . . to turn them into galleries', a petition that was supported by a document giving the 'consent of the parish' to the players in exchange for contributions of 20*s*. a month towards poor relief and an astonishing £500 for highway maintenance (Berry 2000*a*: 157; Bentley 1941–68: vi. 215–16).[4] Though Slater's petition was initially denied, after a lengthy delay Holland converted the inn into a full-time theater sometime between 1605 and 1607 and it was being used by the Queen's Men at least by autumn 1607, when the title page of Thomas Heywood's *Rape of Lucrece* advertises its performance at the playhouse.

Although locating the new theater in Clerkenwell undoubtedly had more to do with the availability of property and legal and financial considerations, the neighborhood proved an auspicious site for the venture. Clerkenwell was a growing suburb north-west of London Wall that, by the beginning of the seventeenth century, boasted three teeming residential neighborhoods around the Charterhouse and the priories of St John and Clerkenwell (Brett-James 1935: 214). The region also had a history of public entertainment, making it in many ways a natural home for a professional theater. The parish of St James's was established in 1175 and soon gained regional recognition when it was selected by the parish clerks of London as the location for the annual exhibition of sacred drama (Pinks 1881: 3; Stow 1598: 119); its rolling hills and grassy fields made it a felicitous site for these mystery and miracle plays and for other leisure pursuits. Given the availability of open land, the community was also home to sledding and ice-skating in winter, May Day festivities, 'leaping, dancing, shooting, wrestling, casting of the stone and ball . . . and [other] merry disports' (Stow 1598: 118–23), and the annual wrestling bouts held during Bartholomew Fair drew the Lord Mayor and his Aldermen to Clerkenwell.

But the success of the playhouse would ultimately stand or fall on the productions that formed the basis of its reputation, both in the early seventeenth century and in the present. Roughly coinciding with the rise and fall of the boy companies, the beginning of the King's Men's seasonal movement between the Globe on the Bankside and a private, indoor house in Blackfriars (in 1608), the Red Bull was first converted to a permanent playhouse at a time when company repertories were

[3] Slater, though mentioned again in relation to Queen Anne's Men, is not mentioned in further disputes about the property, making his claim to the lease somewhat dubious (Ingram 2002: 119).

[4] There is reason to doubt the amount of these highway payments owing to the extraordinarily large sum as well as the ambiguous wording of the document itself (Ingram 2002: 124–5).

undergoing noticeable differentiation, seeking to appeal to a slightly more specialized audience rather than the heterogeneous crowds that were the norm at the public theaters during the 1580s and 1590s, when the industry was still in its infancy (Knutson 1991: 360; Gurr 1996*b*: 138–9). It was a trend that would become more pronounced in future decades and eventually resulted in a rather pronounced bifurcation between public theaters like the Fortune and the Red Bull, attended by artisans and apprentices, on the one hand, and the private houses like the Blackfriars and the Cockpit, home to the gentry and the upwardly mobile, on the other. Although these trends obviously developed over time and were probably an evolving response to market conditions rather than a conscious strategy on the part of the theatrical companies, even the earliest productions at the Red Bull begin to signal a departure from the status quo. In many ways, Heywood's *Rape of Lucrece*, perhaps the first play staged at the Red Bull in 1607, is not unlike the tragedy staged at other playhouses. Although much has been made about the differences between Heywood's play and Shakespeare's poem of the same name (Belling 2004), the play nevertheless confronts the same difficult political, moral, and emotional issues, including the proper response to tyrannous monarchs and the conflicted subjectivity that tempts people to mortal sin even while they remain fully conscious of their own actions and their dire consequences. Yet, coincident with the 'true roman tragedie', Heywood's play also contains spectacular stage action and intricate battle scenes, comic relief and satire not often associated with tragedy, as well as 'the severall songes in their apt places, by Valerius, the merrie lord amongst the Roman Peeres' (1609, A1^{r}). These comic scenes seem to be designed to lighten the atmosphere within the theater even while the play itself moves inexorably towards its tragic denouement; they draw a firm distinction between the intrigues of the Machiavellian court and the conviviality of the commons, inviting the audience to 'be merry, | court Ladies, sing, drinke, [and] dance' (1609, C2^{r}). The play would seem, then, to appeal to those who are intellectually and emotionally engaged with the plot and its characters, while still offering something edifying and entertaining for those who attended the playhouse for more effervescent amusement and fellowship.

It is these latter images of clowning and spectacle that have come to be associated with the Red Bull, and it is these features that gradually become more pronounced in its repertory. At a time when Shakespeare's company began experimenting with a new, highly satirical, cerebral, and acerbic type of clown to capitalize on the skill of its playwrights and the talents of Robert Armin (Wiles 1987: 140), the Red Bull countered with Thomas Greene, the Queen's Men's leading actor, and a throwback to a previous type of clown typified by Richard Tarlton and, later, Will Kempe that specialized in farce, visual humor, improvisation, and dancing. If the title of John Cooke's *Greenes Tu Quoque* (*c*.1611) is not in itself a clear indication of the drawing power of Greene at the Red Bull, then surely this exchange from the play speaks to his popularity at the venue, as well as that of the type of comedy he personifies:

RASH. But what shall's doe when wee have dinde, shall's goe see a play?
SCATTERGOOD. Yes fayth brother: if it please you, let's goe see a play at the Gloabe.

BUBBLE. I care not; any whither, so the clowne have a part: for ifayth I am nobody without a foole.
GERVASE. Why then wee'le goe to the Red Bull; they say Green's a good clowne. (Cooke 1614, G2^{v})

These lines illustrate not only that comedy was more prominent at this playhouse than its rivals, but that playgoers distinguished between the type of comedy on offer at the various public theaters, with some clearly preferring the nostalgic approach of the Queen's Men well after it had gone out of fashion elsewhere in the city. Even while the King's Men at the Globe and the Prince's servants at the Fortune staked their reputation on the *dramatic* abilities of Edward Alleyn and Richard Burbage, who were capable of overwhelming spectators through their virtuoso embodiment of a title character like Hamlet or Faustus, the leading actor at the Red Bull during these years was a clown who's own humor and ability to improvise was often sufficient to steal the show.

The reputation of the Red Bull, however, did not rest on comedy alone, but, as William Turner noticed, its actors also notoriously 'played the man'. This other type of drama is perhaps best represented by Thomas Heywood's five-part cycle of plays known as *The Ages* (*c.*1609–13), which treat mythical history 'from Jupiter and Saturn, to the utter subversion of Troy, with a faithful account of all these Princes of Greece, who had hand in the fate thereof' (Heywood 1632, A4^{r}). Unlike other dramatic versions of these events, notably Shakespeare's *Troilus and Cressida*, these plays tell their story through a series of vignettes punctuated by breathtaking special effects that include fireworks, otherworldly settings that range from the heights of Olympus to the depths of hell, and stage properties that include magic snakes, the seven planets, and even the Trojan Horse, the very 'lowd clamors', 'guns, trumpet... drum', and 'dayly tumults' that, according to the Prologue to J[ohn] C[ooke]'s *The Two Merry Milkemaids*, were a fixture at the playhouse (1914, A4^{v}). Like the comedy staged at the Red Bull, it would be easy to dismiss these plays as of little lasting value or critical interest.[5] Yet they were clearly intended to substantively instruct and convey some kind of moral lesson specifically for the artisans and apprentices of suburban London who, if the numerous contemporary references can be trusted, comprised such a large percentage of the Red Bull's audience. Speaking the Epilogue to the *Brazen Age*, the narrator, Homer, suggests that the actors were

> Striving to illustrate things not knowne to all,
> In which the learned can onely censure right:
> The rest we strive, whom we unlettered call,
> Rather to attend then judge: for more than sight
> We seeke to please...
>
> (Heywood 1613, L3^{v})

[5] Many prominent critics have done just this: T. S. Eliot condemned Heywood for lacking 'the artist's power to give undefinable unity to the most various material' (1934: 107), while, even more curtly, L. C. Knights dismissed the dramatist as a 'minor nuisance' (1937: 256).

Through these eye-catching productions, Heywood and the players sought not just to entertain, but also to inform and improve their largely 'unlettered' audience in ways that go beyond a mere pleasing 'sight', realizing, perhaps, that the lavish spectacle is only a strategic component of a larger moral purpose, that the manner in which these heroic events were depicted could potentially galvanize an audience in unexpected ways.

It would be misleading to assume that all productions at the Red Bull fall around one of two poles, either farcical citizen comedy or bombastic chronicle history. Many plays staged there confront religious controversy in the unsettled aftermath of the Protestant Reformation (Heywood's *If You Know Not Me* (*c*.1605), Dekker's *The Virgin Martyr* (*c*.1620), Shirley's *Martyred Soldier* (*c*.1619)), while still others treat people and places of specifically local notoriety (Heywood's *Wise-woman of Hogsdon* (1605) and, later, Thomas Jordan's *Walks of Islington and Hogsdon* (*c*.1641)), all subjects that could potentially be a source of meaningful social bonding for the types of playgoer who frequented the Red Bull, and, in many cases, helping 'to express and reinforce a kind of plebeian class awareness' (Heinemann 1980: 159). Yet the playwrights who did write for the theater were probably well advised not to deviate too far from this norm. John Webster, whose intricate tragedies proved popular at several other venues, complained about the poor reception of *The White Devil* (1612) at the Red Bull, suggesting 'it was acted in so dull a time of winter, presented in so open and black a theater, that it wanted a full and understanding auditory' (lines 4–7).[6] The weather may indeed have contributed to the play's lackluster opening, but it's difficult to imagine the elements regularly conspiring against a play that was most certainly performed on several occasions. A more pertinent clue is registered in the author's disparagement of the Red Bull's audience. His claim that the play lacked an 'understanding auditory' suggests that Webster may have overestimated the intelligence and attention span of the audience to comprehend and enjoy such a long play with an unusually intricate plot, dense courtly dialogue, and frequent use of Latin. It would be the last time that Webster would write a play performed at that theater.[7]

Even as the Red Bull was building a solid reputation among an important segment of London's playgoers and, apparently, prospering financially, its ownership and its resident theatrical troupe were mired in ongoing legal turmoil. Under the terms of the original lease, Queen Anne's Men paid £17 10*s*. annually as well as a modest share of the profits to Holland, naming a player, Thomas Swinnerton, as the gatherer, responsible for collecting the daily box-office receipts, for which he was entitled to an additional one-eighteenth of the proceeds. In February 1608, however, a new

[6] Quotations from John Webster's *The White Devil* (1912), Francis Beaumont's *The Knight of the Burning Pestle* (1613), and Philip Massinger's *A New Way to Pay Old Debts* (1633) are taken from New Mermaids editions edited by Christina Luckyj (1996), Michael Hattaway (1986), and T. W. Craik (1993) respectively, all published in New York by W. W. Norton. Quotations from all other plays are from the first editions printed in London (dates are noted within the text).

[7] He did, however, write for the Queen's Men after their move to the Cockpit, where *The Devil's Law Case* was first staged around 1618, suggesting that it was more a dissonance between Webster and the Red Bull and its audience than any quarrel with the company that provoked the author's rebukes.

agreement was drawn up, presumably on the same terms, making Philip Stone the gatherer, who, four years later (in June 1612), sold his stake for £50 to a merchant, Thomas Woodford, who left a fiduciary, Anthony Paine, solely in charge of this aspect of his financial affairs (Wallace 1909*b*: 294).[8] This time Paine proved a less than capable financial agent. Three months following the transaction, Paine failed to pay his employer's share of the rent on time (£2 10*s*. annually), prompting Woodford to enter a case in the Court of Requests demanding not only an eighteenth of the gallery proceeds, but the lucrative gatherer's place (worth an additional 3*d*. a day), something Woodford claimed he was entitled to with the purchase of Stone's share. Woodford was never awarded any damages, and his repeated lawsuits can persuasively be read as another account of the colorful figures and intricate financial disputes that so often characterized the Jacobean theatrical marketplace (for a more detailed description of the ongoing litigation, see Wickham et al. 2000: 564–94; Wallace 1909*b*). But these disputes also attest to the popularity of the Queen Anne's Men at the Red Bull, suggesting that Holland had underestimated the theater's earning potential in 1605, perhaps believing the playhouse had grown more profitable than the value of the building itself reflected.[9] Although the courts repeatedly voted in Holland's favor, the legal expenses proved too much and in November 1623 he sold his lease on the land together with his stake in the playhouse for £100 and an annuity, a good deal less than he assumed the property to be worth (Wickham et al. 2000: 566).

And it was not just the investors in the Red Bull that were involved in legal wrangling. The Queen Anne's Men, the resident dramatic company, were also involved in a series of lawsuits that would eventually break them. For nearly the first decade of their existence, Thomas Greene, the troupe's most popular performer, was also their leader; on many accounts, he was responsible for the company's initial popularity at the Red Bull (J. Q. Adams 1917*b*: 298), and he is also listed as the payee for each of their court performances between February 1604 and January 1612 (Chambers 1923: iv. 170–9).[10] Greene, however, died in August 1612, and his absence not only left the group without their main artistic draw, but it created divisions among its personnel and exposed and exacerbated nascent financial difficulties. Salient among these was £117 owed to Susan Baskervile, Greene's widow (remarried to James Baskervile in June 1613), for his stake in the company (valued at £80) as well as £37 for undisclosed expenditures made on the company's behalf. Apparently

[8] Woodford's interest in the venture was clearly speculative; that he viewed playhouses as a 'source of easy wealth' is evident in his pattern of using the courts to recoup losses from risky investments. He had been involved in the Paul's boys in 1600 and financing the troubled private theater in Whitefriars from 1607 to 1614. All evidence suggests that he was a man of ill repute. In addition to his questionable ethics during his career as a moneylender, he was cited by the Admiralty for 'piracy', and by the Middlesex justices for passing counterfeit coin (Ingram 1985: 213, 228).

[9] That Holland would miscalculate the building's potential to turn a profit is not difficult to imagine. George F. Reynolds suggests that, because he was 'utterly unlearned and illiterate', he was easily and routinely taken advantage of in business transactions (1940: 6).

[10] There is one exception, a payment of £10 to 'John Duke one of the Quenes Ma^{tes} plaiers' on 10 December 1604 (Chambers 1923: iv. 171).

Christopher Beeston, the company's new manager, was unable to make arrangements for a lump-sum purchase of Greene's former share from Susan, and, after negotiations in June 1615, agreed on a large amortized payment of 1*s.* 8*d.* a day, six days a week, as long as the company was playing and Susan and James lived. The company did not, and probably could not afford to, live up to its end of the bargain, and a further arrangement was made in June 1616 whereby, in exchange for a further investment of £38, Queen Anne's Men would pay a pension of 2*s.* to either Susan or her son from a former marriage, Francis Browne. This agreement was further modified a year later, but litigation continued intermittently until June 1626, when the players' counter-suit was ultimately dismissed (for more detailed accounts of this saga, see Bentley 1941–68: i. 158–60; Gurr 1996*b*: 323–5; Sisson 1954).

It is difficult to determine what effect, if any, these ongoing lawsuits had on day-to-day operations at the playhouse. We can learn, from the amounts mentioned by the deponents, that the Red Bull was at least as popular as its competitors, and that, like most public theaters, the proceeds were split between the players and the playhouse owners, with the former collecting the money from the yard and a portion of that taken from the galleries, with the remainder going to Holland and his investors. Figures gleaned from the various lawsuits suggest that revenue generated by the theater amounted to about £3 a day for each group, an amount only slightly less than Heywood's estimation that the entire playhouse earned about £8 or £9 a day (Wickham et al. 2000: 565). Despite the theater's profitability, the legal turmoil was obviously detrimental to the company, and perhaps contributed to Beeston's decision to move the troupe to the Cockpit, where they would no longer be liable to the Baskerviles since the lawsuit stipulated that the annuity owed to Susan was void if the troupe was no longer playing at the Red Bull. The move to the Cockpit, however, only precipitated further crises, financial hardships, and legal difficulties. After the riot, Beeston and his company not only lost revenue from playing, but were also forced to finance repairs to the Cockpit, and absorb the cost of the stage properties, playbooks, and apparel damaged or destroyed in the altercation. The move also led to further legal action against Beeston, who was charged before the Sessions of the Peace in Middlesex for being in arrears on the company's highway contributions, thinking that, since the troupe was not actually using the theater at this time, they should be exempted from making these payments (Jeaffreson 1972: ii. 235). The final measure of the company's financial hardship during this period originated with some of its own hired men, who also took the company to court claiming that they were owed a significant sum in back wages dating several years (Sisson 1954: 63–4). It seems, then, safe to argue that the compound effects of these lawsuits and the unexpected circumstances attending their move to the Cockpit eventually broke the company, even though remnants of its membership continued to perform at the theater for years to come.

The legal and financial woes of the Queen's Men, though obviously decisive in the history of that troupe, seemed ultimately to do little to dampen the popularity of the Red Bull or significantly change its reputation for specializing in plays for tradesmen and apprentices. Although it's impossible to determine whether actors and dramatists made a concerted effort to lure this segment of the theatergoing audience, or whether the preponderance of artisans that frequented the Red Bull prompted them to fashion their repertory accordingly, the convergence seemed mutually advantageous. One could argue, in fact, that the company's woes actually solidified the social niche occupied by the Red Bull. The events of Shrove Tuesday 1617 demonstrated to theatrical professionals that plebeian playgoers represented a distinct, lucrative, and vocal segment of the theatrical market whose allegiance could be courted and whose preferences could be dismissed only to their detriment, even while this group of playgoers recognized their own ability to influence demand. The Red Bull was already uniquely positioned to cater to this portion of the audience because of its location in the city and the character of its repertory. Because its yard was approximately 13 per cent larger than the Fortune's, it also could accommodate significantly more of the lowest-paying clientele than their closest competitors, its proprietors hoping of course that volume would make up for a reduction in the marginal revenue earned when patrons sat in the galleries.[11] These larger dimensions also raise the possibility, noted by George Reynolds, that the Red Bull had a larger stage, an extra stage door, and elaborate machinery to orchestrate more complicated stage business than other playhouses and to handle the innovative special effects—especially pyrotechnics—for which the theater was renowned (Reynolds 1940).[12]

While some of the drama staged at the Red Bull during the last years of James's reign continued the proclivity towards zany comedy and magisterial chronicle history, other plays of this period call into question the extent to which its reputation was based solely on its repertory, and force us to rethink the labels that have become so strenuously attached to certain playhouses. Because of the unique circumstances attending their residence at the Cockpit, Christopher Beeston was forced to transfer plays and personnel between these two very different theaters, meaning that these productions had to appeal to two radically different audiences. One such play was Massinger's *A New Way to Pay Old Debts* (*c*.1621), which manages to circumvent the exclusionary entailments of most satire presented at the private theaters[13] by singling out a figure of universal opprobrium with which audiences of widely divergent class

[11] These calculations were made for the Red Bull based on the dimensions given on the 'Plott or Survey' of the Seckford estate (Griffith 2001), and for the Fortune from the contract with its builder, Peter Street (Foakes 2002: 302). The yard at the Globe, owing to its roughly circular shape, was larger than both (28 per cent larger than the Fortune and 17 per cent larger than the Red Bull), but the stage would have covered a greater area than at the others, reducing the space allotted to paying customers (measurements at the Globe are based on the archeological survey used to reconstruct it in 1997; Orrell 1997–8: 61).

[12] Reynolds also raises the possibility that the Red Bull might have been made of brick in order to accommodate the heavy use of pyrotechnics used in the plays staged there, especially Heywood's *Ages*. Such a possibility is especially enticing given that Jacobean building codes prohibiting the construction of new timber buildings in London and its suburbs during the years when the Red Bull was first converted to a full-time playhouse (Reynolds 1940: 171; Griffith 2001: 19). In the late 1630s several actors from the Red Bull migrated to an indoor theater in Dublin, where they brought their expertise in fireworks with them to stage *St. Patrick for Ireland* (*c*.1639), an unusually spectacular play by the ordinarily more sedate James Shirley.

[13] Most of the city comedies staged at the private theaters contain acerbic references to citizens and their pursuits. Francis Beaumont's *Knight of the Burning Pestle* explicitly satirizes the tastes of a certain type of playgoer, noting ''tis stale [since] it has been had before at the Red Bull' (IV. iv. 31).

positions could comfortably identify: the moneylender. Sir Giles Overreach is the quintessential usurer; like Mammon himself, he professes 'the art of undoing men' (III. i. 33; II. iii. 5–56), revels in foreclosure (II. iii. 4), and covets monopoly power whereby he will 'have all men sellers, | and I the only purchaser' (II. ii. 32–3). And it was not just those who were already wealthy who were implicated in this credit crunch: from the plebeians frequenting an alehouse like Tapwell's whose debts were recorded 'in chalk' on a board (I. i. 24), to landowners forced to mortgage their property at exorbitant rates at great risk of foreclosure whose economic and social status was effectively reduced to that of 'the common borrower' (I. i. 55), reliance on credit was the common denominator between rich and poor (Leinwand 1999: 43). The demise of the usurer at the play's conclusion, then, represented a wish fulfillment that could unite the artisans and apprentices of the Red Bull with the wealthy elites at the Cockpit, illustrating that, even in a dramatic market that was becoming increasingly polarized, the dream of a homogeneous audience still held some promise, even if these disparate groups were witnessing the plays at very different venues.

During Charles's reign the differences between the northern amphitheaters and the indoor playhouses scattered throughout London and Westminster become more pronounced, but again it is best to understand this primarily as a widening social fissure rather than the product of company restructuring or repertory management; 'company loyalty', according to Andrew Gurr, 'was never as fixed as audience loyalty' (1996*b*: 437). During this time, the reputations of the Red Bull and the Fortune become even more closely intertwined than in previous years, not just because both specialized in staged entertainment for the 'meaner sort', but because there was significant overlap in plays and actors at the two playhouses. When playing resumed after the lengthy closure following James's death, a group known as the Revels company was formed from the remnants of Queen Anne's Men and two other companies, all of which underwent significant reorganization at this time. Even though Beeston took most of the best actors with him to the Cockpit, the Red Bull's popularity does not seem to have diminished significantly, nor did its audience evaporate a decade later when the Revels group and Prince Charles's Men—previously at the Fortune—simply swapped venues, a move that likely entailed a change in repertory (Gurr 1996*b*: 442–3). Such shifts in plays and personnel, though meaningful to investors, impresarios, and other theatrical professionals—and significant to theater historians today—were probably relatively insignificant to playgoers so long as the atmosphere at the Red Bull, and its day-to-day operations, remained similar, again illustrating the perils of understanding playhouses strictly through legal sources and the comments of a small minority to the neglect of the audiences who were the ultimate guarantors of its stability.

Despite the administrative changes of the late 1620s and 1630s, the types of play staged at both the Fortune and the Red Bull did not deviate markedly. Even while the Cockpit and the Blackfriars competed to stage the latest dramatic fashions for their elite audiences, the northern amphitheaters in many ways defied these innovations in taste and stuck with the same formula that had brought them success in the past, offering a combination of spectacle, romance, and farce, often within the same play.

Performers at the Red Bull soon realized that even a steady stream of new plays was unnecessary, that favorites from the past—even those that had premiered decades earlier—could ensure a packed house. Reliance on old favorites had the added advantage of appealing to older playgoers who grew up with Marlowe, Heywood, and their contemporaries, while initiating a whole new generation of younger playgoers in the forms of Elizabethan and early Jacobean drama that the court and other elites had since forsworn (Butler 1984*a*: 183). Some new plays, of course, were written for performance at the playhouse, but even these more closely resembled the cherished blockbusters of the past than anything being written for the private houses. One of the last new plays written for performance at the Red Bull before the 1642 closure, John Kirke's *Seven Champions of Christendom* (1638), closely recalls many of the ambitiously panoramic plays by Heywood staged at the same venue decades earlier, and explicitly advertises its eclectic inclusion of elements drawn from several generic and dramatic traditions from years past, the same kind of 'mingling of kings and clowns' that had gone out of favor with more fashionable playgoers. Kirke writes that his play 'consists of many parts, not walking in one direct path, of comedy, or tragedy, but having a larger field to trace' (1638, A3^{v}–A4^{r}). It incorporates several features that those familiar with the Red Bull over the long term would easily recognize; its rapid movement between far-flung locales recalls *The Four Prentices of London* (1615), its motley array of otherworldly characters and pyrotechnics is reminiscent of the *Ages*, while occasional musical interludes and comic vignettes hearken back to *The Rape of Lucrece*, perhaps the first play ever staged at the theater. We're used to assuming that successful cultural institutions thrive through constant change and innovation, but the Red Bull is certainly an exception, proving that a stable audience, one that revels in the social opportunities made possible by the theater without quibbling over the content and style of the drama, is sufficient to sustain a cultural enterprise on a very large scale simply by giving patrons what they clamored for. And giving it to them over and over again.

Most narratives of the early modern theater end in September 1642, when a series of parliamentary statutes prohibited public playing and ordered the theaters dismantled. The Red Bull, however, was not demolished and remained an intermittent venue for plays and other popular entertainment even through the Interregnum and into the Restoration. At these clandestine performances, the theater seemed to cater to the same downmarket audience that had made it so popular throughout the first decades of the seventeenth century, a fact that might have mitigated the government's reaction since they did not judge the drama staged at the Red Bull to be particularly subversive. Although the playhouse was frequently raided throughout the period, the actors often escaped with little, if any, punishment and continued their almost daily performances, while the spectators, themselves officially subject to a fine of 5*s*. for each visit to a playhouse, were regularly exempted from the penalty, especially if they could demonstrate that they were, in fact, indigent. This account in the September 1655 *Weekly Intelligencer* describes a situation that must have become normative given the numerous reports of continued playing at the Red Bull:

This day proved Tragicall to the Players at the Red Bull, their acting being against an Act of Parliament ... it never fared worse than the spectators at this present, for those who had monies paid their five shillings apiece, those who had none to satisfie their forfeits, did leave their cloaks behind them ... all which their poverty being made known, and after some check for their Trespasse, were civilly restored to the Owners. (quoted in Bentley 1941–68: vi. 236)

Despite the harsh condemnation of plays and the claims for the success of the government's stern policy against actors and playgoers, the report actually confirms the failure of the authorities to eradicate playing or to diminish its popularity among a large and diverse audience of tradesmen and apprentices. Not all these performances were plays. Again demonstrating continuity with the past, the Red Bull during these years became known for the same kinds of jig and droll that earlier actors like Thomas Greene had popularized at the theater nearly fifty years earlier.

Because of the regularity of performance through the 1640s and 1650s, the Red Bull would seem poised to be at the vanguard of London's professional theaters when legal playgoing resumed. But Davenant and the other noteworthy impresarios of his era took their more innovative productions to the more lucrative private theaters, leaving the Red Bull again to stage its usual fare for the citizens, illustrating again that it seems to be the social atmosphere, comforting nostalgia, and mutual conviviality offered by attendance at the theater rather than a serious artistic appraisal of its performances that lured its spectators. Those familiar with the Red Bull tended to remark on the quantity of its spectators rather than the quality of the plays staged. Francis Kirkman's 1673 collection of drolls entitled *The Wits* differentiates these plays from those 'Dramatick Poems' that have 'so much Art and Learning ... in them' with those in his own collection that 'are but diversions'. Though he admits that this drama cannot offer 'any long learned discourse', it nevertheless packed the house: 'I have seen the Red Bull Playhouse which was a large one, so full, that as many went back for want of room as entered' (1673, A2^{r-v}). Even while the more noteworthy drama of the Restoration dealt in sophisticated social and political satire, the Red Bull continued to satisfy the ever-present market for popular entertainment for the laboring classes, and its reputation continued to be defined by its more elite detractors. The royalist playwright Edward Howard's retrospective assessment of the Red Bull (in 1671) as 'the most irregular, illiterate, obscene, and insipid plays crowded with audiences' is, after all, virtually indistinguishable from that of his predecessors (Bentley 1941–68: vi. 246).[14] Not surprisingly, then, the Red Bull ended its life with the same ignominy that plagued so much of its history, and, true to form, the last reported event at the theater was not a play but a fencing match that took place on 30 May 1664 (Van Lennep 1962: 134). The theater was probably destroyed or damaged beyond repair during the fire of 1666.

Understanding the place of the Red Bull in the large and variegated early modern theatrical marketplace cannot simply mean repeating the trivializing conclusions so

[14] Samuel Pepys, who attended a play at the Red Bull on 23 May 1661, echoed Howard's genteel sentiments concerning the quality of the performance, dismissing it as 'poorly done' and the actors as 'common fellows', but disagreed with him regarding attendance, reporting that there was 'not a hundred in the whole house' (quoted in J. Q. Adams 1917*b*: 309).

often drawn from heavily biased evidence; nor, of course, can these reports be dismissed entirely. In my discussion of this playhouse, I have followed a slightly different tack from some historical accounts of the same theater. Rather than concentrating on the physical edifice itself, as others have done (Reynolds 1940; Dessen 1984; Griffith 2001; Berry 2002), I have sought to give some account, however sketchy, of the people who went there and what the theater might have meant to them; and rather than giving a detailed accounting of the individuals involved in its day-to-day operation, I have tried to look at the plays that they performed, the ultimate point where the suppliers of theatrical entertainment and the audiences that demanded it intersect. Frequent altercations in the theater and the disputes surrounding it attest that relations between these two parties were by no means always harmonious, yet the Red Bull survived and prospered for over fifty years, and did so in a manner unique in the playgoing culture of the city. Throughout its existence, it truly remained a citizen staple, but in so doing it demonstrated the immense market power of this often-neglected group in sustaining large-scale popular entertainment.

CHAPTER 14

THE PHOENIX AND THE COCKPIT-IN-COURT PLAYHOUSES

FRANCES TEAGUE

The Cocke and the Phoenix

Among London's playhouses, none is so ornithological as the Phoenix, although the Cockpit-in-Court at Whitehall comes close. The Phoenix began as a cockpit: the Drury Lane property that was the precursor to the playhouse included 'Cockepittes and the Cockhouses and shedds' (Bentley 1941–68: ii. 48). The manager, Christopher Beeston, converted it to a theater to improve his company's profits in Jacobean London; under his management (and then under his son's) the playhouse was particularly successful before the Civil War. Performances of quasi-legality continued in the Commonwealth and legally in the Restoration, until the newer Drury Lane Theatre put it out of business. Initially called the Cockpit theater, it was renamed the Phoenix after a disastrous fire. As for the Whitehall cockpit, George Wilson remarks in *The Commendation of Cockes and Cock-Fighting* (1607), 'our late Prince of famous memorie King Henrie the Eight, did take such pleasure and wonderfull delight in the Cocks of the game, that he caused a most sumptuous, and stately Cock-pit to be erected in Westminster, wherein his Maiestie might disport himselfe with Cocke-fighting, among his most noble and louing subiects' (Wilson 1607, C3^{r}). According to John Stow, the property included 'diuers fayre

Tennis courtes, bowling Allies, and a Cocke-pit, all built by king *Henry* the eight' (Stow 1598: 374–5), suggesting a site devoted to amusements for well-to-do sportsmen. The cockpit was altered into a playhouse in the years 1629–30 under the direction of Inigo Jones and then remodeled in 1660–2. Performances for the court were given until the Civil War; after the Restoration, the theater was used until 1664 or so. Most discussions about both playhouses suggest that their original purpose as a cockfighting pit shaped the physical space.

While both the Phoenix and the Cockpit-in-Court were converted cockpits, they were not the only such London sites (Wickham 1959–81: ii/2. 45 ff.). In a cockpit, a raised platform in the center of the eight-sided building held a pair of gamecocks that spurred and tore at one another, while all around men watched and wagered. A watercolor, painted for a visitor between 1614 and 1615, shows James I watching a fight between two cocks at a purpose-built cockpit with a lantern roof.

> One [watercolor] that is especially familiar to theater historians is a view of a cock pit, labeled 'Het Haene gefecht In Engelandt' ['A Cockfight in England']. . . . Within the theater-like structure, with brick foundation and tiled roof held up by columns, are two rings of well-dressed spectators seated or standing around the table. Gold coins are in front of them and two cocks are in the middle, fighting. A figure to the left, the only one wearing a hat and seated in a chair, is almost certainly King James. (Schlueter 2006: 310)

This picture cannot be certainly identified as the interior of either the Phoenix or the Cockpit (Whitehall), of course, yet it does suggest features that each building must have had before becoming a playhouse exclusively. Specifically, the painting shows how similar game-pits (whether for bull- and bear-baiting or for cockfighting) were to theatrical stages with seating around the stage so that observers could play close attention to the contest on which they had wagered. In a cockpit, of course, the stage was relatively small, while an arena with a bear-baiting ring was more the size of a large public playhouse. Thomas Platter, a visitor to London, described one such cockpit in 1599:

> There is also in the city of London . . . a house where cock-fights are held annually throughout three quarters of the year (for in the remaining quarter they told me it was impossible since the feathers are full of blood), and I saw the place, which is built like a theatre. In the center on the floor stands a circular table covered with straw and with ledges round it, where the cocks are teased and incited to fly at one another, while those with wagers as to which cock will win sit closest around the circular disk, but the spectators who are merely present on their entrance penny sit around higher up, watching with eager pleasure the fierce and angry fight between the cocks, as these wound each other to death with spurs and beaks. And the party whose cock surrenders or dies loses the wager; I am told that stakes on a cock often amount to many thousands of crowns, especially if they have reared the cock themselves and brought their own along. For the master who inhabits the house has many cocks besides, which he feeds in separate cages and keeps for this sport, as he showed us. He also had several cocks, none of which he would sell for less than twenty crowns; they are very large but just the same kind as we have in our country. He also told us that if one discovered that the cocks' beaks had been coated with garlic, one was fully entitled to kill them at once. He added too, that it was

nothing to give them brandy before they began to fight, adding what wonderful pleasure there was in watching them. (Platter 1937: 167–8)[1]

Platter notes that the cockpit and the theater are alike and mentions the elements of violence, money, and status that recur in the history of the two theaters that sprang from cockpits. The Phoenix theater opened to a deadly riot, was built largely to enrich one man and his family, and became a popular upper-class theater under Charles I. The Cockpit-in-Court was expensively and elaborately created, provided amusement to the court, and closed for the Civil War.

The names of the playhouses can be tricky. Before either cockpit was a playhouse, George Wilson argued that both the cock and the phoenix were excellent birds:

The Phoenix is much prized of many, but not more praysed of all then the Cocke is, for the one is not so worthy of commendations for her rarenesse and chastity (which commeth of necessity, because there is no more of that kind) as the other is for his courage and constancie, who (though he hath greate societie) will rather die, then derogate from any of his company. (Wilson 1607, C1^{v})

Wilson's refusal to choose between the two birds is analogous to the naming practice of scholars, who call the theater made from the cockpit in Whitehall the Cockpit, the Royal Cockpit, or the Cockpit-in-Court, while the theater made from the cockpit in Drury Lane is called the Cockpit theater, the Drury Lane Theatre, or the Phoenix theater. A further complication exists as Eleanore Boswell points out in her discussion of the Cockpit-in-Court (Whitehall): 'The whole heterogeneous mass of lodgings, tennis court, playhouse, and chapel, lying between "the Street" and the park, and south of the Holbein Gate, were constantly referred to and even marked on maps as "the Cockpit"' (Boswell 1932: 11).[2]

As a name, then, 'the Cockpit' can describe a collection of properties as well as a structure or either of the playhouses under consideration. I shall use 'the Phoenix' to keep the first theater in Drury Lane distinct from all those other entities, and 'the Cockpit-in-Court' for the theater fashioned from the royal cockpit in Whitehall.

The Structures of the Playhouses

Both the Phoenix and the Cockpit (Whitehall) have histories well documented in comparison to other early modern playhouses, yet scholars interpret those

[1] On cockfighting as a powerful cultural site, one cannot do better than the anthology *The Cockfight* (Dundes 1994).

[2] See also Wickham (1959–81: ii/2. 45–8, 78).

documents in a variety of ways. A complicating factor is that both playhouses were renovated. Thus, when one considers what the Phoenix looked like, one must consider that the playhouse first went up in 1616–17, but was burned down, and was then rebuilt in 1618. The Cockpit-in-Court was built in 1629–30, underwent small renovations over the years, and a major renovation in 1660–2. Thus, the question is never 'What did the playhouse look like?' but rather 'What did it look like when?'

One can begin with the locations: the Phoenix was on the east side of Drury Lane. The site was long preserved by the name of Cockpit Alley, afterwards Pitt Court, running from Drury Lane to Wild Street. A 1676 royal grant carefully describes the location of the Cockpit-in-Court. To the south stood Hampton House and its garden, on the east stood the Tennis Court, and St James's Park was on the north and west. The land was 210 feet long, and the breadth varied from 140 feet at the southern end to 80 feet at the north (Boswell (1932: 21) found the 1676 and 1684 grants that describe the property).

No other Renaissance playhouse has such a rich pictorial history as the Cockpit-in-Court. One can identify it in several contemporary drawings, such as the Agas map (*c.*1561) and Antony van den Wyngaerde's *Panorama of London* (*c.*1544).[3] The Agas map shows a building that is polygonal on the far left-hand side toward the bottom of the sheet. Just below St James's Park is a cluster of buildings, and at their center the lantern roof of a cockpit.

A rich source of speculation about the appearance of the Cockpit-in-Court and the Phoenix comes from plans that were done by either Inigo Jones (1573–1652) or his assistant and son-in-law John Webb (1611–72), although scholars do not agree on whether these materials depict buildings to be built or renovated, plans that may or may not have been realized, nor, indeed, if they even represent the buildings in question. The documents were part of the library of the eighteenth-century architect George Clark, who left them to Worcester College, Oxford, in 1732 (Harris and Tait 1979).[4] In a catalogue of the collection, James Harris and A. A. Tait (1979) identify three sets of drawings. The first of these is Gotch 1/27, the plan, plan of stage, and section through apron stage or proscenium of a playhouse (Figure 14.1). The others are Gotch 1/7B, a plan and elevation for a theater, and Gotch 1/7C, two transverse sections of the same theater (Figures 14.2 and 14.3). Gotch 1/27 is believed to be for the Cockpit-in-Court, while Gotch 1/7B and Gotch 1/7C may be for the Phoenix theater.

[3] For information on the Agas and van den Wyngaerde maps, I have consulted Fisher (1981). The materials provided in various publications of the London Topographical Survey are also excellent.

[4] This work uses the numbers originally assigned by J. A. Gotch. The square design associated with the Cockpit-in-Court is reproduced as Harris and Tait (1979, pl. 5) (Gotch 1/27). The designs for the U-shaped theater thought to have been the Phoenix are plates 11 and 12 (Gotch 1/7B, 1/7C). I am grateful to Joanna Parker, head librarian at Worcester College, Oxford, and her colleague Natalia Perevezentseva for allowing me to examine these materials.

The Phoenix Theater

The latter items are the more mysterious. Harris and Tait comment that 'These two designs are not only the oldest surviving theatre designs in England, but are of seminal importance for the development of the English stage' (1979: 15), which is true under certain conditions. If these drawings show a theater designed by Jones in 1616–17, they show the state of the art in playhouse construction for Jacobean London. But if they were produced by a far less important designer, John Webb, in the Restoration, then the claim seems too strong. The drawings do indeed show a playhouse that could have been converted from a cockpit. The structure is shaped like a U with a line drawn across it halfway up the letter; the audience sat on tiered benches in the rounded part at the bottom of the U, while the stage and backstage, with an area for perspective scenery, filled a nearly square rectangle in the upper part of the U. The tiered seating in the rounded part is much like the traditional seating in cockpits, so a conversion would have simply knocked open the side of the rounded cockpit and extended it to form the U and add a stage. We actually know more about the sketch, for Iain Mackintosh observed that *The Siege of Rhodes*, first performed in Rutland House in 1656, was produced on a stage corresponding exactly to the one in Gotch 1/7B and C. Since that opera was also staged at the Phoenix in 1658–9, the temptation was to claim the drawings as being for that playhouse, although Graham Barlow objected that the building in Gotch 1/7B and C would not have fit on the Phoenix site. Nevertheless, the drawings are often found reproduced with captions, using various qualifiers or with none at all, that identify them as the Phoenix theater.

Unfortunately for the theory, Gordon Higgott has been able to identify characteristics of the inking, especially the shading, and the handwriting as John Webb's work after the Restoration. Moreover, rather than showing the theater as it was when Sir William Davenant's opera was staged at the Phoenix, Higgott suggests that the drawing is one that Webb did for Davenant when he sought to convert an old barn to the Salisbury Court playhouse in 1660 (Higgott 2006).[5] In short, the drawings, splendid as they are, probably tell us nothing about the appearance of the Phoenix theater.

Little other evidence remains about the structure of the Phoenix theater after 1618. John Orrell remarks that it must have been 'made of brick, with a tile roof, in conformity with the Jacobean Proclamation on building' (Orrell 1988: 43). Herbert Berry notes that in 1699 the Phoenix was said to be the 'same shape and size as Blackfriars (which was a rectangle 66′ × 46′) and Salisbury Court Playhouse' (Berry 2000*b*: 629), although he is skeptical. The idea of a rectangle may be mistaken, however, for the playhouse may appear in Wenceslaus Hollar's Great Map (*c.*1658)

[5] I am deeply grateful that Gordon Higgott was willing to share a copy of his work with me since it rescued me from confusion and saved me from error. Higgott's argument that the plans actually show the Salisbury Court playhouse follows one that John Orrell had made earlier in *The Human Stage* (Orrell 1988: 188).

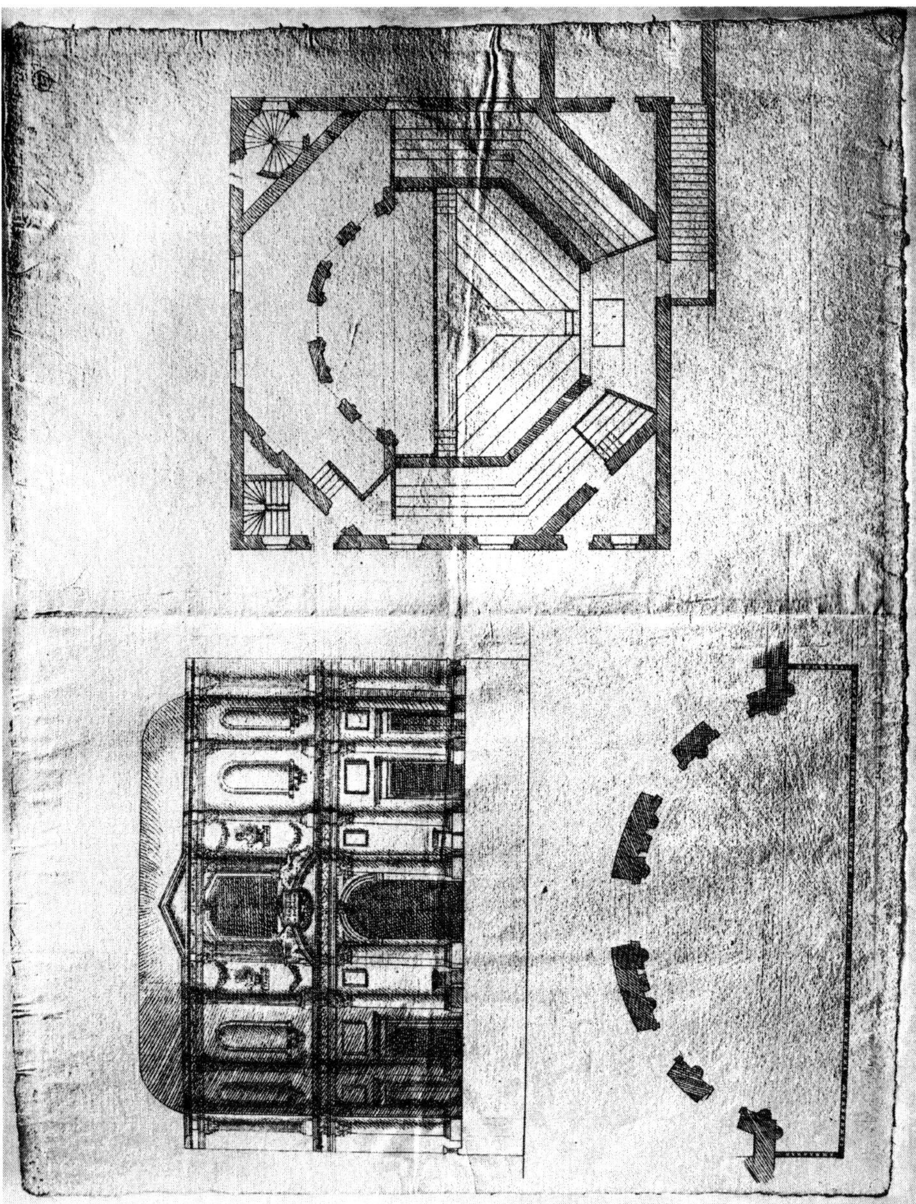

Figure 14.1. Gotch 1/27, the plan, plan of stage, and section through apron stage or proscenium of a playhouse; possibly John Webb's Restoration plans for the Cockpit- in-Court, never realized.

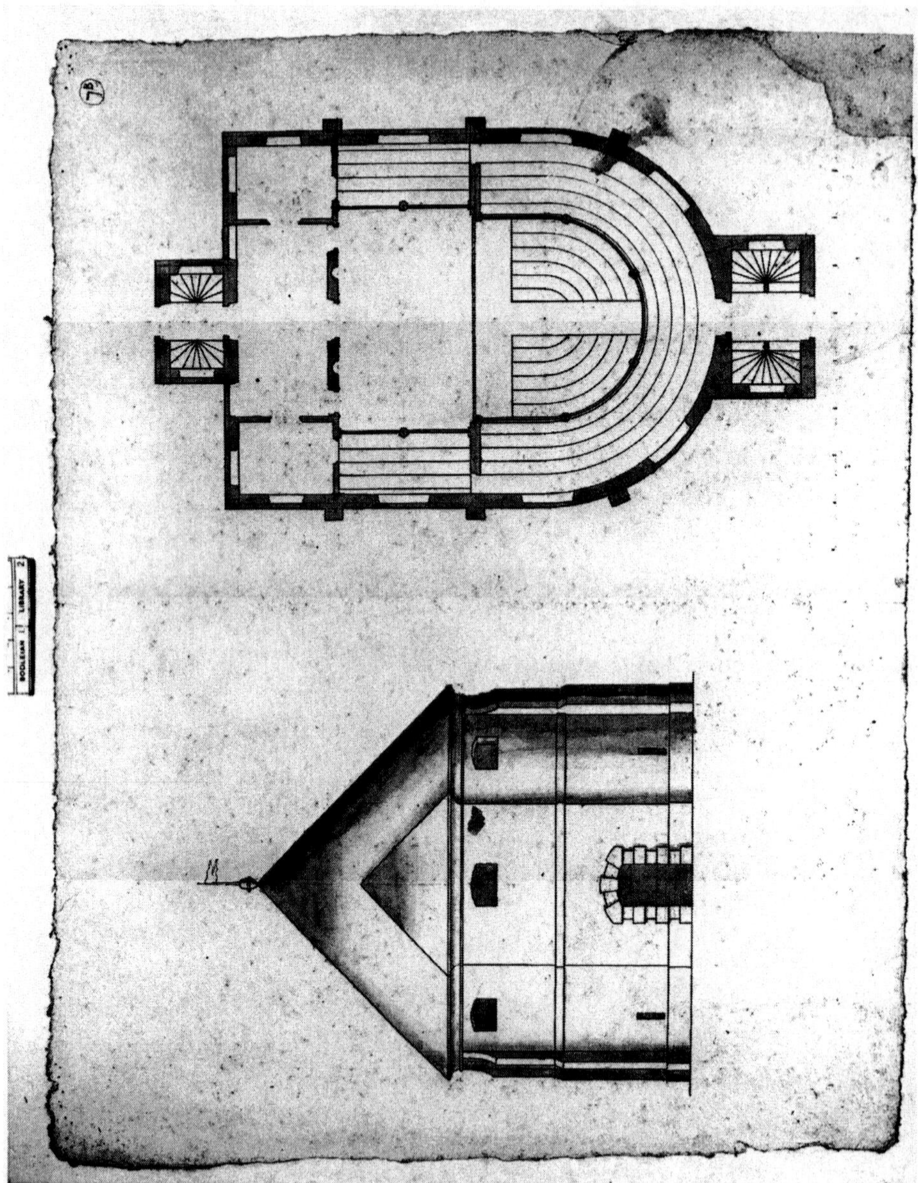

Figure 14.2. Gotch 1/7B, a plan and elevation for a theater; possibly John Webb's proposed plans for the Salisbury Court theater or the Phoenix.

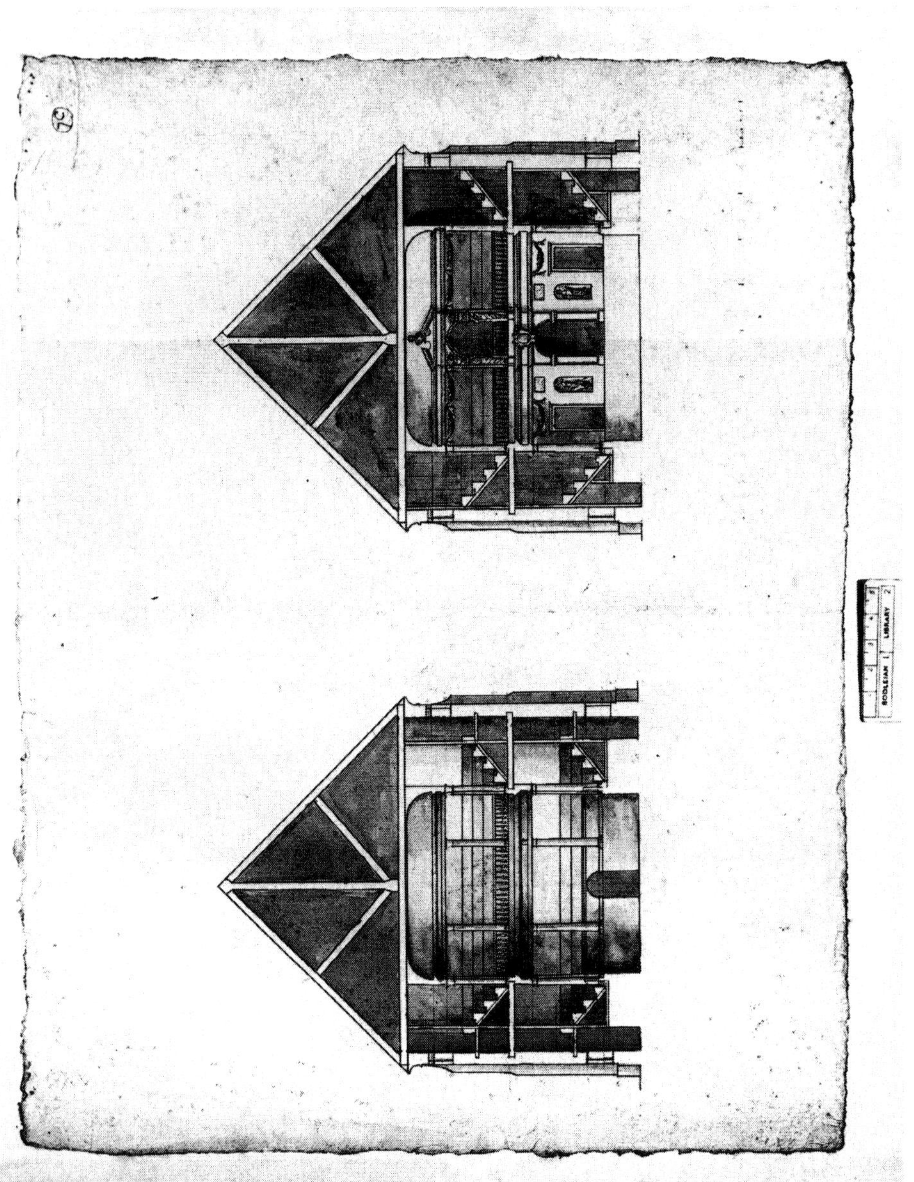

Figure 14.3. Gotch 1/7C, two transverse sections of the same theater; possibly John Webb's proposed plans for the Salisbury Court theater or the Phoenix. I am grateful to the Provost and Fellows of Worcester College for permission to reproduce these designs.

as a square building with three pitched roofs.[6] Such an external structure need not have erased all traces of its cockpit origins, for the octagonal shape might have been retained inside the square exterior, as was the case with the Cockpit-in-Court.

A small amount of additional information about the theater comes from the work of Thomas King, who inventoried all the plays known to have been performed at the Phoenix and every reference to its physical appearance (King 1963). He concluded that the stage had two or three doors, hangings, an acting area above the stage, and that the company used booth structures to create peripheral playing space for some works. Perhaps his most important observation is that no evidence exists for scenery before 1658, when Davenant restaged his *Siege of Rhodes* there, and that the Phoenix plays 'reveal no "anticipation" of the developments in stagecraft seen in the Restoration theatre' (King 1963: 174).

The Cockpit-in-Court

Hamilton Bell argued in 1913 that Gotch 1/27 was an architectural design for the Cockpit-in-Court, a generally accepted argument.[7] While Gotch 1/27 was once attributed to Inigo Jones, scholars now follow the attribution of the drawings to John Webb. But when did he do them? The answer to that question determines whether these plans show a realized Caroline stage or an unrealized Restoration one. Jones, as Surveyor to the King, was in charge of the project to turn the royal cockpit into a royal theater in 1630–2, and one argument is that 'Webb's drawing provides reliable evidence of the Cockpit-in-Court as reconstructed in 1629–31 according to the "Designes and Draughts given by the Surveyor"' (Bell 1913; Harris and Tait 1979: 11). Yet features such as the stage railing and chimneys make the designs more apt to be from 1660–2, and we know that Webb sought charge of that later renovation. Recently Gordon Higgott has both demonstrated that the plans are Webb's and dated them conclusively to 1660 (Higgott 2006). Since Webb was not chosen to handle the renovation of the Cockpit-in-Court's auditorium, they show an unrealized project. That is not to say that they are without information, since they presumably incorporate features of the earlier structure, but since we cannot be certain which features originated with Jones and which came from Webb, the sketches are principally helpful in evoking speculation. Glynne Wickham remarks of the playhouse that 'So much is now known about the Cockpit-in-Court that it would be of more use to consider rebuilding this theatre on a basis of 90 per cent fact and 10 per cent surmise than to persist in attempts to rebuild the first Globe with the proportions of fiction and fact reversed' (Wickham 1959–81: ii/2. 119).

[6] Leslie Hotson (1962) first made the suggestion that the Phoenix is the three-gabled building shown in the Hollar map, although no one else seems to have followed his idea until Berry. See Berry (2000*b*).

[7] The design that Bell considered is reproduced as Harris and Tait (1979, pl. 5).

Wickham goes on to provide a detailed conjectural reconstruction of the theater (1959–81: ii/2. 121) although his account of the dimensions does depend heavily (and reasonably) on Gotch 1/27. The auditorium is an octagon, with a width of 58 feet, in a square. The pit at its center is 36 feet wide, and the stage area is 16 feet deep. (For the sake of comparison, a standard tennis court for a doubles match is 78 feet by 36 feet.) These plans show an octagonal building, a shape that reflects its original use as a cockpit and demonstrates that the power of its origin continued in its first transformation, as well as in its renovation thirty years later. Presumably the renovations planned in 1660–2 retained features of the 1630–2 refitting.

A sketch for a theatrical scene is marked 'for ye Cock-pitt for my Lo Chãberlin 1639' in Inigo Jones's handwriting. (This design, possibly for William Habington's *Queen of Aragon, or, Cleodora*, is in the Duke of Devonshire's collection at Chatsworth House.[8]) Orrell describes it as 'a freely drawn sketch of a full scenic stage set up behind a proscenium arch, with wings, cloud borders in an upper stage, and a "citti of rileve" before a backcloth'. But what the notation means is unclear. This sketch may have been intended for a performance at the Cockpit/Phoenix in Drury Lane or for the Cockpit-in-Court in Whitehall; the note might also be a simple direction since the Lord Chamberlain's lodgings were at the Cockpit in Whitehall (Orrell 1985: 62). If it were a sketch for a performance at the Cockpit-in-Court, perhaps the likeliest explanation, it would provide valuable information about the capabilities of the stage there. Unfortunately, the sketch does not fit well with Gotch 1/27. Nevertheless, Higgott believes that since the Worcester College drawings show what Webb hoped to provide in the 1660 renovation, the sketch probably does represent the Cockpit-in-Court stage in the Caroline period. If that be the case, then the theater was able to use scenery of a certain kind, although not so elaborate as might be used on the stage pictured in Webb's speculative plans of 1660.

Documents from the Office of Works accounts show much about the interior furnishings. The Cockpit-in-Court's function as a venue for royal entertainments means that work orders for renovations and repairs were sometimes kept, and these offer fascinating details.[9] The space must have been gorgeous. The initial transformation of cockpit to playhouse (1629–31) called for the addition of light from 'three wyndowes of Stones for ye newe staires' and the purchase of at least fifteen 'Candlestickes of Iron beautified wth branches Leaues and garnished wth other ornament'. Later the workmen added 'divers Statues ... Corynthian Capitalls for Collomes', painters worked at 'repayring & mending twoe great peec[es] of paynted woorke that were done by Palma, thone being the Story of Dauid and Goliah, thother of Saules Conuersion' as well as 'vij^{en} of the greate Emperours Heades that were done by Titian' (Bentley 1941–68: vi. 271–3).[10] Overhead the entire roof was hung with blue calico decorated with gilt stars cut from assidue (arsedine), and the eight walls were painted blue as well, although it is called a 'fayre blew', a phrase that suggests a lighter color than the calico.

[8] A good reproduction may be found in Orrell (1985: 61).

[9] Bentley prints the main details of these work orders (1941–68: vi. 271–81).

[10] Palma is the Venetian Jacopo Palma il Vecchio (1480–1528).

Figure 14.4. Design by Inigo Jones, possibly for William Habington's *Queen of Aragon, or, Cleodora.*

After the Restoration, refurbishing and a further series of renovations began, which include adding boxes, covering the stage with green baize lined with canvas, using more green baize in the upper tiring room, 'the walles being unfitt for the rich Cloathes'.[11] Because the playhouse now included actresses, the playhouse required curtains to separate men from women in the dressing room, and 'One looking glasse of twenty seaven Inches for the Weomen Comedians dressing themselues'. Finally, the Restoration work included a dais for the monarch, covered by a 'Crimson velvett Canopie' (Bentley 1941–68: vi. 280). The Commonwealth strictures on performance were gone, and Charles II was ready to sit in regal splendor and watch the pretty actresses.

[11] That last item may be the source of the term 'green room'.

The History of the Cockpit-in-Court

While we know more about the appearance of the Cockpit-in-Court than we do about the Phoenix, the history of the former playhouse is less interesting. Although it was not a purpose-built playhouse until 1630, the cockpit had occasionally functioned as a theater before that date. When the first performances took place is unclear, but Bentley says, 'plays for the court had been presented there on numerous occasions before 1616'; court accounts show a dozen or fifteen entries about the preparation of the building for an entertainment, although they 'often fail to record the character of the entertainment' (1941–68: vi. 268). Some of these entries do specify plays instead of cockfighting (although the smell of the game-pit would have been ever present). It seems to have taken a supervisor and between eight and twelve workmen two days to make the change. By covering the pit and hanging a curtain to divide the platform into a backstage area and a performance stage, a temporary playing space emerged, as Wickham has pointed out, that would have closely resembled the *Roxana* and *Messalina* vignettes both in appearance and in scale (Wickham 1959–81: ii/2. 80–3).

When Inigo Jones transformed the cockpit into a single-purpose playhouse, the venue opened on 5 November 1630. A playbill that survives lists the works that the King's Men presented in the first season that the playhouse was open: Thomas Heywood, *An Induction for the House*, and John Fletcher, *The Mad Lover* (5 November); John Fletcher, *Rollo, Duke of Normandy, or, The Bloody Brother* (7 November and 21 February); Ben Jonson, *Volpone* (19 November); John Ford, 'Beauty in a Trance' (28 November, now lost); Fletcher, *Beggars' Bush* (30 November); Francis Beaumont and John Fletcher, *The Maid's Tragedy* (9 December); Francis Beaumont and John Fletcher, *Philaster* (14 December); John Webster, *The Duchess of Malfi* (26 December); Beaumont and Fletcher, *The Scornful Lady* (27 December); Fletcher, *Chances* (30 December); *Oldcastle* [*1 Henry IV*?] (6 January); Nathan Field and Philip Massinger, *The Fatal Dowry* (3 February); Beaumont and Fletcher, *King and No King* (10 February); Thomas Dekker, *The Merry Devil of Edmonton* (15 February); Jonson, and *Every Man in His Humor* (17 February). This list means we know what was offered at the Cockpit-in-Court in its first season; while other lists of plays for the court do exist, the 1630–1 list is the only one to indicate venue. Hampton Court also had plays for the court audience, and in the 1630–1 season four were staged there. For productions that featured spectacular effects or for masques, the Cockpit-in-Court was inappropriate: 'Clearly spectacle was reserved for the Halls in Denmark House and Whitehall, the Banqueting House, and the Masquing Houses' (Bentley 1941–68: vi. 282). These Cockpit-in-Court plays appealed to the taste of the court, with Jonson and Beaumont and Fletcher leading the 1631–2 list. Records of other plays that the King's Men presented at court, whether at Hampton Court or the Cockpit-in-Court, suggests that little changed in court tastes: as a rule, the plays are older, popular, but not challenging.[12] When the Civil War drew nearer, the number of

[12] Andrew Gurr lists court performances in Gurr (2004c: 302–7).

plays offered dropped. During the war and the Commonwealth, the theater was unused, although the lodging rooms at the Cockpit in Whitehall continued to see use.

Following the Restoration, the playhouse was renovated, and payments were made for new matting, candleholders, and upholstery. Pepys records several visits to the Cockpit in Whitehall: to meet those who lodged in the buildings there, like his friend Jeremiah Mount (23 January 1660, 25 February 1661) or General Monk (20 June 1660); as well as to see plays: *The Loyal Subject* (18 August 1660), an unnamed play (20 November 1660), *The Humorous Lieutenant* (20 April 1661), *The Cardinal* (2 October 1662), *The Scornful Lady* (17 November 1662), *The Valiant Cid* (1 December 1662), and *Claracilla* (5 January 1662/3). The notes Pepys makes suggest that audience-watching was as important as play-watching. He mentions whether or not the King is present and visible, while his observation of the Duke and Duchess of York during *Claracilla* was that they 'did show some impertinent and, methought, unnatural dalliances there, before the whole world, such as kissing, and leaning upon one another); but to my very little content, they not acting in any degree like the Duke's people' (Pepys 1893). Boswell suggests that no plays were produced there after 1664 (Boswell 1932).

The History of the Phoenix

The Phoenix has a far livelier record. A document in a 1623 lawsuit gives this abbreviated history: a grocer, John Best, added buildings to the property sometime after acquiring it on 9 October 1609, and by 1610 Best received payment as Prince Henry's cockmaster (Orrell 1985: 48). One of those buildings was a 'messuage, house or tenement called a cockpit and afterwards used for a playhouse and now called the Phoenix' (Berry 2000*b*: 626). We also know that Best leased the property to Christopher Beeston in 1616.

At the start of March 1617, Christopher Beeston prepared to open a new playhouse. For nearly two decades he had worked in London theaters, first as an actor and then as business manager for Queen Anne's Men at the Red Bull inn. Their chief rival, the King's Men, had a second indoor venue at the Blackfriars and enjoyed more success because the company could perform in winter. So Beeston's leasing of the Drury Lane property that autumn was his initial move toward a second performance space. Queen Anne's Men continued to perform at the Red Bull, while Beeston struggled to create a permanent and elegant stage house that would let the Queen's Men cut into the King's Men's profits.

Beeston began with the lease, soon moving onto the site to supervise the work. The Jacobean proclamations on building had forbidden new buildings in the city, while permitting renovations that did not require new foundations (like the playhouse), but Beeston must have thought he could quietly erect a new tenement in the midst of the other work under way to renovate the cockpit and tear down some of the outbuildings (Orrell 1985: 43). At the same time as all this construction and demolition, Beeston continued to manage the Queen's Men and their performances at the Red Bull. Adding to his already complicated situation came an order in early September that sent his bricklayer John Shepperd to jail for 'working on a new foundation in Drury Lane' (Bentley 1941–68: ii. 366). The same record insists that 'Mr. Beeston' must 'appear before the Lords of the Council at their first sitting in Whitehall' to explain himself. By 18 September the Privy Council sent a letter to the High Sheriff of Middlesex declaring that 'Christopher Beeston hath erected a base tenement, not of bricke, and, having formerly been prohibited, did promise to make it only an addition to his owne dwelling howse, but since hath made a tenement of it, distant from his howse, and neere to his Majestys passage. To be pulled downe' (Bentley 1941–68: ii. 366–7). Having set out on the renovation, and then slipped in the construction of a new building, Beeston was now blocked completely. The ensuing confusion over his illicit tenement scheme slowed the legitimate work on the playhouse.

By 15 October new trouble arrived in the form of a complaint filed by the benchers of Lincoln's Inn, who objected to a playhouse being developed so close to their property (Berry 2000*b*: 627). The complaint was doubly unfortunate since Inns of Court men were precisely the audience that Beeston hoped to appeal to with his new venue. The complaint came on the heels of a demand on the company's treasury for arrears of funds that the Queen's Men owed for highway repairs. Somehow Beeston managed to find the needed funds and placate Lincoln's Inn, the Sheriff of Middlesex, and the Privy Council. He was undissuaded as his plan met delays.

The cockpit itself would have been an octagonal building with a central circular cockpit that was raised above the ground and surrounded by amphitheater seating. The renovation would have, at a minimum, required Beeston's workers to clean the space thoroughly, cover the pit with a platform for the stage, replace the benches in the amphitheater, hang curtains, and paint. A more extensive renovation would have them level the interior space, relocate the stage, and build boxes and permanent seating. The delays caused by Beeston's desire for a new building and his other troubles evidently left him behind schedule. Certainly the construction stopped during the winter, for the playhouse that he had sought specifically for winter performances went unopened in 1616. On 23 February 1616/17 the Queen's Men remained at the Red Bull. But the transformation proceeded and by the spring the company was ready to move into its new playhouse. Beeston may have felt a sense of relief, hoping the company's troubles were finally at an end. If so, he was wrong.

Shrove Tuesday fell on 4 March in 1617, a holiday when London apprentices ran wild. Unhappily for Beeston, his brand-new playhouse became the focus of their displeasure, perhaps because they preferred the lower prices at the Red Bull or disliked the possibility that cockfighting would end in Drury Lane. John Chamberlain wrote to Sir Dudley Carleton about what happened (8 March 1617):

On the 4th of the present being our Shrove Tewsday the prentises or rather unruly people of the suburbs played theyr parts, in divers places, as Finsburie fields, about Wapping by St. Katherines, and in Lincolns Ynne fields, in which places being assembled in great numbers they fell to great disorders in pulling downe of houses and beating the guards that were set to kepe rule, specially at a new play house (somtime a cockpit) in Drurie Lane, where the Quenes players used to play. Though the fellows defended themselves as well as they could and slew three of them with shot and hurt divers. Yet they entered the house and defaced yt, cutting the players apparel all in pieces, and other theyre furniture and burnt theyre play bookes and did what other mischiefe they could ... (McClure 1939: ii. 59)

A later letter (29 March 1617) reports:

Our prentises that committed the disorders on Shrovetewsday have been arraigned and acquitted for theyre lives, but found guilty of a fowle riot, and some of them fined in summes they can never pay, and to imprisonment for a yeare, two or three according to the greatnes of theyre offence. (McClure 1939: ii. 65)

Chamberlain's account, though it may be an exaggerated report, is congruent with that of Edward Sherburne in another letter to Carleton. Sherburne adds that, after vandalism inside the playhouse, the rioters 'got on the top of the house and untiled it, and had not the justices of peace and sheriff levied an aid and hindered their purpose, they would have laid that house likewise even with the ground' (Berry 2000*b*: 629). Meanwhile, the Privy Council wrote on 5 March 1617 to London's Lord Mayor, Sir John Leman, about 'tumultuous outrages' carried out by 'a rout of lewd and loose persons, apprentices and others, especially in Lincoln's Inn Fields and Drury Lane, where, in attempting to pull down a playhouse belonging to the Queen's majesty's servants, there were divers persons slain and others hurt and wounded, the multitude there assembled being to the number of many thousands, as we are credibly informed' (Berry 2000*b*: 628). Beeston's triumph in creating a new playhouse was short-lived. Disaster had come to the company, who lost their new playhouse as well as those more valuable commodities, costumes and playbooks. Later in the month fifty rioters were charged in the Middlesex Sessions, but if they were unable to pay the fines, as Chamberlain suggests, the company saw no compensation.

One can only admire Beeston's tenacity. The riot damaged not only his new playhouse, but also 'his owne dwelling howse', where he and his wife were raising their son William, who was 6 or 7. Formidably, he began again. Three months later the theater, renamed the Phoenix, opened 'on or about the third day of June' 1617. With Shrove Tuesday came rumors that those who had rioted the previous year would take revenge and destroy it again; the Privy Council warned the authorities to take precautions to prevent a second riot. While no new riot occurred, the company seems to have struggled at the Phoenix: in Middleton's *Inner Temple Masque*, a character remarks of the Cockpit (i.e., the Phoenix) that 'the poor players ne'er thrived in't' (line 212).[13] From 1616, when construction began, through the various complaints, the riot, and the threat of a riot, Beeston had persisted, but at some point he must have wondered if the scheme was worth the trouble, particularly if the

[13] Quoted from *The Inner Temple Masque*, ed. James Knowles, in Middleton (2007: 1320–30).

company did poorly. Yet over the next twenty years he would lead the playhouse and its personnel to great success.

In 1619 Beeston began a series of machinations about the company working at the Phoenix. One can regard these various shifts as sharp practice by a greedy and unprincipled man, or as astute decisions by a man who saw more clearly than his fellows what excellence required. Briefly, the company at the Phoenix was Queen Anne's (1617–19), Prince Charles's (1619–22), Lady Elizabeth's (1622–5), Queen Henrietta's (1625–37), and finally Beeston's boys (1637–9). In each instance Beeston initiated the change in company; he always retained control of the theater, while some (though not necessarily all) of the actors were evicted. The comments that survive about these changes come from lawsuits, often from actors who suddenly found themselves without a playhouse, so much contemporary comment is aggrieved.[14] Yet, by making these changes, Beeston moved the Phoenix and its companies into the top rank of London theaters. From his initial attempt to skirt the building rules or to rebuild a ruined playhouse, he led the Phoenix into its place as the only serious rival to the King's Men and their Blackfriars theater.

If the Queen's Men did fail to thrive at the Phoenix, Beeston had an excellent chance to make a change when Queen Anne died on 2 March 1618/19. He seized the moment and dismissed his old company, reforming the players as Prince Charles's Men. The troubles of Queen Anne's Men were evidently long-standing, since a deposition for a 1620 lawsuit said the company had begun to break up three years previously and complained that Beeston had sold the company's costumes. In another suit, from 1619, a witness complained that Beeston had been cooking the books for his own benefit; in a further 1623 lawsuit the actors who were all that was left of the company had more complaints about Beeston's management. Yet no complaint is clearly supported, while no disinterested party made any claims that Beeston behaved badly.

Within a few years, however, a second company change occurred, as Beeston shifted patrons from the Prince of Wales to his sister Princess Elizabeth, wife of the Elector of Palatine. The company of Prince Charles's Men seems to have departed amicably, going to the Curtain, and Hotson suggests that Beeston may have controlled this playhouse as well (Hotson 1962: 92). Beeston replaced them with a provincial company, the Lady Elizabeth's company. Bentley says that Beeston used only one performer from the previous company, so the manager was in effect establishing a completely new troupe. The new company seems to have succeeded: on the company's behalf, Beeston both provided substantial gratuities to the Master of the Revels and gave generously to the parish church. Furthermore, allusions in the front matter to Shakespeare's First Folio, in the text of *The Obstinate Lady*, and in a letter by James Howell all couple the Phoenix with the Blackfriars as the leading London theaters.

[14] Accounts of the litigation can be found in Bentley (1941–68: ii. 47–77, 363–70) and Hotson (1962: 88–100).

In 1625 two things happened. First, the plague closed the theaters; then the monarch died. Rather than remaining affiliated to Princess Elizabeth, Beeston found a new patron in a more powerful woman, as the company became Queen Henrietta's Men. This sponsorship was a fortunate one, and, as Queen Henrietta's men, the company and the playhouse became prosperous and successful. Some of the Lady Elizabeth's Men reappear in the new company, so the change was less radical than Beeston's earlier company changes. They were granted royal livery in 1630 and were frequently called to perform at court. In commendatory verses (1629) for Sir William Davenant's *The Iust Italian*, Thomas Carew speaks querulously of 'men in crowded heapes that throng / To that adulterate stage' of the Red Bull or the Phoenix playhouses, and this complaint of a rival suggests the Phoenix was flourishing (Davenant 1630, A4^{r}). Bentley notes that not only the Duke of Buckingham but also the King and Queen attended performances there (1941–68: vi. 63). Nor is such success due simply to the actors or venue. The playhouse dramatists included James Shirley, John Ford, and Thomas Heywood, so the material that the company performed was particularly good.

Beeston's own management deserves praise as well. He was the one who bought for various companies such mainstays of the canon as Dekker, Ford, and Rowley's *The Witch of Edmonton* (1621), Middleton and Rowley's *The Changeling* (1621), Dekker and Ford's *The Spanish Gypsy* (1621), Heywood's *The Captives* (1624) and *The English Traveller* (1625), Massinger's *A New Way to Pay Old Debts* (1625), Shirley's *The Witty Fair One* (1628), Ford's *'Tis Pity She's a Whore* (1629?–1633) and *Perkin Warbeck* (1629–34), and Brome's *A Jovial Crew* (1641). And it was Beeston who smoothed the paths of his company by giving gratuities to the Master of the Revels, Sir Henry Herbert, of around £60 a year (as well as giving gloves to Herbert's wife). Bentley suggests that Beeston even made Sir Henry Herbert a shareholder (1941–68: vi. 64). Furthermore, Beeston contributed with great generosity to the parish church on behalf of the performers. Such contributions would go far to disarming any neighborhood irritation with the playhouse. After the initial riot, whatever company Beeston had in residence faced relatively little trouble.[15] An incident in 1632 illustrates Beeston's success in making his company secure. Herbert notes:

> 18 Nov. 1632. In the play of The Ball. Written by Sherley, and acted by the Queens players, ther were divers personated so naturally, both of lords and others of the court, that I took it ill, and would have forbidden the play, but that Biston promiste many things which I found faulte withal should be left out, and that he would not suffer it to be done by the poet any more, who deserves to be punisht; and the first that offends in this kind, of poets or players, shall be sure of publique punishment. (Bentley 1941–68: vi. 63)

As Bentley notes, the status of the audience is suggested by Herbert's belief that spectators could penetrate the imitations of court figures. It seems likely that the play would have been sufficient to close another company, but Herbert not only permitted

[15] The principal complaint against the playhouse came from William Prynne, who linked the playhouse and bawdyhouses.

Queen Henrietta's Men to continue, but allowed Beeston to produce a revised version of the play.

Beeston had a special position, and while the source of his success may have been the financial sweeteners, it is tempting to speculate that he may have enjoyed special privileges because of the Queen. Both Henrietta Maria and Beeston were Catholic, and while membership in London's Catholic community scarcely ensured a personal knowledge of the Queen, he might well have shared acquaintances who recommended the manager to the monarch. One notes that the Queen's influence brought a troupe of French performers to London in February 1634/5. They performed first at court and then at the Phoenix 'only on those days in Lent which were customarily forbidden to the English actors' (Bentley 1941–68: vi. 65). Evidently the company was well received, unlike their experience on an earlier visit when the spectators at the Blackfriars hissed and threw fruit. Beeston may have offered his playhouse as a favor to his patron, while the atmosphere there may have been more friendly to their performance than elsewhere. In any case, he is unlikely to have lost money on the deal. Bentley also quotes an odd piece of gossip from 1637: 'Here hath been an horrible Noise about the Lady *Newport's* being become a *Romish* Catholick; she went one Evening as she came from a Play in *Drury-Lane* to *Somerset-House*, where one of the Capuchins reconciled her to the *Popish* Church, of which she is now a weak Member' (1941–68: vi. 69). Beeston might have permitted other recusants to pass messages at the venue. Still, this analysis is speculation, although it might help explain the anomaly that, while Beeston turned his other companies out of the playhouse in three years or so, Queen Henrietta's Men remained for a decade.

The recurrence of the plague, however, led to the final change that Beeston made. On 10 May 1626 the Privy Council closed the playhouses, and this suspension of performance would last over a year. In the months of forced inactivity, Beeston decided to repeat his tactic of changing his company, perhaps from financial need. In a 1640 document, a witness said that 'Mr. Beeston, being master of said playhouse [the Phoenix] ... takes occasion to quarrel with the company to the end that he might have a company that would take what he would be willing to give them' (Berry 2000*b*: 633). Beeston sent Queen Henrietta's company away and began recruiting children. A sign of his confidence, or of his desperation, was his decision to present the first production by Beeston's boys in May 1637, despite the plague prohibition, only to have the Privy Council shut them down. In October playing was finally permitted and the company officially launched. They would enjoy great success in the years before the Civil War, but Beeston would not see it. By 10 August 1639 Christopher Beeston was dead.

His son William inherited the company, or rather shared with Beeston's widow in the shares that Beeston had. William had lived in and around the Cockpit for almost all of his life, since Christopher Beeston was resident at the site from 1616, when William was a child. (It is worth noting that the Beestons leased and did not own the property, however.) Richard Brome praised William's skill as a manager, and certainly he inherited control over one of the two most important London companies. While Christopher Beeston could bargain with Sir Henry Herbert about Shirley's *The*

Ball or placate the Privy Council after directly violating their orders, William was less effective. In May 1640 the company gave offense by performing an unlicensed play that referred to 'the K.s journey into the Northe, and was complayned of by his Majestye'. Bentley suggests that the work was Richard Brome's *The Court Beggar*, which mocked members of the Queen's circle, such as Suckling and Davenant (1941–68: iii. 61–5). As a result, Beeston found himself dispossessed of his company and sitting in prison. The Master of the Revels handed the company over to Sir William Davenant, one of the playwrights who worked regularly for the Phoenix and the target of Brome's satire. While it seems implausible that William Beeston could regain the position he had held, that reversal is precisely what followed. During 1641 he was released from prison, Davenant was in prison for his political activities, and the company once again changed hands, going from Davenant to Beeston. The former would be too busy once the Civil War broke out less than a year later, while after 1642 the latter was a theatrical manager forbidden to produce.

Though William Beeston made some effort during the Commonwealth years to purchase the Phoenix, he never succeeded; John Rhodes leased the property around 1649 and was still in control at the Restoration (Hotson 1962: 99). By 1646 the playhouse was evidently used as a school since records note that sixpence was paid 'to the teacher at the Cockpitt of the children' (Hotson 1962: 24 n. 88). Yet the shift to pedagogy was quickly set aside for illicit performances. According to the royalist news-sheet *Mercurius Elencticus*, 'Threescore [coaches] are observed to *wheele* to the *Cockpit*, which is very offensive to the Brethren' (January 1647/8; Hotson 1962: 29). One finds several other references to performances and to raids on those performances. For example, James Wright in *Histrio Histrionica* says a company that included Lowen, Taylor, Pollard, Burt, and Hart was giving secret performances (Wright 1699). While the company was performing Fletcher's *Rollo, Duke of Normandy, or, The Bloody Brother*,

> a Party of Foot Souldiers beset the House, surprised 'em about the middle of a Play, and carried 'em away in their habits, not admitting them to Shift, to *Hatton-House*, then a Prison, where having detain'd them some-time, they Plunder'd them of their Cloths, and let 'em loose again. (Hotson 1962: 40)

Finally, the government's refusal to permit playing throughout the 1640s led the actors 'of Black-Friers and the Cock-Pit' to petition Parliament around 1650 for permission to play (Hotson 1962: 43–4):

> To the Supream Authoritie the Parliament of the Commonwealthe of England The humble Petition of diverse poor and distressed men, heretofore the Actors of Black-friers and the Cock-Pit. Sheweth,
>
> That your most poor Petitioners, having long suffered in extream want, by being prohibited the use of their qualitie of Acting, in which they were trained up from their childhood, whereby they are uncapable of any other way to get a subsistance, and are now fallen into such lamentable povertie, that they know not how to provide food for themselves, their wives and children: great debts being withall demanded of them, and they not in a condition to satisfie the creditours; and without your mercifull and present permission, they must all inevitably perish.

May it therefore please this Honourable House to commiserate their sad and distressed condition, and to vouchsafe them a Libertie to Act but some small time (for their triall of inoffensiveness) onely such morall and harmless representations, as shall no way be distastfull to the Commonwealth or good manners. They humbly submitting themselves to any one of knowing judgement and fidelitie to the State, appointed to oversee them and their actions, and willing to contribute out of their poor endeavours, what shall be thought fit and allotted them to pay weekly or otherwise, for the service of Ireland, or as the State shall think fitting.

And as in dutie they are ever bound, shall pray, &c.

Despite the overwrought petition and the offer to allow Parliament close supervision of their 'morall and harmless representations', the actors' petition failed. No plays were permitted.

Operas, however, were an entirely different matter. Oliver Cromwell's regime encouraged operatic performances.[16] Captured and imprisoned after the war, Sir William Davenant had been released in 1652, returning to London to live. He decided to stage entertainments with music, finding support from the Lord Keeper of the Great Seal, Sir Bulstrode Whitelocke, and John Thurloe. His first such production was the *Entertainment at Rutland* (1656), soon followed by the first English opera, *The Siege of Rhodes* (1656). These were successful, but Davenant required a larger venue to make more money from his new form. Since he had once been the manager at the Phoenix, and since it had been in good enough condition to hold illicit performances in the 1640s, he moved his activities there. First, he staged a revival of *The Siege of Rhodes* (1658), following it with *The Cruelty of the Spaniards in Peru* (1658), and *Sir Francis Drake* (1659). While the government of Richard Cromwell was increasingly suspicious about Davenant's entertainments, their downfall made their concerns irrelevant. In 1660 the theaters opened again and the Phoenix was back in business with John Rhodes as the manager.

Yet the reopening of the theaters destroyed the Phoenix as the Puritans could not. It remained open for a while: in October 1660 Pepys saw *Othello*, Beaumont's *Wit Without Money*, and Fletcher's *The Tamer Tamed*. But this initial success soon met with competition. The Drury Lane Theatre was open by 1663 and the Phoenix was soon out of business for good.

16 On Cromwell and opera, see Sherwood (1977).

PART III

OTHER PLAYING SPACES

CHAPTER 15

'HE WHO PAYS THE PIPER CALLS THE TUNE': HOUSEHOLD ENTERTAINMENTS

SUZANNE WESTFALL

Oh it ain't no myst'ry
If it's politics or hist'ry,
The thing you gotta know is
Everything is show biz.

Mel Brooks, *The Producers*

As William Ingram indicates in the Introduction to this volume, early modern theater history has been enjoying a healthy turmoil during the last fifty years, with scholars offering various and divergent narratives to explain the mounting piles of primary source documents emerging from local record offices and family archives. Nowhere is this revisionism more evident than in patronage studies, particularly when those patrons are not royal households but rather members of the nobility and landed gentry whose seats are in the provinces far from London.

At present the question about gentry household drama has ceased to be not where, but wherefore. Or, more significantly, who benefits? I have described household structures and discussed their retained entertainers at length elsewhere (Westfall 1990), so I will not dwell on these details here. Rather, I would like to explore what we have learned during the past decade about household theater in the provinces, and present a few examples of household performances to open a discussion of the motivations of patrons and the rationales of performances.

Because of the sketchy nature and the various types of evidence that survive, this discussion is problematical. Account books mention names of touring companies and payments to them, family papers occasionally preserve a few random details of performance, published accounts of royal progresses offer us texts and descriptions of the events but do not explain their *raison d'être*, and household ordinances dictate procedures but omit content. Reviewing and combining what we can infer from these records helps us to envision more fully the provincial household revels.

The *Records of Early English Drama* (REED) Patrons and Performances web site[1] is beginning to make searching patrons, events, venues, and troupes from the published records a bit more efficient, but we still know very little about repertoires, audiences, or writers. Most of the evidence about patronized entertainers comes from civic, ecclesiastical, and college financial accounts, along with a few surviving family letters and accounts that record the rewards expended to visiting troupes. We have for some time known that scores of minstrel and player troupes (as well as a variety of other entertainers) were traveling in the protective livery of a patron, and that these troupes visited hundreds of performance spaces from the fourteenth to the seventeenth centuries. Indeed, as Peter Greenfield points out:

> A popular misconception has it that players toured the provinces only when they could not perform in London . . . In fact, touring the provinces was the rule rather than the exception for companies of actors in this period. In 1572 they [Lord Berkeley's troupe] asked their patron for a licence 'to certifye that we are your houshold Servaunts when we shall have occasion to travayle amongst our frendes as we do usuallye once a yere'. This pattern of annual tours continues even after the company constructed their own purpose-built theater in the capital. (Greenfield 2004: 186–7)

Greenfield goes on to show how profitable a tour might be (Greenfield 1983: 16), also quoting a Shropshire record of a traveling singer who testified in court that 'performers might live entirely by going "from gentilmans house to gentilmans house vpon their benevolence"' (Greenfield 2004: 191). This sort of evidence indicates not only regular and lucrative touring, but also an active theater scene in the provinces, in the houses of 'frendes' and 'gentilmen', who, as Clifford family accounts indicate, provided payment, meals, and lodging for the troupes, which could number from five to fifteen players (Greenfield 2004: 196).

The REED volumes and the attendant patrons database list 149 documented private venues, of which ninety-three are private residences of various sorts: castles, halls, manors, houses, and parks. Each of these locations was either visited by a traveling troupe or owned by a patron whose entertainers show up in other records. While most household accounts for Tudor and Stuart gentry do not survive (or have

[1] A work in progress at <http://link.library.utoronto.ca/reed>.

not yet been found), those that do indicate, almost without exception, payments to visiting entertainers. Civic and ecclesiastical accounts, which are more plentiful, allow us to connect patrons to players and musicians who, we assume, went home occasionally to entertain.

An aristocratic household is itself a paradoxical establishment, embodying binary oppositions such as static–active, private–public, and domestic–commercial. Moving from property to property, from manor to castle to London townhouse, a superstructure of servitors and household 'stuff' (known as the 'riding' household) would progress periodically throughout an aristocrat's far-flung holdings. Family 'seats' were rather public private homes to the resident household—a nobleman, his extended family, his staff and their families, as well as all of their servants, a number sometimes reaching 250. And of course a household was an economic unit, a corporation of managers and workers who happened to live (occasionally) under the same roof. Consequently, entertainments in the noble households tended to represent a curious mixture of the public and the private, an opportunity for the formal pretensions of largesse as well as the casual celebration of personal leisure. In addition, such fluidity encouraged a circulation of influences, alliances, and interests, which in turn affected the nature and motivations for household entertainments.

The townhouses, country manors, and provincial castles of the gentry and nobility provided a variety of performance spaces. Certainly great halls, with their screens at one end, so-called 'minstrel gallery' above, and large open dining area, provided ample public space for interludes, masques, dances, and concerts; many believe that this household architecture inspired the shape of the Swan and other public theaters. Richard Southern's *The Staging of Plays before Shakespeare* discusses the possibilities at length, concluding that the doors in the hall screens (which separated the hall from the kitchens or outside doors) were particularly useful for entrances and exits, and that the screen itself might provide a backdrop (Southern 1973). More recently Alan Nelson has provided copious primary evidence to reverse this conjecture completely, using records from Cambridge and Oxford colleges to demonstrate that stages were built nearer to the dais, which provided seating for upper ranks, while commoners sat further down the hall and perhaps even in the minstrels' gallery; doors in the hall screens, he argues, would be more useful for audience entrance than for actors (A. Nelson 1992: 57–65). According to Nelson's evidence, at colleges and civic halls, constructed stages were placed in front of the dais, a configuration that makes sense for great households as well—for aesthetic as well as social effect. John Astington's examination of a surviving groundplan of the Great Chamber at Whitehall, set with a throne for the Queen, seating for audiences, and a central stage for performers, confirms Nelson's view (Astington 1991*b*: 6).

Another natural playing space was the chapel, where the Earl of Northumberland's Chapel Children and Gentlemen were directed to perform holiday plays (Grose 1809: 256; Westfall 1990: 18–27), and where in 1564 students of King's College, Cambridge, performed plays for the Queen (A. Nelson 1992: 66). Clearly the loft and rood-screen area could provide convenient audience seating, and the nether chapel could serve as stage space. Certainly churches had been serving as performance spaces for centuries, and in great and royal households chapels continued to be used as performance spaces.

During royal progresses, entire estates served as playing spaces, often with elaborate sets, tents, and scaffolds constructed in the park for specific performances (Nichols 1823). And during family festivals like weddings, baptisms, or funerals, the entire house would serve as a stage for elaborate ceremonies and processions in addition to music and theater. All of these playing spaces—halls, chapels, parks, and even bedchambers (Henry VIII once surprised Queen Catherine with a Robin Hood masque in her bedchamber)—prevent a modern 'fourth wall' approach to performance because boundaries are so permeable, which would encourage interaction among all participants. Indeed, the opening dialogue in Medwall's *Fulgens and Lucrece* reflects and satirizes this proximity of actor and audience, as one actor identifies himself with the spectators rather than the disreputable players (A. Nelson 1980: 43).

Exactly what was performed in these spaces, particularly during the early Tudor period, is difficult to say. During Elizabeth's reign, when publication of play-texts became more common, troupe repertoires are a bit easier to determine, but we still simply do not know what most players played during much of the sixteenth century, even if we know where and when they did so. Household accounts were, of course, concerned with paying the pipers rather than recording the tunes they played. In very few cases have we been able to connect a play title with a household, but in most of these cases the plays are no longer extant. We know, for example, that Lady Honour Lisle was seeking an interlude in 1538. On 5 October her purchasing agent John Husee writes:

> I have been with Felsted, and given him earnest for a suit of players garments, which he will keep for you, and an interlude which is called Rex Diabole. Sparke knowth the matter. I will do my best to get some of these new Scripture matters, but they be very dear; they asketh above xx^{s} for an Interlude. (Brewer et al. 1862–1914: i/2. 1362; St Clare Byrne 1981: v. 238)

Two days before Husee had been 'in hand with Felsted, silk dyer, for the players' garments, and also to procure some good matter for them. But these new ecclesiastical matters will be hard to come by' (St Clare Byrne 1981: v. 237). Lady Lisle was supplying the household players, who numbered five (St Clare Byrne 1981: i. 163), with a topical script, perhaps with a didactic slant from Henry's reformed church. The garments might, of course, be livery, but since they are of dyed silk, it is more likely that they are costumes to play the script. Although the patron, rather than the players themselves, went to great trouble and expense to produce this interlude, it is impossible to determine the occasion (Easter fell on 6 April that year, so the play was apparently not intended for the usual Shrovetide festivities) or the specific motivation. The performance reflects the politically correct religious views, which Viscount Lisle, Warden of the Cinque Ports in Kent, would be keen to demonstrate. His entertainers also appear in civic accounts as 'Lord Lisle's Minstrels' or the 'Lord of the Cinque Port's Players', indicating that the record keepers were very aware of his influence at court (Hays et al. 1999: 240, 473; Pilkinton 1997: 49; Wasson 1986: 135, 224).

At about the same time, John Bale and his company, probably under the patronage of Thomas Cromwell, were performing Bale's virulently anti-Catholic plays, many of which are extant. Paul Whitfield White has explored at length the relationship between theater and Protestant propaganda, and the patronage of the King's chief minister and Protestant reformer to a troupe of players spreading anti-Catholic scripts on tours supports the assumption that patrons sponsored plays that communicated their personal ideologies and political platforms (P. White 1993: 12–41). White goes on to speculate about various repertoires of leading Protestant patrons like the Duchess of Suffolk, the Earl of Warwick, and the Earl of Leicester, admitting that, although the companies acting in the livery of these patrons would have needed scores of interludes to perform on tour, unfortunately 'not a single play can be certainly ascribed to Leicester's Men prior to 1573' (P. White 1993: 64). A few titles of touring plays, which appear to be moral interludes, have, however, survived: Norwich records about 1551–2 refer to a play 'at the gyldhall of Zacheus', probably by the Marquess of Dorset's players (Galloway 1984: 31). Suffolk's Men, about 1542, were performing a play 'of the battle betwixt the Spirit, the Soul and the flesh' (Brewer et al. 1862–1914, *Addenda*, pt 2, 1547). And on Shrove Monday, a traditional time for plays according to Northumberland's ordinances, Sir Thomas Chaloner's household saw the King's players perform the 'play of Self-Love'; 10*s*. were also expended 'among the maskers at dyn', which supports the idea that masques were performed as 'interludes' between courses at a feast.[2]

In the absence of texts or concrete evidence from eyewitnesses in letters or financial expenditures in account books, some theater historians have chosen a different tactic to speculate about the sorts of play that might have been performed in households, examining extant interludes for internal evidence of private auspices. T. W. Craik has suggested that the political interlude *Wealth and Health* was written for Queen Mary's players (Craik 1953). Ian Lancashire has connected *The World and the Child* to the Earl of Kent (I. Lancashire 1976), *The Interlude of Youth* to the Earl of Northumberland, and *Hickscorner* to the Duke of Suffolk (I. Lancashire 1980*b*). Alan Nelson suggests that *Fulgens and Lucrece* and *Nature* were performed at Cardinal Morton's household, where their author, Henry Medwall, was chaplain (A. Nelson 1980).

During the later Tudor period, texts are easier to associate with specific companies because plays and verses for entertainments were more likely to be published in London, where professional companies under titular patronage of the royal and noble households were based. Scott McMillin and Sally-Beth MacLean have tracked down the repertoire of plays that the Queen's Men, the most important touring company in England, would have taken to cities and households at the end of the century. As McMillin and MacLean point out, 'the plays of the Queen's Men were among the first to reach print from the adult professional companies', and we assume that those plays that were printed were the plays that the company was performing in the provinces. McMillin and MacLean further connect *Three Ladies of London* to

[2] Chambers (1903: ii. 201); British Library, Lansdowne MS 824, fo. 17.

Leicester's Men, *Tamburlaine* to the Admiral's Men, and *Rare Triumphs of Love and Fortune* to Derby's Men (McMillin and MacLean 1998: 84–6).

But far from the royal and London-based companies, the northern and East Anglian nobility, sometimes recusant, maintained strongly independent households out of sight of royal eyes. Consequently, Norwich and Lancashire accounts are particularly interesting for patronage studies; Thomas Howard, fourth Duke of Norfolk, is a case in point. The Norfolk family, the richest and most powerful in England, had remained Catholic, and may have fancied themselves legitimate heirs to the throne. So it should come as no surprise that Norfolk, for his own protection, would cultivate his local power.

We know that Norfolk's chapel children performed for Christmas at his palace at Norwich in 1564 and 1565, where he was in residence. The Mayor and Aldermen dined at the palace, which indicates that one purpose for household entertainment was political: the Duke was strengthening his community ties, celebrating the most important liturgical holidays of the year far from the royal court at London (Galloway 1984: 51, 54–5). The 1564–5 holidays must have been personally and politically fraught; Norfolk was barely in Elizabeth's favor, even though he was a member of her Privy Council. In August he had attended the Queen at Cambridge, but was quarrelling with Leicester over her marriage contracts (Matthew and Harrison 2004: xxviii. 431). By December of that year he had written to Burghley that 'her Hyenes hardlye thynkes enye Thyunge well bestowyd apon me, be yt never so small' (Hayes and Murdin 1740–59: 442). Small wonder that Norfolk preferred to tend his own household rather than paying court to the Queen. Three years later, implicated in the Northern Rebellion and the Ridolfi plot, he was in the tower, finally attainted and executed in 1572 (Matthew and Harrison 2004: xxviii. 431–2).

Thomas Howard, like his forebears, was a documented patron of entertainers who, with the exception of his chapel, traveled the country. Civic accounts preserve payments to his bearward (Pilkinton 1997: 76), minstrels (Wasson 1986: 38), 'performers'—likely musicians (Galloway 1984: 37, 45; A. Nelson 1989: 200; Wasson 1986: 147), and players (Galloway 1984: 37, 45; A. Nelson 1989: 200). Given his stature, we would expect Christmas celebrations at his palace (which also boasted a tennis court and bowling alley), in the heart of his own cultural community, to be lavish; away from London he could also celebrate mass and entertain with impunity those he chose, including local recusants. Although we cannot speculate with any accuracy about these occasions, it is clear that the ambitious duke was highly motivated to build his own power base, and to use his retained entertainers to demonstrate that his court rivaled the royal court.

We are fortunate that household accounts do survive from other provincial families. Accounts dating 1612–36 for Dunkenhalgh Hall, Lancashire, the home of Thomas Walmesley, a wealthy judge of Common Pleas, record fifty-one performance events at the hall, including visits from entertainers of prominent protestant patrons: King James, Prince Charles, the Earl of Derby, Lord Dudley, Lady Elizabeth Stuart, and Lord Stafford, as well as non-nobles, Mr John Warren, Sir Edward Warren, and Sir Cuthbert Halsall (George 1991: 184–212). Accounts for his neighbor, Sir Richard

Shuttleworth of Gawthorpe Hall, also survive from 1609 to 1618 (George 1991: 170–9); Shuttleworth, a barrister and serjeant-at-law who served as Chief Justice of Chester and High Sheriff of Lancashire, was so wealthy that he was asked to lend money to the Queen. At Gawthorpe, Shuttleworth saw players and musicians of the Earl of Derby, Lord Stafford, Lord Dudley, and Lord Monteagle, whose players received an exceedingly generous reward of 50*s*. in August 1612 (George 1991: 173).

Another recusant family, the Houghtons of Houghton Tower, provide yet another perspective on household revels, for Alexander Houghton's 1581 will 'bequeathed play clothes and instruments, and recommended William Shakesshafte and the actor Fulk Gillom "now dwelling with me" to Sir Thomas Hesketh, asking him "either to take them unto his service or else help them to some good master"' (Findlay and Dutton 2003: 1; quoting Honigmann 1998: 136–7).[3] Stanley family accounts also indicate a strong connection both with other noble households and with the royal court. At Knowsley Hall and Lathom House in Lancashire, players of the Earl of Leicester, Lord Strange, the Earl of Hertford, the Earl of Essex, and the Queen herself visited with regularity. At one event, the Queen's players performed during the evening of 6 September 1589 and in the afternoon the following day, with Essex's players performing during the same evening (George 1991: 181). The following year the Queen's players stopped in again at Knowsley en route to Scotland to perform for James VI (George 1991: 182). Frequently records refer once again to Christmas holidays as times when the patron's retained troupes were in residence in their own household.

REED collections, particularly the family accounts, have brought to light a number of other references to provincial household entertainments. *Shropshire* includes a notice of the Earl of Pembroke's 1596 'King Arthur' entertainment at Ludlow Castle (J. Somerset 1994*a*: ii. 395). In Herefordshire we find the 1637–42 accounts of Joyce Jeffrey, an unmarried woman of independent means who ran her own royalist household, paying waits and fiddlers, and purchasing a copy of 'verses upon Benjamin Ionsons death' in 1638–9 (Klausner 1990: 189–93). A Cornwall record mentions that Francis Tregian of Golden Manor hosted an interlude that led to his trial and conviction for recusancy (Hays et al. 1999: 531–3), further evidence that religious ideology affected patronage and choice of plays.

Indeed, performances motivated by religious ideology helped send Sir John Yorke and twenty of his household to Star Chamber in 1611 after a Christmas 1609 performance at his home at Gowlthwaite Hall. Phoebe Jensen has closely examined

[3] It is indeed tempting to identify 'Shakesshafte' with Shakespeare; certainly Shakespeare's plays reflect a detailed knowledge of great households and their procedures (Findlay and Dutton 2003: 2–3), with *Hamlet*, *The Taming of the Shrew*, and *A Midsummer Night's Dream* in particular recording in detail relationships between player troupes and noble courts (Westfall 1989). We have long wondered about Shakespeare's 'lost years' between Stratford and London, and the intimation of relationships between William Shakespeare and the recusant northern households has fueled recent discussions of Shakespeare's own recusancy. From Stephen Greenblatt's ruminations in *Hamlet in Purgatory* (2002) to John Shakespeare's Catholic 'testament of faith' found in the Henley Street birthplace in 1757, to the 1999 Lancastrian Shakespeare conference held at the University of Lancaster, scholars are focusing increasingly on cultural neighborhoods outside London and outside the official ideology of Elizabethan England.

this incident, exploring the nature of recusancy and toleration in the northern families, and drawing on copious evidence to show how complex the politics among neighbors and households might be (P. Jensen 2003: 101–2). As Jensen notes, Sir John frequently entertained during the holidays, including Christmas, May day, Easter, and Ascension day, and the nine players of the offending Simpson troupe had visited before. In 1609 the troupe's repertoire had included *The Travels of Three English Brothers*, *Pericles*, *King Lear*, and *Saint Christopher.* According to Star Chamber accounts, about one hundred people, screened by Sir John's servants to refuse admission to non-Catholics, viewed a Catholic play about St Christopher within the context of a longer play which, according to witnesses, was performed 'to the great scandal of true religion' (P. Jensen 2003: 103).

Some have speculated that the longer play was perhaps Shakespeare's *King Lear*, performed with a pro-Catholic and therefore an anti-royalist slant. Most recently Stephen Greenblatt has suggested that the scene of Gloucester's torture comprises a denunciation of royal abuse of power (Greenblatt 2007: 81–2), which would have reminded the northern recusant families of King James's persecution of Catholics. Indeed, an unrepentant Sir John Yorke continued to welcome polemical plays into his household, including one in 1628 in which a devil carried King James to hell (Chambers 1923: i. 328 n.; quoted in P. Jensen 2003).

What seems clear here is that Yorke was accustomed to frequent entertainments at and for his household, particularly on holidays. He was also unafraid of controversy, for he continued to sponsor plays that promulgated his own ideology, even at the threat of prosecution and with the resistance of his neighbors. One hundred guests for a knight's celebration gives us an idea of audience size and type, particularly if Yorke controlled admission by restricting the performance to his own retainers and invited guests who shared his politics. All of these facts indicate that household patrons, like Theseus in *A Midsummer Night's Dream*, took an active role in the selection of plays and companies. Here we see a patron who is certainly defiant, perhaps devout, but overwhelmingly confident of local support; even after a stint in the Tower he was willing and able to continue his patronage of seditious material.

Another example of a different sort of household entertainment, this less polemical, occurs in Kent, where we find Sir Edward Dering of Surrenden Dering, who owned hundreds of playbooks (including Ben Jonson's and William Shakespeare's Folios) and paid several times to have his playbooks bound together (Gibson 2002: ii. 913–22). Dering has been much discussed, since he was apparently a patron of amateur theatrics in his household, whose manuscript copy of a collated *1* and *2 Henry IV* has been mistaken for Shakespeare's foul papers (J. Baker 1996), although it is more likely a script that Dering himself was putting together for private performance (G. W. Williams 1976). His papers also include a cast list for John Fletcher's *The Spanish Curate*, in which Dering himself took a part, along with family, friends, and a servant called Jack of the Buttery. On 4 December 1623 he paid a shilling for six copies of a drollery called 'Ruff and Cuff', an example of a popular university allegorical form in which various articles of clothing argue with each other. Martin Wiggins surmises that Dering needed the six copies to cut and paste into performance scripts

(2005: 20); an early December purchase date indicates to me that Dering was planning, like most country gentry, his Christmas holiday.

Dering's theatricals add yet another motivation to gentry revels: simple pleasure in the act of playing, like Henry VIII, who took the lead in his own masques. It is not entirely unusual for the nobility to take part in plays, but it is bold; when Henry VIII first led a masque, Hall (1809) reports that the spectators were scandalized. And the royal family took roles in Jonson's masques, though their parts required no great theatrical skills. We have no evidence that earls and dukes and princes ever performed scripted roles in plays, which they might well have considered beneath their station (we could argue that they were, in fact, constantly performing), although they certainly were willing to dance and wear extravagant costumes, since they did so in everyday life. When lines are to be spoken or business learned, the chapel or professional players and not the noble masquers stepped up. But here we have Sir Edward himself indulging in acting roles, a taste he may have acquired during his student years at Cambridge. I would also suggest that such amateur theatricals, and the flourishing salons with which women like Mary Sidney Herbert, Elizabeth Cary, and Margaret Cavendish were involved (Barroll 2002; Bergeron 2006; Fitzmaurice 2006), formed an important part of provincial entertainments, particularly during the Elizabethan and Jacobean periods. Indeed, during the Interregnum, when 'legitimate' city theaters were closed, country houses continued to host readings and private performances of plays (Astington 2003*b*).

We are also beginning to notice connections between great households and local civic plays. The fifth Earl of Northumberland's almoner was also a playwright, and had a hand in the local Beverley plays (I. Lancashire 1980*a*: 13). Recently, Alexandra Johnston has been working to connect the Savile and De Lacy families of Thornhill both geographically and artistically with the Wakefield and York cycle plays, and I have argued elsewhere that 'The Second Shepherds Play', which indicates winter indoor performance and refers specifically to local villages and streets, is a household piece (Westfall 1990: 49–52).

I turn now to another species of household revel—the royal progress, with the lavish entertainments by the Earl of Leicester at Kenilworth and the Earl of Hertford at Elvetham being perhaps the most familiar. The Tudors, particularly Elizabeth, often traveled in the summer months to escape the heat and plague in the city, to show themselves to their subjects, to assess the loyalty of their courtiers, and, most importantly, to sponge off local pantries while they conserved their own household expenses. Provincial gentry were expected to entertain lavishly and support the royal riding household, which could number more than a hundred, plus extra baggage wagons, horses, and additional support staff.

Many of Elizabeth's progresses have been well documented, and I do not mean to conduct a thorough examination of the genre here since it is far too complex a topic for this essay, though recently the progresses have been the subject of interesting analysis. These events do merit some mention, however, if only because we have scripts specifically associated with performance at provincial houses, published in London (Nichols 1823). These texts of the verses composed and descriptions of the activities demonstrate many of the production values and motives I have discussed above, and suggest a few new thoughts about the potential profit of such ostentatious theater. Two such events, the 15 August 1591 entertainment for Queen Elizabeth at Cowdray of Sir Anthony Browne, Viscount Montagu, and the 20 September 'Honourable Entertainment' produced the same year by Edward Seymour, Earl of Hertford at Elvetham, exhibit many of the elements of other great house entertainments (Nichols 1823: iii. 90–6; Dunlop 1962; J. Wilson 1980; Breight 1989, 1992; Dovey 1996; Cole 2000; Louis 2000, pp. xlvii, 188–97).

Progresses are interesting entertainments since they are very public hospitality, and very localized events, but were also printed in London, and so intended for a complex and diverse audience of both readers and spectators. More than just a summer holiday, the progress had purpose: to sustain the illusion of harmony in the kingdom. They are also significant in that they indicate clearly that entire estates—houses, roads, deer parks, and gardens—provided settings for plays and entertainments. Cowdray is also particularly worthy of note because it was offered by Montagu, a prominent Elizabethan courtier who was openly Catholic and somewhat under siege. As Cameron Louis points out, he had opposed the 1559 Act of Supremacy, kept priests in his house, and was related to Arundel, Northumberland, and Norfolk, all of whom had suffered for their recusancy[4] (Louis 2000, pp. xxxii, lii); Curtis Breight explores at length the chequered career of the Viscount, whose power and reputation had suffered since his 1585 removal as Lord Lieutenant of Sussex, an action that could have dimmed his local reputation. Nevertheless, the Queen's own performance at Cowdray implied that Montagu had retained the Queen's trust and favor. In this elaborate charade, by lies that flatter, his Sussex household was assured that their local lord would continue to be honored (Breight 1989).

Montagu and other recusant lords continued to retain power and influence in their own cultural neighborhoods, and perhaps the entertainment at Cowdray is one of the reasons. It is equally possible that Elizabeth wanted to 'check up on suspect counties and two suspected aristocrats who might parlay discontent into political advantage' (Breight 1992: 22). The entertainment was printed twice by Thomas Scarlet and sold in London by William Wright, the first edition perhaps a program for the event, and the second a report that preserves the Queen's reactions (J. Wilson 1980: 88). Certainly this extensive publication for a rather modest entertainment indicates that Montagu was trying to get maximum exposure for his efforts, to challenge his detractors at court while ensuring that his local patronage remained sound.

[4] Recusancy, particularly among the nobility, was a difficult balancing act. The Act of Supremacy and its accompanying Act of Conformity made the Catholic mass illegal, fined those who did not attend Anglican services, and required a pledge to the Queen as head of the Church. At least on paper. Theoretically, Catholics could not hold office, or even serve as lawyers and schoolmasters. By the 1593 Act Against Recusants, the regulations were even more stringent, dictating 'that every person above the age of sixteen years, being a popish recusant . . . shall . . . repair to their place of dwelling . . . and shall not, any time after, pass or remove above five miles from thence' (Gee and Hardy 1896: 499–500).

The event comprises all the elements common to great household revels: music, dance, speeches, properties, sets, feasts, hunts, as well as an audience of mixed classes and habitations. Even though the dramatic production was not terribly elaborate, it must have been very expensive to support the Queen and her household for the week they remained at Montagu's 600-acre estate of Cowdray. The text is a fusion of styles that also reflects the binaries of the household: country folk elements like wild men, porters, fishermen, and rustic dances, combined with courtly elements like phrases in Latin as well as classical, biblical, romantic, and pastoral references that we expect more from plays penned by John Lyly; indeed one editor attributes the Cowdray verses to him (Lyly 1902: i. 404). The tone, like most Elizabethan court performances and progresses, is as obsequious as Uriah Heep, complete with copious (and perhaps scripted) weeping by Lady Montagu as she welcomed the Queen to her home, and constant protestations of everybody's loyalty in the verses.

In fact, the entire entertainment emphasizes—in text and performance—the concept of Montagu's 'honour'; the speeches stress that the entire shire of Sussex, represented by the broad audience that Montagu had collected, is supremely loyal unto death to the cause of the Queen. Thus, Montagu aggrandizes himself and his local power, impressing those both above and below his station, using entertainment to delineate and reinforce his position in the political hierarchy, yet another chief motivation for household entertainment. As Breight points out in his meticulous examination of the religious–political context of the event, Montagu had great need of such a stratagem (Breight 1989: 147). For example, the heraldic decorations, arms of the Queen hung on an oak tree (long a national symbol of strength and loyalty), together with the 'armes of the Noblemen, and Gentlemen of that Shire' (Louis 2000: 191), emphasize the oak's importance as a martial and conciliatory icon.

A dialogue between an Angler and a Fisherman at the fishpond reflects the heterogeneous audience, for the Angler suggests solitary sport while the Fisherman suggests a working trade. Their speeches employ, with some comic effect and compliments to Elizabeth as the goddess Venus, the stereotype of city hypocrisy versus country honesty. The Angler pleads with the Queen not to listen to the 'carpers' and detractors of the loyal Montagu, once again reinforcing the political motivation for the entire entertainment. Later, the 'countrie people' danced to pipe and tabor, joined by Lord and Lady Montagu, not only a cunning demonstration of class harmony but also an opportunity for Montagu to demonstrate to his own local subjects the high regard in which the Queen held him, and to the Queen the high regard in which the locals held him. The following day, after knighting Montagu's son, son-in-law, and four others (prominent Protestants, in fact), Elizabeth rode on.

I explore at length the entertainment at Cowdray partially because we have such a complete description of the activities and text of the speeches. But it is also important to realize that this production represents not only a sampling of the kinds of activity that we should expect at a great house revel, but also the complex causes and effects of those revels. The not-for-profit entertainment (at least in a financial sense) serves a very large and diverse audience in a large and diverse setting. Political allegories were carefully enfolded in Montagu's entertainments, and the text, with its veiled references, allegories, suggestions of subterfuge, and double meanings that required interpretation from the audience (the Queen was particularly adept at and fond of this exercise), preserves for us a fine example of 'court-speak' in the great households. In addition, topical allusion to sea battles and the coast, with the oak tree standing in for a ship, reminds us of the foreign wars in which the English were engaged, and encodes perhaps a veiled warning that it behooves Her Majesty to take good care of her Sussex subjects (J. Wilson 1980: 86; Breight 1989: 148).

As the Queen rode on, she would, on 20 September, experience one of the most spectacular entertainments on record, Edward Seymour's at Elvetham. There she saw an entertainment, as Wilson puts it, 'organically related to the countryside', a synthetic theme we have come to expect in provincial progresses. In addition, the text resonates with Sidney's 1579 *The Lady of May*, and Spenser's *Faerie Queene*, published the previous year (J. Wilson 1980: 96–9). Many editors, picking up on Edith Rickert's suggestion that the 'changeling child' of *A Midsummer Night's Dream* represents Hertford's attempts to legitimize his son by Katherine Grey, believe that the 'love in idleness' episode that Shakespeare would write four years later was inspired by the entertainment at Elvetham, which young Shakespeare might have seen (Chambers 1916; Rickert 1923; Calthorpe 1942; Titherley 1952; Griffin 1972; M. Taylor 1973; Purdon 1974; Patterson 1989; Paster and Skiles 1999: 31).

Hertford's small estate at Elvetham could not sustain extensive riding and hunting. To compensate, 'his honour with all expedition set artificers a work, to the number of three hundred, many dais before her Majestie's arrival, to inlarge his house with newe roomes and offices', including an elaborate presence chamber and 280 service rooms. But the most extravagant set piece, perhaps the most famous excavation of all the progress venues, was the 'goodly Pond, cut to the perfect figure of a half moon', a very concrete allusion to Elizabeth in her aspect of Diana, or Cynthia, as Lyly had immortalized her three years previously in *Endymion*. Once again the revels demonstrate the interrelationship of court and country, of topical allusions with classical. On the crescent pond floated a 'ship Ile', with three masts and cannon, a fort or castle island, and a 'Snayl Mount', a spiral with four levels of hedge. The pond also had room for boats of musicians, a fully rigged ship with more cannon, and scores of performers. Around the pond were ranged a throne and retiring chamber for the Queen and her retinue in addition to tiring houses for the players who were to perform in the masque (J. Wilson 1980: 100–1).

Accompanied by a train of 200 mounted servitors decked in chains of gold, the Earl escorted the Queen to his own personal theme park and four days of magnificent entertainment—dining, music, dancing, tennis, fireworks, Latin orations, and dumb-shows. One particularly extravagant ceremony entailed a 'banket' (several courses of sweets, including the royal arms in sugar), served on the best household plate from the hillside by 200 of Hertford's gentlemen lit by 100 torchbearers (J. Wilson 1980: 115). Such a sizeable gathering of servitors, not only for escort and service but also for the site construction (the works crew numbered 300), was well over the number permitted by the Act Against Retainers, and might be construed as a not-so-subtle display of power and force. Breight even suggests that Elizabeth chose to visit Hertford at

Elvetham precisely *because* it was a small, unfortified house as opposed to the Earl's larger and more fortified properties (1992: 34–5). Hertford had, by his clandestine marriage to a person of royal blood without the Queen's permission, already challenged Elizabeth's crown, so his excessive mustering of men might easily have further threatened the Queen. The entertainments, however, like those at Cowdray, were constantly conciliatory to the point of sycophancy.

The three editions published of the Elvetham entertainment, like those of Cowdray, suggest an aggressive rhetoric, a public relations move; the text, which unswervingly compliments the Earl and emphasizes his family connection to Elizabeth, certainly supports this allegation. Themes of sexuality, fecundity, and chastity spoke to Hertford's secret marriage to Katherine Grey, which Elizabeth had annulled, and the birth of their two sons, who were, as great-grandsons of Princess Mary Tudor, viable contenders for the throne. Hertford never stopped petitioning to legitimize his sons by Katherine, an attempt that did not succeed until three years after Elizabeth's death (Matthew and Harrison 2004: xlix. 889–91).

In the absence of other descriptive accounts of great household entertainments, these published versions of royal progresses provide us with important indications of the purpose and style of such occasions. Clearly the entertainments at Cowdray and Elvetham had multiple audiences and intricate themes. Both were directed to readers as well as spectators, and the spectators comprised diverse classes, heterogeneous cultural neighborhoods, divergent polemical ideologies, and conflicting alliances. The texts, multi-medial and layered, aimed to achieve many effects: pleasure, certainly, as well as political maneuvering, aesthetic and textual sophistication, largesse, and displays of grandeur, luxury, majesty, and power. They required the cooperation of virtually the entire household, from John of the Buttery to the household chamberlain. Musicians, singers, actors, writers, and designers had to collaborate and rehearse to produce a very limited-run show. Perhaps most importantly, the patron subsumed the entire expense of the entertainment without charging admission to offset production costs. Any profit he might garner would not land in the family coffers, at least not directly. Both Montagu and Hertford were seeking more abstract coin, a different return on their investments.

It might appear that a royal progress was unique in its extravagance, but we do have evidence in household ordinances that ceremonies at which the monarch was not present could claim similarly high production values. I turn finally to another sort of documentation, to the second Northumberland household book,[5] which preserves for us the form but not the content for several different family occasions, such as weddings, christenings, and Twelfth Night celebrations. This book is the 'stage manager's bible' as opposed to the producer's 'script', and records no specifics of what guests enjoyed, but does preserve the process by which the household organized and produced the events. The ordinances demonstrate clearly that household entertainment was produced with precision, far from the popular culture phenomenon of the unruly 'Renaissance banquet'.

[5] Bodleian Library, MS Eng. hist. b. 208.

Extant household accounts and ordinance books from the royal courts and a few noble courts (King Edward IV, and the Stafford, Percy, and Howard families, for example) stipulate that retained players, minstrels, harpers, bearwards, and waits were expected to perform for important religious and family occasions, then to vacate and earn their livings by touring to prevent their being a drain on household revenues. Indeed, the household ordinances of Henry Algernon Percy, fifth Earl of Northumberland, stipulate that his chapel performs the 'Play of the Nativity uppon Cristynmes-Day in the morning', as well as the 'Play of Ressurection upon Estur-Day in the Mornynge', and the 'Play befor his Lordship upon Shrofteusday at night yerely' (Grose 1809: 256–8). According to Edward IV's household ordinances, festival attendance at home by retained performers had been the custom for over a century: the King's string minstrels would attend the court 'at v festes of the yere, and than to make theyre wages of houshold after iiij^{d} ob. a day if they be present in court; and than they to auoyde the next day after the festes be don' (Myers 1959: 131–2).

Ian Lancashire has transcribed and edited the Earl of Northumberland's ordinance for Twelfth Night, the end of the households' Christmas season, during which feasts, masques, concerts, and processions occurred on an almost daily basis (I. Lancashire 1980*a*). When we combine these ordinances with household accounts, we get a clearer idea of what the Christmas season entailed: Percy rewarded an Abbot of Misrule, the chapel provided a boy to play St Nicholas and other boys from Beverley or York acted the Boy Bishop. On Christmas day and on Twelfth Night, the chapel processed with the rest of the household, and sang secular carols at the feast, which was served while household musicians played. Between courses, the family watched disguisings and a morris dance performed by the Earl's henchmen (Grose 1809: 254–7; I. Lancashire 1980*a*: 14–15).

Another occasion, a wedding, was also celebrated with ceremony. Like Christmas, this was both a secular and a religious festival, but at a family wedding politics plays a much more prominent role. The orders for the marriage of an earl's daughter were probably followed for the marriages of the fifth Earl's sister and/or his daughter, between 1511 and 1515 (I. Lancashire 1980*a*: 10). No guest lists, descriptions, or accounts for the occasions survive, so it is difficult to speculate about the size of these particular occasions. If Percy celebrated weddings in similar fashion as his brother-in-law Buckingham did, the weddings were likely to be expensive. During 1518 and 1519, when Buckingham married off a daughter and a son, and entertained Henry VIII at his household at Penshurst, Buckingham's household expenditures for provisions rose £1,000 and wardrobe expenditures rose £1,500 for each of the two years (Rawcliffe 1978: 134–5).

At first glance, a family wedding may seem a private and secular event, and in comparison to the great religious feasts, it certainly is. Nevertheless, when two aristocratic families merged, the marriage became a public event, at which the family produced a show of their 'private' life, displaying family treasures of plate and arras, providing lavish feasts with every variety of food the Earl's far-flung properties could provide or exotic delicacies his unstinting purse could purchase. In addition to these displays, entertainments by the Earl's retained artists demonstrated the sophistication of his court, the dignity of his household, and the honor of his family.

The twelfth order of the second Northumberland household book shows that the Earl took the opportunity to display his wealth as set decoration for the theater that was to come. His high altar, his choir, the body of his chapel, and the side altars were to be covered with 'the best stuf that they have', hung with 'arras or counterfeat arras'; carpets covered the floors, and Percy's plate, including 'a crosse vppon a stage', 'ymages' of saints, silver and gilt candlesticks, basins, ewers, cruets, and chalices, was displayed. In the midst of this 'set' of shining white linen, colorful tapestries, and glowing plate, Percy's chapel singers sang a high mass, in the rood loft 'yf the Queir beneth be not sufficiaunte of Rowme', since it was probably filled with guests.[6]

While the Chamberlain (responsible for hierarchy, precedence, and protocol) was arranging the bride and her attendants in the proper order, the lord himself was waiting in the choir to give the bride away 'yf their be not A better to yef her that Day'.[7] This last comment is particularly interesting, for it indicates that rank trumped kinship, that the family patriarch customarily relinquished his paternal right if a guest of higher status were in attendance, clear evidence that the private, domestic aspect of marriage was, in aristocratic nuptials, turned inside out, with the private publicly reconstructed and displayed.

Besides careful attention to rank and timing, the order also dictates procedures based upon the past marital status of the couple involved, detailing the bride's hairstyle, the rank of her attendants, and whether or not she would consume food in sight of the guests (virgins ate behind a cloth held by attendants). This performance signified to the assembled audience the most intimate details of a woman's life—her virginity or widowhood—perhaps to short-circuit later accusations of pre-contract or false testimony.

The wedding supper required the service of cooks and servants, an afternoon of dancing, for which the minstrels played, and an evening of entertainment: 'When they have souped that then they be brought into the great chambre again to se suche passe tymes as is their ordirid for theim As Disguisinges enterludes or playes'. Supper was followed by more dancing and a banquet of sweets.[8]

Although the menu is, of course, non-extant, Percy's household accounts provide some indication of the foods that may have been served. Over the twelve days of Christmas, the revelers consumed venison, swans, cranes, herons, pheasants, peacocks, and other birds (Grose 1809: 103, 167). In 1552, when Sir William Petre celebrated his daughter's wedding, he hired a master cook and four apprentices, and entertained 400 guests for two days (Emmison 1964: 32).

Concerned with the logistics of the evening rather than with the content, the Northumberland wedding order preserves no details of dramatic entertainments, but descriptive accounts from other noble weddings provide some indication of the form the wedding revels might take. In 1536 the Earl of Rutland celebrated a triple wedding that united the houses of Oxford, Westmorland, and Rutland. After a dinner of 'diverse greate dishes and delicate meates with sotteltes, and diverse manner of instruments playinge at the same', the King himself 'came theder in a maske, rydynge

[6] Ibid., fo. 33. [7] Ibid., fo. 24. [8] Ibid., fos 28–30.

from Yorke Place, with 11 more with him, wherof the Kinge and 7 more with him ware garmentes after the Turkes fashion... and so they daunsed with the ladyes a good while' (Hamilton 1875: 50–1).

Few descriptions of noble wedding revels from the early Tudor period survive, but some references to such festivities during the reign of Queen Elizabeth testify that the banquet–disguising structure continued to be popular at noble marriages. 'Mummeries and masks' were performed on each of the four days of the wedding revels that united the houses of Talbot and Herbert at Baynard's Castle in 1563. In 1565 Sir Francis Knollys and Sir Ambrose Cave celebrated the marriage of their children with two disguisings lasting until 1.30 a.m. at Durham Place. The 1566 wedding guests of the Earl of Southampton and the daughter of Lord Montagu saw a disguising with an oration. During July of the same year a disguising of Venus, Diana, Pallas, and Juno (classical ladies perfectly suited to the themes of love, chastity, and fidelity intrinsic to courtly marriage) was performed at the wedding of the Earl of Sussex's sister (Chambers 1923: i. 160–2).

The masque or disguising, sometimes including rhetoric with music and dance, continued in popularity as a wedding entertainment throughout Elizabeth's reign. George Gascoigne wrote verses for one at the house of Lord Montagu in 1572, the costumes for which were hired from the Revels Office. In 1595 the marriage of Burghley's granddaughter to the Earl of Derby was celebrated with a disguising. In 1600 the Queen's own maids of honor performed a disguising of eight Muses in search of their sister when their companion Elizabeth Russell married the Earl of Worcester's son. The painting of the marriage of Sir Henry Unton (*c.*1580) at the National Portrait Gallery depicts a disguising of classical goddesses and child cupids (Chambers 1923: i. 162–8).

Several facets of performance unique to the disguising made it extremely popular as a great household entertainment, particularly for weddings. Like a royal progress, a disguising could be commissioned to celebrate a specific occasion by referring to particular events and people and by employing allegory complementary to the themes of the marriage. Chapel gentlemen and children, singing and perhaps speaking, joined with minstrels and dancing gentlemen and gentlewomen in the context of a feast to create a visual and aural extravaganza.

Other qualities of the disguising made it an ideal entertainment for a patron who wished to impress his guests. A disguising was expensive, including costs for costumes and scenic devices, and was never to be re-created. In addition, the disguising was interactive, involving the guests in a fashion that a play did not: as performers themselves. If commoners were present, as they were at Cowdray and Elvetham, they would focus on the power and luxury of their overlords. In addition, the disguising not only entertained the elite but flattered them as well, complimenting their intellect with its classical themes, and reflecting their own courtly lifestyle. The sole profit to the patron, the grandeur of the impression, made it a splendidly wasteful display.

It is obvious from the variety of provincial performances I have touched on here that these private occasions, while less frequently analyzed than public theater, are nevertheless vital to our understanding of how performances, ceremonies, and revels designed for specific occasions communicated cultural values and intricate ideological relationships. We also find unique production values, motivations, and styles; like civic producers, households strove to produce multidimensional entertainment by enlisting the cooperation of many people. Unlike civic producers, the households' production team was far more diverse: cooks, minstrels, gardeners, composers, priests, players, dancers, and chamberlains, all retained in the place they were to perform, were paid salary to practice their craft in the service of their patron. In the for-profit public theater, this sort of collaboration was definitely out of the question.

The wedding revels and royal progresses I have discussed above illustrate how, through a cooperative effort of these household servants, personal ideologies and aesthetics, principles of hierarchy and power, were expressed through movement, speech, music, and *mise-en-scène*. The records also indicate that stage management was precise and controlled, not loosely organized or haphazard; whether the Earl of Northumberland's chamberlain was arranging a procession or Sir John Yorke's doorkeepers were denying admission to a local Puritan, household theater was micro-managed, perhaps because it was often risky, but particularly because it usually had a specific social, political, or religious objective. Nothing, not even Lady Montagu's tears, was left to chance. At the same time, the revels commingle public and private space, enacting the hospitality that was expected of the noble classes for the various cultural neighborhoods that met at festival occasions. Audiences for household theater were also unique: disparate classes, including household servants as well as local residents, and in some cases readers far away in the city, interpreted the occasions in very different ways. The Queen might see a critique in masques at Elvetham that local folk might view as courtly mythology.

All theater is, of course, ephemeral. A performance of *Hamlet* will never unfold in precisely the same way twice. But household theater was never intended to be performed more than once, and so presents us with a different sort of ephemerality, an intentional transience. Certainly the more elaborate occasions were too expensive, too complex, and too specific to be repeated, which made it that much more extraordinary. In contrast to the urban public theater, which staged popular plays with regularity, with thrift, and with profit in mind, the provincial patrons of early modern England counted their profit not in pounds and shillings, but in status and power.

CHAPTER 16

THE UNIVERSITIES AND THE INNS OF COURT

ALAN H. NELSON

Oxford and Cambridge, England's two historical universities, along with the Inns of Court in London, supplied significant impetus to the drama of early modern England.[1] Connections and influences, however, were often indirect and complex.

Oxford and Cambridge lay distant from London (and from one another) one very long day at a fast pace by horseback, or two or even three days at a more typical pace. The Inns of Court, by contrast, lay just beyond London's western wall, where it was an easy walk to the Royal Courts of Justice at Westminster (Whitehall), and a mile or two on foot to the theaters which lay just beyond the London Wall to the north-east, or by water to the theaters and bear-baiting rings on the far bank of the Thames near Southwark.

Oxford University traces its origins to 1230, Cambridge to 1260. The two universities are best thought of, however, as federations of constituent colleges, each of which had its own history and character. All four Inns of Court, which are not 'inns' in the usual

[1] Unless noted otherwise, information in this essay is from one of three collections in the Records of Early English Drama (REED) series: Nelson (1989); Elliott et al. (2004); and *Inns of Court* (forthcoming). I wish to express my appreciation for the work of the late John R. Elliott, Jr, who prior to an incapacitating stroke (in 2002) and his subsequent death was editor of both *Oxford* and *Inns of Court.* I have extracted information generously from the introductions and appendices attached to each of the three collections, which variously represent his work and my own. Specific information in the three collections can generally be located by consulting their indexes. References to the Cambridge play *Return from Parnassus* are from Leishman (1949), and those to *Every Man Out of His Humour* are from Jonson (1616).

meaning of the word but voluntary societies dedicated to the practice and teaching of English common law, trace their histories back to the fourteenth century. (Lacking charters, none claims a specific foundation date.) In alphabetical order (for no Inn will grant precedence to any other), the four are Gray's Inn, the Inner Temple, Lincoln's Inn, and the Middle Temple. England's two universities have usually been judged—by unbiased observers—as roughly equal in achievement and reputation. London's Inns of Court, which have always enjoyed a similarly high reputation, were known in the sixteenth and seventeenth centuries as England's 'third university'.

The typical college, being quasi-monastic in origin, lay within a walled and gated enclosure, with a chapel, hall, walks, and gardens, and one or more residential blocks, often laid out in quadrangles. The typical Inn of Court was similarly situated and similarly provided, but with residential blocks comprised of elaborate 'chambers' rather than simple 'rooms'. (The Inner Temple and Middle Temple were surrounded by one wall, and shared one chapel.)

Each college and each Inn which set out to perform or to host a play (or a masque) had a hall fit for the purpose. At Oxford, moreover, Christ Church Hall, built in 1529, served the entire university for royal visits of 1566, 1594, 1605, and 1636. At Cambridge the splendid and spacious King's College Chapel was fitted out with a large stage in August 1564 for plays performed before Elizabeth I; after the completion in 1607 of its resplendent hall, Trinity College served as the university-wide venue for royal or aristocratic performances in 1615 and subsequent years. Among the Inns of Court, the Middle Temple boasted by far the finest hall. Constructed during the reign of Elizabeth, Middle Temple Hall served for major performances in 1601–2 and 1635–6.

Up to 1642 records survive of some 384 entertainment events at Cambridge, 185 at Oxford, and 125 at the Inns of Court. These are minimum numbers as records are far from complete. The earliest known dramatic or quasi-dramatic activity at Cambridge can be traced to 1456–7 (a disguising); at Oxford, to 1485–6 (player(s)). The earliest such activity at any of London's legal societies occurred at an Inn of Chancery, Furnival's, in 1407; for the four major Inns, the earliest known dramatic or quasi-dramatic activity can be traced to 1489–90 (disguisings at Gray's Inn and the Inner Temple). Though full details are wanting, these and other sorts of secular entertainment proliferated, to the point that a royal commission appointed near the end of the reign of Henry VIII (*c.*1540) reported that over the Christmas season the Inns of Court 'have all manner of pastimes, as singing and dancing; and in some of the houses ordinarily they have some interlude or Tragedy played by the Gentlemen of the same house, the ground, and manner whereof, is devised by some of the Gentlemen of the house'. About 1522–3 Cambridge students, probably of Trinity Hall, performed Plautus' *Miles Gloriosus*, just the kind of play one would expect in an academic setting. The performance of William Stevenson's *Gammer Gurton's Needle* at Christ's College, Cambridge, in 1550–1 is a salutary reminder that most university plays were not sober enactments of high culture, but rollicking, ribald productions, often in English, and usually more Chaucerian or Skeltonic than 'classical'. But the plays of Plautus and Terence, however moralized by academics and theologians, were themselves often lascivious and even obscene.

Dramatic activity flourished everywhere in the 1560s, the first full decade of the reign of Elizabeth I. Over the 1561–2 Christmas season Inner Temple gentlemen performed the famous *Gorboduc* alias *Ferrex and Porrex*, written by two of their number, Thomas Norton and Thomas Sackville. This was only one event in a season of revels which lasted from All Souls' day (1 November 1561) to Candlemas (2 February 1561/2), and the play was performed both in Inner Temple Hall and at court. Over the same Christmas season the Inner Temple performed a masque of 'Beauty and Desire' by Arthur Broke (or Brooke), who, for his pains, was made an honorary member of the society. Several years later, evidently in 1566, the Inner Temple performed George Gascoigne's *Supposes* and *Jocasta*. In August 1564 Cambridge University and its constituent colleges pulled out all the stops for the royal visit of Elizabeth, performing tragedies and comedies in King's College Chapel, along with academic debates and the formal granting of degrees in St Mary's Church on the Market. Not to be outdone, Oxford performed three plays for Elizabeth in September 1566 in Christ Church Hall, including a two-part dramatization of Chaucer's *Knight's Tale* in the form of *Palamon and Arcite* by Richard Edwards.

Subsequent plays of particular consequence at Cambridge included Thomas Legge's three-day extravaganza *Richardus Tertius* at St John's (1578–9), *Laelia* at Queens' (1594–5), the three *Parnassus* plays at St John's (1598–9 to 1601–2?, of which more below), George Ruggle's *Ignoramus* by Clare College, and Thomas Tomkis's *Albumazar* by Trinity College (both performed at Trinity College Hall, 1614–15), Thomas Randolph's *The Conceited Pedlar* by Trinity College (1627–8), and Peter Hausted's *The Rival Friends* by Queens' College and Thomas Randolph's *The Jealous Lovers* by Trinity College (both performed at Trinity College Hall, 1631–2). Oxford plays included numerous but long-forgotten works from the pen of William Gager (Christ Church, 1582–3 to 1591–2), but also an important sequence of plays mostly performed in Christ Church Hall: Samuel Daniel's *The Queen's Arcadia* (1604–5), Barton Holiday's *Technogamia* (1617–18 and 1620–1), Robert Burton's *Philosophaster* (1617–18), and three plays for the royal visit of 1635–6: William Strode's *The Floating Island*, George Wild's *Love's Hospital* (performed at St John's), and William Cartwright's *The Royal Slave*. Only one post-1560s internally produced play is recorded for the Inns of Court, *The Misfortunes of Arthur* by Thomas Hughes (1587–8).

Indeed, while Cambridge and Oxford colleges went on performing plays until the 1640s, the Inns of Court turned rather to revels and masques. From the fifteenth century and perhaps earlier, gentlemen of each of the four Inns appointed a Master of the Revels and 'reveled' (mostly drinking and dancing) each year that such activity was not precluded by the plague. Revels on a grander scale occurred at the Inner Temple in 1561–2 (as we have seen), but are best represented by the *Gesta Grayorum*, published in 1688 but recording events at Gray's Inn over the entire Christmas season—1 November to 2 February and beyond—of 1594–5. Such grand revels, which included the election of a Christmas Prince and the presentation of a long sequence of varied entertainments, were extremely rare, only six or seven being recorded between 1561–2 and 1635–6. (One full Christmas revels is known to have been performed by university students: this was *The Christmas Prince* at St John's

College, Oxford, in 1607–8.) Two further Inns of Court revels were performed in the years following the Restoration of 1660. The first was printed in 1662/3 as *Eykυk-λορεὶα, or, Vniversal motion being part of that magnificent entertainment by the noble prince, De la Grange, Lord Lieutenant of Lincolns Inn, presented to the High and Mighty Charles II, Monarck of Great Brittain, France and Ireland, on Friday 3 of January 1662*; the second is a less richly documented revels from Gray's Inn, February 1682/3. From the latter survives the image of an entrance 'ticket' (Green 1931, opp. p. 136). This was not the first of its kind, however, as tickets were issued to control admissions to an Inns of Court masque as early as 1633/4 (*Triumph of Peace*).

Masques, which were got up by the various Inns of Court in emulation of royal court entertainment, were something like modern musicals: less a complex plot or double-plot with roles assigned to actors, and more an occasion for poetry, song, spectacle, and dance. Gray's Inn performed several masques in the 1590s, though details are sparse; later, from 1612–13 to 1635–6, the four Inns performed nearly a dozen masques. The marriage of Princess Elizabeth to the Palsgrave Frederick of Bohemia, on Valentine's day, 14 February 1612/13, having been announced long in advance, elicited three masques in the week following the wedding. One, known as *The Lords' Masque*, was organized by courtiers, while two were organized by the Inns of Court: *The Memorable Masque*, by George Chapman, was performed on 15 February by Lincoln's Inn and the Middle Temple, while *The Masque of the Inner Temple and Gray's Inn*, by Francis Beaumont, was performed on 20 February. All three masques were performed at Whitehall, in the 'old' Banqueting House. *The Memorable Masque* was accompanied by a processional 'riding' of gentlemen on horseback, while (for the sake of variety and because the wedding was conceived to unite the Thames and the Rhine) *The Masque of the Inner Temple and Gray's Inn* featured a flotilla on the river. Though an exception may have been made for these two masques of direct national significance, most Inns of Court masques and—earlier—most Inns of Court plays were performed twice, once in the hall of the sponsoring Inn, and once at court, whether at Whitehall or at Greenwich.

By far the most ambitious of all Inns of Court masques was *The Triumph of Peace*, performed February 1633/4 in response to a perceived insult to Queen Henrietta Maria in the *Histriomastix* of William Prynne (1633), a member of Lincoln's Inn. Organized by all four Inns, and reported by contemporaries to have been the most expensive masque ever devised at a cost of more than £20,000, *The Triumph of Peace* was the product of months of preparation. Sets and costumes were designed in large part by Inigo Jones, with music commissioned from William Lawes and Simon Ive. A procession through the streets of London involved 100 men on horseback, intermixed with musicians and others disposed into sixteen chariots. The masque was performed at the Banqueting House in Whitehall (designed by Inigo Jones, *c.*1620) and repeated at Merchant Taylors' Hall (within the walls of London).

Records gathered up in the Records of Early English Drama (REED) series contain an astonishing amount of information concerning dramatic and quasi-dramatic performances in the two universities and the Inns of Court. Theater historians who devote their lives to reconstructing the playhouses and play repertories of the London professional companies must perforce turn green with envy. To give just four examples, full cast lists survive for approximately twenty-five Cambridge plays; the scaffolded stage-cum-auditorium of Queens' College, Cambridge, probably decades old when it was decommissioned in 1638, can be reconstructed down to the last piece of timber (A. Nelson 1994); a detailed architectural drawing in the hand of Inigo Jones survives for the perspective auditorium built in the hall of Christ Church, Oxford, in 1605 (Orrell 1982); while the Inns of Court *Triumph of Peace* of February 1633/4 can be reconstructed almost down to the last penny spent, along with the name, instrument, personal signature, and standing place of each of nearly sixty musicians. The question must be, of course—and it is a question which I will leave open—whether all this information can be applied either directly or indirectly to the theaters of the London professional companies.

Certain connections can certainly be made. For example, the texts of nearly all seventeenth-century Inns of Court masques were commissioned from professional playwrights. In order of performance chronology these include George Chapman, Francis Beaumont, Thomas Middleton, James Shirley, and William Davenant. Members of the King's Men assisted in the performance of the Inner Temple *Masque of Heroes* in January or February 1618/19, while the same company performed Cartwright's *The Royal Slave*—from Oxford University—at Hampton Court on 12 January 1636/7. More significant, no doubt, in the larger picture are performances of professional plays in districts or venues under institutional control. At Cambridge and Oxford the jurisdiction of the university extended to a radius of 5 miles from town center. While Cambridge tended to exclude players, Oxford was more welcoming. The title page of the 1603 (First) Quarto of *Hamlet* boasts that the play had been 'diuerse times acted...in the two Vniuersities of Cambridge and Oxford', less likely perhaps for the former than for the latter. The King's Men (Shakespeare's company) certainly performed *Othello* at Oxford in 1610, in a public venue but to enthusiastic scholarly acclaim.

Far more Oxford than Cambridge colleges performed plays written by outsiders: plays by John Foxe were apparently performed at Magdalen College about 1560–1, Richard Edwards's *Palamon and Arcite* (based on Chaucer's *Knight's Tale*) and *Damon and Pithias* were performed at Christ Church and at Merton College in 1565–6 and 1567–8 respectively, and George Gascoigne's *Supposes* (earlier performed at the Inner Temple *c.*1566) was performed at Trinity College on 8 January 1581/2.

The Inns of Court hosted professional performances as early as the 1560s. Lincoln's Inn hired the Children of the Chapel at least three times, first in 1564–5 and 1565–6 under the direction of Richard Edwards, and then in 1579–80 under the direction of Richard Farrant. Gray's Inn famously procured Shakespeare's *Comedy of Errors* on 28 December 1594, as described in the *Gesta Grayorum*. The anonymous chronicler noted that the play gave its name to the night of its performance: 'a Comedy of Errors (like to Plautus his Menechmus) was played by the Players. So that Night was begun, and continued to the end, in nothing but Confusion and Errors; whereupon, it was ever afterwards called, The Night of Errors.' The chronicler's comparison to the *Menechmi* of Plautus constitutes the earliest recognition of a Shakespeare source. To allay the disappointment of guests including members of the Inner Temple and—perhaps surprisingly—women, Gray's Inn patched together an entertainment for the following night which lay the blame on 'a Sorcerer or Conjurer that was supposed to be the Cause of that confused Inconvenience':

Therein was contained, How he had caused the Stage to be built, and Scaffolds to be reared to the top of the House, to increase Expectation. Also how he had caused divers Ladies and Gentlewomen, and others of good Condition, to be invited to our Sports; also our dearest Friend, the State of Templaria, to be disgraced, and disappointed of their kind Entertainment, deserved and intended. Also that he caused Throngs and Tumults, Crowds and Outrages, to disturb our whole Proceedings. And Lastly, that he had foisted a Company of base and common Fellows, to make up our Disorders with a Play of Errors and Confusions; and that that Night had gained to us Discredit, and it self a Nick-name of Errors.

Each part of this reminiscence supplies invaluable detail to the theater historian: the high scaffolds to accommodate a larger audience; the mixed nature of that audience; the disorder caused by uninvited guests; the gentlemanly condescension to the professional players, presumably the Lord Chamberlain's Men with Shakespeare among them, characterized as 'a Company of base and common Fellows'.

To the Middle Templar John Manningham we owe a similar report on *Twelfth Night*, performed on Candlemas (2 February) 1601/2:

At our feast wee had a play called *Twelve Night or What You Will*, much like the *Commedy of Errores* or *Menechmi* in Plautus but most like and neere to that in Italian called *Inganni*. A good practise in it to make the steward beleeue his lady widdowe was in Love with him by counterfayting a letter, as from his lady in generall termes, telling him what shee liked best in him and prescribing his gesture in smiling his apparaile &c. and then when he came to practise making him beleeve they tooke him to be mad. (Manningham 1976: 48)

Manningham correctly recognizes Shakespeare's *Comedy of Errors* (and its source, Plautus' *Menechmi*) as generally analogous to *Twelfth Night, or, What You Will* (note the full title and subtitle); more particularly he recognizes the Italian *Inganni* as an explicit source. On details Manningham is famously selective (he makes no reference to the cross-dressed Viola!) and is slightly inaccurate: Olivia is not in fact a widow, and mourns the death not of a husband but of a brother. The greatest impression is made by the steward (Malvolio). The Middle Templar Manningham is also the source of a notorious (if dubious) anecdote concerning Richard Burbage, William Shakespeare, and a 'citizen'—that is, the wife of an established Londoner:

Vpon a tyme when Burbidge played Richard 3 there was a citizen goene [gone] soe farr in liking with him, that before shee went from the play shee appointed him to come that night vnto hir by the name of Richard the 3 | Shakespeare overhearing their conclusion, went before, was intertained, and at his game ere Burbidge came. Then message being brought that Richard the 3d was at the dore, Shakespeare caused returne to be made that William the Conquerour was before Richard the 3. (Manningham 1976: 75)

In addition to being an exemplary joke, the anecdote reveals that Burbage and Shakespeare, in their capacities as actors on the public stage, were something like modern rock stars.

When archival records begin to survive in greater numbers in the years after 1603, it becomes clear that the performance of *Twelfth Night* on Candlemas 1601/2 was not anomalous, but typical of Inns of Court play performances. The records demonstrate that at least two Inns hired in professional plays twice each year, for performances on 1 November (All Saints') and 2 February (Purification of the Virgin, alias Candlemas). The Inner Temple contracted with the King's Men, while the Middle Temple contracted with a succession of companies, or rather with one company under a succession of names: the Palsgrave's Men (1615–16), the Prince's Men (1618–19), the Cockpit players (1627–8), the Queen's Men (1632–3 to 1638–9), and Beeston's boys (from 1639–40). Professional plays identifiable by title, beyond the two by Shakespeare already mentioned, are 'The Oxford Tragedy', Inner Temple, 2 February 1607/8; 'The Bridegroom and the Madman', Middle Temple, 2 February 1618/19; *Hyde Park*, by James Shirley, Middle Temple, 1 November 1632; and 'The City Shuffler', Middle Temple, 1 November 1633. Of these four plays, the texts of all but *Hyde Park* are lost. Performances by professional playing companies resumed at the Inns of Court about the time of the Restoration of 1660, and continued until 1687 (Green 1931: 154–6).

This (newly discovered) pattern of professional playing has implications both for the Inns of Court and for the professional companies. For the Inns of Court it meant that plays later than *The Misfortunes of Arthur* in 1587–8 were not played by students (or, as they were called, gentlemen) of the four Inns. For the professional players it meant that two of the major London companies must have kept their annual calendars clear to enable performances in the Inns of Court—and not on the road—every 1 November and 2 February. The standing arrangements suggest, moreover, that professional playwrights must always have written plays with the gentlemen of the Inns of Court in mind, along with the distinctly different audiences of the public theaters, whether open-air or (later) enclosed; the royal court; provincial towns; and country houses. Most plays must have been written, in other words, for a variety of venues, and not for a single, particular playhouse.

Some plays from the universities and the Inns may have influenced professional playwrights over the years. Obvious examples include *Gorboduc*, on a theme close to that of *King Lear* (and with a tragic ending *à la* Shakespeare); *Richardus Tertius*, an obvious analogue of Shakespeare's *Richard III*; and *Laelia*, from Queens' College, Cambridge, yet another analogue of *Twelfth Night*. Textual comparisons have been made much easier in recent years by such projects as the Renaissance Latin Drama in England series, with one sequence devoted to Oxford, one to Cambridge, and one to 'other' plays; while editions and translations have also multiplied greatly in recent years, including on the Internet.[2] For students of the Inns of Court, comparisons are simplified by the fact that all surviving texts of plays and masques are in English. (Inns of Court masque texts are reproduced in the Appendix of REED Inns of Court.)

The two universities and the four Inns of Court supplied many playwrights to the professional stage: from Cambridge (to name but a few), John Fletcher, Robert Greene, Christopher Marlowe, and Thomas Nash; from Oxford, Samuel Daniel,

[2] See Sutton, Philological Museum, <http://www.philological.bham.ac.uk/bibliography/index.htm>.

Thomas Lodge, John Lyly, Philip Massinger, Thomas Middleton, and George Peele; from the Inns of Court, Francis Beaumont, John Ford, and John Marston. (Cambridge and Oxford playwrights are often identified, somewhat anachronistically, as the 'University Wits'.) Despite this flood of dramatic talent, however, two of the finest playwrights of the age were 'outsiders'. This fact is acknowledged in Act IV, scene iii, of the Cambridge play *Return from Parnassus* (*c.*1601–2; printed 1605, 1606; Leishman 1949). The same scene begins with an invaluable comparison between university and professional styles of acting. The speakers, appropriately, are Richard Burbage and Will Kempe of the Lord Chamberlain's Men, Shakespeare's company (spelling modernized):

BURBAGE. Now, Will Kempe, if we can entertain these scholars at a low rate, it will be well, they have oftentimes a good conceit in a part.

KEMPE. Its true indeed, honest Dick, but the slaves are somewhat proud, and besides, it is a good sport in a part to see them never speak in their walk, but at the end of the stage, just as though in walking with a fellow we should never speak but at a stile, a gate, or a ditch, where a man can go no further.

Burbage and Kempe are at the point of letting two Cambridge scholars try out as actors, anticipating that they will work for small wages. While Burbage is hopeful, Kempe laughs at the student actors' proclivity for speaking only at the front edge of the stage, rather than during their walk. Kempe continues:

I was once at Comedie in Cambridge, and there I saw a parasite make faces and mouths of all sorts on this fashion.

Apparently Kempe pulls a face, demonstrating the student actors' inclination to grimace. All in all, university productions seem to have been stylistically stilted and exaggerated, professional productions more naturalistic. Burbage is again the optimist, and hopes that Cambridge will supply him with playwrights as well as actors:

A little teaching will mend these faults, and it may be besides they will be able to pen a part.

KEMPE. Few of the University men pen plays well, they smell too much of that writer Ovid, & that writer Metamorphoses, and talk too much of Proserpina and Jupiter: why here's our fellow Shakespeare puts them all down, aye, and Ben Jonson too. O that Ben Jonson is a pestilent fellow, he brought up Horace giving the poets a pill, but our fellow Shakespeare hath given him a purge that made him bewray his credit.

Kempe's final speech in this exchange is both extraordinarily informative and difficult to parse. His ignorance is palpable, as *Metamorphoses* is not a 'writer' but the title of a work by Ovid. So *Return from Parnassus* has a joke at Kempe's expense. Truth nevertheless survives comic irony, as Kempe is undoubtedly correct when he boasts that 'our fellow Shakespeare puts them all down'. Whether the continuation of his sentence, 'aye, and Ben Jonson too', means that Shakespeare also puts down Ben Jonson, or that both Shakespeare and the non-university-educated Ben Jonson put down all other playwrights, the compliment to the non-university-educated Shakespeare is palpable.

All parts of the *Pilgrimage to Parnassus* trilogy show clear links between the world of the provincial university and the more diverse and variously attractive world of London. Each of the three plays demonstrates that students in Cambridge, upon whom the various literary and dramatic allusions cannot have been lost, were intimately acquainted with London authors, including playwrights, and with performance techniques of professional companies.

A significant part of the impact of the two universities and the Inns of Court on the development of early modern drama may have come not from within the walls of these academic or quasi-academic institutions, but rather from the eagerness with which university students and gentlemen of the Inns of Court escaped their institutional confines to attend performances at public theaters. As Oxford and Cambridge lay at a considerable distance from London, attendance at professional plays was not easy. Nevertheless, Kempe and Burbage, Shakespeare and Jonson, were household names, as familiar and as recognizable to Cambridge students as Thomas Hobson, the carrier who provided horses and carts for travel back and forth between the capital and the provincial town. (Sir Martin Stuteville, residing in rural Essex, received news about London from Joseph Mede of Christ's College, Cambridge!) Conversely, Londoners were quite aware of events in Oxford and Cambridge: witness Francis Meres, who in his 1598 *Palladis Tamia* recorded among those notable for comedy and tragedy not only playwrights active in London, but Dr Legge of Cambridge, and Drs Edes and Gager of Oxford.

For gentlemen of the Inns of Court, access to professional theater was obviously easier. About January 1579/80 the patronage of a minor playing company passed from Ambrose Dudley, Earl of Warwick, to Edward de Vere, Earl of Oxford. On 6 April 1580 an earthquake startled players and playgoers alike at the Theatre, giving fodder to moralizers, who rushed condemnations of all things theatrical into print. Four days later, on 10 April, two 'servantes unto the Erle of Oxford, were committed to the Mareshalsea for committing of disorders and frayes appon the gentlemen of the Innes of the Courte'. The gentlemen composed and circulated a poem satirizing the players, calling them 'Camœlions' rather than 'Comœdians' for their easy transfer of loyalty. This poem anticipates a dozen more, of which most were printed, ranging in date from 1598 to 1633, satirizing Inns of Court gentlemen who abandoned their studies to watch plays. Two examples may suffice, the first by John Earle, *Micro-cosmographie, or, A peece of the world discouered in essayes and characters* (1628), on 'A Player' (sig. E4): 'Your Inns of Court men were vndone but for him, hee is their chiefe guest and imployment, and the sole business that makes them After-noones men.' The second is from Francis Lenton's *The Young Gallants Whirligigg, or, Youths Reakes* (1629), concerning a young man sent to school, then to university, then 'to the Innes of Court, to study Lawes' (sigs B2^{r-v}):

> Instead of Perkins pedlers French, he sayes
> He better loves Ben: Johnsons booke of Playes,
> But that therein of wit he findes such plenty,
> That hee scarce understands a jest of twenty.

Again (sigs $B4^{r-v}$):

Your Theaters hee daily doth frequent
(Except the intermitted time of Lent)
Treasuring vp within his memory
The amorous toyes of every Comedy
With deepe delight; whereas he doth appeare
Within Gods Temple scarcely once a yere,
And that poore once more tedious to his minde,
Then a yeares travell, to a toiling Hynd. ['travell': 'travail, labour']
Playes are the Nurseries of vice, the bawd,
That thorow the senses steals our hearts abroad,
Tainting our eares with obscaene Bawdery,
Lacivious words, and wanton Ribaulry.

Again (sigs $C3^{r-v}$):

The Cockpit heretofore would serve his wit,
But now upon the Fryers stage hee'll sit,
It must be so, though this expensive foole
Should pay an angell for a paltry stoole.
His silken garments, and his sattin robe
That hath so often visited the Globe,
And all his spangled rare perfum'd attires
Which once so glistred in the Torchy Fryers, ['Fryers': Blackfriars theater']
Must to the Broakers to compound his debt,
Or else be pawned to procure him meate.

An unpublished and undated (but late) manuscript poem, 'A Poeticall Reuenge', makes a similar point, referencing Shakespeare:[3]

A Semi-gentleman of th'Inns of Court
In sattin cloathes, redeem'd but yesterday.
One who is ravish'd with a Cocke-pit Play;

. . . . . .

Away got I; But ere I farre did goe,
I flunge the darts of woundinge Poetrie
These 2 or 3 sharpe Curses back: May he
Be by his father in his study tooke
At Shakespeares Playes instead of the Lord Cooke.

Fleshing out such literary reports, Professor John R. Elliott, Jr, has assembled detailed evidence from the diaries of four Inns of Court gentlemen, 1628 to 1635, demonstrating habitual—and perhaps more serious—attendance at professional plays (Elliott 1993).

Playwrights were quite aware that Inns of Court gentlemen would be in their audiences and among the readers of their published works. Thus, Ben Jonson dedicated *Every Man Out of His Humour* (1616) to 'The noblest nurseries of humanity and liberty, in the Kingdome: the INNS OF COURT':

[3] British Library, Add. MS 22603, fos 11–12.

I Vnderstand you, Gentlemen, not your houses: and a worthy succession of you, to all time, as being borne the Judges of these studies. When I wrote this Poeme, I had friendship with divers in your societies; who, as they were great Names in learning, so they were no lesse Examples of living. Of them, and then (that I say no more) it was not despis'd. Now, that the Printer, by a doubled charge, thinkes it worthy a longer life, then commonly the ayre of such things doth promise, I am carefull to put it a servant to their pleasures, who are the inheriters of the first favour borne it. Yes, I command, it lye not in the way of your more noble, and vse-full studies to the publike: For so, I shall suffer for it. But, when the gowne, and cap is off, and the Lord of liberty raignes; then, to take it in your hands, perhaps may make some Bencher, tincted with humanity, reade: and not repent him.

Jonson seems to say that Inns of Court gentlemen prominently attended the earliest performances of the play, apparently in 1599. From Jonson's dramatis personae we learn that the play was performed by the Lord Chamberlain's Men, with William Shakespeare among the actors.

We have already noted that two of Shakespeare's plays, *The Comedy of Errors* and *Twelfth Night*, were performed within the Inns of Court. An Inns of Court connection has also been urged for Shakespeare's *Troilus and Cressida*, based primarily on the report in the variant first edition that the play was 'never stal'd with the Stage, never clapper-clawd with the palmes of the vulger... not being sullied, with the smoaky breath of the multitude', that is, apparently, never performed publicly. So perhaps it was performed privately, at an Inn of Court, for whom its debates and certain legal allusions would have been appropriate (Arlidge 2000: 108–11; Elton 2000). Other plays which have been associated by scholars one way or another with the Inns of Court include Richard Edwards's *Damon and Pithias* (*c.*1565); Edward Sharpham's *The Fleire* (*c.*1606); *Histriomastix, or, The Player Whipped* (1610); and *Tom a Lincoln* (after 1607 but before 1611). This list might easily be doubled or tripled, with many Shakespeare plays added. But evidence for a genuine connection is usually slight.

For most theater historians, especially in light of the discovery that performances of professional plays at the Inns of Court were routine, the question must not be whether a particular play was performed at an Inn of Court, but whether it was performed there initially and perhaps exclusively. Would any one of the Inns, in other words, have commissioned a play from Shakespeare or any other dramatist? The proposition seems unlikely. Masques were certainly commissioned from professional playwrights, but masques were by definition occasional and meant to be performed only once or twice. No professional play is known to have been intended for a single performance only. The effort which went into composing a play was hugely greater than that required to compose a masque. Plays, moreover, were always (so far as we know or can infer) expected to be performed in the full range of venues already discussed.

Much conjecture has gone into discovering how much each performance at a public theater might add to the coffers of a playing company. Whatever the answer, we know from Leonard Digges's comparison between Jonson and Shakespeare that larger audiences meant larger revenues (Shakespeare 1640):

And though the Fox and subtill Alchimist,
Long intermitted could not quite be mist,
Though these have sham'd all the Ancients, and might raise
Their Authours merit with a crowne of Bayes.
Yet these sometimes, even at a friends desire
Acted, have scarce defrai'd the Seacoale fire
And doore-keepers: when let but *Falstaffe* come,
Hal, Poines, the rest you scarce shall have a roome [originally *Hall*]
All is so pester'd: let but *Beatrice*
And *Benedicke* be seene, loe in a trice
The Cockpit Galleries, Boxes, all are full
To heare *Malvoglio* that crosse garter'd Gull.

Evidence compiled by REED demonstrates that income from touring was far from negligible. Exchequer records reveal that, in the 1590s, professional companies received £10 (payment plus gratuity) for each play performed at court. And from Inns of Court archives we now know that from the second decade of the seventeenth century onward, professional companies received the same £10 for each play performed.

James Shirley received £100 plus gratuities as 'poett' for the 1633–4 *Triumph of Peace*. Would Shakespeare have taken much less to compose the much lengthier *Twelfth Night* in 1601/2? It seems far more likely that the play was already in repertory at the time of its performance in Middle Temple Hall; certainly, Leonard Digges confirms that '*Malvoglio* that crosse garter'd Gull' was among the Shakespeare creations which guaranteed the fortunes of the King's Men over the years. Similarly, *The Comedy of Errors* is recorded not only in the *Gesta Grayorum*, but later at court.

We may conclude that Cambridge and Oxford produced plays mostly—but not entirely—for internal consumption. The Inns of Court, by contrast, produced a few plays and a few masques for their own entertainment, but looked primarily outward, to the court and to public theaters, producing masques but consuming plays.

CHAPTER 17

TOURING

PETER GREENFIELD

LONG before they had the Theatre, the Rose, or the Globe in London, playing companies had toured the country, following a centuries-old pattern established by traveling minstrels. Their itineraries took them to the farthest reaches of England (and occasionally beyond), where they performed in towns and great houses from Dover to Devon, and from Southampton to the Scottish border. In 1572 the Earl of Leicester's Men wrote their patron that they expected once again to 'travayle amongst our frendes as we do usuallye once a yere', and they continued their annual tours even after James Burbage constructed the Theatre to be their London base in 1576 (Wickham et al. 2000: 205). Shakespeare's company may have made their name in London at the Globe and Blackfriars, but they, too, regularly journeyed into the provinces. In fact, many acting troupes resembled Lord Berkeley's Men, who had no permanent base (even in their patron's household) and functioned exclusively on the road. Scholars who focused on the London theater used to think that actors would take to the road only when forced to do so by the closure of the public theaters due to plague or political unrest. Research on performing outside London has instead found much new evidence to show that touring was a regular, expected practice of even the most successful companies.[1] Moreover, the players' practices in everything from how they used the stage space to how they organized themselves as companies derived from the conditions of touring (Gurr 1996*b*: 36).

Touring certainly involved hardships. The road itself was dusty, muddy, or frozen, according to the season, and players could never be certain what comfort and remuneration the next stop might offer. Actors must have relished the chance to

[1] See esp. Palmer (2005). The impetus for this new understanding of the importance of touring, and dramatic activity outside London in general, has come largely from the Records of Early English Drama (REED) project, both in the series of volumes publishing the edited records and through the interpretative essays of those involved in the project.

mock these hardships in plays like *Histriomastix* and *A Mad World, My Masters.* In the former, Sir Oliver Owlett's Men complain that they 'travell, with pumps full of gravell... And never can hold together' (Marston 1934–9: iii. 264).[2] In the latter, Sir Bounteous Progress is told that 'certain players' have arrived 'and desire to interlude before your worship', to which he responds:

> Players? By the mass they are welcome; they'll grace my entertainment well. But for certain players, there thou liest, boy; they were never more uncertain in their lives. Now up and now down, they know not when to play, where to play, nor what to play; not when to play for fearful fools, where to play for Puritan fools, nor what to play for critical fools... (Middleton 1995; v. i. 24–31)

Shakespeare, too, expressed his reluctance to leave the relative comfort and financial security of London in Hamlet's question about the troupe that visited Elsinore: 'How chances it they travel? Their residence, both in reputation and profit, was better both ways' (II. ii. 330–1). And yet travel they certainly did, despite the difficulties.

Then as now, players would have agreed with Hamlet that 'the purpose of playing' was 'to hold the mirror up to nature'; that is, they played because that is what players do: they act. As for the purpose of touring, if they had no permanent home, then they had to take to the road to continue to practice their art. At a more pragmatic level, the purposes of touring were to make a living and serve their patrons' interests, both of which required travel.

The Economics of Touring

Players endured a different kind of relationship with their patrons than did other artists. Poets might receive substantial monetary gifts from their patrons, and musicians often lived as regular members of a lord's household, receiving wages in addition to their room and board. Players, however, might occasionally satisfy their own lord's appetite for dramatic entertainment, but were expected to earn their living by performing for others. Lord Berkeley gave his musicians annual New Year's gifts and occasional rewards throughout the year, but over the five years from 1600 and 1605, he paid his players only twice, in January 1603 (Greenfield 1983: 18–23). When Berkeley's Men performed in their own lord's household, they could expect a reward, and perhaps a more generous one than other companies received. But for long stretches of time they were on their own. Carrying their patron's name and license protected players from arrest as vagabonds, and put pressure on local authorities to allow them to play, but financial success and even survival depended on what they could earn on the road.

[2] Quotations from plays are from the following editions: John Marston, *Histriomastix*, in Marston (1934–9: iii. 243–302); Thomas Middleton, *A Mad World, My Masters, and Other Plays*, ed. Michael Taylor (Oxford: Oxford University Press, 1995); Shakespeare (1997*a*).

The players' finances were 'uncertain', then, for they depended on audiences bringing their purses, and opening them generously. For some companies at least, it must have been a hand-to-mouth existence, never knowing whether the take from an afternoon's performance would be enough to pay that night's bill at the inn. At worst a company might suffer the same fate as Pembroke's Men did when their tour aborted in 1593. They had to return to London and sell their costumes to pay their debts. Still, most companies did manage to 'hold together' and a few may have managed to prosper on tour.

We cannot reconstruct the finances of individual companies from the surviving evidence, but we can get a general sense of the economics of touring. The principal costs of touring were for food and lodging, at an estimated shilling per day per person around 1600. Horses, either to ride or to pull a wagon loaded with costumes and props, cost another shilling a day for each horse (W. Ingram 1993: 58–9). Thus, a well-equipped company like the Queen's Men would have spent around 25*s.* a day to feed, lodge, and horse twelve actors when, for example, they toured through Coventry in July 1594. The 12*s.* they received from Lord Berkeley at Caludon Castle on 1 July and the 40*s.* reward from the Mayor of Coventry on the 4th would have covered barely half their expenses of 100*s.* for the four days. No company could survive such losses for long.

Luckily for the players, these figures do not tell the whole story. Scholars have only recently begun to examine the evidence of performing in great houses, and to appreciate how important visiting those houses was to the success of a tour.[3] If welcomed into a household to perform, the players could count on being 'well bestowed', as Hamlet puts it. One itinerant singer claimed that he could survive just by moving 'from gentilmans house to gentilmans house vpon their benevolence' (Somerset 1994*a*: i. 280). In addition to whatever rewards they received for performing, entertainers were given a reasonably comfortable place to sleep and places at meals (probably more plentiful than they could afford to purchase on their own). Moreover, players might enjoy the lord's hospitality for several days while giving only one or two performances. If, for instance, the Queen's Men spent three of the four nights in question at Caludon, they would have had to pay only for a single night at Coventry, turning a crippling loss into approximately £1 in profit.

The profit was probably even larger than that, since the players had other, unrecorded sources of income in addition to the rewards that appear in civic and household accounts. In households, the reward from the lord of the household might be supplemented by gifts from others who were gathered there. Lord Berkeley gave rewards to performers in the households of friends like Sir John Hungerford, with whom he stayed while traveling between his estates (Greenfield 1983: 20). Friends visiting Berkeley at Caludon in July 1594 may have done the same, augmenting Berkeley's 12*s.* payment to the Queen's Men. Similarly, the unrecorded income for performances in towns must often have matched or exceeded the official reward from the mayor. The 40*s.* the Queen's Men received from Coventry may have been for a

[3] See esp. Palmer (2005); Greenfield (1983, 1996); George (1991: 184–212).

'mayor's play'—like the one at Gloucester R. Willis describes in *Mount Tabor*, 'where every one that will comes in without money, the Mayor giving the players a reward as he thinks fit to shew respect unto them' (Douglas and Greenfield 1986: 363). In that case, the 40*s.* would have been the company's full take for that one performance. However, Willis also indicates that a mayor's play was a company's first performance in the city, and at Gloucester a 1580 ordinance explicitly granted the Queen's Men three performances over three days (Douglas and Greenfield 1986: 307). For the other two performances, they presumably charged an admission fee, as the London theaters did. That the Queen's Men did charge at the door for tour performances comes from the court case over an 'affray' at the Red Lion Inn in Norwich in 1583, when someone tried to get into one of their performances without paying, and sword-bearing actors went to the aid of the gatekeeper (Galloway 1984: 71). Even if no one paid more than a penny, two modest crowds of 120 each would have added 20*s.* more to the mayor's reward. A company needed only to put together an itinerary that combined enough lucrative paydays in larger towns with the minimal expenses at great houses to offset the costs of traveling between them.

The Patron's Interests

Of course, the players were also concerned to serve their patron's interests. Some patrons used players to advance specific political programs. Protestant patrons like Thomas Cromwell sent their companies out to perform polemical interludes in support of the Reformation in the 1530s and 1540s (P. White 1993). Fear of the public impact of inflammatory dramas during the political and religious turmoil of the 1550s led to censorship of such overtly political content, but more subtle messages remained possible. Certainly Gascoigne's *The Princely Pleasures at Kenelworth Castle*, performed for the Queen's visit to the Earl of Leicester at Kenilworth in 1575, argued for the Queen's marrying the Earl, and Leicester may well have asked his company to perform material that advanced his political career and interests (MacLean 2002: 268).

Whatever the content of their plays, players could serve their patron's interests simply by spreading the patron's name and influence. Audiences—at least those who authorized and paid for the performances—identified players as representatives of their patrons. Willis tells us that when players came to Gloucester, they visited the mayor 'to enforme him what noble-mans servants they are, and so to get license for their publike playing'. Then, 'if the Mayor like the Actors, or would shew respect to their Lord and Master, he appoints them to play their first play before himself and the Aldermen and common Counsell of the City'. Gloucester also determined how often a company could perform by their rank of the patron: a 1580 ordinance permitted the Queen's players to perform three times over three days, but players whose patron held the rank of baron and above could perform only twice over two days, and other players could play only once (Douglas and Greenfield 1986: 308).

Patrons' rank and influence were also reflected in the amounts of the rewards their companies received, with the largest rewards nearly always going to the players of the monarch, and then to those of the higher nobility. At Gloucester in 1582–3, the Queen's Men received 30*s.*, while the Earl of Oxford's players got 16*s.* 8*d.* and Lord Stafford's only 10*s.* Local influence might count as much as rank, however, for Gloucester gave 20*s.* to the players of Lord Chandos, who lived nearby at Sudeley Castle and represented the county in Parliament. Lord Berkeley also had extensive local holdings but was less in favor at court than Chandos, so his players received only 13*s.* (Douglas and Greenfield 1986: 306–7). Certainly Beverly recognized the Earl of Leicester's influence when it gave his company 30*s.* in 1572, more than the city had given even to the Queen's own players. The Earl had previously held the lordship of the manor of Beverly, and when the town received a new charter the following year, it recorded its gratitude that the charter had been granted 'at the sute and requeste of our most benigne lorde therle of Lacyter' (MacLean 2002: 253). No doubt Beverly felt its 30*s.* investment in the Earl's players money well spent.

Thus, traveling to different parts of the country to present visual and verbal images of the patron's power and influence had great value at a time when mass communication did not exist. Indeed, the Tudor and Stuart monarchs depended largely on theatrical means to maintain their power. Without the means to impose order through a standing army or national police force, the Crown relied on coercive belief created by the theatrical spectacle of royal progresses. Royal entries presented their audiences with pageants depicting the monarch's ability to compel order and the town's acceptance of the monarch's authority (Greenblatt 1980: 44). Performances by traveling players did not so obviously stage power relationships, but still made use of the close connection between theatricality and power in the period to spread and reaffirm their patron's influence. A particular company's visit to a town or household functioned as a gift, a sharing of the patron's personal entertainment with the audience, albeit one intended to remind the audience that the patron had the position and authority to license players. By allowing the players to perform and giving them a reward, the civic officials or lord of the household expressed recognition of that position and authority, thus reaffirming the hierarchy of social relationships.

A tour performance could also reaffirm the local social hierarchy. Urban elites badly needed such symbolic reinforcement of their authority in the later sixteenth century. Most provincial towns were suffering from the combination of economic decline with increasing population, resulting in widespread poverty and social tension. At the same time, the Reformation had eliminated much of the ceremony that had previously symbolized the civic hierarchy, especially the great civic processions at Corpus Christi and Midsummer (James 1983; Phythian-Adams 1972). Towns had to find new symbolic measures to ensure (in Robert Tittler's words) 'the civic deference necessary for effective government'; among those measures were rebuilding the town hall and providing a special chair of office for the mayor (Tittler 1991: 98–128). When visiting players performed in the town hall, with the mayor's permission and with the mayor himself seated prominently in his chair, the symbolism of gift exchange was extended to cover the civic structure of authority. Performing in the hall of a great house offered a similar symbolic recognition of the head of the household.

Playing Places on Tour

Town halls and the halls of the great houses thus provided the usual playing spaces for itinerant players. Unlike the London playhouses, many of these playing spaces still stand, some of them relatively unchanged, including the guildhalls at Leicester and Southampton, and the great halls at Gawthorpe Hall, Hardwick Hall, and Berkeley Castle.[4] Only a few buildings called 'playhouses' represent provincial attempts to follow London's example of identifying structures specifically for staging plays. In the early seventeenth century Bristol had two—the Wine Street Playhouse and Redcliffe Hall—and York had one. These were not purpose-built theaters like the Globe but existing buildings adapted to some extent for theatrical purposes. None of them seems to have seen much use nor lasted very long (Pilkinton 1997, pp. xxxvii–xl; Johnston and Rogerson 1979: i. 530–1). Much smaller towns—Prescot, Tonbridge, Witton—also had structures they called 'playhouses' that were probably used by schoolboys, rather than professional companies (George 1991: 80–2; Gibson 2007; Baldwin et al. 2007).

Players no doubt preferred the town hall because it was usually the largest space available, and thus potentially the most lucrative venue. Civic authorities preferred the town hall for its symbolism, but also because the hall was the space most under their control. Only when one or both of those attractions was lost did civic authorities tend to prohibit playing the hall. Southampton prohibited performing in the Town Hall in 1620, blaming players for broken benches, 'fleas and other beastlie things', and ordered 'That hereafter yf anie suche staige or poppett plaiers must be admitted in this towne That they provide their places for their representacions in their Innes'. Whether the players tried acting in inns is not recorded, but they must have continued to use the Town Hall, since the council had to reissue its prohibition just four years later.[5] At Norwich players performed at the Common Hall, but also at the Red Lion inn, as we know from the court testimony regarding the 'affray' there in 1583 (Galloway 1984: 71).

[4] McMillin and MacLean (1998: 67–83) (includes photographs of the Norwich Common Hall, Leicester Guildhall, and other surviving venues); Somerset (1994: 54–60); REED Patrons and Performances web site, <http://www.reed.utoronto.ca/#ppdb>.

[5] Southampton City Archives (SCA), Southampton Court Leet Book (SC6/1/37), fo. 16^{v}; SCA, Assembly Book (SC2/1/6), fo. 212R.

At times, however, players must have performed in the houses of prominent citizens, for ordinances regulating players from Gloucester and Canterbury include provisions that individuals must have the mayor's permission to host plays in their houses (Douglas and Greenfield 1986: 307; Gibson 2002: 232). In some cases these houses may have been inns, in others private residences. Performances also occurred outdoors and in church buildings, although such places were clearly the exceptions. That a 1590 performance by the Queen's Men happened in the 'Colledge Churche yarde' of Gloucester Cathedral was no doubt recorded because the location was so unusual; players normally acted in the town hall, known as the 'Bothall' (Douglas and Greenfield 1986: 311). In smaller towns or parishes, the players might use the church house, as at Sherborne, Dorset, or even the church itself, as at Doncaster (Hays 1992: 12–23; Wasson 1997: 36).

Few if any touring venues approached the dimensions of London theaters like the Fortune, which was 80 feet square and had a stage 43 feet wide (Wickham et al. 2000: 535). Guildhalls and great halls of the period more commonly measured 25–30 feet wide by 50–60 feet long, and some were as small as the 20 by 30 feet of Gawthorpe Hall, Lancashire, where traveling performers entertained the Shuttleworth family.[6] Towns occasionally provided raised stages: Gloucester spent 8*s*. in 1567–8 for 'elme bourdes for a skaffold for pleyers to playe one' (Douglas and Greenfield 1986: 300). Most of the time the players must simply have performed on the hall floor. Some halls offered a screen with two doors, providing a façade closely resembling that of the London theaters.[7] Others were much less convenient. Southampton's Bargate Hall, where the mayor and council met, could offer only a single entrance up a steep stone staircase. Players would have been severely restricted unless they could construct a curtained space to act as a 'tiring house'. Adapting to the variations in the size and arrangements of these playing spaces called for flexibility and ingenuity from the players.

The Touring Repertory

On the other hand, a company needed only a small number of plays, since it would have performed a few times at most in each town or household. In fact, that small repertory may have been one of touring's few attractions, since the London audience required a steady stream of new plays that had to be learned and rehearsed (Somerset 1994*b*: 59–60). Unfortunately, the titles of touring performances appear in the records only rarely. Most of the evidence comes from the accounting records of towns and households, and the accountants showed little interest in details beyond whom they

[6] REED Patrons and Performances web site.

[7] See Figure 31.4 in this volume, an illustration of the Middle Temple hall.

paid and how much. Only on unusual occasions—when someone was sufficiently intrigued by the performance to mention it in a letter or when a disturbance at the performance led to a legal dispute—are we likely to find out more.

Bristol's records from the late 1570s are thus exceptional in mentioning 'the red Knight', 'Myngo', 'the *Queen* of Ethiopia', 'quid pro quo', 'what mischief workith in the mynd of man', and 'the court of comfort' (Pilkinton 1997: 112, 115–17). None of these plays has survived, but the last two are reminiscent of *The Cradle of Security*, performed at Gloucester around the same time, and the only touring performance to be described in considerable detail:

> The play was called (the Cradle of security,) wherin was personated a King or some great Prince with his Courtiers of severall kinds, amongst which three Ladies were in speciall grace with him; and they keeping him in delights and pleasures, drew him from his graver Counsellors, hearing of Sermons, and listning to good counsell, and admonitions, that in the end they got him to lye downe in a cradle upon the stage, where these three Ladies joyning in a sweet song rocked him asleepe, that he snorted againe, and in the meane time closely conveyed under the cloaths were withall he was covered, a vizard like swines snout upon his face, with three wire chaines fastned thereunto, the other end whereof being holden severally by those three Ladies, who fall to singing againe, and then discovered his face, that the spectators might see how they had transformed him, going on with their singing, whilst all this was acting, there came forth of another doore at the farthest end of the stage, two old men, the one in blew with a Serjeant at Armes, his mace on his shoulder, the other in red with a drawn sword in his hand, and leaning with the other hand upon the others shoulder, and so they two went along in a soft pace round about by the skirt of the Stage, till at last they came to the Cradle, whereat all the Courtiers with the three Ladies and the vizard all vanished; and the desolate Prince starting up bare faced, and finding himself thus sent for to judgement, made a lamentable complaint of his miserable case, and so was carried away by wicked spirits. This Prince did personate in the morall, the wicked of the world; the three Ladies, Pride, Covetousnesse, and Luxury, the two old men, the end of the world, and the last judgement. (R. Willis, in *Mount Tabor, or, Private Exercises of a Penitent Sinner* (1639); quoted in Douglas and Greenfield 1986: 363)

The Cradle of Security was a moral interlude of a kind that had been popular for decades, but some of the other titles from Bristol suggest plays of a newer sort. Shakespeare's parodying of an older style of play in *The Murder of Gonzago* has led some scholars to imagine the touring repertory lagged behind London fashion, but much evidence shows that the London companies took current favorites on the road. When Edward Alleyn and Lord Strange's Men performed 'hary of cornwall' at Bristol in 1593, they had already performed it several times at the Rose (Pilkinton 1997: 144; Foakes and Rickert 1961: 16–18). Alleyn presumably played Tamburlaine and his other famous Marlowe roles on tour, and Shakespeare's company took his plays to the provinces. The Lord Chamberlain's Men were no doubt the actors from London who performed *Titus Andronicus* at Sir John Harington's Rutland estate on New Year's day 1596 (see Gurr 2004*c*: 282 for his reference).

In fact, even regionally based companies might play recent London hits. At Christmastide 1609–10, Sir Richard Cholmley's players visited the household of Sir

John Yorke at Gowthwaite Hall in Yorkshire.[8] They offered Sir John a choice of four plays: *King Lear, Pericles, The Travailes of Three English Brothers,* and *The Play of St. Christopher.* Sir John chose the St Christopher play, setting off a conflict with his neighbors over the play's religious content that eventually led to a case in Star Chamber. The other three plays had premiered on London stages only a few years earlier—*Lear* and *Pericles* with Shakespeare's company, the King's Men, and *The Three English Brothers* with the Queen's Men. Late in the period, Beaumont's *The Knight of the Burning Pestle* and Massinger's *A New Way to Pay Old Debts* were performed for Henry Clifford's household at Skipton Castle in February 1636 (Palmer 2005: 276, 302).

Some scholars have assumed that plays designed for the Globe or the Rose must have been cut for touring performance, but the evidence indicates that touring companies had sufficient actors to do those plays as published. Cholmley's company may have traveled only locally, near Cholmley's North Yorkshire seat at Egerton, but they numbered fifteen. They could have handled a play like *King Lear* without cuts and with only such doubling of parts as was common on the London stages. Certainly some traveling troupes were smaller, especially early in the period. *The Cradle of Security* requires a cast of six, and *The Murder of Gonzago*—clearly meant to represent an older kind of play than *Hamlet*—calls for a company of from five to seven. The companies of Lord Clinton and Sir Richard Berkeley both numbered six when they visited Southampton in 1577. Such companies may indeed have used cut-down versions of popular London fare, as well as older plays and plays written specially for their small numbers. On the other hand, as early as 1577 the troupes of Lord Delawarre, Lord Stafford, and the Earl of Worcester had ten actors each, Lord Bath's eleven, and the Earl of Leicester's twelve, the same number as the Queen's Men at their formation in 1583.[9] Most seventeenth-century touring companies numbered between ten and fifteen (Palmer 2005: 276).

A company's touring repertory may well have been shaped less by the size of the company than by the costume and property requirements of particular plays. No troupe could have carried everything needed to stage a full London season, and even an individual play might tax their ability to carry it on the road if it involved the bulky, spectacular props of *Friar Bacon and Friar Bungay,* which include not only the brazen head, but also the tree of the golden apples of the Hesperides, guarded by a fire-breathing dragon. A company traveling on foot, or only with what they could pack on a horse, would have been quite limited in what they could carry. Bringing a wagon would have meant slower progress, though it might have been worth the trouble. Of five payments to players Exeter made in 1576–7, the largest reward went to 'the plaiers wth the waggen', suggesting that the wagon had allowed them to do something

[8] Although Chambers 1923 (i. 328) briefly mentions these plays at Sir John Yorke's, the best source to date on these plays and the Star Chamber case is Boddy (1976). Complete records of this case will appear in the REED edition for the West Riding of Yorkshire and Derbyshire, edited by Barbara D. Palmer and John Wasson.

[9] The figures appear in the Book of Fines, the accounts of the mayors of Southampton (SCA, SC5/3/1, fos 158^{v}, 165^{v}, 167; McMillin and MacLean 1998: 60).

remarkable (Wasson 1986: 156). The will of the actor Simon Jewell mentions a wagon to be taken on tour, and Berkeley's Men got into some sort of altercation with the people of Faversham over theirs in 1597–8 (Edmond 1974; Gibson 2002: 563). Even if they took a wagon, the players must have considered which plays could use many of the same costumes and props when they decided on a touring repertory.

Touring Itineraries

Four main factors affected the players' itineraries: in addition to money and patrons' interests, topography and the calendar guided their choices. Populous cities like Norwich and Bristol promised lucrative visits, as did the country residences of the wealthy and powerful. Coventry was a particularly attractive destination, not only because of its location in the center of the country at the intersection of important roads, but also because the city always welcomed players, as did Henry, Lord Berkeley, whose seat at Caludon Castle lay just outside Coventry. Smaller towns and households served as stepping stones between the larger ones. Stratford upon Avon no doubt owed the players' occasional visits there to its proximity to Coventry and Warwick. Little Ashburton in Devon no doubt saw players because it lay on the road from Exeter to Plymouth. The relatively minor households at Ticknall Hall (Derbyshire) and Wollaton Hall (Nottinghamshire) were conveniently located for companies making their way from Coventry and Leicester north to Hardwick Hall, Chatsworth House, Doncaster, and York.

Since their patron's influence in an area might affect a company's reception, itineraries also reflected the geographical spread of a patron's influence. The players of minor patrons tended to focus on the region immediately surrounding their master's residences and holdings. Sir Richard Cholmley's players stuck close to his seat at Egerton. Lord Berkeley's players were most often found in Warwickshire and Gloucestershire, near his estates at Caludon and Berkeley; when they ranged more widely, it was often to areas dominated by his wife's family, the Howards. Companies with royal patrons obviously took the entire country as their territory, matched only by companies with patrons who had royal or at least national ambitions, like the Earl of Leicester.

Topography and the ease of travel on major roads and watercourses helped to shape itineraries. Players reached Oxford by following the Thames through Reading, Wallingford, and Abingdon, and then continued north through Banbury to Coventry. They rarely took the road that connected Gloucester to Oxford, which required climbing the steep Cotswold Edge. Instead, when visiting Gloucester they tended to follow the Severn valley from Bristol through Gloucester to Worcester and Shrewsbury, or perhaps to turn north-east along the Avon beyond Gloucester, to Stratford, Warwick, and Coventry. They may even have traveled by water. When roads were muddy and all but impassable, they could still make their way by boat on the river or the sea. The south-eastern circuit that led along the Kentish coast to Rye might well have been accomplished by water, and travel along the Dorset and Devon coast—from Southampton to Poole to Lyme and eventually Plymouth—would have been a good deal easier by sea.

London-based companies took to the road most often in the summer, particularly as that was the season when the authorities sometimes closed the playhouses down owing to the increased threat of plague. Other companies toured throughout the year, as the Southampton Mayor's accounts for 1593–4 suggest: the Mayor rewarded the Earl of Worcester's players on 18 October 1593, the Queen's players on 26 November, and Lord Chandos's on the 28th. Lord Monteagle's players visited Southampton in March 1594, those of Lord Morley and the Earl of Derby in May. The Queen's players returned in August, and Worcester's in September.[10] Two years earlier the Queen's Men had also visited in August, and Lord Morley's in May, showing that the itineraries particular companies habitually followed frequently brought them to the same places at the same time of year.[11] When they could, companies no doubt timed their visits to coincide with fairs, meetings of the assizes, and other events that brought crowds, and especially those with money to spend, to town. The Christmas season was a particularly good time to visit provincial households. A company might be commanded to return to their patron's seat to celebrate Christmas, the New Year, and Twelfth Night. Players earned fine rewards in their patron's and other households by contributing to the holiday festivity.

The itineraries of the major London companies predictably looped out from London like flower petals. An East Anglian loop made a good short tour, taking in Cambridge and Ipswich on its way to Norwich, England's second-largest city. Another brief tour led south-east through Canterbury, then followed the Kentish coast from Sandwich to Rye before returning to London. A longer loop went south-west to Southampton, then west to Exeter and perhaps Plymouth, before curving back to Bristol, the nation's third-largest town. From there the players might turn back east to London, or they could extend their tour to the north through Gloucester, Worcester, and Shrewsbury, as far as Kendal, York, and the northern households before returning south through Coventry and Leicester. These routes were obviously planned with care. When Lord Strange's Men went on tour in 1593, they knew their itinerary well enough that Edward Alleyn could write to his wife from Bristol and confidently ask her to send to him at Shrewsbury or York (Foakes and Rickert 1961: 276).

Touring under the Stuarts

Under the Stuarts, the traditional itineraries began to break down, and touring had nearly died out completely by the time Parliament closed the London public theaters in

[10] SCA, SC5/3/1, fos 247^{v}–250^{v}. [11] Ibid., fo. 237^{r}.

1642. The number of recorded tour performances across the country decreased with each decade up to the Civil War, even at Coventry, which was perhaps the most welcoming of towns. Coventry rewarded six visiting companies per year on average in the 1590s, the last full decade of Elizabeth's reign. The average actually increased to eight a year for the first decade of the seventeenth century, but dropped to four a year between 1610 and 1619, and then to only two a year through the 1620s and 1630s (R. W. Ingram 1981).[12] The number of different companies touring the provinces also decreased through the four decades of Stuart rule. The King's Men continued to tour, as did the other companies that had patrons from the royal family and their own London theaters. Companies with non-royal patrons, which operated exclusively in the provinces, began to disappear. Many individuals who had taken on acting troupes under Elizabeth continued their patronage under the Stuarts. Lord Berkeley's Men and those of Lord Eure kept at it until their patrons' deaths—in 1613 and 1617, respectively. The players of Edward Sutton, Lord Dudley, toured until 1633, and those of William Stanley, the Earl of Derby, did not give their last recorded performance until 1635. Yet many long-lived provincial companies ended their runs much earlier: Morley's in 1603, Mountjoy's in 1606, Chandos's in 1610, Monteagle's in 1615.[13] Moreover, no new patrons who were not members of the royal family came forward to give their names to companies that toured widely. Prior to Elizabeth's death, new patrons got involved at a steady rate, forming new companies, or taking players over from fathers or brothers, or from other nobles who had died or lost interest. Under James and Charles, however, companies did not find replacement patrons, and their numbers dwindled.

James's bringing the main London companies under royal patronage shortly after taking the throne undoubtedly contributed to this decline in the number of patrons. While it remained legal for anyone of the rank of baron or above to license players, James reduced the attraction of patronizing players. Before 1603 even the patron of a relatively minor provincial troupe, like Lord Berkeley, could hope to see his company achieve lucrative success in London and perhaps be called to court, supporting his own ambitions. After 1603 any prospective patron would have known that the companies under royal patronage held a virtual monopoly on playing in London and at court. It is hardly a surprise that nobles should have been discouraged at the thought of lending their names to actors who would have to make their living entirely in the provinces, where some locales had already become less receptive. Actors must have felt much the same way: when a company broke up, the only sensible options would have been to join one of the royal companies or to go into a different line of work.

[12] Andrew Gurr (1994*b*) has theorized that the declining numbers result from changes in the Crown's regulation of playing that meant mayors no longer had to license each company that came to town. Since the mayor did not need to preview the players' work, he would not have given the rewards that provide most of the evidence of the players' activities. Coventry, however, continued to record players' visits right through the period, as did a number of other towns, some of them—e.g. Canterbury and Hythe—restoring through their own ordinances the mayor's responsibility to license any visiting players (Gibson 2002: 231–2, 635–6; see also Gibson 1995). Household accounts also indicate a decline in touring activity, and no similar change in regulatory or accounting practices would explain that trend.

[13] REED Patrons and Performances web site.

James's 'royalizing' of the London companies added to the difficulties of players who, in Sir Bounteous's words, were already experiencing uncertainty over 'where to play for Puritan fools'. As the reformed religion spread strongly among urban elites in the second half of the sixteenth century, the views that would come to be called 'puritan' affected civic authorities' treatment of itinerant players. At first, provincial mayors' desire to 'shew respect' to the players' patrons and to appropriate the symbolism of a tour performance in the guildhall to reaffirm their own authority took precedence. Civic ordinances concerning players focused on regulating the time and circumstances of performance to ensure the maintenance of public order. The 1580 Gloucester ordinance that restricted the number of performances a company could give put restraints on players because they 'allure seruauntes, apprentices and iorneyman & other of the worst desposed persons to leudenes and lightnes of life'. Moreover, the players 'Drawe awey greate Sommes of money from diuerse persons' and encourage 'the maintenance of ideleness' among those servants, apprentices, and journeymen who should be at work, contributing to their masters' prosperity. The ordinance also prohibited performing 'in the nighte season nor at any vnfeet tyme', but the number of companies visiting Gloucester and receiving rewards grew, despite the restrictions (Douglas and Greenfield 1986: 307).

A 1595 order of Canterbury's Burghmote Court at first appears to resemble the Gloucester ordinance in restricting any company to playing in the city only two days per visit, and in its rationale that 'the contynuance of them [the players] so longe tyme as commonly hathe byn vsed ys deemed verie inconvenient and hurtefull to the state and good quiet of this Cittie and Impouerishinge thereof'. But the Canterbury ordinance reveals a new religious emphasis in prohibiting playing on Sundays: 'to suffer players to playe on the Sabaothe daie ys a prophaninge of the Sabaothe & a matter highely displeasinge to god'. The ordinance also required performances to end by nine in the evening, and prescribed heavy penalties for violations; companies that did not comply would never be allowed to perform in Canterbury again (Gibson 2002: 231–2). These provisions, and the city's reception of players in subsequent years, show that the civic leadership hoped to suppress playing altogether, and not merely to regulate it. For many years prior to passage of this ordinance, the Queen's Men had visited Canterbury annually, and rewards to one or two other companies a year were normal. After 1595 the city gave only eight more rewards for performing, the last one coming in 1613, after which Canterbury paid players only to leave town without playing (Gibson 2002, p. lvi).

The seventeenth century saw the interests of the urban elite in many towns diverge from those of the Crown, so that towns no longer felt the need to 'shew respect to [the players'] Lord and Master'. Still, civic attitudes toward touring players did not develop uniformly, and as long as places like Canterbury were relatively rare, players could still survive on the road, performing where they could, and making brief forays into less receptive towns to pick up their payments not to play. As more and more towns paid them not to play, traveling became less and less viable, since the official rewards alone had never met expenses. The south-eastern loop out of London that included Canterbury had long been popular with itinerant entertainers, no doubt because a relatively short tour could visit a large number of closely spaced towns: Maidstone, Faversham, Canterbury, Fordwich, Dover, Folkestone, Hythe, New Romney, Lydd, Rye, and Tenterden. Though none of the towns was as large as Bristol or Norwich, they were less than a day's journey apart, and the monetary rewards sufficient to bring increasing numbers of companies to the Kent coast. Nearly 200 payments to traveling players appear in borough accounts for the quarter-century between 1550 and 1574, and between 1575 and 1599 the number approached 275. For 1600 to 1624, however, the figure dropped back to 200 (many of them payments not to play), and most of those payments were recorded in the first decade of the seventeenth century. Between 1625 and 1642 well under fifty rewards were given, only a handful for actually performing (Gibson 2002, pp. liv–lvi). As long as only Canterbury so strongly resisted the players, the south-eastern circuit could still offer a lucrative tour. When Hythe instituted restrictions similar to Canterbury's, and Dover, Hythe, and other towns joined in paying companies to leave without performing, setting off for the Kentish coast became a risky venture indeed.

The only companies to tour with much success in the 1620s and 1630s were the King's Men and some puppet players led by William Sands. The Sands troupe became known for their elaborate show *The Chaos of the World*, which required twelve puppeteers to perform seven episodes from the Old and New Testaments. Sands and his puppets appeared across southern England—at Oxford, Beaminster, and even on the Isle of Wight—but Sands himself came from Lancashire, in the one part of England where dramatic activity continued to flourish under the Stuarts.[14] The towns and especially the great houses of Lancashire, Cumberland, and Westmorland—places dominated by the old faith and a love of traditional customs and entertainments—remained receptive to visiting performers. Players who were lucky to receive even a token payment not to play at Canterbury or Norwich found consistent welcome at Kendal and Carlisle, at Workington Hall, Dunkenhalgh Hall, Gawthorpe Hall, and Skipton Castle. The King's Men still journeyed that far north from London, and the few remaining provincial companies, like Derby's and Dudley's, appeared more often in the north-west than anywhere else in the country. The north-west counties also developed their own regional touring activity, provided by companies like those of Lord Wharton, whose players never traveled far from his seat at Wharton Hall in Westmorland, or those of Lord Strange, whose main holdings were in Lancashire. These lords and others created a regional entertainment network, exchanging performances and providing for each other what the rest of the country could no longer offer.

Even in the north and north-west touring activity waned in the late 1630s. Doncaster rewarded a single King's player in June 1642, but Carlisle gave its last reward to touring players in 1638, and Kendal its in 1637, while 1636 saw the last payments for play performance at York, as well as at Norwich and Bristol.[15] Gloucester had not

[14] Bawcutt (1995); George (1994). Newport, on the Isle of Wight, prohibited 'the showe of the Chaos' owing to plague in 1627–8; my thanks to Jane Cowling for sharing her transcription of the Convocation Book, Isle of Wight Record Office, NBC/45/16a, p. 232.

[15] Palmer (2005: 303); REED Patrons and Performances web site.

rewarded players for years when the Mayor and justices gave 20*s*. to 'Stage players... when they went to see the Accte' in 1640–1, only months before the city's staunch resistance to a royalist siege (Douglas and Greenfield 1986: 328). Only Coventry remained welcoming to the end, though William Vincent and his company were paid not for a stage play, but 'to daunce vpon the ropes & shew other trickes of legerdemeane'. That was in December 1641, and the war that ended touring for good appears in the last item of the same set of 'Reward*es* to players': 'given to the trumpeters of the troopes w*hi*ch came with the Lord Brooke & the lord Gray x s. the xxviijth of August 1642' (R. Ingram 1981: 447–8).

CHAPTER 18

COURT THEATRE

JOHN H. ASTINGTON

In 1598 Shakespeare's 'pleasant conceited comedy' *Love's Labour's Lost* appeared in print, proclaiming on its title page that the play might be read 'As it was presented before her Highness this last Christmas'. To modern eyes this would signify December 1597, but since Elizabethans changed the dating of the year in late March and we do not know in what month the play appeared in the bookshops the court performance may have been in the season 1597–8 or that of 1598–9. In both years, however, the Chamberlain's Men played at court on 26 December and on 1 January, and in the earlier year also on Twelfth Night, 6 January, the end of the period of Christmas revels. On whichever of these days his comedy was presented, Shakespeare, we may take it, appeared as a member of the cast performing before the Queen in the company of her assembled court, at Whitehall Palace in the evening. Since the reign of Queen Elizabeth's father, Henry VIII, Whitehall, next to the older medieval palace of Westminster, had become the chief royal seat. Apart from a few architectural fragments the buildings known to Queen Elizabeth and to Shakespeare are gone, replaced by later structures devoted to the administration of the state. The modern thoroughfare called Whitehall follows the line of the Elizabethan King Street, which ran from Charing Cross to Westminster, directly through the precincts of Whitehall Palace. Most of its principal buildings lay on the eastern side of the road, fronting the river, with two docks, one public and one private, for travel by water.

Shakespeare and his fellow actors were licensed to perform as servants of Queen Elizabeth's lord chamberlains, Henry Carey, Lord Hunsdon (until 1596), and George Carey, his son (from 1597). Since the Lord Chamberlain oversaw the organization of the court, and particularly arrangements for entertainments for the monarch, Shakespeare's troupe might be understood to have held a very important position in the hierarchy of Elizabethan performers. The patronage of the court in and around the London area, it has long been acknowledged, had a good deal to do with the growth of the professional theatre in the metropolis during the sixteenth century.

Since court performances were given in the evening, and Whitehall was a relatively short journey by land or water from the city of London, actors in the 1590s might have considered performing in their playhouses in the afternoon of the same day, at the time they habitually did for the paying public, perhaps giving a further run-through of the piece they were to present before the court at night. *Love's Labour's Lost*, then, may have been acted at the company's current playhouse—probably the Curtain theatre in Shoreditch—to an audience of a thousand or more, some hours before it was seen by the Queen at night. The Curtain playhouse was a 'wooden O', roughly circular in plan, open to the sky in the centre, and with a fairly large stage abutting one side of the O, lit by the daylight from above, perhaps helped at the end of the darker afternoons of winter by some torchlight towards the end of the show. Once the play was over, the actors might have packed their costumes and properties in bags and baskets and made their way the 2 miles or so from their theatre to Whitehall.

The subsequent performance of *Love's Labour's Lost* would have been mounted in conditions rather different from those at the Curtain. It seems most likely, though we do not know for certain, that the Hall, the largest of the chambers at Whitehall, was the venue for the Christmas revels. A large, rectangular space, with a high pitched roof, it closely resembled the surviving Great Hall at Hampton Court Palace, which is 40 feet wide by over 100 feet in length, and 65 feet from the floor to the peak of the

Figure 18.1 Whitehall Palace viewed from the river, etching by Wenceslaus Hollar, late 1640s. At the centre rear is Inigo Jones's Banqueting House (early 1620s); the darker roof to its right, crowned with a lantern, is that of the Hall (early sixteenth century).

roof. The cubic area of the space the actors had to fill with their voices was roughly double that of an Elizabethan playhouse like the Curtain, although, unlike a wooden O playhouse, it was entirely enclosed. While the space was larger, the audience was smaller: probably no more than 500 people. They were, unlike a public theatre audience, mostly seated, and no one would have occupied the space between the Queen's seat, set on a dais somewhere near the centre of the auditorium, and the actors' stage, a custom-built platform set across one end of the space, and possibly as large as their playhouse playing area. The court audience would have sat not in three storeys ringing the stage and the ground-level area, as at the Curtain, but in sloping banks of seating set against the side walls and the rear wall behind the Queen's seat, creating more of the effect of a modern sports arena. The chief difference as one looked out from the stage, Shakespeare's point of view, would have been the effect of the glow and shimmer of numerous candles, suspended on decorated chandeliers hung from the roof, and burning in candleholders set against walls and posts all around the room. The aura of this scintillating lighting would have been picked up in the jewels and spangled fabrics of the richly dressed and high-born audience assembled to watch the play. Brilliance was the mark of court performance.

Actors and playwrights contributed their work to the splendour of the court, and the entertainment they offered, paid for out of the royal purse, formed part of the magnificent hospitality English kings and queens provided for their entourage and guests, signifying wealth, largesse, and generosity, deliberately cultivated as a political strategy. Queen Elizabeth's grandfather King Henry VII, founder of the Tudor dynasty, had carefully fostered a programme of conspicuous artistic patronage, and his son enthusiastically took it over and expanded it. The style of the English court was firmly established under King Henry VIII, and in many respects it was to persist for almost a hundred years following his death in 1547.

A court might be understood as a building, like Whitehall Palace, or as a group of people: the monarch and his or her family, servants, and attendants, and those who held high office in administering the country's finance, its laws, its foreign relations, its military defence, and other matters, and who sat on the chief advisory and administrative body supporting the king or queen, the Privy Council. The court as a place was hence a mixture of personal residence and a high-powered office building; official court appointments might reflect the confusion between personal attendance on a monarch and high executive office. Access to the king or queen's private quarters invariably brought with it political and financial rewards.

Since medieval times the group of people constituting the court had been peripatetic, moving from place to place to transact business or to maintain political power. As a result the Crown owned many buildings throughout England, Wales, and Ireland, any of which might temporarily become a court in the sense defined by the presence of a group of important people. The Palace of Woodstock, just beyond Oxford on a main Elizabethan route from London to the midlands, the site of which is now occupied by Blenheim Palace, was such a place. Its medieval buildings continued occasionally to be used by King James and by King Charles I, and theatrical entertainments were sometimes mounted there. By the Elizabethan years, however, the movement of the court during the winter months was confined to the greater London area, and four palaces, all largely early Tudor creations and all built alongside the river Thames, constituted the principal places where the court might be found between, roughly, October and the following May. From east to west they were Greenwich, Whitehall, Richmond, and Hampton Court. The old medieval castle of Windsor, further to the west, was also sometimes used as a residence, usually for shorter periods, and it retained an important ritual significance as the centre of the chief English honorary Order, that of the Garter, whose ceremonies provided an important event in the court year throughout the period considered here.

Hampton Court, in Shakespeare's day the most remote and rural of the sixteenth-century buildings, is the only larger palace of its date to survive substantially today, and a visit will give a strong impression of the physical environment of Tudor and Stuart courts. Standing in the Hall, one is surrounded by a space where Shakespeare's troupe performed. The distance of Hampton from the city made it a retreat in years of bad plague epidemics: James I held his first Christmas court as King of England at Hampton, in 1603–4. It was also frequently the point of departure for the monarch's summer progresses, the remarkable journeys through the kingdom, often lasting many months, which marked three of the four decades of Queen Elizabeth's reign and which were also practised, if less exhaustively, by her successors. Hampton Court also often was the point of return from progress, marking the beginning of the London season.

Richmond, further downriver towards London, was largely the creation of Henry VII, and built on an ambitious scale. Pictures of the now vanished palace show it to have been perhaps the most elegant and impressive of the Tudor courts, and it was a favourite of Queen Elizabeth, who died there in March 1603. Actors summoned to play at either Hampton Court or Richmond faced a considerable journey, whether by the winding route of a boat on the river, or by the more direct roads, and by the later Stuart period they were receiving larger fees for their trouble, since they did not have time to follow the practice I describe above, and precede their court performance with an afternoon show at the playhouse. In the Christmas season of 1636–7, during a period of bad plague, the King's Men took up residence at Hampton Court for several weeks, to provide entertainment for the King and the court. The theatres were closed, as they always were at such times, and the court authorities must have decided it was safer to keep the actors away from potentially infectious contacts in the city.

The third outlying palace lay to the east of the riverside suburbs of the city at Greenwich, a favourite of King Henry VIII, and also frequently used by his younger daughter, Elizabeth, when she became queen. It enjoyed a splendid site, now occupied by the Royal Naval Hospital and the Maritime Museum, built directly on a bend of the river, with gardens and parkland on rising ground behind it. At the right state of the tide it did not take long to travel by boat between London and Greenwich, and actors performed there often before 1603. The Stuart kings gave the use of the palace to their queens, and the festive holiday courts were not held there.

Queen Elizabeth's domestic arrangements never included a spouse and children, although her 'family' of trusted advisers and female companions included a number of blood relatives. King James arrived from Scotland with a wife and three children, and the official entourage which accompanied each of these important individuals expanded the size of the court, or group of connected courts, and made further demands on space. Concurrently the enlarged royal household increased the opportunities for patronage of the arts, one conspicuous and immediate sign of which was the well-known renaming of all the principal troupes of actors with royal titles, so that Shakespeare's fellows became the King's Men, and he himself was sworn as a member of the King's household, a Groom of the Chamber in Ordinary. Such a direct relationship, linking the allegiance of actors firmly to the Crown, was to persist for a long time, surviving the disturbance of the civil wars and the Interregnum.

The need for new space for the larger Stuart courts was met by calling into service the other royal houses not far from Whitehall: St James's Palace, another building project of Henry VIII which survives today, and Somerset House, former residence of the dukes of Somerset, forfeit to the Crown in 1552, which stood on the site of the current building of that name, between the Strand and the river, in a row of large aristocratic residences which lined the Thames between Whitehall and the city limits. In honour of James's queen, Anne of Denmark, the building became known as Denmark House in the Stuart period. It served as a distinct London court of the queens of both King James and King Charles, and a number of entertainments were mounted there. St James's Palace, a relatively small establishment (though it retains its Tudor chapel, it never had a great hall), served as the London court of the Prince of Wales, the heir to the throne. Prince Henry died there in later 1612, and Prince Charles lived there afterwards for the dozen years before he became king. In the 1630s the palace became a distinctly Catholic establishment for Queen Henrietta Maria's French entourage, but throughout the Stuart years plays and entertainments were presented there, particularly in the 1630s. The Queen's Presence Chamber, where the actors performed, survives as the Armoury Room in the remaining buildings at St James's. Its modest dimensions—roughly 20 feet wide by 40 in length and a ceiling of some 15 feet—provide quite a different model of a space which became a temporary court theatre: compared with the Hall at Whitehall, it was truly a chamber theatre.

The naming of the King's Men in 1603 had a long tradition. Medieval kings had patronized players, although the troupes were smaller than that of the nine actors 'and the rest of their associates' named in the royal patent of 1603. Twenty years earlier Queen Elizabeth had created the Queen's Men, a company of twelve actors, including the famous clown Richard Tarlton, reviving a Tudor tradition of the patronage of actors which had begun in the 1490s. By Queen Elizabeth's day, at least, royal players were not expected to be permanent residents of the court, nor was their troupe the only one to offer dramatic entertainments there. Although Shakespeare and his fellows swore an oath of loyalty to the Crown in becoming minor members of the royal household and were certainly expected to respond to any summons to attend court from the representatives of their patron, they were regarded as royal servants 'out of court', and were free to pursue professional lives in theatres and playing places, working on their own account for a paying public. As royal artists they were associates, rather than residents.

Their position might be compared with that of musicians, a considerable number of whom were required to reside permanently at court, as music directors and choristers in the royal chapels, where service was held daily, or as the providers of ceremonial flourishes (trumpeters and drummers) or of, for example, accompanying music at formal meals (string players). Graphic artists tended to be commissioned for particular tasks, although the department of the royal household devoted to building and upkeep, the Office of the Works, included among its staff many accomplished painters, carvers, masons, and architects: Inigo Jones was the Surveyor of the Works from 1615 onwards. His drawings and plans for royal entertainments during the first four decades of the seventeenth century form the richest source of our knowledge of the appearance of court theatre.

Dramatic entertainments provided by actors were merely one part of the range of spectacles, games, contests, and musical entertainments collectively known as revels which marked traditional holidays and feasts, or else such special court events as royal marriages, foreign treaties, diplomatic expeditions, and important anniversaries: that of the monarch's accession to the throne, for example. Some of these shows were produced within the court itself, and some—like those of both amateur and professional actors—were invited or commissioned. The management of the wide variety of costumed parades, entries, disguised dances, and the like, many of which featured elaborate scenic effects as well as exotic and extravagant costumes, fell to the responsibility of a court officer, at first appointed ad hoc for particular occasions, but increasingly under King Henry VIII institutionalized as the task of one individual, and recognized at the end of the reign by the creation of the post of Master of the Revels, in 1545.

The position survived until the Restoration, although its responsibilities changed considerably. Chiefly, King Henry's successors, Edward (1547), Mary (1553), and Elizabeth (1558), inherited a strong tradition of court entertainment, and all three were served by their father's Master of the Revels, Sir Thomas Cawarden. The surviving accounts for the expenditure of the Office on costumes, properties, and scenery, from the middle years of the century through to the late 1570s, provide a great deal of information about court revels during the first half of Queen Elizabeth's long reign. The Revels Office maintained a large wardrobe of costumes, which it stored for many years after it no longer prepared a new stock of costumes each season. In its active years of theatre business, in addition to tailors and seamstresses it also employed designers, property makers, scenic artists, and machinists, as well as stage carpenters who constructed the 'houses', built of wooden frames and canvas, which were commonly provided for the performance of plays: a version of what Elizabethan players would have called the tiring house, a combined dressing room and common entry point lying behind the upstage limit of the playing area. It is clear from the accounts that particular spectacular pieces of machinery—a collapsing tower in early 1548, and a rock emitting smoke and fire, and containing a mechanical chair, in 1579—were built for players visiting the court. At least some visiting actors were also provided with costumes. Until the early 1580s, when economies and reorganization changed the functioning of the Revels, it was a major patron of theatre artists of all kinds, and undoubtedly a chief influence on the developing theatre culture of London. The kinds of theatrical preparation apparent in the memorandums of Philip Henslowe, between the later 1580s and the early 1600s, might be profitably compared with the similar material in the Revels accounts of the preceding decades.

The Office instituted by Henry VIII gave its Master authority over all and singular 'jests, revels, and masks', and this last term deserves some attention in any account of the range of performative activity at the Tudor and Stuart courts. Masques, so spelt, we associate with the English court after 1603, and particularly with the creative partnership of Ben Jonson and Inigo Jones. But the older Tudor masks shared many features with the Jacobean and Caroline shows: central to both was an entry, to music, of identically disguised dancers, frequently prominent members of court society, with attendant torchbearers. The maskers performed, first, rehearsed choreographed dances, and then took out members of the audience to dance, before leaving the gathering again, in procession. The entertainment was a musical variation on the 'disguising', a cultural practice with many manifestations at all levels of society, across the breadth of European civilization in the Middle Ages and later; masking was not confined to the royal court. Elaborate dramatization was not an essential ingredient of masking, although a framing speech or dialogue might be delivered to explain the sudden irruption of the exotic 'strangers' into the social circle they visited. Such an explanation is attempted, at least, in *Love's Labour's Lost*, when the King and lords of Navarre appear in disguise as 'Muscovites' (also wearing masks on their faces), and invite the French ladies to dance. So 'masks' and 'masques' are essentially the same thing; the spellings usefully distinguish the Tudor and Stuart forms, however, and I retain them here.

Exotic costumes, like those of the Shakespearean Muscovites, were characteristic of Elizabethan, and earlier, masks: barbarians in early 1560, satyrs in 1565, lanceknights (Germany mercenary soldiers, with their extravagant slashed doublets and breeches, like the papal Swiss Guards) in 1573. The simplest physical provision for masking, apart from costumes, for which the Revels Office was responsible, was a cleared space in the hall or chamber on which the maskers might perform: the dancing floor, traditionally covered with green baize, like a very large billiard table, remained the central physical feature of the Stuart masques, despite their scenic elaborations and proscenium stages. Most Elizabethan masks appear to have been fairly simple as regards any associated scenery, although the show mounted by the legal students of Gray's Inn at Whitehall in March 1595 featured a large rock which opened and from which the maskers made their entry, following a framing dramatic debate which released them, through the power of Elizabeth herself.

The mask of *Proteus and the Adamantine Rock* was presented at Shrovetide, the festival period immediately before Ash Wednesday and the Lenten period following. Shrove was a traditional holiday season invariably marked at court by revels; the other, invariably, was Christmas, observed for each of the twelve days between 25 December and 6 January. Both were winter festivals, and although they were part of the Christian calendar they also had deep pagan roots in communal eating and drinking, celebration of light and heat, and various forms of sanctioned rough, wild, or mocking behaviour. The mask that the gentlemen of Gray's Inn brought to the royal court actually marked the end of a protracted jest, the rule of the 'Prince of Purpoole', a mock monarch who presided over a facetious court among his fellow legal students. He had been elected on the preceding All Saints' day, 1 November 1594, and his long reign demonstrates how winter festivals might run together to provide an extended season. It is also a reminder of the widespread observation of holiday revelling, even, in the case of Gray's Inn, extending to the patronage of players: Shakespeare's troupe presented *The Comedy of Errors* in the hall there on the night of 28 December 1594, a Christmas visit to a rather different court from that of Whitehall. The heads of any large household would have been expected to provide hospitality for their dependants and servants at times of festival, with feasting and revelling. Monarchs fulfilled such a role at the traditional festive seasons of the court.

If we compare the calendar of entertainments at court during the last decade of Queen Elizabeth's reign with that of the first decade of King James's, we can observe that the Jacobean season expanded to fill the longer period, between late October and early March, defined above, whereas Elizabeth had commissioned entertainments chiefly within the limits of the two weeks of Christmas and the two or three days of Shrovetide. In 1604 the King's Men played *Othello* at Whitehall, in the old Elizabethan Banqueting House, on All Saints' day, 1 November, and concluded the season of plays attended by the King with *The Merchant of Venice*, on 15 February 1605. There were only a few intervening weeks when the actors did not visit the court. The 1611–12 season was a particularly expansive one, with many visits by a range of players between 31 October and 26 April, approaching six months in length. Part of this increase may be accounted for by a wider range of patrons: Prince Henry and Princess Elizabeth, the King's older children, commissioned performers on their own account, and watched them in the company of their individual entourages, rather than that of the larger audiences which would assemble for the holiday courts of Christmas and Shrove.

In the following winter season, February 1613, Elizabeth was married to Frederick, Elector Palatine, and as a part of the celebrations the court saw many plays, in addition to three distinct masques. Marriage celebrations had not been a chief part of Elizabethan court culture, although the Queen had on occasion sponsored entertainments for the weddings of prominent or favoured courtiers. King James marked the paternal character of his new court by including wedding revels for leading noblemen within the Christmas season, celebrating the occasion with a masque. The teenage Earl of Essex, an intimate of Prince Henry, and son to the executed Elizabethan favourite, was married at court on 5 January 1606, and Jonson and Jones's *Hymenaei* was presented in the evening, with leading men and women of the court as costumed dancers, dressed in crimson and white, with plumes and jewels. Next day, Twelfth Night, in further honour of the marriage a barriers—a martial contest with swords and pikes, fought across a dividing bar—was presented in the Hall; Jonson wrote framing speeches and arranged special theatrical effects for the fighting, between the forces of Truth and Opinion, and the participating thirty-two nobleman were once again elaborately and colourfully dressed. (A roughly contemporary illustration of such an event, at the court of Lorraine in 1627, was made by the French artist Jacques Callot.)

The theatricalization of martial contests between royal and noble participants had a long history; though it had been particularly favoured in the court of King Henry VIII it survived in the Elizabethan years in the elaborate and showy tilts mounted on the Queen's Accession day, 17 November. Elaborate shows also accompanied Elizabethan tiltings to honour foreign visitors; the text of the speeches and descriptions of the action of the show *The Four Foster Children of Desire*, presented in the Tiltyard at Whitehall in 1581 for the visiting Duke d'Alençon, may have been partly written by Sir Philip Sidney, who took part in the jousting. For the same occasion a rather grander Banqueting House, the third in an Elizabethan series of such buildings at Whitehall, was erected. Principally large temporary chambers, decorated in pastoral style, for use in the warmer months of the year, their chief function is indicated by their title, although they were also occasionally used for various kinds of theatrical show, a tradition which led to their eventual successor, designed by Inigo Jones, becoming the chief venue for court masques for several years after 1622.

In the year following the Essex wedding, on Twelfth Night 1607, James, Lord Hay, a Scottish follower of King James and a prominent member of the court for the subsequent three decades, married Honora Denny in the Chapel at Whitehall, and in the evening a masque was presented in the Hall, with both words and music written by Thomas Campion. Among the nine male dancers, dressed as the Knights of Apollo, was a future Master of the Revels, Sir John Astley. (Hay himself had a lively interest in the arts, and mounted at least one masque at his London residence.) The Stuart courts also took notice of significant anniversaries aside from that of Accession day; plays were frequently shown on royal birthdays.

The increase in entertainments at court after 1603 was not matched by any expansion of the Office of the Revels, which during the 1580s had largely lost its earlier role as an initiator and supporting producer of theatrical shows. Much of the Master's attention thereafter was given to the licensing of plays for performance, although the Office retained chief responsibility for court visits by the actors, as it also hung on to some residual production responsibilities, discussed below. The Revels officers continued to claim money for looking after a theatrical wardrobe, although whether it was much used after the 1580s seems doubtful. Notably, the preparations for the newly elaborated form of the Jacobean masques, supported by the patronage and participation of Queen Anne, lay outside the area of Revels responsibilities. The principal designer of the new style of show, Inigo Jones, seems to have had more connections with the Office of the Works, even before his appointment as Surveyor. Much of the cost of the masques went on the very elaborate costumes constructed for them, but the expectation would have been that the rich and noble participants would each have paid for his or her own.

Scenic and lighting effects—insofar as the latter were possible with the limited resources of candles and lamps—were among the leading spectacular attractions of the Stuart masques, and effects of transformation and revelation were commonly written in to the fictional situations of the shows. Surprising and showy effects produced with stage machinery were hardly new—the Revels Office had employed skilled machinists before Queen Elizabeth's reign—but there are signs that Jones and the workmen who translated his ideas into action were capable of quite sophisticated techniques. A letter describing the scenery for *Hymenaei* in 1606—no designs survive—speaks of the descent of the lady masquers from an upper level in 'two great clouds' which moved 'not after the stale downright perpendicular fashion, like a bucket into a well; but came gently sloping down'. Where the Globe had a stage machine which might produce gods from the heavens bucket-fashion, the fuller resources of the court allowed for a wider visual and spatial inventiveness in theatrical pictures, yet there is not much indication that these resources were expended on the production of plays at court, at least in the Jacobean years.

The settings and stage effects of Stuart masques were expensive only in relative terms: timber, rope, and paint were cheap in comparison to silks and brocades. They were constructed for only one single performance (though on some occasions masques were given a second showing), and then theatre and stage were taken apart. Professional actors would not have considered such expense or trouble; playhouse stages, once built, were expected to serve a wide repertory of plays with the least possible physical adaptation, while plays themselves had to be adaptable to a variety of staging conditions when the actors toured, or played in court chambers of one kind or another. The specificity of masques, then—the ways in which they were written, conceived, and designed to serve one particular occasion—made them quite unusual theatrical phenomena. They were also designed for amateur performers, supported by professionals. At the centre were the dancers, trained as well as shared talent allowed over the course of a week or two with a dancing master. The musicians, instrumentalists and singers, were royal servants, as were the actors who took speaking parts.

Aside from the circumstance that the speeches in many masques make direct reference to their principal patron, the King, sitting prominently on a dais in the centre of the theatre, the participation of Queen Anne and the leading noble ladies of her court in the early masques of the Jacobean years—for example, *Blackness* in 1605 and *Beauty* in 1608—made the reception of the performances very different from that, say, of the 1604 *Othello*, an entirely enclosed fiction performed by actors concerned to make it convincing, exciting, and moving. Even behind the negro make-up she applied to dance as a Daughter of Niger the Queen would have been apparent as the prominent personage she was, and the audience watching her had come to see her at play, as it were. That audience was invited, its access to the performance guarded, and it was constituted chiefly of the highest-ranking members of the court and their immediate families: husbands, fathers, brothers, wives, sisters, mothers, and cousins of those taking part as masquers, in fact. Masque occasions therefore had something of the air of a family party, particularly accentuated when children were included as performers, as they frequently were.

While masques were undoubtedly meant to be impressive, and included in their audiences the ambassadors of the major European powers, to confer honour and to display the splendour of British culture, they also had a certain amount of the shared game about them, in which both performers and audience enjoyed dressing up and showing off. Critical solemnities about the symbolic royal empowerment enacted by the remaining texts of the masques rather miss, I think, the general sense of fun and pleasure which both rehearsals and performance must have generated among a group of people who knew each other well, and who did not go to the evening of the masque in a mood of especial solemnity.

If masques, produced uniquely within court for a selected elite audience, and plays, shared with a wide public through their performances in the playhouses, were different, at court they shared common conditions of production. The theatres provided for either were temporary structures, built within court spaces that had many other functions throughout the year. From the beginning of Queen Elizabeth's reign until the outbreak of the Civil War a traditional sound at court in the days before and after the holiday feasts would have been the clattering and hammering of carpenters unloading piles of planks and scaffold poles in one or another large, echoing chamber, then nailing and lashing them together to form a theatre, and pulling it apart again when the revels were ended. When the professional players performed in a room such as the Hall at Whitehall, most of the space would have been dedicated to seating for the audience, constructed of rising ranks of benches ('degrees') supported on a wooden framework braced against the wall. More exclusive seating for particular groups might have been provided as boxes, closed off from the open rows with partitions, and sometimes raised on posts. Ranks of raised wooden seating bearing the weight of a few hundred important people could not have been allowed any risk of collapse, so we may take it the construction was well engineered and substantially built.

Rectangular chambers imposed a certain form on the theatres built within them. Stages were usually built across one end of the width of the rectangle. The elaborate proscenium stage Inigo Jones designed for the French pastoral play *Florimène* at Whitehall in December 1635 was built in front of the Tudor hall screen (the 'low' end of the Hall) and occupied the full width of the room, and nearly half its length. The surviving plan of the theatre shows raised seating arranged against the three walls surrounding the central royal dais, positioned about 20 feet from the downstage edge of the playing platform. This was a specially mounted production, provided by Queen Henrietta Maria and her French entourage in honour of the King's birthday. English actors at this date did not usually perform their plays on stages with painted scenic wings and back shutters, although under the influence of the Queen certain experiments in doing so were undertaken. Far more usually, the actors could have made do with smaller platforms than that built for *Florimène*, and when they played in smaller chambers they would have perforce to have done so. The Works accounts rarely give the dimensions of the structures built by their workmen, but one Elizabethan document describes a platform built in the Great Chamber at Richmond for the Christmas season of 1588–9 which was 14 feet square, and used by the Queen's Men, the Admiral's Men, and Paul's boys in presenting at least four distinct plays before the Queen and court. That stage was about half the size of the playing space at

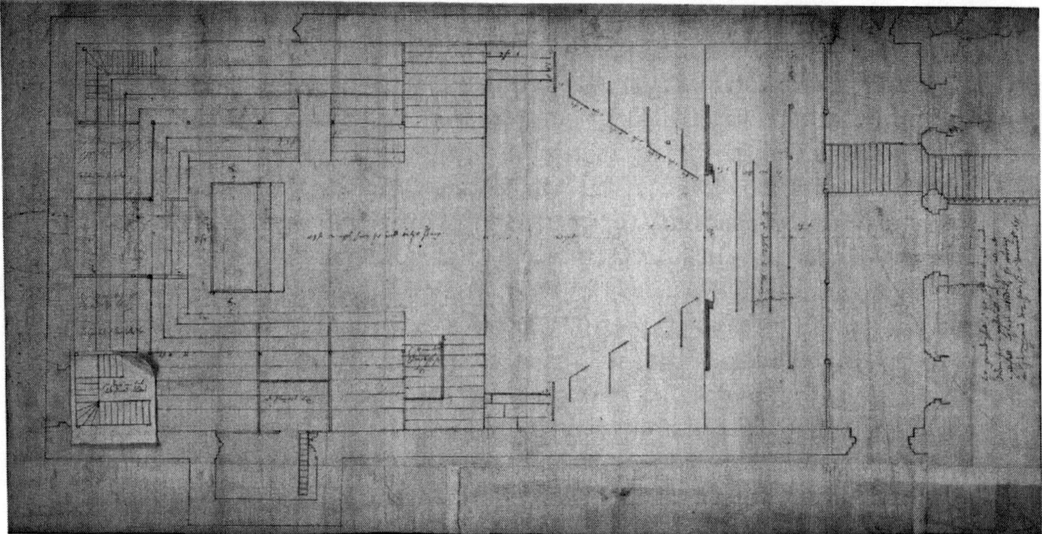

Figure 18.2 Plan of the Hall at Whitehall set up for the French pastoral *Florimène* (1635). A proscenium stage with scenery has been placed in front of the screen (right); facing it is the royal state, surrounded by degrees and boxes for the court audience.

the newly opened Rose playhouse, for example, but it was evidently large enough to serve, and its dimensions provide an exemplary reminder about the adaptability of early modern performers to local conditions.

In addition to a stage, the actors would certainly have expected a tiring house to have been provided immediately behind it: the Elizabethan 'backstage', dressing room, and point of entry and exit for the performers. Court records do not frequently mention this essential provision, with the exception of the Revels accounts describing scenic 'houses' from the earlier Elizabethan years. As the Revels Office retained responsibility for the lighting of theatrical shows at court, they perhaps also continued to look after completing the stage arrangements. In 1604–5 they bought canvas for 'the Tiering house', and in 1611–12 supplies for 'ye Tiering Chamber'. A range of records suggests that curtaining 45 feet in length was provided for the front of it (long enough for the width of large court chambers?), and that actors at court made their entrances through curtains behind the stage; a curtained façade, probably painted with some patterned or figurative decoration, lay in the audience's view as they waited for the play to begin. The tiring house was probably two storeys in height, as it would have to have been to match the staging requirements of some plays: the opening of *Othello*, for example. A practicable floor above the stage level of the tiring house in turn suggests that a fairly substantial frame must have been built for the entire structure (as well as backstage stairs or ladders). Revels records of the same date as those above make several references to 'music houses'; that provided in

1611–12 was decorated with a 'Paynted Clothe'. In terms of the language of the contemporary playhouse, music rooms or houses were raised over the stage; in 1638 Jasper Mayne commended Jonson's plays for not laying siege to the music room, or the 'walls', where the scaling ladders in battle plays were set. In summary, then, it seems that in Shakespeare's day a painted wood and canvas structure lay behind the actors' stages at court. Music produced by the theatre musicians, possibly supplemented with court players, was heard from the upper level of the theatrical façade before the show began, and probably also at suitable intervals as it proceeded.

Once auditorium, stage, and tiring house had been set up, the Revels workmen could proceed, with the aid of high ladders, to the job of straining long wires across the width of the roof of the chamber, and then suspending the array of chandeliers, decorated with twinkling reflective pendants, which provided the traditional illumination of court theatres. The decoration of the theatre auditorium itself, probably the responsibility of the Offices of the Works and the Wardrobe working together, was likely to have been completed by covering perpendicular surfaces with woven hangings, a feature of higher-status domestic interiors since the medieval period. The state rooms at all the royal palaces were decorated with a rich variety of hangings and tapestries; King Henry VIII had assembled an enormous collection of very valuable and artistically sophisticated tapestries, and their display was one of the chief impressive visual effects of the English court. While damage to the very richest of these fabrics would have been avoided, court plays and masques were occasions of demonstrative magnificence, and every effort would have been made to decorate the temporary theatre with appropriate style. Actors and audience might have been surrounded, then, not only by woven figurative and allegorical scenes on historical, classical, and biblical themes, but by the shimmering and glittering reflection of candlelight on the many gold and other metallic threads woven into the designs of the hangings. The court play was presented within a 'feasting presence, full of light'.

The expense and trouble of erecting and demolishing these temporary theatres for masques and plays must eventually have suggested that spaces devoted to the theatre arts might form a suitable part of the palace. By the eighteenth century such planning was common, in the rest of Europe if not in England, but by the start of the preceding century theatre-loving rulers in northern Europe were beginning to experiment with their own theatre buildings. King James was largely a passive consumer of court theatre; his wife and children were more enthusiastic observers of and participants in theatrical events. King Charles, who came to the throne in 1625, had his court architect draw up plans for an extensive rebuilding of Whitehall Palace in an up-to-date and elegant Italianate style, in key with Jones's major architectural achievement, the Banqueting House, which had been completed in 1622, and still stands on the site of its various predecessors, more insubstantial wooden buildings, the last the victim of fire in 1619. If Charles dreamt of finding Whitehall brick and leaving it marble, he had neither money nor time to launch the scheme, but he did direct Jones to carry out a relatively cheap conversion of a Tudor gaming house into an impressive small theatre.

Not a wooden O but a brick octagon, the Cockpit at Whitehall had been built by Henry VIII for courtly cockfighting, as part of a range of buildings devoted to pastimes and sports on the edge of St James's Park. It featured a central table or fighting arena surrounded by rings of seats and a gallery, and was lit by a central lantern window at the peak of a sloping octagonal roof. From the early 1600s onwards it had been occasionally set up for plays shown to Prince Henry, and then to Prince Charles, to whom it subsequently suggested itself as a permanent theatrical facility. Jones's conversion, completed in 1630, divided the plan of the building along its centre line, devoting roughly half to auditorium, and half to stage and backstage space. The style of the permanent façade was elegant classicism—Jones had visited Palladio's Teatro Olimpico at Vicenza—with decorative columns, arches, busts, and swags. What actors would have called the tiring-house wall described a concave curve around the back of the stage, following the line of the octagonal layout of posts supporting the gallery, and disguising it. At the upper level the façade featured one large central window—an acting station or a music house—but at the stage level there were five symmetrical entry doorways, the largest at the centre, directly below the opening above. If the scale on the surviving plan is to be trusted, the acting area was 34 feet across at its widest, and 15 to 16 feet deep to the central backstage door: smaller than the stage at the Globe, but quite comfortably comparable to the area, if not the shape, of the stages of the smaller indoor playhouses of Stuart London.

For the last decade of his London court, then, King Charles had at his disposal an elegant small theatre which could be used at short notice, without the need for elaborate preparation. It probably held an audience of about 350 people, and must have been regarded as large enough, since it became the principal venue for plays when the court was at Whitehall. Plays acted there by the King's Men in its first season of use included *Volpone*, *The Maid's Tragedy*, and *The Duchess of Malfi*, and on the basis of the published texts of those plays we can make some guesses at how they might have been translated into action on Inigo Jones's stage in late 1630.

Beginning with Twelfth Night in 1622 the preferred place for the presentation of masques was another building by Jones, the new Banqueting House. The show on that date was Jonson's *Masque of Augurs*, featuring Prince Charles as principal dancer. Surviving designs for stages and scenery for the masques of this period can therefore be referred to an extant building, the interior of which was temporarily adapted in the traditional manner by the Office of the Works: in 1622 they built eleven 'bays of degrees' on each side, each 16 feet long and two storeys high, the upper gallery supported on posts. The seating produced by this arrangement would have accommodated 1,300 spectators, calculating by contemporary measures, a figure which tends to emphasize the function of masque as a grand occasion where the play, at such places as the Cockpit theatre, was a more intimate event.

The Banqueting House continued to be used as a theatre for masques for fourteen years. In later 1635 Rubens's great paintings were installed in the ceiling, where they may still be seen, and concern about damage to them from the smoke from the many candles and torches used in the masques led to the commissioning in 1637 of a building dedicated to masque production, also designed by Inigo Jones: a large wooden structure fitted into the courtyard to the east of the Banqueting House, and reduplicating the size and layout of that building, with space above and below the stage for theatre machinery (and presumably with fixed seating, as at the Cockpit). Its considerable height (walls of almost 60 feet to the eaves) may have had something to do with a ventilation system, to disperse the smoke from the lights, and to avoid the fires which had destroyed similar buildings in the past. (It was, reportedly, very draughty in cold weather.) It was used for the production of the last three masques at Whitehall, in 1638 (*Britannia Triumphans* and *Luminalia*) and in January and February 1640 for *Salmacida Spolia*, in which both King and Queen appeared as masquers, the Queen and her ladies descending to stage level in a flying machine to accompanying music and a song of praise.

Although September 1642, the date of Parliament's Act suspending the activities of the London players and closing the theatres, is often taken as a terminus in the history of the English theatre, theatre at court effectively ended in the Christmas season of 1640–1. The following year the King's Men went to Whitehall once only, on Twelfth Night 1642, to play Fletcher's old comedy *The Scornful Lady* before the young Prince Charles and his attendants at the Cockpit, the court season having been otherwise abandoned. Visits to court to play before an audience of the most powerful men and women of the country had been a regular part of the lives of professional actors for a century and more. Most often these were players directly under royal command or that of leading court noblemen, and usually, although not invariably, they were based for most of their working year in and around London, seeking audiences at playhouses and other playing places from the large metropolitan population. To be chosen to play at court was undoubtedly a sign of favour and status, which could help in the commercial marketplace, and it was also reasonably profitable. A fee of £10 would have been divided out in the agreed way among the sharers and hired actors of the playing company; under King Charles players visiting Hampton or Richmond received twice that amount, while a troupe which accompanied the King on summer progress for six weeks in 1634 received 'progress money' of £100, in addition to accommodation en route.

Court performance was also marketable in the case of plays, affecting the reputation of playwrights, and commonly proclaimed on title pages when plays were published. Many of Shakespeare's plays were shown at court soon after they were written, and court taste in the 1620s and 1630s did a good deal to canonize his writings. The dedication of the 1623 Folio is addressed to two successive lord chamberlains of the Stuart courts, and a copy of the book was among King Charles's reading material as he awaited his eventual trial. The court playwright, however, was truly Ben Jonson, who wrote specifically for royal shows for twenty-five years, and was rewarded with a royal pension. Actors who visited court regularly, as the King's Men increasingly did, were also well-known and welcome presences, like Hamlet's visiting players. By the time Richard Burbage died in 1619, William Herbert, Earl of Pembroke (one of the dedicatees of the Folio) regarded him as 'my old acquaintance', and could not bring himself to watch a performance of the King's Men without their senior star. As he read his Shakespeare, King Charles too perhaps recalled Burbage's voice.

The ironic juxtaposition between the ideal world of rule celebrated in Davenant's text for *Salmacida Spolia* in 1640 and the contemporary crisis facing the King and country has often been remarked upon. The violent political disruption of the next nine years ended the traditions of court theatre as they had developed from the sixteenth century, as it also interrupted those of the English professional theatre; when it resumed in 1660, the actors took up the international style which the court theatre of the masques had absorbed early in the seventeenth century. It was court theatre, not the playhouses, which kept English culture in touch with the baroque avant garde, and produced shows which might be compared to those of Aleotti, Parigi, and Torelli. After 1640 court masques were never again performed, and the Whitehall Masque House was pulled down in 1645 at the command of Parliament, the lumber sold off to pay royal debts. The Cockpit theatre survived the Interregnum, and was restored, though never much used. Charles II, who had as a boy been patron of a troupe of players and had watched plays staged by the pre-war companies in his father's court, revived the court playhouse, but in 1665 translated the old Tudor Hall at Whitehall to accommodate the newer form of scenic stage. The conversion, by Jones's pupil John Webb, was not particularly successful, and the cultural world of the court had changed; the King now visited the playhouses more frequently than the players came to court. Charles's death in 1685 and a devastating fire which destroyed most of Whitehall Palace in 1698 together put a definitive end to English court theatre.

CHAPTER 19

LONDON STREET THEATER

ANNE LANCASHIRE

In London from 1500 (and long before) to 1642, street theater—involving the city's major thoroughfares and including among those the river Thames—was a significant part of urban life for the majority of the city's inhabitants: in its major manifestations not only entertainment but also a participatory ritual of civic affirmation, and/or of national politics intertwined with civic participation in international trade and diplomacy.

The three most significant kinds of street theater, during this period of approximately 150 years, were the Midsummer Watch, the Lord Mayor's Show, and the royal entry.[1] The Watch and the royal entry were at their peak in the first half of the sixteenth century; the Lord Mayor's Show reached its height in the early seventeenth century. All three theatrical forms were city-sponsored, occasional (i.e. focused on specific occasions), and thoroughly inclusive in their entertainment display, political aims, and city-wide audiences. Along with these major street theater forms existed a number of minor ones, such as, at various times during the period: Maying entertainments, with giants, morris dancers, musicians, and representations such as of St George and the dragon, performed all the way from 1 May to midsummer (Lancashire 2002: 168–9); special theatrical entertainments for formal civic occasions, such as Middleton's Running Stream, or New River, entertainment for the 1613

[1] I use the term 'royal entry', as most London theater historians do, to refer to the elaborate ceremonial processions through the city, involving decorations, pageant stages, costumed performers, and musicians, on major occasions such as coronations and formal visits by foreign monarchs. Lesser ridings through the city not involving pageants and performers, even when by royalty, are not included within the term.

opening of a new city watercourse; and royal entertainments, such as mock naval battles and fireworks displays, on the Thames (see e.g. Nichols 1828: ii. 525–41). The minor forms of street theater were comparatively localized in performance; the major forms took the entire city as their stage. Other kinds of secular street display, not involving constructed pageants and/or role-playing, also occurred: for example, punishment display of convicted lawbreakers, and routine royal, ambassadorial, or aristocratic ridings through the city; other street celebrations also took place, as in March 1525, when the French king was taken in battle by the Emperor and his allies, and Londoners were ordered by their civic government to light bonfires in certain street locations and to gather around them, 'after the maner of May Games', with minstrelsy and with parish clerks' groups of singing child choristers.[2] Accession entries—when a new monarch entered the city for the first time, immediately after acceding to the Crown—also involved, at least by the mid-sixteenth century, formally positioned choristers and civic officials on stages in the streets, welcoming the monarch upon his or her first approach into London en route to the Tower (Lancashire 2002: 137–8). In what follows, however, I will deal only with the major and the theatrical (the latter of which I define as involving constructed representations and/or role-playing performers), which in the forms of Lord Mayor's Show and royal entry were also associated with the professional theatrical writers, performers, and designers and craftsmen of the times, the last three groups also being involved in the Midsummer Watch.

The London Midsummer Watch, which had begun to be a decorative processional spectacle as early as the late fourteenth century, by the 1520s and 1530s had reached the performance peak which John Stow has famously described in his nostalgic 1598 and 1603 history and urban geographical account *A Survey of London*. Stow's description is generalized and idealized, rather than being an accurate description of any one Watch; but it conveys the overall nature of the event more clearly than do any of the extant records of a specific Watch.

In the Moneths of Iune, and Iuly, on the Vigiles of festiuall dayes, and on the same festiuall dayes in the Euenings after the Sunne setting, there were vsually made Bonefiers in the streetes.... On the Vigil of Saint *Iohn Baptist,* and on Saint *Peter* and *Paule* the Apostles, euery mans doore being shadowed with greene Birch, long Fennel, Saint Iohns wort, Orpin, white Lillies, and such like, garnished vpon with Garlands of beautifull flowers, had also Lampes of glasse, with oyle burning in them all the night, some hung out braunches of yron curiously wrought, contayning hundreds of Lampes light at once, which made a goodly shew, namely in new Fishstreet, Thames streete, &c. Then had ye besides the standing watches, all in bright harnes in euery ward and streete of this Citie and Suburbs, a marching watch, that passed through the principal streets thereof, to wit, from the litle Conduit by Paules gate, through west Cheape, by ye Stocks, through Cornhill, by Leaden hall to Aldgate, then backe downe Fenchurch streete, by Grasse church, aboute Grasse church Conduite, and vp Grasse church streete into Cornhill, and through it into west Cheape againe, and so broke vp: the whole way ordered for this marching watch, extendeth to 3200. Taylors yards of assize, for

[2] Corporation of London Records Office (CLRO; MSS temporarily held at the London Metropolitan Archives), Letter Book N (1515–26), COL/AD/01/013, fo. 280^{r-v}.

the furniture whereof with lights, there were appointed 700. Cressetes, 500. of them being found by the Companies, the other 200. by the Chamber of London : besides the which lightes euery Constable in London, in number more then 240. had his Cresset, the charge of euery Cresset was in light two shillinges foure pence, and euery Cresset had two men, one to beare or hold it, an other to beare a bag with light, and to serue it, so that the poore men pertayning to the Cressets, taking wages, besides that euery one had a strawne hat, with a badge painted, and his breakfast in the morning, amounted in number to almost 2000. The marching watch contained in number about 2000. men, parte of them being olde Souldiers, of skill to be Captains, Lieutenants, Sergeants, Corporals, &c. Wiflers, Drommers, and Fifes, Standard and Ensigne bearers, Sword players, Trumpeters on horsebacke, Demi-launces on great horses, Gunners with hand Guns, or halfe hakes, Archers in coates of white fustian signed on the breast and backe with the armes of the Cittie, their bowes bent in their handes, with sheafes of arrowes by their sides, Pike men in bright Corslets, Burganets, &c. Holbards, the like Bill men in Almaine Riuets, and Apernes of Mayle in great number, there were also diuers Pageants, Morris dancers, Constables, the one halfe which was 120. on S. *Iohns* Eue, the other halfe on S. *Peters* Eue in bright harnesse, some ouergilte, and euery one a Iornet of Scarlet thereupon, and a chaine of golde, his Hench man following him, his Minstrels before him, and his Cresset light passing by him, the Waytes of the City, the Mayors Officers, for his guard before him, all in a Liuery of wolsted or Say Iacquets party coloured, the Mayuor himselfe well mounted on horseback, the sword bearer before him in fayre Armour well mounted also, the Mayors footmen, & the like Torch bearers about him, Hench men twaine, vpon great stirring horses following him. The Sheriffes watches came one after the other in like order, but not so large in number as the Mayors, for where the Mayor had besides his Giant, three Pageants, each of the Sheriffes had besides their Giantes but two Pageants, ech their Morris Dance, and one Hench man their Officers in Iacquets of Wolsted, or say party coloured, differing from the Mayors, and each from other, but hauing harnised men a great many, &c. (Stow 1908: i. 101–3)

This London Midsummer Watch had begun as a purely military display, presumably in response to the 1285 Statute of Winchester—reissued from time to time by successive monarchs and not repealed until 1558 (Boynton 1967: 7–8)—which required cities and towns throughout England to hold twice a year a viewing of citizens' arms, to ascertain military preparedness to serve in time of war (Stubbs 1882: 469–74). The Midsummer Watch, unlike ordinary 'standing watches' throughout the various wards of London, was a night-time 'marching watch' along a set route (as outlined by Stow) through major city streets. The processing armed men were accompanied by bearers of cresset lights (fires burning in iron dishes fixed on the tops of poles); and this Watch took place twice within five days, on the eves to early mornings of the feasts of St John Baptist (24 June) and of Sts Peter and Paul (29 June). Celebrating Londoners turned out to be entertained by the display, as (at least sometimes) did royalty. The first record of a purely non-military display element in the Watch comes in 1378,[3] perhaps because this was the first Watch of the reign of Richard II, who loved ceremonial spectacle. The city may have been responding to royal expectations, just as in its royal entries and later Lord Mayor's Shows (see below) it mixed civic ceremony and entertainment with politics. The watchmen in 1378 held red, white, and black lances, some decorated with wreaths or

[3] CLRO, Letter Book H, COL/AD/01/008, fo. 79^{v}.

stars, and were accompanied by cresset-bearers. In 1445 the Watch, coming shortly after the 30 May coronation of Margaret of Anjou, queen to Henry VI, was described by the chronicler Robert Bale as the 'royallest wacche th*a*t ever was seyn ther a fore', with royalty and the nobility present (Bale 1911: 120), which suggests that on this occasion Watch display went considerably beyond what the records show to have occurred in 1378. There may have been elaborate display, but unrecorded, at other times as well. In 1477 the King, wanting to impress visiting ambassadors from France and Scotland, requested a 'greater watch'; and the city provided 510 marching men, a morris dance, and a portable pageant—apparently a wood and canvas construction featuring the nine worthies—carried in the procession by fourteen porters.[4] London's Midsummer Watch in 1477 was clearly in part theatrical, and an event not only of local importance but also with national and international political effect.

Watch records before the sixteenth century are sparse; but from 1504 on, and especially from *c.*1519, we have records for most years of the kind of Watch described by Stow (see Robertson and Gordon 1954: 1–36). Possibly the major Watch display recorded from 1504 was inspired, at least in part, by the city's elaborate 1501 royal entry for Catherine of Aragon. The city sold off its entry pageant stuffs in 1502;[5] perhaps some of the companies made purchases. The city and its livery companies arranged and paid for a general Watch display of men and lights each year, but the arrangements and costs fell especially in any given year to the companies from whose membership came that year's mayor and two sheriffs. The mayor and sheriffs were elected annually, but the same companies tended to be repeatedly involved, as the mayor had to be from one of the so-called twelve Great Companies (the most prestigious and influential companies) and the sheriffs usually were also from these companies. These companies were expected to provide portable constructed pageants, on biblical, historical, mythological, and/or allegorical subjects: usually up to four for the mayor and up to three for each sheriff (though the numbers varied somewhat over the years of the Watch),[6] along with armed men and, with variations, features such as a giant, swordplayers, morris dancers, and musicians. When in 1539 Henry VIII suggested to the city that its money might be better expended in military musters for the King's benefit, the city replied in part that the Watch was a spectacle admired by all, bringing honor to the city and country 'thorowe all the Realmes of Crystendome', and also a great benefit to the poor who were hired to bear lights and to perform other Watch tasks.[7] For the Watch in 1521, for example, the Drapers' Company provided a large number of armed men, four constructed wood and canvas pageants carried by porters (the Castle of War, the Story of Jesse, St John the Evangelist, and the Assumption of Our Lady), a King of the Moors accompanied

[4] Mercers' Hall, London, Mercers' Company MS Acts of Court 1, fos. 32^{v}–33r (the MS reference to St Peter's night is clearly meant to be to the eve); CLRO, Journal 8, COL/CC/01/01/008, fo. 155^{v}; Drapers' Hall, London, Drapers' Company Wardens' Accounts 1475–1510, MS +403, fo. 9^{r-v}. What here was routine Watch display, and what was 'greater', is not recorded (though see Lancashire 2002: 156).

[5] CLRO, Repertory 1, COL/CA/01/01/001, fo. 100^{r}.

[6] Three was the limit for sheriffs in 1542 (CLRO, Repertory 10, COL/CA/01/01/010, fo. 259^{r}).

[7] CLRO, Letter Book P, COL/AD/01/015, fo. 194^{r-v}.

by numerous other Moors and wildfire, a mechanical giant (newly oiled), morris dancers, and musicians. The King of the Moors wore a red satin mantle and silver-paper shoes; the Castle pageant incorporated a drawbridge, gunpowder, paper gunstones, and four child actors (children were extensively used in processional pageantry) in silver-paper and canvas harness and with swords (See Robertson and Gordon 1954: 5–11.) Stow's generic description of the Watch is both idealized and static, and oriented towards the community context rather than towards the pageantry itself; the surviving records tell us about the practical details of pageant constructions, performers, and costs, and show the fluctuations in the event display from one year to the next. For example, there were no pageants for a Draper mayor in 1515, 1522, or 1525; but in some years greater than usual elaboration took place as a result of political factors, such as potential or actual royal spectators (see, for example, Robertson and Gordon 1954: 13, 28).

The Watch seems to have focused on entertainment; but, as previously noted, as a display of armed preparedness and of organized spectacle it had national and international political importance; and the Watch was also locally political, in that its pageantry provided an opportunity for the London companies to demonstrate, through the lavishness of the spectacle they provided, their economic status within the city and their charity towards its poorer inhabitants. Pageant types, such as the castle, were recycled,[8] but particular pageant subjects may have been used at times as indirect political commentary. A pageant of 'Lady M' in 1534, for example, has been the subject of some modern critical speculation on political meaning, given Anne Boleyn's recent displacement of Catherine of Aragon and her daughter Mary, though Lady M could simply (or also) be the Virgin Mary.[9] The Watch also had political importance as a unifying cultural ceremony; Lawrence Manley has written (Manley 1995: 238–9) about the Watch as community ritual, with a ceremonial route incorporating the city's two main royal entry routes and emphasizing—in its movement both to the east and back to the west—the 'hallowed' stretch, traversed in both directions, between St Paul's Cathedral and St Peter's Church near Leadenhall.

For about 150 years the Midsummer Watch was London's major recurring street theater event, until in the 1540s the costs imposed onto London for Henry VIII's wars in France became so heavy that, for at least three consecutive years (1544–6), the Watch was cancelled: after which, despite a 1548 revival mandated by the King's Council, the Watch in its civic pageant-focused form became extinct, though for some time the mayor still rode through the city at midsummer (Lancashire 2002: 165–9) and we have records of occasional pageantry provided then from other sources: for example, in 1567 'diuers prety showes done at the charges of yongemen in certayne Parishes' who 'aweighted on the Lorde Maior' as he rode from Guildhall

[8] See e.g. Robertson and Gordon (1954: 2 and 9 (castle), 9 and 18 (Jesse)). For general work on Watch pageant recycling, see Lusher (1940: i, esp. 50–8).

[9] Lusher (1940: i. 81–2) suggests the (royal) Mary reference; the Virgin Mary is assumed in Robertson and Gordon (1954, p. xxii). Since Anne was pregnant in June 1534 (Ives 2004: 191), a pageant reference then to Catherine of Aragon's daughter—whose existence was a continuing threat to Anne (Ives 2004: 197–8)—would have been risky, though possible under the guise of a Virgin Mary reference.

along Cheapside to Aldgate and back again (Stow 1570, fo. 411r). A final attempt in 1585 to revive the Watch as a major city-sponsored event (Lancashire 2002: 158 and n. 19) had no success, however, leaving the occasion to Stow's elegiac *Survey* description.

But, by the 1550s, another form of street theater incorporating music and pageants—the Lord Mayor's Show (as it is called, from this date, by theater historians)—had become London's major annual street theater occasion. From the early thirteenth century the newly elected mayor of London had processed, usually on 29 October each year, at first by water or land, and then regularly by land, from the city to Westminster and back, to take his oath of office before the King or his representatives, the Barons of the Exchequer. Accompanying the mayor were other city officers, gowned senior members of the city's major craft guilds, and (at least from 1369[10]) musicians. In 1453 the land procession began regularly to incorporate a river procession to and from Westminster. The land procession may have included theatrical elements from early on; but we have no records of them until 1481, when it was forbidden to have a 'disguysyng' or a 'pageon' on land on this occasion, 'like as it hath ben used nowe of late'.[11] The city prohibition gives no details; but the display 'to the water' and 'from the water' apparently involved performers in costume (a disguising) and probably one or more portable constructed pageants such as the one carried in the 1477 Midsummer Watch, as although the word 'pageant' at this time could be used for any kind of decorative display, including elaborate banners, presumably the city would not have prohibited routine display such as banners. After the 1481 prohibition, lack of records of pageants in the mayoral processions, despite sometimes extensive records of them in the Midsummer Watch, would suggest that from 1481 until the mid-sixteenth century constructed portable pageants were confined to the Watch.

In the 1550s, when accounts and other records begin of constructed portable pageants for the mayor's annual oath-taking,[12] the mayor's inauguration procession finally became continuously 'street theater', though its pageantry was seemingly, until the seventeenth century, less extensive than that of the Watch at its height. One constructed pageant only (such as one involving famous historical and mythological harpers, for the incoming mayor, William Harper, in 1561) is recorded as having been carried in the land procession in the sixteenth-century years for which we have records, although there were also other elements of spectacle such as fireworks, wild men, and devils (see Machyn 1848: 47–8, 72–3, 96). Three caveats are necessary: published records of the Show before the seventeenth century are minimal, and further manuscript research may indicate a more extensive sixteenth-century Show than has been assumed until now; some elaborate displays were probably included which in the records were not called 'pageants', and also the water procession may have been elaborate. Civic-sponsored royal entry water processions by the late

[10] Goldsmiths' Hall, London, Goldsmiths' Company Wardens' Accounts and Minutes 1334—1443, MS 1518, p. 39, col. b.

[11] CLRO, Letter Book L, COL/AD/01/011, fo. 169r.

[12] For the uncertainty about the starting date of sixteenth-century mayoral oath-taking pageants, see Lancashire (2002: 171–84).

fifteenth century involved major pageant displays; and in the printed text of George Peele's 1591 Show, *Descensus Astraeae*, the mayor is greeted at the waterside, preparatory to his journey up the Thames to Westminster, by a performed episode of a nymph presenting to him a pinnace on the water, laden with gold and other treasures and carrying fictional foreign visitors from the treasures' geographical origin. We know about the pinnace only because Peele wrote a speech for the nymph; considerable non-speaking performance display on the water may have taken place in other sixteenth-century years, from the 1550s to 1599.

Just as, however, the Midsummer Watch may have been stimulated into becoming a major street pageantry event by the 1501 royal entry of Catherine of Aragon, so the Lord Mayor's Show may similarly have begun to incorporate more extensive street pageantry because of the lavish March 1604 royal entry into London of James I, London's first royal entry since 1559 (see below).[13] Certainly after 1604 we have both records and printed Show texts demonstrating that the Show was an extensive and highly elaborate annual display: rivaling and in some elements surpassing, in its entertainment spectacle on both land and water, the lavish visuals of James's court masques. By the early seventeenth century a typical Lord Mayor's Show would involve a morning procession by the mayor and his entourage from his residence to the Guildhall, then a full civic procession to the Thames, where a fleet of barges, with livery company members in their gowns, escorted the mayor to Westminster, accompanied by vessels firing salutes and by water pageants: displays at the waterside and/or mounted on barges, with costumed actors and sometimes speeches. In 1609, for example, the water pageants included a mermaid, and a whale spouting fireworks from its mouth and venting water (Robertson and Gordon 1954: 72–3). After the mayor's oath at the Exchequer, the water procession returned with the mayor to a wharf below St Paul's, where the land procession began again, usually with a water pageant wholly or in part moving onto the land to join it. Another pageant might be stationed at Paul's Chain, just south of the cathedral, and/or at Paul's churchyard; and one or more others would be situated along Cheapside, on the route from the cathedral to the Guildhall (where an elaborate formal dinner was served). Along with the pageants, which largely moved into and became a part of the mayoral procession as it traveled along its set route, the accumulating procession featured musicians, wild men, devils, fireworks, and the like (see, for example, Robertson and Gordon 1954: 92). After dinner at the Guildhall, the mayor and procession returned to St Paul's for religious services, and the day ended at the mayor's house with a final pageant display and one or more speeches.

The Lord Mayor's Show was an episodic theatrical form, structured not as a linear narrative but as a processional progressive series of moral, historical, and political displays and lessons set within the context of the overall mayoral procession. The displays involved emblematic constructions such as castles, arbors, and mounts, allegorical figures such as Fame, Error, and Time, historical personages such as early

[13] It may also be relevant that—as after 1501's royal entry—after the 1604 entry the city sold off the pageant materials (CLRO, Journal 26, COL/CC/01/01/027, fo. 186[r]).

London mayors and English kings, classical mythological figures such as Jason and Hercules, and religious figures such as livery company patron saints. The speeches, largely directed to the mayor but as expressions of communal intellect and emotion, elaborated upon the visuals, drawing from them points both specific and general. The figures, colors, movements, and speeches simultaneously entertained the crowd along the processional route, the mayor, and his procession, and placed the mayor within a ritualized civic context of moral, social, and political expectations. This context included the specifics of the processional route: the Thames (London's main commercial artery, linking it through trade with the riches and cultures of the known world), Westminster (main seat of the monarchy, which both ruled London and was dependent upon its commercial wealth and connections), St Paul's (the center of city religious ceremonial since the seventh century), and Cheapside (London's central market area from the eleventh or twelfth century, just south of the Guildhall, and from the Middle Ages the city's widest thoroughfare, used for major ceremonial displays). The Lord Mayor's Show was a ceremonial genre, both in its traditional features and in its route; and like the sonnet form for poets, formally restrictive, the established form of the Show invited pageant writers, designers, and craftsmen to express their creativity within a set of highly limiting conventions and requirements.

From the late sixteenth century, at least, until the 1630s, the pageants and pageant speeches of London's Lord Mayor's Shows seem largely to have been conceptualized and written by individuals with some form of special civic status, such as London birth, London citizenship through membership in a London livery company, and/or the holding of a city office or position (hence perhaps Shakespeare's absence from the list of Show authors). Before 1600 references to Show authors are scarce, but Richard Mulcaster—who wrote speeches for the 1568 Show and perhaps also for 1561's—was the first headmaster (from 1561) of Merchant Taylors' School (Robertson and Gordon 1954: 47, xxxiv). James Peele, father of the dramatist George Peele, worked on the Shows for 1566 and 1569 (though the latter Show in the end did not take place); he was chief administrative officer of Christ's Hospital from 1562 to 1585, and a member of the Salters' Company (Horne 1952: 10, 13–15, 21; Matthew and Harrison 2004). His son George, London-born, wrote the Show's pageant speeches in at least 1585, 1588 (text not extant), and 1591, and perhaps in several other years as well; possibly George was also a Salter through his father's membership.[14] T. Nelson, author of the 1590 Show, was probably Thomas Nelson, a bookseller free of the Stationers' Company (Meagher 1973: 95). In the seventeeth century, up to 1630, Show commissions were above all received by three London-born professional dramatists: Anthony Munday, nine Shows (two not extant; plus in one year the water show only); Thomas Dekker, four Shows (one not extant); and Thomas Middleton, seven Shows.[15] Munday was also a Draper by patrimony, and after the death of John Stow in 1605, as a historian of

[14] See the unpaginated chronology in Braunmuller (1983). Horne states (Horne 1952: 72) that George Peele was a Salter, but cites no record for this.

[15] Dekker was to have written one more Show—in 1630—but was paid off when it did not go forward (Robertson and Gordon 1954: 120). Munday received a small payment in relation to yet another Show, in 1604, but this may have been for preparation of a design not chosen (Robertson and Gordon 1954: 61, 63).

the city he continued Stow's *Survey of London* (Matthew and Harrison 2004). Middleton became city Chronologer in 1620 (Matthew and Harrison 2004). Thomas Heywood, with seven Shows all in the 1630s, breaks the pattern; he was not London-born, and there is no record (so far) of a company membership or a city office.

Regardless of company membership or otherwise, the dramatists to whom Show commissions were regularly awarded all wrote for a variety of companies. The companies (at least by the seventeenth century) entertained bids for Show production from interested parties; and Munday, a Draper, wrote Shows for all of the Drapers, Fishmongers, Goldsmiths, Ironmongers, Mercers, and Merchant Taylors. Dekker wrote for the Haberdashers, Ironmongers, Merchant Taylors, and Skinners; Middleton, for the Drapers, Grocers, and Skinners. Heywood's seven Shows, from 1631 to 1639, were for the Clothworkers, Drapers, Haberdashers, and Ironmongers. Four other individuals over the forty-year period 1600–39 are known to have written one Show each: London-born Ben Jonson, a Tyler and Bricklayer, in 1604 (text not extant) for the Haberdashers;[16] John Squire, perhaps the vicar of Shoreditch,[17] in 1620 for the Haberdashers; London-born John Webster, a Merchant Taylor, in 1624 for his own company; and John Taylor, a Waterman, in 1634 for the Clothworkers.[18] The Show author would develop the Show's theme (approved by the company in selecting his Show proposal), write the Show's speeches, conceive the pageants, work with a designer to manage the detailed physical designs and actual constructions, and see to the printing of the Show's pageant text, in a limited run, apparently mainly for private distribution to the members of the mayor's company. Each Show simultaneously honored the incoming mayor and his company, entertained the London public which lined the processional route (including on the banks of the Thames and in boats), demonstrated the wealth and importance of the company concerned, and demonstrated as well the financial, cultural, and social strength of the city as a whole. Each Show was in part a gift to the mayor from his company, in part company publicity, and in part, as general civic entertainment, a gift to the whole city. Some Shows, at least, and probably more of them than has been recognized to date, also were significant political commentaries on current major social and political problems. Most obviously, for example, Munday's 1605 Show, *The Triumphs of Reunited Britannia*, commented on the issue of the union of England and Scotland under James I, and in pre-Civil War 1639, as political and social tensions increased, Heywood's *Londoni Status Pacatus* focused on the calamities of war and blessings of peace.[19] Most Shows probably also contained a good deal of city-specific political

[16] Jonson's involvement with a mayoral Show in 1604 (and only then) may have been related to his work for James I's 1604 royal entry.

[17] See Fairholt (1843–4: i. 46, ii. 261), though his Nichols citation is incorrect. I am grateful to Caitlin Finlayson for the reference. Squire is discussed, though without reference to a mayoral Show, by Ellis (1798: 17, 26–9).

[18] For all of these Show authors and dates, see Harbage (1964) from 1600 to 1639, and Robertson and Gordon (1954: 58–131) under the relevant years.

[19] See also Robertson and Gordon (1954, p. xli) on the 1624 Show, and Bradbrook (1989: 105–7).

commentary (see e.g. Bradbrook 1989: 103–4), available to modern readers only through detailed scholarly investigation, too little of which has yet been done.

Although Thomas Dekker's 1612 *Troia Nova Triumphans* and Thomas Middleton's 1613 *The Triumphs of Truth* are often cited today as the creative peaks of London's Lord Mayor's Show, the modern esteem in which they are held comes from the fact that they are the most narratively and dramatically designed—the most playlike—of extant Lord Mayor's Shows. *The Triumphs of Truth*, for example, is a kind of morality play in which Truth and Error do battle in relation to a mayoral everyman. Error tempts the mayor with the satisfaction of appetites, power, and profits, but at the day's end is finally destroyed by Zeal, the champion of Truth. The Lord Mayor's Show genre, however, may only uneasily have incorporated the morality play design of the 1613 and, to a lesser extent, 1612 Shows: for this kind of narrative and dramatic design did not continue past 1613. Perhaps this was because dramatic narrative, much of which typically depends, as in *The Triumphs of Truth*, on oppositions, was in general not a form well suited to the overall aim of a Show: the bringing together of civic London, and its actual and potential tensions and oppositions (in politics, economics, religion, and so forth), in a communal act of honoring, celebrating, and promoting itself and its long-continuing civic institutions through the inauguration festivities for its new mayoral representative.[20] A good Lord Mayor's Show would be inclusive, not exclusive;[21] it would be intended to bring London into a harmonious whole, at least aesthetically and theatrically, and, at least for the Show's duration, serving as a model of the cohesiveness to which—at least from its rulers' viewpoint—the city should aspire. Other Show desiderata also worked against the privileging of a narrative–dramatic structure. A well-designed Lord Mayor's Show, for example, would also have incorporated variety (a central theatrical pleasure of the period, as Kathleen McLuskie has pointed out; McLuskie 1994: 10), and each pageant would presumably have been self-contained in meaning, though also relating to the accumulating processional whole, as Show spectators (other than the mayor and his entourage), strung along the processional route, would each have experienced the performance of only one pageant (at most) at his or her particular location. (It is also true, however, that the further along the route a spectator was positioned, the more pageants in the lengthening procession would have moved past him or her; and also a spectator could move from one location to another, along the processional route, over the course of the day.) The appropriateness of a pageant to its initial physical location, in the context of material London, would also perhaps have been more important than its place in any dramatic narrative; and a dramatic structure would also less easily have accommodated the non-pageantic features of the mayoral procession than a more episodic, thematic structure (see Knowles 1993: 157–9).

[20] Lobanov-Rostrovsky (1993: 880) has suggested that the design of the 1612 and 1613 Shows did not continue past 1613 because it turned the mayor, unwelcomely, into an actor in a play; but this would seem most unlikely to have been a problem, since the monarch himself or herself as actor had traditionally been a positive trope in London theater and politics, as in Richard Mulcaster's description (Mulcaster 1999: 22) of the 1559 coronation entry of Elizabeth.

[21] See e.g. Manley (1995: 214–21).

A more typical, well-designed Show than 1612's or 1613's would be Anthony Munday's episodically and thematically designed *Chrusothriambos: The Triumphs of Gold*, for the inauguration of the Goldsmith mayor James Pemberton in 1611. (One of the sheriffs in this mayoral year was also a Goldsmith.) On the water to and from Westminster, the mayor's barge is accompanied by ships fictionally arrived home from the gold mines of India, on one of which are the golden king and queen Chiorison and Tumanama, come to see both England and the Show. Sea skirmishes take place going both up and down the river. The commerce upon which London and its mayoralty are based is thus celebrated at the start of the mayor's literal and symbolic journey into office, with foreign trade and politics brought into the ordering milieu of London and its mayoral celebrations.[22] At Baynard's Castle wharf, below St Paul's, the mayor—now duly accepted into office by the Crown—is met by a martial guard and the figure of Leofstan, a goldsmith (like Pemberton) and first provost of London; Pemberton, that is, now joins a historical governance chain.[23] Chiorison and Tumanama disembark and, mounted on two golden leopards pulling a chariot (the leopards come from the leopards' heads on the Goldsmiths' arms), join the mayoral procession, thus linking and harmonizing the water and its foreign (trade) commercial associations with the land and its domestic history of ordered governance. The procession then moves up the hill from the water to a tomb set-piece near St Paul's, where Time addresses the tomb's occupant, the famous fourteenth-century Goldsmith mayor Nicholas Faringdon, and explains also the presence in the chariot of Richard I and King John. The two Kings, who have appropriately been accompanying the mayor since his return from his Westminster oath-taking to the Crown, in the twelfth to thirteenth centuries gave London its mayoralty; here, past the time of Leofstan, they represent a 400-year, mutually supportive binding together of monarch and mayor, essential also to the city's trading power and prosperity (as indicated by the continuing presence of Chiorison and Tumanama). Past and present, mayoralty and royalty, are drawn together, at the physical structure of St Paul's, in a historical, political, commercial, religious, and material continuum.

The next and largest pageant, situated where St Lawrence Lane runs into Cheapside, south of the Guildhall, is an 'orfery' (a display of goldsmithery: from 'orfevrerie' or 'orfevery', goldsmiths' work, and perhaps 'orphrey' or 'orphery', gold embroidery), a constructed mount of gold, with miners, refiners, coiners, goldsmiths, and the like, surmounted by Vesta, mother of all minerals and metals, with her daughters Gold and Silver. The 'realistic' gold workers are combined with mythological and allegorical figures in a vertical structure privileging the allegorical–emblematic, or abstract, just as the mayoral processional display itself has moved upward (literally as well as

[22] The mayor is in fact already part-way through his inauguration, having sworn an oath of office at the Guildhall the preceding day; now the dimension of royal approval is being added.

[23] Munday also refers to Henry fitz-Ailwyn, the first mayor of London, as a Goldsmith. Later, in his 1614 Show for the Drapers' Company, *Himatia-Poleos*, Munday apologized for having portrayed fitz-Ailwyn as a Goldsmith when he was instead a Draper. (There is in fact insufficient evidence that fitz-Ailwyn was indeed a Draper; Lancashire 2004: 311 n. 8.)

symbolically, given London's geography) from the Thames, with its commercial trading vessels and sea fights, to St Paul's and historical figures of royal and civic governance, to here a representation, both concrete and abstract, of the prosperity created by the balanced harmonization of what has been shown in the previous pageants, which are now all part of the cumulative mayoral procession. Before the mount, or orfery, is another, though lesser, balanced harmonization: a merman and a mermaid, each with a unicorn, in heraldic style, representing the traditional and special historical amity between the Goldsmiths' Company and the Fishmongers' Company. Water and land once again here come together, in a specific company context.

The printed Show text gives Leofstan, the presenter to the series of pageants, a brief speech at the orfery indicating that there is insufficient time for its presentation before the Guildhall dinner and that the presentation will therefore be delayed. The printed Show text is almost certainly incorporating a performance change here, thus giving us an example of the necessary flexibility, at the intersection of the practical and the ceremonial, required of a processional, time-dependent theatrical spectacle. Such flexibility is maximized in *Chrusothriambos* by the use of a presenter, and by thematic rather than narrative connections of pageants. Leofstan then presents the orfery after the Guildhall dinner, when the mayoral procession moves back towards St Paul's for religious services; and Time and Faringdon also speak again, as at the earlier tomb location, adding to the Show's cumulative effect. When, after the services, the procession finally reaches its last stop, at the gate of the mayor's house, Leofstan, Time, and Faringdon all speak again, as twice before, while presumably the physical presences, still, of Chiorison and Tumanama continue to unite the water show with the land show. The original plans for the Show had not included a significant water segment; one was added only in the final two weeks of preparation, when Queen Anne had declared her intention to view the Show both on land and on water (Robertson and Gordon 1954: 83), hence perhaps the land-unified structure of three main locations with three speakers at each one, tighter when the water show is not also considered. The land pageants are also dependent not only on a three-times patterned order of speeches by Leofstan, Time, and Faringdon, but also on consistent verse form differentiation among the speakers.

The 1611 Show is significant not only for what it tells us about the ways in which an episodic, thematically ordered processional theatrical display may be coherently structured, but also for what it tells us about links, both physical and creative, between the professional theater and the Shows. Munday himself had been a prolific public theater dramatist, though by now focusing on other kinds of writing; but more significant are the connections—in form, in content, and in intent—between public theater performances of 1607–11 and *Chrusothriambos*. Goldsmiths' Company records tell us that King's Men actor John Lowen, himself a Goldsmith, was required by his company to play the key role of Leofstan (Robertson and Gordon 1954: 81); and the use of a narrator–presenter from ancient times to bridge discontinuous theatrical episodes is reminiscent of the King's Men's *Pericles* (printed in 1609), in which the story is presented by the fifteenth-century poet Gower, who uses the distinctive verse form—four-beat rhyming couplets—also used by *Chrusothriambos*'s Faringdon. Also Time is a minor but structurally and thematically key character in *The Winter's Tale* (*c.*1609–11), and a tomb sequence with a resurrection is central in Middleton's 1611 *Second Maiden's Tragedy.*[24] Sea journeys and foreign exotica are also of key importance in *Pericles*; and water–land contrasts, eventually harmonized, have thematic links as well to *The Tempest* (performed at court in 1611). Links with other plays of the period could also be cited.[25] This is not to say that the 1611 mayoral Show is put together with bits and pieces of the theatrical plays of the day; far from it. The point is that theatrical ideas about presenters, time, history, sea journeys, and significant emblematic displays appear to have been circulating for use, in different genres, in early seventeenth-century London; and the initial inspiration for the structures and forms of some of the plays could even have come in significant part from the Shows, in which display presenters, water–land combinations, emblematic spectacles, and literal and symbolic water journeys had been in use at least since the late sixteenth century. The added water show in *Chrusothriambos*, for example, in its golden-trade motif looks back at least as far as the water pageantry for Peele's 1591 Show, *Descensus Astraeae*;[26] and the dark-skinned foreigners of late sixteenth- and early seventeenth-century plays—perhaps including the native Caliban in *The Tempest*—have their counterparts in the Moors and foreign islanders of the Shows, which in turn go back to royal entries such as the water show for Anne Boleyn's coronation entry in 1533, which included a 'Moorish' diver.[27] A Lord Mayor's Show such as *Chrusothriambos* was fully a participant in the theatrical world of its time, and significantly the Shows and Shakespeare's late romances had a goal in common: the achievement of reconciliation and integration, in part through the magic of ceremonial spectacle and ritual.

The Midsummer Watch and the Lord Mayor's Show, although receiving more critical attention of late than in earlier centuries, have not traditionally been as prominent in studies of London street theater as have royal entries, which began as processional spectacles as early as the thirteenth century (Lancashire 2002: 43–4). By at least the fourteenth century a monarch (foreign or native) or similarly important figure would normally be met outside the city, south across the Thames, by London's mayor, aldermen, and other civic officers and senior members of London companies, usually with musicians, and escorted in procession through city streets decorated

[24] David Bergeron has long suggested a link between *Chrusothriambos* and *The Winter's Tale* (see e.g. Bergeron 1985: 66, referring back to 1978), noting the resurrections both of Faringdon here and of Hermione there—though there is no tomb in *The Winter's Tale.*

[25] David Bergeron has for some time pointed out (e.g. Bergeron 1985: 65–6, with several examples) the 'steady commerce' between early modern plays and pageants. See also Bergeron (2003: 7–9).

[26] Looking at earlier water shows for specific sources is potentially misleading when we have so little information about them, but Peele's 1591 text at least shows the golden-trade motif to have existed two decades before the 1611 mayoral Show. *Chrusothriambos's* mock water battles were also part of a long tradition (see e.g. Machyn 1848: 196 on a mock battle on the Thames as a 1559 Maying entertainment, and Nichols 1828: i. 415 on the 1604 water show apparently before James I's land entry through London)—though perhaps here drawn in part from the 1610 celebrations for the creation of Prince Henry as Prince of Wales, as recorded in the text of Munday's water show for the occasion, *London's Love to the Royal Prince Henry.*

[27] For the diver, see Furnivall (1868: 373, 380; from the British Library's Royal MS 18 A.lxiv).

with rich hangings and banners (Lancashire 2002: 46–7). By this time, if not earlier, a formal royal entry also included stationary pageants constructed along the traditional processional route through the city: a route which led, for non-coronation entries, across London Bridge, up Bridge Street and (New) Fish Street, to Gracechurch Street and to Cornhill, then west along Cornhill and Poultry to Cheapside and along Cheapside to St Paul's, leaving the city at Ludgate and passing Temple Bar on the way to Westminster. The pageant stages were built and financed (through a special levy) by the city and also by groups such as the Italian merchants resident in London, and were regularly constructed at London Bridge itself and at other locations such as the conduit in Cornhill at Gracechurch Street, the Great Conduit in Cheapside, and—by the late fifteenth century—the Little Conduit, at the western end of Cheapside, just north of St Paul's.[28] The royal entry of the emperor Charles V in 1522 included, for example, nine pageant stages along the processional route (see Anglo 1997: 191–202). The displays were often emblematic, featuring, for example, a castle, an arbor or garden, a wood, a heaven, with choirs singing; classical mythological and historical displays, allegorical representations, and mechanical devices were used; and individual performers (usually children) made speeches. For coronations, entries took two days, the first involving a procession, by land or (frequently from 1483) by water, to the Tower of London (royal territory, though within city walls, just to the north-east of the Bridge), and the second (by the sixteenth century not the immediately following day) involving the usual processional route through the city after an initial different stretch from the Tower (rather than from the Bridge) to Gracechurch Street. Lawrence Manley has written (1995: 223–9, 237–41) on the ritualistic aspects of the routes, and Gordon Kipling (1998) has demonstrated the religious and political meanings of the pageants, which were designed to fit together, for any one entry, into a thematic whole. The 1501 entry of Catherine of Aragon, for example, was structured as a journey from the earth through the cosmos to the throne of honor in heaven (Kipling, in Anon. 1990, p. xv), and the 1533 coronation entry of Anne Boleyn was simultaneously a type of the assumption and coronation of the Virgin and a celebration of the Golden Age returned (Kipling 1997: 57–65). The 1559 coronation entry of Elizabeth I was focused on 'epiphany' gift-giving (Kipling 1998: 125–9) and had a Reformation theme (see e.g. Smuts 1989: 81). A coronation entry both acknowledged London's duty to the Crown, celebrating both the monarch and the city's fealty to him or her, and implicitly insisted upon London's support as a condition of the monarch's rule.

The pageantic royal entry was as much a self-defined genre as was the Lord Mayor's Show, with particular kinds of pageants recurring, sometimes in relation to particular locations, but varied to suit the specific entrant and occasion. Bridge pageantry, for example, habitually involved one or more giants as city gatekeepers, along with a choir of singing, costumed children; and a heavenly castle, varied as appropriate, was commonly featured centrally on the processional route (Kipling 1997: 52 describes some of the varied castles, 1377–1522). As in the mayoral Show, the

[28] Manley (1995: 226–7) provides a useful map of locations.

elaborately robed entrant him- or herself, accompanied by a long train of dignitaries dressed with similar richness, was central to the whole: an ordering presence structurally, thematically, emotionally, and aesthetically. Unlike the mayoral Show, however, the royal entry did not processionally accumulate its pageants, which remained fixed in their locations and therefore arguably allowed the royal entrant more contextual freedom than the Show pageants allowed to the processing mayor. Novelties, such as acrobatic entertainments in 1547, 1553, and 1554, were also sometimes introduced.

Originally the royal entry seems to have taken place only on land; but in the late fifteenth century at least two royal entries involved both land and water (as did some in the next two centuries). Richard III in 1483, perhaps for reasons of security, went by water rather than land to the Tower of London before his pre-coronation procession (about which we know very little) through the city of London to Westminster (Grafton 1809: ii. 113; Hall 1809: 375). In 1487 Elizabeth of York also came to the Tower on the water, with a spectacular water show involving a pyrotechnical display of a red dragon (Leland 1774: 218), the badge of the Tudors. The next day she processed through the city, probably with pageant display, but we have information only about the water show. In 1501, however, the entry of Catherine of Aragon was entirely—and traditionally—by land; and since London had been preparing for the entry for two years, it was spectacular and costly, featuring elaborate pageants at six locations (see Kipling, in Anon 1990: 12–36).

The sheer number of royal entries into London, 1485–1559, is significant. During the sixty-three years of the reigns of Henry VII (1485–1509) and Henry VIII (1509–47), London mounted at least four major royal entries, or approximately one every fifteen years. We have no records of a pageantic entry for the coronation of Henry VII in 1485 or of Henry VIII in 1509; but there was extensive display spectacle, as already noted, for the coronation of Elizabeth of York (1487) and for the entry of Catherine of Aragon to marry Prince Arthur (1501); and also the entry of the emperor Charles V (1522) and the coronation of Anne Boleyn (1533) were occasions of magnificent processional theatricality. For Anne Boleyn the city provided a dragon spouting wildfire, monsters, wild men, a mount with a falcon and singing virgins, and a Moorish diver, all on the water (Lancashire 2002: 144), while on land there were six pageants and six additional stages (Kipling 1997: 44). Then, between 1547 and 1559, i.e. over a span of only twelve years, London mounted four more major royal entries: for Edward VI's coronation (1547), for Mary's coronation (1553), for the welcoming of Philip of Spain (1554), and for the coronation of Elizabeth I (1559). The seventy-five-year period from 1485 to 1559 seems to have been the peak of the royal entry as a London theatrical genre, with a special intensity of focus—and costs—from 1547 to 1559.[29]

But, after 1559, the decline in the pageantic royal entry genre in London was precipitous. Between Elizabeth's coronation in 1559 and James I's in 1603, there was no city-sponsored royal entry, as such, in London. Since Elizabeth liked to go on

[29] For sources of information on the entries from 1547 to 1554, see Lancashire (2002: 193–4). Manley (1995: 248–52) gives an account of Elizabeth's entry.

progresses through her realm, there were royal entries in the provinces, but London remained entry-free (though the Queen rode sometimes through the city; see Smuts 1989: 90); and after James's formal royal entry, postponed, because of plague, from his 1603 coronation until 1604, records to date are of only a few occasions between 1605 and 1642 upon which some civic royal entry pageantry was provided: the entry of Christian of Denmark in 1606 from Tower Wharf through the city (Nichols 1828: ii. 64–9, 86–7; iv. 1074–5), the creation of Prince Henry as Prince of Wales in May 1610 (pageantry entirely on the water, not on the land, with water speeches written by Munday and performed by King's Men actors Richard Burbage and John Rice[30]), and the creation of Prince Charles as Prince of Wales in 1616 (again with pageantry entirely on the water (Nichols 1828: iii. 207–11): Middleton's *Civitatis Amor*). There was apparently no royal entry for the Count Palatine arriving in October 1612 to marry James's daughter Elizabeth; and Charles I, upon his accession in 1625, refused to make a royal entry through London, although preparations for one had been made.[31] Royal entries, upon which London theater professionals worked as designers, speech-writers, craftsmen, and performers, had been an important aspect of London street theater, and an important aspect of London theatrical development, from the thirteenth century to 1559: given the influences which must have existed back and forth between entries and plays, as in the 1550s to 1639 between Lord Mayor's Shows and plays, when the same personnel worked on both. From 1560 to 1642, however, the royal entry as a theatrical form cannot have contributed much to London theater when it so seldom occurred. Hence the Lord Mayor's Show, which took place reliably every year, became the major form of street theater in the city: increasingly lavish in its visual effects, usually designed and written by professional dramatists, and thus intertwined with the development of Elizabethan, Jacobean, and Caroline playhouse theater, with the influences flowing in both directions.

The 1604 royal entry, however, as the first such London event in several decades, must individually have been hugely influential, with its extensive pageantry involving many designers, writers, craftsmen, and performers. As previously noted, it was perhaps also in part responsible—together with the gap created by the paucity of following royal entries—for a major increase in the lavishness of Lord Mayor's Show pageantry. As the first royal entry into London in over forty years, James's entry provided theater professionals with an opportunity, unparalleled since 1559, for showcasing and further developing their talents; and the entry's postponement from spring–summer 1603 to March 1604 provided more time for pageant development. Dekker, Jonson, and Middleton all wrote pageant speeches which are still extant, and the artificer Stephen Harrison's drawings of the elaborate pageant arches have also survived in print. The arches, begun in 1603 and remaining in the streets until completed for the March 1604 entry (Nichols 1828: i. 328–9), featured figures such as Monarchia Britannica, Henry VII, Divine Providence, Fame, and Peace, and

[30] Munday, *London's Love to the Royal Prince Henry*, in Munday (1985: 35–48; for Burbage and Rice see p. 46); Withington (1980: i. 230–2).

[31] See Withington (1980: i. 234–5) and Bergeron (2003: 111–13). The preparations included pageants.

devices such as a garden, a globe, and a heaven. Dekker describes the entry itself, in his 1604 printed account of it (*The Magnificent Entertainment*), in terms of a passage through various rooms in the King's 'royal court' of London.

Royal entries and Lord Mayor's Shows alike were inherently political; and with the disappearance of major royal entries in pre-Restoration London after 1606, the Lord Mayor's Show remained the one kind of major street theater for the communal expression of political ideals and opinions. The royal entry—a civic-sponsored, communal performance event—had been replaced by the elitist court masque, provided by the court for itself and thus cut off from wider political trends and public opinion. The Lord Mayor's Show continued annually as an outdoor, accessible, communal public expression of social and political ideals and opinions, until its pre-Restoration ending in 1639, its theatrical dominance of the streets foreshadowing the coming dominance of Parliament over the monarchy.

In 1603, perhaps as part of the pent-up hunger for elaborate royal-focused civic pageantry after some forty-five years of no royal entries, the city seems to have tried to present a pageant at James I's accession entry: i.e. at his first entrance into London after his accession to the throne, on the way to the Tower of London. Accession entries involving speech-making, and choirs of children singing, had taken place both for Mary in 1553 and for Elizabeth in 1558, as they came into the city and to the Tower immediately following their accessions (Lancashire 2002: 137–8), but we have no records of pageants in either case. In 1603, however, perhaps because the King's slow progress from Scotland provided considerable preparation time, the city apparently had the dramatist Thomas Dekker write a theatrical presentation for James I's accession entry from the north, which was expected to involve Bishopsgate. Dekker's pageant was to be presented, his printed text tells us, at the Bars beyond Bishopsgate.[32] James, however, went first to the Charterhouse, north of Aldersgate, and then, probably because of the plague developing in the city, not through London to the Tower but from the Charterhouse to Whitehall, and by boat to the Tower (Nichols 1828: i. 113–18). The accession pageant was 'layd by',[33] although later adapted for the 1604 entry and printed (in its original form) along with the 1604 pageants in Dekker's *Magnificent Entertainment*.[34] The 1603 fate of the accession entry pageant was premonitory; 1603–4—despite the extraordinary excitement and spectacle—was the beginning of the end for civic-sponsored street theater focused on the Crown.[35]

32 Elizabeth I at her accession had processed from the Charterhouse through Cripplegate, along London Wall to Bishopsgate, and then south to the Tower (Lancashire 2002: 194). Dekker apparently expected James to enter through Bishopsgate.

33 Dekker, *The Magnificent Entertainment* (1604), in Dekker (1953–61: ii. 257).

34 See Lancashire (forthcoming *b*).

35 I gratefully acknowledge generous provision of access to MSS, for research on London street theater, by the Worshipful Companies of Drapers, Goldsmiths, and Mercers, and by the Corporation of London.

PART IV

SOCIAL PRACTICES

CHAPTER 20

NOT JUST SIR OLIVER OWLET: FROM PATRONS TO 'PATRONAGE' OF EARLY MODERN THEATRE

ALAN SOMERSET

THIS essay cannot be any more than a sketch, a work-in-progress towards a complete account that will be some years yet in the making. The evidence that I will be using is largely drawn from the Records of Early English Drama (REED) Patrons and Performances web site, and this is itself necessarily incomplete. The data upon which the web site rests, at this point, are taken from the first fourteen collections published by REED—that is, we have not incorporated *Sussex* (Louis 2000), *Kent, Diocese of Canterbury* (Gibson 2002), or *Oxford* (Elliott et al. 2004). *Wales* (Klausner 2005) and *Cheshire, including Chester* (Baldwin et al. 2007) were entered simultaneously with publication (as all future volumes will be). The records from Wales contain very few references to professional companies or their patrons, and the same is true of Cheshire. As a result our present dataset is skewed towards records from the west, south-west, and north, with the exception of those found in *Cambridge* (A. Nelson 1989) and *Norwich* (Galloway 1984); a lot of professional dramatic activities took place in the east and south-east, and their inclusion would, I am sure, materially alter the picture of patronage presented here, as would completion of the data from the north. To give an idea about the riches that remain to be included from the north, and what I mean by 'incomplete', Barbara D. Palmer's recent comprehensive article presents some of her unpublished data from Yorkshire. For example, she includes, for 1610 to 1619, forty-two performance records, of which only four (the entries from York) are in the database. Equally strikingly, Palmer tallies 105 hitherto unknown payments from households; she notes, tellingly, that, for the decades 1590–9, 1610–19, and 1620–9, performances in households outnumber those recorded from towns and cities in Yorkshire—a discovery I will return to later. Palmer's article supplies a wealth of detail about household arrangements, audience sizes in great houses, and the frequent resort to London playhouses by these northern peers and gentry (Palmer 2005: 259–305).

I don't wish here to present a counsel of despair, because, although incomplete, the REED database is at least based on solid evidence presented according to uniform principles. At the time of writing, the database contained the names of 617 patrons, of whom 478 were not 'shadowed' (that is, they appear on the public web site, while the shadowed ones are available only on our private administrative web site while they are being investigated and worked upon). That is surely enough patrons to allow us to ask questions, beginning with some about particular patrons and their biographies. Then we can move beyond thinking about the lives and activities of particular patrons to work towards some conclusions about the phenomenon of patronage in general. Finally, we will be able to speculate about the effects of the patronage system upon the quotidian lives of professional actors under patronage.

I

Many of the most active companies in London are traceable in the provinces as well, which allows us to think more generally about theatrical patrons, including in our discussion those prominent patrons (all men, except for a few queens and princesses) whose important companies and London playhouses have been, for many years, considered to be the pinnacles of early modern theatre. First, we may consider some aspects of patrons whose companies were far more active than the average. I will ask some questions here about two such patrons, one well known and the other much less prominent, as a means of suggesting the range of information that the REED Patrons and Performances web site can (or will be able to) make available about the lives of particular patrons. As if REED were the online *Oxford Dictionary of National Biography* (*ODNB*; a resource we use constantly), we have been for many years assembling information about patrons' lives. We try to get straight such aspects as birth and death dates, and family details (parents, siblings, marital or other conjugal relationships, and children). This material will appear on the main page for each patron; it will present a 'family tree on the fly' with hyperlinked elements to follow the fortunes of any relation, and it will indicate those among their relations who were patrons themselves. The patron's main page also offers links to pages that return (1) dates of accessions to, and relinquishment of, titles (if any); (2) details of properties held, particularly principal or frequent residences, and especially places that might have been or certainly were playing venues; (3) lists of offices held, including dates of appointments and duration of tenure; and (4) listings of the troupes and single performers under that patron's patronage. This provides a 'footprint' for the patron (some comprehensive, others less so but at least as complete as we can provide), thereby making it possible to think about links between a patron and his (usually) or her troupes. Particularly important are the offices held by these patrons, because office had become, by the seventeenth century, a primary means of advancement. As Barbara Palmer points out (quoting H. R. Trevor-Roper), from '1603 to 1629, seventy-two commoners were elevated to the peerage, and "almost every peerage in the period . . . can be shown in turn to have rested, economically, not on lands but on offices"' (Palmer 2005: 288).

I begin with a patron whose company, although rumoured to be defunct, refused to disappear. Its patron held an important office and an earldom. Henry Herbert, Earl of Pembroke, Lord President of the Council in the Marches of Wales (1538–1601), had a company of players that entered what E. K. Chambers has termed the 'charmed London circle' because of two court performances, on 26 December 1592 and 6 July 1593. Chambers goes on to notice seven provincial performances in the summer of 1593, about which he surmises that the company 'had little success'. (As I will argue later, seven performance records in a season is, in fact, a remarkably large number.) Chambers, and others since, have lost interest in the company because, in September, the company was 'disappeared' by Henslowe, who in a famous letter to his son-in-law commented, or gossiped: 'As for my lorde a Penbrockes wch you desire to knowe wheare they be they ar all at home and hausse ben this v or sixe weackes for they cane not saue ther carges wth trauell as I heare & weare fayne to pane ther parell for ther carge' (Chambers 1923: ii. 128). Two facts persuade us to doubt the accuracy of this report. First, Pembroke's troupe appeared in the provinces not seven times, as Chambers indicated, but eighteen times (in the database; twenty-one in total), and, of these, sixteen appearances occur *after* June–July 1593, when they were supposedly forced to disband. We encounter them, among other places, in 1593–4 in Bewdley, Worcestershire, in 1596–7 and 1597–8 at Bath, in 1598 (twice) at Coventry, and in 1598–9 at Norwich, Bristol, and Newcastle. Barbara Palmer has recently unearthed three records, two from Londesborough, Yorkshire, and one from Hardwick Hall, in 1599–1600 (Palmer 2005: 297). Energetic travels, for a supposedly broken company. And secondly, looking at all twenty-one records, Pembroke's Men enjoyed the second-highest average reward per visit, second only to the Queen's Men, before they disbanded upon the Earl's death in 1601. Is it possible that Henslowe, like many gossips, was misinformed? And might it be that Chambers, having been assured of the company's demise, did not look further for evidence of their provincial

Table 20.1. 'The charmed London circle'

Patron	No. of provincial performances	Date range of performances
Robert Dudley, Earl of Leicester	69	1558–88
Richard Rich	2	
Robert Rich, first Baron Rich	2	
Henry Neville, Lord Abergavenny	2	
Thomas Radcliffe, third Earl of Sussex	26	1570–82
Henry Radcliffe, fourth Earl of Sussex	27	1587–93
Robert Radcliffe, fifth Earl of Sussex	6	1608–9
Sir Robert Lane	1	
Edward Fiennes, first Earl of Lincoln	1	
Henry Fiennes, second Earl of Lincoln	15	1576–1609
Ambrose Dudley, Earl of Warwick	15	1559–75
John de Vere, sixteenth Earl of Oxford	0	
Edward de Vere, seventeenth Earl of Oxford	28	1580–6
Walter Devereux, first Earl of Essex	8	1572–6
Lettice, Countess of Essex	3	
Robert Devereux, second Earl of Essex	39	1575–94
William Vaux, third Lord Vaux	0	
Edward Vaux, fourth Lord Vaux	2	
Henry, Baron Berkeley	43	1557–1610
Queen Elizabeth	63	1558–83
The Queen's Men	160	1583–1603
Henry Fitzalan, twelfth Earl of Arundel	0	
Philip Howard, thirteenth Earl of Arundel	2	
Edward Seymour, Earl of Hertford	13	1590–1606
Mr Evelyn	0	
Henry Stanley, fourth Earl of Derby	20	1564–83
Ferdinando Stanley, fifth Earl of Derby	24	1576–93
William Stanley, sixth Earl of Derby	55	1590–1635
Henry Herbert, second Earl of Pembroke	18	1592–1600
Charles Howard, Earl of Nottingham	35	1578–1603
Henry Frederick, Prince of Wales	5	
Frederick, Count Palatine, King of Bohemia	7	1617–23
Henry Carey, Lord Hunsdon	19	1564–95
George Carey, second Lord Hunsdon	3	
King James I	44	1603–24
William Somerset, third Earl of Worcester	46	1555–85
Edward Somerset, fourth Earl of Worcester	33	1589–1611

(*Continued*)

Table 20.1. Continued

Patron	No. of provincial performances	Date range of performances
Henry Somerset, fifth Earl of Worcester	0	
Anne of Denmark, Queen of England	86	1602–28
Ludovic Stuart, first Duke of Lennox	5	
Charles, Duke of York, Prince of Wales	5	
Elizabeth, Queen of Bohemia	52	1610–31
King Charles I	42	1614–38
Queen Henrietta	0	
King and Queen of Bohemia's	0	
Red Bull–King's Company	0	
King's Charles's Revels	19	1624–36
Prince Charles's Charles II	3	
King's and Queen's Young Company	1?	
Total	1,049	

Sources: Chambers (1923: ii); Bentley (1941–68: i); REED Patrons and Performances web site, <http:// link. library.utoronto.ca/reed>.

activities? All the evidence, taken together, suggests that Pembroke's was a remarkably successful and active company.

Important and widely travelled companies may be found under the patronage of persons who are really very obscure, when considered from the point of view of national importance, public offices, etc. The REED patrons' researches are filling a vital need because they supplement the riches of the online *ODNB*, supplying details about patrons who are not included in that source but who may be very prominent in the world of patronage. My favourite example (because I am currently editing the REED material in his household records) is Lord Henry Berkeley (1534–1613), who stands eleventh in the count of provincial performances per patron at present, linked to forty-six records of performance (when all types of performer are considered), or fifth in the count with forty-three records of performances when we look only as his players or men. That is only one fewer record than survives for King James's Men–King's Revels, and Lord Berkeley's number will certainly grow when his own household records, including payments to 'the players', are factored in. His was a very active troupe, although it is known as a London company only because of a reference to a brawl in 1580–1 involving members of the company with Inns of Court men. Chambers goes on to list thirteen provincial records for the troupe, a very incomplete picture (Chambers 1923: ii. 103–4). Lord Henry Berkeley lived a provincial life of comfortable and cultured obscurity. He lived well beyond his means, held a few very minor local offices, was involved in extensive litigation to recover the alienated

Berkeley properties, was addicted to card-playing (at which he usually lost), and was an avid hunter, all over southern England—his chief interest. His contemporaries nicknamed him 'Lord Henry the Harmless'; presumably they didn't consult the deer population. Fortunately for us, a contemporary, John Smyth of Nibely, knew Berkeley well because he began his professional career as Berkeley's household steward at Caludon Castle and later became the steward of the contested Berkeley Castle estates. Smyth wrote a voluminous history of the Berkeley family, and recorded many vital details about this unremarkable but interesting man (Smyth 1883–5). Smyth's pages trace Berkeley's talents and interest in music and other gentry pastimes, just as his household accounts amply display a continuing and energetic 'patronage' in another sense, as a welcoming payee of dozens of visiting troupes. Looking in detail at such provincial patrons valuably fills out our picture of life in the provincial boroughs, cities, and households of England, which is very important when considering the full picture of patronage.

II

We turn next to ask more generally about patronage, its distribution, and its existence. E. K. Chambers's research, we all realize, was very London-centred; he writes, for example, that the Earl of Sussex's Men 'enter the charmed London circle with a Court performance on 2 January 1592' (Chambers 1923: ii. 94). (The 'charmed London circle' is a phrase that Chambers repeats elsewhere; I emphasize it here again because it illustrates a perhaps unconscious preconception.) He presents us with information about twenty-four companies that had traceable London connections, including Pembroke's and Berkeley's, usually because of the companies' appearances at court or their having become the subject of exchanges about disorders in theatres. Of course, particularly in the earlier period companies' activities in or near London might pass quite unrecorded. Who performed at the Boar's Head inn, Whitechapel, for example? Or at the first theatre, built at the Red Lion, Mile End, in 1567? Or at what Herbert Berry calls the 'Four Inns'—made into playhouses but continuing as inns, all open for business in the 1570s (Wickham et al. 2000: 290–306)? In any event, these twenty-four 'charmed' London companies had, during their careers, a total of forty-six patrons, which represents 7.7 per cent of the total of patrons so far identified. Chambers presents very brief biographical information about each patron in a headnote to his account of the activities of each company. Without supplying similar biographical details, G. E. Bentley adds, for us, companies that were first formed after 1625: Queen Henrietta's, the King and Queen of Bohemia's company (as opposed to their separate companies, formed earlier), the Red Bull–King's company, the King's Revels company, Prince Charles's (Charles II) company, and the King and Queen's Young Company (Bentley 1941–68: i. 218–43). This list adds only two additional patrons to our number (both of them royal), so theatre activities in London, so far as we know, were performed by thirty companies under the patronage of only forty-eight individuals, thirteen of whom were members of the royal families of England.

What proportion of provincial dramatic activity, thus far recorded in the REED dataset, is attributable to the twenty-one of these thirty companies which appear in records outside London? It is surprising how few theatrical companies in the 'charmed circle' appear to have performed widely and frequently outside London, although some were very active. Only thirteen patrons are found in connection with more than thirty records of provincial performance, and only two, Queen Elizabeth and Robert Dudley, occur more than sixty-five times. Elizabeth's companies, particularly the Queen's Men from 1583 to 1603, are really remarkable, accounting for 13.6 per cent of all recorded activities. Table 20.1 is a list of the patrons named in Chambers and Bentley, in the order given by them, with the number of provincial performance events recorded, for the players of each, in the REED Patrons and Performances web site. Where a patron is associated with six or more provincial records, the date range of the occurrences is given.

The activities represent 64 per cent of the total of 1,633 performance events by players recorded in the databases thus far; so far excluded from that number are the numerous records in which, for whatever reasons, the name of the patron is omitted. We can conclude that companies known to have performed in London were an important part of the picture in the provinces, but they are not the whole story. Similarly, the 'charmed circle' of these forty-eight patrons represent only 7.7 per cent of the total of 617 patrons in the REED database. Many of the patrons with whom we're dealing had companies that never appeared in London (or, like Berkeley's, did so very seldom), just as 30 per cent of the companies in the 'charmed London circle' are so far unrecorded outside London.

What was an 'average' or typical patron of provincial playing? This was the subject of a paper I gave in 2005; briefly, I will summarize its conclusions here because they relate to the overall picture of patronage that I wish to develop. My profile of an 'average' patron is gathered by analysis of the number of performance events recorded for each patron. First, the distribution of patronage is very uneven. There are at present a total of 478 unshadowed patrons linked to performances in the databases; of these, 220 patrons (46 per cent), including three in the 'charmed London circle', are linked only to single-performance records from the provinces, suggesting that patronage of provincial playing was widespread but intermittent. The proportion of 'single-event' patrons remains approximately the same in the later period, so it is not true that the singular patrons occur in the fourteenth and fifteenth centuries only, when the records are sparser and performance activities not as widespread. Of the 216 patrons born after 1525, 102 of them occur in performance records only once; of the forty-seven patrons born in 1575 or after, twenty-three of them are likewise singular.

The large number of 'single-event' patrons from across the period obviously skews averages and results. Between patrons of performers of numerous events and those many whose players occur only once, what is the average? If one limits the survey only to patrons linked to players, the average is 7.9 events per patron, and there are thirteen patrons who are at or close to that average. If we look at these 'average' patrons, with regard to their family and kinship relationships, their public offices, and the geographical range of their companies' performances in relation to the areas of the patrons' influence, do any common elements emerge?

Let us look in a little detail at just two 'average' patrons (neither from among the 'charmed London circle'), and from elements common to them we can widen our net somewhat. I will then move beyond looking at the behaviour of particular patrons to thinking about what patronage apparently entailed for the patron, and what its advantages and drawbacks were for the professional actors who formed the troupes.

Sir William Compton, Earl of Northampton (1572–1630), was a midlands magnate who held a number of offices in that area, many of them no doubt administered by deputies; he is not in the *ODNB* although he held one office of national importance as a Privy Counsellor from 1629. He lived in some style, and died £10,000 in debt; he was patron of a wider variety of entertainers than just players. I don't think the debt and the patronage are necessarily connected, although that is a possibility. Significantly, all the performances are at Coventry, the centre of Compton's influence; the confluence of patronage and influence is notable. One may wonder what Compton, as Lord Lieutenant of Warwickshire and Coventry, was doing as a patron of players in 1605 and 1608, because such patronage became illegal in 1604—but Compton had plenty of company among non-royal patrons, supposedly 'illegal' after 1604. We also note that he apparently switched his interest to bear-baiting between 1611 and 1616, and to musicians (waits) after 1621; then he disappears from the records although he lived another nine years. Did he lose interest in patronage? Compton was never a particularly active patron of actors (or, to put that another way, Compton's troupe of players was not very active); two performance records over three years is a very sparse result. This raises a question as to how long a silence in the records must occur before we consider a company to be defunct. What occurrence of activities is necessary to allow us to envision a 'live' company? Was the company of 1608 the company of 1605? If so, what were they doing during that three-year silence? Or were they a different company, hired for a different occasion?

In terms of concentration of effect, the records of the entertainers of William Bourchier, Earl of Bath (1557–1623), are remarkable. He began to become active in public life in the local administration of the south-west when he was in his mid-thirties. The events recorded for his players are earlier, and concentrated upon the south-west, Bourchier's centre of influence and residence, except for one appearance at Coventry by his actors and his musicians. The records are exclusively clustered in his youth, just graduated from Cambridge University; in the period between 1576 and 1578 there occur six performance events by his actors and one by his musicians. It is likely that Bourchier was under the jurisdiction of the Court of Wards from his father's death (when he was 3) until he attained his majority in 1575; his players began to appear a year later. But apparently, for some reason, Bourchier decided to give up as a patron of the performing arts before his twenty-first birthday, so he acted as a patron for only a short time and in a limited locale. Again, one can only wonder why the Earl of Bath decided, so quickly, to cease being a patron of players. Did he swear off them, or join Patrons Anonymous? More seriously, one would like to know what lay behind such short-term commitments to patronize troupes, because it appears to be a common phenomenon among these 'average' patrons. Could we guess that this evidence suggests that being a patron entailed financial and/or other commitments that some patrons found themselves unwilling to commit themselves to over the long haul? I will return to these questions later, and to asking what were the implications for a troupe of actors like Bourchier's.

The fortunes of a far more active troupe, latterly patronized by Edward de Vere, seventeenth Earl of Oxford, lead again to the suggestion that being a patron might have entailed some financial responsibilities. This company was first under the patronage of Ambrose Dudley, Earl of Warwick, where it appears in provincial records from 1559 until 1564, reappearing in 1572–3 and 1574–5, after which date it disappears from provincial records but is known from annual performances at court until 1580. This indicates that the reappearing company may have been a new creation, particularly since one member, Laurence Dutton, had been in Lord Clinton's service before 1575 (Chambers 1923: ii. 98). Dudley's cessation as patron raises questions, chief of which is why Dudley, who was to live until 1590, decided to relinquish his position as patron in 1580 (or perhaps even earlier), at which point Edward de Vere, Earl of Oxford, became its patron. One factor may have been Dudley's failing health in the late 1570s. Chambers suggests that this migration constituted a desertion by the Duttons, as is attested by a contemporary poem whose title begins: 'The Duttons and theyr fellow-players forsaking the Erle of Warwycke theyr mayster, became followers of the Erle of Oxford' (Chambers 1923: ii. 98). Were the Duttons and their company available to the highest bidder, or did Oxford promise them more prominence? Was their eye on the main chance? Laurence Dutton was particularly peripatetic, having been in the troupes of Sir Robert Lane (1571) and Henry Clinton (1572); he was ultimately chosen to be one of the Queen's Men in 1583.

Certainly, under Oxford the company was very busy, and it quickly became notorious because of an affray at the Theatre involving it and members of the Inns of Court. The company's first recorded performance at court occurred in 1584. The web site has twenty-eight events currently listed for Oxford's players in our database. Since the company was in Chambers's 'charmed London circle', there is a narrative of its activities there (plus a few additional provincial records) in his account (Chambers 1923: ii. 99–102). Alan Nelson, in his monumental biography of Oxford, draws from Malone Society Collections volumes, plus records from unpublished REED collections, to add a further eight provincial records, for a total of thirty-six

(A. Nelson 2003: 239–48). The company's activities begin in London in 1580, when the Earl was 30 years old, so the decision to patronize a company seems to have been a conscious and mature one. One wonders why Oxford, at the age of 30, decided to become a patron. The company was active, averaging six records per year under Oxford's patronage (eleven, a very large number, in its busiest year, 1584–5), and its performances are widespread across the country. Its activities were fostered by Oxford, who obtained his father-in-law's help, for example, to ask the Cambridge authorities for permission to play (A. Nelson 2003: 244). But the company was active for only a few years. Its activities were in steep decline after 1584–5, and it had disappeared from provincial records by 1586–7. There exists a letter of 25 January 1587, from Maliverny Caitlin to Sir Francis Walsingham, which suggests that the company continued to thrive in London, but this letter raises suspicions on several grounds: it is malicious, biased, and certainly exaggerating in its suggestion that one could see 'two hundred proude players iett in theire silkes' through the streets of London (A. Nelson 2003: 246). The writer's anti-theatrical sentiments echo those of John Stockwell and other Puritan sermon writers, setting up the usual contrast between overflowing playhouses and 'naked' churches, and may not reflect actual experience. I think it is safer to assume that the total cessation of provincial records of the company (after six years of very active touring) reflects the end of Oxford's patronage. Again, one wonders, why? Oxford did not die in 1586–7, but went on to live until 1604, and was mentioned by Francis Meres as one of 'the best for comedy among us' (Chambers 1923: ii. 100). If he had plans to write plays, why cease to be a patron? Nelson would clearly welcome evidence of the continuance of Oxford's Men but he is forced to admit that 'Oxford's Men—his adult players—seem to have practiced a kind of disappearing trick' during the 1590s (A. Nelson 2003: 248). He provides clues that may answer my questions about Oxford's involvement as a patron, particularly its early cessation. Simply, from having been on the make at court in 1580, assuming patronage of an acting company, and presenting Queen Elizabeth with a rich New Year's Gift, by 1585 Oxford was flat broke, so broke that he called himself in a letter to his father-in-law 'thus disfurnished and unprovided to follow her Magesty as I perceive she will loke for' (A. Nelson 2003: 300). He was forced to borrow from his father-in-law, Lord Burghley, with whom he was not on good terms. He had, as one contemporary, Thomas Wilson, noted, 'prodigally spent and consumed all even to the selling of the stones and timber and lead of his castles and howses' (A. Nelson 2003: 301). Finally, the Queen granted him an annuity of £1,000 per year, to keep the wolf from the door. This sounds like a lot of money; however, Lawrence Stone estimates Oxford's annual expenditure to have been £7,000, so this represents a considerable belt-tightening (Stone 1965: 272). It is not unlikely that Oxford gave up his players because he couldn't afford to keep them, and this in turn suggests that there was a cost to keeping an acting company under one's patronage.

Those two 'average' examples, plus the case of the prominent Earl of Oxford (patron of an active but short-lived troupe), lead me to want to enquire into the timing and duration of all patrons' activities, by looking at all patron biographies, considering these in relation to the duration and geographical scope of their troupes' activities. When involvement as a patron appears to be sporadic or short-lived, is there a discoverable reason, or grounds for surmise? Looking at all 617 patrons is far beyond the scope of this essay; however, the REED web site allows one to conduct a sample survey, by looking at evidence about troupes whose identities are arranged under the names of their patrons and whose troupes appear in between five and twenty performance records. A significant pattern emerges, which suggests that the experiences of the troupes of the earls of Oxford and Bath are not untypical. One can look at each patron in turn, assess the activity pattern of the troupe(s) under patronage, and then look in biographical and other sources (particularly the online *ODNB*) to see if any reasons for the patronage patterns suggest themselves. In some cases, the reason for a cessation of patronage is self-explanatory: the patron's death date occurs in the year that records cease, or the company passes under royal patronage (e.g. Queen Anne's Men). In some cases one might wonder why a decision was taken late in life to become a patron. Perhaps we all think we will live for ever. In other cases the issues are more questionable, and in most cases the reasons for the inception or cessation of patronage relationships are unexplained but intriguing.

For clarity and brevity I will tabulate the 'patterns' of patronage of sixteen patrons, with commentary to clarify their activities in connection with life records, where possible. Those in the 'charmed London circle' are indicated by an asterisk. They are arranged in order of birth dates:

Henry Fortescue (1515–76)

Five (perhaps up to eleven) events, 1560–8

Sometimes styled a knight, this obscure patron had no known connection to the south-west. Eleven events are recorded there between 1561–68, and in five of them the players are named as Sir Henry Fortescue's; in the other six records the patron is given as 'Mr Fortescue' and so may be traceable to Mr Richard Fortescue (1517–70), a man who held three minor offices in Devon. As well, one record (Dartmouth, 31 January 1561) explicitly names 'Mr Richard Fortescue', so it is indisputable that there were two different troupes operating there during the same decade. Richard's troupe records end near his death, while the latest that Sir Henry's troupe is known is from 1569.

Katherine Willoughby (1519–80)

Seven events, 1560–2

A strong Protestant, Katherine Willoughby, Duchess of Suffolk, returned from Continental exile in 1558; this accounts for her late inception as a patron, but not her early cessation. As the *ODNB* says, 'Upon her return [from the Continent] the duchess resumed her extensive patronage, which rapidly assumed a puritan cast that set her apart from Cecil and Elizabeth, who had had to make accommodations to Mary's regime to ensure the ultimate survival of English protestantism.' Her commitment did not cease in 1562, so the reasons why her troupe ceased to exist in the records are obscure.

James Fitzjames (1520–79)

Five events, 1575–7

Holder of nine offices in Somerset and Dorset, Sir James lived at Redlynch, Somerset. His troupe is recorded five times in Devon and Somerset between 1575–7, leaving one to wonder why he became a patron so late in life, and for so short a time.

***Henry Stanley (1531–93) and *Ferdinando Stanley (1551–94)**

Henry, as Lord Strange: five events, 1564–9; as Earl of Derby: fifteen events, 1573–83. *Ferdinando, as Lord Strange: twenty-two events, 1576–93; as Earl of Derby: one dated event, 1593*

I consider the Stanleys, father and son, together because the family habit of using the patronal courtesy title during the father's lifetime makes for confusion. One may also wonder if actors might have migrated from one troupe to another. The matter to concern us here is the cessation of patronage by Henry Stanley in 1583, ten years before his death. Perhaps, as evidence in *ODNB* suggests, Henry gave up his company because of serious debt problems; however, he had financial problems before he began as a patron; *ODNB* states that 'by 1570 his diplomatic missions, with a train of eighty gentlemen and yeomen and an entourage of 220, brought him close to insolvency'.

Thomas Howard (1538–72)

Six events, 1556–9

Thomas Howard succeeded his grandfather as Duke of Norfolk in 1554, and while still in his minority he began to assume public offices. His company is first recorded when he was 18, and last when he was 21; he continued a career of high public service for many years. Possibly more records will surface when REED publishes its volumes from East Anglia, since four of the five events so far known (as well as two performances by the children of his chapel, in 1564 and 1565) are all from Norwich or Cambridge.

Henry Compton (1538–89)

Five events, 1573–8

Created first Baron Compton, and holder of three minor provincial offices, Compton barely makes it onto the radar here. The point of interest here is that his players disappear after only five years, but his bearward or bearwards continue to perform up to Compton's death in 1589, suggesting that his cessation of patronage to players was a conscious decision.

***Walter Devereux (1539–76)**

Eight events, 1572–6

Created Earl of Essex on 4 May 1572, Devereux was much involved from July 1573 to October 1575 in a disastrously unsuccessful attempt to colonize Ulster. He had returned to Ulster by July 1576, and on 22 September he died in Dublin. It is hard to explain why Devereux assumed patronage of a company of players (as well as musicians and minstrels) so late, during this tumultuous period of his life when he was away for much of the time in Ireland.

***Henry Clinton (aka Henry Fiennes; 1539–1616)**

Fifteen events, 1576–1609

A company styled Lord Clinton's players appears twice, in 1576–7; next, Clinton succeeded as Earl of Lincoln in 1585, and a company called the Earl of Lincoln's players occurs thirteen times between 1599 and 1609. Clinton appears, therefore, to have ceased being a patron twice, and neither decision is easily explainable (he is not recorded in *ODNB*). If the second company was transferred to Henry from his father, Edward, the fourteen-year gap between Edward's death and the first datable record of Henry's company is difficult to explain.

***Edward Seymour (1539–1621)**

Thirteen events, 1590–1606

Edward Seymour, Earl of Hertford, had a difficult career during the 1590s, and this may be reflected in the interruptions in events recorded by his troupe, from 1592 to 1596 and 1597 to 1601. Or perhaps we should think of separate troupes, each having a brief history under Seymour's patronage. His fortunes rose under King James, so it is unexplained why he apparently ceased being a patron in 1606.

Phillip Wharton (1555–1625) and Phillip Wharton (1613–96)

The former: eight events, 1600–23. The latter: eight events, 1626–38

The Wharton patrons, grandfather and grandson, exhibit markedly different patronage patterns; the grandfather ceased being a patron shortly before his death, and the grandson presumably assumed patronage of the troupe, which he apparently abandoned twelve years later. Under neither's patronage was the company particularly active, and they were localized to the patronal area of influence, Cumberland and Westmorland. The younger Phillip was not embarrassed by lack of money, having come into his estate in 1634; perhaps his attention was diverted after 1638 by the first Bishops' War, the Short Parliament, and other portents of the coming Civil War, in which he was to be a prominent Parliamentary supporter.

***Robert Devereux (1565–1601)**

Thirty-eight events, 1575–94

With thirty-eight events, the Earl of Essex's players were very active, under his patronage very early (when Devereux was 10 years old), and apparently inactive after 1594. I include him here because the continued activity of his drummers (recorded in 1598–9), his musicians (recorded after November 1600), and his trumpeters (recorded in 1598–9) suggests that the decision to cease being a patron of players was a conscious one. He did have one further occasion to require players: the Lord Chamberlain's Men, who were paid 40*s*. for a performance of *Richard II* at the Globe, on the eve of Essex's abortive rebellion.

Edmund Sheffield (1565–1646)

Fifteen events, 1577–86

It is hard to imagine a patron of 12 years old, but perhaps harder still to conceive of an Oxford student who entered the university at age 9 and left at age 14! Sheffield apparently matured early; he was married at 16 years old, was employed on a royal embassy at 17, and was commander of three ships against the Armada at 23. His company of players disappears when he was 21, sixty years before his death after a chequered career, beset by financial woes, in the north.

Edward Stafford (1572–1625)

Eleven events, 1603–18

Stafford may have taken over the troupe patronized by his father, whose death on 18 October 1603 occasioned his son's succession as Baron Stafford. This preceded by two months the first record of a troupe bearing the son's name, at York on 18 December. The troupe is not again recorded until 24 April 1609, so it probably did not live an uninterrupted existence. After 1609 the troupe appears a further nine times in Lancashire and Cumberland, and then disappears in 1618. Stafford is not included in *ODNB*, and is otherwise unrecorded.

*__Robert Radcliffe__ (1573–1629)

Six events, 1602–17

Radcliffe succeeded his father as fifth Earl of Sussex in 1593, and enjoyed a troubled career never free from debt. There is no discernible relation between his personal circumstances and his career as patron. There are large gaps in the troupe's activities; 1603–8 and 1609–17 are voids, which leads one to wonder if there may have been three separate troupes, each active for only a short time.

*__Ludovic Stuart__ (1574–1624)

Five events, 1604–9

Ludovic Stuart, Duke of Lennox, son of Esmé Stuart, was steward of the King's household until his death in 1624, and one of James I's three Scottish Privy Counsellors. His late start as a patron is explained by his late arrival in England in 1603, but the reasons why his troupe disappears after 1609 are obscure.

James Stanley (1607–51)

Six events, 1634–6

The occurrence of patronage in the midst of Stanley's long and varied career is impossible to explain, particularly since the records (all concentrated in the north-west) occur during a period, in the 1630s, when Stanley had withdrawn from court because of disagreement with the King's ecclesiastical policies.

The patronage histories whose patterns can be clearly seen here admit of no simple explanations, nor are we ever likely to be able to answer the questions that have been puzzling us through these accounts of patrons. The patrons discussed above comprise those for whom I can as yet, from the records available, discern some inexplicable irregularities in patterns of patronage, and I conclude that such seems to be a not unusual pattern among troupes whose tenure with a particular patron was short-lived.

III

There are two implications to these records that we need to think about. First, being academics enjoying the benefits of tenure, we are accustomed to the experience of spending long careers in one university, so we may tend to accept as the norm the experience of members of Shakespeare's company, the Lord Chamberlain's/King's Men (1594–1642), or the Queen's Men (1583–1603). Looking at the company histories that I have been surveying, as well as glancing over the dates given for the provincial activities of the troupes in the 'charmed London circle', show us that adaptability and variety was the more likely lot of most actors in early modern England. It is certainly the norm for actors in our own time, who face great uncertainty as one engagement comes to an end and a period of 'resting' seems to be in the offing. (There are now, I understand, over 12,000 members of the British actors' union, Equity, of whom only a tiny minority is employed at any given time.) Where, to take just a few examples, did Warwick's—Oxford's Men go next, after Oxford's patronage apparently was withdrawn (presuming, as we should not, that the company remained intact)? Or after two years' employment under the patronage of the Earl of Bath, what did members of that company do next? How did playscripts migrate from company to company? It is possible to construct such speculations negatively, envisaging tenuous existences, barely keeping out of the hands of bailiffs, constables, or churchwardens. This was the normal mode of thinking a generation ago, sparked by such vignettes of touring provincial life as are offered by, for example, John Marston in *Histriomastix*, who presents us with Sir Oliver Owlet's Men (the patronal name forms part of my title). No doubt life was extremely difficult for some troupes, as Marston suggests in his satire. However, must we take such tenuousness, such a need to be adaptable, only negatively? As well as comfortably tenured professors, at one extreme, and often unemployed actors eking out a living at the other, might there not be other possibilities? Think, for example, of the careers of talented professional athletes, or screen actors: change provides opportunities as well as challenges. Barbara Palmer offers an intriguing and attractive model to think about: 'the professional entrepreneur who seized opportunities, exploited advantages, dodged disasters, invested wisely, and generally profited from a shrewd sense of the market' (Palmer 2007: 1). Palmer traces the activities of two such successful players, Richard Bradshaw (active 1594–1633) and 'Disley (Distle, Dishley, Distley)' the player (active 1599–1633) through long careers 'playing from town to town, great household to great household, and, on occasion, from company to company, patron to patron'. Another example of this, already noted, is Laurence Dutton. Life might be tenuous and uncertain, but to the really talented such conditions offer opportunities, not brick walls.

Another important question that these examples point towards is best expressed as a question, albeit an unanswerable one: how complete are the records that we have? Or, to put it another way, how did these many companies of players make a living? When we consider the 'charmed London circle', we cannot go beyond suggesting that those companies with London connections might have made the bulk of their income from London performances (and not have toured every year), because, when one looks at the average number of provincial appearances per year by each troupe, the results are not encouraging. Taking the performance records per patron per year of the troupes in Table 20.1 that appeared more than six times (i.e. those given a date range), and averaging that result, one comes up with a disappointing average of 1.67 performances per year. (This average leads me to conclude that the records of Pembroke's Men in the summer of 1593—seven performances over a few months—provide evidence of energetic activity and remarkable success, not incipient failure!) Things are little better when one looks at the ten troupes in Table 20.1 for whom no London records are found; their average is 1.74 performances per year. Again, to cite such averages one must acknowledge that an average conceals individual differences, such as would occur when a company chose, in a particular year, not to tour, to fold up activities, or what have you. If one takes the period 1575—1642, and looks at all performance records by all player troupes across the cities, towns, and households of England and Wales so far recorded in the REED performance database, the annual average number of performance records by all troupes under patronage is only 17.5 per year. Changing the date range to 1575—1620 improves the yearly average somewhat, but only to 22.7 performance records per year. We can hope that the completion of the REED research, particularly in eastern England, will substantially increase these totals and averages, but even if they were to be at least tripled, one can see that the record set will remain incomplete and inadequate.

What an annual total might be from a complete survival of records is anybody's guess, but it has to have been far, far higher than these results. If we begin at the 'high' end, and look at the Queen's Men from 1583 to 1603 (average of eight performance records per year), or the Earl of Pembroke's Men in 1593 (seven performances recorded in the summer tour), or Oxford's Men (six performances per season, with a high of eleven in one season), we may have a basis for the most optimal speculation. If we were to triple such totals (supposing, as I suggested, that completion of the REED project might optimally lead to such a result), we would be faced with eighteen to twenty-four performance records per year for an optimally successful company. What relationship might such a number have to the number of performances per year that would be necessary for a company to thrive (as at least two of them, Pembroke's Men and the Queen's Men, evidently did)? Looking at average rewards per performance and considering these high achievers, let us recall what William Ingram has led us to believe were the costs of touring. We have to suppose, given the costs of horsemeat, food, lodging, and other necessaries, that on average a troupe needed to perform twice a week to survive (say, 100 performances per year), but our results come nowhere near this (Ingram 1993: 57–63). The proportion of records that survive, as opposed to those that must be missing, appears to be between 1:5 and 1:4. Where might these 'lost' performances have occurred?

Writing in 1990, Ingram discounted one possibility:

> The best sort of occasion for playing would be an invitation from a great house, where food and lodging would be provided along with the lord's monetary gift. There's no way for us to estimate how often such an invitation might have arisen during the course of a particular tour, so I have ignored the great-house option . . . (Ingram 1993: 58)

As I indicated at the beginning of this essay, Palmer's research into household records in Yorkshire clearly indicates that the 'great-house option' cannot be ignored: remember that, for the decades 1590–9, 1610–19, and 1620–9, performances in Yorkshire households outnumber the records from towns and cities in Yorkshire. This evidence can be replicated in other localities, for other families, such as the Shuttleworths of Gawthorpe Hall and Smithills Hall, in neighbouring Lancashire. Nor is it only a northern phenomenon, as my own research into families in Warwickshire has shown. Consider Lord Berkeley, whose residence at Caludon Castle, just north-east of Coventry, was a major venue. Looking at just one year, between November 1605 and November 1606, Berkeley rewarded entertainers on eighteen occasions, seven of them being companies of players. In the same period the city of Coventry made six payments to entertainers, five of them companies of players (including some of the same companies rewarded by Berkeley). Apparently Caludon Castle was a far livelier entertainment centre than the large city to the south-west—and Coventry was, as we know, an extremely active and welcoming venue, with more entertainment payments between 1572 and 1642 than most boroughs. Or consider another Warwickshire example, Sir Thomas Puckering of Priory Park, Warwick, whose household accounts survive for only a single year, 1620–1. These contain handsome rewards for plays at Christmas, to Lord Dudley's players (20*s.*) and Lady Elizabeth's players (22*s.*); at other seasons there are two smaller performance rewards, to the Prince's players (2 August, 2*s.* 6*d.*) and the King and Queen of Bohemia's players (27 November, 2*s.*). Like the Shuttleworth family, Puckering was not a patron of a company of players; however, they were both 'patrons' of playing in another important sense. These people, and no doubt many others, provided venues, audiences, and rewards to travelling professional troupes under the patronage of others. Knowing more about them valuably fills out our picture of provincial life; we cannot discount the 'great-house option'.

But would all the great houses of England, even if their records all survived, provide sufficient performance rewards to account for the deficiency I suggested, the 'lost' performances? While optimism might want to keep such a speculation alive, realism intrudes with the knowledge that there were not likely enough great houses to go round. Where else might we look for 'lost' performances to make up the deficiency? What could allow us to provide evidence that touring professional actors under gentry, noble, or royal patronage were able to make a decent, even a comfortable, living? First, civic account entries do not always mean that one record is evidence for one performance. I offer two examples. First, at Norwich the Mayors' Courts regularly licensed companies to perform more than once; for example, Pembroke's Men, 1598–9, licensed for two days and two nights (implying possibly four performances) (Galloway 1984: 113). Secondly, at Shrewsbury in 1613 there occurred a civic reward to the Lady Elizabeth's Men, dated 26 November, a Friday, presumably for a civic performance on the preceding Wednesday or Thursday. On the day following the payment date, Saturday night, the town exchequer was robbed after an evening performance by the same company (Somerset 1994*a*: i. 303–5). No doubt, once again, examples of multiple-performance visits could be multiplied, both from civic venues and from great houses. Might they make up the deficit, or do we need more?

I would like to end with speculation, by suggesting that there is an unknown, virtually unknowable, but likely important source of records that we cannot do more than wonder about: records of performances in provincial inns. I step warily here into a lively debate between those, such as William Ingram and Andrew Gurr, who assert that inns were a 'standard venue' particularly in the later period. Ingram points out that the strolling players in John Marston's *Histriomastix* played and stayed at an inn but neglected to pay their bill (Ingram 1993: 58). Gurr suggests that when borough authorities began to prohibit playing in civic halls, inns likely provided the alternative venues (Gurr 1994*a*: 2–19). Others, such as Barbara Palmer, are deeply sceptical: 'what does not make sense is the repeated assertion that players regularly stage plays at inns' (Palmer 2005: 282). Palmer does present the scattered evidence that survives, from Norwich (the 1582 affray at the Red Lion), Dorchester (the George inn), Barnstaple (the mayor's play, occasionally), Leicester (Derby's and Dudley's Men, in 1599), and elsewhere. It's not an impressive array of evidence. There are other records that point to the possibility of performances in inns, such as the city of York's prohibition against playing in the Common Hall, which is accompanied by permission to use a private alternative in the city (Palmer 2005: 273). Sometimes, as at Stratford on Avon, a prohibition against playing in public space is not accompanied by such an invitation to explore alternative venues, but perhaps one is implied because the players are not forbidden the town, just the guildhall. (This reference, from 1602, will appear in my REED edition of the records of Staffordshire and Warwickshire.) I propose to approach this issue from another direction, by looking at the county with whose records I am deeply familiar: Shropshire. In Shropshire, at Bridgnorth, we have permission granted, in the course of forbidding players the use of the council house or Town Hall, for players to 'playe in their Innes, yf it so please them' (Somerset 1994*a*: i. 21). Ludlow is a more fruitful ground, perhaps because that borough lacked a commodious guildhall (the Palmers' guildhall, used civically, was aisled and unsuitable; a new hall begins to appear in the records in the 1580s). Civic payments were made to the Lord Privy Seal's players, including money spent on them 'at Mr Wyttalls' (1537–8), to the Prince's players for their play 'played at Alsopps' (1540–1). An affray took place in 1627–8 involving the King's Men, who were acting 'in the said howse' (likely to have been an inn) when a disturbance occurred at the door. The indictment locates the house in a ward called Oldstreete and Galdford. The county's total records of plays in inns, four, does not look very promising, but we have to consider it in relation to one fact about which I am categorically sure: not one single scrap of paper or parchment bearing any accounting or other type of record from an inn survives in the Shropshire County Record Office. Nor is there any such in the archives of Staffordshire or Warwickshire. I have been reading documents in record offices for thirty years, and have found nothing whatever related to innkeeping, except for scattered entries in household accounts, of payments for music at inns by travelling gentry. The dilemma is, without documents there can be no history, either negative or positive. Scholars, particularly London-centred ones, used to think that nothing happened in the provinces because there was no evidence. The Malone Society, and then REED, came along, adduced the copious remains in county record offices, and disproved that misconception. Even then another misconception persisted (reflected by Ingram) that nothing much took place in great houses because the REED project, in its early days, omitted to investigate those record sources owing to difficulty of access. Now being mined assiduously, the records of the nobility and gentry are proving to be fruitful sources for records of theatrical activity. I cannot call for a systematic effort to mine the (non-existent) records of innkeepers; all that can be said is that in the face of silence, we have to remain silent, at the same time as we continue to wonder how complete are the records that we have, and how the hundreds of patronized troupes made their livings from their craft.

CHAPTER 21

THE COURT, THE MASTER OF THE REVELS, AND THE PLAYERS

RICHARD DUTTON

HAMLET. What players are they?
ROSENCRANTZ. Even those you were wont to take such delight in, the tragedians of the city.
HAMLET. How chances it they travel? Their residence, both in reputation and profit, was better both ways.

(*Hamlet*, II. ii. 324–9)[1]

As the essays of John Astington, Peter Greenfield, Suzanne Westfall, and others attest elsewhere in this volume, this rationale for 'the tragedians' to travel is a fiction on several levels. The players sometimes had their own reasons for preferring to travel, as opposed to performing in the city, perhaps connected with patronage traditions. But there is no evidence that a major company was ever forced out on the road by competition from the boy actors or anyone else. And if they did take to the road, they most certainly did not drop in at court on the off-chance of giving a performance.

[1] References to *Hamlet* are to Harold Jenkins's Arden edition (London: Methuen, 1982); those to *As You Like It* are to Juliet Dusinberre's Arden edition (London: Thomson Learning, 2006); those to *Henry V* are to John H. Walter's Arden edition (London: Methuen, 1954); that to *Bartholomew Fair* is to E. A. Horsman's Revels edition (London: Methuen, 1960).

In the era of Elizabeth and James, the English court did indeed sometimes spend the revels season at a distance from London—at Greenwich, say, or Hampton Court. But the players did not simply travel out there unannounced, as they do in *Hamlet*. Whatever the courtly venue, they would at some point, as Thomas Heywood tells us, first have visited 'the office of the Revels, where our Court playes have been in late daies yearely rehersed, perfected, and corrected before they come to the publike view of the Prince and the Nobility' (1612, E1^{v}). What I want to explore here is what exactly that 'perfected, and corrected' actually meant to the players. How did it impact on their relationship with the Master of the Revels and the court more generally? What legacy might it have left in respect of the scripts of their plays that have survived? I shall be suggesting that the call to perform at court was always of more professional significance than traditional accounts of early modern theatre have allowed, even in the 'Shakespearean era' (*c*.1590–*c*.1613) when the proto-capitalist nature of theatrical enterprise is often regarded as its most distinctive motor. That being the case, the court was always a distinctive arbiter of theatrical taste and practice, long before it became an unavoidable fact of life in the Caroline era. It helped to set the theatrical agenda and did not merely consume what happened to be available. And the key negotiating figures in all of this were the Masters of the Revels—specifically Edmund Tilney, who served from 1578 to 1610; Sir George Buc, 1610 to 1622; and Sir Henry Herbert, 1623 to the closing of the theatres and into the Restoration (Dutton 1991).[2]

The first process mentioned by Heywood—'rehersed'—is unproblematic. By the end of the sixteenth century—say, the period covered by Philip Henslowe's so-called diary—Tilney had abandoned his earlier practice of seeing in person rehearsals of all plays before licensing them for public performance. Possibly the sheer number of new plays that were produced made this impractical, once key companies settled in permanent London theatres and needed a regular turnover of fresh material to keep pulling in audiences. From 1581 Tilney held a special commission which instigated a system for the regular licensing of plays—something he now did on the basis of 'perusing' the script, requiring such changes as he saw fit, and then appending his licence to what became the 'allowed' copy. But if there was a question of a play being performed at court, he still insisted that it be 'rehersed' before him. As Heywood makes clear, this was done in his spacious quarters in the former Priory of St John, in Clerkenwell: the actors came to him, not vice versa.[3]

While Tilney's special commission had the effect of instituting censorship and licensing for most of the plays performed in and around London—the outcome for which it is best remembered—this was actually a secondary consequence of a more fundamental motivation: to acquire high-quality entertainment for the court as readily and as cheaply as possible. To that end Tilney was given plenipotentiary

[2] Sir John Astley became Master when Buc went mad in 1622 and served briefly in person; but Herbert bought him out of the office and was recognized as de facto Master by 1623, though technically he served as Astley's deputy until the latter died in 1640 (Dutton 1991: 273 n. 6).

[3] Tilney was required to move in 1607, when James I presented the priory to his cousin Lord D'Aubigny as a wedding present. Thereafter the Revels Office moved around several quarters near the Blackfriars.

powers, not only over the players but over any workmen who might be necessary for the court's purposes. He was authorized:

to warn, command and appoint in all places within this our Realm of England, as well within franchises and liberties as without, all and every player or players with their play-makers either belonging to any nobleman or otherwise bearing the name of using the faculty of play-makers or players of Comedies, Tragedies, Enterludes, or what other shows soever from time to time and at all times to appear before him with all such plays, Tragedies, Comedies or shows as they shall in readiness, or mean to set forth and then to present and recite before our said Servant or his sufficient deputy whom we ordain and appoint and authorise by these presents of all such shows, plays, players and playmakers, together with their playing places, to order and reform, authorise and put down, as shall be thought meet or unmeet unto himself or his said deputy in that behalf. (Wickham et al. 2000: 71)

The fact that Tilney could henceforth enhance his income by licensing plays and playhouses doubtless induced him to develop that side of his activities, but it was never at the expense of this central role at court. As early as 1578, while he was still only Master on a yearly renewable basis, the Privy Council defined his primary duties. They wrote to the Lord Mayor of London, requiring that certain companies be allowed to perform in public, under Tilney's authority. Their minutes note:

A letter to the Lord Maiour, &c, requiring him to suffer the Children of her Majesties Chappell, the servauntes of the Lord Chamberlaine, therle of Warwick, the Erle of Leicester, the Erle of Essex and the Children of Powles, and no companies els, to exercise playeng within the Cittie, whome their Lordships have onlie allowed thereunto by reason that the companies aforenamed are appointed to playe this tyme of Christmas before her Majestie.[4]

This sets a pattern which did not change in essentials until the accession of James I. The privileged adult companies were all patronized by members of the Privy Council (the earls of Sussex (the Lord Chamberlain), Warwick, and Leicester) except for the company of the young Earl of Essex, whose mother, Lettice Knollys, was a cousin of the Queen. Also to be allowed were the two children's companies, who in earlier years had been firm favourites at court, playing within the city albeit outside the control of the city authorities. Patrons died and new companies flourished. Specific circumstances intervened, such as the creation of the Queen's Men in 1583 and their temporary dominance at court (described in Sally-Beth MacLean's chapter in this book), and the inactivity of the boy companies for most of the 1590s. But for much of the period a select group of four to six companies had privileged performing rights in or around London. Apart from the Queen's Men and the boy companies, these included groups patronized by Privy Counsellors. At the end of Elizabeth's reign, for instance, these were Hunsdon's, Nottingham's, and Worcester's Men; just occasionally troupes with especially powerful patrons who were not Counsellors, like the Stanleys, were also sanctioned—Strange's Men around 1590, the Earl of Derby's Men in the late 1590s.

But the point, in all of these instances, is that these privileged London performing rights were only extended to a limited number of companies at any time, and always

[4] Dasent et al. (1890–1964: xi. 73), as quoted in Gurr (1996*b*: 55).

(in effect) 'by reason that the companies afore-named are appointed to play this time of Christmas before her Majesty'. This argument was trotted out repeatedly by the Privy Council in response to appeals by city authorities who wanted to curtail the activities of players in the region, and it has sometimes been regarded as a rather mechanical excuse aimed at defending theatre in general. But there is good reason to suppose that it was always a serious and self-interested argument. The Privy Council was not interested in defending all theatre, only in ensuring that there would be sufficient high-quality drama to entertain the court during the revels season and at times when important visitors needed recreation. The Lord Mayor tried to call what he perhaps thought was their bluff on this in 1592, writing to Archbishop Whitgift:

> And because we understand that the Queen's Majesty is and must be served at certain times by this sort of people... [we] are most humbly and earnestly to beseech your Grace to call unto you the... Master of Her Majesty's Revels, with whom we have also conferred of late to that purpose, and to treat with him, if by any means it may be devised, that Her Majesty may be served with these recreations as hath been accustomed (which in our opinions may be easily done by the private exercise of Her Majesty's own players in convenient place), and the City freed from these continual disorders. (Wickham et al. 2000: 96)

The challenge was effectively that Elizabeth had the Queen's Men; they were all that were needed, they could rehearse and perform quite adequately within royal property, and would do so at the Queen's expense. The Lord Mayor was prepared to buy out Edmund Tilney, who by this time made a significant income from the situation engineered by the Privy Council. But, for the rest, he felt the court could and should fend for itself.

The Privy Council did not see it this way and nothing came of it. It must have suited them to 'outsource' court entertainment this way: the players essentially earned their own living by performing in public, provided most of their own sophisticated props and costumes (an expensive responsibility formerly incumbent upon the Revels Office), and required only the modest sum of £10 for their court performances. The Lords of the Council may, moreover, have seen problems in restricting the choice of royal entertainment to a single troupe, however talented. The Queen's Men carried all before them for half a dozen years, but they faltered when key players left: Robert Wilson rejoined Leicester's Men in the Low Countries in 1585; William Knell died in a sword-fight in 1587; the incomparable Richard Tarlton of natural causes in 1588. So competition from Strange's Men must have suited their lordships in the late 1580s. On the other hand, the Privy Council would not sanction a free-for-all. By 1598, when the roster of privileged companies had shrunk temporarily to two, they made efforts to keep out interlopers, writing as follows to Tilney and similarly to the magistrates north and south of the Thames, in Middlesex and Surrey:

> Whereas licence hath been granted unto two companies of stage players retained unto us, the Lord Admiral and Lord Chamberlain, to use and practice stage plays, whereby they might be the better enabled and prepared to show such plays before Her Majesty as they shall be required at times meet and accustomed, to which end they have been chiefly licensed and tolerated... and whereas there is also a third company who of late (as we are informed) have by way of intrusion used likewise to play, having neither prepared any play for Her Majesty

nor are bound to you, the Master of the Revels... We have therefore thought good to require you upon receipt hereof to take order that the aforesaid third company may be suppressed, and none suffered hereafter to play but those two formerly named. (Wickham et al. 2000: 104)

It is unlikely that anyone expected the Admiral's and Chamberlain's Men to be the *only* companies to perform around London between 1594 and 1599 (when Derby's Men briefly joined the charmed circle). But they were probably expected to be the only ones in permanent residence, and were certainly given exclusive access to court. In 1598 the Privy Council would have been particularly mindful of what happened the year before, when Pembroke's Men set up in the Swan on a year's contract, and started recruiting personnel from the Admiral's Men—giving every impression of muscling in and becoming serious rivals, not just playing a brief season. If so, they miscalculated badly in staging 'The Isle of Dogs', which caused such a scandal as to condemn many of them to prison for a time, effectively bringing the enterprise to a close.[5] The action in 1598, which was followed shortly after by moves to tie the two 'allowed' companies to specified 'houses' (eventually the Globe and the Fortune) and so institutionalizing their presence, was doubtless designed to prevent a repetition.

It is noteworthy in all this that Tilney seems not to have been involved in the 'Isle of Dogs' affair. Pembroke's Men were not one of the 'allowed' companies, and it had not fallen to him to police them; that would be the responsibility of the Surrey magistrates. Only from 1598 was he expected to keep unwelcome 'intrusion' at bay, in conjunction with the county magistrates. While he might issue licences to all manner of companies for use in their travels outside the capital (to the growing distress of provincial officials, who resented the encroachment of court authority over their traditional responsibilities), his professional attention in the London region was firmly focused on the 'allowed' companies and their potential for use at court. This must have been a notably symbiotic relationship: he needed them to perform his key duties at court; they needed him to be allowed to continue to perform in public in what, by the time James came to the throne, must indisputably have been the most lucrative locations in the country. In this context, the unspectacular £10 for a court performance can be seen for what it was: a mere token in a much larger gift-exchange economy.

In saying this I challenge an orthodoxy which held sway for a good deal of the twentieth century, one which made the public theatres—rather than the court—the principal focus of their playing, because they generated the great majority of their profits. Bernard Beckerman here summarizes the view of several generations:

From Elizabeth, and later from James, the Chamberlain–King's Men received £873 between 1599 and 1609, of which amount £70 was for relief of the company during plague time, and £30 for reimbursement for expenses incurred during unusually lengthy travel to and from the

[5] A more cynical interpretation of these events would have it that the Privy Council were looking for an excuse to close down Pembroke's Men, and employed their chief spy-catcher and notorious torturer, Richard Topcliffe, to find it—which he conveniently did in 'The Isle of Dogs'. The whole incident is described in Gurr (1996*b*: 106–8), and its wider ramifications are considered in Ingram (1978: 167–86, 313–14).

> Court. Thus the annual average for playing was £77.6s., with the court payments in the later years substantially greater than in the early one. Grants from Elizabeth never totaled more than 5 per cent of the income the company earned at the Globe.[6] Under James the percentage rose to a high of about fifteen by 1609. The increase in Court support, evident in these figures, ultimately led the Globe company to appeal increasingly to an aristocratic audience. But throughout the decade we are considering, the actors depend on the pence of a large, heterogeneous public more than upon the bounty of their prince. (Beckerman 1962: 22–3)

Beckerman concedes that 'The players certainly tendered courtesy and respect to the Court, which after all was their main defense against puritanical suppression' (1962: 23), but the economics of the situation required them to cater first and foremost to 'a large, heterogeneous public'. This, I suggest, is the logic of the twentieth century, not of the sixteenth and seventeenth centuries. It was not only Puritans who wanted to 'suppress' the theatre. The city of London authorities had genuine public order and health concerns, in an era before modern policing, about auditoriums that held upwards of 2,000 people at a time. The Lord Chamberlain's Men only existed at all, and certainly only flourished in their privileged metropolitan situation, because they were servants of the court, providing entertainment when needed for the Queen and her guests. This was their *raison d'être.* The patronage situation of the players may have moved out of the domestic contexts in which it was originally formulated, but it was far from a cipher: they wore their patrons' livery most of the time, and they prayed for him (or her) at every public performance. Money, in and of itself, was not the simplistic bottom line.

This being the case, Beckerman's claim (again symptomatic of its era) that the increasing proportion of income that the King's Men derived from the court 'ultimately led' to their appealing 'increasingly to an aristocratic audience' seems to me back to front. The aristocratic audience was always their first concern—and that of the overwhelming majority of companies whose plays have survived from this era. Similarly, the old canard that the bringing of the three leading companies under royal patronage in 1603–4 marked a decisive break with 'popular' Elizabethan theatre is misconceived: they were already royal companies in all but name. There is, moreover, evidence—from the 1590s and beyond, when we have Henslowe's diary and a much higher proportion of play-texts have survived—that what was performed at court was not always exactly the same fare as graced the public theatres. It remains a moot point whether plays such as *A Midsummer Night's Dream* or *Merry Wives* were originally written expressly for the court, or for court-related events (though my argument in general makes such claims more credible). What we know is that some plays were *revised* expressly for court performance. In Heywood's terms, they were 'perfected, and corrected'.

The significance of this may not be immediately apparent, since the common perception remains that the revision of plays throughout this period was a necessary consequence of repeatedly bringing them back into the repertoire. As G. E. Bentley put it, 'the refurbishing of old plays in the repertory seems to have been the universal

[6] Beckerman cites Chambers (1923: iv. 166–75).

practice in the London theatres from 1590 to 1642' (Bentley 1971: 263). But Roslyn Knutson has demonstrated that this is simply not the case in the one set of documents, Henslowe's diary, where we have tangible evidence of the companies' practices: 'we may argue that the repertory companies in the 1590s did not see the payment for revisions to accompany a revival as a commercially necessary or profitable venture' (Knutson 1985: 11). She acknowledges such famous instances of revision as those of *The Spanish Tragedy* and *Dr Faustus* in 1601–2 but suggests that they relate to 'a period of unusual business activity' (1985: 14) and concludes that

> From the evidence in the diary, the Admiral's Men and Worcester's Men (and by association, all adult companies) operated their businesses as economically as possible. If they invested in substantial revisions, they did so because of pressing circumstances in their commercial world. The normative and preferred practice in the Elizabethan playhouse is seen in the revivals of such plays as *The Jew of Malta* and *The Wise Man of West Chester*, which could be returned to the stage every few years at essentially no cost. (Knutson 1985: 15)

Yet in the course of this argument she notes other specific occasions 'for which the Admiral's Men commissioned alterations, mendings, and additions. Of the sixteen plays in these entries, most were altered either during their maiden run or for a presentation at Court,' observing that the cost of such revisions was typically negligible. 'In several cases, however, the company paid sums seemingly out of proportion with the return they could have expected for a single performance at Court... Possibly the players transferred the dramas to the public stage in order to recover expenses' (Knutson 1985: 12). It is these 'out of proportion' cases with which I am concerned; most of them were demonstrably related to court performances (and others may have been too). They defy the economic laws of business which, as she so ably shows, pertained in relation to most of the companies' commercial affairs. While it is very likely that they did indeed try to recover costs by subsequently using these revisions on the public stages, we may wonder why they did not simply use the money to invest, as they usually did, in their most lucrative products—new plays. I suggest that the answer to this is tied up with the companies' intimate dependence upon, and patronage relationship to, the court.

Let us examine some examples of revision for the court. Henry Chettle was paid 10*s*. for 'mendynge of the first pt of Robart hoode' on 18 November 1598, and received a further 10*s*. exactly a week later, in part 'for mendinge of Roben hood. for the corte' (Foakes 2002: 101–2).[7] A parallel sequence occurs in 1600, in respect of the play 'Phaeton' (for which Henslowe originally paid Thomas Dekker in January 1597, and also lent money for 'a sewte' and 'a whitte satten dublette'). Now, on 14 December, he paid Dekker 10*s*. 'for his paynes in fay^e^ton... for the corte' and eight days later a further 30*s*. 'for alteryng of fayton for the corte', while on 2 January 1601 William Bird was advanced 20*s*. 'for divers thinges a bowt a bowt [*sic*] the playe of fayeton for the corte' (Foakes 2002: 137–8). The reference to 'the first pt of Robart hoode' presumably

[7] For those unused to the money, 10*s*. was half of a pound (£). The usual fee for a new play was between £6 and £8, plus a share in the take for an early performance; 10*s*., then, presumably represents relatively minor work.

identifies it as *The Downfall of Robert, Earl of Huntingdon* (rather than its sequel, *The Death of Robert, Earl of Huntingdon*), for which Anthony Munday was originally paid in February 1598. But nothing in the text as published in 1601 singles it out as a version performed at court; nor is it clear if the text reflects either set of Chettle's 'mendings' of Munday's original. 'Phaeton' has not survived at all.

We are on somewhat surer grounds with *Fortunatus*, a text of which *has* survived, though the issue is muddied by the question of whether we are dealing with one play or two. All entries may relate to the play of that title recorded by Henslowe as performed several times in the winter of 1596, but given the sums involved, some of the later payments may relate to a sequel or at the least a complete rewriting. On 9 November 1599 Dekker was advanced 40*s*. 'in earnest of abooke cald the hole hystory of ffortunatus' (Foakes 2002: 126); on 24 November he was advanced a further £3. On 30 November he received 20*s*. 'in full payment of his booke of fortunatus' (Foakes 2002: 127). That is, over the month he received a total of £6, commonly the fee for a new work. But the very next day (31 November, in Henslowe's sometimes erratic reckoning) he was paid a further 20*s*. 'for the altrenge of the boocke of the wholl history of fortewnatus', and shortly thereafter Henslowe records: 'pd unto m^r deckers the 12 of desember 1599 for the eande of fortewnatus for the corte . . . the sum of . . . 40s' (Foakes 2002: 128). So, in December, Dekker received a total of £3, half as much again, apparently to revise a play which he either had just written or had completely revamped from an earlier version.

We can set some scale to the amount of work involved here, from the fact that in 1602 Chettle was to receive 5*s*. 'for a prologe & a epyloge for the corte' for an unspecified play, while the year before Dekker received 10*s*. for a similar commission for 'the playe of ponescioues pillett [Pontius Pilate?]' (Foakes 2002: 207, 187).[8] Chettle's two stints of work on 'Roben hood' equated to at least twice the effort of supplying a prologue and an epilogue. But Dekker's payments for both 'Phaeton' and *Fortunatus* were of a different order again. He received a total of £3 (beside the £1 that went to Bird) for work on 'Phaeton' expressly for the court; and even if we discount the £6 that he first received in 1599 for *Fortunatus*, he seems to have received a further £3 to work on the play again for the court.[9]

These payments amount to half of what was commonly paid for a new play, and so represented a significant investment on the part of the Lord Admiral's Men. And we may add to this that, in an undated entry in the diary (between entries for 3 and 12 December 1599), Thomas Downton, an actor with the company, acknowledged receiving the princely sum of £10 'ffor to by thinges for ffortunatus' (Foakes 2002: 128). No expense was to be spared in making an impression with this play. In the case

[8] The 5*s*. payment may be an underestimate, in that on the same day (29 December) he was paid another 5*s*., via the same member of the Lord Admiral's Men, Thomas Downton, this time specifically for part-payment in respect of *The Tragedy of Hoffman*. Maybe the two payments together represent extra, court-related work on the same play.

[9] If what Dekker was paid £6 for was a sequel to the original *Fortunatus*, it is possible that the further £3 was for revising the original. But, one way or another, it is inescapable that he received £3—half a usual fee for writing a play—for rewriting *some* version of *Fortunatus* for the court.

of *Fortunatus* we indisputably have the finished product of at least some of these revisions, *The pleasant comedie of old Fortunatus As it was plaied before the Queenes Maiestie this Christmas* (printed 1600). The Prologue for the Court and the Epilogue, dialogues spoken by two old men, are clearly new. The Prologue begins with one asking the other, 'Are you then traveling to the temple of Eliza?', locating the whole play within the late mythologizing of the Virgin Queen, and defining the actors as her humble and overawed subjects. W. L. Halstead has also plausibly suggested that the Vice–Virtue subplot was a result of the late alterations (Halstead 1939: 352).

Something of a pattern seems to be apparent in Henslowe's accounts: the company revived a play in November. (The Elizabethan revels season rarely began before Christmas, though it often began early in November for James, so this schedule presumably changed.) The play might not necessarily be all that old ('Roben Hood', 'Phaeton'), but they would make modest efforts to spruce it up. Or they aimed for something more substantial, a sequel or a complete revamping of something slightly older (*Fortunatus*). There is no way of knowing at what point Edmund Tilney had a say in these decisions, but the very fact of revision rather than new work makes it likely that it was quite early: a tried and tested product, with court potential, is to be transformed into something even more impressive. Certainly *after* revisions the company must have 'rehersed' it in front of him, hoping that it would clinch selection for court. If he felt it had potential, he would perhaps then make his views known as to how it might be further 'perfected' and 'corrected'.

To that end, the company might call in one of their regular writers to revise it further, in line with Tilney's suggestions: perhaps again modestly, but perhaps even more extensively. The loans to Bird over 'Phaeton' 'for divers things' and to Downton 'ffor to by thinges for ffortunatus' suggest that Tilney's advice might have included suggestions on new properties as much as rewriting—a play on such a subject surely involved some spectacular effects. All of this confirms yet again the trouble and expense the company was prepared sometimes to go to in order to make the court performance as impressive as possible. Of course, these properties would remain with the company to recoup their costs in public performances at the Rose or the Fortune. But the entry in respect of 'Phaeton' expressly links the purchase with court performance in the first instance, and the timing of that for *Fortunatus* also makes such a link highly likely.

Is it significant that we hear nothing in Henslowe about specific revisions 'for the corte' before 1598? In and of itself the diary does not give us reason to suppose so. Henslowe changed the nature of his entries in the diary more than once, and although it details theatrical business going back to 1591, it is not until late 1597 that he starts listing payments and loans to writers for particular plays (Foakes 2002: 72). And it is only from 1598 (starting with Chettle's work on *Robart hoode*) that we get any reference to changes of any sort to existing plays, whether described as additions (including those identified as prologues and epilogues), alterations, or mendings. Moreover, within these references, there is no necessary consistency about Henslowe's entries. There are, for example, three references to work by Dekker on *Tasso* (presumably the *Tasso's Melancholy* listed as 'ne' on 11 August 1594 and popular for some little while thereafter). He was advanced 20*s.* 'toward the alterynge of tasso' on 16 January 1601, a further 40*s.* 'for mendinge of the playe of tasso' on 3 November 1602, and a final 20*s.* 'in pt of payment for tasso' on 4 December 1602 (Foakes 2002: 187, 206). This would seem to represent two instances of revamping, one relatively light and the other (1602, involving a total of £3) much more substantial. Either of these might plausibly have been for court purposes, given their seasonal datings. But if so, Henslowe did not choose to record the fact.

As I say, the fact that Henslowe does not expressly record alterations to plays before 1598 may be an accident of accountancy practice. But it is intriguing that, when we look to the repertory of the Chamberlain's Men in this period (for whom, of course, we have no such accounts), we find printed for the first time *A pleasant conceited comedie called, Loues labors lost As it was presented before her Highnes this last Christmas. Newly corrected and augmented by W. Shakespere., Imprinted at London: By WW for Cutbert Burby, 1598.* This is the earliest play by Shakespeare to be printed with his name on it; it is also the earliest instance of any Shakespeare play that we *know* to have been performed at court—though it must be highly likely that others were before this. And it is one of the earliest of all plays by a dramatist writing for an adult company to make the fact of performance at court a selling point on the title page.[10] Given the uncertainties about Old and New Style dating, however, the title page is ambiguous. As John Astington says in this Handbook: 'the court performance may have been in the season 1597–8 or that of 1598–9'. The former would make it a year earlier than 'Roben Hood'; the latter would put it in the same revels season. But either puts the two plays in sufficiently close proximity to make us suspect that it may be part of the same phenomenon of being 'rehersed, perfected, and corrected' for the court. *Love's Labour's Lost* is printed as *Newly corrected and augmented by W. Shakespere* as well as being *As it was presented before her Highnes this last Christmas*, as if the two facts are linked.

Might this extra effort of rewriting for court be connected with the privileged status explicitly conferred on the Admiral's and Chamberlain's Men in 1598? ('Whereas licence hath been granted unto two companies'—and implicitly *only* two companies—'of stage players retained unto us, the Lord Admiral and Lord Chamberlain, to use and practice stage plays'.) The companies had implicitly had such status since 1594, but now it was explicit and was shortly to be compounded by the formal identification of each company with a prestigious playing space, the Chamberlain's Men with the Globe in 1599 and the Admiral's Men with the Fortune in 1600. I have suggested before that the repertories of the two companies at this time, the one full of references to the globe or world (as in Jaques's 'All the world's a stage' speech), the other to fortune (as indeed in *Fortunatus*), are self-congratulatory about their enhanced status, for which they were entirely beholden to the court. Is it

[10] There are, of course, a number of earlier extant plays written for the children's companies which were performed at court. Only Robert Greene's *Orlando Furioso* (1594), of plays apparently written for an adult company, makes an earlier claim to court performance on its title page. See Alan Farmer and Zachary Lesser, DEEP Database of Early English Playbooks, <http://deep.sas.upenn.edu>.

possible that the practice of *Newly correct[ing] and augment[ing]* plays for performance at court specifically arose at this time as a reciprocal gesture of thanks, an obeisance to their most important patrons?

Support of a kind for this suggestion comes with Juliet Dusinberre's recent argument that *As You Like It* was performed at court on Shrove Tuesday (20 February) 1599 New Style (Dusinberre 2003: 371–405; see also her 2006 Arden edition, 36–46). The key evidence here is an epilogue 'to ye Q. by ye players' preserved in the commonplace book of Henry Stanford, an adherent of the Hunsdon family, which makes it most likely to derive from the Lord Chamberlain's Men.[11] We cannot be certain that the epilogue relates to Shakespeare's play, but it does fit it well and explicitly refers to Shrovetide that year, when we know that the Chamberlain's Men performed at court. The Shrovetide context, moreover, would be particularly apt for Touchstone's joking about pancakes and mustard (I. ii. 72–7; see Dusinberre's Arden edition, 40). If we accept this dating of a court performance, we may note that Jaques philosophized at court about all the world being a stage the night before Richard Burbage, his brother Cuthbert, and five of the leading Chamberlain's Men signed the lease for the Globe theatre, then being constructed on the Bankside (Ash Wednesday (21 February) 1599).

What we cannot know here is whether the play was specifically written for that performance or performed in the public theatres first and then 'perfected, and corrected' for the court. Dusinberre argues for the former: 'Without being in any specific sense an "occasional" piece, *As You Like It* is geared to Elizabethan court taste' (Arden edition, 41). What seems reasonably probable is that the Stanford epilogue is evidence of particular care for court performance, either when it was first staged or when it was revised. Rosalind's much more familiar and 'egalitarian' epilogue (Arden edition, 42) seems to speak to a more popular audience, presumably in the public theatres. Shakespeare and his actors took care to differentiate and to incorporate for the court Shrovetide material that would be very lame in other contexts. There is every reason to suppose that Edmund Tilney must have been consulted about such differences.

Another Shakespeare text with indisputable court associations appeared in 1602: *A most pleasaunt and excellent conceited comedie, of Syr Iohn Falstaffe, and the merrie wiues of Windsor Entermixed with sundrie variable and pleasing humors... By William Shakespeare. As it hath bene diuers times acted by the right Honorable my Lord Camberlaines seruants. Both before her Maiestie, and else-where.* This seems to imply that the Queen saw the same *Merry Wives* as did the patrons of the Globe, but, as we have seen with other plays of that era, performances were unlikely to have been absolutely identical.[12] Jonson's *Every Man Out of His Humour* is another case in

[11] It was first printed in Stanford (1988: 166, annot. 373). Dusinberre reproduces it in her Arden edition of *As You Like It*, 38–9.

[12] Myth has it, of course, that *Merry Wives* was expressly written for the court, at the Queen's request. So revisions would not have been required. But that is probably a speculation too far. The differences between the Quarto and Folio texts of this play indicate that it was certainly revised at some point, for some reason.

point. Someone objected (as he tells us, in a characteristic flourish of Greek) to the representation of the Queen in the original version on the public stage—presumably a boy actor made to look like Elizabeth. When the play was presented at court in 1599 Jonson was able to restore something like the original ending, invoking the actual Queen rather than a representation of her—but adding a special address to Elizabeth herself. The 1600 Quarto of the play jumbles together a theatrical version (addressing 'The happier spirits in this faire-fild Globe') and the special address, making it unclear where the final Grex, or chorus, stood in the running order.[13] At all events, Jonson and the Chamberlain's Men would certainly have had to negotiate the precise terms of the 1599 court version with Tilney. And they must have had to renegotiate those terms in 1605 when the play was again performed at court, before a different monarch—though, intriguingly, no evidence of that is preserved in the 1616 Folio text or any other surviving version.

We may also consider two other plays revived in that 1604–5 court season, Shakespeare's *Henry V* (7 January) and Jonson's *Every Man in His Humour* (2 February). What state were their texts in on those occasions? In particular, could the former have contained the famous lines in the Chorus to Act V about 'the General of our gracious Empress' (lines 29–34). Was the latter in its original, Quarto state, or was this the occasion for the revision which appeared in the 1616 Folio? In both cases we can only speculate, though the fact that the Prologue to the revised *Every Man In* 'speaks to' the choruses of *Henry V* ('Where neither *Chorus* wafts you ore the seas'; Jonson 1616, A3, line 15) makes it a particularly intriguing speculation that the later version was performed in each case, within a month of each other. Whether by Tilney's intervention or Jonson's calculation, the court audience would have been invited to compare two very different styles of drama performed by the same acting company. In the case of *Henry V*, however, while the court may well have seen something like the 1623 version of the play, it is surely unlikely that they heard the lines about 'the General' as we have them. They are couched in an uncomfortable conditional mode: 'Were now... As in good time he may'. Whether they refer to the Earl of Essex or to Lord Mountjoy, that conditional mode has now past (Dutton 2005; Bednarz 2006). If the lines did originally refer to Essex, whose memory had been rehabilitated under James I, it would have been graceless to recall one of the most ignominious phases of his career. If they referred to Mountjoy, he had already 'Br[ought] rebellion broached on his sword' (line 32) and might well have been in the audience that night, now a member of the Privy Council. Either way, the original lines were inappropriate and we must assume that Tilney would have required them to be changed. He may also have given careful thought to the fact that the French Herald in the play is called Montjoy (several times in the Folio text printed as 'Mountjoy'), but probably saw no reason to change it. As we shall see, there are several clear instances of court performance texts 'glancing' at members of that court who were very likely present, and not always in obviously flattering ways. It must

[13] The Folio text tidies this up, but may represent no version as it was actually acted: the address to the theatrical audience is cut, while the special address to the Queen appears as a postscript.

have been one of the incidental pleasures of these intimate private performances, but as such carefully policed by the Master of the Revels. My key point here, however, is that *any* revival of a play for performance of court must have required careful monitoring to avoid giving inadvertent offence, and this in turn may have prompted a degree of rewriting to square with current realities. It must have been something of a matter of chance how much of this, if any, was preserved in printed texts.

In the case of *Every Man in His Humour* there are two distinct trains of thought about when and why it might have been revised. One, first proposed by Johan Gerristen, seconded with reservations by James A. Riddell, and supported on other grounds by Hugh Craig, argues that the 'revision was prompted by the forthcoming folio of [Jonson's] collected plays' in '1612 or so' (Craig 2001: 24, 14). This would be linked to the fact that, though the printer, William Stansby, started setting *Every Man In* as the first play in the Folio, he stopped at I. iii. 104 and did not complete it until he had set all the other plays (Gerritsen 1959; Riddell 1997). The other school of thought was championed by J. K. Lever in his 1971 edition of the play, where he cites E. K. Chambers's view that the '"natural time for a revision" would have been prior to 2 February 1605, when *Every Man In His Humour* was revived for performance at court'.[14]

The two arguments, of course, need not preclude each other. Jonson might have revised the play more than once. Indeed, it is implicit in my argument throughout that the revision of plays—*for court performance*—was far more common than we often assume. For which reason we need to be far more circumspect about the dating and venue of the texts that have survived than we often are. In the case of *Every Man In*, one thing that makes the *c.*1612 revision argument so beguiling is that it plays so readily into our view of Jonson as the champion of print culture, apparently revising an old play simply to make it fit to stand at the head of this monumental collection of his works. Jonson was, of course, cushioned by the income he received from the court masques, and of all the dramatists of the era could have chosen to do it if he wished. But if we look back to 1604–5, an equally compelling but less familiar narrative emerges. Jonson is making his first assault on the Jacobean court. His *Masque of Blackness* has been chosen by Queen Anna over anything proposed by Samuel Daniel, who had secured the commission the previous year. The King's Men, with Tilney's agreement, are reviving both of his *Humour* plays for the court. He has an opportunity to make a real mark. *Every Man Out*, as I have already said, must have been revised to some degree. What better occasion to revise *Every Man In* as well, to show off his polished New Comedy credentials, snub Shakespeare's old-fashioned chronicle histories, and presumably get paid for it by the actors into the bargain?

There is, finally, no way of knowing which of these narratives is true (or indeed if both of them are). My point, however, is that if we recognize the revision of plays for the court as a regular and substantial element of the era's theatrical economy we need

[14] Ben Jonson, *Every Man in His Humour*, ed. J. K. Lever, Regents Renaissance Drama Series (Lincoln: University of Nebraska Press, 1971).

also to rethink some of our ideas about dramatic authorship.[15] In Jonson's case nothing brings this into sharper focus than *Bartholomew Fair*, which was certainly written while the 1616 Folio was being prepared, though it was not printed there. The discrepancies between the Induction's account of the play's playing time and the actualities of the surviving printed text can only be accounted for by supposing that there were at least two distinct versions of the play. Lukas Erne observes of this:

> the 'Articles of Agreement'... promise a playing time of 'two houres and a halfe, and somewhat more'... Even by Jonsonian standards, *Bartholomew Fair*, at 4344 prose lines is very long... Performed at... the average speed of the Royal Shakespeare Company, the unabridged play would take more than five hours to perform. At the higher speed at which Elizabethan players may well have delivered their lines, a performance of the full text would have taken close to four hours. Jonson's precise indication thus suggests that when *Bartholomew Fair* was acted, performances were some seventy to eighty minutes shorter than they would have been if the play had been performed in its entirety. (Erne 2003: 143–4, citing Hart 1934: 103 and Klein 1967)

But Erne, who is concerned here to argue that the longer texts of Jonson and Shakespeare were written with a *reading* audience in mind, ignores the unique production circumstances of the play. We know of only two Jacobean performances: on 31 October 1614 at the Hope theatre, for which the Induction was expressly written; and the following day at court, for which a separate prologue was provided, directly addressed to King James.

Looking at the Induction and the text together, the only reasonable conclusion is that we have a misfit: a preface to a show of 'two houres and a halfe, and somewhat more' and an acting text which takes from four to five hours to perform. The overwhelming likelihood is that the Induction was meant for a shorter, commercial theatre version of the play, which has not survived; and that the printed text was that used at court the following day. Jonson by this time had all but stopped writing for the public theatre, so his practice here (apparently producing both versions at the same time) must be anomalous. It would be no small challenge for the actors to switch from one to the other, virtually doubling the length, which would have made the Hope performance somewhat less than satisfactory as dress rehearsal. Yet the schedule of revisions which we have observed Dekker making to 'Phaeton' and *Fortunatus* for the court, where the texts seem to have been extensively revised, must have placed similar burdens upon the actors in terms of last-minute learning of new lines, business, running sequence, etc. And we must suppose that Sir George Buc was kept closely apprised of *all* versions of *Bartholomew Fair*, which opened the 1614 revels season at court. The true dress rehearsal for that event would have been at his quarters (by then removed to the Blackfriars district) rather than at the Hope. It would have been under his watchful eye that the parallels between Justice Overdo and King James remained on the right side of respectful jocularity. Overdo's denunciation

[15] This is especially the case in relation to Shakespeare, who by any standards was the most successful court dramatist of the era. Records of the titles of plays performed at court are notoriously patchy, but in the period 1604–13 we can identify sixty-two plays, including repetitions: twenty-one are by Shakespeare, more than a third, against forty-one by all others combined (figures from Astington 1999*a*).

of tobacco in particular—'who can tell if, before the gathering and making up thereof, the aligator hath not pissed thereon?' (II. vi. 24–5)—steers sufficiently close to the King's *A Counterblaste to Tobacco* (1604) that the point could hardly be missed (McPherson 1976).

The issue of suiting a text for the court audience involved matters either great or small—from a five-shilling prologue, to jokes about Shrovetide in *As You Like It*, to the refashioning of the end of *Every Man Out*, to the fuller fleshing out of *Fortunatus* with purpose-written head- and tailpieces, to (it would appear) the whole text of *Bartholomew Fair.* The latter may have been written at the behest of Jonson's former 'scholar' Nathan Field, the leading figure with Lady Elizabeth's Men at the Hope, but it seems likely that Jonson always had the fuller court version in mind.[16] This begs the question of whether other plays of the era were similarly *conceived* with court performance in view, rather than adapted for it after the fact. Such plays of course became commonplace from the pens of the courtier dramatists of the Caroline era, but it has been usual to assume that such a practice would be contrary to the economic interests of the professional acting companies in the Shakespearean era. My argument, of course, calls that usual understanding of the economic interests of those companies into question.

The court revels season of 1606–7 is interesting in this regard. We only know two of the texts presented then. One was *King Lear*, which opened the season on the day after Christmas: *As it was played before the King's Maiestie at Whitehall upon S. Stephans night in Christmas Hollidayes* (title page, 1608 Quarto). Leah Marcus has adroitly explored the 'local readings' of the text of *Lear* and of the event of its court performance (Marcus 1988: 148–59). Prince Henry was also Duke of Cornwall, Prince Charles was Duke of Albany, so that the division of ancient Britain between Cornwall and Albany in the play could hardly but have spoken to James's ambition formally to unite England and Scotland. And, as Andrew Gurr puts it: 'It is difficult not to assume from this that the Master of the Revels could only have approved *King Lear* for a performance at court because he thought the play supported the king's position over the... uniting of the kingdoms' (Gurr 1996*b*: 33). Indeed Tilney, as an expert genealogist, would not have missed the point. But in the broader context that I am adumbrating Tilney would not merely have been a passive gatekeeper in such matters. There is every likelihood that he collaborated with Shakespeare and the company to produce this explicitly court version of the play. What unfortunately we cannot know is how this compared with whatever version of *King Lear* the patrons of the Globe saw. This is a text (like *Bartholomew Fair*) which significantly transgresses our usual assumptions about the 'two hours' traffic of the stage' and it must be likely that the Globe version was significantly shorter (Erne 2003: 131–73). But whether it came *before* the court version and was expanded, or *after* it and was carved from it, we have no way of knowing.

The other known text from the 1606–7 season is the far less familiar *The Devil's Charter* by Barnabe Barnes, which was printed *As it was plaide before the Kings*

[16] Field received the company payment for the court performance.

Majestie, upon Candlemasse night last: by His Majesties Servants. But more exactly revewed, corrected, and augmented since by the Author, for the more pleasure and profit of the Reader. Several issues arise here. In the opening line of the play proper (after an induction of diabolical magic) King Charles of France greets 'Renouned Lodowik our warlike Couzen' (Barnes 1607, A3^r). Lodowick Sforza was an actual historical figure, but at Whitehall in early 1607 the name—it is repeated several times thereafter—must surely have evoked King James greeting his own cousin Lodowick Stuart, Duke of Lennox; shortly thereafter, if there was any doubt, King Charles receives news from someone called 'Daubigny', which must in turn have evoked Lennox's younger brother Esmé Stuart, Seigneur D'Aubigny (Barnes 1607, A3^v). Leaving aside wider political agendas, Shakespeare's play pays a tribute of sorts to the King's sons, Barnes's to his cousins—gracious touches for the court performances, which must have been negotiated with Tilney, if not actually required by him. They can hardly have been accidental—but nor need they have been deeply meaningful.

It is surely not accidental, either, that these two plays have other features in common. Both are about dealing with devils: in *Lear*, Edgar as Poor Tom famously draws on Samuel Harsnett's *Declaration of Egregious Popish Impostures* for his language of diabolic possession; *The Devil's Charter* is about a pact with the Devil, who drags the Borgia Pope, Alexander VI, to hell before his expected time. The play is a rabidly anti-papist cross between *Dr Faustus* and *The Revenger's Tragedy*, perhaps calculated to speak to anti-Catholic feeling in the wake of the Gunpowder Plot. But, as everyone knew, demonology was a subject on which James had written, and in which he continued to take a lively interest. Could it have been pure chance that two plays on that subject were chosen for the same revels season? Was this a result of the players anticipating the court taste? Or might Tilney have prompted them, and if so, at what point in the writing and revision process? An intriguing dimension in all of this is the figure of Barnabe Barnes. He was a colourful character (once tried in Star Chamber for trying to poison someone) and clearly looking for advancement at court, since in 1606 he dedicated his *Foure Bookes of Offices* to the King, a substantial work on the four cardinal virtues for the benefit of princes. He dedicated the text of *The Devil's Charter* to Sir William Herbert and Sir William Pope in 1607, again apparently seeking patronage. No other play by Barnes has survived, and this may in fact have been his only work for the stage.[17] Plays by courtiers and other amateurs were regularly staged by professional players in late Jacobean and Caroline times. But this is a strikingly early instance. Would it have been Barnes himself, or acquaintances among the King's Men, or even conceivably Tilney, who proposed that he write a play so closely tuned to courtly preoccupations and linked thematically with the lead play of the season?

There is also evidence elsewhere of the court revels season being structured or thematized beyond what could reasonably have been expected if the Masters of the Revels had simply trawled whatever happened to be in the repertoire of the current 'allowed' companies. The 1604–5 season, for example, opened with *Othello*—and the

[17] There may have been a lost 'The Battle of Evesham' (or Hexham). See M. Eccles (1933).

Twelfth Night masque was *The Masque of Blackness*, in which Queen Anna and her ladies all wore black make-up, as Richard Burbage would have done in the play. In 1633 Shakespeare's *The Taming of the Shrew* and Fletcher's continuation, *The Woman's Prize*, were acted before the King and Queen at St James's Palace on 26 and 28 November respectively. In that case we can say categorically that the pairing was not planned more than a month beforehand, since it was only on 19 October that the Master of the Revels, Sir Henry Herbert, heard about the revival of Fletcher's play and peremptorily ordered the King's Men not to play it until it had been revised to his satisfaction—one of the more notable flashpoints in relations between the players and the Master, and all the more striking for being so unusual (Dutton 2000: 41–61). Another intriguing pairing is Thomas Heywood's two-part *Fair Maid of the West*; both parts were published together in 1631, with identical phrasing on their title pages: 'As it was lately acted before the King and Queen, with approved liking. By the Queens Majesties Comedians'. All the evidence suggests that the first part had been revived after some thirty years, since it was clearly written at the end of Queen Elizabeth's reign; the second part may well, however, be Caroline. As G. E. Bentley puts it: 'The fact that both title pages boast of a court performance suggests that they were acted together, a suggestion apparently confirmed by the fact that there is no epilogue for Part I and no prologue for Part II, but only a prologue addressed to the court before Part I and an epilogue obviously to the court to Part II' (Bentley 1984: 273). Was it Heywood's own idea to write the continuation, some thirty years later? We know that Herbert must at least have agreed to the court performances. Is it possible that he was involved earlier, encouraging if not actually instigating this theatrical double-header?

This is only one of many questions that require further investigation, and this essay is only an early foray in a much wider project on which I am embarked. Instances such as *Bartholomew Fair* and the possibility that the two parts of *The Fair Maid of the West* were staged at court as a double-header may well make us wonder if some performances at court—I do not suggest all—were not significantly longer than those in the public playhouses. Reviewing the revised *Fortunatus*, for example, W. L. Halstead observed that 'after altering, the play was nearly 3000 lines long, and this was too long for performance in the London theatres' (Halstead 1939: 352 n.).

To close here, I return to *Hamlet* and the actors at Elsinore. One of the multiple theatrical in-jokes in the play is that Hamlet here, among his myriad other roles, becomes Denmark's Master of the Revels, a Philostrate to Claudius. It is he, not the actors, who proposes that *The Murder of Gonzago* be performed. He has them 'reherse' at least enough of it to be assured of their quality. 'This is too long,' complains Polonius (II. ii. 494), blithely unaware of the subtext. Hamlet requires them to 'perfect' it with the addition of 'a speech of some dozen or sixteen lines, which I would set down and insert in't' (534–5). He 'corrects' their style with a detailed critique of acting method ('Speak the speech, I pray you, as I pronounced it to you, trippingly on the tongue'; III. ii. 1–2 ff.), assures Claudius there is 'no offence in't', and presides over the performance itself, 'your only jig-maker' and 'as good as a chorus' (III. ii. 227–8, 123, 240).

So he contrives to perform all the functions that Tilney would have been expected to perform when *Hamlet* itself was performed at court—except, of course, that he lies when he says there is 'no offence in't'. It is stretching the analogy somewhat to think of Tilney himself writing lines for a play, but in a wider sense the Master of the Revels was the 'author' of the whole event, the impresario who sponsored and supervised it, certainly requiring others to add or revise text, defining its acceptable parameters.[18] Thus, in court performances, he was in every sense a collaborator—the *key* collaborator—with the actors and their dramatists. And, given that the overwhelming majority of playbooks which have survived came from his 'allowed' companies, we have yet to weigh squarely how great his influence upon those texts may have been since—for whatever reason—the booksellers did not always choose to advertise that the version they printed was one performed at court.

[18] Tilney, Buc, and Herbert were all authors. Tilney published *The Flower of Friendship* in 1568. Buc was a historian, who wrote a remarkably sympathetic account of Richard III. Herbert was the brother of the poets Edward, Lord Herbert of Cherbury, and George Herbert. He wrote an unpublished play, *The Emperor Otho*, the autograph manuscript of which shows him carefully counting the lines, as if he wanted it to be suitable for professional presentation.

CHAPTER 22

THEATER ENTREPRENEURS AND THEATRICAL ECONOMICS

S. P. CERASANO

THE theatrical culture of early modern England is remembered primarily for its plays and playwrights; however, it would never have flourished had it not been underwritten by investors for whom the enticement of financial success outweighed the risk of economic ruin. Nevertheless, while scholarly discourse over the past two centuries has paid great attention to the conditions of performance, conversation surrounding theatrical economics has emerged relatively recently. Part of this can be attributed to our growing awareness of theater as a developing institution, one that functioned within a cultural framework affected by a complexity of influences. Yet equally important developments within socio-economic history have sharpened our perceptions of theater as a business that was fully integrated into the economic climate of its time. Not least of all, the shift in scholarly inquiry, away from obvious theatrical sources—particularly play-texts—and towards manuscript sources that reveal more about the lives of playhouse owners has suggested many new contours for investigation.

Any description or discussion of theatrical economics is fraught with difficulties. While a basic understanding of theatrical economics was articulated early in the twentieth century, much less is known about the details of theatrical commerce or how business practices might have altered over time. (For instance, we understand that a shareholding system evolved within the practices of the merchant trading companies, and that this subsequently served as a model for the joint ownership of some theaters by actors, such as the first Globe, constructed in 1599. But because this model was not employed in all situations (or employed in the same fashion) it is often difficult to ascertain every detail concerning how the other playhouse investors functioned.) Additionally, the biographical and historical circumstances surrounding early playhouse owners are turning out to be more complex than we ascertained previously; and some of the individuals who participated in financing theater never achieved name credit in their time, and have consequently been lost to the annals of history. So historians face the not unusual problem of investigating an area in which they know far more than they did fifty years ago, and yet their understanding of the situation is, in some respects, still rather rudimentary. While we continue, even now, to sort through the details of certain questions (for instance, the level of profits that could be expected relative to particular plays, or the work of particular playwrights) the discourse surrounding theatrical commerce is still in its infancy. What is more, the outlines of the conversation continue to shift and develop.

Taken together such difficulties would seem to make it almost impossible to discuss the economics of the early modern theater in any coherent manner, especially since those who qualify as 'financiers' seem so dissimilar in background, and their motivations were, for the most part, so unarticulated in their own time. Apart from the quest for increased wealth it is difficult to attribute any other motives to investors, especially because few were involved in the artistic side of performance. Yet the lack of any obvious interest in theater as an artistic medium is actually typical of those who built, subsidized, and even operated a substantial number of the early modern London playhouses. For just as the motivation to construct a permanent, purpose-built playhouse was new in the sixteenth century, so too was the concept of the 'theater entrepreneur'. But regardless of all the difficulties embedded in this research, and the very real limitations barring our access to historical data, attempting to understanding economic issues remains central to our discussion of theatrical culture. Without 'investors'—a term that, in its broadest sense, encompasses a broad range of individuals, from playhouse owners to actors to spectators—the sheer quantity of theatrical activity would have been far less, and its corresponding influence much reduced in significance, if we reconsider early literary and theatrical history. Those who were involved in theatrical economics were absolutely fundamental to the development of the late sixteenth- and early seventeenth-century theater.

Trade, Commerce, Economics

For those who were involved in the early modern theater the dependence of art upon commerce was abundantly clear. Plays of the period are replete with references to economic matters, and the occasional failures of theatrical ventures were a reminder that theater was, before all else, dependent upon financial considerations. Moreover, because issues raised by investing, credit, and merchandizing were central to everyday living, these were also fundamental to the organization, operation, and perpetuation of theater and its related artistic activities.

The first scholar to acknowledge in print that economic matters were central to theatrical practice was Edmund Malone. In the introduction to his 'Historical Rise and Progress of the English Stage' (which was printed as a preface to his edition of *The Plays and Poems of William Shakespeare* (1790)) Malone acknowledged the promise held by the then recently discovered Henslowe papers and of Henslowe's diary, in particular, as sources that allow scholars to understand more fully the financial workings of the Rose playhouse (1587–1600). (However, Malone also claimed that these had not come to light in time for him to make use of the materials fully in writing his history.) Fifty-five years later, in 1845, the Shakespeare Society published the first full transcription of Henslowe's diary, and during the twentieth century two more editions followed, by W. W. Greg (1904–8) and R. A. Foakes (1961; repr. 2002).

Equally important to the evolution of the conversation is the dense chapter entitled 'The Actor's Economics' in E. K. Chambers's *The Elizabethan Stage*, which appeared in 1923 (i. 348–88), in which, for the first time, a historian attempted to provide a comprehensive analysis of shareholding arrangements, as well as to probe a series of related issues. Interestingly, however, Chambers's discussion begins not with a disinterested examination of shillings and pence, but with an assertion that would seem to be more fitting as part of a psychological examination of playhouse owners: 'Withal the actors, or the more discreet of them, prospered' (1923: i. 348). From this and other indications it is clear that, to Chambers and his original readers, theater was more of a static construct than a living, breathing business. In the course of his chapter Chambers provides interesting details relating to shareholding and householding, to court payments, players' debts, the players' social ambitions, and the potential for profits (Ingram 1992: 32–4). Nevertheless, despite all of the information gathered from his many accounts of actors and theaters, Chambers's description of theatrical commerce tends, ultimately, to be reductive, setting up a central dichotomy that pits the Burbage playhouses (the Theatre and, by extension, the first Globe) against those owned by Philip Henslowe and Edward Alleyn (in this case, the Rose and the first Fortune). In the process and in a manner that is utterly predictable, Chambers sees the former as superior to the latter because the Burbages were associated with William Shakespeare; and by the end of his chapter Chambers is fully dedicated to the Chamberlain's/King's Men. His closing statement focuses on the late career of one of the most notable members of the King's Men in retirement: 'we have one glimpse of the last of Shakespeare's fellows, John Lowin, keeping an inn, the Three Pigeons, in Brentford, where he died very old, and his poverty was as great as his age' (Chambers 1923: i. 388).

Such 'Shakespeare-centric' discussions are, of course, typical of scholarship written in the early twentieth century; however, Chambers's discussion falls short of even suggesting the rich complexity of theatrical commerce in early modern London. It does little to orient readers to the ways in which theater, as a business, was embedded in, and subject to, larger, commercial interests and influences. It does not flesh out the individual interests and motives of investors. And, consciously or not, Chambers also maintains former (mis)impressions concerning theater as a London-based business without considering other cash-producing performance opportunities, such as provincial touring or performing at court. He also assumes (mistakenly) that the London playhouses must have been closed (and therefore profitless spaces) when their companies performed at court. Therefore, although Chambers provides a useful gateway into the conversation concerning theatrical economics, his chapter cannot be taken as anything approaching a comprehensive account.

To our benefit the recent attention focused on medieval and early modern commerce, prompted largely by economic and social historians, has encouraged scholars to reconsider theater owners as engaged in something quite apart from any artistic enterprise. In so doing we have begun to shift our attention to the utterly pragmatic terms and conditions of owning and operating a business during a time in which the sheer scale, range, and influence of commercialization was being felt throughout English society in an unprecedented way. Furthermore, in the last twenty-five years scholars have come to realize that not only were the early London playhouses new investment opportunities, but the entire concept of play performances as 'commodities' that could be 'sold' for profit on a regular basis was also innovative in the second half of the sixteenth century. This is not to say, however, that theater was somehow 'non-commercial' in previous centuries. In reality, theatrical performances always had to be paid for by someone, whether it was the court, a wealthy patron, the mayor and citizens of a village, a group of bystanders in an inn-yard, the master and wardens of a trade guild, or, in earlier times, by the Church. But what altered radically, from the late 1560s onward, was not only that the construction of permanent playing places made it possible for actors to become professionals who could, in turn, make a profit by performing in a stable setting, but that, with this, many supporting business practices (such as the need to hire gatherers to collect money at the playhouse doors) also developed in tandem. If nothing else, both actors and theater owners quickly discovered that the requirements for owning and operating a large-scale performance space were different from leasing, on a temporary basis, other performance spaces. Economic practices for the occasional performance in a guildhall, inn-yard, or great hall were informal, taking place within the confines of pre-established structures; however, some economic practices had to be adapted or invented anew in order to accommodate permanent theatrical businesses. Consequently, the construction of the public playhouses and the establishment of acting as a profession encouraged a new kind of independent industry to develop, and with this, new administrative and managerial structures emerged that were conducive to promoting entertainment as trade. In these transitions investors emerged who would differ radically from former patrons. Furthermore, given the financial landscape of the late sixteenth century, the terms of theatrical 'trade' would come to be defined within a rapidly changing economic matrix.

Not least of all, re-examining the role of theater within London society during the time of its emergence points up unique difficulties in defining commercial practices and conditions; for in many ways theater has always been a distinctive type of business, and during the early periods it attracted a wide variety of supporters, some of whom were performers. On one level becoming an actor was similar to any other trade in that boys could acquire training by becoming apprenticed to professionals. However, it differed greatly from learning a trade in that the possession of exceptional, perhaps even unique, talent was the overwhelming determinant for success, and, also, the numbers of positions (for both young and older men) within the London playing companies were incredibly limited. Given such realities, it is likely that only young men of rare ability could have found an apprenticeship with a master actor; and positions within playing companies for adult actor–shareholders would have been even more difficult to procure. Also, the playing companies differed from guilds in other ways. During the second half of the sixteenth century, when the public playhouses were coming into prominence, 'theater' was not an organized 'industry' in the same way as other trades. While musicians had enjoyed the privileges and security of guild membership since the thirteenth century, there was no actors' guild to provide a well-established model for training, to protect its members or guarantee wages, or to adjudicate disputes within the profession. (Regardless of the fact that many players were freemen of well-established trade guilds, most actors guarded their status as 'gentlemen' in legal records; and their guild membership did not necessarily extend, professionally speaking, into the playhouse environment.)

In other ways, as well, theatrical businesses differed from more traditional commercial settings. Because there really was no organized theater 'industry', playhouses did not operate within a framework that regulated standards, nor were they bound by higher authority to adopt practices that were mutually beneficial to all actors and theater owners. Although some parts of their operation were taken from existing practices in commercial establishments, other elements—such as the management of repertory schedules, or the determination and size of probable markets—were doubtless learned through experience. Likewise, the challenge of envisioning a new kind of commercial space called upon the ability of investors to unite different, but complementary, businesses that were profitable for all interested parties. A playhouse required performance space for acting and areas for the storage of costumes and playbooks; but other kinds of commercial space (such as a tap house) or residential space (for actors or caretakers) might well be factored into the plan, as it was in constructing the first Fortune playhouse in 1600. These challenges made playhouse ownership unique, differentiating it, in important ways, from other businesses.

Lastly, for both their original supporters and for modern historians, determining the ways in which theater can be viewed as 'commercial', on both a theoretical and a practical level, presents its own particular set of difficulties. Playhouses provided a place for 'buying' and 'selling'; yet they did not produce a material 'product' in the same manner as other trades. Concurrently, because a live performance is, by nature, transient, it is inaccurate to think of the players as delivering a 'service'. While, on the one hand, any theatrical business seems to have been motivated by sheer practicalities—providing as it did, a permanent place where every spectator could be charged an entrance fee and where, over time, the playing companies became associated with a particular locale—on the other hand, to charge money for a performance was to be in the business of 'selling' a fantasy, one that ended as soon as the performance was over. Of course, as academic questions relating to the commercial playhouse are now framed no economic historian could argue that attending performances in the public playhouses—any more than bear-baiting, prizefighting, or archery matches, all popular entertainments within the greater London area—were a necessity of life; so, by default, such activities become categorized as luxuries. Yet, simultaneously, we need to consider the fact that these entertainments were within the reach of large groups of people, some native and some foreign. For this reason, as I have argued elsewhere, they were—conceived of in the commercial sense of the times—probably considered 'affordable luxuries', functioning within a more abundant and richly textured consumer-driven network (Cerasano 2006: 18–19). Although clearly peripheral to life's necessities, an admission fee to a public playhouse was much less expensive than a bolt of silk or a pair of ornamented gloves. At the customary rate—one penny for standing in a playhouse yard—such a treat was affordable to many individuals, even those who might forgo a loaf of bread in exchange for the experience of seeing Tamburlaine, decked out in his great chariot, conquering his way across the known world. Therefore, 'selling a performance' not only offered the potential for great profits, but the very nature of theater reinforced the owners' potential to make money. In order for a spectator to enjoy a performance, he or she had to pay for admittance to see the play; and because of the evanescent nature of the performance, the spectator was required to pay admission again if he or she wished to see either a different play or a repeat performance of the same play. As the players who performed in London inns, previous to the construction of the permanent playhouses, doubtless recognized, the very existence of permanent purpose-built playhouses came to provide a key element in the development of playing into a commercialized profession. At the same time, the London authorities, in their rather frenzied attempts to regulate playing (and perhaps even in their persistent harassment of the theaters) probably ended up inadvertently encouraging the very institutionalization of playing, and along with it the development of theater as an increasingly sophisticated commercial enterprise.

All this occurred within a fluctuating commercial climate that was neither robust nor stable. By the 1590s, when theaters and acting companies were being transformed into mature entities, disruptions such as an outbreak of plague could easily force the closure of playhouses for months on end. At Henslowe's Rose during the entirety of 1593 and even into part of the following year, the theater was dark owing to a series of plague closings, and the resulting loss to the Lord Admiral's Men was substantial. Then, in 1603, three years after the company moved to the Fortune playhouse, they suffered the same fate again (Foakes 2002: 19–23, 297–8). And other influences also worked against the establishment of economic stability. During the 1590s the entire English economy labored under a dire combination of overwhelming debt (generated largely by the Irish wars), severe inflation, a major grain shortage, and a shortage of coinage; and some of these factors remained largely unchanged in the early part of new century. Regardless of such dismal circumstances, however, a few individuals were able to raise the large sums of money necessary to finance a successful theater business, and they seem to have been rewarded by an unending stream of spectators.

Markets, Merchandizing, Consumers

During the early modern period theatrical investment in England was always financed by private individuals. While the acting companies enjoyed, at first, the privileges of noble patrons and, after 1603, of royal patrons, they did not receive financial support from them; nor did patrons agree to underwrite the actors' expenses if business was flagging. In this way theater was subject to the vacillation of the marketplace, much like other businesses of the time. However, two critical features differentiated it from other business settings: the lack of any professional regulation and a lack of any commercial protection. In and of themselves these factors exposed investors to types (and levels) of risk that could not easily be foreseen or controlled. Therefore, the ability of theatrical investors to contain and manage various kinds of risk was a primary factor in differentiating the successful from the unsuccessful. In this sense, E. K. Chambers's parallel between the shrewdness of 'discreet' theater owners and their ultimate success is absolutely pertinent.

Risk manifested itself in various ways, and by its very nature the business of theater ownership was perilous. To begin with, for the London entrepreneurs the amount of money required in order to construct individual playhouses was substantial. The Theatre, built in 1576, ended up costing its investors around £700, as did its replacement, the first Globe, which followed in 1599. (For transcriptions of the manuscripts documenting the construction of the Globe, see Berry 1987: 195–240, especially 221.) The first Fortune cost £520 in 1600, before the costs of the property lease, a tap house, and outbuildings were added into the total expense. In comparison, the second Globe cost £1,400 in 1614, and the second Fortune, architecturally different from its predecessor, cost roughly £1,000 to build in 1622–3. In order to raise such sums, investors had to find the money by shifting or selling other investments, or borrowing money, or organizing a group of investors who could back such a project. In the case of the first and second Fortune playhouses two co-owners constructed the building themselves, leasing it out to a company of players. Alternatively, the first Globe playhouse was financed by a syndicate of individuals who were fellow actors in the Lord Chamberlain's Men.

Moreover, the costs of the initial construction constituted only part of the financial project that theater investors undertook. They had to subsidize many ongoing hidden expenses as well. Owners paid for the basic upkeep of the theater building, both within and without, which could result, over time, in considerable costs, especially in a large structure, exposed both to the elements and to the wear and tear of heavy use. (In 1592, only five years after the Rose playhouse was built, its owner, Philip Henslowe, spent over £100 to enlarge and improve the galleries. That most public playhouses appear to have held a thousand (or more) spectators accounts for some of the damage that would have occurred normally; that all of the structures in greater London were subjected to considerable damp rendered the wooden portions of the playhouses susceptible to erosion as well.) Not only this, but theater owners maintained the grounds surrounding the playhouses, including the adjacent walkways, bridges, fences, sewers, and, depending upon the location, perhaps even wharves; and to complicate the picture even further, all of these expenses varied from year to year.

In addition to the costs of maintaining the physical fabric of the playhouse and its environs were expenditures related to performance. The acting company spent money on playbooks (roughly £6 apiece in the 1590s, and perhaps as much as £84 per annum, if the 1595 calendar year at the Rose playhouse represents a typical year's expenses); and the company paid scribes for copying out parts for the individual actors. Additionally, they paid the Master of the Revels £3 to license every play before it was performed. Beyond this, the actors paid for costumes, which frequently comprised the most expensive portion of their outlay. They also had to budget for travel expenses if they were invited to perform at the house of a noble or at court (wherever the court was sitting at the time). (And for the actor–householders at the first Globe, all such expenses would have been additional to those accrued as owners of the playhouse.) Nevertheless, while we can deduce that the magnitude of the total outlay at the best-known public playhouses was considerable, it is impossible to determine precisely how much money was laid out on an annual basis. Costumes were often used and reused, or purchased second-hand; playscripts, though retired after a time, were occasionally brought back into production, sometimes with additions and alterations (all which had to be paid for). The reward paid to a company for performing a play at court was generally £10 per play in the 1590s, but travel expenses on these occasions would have varied (Chambers 1923: iv. 163–6).

As even a general outline suggests, then, over a five- or ten-year period the ongoing investment in a playhouse or a company was substantial. (In 1600 the shareholders in the Lord Admiral's Men owed their financier £300.) And even though it appears that the owner of the Rose potentially collected as much as £100 per annum for his share of the receipts, the factors that could interfere with a steady influx of income were many. Added to the negative effects of plague closings, which, as mentioned earlier, occurred rather commonly during the warmest months of the year, were restrictions on public performances during the Lenten season, the departure or deaths of actors from the companies, destruction caused by fire (which brought down both the first Fortune and the first Globe), the changing tastes of the London market, and the necessity for companies to turn over a certain number of performance texts, on a regular basis, in order to keep their repertories fresh and alive. This 'need for newness' would seem to imply that, despite the large amount of traffic in and out of London, a portion of the spectators in the playhouses must have been repeat customers who were eager for original plays. It is also some indication of the sophistication of the London audiences at the time; and it further suggests that the actors who served as company managers had to be shrewd in cultivating a repertory that included plays that were, after all, 'good investments'; that is, a combination of plays that stood the test of time and remained popular, together with those that simply played to the moment, offering variety and novelty (Knutson 2001: 20).

But despite the fact that the levels of income and outlay can be estimated, these fail to characterize completely what the playhouses were finally marketing to their audiences, which raises another question related to theatrical commerce. Descriptors of individual plays, such as 'tragedies' and 'histories', tell us a bit more about the nature of the plays that constituted individual repertories; however, they do not describe fully what the playhouses were ultimately 'selling'. Because the 1590s saw the first concentrated 'wave' of celebrity actors on the London stage (with players such as Edward Alleyn and Richard Burbage leading the pack), the companies were clearly in the business of marketing both dramatic talent and charisma, and therefore they defined their repertories around those actors who were the most able to bring in crowds (Cerasano 2005*a*: 55–6). Over time, however, differences even in the format of playhouse entertainments lured spectators to one theater or another. Some companies showcased a single play only at each performance, while the entertainment at the first Fortune playhouse (1600–21) was choreographed around a complex series of events, including a play, and ending with a jig (a short interlude featuring clever music and dancing).

Even the choice of a location or the settings of individual playhouses—which differed greatly, one from another—could potentially have a financial impact upon the success or failure of a venture. The Rose playhouse stood on a small parcel of land, barely large enough for the playhouse; conversely, the first and second Fortune playhouses were surrounded by a large (and a well-developed) yard. (In July 1621 the Spanish ambassador and his train went to the Fortune to see a play and later attended a banquet put on for them in the playhouse gardens.) By contrast, the Blackfriars playhouse—located among a thicket of city structures, including many elite residences—offered not only indoor seating for a small audience of elite theatergoers, but proximity to the shops that would have served a well-to-do clientele. All these factors influenced the success of a playhouse enterprise. An investment in a playhouse was dependent on more than simply the quality of the plays that could be purchased and performed. Historians might hypothesize that popular plays brought high profits; however, many other factors—some controllable and some less easily controlled—might intervene to make one week's receipts high or low. The healthy handful of playhouses whose lives were short suggests that the balancing act for success was delicate. Nonetheless, over time an increasingly sophisticated sense of how to handle theatrical management appears to have benefited theatrical prospectors in general. Owners and investors seemed to profit, in some significant way, from the hard-earned experiences of the first generation of Elizabethan public playhouses. By 1600 London's theatrical culture appears to have become sufficiently well developed, within individual enterprises, that the investors became competent both to predict success and to direct their financial and human assets in the most purposeful directions, thereby minimizing risk. Individual texts or dramatists might come and go, but after 1600 investors seem to have made few dire mistakes.

At the very center of commerce was a large and changing market; but because a theater was, in many ways, a business that depended upon the cultivation of broad appeal, it actually relied on many different markets. Visitors to London from the Continent potentially represented a different market sector than the home-bred London audience. The spectators drawn to London from the country possibly constituted yet another market; and those gathered at court for the Christmas and New Year festivities, ranging from English nobility to foreign ambassadors, perhaps constituted a third type of market. London's residential playgoers—the students at the Inns of Court, the tradesmen who formed the backbone of the urban economy, the foreign agents who were stationed in London by merchant trading companies based elsewhere in Europe—formed audiences that were both socially and culturally diverse. As such, London's theatrical marketplaces were potentially influenced by many other 'economies': the local economy, the economy of England (defined more broadly), and larger market forces located outside of the country. Therefore, one of the issues faced by investors, especially during the years when theatrical culture was developing, had to do with ascertaining the range and depth of the potential marketplace. This was important, not only because it related to income, but also because it was a factor in balancing income against outlay, and owners had to account for the fact that market forces frequently worked in more than one direction. For example, fluctuating market forces abroad might affect the costs of making costumes if the prices of imported fabrics vacillated, thereby resulting in fewer costume purchases; but, equally importantly, during a season when a company's income was diminished their ability to purchase new costumes was doubtless reduced. Consequently, a single or even multiple influences could potentially come into play in producing some vacillation within the finances of a particular playhouse or acting company. Similarly, wider influences also took their toll on profits. For instance, income might well have fluctuated in the late 1580s if there was a decrease in the number of visitors coming to London from the Low Countries when they experienced a period of heightened military activity. Likewise, political tensions between England and various other countries on the Continent might well have lessened the traffic of foreign visitors during different periods.

Not only must such patterns be taken into account in scrutinizing the theatrical marketplace, but part of the continuing challenge to historians in reconstructing a full picture of theatrical commercialism emanates from the fact that our knowledge of economic practices is drawn from a diverse group of playhouses. Even by the late 1590s, when the Theatre and the Rose appear to have become fairly permanent fixtures within the theatrical landscape, the public playhouses, as entities, had not achieved anything approaching commercial stability. Nor would they be in so fortunate a position at any time during the period leading right up to the 1640s when the theaters were closed down altogether. Owing to their susceptibility to the changing demands of audiences, their defenselessness against conservative religious-cum-political trends, and their sheer vulnerability to changing human circumstances, the public playhouses were never finally able to acquire the same kind of permanence as other, more ordinary, businesses.

Over time, many investors who held a significant interest in individual playhouses seemed to develop techniques for managing risks and maximizing profits. Predictably, perhaps, most of these techniques were grounded in sheer practicality (as much as, or perhaps even more than, they were grounded in some of the political and artistic concerns that we have traditionally cited in order to explain management decisions). Theater owners built performance spaces with an eye to the potential size of the audience that could be attracted, not only during times when popular plays were in repertory, but allowing as well for the times when less popular fare was offered. Following along with these lines, the playhouses had to be 'performance-friendly', creating circumstances in which the actors could speak and be heard comfortably. The site chosen for a public theater was also an important financial consideration. Thus, wise investors seem not to have been interested in placing the large public theaters within prime real-estate districts because the expensive nature of the ground leases for the property on which the playhouses stood would have absorbed large amounts of their profit (and the public playhouses were writ large precisely to maximize profit). Yet, simultaneously, neither could a theater be located so far afield from the major roads that large numbers of potential spectators would have found it a great inconvenience to travel to the playhouse. Consequently, the challenge was to construct a playhouse in a place where it was accessible to a large portion of the market sector, but where the ground rents were as cheap as possible. To cite one useful example, when Edward Alleyn and Philip Henslowe chose a site for the construction of the first Fortune playhouse, they sought a location north of Cripplegate, which was convenient to the road that ran north through the city, a place where they could rent a sizeable plot of land inexpensively, and a site that was clear and ready for construction (thus minimizing their expenses in preparing the site). That the site was outside the jurisdiction of the City authorities was an additional benefit, as was the fact that it also lay not far from older playhouses and inns at which plays had been performed for over a generation. At the same time, the Fortune site was located near to Holborn, an area that was rapidly becoming gentrified. Moreover, an additional advantage lay in the fact that Alleyn was well acquainted with the rector of the parish in which the new theater was built, and could be instrumental in offering assistance for poor relief in the parish. Such mutual benefits helped to assuage any fears from nervous neighbors; they created a buffer between the playhouse community and the local authorities as well (Cerasano 2008: 7–14).

Correspondingly, the acting company that occupied the Fortune clearly learned how to maximize their profits, from not only a commercial but also an artistic perspective.

The business managers (all of whom were actors) of the company (the Lord Admiral's/ Prince's Men) purchased playbooks that seemed to complement their established reputation for heroic romance, foreign history, and domestic comedy. As at their previous house, the Rose, where the success of *Tamburlaine the Great, Parts 1 and 2*, demonstrated the commercial virtues of sequence plays, the company at the Fortune went on to purchase *Fortune's Tennis, Parts 1 and 2*. Where it served their advantages, the company also carried over former 'hits', probably including the Marlowe repertory and blockbusters such as *Jeronimo*. Again, if the company's commercial patterns in the 1590s taught them anything, it was to maximize the performance schedule following theater closures, as they did following the 1593 outbreak of plague (Foakes 2002: 22–7). The company at the Fortune would, additionally, have kept a tight rein on expenses for costumes and props; and, if the archaeology of the Rose playhouse site is at all telling, the props and stage furniture would have been of modest quality. Plays prepared for court performances would have consisted of the same plays that were performed in London, but they were spruced up with new prologues and perhaps a few new costumes or accessories, as was the case with 'Phaeton', performed before the Queen at Whitehall early in 1601 (Foakes 2002: 137–8). In many ways, not only was the prospect of maximizing profit advantageous for its own sake, but it was desirable, as a rule, because actors and investors were constantly testing the financial waters of theater ownership as they worked out methods for better management. They might well have inherited the shareholding system as a model that operated within the merchant trading companies, and doubtless they had learned from the long experience of trade guilds that family businesses (the rule rather than the exception) might, over time, create an ongoing commercial legacy. However, in many ways the theater owners of Shakespeare's time were charting unknown territory and were learning, through hard-won experience, what practices did or didn't work.

Among other things, the concept of 'making a living' vis-à-vis theater was being tested for the first time during this period. Because actors did not enjoy a fixed salary (except for those few young boy apprentices whose parents received a regular fee), their income was variable. Evidence supplied by actors' wills (while not exhaustive) suggests that most of them did well enough overall to sustain themselves; and some apparently did quite a bit better. Robert Armin (d. 1614), a member of the Lord Chamberlain's Men who is remembered for his clown roles, bequeathed a 'seale ringe of golde w*i*th [his] Armes on it'. Alexander Cooke, a lesser-known member of the same company (also d. 1614), left £50 each to three children in addition to window cushions, a cupboard cloth, and a chimney cloth 'being all bordered about with needleworke'. Edward Sharpham (d. 1608), a dramatist who wrote for the Children of the Revels, bequeathed to his brother his 'damson Colloured Cloake lined throughe with blacke veluett and [his] Rapyer beinge hatched w*i*th syluer', in addition to a 'cheyne of smalle pearle and my goulde ringe with the Dyamond therein' and 'palle Carnac*i*on sylke stockings' (Honigmann and Brock 1993: 77–9, 94–8). Sharpham also had a coat of arms and set his seal to his will.

Adventurers, Investors, Owners: Three Case Studies

Any consideration of the most influential theater owners of the sixteenth century must take into account James Burbage, Frances Langley, and Philip Henslowe, the owners of the Theatre, the Swan, and the Rose (which were all built in the London suburbs). And although other investors might also serve as models, I will concentrate on the most prominent ones here. James Burbage, perhaps because he was one of the first investors, has also become something of a model against which historians, like E. K. Chambers, tend to compare all others. The fact that his son the actor Richard Burbage went on to perform in Shakespeare's plays has meant that the Burbage enterprises have naturally attracted more scholarly attention than others. Nevertheless, there is nothing in James Burbage's early career to suggest that he would have become involved in theatrical affairs. As far as we know, Burbage was born into the trade class, and he belonged to the London Joiners' Company, whereby he presumably earned a living early on in his life. (He is twice identified as a 'joiner' in the parish register of St Stephen, Coleman Street, in 1559.) In that year he married Ellen Brayne, the daughter of a tailor who was freed of the Girdlers' Company. So it is reasonable to say that Burbage's beginnings were very average indeed. However, by 1572 he was identified as a player in the Earl of Leicester's Men in a petition from the troupe to their patron begging him to allow them to continue wearing his livery; and in May 1574 a royal patent was issued to the company granting them the privilege to perform in London and in the country (Edmond 2004). Two years later, Burbage seems to have begun building the Theatre in Shoreditch, largely with the financial support of his brother-in-law John Brayne, a wealthy grocer, who financed most of the construction. (Brayne had, a decade earlier, been involved in the financing of the Red Lion playhouse, a conversion of an existing inn; but his involvement with Burbage seems to have come later.) Unhappily, the business arrangements between Burbage and Brayne at the Theatre went sour early in the construction phase of the project, and in 1586 Brayne died out of the arrangement altogether, prompting an extended family quarrel that was never settled satisfactorily (Berry 2004). Nevertheless, the companies that occupied the Theatre eventually came to include several key members of the Lord Chamberlain's Men—not least of all, Richard Burbage and William Shakespeare—and the physical fabric of the playhouse became the nucleus for the newly constructed Globe in 1599. Thus, the initial financial investment that Brayne made in the Theatre in 1576 outlived both him and his brother-in-law James; and, even twenty-five years later it continued to support the Lord Chamberlain's Men.

A second model of theater ownership is suggested by Francis Langley, one of seven children of a tenant farmer in Lincolnshire. After he was orphaned at an early age, Francis and his younger brother were sent to London, where they were raised by a prosperous uncle, John Langley, who was a member of the London Goldsmiths' Company. Attracted to the affluence that the City offered, and surrounded by businessmen who were putting their acumen to good use, Langley eventually took up the office of City Alnager (searcher and sealer of woolen cloths) in 1585. Several years later he acquired the lordship and manor of Paris Garden, on the south side of the Thames, across from London, a property that he began to develop with the construction of rental tenements. By 1594–5 Langley perceived that there was money to be made by investing through the rental of theatrical properties, and so he constructed the Swan playhouse on the eastern side of the manor, moving in the direction of Southwark, which would eventually become the home to several playhouses, the bear-baiting arena, and other entertainment spots (Ingram 2004). According to its most famous spectator, Johannes DeWitt, the Swan was the largest and most impressive playhouse of its time. Clearly, Langley's ambitions were reflected in this; however, the venture failed partly owing to Langley's miscalculation in the number of playing companies that were available to rent the Swan on a consistent basis. Although the playhouse was apparently occupied in its early days (by an unnamed company), the Earl of Pembroke's players (who performed there in 1597) seem to have brought Langley's success to a halt when they performed 'The Isle of Dogs', a allegedly 'seditious' play that caused the theater to be shut down and tore the acting company apart (Ingram 1978: 167–96). Despite the fact that the Swan eventually reopened, the incident cast a bad light on the playhouse and its owner, who subsequently became a personal target of Sir Robert Cecil. Langley ended his life in 1602, having been forced out of his position as City Alnager. By this time the Swan had fallen into disuse and decay, and its owner was bankrupt, his other business investments having failed similarly, from all of which we might reasonably conclude that Langley lost a tremendous amount of money. But whereas James Burbage and his son Richard had practical experience with theater as a business, Langley did not. And, although nobody examining their origins could have predicted that they would have become investors in commercial theater, the Burbages clearly had the advantage.

In contrast to these models is another, exemplified by Philip Henslowe (1558–1616) and Edward Alleyn (1566–1626), whose careers in the theater world might also be something of a surprise. If we examine their early lives, there is little indication that they would have become invested in the business of playhouse ownership. Henslowe was the son of Edmond Henslowe, who was appointed Master of Ashdown Forest by the Crown. Consequently, the family lived near Lindfield, Sussex, where Philip's uncle held a royal license to mine iron for the Royal Ordnance. As a young man Philip was apprenticed to a London dyer; and it may be that his earliest interaction with the theater business consisted of supplying cloth for costumes, or even finished garments (Cerasano 2004*b*). (Henslowe later ran a pawnbroking business, where he took in clothing, among other items.) He never—as far as we know—wrote a line of poetry or acted in a play. By contrast, Alleyn, the son of Edward Alleyn senior, a Porter to Queen Elizabeth I, seems to have been an actor from his teenage years, and his elder brother John also engaged in playing for a time with Lord Sheffield's Men. One of the businesses that Edward Alleyn senior was involved in related to the administration of Bethlem Hospital. Additionally, the Alleyn family owned an inn in Bishopsgate, not far from the hospital, and not far from other inns in which plays were frequently performed. However, there is no evidence that Edward Alleyn senior ever helped to sponsor players. Nevertheless, the family's location in London, near to other inn-yard playhouses and not far from the Theatre and its near neighbor the Curtain (built in 1577), meant that the Alleyn brothers had ample opportunity to see plays performed from an early age in playing spaces that evidenced some level of ongoing success (Cerasano 2004*a*). Doubtless, this helped them to develop both an artistic and a financial sensibility.

Nonetheless, the fact that Henslowe and Alleyn were both from armigerous families who had clear social aspirations and a level of recognized achievement at court would seem to militate against their involvement in theater, which was not, at this time, a natural place for young men with gentrified backgrounds to go. Years later, however, it is clear that Henslowe and Alleyn had managed to combine the logical expectations dictated by their backgrounds with the emerging models created by new investors. Having jointly managed the Rose playhouse in the 1590s, they went on to build two other playhouses, the Fortune (1600) and the Hope (1613), and to obtain jointly the royal patent for the Mastership of the Bears, Bulls, and Mastiff Dogs. In addition to this license, which brought with it the privilege of owning and operating the bear-baiting arena in Southwark (near to the Rose and the Globe), a very lucrative investment, Henslowe and Alleyn financed other businesses; and Henslowe also managed to obtain positions at court as a Groom of the Chamber and a Sewer (Steward) of the Chamber. He was also granted a pension by James I (Cerasano 2005*b*: 338). In contrast, Alleyn acquired substantial property holdings, including Dulwich Manor (1,200 acres) and a manor in Yorkshire. Although Alleyn's conspicuous success on stage, in the signature roles of many of Christopher Marlowe's plays, would equate him with the Rose playhouse, and therefore make him a more probable candidate for theatrical investment than Philip Henslowe, neither Alleyn nor Henslowe was interested solely in theatrical investment as an end in itself. In both of their lives an involvement in theater seems to have been a means to a greater end, as purveyors of entertainment to the royal household, and to allow them to create for themselves a unique niche at court at a time when most of the positions there were occupied by men who had distinguished themselves through military or diplomatic service (Cerasano 2005*b*: 333–41; 2007: 49–57).

Consequently, the Burbages, Francis Langley, and the Henslowe–Alleyn partnership all seem to have approached theatrical investment with different goals and purposes, and with different talents and levels of experience (or inexperience, for that matter). For Langley, the Swan was part of a grand scheme devised by a young man with a taste for wealth, who saw the opportunity to make money in what seemed to be a unique and expanding sector of the economy. For James Burbage, the Theatre was the first step in what eventually became a theatrical empire, one that included the Globe, a public playhouse in the Blackfriars, and a second Globe when the first burned down in 1613. Whether James Burbage could have seen his initial investment leading to the others that followed is debatable; however, what he could have seen initially was the need for a large permanent, purpose-built space in which to perform.

In time, he would also have recognized the growing success of his son Richard as an actor, and finally, he would have realized the potential of the Lord Chamberlain's Men as a performing entity. James would also have deduced that the company could have utilized a private playhouse, so he leased part of the Blackfriars for that purpose, on 4 February 1596, just a year before his death. Among other things, we might credit James Burbage with an excellent sense of vision—for envisioning theater as a developing business. And within this context he managed to maintain the kind of fortitude that was necessary in order to get the Theatre up and running, and he also imagined another possibility, for private theater, which was intended to appeal to a more upmarket audience within the rapidly expanding city.

Afterword

In examining the commercial landscape of the public playhouses in greater London—with its high-stake financial risks, sociopolitical complexities, and stories of devastating failure—we might periodically wonder whether the players who made their living on tour didn't end up enjoying the best of all worlds. As we now understand from the studies of the Records of Early English Drama, in general, and from individual researchers, such as Barbara D. Palmer, who work closely with those records, traveling players had very satisfactory careers. They earned a good living, were generally welcomed by spectators and aristocratic patrons, were assured of a certain regularity of employment, and benefited from a kind of financial freedom that was inherent in the peripatetic nature of their existence (Palmer 2005: 259–305). By comparison, many of the London-based playhouses came and went. For every playhouse like the Rose and Globe that succeeded, there were others, such as the Swan (which was brought to closure following the disastrous staging of 'The Isle of Dogs', and eventually vacated; Chambers 1923: ii. 412) or the Boar's Head (which never really attracted a permanent company and so floundered and eventually folded). And although historians have been reluctant to associate the actor Robert Browne with the man of the same name who owned the Boar's Head playhouse, Joan Alleyn, writing to her husband, Edward, in October 1603, stated that 'Browne of the Boares head is dead & dyed very pore' (Chambers 1923: ii. 412–13, 445). So despite the fact that the characteristics shaping the success of the dominant acting companies and the playhouses they occupied seem to be growing clearer with each successive generation of scholarship, it well might be that the failed ventures—had we more knowledge of them—would also have much to teach us about the commercial environment of the public theaters in Shakespeare's time. But that is the subject of a different essay.

CHAPTER 23

THE CITY OF LONDON AND THE THEATRE

IAN W. ARCHER

THE subject of the City of London's regulation of the theatre has been well served by historians and critics. Most of the relevant documents are in print, the editors of successive volumes of the Malone Society Collections having transcribed the key exchanges of correspondence between the Privy Council and the Lord Mayor and Aldermen, and the relevant minutes from the courts of Aldermen and Common Council. Much of the material they edited, and more too, was incorporated into the monumental work of E. K. Chambers (1923), and latterly into the compendium of materials assembled by Wickham, Berry, and Ingram (2000). However, it should be noted that the dependence on these early transcriptions has not been without problems. Occasional errors in transcription are repeated, with the result, to take a significant example, that the identity of one of the early sponsors of playing in the city has until recently been consistently mistaken. As we shall see, one or two key documents have been missed, and the significance of the hard line taken by the city authorities in 1579 passed by. Moreover, the lack of interest in the personnel of city government meant that the editors rarely identified individual signatories to letters, and this failing has been carried over into the more recent compilations. The successive lord mayors remain faceless cardboard cut-outs, the 'city fathers', who

A version of this chapter was read at the Literature and History seminar run by Paulina Kewes and Susan Brigden in May 2008. I am grateful to the comments of participants, as also to David Kathman and Lawrence Manley, who provided some last-minute corrections.

adopted a unitary stance against playing from the later 1570s onwards, allegedly issuing the same complaints year after year.

We also need to bear in mind the limits of the underlying city archives. The remembrancia do not record all the correspondence between the City and the Privy Council; what, for example, has happened to the letter for the pulling down of the Theatre and Curtain in April 1584 mentioned by Fleetwood, the city's Recorder? Some of the most significant exchanges between the city and Privy Councillors were conducted face to face rather than by correspondence. How much one would love to know what happened when the high-powered delegation of Aldermen appeared before the Privy Council in November 1587 'to move theyre honours for the suppressinge of playes and interludes within this Cittye'.[1] We know nothing of what transpired. It is also difficult to get a real sense of the complexities of the decision-making process at the Guildhall. The documents generated by city government put a premium on civic unity. The minutes of the Aldermen and Common Council are essentially records of decisions taken, and there is hardly any indication of the terms of debate, nor of the scale of internal opposition. The nature of the records has encouraged historians to concentrate too much on the homogeneity of the elites, the structures of government, and the processes of interaction between institutions seen as rather monolithic blocks (Aldermen, Common Council, livery companies, and parishes within the City), and between all these bodies and the Privy Council. Because of the nature of the sources, the personalities and prejudices of individual citizens remain highly elusive: we have very little in the way of personal correspondence, diaries, or account books for members of the civic elite. So, the dominant narrative established by E. K. Chambers has been that the city government consistently opposed the theatres, but that its efforts were stymied by the ambivalent stance taken by the Privy Council, which, while recognizing the threat that large gatherings might pose to public health and public order, nevertheless also saw the need to foster theatrical entertainments in the City so that the players could try out in public the entertainments that were intended for the recreation of the Queen (or, as the Council put it in 1582, 'to the ende [the players] might thereby attaine to the more dexteritie and perfection in that profession, the better to content her maiestie'), and therefore consistently undermined the more hardline stance taken by the City.[2] For a long time this was the standard view, but more recently some critical voices have been raised. It has been suggested, for example, that the Privy Council's objective may have been the containment of playing by limiting the numbers of companies licensed to perform. Thus, the formation of the Queen's Men in 1583 at Walsingham's instigation can be seen as an effort not only to concentrate theatrical talent by creaming off the best performers from existing companies, but actually as a measure to limit the number of companies able to perform in the city (McMillin and MacLean 1998: 8–17). Likewise, Andrew Gurr (1996*b*) sees the emergence of the duopoly in 1594 confirmed in 1598, as a means of ensuring a regular flow of plays for the Queen, while limiting the potential for disorder that lay behind so many of the City's concerns. If this is the case, then there

1 London Metropolitan Archives (LMA), RCA 21, fo. 503^{v}; Chambers (1923: iv. 305).

2 LMA, Remembrancia I, no. 317; Chambers (1923: iv. 287–8).

may well have been more common ground between the City and the Privy Council than the conventional narrative suggests.

More interestingly still, some of the new work is beginning to question the notion of the City united in implacable opposition to the theatre. It has, of course, long been recognized that the stance taken by the city's leaders was not shared by all those that they ruled. The fact that Londoners flocked to the theatres clearly demonstrates that the prejudices of the elite were not shared by the wider citizenry. But the debate over audiences has been conducted in sometimes unhelpfully bipolar terms. In an effort to disprove Anne Jenalie Cook's notion that the theatres were another gentry-orientated service industry, we have all rushed to find examples of London lowlife flocking to the plays, and there is no doubt that they were there (Cook 1981; Butler 1984*a*; Gurr 2004*b*; Whitney 1999; Capp 2003). But in establishing the presence of servants and apprentices we run the risk of reinforcing stereotypical images of the grave city fathers, respectable bourgeois to a man, pitted against the evils of the theatre, which proved irresistible to the masses, in other words buying into the rhetoric that the audiences were the 'refuse sort of evill disposed & vngodly people about this Cytie'.[3] This view runs counter to several rather elementary points. First, because, for the majority, apprenticeship was essential to citizenship, there were in the elite guilds a large number of people recruited from gentle backgrounds, predominantly younger sons. Secondly, the preachers who fulminated against the flight from the churches to the theatres were targeting middling Londoners, not the poor and the rootless. When John Field enumerated the victims of the Paris Garden disaster in 1583 (the scaffolds at a sabbath day bear-baiting had collapsed, causing the godly to go into overdrive on the providential lessons to be drawn), showing that they were mostly humble tradesmen and servants, he drew a distinction, as Patrick Collinson has pointed out, between 'these of such sorte' (them) and 'us', his reasonably affluent literate readers, to whom the fate of the poor was 'an example' (Collinson 1982: 221).

This is not to deny that there were lower-class theatregoers, but rather to warn against too ready an equation of the audiences with London lowlife. It is also intended to raise the question about how often 'respectable' citizens visited the theatres. Did the City fathers never show up? It is probably impossible, given the nature of the evidence, to prove the case either way. But it is surely significant that when Beaumont and Fletcher choose to satirize citizen taste in the meta-theatrical *Knight of the Burning Pestle* they show the apprentice Rafe attending the theatre in the company of his master and mistress (Munro 2005: 55–95). His master is free of the Grocers' Company, and it would not be unreasonable to suggest that both apprentice and master would have been younger sons of the gentry (no less than 36 per cent of apprentices in the Grocers' Company were recruited from gentle backgrounds in the 1630s), and that the master was the sort of prosperous middling citizen who would have found his way onto the City's Common Council (Brooks 1994: 57). Martin Butler has identified several examples of members of the elite like the Essex gentleman Humphrey Mildmay with extensive city contacts who were avid theatre fans in the 1630s (Butler 1982). Did he never attend the

[3] LMA, Remembrancia II, no. 103; Chambers (1923: iv. 318).

theatre with those citizens with whom he was socializing in other contexts? The rising city merchants Arthur Ingram and Lionel Cranfield were members of the literary circle that gathered at the Mermaid tavern in the 1600s, rubbing shoulders with Inns of Court men like Richard Martin (himself the son of an alderman, of whom we will hear more shortly), and poets like Ben Jonson (O'Callaghan 2004). It is barely credible that they never went to one of Jonson's plays. One of Cranfield's associates in customs farming was the London alderman Sir John Swinnerton, Lord Mayor in 1613, who as a 'great cherisher of the Muses' was the dedicatee of a play by the rouge dragon pursuivant William Smith, *The Hector of Germanie, or, The Palsgrave Elector*, in honour of the marriage of Princess Elizabeth and the Elector Palatine, and performed at the Red Bull and at the Curtain (Smith 1615, A1R). A dedication does not necessarily mean that Swinnerton had actively patronized the play, but his broader connections with dramatists, poets, and pamphleteers are suggested by the fact that it was to him that the Merchant Taylors' Company turned for advice in their negotiations with Ben Jonson over the entertainment at Merchant Taylors' Hall for Prince Henry in 1607, and that Anthony Munday described him as 'the foster-father of his meane desarts' (T. Hill 2004: 38, 86–90; Knowles and Heaton 2003). Swinnerton is likely to have been ambivalent about the drama—his dealings over the sweet wines and his cosy relationship with the late Lord Treasurer Robert Cecil, Earl of Salisbury, were satirized in another play performed by apprentices at the Whitefriars theatre in 1613, *The Hog Hath Lost His Pearl*—but the circumstantial evidence suggests that this particular city father was a patron of the theatre (Kathman 2004*c*).

How many more such civic Maecenases were there? Perhaps not many. But from the other end of our period, we have the case of George Tadlowe, citizen and haberdasher, who at a meeting of the Court of Aldermen on 2 April 1543 was bound by recognizance not to permit playing in his dwelling house (possibly the White Horse tavern in Lombard Street in St Mary Woolnoth, which he leased from 1539) without permission of the Lord Mayor. Tadlowe's identity has eluded historians of the theatre because of a mistranscription in the relevant volume of the Malone Society, where the name is rendered 'Gadlowe' (Chambers 1931: 290).[4] George Tadlowe (d. 1557) is a rather interesting figure. He is the prominent Common Councillor who was immortalized in the pages of both Foxe's *Book of Martyrs* and Holinshed's *Chronicle* for his speech at Common Council on 8 October 1549, using examples from Fabian's *Chronicles* to warn his fellow citizens against the perils of choosing the wrong side in conflicts between the Crown and the nobility (Holinshed 1807–8: iii. 1018; Foxe 1837–41: vi. 289–90). He was sufficiently prominent to be elected a Member of Parliament on four occasions in the reigns of Edward VI and Mary, probably with the patronage of William Paulet, well connected in the city through his marriage to the daughter of a former Lord Mayor (Bindoff 1982: iii. 417–18). Tadlowe is also identified by Ralph Robinson in 1551 in the dedication of his translation of More's *Utopia* as the man who persuaded him to undertake the work:

[4] He was, however, correctly identified by Susan Brigden and Paul Whitfield White, as David Kathman reminds me (P. White 1993: 206; Brigden 1988: 344–5).

This thing I well pondering & wayinge wt me self, & also knowing, & knowledging the barbarous rudenes of my translation was fully determined neuer to haue put it forth in printe, had it not bene for certein frendes of myne, & especially one, whom aboue al other I regarded, a man of sage & discret witte, & in wordly matters by long vse well experienced, whoes name is George Tadlowe: an honest citizein of London, & in the same citie well accepted, & of good reputation: at whoes request, & instaunce I first toke vpon my weake, & feble sholders ye heauie, and weightie bourdein of this great enterprice. This man w^{t} diuers other, but this man chiefely (for he was able to do more wt me, then many other) after that I had ones rudely brought ye worke to an ende, ceassed not by al meanes possible continualy to assault me, vntil he had at ye laste, what by ye force of his pitthie argumentes & strong reasons, & what by hys authority so persuaded me, that he caused me to agree & consente to the impryntynge herof. He therfore, as the chiefe persuadour, must take vpon him the daunger, whyche vpon this bolde, and rashe enterpryse shall ensue. (More 1551, 4^{v}–5)

Tadlowe emerges not just as an opportunistic London tavern keeper exploiting the commercial potential of dramatic performances, but as a cultivated man at ease in humanist circles, and aware of the uses of history.

There are other reasons for supposing that the city elite may have been less united over its attitude towards the drama. Much of the recent work on the business of playing has emphasized the degree to which theatre entrepreneurs and actors were embedded in the city's neighbourhoods and its economic structures. David Kathman, in particular, has demonstrated the way in which a host of actors, musicians, playwrights, and the leaders of the children's companies were apprenticed through the London guilds, taking advantage of the relatively liberal rules, which meant that guildsmen were not expected to follow the occupation suggested by their guild affiliation. Likewise, those who financed and owned the theatre venues also regularly turn out to be deeply embedded within the guild structures of London (Kathman 2004*a*, 2005*a*). Kathman's case will be strengthened once more work is undertaken beyond the guild records. For example, Robert Fryer, the goldsmith who was bound not to allow plays to be played in his house before 4 p.m. on Sundays and 3 p.m. on other days, was, like Tadlowe, a prominent and active Common Councillor.[5] They were not alone among the members of the theatrical profession in their prominence in local government. Prejudices against the theatre might be deployed in the bickerings to which local communities were prone. Some of the local opponents of Henry Condell, actor, sharer in the Chamberlain's Men, and editor of Shakespeare's First Folio, sought to prevent him from becoming churchwarden of St Mary Aldermanbury in 1617 'onely in regard of his profession he being a player', but they did not succeed, as others testified that he had been 'a parishioner of the parishe of St Mary Aldermanbury by the space of xxj yeares & more, hath in that parishe borne all offices vp to the place of churchwarden and always held in good repute & estimacion amonge his neighbours'.[6] Likewise anti-theatrical prejudice did not prevent Edward Alleyn and Philip Henslowe from serving on the highly select vestry of St Saviour's, Southwark, from 1607.[7] The Southwark vestries were very much the linchpin of local

[5] LMA, RCA 16, fo. 42^{v}; Chambers (1931: 301).

[6] LMA, DL/C/314, p. 95, cited by Erler (2008: 210–11, 398).

[7] LMA, P92/SAV/450.

government in the borough and dominated by the parish elite. Men like Condell, Henslowe, and Alleyn were thoroughly integrated into the structures of local government and upper-middling sociability. The pursuit of the theatrical entrepreneurs and actors into their local communities is thus a healthy corrective to the emphasis in certain strands of literary criticism on the theatre's marginal status (Mullaney 1988). As Stephen Gosson, no friend of the theatre, conceded, 'some of them are sober, discreets, properly learned honest housholders and Citizens well thought on amonge their neighbours at home' (Gosson 1579*b*: $22^{r–v}$). The theatre was very much part of the City economy, its actors, managers, and financiers well known in their guilds and neighbourhoods (Knutson 2001: 21–47).

Another reason for suggesting that attitudes among the city elites towards the theatre may have been more ambivalent was that City policy seems to have been divided between the advocates respectively of regulation and prohibition, though the latter were to become increasingly ascendant in the city's counsels. Even the critics of the theatre were less uniformly hardline than one might think from the conventional accounts. The earliest denunciations by the preachers at St Paul's Cross seem to have concentrated their fire on the issue of playing on Sundays, leaving open the possibility of performances on work days. Thus, John Stockwood in his sermon at the Cross on 24 August 1578 drew back from a full-blooded denunciation: 'I will not here enter this disputation, whether it be vtterly vnlawfull to haue any playes, but will onelye ione in this issue, whether in a Christian common wealth they be tolerable on the Lords day' (Stockwood 1578: 133). For those who worried about the content of the drama, it was possible to argue that not all playing was bad, but that the abuses must be reformed. This was Stephen Gosson's initial position in *The Schoole of Abuse*:

> And as some of the Players are farre from abuse: so some of their Playes are without rebuke: which are as easily remembred as quickly reckoned. The twoo prose Bookes plaied at the Belsauage, where you shall finde neuer a woorde without wit, neuer a line without pith, neuer a letter placed in vaine. The *Iew* & *Ptolome,* showne at the Bull, the one representing the greedinesse of worldly chusers, and bloody mindes of Usurers: The other very liuely discrybing howe seditious estates, with their owne deuises, false friendes, with their owne swoordes, & rebellious commons in their owne snares are ouerthrowne: neither with Amorous gesture wounding the eye: nor with slouenly talke hurting the eares of the chast hearers. The *Blacke Smiths daughter,* & *Catilins* conspiracies vsually brought in to the Theater: The firste contayning the trechery of *Turkes,* the honourable bountye of a noble minde, & the shining of vertue in distresse. (Gosson 1579*b*: 22^{v}–3)

George Whetstone, himself of impeccable citizen stock, dedicating his probably unperformed play *Promos and Cassandra* (the source play for *Measure for Measure*) in 1578 to William Fleetwood, the godly recorder of London (intriguingly, otherwise known as the City's iron man of law enforcement, and persecutor of the players), was anxious to distance himself from the contemporary abuses of the drama: 'Manye tymes (to make mirthe) they make a Clowne companion with a Kinge: in theyr grave Counsels, they allow the advise of fooles: yea they use one order of speech for all persones' (Whetstone, 1578, in Smith 2004). Whetstone was also the author of a number of tracts calling for moral reform in the City, and urging London's magistrates to follow the example of the emperor Severus in rooting out vice. It is significant that he does not identify the theatre as among those vices, reserving his fire for prostitution, taverns, and dicing houses (Whetstone, 1584, in Smith 2004). His more liberal position may be all the more striking in view of the possibility that the play *Promos and Cassandra* (in the author's words about the 'unsufferable abuse, of a lewde Magistrate', Promos, whose advocacy of moral reformation is undercut by his designs on the chastity of Cassandra) had specific topical reference to the controversy raging over Bridewell's campaign against prostitution in the later 1570s, where the treasurer was accused of having framed prominent citizens on charges of sexual incontinency (Griffiths 2003). His insistence on his conformity to the classical rules of dramaturgy may have deflected attention from the play's more topical applications, which might have made it less than welcome on other grounds to the city magistracy.[8]

The context of playing was also important. It was public performances for commercial gain which drew forth most opprobrium, while private performances before select groups were non-problematic. Orders banning plays, like that of February 1545, repeated in the following year, generally made exceptions for performances in the houses of noblemen, or the Lord Mayor, sheriffs, and Aldermen. The exceptions of 1545 were in fact still more permissive, for they extended also to performances in the houses of 'the substancyall & sad Comminers or hed parrisheners of the same Citie or in the open streets of the said citie as in tyme paste it hathe bene vsed or in the commen halles of the Companyes fellowshipps or brotherheddes of the same Cytie'. Not only was the category of citizens entitled to enjoy private performances extended to Common Councillors and members of the parish elites (rather vaguely defined), but plays were to be allowed in the livery company halls, and most surprisingly, in the open streets.[9] Presumably the Aldermen were thinking of the kinds of performance which had traditionally supported the parish church. The 1574 Act of Common Council also made exceptions for performances in private houses of 'anie nobleman, Citizen, or gentleman' associated with 'the festyvitie of anie marriage, Assemblye of ffrendes, or otherlyke cause withowte publique or Commen Collection of money of the Auditorie or behoulders theareof'. The extension of this privilege to citizens again was quite broad, though the Lord Mayor and Aldermen reserved to themselves the discretion to determine what constituted 'a playenge or shewing in a private place'.[10] The hostility to the commercialization of the theatre is also evident in the repeated attempts to ban advertising: there were orders to pull down bills in 1543, 1547, and 1581.[11]

If the content of plays was sometimes thought to be objectionable, then perhaps censorship would have provided the solution. In May 1559 a royal proclamation regulating dramatic performances laid down that local magistrates should 'permyt none to be played wherin either matters of religion or of the gouernaunce of the

[8] This reading of the play is offered as a suggestion.

[9] LMA, JCC 15, fos 241^{v}–243; Chambers (1931: 291–2).

[10] LMA, JCC 20, fos 187–8; Chambers (1923: iv. 273–6).

[11] LMA, RCA 10, fos 322^{v}–323; RCA 11, fo. 315^{v}; JCC 21, fo. 151^{v}.

common weale shalbe handled or treated, being no meete matters to be wrytten or treated vpon, but by menne of aucthoritie, learning and wisedome, nor to be handled before any audience, but of graue and discreete persons'. However, the tolerance shown towards such performances in private settings before appropriately elite audiences reminds us of the wide latitude that was in fact contemplated: what critical sentiments could be voiced depended on the audience before which they were uttered. The proclamation envisaged that all 'interludes to be playde eyther openly or priuatley' should be first approved by the mayor or 'other chiefe officers' (Chambers 1923: iv. 263–4). Likewise, the city's Act of Common Council regulating playing in December 1574 required that no plays be allowed within the City 'whearin shalbe vttered anie wourdes, examples, or doynges of anie vnchastitie, sedicion, nor such lyke vnfytt and vncomelye matter', and required that no plays should be 'openlie' shown unless first perused by the appropriate persons designated by the Lord Mayor and Aldermen.[12] However, there is no evidence that the provisions of either the 1559 proclamation or the 1574 Act of Common Council with respect to the licensing of plays were carried out. It is not inconceivable that the city bureaucracy could have mounted such an operation, for in November 1549 the Aldermen, apparently in response to an intervention from William Paulet, the Lord Great Master of the Household, had ordered that the two secondaries of the counters, Mr Atkyns and Mr Burnell, should 'pervuse all suche enterludes as hereafter shalbe played by eny comen pleyr of the same within the Citie'.[13] The secondaries were important legal officials with major responsibilities in the sheriffs' courts (Masters 1968). We can assume that they were pretty well educated, and at ease with the culture of playing through their Inns of Court connections. But this minute from 1549 is the only such reference to the mechanics of civic censorship. It may be that the limitations of the civic licensing system contributed to the centralization of authority over censorship of performances in the hands of the Master of the Revels in Edmund Tilney's patent of 1581. It is true that civic involvement in censorship was again mooted in 1589 in the wake of the furore over Martin Marprelate with a proposal that a nominee of the Lord Mayor join with Tilney and a nominee (a 'fitt persone well learned in divinity') of the Archbishop of Canterbury in licensing plays, but again there is no evidence that this was ever more than a paper proposal (Dutton 1991: 77–8).

Efforts were also made to limit the threat that plays posed to attendance at religious services, while retaining some space for playing, but there was very considerable room for disagreement over how that was to be done. In March 1553 the City had banned playing on Sundays or holidays before 3 p.m., but there were other considerations to bear in mind about plays starting in the late afternoon for it would be dark when they finished, and darkness in the contemporary discourses of criminality was associated with disorder.[14] So, in 1569 a series of orders required that playing should cease by 5 p.m., giving a two-hour window within which performances

[12] LMA, JCC 20, fos 187–8; Chambers (1923: iv. 273–6).

[13] LMA, RCA 12 (i), fo. 162^{v}; Chambers (1923: iv. 261).

[14] LMA, JCC 16, fo. 254; Chambers (1931: 294–5).

could take place.[15] But the problem with this was that the people tended to be taking their seats or enjoying refreshments for some time before the play began, thereby keeping them away from church services, 'attending to serue Gods enemie in an Inne'. The dilemma was elaborated upon by the Lord Mayor in a tetchy letter to the Privy Council in April 1582: 'if for remedie hereof I shold also restraine the letting in of the people till after seruice in the chirche, it wold driue the action of their plaies into very inconuenient time of night, specially for seruantes and children to be absent from their parentes and masters attendaunce and presence'.[16] The City therefore increasingly moved to the position of outright bans on both sabbath and holiday playing (there were orders to that effect in 1557 and 1582); although the Council seems to have backed the sabbath ban, it was less happy with the holiday ban. In 1583 Walsingham rather unhelpfully opined that playing should not be allowed save on the sabbath and 'other daies wherein sermons and lectures are comonly vsed': in godly London, lectures could take place on any day of the week, those at St Antholin's being held every weekday.[17]

It was also common ground that playing should be suspended during periods of plague, though there was disagreement over what constituted a dangerous level of mortality, and the city (or at least some sections of city opinion) offered sometimes different grounds for action (Barroll 1991; Freedman 1996). From the point of view of the more hardline elements in the city, the public health argument was often a rhetorical strategy designed to bring round the more hesitant elements on the Privy Council, perhaps never more pointedly than when the City argued in a petition to the Council in 1584 that it was dangerous to allow actors 'playeing in the throng of a multitude of some infected, to presse so nere to the presence of her maiestie'.[18] Whereas the players tended to argue for the early restoration of playing as plague abated, the city more cautiously pointed out the distinction between morbidity and mortality, and painted graphically ghoulish pictures of people 'enfected with sores running on them' thronging to the theatres.[19] The figures collected in the bills of mortality took no account of 'those that recouer and cary infection about them either in their sores running or in their garments', and the Aldermen also cast doubt on the reliability of the reporting of the causes of death by the parish clerks. Rather than using the number of deaths recorded as being from plague as a threshold for licensing the resumption of playing, the Aldermen suggested that playing only be allowed when the total level of mortality had stood below 50 per week for twenty days.[20]

But it was not only that one could argue over the appropriate time to resume playing; the more hardline position was that because plague was understood in providential terms as a punishment from God, playing would merely provoke God's wrath. As the Aldermen put it in their rebuttal of the players in 1583: 'To

[15] LMA, RCA 16, fo. 442^{v}; JCC 19, fo. 138^{v}; *Malone Society Collections*, ii/3 (1931), 302–3.

[16] LMA, Remembrancia I, no. 319; Chambers (1923: iv. 288).

[17] LMA, Remembrancia I, no. 553; Chambers (1923: iv. 296–7).

[18] British Library (BL), Lansdowne MS 20/12; Chambers (1923: iv. 300).

[19] LMA, Remembrancia I, no. 538; Chambers (1923: iv. 294).

[20] BL, Lansdowne MS 20/12; Chambers (1923: iv. 301–2).

play in plagetime is to encrease the plage by infection: to play out of plagetime is to draw the plage by offendinges of God vpon occasion of such playes.'[21] The City was more ready to invoke the providentialist argument than the Privy Council. The Act of Common Council of 1574 fretted over the possibility that the people

> vppon Goddes mercyfull withdrawinge his hand of sycknes from vs (which god graunte)... sheould with sodayne forgettinge of his visitacion, withowte feare of goddess wrath, and withowte deowe respecte of this good and politique meanes that he hathe ordeyned for the preservacion of Commen weales and peoples in healthe and good order, retourne to the vndewe vse of such enormities to the greate offence of God, the Quenes maiesties commaundementes and good gouernaunce.[22]

To Sir Nicholas Woodrofe, Lord Mayor in 1581–2, plays carried a 'doble perill, both naturarly in spreding the infection and otherwise in drawing God's wrath'.[23]

If the city fathers were more prone to deploy the providentialist argument, it was perhaps because they were themselves subject to the lashings of the godly from the City pulpits. Their position is summed up in Thomas White's blunt syllogism: 'the cause of plagues is sinne: and the cause of sinne are playes: therefore the cause of plagues are playes' (White 1578: 46). One should not underestimate the force of the Paul's Cross admonitions, often direct addresses to the City authorities, seated in place of honour before the vast open-air congregation, but forced to endure none-too-veiled criticisms of their lack of zeal. John Stockwood called on the Lord Mayor and Aldermen to keep 'a carefull and diligente watche' against 'all such abuses as highly offende God', including the 'flocking and thronging to baudie playes by thousandes'. He drove home the message with a warning that 'ye higher their callinge is, the higher shal their place bee, and greater paynes in Hell, in thys behalfe they omitted theyr dutie. For the myghtye men shall suffer mightie tormentes, and hee that knoweth hys maysters will and doeth it not, shall be beaten with many stripes' (Stockwood 1578: 85–7). The Aldermen did indeed squirm. Lord Mayor Thomas Blanke bemoaned their position in 1583: 'These thinges ar obiected to vs, both in open sermons at Poules crosse and elsewhere in the hearing of such as repaire from all partes of to our shame and grief.'[24] William Webb, Lord Mayor in 1592, remarked to Archbishop Whitgift that 'the preachers & ministers of the word of God about this Citie... have long time & yet do make earnest continuall complaint vnto vs for the redresse hearof'.[25]

The moralists' campaign against the theatres seems to have gathered momentum from 1577, presumably in response to the suddenly increased visibility of playing with the opening of the Theatre and the Curtain in 1576–7. The campaign may have owed something to the patronage of the city elite (or at least elements of it). Thomas White, who sounded forth from Paul's Cross in November 1577 against the

[21] BL, Lansdowne MS 20/12; Chambers (1923: iv. 301).
[22] LMA, JCC 20, fos 187–8; Chambers (1923: iv. 274).
[23] LMA, Remembrancia I, no. 40; Chambers (1923: iv. 281).
[24] LMA, Remembrancia I, no. 520; Chambers (1923: iv. 294–5).
[25] LMA, Remembrancia I, no. 635; Chambers (1923: iv. 307–8).

'sumptuous Theatre houses, a continuall monument of Londons prodigalitie and folly' (White 1578: 46), had been the vicar of St Dunstan-in-the-West since 1575, and was already sufficiently well trusted by the Mercers' Company to act as an examiner at St Paul's School. John Stockwood, who preached against the theatres in the following year, had since 1574 been the schoolmaster of Tonbridge School, the foundation of the London Lord Mayor, Sir Andrew Judd, the patronage of which lay in the hands of the Skinners' Company. It has also been speculated that the lay pamphleteers against the theatre may have been patronized by the city. Stephen Gosson's *Schoole of Abuse* (1579*b*), it is suggested, had such an extensive print run that there must have been some backing, and the work was dedicated to the Lord Mayor Sir Richard Pipe. Anthony Munday, who entered the lists with *The Second and Third Blasts*, claimed that he was writing 'by auctoritie' and appended the City's coat of arms to his work. But just how far this official sponsorship extended, or indeed whether it existed at all, is not clear (Ringler 1942; Kinney 1974; Lake and Questier 2002: 425–79; T. Hill 2004: 106–12). Gosson's tract used classical arguments rather than the ones deployed by the city. Munday's scriptural and providentialist rhetoric is closer to the city's and that of the preachers. He ended with an appeal to the London magistrates to show similar foresight to those of Marseilles in banning players. 'The permission of plaies hath already corrupted this citie; and brought the name of the citizens into slander; the examples of Gods iudgment is at this present an example in this citie' (Munday 1580: 152). But Munday was a shameless opportunist, and the act of *lèse-majesté* involved in appropriating the City's arms may not have been beyond him. Some of his arguments, in particular the attack on the noble sponsors of the theatre 'that to pleasure as they thinke, their seruants ... they should restraine the magistrates from executing their office' (Munday 1580: 128), were impolitic, and not the sort of thing the city fathers should have been encouraging!

However, it is not implausible that elements of the city elite should have backed the pulpit and pamphlet wars against the theatres, because some of the London elite must undoubtedly be counted among the 'forward' elements of protestantism. We must be wary of ascribing the blanket label 'Puritan' to the city fathers, for, as David Hickman has shown, the Aldermen and Common Councillors subscribed to a variety of religious positions, with as many conformists as forward Puritans (Hickman 1999). But insofar as we can identify the religious positions of individuals associated with the developing anti-theatrical campaign of the 1570s and 1580s, the results are telling. In April 1574 the Aldermen appointed a committee to consider a 'bill for playes'. The committee comprised Aldermen Francis Barnham, James Hawes, and Nicholas Woodrofe, with two lawyers, Thomas Norton, the Remembrancer and key intermediary between the city and Privy Council, and John Marsh, formerly the city's Common Serjeant. We know little of Hawes's or Woodrofe's religious position, but Barnham left money for sermons to be preached by the Dean of St Paul's Alexander Nowell and John Foxe, the martyrologist.[26] Norton's godly stance is well known, and in spite of his authorship of *Gordobuc*, he urged the incoming Mayor (the same James

[26] The National Archives (TNA), PROB 11/58, fo. 76^{v}. See also Orlin (2007) for Barnham.

Hawes) in November 1574 to take action against 'that unnecessarie and scarslie honest resort to plaies' (Graves 1994; Chambers 1923: iv. 273). Marsh was consistently identified with the godly, an opponent of Mary's religious policy in Parliament, and no friend to the Spanish as governor of the Merchant Adventurers in the 1560s (Hasler 1981: iii. 20–2; Ramsay 1975). The measure that emerged from this group's deliberations is presumably the Act of Common Council of December 1574, which is nowadays seen as more permissive. Although its preamble ratcheted up the rhetoric, setting out the case against playing in rather elaborate terms, its provisions amounted to a licensing of plays under a regime of civic censorship with provision for payments by the theatrical companies to the hospitals. Maybe this Act represented the sort of compromise that emerged in committee between hardliners and pragmatists (Ingram 1992: 123–38).

We are on firmer ground with the measure of 1579, curiously missed by most commentators on the subject. The Act of 1574 had been a dead letter; there is no evidence that the licensing regime was implemented; Christ's Hospital, which was supposed to collect the fees from the players, took the high-minded view that the scheme was a 'matter very vnconvenient', and recommended that plays 'shold be altogether restrained, and that in any wyse they wold not haue any monie so gotten to releue the poor withall'.[27] In the meantime, the availability of theatrical performances had mushroomed with the building of the suburban amphitheatres and the regular use of the city inns for playing from 1575, and the preachers' campaign had been moved up a gear. The later 1570s were a critical period in the evolution of social policy, as some of the principles which underlay the mid-century hospital project came to be questioned, and in 1579 committees of Common Council laboured to produce an overhaul of the City's welfare with emphasis placed on the provision of work for the able-bodied. The result was an Act of Common Council which embodied the subsequently printed *Orders Appointed to be Executed in the Citie of London for Setting Rogues and Idle Persons to Worke and for Releefe of the Poore.* Because the printed version is usually ascribed to 1582, the dating of the measures is sometimes mistaken. What is more, it looks like the committee appointed to consider the measure tacked on some extra provisions which included an absolute prohibition on playing within the City as ungodly: the relevant clause rehearsed the arguments about the corruption of youth, the dangers of infection, and the waste of resources by the poor, but added the risk of the 'great prouoking of the wrath of God the ground of all plagues... and daily cryed out against by the graue and earnest admonitions of the preachers of the word of God'.[28] Committees to consider the 'book deuised for the relief of the poor' were appointed on 11 February 1579; they reported on 19 May, and the book being 'well liked' by Common Council was to be preferred to the Privy Council, but when the measure with its fifty-three clauses came back to Common Council on 4 August, new articles were agreed, among them the ban on playing. Still more intriguingly, the minute in the Common Council journal

[27] Guildhall Library, London, MS 12806/2, fo. 140.

[28] *Orders Appointed to be Executed* (1582), Art. 62; Chambers (1923: iv. 291).

justifies the absolute ban by claiming that the existing ban on Sunday, holiday, and Lent playing ran the risk of being 'depraued to a superstitious construction' by the papists.[29] The measure of 1579 calls into question the notion that John Spencer was adopting a novel position in 1594–5 in calling for 'the present staie & finall suppressing of the said plaies'.[30]

So, who were the committee members who pushed through this radical hardening of the City's line? Hawes, Woodrofe, and Norton, the veterans of the 1574 committee, were there. So too was the ubiquitous Alderman Rowland Heyward, whose religious position is maddeningly elusive. But with Alderman Martin we are on firmer ground. Richard Martin, Master of the Mint and goldsmith to the Queen, and his wife, Dorcas, were well known as patrons of the critics of the Church; they gave money to the stranger churches; they had harboured Thomas Cartwright shortly before his exile in 1573; in 1589 Martin Marprelate was to tease the authorities about the location of the secret press by suggesting they should look to Alderman Martin's house (Collinson 1984: 270, 283; Lake and Questier 2002: 514). Nor is there any doubting where the Common Councilmen on the committee stood. Martin's fellow goldsmith Andrew Palmer witnessed John Field's will and appointed the Presbyterian William Charke as his overseer.[31] Thomas Aldersey, founder of a lectureship and school at Bunbury in Cheshire, had been in trouble with the Marian regime and was a patron of godly clergy (Archer 1991*b*; R. Baldwin 2004). Walter Fish was the Queen's tailor and a supplier of costumes to the Revels Office, but in his will he refused funeral blacks 'or suche like vayne pompe or ceremonye', which 'in myne owne opinion doe rather agree with poperie and paganisme then with the rule of the Ghospell of God'.[32] Richard Young, member of the Grocers' Company and a collector of customs, was the notorious justice and pursuivant who terrorized Catholics, the rack becoming known as Young's fiddle. (To their great delight Young met his end while in hot pursuit of a Catholic at Lambeth, falling down 'on a suddayne' and 'foaming at the mouthe [he] presently died'!; T. Hill 2004: 34–6; Kilroy 2005: 14, 22–3.) The committee seems to have been dominated by godly diehards. The episode is perhaps characteristic of the ability of the members of the godly minority by dint of their enthusiasm for moral reformation to thrust themselves into the driving seat.

Hardline measures like that of 1579 were unlikely to have commended themselves to the Privy Council, and, as we have seen, it looks like the measure had not been cleared with them in advance. The policy is also unlikely to have commanded universal assent within the City, given its origins in the godly nexus. And one might doubt how far men like Martin or Fish may have been willing to turn their forward protestantism into 'froward' opposition, given their dependence on the court for their livelihood. In the years ahead the City reverted to the policy of seeking to regulate playing as far as possible. Thus, in 1584 the Aldermen argued vigorously for the enforcement of the existing Acts of Common Council, but there is a defeatist

29 LMA, JCC 20 (i), fos 468, 486, 502^{v}–506^{v}; BL, Add. MS 48019, fos 143–52.

30 LMA, Remembrancia II, no. 103; Chambers (1923: iv. 318). Contrast Whitney (2001: 176–7).

31 Hasler (1981: iii. 167–8).

32 TNA, PROB 11/68, fos 421^{v}–422; Archer (2006).

tone. Playing should be confined to private houses, but 'if more thought good to be tolerated', then they should observe the following restrictions: no playing on the sabbath, no playing on holidays until after evening prayer, no playing in the dark, and playing by the Queen's players only, and playing only when mortality levels have been below fifty per week for three weeks.[33] In the meantime, the Aldermen took advantage of every polemical opportunity circumstances afforded to press their case for tightened restrictions. In April 1580 an affray breaks out at the Theatre between the Earl of Oxford's Men and some Inns of Court gentlemen; the Lord Mayor writes to the Lord Chancellor denouncing plays as 'vngodlye and perilous'.[34] Another broil between Lord Berkeley's players and the gentlemen of the Inns of Court flares up in July 1581; within days the Aldermen suspend playing in the city.[35] The 'greate mysshappe' at Paris Garden on 13 January 1583 kills spectators at a bear-baiting; the Lord Mayor immediately writes to Burghley 'to give order for redresse of suche contempt of gods service'.[36] The Privy Council laments the decay of archery in July 1583; the City responds by pointing out the problems posed by all the unlawful sports tolerated in the city's environs.[37] Quarrels between servingmen and apprentices outside the Curtain in June 1584 escalate into huge riots; within days the Aldermen dispatch a delegation to the Privy Council for the pulling down of the Curtain and the Theatre.[38] Again, in June 1592, felt-makers riot in Southwark; the Lord Mayor writes to Burghley to point out that they 'assembled themselves by occasion & pretence of their meeting at a play', and the Privy Council responds with an order for the suspension of playing.[39] After plague, the order card was the most powerful one in the Lord Mayor's hands.

Another of the problems of a full-scale ban was the difficulty of getting it enforced over the playhouses in the Middlesex and Surrey suburbs. The Aldermen could regulate playing only in the city inns, which had become popular venues from the mid-1570s. So, when the Common Council decided it wanted to ban playing in 1579, it also suggested an approach to the Privy Council for action against the suburban theatres.[40] The following year Sir Nicholas Woodrofe identified for Burghley a list of 'such matters as I do lack power to redresse', including the 'hauntyng of playes out of the liberties'.[41] The Middlesex and Surrey justices are generally seen as the weak link in the machinery of regulation, 'closer to Shakespeare's Shallow and Dogberry than to Jonson's Adam Overdo' (Rutter 1984: 11), but these judgements are misleading, and have contributed rather too much to the discourses of the theatre's marginality. The metropolitan magistracy may not have been so hopelessly uncoordinated. There was in fact considerable overlap between the Middlesex and London authorities. Gaol

[33] BL, Lansdowne MS 20/12; Chambers (1923: iv. 300–2).

[34] LMA, Remembrancia I, no. 9; Chambers (1923: iv. 279–80).

[35] LMA, Remembranica I, no. 224; RCA 20, fo. 192; Chambers (1923: iv. 282–3).

[36] BL, Lansdowne MS 37, fo. 8; LMA, Remembrancia I, no. 458; Chambers (1923: iv. 292).

[37] LMA, Remembrancia I, nos 519–20; Chambers (1923: iv. 294–5).

[38] BL, Lansdowne MS 41, fo. 31; Chambers (1923: iv. 297–8).

[39] BL, Lansdowne MS 71, fo. 28; Dasent (1890–1964), xxii. 549; Chambers (1923: iv. 310–11).

[40] LMA, JCC 20, fos 505^{v}–506^{v}.

[41] LMA, Remembrancia I, nos 40–1; Chambers (1907: 40–1).

deliveries in Middlesex were taken by the Lord Mayor, Recorder, sheriffs, and senior Aldermen of London along with representatives of the central judiciary. Many Middlesex justices had strong city connections. In the 1580s the two most active Middlesex justices were in fact Humphrey Smith, the Under-Sheriff of the city, and none other than Richard Young, member of the 1579 committee and terror of recusants (Archer 1991*a*: 227, 230; 2001: 140–2). It was to Young that the Lord Mayor turned in April 1583 for action to prevent the playing of a fencing competition at the Theatre on May Eve; it was to him that Burghley wrote in November 1589 for the restraint of playing.[42] Fleetwood's letters make it clear that there was very considerable informal interaction between the metropolitan magistrates. On 4 October 1577 he dined at the Lord Mayor's along with a number of the Middlesex justices, including Barnard Randolph, the city's Common Serjeant, and John Southcot, both workhorses of the Middlesex bench, and Sir Owen Hopton, Lieutenant of the Tower, and Sir William Cordell, Master of the Rolls, both of whom took an active interest in metropolitan policing. After dinner they heard a 'brable ... for a matter at the Theater'.[43]

So, if the campaigns against the theatres faltered, it was probably as much owing to the lack of political will as to administrative failings. In 1584 in the wake of the Curtain riots the Lord Mayor secured an order from the Council for the pulling down of the Theatre and Curtain, a triumph for the hardliners. Apparently only the Lord Chamberlain and Vice-Chamberlain had opposed it; when Fleetwood tried to summon James Burbage before him, he refused to come, standing on his being a servant to Lord Hunsdon, to whom only would he answer; Burbage maintained his opposition even after the Under-Sheriff had fetched him before the Recorder, refusing to be bound over.[44] The denouement is unclear, but the playhouses were not pulled down. One suspects that the Privy Council's will was sapped once it was clear that the disorders had been quieted, and that the opponents of suppression were able to gain the upper hand once more. Given his theatrical patronage, Lord Admiral Charles Howard's position as Lord Lieutenant of Surrey from 1585, not Dogberry constables and Shallow justices, would have stymied action in Southwark thereafter (Gurr 2005: 62).

Andrew Gurr has forcefully argued that in the wake of the disruption of playing arrangements by the plague of 1592–3 and the break-up of several theatrical companies, a deal was struck with Lord Mayor Cuthbert Buckle in May 1594 by which the Lord Admiral's Men and the Lord Chamberlain's Men established a duopoly over playing, with each company having a fixed playhouse in the suburbs (the Rose and the Theatre respectively), while playing was banned in the City. Unfortunately, there is no direct evidence of a ban at this date in the city, and the argument rests on inferences, albeit powerful ones: the fact that after 1594 orders relating to playing are sent only to the Middlesex and Surrey justices, the fact that in November 1596 the

[42] LMA, Remembrancia I, no. 498; BL, Lansdowne MS 60, fo. 47; Chambers (1923: iv. 293, 305).

[43] BL, Lansdowne MS 24, fo. 196; Chambers (1923: iv. 277).

[44] BL, Landowne MS 41, fo. 3; Chambers (1923: iv. 297–8).

residents of the Blackfriars claimed that the Lord Mayor had banished playing within the city (Chambers 1923: iv. 319–20), and the fact that Hunsdon asked the Lord Mayor for permission for his company to play a winter season at the Cross Keys in October 1594, which would not have been necessary unless a ban was in force. The loss of the Privy Council minutes over a crucial period (August 1593 to October 1595) makes it difficult to be certain exactly what was going on, but Gurr suggests that the order of 3 February 1598,[45] which did refer explicitly to the duopoly, was in effect reaffirming in the face of a rival third company a decision taken four years previously. As for Hunsdon's October 1594 letter, this is ingeniously seen as an attempt to test the terms of the new agreement before the new Lord Mayor, John Spencer, a known hardliner on theatrical matters, took office at the end of the month (Gurr 2005; Whitney 2001).

This interpretation is consistent with my own sense that we need to be wary of assuming that the City was monolithic in its opposition. Gurr rightly notes the ability of individual lord mayors to set their own agendas, and the differing levels of hostility towards the theatre expressed by different lord mayors. Spencer's letter of 3 November 1594 definitely represented another ratcheting up of the anti-theatrical rhetoric, and it was typical of his abrasive personality, perhaps the most controversial Lord Mayor of the entire century, that he should have taken such a hard line within days of assuming the mayoral office. The letter was occasioned by Francis Langley's building of the Swan, but Spencer revived the call for an outright ban on all theatres, thereby seeking to undo the Buckle concordat, if such it was. Gurr implies that the recipient of Hunsdon's October 1594 letter, Lord Mayor Sir Richard Martin (who had replaced Buckle when he died in office in July), may have been more sympathetic to playing, because there is no anti-theatrical letter extant from him, but it is clear that Martin's answer, though not recorded, was no. Where my interpretation diverges from Gurr's is in the weight I have placed on ideological opposition, and I have accordingly placed Martin (on grounds as inferential as Gurr's—namely his membership of a key committee) among the hardliners. What cannot be determined at present is the degree to which Spencer's opposition had an ideological edge (he died intestate, and there seems to be no evidence either way, although the providentialist argument was more muted in his letter than in most), or whether it simply reflected his general contrariness. Spencer was a nasty piece of work: it is striking that Aldermen frequently identified each other as friends in their wills; but no Alderman dying in the 1590s wished to be associated with Spencer. Gurr may therefore be right that Hunsdon saw Martin as more biddable than Spencer; as a supplier of luxury goods to the court, Martin would surely have learned a certain courteous flexibility irrespective of his Puritan sympathies.

The City had won a victory of sorts. Possibly in 1594, and certainly by 1600, playing within the city inns had been eliminated, and this had been done with the agreement of the Privy Council. Playing in the private theatres at Blackfriars and St Paul's was permitted, but as private venues the applicability of the regulations was in doubt, and the Blackfriars theatre continued unmolested even after the incorporation of the

[45] Dasent (1890–1964), xxviii. 327; Chambers (1923: iv. 325).

Blackfriars liberty into the city's jurisdiction by King James's charter of 1608 (Gurr 1996*b*; Dillon 2000: 96–108). The City had in essence won the ban on public playing for which its hardliners had been pressing since the mid-1570s. But, as Whitney has noted, the effect of the City's continuing opposition to the suburban theatres was to 'write the city out of anything resembling a partnership in regulation' (Whitney 2001: 178). The Privy Council's regulation of the theatres now bypassed Guildhall altogether, and the subsequent development of theatres was determined more by the dynamics of the interaction of court interests with each other and with commercial forces than by the city's own priorities. The City authorities had indeed driven the players into the suburbs; they had perhaps protected themselves from the attacks of the preachers at Paul's Cross, but the theatres remained easily accessible to the citizens, a brief walk beyond the bars or a short river crossing away.

CHAPTER 24

PLAYERS, LIVERY COMPANIES, AND APPRENTICES

DAVID KATHMAN

Apprenticeship was a key feature of early modern playing companies, yet it is easily misunderstood by modern observers. Male apprentices were important because they played all the female roles on the professional English stage before 1660, but the institution also served as a training ground, with many (perhaps most) theatrical apprentices going on to become adult players. In this sense, theatrical apprenticeship was much like apprenticeship in more traditional trades, and the similarities became more notable as the professional theater became more stable and structured. In fact, many professional players were members (or freemen) of the livery companies that collectively oversaw most of the trades in London, and theatrical apprentices were often formally bound as goldsmiths, grocers, drapers, or some other trade, even when all their training was on the professional stage.

In the past, discussion of boy players and apprentices in histories of the Elizabethan stage has often been cursory, based largely on guesswork, with an underlying assumption that the details are lost to history. However, recent years have seen a tremendous increase in our understanding of apprentices in the pre-Restoration English theater, both in general terms and in terms of the lives of individual apprentices and their masters. We can now put theatrical apprenticeship more firmly in a broader social context, and can see the long-forgotten but crucial role that London livery companies played in the binding of apprentices for the stage. We now know the names of dozens of apprentices in the major adult playing companies, including most of those in the Chamberlain's/King's Men (Shakespeare's company) from the late 1590s onward; we know that these apprentices were typically bound around age 13 or 14, transitioning to male roles in their late teens or early twenties; and we have a much better idea of where they came from (both geographically and socially) and what happened to them after their apprenticeships ended.

Apprenticeship in Elizabethan England

The English apprenticeship system developed in order to formalize training in the various skilled trades, and its essentials remained the same for hundreds of years.[1] An apprentice would be bound to a master, typically living in the master's household for a specified term of years and receiving free room and board while learning the master's trade. If the apprentice served to the end of his term, he would typically be considered a member of the trade, and would become eligible to bind apprentices of his own. By the late sixteenth century, a number of laws and traditions governed relationships between masters and apprentices, and some knowledge of these traditions is necessary for a full understanding of theatrical apprenticeship.

The development of apprenticeship paralleled the development of trade guilds, more properly known in London as livery companies. The London livery companies were important because they regulated the city's major trades, but also because they controlled who could be a citizen, or 'freeman', of London, a status that involved many economic benefits. Anyone who wanted to become a citizen of London had to do so through one of the dozens of livery companies, so that such a person would necessarily be a 'citizen and grocer' or 'citizen and draper' or something similar, and was then said to be 'free of the grocers' or 'free of the drapers'. This status could come via patrimony, redemption, or servitude. Any son of a freeman could claim membership in his father's company by patrimony once he turned 21 (and paid the necessary fees), and a small number of the sufficiently wealthy and well connected could buy their freedom by redemption. The great majority of London citizens, however, gained their freedom through servitude, i.e. apprenticeship. Rappaport (1989: 292–4) estimates that 87 percent of citizens in sixteenth-century London became free through apprenticeship, with 9 percent through patrimony and 4 percent through redemption.[2]

[1] Hanawalt (1993: 129–53) has a good overview of apprenticeship in London in the fourteenth and fifteenth centuries. Archer (1991*a*: 124–40) and Rappaport (1989: 291–322) discuss the situation in sixteenth-century London, though Rappaport's account must be significantly qualified. I will use the masculine pronoun to refer to apprentices, even though it was not uncommon for girls to be bound in some trades, mainly those having to do with domestic activities such as making clothing.

[2] Until the early fourteenth century, freedom by redemption was far more common; Barron (2004: 204–20) notes that 72 percent of all freedom admissions in 1309–12 were by redemption, and describes how the crafts soon afterward forced changes that gave them much greater control over who gained the freedom of London.

While most apprentices in Elizabethan London were bound to freemen of livery companies, by no means all were. The 1562 Statute of Artificers, which codified many regulations involving trades across England, specified that any householder over the age of 24 who practiced 'any Arte Misterie or Manuell Occupacion' could bind apprentices (Statutes of the Realm 1993: iv/1. 414–22). Many 'strangers' (foreign-born craftsmen) and 'foreigners' (non-freemen from other areas of England) practiced trades and routinely bound apprentices; these apprentices would learn their master's trade, but were not eligible to become citizens at the end of their term, as apprentices bound to freemen were. Despite numerous attempts to legislate tighter restrictions on strangers and foreigners, their numbers increased dramatically in the sixteenth century, and significant numbers of them continued to bind apprentices (Archer 1991*a*: 131–40). Even so, there were still many social and economic advantages to becoming a freeman, for those able to do so.

The Statute of Artificers set some restrictions on apprenticeship that were generally enforced, notably the requirement that apprentices be bound for a minimum of seven years. In London further rules developed through long-time custom, though enforcement was often erratic, and city custom generally trumped statutory provisions when the two conflicted. Thus, while the 1562 statute specified that no apprentice could become free before the age of 24, in London the effective minimum was 21 (also the minimum age for claiming freedom by patrimony), and it was not unheard of for apprentices to become free at 20 (Kathman 2004*a*: 7). The customary minimum age for apprentices in London was 14, though here, too, the rule was broken, or at least bent, with some regularity (Kathman 2005*b*: 226–7).[3]

There were other types of service besides apprenticeship available to young people in their teens and early twenties. Most of these involved serving a master and living in his household, like an apprentice, but also receiving a regular wage, unlike most apprentices (Hanawalt 1993: 173–5). These other forms of service were generally for shorter terms, ranging from a few months to a few years, and were far less prestigious than apprenticeship, which explicitly involved training in a trade and the promise of a higher social status at the end of the term. London apprenticeships were so desirable, especially in the major livery companies, that parents would usually pay a master for the privilege of having their son or daughter bound (Hanawalt 1993: 133–4; Rappaport 1989: 306–7). The right connections were also important, so that it is common to find a London citizen binding apprentices from his home town or home county. For example, Richard Ibotson, a freeman of the Brewers who ran the Cross Keys inn in Gracechurch Street (where plays were performed in the late sixteenth century), was born in Kettlewell in Craven, Yorkshire. Between 1568 and 1578 Ibotson bound seven apprentices, two of whom were from Kettlewell in Craven, and another four of whom were from nearby towns in Yorkshire (Kathman 2005*a*: 43–4).

Once a master had agree to take on an apprentice, an indenture specifying the terms would be drawn up in two copies, one for the master and one for the

[3] In companies requiring a lot of physical labor, such as the Carpenters, it was usual for apprentices to be bound later, in their mid- to late teens (Rappaport 1989: 295–7). However, this was not the case for theatrical apprentices, as we will see later.

apprentice and his parents. A number of original apprenticeship indentures survive from the sixteenth and early seventeenth centuries, and they are remarkably uniform, both in physical appearance and in content. They are small, generally about 8 inches wide by 5 inches long when unfolded, written usually on parchment but occasionally on paper, with a wax seal hanging from the bottom edge. Some indentures are written in English, while others are in Latin. The opening always gives certain key information: the name of the apprentice, his father, and (usually) the father's occupation and home town; the name of the master and his occupation or livery company; and the length of the apprenticeship term. Following this is a description of what was expected of the apprentice and a list of prohibited activities, both of which changed very little over the years.

For example, when John Harrietsham was apprenticed to Robert Lucy as a Merchant Taylor in 1451, the indenture specified that Harrietsham was to keep his master's secrets, do him no injury, and avoid excessive waste of his goods. Harrietsham was not to commit fornication 'in or out of his master's house'; make any contract of matrimony; play at dice, tables, checkers, or 'any other unlawful games'; or frequent taverns. More than a century later, in 1583, Robert Savill apprenticed himself to John Archer, citizen and fishmonger, under an indenture containing nearly identical terms. Savill was to serve his master faithfully, fulfill the master's lawful and honest commandments, and do him no harm; he was not to waste his master's goods or lend them unlawfully; and he was not to commit fornication 'in the house of his master or without', contract matrimony, play 'at the dice or any other unlawfull game', or haunt taverns or alehouses. The language of apprenticeship indentures became so standardized that some scriveners wrote them out ahead of time, with blank spaces for the names of the apprentice and master, the length of the term, and the date. One such boilerplate indenture from 1633 includes all the major prohibitions noted above, specifying that the apprentice will keep his master's secrets, will not do damage to his master or waste the master's goods, and will not 'committ fornicacion', 'contract Matrimony', 'play at the Cardes Dice Tables or anie other unlawfull games', or 'haunt Tavernes'.[4]

Theatrical Training in Sixteenth-Century England

The apprenticeship system outlined above eventually became the framework for the system used by the professional stage in the late sixteenth and early seventeenth centuries, but only after much trial and error. In the mystery plays of the fifteenth

[4] Harrietsham's indenture from 1451 is abstracted in Hanawalt (1993: 134–5); Savill's indenture from 1583 is in the National Archives (TNA), E40/5697; the 1633 boilerplate indenture is TNA, C115/71/6510.

and early sixteenth centuries, documentary evidence shows that female roles were played by male performers, at least some of whom were probably in their late teens or early twenties (Twycross 1983; Rastall 1985: 29). To the extent that we can guess at their status, however, they appear to have been not apprentices, but servants of guild members involved with the plays. In 1496 'Ryngolds man Thomas' played Pilate's wife in a mystery play put on by the Coventry Smiths' guild, and in 1544 'rychard ye capp*er* borsleys man' played Anne in a production of the 'Purification' put on by the Weavers of Coventry (Twycross 1983: 124–5).

Our earliest concrete evidence about theatrical training by professional players also involves not apprentices, with their minimum seven-year term, but covenant servants with much shorter terms. This evidence comes from a lawsuit by George Maller, one of King Henry VIII's players, against his former servant Thomas Arthur. According to Maller, on 23 November 1528 Arthur signed a contract promising to serve Maller for one year, during which Arthur was to receive meat and drink and wages of 4*d.* a day; Maller was to teach Arthur in playing of interludes and plays, 'whereby he might attain and come to be one of the King's players' (Wickham et al. 2000: 275–7). Maller claimed that Arthur was 'right hard and dull to take any learning', and that seven weeks into the contract, Arthur 'procured three of the covenanted servants of your orator [Maller], being expert in playing', and went touring around England, earning £30 from playing. Maller claimed that this money should be his, 'by the reason of their said covenant, promise, and service', since he had 'taught the said Arthur and others'.

Another lawsuit from a half-century later shows that short-term indentures were still being used for such purposes in the 1570s. The lawsuit in question arose out of complicated litigation between James Burbage and John Brayne, who had financed and built the Theatre in 1576, and John Hind, citizen and haberdasher.[5] In 1577 Burbage and Brayne signed an indenture specifying that John Hind's two sons John and Augustine would be available to them as boy actors over a six-month period from 13 October 1577 to Low Sunday (6 April) 1578. Burbage and Brayne were to pay the senior Hind 7*s.* for each week the company was on tour, in addition to the boys' room and board, and 12*s.* for each week it was not on tour; in exchange, the boys were to be available up to twice a week, on reasonable notice, to perform in plays and other theatrical performances. The indenture also specified that the boys were expected to learn their lines in the aforesaid plays, and to play the cithern and sing on stage. They were also to receive no wages if they became ill or if the company was prevented from playing.

The Hind boys were teenagers at the time of the dispute; Augustine was christened at St George's, Botolph Lane, on 14 October 1560, and thus turned 17 on or about the indenture's start date. They must have been star-quality performers, since, as Mateer (2006: 348) points out, they were paid more than many skilled tradesmen. Yet even though both Burbage and Brayne were freemen of London (Burbage through the Joiners, Brayne through the Grocers), they did not bind the Hind boys as apprentices;

[5] This litigation is described fully in Mateer (2006), on which the following summary is based.

instead, they bound them for only six months, similar to George Maller's contract with Thomas Arthur a half-century earlier. This is not too surprising given Burbage and Brayne's perilous financial condition at the time, which put them in no position to make a long-term commitment.

However, things were changing. In 1577 there was plenty of room to doubt whether Burbage and Brayne's Theatre would ever be financially viable, but in hindsight it symbolized a turning point in the growth of the Elizabethan professional theater, after which playing became increasingly respectable—a potential path to wealth, or at least financial stability. Such stability made the idea of a theatrical apprenticeship, with its minimum seven-year commitment, increasingly viable. Adding to the attractiveness of the idea was the fact that many professional players were freemen of the City of London, and thus were able to bind apprentices in their livery companies if they so chose. This situation was made possible by the custom of London under which a freeman was allowed to practice any trade he chose, not just the one he had been trained in. This custom had always resulted in some citizens whose trades did not match the name of their company—a freeman of the Goldsmiths making a living as a grocer or a tavern keeper, for example—but such cases became much more common in the course of the sixteenth century owing to changing economic and demographic trends (Archer 1991*a*: 114–15; Rappaport 1989: 110–17). For the most part, such a freeman could formally bind apprentices in his livery company but then train them in his actual trade, or any other trade he wished; if these apprentices served out their terms and became freemen themselves, they could bind more apprentices in the same company, and so on.[6]

Some professional players had been freemen of London in the first half of the sixteenth century—George Maller, the King's player who had the dispute with Thomas Arthur, was apparently a Merchant Taylor, and John Young, a court interluder from 1539 to 1553, was free of the Mercers (Kathman 2004*a*: 34–5, 43). However, there is no evidence that they bound apprentices for theatrical purposes, and in fact the evidence we saw above suggests that Maller trained short-term covenant servants rather than apprentices. The earliest professional player whom we can specifically document binding apprentices is Richard Tarlton, the famous clown who became the star of the Queen's Men in the 1580s.[7] Tarlton served an apprenticeship as a Haberdasher, was freed in 1576, and in 1584 successfully petitioned to be translated to the Vintners, probably because of his sideline as a tavern keeper. He bound at least one apprentice in each of these companies: Phillip Woodward, bound as a Haberdasher sometime before 1582 and freed in 1589 after Tarlton's death, and

[6] To give one illustration, in the early sixteenth century, several freemen of the Drapers became printers or booksellers and trained their apprentices in those trades. By the end of the century, there were so many Drapers in the book trade that it caused major conflicts with the Stationers' Company, who forced some of these Drapers to transfer to the Stationers (G. Johnson 1988).

[7] John and Lawrence Dutton, leading players with several companies in the 1570s and 1580s, were freemen of the Weavers, but no apprenticeship records for the company survive from that time. The Duttons' sometime colleague Thomas Goughe was freed as a Barber–Surgeon in 1572 and freed an apprentice, Richard Alderson, in 1588, but that was fifteen years after the last record of him as a player (Kathman 2004*a*: 24–5, 28).

Richard Haywarde, bound as a Vintner in 1584 but never freed (Kathman 2006). Neither of these boys shows up in the scanty theatrical records of the 1580s and 1590s, but given Tarlton's status, it seems very likely that they were boy actors in the Queen's Men alongside their master.

A decade later, we find the first evidence of a professional player binding apprentices who can clearly be traced on the stage. This was John Heminges, friend of Shakespeare and co-editor of the First Folio, who was freed as a Grocer in 1587 after serving an apprenticeship under James Collins. In the 1590s, while he was a leading member of the Lord Chamberlain's Men, Heminges bound two apprentices as Grocers: Thomas Belte, bound on 12 November 1595 for a nine-year term, and Alexander Cooke, bound on 26 January 1597 for an eight-year term (Kathman 2004*a*: 8). Belte is undoubtedly the 'T. Belt' who is listed as playing a servant and Panthea (a female role) in the manuscript 'plot' of *The Second Part of the Seven Deadly Sins*. This plot has traditionally been assigned to a performance by Strange's Men in the early 1590s, but much evidence suggests that it actually belonged to the Chamberlain's Men around 1597–8 (Kathman 2004*b*). In the same plot, 'Saunder' played the major female roles of Queen Videna and Progne, and this was probably Alexander Cooke. Whether or not that assignment is correct, Cooke definitely acted with the Chamberlain's/King's Men in the early seventeenth century, and was freed as a Grocer by Heminges on 22 March 1609, five years before his death.

However, apprenticeship was not yet a universal feature of the professional theater. A recent discovery by David Mateer shows that, right around the time that Heminges was apprenticing Belte and Cooke, Edward Alleyn of the rival Admiral's Men was binding a boy to a shorter contract as a covenant servant.[8] On 26 November 1596 Richard Perkins contracted to serve Alleyn for a term of three years; this must be the Richard Perkins who later became a well-known leading man, and who was 17 years old in 1596. Perkins was thus the right age to be an apprentice, and was presumably being trained by Alleyn, but he was not a true apprentice. There is other evidence that Alleyn trained boys; John Pig, a boy player with the Admiral's Men, referred to Alleyn as his 'master' in a letter, and 'mr allens boy' played a Moorish page in *The Battle of Alcazar* for the same company (Kathman 2004*a*: 18). The exact status of these other boys is unclear; it is natural to suspect that they were non-apprentice servants like Perkins, though Pig appears to have been an Admiral's boy for at least five years, making it more likely that he was an apprentice.[9]

Soon after Alleyn bound Perkins, we find some interesting evidence in the 'diary' of Alleyn's step-father-in-law, Philip Henslowe, the owner of the Rose playhouse. On 18 December 1597 Henslowe recorded that he 'bowght my boy Jeames brystow of

[8] The relevant information is preserved in a lawsuit which Mateer described in a paper for a seminar at the 2007 Shakespeare Association of America meeting in San Diego. A version of this paper is planned for later publication.

[9] Pig's letter is undated, but probably from 1593, and Pig appears to have been still playing female roles in 1597–8 (Kathman 2005*b*: 229–30). Alleyn was apparently not a freeman of London, though his father and brother were both freemen of the Innholders, and as a householder he could have bound apprentices if he so chose.

william agusten player' for £8. Other evidence in the diary shows that Henslowe essentially rented Bristow out to the Admiral's Men, who occupied the playhouse; in 1600–1 the players owed Henslowe money for Bristow's wages, and a boy named James, probably Bristow, played various minor roles for the company (Kathman 2004*a*: 15). Henslowe had apparently bought Bristow's contract from Augustine as an investment. It is not clear whether this contract was an apprenticeship indenture, à la Heminges, or a service indenture for a shorter term, à la Alleyn. The diary shows Henslowe binding several minor adult players (hired men) as covenant servants with terms of two or three years (Henslowe 2002: 238–43, 268–9), but Henslowe was also a freeman of the Dyers, which might have made it advantageous to bind Bristow in his livery company.

Finally, some very interesting evidence about theatrical apprenticeship comes from the town accounts of Bridgwater, Somerset. In July 1597 these accounts show the town paying 26*s.* 8*d.* (2 marks) 'to the pleares [players] wth stoles sone w^{che} one of them tocke [took] prentyse' and 13*s.* 4*d.* (1 mark) 'for the pleaye the same tyme'. Here 'stoles sone' is an orphan who had become a ward of the town. The parish registers of the town suggest that the boy must have been Robert Stole, who was baptized on 9 November 1582 and thus 14 years old in July 1597, and whose mother and father had both been buried within the previous three years (Berry 1983: 74–5). We cannot easily guess the identity of the playing company, but it was probably one of the minor traveling companies rather than one of the major London ones. The important thing for our purposes is that this is an example of a boy being apprenticed to a player in the country, in Somerset, suggesting that the practice had become widespread in England by the end of the sixteenth century. This is also one of the few instances where we can see the amount of the premium paid for binding an apprentice to a player; the amount in this case suggests that such binding was at least somewhat desirable (Berry 1983: 76).

Apprenticeship and the Seventeenth-Century Stage

After the death of Queen Elizabeth in 1603, evidence about theatrical apprenticeship becomes much more plentiful, corresponding with the increasing popularity and financial stability of the professional stage. With several major playing companies active in London and some players having careers that lasted for decades, various conventions grew up around theatrical apprenticeship, and it becomes possible to describe the system in some detail.

Apprenticeship per se was only a feature of the adult professional theater, and not of the all-boy companies that thrived in the first decade of the seventeenth century (and intermittently thereafter). Boys in such companies were typically bound by indentures with terms of three years, similar to what we saw above for Edward Alleyn's binding of Richard Perkins. For example, in November 1606 Thomas Kendall, one of the leaders of the Queen's Revels boy company, bound Abel Cooke for a term of three years, with the indenture specifying that Cooke was to 'practice and exercise himself in the quality of playing, as one of the Queen's majesty's children of her Revels' (Wickham et al. 2000: 268–9; Kathman 2004*a*: 32–3). Cooke left six months into his three-year term, leading to a lawsuit through which the indenture is preserved. In 1608 the veteran player Martin Slater signed articles of agreement with the leaders of another boy company, the Children of the King's Revels, to oversee and train the boys; among the articles was one specifying that 'all the children are bound to the said Martin Slater for the term of three years' (Wickham et al. 2000: 271).

Such indentures were broadly similar to apprenticeship indentures in that they had a pedagogical component, and Slater's articles of agreement even use the word 'apprenticeship' at one point. However, these were not apprenticeships in the legal sense, since, among other things, their three-year terms were well below the seven-year minimum for true apprenticeships. Although Kendall and Slater were both freemen of London (via the Haberdashers and the Ironmongers respectively), the indentures described above were not recorded in the apprenticeship records of their companies (Kathman 2004*a*: 32–3, 38). As a result, these indentures were not governed by the rules concerning apprenticeships, including the customary minimum age of 14. The boys in the all-boy companies at the height of their popularity were often younger than that minimum, with many being 10 to 13 years old (Kathman 2005*b*: 222–3, 239).

It is possible that some players in adult companies continued to bind boys with short-term indentures in the seventeenth century, as Edward Alleyn had done, but the evidence that they did so is scant. Rather, the evidence indicates that these players bound their boys as apprentices, subject to all the customs and restrictions that entailed. Not all of these players were necessarily freemen of London, as Richard Tarlton and John Heminges were; recall that any householder above the age of 24 who practiced a trade was technically able to bind apprentices. One example of a theatrical non-freeman binding apprentices is Augustine Phillips of the Lord Chamberlain's/King's Men. Phillips is not traceable in the surviving records of any livery companies, and in his 1605 will, where status as a citizen of London was almost always declared, he calls himself a 'gentleman'. In that same will, however, he leaves bequests to 'Samuel Gilborne my Late Aprentice' and to 'Iames Sandes my Aprentice', as well as to 'my servaunte Christopher Beeson', perhaps another former apprentice (Honigmann and Brock 1993: 72–5). Samuel Gilburne was one of the actors listed in the Shakespeare First Folio, and Christopher Beeston became a prominent actor and theatrical entrepreneur until his death in 1638.

A somewhat similar example is the 1615 will of the player and theatrical sharer William Hovell. He had been apprenticed as a Brewer to Nicholas Long on 11 October 1593, but never gained his freedom, and in his will he calls himself 'gentleman'. In the will he mentions 'my apprentice Michael Bowyer' (later a prominent member of

Queen Henrietta's Men), 'my apprentice William Wilson' (who wrote to Edward Alleyn in 1617), and 'Nicholas longes somtyme my servant' (the son of Hovell's former master, later a traveling player); he also leaves to Nathaniel Clay and John Podger 'my fyfte part of my stocke of apparell and other thinges which I haue in the companie wherein they playe' (Honigmann and Brock 1993: 98–101). Of Hovell's two apprentices, Bowyer does not appear in any known livery company apprenticeship records, but Wilson had been apprenticed as a Brewer to John Sakry on 25 January 1614. This suggests that Hovell, though not free of the Brewers himself, maintained contacts in that company from his apprentice days, and was somehow able to gain control of Wilson's indenture from Sakry. Later we will see clearer examples of apprentices who were formally bound to one person but controlled by someone else, often after money changed hands.[10]

Non-freemen such as Phillips and Hovell appear to have been the exception rather than the rule, though, because most of the details we have about theatrical apprentices in the seventeenth century come from the records of the London livery companies. At least a few members of every major acting troupe were freemen of such companies, as we saw earlier with Richard Tarlton and John Heminges, and would formally bind apprentices in those companies even if they intended to train the boys entirely on the stage. The most explicit statement of how this system worked comes from a set of depositions taken on 1 February 1655, more than a dozen years after professional theater had been outlawed at the start of the English Civil War.

The lawsuit that led to these depositions, *de Caine* v. *Wintershall*, was a dispute over an £80 bond from 1624 between Richard Gunnell, the part-owner of the Fortune playhouse, and six sharers in the company that played there, including Andrew Cane. Gunnell's daughter Margaret and her husband, William Wintershall, claimed that they were owed £40 from the 30-year-old bond, but Cane, the only survivor of the original six sharers, denied this. He said that bonds such as the one in question were meant to bind the players to a given playhouse, and that the payment mentioned in the bond was a legal fiction, necessary because 'itt was held vnlawfull' for a bond to bind players explicitly to a specific playhouse. To illustrate that such legal fictions were common in the theater world, Cane's lawyers asked his witnesses about theatrical apprenticeship. Cane's former acting fellow Ellis Worth deposed that 'itt was an vsuall vsage & Custome with & Amongest the Masters & Chiefe Actors of the ffortune Playhouse . . . to take youthes & boyes to bee their Apprentices or Covenant servants', that these chief actors 'Did vsually bynde such boyes & youthes as Apprentices to themselfes or some others that were freemen of some trade or other And that such boyes and servants Did vsually Acte & play partes in Comidies and Tragidyes', even though they 'were not bound to Acte playes by Covenant in Expresse words' (Kathman 2004*a*: 5).[11]

[10] Hovell's apprenticeship is recorded in Guildhall Library, City of London, MS 5445/9 (Brewers' Court Minutes, 1590–7), and Wilson's is in Guildhall Library, MS 5445/11. Nicholas Long Jr. does not appear in the Brewers' records.

[11] The mention of 'Apprentices or Covenant servants' suggests that shorter contracts of the Alleyn–Perkins type for boy actors may have survived into the seventeenth century; however, the reference may be to hired men, who were generally bound as covenant servants, as we saw above under Philip Henslowe.

Another deponent, John Wright, testified 'that hee himselfe was bound as an Apprentice to the said partie [Cane] for A certaine number of yeares to Learne the trade of A Goldsmith, And hee sayeth that hee this Deponent Did vsually Acte & play partes in Comidyes & Tragedies in the tyme of his Apprenticeshipp and was afterwards made free of the Trade of A Goldsmith' (Kathman 2004*a*: 6). Here we have explicit testimony from a former apprentice, and all of it is confirmed by the documentary record. The Goldsmiths' apprentice book shows that Andrew Cane bound John Wright as his apprentice on 27 November 1629 for a term of eight years, and the 1632 Quarto of Shakerley Marmion's *Holland's Leaguer* shows that Wright played Milliscent in that play's first production, alongside Cane as Trimalcho. The same quarto shows another of Cane's apprentices, Arthur Savill (bound 5 August 1631) playing the gentlewoman Quartilla. Other Goldsmiths' records show that Wright was eventually freed as a Goldsmith on 13 March 1646, just as he testified. Cane bound a total of nine apprentices in the Goldsmiths between 1612 and 1654, but only Wright and Savill can definitely be traced on stage, mainly because the *Holland's Leaguer* cast list is the only one we have for any of the companies Cane acted with.

The evidence is more plentiful when we turn to the King's Men, the leading playing company from 1603 until the closing of the theaters in 1642. John Heminges was one of that company's leading members in the first three decades of the seventeenth century, and, as we saw earlier, he was a freeman of the Grocers who bound two apprentices in the 1590s (Thomas Belt and Alexander Cooke) who acted on the professional stage. Between 1607 and 1628 Heminges bound eight more apprentices as Grocers, to terms ranging from eight to twelve years. At least six of the eight are known to have acted with the King's Men (Kathman 2004*a*: 8–11).[12] George Burgh (bound 4 July 1610) was with the King's Men from 1619 to 1625, and is probably the 'Richard Birch' who played two female roles for the company around 1616. John Wilson (18 February 1611) played Balthasar in a revival of *Much Ado About Nothing*, was freed as a Grocer on 29 October 1621, and later became a well-known musician and composer. Richard Sharpe (21 February 1616) played the title role in *The Duchess of Malfi* around 1620 and adult roles for the King's Men from 1626 to his death in 1632. Thomas Holcombe (22 April 1619) played the Provost's wife in *Sir John Van Olden Barnavelt* in 1619, and Robert Pallant (9 February 1620) played Cariola in *The Duchess of Malfi* alongside Sharpe. William Trigge (20 December 1625) played numerous female roles for the King's from 1626 to 1632, and in the latter year successfully petitioned to get out of his apprenticeship indenture. In his petition to the Mayor's Court, Trigge explicitly stated that he had been apprenticed to Heminges 'pur apprendre larte d'une Stageplayer' ('to learn the art of a stageplayer'). He argued that the indenture was invalid because he had only been 13 years old at the time,

[12] Even Heminges's two apprentices who cannot be definitely traced on stage had possible theatrical connections: Nicholas Crosse (25 May 1614) may be the boy of that name who was a chorister at St Paul's in 1607, and William Patrick (10 December 1628) is probably the son of the minor actor of the same name who was with the King's Men in the 1620s. The William Patrick who appeared with the King's Men in the mid- to late 1630s may have been either father or son.

rather than the customary London minimum of 14, though his real reason for wanting to get out was undoubtedly the fact that Heminges had died in 1630.

Several other freemen in the King's Men also bound apprentices during this time, some of whom can be found in theatrical records. Robert Armin, the company's clown, had been apprenticed as a Goldsmith in 1581 but did not claim his freedom until 27 January 1604, after he had become a sharer in the King's Men. Armin bound one apprentice as a Goldsmith, James Jones, on 15 July 1608, but three years later Jones was reapprenticed to William Perry, a citizen and Draper who led various traveling playing companies (Kathman 2004*a*: 12, 18). John Heminges's apprentice Alexander Cooke was freed as a Grocer on 22 March 1609, after he had been active with the King's Men for several years, and on 28 March 1610 Cook bound an apprentice of his own, Walter Haynes (Kathman 2004*a*: 8). John Lowin, who joined the King's Men in 1603 and stayed with them for fifty years, was a freeman of the Goldsmiths like his fellow Armin. Lowin bound three apprentices as Goldsmiths: Michael Bedell (bound 24 January 1612), Thomas Jeffrey (15 April 1614), and George Varnum (9 May 1617). Of these, Bedell was probably the 'Mighell' who played a huntsman and a captain in *Sir John Van Olden Barnavelt* in 1619, and Varnum (as George 'Vernon') was a minor player with the King's Men from 1624, when his apprenticeship would have ended, to 1630 (Kathman 2004*a*: 33–4).

Most of these boys were presumably trained by the masters who bound them, but this was not always the case. Apprenticeship indentures could be bought and sold, and a master could lend or rent out his apprentices to a third party. We have already seen some possible examples: Philip Henslowe buying the contract of the boy James Bristow and renting him out to the Admiral's Men, and William Hovell keeping William Wilson as his apprentice even though Wilson had recently been bound as a Brewer to John Sakry. Henslowe had paid £8 in 1597 for Bristow's contract, but by the 1630s a talented boy was worth several times that amount. Significant evidence on this point comes from a 1635 petition by John Shank, who joined the King's Men around 1615 and was free of the Weavers. Shank wrote that he had, 'of his own purse, supplied the company for the service of his majesty with boys, as Thomas Pollard, John Thompson, deceased (for whom he paid £40), your suppliant having paid his part of £200 for other boys since his coming to the company—John Honyman, Thomas Holcombe and divers others—and at this time maintains three more for the said service' (Wickham et al. 2000: 225; Kathman 2004*a*: 37). All four of the boys named here are otherwise known to have performed with the King's Men. Pollard and Thompson were apparently apprenticed to Shank, presumably as Weavers (the company's apprenticeship records do not survive for this period). Shank had to pay £40 for the privilege of binding Thompson, who was one of the company's leading boy actors in the 1620s, and 'his part of £200' for other boys. Shank and the other company members apparently had to share the considerable cost of binding these other boys, even though one of them, Thomas Holcombe, was apprenticed to John Heminges, as we saw above.

A 1632 lawsuit over the apprentice Stephen Hammerton gives some insights into how the King's Men obtained such boys. Hammerton had originally been apprenticed to William Perry, a freeman of the Drapers and long-time leader of traveling players whom we saw above in 1611 binding Robert Armin's former apprentice James Jones. By a deed dated 15 October 1629, Perry turned Hammerton over to William Blagrave for use at the Salisbury Court playhouse, in which Blagrave was a sharer, for the remaining nine years of his apprenticeship. In the autumn of 1631 Christopher Babham allegedly stole Hammerton and his contract (which Blagrave estimated to be worth £30) for the use of the King's Men at the Blackfriars. Babham denied stealing Hammerton and said that the boy was apprenticed to William Waverley, citizen and Merchant Taylor, who was allowing him to remain with Babham (and by extension the King's Men) by his own good will (Bentley 1977).

The Merchant Taylors' records confirm that Waverley did indeed bind Hammerton as his apprentice on 5 December 1631, but Perry had apparently not bothered to register his earlier binding of Hammerton with the Drapers, since the company's records show no trace of the deal. This distinction turned out to be important, for Hammerton was allowed to remain with the King's Men, and eventually became an adult leading man with the company (Kathman 2004*a*: 13–15). This episode demonstrates one of the advantages of binding apprentices in a livery company, since such apprenticeships were recorded both by the company and by the city of London, providing backup documentation in case of disputes. The case also suggests that the King's Men were powerful enough to get virtually any boy they wanted, and that they sometimes used friendly third parties to help bind these boys.[13]

The Player and his Boy

We can sum up this survey of theatrical apprenticeship by looking at the boys themselves. Where did they come from, how old were they, and what happened to them after their apprenticeships were over? A wealth of evidence uncovered in recent years makes it possible to answer such questions more thoroughly than ever before.

Many apprentices attached to the London playing companies were London natives themselves, as one might expect. John Wright, whose testimony about his apprenticeship to Andrew Cane was discussed above, was the son of John Wright, baker, of St Giles, Cripplegate. Arthur Savill, who was apprenticed to Cane two years later and appeared in *Holland's Leaguer* alongside Wright, was the son of Cordell Savill, gentleman, of St James's, Clerkenwell, and Robert Stratford of the same cast was the son of William Stratford of St Giles, Cripplegate, a player who had been a fellow of

[13] On 6 June 1631, six months before he bound Stephen Hammerton, William Waverley bound Thomas Cockson as his apprentice, after having bound no apprentices in the previous twelve years (Guildhall Library, MS 34038/10, pp. 150, 180). The circumstances make it look as though Cockson may have been bound for similar reasons as Hammerton, though specific evidence is lacking.

Andrew Cane (Kathman 2005*b*: 224). St Giles, Cripplegate, and St James's, Clerkenwell, were both parishes where many theater people lived, so it is not surprising that numerous boy actors were born there, and in similarly theatrical parishes such as St Leonard, Shoreditch. A number of these boys, like Robert Stratford, were sons of professional players. For example, Robert Pallant, whom we saw earlier as one of John Heminges's apprentices, was the son of Robert Pallant senior, and Alexander Goughe, who played female roles for the King's Men in the 1620s, was the son of Robert Goughe. Both Pallant senior and Robert Goughe had been in the Lord Chamberlain's Men with Heminges, and their sons were both baptized in St Saviour's, Southwark, where the Globe was located (Kathman 2005*b*: 225, 233–4).

However, some theatrical apprentices, like apprentices in all trades, came from elsewhere in England. Stephen Hammerton, the subject of the dispute between Salisbury Court and the Blackfriars, was from Hellifield, Yorkshire. Thomas Belte, John Heminges's first apprentice, was apparently the son of a wait (civic musician) who had been expelled from Norwich; Thomas Holcombe, one of Heminges's later apprentices, was born in Sherbrooke, Devon. Robert Armin's apprentice James Jones was from Kreinton, Huntingdonshire, and John Lowin's apprentice George Varnum was from Langham, Cheshire (Kathman 2005*b*: 230, 233, 235; 2004*a*: 18, 34). It is interesting to note that nearly all of the London-based theatrical apprentices we can confidently identify as coming from outside London were associated with the King's Men. To some extent this is because we know more about that company's apprentices than apprentices in other companies, but it also reflects the King's Men's status as the most popular and powerful playing company in England. This status allowed them to recruit boys from all over England, sometimes after the boys had previously been bound in a minor company, as we saw with Stephen Hammerton.

How old were these theatrical apprentices? This question has often been a subject of contention, weighted down by assumptions about what would or would not have been plausible. One way to address the issue is to see how old boys were when they were apprenticed to actors who were freemen of livery companies. We saw above that William Trigge said in his petition to the Mayor's Court that he had been 13 when he was apprenticed to John Heminges of the King's Men. Of Heminges's other apprentices, Alexander Cooke and Thomas Holcombe were also 13 when they were bound; Richard Sharpe and Robert Pallant were 14; John Wilson was just short of 16; and Thomas Belte was 16.[14] We find a similar range elsewhere, with 14 the most common age. Recall that Robert Stole was 14 when the town of Bridgwater, Somerset, apprenticed him to some traveling players. John Wright and Arthur Savill were both 14 when they were bound to Andrew Cane, as was William Bartlett, a boy bound in 1630 to John Bugge, a player with the Queen of Bohemia's players who was free of the

[14] The birth dates of Cooke, Wilson, Sharpe, Holcombe, and Pallant are discussed in Kathman (2005*b*); the record of Belte's baptism was discovered by Lawrence Manley, and will be described in a future publication.

Apothecaries. William Allam and Henry Savage were 15 and 13 when they were bound to Francis Walpole, a player who was free of the Merchant Taylors.[15]

A distinct but related question is the age of actors known to have played specific female roles on the professional (adult) stage. The lower age limit found for such actors is roughly 13, corresponding closely to the typical age of binding that we just saw (Kathman 2005*b*). In the 1631 *Holland's Leaguer* cast with Andrew Cane noted above, Arthur Savill was 14, having just been apprenticed to Cane a few months earlier, and Robert Stratford was 13. (John Wright, who also played a female role in that cast, was at least 16 by then, having been apprenticed to Cane two years earlier.) Several other boys of 13 and 14 can be identified playing women on stage, including Richard Robinson in *The Second Maiden's Tragedy* (1611) and Thomas Holcombe in *Sir John Van Olden Barnavelt* (1619). None definitely younger than 13 can be identified; Alexander Goughe may have been as young as 12 when he played a concubine in *The Roman Actor* for the King's Men, but he may have been as old as 15 (Kathman 2005*b*: 232–3, 245).

At the upper end of the age range, the oldest performers playing female roles were in their early twenties. Theophilus Bird may have been as old as 22 when he played Toota in *The Fair Maid of the West* for Queen Henrietta's Men; William Trigge was 20 when he played Rosalura in *The Wild Goose-Chase*; Richard Sharpe was between 17 and 21 when he played the title role in *The Duchess of Malfi*; and John Thompson and Hugh Clarke were probably in their very early twenties when they played their last known female roles for the King's Men and Queen Henrietta's Men respectively (Kathman 2005*b*: 245). Not coincidentally, the age range for performers of female roles, roughly 13 to 22, is also the typical age range for apprentices. Not all apprentices continued to play women into their twenties; some started playing minor male roles in their late teens, and all apprentices made the transition to male roles eventually. The age of the transition no doubt depended on a given apprentice's ability to continue playing women convincingly.

Some theatrical apprentices, like apprentices in all trades, did not serve out their terms for one reason or another. Of those who did finish their terms, most stayed with the companies where they had been apprenticed. Some appear never to have advanced beyond the status of hired men; John Lowin's former apprentice George Varnum is one example. A greater number eventually became sharers; examples from the Chamberlain's/King's Men include Alexander Cooke, Nicholas Tooley, Richard Robinson, George Burghe (or Birche), and Richard Sharpe. Only a relative handful moved on to different companies. One apparent example is Christopher Beeston, Augustine Phillips's 'servant' in the Chamberlain's Men, who moved on to Worcester's/Queen Anne's Men before becoming a theatrical entrepreneur. John

[15] For Bugge and Walpole and their apprentices, see Kathman (2004*a*: 20, 41). I found the baptism records of Bartlett (20 March 1616), Allam (8 April 1600), and Savage (3 January 1609) in the International Genealogical Index, matching the fathers' names and home towns found in their binding records. Walpole's third apprentice, Edward Catesby, may be the boy of that name baptized in Westminster in October 1604, which would make him 11 when he was bound to Walpole; however, the binding record says that Catesby's father was from Hackney, making the identification uncertain.

Rice, the most important King's boy in 1607–10, was lured away in 1611 to be a sharer in the new Lady Elizabeth's company, consisting mainly of recent boy actors now in their early twenties, but he eventually returned to the King's and became a sharer there (Kathman 2005*b*: 231–2). In the late 1630s a similar company popularly called Beeston's boys also consisted mainly of former apprentices, including John Heminges's apprentice William Trigge.

All this became largely moot when the English Civil War and its aftermath closed the theaters between 1642 and 1660, causing severe financial hardships for all professional players. There was some surreptitious playing, and some players continued to bind apprentices in livery companies, notably Andrew Cane, who bound three apprentices as Goldsmiths between 1649 and 1654 (Kathman 2004*a*: 22; Astington 2003*a*). Cane was a working goldsmith during these years, but he also took part in underground playing, so it is possible that some of his apprentices may have appeared on stage. John Rhodes, a citizen and Draper with some minor theatrical experience before the war, bound four apprentices in the 1650s; two of them, Edward Kynaston and Edward Angell, played female roles when the theaters officially reopened, and Kynaston went on to become a famous male actor (Kathman 2004*a*: 43–6).

However, the introduction of actresses soon after the reopening of the theaters made apprentices unnecessary for female roles. The elaborate apprenticeship system of the pre-war theater never fully returned after the Restoration, and was soon largely forgotten. While the knowledge that boys played women in the pre-Restoration theater was never lost, only in the early twenty-first century have most of the details been rediscovered, including the identities of many theatrical apprentices. Given their importance for the original theater of Marlowe, Shakespeare, and Jonson, it is fitting that these boys can now receive some of the recognition they deserve.

CHAPTER 25

MATERIALITY AND THE MARKET: THE LADY ELIZABETH'S MEN AND THE CHALLENGE OF THEATRE HISTORY

KATHLEEN E. MCLUSKIE

I

Shakespeare in Love has a lot to answer for. The opening scene of the film in which the angry entrepreneur roasts the feet of a defaulting debtor offers a wonderfully comic account of a founding myth of capitalism: the myth of a direct relationship between a man and his money. In that scene, the terrifying complexity of modern economic relations, hedge funds, sub-prime mortgages, and commodity bargaining is swept aside in a fond, imaginary return to a time when debt was not tolerated, private property was sacrosanct, and the tedious regulating state was represented only by the charming autocracy of Judi Dench as Queen Elizabeth.

To be sure, there were negative sides to that version of the past. The streets were not very clean, the Queen's court was full of spies, fathers were intolerant of their daughters' disobedience in emotional matters, but with a little good will all this could be resolved. In this robust market, more primitive accumulation than capitalism, there was, of course, room for art. Shakespeare could be tolerated and even successful because he spoke to the people who paid their pennies to hear his poetry. 'Ethel the Pirate's daughter' could be seamlessly transformed into *Romeo and Juliet* driven by the inspiring power of true love.

The film offers a satisfying synergy between the image of the young Shakespeare, 'biting his truand pen', scattering ink and manuscript around a sunlit garret, and the weeping or laughing audience, including the Queen, united in appreciation of the performance on stage. The smooth transfer from the poet's imagination to the audience's pleasure is untrammelled by the mediating role of organizations and their financiers, who are represented only by the colourful arrival of the players in the town (more the players in Hamlet than the Chamberlain's Men), and the intransigent entrepreneur, whose rapacious drive for profit (or at least his money back) could be won over with a bit part in the magic of theatre.

The continuing appeal of this myth of the commercial theatre is that it provides a single coherent and reified image of how it was and how it must have been for everyone. It has informed discussion of the economics of theatre since the early twentieth century (Ingram 1992), it has allowed the imagined audience of Shakespeare's theatre to be the touchstone against which the commercial arts from movies to the Internet were measured and found wanting, and it is the informing principle of state subsidy of the arts (at least in the UK) as it lurches uneasily from the values of what arts policy-makers call 'artistic excellence' (currently meaning innovation) to the democratic imperatives of 'access for all' (currently defined as multicultural youth and state-educated children).[1] If the plays of Shakespeare could have united Queen and people, they might also be used to enhance social cohesion in the modern world, and if the market in plays could have been managed by Shakespeare's company, then theatre might also find a place in a regulated modern artistic economy.

This conflation of the early modern theatrical repertory and the material conditions of theatrical production has been recently contested in detail by Leeds Barroll's carefully argued case for a 'Shakespeare without King James' (Barroll 1991). His suggestion that the King's Men's change of title has more to do with court politics than a royal taste for the drama, or that the players were at Wilton with the King of Denmark in 1604, not to perform a play, but to act as attendant servants, opens an important gap between the aesthetic qualities or topical significance of the company's repertory and their significance in early modern culture. The separation between playing companies and influence at court is further extended in Susan Cerasano's suggestion that Henslowe's theatre interests may have been an instrument of his more immediate concerns over courtly support for his brother's iron-mining activity in Sussex or his own aspiration to act as regulator of the wool trade in Essex and Kent (Cerasano 2005*b*: 337).

The effect of this separation between theatrical commerce and the theatre repertory has serious implications for the history that informs our readings of early modern drama. Theatre history has, for the most part, been used to establish the

[1] See 'Our Agenda for the Arts' at <http://www.artscouncil.org.uk>.

framework within which to place literary analysis of the plays' manifest content and to provide the route into the plays' contemporary significance. Literary accounts of thematic attention to contemporary politics seem to be historically endorsed by the connection between a company and its assumed court patronage (Orgel 1999), while the representation of the market in plays' narratives is routinely connected to the market for plays in the life-world of early modern England (McLuskie 1996).

These readings of play-texts often produce an elegant and persuasive synergy between literary and theatre history, closing the often troubling and frustrating gaps in our knowledge of the day-to-day operations of a theatre company and the even more elusive evidence of the reception of early modern drama. However, these historicist readings obscure the essential relationships between playing companies, playwrights, and their plays in two important respects. By insisting that the circuit of commercial activity centred on the theatre they disguise the significance of print in ensuring the longevity of a particular repertory (and its availability for literary analysis), and by continuing to use Shakespeare and the Chamberlain's/King's Men as the default model they obscure the very particular combination of resources, personnel, and luck that produced the most commercially successful and, fortuitously, the most artistically successful company that dominated the theatrical scene from the 1590s to the closing of the theatres.

Recent work by Lukas Erne and others has begun to drive a wedge between the ideas of the playwright as dramatist and the playwright as writer of printed texts, and it is some years since Rosalyn Knutson first pointed out the interesting correlation between the printing of Chamberlain's Men quartos and the evidence for revival of their plays in a maturing repertory.[2] The implications of that work are extremely significant in that they draw the commerce of print into the commerce of theatre and reinforce the attention on the extant plays. Printed play-texts can stand in for the material objects that passed from stage to page, and the extant repertory can thus establish comfortable boundaries for the discussion of the early modern drama as a historical phenomenon.

These boundaries, of course, marginalize a number of key players: the companies whose activity crosses the borders between the city, the country, and the court, the plays whose print history cannot be easily mapped onto performance by a single company, and the dramatists whose eclectic, and often collaborative, output suggests a more opportunist, not to say chaotic, relationship to the regulated market. These outliers among companies, plays, and dramatists are hardly insignificant. As the work of the Records of Early English Drama (REED) investigators has identified, a significant proportion of theatrical activity in early modern England took place outside London and much of it involved plays whose titles are unknown (Knutson 2006). While the plays, such as those of Shakespeare and Jonson, that moved relatively smoothly from performance to print might define a market in which the product was managed for literary self-fashioning or company commerce, the 'lost' plays, the plays that were printed more than ten years after the record of their first

[2] See Erne (2003); Brooks (2000); Lesser (2004); Knutson (1991).

performance, and the plays that changed company ownership suggest that the stable economic institution (Cerasano 2005*a*) of London-based theatre that may have underpinned the major companies in the 1590s had gained only a tenuous and preliminary hold on the means of production, consumption, distribution, and exchange in the early modern theatrical market.

Focusing on the outliers rather than the dominant model does not completely overturn the emerging patterned connection between company, play-text, and dramatist. It might, however, insert a small wedge into the assumed connection between the practices of a particular couple of playing companies and the grand narrative of market forces. It might alert us to the difficult struggle that entry into the market presented to companies, and the fundamental dissonance between plays as commodities and plays as literary objects. By paying attention to a company that worked in both the metropolis and the provinces and whose repertory (both known and lost) was claimed by different playing companies we might perceive and understand one point of pressure on the market model that dominates the current history of the early modern stage.

II

It may seem perverse to take the Lady Elizabeth's Men as a case study for the development of drama and theatre in the first half of the seventeenth century. The company is accorded less than a whole chapter in Professor Andrew Gurr's magisterial summary of existing knowledge of the Shakespearean playing companies (Gurr 1996*b*), largely because their fortunes as a company—or at least the existing evidence of those fortunes—seem impenetrably entangled with those of Prince Charles's Men, the children of the Queen's Revels, and the later companies managed by Christopher Beeston. The purpose of this chapter is less to identify the full range of their activities than to use them as an example of how the evidence from some of their plays and playing, both well known and lost, illustrate the complex relationships of patronage and commerce, service and entertainment, that characterized the activity of playing companies other than the King's Men in the early years of the seventeenth century.

The Lady Elizabeth's Men were formally constituted as a company by a patent of 1611 that allowed them to perform 'In and about our Cittie of London in such usuall howses as themselves shall prouide. And also within anie Towne halles, moote-halles, Guyld-halles, School howses or other convenient place...' (Chambers 1923: ii. 246–7). This licence to perform, however, indicates the key problem for playing companies: that of finding a venue in which to perform. The Admiral's/King's Men had been unusual and lucky in having family and kin relations underpinning the initial connection between company and theatre and then having a sufficiently established group able and willing to stump up the cash for the new organization that built the

Globe and bought the Blackfriars, thus releasing the players from the continual headache of finding somewhere in London to play. For other companies the link between playing and a place to play involved a mix of travelling in the provinces, performance at court, and negotiating a relationship with an owner of a theatre building to use their space. In other words, the innovation that drove the theatre business in late sixteenth- and early seventeenth-century London was less a matter of charging punters to see a show than a more complex business of finding somewhere to play, acquiring the plays and other necessities for putting on performances, and, in some cases, an eventual relationship with printers that made the plays available for the public (and for posterity).

None of this proved simple for the Lady Elizabeth's Men. In 1611 two of their company, John Townsend and Joseph Moore, entered into a bond with Henslowe that may have assured him of their commitment to his theatre spaces.[3] By 1613 they were in dispute with him over the terms of the bond that dealt with the employment of hired men, the payment for court performance, the company's stock of costumes, and their playbooks. The amalgamation between the Lady Elizabeth's Men and the Children of the Queen's Revels had provided them with new performers in the fast-growing child actors, together with a new repertory of the children's company plays. This entrepreneurial initiative may have given the Lady Elizabeth's Men more resources and the potential for a wider range of theatrical activity,[4] but for the writers of the Articles of Grievance against Henslowe it amounted to 'the breaking of our Companie'.

The fluidity of the group of people who at different times were associated with the Lady Elizabeth's Men demonstrates how shaky an entity a 'company' could be as they appear in court and country records. Far from being a self-regulating business of coherent 'capitalist' companies, the margins of theatrical enterprise are shot through with individuals on the make, looking, often without any systematic business case, to gain a marginal advantage and short-term financial gain from this highly volatile business. Underneath the macro regulation by the Privy Council and the city authorities was a much more hand-to-mouth business characterized by low levels of investment and considerable instability for the individuals involved.

None of this instability is evident from the content of the plays that are associated with their repertory. Indeed, many of the plays that they performed included confident addresses to a putative audience that invited them to attend to the plays' ideas and pleasures in ways that distanced them from the commercial activity that made them possible. The most celebrated of these, Ben Jonson's *Bartholomew Fair*, begins with an Induction that presents a literary manifesto for innovation, together with a critique of a reductive commercialization of literary judgement. The play itself

[3] Gurr suggests that this bond may have been for 'for loans to help the company purchase plays and other properties', but the closest analogy to this bond is the one that Henslowe insisted on when he took the Admiral's Men's players back after the debacle over Langley's investment in the Swan Theatre (Gurr 1996*b*: 295). See Ingram (1978: 17).

[4] See Alfred Harbage's speculation that Henslowe was intending to set up a double-venue company at Whitefriars and the Hope to compete with the King's Men at the Globe and Blackfriars (Harbage 1952: 27).

satirizes, among other things, the replacement of social values by, on the one hand, those of the market and, on the other, the regulatory impulses of the new middling sort, represented by the puritan Zeal of the Land Busy. The theatre itself is represented as the action ends with a parodic performance of a romance narrative that offers a defence of puppet shows against fundamentalist religious provincialism. The play gathers together all the participants in the fair and becomes, in the finale, an occasion for communal feasting that will transcend the intolerant and incompetent regulation of social life. Jonson's play seems to offer a perfect fit between the preoccupations of the play, its author's management of audience expectations, and the large themes of patronage and commerce that inform current scholarly analysis of the cultural contexts of playing.

As everyone also knows, the play was also presented before the King. It is not known whether the King's performance was begun with the Induction. The references to the bears and the stinking nature of the Hope theatre might have seemed less relevant in Whitehall. What the text of the play does offer is the elegant 'Prologue to the King's Majesty', which offers him 'for a fairing true delight', the fantasy that the players had brought him to the pre-commercial market of honest barter in primary goods. A clearer representation of the world of *Shakespeare in Love* is hard to imagine. King and commoner engaged in the same theatre world, sharing the denunciation of puritanical meddling and the market values that go with it.

What is less often discussed, because Jonson's play makes no mention of it, is the fact that this season at court included, alongside *Bartholomew Fair*, eight unnamed plays by the King's Men, three unnamed plays by the Queen's Men, and two by the Elector Palatine's Men, as well as plays provided by the Revels Office for the King's entertainment at Cambridge (Streitberger 1986: 68). Jonson's *Bartholomew Fair*, which seemed so aptly to sound to present occasions, was only one in a season. The Lady Elizabeth's Men were in competition with other companies and may have needed Henslowe's help in getting a place in the court season.[5] The court audience too had alternative distractions of other plays that might have got in the way of a full appreciation of any connection between the play's message and the current political issue surrounding James's handling of the Puritan opposition via the *Book of Sports*.[6] Whether being teased at the Hope theatre with a reminder of the commercial terms of their entertainment or being welcomed to the court as part of a more exclusive event, the audience addressed by the Prologue and Epilogue of Jonson's play remains both elusive (we never know of the existence of more than one or two people attending any particular early modern performance) and overdetermined in that scholars use the Prologue and the Epilogue to reinforce pre-existing but contradictory assumptions about the relations between the public and the performance. The richness of the text of *Bartholomew Fair* allows us to posit two different kinds of public: one resolutely commercial and the other participants in an occasion constructed by the social relations of courtly patronage.

[5] See the item in the Articles of Grievance that refers to the company's resentment that Henslowe had pocketed 'the profit of a warraunt of tenn pounds due to us at Court' (Chambers 1923: ii. 250).

[6] Suggested in, for example, Leah Marcus's subtle reading of the play and its politics (Marcus 1995).

Yet both of these constructions of the theatrical public are a function of the play's textual strategies. As Robert Weimann has reminded us: 'the political economy of the early modern market was... intercepted or mentally anticipated in a discursive practice that felt *authorised* by itself to reorder its own procedure, its aims and strategies' (Weimann 1996: 14). Playwrights, in other words, were exercising their own interest in the commerce of playing, establishing their role as arbiter of taste, setting the terms of the plays' reception, and, in the case of Ben Jonson, managing the plays' publication so that their version of events and relationships dominates the view of posterity.[7] The supply side of the business of playing, producing plays, providing a venue whether in a theatre or at court, was subsumed in the playwright's prologues and epilogues into a discussion of taste and differentiated audiences. In the face of the instability of the supply side, the writers created an illusory demand side with which the supply of plays could be managed.

That management of the demand side of the playing business may have been especially necessary for the writers who found themselves working for the innovative and unstable end of the business. The innovative, sexually explicit, and satirical drama that had characterized the repertory of the boy player companies may well have been designed, as Richard Dutton has suggested, to create a new audience that could see itself as 'young male, affluent, witty, educated, morally relaxed'.[8] However, the plays were also the resources whose ownership had been the subject of conflict between Henslowe and the Lady Elizabeth's Men. Court and printing records connect the company to some of the most interesting plays of the period, including the court revival of *Eastward Ho*, *A Chaste Maid in Cheapside* (if the extant text, not printed until 1630, is to be believed), and *The Dutch Courtesan*. Once this repertory moved to the Lady Elizabeth's Men, the link between text, company, performance, and public is harder to trace.

Following their patent being issued, the Lady Elizabeth's Men had a few good seasons at court: their performance of *Bartholomew Fair* in 1614 was their solitary show, compared with the four plays they presented in 1611, soon after their patent was approved. In 1612 they had three and in 1613, two, including a revival of *Eastward Ho* that did not seem to arouse any of the outrage that it had caused in 1605 (Streitberger 1986). Their next major season at court, from 1622 to 1625, shows them using the same pool of dramatists as the King's Men, including revivals of plays written by Beaumont and Fletcher, Davenport, Dekker, Heywood, Massinger, Middleton and Rowley, and Shirley. However, before we construct their repertory as an alternative to the rival tradition of the King's Men, we should also be aware that many of their court performances also involved unnamed plays, and on the rare occasions that they were

[7] *Bartholomew Fair* was not published until the second Folio of Jonson's *Works* in 1640, some fifteen years after it was seen on stage at the Hope and the court. The Folio includes a title page from an earlier printing 'for Richard Meighen', which suggests that the transfer from stage to print was complicated by the print market of the 1630s.

[8] Tracking the complex repertory and connection of the company that took over the Whitefriar's theatre in 1609, Richard Dutton uses the test case of *Epicene* and finds that 'This most misogynist of plays seems to identify the target audience of this new company' (Dutton 2002: 350).

named, they included *Raymond Duke of Lyons* at Shrovetide in 1612/13 as well as the performance of the better-known *The Dutch Courtesan* in February and November 1613. *The Dutch Courtesan* was listed as *Cockledemoy*, suggesting, as in one or two other cases, that the sub-plot, in this case involving Mulligrub the trickster, might have been more memorable than the central action.

The mix of new plays and revivals that seems to have constituted the Lady Elizabeth's Men's repertory is not unusual. The company's commercial existence, as the Articles of Grievance had shown, depended on performing the plays to which they had access wherever they could. Any further political or ideological connection between the plays' content and the supposed audience must have been a secondary matter. The company, moreover, seems to have been eclectic in taking up opportunities for paid work wherever they could, playing to a variety of different constituencies. The commercial nature of the theatre companies was signalled as much by their trade in drama through revivals and their transfer of plays from one venue to another as in the provision of an entertainment service that tied the play to the particular public.

III

The transferability of plays, the sense that they could be offered to quite distinct publics, also presents an important angle on the Lady Elizabeth's Men's active role in the provincial drama that is accumulating as the REED volumes and their ancillary commentary have emerged. The editors of the REED volumes have long since laid to rest the metropolitan prejudice that trailing round the country with their pumps full of gravel was a last resort for a failing company. The records of the Lady Elizabeth's Men on the touring circuit presents an intriguing picture of a company making the most of the opportunities offered outside London, which included a variety of different business models for the company's fortunes. In 1613, between the court season, in which they presented *Eastward Ho*, and the 1614 one, when they presented *Bartholomew Fair*, they were in Canterbury, accompanying the Lady Elizabeth on what might have been a marriage progress. On that occasion, they were paid 10*s*. by the City Chamberlain but there was no indication that they performed a play (Gibson 2002: 262). The sum of money may have been a generous tip—part of the costs of entertaining the royal visitor and her retinue. Part of the playing company's role on that occasion may, quite literally, have been as the Lady Elizabeth's servants.[9]

The sense that the company's court performance involved them in further commercial opportunities may also have lain behind the note that the Lady Elizabeth's

[9] Their position in the Princess's retinue may also have boosted the company's standing in Kent since they visited Canterbury every year from 1611 to 1624–5 (apart from 1614–15), earning an average of 20*s*. a time (though there were eleven other companies working the Kent circuit, to whom courtly patronage does not apply).

Men presented three unnamed plays before the King on his journey to Scotland in March 1617 (Streitberger 1986: 75; Cook and Wilson 1961: 62). The job for the King was part of a bundle of engagements that year and may not have required them to remain in his retinue all the way. As Barbara Palmer's work has shown (Palmer 2005), they had regular dates at the Clifford country seats in the north of England and stayed on to play for ten days in Doncaster from 4 to 14 April 1617. It is perhaps worth noting that the Doncaster authorities paid them 20*s*., the Clifford household seem to have offered regular payments of £2 per play, while the Office of the Revels forked out £30 (Cook and Wilson 1961: 62).

There is no space in this essay to track the implications of all the different venues and sums of money earned by the Lady Elizabeth's Men in the country—that is, for a new phase of work made possible by the REED project. The accumulating evidence, however, suggests that the firm links between authors, plays, companies, and printed texts was, by the early years of the seventeenth century, beginning to be complicated by entrepreneurial (and possibly illegal) activity on the part of assorted companies, together with the circulation and reperformance of some printed texts by groups who may have been ad hoc and opportunist. The Clifford family, for example, paid a 'certeyn company of Roughish players' who had played *The Knight of the Burning Pestle* and *New Way to Pay Old Debts* in Skipton Castle at Shrovetide in 1635–6 (Palmer 2005: 277). *The Knight of the Burning Pestle* had recently been revived at the Cockpit in London by Queen Henrietta's Men (who had taken over many of the Lady Elizabeth's Men's plays) (Gurr 1996*b*: 432). It was played at court in the 1635–6 season and had been reprinted in 1635. The 'Roughish players' may have been a residue of the Queen's Revels company, who first performed the play at Blackfriars in the first decade of the century. A company calling themselves the Children of the Queen's Revels was performing in Doncaster in 1615; they may also have been associated with the Lady Elizabeth's Men, who had acquired the Queen's Revels repertory when they merged, or they may have acquired the play from a member of Queen Henrietta's Men. Equally, they could have acquired a printed copy and put together a performance from scratch. The market in plays, in other words, involved not only the financial underpinnings of companies by entrepreneurs, but the entry of a number of different kinds of players (in the entrepreneurial as well as the theatrical sense) into the entertainment market. When, unusually, the records reveal the titles of the plays presented, it is tempting to over-read the religious or political significance of the event in terms of what we know of the developing ideological conflicts of the seventeenth century, but from the perspective of a playing company, a play may have been more significant as the necessary resource needed to continue playing.

Equally intriguing is the evidence that the entertainment was following other luxury trades in creating commercial relations between London and the provinces. Barbara Palmer has noted that 'The Cliffords seem to have heard their London plays at court; no payments for public theatre play-going have been found to date' (Palmer 2005: 278). A similar question about how London-based companies were connected to their provincial patrons is raised by another record that may refer to the Lady Elizabeth's Men. In April 1620 Thomas Puckering, of the Priory House in Warwick, paid to see a play in London. The following Christmas season he records a payment of 20*s.* to 'lord Dudley his players for playing a play in my house this night', and on 11 January he records that on 6 January (Twelfth Night) he had paid 22*s.* 'to the Queene of Bohemia's Players, playing that night at my house' (Werstine 2006: 112). The Queen of Bohemia was, of course, the Lady Elizabeth's name after her marriage to the Elector Palatine in 1613 but the connection between the Queen of Bohemia's players and the Lady Elizabeth's Men may be more complex. As Andrew Gurr has pointed out (Gurr 1996*b*: 400–6), their fortunes as a metropolitan playing company not only were tied to Prince Charles's Men but also seem to have been influenced by the new theatrical entrepreneurs Jacob Meade and Christopher Beeston.

Nonetheless, this example of provincial playing is particularly interesting, not only because of the company who played but also because of the rare existence of ancillary evidence about the significance of playing that is separate from the content of the unknown play that they performed. Puckering's account book, from which this entry is taken, shows that he bought more in London than plays. As Catherine Richardson has described,

> Puckering lodged with a cutler in The Strand between January and April, purchasing tiles for his banqueting house, but also sugar, spice, fruit, soap, sturgeon, Westphalia bacon, anchovies, Bologna sausages and starch. From London to Warwick went melons, a china-work fruit table, two tin watering pots for the garden, painting materials for the banqueting house, a featherbed tick and bolster, reams of paper, Dutch lights, three wroughtwork purses for Puckering's nieces and nephews and 'weekly collections of the news from diverse foreign parts' from Mr Hoevenaer the Dutch merchant. (Richardson 2008)

If we relied entirely on the drama to read this character, he would appear like a cross between Bartholomew Cokes and the clown with the shopping list in *The Winter's Tale*. Puckering, however, was no provincial simpleton, He had been educated at the Middle Temple and was for some years a companion to Henry, Prince of Wales, before completing his education in Paris (Matthew and Harrison 2004). He entered Lincoln's Inn in 1621 and sat as MP for Staffordshire as well as, later, for Warwick. He was much more typical of the country gentry like Edward Dering, who bought play-texts and had at least one reworked for performance at his house in Kent (Williams and Blakemore 1974; Yeandle 1986). These provincial gentry sat in Parliament and on the bench in their region, took part in civic ceremonial, welcomed the circuit judges to the town, and, insofar as they engaged in politics, were bitterly divided by the tumults of the Reformation and the Civil War. Attending plays was not an especially significant part of either their total costs or their time. However, buying a play performance, like the other luxury goods, from London did provide an opportunity for display and hospitality, an ability to make the kind of statement about status and community that historians of material culture have shown to be so significant in the period. Whether Puckering got the play from Lord Dudley's players or from the Queen of Bohemia's Men in London may not have made much difference. The Queen of Bohemia's Men was given the prime Twelfth Night slot, but they were paid the same sum as Lord Dudley's players.

What is most frustrating for the literary critic is, of course, that we have no idea what Puckering and his guests might have thought about the play or even which play it was. The repertory of the Lady Elizabeth's Men is a matter for debate as the plays were traded over by Daborne and Henslowe, Meade and Beeston. Scholars differ over the allocation of the contested playbooks to companies that included the Palsgrave's Men and Prince Charles's Men, and there is even debate about whether the Lady Elizabeth's Men was the same company in the country and the court. The circulation of plays from Lady Elizabeth's to the succeeding companies and the availability of plays in print for other groups to perform suggest that the hermeneutic endeavour that connects a play such as *Bartholomew Fair* to its conditions of early performance may, in this case, be misplaced. The content of the play may not have been as significant as we might wish it to be since it was the event, the coming together of a significant provincial figure and his clients, that mattered.

This is not to suggest that the event was without artistic appreciation. Nathaniel Tomkyns's commentary on his visit to the London performance of *The Late Lancashire Witches* (Berry 1984; McLuskie 2006), the French tutor's account of the performance of *Titus Andronicus* at Sir John Harington's country seat at Burleigh on the Hill (Ungerer 1961), Lady Southwell's letter on some books sent from London (Cavanaugh 1984), or Joyce Jeffries' payment for 'pamphilletts', including one on the death of Ben Jonson (Klauser 1990), all show provincial gentry to be sophisticated, if conventional, in their reading of the literary material that they had at their disposal. What is more important for our understanding of the development of a commercial theatre is that these provincial people were buying these artistic goods from an existing metropolitan market rather than making them at home. The performance at Warwick Priory, though it can be characterized as a patronage event, was fully commercial, and the play involved had been traded as much as the raisins and wine that might have accompanied it.

We cannot, of course, leap from this example to any kind of generalization about the commodification of drama in the early modern period. The plays presented by the Lady Elizabeth's Men, in common with those of other companies, did not attract the same fee in every location, and those fees ranged from the 2 guineas paid by Thomas Puckering to the £30 paid by the King on his journey to the north. All we can note at this stage was that the drama provided a significant opportunity for Puckering to create a local event that displayed his cosmopolitan taste and his connection to the world of London and the court. In the absence of a text, the event of the performance must come into prominence, with the social and regional significance taking precedence over the content of the play.

Alan Somerset's wonderful maps of touring routes, which are tracing the country as the REED evidence begins to cover more and more of England, are making clear that these routes seem to have been directed as much by the opportunities provided by performances in country houses as by the opportunities for provincial audiences in county towns.[10] What we can tentatively ask is whether the practice of bringing

[10] To be found on the REED web site, <http://www.reed.utoronto.ca>. Compare P. Davidson (2000); see also Somerset (1999).

London plays to the country seems to have been on the increase and to be supplanting home-grown products, or indeed the more locally focused games and revels that linked the country communities in seasonal festivity. Plays by London companies were in a market, but the market relations in which they operated were varied according to location and occasion. The anxious efforts of Ben Jonson and others to insist on a direct relationship between the costs paid and the right to judgement could not function in early modern culture once the plays had been removed from their original moment of production. The multiple publics at the Hope, the Swan, the royal court in both London and the provinces, and in the county towns and country seats may have made different uses of the plays they attended. And the interests of playing companies, playwrights, and playhouse owners were not the same, as the market in plays pulled each of them in different directions. The London playwrights might have tried to cultivate sophisticated metropolitan taste in the short term but once the Lady Elizabeth's Men secured the repertory, they took their chances and performed them where they might. In doing so, they might have spread the taste for sophisticated forms of narrative drama and contributed to the decline of the more communal festive forms fantasized in the endings of both *Bartholomew Fair* and *Shakespeare in Love.*

At this stage of the research on the full story of early modern theatre in London and the provinces, even that conclusion seems dangerously teleological. We might recognize instead that the market for plays was meeting a variety of different needs. It was necessary to sustain the playing companies who traded in it, and it provided material for different kinds of social and commercial event in different venues. Understanding the social relations that surrounded those events should make us more sceptical about interpretations of dramatic texts from the perspective of an audience and pay more attention to the social relations that were embedded in the deeper changes taking place in the patronage and commerce of early modern England.

CHAPTER 26

'FOR THE AUTHOR'S CREDIT': ISSUES OF AUTHORSHIP IN ENGLISH RENAISSANCE DRAMA

HEATHER HIRSCHFELD

DURING the course of the elaborate meta-theatrics that constitute the fourth act of Thomas Kyd's *The Spanish Tragedy*, the protagonist, Hieronimo, whose tragic play is to be performed before the court, 'knocks up the curtain' (IV. i, s.d.).[1] The Duke of Castile observes the exertions, which he takes to be unusual, and questions Hieronimo. 'Where's your fellows | That you take all this pain?' he asks. Hieronimo's reply suggests that he is prepared to take upon himself a number of responsibilities in addition to the scripting, assigning, and learning of parts with which he has already been occupied: 'O sir, it is for the author's credit | To look that all things may go well,' he says (IV. iii. 1–2, 3–4).

[1] References to *The Spanish Tragedy* are from J. R. Mulryne's 2nd edn (New York: A & C Black, 1989).

Hieronimo, knight marshal to the Spanish king, works on plays only for special occasions and for special audiences. But his association of certain burdens (as well as potential benefits) with being an 'author' bespeaks a more widespread effort by participants in and watchers of the early modern drama to define and assess, as well as to shape, the meaning and value of writing for the stage. Hieronimo's interest in identifying the author and his worth is evident, for instance, in the writing of Francis Meres, who judges contemporary playwrights against classical forebears in a form of nationalist praise:

As these Tragicke Poets flourished in Greece, Aeschylus, Euripedes, Sophocles... and these among the Latines, Accius, M. Atilius, Pompon[i]us Secundus, and Seneca: so these are our best for Tragedie, The Lorde of Buckhurst, Doctor Leg of Cambridge, Doctor Edes of Oxford, Master Edward Ferris, the author of the *Mirror for Magistrates*, Marlow, Peele, Watson, Kid, Shakespeare, Drayton, Chapman, Decker, and Beniamin Iohnson.... the best for Comedy amongst vs bee Edward Earle of Oxforde, Doctor Gager of Oxforde, Master Rowley... Maister Edwardes... eloquent and wittie Iohn Lilly, Lodge, Gascoyne, Greene, Shakespeare, Thomas Nash, Thomas Heywood, Anthony Mundye, our best plotter, Chapman, Porter, Wilson, Hathway, and Henry Chettle. (Meres, in G. Smith 1904: ii. 319–20)

Meres's impulse to evaluate is echoed, though much more negatively, in the writing of anti-theatricalists such as Anthony Munday (himself ironically listed as Meres's best plotter!), who complained in 1580 that writers for the stage had been 'so led awaie with vaineglorie, that their onlie endeuor is to pleasure the humor of men; & rather with vanitie to content their mindes, than to profit them with good ensample' (Munday 1580: 104). These Elizabethan commentaries remind us that in the early modern period the role of dramatist was a site of ideological negotiation for playwrights and cultural commentators alike; they assumed neither a single definition nor a simple explanation of what the dramatist did and why.

The same is true at the start of the twenty-first century. Contemporary scholarship, spurred by insights gleaned from literary theory as well as from the archive, has begun to take account of the multiple meanings and functions of Renaissance dramatic authorship, complicating earlier assumptions about the playwright and his relation to scripts both on stage and in print. The dominant effect of this kind of criticism has been to explain the role of the dramatist as a social or discursive construct embedded in particular historical conditions and disciplinary needs. In the essay that follows, I discuss a number of those conditions and needs as they have been elaborated in recent scholarship. Such contexts reinforce a growing sense that the development of the dramatist as a literary and cultural figure was intimately linked to the rapid emergence and institutionalization of the public theater in the late sixteenth and early seventeenth centuries. The end of the essay thus argues that in such a climate—what Pierre Bourdieu has theorized as a 'cultural field'—playwrights became increasingly aware of and concerned with the ways in which their work might redound to what Hieronimo calls the 'author's credit': to financial reward but also to gains in professional reputation and status.

Studies of the early modern drama, starting perhaps with Coleridge's essays on Shakespeare, have depended upon certain standard notions of the playwright and his relation to his work. Such notions range from ideas about the playwright as expressive artist, concerned with portraying essential human emotions in coherent characters, to those of the playwright as political propagandist, offering in his work a consistent critique of the social or political order. Chronologically and methodologically wide-ranging as these approaches are, they share an understanding of the author as an autonomous creator who enjoys a privileged, usually possessive and regulatory, relation to his work and its meaning. This understanding, implicitly refuted by New Critics and their theoretical objections to the intentional fallacy, has been thoroughly critiqued by the deconstructive and genealogical approaches of Roland Barthes and Michel Foucault, both of whom have made clear its historical and ideological—rather than given or transcendental—origins. As Foucault explains, the author represents a 'principle of thrift' or 'a certain functional principle by which, in our culture, one limits, excludes, and chooses; in short, by which one impedes the free circulation, the free manipulation, the free composition, decomposition, and recomposition of fiction' (Foucault 1979: 159). This reading, as well as more recent modifications to it that stress the consequences of a text's conditions of production over the writer's individual subjectivity, have been fundamental to the redefinition over the last two and a half decades of the links between playwright, sociocultural environment, and text.

Foucault's discussion calls for the historicization of the 'author-function', for the explaining in material and ideological terms the role that the author plays in both 'manifest[ing] the appearance' and 'indicat[ing] the status' of acceptable discourses. Such historicization, I would argue, was already under way, although certainly with very different suppositions and goals, in the work of Shakespeare and drama scholars such as T. W. Baldwin, E. K. Chambers, and G. E. Bentley, whose archival forays have provided much of the basic information by which subsequent critics have been able to interpret the contexts and significance of Renaissance dramatic authorship. Bentley's seminal *The Profession of Dramatist in Shakespeare's Time*, for example, proclaims at the outset that it is 'an explication of the normal working environment circumscribing the activities of those literary artists who were making their living by writing for the London theatres' (Bentley 1971, p. vii). If his rigid distinction between amateur and professional writers as well as his generalizations about a consistency of interests among playwrights from the late 1570s to the 1630s are conclusions we challenge today, nevertheless the contents and aims of Bentley's book are indispensable to the discussion of early modern dramatic authorship. Drawing from a variety of documents including court records, Henslowe's papers, and the Stationers' Register, Bentley provides information about the basic environment of the stage-writing life: what dramatists were paid, how quickly they were asked to write, what kinds of contractual arrangement they enjoyed with different acting companies. This is not the kind of biographical research that can be dispensed with as what Foucault calls 'man-and-his-work criticism'; rather, the book provides data about the material conditions of playwriting in the period, about 'the inescapable realities of the theatre', and in so doing it reorients any simple connection between the autonomous individual and textual production (Foucault 1979: 141; Bentley 1971: 9).

But if Bentley does not reinforce a naive notion of man-and-work, his book is nevertheless governed by an assumption that his data fully and immediately expresses what it meant to be a playwright in the early modern period. Bentley assumes, that is, that his description of *what* the dramatists did is equivalent to an assessment of the *significance of what they were doing* as well as *how they and their contemporaries conceived of what they were doing*. But it is impossible to treat Bentley's description as a mirror image of a cultural position or enterprise, since the dramatists' objective practices or material contexts have meaning only in relation to their symbolic frames or ideological uses. Bentley's myriad 'facts' about the profession of writing of plays in the early modern period cannot be translated transparently into the meaning or role of the dramatist; rather, they ought to prompt what Jeffrey Masten calls a 'denaturaliz [ation of] authorship and common-sense notions of writing' (Masten 1997: 7).

One of the goals of contemporary discussions of authorship is to explain, even puncture, those ideological uses by investigating their discursive and institutional contexts, as Laurie Maguire does in her discussion of the making of the 'Author' of Shakespeare's First Folio (Maguire 2000: 134–53). Such contexts serve as important checks on our assumptions about the cultural standing of Shakespeare and his contemporaries; as Peter Thomson writes, 'there was nothing holy about a playscript and nothing lofty about the status of its author' (P. Thomson 2003: 45).[2] Nevertheless, what we now take to be the dramatist's lack of license for a playscript or of immediate cultural eminence did not preclude a range of investments by members of the theatrical community in defining the place—often as part of an assertion of eminence—of the dramatist and his work.[3] The playwrights' investments in constructing and conceptualizing their roles are evident in period documents as well as in the plays themselves. John Marston's turn-of-the-century *Histriomastix* (Marston published 1610), for instance, offers different versions of the working dramatist: one, Posthaste, a 'hack' who becomes a playwright because he lacks other employment and can churn out plays quickly, and another, Chrisoganus, considered an elitist 'translating-scholler' who defends his belabored productions: 'poore Art shall weare a glorious crowne, | When her despisers die to all renowne' (Marston 1610, B4^{v}). Posthaste and Chrisoganus represent two extremes of authorship—they are caricatures, really—and their portrayal implicitly invokes the possibility of alternative versions of the dramatist shaped against the extremes. Efforts such as *Histriomastix* to represent the scope and significance of authorship for the stage were, of course, part of global shifts in notions of authorship as they related to the production of non-dramatic manuscripts and published works and as they were influenced by

[2] For discussions of the acting company as owner of playscripts, see Bentley (1971: 62). Richard Dutton discusses the acting company's copyright in relation to the printing of plays in Dutton (1997*a*: 154–7).

[3] Consider Paul Yachnin: 'The commercial dramatists attempted to redescribe playwriting in legitimate terms, wresting positive meanings from the debased language surrounding their paid work in the common playhouse' (Yachnin 1997, p. xii).

contemporary associations of authority—*auctoritas*—with personal and political control, power and autonomy.[4] But these investments also took shape against, in Paul Yachnin's words, 'the viewpoint of the interests of the theater' (Yachnin 1997, p. xii). Three of those 'viewpoints' are considered below: the connection of playwrights and players; the intersection of the playwright with the emergent book trade; and the demand for collaborative playwriting.

Playwrights and/as Players

When Hieronimo is spied by the Duke of Castile assembling curtains for performance, he is busy with theatrical activity beyond scriptwriting. Indeed, Hieronimo's most essential role in the tragedy is that of actor, in the part of the murderous and suicidal bashaw. Scholars have long known that writers of plays were involved in multiple aspects of the theater business, particularly as players and members of acting companies. The most cited, of course, is Shakespeare, an actor as well as shareholder in the Chamberlain's and then King's Men, but he is only one among a range of others who occupied multiple roles in the world of the public theater: John Lyly, Ben Jonson, Thomas Heywood, John Marston, Samuel Daniel, Nathan Field. Their multiple roles or duties, scholars have suggested, would have had numerous effects on the playwrights, who would have been especially aware of their obligations to write for a particular stage, for particular actors, for particular audiences. Such multiple duties take on particular interest when they seem to be in some kind of conflict: Samuel Daniel, as licenser for the Children of the Queen's Revels, wrote the famously censored *Philotas*; Thomas Heywood, a sharer and performer for Worcester's, which became the Queen's Men, wrote plays for other companies. For Bentley, Heywood is simply an example of the limits of company contracts and of the way that the professional playwright worked to maximize his economic opportunities. But recent scholarship has tried to tackle the multiple roles of the dramatist in relation to the acting companies in different ways. Lucy Munro's approach in her excellent *Children of the Queen's Revels*, which presents itself as the 'biography' of a company rather than a playwright, suggests that Daniel was at the very least ambivalent about his position with a boy company; she quotes a letter from Daniel to Sir Thomas Egerton in which he complains, 'whilst I should have written the actions of men, I have been constrained to live with Children' (Munro 2005: 20). And Heywood's work for multiple companies—he trumpeted a 'finger' in some 200 plays—seems as much a part of a philosophy of the stage community's worth, as articulated in his *Apology for Actors*, as an effort to make money.

[4] Scholars have accounted for a variety of factors influencing the changing notion of authorship over the period. See e.g. Goldberg (1983); Guillory (1983); Wall (1993); Marotti (1995); Halasz (1997); Kezar (2001).

Recent scholarship has also put fresh pressure on the role of the player–playwright. Often this means dispelling assumptions about the oppositional stance between players and playwrights, whose interests in 'owning' a performance are often seen to be at odds. The evidence cited for this animosity is often linked to moments of dramatic censorship, when it behooved the actor and author to emphasize their creative differences. In contrast, satirists of the theater, like John Davies, see connections between actors and authors—but only in terms of their shared depravity:

Fucus, the furious Poet writes but Plaies
So playing writes; that's, idly writeth all:
Yet, idle Plaies, and Players are his Staies;
Which stay him that he can no lower fall:
For, he is fall'n into the deep'st decay
Where Playes and Players keepe him at a stay.

(J. Davies 1611: 56)

But it is possible and useful to see their work and interests as mutually constitutive, making authorship less about policing scripts and more about what Nora Johnson identifies as 'the theatricality of authorship itself' (N. Johnson 2003: 4). As she says, 'authorship is performance, on stage or in print' (N. Johnson 2003: 78–9). Concentrating on the various performances—written as well as acted—of Robert Armin, Nathan Field, and Thomas Heywood, Johnson explains dramatic authorship as a matter of neither ownership nor literary intention but rather of 'textual appropriation': the actor–author uses stage and page to cultivate a celebrity that makes him immediately recognizable to audiences (Johnson 2003: 17).

For Johnson, the cultivation of this celebrity depends on the 'continuity between stage and print' (N. Johnson 2003: 17). I take up the recent interest in playwrights as writers for the printing press below, but it is worth noting Johnson's distinct approach to the nexus of acting, writing, and publication: for her, theatrical performance, as the result of a complex series of negotiations, establishes the criteria for printed authority. John Marston gives us a taste of the range of such negotiations in his Prologue to *Jack Drum's Entertainment*, when the stage-keeper argues with a child actor about the intentions of the playwright. 'I thinke we shall be forced to giue you right Iohn Drums entertainment,' the Tyer-man apologizes, 'for hee that composed the Booke, we should present, hath done vs very vehement wrong. He hath snatched it from vs, vpon the very instance of entrance, and with violence keepes the boyes from coming on the stage.' But the child actor defends the author:

You mistake his Action Tyer-man
He vowes, if he could draw the musick from the Spheares
To entertaine this presence with delight,
Or could distill the quintessence of heauen
In rare composed Sceanes, and sprinkle them
Among your eares, his industry should sweat
To sweeten your delights.

(Marston 1601, A2^{r-v})

This introduction is a reminder of the intense meta-dramatic quality of early modern plays, the ways they ceaselessly called attention to their own practices. For some, this kind of meta-drama, particularly its attention to the actor–author relation, is precisely what makes the Renaissance stage so exceptional. Robert Weimann, for instance, argues that the Shakespearean theater not only self-consciously represented the interchange of playwright–player, but interrogated its *irreducibility*:

> Was it perhaps, one is left wondering, that one unique strength of Shakespeare's theatre derived from superbly acknowledging this difference [between writing and playing], from hiding it and seeking it, from playing with it even in *displaying* it? Whatever the answer to this question, the historical thrust of 'this unworthy scaffold' was inseparable from the dynamic in the sense of (dis)parity between what was represented in the text and what went into the toilsome, playsome practice of performing it. (Weimann 2000: 17)

Our notion of the playwright is further complicated by work on Renaissance acting practices. Tiffany Stern, for instance, explains in marvelous detail rehearsal procedures from the period; she documents the dominance of private 'study' of individual parts over group rehearsal with an entire script. Although Stern's focus is the impact on actors of the emphasis of parts over wholes (it would have had, she says, 'a strong effect both on the way they conceived of their roles, and on the way texts changed in general'), her findings have important implications for notions of dramatic authorship (Stern 2000*a*: 11). According to Stern, the dramatist's control over a text would have been curtailed by a system that relied on the actors learning only their own lines, occasionally receiving advice or input from others: 'Individual instruction gave mixed authority to the playwright involved in the production,' she writes; 'it allowed him to settle particular performances but not all performances, so that he was responsible for threads running through the play... but not responsible for the action of the whole' (Stern 2000*a*: 70). Stern's suggestions here are based on an implicit, and at times confining, assumption that dramatic authorship is defined by the ability to govern a play-text and its presentation. But her findings, if seen to describe not only the limiting conditions of authorial control but also the *enabling contexts* of dramatic writing, leave open new possibilities for understanding the demands on the writer of dramatic dialogue for characters that were recognized not as whole, coherent identities but as discrete parts.

Playwrights and Print

The enactment of Hieronimo's play reinforces Stern's discussion of the limitations of authorial control: Bel-Imperia, contrary to her scripted part, kills herself after stabbing Balthazar ('Poor Bel-Imperia missed her part in this: | For, though the story saith she should have died, | Yet I of kindness, and of care to her, | Did otherwise determine of her end'; IV. iii. 140–3). But Hieronimo's concern for the text of his play—he presents the Duke of Castile with what he refers to as both the 'copy of the play' and the 'argument of what we show'—belies recent critical insistence on the priority of performance over script, an insistence that has tended to downplay the role of the dramatist in the performance and meaning of a dramatic production. Renaissance plays offer ample evidence of the practice of providing a royal audience with an outline of a courtly play or masque, but Hieronimo gives the impression here that he offers not only a summary or 'argument' but a more complete '*copy* of the play' as well. The actual status (a status complicated, of course, by the fact that the play is to be acted in 'unknown languages') of Hieronimo's 'copy' may be impossible to resolve. But his attachment to it as a written document—indeed, he developed his play for the court from a manuscript he had with him from his university years—represents an obvious link between writer and text that informs the 'author's credit'.[5]

Recent scholarship in book and manuscript culture has prompted scholars to call fresh attention to the role of the play-text in early modern concepts of dramatic authorship. Grace Ioppolo's *Dramatists and their Manuscripts in the Age of Shakespeare, Jonson, Middleton and Heywood*, for instance, scrutinizes the kinds of behind-the-scenes exchanges of play manuscripts in their journeys from composition to performance. But the play-text of primary interest has not been the manuscript copy or argument but rather the printed, published editions of plays. The result has been a thoroughgoing reassessment of the drama's relation to early modern England's emergent print culture, which has allowed us to see the printing house as a key element in the construction of dramatic authorship from 'the viewpoint of the interests of the theater'. Such a reassessment has been shown to be necessary for dramatists other than Ben Jonson, whose legendary involvement in the publication of his plays as 'works' has usually been assumed an anomaly in a theatrical environment in which acting companies, not playwrights, had legal rights to playscripts and tried to keep them from the press to protect their investment.

Challenges to standard assumptions about the licensing of playscripts and companies' resistance to publication have made it possible to see profound relations between the early modern printing press and the meaning of dramatic authorship—to see, that is, the ways that 'the authorship of drama in the period was shaped by emergent modes of textual production' (D. Brooks 2000, p. xiii). Often these ways harkened back to classical concepts of literary fame refashioned by courtly models devoted to poetry. As Lukas Erne, for instance, writes, 'By the time Shakespeare started writing poetry and plays, the printing press had made the creation and perpetuation of literary fame a distinct possibility,' a possibility that can be traced in citations from plays such as *Richard II* in anthologies such as *England's Helicon* (1600) (Erne 2003: 7). As Erne says, 'It is one of the greatest paradoxes of English literary history that even though print had become an agent of the greatest importance in the construction of literary reputation by the late sixteenth and the early seventeenth centuries, scholarship has long

[5] 'When in Toledo there I studied, | It was my chance to write a tragedy—see here, my lords—[*He shows them a book.*] Which, long forgot, I found this other day' (IV. i. 77–80).

taught us that Shakespeare and many of his contemporary dramatists remained largely unaffected by these developments' (Erne 2003: 2). Instead, Erne insists that the very survival of printed plays 'bears witness to the fact that, during Shakespeare's time, many plays started having more than one kind of public existence: on stage *and* on the page' (Erne 2003: 10). The possibility of a play's 'second existence' in print made writing for the stage, at least by the 1590s, a distinctly literary endeavor, one undertaken with the prospect of making a name for oneself to multiple audiences (Erne 2003: 7). By the 1630s this notion could be seen explicitly in places such as a commendatory epistle to Philip Massinger's *The Bond-man*:

> The Avthor (in a Christian pitty) takes
> Care of your good, and prints it for your sakes.
> That such as will but venter Six-pence more,
> May *Know*, what they but *Saw*, and *heard* before.
>
> (Massinger 1624, A4)

The epistle further implies that playwriting had become nearly synonymous with poetic undertakings of a highly literary kind: 'And in the way of *Poetry*, now adayes, | Of all that are call'd *Workes* the best are *Playes*' (1624, A4).

The idea that plays are works was inaugurated, scholars have argued, by Ben Jonson in his Folio *Workes* of 1616. Jonson's scrupulous attention to the publication of his texts, his explicit laureate aims, his pursuit and commitment to aristocratic patronage, and his deeply ambivalent relation to theatricality all testify to a highly developed sense of the dramatist's place in writing for what he would call, in the 1620s, the 'loathed stage'. Although it is risky to take Jonson as paradigmatic, it is certainly possible to see in him an especially self-conscious or extreme version of what Joseph Loewenstein has called '*bibliographic authorship*, a gesture by which the author is presented as an editor of his own works, and thus as perhaps the pre-eminent reader of his works' (Loewenstein 2002: 134). But there were other 'pre-eminent readers' of Jonson's works: his dramatist colleagues such as Francis Beaumont and John Fletcher, whose commendatory writings for his printed editions remind us that the Jonsonian model was an important, available influence for other playwrights. Beaumont's epistle to *Volpone* recognizes the distinctly artistic, literary quality of the play as well as its theatrical virtues:

> I would haue showne
> To all the world, the Art, which thou alone
> Hast taught our tongue, the rules of Time, of Place,
> And other Rites, deliuer'd, with the grace
> Of Comick stile, which onely is farre more,
> Then any *English* Stage hath knowne before.
>
> (Jonson 1607, A2)

At the heart of readings such as Erne's and Loewenstein's is a commitment to the centrality or priority of the playwright in the context of early modern England's emergent print culture. Looking at dramatic authorship in the light of publication, in other words, can thus reinforce—even as it can historicize—modern notions of the dramatic writer as possessor of his work. This does not, however, have to be the case, as it is possible to approach the publishing industry and its connection to the theater in ways that reinforce the 'death of the author'. Zachary Lesser, for instance, effectively replaces the dramatist with the publisher as the 'pre-eminent reader' of dramatic works, advocating a new approach to the reception history of early modern drama grounded in the study of the reading practices of publishers—the people who 'staked their money on their readings of plays' (Lesser 2004: 4). The goal here—opening up new readings of plays based on insights gleaned from publishers' strategies—has important implications for the meaning of the dramatist: 'When authors played a part in this process [of publication],' Lesser writes, 'it was less as the originators or guarantors of meaning than as one element among many in a publisher's specialized corpus. The politics of playbooks thus come into focus only as the authors of plays are decentered from their position as the organizing principle of meaning' (Lesser 2004: 21). But if Lesser decenters the author, it is only in order to replace him with the publisher as the barometer of meaning. Such a reading, of course, like Erne's and Loewenstein's, depends on seeing the notion of dramatist primarily in relation to print and the printed text.

Playwrights and Collaboration

When the Duke of Castile discovers Hieronimo setting up the stage, he is surprised to see him working alone: 'Where's your fellows | That you take all this pain?' he asks. The language of theatrical fellowship was standard at the time, a way of describing the multiple vectors of company relations as opposed to the tête-à-tête sensibility of courtly friendship.[6] Whether Castile expected to see Hieronimo with other writers, actors, or set designers is not specified (the latter is implied), but clearly he assumes that the knight marshal should have fellows around him, collaborators in his enterprise.

The scholarly interrogation of the collaborative world of the early modern theater has done more than any other critical sub-specialty to redefine our understanding of dramatic authorship. The image of the Renaissance theater as an organization that both necessitated and facilitated close relationships among players and writers has been a staple of drama criticism. As T. W. Baldwin explained in his influential early study, the theater business 'was founded, especially in Shakespeare's day, both in theory and in practice on a closely knit, self-propagating society of friends, whose whole aim in life was to make their mystery a success' (Baldwin 1927: 161). But it is only recently that critics have tried to extrapolate theoretically the implications of

[6] See Hirschfeld (2004: 89–117).

such a structure for the construction of the dramatist and dramatic authority, an effort that has involved scholars in exploring the theater's connection to the discourses and institutions that surrounded and supported it. As John Cox and David Kastan, for instance, remind us, 'drama is always radically collaborative, both on stage and in print'; it is therefore 'motivated and sustained' by 'networks of dependency, both discursive and institutional' (Cox and Kastan 1997: 2). This kind of dependency, they argue, necessitates the 'dislodging of authors and scripts from the center of drama history' (Cox and Kastan 1997: 5).

The dislodging of author and script, just like their overvaluation, is an anachronism for the early modern theater; as this essay has shown, the theater enterprise had many 'centers', and the playwright—or the idea of the playwright—occupied several of them. But certainly the cooperative sensibility of the stage—the fact that, as Grace Ioppolo reminds us, 'Dramatists and those using their texts worked with and not against each other in the most financially and artistically productive, and cost-effective and time-efficient, ways possible'—demands a rethinking of the roles and meanings of the dramatist and his work (Ioppolo 2006: 11). And no practice demands this rethinking more than the fact of collaborative writing—the scripting of a play by more than one dramatist. The records in Henslowe's diary, which charts the theater entrepreneur Philip Henslowe's payments to players on behalf of the Admiral's and Worcester's Men between 1592 and 1604, make it abundantly clear that multiple playwrights contributed to a single play, as do the title pages of plays such as *Eastward Ho* (1605), which proclaims that it was 'Made by Geo: Chapman. Ben: Iohnson. Iohn Marston'. Bentley suggests 'that it would be reasonable to guess that as many as half of the plays by professional dramatists in the period incorporated the writing at some date of more than one man' (Bentley 1971: 199).

Often explained in terms of simple economic convenience—that is, as a way to speed up the composition of a play—dramatic collaboration is a much more complex phenomenon that, as Jeffrey Masten has written, poses 'historical and theoretical challenges... to the ideology of the author' (Masten 1997: 19).[7] Masten's work in *Textual Intercourse* has been tremendously influential for the field of authorship studies, offering as it does a methodological model for understanding collaborative work—he connects it to broader cultural discourses of gentlemanly male friendship—and an overarching argument about its place in a genealogy of authorship—he traces in the trajectory from Shakespeare's *Two Gentlemen of Verona* to the Beaumont and Fletcher Folio of 1647 the movement from non-proprietary to possessive composition. Additionally significant has been his sustained critique of attribution studies, the dominant critical approach to collaborative writing that tries to determine, based on various external or internal criteria, who wrote which scenes or lines of a joint play. Masten offers powerful arguments against the anachronism of locating individual hands in co-authored or multi-authored plays: 'Collaboration is... a dispersal of author/ity, rather than a simple doubling of it; to revise the aphorism, two heads are different than one' (Masten 1997: 19).[8] Decomposers, for

[7] For the economic argument, see McLuskie (1981: iv. 169–70).

[8] For an earlier critique of the evidentiary inconsistencies of such approaches, especially in light of early modern printing practices, see Schoenbaum (1966).

Masten, depend on a modern notion of authorship inappropriate for the assessment of collaborative work, a practice of blending or sharing texts that reminds us of how very distinct Renaissance assumptions about the playwright were from ours today.

Despite Masten's critique, efforts to detect discrete hands—to 'decompose' the text—continue apace, enabled by advances in sociolinguistics as well as statistical technologies and the advent of digitized texts.[9] Such advances, however, have not changed the relatively limited set of assumptions and goals of attribution studies, whose focus on identifying authorial contributions makes it less sensitive to the historical and institutional issues that joint work raises: questions about why, for what purpose, or with what effects particular dramatists joined forces. But joint work, it is important to note, was a pragmatic matter as well as a symbolic practice with distinct and shifting meanings, meanings influenced by the early modern theater milieu itself. In my own study of collaboration, I sketch some of the theatrical conditions of a given joint play—including its venue, its potential audience or patrons, its playwrights' past histories of joint work—in order to 'offer readings that challenge accepted rationales for collaboration by exploring the diverse implications of joint work, both for a given play as well as for the broader theatrical infrastructure' (Hirschfeld 2004: 6). This method, by focusing on the institutional grounds of collaborative playwriting, offers a corrective to Masten's largely discursive emphasis, especially as it illustrates the sheer variety of collaborative configurations between different dramatists as they responded to different professional circumstances at different times.

While it does not endorse a view of the proprietary, autonomous author eschewed by Masten, this approach does treat the 'dramatists as agents operating, both consciously and unconsciously, within a set of institutional practices and protocols' (Hirschfeld 2004: 153). For this reason it shares, although with obvious differences in goals and philosophy, a fundamental premise of attribution studies: that dramatists had personal 'fingerprints'—styles that they expected their fellows and audiences to recognize. Indeed, I would argue, early modern dramatic authorship is best understood not in terms of ownership or in terms of hermeneutic priority, but in terms of the presentation and identification of rhetorical style. In a culture obsessed with rhetorical performance and self-presentation, an obsession inculcated by grammar school training and borne out in handbooks by writers such as Henry Peacham and John Hoskyns, dramatists and their audiences were highly conscious of the intricacies of stylistic expression and were invested in their own and others' writing style(s). Of course, for them 'style' had a much more capacious meaning than it does for contemporary stylometrists, who are interested in traceable linguistic phenomena such as the repetition of function words or vowel collocation. Style referred to a wide range of textual effects, from generic choice to imitation of earlier models to

[9] For a sociolinguistic approach, see Hope (1994); for computer-aided stylistics, see e.g. Vickers (2002) and Jackson (2004).

arrangement of plot or argument (Munday, recall, was Meres's 'best plotter') to word choice. Or as George Puttenham explains:

Stile is a constant and continual phrase or tenour of speaking and writing, extending to the whole tale or processe of the poeme or historie... [it] is of words speeches and sentences together, a certaine contriued forme and qualitie, many times naturall to the writer, many times his peculiar election and arte, and such as either he keepeth by skill, or holdeth on by ignorance, and will not or peradventure cannot easily alter into any other. (Puttenham 1589: 160)

Puttenham goes on to stress the relation between style and speaker or writer:

So we say that *Ciceroes* stile, and *Salusts* were not one, nor *Cesars* and *Liuies*... And because this continuall course and manner of writing or speech sheweth the matter and disposition of the writers minde... therefore there be that haue called stile, the image of man [*mentis character*] for man is but his minde, and as his minde is tempered and qualified, so are his speeches and language at large. (Puttenham 1589: 160–1)

Indeed, the tight association of style with a particular writer or speaker was inherited from classical authors such as Cicero ('so much is done by good taste and style in speaking, that the speech seems to depict the speaker's character (*mores oratoris*)') and refashioned for the time by pedagogues such as Joseph Brinsley, who recommended double translation so that students learned to 'attaine to the phrase, stile & Composition of any Authour which they vse to reade ouer, & to make it their own' (Cicero 1948: i. 39; Brinsley 1612, $Q1^v$).

The habit—even the compulsion—of identifying specific styles of dialogue with specific dramatists was an important part of the period's print and dramatic cultures. Robert Allott's commonplace book *England's Parnassus* (1600) features quotations from *Richard II* and *Old Fortunatus* which it ascribes to Shakespeare and Dekker (the play titles are not named). The accuracy of the attribution is less important here than the impulse to attribute, an impulse that we have already seen in Meres's survey of his contemporaries and their theatrical predispositions. More interesting are instances of the impulse in the drama. A scene from the second part of the Cambridge play *Return from Parnassus*, for instance, features characters commenting on poets' and playwrights' styles. They associate Christopher Marlowe with the genre of tragedy as well as the plot of damnation:

he was happy in his buskind muse,
Alas vnhappy in his life and end.
Pitty it is that wit so ill should dwell,
Wit lent from heauen, but vices sent from hell.

(Leishman 1949; I. ii. 293–9)

But nowhere is the urge to identify more explicit than in the turn-of-the-century Poets' War, or 'Poetomachia', as it was termed by Thomas Dekker, in which different dramatists caricatured their fellow writers; that is, they literally brought other dramatists 'on stage' by imitating their diction or writing habits. Often seen as merely a commercial gimmick, the Poets' War also confronted a 'basic philosophical issue—a debate on the theory of literature', and it testifies to a belief in the existence and identifiable distinctiveness of a playwright's style, to his peers as well as to his audiences of men and women (Bednarz 1991: 23). The Poetomachia, with its expectation that audiences would recognize playwrights dramatized or characterized by their diction, suggests that identification of playwright and style was not limited to readers of printed editions. With this context in mind, it is easy to see why, as Suzanne Gossett has written, collaboration would have presented 'differing professional and psychological challenges to the authors involved, with effects on their working methods that we may never be able entirely to reconstruct' (Gossett 2004: 195).

I am not suggesting that we limit a discussion of early modern dramatic authorship to a strict equation between style and writer, one that reinforces the playwright as a romantic individual composing in private or one that simply adopts the cultural connection of person and style or person and book. Such an equation is impossible not only because playwrights experimented with different genres, created different characters with different forms of expression, and imitated classical authors as well as their peers, but also because any use and attribution of style, as Richard Halpern has shown, is always part of a 'global process for ideological production of social subjects'; any discussion of an author's style, in other words, always involves consideration of the style's broader social and cultural resonances (Halpern 1991: 33).

Indeed, some writers of the time did their best to police the stage precisely by using style as a symptom of class and thus an arbiter of who could properly write for the theater. Thomas Nashe's introductory epistle to Robert Greene's *Menaphon* (1589*a*) is exemplary:

> I am not ignorant how eloquent our gowned age is grown of late; so that euery Mechanicall mate abhorreth the English he was borne to and plucks w a solemn periphrasis, his *ut vales* from the inke-horne: which I impute, not so much to the perfection of Arts, as to the seruile imitation of vaine-glorious Tragedians, who contend not so seriously to excell in action, as to embowell the cloudes in a speech of comparison. (Nashe 1589, **)

But to see dramatic authorship as the staging of an identifiable style allows us to describe or define the term largely in relation to performance and audience, to the theatrical milieu itself, without needing recourse to expectations or desires for publication to determine the playwright's aspirations. Such an approach seems especially appropriate in light of recent work on the early modern theater as an entertainment industry with its own set of residual and emergent conventions and practices. It is also congruent with other approaches to the functionality of authorial ascriptions. Marcy North, for instance, in her compelling work on Renaissance anonymity, reminds us that the ascribing of texts to 'Anon.', or with pseudonyms, acronyms, or other puzzles, was a deliberate and interpretable practice: 'Anonymity's many variations in early modern books and manuscripts speak to its popularity and usefulness and also to the fact that it formed a coherent enough set of conventions to allow authors and book producers to borrow, compare, conflate, and make surprisingly fine distinctions among its forms and potential meanings' (North 2003: 3).

The early modern theater milieu served as what Pierre Bourdieu has called a 'cultural field,' a realm of creative or symbolic production that sits alongside but remains distinct from other political or economic arenas (Bourdieu 1993: 132–9). According to Bourdieu, cultural fields function as 'economies' governed not only by the exchange of material goods but also by the accumulation and distribution of symbolic or 'cultural capital', so that being an author involves taking various 'positions' meant to enhance one's symbolic as well as real interests and investments. In the world of the early modern theater, to be *identified* with a script and its style, as opposed to being, anachronistically, its 'owner' or 'director', was the primary means of establishing or expanding cultural capital. Dramatic authorship, in other words, was closely linked to establishing and manipulating a style in its broadest sense, so that one's work would be recognizable (or, as North suggests, 'disguisable') to specific audiences: to theatrical peers, to a special coterie, to general theatergoers. Dramatic authorship was about accumulating cultural capital, whether that capital was linked to further investment in or beyond the stage itself. Hieronimo calls such capital 'the author's credit': for him it is not a concrete financial reward but the fund of reputation that guarantees his place at court and his future as an occasional Master of the Revels.

Part of the wonder of the Elizabethan stage is the way in which it questions or deconstructs the stability of this very model of dramatic authorship. Both the facts of theater history and the plots of theater fiction demonstrate that to invest, whether literally or symbolically, in the position of playwright always involved the possibility of losing or being robbed of that investment. For a figure such as Hieronimo, the loss is both symbolic and real: a fictional character, he uses his play within a play to actually slaughter two young men and slice out his own tongue before stabbing himself. If the theater milieu was rarely as bloody, Hieronimo's ending reminds us just how much was at stake in the 'author's credit'.

27

WOMEN IN THE THEATER

NATASHA KORDA

> Whatever alleged 'exceptions' might have existed in early modern culture to the implicit but nonetheless *systematic* prohibition against female mimesis, there were no women on Shakespeare's stage.
>
> Dympna Callaghan, *Shakespeare without Women*

> Women were everywhere in Shakespeare's England, but the variety of their roles in life and in the scripts of plays too often goes without notice.... there were many women who performed in the guild plays, May games, and civic entertainments that were regular features of village life, and there were many women among the itinerant musicians, acrobats, and other performers who toured the English countryside.
>
> Phyllis Rackin, *Shakespeare and Women*

In juxtaposing the epigraphs above at the start of this essay, my aim is to highlight divergent approaches to the subject of 'women in the theater' in Shakespeare's England, as well as the apparent impasse produced by this divergence. For the purposes of this essay, I will somewhat reductively refer to these two perspectives as 'female absence' and 'female presence' respectively. Simply put, proponents of female absence hold, as Dympna Callaghan succinctly puts it in *Shakespeare without Women*: 'there were no women on Shakespeare's stage' (2000: 7), while advocates of female presence maintain, as Phyllis Rackin argues in *Shakespeare and Women*, 'Women were everywhere in Shakespeare's England' (2005: 25), including the theater.[1] The former position has, until quite recently, unquestionably predominated as

[1] In her introduction to *The Impact of Feminism in English Renaissance Studies*, published after this essay was written, Callaghan similarly describes 'two divergent perspectives' that have produced an

the governing paradigm of Elizabethan and Jacobean theater history. It might be argued that the longevity of this paradigm can be attributed to women's relative invisibility (until the advent of the new social history) within historical studies more generally; yet this argument would still have to account for the foundation upon which the paradigm of the 'all-male stage' rests, namely, the undeniable 'fact' of women's exclusion from the commercial stages and professional playing companies of Shakespeare's time. Callaghan's book makes a strong claim, moreover, that the paradigm of the 'all-male stage' is not in itself anti-feminist, arguing that we must look unflinchingly at 'the exclusion of women from the Renaissance stage as the determinate material condition of the theatre's production and representation of femininity', in order to grasp the implications of 'what was rather than what should or might have been' (Callaghan 2000: 31, 18). The 'absence of women' (Callaghan 2000: 7) from the commercial stage is from this perspective quite simply historical fact—'what *was*', rather than what might have been. Contrary or qualifying examples of female theatrical activity are considered to be exceptions that prove the rule.[2] Such attempts to mitigate the fact of women's exclusion merely work to deny or dilute the harsh reality of women's absence from the stage.

Like all 'facts', however, the historical account of the 'all-male stage' is a product of perspective, that is, of the disciplinary parameters scholars have established in defining what are considered to be the proper objects of theater history. If we shift our perspective, alter our established parameters, things may begin to look rather different. Recent scholarship emphasizing female presence has done just this. In an effort to displace the paradigm of the 'all-male stage', such scholarship has redefined our most basic understanding of what constitutes a 'stage' (or, for that matter, a player, playhouse, or performance), and, in so doing, has unearthed a growing body of evidence detailing female presence in a wide array of performance practices. The title of Phyllis Rackin's book nicely sums up this shift in perspective from absence to presence by countering the bluntly privative preposition *without* in Callaghan's title with the equally bluntly affirmative conjunction *and*.

What distinguishes these two arguments is not so much a disagreement with regard to historical facts, but rather a difference of emphasis and perspective. Thus, scholarship emphasizing female absence has tended to confine its definition of the 'stage' to the commercial theaters and professional playing companies in London and to minimize the significance of women's participation in theatrical production outside of this purview, branding the latter as exceptional or of lesser significance. Conversely, scholarship asserting female presence has tended to minimize the significance of women's absence from the commercial theaters and professional playing

'impasse' in recent feminist early modern studies (Callaghan 2007: 7, 13). The first, which emphasizes female presence and participation in culture, she terms 'revisionism', while the second, which emphasizes female absence and subjugation, she terms 'exclusionism' (Callaghan 2007: 5). She likewise argues for a 'post-revisionist' approach that analyzes 'women's simultaneous participation in *and* exclusion from early modern culture' (Callaghan 2007: 13, 7).

[2] Thus, Callaghan argues, 'The exception does not mitigate the patriarchal rule. We must keep looking at exceptions, but it is equally urgent that we keep in mind that they were just that' (2007: 13).

companies in an effort to shift our perspective from the center (London) to the periphery, from professional to amateur or unpaid performers, from England to the Continent, from city to court, and so on, in order to emphasize female participation in theater, broadly construed.

In what follows, I will first briefly survey what is known regarding 'women in the theater' in Shakespeare's England, and the ways in which the evidence has been interpreted by scholarship emphasizing female absence and presence respectively. I will go on to suggest, however, that the dichotomy of absence versus presence, although it has produced important scholarship regarding women's exclusion from the professional playing companies and inclusion in other modalities of performance and spheres of theatrical production, has tended to occlude investigation of this gendered division of theatrical labor itself. If we wish to understand better how the rise of the commercial theaters and the professionalization of playing affected the forms of female participation in theatrical production, I argue, we must first grasp how the latter related to the gendered division of labor within the economy at large.

Scholars emphasizing female absence and presence agree that women were present as spectators in the theater, but disagree over the significance of this presence. The latter argue that women 'constituted a sizeable proportion of the paying customers in the public playhouses' and that 'the offstage presence of women would have exerted a powerful influence upon playscripts' (Rackin 2005: 46; see also Neill 1978; Gurr 2004*b*; R. Levin 1989; A. Nelson 1990; J. Howard 1994; Cerasano and Wynne-Davies 1996: 157, 161–7).[3] The former, by contrast, maintain that women's role as spectators exemplifies their status as 'the objects and the consumers of the very representations they could not produce, and by extension, [as] the bearers, not the makers, of meaning' (Callaghan 2000: 15). Female spectatorship is from this perspective but another instance of women's secondary status and exclusion from the stage. Even if

[3] Andrew Gurr's *Playgoing in Shakespeare's London*, the first study to gather and examine the evidence for female spectatorship in the public and private theaters in London throughout the period from 1567 to 1642, posits a 'high proportion' or 'plentiful supply' of 'women from every section of society', but concludes that 'few assertions, beyond the bare fact that women were present, can be trusted entirely' (Gurr 2004*b*: 65, 67). Richard Levin examines the evidence provided by prologues, epilogues, prefaces, and commendatory verses of printed plays in an effort to discern whether women 'were regarded by the playwrights and acting companies as a constituency whose interests and feelings should be considered' (R. Levin 1989: 165), concluding rather tentatively that women's 'interests and feelings seem to have been taken into account by at least some of the playwrights of the period' (p. 174). Alan H. Nelson uncovers evidence of female spectators at university plays, asserting that their presence 'increase[d] the pressure for plays in English', but says little about how their presence may have affected content, beyond the observation that 'women characters in Cambridge plays were often presented sympathetically' (A. Nelson 1990: 335). Other scholars have ascribed greater cultural significance to female theatrical spectatorship, asserting that it had a profound and shaping influence on the drama of the period. Michael Neill suggests that female spectatorship was 'an important factor in shaping Caroline taste' with regard to plays staged in the private theaters (Neill 1978: 343). More recently, Jean E. Howard argues that anti-theatrical writers' preoccupation with female spectatorship is a manifestation of male anxiety in response to certain forms of autonomy the theaters afforded female spectators, such as licensing them to look actively, thereby positioning them as subjects, rather than objects, of the gaze, and even to make 'themselves into spectacles' (J. Howard 1994: 79). See also A. Cook (1981) and Osborne (1999).

one defines the female spectator's presence as productive, Callaghan argues, 'the productions of the audience are not equivalent to the production on the stage' (2000: 165). The latter claim is grounded in the long-held view that women were 'not represented at the production end' (R. Levin 1989: 174) of the theater industry, insofar as the commercial theaters were thought to have 'had no women shareholders, actors, writers, or stage hands' (McLuskie 1985: 92).

Recent scholarship emphasizing female presence has begun to put pressure on this assertion, however, arguing that if we broaden our conception of what constitutes early modern theatrical production beyond the onstage activities of the professional playing companies in London's commercial theaters, we discover that women indeed participated in various kinds of performance and various aspects of production. The bulk of this scholarship has been devoted to deepening our knowledge of a broad array of female performance practices (Brown and Parolin 2005; Findlay and Hodgson-Wright, with Williams 2000; T. Graves 1925; Cerasano and Wynne-Davies 1996: 168–72; Orgel 1996: 3–9; Thompson 1996), and may be subdivided into three main avenues of research. The first of these focuses on the ways in which female performers on the Continent influenced both dramatic representations of women and female performance styles in England (P. Brown 1999; Barasch 2000, 2001; Campbell 2005; Clubb 1989; Gough 2005; Katritzky 2005; Parolin 2000; Poulsen 2005). The second focuses on women who performed outside of the commercial theaters in England, a category that may be further subdivided into scholarship on elite women who performed in masques and other court and manor entertainments (Barroll 2001; Gossett 1998; Gough 2003, 2005; McManus 2002; Tomlinson 1992, 2003, 2005; Wynne-Davies 1992); on women of the middling sort, who performed in parish drama and festive pageantry in both rural and urban settings (Erler 1991; Sale 2004; Stokes 1993, 2005; Gweno Williams et al. 2005); on poor women who performed as itinerant entertainers, ballad singers, mountebanks, and criers of wares in streets, alehouses, market squares, etc. (S. Clark 2002; T. Graves 1925; Mirabella 2005; Korda 2008; Rollins 1919: 307–10; Thompson 1996: 104–6); and, finally, on women at all levels of society who engaged in theatrical behavior more broadly defined, from the self-staging, public proclamations of queens (C. Levin 1998) down to the bawdy jests and billingsgate of 'queans' or prostitutes and fishwives (P. Brown 2003, 2005). The third area of research focuses on the rare instances of women, such as Mary Frith, who are known to have performed in the commercial theaters in London (Dowling 1934; M. Eccles 1985; Korda 2005; Orgel 1996: 8–9, 139–53; Ungerer 2000). This multifaceted yet 'relatively hidden tradition of female performance' (Thompson 1996: 103), in the view of scholars emphasizing female presence, 'does not support any blanket claim that women were excluded from the stages of Renaissance England' (Orgel 1996: 8–9). From the perspective of those emphasizing female absence, however, such scholarship fails to undermine the paradigm of the all-male stage (as defined by the professional playing companies and commercial theaters): 'Exclusion from the stage', in Callaghan's view, 'bespeaks an aspect of women's secondary social status and is not remedied by those rare instances of female performance' (2000: 8) noted above.

The significance of women's participation in other aspects of theatrical production is likewise viewed differently from the two perspectives. Scholars emphasizing absence consider 'closet drama' (by female playwrights such as Mary Sidney, Elizabeth Cary, and Mary Wroth) to be a genre having little to do with plays written for production in the commercial theaters, and to be yet another instance of women's exclusion, secondary social status, and confinement to the domestic sphere. Scholars emphasizing presence, by contrast, contend that 'lack of evidence does not preclude the possibility that plays by women were produced at the time of their composition, or were intended for performance' (Findlay and Hodgson-Wright, with Williams 2000: 2; see also Acheson 2001; Cerasano and Wynne-Davies 1996, 1998; Cotton 1980; Raber 2001; Straznicky 2002, 2004). Rackin goes one step further in arguing that a lack of evidence should not preclude the speculation that women may have written for the commercial theaters as well: 'it would not be surprising to discover that some of these many anonymous plays—as well as some of the plays sold to the players as the work of men whose names are now associated with them—may actually have been written in whole or in part by women' (2005: 45). When it comes to women's social history, such scholarship reasons, an absence of evidence does not necessarily indicate evidence of absence.

Scholarship on women who worked behind the scenes as patrons or providers of credit, although less developed than that on female players and playwrights, leads to a similar critical impasse within the absence–presence dichotomy. Advocates of presence argue that female participation in theatrical production offstage should be regarded as a 'significant index of the importance of women for the drama' (Bergeron 1981: 277). Such scholarship includes work on women as sponsors or patrons of theatrical activity and recipients of dramatic dedications (Bergeron 1981; see also Westfall 1990, 1997), as providers of small- and large-scale credit to players and other entertainers (Korda 1996, 2004), as gatherers (who collected entrance fees) or inheritors of shares in playhouses and playing companies (Honigmann and Brock 1993; Cerasano and Wynne-Davies 1996: 173–5; Rackin 2005: 42), as wives and widows who participated in theatrical commerce (Sisson 1936, 1954; Wallace 1912: 152–68), and as 'sempstresses', or seamstresses, and dealers in second-hand cloth and clothing (Stallybrass 1996; Jones and Stallybrass 2000; Korda 2002, 2004). Although such scholarship has demonstrated that women contributed to theatrical production in a variety of ways behind the scenes, from the perspective of those emphasizing female absence this contribution fails to meet the standard of full inclusion or presence, in so far as production behind the scenes is—recalling Callaghan's expression—simply 'not equivalent to . . . production on the stage' (2000: 165).

The preceding survey illustrates, I hope, that scholarship on female absence from and presence within different modalities of performance are equally necessary to an understanding of women in the theater, but that the polarization of these two perspectives has tended to occlude analysis of this gendered differential itself. While traditional theater history, with its focus on the all-male professional playing companies and commercial stages in London, rendered this differential invisible, recent scholarship emphasizing female presence (including my own), in its excitement over the revelation of female participation in what had formerly been viewed as an all-male playing field, has focused almost solely on detailing the forms of this participation, rather than on understanding the gendered division of theatrical labor it has thereby revealed. Stephen Orgel's ground-breaking *Impersonations* was something of an exception, in that it explored *both* the anomaly of women's absence from the commercial stage in England, *and* the 'relatively hidden' tradition of female performance, in an effort to address the question 'Why did only the English public theater resist the introduction of women on the stage?' (Orgel 1996: 35). Orgel states his reluctance, however, to offer an answer to the question thus posed: 'As I have indicated, any attempt to answer this question by simply producing an explanation, whether social, religious, or political, will only close off the ramifications of the question. But the context within which the issue can be understood must have to do with culture-specific attitudes toward women, and toward sexuality' (1996: 35). Orgel quite rightly suggests that any answer to the puzzle of women's exclusion from the commercial playing companies (and, concomitantly, of their inclusion in other spheres of theatrical activity) must consider the broader terrain of the early modern sex–gender system (i.e. its 'culture-specific attitudes toward women, and toward sexuality'). Yet, as his book unfolds, it becomes clear that his primary interest is in the way the former (the gendered division of theatrical labor) illuminates the latter (the sex–gender system), rather than vice versa.

Michael Shapiro likewise considers the question of why women were excluded from the commercial playing companies, in spite of the fact that 'There was never... any legal statute prohibiting the appearance of women onstage' (M. Shapiro 1999: 187). He departs from Orgel's focus on the early modern English sex–gender system, however, arguing that similar attitudes towards women existed in France, Italy, and Spain, where professional actresses were employed as early as the 1560s. For this reason, he directs his inquiry 'away from cultural attitudes toward gender and toward the economics of the English commercial theater' (1999: 178). Although Shapiro purports to privilege questions of economy over cultural attitudes towards gender, the argument he proposes makes clear that the two are not so easily separable: 'Perhaps the strongest reason for the continued exclusion of women from the stage', he maintains, 'was a desire on the part of male actors to preserve the profession of acting as a site for male employment' (1999: 185). Shapiro thus views women's exclusion from the commercial theater as but an extension of their exclusion from employment within the economy at large. He cites no specific evidence to support this assertion, however, apart from the general observation that 'For most of the sixteenth century, women were being pushed out of economic niches they had occupied earlier' (1999: 185).[4] The latter claim, first put forth in Alice Clark's ground-breaking *Working Life of Women in the Seventeenth Century* (1919), and

[4] Shapiro likewise argues that women would have been 'liabilities for itinerant acting troupes' (M. Shapiro 1999: 189) without citing evidence to support this claim, and in spite of the fact that Continental touring companies included women, as did troupes of itinerant entertainers of other sorts in England (see T. Graves 1925; Thompson 1996).

taken up more recently in relation to London's citizenry in Steve Rappaport's *Worlds within Worlds* (1989), has been subject to critique in a number of important ways by more recent scholarship on women's economic history.

Clark's book remains 'the leading exposition of the pessimistic view that capitalist industry seriously eroded women's status, which had been higher in the pre-capitalist and pre-industrial past' (Erickson 1982, pp. vii–viii). More recent scholarship on women's social and economic history in the early modern period has significantly revised Clark's sweeping thesis, however, and revealed a more complex picture. Women's exclusion from certain crafts, trades, and occupations, for example, did not follow a strictly linear development, but occurred unevenly in different regions, and fluctuated in response to economic conditions such as labor shortages (Erickson 1982, pp. xv–xxxii). Like Clark, Rappaport cites examples of restrictions placed on female labor by several livery companies, such as the Clothworkers' Company, which in 1548 warned every company member not to 'suffer either his wife or any of his maiden servants to work openly either in his shop or at his tenters [wooden frames on which cloth is stretched to dry]'. The order was repeated four months later in even stronger terms: 'no man shall suffer nor set to work any maiden or womankind to the handicraft in any shop, tenter, or other open place' (cited in Rappaport 1991: 38). The intermittent appearance of such orders should not, however, be taken as proof of women's wholesale exclusion from such crafts or trades; for the very necessity of such orders, and of their repetition, points to female participation in activities that were from time to time, in accordance with other economic factors, curtailed, hidden, and sometimes proscribed in various ways. It is clear from the heading written in the margin by the Clothworkers' Company clerk, for example, that the above orders were aimed not at women working in the craft per se, but only at 'women working *openly*' (cited in Rappaport 1991: 38; my emphasis).[5] Rappaport himself acknowledges that proscriptions on women's work by London's livery companies 'should not be construed as evidence that most women did not participate directly in the city's economy', and further argues, 'it is likely that in the early modern period most women were actively engaged in the production and distribution of goods and services' (Rappaport 1991: 41).

The *form* of women's participation in the economy, however, differed from that of men. In order to grasp the significance of this difference, and how it may have influenced the gendered division of theatrical activity in early modern England, we will therefore need to gain a more complex understanding of the gendered division of

[5] The Weavers' Company records offer additional evidence of this dynamic. In spite of several oft-cited Company Ordinances restricting women's work in 1555, 1577, and 1596 (Consitt 1933: 230, 292, 320), it is clear that women were employed both on the looms and in subsidiary activities (although it is impossible to determine in how great numbers), as many freemen were fined for employing women. Thus, for example, Richard Sampson was fined for having six looms 'and two maidens at work in two of the looms', and John Hogg was fined for keeping a 'wench at work for a whole year contrary to the Ordinances'. Another weaver was ordered to discharge 'four wenches who were working in his looms'. Company members came up with a variety of prevarications to explain the presence of women in their workshops, such as passing young women off as the master weaver's daughter, or claiming they were not put to work in the looms, but only to 'wind silk and [do] other household business' (Plummer 1972: 61–2).

labor within the economy at large, and how the gendering of work was defined in relation to the gendering of play (and vice versa). For women's inclusion in and exclusion from different types and areas of theatrical activity were tied not only to contemporary attitudes towards women players (Brown and Parolin 2005: 2–3; Rackin 2005: 43–4), as previous scholarship has demonstrated, but towards women workers as well. Indeed, cultural attitudes towards what, in any given historical period, counts as 'work' and as 'play' are inseparable, as each term will invariably be defined in relation and/or opposition to the other.

The Clothworkers' Company restrictions on 'women working openly' provide an important insight into the particular form of women's participation in the early modern English economy; for they suggest that such participation was often informal or hidden. This was particularly true of both married women and 'maids' (or never married women), as widows (particularly widows of freemen) had special rights and privileges that allowed them to work openly in ways that were often proscribed for other women. Thus, for example, a Weavers' Company Ordinance of 1596 stipulated 'no woman or mayd shall use or exercise the Arte of weaving upon any Loome, Sapyn or Benche excepte she be the widowe of one of the same Guilde' (Consitt 1933: 320; see also note 5 above). Masters' widows inherited the tools, stock, and apprentices of their husbands' businesses (A. Clark 1919: 153–4), and although such women were highly sought after commodities on the marriage market (many married men much younger than themselves in the same or allied crafts), some continued to work as independent craftswomen, while others deployed their inherited capital and financial acumen as rentiers, mortgage brokers, moneylenders, and general 'facilitators of urban credit' (Brodsky 1986: 144; on women and credit, see also Froide 2005; Holderness 1984; Lemire 2001; McIntosh 1988; Muldrew 1998; P. Sharpe 1999; Spicksley 2003; Tittler 1994). The labor of wives is still more elusive to the eyes of the historian. Although crafts- and tradesmen's wives sometimes worked actively alongside their husbands, either in manual labor or taking charge of the financial end of their businesses (receiving payments, acting as buyers, and so forth), their labor was unremunerated and therefore largely unrecorded. As such, it belonged to a hidden, yet nonetheless crucial, shadow economy (A. Clark 1919: 156). The diverse forms of female labor (including theatrical labor) within this shadow economy have been further obscured, moreover, by the paradigm of absence–presence, which fails to account for work that is present, yet unacknowledged—because unremunerated, unrecorded, stigmatized, or otherwise placed under erasure.

A dramatic glimpse into the workings of this shadow economy may be gleaned from Thomas Middleton and Thomas Dekker's play *The Roaring Girl* (1611), in which the following exchange takes place between Master Openwork, a 'sempster', or seamster, and his wife:

OPENWORK. Ha' you done with my lord's shirt?
MISTRESS OPENWORK. What's that to you sir?
I was this morning at his honour's lodging

Ere such a snail as you crept out of your shell.
OPENWORK. O, 'twas well done, good wife.
MISTRESS OPENWORK. I hold it better, sir,
Than if you had done't yourself.
OPENWORK. Nay, so say I.
(II. i. 160–4[6])

Mistress Openwork chides her husband for inquiring into the day-to-day operations of his own seamster's shop. She makes it quite clear that her own labor-power is crucial to the successful running of the family business. Moreover, the gendered division of labor within the shop does not confine her merely to menial or unskilled tasks: both agree that she is the more accomplished seamster. She likewise exercises a degree of managerial control over the shop (indeed, a degree apparently greater than that of her husband). The humor of the exchange arguably depends upon the scene's revelation (and, perhaps, comedic exaggeration) of wives' contributions to their husbands' business affairs, a revelation echoed in the family name, Openwork. Within the culture at large, this contribution would seem to have had the status of a kind of open secret, one that does not easily fit into a strict absence–presence dichotomy.

Never married single women, who are variously estimated to have comprised some 20 to 30 per cent of all adult women in seventeenth-century England (Kowaleski 1999: 53; Froide 1999: 237), had little opportunity to participate in the formal sector of the economy regulated by the livery companies (Rappaport 1991: 38). Those who could not find work as servants were forced to enter the informal economy of makeshifts, as hawkers, hucksters, frippers (second-hand clothes dealers), botchers (menders of old clothes), pawnbrokers, unlicensed ale-wives, prostitutes, and so forth (Mendelson and Crawford 1998: 171–2, 263–81; Froide 1999: 243–52). Yet wives and widows who could not make ends meet within the formal economy likewise turned to informal commercial practices. Such women included the wives and widows of foreigners and aliens, who migrated to London in large numbers during the late sixteenth and early seventeenth centuries (see Kirk and Kirk 1900, 1907; Pettegree 1986), and other women who supplemented their husbands' incomes by working in the informal sector. In a study of the female labor market in London in the late seventeenth and early eighteenth centuries, Peter Earle has found striking evidence of the vitality of this practice.[7] His study suggests that 'a very high proportion of London women were wholly or partly dependent on their own earnings for their living'[8] (at least in the

[6] References to Middleton and Dekker's *The Roaring Girl* are from Thomas Middleton and Thomas Dekker, *The Roaring Girl* (1611), ed. Paul Mulholland, The Revels Plays (Manchester: Manchester University Press, 1987).

[7] Earle's evidence is culled from the depositions of 851 female witnesses who testified in the London Church courts, who were asked in interrogatories (in an effort to ascertain their status and credibility): 'How and by what meanes doe you gett your living and are you maintained?' (P. Earle 1989: 330). Such evidence is a valuable supplement to that provided by guild records, in so far as it renders visible the flexibility of female labor (many list more than one craft or trade), as well as the separate work identities of husband and wife.

[8] Only 28 percent of Earle's sample claimed to be unemployed. Most of the latter were the wives of gentlemen, professionals, and skilled artisans (whose wives, according to Earle, may have 'helped their

predominantly artisan and working-class population represented in his sample; P. Earle 1989: 337–8), and that women often worked in crafts or trades different from those of their husbands. Much of the work performed by the employed women in early modern London, he finds, was 'of a casual nature and *none of it organized by gilds or livery companies*' (P. Earle 1989: 342; my emphasis).

This brief survey of the gendered division of labor in early modern London makes clear that a dichotomous view of female absence–presence cannot account for the complex forms of working women's participation in the informal sector. Precisely how to define informal commerce, however, remains a difficult question. The blurred contours of this sector of the market have given rise to a host of descriptive terms—informal, irregular, black, hidden, shadow, parallel, secondary—that reinforce its penumbral or marginal status. Recent scholarship has seized on the purely relational aspect of what is termed 'informality', arguing that it is not so much a bounded sector of the economy as 'a specific form of relationship of production' whose contours or boundaries are in constant flux with respect to the formal economy, varying in accordance with the vicissitudes of politico-economic regulations (Castells and Portes 1989: 12). Hence, they maintain, 'what is informal and perhaps persecuted in one setting may be perfectly legal in another' (Portes et al. 1989: 298); and the same economic activity will continually shift its relative location across the formal–informal divide (Castells and Portes 1989: 26; see also Hoyman 1987: 81). Conceived in this way, informality is far from marginal; rather, it is 'a fundamental politico-economic process at the core of many societies' (Castells and Portes 1989: 15), often serving to 'fill in where the conventional economy falls short or fails' (Gaughan and Ferman 1987: 15; see also Henry 1987). Participants in the informal sector likewise vary, incorporating a broad range of economic agents, from those who have been excluded from the formal economy and who may have no other means of survival (e.g. the poor, women, immigrants), to informal entrepreneurs seeking ways to profit from the economic dynamism of unregulated commerce. Because informality 'cut[s] across the whole social structure', encompassing a broad range of heterogeneous economic activities and agents, it may simultaneously incorporate relations of production that are progressive and exploitative (Castells and Portes 1989: 11–12; see also Gaughan and Ferman 1987: 23; Roberts 1990: 23–42). As such, it provides a useful framework within which to understand the varied contributions of both impoverished workers and informal entrepreneurs to the rise of the commercial theaters in London. It will also help us to grasp how the gendered division of labor within the nascent entertainment industry was shaped by shifting definitions of what constituted legitimate (and illegitimate) work.

husbands, but received no money for their help and so did not think that such work was relevant'; P. Earle 1989: 338). Of married women working in occupations separate from those of their husbands, excluding servants (who made up 25.4 percent of the sample), most worked in the textile and clothing trades (24.8 percent). The rest worked in a diverse range of occupations, such as itinerant and market retailing, shopkeeping, manufacturing, and victualling and alehouse-keeping (P. Earle 1989: 340–1).

The concept of informality renders visible a broad array of economic activities occluded by the 'apparently all-pervasive' formal economy (Ferman et al. 1987: 13) regulated in early modern London by livery companies and City officials. In the present context, these might include activities as diverse as the unrecorded labor of theater wives, widows, daughters, and maidservants; the informal lending practices of petty pawnbrokers, upon which actors frequently relied; the resale of second-hand clothing, costumes, comestibles, and other goods by female frippers, hawkers, and hucksters to actors, audiences, and theater managers (Jones and Stallybrass 2000; Korda 1996, 2002, 2004, 2005, 2008; Stallybrass 1996); the sex work of prostitutes, bawds, and brothel-keepers in the environs of the theaters (Dawson and Yachnin 2001; Griffiths 1993; Shugg 1977; Ungerer 2003; Varholy 2001); and even the activities of petty female criminals, such as dealers in stolen goods, in and around the theaters (Ungerer 2000; Walker 1994). As the diversity of these practices makes clear, the concept of informality 'challenges our very definitions of what is economic and demands a new understanding of what constitutes work' (Gaughan and Ferman 1987: 20)—just as the diversity of female performance practices in early modern England has challenged our very definitions of what is theatrical and demands a new understanding of what constitutes 'play'. Indeed, it is the very instability of the boundary between what counts as work and as not-work (e.g. as play, pastime, leisure, sport, or, more pejoratively, as idleness, sloth, or outright crime) in a given historical context that makes it essential to consider the two categories in relation to one another.

Historians generally agree that the informal sector expanded rapidly in late sixteenth-century London, when the increasing scale of immigration to the city (and in particular to its rapidly expanding extramural parishes and suburbs) resulted in large numbers of impoverished migrants taking up occupations outside of guild control, thereby swelling the ranks of 'foreigners' or unfree laborers (Archer 1991*a*: 52–5, 61–3, 202–3, 242–5; Archer et al. 1988: 11; Kellett 1958; Muldrew 1998: 48).[9] The flourishing of such informal commerce in London's suburbs and liberties may be attributed as well to the limited capacity of City authorities and livery company officials to enforce labor standards and market regulations there (Archer 1991: 225–6, 234; D. Johnson 1969: 87–92, 313–15; Kellett 1958: 381–2; Unwin 1908: 245–6, 251). City authorities nonetheless tried to curb the expansion of informal trade through numerous legislative initiatives. Such initiatives targeted a broad range of informal commercial activities and actors, from 'hucksters hawkers [and] haglers', who peddled their wares in the streets, thereby evading market regulations, to 'upstart Brokers', a term that included both pawnbrokers and dealers in second-hand goods and clothing. Those who worked in the informal sector were typically accused of 'framing themselves to leade a more easie lyfe than by labor' (cited in Archer et al. 1988: 15), and of 'findinge thereby... a more idle and easier kinde of Trade of livinge, and... a more readie[,] more greate[,] more profitable[,] and speedier Advantage

[9] On the continued growth of the informal sector in late seventeenth- and eighteenth-century London, see C. Smith (2002). On women's role in the informal sector in England during this period, see Lemire (1997) and P. Sharpe (1998). For comparison with early modern France, see Hufton (1974).

and Gaine then by theire former manuall Labours and Trades'.[10] As the language of such legislation makes clear, work in the informal sector was not only considered illegitimate, it was not considered to be 'work' at all. Unfree labor was routinely relegated to the status of mere 'idleness'.

The frequency of such legislative initiatives during the late sixteenth and early seventeenth centuries, together with their repeated assertions that the number of such informal traders was 'greate & excessive' and growing, rather than abating,[11] suggests that efforts to rein in the rising tide of informal commerce during the period met with little success. Attempts at regulation, however ineffective, nonetheless provide an important source of evidence regarding both the growth of the informal sector, and women's work within it. The Repertories of the Court of Aldermen and the Journals of the Court of Common Council for the City of London are filled with attempts to control such trade, attempts that were frequently directed specifically at women, such as the 'womon brokers' who were ordered not to carry 'abowte the streets of the cyttye any manner of apparel to be solde', and other unlicensed, itinerant hawkers of food and other commodities).[12] In 1602 an Act of Common Council specified that the 'Huxters, Pedlers and Haglers' who 'walke upp and downe the streetes hawkinge w[i]th wares and offeringe the same to be soulde openlie to all sortes of people . . . be for the most p[ar]te women'.[13] Similar orders regarding the population of itinerant criers who sell 'oysters ffishe fruites . . . and other victuals' in the streets describe that population as made up predominantly of 'wives, widdowes weomen' and 'maides'.[14] A mayoral order of 1590 claimed the numbers of such women 'are of late yeres . . . wonderfully encreased'.[15] Such legislation suggests that in the early modern period, as in the present, occupations within the informal economy may well have been 'female dominated' (Hoyman 1987: 69). Indeed, some have argued that women's contributions to the informal economy have historically been 'so dramatic—although invisible—that if ever recorded, it would usher in a new chapter in the book of women in the work force' (Hoyman 1987: 82). Although we may never know the precise extent of women's work in the informal sector in early modern London, what seems certain is that 'any analysis of women's contribution to work [and, I would add, play] that does not take account of the informal economy will be seriously flawed' (Hoyman 1987: 82).

It is no accident that the success of the commercial theaters coincided with the expansion of informal commerce, nor that the theaters were located in the very same suburbs and liberties of London in which such commerce thrived. For the

[10] *Statutes of the Realm* (1810–28: iv. 1038).

[11] A 1603–4 statute, for example, held that informal brokers 'are growen of late to many Hundreds within the Citie of London, and other places next adjoining to the Citie and Liberties of the same, and are like to increase to farre greater multitudes' (*Statutes of the Realm* 1810–28: iv. 1039).

[12] London Metropolitan Archives (LMA), Corporation of London MSS, Repertories, 20 (1579–83), 237; see also Archer et al. (1988: 23–4).

[13] LMA, Corporation of London MSS, Journal 26, COL/CC/01/01/026, 7.

[14] LMA, Corporation of London MSS, Journal 22, COL/CC/01/01/022, 378^{v}; see also 28, COL/CC/01/01/028, 300–2.

[15] LMA, Corporation of London MSS, Journal 24, COL/CC/01/01/024, 98^{v}.

professional playing companies and the entrepreneurs who backed them took maximum advantage of the flexible forms of trade that characterized the informal sector (see Agnew 1986: 54). Many of those involved in the nascent entertainment industry were guild members who had earned their freedom from one of the established livery companies, and had then opted to leave these traditional occupational backgrounds (Forse 1993: 8–9; see also Lawrence 1926; O'Neill 1926). In doing so, they took opportunistic advantage of a custom of London whereby 'every Citizen and Freeman of London, which hath been an Apprentice in London unto any trade by the space of seven years, may lawfully and well relinquish that trade and exercise any other trade at his will and pleasure' (Tawney and Power 1924: i. 379; on this custom, see also Kellett 1958: 384; D. Johnson 1969: 314; Unwin 1908: 262–4). These men effectively kept one foot firmly planted in the security of the formal economy, while taking a giant step with the other into the risks and benefits of unregulated commerce. Certain aspects of the older economic structures were imported into the new, such as the apprenticeship system (Orgel 1996: 65). Yet there were important differences between the playing companies and the guilds; for the former had 'no central organization, no court system, and no regulations that governed all of them... and [they] certainly did not have the social prestige of the ancient guilds, like the Goldsmiths or the Mercers' (Streitberger 1997: 347). By importing structural aspects of the guild system into their new economic ventures, however, these men 'subtly... relat[ed] the work of acting to the crafts and professions, and thereby implicitly [laid] claim to their rights and privileges' (Orgel 1996: 65). The commercial playing companies were in this sense transitional economic formations, in certain respects retaining the residual structure of the guilds while at the same time assuming the emergent form of innovative capital ventures. Situated on the cusp of formal and informal market activities, they enjoyed a hybrid status, which allowed them to take opportunistic advantage of both. While many of those involved in the 'early entertainment industry' sought status and protection by gaining their freedom from the established livery companies, they were thus also 'freelancing entrepreneurs in an underground economy', who took maximum advantage of the many forms of 'deracinated' and ad hoc commercial activity thriving in early modern London (Bristol 1996: 38–9).

How did the commercial theaters' peculiar hybrid status influence the forms of female labor within the nascent entertainment industry? As one might expect, the gendered division of theatrical labor in certain ways reflected that of the economy at large. Thus, theater wives sometimes worked actively alongside their husbands, participated in the financial end of their husbands' business ventures, and continued to work in these capacities, at least for a time, into their widowhoods. Evidence of married women's involvement in their husbands' theatrical affairs, although scarce, is by no means non-existent. The evidence we do have has sometimes been ignored, or its significance diminished, by theater historians. Thus, for example, Margaret Brayne's contribution to theater history has been limited to her financial dealings and litigation with James Burbage, following the death of her husband (and Burbage's partner), John Brayne. In focusing solely on Margaret's financial dealings with Burbage, Skiles Howard maintains, theater historians have ignored the significance of her collaboration with Brayne in the building of the Theatre. For, according to Robert Miles's testimony in the litigation with Burbage, John Brayne, who was the primary investor in the project, although a financially successful grocer, was soon overwhelmed by the building expenses, and forced to sell his house and stock, and give up his trade as a grocer, pawn his own clothes and Margaret's, and

> to run in debt to many for the money to furnishe the said Playe house | & so to employe himselfe onlye uppon that matter...to his utter undoing | for...in the latter end of the fynishing therof | the said Braynes and his Wyfe...were dryven to labor in the said workes | for saving some of the charge | in place of ii laborers. (S. Howard 1998; Wallace 1969: 141)

While the once wealthy Brayne and his wife were clearly driven to this arrangement by the extremity of the situation, the testimony suggests a pattern of collaboration between husband and wife that may have carried over from the Braynes' years as grocers. Nor was it unheard of for women to work as carpenters or joiners in the period (A. Clark 1919: 172–8; Snell 1985: 286). The Braynes provide a good example of the kind of flexibility and improvisation required of crafts- and tradesmen and women in launching these new theatrical enterprises.

Evidence of married women's involvement in the financial end of their husbands' theater affairs includes the theater entrepreneur Philip Henslowe's wife, Agnes, who appears to have been involved in her husband's pawnbroking and moneylending activities, as she is listed several times in his accounts lending money to actors, as well as friends, family, and other employees (Henslowe 1961, fo. 28^{v}; see also fos. 28^{r}, 38^{v}, 42^{v}, and 124^{r}). Henslowe owed his initial investment capital for his business and theatrical ventures largely to his provident marriage to Agnes, who had been his former master's widow; so it is certainly not surprising that she should have taken an active interest, and even played an active role, in his business affairs. Another example of a theater wife and widow who was intimately involved in her husband's financial affairs is that of Elizabeth Hutchinson, wife of Christopher Beeston, an actor and theater entrepreneur who owned the Cockpit theater. Beeston appointed his wife 'full and sole executrix' of his estate 'by reason I doe owe many greate debtes, and am engaged for greate sommes of money, which noe one but my wife understandes, where or how to receaue pay or take in'. Beeston's will suggests that his wife was involved not only in his credit activities, but in the procurement of costumes as well; it directs 'that my said executrix shall...prouide and finde for the said Companie [the King's and Queen's Young Company], a sufficyent and good stock of apparell fitting for their vse' (Honigmann and Brock 1993: 192–3). It seems unlikely that Beeston would have entrusted his wife with this task if she had had no prior experience in the procurement of costumes for the stage.

Yet the theater's peculiar hybrid status also differentiated the opportunities it created for women from those available within the economy at large, in certain ways for the better, and in others for the worse. Certain of these opportunities were relatively unique, simply because the purpose-built theaters were themselves relatively unique. Thus, for example, women participated in the financial end of the theater business as gatherers, who collected the penny fee for general admission, and further fees for entrance to the interior galleries. There is relatively plentiful evidence that 'not a few of the gatherers were women' (Thaler 1919: 195). Mary Phillips was paid a 'stipend' by Thomas Greene, the leading actor of Queen Anne's Men, and his fellows in the winter of 1606–7 'for keeping the gallarie dores of the [Boar's Head] playhowse' (M. Eccles 1991*b*: 456). In 1612 Robert Browne wrote to Edward Alleyn on behalf of a 'Mr Rose', an impoverished hireling of Prince's Henry's Men, 'to p[ro]cure him but a gathering place for his wife' (Greg 1907: 63; see also Chambers 1923: i. 356, ii. 187). The Globe and Blackfriars had at least one female gatherer in 1627, according to the will of Henry Condell (an actor and manager of the King's Men, and housekeeper in the two theaters), which bequeaths to his 'old servant Elizabeth Wheaton... that place or privilege which she nowe exerciseth and enioyeth in the houses of the Blackfriars London and the Globe on the Banckside for and during all the terme of her naturall life yf my estate shall soe long continue in the premises' (Bentley 1941–68: ii. 616). Scholarship emphasizing female absence has characterized such female employees in the commercial playhouses as trivial and peripheral. Yet the role of gatherers was neither insignificant, nor limited to the collection of fees. An undated letter from William Birde to Edward Alleyn (*c.*1617) suggests that gatherers performed a variety of functions, being reassigned as 'nessessary atendaunt[s] on the stage' or 'to mend [players'] garments' as needed (Greg 1907: 85). Birde's letter likewise conveys the sense that the gatherer's role was taken quite seriously, which should come as no surprise, given that the safekeeping and proper allocation of the nightly takings was essential to the financial well-being of company sharers and theater 'housekeepers'. The demonstrated trustworthiness of the gatherer was a central concern in her or his appointment; Browne's letter thus testifies of Mrs Rose, 'she shall so carry her self in that place as they shall think it well bestowed by reason of her vpright dealing in that nature' (Greg 1907: 63). Yet it was not simply the honesty of gatherers that was at stake in their assignment, but their allegiance as well. For the gatherers effectively functioned as agents or representatives of diverse financial interests in a given theatrical enterprise. The deed of partnership in the Rose theater, for example, allows each of the partners, Henslowe and Cholmley, if they cannot be 'there p^{r}sent' as doorkeepers themselves, to 'appoynte theire sufficiente debutyes or assignes... at theire Choyse to Coleckte gather and receave all suche some and somes of moneye of every psonne & psonnes resortinge and Cominge to the saide playe howse' (Greg 1907: 3). When disputes between various financial interests arose, the allegiance of these 'debutyes' was crucial (see Chambers 1923: ii. 389–91; Bentley 1941–68: vi. 128).

To the extent that the commercial theaters relied on the labor of those who worked within the informal sector, they created employment opportunities for women, whose labor, as we have seen, was largely concentrated in this sector. There is evidence, for example, that their reliance on what Jones and Stallybrass call the 'clothing economy', and in particular on the circulation of second-hand clothes, created new opportunities for the many women who worked as spinsters, seamstresses, and dealers in cloth and second-hand clothing (Jones and Stallybrass 2000;

Stallybrass 1996). I have argued elsewhere that the historical Mary Frith—upon whom Middleton and Dekker's *The Roaring Girl* is based, and who is known from a record in the Consistory of London Correction Book to have made an appearance during the play's run 'at the ffortune [theater]', where she sat 'vppon the stage . . . in mans apparrell & playd vppon her lute & sange a songe' (cited in Mulholland 1977: 31)—may well have been brought into contact with Prince Henry's Men and the Fortune theater through her work as a broker in second-hand and stolen goods and apparel (Korda 2005). Elizabeth Hutchinson, mentioned above, would likewise most probably have relied at least in part on the second-hand clothing trade to 'provide and finde' the 'stock of apparell' for the King's and Queen's Young Company. As Susan Cerasano has argued, 'players kept costs to a manageable level by buying second-hand garments and purchasing new costumes for only the major actors (or the unusual characters . . .) for each production' (Cerasano 1994*a*: 51).[16] There are many instances in Henslowe's diary of Henslowe lending money to the Admiral's Men to purchase second-hand costumes, and of his selling them used costumes himself (Jones and Stallybrass 2000: 184–6). The work of altering apparel frequently fell to women, particularly when it involved remaking rather than making up new, as was often the case with the production of costumes for the public theaters (Korda 2004: 209–10; 2005: 73, 84–5). Finally, there is evidence that the commercial theaters' heavy dependence on large- and small-scale credit provided opportunities for the many women who worked in the informal sector as pawnbrokers and moneylenders (Korda 2004: 211–16). All of the above evidence regarding the opportunities created for women who worked in the informal sector by the rise of the commercial theaters, however, does not change the general 'fact' of their exclusion from the stage itself.

What light is shed upon this exclusion by contemporary attitudes towards what constituted legitimate and illegitimate forms of male and female labor? To the extent that the commercial playing companies relied upon and imitated the formal economy regulated by the livery companies and City authorities in an effort to buttress the status of 'playing' as a legitimate profession, they may well have been motivated to exclude women from the most visible work space of that profession, namely, the stage itself, and to distinguish their own theatrical practices from those of female amateurs (see Korda 2008). It is well known that City authorities and Puritan preachers who inveighed against the rise of the commercial theaters accused the players of being effeminate themselves, and of effeminizing their audiences. The gendered form of such attacks has most often been understood to refer to the practice of cross-dressing—which it at times explicitly did (see Pollard 2004: 101, 173–4). Yet the charge of effeminacy was also frequently linked to what was

[16] It seems to have been common knowledge, and the butt of many a satirical jibe, that the upper ranks of society were in the habit of bringing their cast-off apparel 'to the theatre to sell' (John Donne, 'Satire IV' (*c*.1597), in John Carey (ed.), *John Donne* (Oxford: Oxford University Press), 36–42, cited in Cerasano 1994*a*: 55). Stallybrass and Jones cite Thomas Platter, who maintained: 'it is the English usage for eminent lords or Knights at their decease to bequeath and leave almost the best of their clothes to their serving men, which it is unseemly for the latter to wear, so that they offer them then for sale for a small sum to the actors' (Platter 1937: 167, cited in Jones and Stallybrass 2000: 189; see also p. 187).

arguably the most pervasive preoccupation voiced by Protestant prelates and City fathers alike in their attacks on the commercial theaters: the charge that playing was an illegitimate or 'idle occupation' (Gosson 1582, B3^{r}). The accusation of idleness, and its gendered dimension, take on new significance within the broader context of the City's preoccupation with the rise of informal commerce in London's suburbs and liberties during the late sixteenth and early seventeenth centuries. Indeed, the language used by anti-theatrical writers to stigmatize the players is identical with that deployed by City authorities to legislate against those who worked in the informal sector: players, like pawnbrokers, were described as parasites, or 'Caterpillers of a Commonwelth' (Gosson 1579*b*; see also Rankins 1587, B1^{v}), and accused of seeking 'a more idle and easier kinde of Trade of livinge... [than] manuall Labours and Trades did or coulde bringe them'.[17] 'Most of the Players', according to Stephen Gosson, are 'men of occupations, which they haue forsaken to lyue by playing' (Gosson 1582, G6^{v}). As Gosson's language makes clear, in the eyes of the theater's opponents, playing was defined as the very antithesis of legitimate work (see Pollard 2004: 81, 117, 193).

The stigmatizing of playing as an illegitimate form of labor, and the charge that the commercial theater was, in Gosson's terms, a 'nurserie of idelnesse' (Gosson 1582, G6^{v}), were frequently linked to the claim that playing caused effeminacy. According to Gosson, players lead 'a softe, a silken, a Courting kind of life, fitter for women than for men', and, as such, are 'vnfit for manly discipline' (Gosson 1582, E2^{r}). Thomas Beard similarly maintains that playing serves 'to no other purpose but to make the people idle, effeminate, and voluptuous' (Beard 1597: 374). The earliest anti-theatrical treatise, John Northbrooke's treatise against dicing, dancing, and 'Vaine Playes or Enterluds', grounds the link between idleness and effeminacy in humoral discourse. Idle pastimes, such as plays, Northbrooke maintains, are like sleep, in that they 'ingendreth much humiditie and rawe humours in the bodie' so that 'all the moystures and humors of the bodie, with the naturall heate, retire to the extreme parts therof', thereby making those who engage in such pastimes 'slouthfull, weake, and *effeminate with ouermuche ydlenesse*' (Northbrooke 1577: 19; my emphasis). Players are effeminate because they are idle and therefore cold and damp like women, while 'good true labourers in the Common wealth' make their living 'with their owne handes, in the sweate of their face', like 'honest men' (Northbrooke 1577: 71). A decade later, William Rankins similarly argues that players' 'idlenesse weakeneth the sences and members of men, that they shall neuer be able to profit their countrie' (Rankins 1587, D1^{r}). To counter such arguments, defenders of the stage sought to establish its legitimacy as a 'manly' and 'honest' profession. In his *Apologie for Poetrie*, Sir Philip Sidney mocks the 'imputations' of effeminacy 'laid to the poore Poets', deriding the claim that 'before Poets did soften vs, we were... the pillers of manlyke libertye & not lulled a sleepe in shady idlenes with Poets pastimes' (Sidney 1595, G4^{r}); to the contrary, he argues, poetry is 'an Art... not of effeminatenes, but of notable stirring of courage' (I2^{r}). In his *Apology for Actors*, Thomas Heywood defends playing as a

[17] *Statutes of the Realm* (1810–28: iv. 1038–9).

'worthy imployment' (Heywood 1612, C3^{r}) by countering the humoral argument of the anti-theatricalists with one of his own. Far from engendering 'humiditie and rawe humours in the bodie', as Northbrooke maintained, the theater serves 'to recreate such as are wholly deuoted to Mellancholly, which corrupts the bloud' and to 'refresh such weary spirits as are tired with labour, or study, to moderate the cares and heauinesse of the minde, that they may returne to their trades and faculties with more zeale and earnestnesse' (Heywood 1612, F4^{r}).

In this very brief survey of the gendered ideologies that contributed to the rise of the commercial theaters and the profession of playing, it has become clear, I hope, why women's absence from the professional stage, as well as their presence in other forms of performance and other areas of theatrical production, should be situated more broadly in relation to the ideologies and material practices that grounded the gendered division of labor within early modern English society at large. Seen from this perspective, female theatrical absence and presence are inextricably linked. For the hybrid status of the commercial theaters allowed the players to take maximum advantage of unregulated commerce in the informal sector, where so many women were employed, while they simultaneously worked to define the theater as a legitimate, 'manly' profession. In this sense, the commercial theaters' hybrid status may well have worked *both* to women's advantage *and* to their disadvantage, opening new opportunities for women who worked behind the scenes, and providing the theaters with costumes, properties, credit, and a hand in their day-to-day operations, while at the same time excluding women from the visible or 'open' work space of the stage itself in an effort to define the 'play' that took place there as legitimate work.[18]

[18] I am grateful to Mary Bly, Adam Zucker, and Amanda Bailey for their insightful comments on an early draft of this essay.

PART V

EVIDENCE OF THEATRICAL PRACTICES

CHAPTER 28

EARLY MODERN NATURALISTIC ACTING: THE ROLE OF THE GLOBE IN THE DEVELOPMENT OF PERSONATION

JACALYN ROYCE

The prose portrait of an actor in the expanded version of Sir Thomas Overbury's *Characters* (published 1615) describes Richard Burbage's acting style: 'what we see him personate, we think truly done before us' (N2^{r}).

To envision the acting style called 'personation' by the Chamberlain's and King's Men requires both mining their scripts for clues and investigating the design of the Globe theater for its contribution to the development of personation and of play-wrighting for that acting technique. Providing the actor with a stage large enough to allow for freedom of movement, yet small enough and close enough to the audience to highlight discrete details of body language, the Globe enabled the actor to counterfeit naturalistic physical behavior. Placing audience members on three sides of that stage focused their attention on the physical body of the actor, marking the contrast between movement that closely resembled that of the everyday world and other performance styles founded in artifice. The Globe's arrangement freed the actor to use his body and voice in an unaffected manner and, at the same time, made it possible for the actor to overemphasize physicality for comic effect. Not only would the Globe's conditions encourage plausible body language and behavior, but also, by visually emphasizing gesture, they might demand it.

'Seems Madam? Nay, it is'

Hamlet's first allusion to acting invokes the relationship between 'custe' (exterior appearance and behavior) and 'kinde' (internal feelings and intentions):

> GERTRUDE. Why seems it so particular with thee.
> HAMLET. Seems Madam? Nay, it is: I know not Seems:
> 'Tis not alone my Inky Cloak (good Mother)
> Nor Customary suits of solemn Black,
> Nor windy suspiration of forc'd breath,
> No, nor the fruitful River in the Eye,
> Nor the dejected havior of the Visage,
> Together with all Forms, Moods, shows of Grief,
> That can denote me truly. These indeed Seem,
> For they are actions that a man might play:
> But I have that Within which passeth show;
> These, but the Trappings, and the Suits of woe.
> (I. ii. 75–86[1])

Hamlet admits that he looks like a man in mourning, or, more accurately, that an actor playing a man in mourning would appear and behave as Hamlet does. Yet, Hamlet claims that what he wears is not a costume. He also asserts the authenticity of his body language and behavior. Sighing, crying, and otherwise 'appearing' dejected emanate from his true personal feelings; the reaction to his father's death is 'particular' with Hamlet. In recoiling from Gertrude's words, Hamlet combines two senses of 'particular'. He claims that this emotional response is particularly his—specifically his both in ownership and in mode—as well as particulate, that is, engrained in his physical being. Hamlet further insists that, while his appearance 'suits' his feelings (punning appropriateness with costuming), that appearance inadequately expresses them: 'I have that Within which passeth show…'.

Hamlet's statement has inspired voluminous inquiries into early modern interiority—self-consciousness as well as subconsciousness. In the pragmatic terms of

[1] I quote the Folio scripts, utilizing Folio punctuation and wording while updating most spelling myself. Line indications, however, are taken from the most recent Arden editions.

stage performance, however, the amount of information that an actor can share with the audience in the space–time constraints of a few moments on stage contrasts sharply with the amount of possible subtext that a reader may imagine in open-ended private examination. Further, subtext was not an Elizabethan theatrical concept, nor were early modern English writers concerned about the subconscious. As a brief entry in the ongoing discussion of players and playing in *Hamlet*, the line translates simply: 'I am not pretending, not "acting".' The list of physical elements that Hamlet insists arise from his true feelings parallels precisely those he later admires the First Player's ability to counterfeit:

> this Player here,
> But in a Fiction, in a dream of Passion,
> Could force his soul so to his own conceit,
> That from her working, all his visage warm'd;
> Tears in his eyes, distraction in's Aspect,
> A broken voice, and his whole Function suiting
> With Forms, to his Conceit? And all for nothing? (II. ii. 545–51)

Hamlet feels on the inside as he appears to feel on the outside. 'Seems Madam? Nay, it is . . .'. The rhyming couplet that completes the speech reiterates Hamlet's initial insistence that his *custe* accurately signifies his *kinde*:

> I have that Within which passeth show;
> These, but the Trappings, and the Suits of woe.

Hamlet is not counterfeiting.

Yet, Hamlet understands acting technique, often uses it as a metaphor, and discusses it with the players. The play-text indicates that what Hamlet describes as good acting echoes what the audience sees at the Globe theater: Burbage personating Hamlet. More accurately, Burbage personates Hamlet not pretending (and in contrast to other characters who *are* pretending). The actor desires seamlessness in portrayal that assists the illusion of truth and enables the staged scenes to maintain the premise of happening in 'real' time and space. The stylization of language, voice, and body that characterizes an actor's presence in non-naturalistic theater has no place here. For the character (Hamlet) to claim without absurdity that *he* is not 'acting'—not using any acting method with the intention of fooling anyone about his emotions and intentions—the actor (Burbage) must hide the artifice completely and achieve the illusion of not *pretending* to be someone he is not. In *Hamlet*, the actor and the character he portrays represent separate but concurrent events, recalling the infinite regression of images that one sees when holding a mirror up to a mirror.

'Personation' names what actors do to achieve the appearance of not 'acting', the illusion of *being* their characters rather than performing them or, even, *seeming* like them. The elements necessary for an actor to create the illusion that he or she is not 'acting' interweave the appropriateness of the character's language as supplied by the author with the physical and emotional investment in using that language made by the actor. 'Counterfeiting' also achieves the appearance of not 'acting', but with the added implication of forgery. An actor counterfeits the body, voice, and passion of a character in order to personate him or her. The goals of personation and modern naturalistic acting are essentially the same (although each approach was developed for different modes of playwrighting, experiences of language, and concepts of psychology): the illusion of 'real' people at 'real' moments in their lives. Either 'to counterfeit' or 'to personate' can apply interchangeably when used to describe the craft of a player.

When used to discuss Shakespeare's characters who adopt the methods of players, however, only 'to counterfeit' remains applicable. In these cases, the element of forgery becomes thematic: Richard III counterfeits; Osric cannot; Coriolanus refuses. The frequency with which so many other characters call Iago 'Honest Iago' indicates his success as an actor. If Iago didn't inform the audience himself, they would be duped by his lies along with the characters. Shakespeare designed the structure of *Othello* so that it does not require the actor personating Iago to provide any physical or vocal markers of fictionality. The script allows Iago to counterfeit 'Honest Iago' well and, at the same time, allows the actor to personate Iago without needing to play some scenes badly by displaying the artifice. Since Iago tells the audience his plans and rationale, the actor playing Iago need not *appear* to be lying during the scenes of forged emotions and loyalties in order for the audience to recognize Iago's forgery. Conversely, if the play required the actor to make it clear to the audience that Iago was lying *while* Iago lied to the other characters, the actor would need to overact or to make mistakes in disguising Iago's intentions. In that case, Iago's 'acting' would fool no one in the story—or, at least, the audience might have trouble believing that the characters are deceived. The combination of good personating by the actor and good counterfeiting by the character makes plausible Emilia's inability to recognize her husband as the instigator of violence.

Shakespeare's scripts provide explanations and examples of methodology for personation. Overt discussions about technique, such as those in *Hamlet*, supplement examples of counterfeiting by characters within the plays. Hamlet tells the actors how; Richard III and Iago just do it. Yet, it is one thing to say that Richard III counterfeits well—that is, to refer to *plot*—and quite another to show how he does it. What is Richard's acting method? Personation requires an approach that combines the dialogue, the mind, and the body in a commitment to creating 'the true and perfect image of life'. The Chamberlain's Men transformed the elaborate verse structure and unnatural physical and vocal style that characterized other Elizabethan theater, rejecting artificial modes of performance to develop a theatrical style more grounded in the variety of language and action of life off the stage.

A Local Habitation

Physical space has consequences. To theorize the original performances requires exploring how the physical performance space shaped acting styles and, in turn, how those styles influenced the writing of the scripts. The Chamberlain's Men designed and built the Globe to serve their repertoire and style after several years of playing in other spaces, particularly the Theatre, presumably in reaction to positive and negative attributes of previous theaters. The performance style that they developed at the Theatre led to the Globe theater's design (and, later, to the company's indoor space at Blackfriars). The style further evolved as the players discovered the unforeseen capabilities of their performance space. A more complete and accurate understanding of the original techniques of acting used to perform Shakespeare's plays involves considerations of the intersection of historical influences and actors' needs that led to the design of the Globe, and how this design then interacted with playwrights and actors to influence style further. In what ways could the actors manipulate the physical and external conditions of performance, and/or how were the actors forced to respond to them? What kind of naturalism was possible under those conditions? The Chamberlain's Men made their theater, and their theater made them.

Early modern English theater-makers did not use scenery and lighting design to provide visually realistic representations of locations; nor could they focus light, and therefore the audience's attention, on the actors and the set. Since several modern conventions for creating the illusion of reality never surfaced during Shakespeare's time, it can be tempting to dismiss the idea that the players ever attempted naturalistic use of body and voice, or that audiences ever suspended disbelief. Arguments grounded in contemporary assumptions about the nature of theatrical realism tacitly suggest that naturalism in acting depends upon the illusion of an environmental reality independent of the theater itself, dark proscenium theaters, and silent, invisible audiences. Yet, the physical conditions of Globe theater performance—an open playing space with a back wall and doors but no additional scenery, along with an audience who do not sit quietly in the dark—neither enforce artificiality of manner and voice nor preclude authenticity in personation. Quite the opposite: the dynamics of the Globe created optimal conditions for a theatrical style that focused on character rather than location: realistic acting without realistic settings. Neither the Globe's players nor their audiences viewed realistic scenery as a necessary component of the illusion of truth on stage; the actors personated characters without requiring the stage to counterfeit locations. The intimate dynamic connection through which the Shakespearean character creates the scene is quite different from the illustrative method of theatrical or cinematic realism. An environment need not be solely created through visible images and appropriately defined space—that is, quantitatively—since a scene depends upon the characters who inhabit it for its quality. The character who speaks the scene both makes the scene and is in it. Upon entering the Globe stage, an actor initiated a relationship with other characters (and/or with the audience) in establishing the scene, rather than simply walking into a picture.

The illusion of life on the Globe stage involved the actors rather than the scenery. People, movement, costumes, and select handprops prevailed over location and stage dressing. This convention seems an obvious outgrowth of touring, for which companies could carry costumes and small props but not scenery. The fantastic scenery designed and built by the guilds for town play cycles could not have been practical for the touring players who were the immediate predecessors of the first London acting companies. Since professional early modern actors worked without scenery, Shakespeare developed other ways of indicating place, time, and atmosphere. The relationships between Shakespeare's characters, and/or the effects of time, place, and atmosphere upon them, are usually more vital to a scene than the location. Situation and dialogue, abetted by the actors' body language, signify these relationships and effects, allowing the flexible space to become a throne room, or dungeon, or heath. The opening lines of each scene set the stage whenever the specificity of the location is important. Occasionally, a narrator character directs the audience's imagination of the setting, as does Chorus in *Henry V.* Frequently, as in the opening of *Hamlet*, Shakespeare combines several tactics that enable the characters to give the audience a complete 'picture' through a naturalistic response to each other and the environment.

Shakespeare appeals to the mind's eye, manipulating the combination of the actor's personation and the audience member's imagination through the words themselves. When Richard III informs us that 'the Lights burn blue' (v. iii. 181)—a superstitious reference to the presence of ghosts—the audience's role in the performance of the play includes imaginative visualizing. As the actor embodies Richard III's reaction to the blue candle flame and its significance, he enables the audience members to accept that it is blue and to see it as blue in their minds' eyes. Shakespeare does not expect his audience to see things that aren't there, but, rather, to enable what is there to represent what the character describes, from the walls of Harfleur to Bosworth Field. Discussing this phenomenon in *Great Reckonings in Little Rooms*, Bert O. States notes, 'Even if nothing has changed scenographically, the play appropriates the stage as part of its qualitative world as established by its poetry. It is much the same process that an actor undergoes when Hamlet appropriates his body on one occasion and Macbeth on another' (1985: 53). States compares the freedom of the actor to personate different characters with the freedom of a flexible theatrical space to represent distinct environments.

Just as an actor must learn to make distinguishable a distinctive use of the body in order to counterfeit the physical behavior of an individual, a neutral space may be adapted through the player's use of it into a representation of a unique place. The actor doesn't become the character but, rather, personates the character through physical behavior, voice, and moment-to-moment specificity in action and reaction. The space doesn't become the location, but the players use it and respond to it in the same way that they would the 'real' place. In this kind of theater, the illusion of authenticity is an effect of physical technique. Through the player's specific use of the body in opening the door, any door becomes the door to Imogen's chamber or Juliet's tomb. The stage neither pretends to be Agincourt nor becomes it, but the players' bodies behave as though that is where they are. The line between pretending and personation may seem blurry, but States's use of the word 'appropriates' provides a clue to the distinction. One could say that the actor lends the character body, voice, and sense memories, while the stage lends the environment a place to exist. The flexible stage expands the available *modi significandi* for the actor to include the space in addition to the body. The actor, then, is able to use the character-specific rhetorical language provided by the playwright, along with the appropriate rhetorical behavior (rhetorical in that it is purposeful and significant) to create an impression of the environment: a rhetoric of space.

The stage as a generalized space made particular by the imagination parallels the interaction between the mind's eyes of the actors and the audiences in response to the words. The highly decorated back wall and 'heavens' of the Globe managed to function both as neutral backgrounds for stories that took place in many locations and as scenery when appropriate: 'This Majestical Roof, fretted with golden fire....'. The ease with which a stage uncluttered by the objects of mundane reality enabled the performance space to represent any location freed theatrical characters to wander all over the world. This flexibility of location may also have contributed to the freedom felt by Shakespeare and others to break the neoclassical rules in regard to both setting and time.

Arguing for formalistic original productions, many critics have contended that the lack of a proscenium arch curtailed the ability of the Elizabethan acting companies to present the two-dimensional visual illusions necessary for audiences to suspend disbelief. The pictorial illusion of proscenium theater requires the 'fourth wall' and the proscenium arch to separate the audience from the set and to hide the machinations creating that illusion. Current conventions of Realism require passive, voyeuristic audiences to assist the illusion by pretending that they do not exist on the other side of the fourth wall. The orientation of the audience, all politely facing front in an attempt to ignore each other, focused by light on the stage and darkness in the audience, contributes to the stability of the fourth wall and, hence, the illusion of location. Directors must take these inherent dynamics into account and submit to them, manipulate them, or work to subvert them. While proscenium theater leaves only one 'wall' open to the audience's view, the Globe's thrust stage kept only one wall closed to them. The Chamberlain's Men could not create a realistic setting in their theater—but it may never have occurred to them to try, since the actors and the dialogue created the illusion of truth on their stage independent of the visual environment.

A naturalistic performance at the Globe theater in 1601 would require quite different skills from those needed today in a proscenium theater (or on film). An actor can rarely make 'cinematic' detail the basis of character portrayal when extreme efforts are required to keep the focus on the stage while a thousand people are crammed in standing around it, eating, drinking, laughing, and jostling each other, with another two thousand people sitting in the galleries, particularly in the rain. The Chamberlain's Men had no built-in focusing mechanism such as directed lighting or a proscenium arch to mitigate this problem, so they had to use their bodies, voices, and words to keep the audience engaged in their characters and stories. Their theater made it possible. It would be difficult to extract an answer to 'Which came first, the round, thrust-stage theaters built by the Burbages or Richard Burbage's naturalistic acting?' If actors had continued to use thrust stages, at least for Shakespeare's plays, we might never have inherited the confused assertion that Burbage and company acted in a formalistic manner. Both thrust stages and Globe-style naturalism, however, fell out of favor in the 1620s with the rise in popularity in England of the 'new' Italianate stage brought about by Inigo Jones. The neoclassical proscenium stage itself provoked the transition to a new, stylized use of the body and voice.

When professional Elizabethan players first began working in permanent theaters, they came from a tradition that had required them to perform with limited materials and under undependable physical circumstances. The conditions of touring restricted elements of visual illusion to costumes and small props. Touring also forced players to adjust to whatever performance space and furniture was made available to them. Records kept by communities in which touring players performed show that most performances happened indoors in town halls, the banquet-style public rooms at inns, and the great-rooms of nobles' mansions. These rooms were usually rectangular, often with a small platform added at one end on which the actors performed. Most of the audience faced the front of the stage, similar to the situation in most modern theaters. Often, stylish courtiers or local dignitaries sat onstage, as much a part of the show as the actors and further restricting the amount of the platform available for the performance. In addition, indoor performance spaces were relatively dim and shadowy, lit only by candles.

The legacy of touring can be seen in the design of London's indoor theaters. The Blackfriars theater, for example, was 66 feet by 46 feet, with a stage at one end of the rectangle.[2] The size of the Blackfriars stage, approximately 20 feet deep and 25 feet wide, was atypical, however. Most indoor performance spaces had much shallower stages: 10 feet deep was common, and the stage at Whitehall was only 5 feet deep. The shallow stages severely restricted movement and physical relationships between characters, especially given the bulkiness of Elizabethan clothes.[3] The addition of furniture to any scene would further exacerbate the problem. Sightlines, combined with limited space, precluded unaffected use of the actors' bodies, such as facing each other directly in conversation. Standing center stage and declaiming the lines was almost the only possible performance style under these conditions. The limitations posed by the conditions of touring and the spaces in which players performed strongly influenced (and restricted) the development of English theater until quite late in the sixteenth century. The pre-Shakespearean dramatic poetry of strict rhythm, and the nearly complete lack of movement in plays such as *Gorboduc*, suited the physical conditions of indoor playing.

The stability provided by James Burbage's Theatre precipitated a change in working conditions that revolutionized theatrical methods, particularly the methods of the company that called the Theatre its home. Staying in London presented conditions that made the shift to naturalistic acting possible. For example, the gradually lessening need for touring allowed more time for rehearsal, while the

[2] Dimensions of early modern London stages are culled from many sources, particularly Orrell (1985).

[3] In experiments with students, I have found it impossible for two women in Elizabethan dresses to pass each other on a 5-foot-deep stage—and difficult to do so gracefully on a 10-foot-deep stage.

ever-increasing pool of 'hired men' to act in bit parts reduced the need for doubling. A company could develop a production that did not need to travel and, thus, the performers could refine blocking to utilize the attributes (and avoid the pitfalls) of a certain playing space. In addition, permanent theaters enabled a few writers to craft plays for the physical structures and qualities of specific playing spaces as opposed to ensuring adaptability for touring. Stage-specific playwrighting may be the most important change signaled by James Burbage's enterprise.

The Theatre was the first open-air amphitheater in London since Roman times and, as such, differed considerably from the halls in which touring actors usually performed. The early Roman amphitheaters that dot the English countryside apparently inspired the design and the name of the Theatre. Many considerations of Elizabethan amphitheater playing spaces assert that the design idea came from inn-yards and/or echoed bear-baiting arenas. Since traveling players, however, rarely used inn-yards—and bear-baiting arenas were, essentially, enclosed pits until a few entrepreneurs built theaters that doubled as bear-baiting venues—the ubiquitous ruins of Roman amphitheaters provide a much more likely source of architectural inspiration. The popularity of drama by Roman playwrights such as Seneca and Plautus may also have contributed to James Burbage's choice to emulate the Roman design of a round open-air theater in which the playing space is almost surrounded by the audience.

After Burbage built the Theatre, he continued to act with Leicester's Men. The Theatre probably became the main venue for the company, since their leader owned it. As performance companies went, Leicester's Men were a remarkably stable group, which may reflect their status as the only company with a home stage. When the playing companies reorganized after the plague of 1592–4, many former members of Leicester's Men were among the founders of the Chamberlain's Men. The company's name change indicates a transition in patronage; it does not necessarily follow that the actors formed a totally new organization. Rather than an ad hoc collective of actors beginning a new enterprise in 1594, perhaps the remaining members of Leicester's Men invited other players to join the company. In that case, one successful company of actors, known in different years as Leicester's Men, the Chamberlain's Men, and the King's Men, according to the identity of their patron, continued to work in London from 1576 until the theaters were closed by the revolutionary government. The stability of the playing company parallels the stability of their performance spaces.

Richard Burbage apparently apprenticed as an actor at the Theatre, under his father. Thus, one vital distinction between Richard Burbage and previous apprentice actors was that he apprenticed to the theater itself, in addition to the master actor. Other players learned to work solely under the conditions of touring, adapting generalized staging concepts to many spaces. In addition to the adaptability required for touring, Richard Burbage learned how to work in and with a particular performance space and set of physical conditions. All young players who apprenticed to Leicester's Men after they settled at the Theatre (and, later, to the Chamberlain's Men and the King's Men at the Globe) benefited from this specialized aspect of actor training. The constancy of both personnel and performance space enabled the company to establish a unique system and to continue to develop their approach to acting.

Much evidence suggests that Shakespeare, like Richard Burbage, apprenticed to the Theatre. Each of Shakespeare's plays requires a stage at once intimate and spacious, and utilizes the same theatrical elements (three doors, a trap, and an 'above'). This combination of conditions was not provided by any other theater. When the Chamberlain's Men first incorporated, they owned all of Shakespeare's early plays, which further indicates that he had always written for the company and, hence, for the Theatre. (Records of performances by other companies complicate this assertion, but do not serve as proof against it.) Just as Richard Burbage's acting was influenced by his experience of a specific playing space, Shakespeare's playwrighting would have been both inspired by and accommodating to the physical dynamics of the Theatre—along with the acting techniques developed there.

As is well known, when the Burbages lost their lease on the land on which the Theatre had stood for over twenty years, six company members formed a partnership to finance and build the Globe. The players apparently favored the idea of continuing to have their own, consistent performance space over renting out other theaters. More than an excellent financial decision, the choice suggests artistic preferences as well. Designed and built to the specifications of the players, the Globe was exactly what they wanted to suit their style and their repertory. The company built the Globe out of the timbers of the Theatre. This fact, in conjunction with the staging requirements shared by all of Shakespeare's plays, indicates that the new design resembled the old design, possibly quite closely. Since the company did not opt for a complete redesign, the players clearly preferred the Theatre's architectural arrangement to that of other London performance spaces. Further, the decision to build the Globe in the same general form as the Theatre implies that the Chamberlain's Men appreciated what their original performance space contributed to their work. It appears, for example, that the company had developed all of their work for a thrust stage larger than the stage in any other English theater. Any design elements that were new to the Globe would have been inspired by what the players had learned from working with the physical conditions and capabilities of their previous space. One possible new feature was the orientation to light that ensured the stage was never in direct sunlight yet always well illuminated by ambient light (Orrell 1997*a*: 55). This arrangement precludes shadows, and thus leaves the time of day or night in which a scene takes place as open to suggestion as the location.

The company must have been very satisfied with the Globe: they spent a fortune to rebuild it after it burned down in 1613, even though they owned another, equally profitable theater. The Burbages' amphitheaters clearly impressed other London theatrical entrepreneurs, as they built several. Aside from the Fortune, which was square, London's open-air theaters followed the Roman plan of an enclosed circle. Audiences stood in front of the stage or sat in the galleries that enclosed the space. The theaters were open to the sky, permitting daylight to fill the entire space (and exposing the groundlings to rain). Unlike modern outdoor theaters in which actors frequently have to shout in order to be heard, the 20- to 30-foot-tall circular enclosures actually would have kept sound from dissipating. The enclosure, combined with the relatively small overall area, the proximity of actors to the audience, and the 'heavens' built over the stage to protect the costumes from rain, made the job of being heard much easier for actors than it is today in many indoor proscenium theaters.

The 1587 design for the Rose, Henslowe's first theater in Southwark, serves as a representable example of early amphitheaters other than the Globe (and, probably, the Theatre). The Rose's fourteen walls enclosed a roughly circular space about 50 feet across. Despite the round space, the audience–stage relationship echoed that of the indoor theaters: the audience faced one end of the area. The Rose's 10-foot-deep stage ran along 37 feet 6 inches of one side of the 'circle' and tapered down to 27 feet 6 inches at the front of the stage. The shallowness of the stage rendered authenticity of movement unlikely. Further, the total usable area of the Rose's stage was smaller than it seems: the stage was 10 feet deep only along the 27 feet 6 inches front edge, tapering back to unusable corners. If facing out front, a player might stand carefully about 2 feet in from the corner and 18 inches downstage, but in that location an Elizabethan dress would hang over the edge of the stage and be crushed against the rear wall. The physical dynamics of the Rose, and nearly every other early London theater, encouraged artificiality of movement and forward-facing presentational style. The stages were too restrictive in size and focus to enable the freedom of movement necessary to counterfeit 'real' people in 'real' places.

Figure 28.1 View from the expensive seats in the Globe theater: the front row of the second balcony, next to the Gentlemen's Box. From up here, especially from the Gentlemen's Box, audiences watch more than participate.

In striking contrast to the other theaters built before 1601, the Globe's performance area was large enough to accommodate the physical variety that characterizes familiar life. On the smaller stages, actors were compressed by the space, but at the Globe their bodies could be put into motion with the words. The design illustrates an important breakthrough in the crafting of theaters for unrestricted use of the actor's body. Nearly perfectly round, the twenty-sided building enclosed a space about 70 feet in diameter, with the stage extending out from three of the sides for a 43-foot width. The stage was 28 feet deep, making true-to-life movement (and exciting swordfights) possible. Although the stage was larger than that at any other London theater yet built, the audience at the Globe was treated to unparalleled intimacy with the performers owing to the theater's unique thrust stage. The Globe's configuration, a large thrust stage encircled by the building as opposed to a small platform at one end of it, allowed the audience to stand on either side and face into the stage, joining the audience members who faced along the front. With the thrust stage, the Chamberlain's Men moved the playing space into the audience. Audiences surrounded the sides of the stage, essentially making up three walls of the set, instead of sitting outside an invisible fourth as they do in a proscenium theater. The Chamberlain's Men used circular space to concentrate the energy of the performance and of the audience in the center of the theater. The downstage center point of the stage was also the center of the building, allowing Hamlet, or any other character talking directly to the audience, to stand (or sit) in the center of the room. Concentrating all of the focus on the center of the theater, the stage managed to be large and intimate at the same time. Actors were easy to see and hear, which enabled them to use subtle movements and vocal shadings; yet, the stage was big enough to accommodate grandeur. The Globe allowed the flexibility to blend the epic and the intimate.

As Marion Trousdale observes, 'modes of composition' reflect 'modes of perception' (1982: 7)—and vice versa. These actors and their actor–playwright intentionally built their theater with physical dynamics different from those at other London theaters. The Chamberlain's Men demanded a unique type of playing space to accommodate their particular repertory and performance style, as well as their manner of interacting with their audience. This statement also obtains in reverse: the playing space demanded a unique style and repertory. The framing of the stage and the arrangement of the audience in the proscenium theater resemble painting and appear two-dimensional. In contrast, the audience surrounding the thrust stage experiences three-dimensional performances. Analogous to the difference between perspective painting and sculpture, the proscenium stage mimics three-dimensional reality, while the thrust stage achieves it. The three-dimensional possibilities of the thrust stage liberated the playwright and the players to craft their work without the restrictions of a two-dimensional view.

In addition, the combination of large stage size and intimacy with the audience enabled myriad choices in the dynamics of scenes. In purely practical terms, the stage was large enough for actors to progress from one part of the stage to another as one scene transitioned into another; to allow for quickly moving from scene to scene by using different parts of the stage and the various exits and entrances; and to have two or three scenes happening at once, as the two different camps at Bosworth Field in *Richard III* and at Agincourt in *Henry V.* For *Sejanus*, Ben Jonson takes advantage of the stage's capabilities to enable believable treatment of asides and to accommodate plausibly the most common of Elizabethan and Jacobean theatrical activities: spying. At the same time, the Globe was small enough for intimate scenes to happen on any part of the stage. The variety of uses available to playwrights and actors ranged from conversation and domesticity to ceremony, masque, and illusions of war. The company responded to these possibilities—to this freedom—by developing personation.

The character on the thrust stage is visible from many perspectives simultaneously, since the audience nearly surrounds the stage. Natural daylight illuminating the playing area intensifies the effect. The space and system of perspective at the Globe accentuated body language and movement, and thus opened up the possibility for the Chamberlain's Men to develop a physically naturalistic style of acting. The arrangement freed the actor to use his body and voice in an unaffected manner. Unlike every other London theater, the Globe did not require the players to 'cheat out', but, rather, allowed for movement in three dimensions and groupings of characters that mimicked the familiar. Nothing about the Globe theater inhibited the actors from achieving the illusion that the action onstage was 'real' or 'true', as well as 'here' and 'now'. Although the size of the Globe stage allowed large physical movements, the combination of the three-dimensional view and the proximity of the audience to the actors also made every small motion by an actor visible. The Globe enabled Shakespeare to write discrete physical details for characters, allowing King Lear to fiddle with tiny objects, like buttons. 'Off, off, you Lendings: Come; unbutton here' (III. iv. 106–7); 'Pray you undo this Button. Thank you Sir' (v. iii. 308).

Not only would the Globe's conditions encourage plausible body language and behavior, the stage might demand naturalism by visually emphasizing gesture. Without the framing and limited audience perspective of a proscenium, posing and such theatrical techniques as 'cheating out' cannot be masked as verisimilar. An artificial body posture, even if it appeared unaffected from in front of the stage, would look ludicrous from the sides. Further, to out-Herod Herod at the Globe would transform tragedy into melodrama. On the other hand, these same conditions could be deliberately manipulated for comic effect. The audience could appreciate every slight movement by a physical comedian, one reason that Jonson's 1605–6 *Volpone*, with its *commedia dell'arte*-inspired physical comedy and posturing characters, was so popular.

The traditional and nearly ubiquitous tendency of scholars to assume a similarity of styles on all Elizabethan, Jacobean, and Carolinian stages—and for all plays, whether comic or dramatic—ignores evidence to the contrary. The 'deep tragedian' whom Buckingham parodies in *Richard III* embodies the part in a style that is clearly the opposite of that used by the actor who played Buckingham:

> Tut, I can counterfeit the deep Tragedian,
> Speak, and look back, and pry on every side,
> Tremble and start at the wagging of a Straw:
> Intending deep suspicion, ghastly Looks

Are at my service, like enforced Smiles;
And both are ready in their Offices,
At any time to grace my Stratagems. (III. v. 5–11)

If Buckingham later showed his own (well-founded) paranoia in a similar gestural manner, he would have predisposed the audience to find him ludicrous. Yet, most scholars' descriptions of acting at the Globe have implied that Buckingham's burlesque actually describes himself.

Shakespeare's dialogue provides much evidence of plausible body language and gesture, capitalizing on the visibility of the actor's body in the Globe's performance space. Descriptions of how characters move both provide information to the actor reading the script for the first time and emphasize the significance of that movement to the audience. Julius Caesar's portrait of Cassius, for example, discusses Cassius' facial expressions and what they indicate.

Yond Cassius has a lean and hungry look,
He thinks too much: such men are dangerous.
. . . . . .
He is a great Observer, and he looks
Quite through the Deeds of men. He loves no Plays,
As thou dost Antony: he hears no Music;
Seldom he smiles, and smiles in such a sort
As if he mock'd himself, and scorn'd his spirit
That could be move'd to smile at any thing.
Such men as he, be never at hearts ease,
Whiles they behold a greater than themselves,
And therefore are they very dangerous. (I. ii. 191–207)

Similar examples of dialogue that can be mined for physicality permeate the play. Shakespeare also uses naturalistic movement to establish scene and atmosphere. Perhaps Shakespeare's most interesting uses of unaffected movement and location-setting dialogue occur when actors physically engaged in changing the set discuss doing so, as do the servants in *Romeo and Juliet* decorating Juliet's house for the masked ball (I. v. 1–15) and the soldiers bringing in the cushions for the Roman senate to sit upon in *Coriolanus* (II. ii. 1–36).

Many factors could have contributed to the players' evolution of staging ideas to supplement those specifically called for by dialogue. The actors' familiarity with each other, combined with the adaptability they acquired through touring and playing at court, would have conditioned them to improvise physically. More importantly, the company always developed their performances on the same stage, with its consistent size, actor–audience dynamics, and setting of three doors, a balcony, and a trap. In direct contrast, modern actors rarely, perhaps never, work in the same configuration of theatrical space twice. The Globe company's intimate knowledge of the stage and its physical properties would have made much of a modern stage director's input superfluous. The playwright visualized working on the Globe's stage as he wrote, and the actors would have imagined performing there as they read and memorized. The imagery and dynamics of the dialogue often appeal to obvious uses of the company's customary space, such as translating the statues at the back of the stage to Paulina's statues in *The Winter's Tale* and the balcony space to the walls of Harfleur in *Henry V.* Through years of experimentation on the same stage, the actors would have known such intangibles as how different physical relationships between bodies in different parts of that stage carried specific messages about interpersonal power dynamics, or, simply, where the actor could appear the most powerful (or least). Playwright and players essentially collaborated with the theater in developing productions.

In addition to offering the audience a three-dimensional perspective, the thrust stage capitalized upon and increased the theatrical potential of the English tradition of talking to the audience. English playwrights had always combined direct address with scenes that pretended that the audience was not there. Scripts indicate that talking to the audience in plays written for spaces other than the Theatre and the Globe tended to be presentational, in keeping with the stylized nature of the rest of the performance. Owing to sightlines and the small acting areas, the stages had offered little other choice. The thrust stage, however, by freeing actors to move and speak without artificiality, enabled them to stay 'in character' and, even, conversational

Figure 28.2 Groundling's-eye view in the Globe theater. Unlike the gentlemen, the groundlings get to see the heavens. Furthermore, the play happens in their midst, enabling the groundlings to participate.

when addressing the audience. The proscenium stage aggressively discourages naturalistic characters from 'stepping out' of the frame. In contrast, the combination of a round space and a thrust stage encompassed by the audience invites transgression of the threshold between the audience and the characters. The characters and the world of the play exist in the midst of the audience; the actor need not leave the character and the world behind physically in order to change the character's focus to the theater and its inhabitants. The character's intermittent acknowledgement of the theater and the audience became a convention of Globe theater personation, which was rooted in the actor's embodiment of the character and not dependent on the pretense of a fourth wall. An after-effect of the physical freedom of the thrust stage is Benedick's ability to use the audience as a sounding board as he works out his attraction to Beatrice.

Since the audience shared the space with the characters at the Globe, the audience functioned as part of the performance. Surrounding the action, the audience became physically involved in it. Frequently, they served as extras in Shakespeare's cast, becoming Richmond's troops when he exhorted them to overthrow Richard III, and Roman citizens when Mark Antony addressed them at Julius Caesar's memorial. Not only was the audience 'in' the forest with Macbeth and Banquo when the characters heard the prophecies, but when the Weird Sisters performed their binding spell in the third scene, they implicated the entire audience in an act of witchcraft. A binding spell is performed in a circle; the audience surrounded the Weird Sisters' circle, and was encompassed by the circle of the Globe as well. Three concentric circles—the one drawn on stage, the audience itself, and the walls of the building—physically reinforced the words of the spell. Demons had been called to the stage; how could one be sure that the demons would know it was only a play? The realistic representation of the Weird Sisters and their spell-casting, as opposed to the comic devils with firecrackers in *Dr Faustus*, illustrates the naturalism of Shakespeare's theater through contrast. Kenneth Muir notes in his introduction to the Arden edition of *Macbeth* that, by the time Shakespeare wrote the play, one could not use devils as characters in tragedies because they had become so associated with comedy (Muir 1951, p. liii). Unlike *Dr Faustus*, *Macbeth* never descends to silly circus tricks and fart jokes, so the audience members are never released from their culpability. When the Porter later welcomed all the 1606 audience to hell, despite the sardonic humor, an element of true danger must have pervaded the atmosphere. Audiences knew what to expect from the Chamberlain's and King's Men, and they learned to play the game, to pretend along with the actors that the people and events were 'true', 'real', and 'now'. The audience had a responsibility in maintaining the illusion that was not required of them at the other theaters, where the focus of production was on spectacle, rather than character. The Globe also enabled the actors to ignore the audience and pretend that the stage had four walls. The actors could even retreat from the predicament of always sharing visual space with the audience, and permit the audience members to quit seeing each other for a while, by moving to upstage center and using the back wall of the stage, and/or the balcony, as a set. At the Globe, the actors could have it both ways.

Shakespeare wrote all of his plays to take advantage of the performance conditions and physical dynamics of his theaters. He wrote his great tragedies as he learned the potentialities of the Globe's stage and its company of actors, crafting *Hamlet* for their second season at the Globe. No other company hired a resident playwright, which seems especially surprising considering the Chamberlain's/King's Men's success with custom-written plays. Since all other playwrights sold their scripts to any company that would buy them, no other playwright had the consistent opportunity to write specifically to utilize the dynamics of a particular space. (Some individual plays were clearly crafted for specific theaters, notably Ben Jonson's Globe play *Sejanus.*) The King's Men, on the other hand, continued their tradition by hiring Beaumont and Fletcher as Shakespeare began to retire.

Following the success of the Globe, Henslowe and Alleyn commissioned a square version of it, the Fortune. With its stage nearly four times the size of the stage at the Rose, the Fortune provided, for example, dramatically expanded possibilities for staging Marlowe's *Dr Faustus.* The enhanced space may account for the 'B' text's additional dances, theatrical tricks, and other expansions of physicality. Prior to the Fortune, if the Admiral's Men performed the dance of the Seven Deadly Sins and the scene of playing tricks on the Pope, they did so on a 10-foot-deep stage. In contrast to the Chamberlain's Men, the Admiral's Men's repertory grew more extravagant and stylized. Henslowe's financial records for the Rose show him spending more and more money on visual elements and plays such as Heywood's *The Golden Age* and *The Silver Age*, which Gurr calls 'colorful and fire-works spangled' and indicative of 'a preference for spectacle over the word' (1992*b*: 323). *Dr Faustus*' devils' 'farting' fireworks, along with other elaborate visuals including machinery for astonishing theatrical tricks such as *dei ex machina*, joined bombastic verse that encouraged actors to out-Herod Herod. In 1613 William Turner wrote in his *Dish of Lenten Stuff* that he liked the military heroics scripts—known as 'drum and trumpet plays'—that characterized the Fortune's repertoire. The Red Bull produced these visual extravaganzas, as well. George Wither attacked the verse and acting style at these theaters in his 1614 monograph *Abuses Stript and Whipt.*

Although some other amphitheaters eventually adapted aspects of the Globe's design, notably the square Fortune, the companies performing in these spaces rarely altered their style accordingly. A study of the domestic tragedy genre plays might encourage an argument that fairly true-to-life characterization was occasionally used by other companies. In addition, although Edward Alleyn was famous for his over-the-top performances of Tamburlaine and Barabas, the eyewitness description of his performance as Talbot in *Henry VI* indicates that Alleyn could also personate. Further, Marlowe's *Dr Faustus*, despite its tricks and devils, provided Alleyn, as Faustus, with opportunities to speak conversationally in private moments with Mephistopheles. Still, the players at the Fortune were often attacked for overacting. Due to Webster's extreme dissatisfaction with the production *The White Devil* received at the Fortune (*c.*1610), he took *The Duchess of Malfi* to the King's Men (1612–13), apparently seeking a less melodramatic mode of performance.

The Chamberlain's/King's Men preserved the potential of the space to 'act' as a location by maintaining its integrity within the world of the play. The company discontinued post-performance jigs just before the move to the Globe, a decision that may account for Will Kempe's choice to drop out of the company. After Kempe left, all dances and songs used in performance related to the action of the plays. After the King's Men added the Blackfriars, they hired Beaumont and Fletcher to craft *Philaster*, a rewrite of *Cupid's Revenge* that eliminated its *dei ex machina* and artificial performance style. As the directions for using props and stage dressing in *Pericles* demonstrate, however, the King's Men gradually joined in the trend toward striking visual elements. Yet, records indicate that the only play ever produced by the Chamberlain's or King's Men that required any kind of machinery (which might potentially mar the illusion of reality by drawing attention to itself) was *Cymbeline.*

The opening of the Blackfriars theater had no immediate effect on the King's Men's style or repertory. The Blackfriars had the largest stage of any indoor theater; it was not conducive to fireworks and cannons, but scaled-down swordfights were possible. The unaffected acting style employed by the Chamberlain's and King's Men, combined with their scrupulous avoidance of non-naturalistic elements from comic jigs to the machinery required for *dei ex machina*, facilitated the adaptation of their plays into smaller spaces. This adaptability accounts in part for the popularity of Shakespeare's plays at court. From 1609 on, the King's Men worked in both theaters—essentially, summers at the Globe and winters at Blackfriars. Adding the indoor theater expanded their audience, rather than changed it. Audience members who could afford higher ticket prices patronized the same plays; they just did so at a different theater. Prior to Burbage's death, the company bought no plays intended only for performance indoors. The company continued to develop plays at the Globe, transferring them indoors when the weather turned poor.

The King's Men used both theaters for thirty-three years, from 1609 until the closing of the theaters in 1642. During these years, English playgoers gradually came to consider themselves spectators rather than audience: they went to 'see' plays, rather than to 'hear' them. After Heminges died in 1630, the company finally gave priority to the Blackfriars over the Globe and allowed their repertory to succumb to the fashion of fantastic visual scenery that appealed to the physical eye over verbal scenery that spoke to the mind's eye. The death of the last member of the original company signaled the demise of their style, although Shakespeare's plays continued to be popular until the monarchy was overthrown and the theaters were closed.

For more than 350 years, no production of a play by Shakespeare was staged in a theater truly similar to the one in which Shakespeare and his fellow actors performed. To produce a script written for the Globe theater in a theater with different physical dynamics requires an act of adaptation, rather than simply another production of the same play. Hundreds of years of productions in other kinds of theater obscures contemporary understanding of how Shakespeare's plays were originally designed to work, as different performance spaces draw out distinct potentialities from both scripts and actors. Formalistic 'classical' acting arose long after Shakespeare's death, as directors and actors adapted the plays to stages that discouraged naturalistic body language and movement, such as the cavernous and footlit proscenium theaters of the nineteenth century. The convention that actors can only maintain authenticity of character and emotion on sets that counterfeit real locations and by pretending the audience doesn't exist arose in theaters that created vastly different actor–audience interactions than those at the Globe. Twentieth-century scholars inherited a conception of original Shakespearean performance as artificial and formalistic for two interlaced reasons: centuries of adaptations to other theaters and modern concepts of the conditions necessary to create a feeling of realism in acting.

The new acting style and method that the Chamberlain's Men developed were indebted to a specific use of the body and of space, and to a unique theater. As authentic characters were more vital to Shakespeare's dramaturgy than accurately represented locations, the Chamberlain's and King's Men employed three-dimensional characters, with bodies and movement in three dimensions, rather than three-dimensional scenery. The space inspired the technique. The Globe theater enabled actors to achieve an unprecedented level of physical verisimilitude by providing a new possibility for 'truth' in the visibility—or visible body—of a character.

CHAPTER 29

ACTORS' PARTS

TIFFANY STERN

WHEN Quince first meets his actors in *A Midsummer Night's Dream*, he tells them who they will be playing and a little about their fictional characters: 'You *Nicke Bottome* are set downe for *Pyramus*... a Lover that kills himselfe most gallantly for love' (TLN 288–92); 'you must take *Thisbie* on you... the Lady that *Pyramus* must love' (TLN 306–8).[1] It is at this moment that he also distributes to the actors their 'parts', the pieces of paper on which their words are written. 'Part' in this instance, then, means not simply the character who will be played by the performer, but also the text from which that character will be learned. Walking away from the meeting, the actors take their paper parts with them for memorizing at home: by the time they next gather together, each player must be word-perfect, as Quince makes clear when he requests everyone 'to con' the lines 'by too morrow night' (TLN 361). So the players are going to learn from a text that is only 'part' of the play—an idea so strange to scholars that it is still regularly called into question. Actually many texts survive that illustrate what Quince gave his actors. This chapter will discuss some of them. It will look at extant actors' parts, consider references to such parts, and look towards the consequences both for actors and for playwrights of writing plays in and for parts.

[1] Shakespeare quotations are taken from the facsimile of *Mr. William Shakespeares Comedies, Histories, & Tragedies* prepared by Charlton Hinman (New York: Norton, 1968), using the through line numbers (TLN) of that edition.

Actors' Paper Parts

A large number of actors' parts are extant, though it can be hard to find them in libraries. They are frequently not recognized: the earliest surviving British cued part—for Secundus Miles (Second Soldier) in an unknown play—was only spotted in the 1970s having for years been taken to be a page of playscript with some oddly situated stage directions (Davis 1979: 81–3). Even when parts are not miscataloged, they hide under one of several names given to these fragmented scripts at different points in history: 'cue-script' (their twentieth-century name), 'side' (their twentieth- and nineteenth-century name), 'length' (their eighteenth-century name), 'part' (their usual early modern name), 'parcel', 'scroll', or 'roll' (alternative early modern names). Among the more prominent of the surviving parts are: eighteenth- and nineteenth-century parts including many belonging to Kemble in the Folger Library, Washington; Macklin's book of 1730s parts in the Harvard Theatre Library; Medbourne's 1662 part in the Houghton Library in Harvard; four parts (bound together) performed by a student at Oxford in the 1620s, now held by the Harvard Theatre Library; and, most famously, Alleyn's 1590s part of Orlando in Dulwich College Library, London. Earlier, medieval, parts also survive; and even fragments of a classical part—for Admetus in Euripides' *Alcestis*, dating from between 100 BC and AD 50—have been discovered (having been misidentified for years as poetic scraps) (Greg 1931: i. 173–5; Hall 2006: 43). A substantial number of medieval and early modern parts are also to be found on the Continent. There are upwards of ten in France and twelve in Germany; Italy has at least four—and these are only the ones recorded in books and articles (Lalou 1991: 63–4; Linke 1988: 532; Palfrey and Stern 2007). In Vevey, Switzerland, twenty-three parts from the sixteenth century have been unearthed, all from the same slender source: squashed together with other waste material, they made up the cardboard wrapping to a book of poetry, and were only revealed in the 1920s when the cover was unglued (Aebischer 1925: 511). Most people who come across parts in one country have been unaware of parts in other countries—and that goes for England too: often people write of the surviving English material as though there is too little of it for academic discussion. But by combining what can be learned from looking at the Continental parts, seventeenth- and eighteenth-century English parts, and surviving references to parts in the literature of Shakespeare's time, it is actually easy to work out more or less what an average early modern part would have looked like and what information it would have contained. There is no difficulty, then, in defining what the principal characteristics of the parts given to Quince's actors will have been: for, as will be shown, parts look roughly the same over time and across country.

Let us start by looking at one of the large numbers of surviving eighteenth-century parts, or 'lengths'—for these show what the early modern theatre part eventually became once it had been formalized, regularized, and made routine over time; seeing what an eighteenth-century part is like teaches us what to look for in earlier parts.

By the early eighteenth century the theatre had been streamlined. Plays were performed in 'runs' of several days, and there was a mechanism for preparing for them: actors would have a minimum of two but sometimes up to five weeks to ready performances (Stern 2000*a*: 203). Yet this is what Macklin's 1730s part—for Lissardo in Susanna Centlivre's *The Wonder: A Woman Keeps a Secret*—looks like:

——————————————Lisardo, Lisardo
Coming Sir, what a Pox will you do?
——————————————I get Out!
Nay, nay you must e'en set your Quarrel aside, & be Content to bee mew'd up in this Clothe's Press together, or Stay where you are & Face it Out—there's no help for't.
——————————————hear me call?
I did hear you, & answer'd you I was coming.
——————————————to see it more.
Hey-day! What's the matter now? {Exit P: 31} PS
{Re-enter to Felix P: 32} OP
at——————————————punish my Infidelity.
Oh sir! Here's your Father DonLopez coming up.

(Book of parts belonging to Macklin)

As the part shows, Macklin is provided with up to four words as a 'cue' (the last words spoken before his own), but is never told who the cue-speaker will be or how much time he must wait between one cue and another. He is, however, given careful information concerning entrances, exits, and the side of the stage on which these should take place ('PS' is 'Prompt Side'; 'OP' is 'Opposite Prompt'); he is also told which fictional character to approach ('to Felix'). The final cue of the passage provided, the one that is preceded by 'at', is a cue of entrance: on this manuscript all entrance cues are heralded so, making them slightly different—though not longer than—other cues; a common pattern in parts. Apart from this, Macklin is given relatively little. In the full text a stage direction explains that, before exiting, Lissardo is to 'open[] the Press' and hide Flora inside, but that information is not written onto this script (Centlivre 1714: 32). Indeed, what Macklin's actions are to be are never particularly clear in the part-book, a fact that obviously disturbed the actor, for on more than one occasion he annotates the text, adding extra stage directions, and, sometimes, swelling his cue line from three words to five. The sense this book of parts gives is that its eighteenth-century actor felt somewhat hampered by the lacunal nature of the part. What is surprising, in the circumstances, is that Macklin received—and used—a part at all. For cross-references here to pages 31 and 32 suggest that the actor at least had access to, if he did not own, a complete playbook for the entire play. That raises an interesting question about the form of the part itself. What was it about parts that made them continue to be written out for actors, when cheap printed full texts were readily available? Was there anything positive about parts; anything that parts provided the actor that the full text did not?

A look at other parts may provide some of the answers. One of the other surviving earlier parts, also in a book, and also for professional performance, dates from the Restoration. It is for the actor Matthew Medbourne, who played Trico in Ferdinando

Parkhurst's *Ignoramus*, a play that was performed by the Duke's company in the Cockpit and in Whitehall in 1662. In appearance, the text is much the same as Macklin's part-book. It is not, however, annotated by the performer.

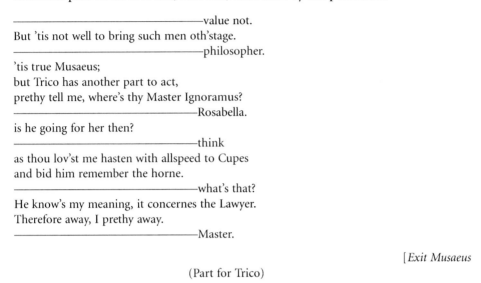

————————————————value not.
But 'tis not well to bring such men oth'stage.
————————————————philosopher.
'tis true Musaeus;
but Trico has another part to act,
prethy tell me, where's thy Master Ignoramus?
————————————————Rosabella.
is he going for her then?
————————————————think
as thou lov'st me hasten with allspeed to Cupes
and bid him remember the horne.
————————————————what's that?
He know's my meaning, it concernes the Lawyer.
Therefore away, I prethy away.
————————————————Master.

[*Exit Musaeus*

(Part for Trico)

As before, the speaker of the cues is not named, and the cues themselves are as little as a word—and, in one instance, elsewhere on the manuscript, a single syllable—in length. Again, entrances and exits remain important so that even the exit for another character is provided, affording the onstage actor a sense of the disposition of the scene. In other respects the part is superficially unhelpful. It makes no distinction, for instance, between a cue that is a bit of what the interlocutor is going to say, and a cue that is everything the interlocutor is to say. On the other hand, Medbourne's stage directions are better than Macklin's: comparison shows that Trico has fuller directions than those supplied in the manuscript playbook of the entire text. So in IV. v the part tells Trico to 'hide', a stage direction that is absent from the complete play. What may account for the difference in stage directions between this part and Macklin's? Perhaps the fact that Macklin has a playbook to hand has lessened the need to provide him with all information available, or perhaps the fact that Macklin will have access to several group rehearsals makes the provision of full directions less important. What is clear is that between the Restoration and the eighteenth century, parts look roughly the same, and that there is generally a discrepancy around stage directions: whether more or less useful, in neither instance are the stage directions the same as those provided by the full text.

Non-professional performers also played from parts—for the part was the unit in which all texts were disseminated. Examples are provided by the four 'University' parts for plays that were performed at Christ Church, Oxford, in the 1620s: the part of Poore (in English, from a lost play), the part of Polypragmaticus (in Latin, from Robert Burton's *Philosophaster*), the part of Amurath (in English, from Thomas Goffe's *The Courageous Turk, or, Amurath the First*), and the part of Antoninus (in

Latin, from the anonymous *Antoninus Bassianus Caracalla*). These parts are bound together in a small book, and each is presented similarly, irrespective of language. They all contain just the words of the speaker interspersed by cues, but here cues are long, extending for as much as one full line of verse; the speaker of the cue-line is also named. Full stage directions are regularly provided—'by his hand he swears', 'privatly to her'—and these extend beyond the actor, so that other people's actions are supplied when they are relevant to the performance: 'Badg: gives him ye l[ett]re', for instance (Bawcutt 1993: 149). Even here, though, the explicit stage directions constitute only some of the action required by the text itself: stage directions tend not to be given when the words of the part itself make the required action clear. Most usefully, a system of dashes indicates when the actor is finishing or starting a verse line. So, for instance, if Poore's text completes a verse line that starts in the cue, a rule follows the verse, and Poore's line is indented:

SNAILE. I nere wrongd you——
POORE.——————nor ere mistrusted him?
SNAILE. No on my life.——
POORE.———————nor wife, I knowe it well
Sir hye you home; if now you meet not wth him . . .
(Part of Poore)

Instructive as these parts are about early modern staging for university performance, they are, clearly, slightly unlike professional theatre parts. They were written for plays that will have been carefully rehearsed for a single performance, as was university custom (Carnegie 1982: 12), and they provide helpful material for people unfamiliar with the conventions of regular playing. Yet though the Christ Church parts cannot be taken as models for the public theatre part, they do indicate the upper limit of the information that might be given actors through the medium of cued scripts.

How, then, does the most important part for early modern theatrical studies, the part of Orlando, fit in? In being cast as Orlando, Edward Alleyn—the great actor for whom the roles of Dr Faustus and Tamburlaine were probably written—received, as usual, the lead character. Orlando gave him the protagonist of Robert Greene's 1590s play *Orlando Furioso*, performed at the Rose theatre in 1591–2, for which we also have a printed playbook (published in 1594). Unfortunately, however, the printed text records a revised and perhaps mutilated form of the play that does not compare directly to the text provided in the part (Greene sold *Orlando* twice to two different companies, the Admiral's Men and the Queen's players; variations between the part and the printed play may be traceable to that fact) (Greg 1922: 128). But although the printed book does not tell us everything about the part, it does provide information the part denies—and deny information the part provides. As ever, the texts are markedly different in stage directions; Orlando is also sometimes more 'correct' than the playbook.

The part of Orlando shows us what was received and used by a professional actor in an early modern theatre production. It is much like the other, later, professional parts. Like Macklin's part-book, Orlando contains on it corrections in the hand of

Alleyn—though those corrections do not add to the content of the part: they are limited to filling in the blank spaces left when the scribe could not read the words in the playbook. Has Alleyn, then, been correcting his part against the full text? Or has he learned the words during his 'instruction' sessions or in rehearsal—of which, more below? Cues on the part are of one to three words, their length determined, it seems, by circumstance: cues are often longer when a shorter cue would be confusing. Here, for instance, is a section of Orlando in which cues are elongated, seemingly to identify them as different from other similar-sounding cues occurring at roughly the same point in the play:

——————————————my lord
I pray the tell me one thing, doest thou not
Knowe, wherfore I cald the
——————————————neither
why knowest thou not, nay nothing thou
mayst be gonne, stay, stay villayne I tell
the Angelica is dead, nay she is in deed
——————————————lord
but my Angelica is dead.
——————————————my lord
and canst thou not weepe
——————————————Lord
why then begin...

(Greg 1922: 156)

As in other public theatre parts, the speaker of Orlando's cues is not named, nor is Alleyn told how long he will have to wait between one cue and another. (Will the actor hear his cue almost immediately after he has finished speaking, or will three people have a five-minute conversation on stage before his next cue comes up?) There is also no indication given to suggest that any of Orlando's verse lines are completions of a verse line begun by another character—either the instance does not arise in the text, or Orlando has to count out the beat of the verse for himself: the reason is unclear. Orlando is, however, supplied with stage directions in a mixture of Latin and English. They are relatively full, ranging from property notes—'enters wth a mans legg'; to action notes—'he walketh up & downe', '<he> singes', 'he whistles for him'; to notes concerning other people whose actions will affect Orlando—'A[rgalio]. begins to weepe' (Greg 1922: 152, 156, 158). When the words to be spoken act as a direction themselves, however, additional direction notes are not always provided. Moreover, one important piece of action is not indicated by notes in the part. Orlando, at one point, has to change clothes off-stage, re-entering dressed as a madman. A specific direction is not provided for this in the part—yet, that said, changes of attire are seldom given in stage directions even to full plays. There was, presumably, a playhouse routine for dealing with dress changes, which may have been the concern of the tireman or -woman ('tire' meaning 'attire) backstage in the 'tiring house' as much as the actor.

Here, then, is a used, working theatrical document—and yet it has often seemed to commentators to be disappointingly lacking in extra-textual information. Reviewing the publication of Greg's *Dramatic Documents*, which contains a facsimile of the part, one famous theatre historian wrote that the part had 'mere antiquarian appeal' and was the 'least important' of all the documents reproduced (Greg 1931; Lawrence 1932). Orlando is so free of detail that it has sometimes been questioned whether it was ever actually used for a production: might it have survived because it was a 'reject' (Warren 1998: 67–91)? For the text contains on it no performance notes scrawled in the margins by Alleyn, no underlining to suggest blocking or stress, and no clearly indicated movement cues. Yet, as has been shown, this impersonal, scrappy part relates closely to other, later parts above, or to the Swiss parts from Vevey, nearly all of which are lacking in actor's notation and are surprisingly 'carelessly written and full of error' for performance documents (Runnalls 1990: 98). Lack of information, and what seems to be a pointedly difficult text from which to perform, are features of most parts in England and abroad both in the early modern period and later.

We return, then, to the question of what actors gain through learning from a part rather than from a full play. In the early modern period, one might argue, parts were written because paper and scribes were expensive: a part was a way of handing only essentials to an actor. But by the eighteenth century, when cheap playbooks were easily available, a part *cost* paper and scribes. So what did parts offer?

One advantage of the part is psychological. An actor with a part is the lead performer of his text—indeed, in the form in which he receives each play, every production appears to star him. This may have aided the player to identify with and internalize his role. When actors like Macklin or Alleyn wrote on their texts, they furthered the process of identifying with the part, inserting themselves into their personal scripts. But in practical terms a part can be particularly useful. Actors with parts are focused solely on their own characters, and thus have the opportunity to become deeply attuned to their characters' habits of speaking—as well as alert to the moments when those habits are changed. In the early modern period, when actors looked through their parts to find their 'passions' and the moments when those passions were altered ('acting' at the time was sometimes called 'passionating'), switches from prose to verse, from asking questions to answering them, from formal to informal speech, are likely to have stood out as, themselves, stage directions. Orlando's angry madness, for instance, is heralded by a change of verbal register: he starts to repeat words, particularly 'villayne'; he loses Spenserian lyricism ('oh thought, my heave*n*; oh heaven yt knowes my thought. | Smyle: [for] joy in hir, that my content hath wrought') in favour of jagged 'mad' verse ('yf he will eate g<old | he shall have it. thre blew bean< s | a blewe bladder, rattle, bladder <> rattle'). A part indeed makes a character the product of his verbal habits. And, as in real life, the actor's character would be constructed not from anything said to or about him but only from the words he himself uttered.

A part-reliant actor could easily have his performance 'directed' in interesting ways through the cues on his text. For these might give him weighted information (Orlando's coming emotional crisis is heralded with 'shall ensewe', 'sorowes dwell', and 'angry brest' as consecutive cues); or might, if repeated several times in a speech, direct the cued player to speak 'early'. A part was not merely a section of something larger, then: it seems to have functioned as an entity containing its own rules and directions with a worth different from that of the full text. Thus, there appears to have been something positive—something useful and telling to the actor—about receiving a play in part form. Indeed, even now, years after the last physical part has ceased to be distributed, the words 'part' and 'role' are still the titles we use to describe an actor's assumed character: an actor's 'part'—is who he is.

Some features of Orlando are specific to their time. Punctuation, for instance, is very light on the part—but in this way it simply resembles surviving play manuscripts of the period. What is perhaps more telling is that Alleyn has not felt the need to add his own punctuation into the text, although he will certainly have had to decide where to pause, where to stop, and where to enjamb lines on stage. Then again, breathing spaces, verse-speaking, and the choice of which words to emphasize were said at the time to be the actor's business; deciding on 'pointing' was, indeed, one of the main aspects an actor would address when learning a part. Thomas Newton tells young men to speak aloud to music in order to achieve the kind of 'bigge tuned sounds' made of 'stoppes and certayne Pauses' that 'Comicall felowes' could so easily produce (Lemnius 1576, G5a–b). Actors were praised or blamed for their skill at 'pointing' well, or their lack of skill ('pointing' badly): 'if there be not a facility in [their] deliverance', writes Gainsford, 'it must needes sound harsh to the auditour, and procure his distast and displeasure' (Gainsford 1616: 118). What we might think of as punctuation, then, was up to the speaker; it did not need to be written into the text itself—as this sparsely punctuated passage shows:

——————————————a ballad
Are not my sweet, thes eyes those sparkling lampes
whereout proud Phebus flasheth forth his light*es*
——————————————wth an othe
but tell me false Angelica
stru*m*pett worse than the whorish love of Mars
traytresse surpassing trothlese Cresida
that so inchast his name wthin that grove
whers medor...

In another way, too, the part of Orlando differs from the later parts looked at so far. Though it is now in strips, it was clearly originally kept as a roll—as the pattern of wormholes running through it makes clear. Each sheet was once joined to the other, top to tail, making a strip that was 18 or so feet in length; this appears to have been anchored at the very top and bottom with rods. The part will then have been wound around its two sticks, creating a text that could be 'scrolled', probably with one hand. Though the later parts are often found in book form, the rolled part seems to have been usual in the early modern period: most of the Swiss parts were clearly once rolls, for instance. Indeed the names given to parts overseas at the time reflect their structure in their title—they are called *roole*, *rollet*, *roullet* in France (from which we get our term 'role'), *Rolle* in Germandy, *rotuli* in Italy. Even in England the word 'roll', like its foreign equivalents, was sometimes used, as when Samuel Gardiner described God as giving a 'rowle' to the Evangelist (Gardiner 1606: 102), or when William Percy in a manuscript poem described the way the candles

> set on high, where as a Playe
> Is to be fare enact, thus seeme to saye,
> See in your rouled Parts, you do not misse,
> For, on you, there be many eyes, I wisse.[2]

The reason for constructing a roll may have been no more than that rolls produced no waste paper: any bit of a page not inscribed could be used to make up someone else's roll. Yet a roll, because of the way it was revealed to its reader, affected the way the part was learned. It is likely to have been learned sequentially, the actor scrolling through his text from beginning to end. Rolls will have made it difficult to compare passages that occur far apart, but will have left the actor with a secure sense of the sequential 'order' of the play. Books, on the other hand, make flipping from one passage of text to another easier; they encourage 'comparison' between scene and scene. They can also threaten the distinction between one text and another: a book that contains several parts—like Macklin's part-book, or, years earlier, the book of University parts—can make all parts seem interchangeable, or at any rate take on 'across-play' dimensions.

The Reading of the Play

One reason why parts were of such importance to productions is the amount of time the actor spent exclusively with them. For, much as in *A Midsummer Night's Dream*, the actors, having received their parts, did not meet again to rehearse until those parts had been fully committed to memory, most of the work that the actor was going to put into a role having already been done by the time group rehearsal occurred. True, the actor had attended a reading of the play given, often by the playwright, to the sharers (hirelings—people paid by the week—would not have been present) at the very beginning of the learning process. But such readings were often as much an 'audition' of the play itself as an occasion for the actors to learn the narrative of the play. So the actor–sharer Robert Shaa writes to Henslowe the financier on 8 November 1599, 'we have heard their booke and lyke yt their pryce is eight poundes, wch I pray pay now' (Greg 1907: 49). Here the play is at a very early stage and the company's main concern is simply to decide whether to buy it or not. There may even have been two varieties of reading: one in which the playwright solicited for approval to write his text, and another, later, in which the playwright read his completed text out loud in order to show what it was about and how he would

[2] William Percy, *Poems*, Huntington Library, San Marino, Calif., MS HM 4, fo. 278.

like it performed. One such example is dramatized in *Histriomastix*, where Posthaste the poet reads to the actors the terrible play he has written. This reading takes place in a tavern, and it is not long before Posthaste is overcome with drink and emotion. Up until that point, however, he recites the text, including stage directions, annotating the verse and highlighting the stylistic qualities of his writing:

> POSTHASTE. Enter to him Dame Vertue:
> *My Sonne thou art a lost childe,*
> (This is a passion, note you the passion?)
> *And hath many poore men of their goods beguil'd:*
> *O prodigall childe, and childe prodigall.*
> Read the rest sirs, I cannot read for teares.
>
> (Marston 1934–9: iii. 259)

Such readings seem usually to have been held in taverns. Henslowe's diaries record how money was lent 'unto the company for to spend at the Readynge of that boocke [*Henry I*] at the sonne in new fyshstrete', or 'Layd owt for the companye when they Read the playe of Jeffa for wine at the tavern' (Foakes 2002: 88, 201). Being held outside the playhouse and in a building that offered ready distractions, readings may not always have been entirely play-focused.

Whether the parts were given to the actors immediately after the reading to the company is unclear; it may have depended on the state of a play's acceptance. That said, a couple of accounts make it clear that parts were sometimes distributed *before* the play had even been completed. 'I have took extraordinary payns wth the end & altered one other scean in the third act which they have now in parts,' writes Daborne the playwright on 25 June 1613, showing that parts could be written and sent out as acts were submitted; Henry Herbert, Master of the Revels, criticizes Edward Knight, the prompter of the King's Men, for letting the players have parts before the play has been approved: 'the players ought not to study their parts till I have allowed of the booke' (Greg 1907: 73; Bawcutt 1996: 183). Both these instances show companies hurrying parts to their actors at the earliest opportunity; sometimes plays had barely been constructed in their entirety before they were rerendered as parts, for parts were essential units of rehearsal—and, indeed, performance—in a way that full texts were not.

Studying the Part

Having received a part, the actor took it home with him to learn: 'the Player so beateth his parte too him selfe at home, that hee gives it right gesture when he comes to the scaffolde', writes Gosson; Dekker in *Jests to Make you Merrie* draws an analogy in which the chief actor goes 'into his bed-chamber, where he [is] fast enough lockt all night, to rehearse his parts by himselfe' (Gosson 1579*a*, K2a; Dekker 1963: ii. 345).

Again, one result is likely to have been psychological: an actor may have felt he 'owned' the lines because he had brought them into his house.

In Fletcher's *Maid in the Mill*, Bustofa is depicted learning the part of Paris at home. The ridiculous passage he is trying to memorize is 'The thundring Seas, whose watry fire washes | The whiting mops: | The gentle Whale whose feet so fell | Flies ore the Mountains tops'.

FRANIO [*within*]. Boy.
BUSTOFA. The thundering—
FRANIO. Why boy *Bustofa.*
BUSTOFA. Here I am—the gentle whale—
[*Enter* Franio
FRANIO. Oh, are you here Sir? where's your sister?
BUSTOFA. The gentle whale flies ore the mountain tops.
FRANIO. Where's your sister (man)?
BUSTOFA. Washes the whiting-Mops.
FRANIO. Thou ly'st, she has none to wash! mops?
The Boy is half way out of his wits, sure:
Sirrha, who am I?
BUSTOFA. The thundring Seas—
FRANIO. Mad, stark mad.
BUSTOFA. Will you not give a man leave to con?
(Fletcher 1966–96: ix. 590)

Bustofa is enraged by the intrusion of his father when he wants to concentrate on the solitary act of 'conning' his lines. And it was 'conning' of this kind—or 'studying', as it was often called—that occupied most of the rehearsal period. *As Maid in the Mill* goes on to show, actors could well be entirely competent in their parts and yet ignorant of the rest of the text. For when Bustofa, who is 'studied in my part', actually performs the play, he does not know or fully understand the story. Gerasto enters the play and takes Venus away, and Bustofa is unclear whether or not this should have happened: 'Ha? what follows this? [he's] carried away my sister *Venus*: | He never rehears'd his part with me before' (Fletcher 1966–96: ix. 601). A similar fictional culmination of part-learning is depicted in the Induction to Marston's *Antonio and Mellida*, where the scripted pretence is that the actors have not had even one group rehearsal and have no idea what roles their fellow actors are playing, let alone the details of the story. They enter onto the stage for performance still holding their parts in their hands, and asking each other: 'Whome doe you personate?', '*Piero*, Duke of *Venice*...', 'whome act you?', 'The necessitie of the play forceth me to act two parts...', 'Wel, and what dost thou play?' (Marston 1934–9: i. 5–6).

Of course, these accounts are fictional. But similar information is provided by a contemporary law case. When the young Thomas Clifton was kidnapped and forcibly made into a boy player in 1600, his father mounted a legal investigation into what had happened. He recounted the events that had followed the capture of his child, including the fact that Giles Robinson and Evans 'did then and there deliver unto his sayd sonne, in moste scornefull disdaynfull and dispightfull manner, a scrolle of paper, conteyning parte of one of theire sayd playes or enterludes, and him, the sayd Thomas Clifton, comaunded to learne the same by harte' (Chambers 1923: ii. 44). Here the father's objection is to the bullies Robinson and Evans, but he incidentally shows how, just as in a *Midsummer Night's Dream*, the boy is to commit his part to memory as soon as he gets it—before he has met his fellow actors or been introduced to the play's story.

So important was this individual learning that most rehearsal time was dedicated to it. Not that this meant the actor was entirely left to his own devices. It was not unusual to be helped in one's individual learning by a superior actor, the playwright, or someone else thought to be rhetorically competent: an 'instructor'. Richard Burbage, the famous actor for whom Shakespeare wrote so many of his key roles, is parodically depicted in a contemporary play 'instructing' a would-be performer. He illustrates how to play Hieronimo in *The Spanish Tragedy* by reciting 'correctly' an important passage: 'observe how I act it, and then imitate me' (Leishman 1949: 341). In *Hamlet* Shakespeare depicts a writer–instructor, perhaps someone rather like himself, who, having written a 'dosen or sixteene lines' (TLN 1581) for a play, similarly recites the words as he would like them pointed: 'Speake the speech . . . as I pronounc'd it to you' (TLN 1850). Thus 'instruction' was an occasion on which 'pronunciation' (pauses and emphases) as well as 'action' (gesture) were decided—and in a rather dictatorial fashion if the instructor felt rhetorically superior. Naturally, given the nature of the preparation, it took place away from the full acting company. So when Alphonso instructs Medice in his part for a masque in a Chapman play, *The Gentleman Usher*, only the two of them are present; indeed when, in that same play, Bassiolo asks Sarpego, 'Are all parts perfect?', Sarpego replies, 'One I know there is': he knows only that his own part has been perfectly learned. In rehearsal and performance, actors who might be very well individually prepared did not necessarily ever have ensemble values.

Learning parts in this fashion put tremendous emphasis on the very elements of the part that are absent from the full text. Particularly visually prominent were a part's cues and the long line that preceded them: these were so distinctive that even printed texts for a reading 'audience' assumed a knowledge of them. When Sir John Mennes published the famous short epitaph for Shakespeare's lead actor Burbage, he presented it as Burbage's final cue—his cue of exit—flanked by his final cue 'tail' (the long line before a cue):

> *On Richard Burbage a famous Actour*
> ————————————Exit Burbage
> (Mennes 1817: ii. 216)

Even outside the theatre, then, a part's division into speeches and cues was familiar. Indeed, even the sight and sound of actors taking cues (or missing them) was familiar enough to make its way into a set of joke definitions: Richard Brathwaite describes how an echo 'were good to make a Player of the Stage' because 'she would take her cues excellently well'—the echo, would, of course, always 'come in on cue' (Brathwait 1634, C11b). Meta-theatrical 'cue' references abound in Shakespeare, from the moment when Beatrice enjoins, 'Speak count, tis your Qu' (*Much Ado*, TLN 704), to the number of cue jokes enwrapped in *A Midsummer Night's Dream.* At the start of the mechanicals' rehearsal, Flute has learned his part by heart, but has not understood its construction. As it seems, he has learned it in its entirety, and starts speaking straight through from speech to cue to speech again, for Quince has to reprimand him with 'you speake all your part at once, cues and all' (TLN 913). Bottom, meanwhile, has learned his part but is slow at coming in: 'your cue is past; it is *never tyre*' (TLN 913–14; my emphasis). Later, in the performance itself, the actors are proud at having finally learned how to use their parts properly. Bottom, playing Pyramus, glosses the words 'O wicked wall, through whom I see no blisse, | Curst be thy stones for thus deceiving mee' with an explanation to the restless audience, '*Deceiving me,* | Is *Thisbies* cue...' (TLN 1983–4). The nature of the part was a fact so elemental to performance that jokes on the subject were available to everyone, whether they were actors or not.

The General Rehearsal

Many stories of the time depict an actor who is individually competent, yet relatively unclear on details of the story he is in or the movements of his fellow actors. For even in the more carefully learned and rehearsed university productions, the actors were brought together on stage usually only once after the learning process before performance itself. Gayton tells an anecdote which illustrates the consequences of knowing a part well and a play badly. He recalls a university production in which two actors had both independently studied their parts of ghosts—without, seemingly, realizing that there would be more than one ghost in the performance:

> two Scholars there were in this Spanish Tragedy (which was the story of *Petrus Crudelis*) whose parts were two Ghosts or Apparitions of some Noble Personages, which that Bloody Prince had Murder'd. These two at the Repetitions spoke their lines very confidently, insomuch, that the Judges thought they would be very good Ghosts; but when the tryall night came, that the Play was to be presented to some few friends before the publicke exhibit, and then these two Scholars were put out of their blacks into white long robes, their Faces meal'd, and Torches in their hands, and some flashes of Sulphur made at their entrance; just as they put their heads through the hangings of the Scene coming out at two severall sides of the Stage, they shook so, and were so horribly affrighted at one anothers ghastly lookes, that no force of those behind them, could get them to advance a foot forward toward the stage, or speak a word of their Parts. (Gayton 1654: 94–5)

What Gayton here describes as the 'tryall' performance is regularly referred to, though it hides under a number of names. Blount records how 'Among Comœdians the tryal or proof of their action, which they make before they come forth publiquely upon the Stage, is their *Essay*' (Gayton 1654: 94–5; Blount 1656, P7a). This 'essay', 'proof', or 'trial'—the 'general rehearse', as the occasion is known in provincial documents—seems to have, usually, been one in number, though there were, of course no rules: if the single rehearsal showed the play to be unready for performance, another rehearsal could always be demanded. Nevertheless, plays within plays from that period generally refer to a maximum of one group rehearsal: Shakespeare's *A Midsummer Night's Dream*, Marston's *Histriomastix*, Middleton's *Your Five Gallants*, each have one; Kyd's *Spanish Tragedy*, Jonson's *Cynthia's Revels*, Beaumont and Fletcher's *Maid in the Mill*, Chapman's *The Gentleman Usher*, Carlell's *The Fool Would Be a Favourite*, Brome's *A Jovial Crew*, all have none. One is also the number usually demanded when provincial actors put a performance together (Stern 2000*a*: 32). At least one collective rehearsal was desirable, but it was also, if necessary, disposable, in ways that conning a part at home was not. Hence professional theatre contracts of the time suggest that not attending rehearsal was a finable offence—illustrating, by so doing, that actors could not be relied on to turn up for rehearsal by choice (the event was, after all, unpaid). These same documents also make clear that collective rehearsal did not happen daily, but only when occasion demanded. On such instances the rehearsal would be announced the night before. Robert Dawes is contracted to

> attend all suche rehearsal which shall the night before the rehearsal be given publickly out; and if that he the saide Robert Dawes shall at any tyme faile to come at the hower appointed, then he shall and will pay to... Phillipp Henslowe and Jacob Meade... Twelve pence; and if he come not before the saide rehearsal is ended then the said Robert Dawes is contented to pay twoe shillings. (Greg 1907: 123)

Complaints that rehearsal is slighted are regular, but then again, there was no director (the actor–manager was not to come into being for over a century), and rehearsals were run only to ensure that the play was ready for performance. So bad men are compared to bad actors, whose lack of attention to study and rehearsal leads to a performance that lets down God—the careful playwright:

> Th'unworthy *Actors*, dull, imperfect skill
> Bred by distemper, grosse neglect in studdy,
> Carelesse Rehearsalls, and a skull so muddy,
> As never minds th'infinite paines and Art,
> Penn'd, to advance and fit him with a part
> That might immortalize...
>
> (Richards 1641: 20–1)

What actually happened at these group rehearsals is open to question. If actors had already learned their lines with the help of an instructor, there was little need for rehearsal to check that they were 'perfect' (as there is for the uninstructed actors in *A Midsummer Night's Dream*, for instance). Passages in plays of the time referring to what is rehearsed often suggest that the verbal content of a play is not the emphasis of collective rehearsal; that a general rehearsal is largely intended to determine action that affects the group: in Jonson's *Every Man Out of His Humour* Carlo speaks of 'a thing studied, and rehearst as ordinarily... as a jigge after a Play'; in Chapman's

Gentleman Usher the boys intensively practise their song for the play together (Jonson 1925–52: iii. 467; Chapman 1970: 146). Jigs, songs, and, perhaps also, dances, swordfights, slapstick, and other complicated action—everything, in other words, that cannot be perfected from the part alone—seem to have been the emphasis of group rehearsal.

Performing from Parts

Naturally the playhouse had certain mechanisms for putting a production together and attempting to unite the separate parts on stage. A prompter standing backstage in the tiring house would direct aspects of the production while it was happening, rather as a modern musical conductor brings separately prepared instrumental performers together during a concert. For prompters, peeping through curtains and grilles, shouted out essential instructions to the players. The prompter's 'Dismisse the Court' in Brome's *Antipodes* is repeated by the actor Letoy: 'Dismisse the Court, cannot you heare the prompter'; his 'Mend your lights, Gentlemen. *Master Prologue*, beginne' intrudes into Jonson's *Staple of News*; while Will Summers in *Summers Last Will* can hear the prompter's cry of 'Begin, begin' (Brome 1873: iii. 292; Jonson 1925–52: vi. 280; Nashe 1958: iii. 233). Thus, various aspects of the action never needed to be collectively rehearsed and learned by the actors at all: they could be prompted in performance. This goes not only for timing and entrances but even for fights and comedy. When Othello says, 'Were it my Cue to fight, I should have knowne it | Without a Prompter' (TLN 301), he makes clear that the prompt to fight might also be the book-holder's responsibility. Moreover, parts, with their actual stage directions and the stage directions implied in them by layout, could themselves 'direct' some of the actor's performance, as has been discussed; used in conjunction with the backstage 'plot' that isolated on it actors' entrances and properties, the actor seems to have had rich access to performance information (though not necessarily to narrative information) about the play.

Nevertheless, actors' part-focus was visible in performances. A second-rate actor might only ever really play his fragment, which is why, in a late account, Burbage is singled out for his ability to maintain character throughout a production, 'never falling in his Part when he had done speaking; but with his looks and gesture, maintaining it still' (Flecknoe 1664, G7a–b). Other (bad) actors had a tendency to stop acting when they stopped speaking: in Brome's *Antipodes* Letoy accuses a player of limiting his performance to the moments when he recites his lines, 'And when you have spoke, at the end of every speech, | Not minding the reply, you turne you round | As Tumblers do' (Brome 1873: iii. 259). For the next two centuries critics would continue to complain about part and cue actors. In the 1730s Aaron Hill in *The Prompter: A Theatrical Paper* wrote of players who 'relax themselves as soon as any speech in their own part is over, into an absent unattentiveness to whatever is replied by another, looking round and examining the company of spectators with an ear only watchful of the cue, at which, like soldiers upon the word of command, they start suddenly back to their postures' (Hill and Popple 1966: 78).

Plays often stage what might happen if the cue-reliant system came under threat. In Shirley's *Hide Parke* Mistress Caroll asks Mr Fairefield whether he has gone off course and needs a 'prompter to insinuate | The first word of your studied oration' (J. Shirley 1637, F2a). Were an actor to give out a right cue at the wrong time, the other actors might not even realize what had happened: only conscious of the required response, they might set off from the cue, the result being that entire passages would be left unsaid. If, on the other hand, an actor gave out a thoroughly wrong cue, the entire production would be paralysed. Hence the terror behind the threat made by Summers in *Summers Last Will*: 'looke to your cues, my masters; for I intend to play the knave in cue and put you besides all your parts' (Nashe 1958: iii. 235).

Naturally, the more a play was performed, the more familiar actors would become with it as a whole. Yet there were no play 'runs', and up to forty plays might be performed in a season: plays will never have been as familiar to actors in their entirety as they were in parts (Stern 2000*a*: 53). Hardly surprisingly, then, plays habitually refer to their own part-related qualities, meta-theatrically embracing the mechanism of the part that was so continually visible in performance. 'Your speech being ended, now comes in my cue,' says Captain Bonvile in Heywood's *The Royall King, and the Loyall Subject*; Dr Makewell in Clavell's *The So[l]ddered Cittizen* declares that 'all's fitted, | If you be perfect, in yor. Cues, and action' (Heywood 1637, C1a; Clavell 1936: 74). So rooted was the idea of the 'part' that plays about non-theatrical—and yet performative—events, tend to make part assumptions, or part jokes. So Viola is sent to woo Olivia in *Twelfth Night* with a speech, presumably written by Orsino, that she has 'taken great pains to con' (TLN 468). When asked 'Whence came you...?' she replies, 'I can say little more then I have studied, & that question's out of my part' (TLN 472–3), as though she is an actor waiting for a different cue. In Shirley's *Humorous Courtier* Depazzi has learned a love speech to recite, to which he *has* even been given a cue—an absurdity, as the Countess to whom he is speaking has no knowledge that he is reciting a text. So when she teasingly asks him whether her face 'looks bad', Depazzi's love recitation grinds to a halt: 'speake your part right[.] | "Oblivion" is my qu. I doe remember.'[3]

Parts had their effect on the way a performance was watched, too. Spectators were conscious of seeing a series of separately perfected parts, and so they individually evaluated the performers of those parts. Excellent players were given 'Plaudits, Showts and Acclamations', while bad ones would 'goe hissed off the Stage. And that is for want of being perfect in those good parts, which are put into them' (Dekker 1630: 3). The danger was that the audience's response to a play might be confounded with their response to the actors of those plays; hissing a lot might make them feel that the play

[3] James Shirley, *The Humorous Courtier* (1640), ed. Marvin Morrillo (New York: Garland, 1979), 142.

itself was bad—and the result was that 'A good play sometimes [was] hissed off the stage, through the fault of the plaier, ill acting it' (Meres 1598, 2K6a). But even when this did not happen, the audience seem regularly to have compared the narrative of the play to its part structure, a method of critical evaluation that is foreign to us. One Caroline writer's response to *Othello*, for instance, is to praise first its story, then its parts: 'a very good play...for...plot. Iago for a rogue and Othello for a jealous husband 2 parts well pend' (Kirsch 1969: 257).

With parts informing so fundamentally the way actors performed and audiences watched, they must also have affected the way playwrights wrote. 'He that writes, resembleth a man acting his part upon a theator or stage, where the spectators have their eyes fixing upon him,' writes William Gray (1649, A3b): writing is like acting, where the part is critically judged by the spectators. As has been shown, plays themselves frequently refer to parts or part-based anxieties. Writers who were conscious of the way their plays would be disseminated—particularly writers who were also actors (like Shakespeare, for instance)—probably had the part in mind as a fundamental unit of construction for their plays (Palfrey and Stern 2007). For the part was an extraordinary piece of paper: its organization and stage directions were unique; it was a text with its own rules that was not the same, and was never the same, as the full play. The part, then, was potentially more than a practical necessity. On occasion the part may have been embedded in the creative core of a play itself, helping to shape not just the way actors learned, but the way they performed, the way audiences watched, and the way playwrights wrote.

CHAPTER 30

STAGE DIRECTIONS AND THE THEATER HISTORIAN

ALAN C. DESSEN

When watching the first performances of *Twelfth Night* or *Hamlet*, what did an Elizabethan playgoer actually see? For the theater historian, that question leads to another: wherein lies the evidence for such an investigation? And, given the dearth of eyewitness accounts, drawings, and other external records of theatrical practice, that second question leads to the internal evidence found in extant manuscripts and printed plays. Hence—*enter* the stage direction.

To build edifices upon these signals in italics, however, can be a daunting task. Sometimes, interpretation is easy, requiring no more than the translation of a Latin word (***manet***, ***exiturus***). Occasionally, directions can be detailed and evocative, as with accounts of ***dumb shows*** (as in *Hamlet*, III. ii),[1] a few battle scenes (as in *Cymbeline*, V. ii), or scenes involving special effects or pageantry (*The Tempest*, *Henry VIII*). More

[1] To streamline this essay I have drawn my examples when possible from *The Riverside Shakespeare* (Shakespeare 1997*b*) and from plays in *The Works of Francis Beaumont and John Fletcher*, ed. Arnold Glover and A. R. Waller, 10 vols (Cambridge: Cambridge University Press, 1905–12); Richard Brome, *Dramatic Works*, ed. R. H. Shepherd (Brome 1873); Thomas Dekker, *Dramatic Works*, ed. Fredson Bowers (Dekker 1953–61); Nathan Field, *Plays*, ed. William Peery (Field 1950); Thomas Heywood, *Dramatic Works*, ed. R. H. Shepherd (Heywood 1874); Ben Jonson, *Jonson*, ed. C. H. Herford and Percy and Evelyn Simpson (Jonson 1925–52); and Philip Massinger, *Plays and Poems*, ed. Philip Edwards and Colin Gibson (Massinger 1976).

typically, however, are directions that lack specific details but instead invoke a formula (***vanish***; *they **fight***; *enter **unready**, **mad***, or *in his **study***) where the implementation of the onstage effect is left to the players or to the imagination of a reader. In some instances such formulas can be fleshed out by invocation of material from comparable scenes elsewhere where more details *are* available, a process analogous to the work of an iconographer who ranges widely in the available literature so as to explicate an image (***booted***, ***rosemary***)—and here is a major asset of a stage direction dictionary. Nonetheless, many texts (*Measure for Measure* is a good example) provide few signals other than straightforward entrances and exits—and the first published version of Ben Jonson's *Volpone*, the 1606 Quarto, provides no stage directions at all.

To use stage directions as evidence is therefore to confront many puzzles and potential sources of confusion. First comes the question of who is responsible for the extant signals? In his landmark 1790 edition Edmund Malone stated categorically that they were 'furnished by the players' and were therefore subject to change by the editor (Malone 1790, vol. i, p. lviii); other candidates have been scribes who copied the manuscripts (notably Ralph Crane, to whom have been attributed the massed entries in *The Winter's Tale* and some unusual items in *The Tempest*), compositors in the printing shop, and bookkeepers in the playhouse who supposedly transformed a playwright's draft into a promptbook suitable for performance. Recent scholarship, however, has demonstrated that a high percentage of stage directions are authorial in origin. Indeed, close attention to the surviving manuscripts and printed texts with playhouse annotations has shown how few were the additions or corrections made by the bookkeeper—most commonly to specify sound effects, spell out which actors are to play supernumerary roles, and anticipate the introduction of large properties (W. Long 1985). Occasionally, one of these practical in-the-theater signals survives in a printed text, as with '*two Torches ready*' (Fletcher, *Love's Cure*, vii. 205).

Questions about origins are linked as well to the issue of *provenance* (place of origin, derivation). Scholars seeking to reconstruct the physical features of a particular theater such as the Globe will concentrate on evidence from plays known to have been performed in that building. If the goal is to tease out the number of stage doors or the presence of flying machinery at the Rose, that scholar will not invoke scenes or

Also cited are Barnabe Barnes, *The Devil's Charter*, ed. John S. Farmer (Barnes 1913); Robert Greene, *Alphonsus of Aragon* (Greene 1926) and *James IV*, ed. A. E. H. Swaen (Greene 1921); Thomas Heywood, *The Escapes of Jupiter*, ed. Henry D. Janzen (Heywood 1978); Thomas Lodge, *The Wounds of Civil War*, ed. J. Dover Wilson (Lodge 1910); Christopher Marlowe, *Doctor Faustus*, ed. W. W. Greg (Oxford: Oxford University Press, 1950); Thomas Middleton, *A Mad World My Masters*, ed. Standish Henning, Regents Renaissance Drama (Lincoln: University of Nebraska Press, 1965); *The Two Merry Milkmaids*, ed. John S. Farmer (Amersham: Tudor Facsimile Texts, 1914); John Webster, *The White Devil*, ed. John Russell Brown, Revels Plays (London: Methuen, 1960); and George Whetstone, *Promos and Cassandra*, ed. John S. Farmer (Whetstone 1910).

For fuller documentation of various items, see the *Dictionary of Stage Directions*, Dessen and Thomson (1999). Terms in my text for which there are dictionary entries are printed in ***bold italics***. As is the practice in the dictionary, when citing stage directions from old-spelling editions I have modernized the spelling. Playwrights' names attached to titles are for the convenience of the reader and do not take into account multiple authorship.

stage directions from a play linked to the Red Bull. When widely scattered stage directions are invoked as evidence, the provenance of individual plays cannot be completely ignored (as when John Marston, writing with a particular theater in mind, refers to *music* ***houses***), but for those whose primary concern is not the reconstruction of a specific theater this distinction becomes less important than other variables.

Similar questions pertain to *chronology* (when were a play and its theatrical signals composed?). Some locutions found in the 1580s and early 1590s are superseded or simplified in the play-texts that follow (***proffer***, ***let***); the earlier signals are often longer, without the shorthand forms that later become commonplace. However, for the bulk of the period up through the 1630s continuity rather than evolution is the norm. To downplay the importance of chronology is not to argue that staging procedures and the terms used to signal those procedures stayed the same in all theaters between the 1580s and the early 1640s. But if (as is often the case) Shakespeare–Heywood and Brome–Shirley make use of much the same terminology, the importance of chronological distinctions is greatly diminished.

Although the theater historian cannot discount provenance and chronology, what needs stressing is the presence in the extant stage directions of a widely shared theatrical vocabulary, especially from the 1590s on. Admittedly, the language used by a professional dramatist may not be exactly the same as that used by a bookkeeper, a scribe, an amateur writer, an academic, or a Ben Jonson refashioning his play for a reader. Still, the major variations in that vocabulary arise less often from different venues or different decades than from authorial idiosyncrasy. For example, George Chapman is more likely than any other professional dramatist to use Latin terms; most dramatists regularly use ***aside*** to mean *speak aside*, but Shakespeare, for one, prefers other locutions (e.g. ***to himself***) and uses *aside* to denote onstage positioning. By proceeding carefully and not building edifices upon unique or highly idiosyncratic usages the scholar can set forth a range of terms that would have made excellent sense to Marlowe, Shakespeare, Dekker, Heywood, Jonson, Marston, Chapman, Middleton, Massinger, Brome, Ford, and Shirley.

Next to consider are the different functions of stage directions. Their major role is traffic control—getting actors and properties on and off the stage—so that the most widely used term by far is ***enter***. A large majority of the extant signals therefore consist of *enter* and some combination of proper names (Hamlet, Faustus, Hieronimo); titles or professions (queen, bishop, merchant); and generic types or collective nouns (army, citizens, others, servants, soldiers, women). Also plentiful are signals that specify the place where or from which the entrance is to be made (***above***, ***below***, ***at several doors***, *in a* ***prison***, ***shop***, or ***study***) and modifiers that characterize the entering figure as ***amazed***, ***bleeding***, ***booted***, ***disguised***, ***marching***, ***mourning***, ***muffled***, ***raging***, ***reading***, ***running***, ***sick***, ***solus***, or ***weeping*** (to cite but a few examples). Equally important are the many uses of ***exit*** and its plural, *exeunt*, along with related terms such as ***manet***–*manent* and ***offers to go***. Even here at the most basic level, however, problems and inconsistencies abound, particularly for mid-scene exits and re-entrances which are regularly omitted.

When one moves beyond *enter–exit* and traffic control, problems increase exponentially. What can be frustrating for both first-time readers and theater historians are the many silences when we today most want specifics about the onstage action. (Is Hamlet aware of the eavesdroppers during the nunnery scene? If so, when?) What *is* characteristic of most playscripts of this period is not explicit detail about how to stage a given moment but some combination of (1) silence and (2) coded signals directed at playhouse professionals who knew their craft well.

As a case study, consider *The Two Merry Milkmaids*, one of the few examples of a printed text (as opposed to a manuscript) of an Elizabethan or Jacobean professional play that has been annotated for performance, in this instance in two different hands (L. Thomson 1996). To set up the play's central trial scene the Quarto first directs: '*Enter the Duke, Judges, Raymond, with others, the form of a Court*' and then '*Enter Dorigen placed at the Bar*' (I3^{r}). The two annotators then *do* spell out several items not available in the Quarto: from one a sound effect (a ***sennet*** at the entrance of royalty) and a table (presumably for the judges and perhaps the Duke himself); from the second a sound effect (***hoboys***), a guard to place the accused at the ***bar***, and an expansion of '*with others*' into several named courtiers. Nonetheless, neither annotator spells out the number of judges (subsequent dialogue has two judges speak), any distinctive costumes, the presence and number of chairs, or how the table and chairs are to be configured. Here, then, for a major ensemble scene that requires at least two significant pieces of furniture, the author of the printed stage direction has left a great deal to the expertise of the players; the playhouse annotators have inserted marginal signals to ensure the availability of large properties and sound effects; but those annotators have not felt it necessary to expand or improve upon '*the form of a Court*'.

In preparing the Quarto for playhouse use the two annotators did not have today's reader in mind—and here is the basic problem that confronts today's theater historian. Certainly, the staging of court and trial scenes may have varied somewhat from theater to theater or even in the same theater over a span of years, but the configuration probably remained roughly the same: a bar; a table; seats and placement for the judges; and something important that is implicit but not spelled out in the many signals: distinctive costumes for judges, sheriffs, advocates, and other court personnel. Indeed, along with the bar, such costumes would probably have been the most significant part of the 'code' to signify 'a courtroom'. An experienced dramatist, however, could assume a theatrical vocabulary shared by both players who knew their craft and playgoers familiar with such scenes; such a playwright could therefore provide few or no details or could fall back upon some formula: '*the form of a Court*'; '*as to her Trial*' (*The Winter's Tale*, III. ii. 9); '*in manner of a Consistory*' (*Henry VIII*, II. iv. 0).

To deal with this scene in *The Two Merry Milkmaids* is to confront a larger problem linked to ***permissive stage directions***, a category wherein key details are left indeterminate or open. By far the most common situation is to leave indefinite the number of actors required for an entrance, a lack of specificity that may result from either (1) theatrical exigency or (2) a necessary lack of precision at the time of writing (as when a playwright is not familiar with the personnel of the theatrical company that is to perform the play). In either case the writer of the stage direction may not be certain how many actors will be available as supernumeraries (for example, early in a show some personnel may be busy taking tickets and unavailable as extras).

The number of figures in an entrance can be left indeterminate by a variety of means. Most common is the use of a collective noun (***army***, *attendants*, *followers*, *lords*, *men*, *others*, **train**, '*and the rest*'). Typical of hundreds of examples are: '*Lucius, Iachimo, and the Roman Army at one door: and the Britain Army at another*' (*Cymbeline*, v. ii. 0); '*Enter Bassanio, Antonio, Gratiano, and their followers*' (*The Merchant of Venice*, v. i. 126). Various modifiers also allow for indeterminancy: ***certain***, ***diverse***, ***sundry***, and most commonly ***several***: '*certain Romans with spoils*' and '*certain Volsces come in the aid of Aufidius*' (*Coriolanus*, I. v. 0; I. viii. 13); '*diverse Spirits in shape of Dogs and Hounds*' (*The Tempest*, IV. i. 254); the Muses '*playing all upon sundry Instruments*' (Greene, *Alphonsus of Aragon*, line 45); '*a Masquerado of several Shapes and Dances*' (Fletcher, *Women Pleased*, vii. 308). Most obvious are the eight entrances that include some version of '*as many as can be*', as in *Titus Andronicus* (I. i. 72).

Other signals leave costumes, properties, or stage business open: '*with as many Jewels robes and Gold as he can carry*' (*2 The Seven Deadly Sins*, line 15; Greg 1931: ii, no. 2); '*The Ghosts use several gestures*' (Massinger, *The Unnatural Combat*, v. ii. 278); '*A Spirit (over the door) does some action to the dishes as they enter*' (Heywood, *The Late Lancashire Witches*, iv. 206). For costume the term of choice is sometimes *proper* (in the sense of 'fitting, appropriate'), as in '*certain Reapers (properly habited)*' (*The Tempest*, IV. i. 138). Occasionally a stage direction calls for a speech or song but leaves the specific words or melody to the performers: '*Jockey is led to whipping over the stage, speaking some words, but of no importance*' (Heywood, *2 Edward IV*, i. 180). The verb ***prepare*** is used to set up an onstage action: '*Prepare to play*' for the fencing in Folio *Hamlet* (v. ii. 265); '*Prepares for death*' at an execution (Heywood, *A Challenge for Beauty*, v. 68); and when special properties are involved: '*An Altar prepared*' (Fletcher, *The Sea Voyage*, ix. 62); '*two prentices, preparing the Goldsmith's Shop with plate*' (Heywood, *1 Edward IV*, i. 63). Most common are versions of '*A banquet prepared*' as in *Macbeth* (III. iv. 0). Again, how to prepare an ***altar***, ***banquet***, ***execution***, ***shop***, or ***trial*** is not specified but is left to the expertise of the players, as is what is *proper* or the number of items or actions encompassed by *certain*, *diverse*, *several*, and *sundry*.

Along with *as many as can be*, the most obvious set of permissive signals consists of those that include an ***or***. These signals are used widely for personnel, properties, costumes, and actions. The most common use of *or* is to leave indeterminate the number of entering figures: '*three or four with tapers*'; '*two or three other*' (*Much Ado*, v. iii. 0; v. iv. 33); '*Enter two or three setting three or four Chairs, and four or five stools*' (Field, *A Woman Is a Weathercock*, v. ii. 0). Comparable locutions are used to leave open the number of repetitions of an action or sound: '*makes a conge or two to nothing*' (Fletcher, *The Nice Valour*, x. 149). Less plentiful are uses of *or* with reference to alternative actions, sounds, and properties: '*makes legs: or signs*' (Jonson, *Epicoene*,

II. i. 10); '*musical songs of marriages, or a mask, or what pretty triumph you list*' (Greene, *James IV*, lines 2051–3). Sometimes at issue is the availability of a particular property or resource: '*Exit Venus. Or if you can conveniently, let a chair come down from the top of the stage, and draw her up*' (Greene, *Alphonsus of Aragon*, lines 2109–10).

The indeterminacy clearly evident in *others*, *as many as can be*, and *or* can also be glimpsed in a much larger group of stage directions that contain coded or shorthand terms that omit significant bits of information so that much is left to the implementation of the players (as is the case with verbs such as *prepare* and ***entertain***). The most visible examples are what can be termed *elliptical* or *metonymic* signals in which the missing details are easy to spot and flesh out. Few readers will take literally a direction such as '*Exit corse*' (*Richard III*, I. ii. 226) or '*The organs play, and covered dishes march over the stage*' (Middleton, *A Mad World My Masters*, II. i. 151), where the attendants who carry the bier or the covered dishes are assumed, not specified. Such a practice is widespread, most notably with signals that call for the entrance of figures bearing a ***body, halberd, musket, torch, drum,*** or ***trumpet***: '*Enter Buckingham from his Arraignment, Tipstaves before him, the Ax with the edge towards him, Halberds on each side*' (*Henry VIII*, II. i. 53); '*Enter four torches*' (Heywood, *1 If You Know Not Me*, i. 234); '*Enter Edgar at the third sound, a trumpet before him*' (Quarto *King Lear*, V. iii. 117). Such shorthand usages are practical, unremarkable, and easy to document (indeed, signals for *halberds* without designated bearers are more common than those for *officers with halberds*).

More tantalizing for the theater historian are those situations where what is omitted is less certain. An ellipsis may be obvious when an object is cited without the player who must carry it, but is much harder to recognize when personnel or effects are signaled without any accompanying costumes or properties. A reader today who confronts such theatrical shorthand will either expand the phrase ('*Exit corse*') or at the least recognize the existence of some coded effect (*enter in a shop*, '*the form of a Court*') even if the exact implementation of that effect remains in doubt. But, as already noted, the vast majority of surviving stage directions consist only of an *enter* followed by one or more named figures or generic types (doctor, forester, friar, jailer, lawyer, lord, merchant, nurse, sailor, servant, soldier) with no information about costume, make-up, and hand-held properties, all of which were presumably the province of the actor (as opposed to an ***altar, bed, bar, bier, coffin, scaffold,*** or ***table***). For example, an apparently straightforward stage direction such as *enter a jailer* or *keeper* may be as elliptical or incomplete as '*Exit corse*' if such a figure would be assumed to have a distinctive costume and be carrying a large set of ***keys*** so as to convey to a playgoer a sense of *enter in prison*.

To borrow from Hamlet, the norm is silence. Signals for the most elaborate ***tavern*** scenes (e.g. *1 Henry IV*, II. iv; *1 The Fair Maid of the West*, Act 1) provide nothing more than entrances for the relevant figures, and the same is true for many comparable busy scenes. Costume signals are plentiful and therefore too complex to characterize easily, but the standard procedure is to have figures that were probably readily identifiable by their distinctive garments or properties (doctor, forester–woodman, friar, gardener, jailer, lawyer, merchant, nurse, scholar) enter with no further details provided. Large properties, as noted earlier, are sometimes *prepared*, but more often an altar, bar, bed, bier, coffin, scaffold, or table is ***borne***, ***carried***, ***placed***, ***set***, or ***thrust in/out/forth***, sometimes with a permissive or coded term attached: '*a Tomb, placed conveniently on the Stage*' (Greene, *James IV*, line 3). Although not elliptical in the fashion of '*Exit corse*', the many signals that call for generic figures or large properties are couched in a form of shorthand that conveyed a great deal to a knowledgeable theatrical professional but is often opaque to a reader today.

Admittedly, not all items left to the implementation of the entering actor remain murky or indecipherable today, as when players are directed to enter ***discontented***, ***drunk***, ***malcontent***, or ***melancholy***. Today's reader or actor can readily understand '*Caliban sings drunkenly*' (*The Tempest*, II. ii. 178), but harder to piece out are the signals and silences linked to madness. Few of the plentiful *mad* scenes that start in the 1580s with plays such as *1 Tamburlaine*, *The Spanish Tragedy*, and *The Cobbler's Prophecy* provide any details in the stage directions, as with '*Enter Lear*' (Folio *King Lear*, IV. vi. 80). The occasional more specific direction is usually generic, most commonly *enter* ***mad*** (ten examples, including Quarto *King Lear*, IV. vi. 80) and *enter* ***distracted***/*distractedly* (eight examples, including Folio *Hamlet*, IV. v. 20). Variations include '*with distracted looks*' (Massinger, *A New Way to Pay Old Debts*, V. i. 88) and '*raving and staring as if he were mad*' (Quarto *2 Henry VI*, III. iii. 0). The use of generic signals that leave the implementation to the actor is best seen in John Webster's *The White Devil* where the speeches of the dying Bracciano '*are several kinds of distractions and in the action should appear so*' (V. iii. 82; see also V. iv. 82). The one detail that is supplied with any regularity is disheveled ***hair*** for mad women, usually phrased as '*with her hair about her ears*' (Folio *Troilus and Cressida*, II. ii. 100; Heywood, *1 The Iron Age*, iii. 269). The variations from silence to specificity can be seen in the three versions of Ophelia's first mad appearance in *Hamlet* (IV. v. 20): '*Enter Ophelia*' (Q2); '*Enter Ophelia distracted*' (Folio); '*Enter Ophelia playing on a lute, and her hair down singing*' (Q1).

Also instructive are the many variations in directions for an actor to *enter* ***unready***. As with *mad*, sometimes a variant of the term can stand alone, so that figures enter: '*unready*' (Fletcher, *The Coxcomb*, viii. 323); '*all unready*' (Heywood, *2 The Iron Age*, iii. 381); '*not full ready*' (Dekker, *1 The Honest Whore*, II. i. 12); or '*as in his Chamber in a morning, half ready*' (Field, *A Woman Is a Weathercock*, I. i. 1–2). To join Danae in bed '*Jupiter puts out the lights and makes unready*' (Heywood, *The Golden Age*, iii. 69). Unlike the situation with such terms as *discontented*, *drunk*, *mad*, and *malcontented*, an even larger number of signals spell out how to stage unreadiness, most commonly by means of costume. Many *unready* situations result from interrupted sleep, as with '*half unready, as newly started from their Beds*' (Heywood, *2 The Iron Age*, iii. 413), so that various items of night attire, especially the nightgown, are regularly specified. The number of actual uses of *unready* itself is then dwarfed by a much larger number of signals that direct an actor to enter in a ***nightgown***, ***nightcap***, ***shirt***, or ***slippers***, and ***trussing***, ***unbraced***, or *half* ***naked***.

If the authors of stage directions leave much to the implementation of the entering actor (for example, details about what we term *make-up* are rare), the same is true for that category of signals linked to the placement of the actors on the stage, an equivalent to what we term *blocking*. A reader today may assume that the two onstage posts or pillars that supported the heavens (at least in the large public amphitheaters) were used regularly for various actions, most notably the many eavesdropping or observation scenes (e.g. *Much Ado*, II. iii and III. i; *Othello*, IV. i; *Troilus and Cressida*, V. ii), but only one such signal survives: '*stands behind the post*' (Barnabe Barnes, *The Devil's Charter*, F3^{v}). Rather, the few theatrical signals that mention a ***post*** call for some distinctive business, as with '*practicing, to the post*' (Jonson, Folio *Every Man in His Humour*, III. v. 141). Given the large number of observation or concealment scenes, surprisingly few specific signals are available, and those few are generic or non-prescriptive, as with '*stand unseen*' (Heywood, *The Escapes of Jupiter*, line 1583). That '*behind the post*' (as spelled out in *The Devil's Charter*) should be understood as implicit in '*stand unseen*' is a possible inference, but such an expansion is far less obvious than a comparable expansion of '*Exit corse*'. The evidence suggests that the staging of such eavesdropping was either (1) a matter of standard practice that did not need specific signals (so that Barnes's usage is anomalous or superfluous) or (2) something to be left to the players.

Other directions for onstage placement are also less than informative to a reader today. Admittedly, references to figures and actions *above/aloft* and *below/under the stage* are common, presumably because such entrances or effects were to be distinguished by the bookkeeper and players backstage from the normal flow of action on the main stage. As already noted, anything to do with traffic control is likely to receive attention, as with widely used locutions such as *enter at one door... and at the other door; enter severally; enter at both doors.* However, the few terms used to denote movement or location on the main stage leave almost everything to the implementation of the actor, as when attendants are directed to '*stand in convenient order about the stage*' (*Henry VIII*, II. iv. 0). Signals that correspond to today's sense of blocking are rare and usually are linked to some special effect or configuration: '*They place themselves in every corner of the stage*' (*Antony and Cleopatra*, IV. iii. 8).

Stage directions linked to onstage placement are therefore open rather than specific. An exception is found in the relatively few signals that invoke the term ***side***: '*the Pope taketh his place, three Cardinals on one side and captains on the other*' (Barnes, *The Devil's Charter*, L1^{r}); '*four stand on one side, and four on the other*' (Folio *3 Henry VI*, IV. i. 6). More permissive and therefore more typical are terms such as ***apart***, ***aloof***, and ***afar off***: '*Enter Hamlet and Horatio afar off*' (Folio *Hamlet*, V. i. 55); '*She espies her husband, walking aloof off, and takes him for another Suitor*' (Heywood, *1 Edward IV*, i. 83). In Dekker's *Satiromastix* Horace enters *aloof* so as to elicit the comment 'Captain, captain, Horace stands sneaking here' (IV. ii. 24, 46); in Folio *3 Henry VI* the French king asks a group 'to stand aside' and '*They stand aloof*' (III. iii. 111).

Similarly, signals for rapid movement, violence or threatened violence, and interrupted exits (as in variations on ***offers to go***) may be widespread, but, except for items already cited, indications of onstage placement are surprisingly few. A number of figures are directed to ***withdraw*** or ***retire***, often to be observers or eavesdroppers: '*withdraw to the other part of the stage*' (Jonson, *Every Man Out of His Humour*, II. iii. 20). The term of choice for such onstage movement is often ***aside*** (to be distinguished from the more familiar use of the same term as applied to speech). Most of the many examples provide only *aside* linked to a verb, most commonly ***go***, ***stand***, *step*, and *take*: '*takes Amy aside, and courts her in a gentle way*' (Brome, *A Jovial Crew*, iii. 426); '*walks aside full of strange gestures*' (Fletcher, *The Mad Lover*, iii. 14).

Although sporadic use of terms such as *aloof*, *apart*, *aside*, *post*, *retire*, and *withdraw* suggest at least some attention to positioning or blocking, a survey of hundreds of plays and thousands of stage directions provides no equivalents for terms we take for granted today: *onstage*; *offstage*; *upstage*; *downstage*; *stage right*; *stage left*. The one consistent signal that *is* to be found is the term ***within***, which is regularly linked to offstage sounds or voices. However, the term ***without***, which would seem to be the logical extension or antithesis, is rare. Similarly, onstage figures are regularly directed ***off***, but rarely is the term *on* invoked to bring actors onto the stage. Rather, the key words in their vocabulary that would correspond to our *onstage–offstage* are ***in***, ***out***, and ***forth***. The problem is that a review of the use of these terms by such seasoned professionals as Shakespeare, Dekker, Fletcher, and Heywood not only yields no clear, consistent distinctions but offers numerous examples of apparent contradictions, sometimes within a given scene. Indeed, in some instances the verb being used (***bring***, ***draw***, ***lead***, ***set***, ***thrust***) appears to be more important than the adverb that supposedly provides the direction.

A few examples can be instructive. Some signals do provide what appear to be clear, consistent distinctions, as with '*He goes in at one door, and comes out at another*' (Heywood, *The English Traveller*, iv. 69). Here *out* clearly corresponds to our *in*–onstage and *in* corresponds to our *out*–offstage. What could be more straightforward? But from another Heywood play comes: '*They march softly in* [off the stage] *at one door, and presently in* [onto the stage] *at another*' (*2 The Iron Age*, iii. 379—and *presently* means 'immediately'), so that the same stage direction can provide two opposite meanings for *in*. Similarly, the same scene in Shakespeare's *1 Henry VI* supplies '*Bedford brought in sick in a Chair*' and '*Bedford dies, and is carried in by two in his Chair*' (III. ii. 40, 114); and the Folio version of *3 Henry VI* provides, first, '*enter Warwick, Somerset, and the rest, bringing the King out in his gown*' and later, '*They lead him out forcibly*' (IV. iii. 27, 57). Similarly, in Jonson's *Bartholomew Fair* Ursula '*Comes out with a fire-brand*', but, when she reappears a hundred lines later, she '*comes in, with the scalding pan*' (II. v. 59, 155); for the same climactic moment in *King Lear* (V. iii. 238) the Quarto has '*The bodies of Goneril and Regan are brought in*' ($L3^r$), but the Folio has '*Goneril and Regan's bodies brought out*' (TLN 3184), so that, in this instance, *brought in* and *brought out* are synonymous.

In citing such examples, my purpose is not to belittle Shakespeare, Heywood, Jonson, and others as sloppy or inconsistent. Rather, my point is that a firm sense of *onstage* and *offstage*, although crucial to *our* theatrical vocabulary and habits of thought, was far less important to them (and the varying uses of *forth* further reinforce this argument). Although I am reluctant to draw any far-reaching conclusions from this evidence, I do sense that their mindset is actor-centered and therefore closely linked to the presence, needs, and perspective of the entering or departing actor. As Bernard Beckerman has argued (Beckerman 1981: 152, 158), today's actors and directors 'expect to turn the stage area into an idiosyncratic world that can house the events of the play in question' so that 'somehow the stage is to be altered to suit the play at hand and *only* the play at hand', but for the Elizabethans 'whatever sense of locale a play or scene showed was derived from what the actors brought on stage' so that 'doors, posts, and walls did not convey information about locale independently'. Rather, 'the players projected an identity upon the individual part of the stage by calling, for instance, the upper level the walls of Corioli or one of the doors Brabantio's house', so that 'the environment that the players projected onto the facade or about the platform needed to be only as detailed as the narrative required for the moment'.

In practice, such an approach can then be oblivious to rigorous distinctions that to us seem logical, even essential. Similarly, signals such as '*Exit corse*' and '*covered dishes march over the stage*' may at first seem amusing or quaint but, especially when combined with permissive stage directions, can point us towards a fundamental problem that underlies any attempt to reconstruct English Renaissance theatrical practice. Admittedly, details *are* available about many onstage effects, but in some areas the inconsistencies can be puzzling and the silences deafening. Because the signals were directed at theatrical professionals who needed no tutoring, exactly how much coded information was conveyed by *enter a friar/doctor/jailer* or '*stand unseen*' is difficult, perhaps impossible, to reconstruct today.

Another hurdle in the path of reconstruction is linked to Richard Hosley's distinction between ***fictional*** and *theatrical* stage directions (Hosley 1957: 16–17). For Hosley *theatrical* signals 'usually refer not to dramatic fiction but rather to theatrical structure or equipment' (*within, at another door, a scaffold thrust out*), whereas *fictional* signals 'usually refer not to theatrical structure or equipment but rather to dramatic fiction' (*on shipboard, within the prison, enter the town*). The same onstage event can therefore be signaled by both *enter above* and *enter upon the walls* (of a city), with the second locution the fictional version of the first.

The most theatrical of signals can be seen in a playhouse annotator's call for a specific property such as a bar or a table. At the other extreme are those fictional directions in which a dramatist slips into a narrative or descriptive style seemingly more suited to a reader looking at a page than an actor on the stage. Some of these fictional signals show the dramatist thinking out loud in the process of writing so that the details anticipate what will be evident in the forthcoming action: '*Parolles and Lafew stay behind, commenting of this wedding*' (*All's Well That Ends Well*, II. iii. 184). Such stage directions can be valuable insofar as they provide evidence about the dramatist's thought processes or his sense of the narrative but often tell us little about what the playgoers saw.

In interpreting such evidence, however, various complications can arise when today's reader cannot be certain if a signal is *theatrical*, and therefore calls for a significant property such as a tomb or a tree, or *fictional*, so that a sense of a tomb or forest is to be generated by means of language, hand-held properties, and appropriate actions in conjunction with the imagination of the playgoer. Such complications are further compounded by the presence of an explicit or implicit *as* or *as if*. A seemingly straightforward fictional signal such as '*Enter Marius solus from the Numidian mountains, feeding on roots*' (Lodge, *The Wounds of Civil War*, lines 1189–90) initially may appear to tell the story rather than provide a signal to an actor, but a starving Marius who has been alone in exile could enter '[*as if*] *from the Numidian mountains*' so that the actor will use '*feeding on roots*' (as in *Timon of Athens*), along with disheveled costume and hair, to signal his mental and physical state. Similarly, '*Enter old M. Chartly as new come out of the Country To inquire after his Son*' (Heywood, *The Wise Woman of Hogsdon*, v. 340) tells the mission of the old man in narrative terms but may also signal some 'country' costume or other property (a staff, a basket). A fictional signal such as *enter on the walls* requires only that the figure enter *above* or *aloft*, whereas other seemingly fictional signals may convey some practical, albeit coded, instructions.

In this context consider the many and varied stage directions that either incorporate or omit the tiny word ***as***, particularly in constructions that involve *enter from* and *enter in*. Uses of *enter from* often show a playwright using a stage direction either to enhance the story being told or to indicate a particular stage door. A selection from Shakespeare's plays includes entrances '*from his arraignment*' (*Henry VIII*, II. i. 53); '*from the murder of Duke Humphrey*' (Folio *2 Henry VI*, III. ii. 0); '*from the Courtesan's*' and '*from the bay*' (*The Comedy of Errors*, IV. i. 13; IV. i. 84); and '*from the cave*' (*Cymbeline*, IV. ii. 0). To see the potential significance of the omission of an *as*, however, one need only set up some pairings: enter '*from hunting*' (*Titus Andronicus*, II. iv. 10) versus '*as from hunting*' (Heywood, *The Late Lancashire Witches*, iv. 171) or '*with her Hawk on her fist*... *as if they came from hawking*' (Quarto *2 Henry VI*, II. i. 0); enter '*from dinner*' (Quarto *Merry Wives*, B1^r^, I. ii. 0) versus '*as from dinner*' (Massinger, *A New Way to Pay Old Debts*, III. iii. 0) or '*as it were brushing the Crumbs from his clothes with a Napkin, as newly risen from supper*' (Heywood, *A Woman Killed with Kindness*, ii. 118). The largest group consists of variations on '*as from bed*' (e.g. Fletcher, *The Lovers' Progress*, v. 128; Heywood, *2 The Iron Age*, iii. 381), a version of *unready*, including such costume signals as '*Dalavill in a Nightgown: Wife in a night-tire, as coming from Bed*' (Heywood, *The English Traveller*, iv. 70). Most of these signals use the *as from* formula with few or no details to set up a recently completed offstage action: '*as from a wedding*' (Fletcher, *The Woman's Prize*, viii. 2); '*as from prison*' (Massinger, *The City Madam*, v. iii. 59). The effect is to create a sense of actions, places, or a 'world' just offstage to be imagined by the playgoer.

Harder to interpret but potentially more revealing are the *enter in* signals. For many scenes the ongoing narrative fiction requires that the action take place *in* a particular place (a ***courtroom***, ***garden***, ***prison***, ***shop***, ***study***, or ***tavern***). As already noted, most of the relevant scenes provide no more than an *enter* followed by a list of proper names or generic types. Some, however, do provide a shorthand signal, as when Brutus is directed to enter '*in his orchard*' (*Julius Caesar*, II. i. 0). A number of figures therefore enter *in prison*, *in his study*, or *in the shop*, and a smaller number enter *in* other venues. To read such signals today is almost inevitably to draw upon reflexes gained from reading novels or watching cinema, television, and modern stage pictures linked to properties, sets, and lighting.

But what if an implicit *as* or *as* [*if*] is factored into this equation? Eleven plays may specify entrances '*in prison*', and a few of these stage directions do provide more details, as with '*in prison, with Irons, his feet bare, his garments all ragged and torn*' (Heywood, *A Woman Killed with Kindness*, ii. 127). However, four Caroline playwrights signal an entrance '*as in prison*' (e.g. Brome, *The Queen and Concubine*, ii. 35). Again, consider the following pairings: enter '*in the woods*' (*Timon of Athens*, IV. iii. 0) versus '*Andrugio, as out of the woods, with Bow and Arrows, and a Cony at his girdle*' (Whetstone, *Promos and Cassandra*, K4[r]); enter '*in his Study*' (Marlowe, *Dr Faustus*, A-text lines 30, 437) versus '*as in his Study*' (Fletcher, *The Fair Maid of the Inn*, ix. 193); '*Enter Luce in a Seamster's shop, at work upon a laced Handkerchief*' (Heywood, *The Wise Woman of Hogsdon*, v. 284) versus '*as in their shop*' (Field, *Amends for Ladies*, II. i. 0). For a related usage compare two versions of *Richard II*, IV. i. 0: '*Enter Bullingbrook with the Lords to parliament*' (Quarto) versus '*Enter as to the Parliament*' (Folio).

As with '*Exit corse*', to omit an implicit *as* from an *enter from* signal does not cause major problems, for a theater-oriented reader can readily imagine the appropriate costume and effects for entrances in a Noel Coward comedy *from tennis* or *from swimming*. However, the same omission from an *enter in* signal can make a significant difference. An entrance *in the woods*, *in a garden*, or *in his orchard* may suggest onstage greenery, but an implicit or explicit *as* suggests that any sense of woods, garden, or orchard is to be generated for the playgoer by the entering actor's costume, hand-held properties, and dialogue. Similarly, the sense of a tavern can be linked to easily recognizable figures (most commonly drawers) in distinctive costumes along with portable objects such as wine, cups, tobacco, and towels. Specific directions to *enter in the tavern* may be scarce, but far more common is a signal such as '*Enter Drawer with Wine, Plate, and Tobacco*' (Field, *Amends for Ladies*, III. iv. 36) which is comparable to *as in a tavern* or perhaps *a tavern prepared*.

To focus upon *as from*, *as in*, and related entrances is then to confront a variety of situations that bring into focus distinctive features of the drama before 1642. Starting in the Restoration but especially in the 1700s, movable scenery became an integral part of both staging and theatrical thinking, so that, from the beginning of the editorial tradition until very recently, scholars, drawing upon their sense of playgoing or imagined performances, have attached specific locales to Shakespeare's scenes, even when such specificity clashed with the original effects. As Beckerman notes, what is assumed in such post-1660 or post-1700 thinking is that an actor arriving onstage enters to a pre-existing, already established 'place'. But, as indicated by the plentiful *as from* and *as in* signals, before the emergence of scenes and sets the pre-1642 actor entered to a neutral, unlocalized space. If the locale was for some reason important, that actor then, whether through dialogue, properties, costume, or distinctive actions, brought that 'place' with him or somehow signaled the place-activity he had left behind him offstage. In short, the locale did not precede the actor; rather, the actor created or signaled the locale. To specify 'place' in our texts (a practice still to be found in editions of Shakespeare) is then to impose a later editorial–theatrical logic upon the received texts so as to eclipse features basic to the original onstage vocabulary.

Another tricky question when dealing with stage directions is their placement in a given scene, particularly for mid-scene entrances and exits—and here is an issue where theater historians and editors may part company. In an influential essay E. A. J. Honigmann describes what he sees as Shakespeare's carelessness with stage directions: 'He often omitted them, or left them incomplete, or inserted them in approximately but not precisely the correct place'; he argues, moreover, that some of these signals 'were added or misplaced by scriveners, prompters, Folio editors or compositors', to the point that the editor or reader 'cannot avoid giving a higher authority to the "implied stage-directions" of the dialogue than to directions printed as such' (Honigmann 1998: 187).

Honigmann rightly calls our attention to omissions or incompleteness in the surviving stage directions, but the line between 'carelessness' and 'permissiveness' (wherein one knowledgeable theatrical professional is talking to another) is a hard one to draw. Of interest here is a recurring phenomenon: that a number of figures in the early printed texts enter one or more lines before they are noticed by those onstage. Readers of Shakespeare who do not work directly with the original quartos or the First Folio will not be aware of many of these potential anomalies (roughly one or two per play), because editors regularly move the signals so as to have them conform to normative usage. To Honigmann and many editors these odd placements represent carelessness (by the dramatist or compositor) or the result of exigencies in the printing shop or an indication of the depth of the Globe stage (so that a few lines were needed for the entering figure upstage to join a downstage group). The latter explanation (that extra lines were inserted for practical reasons) makes good sense until one asks: Why is such a special allowance granted to one entrance but not to the fifteen to thirty comparable moments in the same script?

Since I devote much of a chapter to this phenomenon (Dessen 1995: 64–77), I will limit myself to one highly visible example, the entrance of a smiling Malvolio in yellow stockings and cross-gartered (*Twelfth Night*, III. iv). Most modern editions (here the Riverside is an exception) place that entry just before Olivia's 'How now, Malvolio?' (line 15), so that she and the playgoer see the entering figure at the same time. In the Folio, however, Malvolio is directed to enter two lines earlier, just after Olivia's 'Go call him hither', so that the only authoritative early printed text of this comedy places Malvolio onstage for her 'I am as mad as he, | If sad and merry madness equal be' (lines 13–14).

To some readers the difference may seem unimportant; to many editors the Folio version appears illogical or impractical. But what happens if we take this placement as seriously as any other bit of evidence in the Folio *Twelfth Night*? For example, what would be the effect upon Malvolio if at his entrance he overhears Olivia talking about her own madness? Could such words reinforce in his mind the evidence gained from the letter in II. v and therefore serve as another building block for the cross-purposes and comic delusion that follow? Or would a playgoer who sees Malvolio enter while at the same time hearing Olivia talk of her own malady be more likely to see an analogy between the two instances of comic madness or self-delusion? Again, how does one distinguish between 'carelessness' and a valid theatrical logic?

To puzzle over the placement or timing of stage directions is to confront a related yet different set of problems. Dealing with permissive or coded signals is regularly to encounter silences in the original manuscripts and printed texts. In contrast, provocative evidence *is* available about early entrances, but those signals are regularly deemed dispensable by many scholars because their placement is out of phase with our paradigms or expectations—and if an editor repositions such a signal, users of that edition will be unaware that such an option even exists. In this instance, provocative evidence may survive, but, whether because of the editorial process or because of the lenses through which today's reader views a Shakespeare play, no one is paying attention. In seeking to recover the original staging practice, the theater historian is therefore bedeviled by both the *absence* of evidence and the *presence* of seemingly anomalous signals that can easily be ignored. Both silences and anomalies, however, can be crucial if the goal is to open up a window that will reveal how Shakespeare's theatrical assumptions and practices differ from ours.

Behind my attempts to open that window lie the twin assumptions that (1) the original theatrical artists knew what they were doing but (2) their methods and working assumptions are not what we take for granted today. Shakespeare and his colleagues were not benighted primitives who lacked our superior know-how and technology, but were highly skilled professionals who for many decades sustained a repertory theater company that is the envy of any comparable group since. However, when putting quill to paper Shakespeare (or Heywood or Fletcher) was crafting his plays for players, playgoers, and playhouses that no longer exist. In reading their playscripts today we enter into the middle of a conversation—a discourse in a language we only partly understand—between a playwright and his player colleagues, a halfway stage that was completed in a performance now lost to us. Although we will never reconstitute that performance, we may be able to recover elements of that vocabulary and hence better understand that conversation, whether the pre-production concept of the playwright or the implementation by the players. Nonetheless, despite such efforts in historical recovery we remain eavesdroppers.

The collaboration that underlies this process and the conversation on which we are eavesdropping have various implications for scholars. Honigmann's argument in favor of 'implied' stage directions in the dialogue or 'signals in the script' (a term regularly invoked by Shakespeare-in-performance critics and teachers) sounds attractive, but anyone who has followed the path of theater history over the last century is aware of various false hypotheses (the postulation of an 'inner stage' quickly comes to mind) linked to a reader's assumptions about how X *must* have been staged, assumptions based upon notions of theater contemporary to that reader and often alien to the 1590s and 1600s. To deal justly with the original stage practice is to unlearn what today we know, or think we know, about how a play should or must work onstage (the absence then of anything comparable to our variable onstage illumination for night and darkness scenes remains the best example). To overcome the significant but often invisible gap between theater practice then and now, the best place to turn remains the stage directions that survive from the professional repertory theater, for to build upon those signals as evidence is to stay within the realm of the possible: what was or could have been done in the original productions.

What emerges from this scattered but nonetheless suggestive evidence is a sense of a collaborative theatrical process where the authors of the surviving stage directions took for granted the professionalism and expertise of the players. The editor or theater historian would much prefer 'spell it all out' signals, but the actual stage directions provided by professionals usually display a 'leave it up to the players' approach characterized by permissive terms, *as if* thinking, and a lack of specificity about gestures, costume, blocking, make-up, and hand-held properties. The abundant presence of permissive, elliptical, and coded signals highlights the collaborative nature of this theatrical enterprise and the need for editors, theater historians, and other eavesdropping readers to attend carefully to a conversation in a language we at best partly understand. The alternative is spelled out by Hermione: 'You speak a language that I understand not' (*The Winter's Tale*, III. ii. 80).

CHAPTER 31

LIGHTING

R. B. GRAVES

WHEN John Webster's *The White Devil* was produced at an open-air playhouse (almost certainly the Red Bull) early in 1612, the play failed not because the dramatist or actors were inept, but because the playhouse was dark and dreary—or so Webster claims in his Preface to the first printed edition. The play was presented '*in so dull a time of Winter*,' he complains, '*in so open and blacke a Theater, that it wanted... a full and understanding Auditory*'.[1] Those who know London in the wintertime can sympathize with Webster and his audiences. In seventeenth-century London, mid-December sunsets occurred around 3.45 p.m.; and with performances not normally beginning until 2 or 3 p.m., even a short, two-hour winter presentation would end in waning daylight. Moreover, the period from 1550 to 1680 was the first phase of what climatologists call the 'little ice age', a period of cooler, more unstable weather than we enjoy today.

The *White Devil* was revived around 1630, and Webster may himself have lived to see the vindication both of the play and of his explanation for its initial failure out of doors. The revival took place at the indoor Cockpit in Drury Lane, which the *Historia Histrionica* of 1699 describes as 'small to what we see now... had Pits for the Gentry, and Acted by Candle-light', whereas large amphitheaters such as the Red Bull and Globe 'lay partly open to the Weather, and... alwaies Acted by Daylight' (Bentley 1941–68: ii. 694). This distinction between two kinds of lighting system is confirmed by several earlier sources that mention daylight at the amphitheaters and artificial light at the hall theaters. But in attempting to reconstruct what early modern English theatrical performances looked like, we must take care not to make more of the distinction than was actually the case. The *Historia* tells us the amphitheaters

[1] Quotations from play-texts are from the following editions: Shakespeare, Quarto *Othello* (1622); Dekker and Webster (1607); Webster (1612).

employed daylight and the hall playhouses candlelight, but it does not follow that the outdoor venues were planned to be especially bright. Indeed, the physical orientation of the amphitheaters vis-à-vis the sun and the frequent placement of a 'heavens' above their stages suggest that attempts were made to shield the stage from the elements, including direct sunlight. As for the hall playhouses, the *Historia* does not say that they 'alwaies' employed artificial light, nor is it true that daily or weekly performances indoors regularly or even occasionally took place at night, as is sometimes asserted. Records of the times of performances at the professional troupes' hall playhouses consistently refer to the afternoon; the number of candles lit was apparently not large; and the evidence we have indicates the auditoriums were well provided with windows, admitting substantial sunshine.

In attempting to understand the illumination of the two kinds of theater, we seek not just to reconstruct the visual experience of early playgoers, but—just as importantly—to understand how particular theatrical environments may have caused both actors and playwrights to alter their methods in order to accommodate those environments and to take advantage of them. It has long been thought, for example, that the new tone of Shakespeare's late romances can be accounted for, in part, by a variety of artistic choices that the King's Men made in 1609 in anticipation of their acquisition of the small, artificially lit second Blackfriars playhouse, in addition to the large, open-air Globe. Evidence of fewer seats, a smaller stage closer to wealthier patrons, and, above all, the splendor of the lighting was adduced to explain the attraction of a more cultured audience requiring a shift in Shakespeare's tone and interests. Despite the King's Men's continuing to play both indoors and outdoors, many scholars assumed that a shift in theatrical style had been caused in some measure by the physical conditions of the Jacobean hall playhouses with their more sophisticated facilities.

Yet in a careful survey of plays written from 1599 to 1642, T. J. King has found that, whatever physical differences distinguished the indoor and outdoor playhouses, staging practices remained more or less the same. 'Although these two kinds of playhouses differed in outward appearance,' he announced, 'analysis of 276 plays probably first acted by professionals in this period shows that there were no significant differences in the staging requirements of the various companies' (King 1971: 2).

For example, one might assume that lighting instruments like candles and torches would be employed in one way in daylight amphitheaters but in a different way in halls that were already lit by candles. Yet it seems that stage property lights carried by actors produced their effect not so much by illusionistic means, as by serving as emblems that signaled such information as when or where a scene takes place. Thus, when Othello enters Desdemona's bedroom '*with a light*' at the end of the play, the audience understood that the scene is supposed to take place at night, even if the scene was acted in broad daylight, because people carry candles only at night. The theatrical statement is that an *instrument* of light was called into use. It was the instrument, or rather the imaginary need for the instrument, and not the light it produced, that represented the darkness. Thus, the emblem could work as well indoors or out of doors.

The candle that Othello carries also serves as a signal that Desdemona's death takes place indoors, because candles were largely an indoor instrument, whereas, in the first two scenes of the play, when characters are rushing through the streets, we hear no less than three calls for torches, an outdoor instrument. Once inside the council chamber, the action is accompanied by only 'lights'. Or again, at the end of the play, Iago carries a torch in v. i, indicating an outdoor scene, whereas Othello brings a candle into Desdemona's chamber in v. ii. Unfortunately there are no contemporary illustrations depicting the possible staging of *Othello*, but the title page illustration to Thomas Kyd's *The Spanish Tragedy* (1615) shows an outdoor scene accompanied by a torch, while the title page of the first edition of *Arden of Feversham* shows an interior scene lit by a single candle.[2] Whether the audience was to think of a scene as indoors or outdoors was determined by the *type* of lighting instrument, not by how it illuminated the stage.

The emblematic utility of these instruments goes even further. Hand-held lighting instruments could occasionally be used to help define a character's social class. For instance, though we may think of torches as fairly primitive lighting devices, early English torches were in fact obligatory at sumptuous court masques, and a passage from *Westward Ho* (1607) gives a truer picture of their status. The authors tell how 'the Cobler, in the night time walks with his Lanthorne, the Lawyer with his Link, and the Courtier with his Torch' (Dekker and Webster 1911, sig. D). Because a courtier uses a torch here, it cannot have been thought a crude device, especially since the phrase quoted implies habitual use. Thus, when considering these lights as emblems, whether of time, place, or character, we must be careful to assign appropriate connotations to them. In the storm scenes of *King Lear*, for instance, the raw power of nature was accompanied not by crude clubs, but by genteel torches whose staves were probably richly decorated.

To be sure, these property lights and other stage properties, not to mention the actors who carried them, had to be seen in order to fulfill these emblematic functions. Even if a scene was supposed to take place at night, there had to be sufficient light on stage for the audience to see the type of lighting utensil used and to understand its indication of time, place, or character. And sufficient illumination would depend on the season of the year, the time of day, the weather, and the amount of light admitted by the structure of the playhouse. Leaving aside the unpredictable effect of the weather, the major variables for the open-air amphitheaters are the position and size of the stage and the 'heavens' above the stage, the altitude of the sun above the horizon, and the proportions of the playhouse. Figure 31.1, based on Richard Hosley's reconstruction of the Swan, demonstrates the principles.

In the mid-afternoon, on average from spring to autumn, sunlight comes from the south-west. In the top row of Figure 31.1, the stage is placed at the north-east side of the playhouse, opposite the sun. In Figure 31.1(*a*), showing the articulation of light in the Swan at 2 p.m. on the summer solstice, it will be seen that at the height of summer the altitude of the sun at 2 p.m. (about 54°) is high enough to light the entire stage. Figure 31.1(*b*) presents a more typical performance situation, however—3 p.m.

[2] The illustration from the 1615 *Spanish Tragedy* is reproduced as Figure 34.9 in this volume.

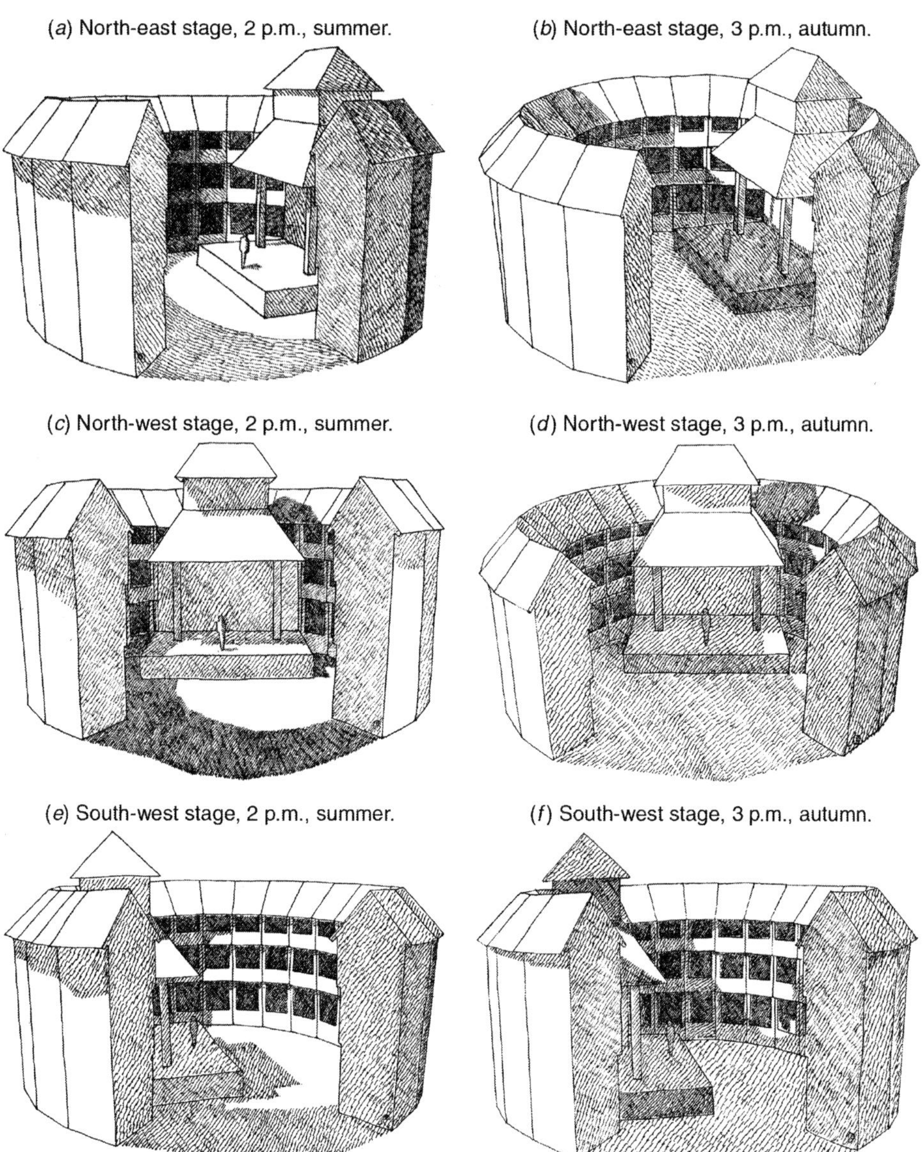

Figure 31.1 Illumination in the Swan playhouse.

on the autumn (or spring) equinox. Here the altitude of the sun is about 27°, and only an area on the tiring house wall is lit directly by the sun. In winter the sun is so low in the sky even at 2 p.m. (only 11° above the horizon on the winter solstice, for instance) that the stage is never lit by direct sunshine.

The middle row of Figure 31.1 shows cross-sections of Hosley's Swan with the stage and heavens at the north-west side of the arena (or the mirror image of its complement, the south-east). On the left (Figure 31.1(*c*)), the early afternoon summer sun can light the forepart of the stage, while the walls of the playhouse and the heavens shade most of the rest. Figure 31.1(*d*) demonstrates that on an autumn or spring day at 3 p.m., veritably no direct sunlight could strike the stage at all.

The bottom row depicts the corresponding situations when the stage is at the south-west, the same compass point from which the sun is shining. It will be seen that even at the height of summer at 2 p.m., no direct sunshine reaches the stage.

To obtain the fullest light, a modern theater or lighting designer would likely put the stage at the north-east side of the yard, as in the top row of diagrams. This, at any rate, is the placement many early theater historians preferred in attempting reconstructions of the amphitheaters. But the practice in Shakespeare's time was less predictable; in many of the amphitheaters, in fact, the orientation appears to have been the exact opposite of what we might expect. For those amphitheaters about which we can draw conclusions regarding the orientation of their stages, the evidence indicates one stage to the north (the Rose), one to the east or west (Red Lion), one probably in the west (Swan), one probably in the south-west (Boar's Head), and three in the south-west (first and second Globes and the Hope) (R. Graves 1999: 88–92). Although there is variation among these, we cannot fail to notice the preponderance of stages situated to the west or south-west.

Thus, the lighting at many amphitheaters seems to have been as depicted in Figure 31.1(*e*) and (*f*), where the stage orientation means that frank sunshine rarely illuminated the actors. On some days, not only would direct sunlight miss the stage entirely but occasionally it would shine fully in the faces of those sitting or standing opposite the stage, locations we should consider the choicest in the house. On an even greater number of days, however, no direct sunshine illuminated any part of the playhouse, as records kept at Kew over many years show that only one in three daytime hours is sunny in London (Brazell 1968: 172). Thus, the most typical light source for an afternoon performance at the amphitheaters was an overcast sky producing an evenly distributed illumination from above, more evenly distributed than any example illustrated in Figure 31.1. The galleries of the playhouses obstructed light from a low angle, while the heavens shaded the stage from a vertical angle. Although the original configurations of the Theatre, Rose, and Boar's Head may have lacked a heavens, or roof over the stage, every outdoor playhouse built or remodeled after 1595 seems to have supported what the Fortune contract calls a 'shadowe or cover over the saide Stadge' (Greg 1907: 5), telling us in the name 'shadow' much of its purpose and effect.

The general effect at the amphitheaters is, therefore, a well-shaded stage without strong contrasts of light and dark due to direct sunlight. As an actor came forward toward the foot of the stage, the light would increase slightly because the heavens overhead intercepted less light. But apart from modern reconstructive conjecture, there is little evidence of any contemporary effort to introduce more light into the amphitheaters. We read nothing of large windows, reflective interiors, noontime performances, or the habitual use of artificial lights for general illumination. We hear rather of painted imitation marble, stained oak, black hangings, and performances stretching into twilight, especially in the winter.

Several researchers, concerned about failing natural light in performances with late starting times and early winter sunsets, have considered the possibility of supplemental artificial light in the amphitheaters. But the evidence is slim, resting largely on the definition of 'falot' in Randle Cotgrave's French–English *Dictionarie* (Cotgrave and Islip 1611): 'A Cresset light (such as they vse in Play-houses) made of ropes wreathed, pitched, and put into small and ope[n] cages of yron.' Assuming Cotgrave is referring to English practice, the playhouses he mentions in 1611 could, in fact, be either amphitheaters or halls.

Because the smoke produced by such crude instruments would likely eliminate their use indoors, the only unmistakable reference to cressets at a professional English playhouse comes from a legal squabble regarding the outdoor Boar's Head playhouse in which testimony was given regarding operating expenses that included 'rushes and cressett lights in Wynter wch some weeks came to ten or twelve shillings a weeke' (Berry 1986: 173). Herbert Berry argued that the pairing of cressets with rushes implies that cressets illuminated the stage because rushes were sometimes strewn there, but rushes were also a fuel typically burned in cressets or by themselves in rush-holders. Thus, the pairing of rushes and cressets more likely signifies only that they were purchased from the same source, and their juxtaposition in a tradesman's legal testimony cannot prove that cressets were placed on or near the stage. It is also possible that, since in certain weeks of winter more cresset lights were needed than in others, one purpose for the cressets was heat rather than light, as the average winter temperature in London varies considerably more from week to week than the average amount of winter daylight. Public establishments like inns and taverns sometimes had cresset lights burning near their doors so that torches for travelers could be lit, and playhouse cressets may also have served such functions for spectators, whether or not the cressets played a part in lighting the stage or auditorium.

Considering the size of the area to be illuminated and the problems English weather might have posed in keeping them lit, it is doubtful that the artificial lights at the actors' disposal played a major role in the general illumination of the amphitheaters. Tiremen would have had to go about the stage and auditorium lighting torches and replenishing cressets. And should any wind or rain come up, these same tiremen would have had to tend to vulnerable instruments. In the private theaters, there were always act breaks during which such duties could be carried out without routinely interrupting the performance. But the custom of inter-act music and act breaks did not spread to the amphitheaters until shortly before Shakespeare's retirement. Just as troublesome would have been the dangers of placing large burning cressets near the stages of these highly inflammable playhouses. The first Globe and Fortune playhouses did indeed burn down, but smoldering cannon fodder started the Globe fire, while the Fortune 'by negligence of a candle was clean burnt to the ground' at twelve o'clock midnight, presumably when a well-lit performance before an audience would not have been allowed (Howes 1631, Iiii^{v}).

The possibility that artificial lights were used outdoors cannot be entirely disproved, of course. But we should admit that the whole question of supplemental light never arose until early twentieth-century scholars, accustomed to the bright and carefully controlled stage illumination of their own era, began to worry about actors performing in the uncontrollable light and twilight of early modern London. These scholars assumed that actors must have done everything in their power to correct the deficiency of natural light and that it was important to perform in as consistently bright an environment as possible. Yet the opposite seems to be true. That the light was on some occasions dim does not appear to have bothered the actors. Indeed, their answer to the problem of stark contrasts and sudden fluctuations of light outdoors was to approximate as much as possible the overall reduced level of light indoors. By placing the stage at the south-west, the actors shaded themselves from the mid-afternoon sun, while toward evening the audience could adjust to a lower level of brightness because the heavens above the stage eliminated glare from the sun as it set in the west. Practical men of the Elizabethan theater apparently sought a stage protected from the elements, including sunshine. Concern about a lack of brightness on the Elizabethan stage must be accounted a modern concern.

In our contemporary theaters, Hamlet and Macbeth are examined more often than not under the blazing glare of spotlights, even as a pervasive gloom gathers around them and spectators in the auditorium. Our stage lighting tends to be highly directional, emanating from two distinct positions in front of the actors, but the overall lighting of the Elizabethan amphitheaters came from many directions, from all around the actors, or nearly so. To the amphitheater audience, there was no impression of light focusing on the actor, no way to expose him to the interpretive scheme of a lighting designer. Early English actors moved in more natural surroundings. At the Swan and Globe, they must have performed in a generally subdued, though ungovernable, light. Like the bare, open stage, the overall illumination permitted not only flexibility in staging but also a sense of continuity between the stage and the auditorium, between the actors and their background.

In contemporary theater practice, an audience's attention can be drawn to specific actors or properties by means of strategically placed pools of light or by color contrasts. Lacking the means to bring about such strong contrasts, early modern actors and playwrights secured theatrical emphasis more often by conventionalized gestures or by literary techniques—soliloquies, ceremonial entrances, poetic set speeches, and the like. The relative uniformity of the light necessitated, in part, the use of more explicit signals and pointers on stage than we care for in narrative drama. Of course, it should be noted that several influential modern theater artists, such as Antonin Artaud and Bertolt Brecht, advocate uniform stage and auditorium illumination in emulation of early English theater lighting. They yearn for an active rapport between spectators and actors, a rapport that an audience, sitting submissively in the dark, they argue, can never establish. Their experiments have had some success, but we must not confuse their aims with Shakespeare's. Light shining on the modern audience is a reaction against Victorian illusion and produces its effect in part by dislodging the spectators' illusionistic expectations. To Shakespeare's public, there was nothing jarring about being as much in the light as the actors and, hence, no dislocation of normal sensibilities and no shocking reminder of the artifices of the theater. It is unhistorical to view Shakespeare's lack of illusion as equivalent to the conscious anti-illusionism of much modern stagecraft. To us, the convention that regularly presented nighttime scenes on a daylit stage may be a 'perverse *tour de force*', as J. L. Styan puts it (1967: 42–4), but it is doubtful that an audience, unfamiliar with the effects of dimmers and rheostats, would have been deeply impressed by a convention which, after all, goes back to the Corpus Christi plays and beyond. The idea that the lighting conventions of the period enabled a continuity between audience and stage is undoubtedly accurate; but that it had the effect of disrupting the audience's expectations is unlikely.

This is not to say that the daylight convention did not have important consequences and uses. Indeed, some plays appear to demand the convention in order to explore the full repercussions of their action. Critics have long spotted the irony when the blind Gloucester jumps, he thinks, off the cliffs at Dover but in reality merely falls to the stage floor in the glare of the day. Here the light on stage comments unmercifully on physiological darkness. Conversely, a similar irony often attaches to scenes presented as taking place in nocturnal darkness. In *Othello*, what to Cassio and Roderigo is dark confusion, for example, is clear to an audience who can see Iago furtively wound Cassio in their fight. Actors at the outdoor theaters may have been more or less powerless to control their light, but they could occasionally employ it to convey meaning.

The title page of the 1622 first edition of *Othello* states that the play was acted not only at the open-air Globe but also indoors at Blackfriars; indeed, Office of Works records at court show that the play was performed in the banqueting house at Whitehall in November 1604. Indoor venues such as Blackfriars and the halls at court and those used by the various boys' troupes could presumably provide more thorough control of the illumination than at the amphitheaters by manipulating window shutters and employing artificial light, such as candles. The best estimate of the number of candles regularly used by professional actors in their hall playhouses comes from an agreement between housekeepers and hireling actors at Salisbury Court in 1639. In that agreement, the housekeepers promised to pay half the cost of the lights, 'both waxe and Tallow, wch halfe all winter is near 5s a day' (Bentley 1941–68: vi. 106). Using this figure, we can make a rough estimate of the number of candles employed at Salisbury Court in the winter. Making some assumptions about their size and the proportion of wax candles to cheaper tallow ones, we can estimate that between two to four dozen candles shone at Salisbury Court—a fair quantity, one would think, but in actual brightness not equivalent even to the power of one 60-watt light bulb. The use of the phrase 'all winter' in the agreement suggests that the candles did not provide the principal source of stage illumination all year, but rather that the purpose of the candlelight was primarily to mitigate winter darkness. For although some hall playhouses were used only in winter (such as the King's Men's Blackfriars), documents record a number of summer performances at Salisbury Court. It seems probable that summertime performances there could do without many burning candles and that wintertime performances relied on a mixture of natural and artificial light.

The well-known *Wits* frontispiece of 1662 (Figure 31.2) shows how such a mixture might appear, even though we have no evidence that lamps served as footlights at pre-Interregnum playhouses. Hanging above a small stage are sixteen candles arranged in two branched chandeliers. The principal light comes from the actors' right, but not from the chandelier there, as the opposite chandelier casts no similar shadow. Apparently daylight was plentiful from that side of the room. Unfortunately, we do not know what kind of playhouse *The Wits* frontispiece represents; but it supports evidence derived from the Salisbury Court agreement that the number of candles was not large and that candles were not the only lighting source. In other words, we should not view the use of candles indoors as regularly fulfilling the functions artificial light normally performs in our modern theaters: providing bright light that is the sole means of illuminating the actors.

Further evidence that actors regularly employed daylight in conjunction with candle-light to illuminate their indoor theaters is provided by the playwright Thomas Dekker, who notes a specific exception to the practice. In *The Seven Deadlie Sinns of London* (1606), Dekker describes a typical London nightfall in this way: 'all the Citty lookt like a private Playhouse, when the windowes are clapt downe, as if some... dismall *Tragedy* were presently to be acted before all the *Trades-men*' (1606, sig. D2). From this passage we learn several things about indoor lighting. For some performances, daylight was specifically blocked out, apparently because the illumination could be used not simply for visibility but to reinforce aesthetic qualities of a play. Dekker specifically links the metaphorical darkness of 'dismall Tragedy' with the technical darkness of closed shutters. And there is the further implication that afternoon performances of other kinds of plays would find the window shutters open. Whether or not Dekker is describing a sort of 'mood lighting' is difficult to say, but we can note that a practicing playwright of the period saw a relationship between illumination under specific theatrical conditions and the emotional requirements of a particular kind of drama. There is no evidence that window shutters were routinely opened and closed or hanging candelabra raised and lowered during performances to indicate that the action of a play moved from day to night, but assumptions that such effects were always handled by word-painting or poetic imagery alone may stand in need of revision.

What kind of windows were these that Dekker refers to? We know enough about the conventions of medieval and early modern architecture to form a good idea of the nature of the windows in the halls converted into playhouses; indeed, the windows of several halls that were sometimes used as theaters still exist today for our inspection. Of these, most interest attaches to the halls at the Inns of Court and several royal palaces, as Shakespeare probably acted in them.

One such venue is the Great Hall of the Middle Temple (Figure 31.3). Plays and other entertainments were frequently performed there; Shakespeare's company performed *Twelfth Night* there in February 1602, for example. The hall is oriented east and west and is divided into seven cross-bays. In the first bay are the magnificent screen, two small windows, and a large end window. In the second through the sixth bays are square-headed windows, five on each side, with transoms and four elliptical-headed lights each. In the seventh bay, lighting the dais, are two large oriel windows. The hall is 39 feet wide and 88 feet from the front of the screen to the opposite wall. In the etching, we can see diffused light filtering down from elevated windows. As in other Tudor halls, such as the great halls at Gray's Inn and Hampton Court Palace

Figure 31.2 Frontispiece to F. Kirkman, *The Wits, or, Sport Upon Sport* (1662).

Figure 31.3 T. H. Shepherd, *Middle Temple Hall*, from *London Interiors* (London, 1841).

(which also hosted performances by Shakespeare's company), light emanates from a band of veritable clerestory windows.

The effect of these high windows, characteristic of all Tudor halls, is the soft, descending nature of the light. The side walls are paneled to a height of over 15 feet and the windows are set higher than that on the walls, their sills nearly 18 feet above the floor. Very little direct sunshine can ever cross-light the space. Indeed the windows are so high that only in the early afternoon at the height of summer does any direct sunlight light more than a narrow strip of the floor along the north wall. But in winter, when the Middle Temple was used as a theater, the sun is never high enough to light any part of the floor directly. Even on bright summer days, a dim, gently diffused light descends from the warm-tinted glass and is partly absorbed and reflected by the magnificent hammerbeam roof.

How do we know that permanent private playhouses were set up in halls like this? For one thing, the resemblance between the early sixteenth-century hall screen and the late sixteenth-century tiring house of the Swan implies that their chronological intermediaries—the tiring house façades of the first hall playhouses—did not differ widely from either. Moreover, the first boys' companies at St Paul's and the first Blackfriars were originally founded for the express purpose of entertaining Queen Elizabeth in halls like these.

We also have information about the kinds of buildings that were acquired for indoor theatrical productions, and this information supports the idea that Tudor halls and early indoor playhouses were similar in design. Two of these theaters, the second Blackfriars and the Whitefriars, were in fact called 'great halls' in legal documents arising out of quarrels within their managements. It is believed that the hall James Burbage bought in Blackfriars was the large Parliament Chamber on the second floor of the Frater in the western range of the old Dominican priory. This was not a characteristic Dominican room, but rather a large hall similar to those at court, with which the Dominican friars enjoyed a close relationship. The nearly equal dimensions and the similar uses to which these halls were put suggest that the Parliament Chamber and the several halls at court were built along the same lines.

In Burbage's deed for the second Blackfriars there is no mention of windows, although all the glass belonging to the premises is included. But in a lawsuit brought in 1609, a sharer of the Children of the Chapel specifically mentions glass and wooden windows on each side of the room (Hillebrand 1964: 183). In this way, we learn that the Blackfriars was 'through-lighted'; that is, it had windows on both sides of the room, as do most Tudor halls. The dimensions of the second Blackfriars are given as 66 by 46 feet, presumably including the tiring house and stage (the theater itself seems to have occupied only part of the original hall). So we can estimate, on the basis of the analogy between this theater and the Parliament Chamber and other halls, and taking these dimensions into account, that the second Blackfriars had fourteen side windows with perhaps only ten in the auditorium itself, five on each side. The south end-window or -windows would have been obstructed by the tiring house.

There is little written architectural theory in English before the Restoration, but what there is supports this pattern of lighting design. In 1624, eleven years after he saw the first Globe burn, Sir Henry Wotton published his *Elements of Architecture*, based largely on Vitruvian principles of architecture. Wotton was a member of the Middle Temple who spent a good part of his life as a diplomat in Venice, where he was influenced by neoclassical architecture. Nevertheless, he held the view that for most styles of architecture the best light was 'a descending Light, which of all other doth set off mens *Faces* in their truest Spirit' (1624, sig. N2). Vitruvius was 'an extreame Lover of *Luminous Roomes*', he admits, but Wotton himself preferred not 'to make a House (though but for civill use) all *Eyes*, like *Argus*' (1624, sig. G4). He believed that, especially in ecclesiastical buildings, 'which were anciently darke, as they are likewise at this day', care must be taken not to distract the eye with too many windows. Because many of the hall playhouses were set up in what were formerly ecclesiastical buildings, it is understandable that a pattern of clerestory illumination took hold.

Another written endorsement of the practice of lighting large rooms from both sides is a short chapter entitled 'Building', published in 1642 by Thomas Fuller. The author (whose interest in theater extended to an early biography of Shakespeare) expresses the opinion that 'Thorow-lights are best for rooms of entertainment, and windows on one side for dormitories' (Fuller 1642, sig. Y4). If Fuller does not refer specifically to theaters, it is probable that he had them and other halls in mind when he spoke of 'rooms of entertainment'. With both contemporary practice and theory

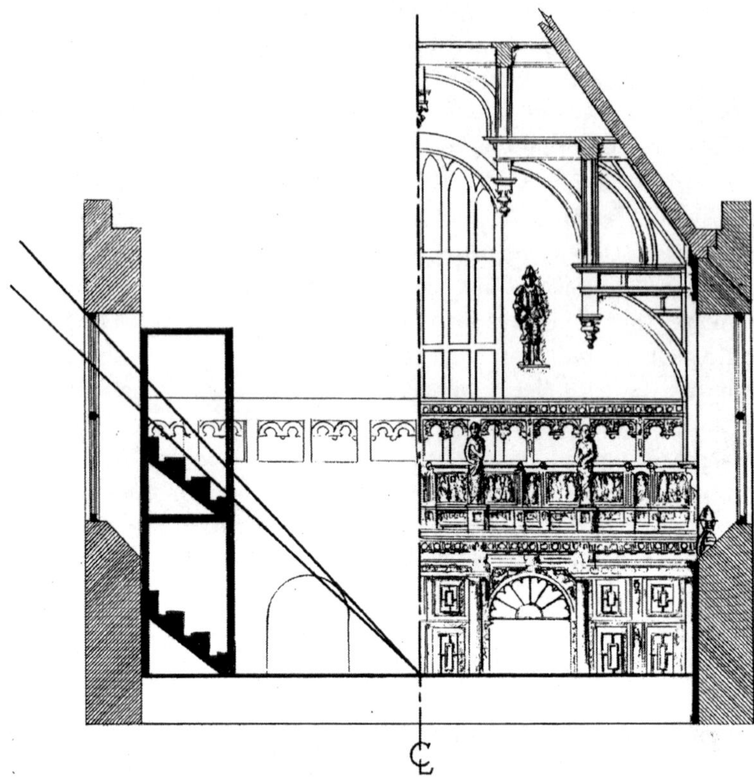

Figure 31.4 Middle Temple hall with 'Webb Playhouse' gallery.

calling for high windows on both sides of such rooms, it is probable that, when the actors sought permanent indoor theater, the illumination available to them resembled that of the halls they had so often played in as guests.

When pre-existing halls were converted into playhouses, certain modifications that affected the introduction of daylight may have been necessary. In Figure 31.4, for example, we see the screen of the Middle Temple sketched as if it were a tiring house façade with a stage placed before it. In order to maximize the number of spectators, the actors erected 'degrees', or the tiered scaffolds for the seating of the spectators, that likely obstructed some window light. Thus, I have superimposed in black a two-tiered audience gallery onto the transverse section of the Middle Temple hall, a gallery modeled after galleries in architectural drawings, now in Worcester College, Oxford, for an unidentified indoor playhouse probably designed by John Webb during the Interregnum or early Restoration (reproduced in Figure 14.3, above). In order to imagine the directionality of daylight entering the hall, diagonal lines have been drawn from the center of the stage to the sills and heads of the south windows of the Middle Temple hall. Of course, the diffused light common to these halls seldom produces beams of light as distinct as the diagonal lines; they serve only to indicate the lowest and highest angles from which daylight, unreflected by the interior of the

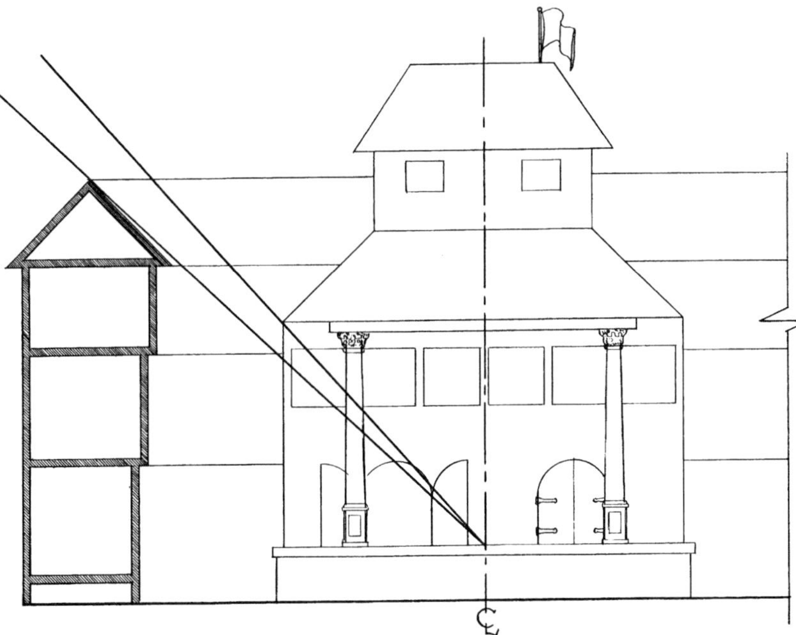

Figure 31.5 The Swan playhouse.

hall, could illuminate actors standing at the center of a stage. For purposes of comparison, I print a similar sketch of the stage and galleries of the Swan, again based on Richard Hosley's reconstruction (Figure 31.5). Once again, the lines drawn from the center of the stage serve only to indicate the directionality of the normally diffused light. Note that, in both indoor and outdoor playhouses, the major source of light enters from a relatively steep angle, crossing the stage from a height approximately equal to the height of the balconies above the stage. On many days in the spring, summer, and autumn, therefore, it was entirely possible that audiences saw afternoon performances at the two kinds of playhouse in similar natural light, with artificial light in the hall playhouses supplementing rather than overpowering the window light.

Near the conclusions of many performances in the depth of winter, however, candlelight in the hall theaters inevitably took on a larger burden of the illumination. Jacobean descriptions of artificial light at court sometimes tell us that the King's halls were 'as bright as day' or words to that effect. But the halls at court afforded nighttime royal entertainments with nearly ten times as many candles as were available at Salisbury Court. Thus, as we picture the ending of wintertime plays indoors at the professional theaters, we should imagine a gradually waning natural light yielding to a warm, but by no means brilliant, artificial light on the actors.

Because subjective brightness is a function of the cube root of actual brightness, the number of candles necessary for even small increases in perceived brightness increases geometrically. To double the apparent brightness of an actor, for instance, one needs to light him with eight times as many candles (from the same distance).

Thus, there are physical and monetary limits to how many candles can be placed close enough to the actors to increase illumination on them significantly. In experiments conducted in various halls, candelabra hung approximately 11 to 12 feet above the stage and a few feet downstage of the main acting area produced less glare and fewer shadows than other locations. Apart from the number of candles and their placement, the reflectance of the ceiling above the stage and its distance from the candles and the actors would be crucial in determining the level of brightness on stage. A light-colored ceiling or cloth stretched above the stage but still fairly close to the candelabra suspended above the stage could increase the amount of light on the actors by as much as 10 to 20 per cent. In addition to any iconographic functions they served, cloths and ceilings above the actors could reflect candlelight and, therefore, help to alleviate glare, the result of attempting to put too many candles close to the actors in the audience's line of sight.

After sunset, the indoor stage would certainly appear brighter than the rest of the playhouse, but we should avoid thinking of the stage as a picture-frame showcase. Apart from some special costumes and stage properties, the environment in the hall theaters more nearly approximated that of a lecture room today, where overhead artificial light supplements and then replaces window light as the day changes to night. In comparing hall playhouse lighting with our own theatrical illumination, we must remember that our psychological associations with candles were not shared by Tudor and Stuart Londoners. There was nothing quaint or romantic about candles to them. Elizabethan spectators may well have found entertainments at court extravagantly lit, but they cannot have thought of the lighting there as precious or theatrical, at least not until Inigo Jones began experimenting with special colored and reflected lights near his Italianate masque scenes at the Jacobean and Caroline courts.

In sum, an overall, indirect light normally obtained in both the amphitheaters and hall playhouses. And because both kinds of venue enjoyed a roughly similar articulation of light, there was the practical result that the actors were not habitually obliged to alter their methods of staging as they moved from one kind of playhouse to another. Some of the smallest indoor halls may have allowed the audience to enjoy subtler acting than was possible outdoors, but reconstructions of the Blackfriars, for instance, show that the majority of spectators there were nearly as far from the stage as those in the largest public theaters, where the audience could surround the actors. Hence, if the general illumination were good, audiences at both kinds of playhouse could discern about the same degree of refinement in the acting.

The steady, overall illumination of the amphitheaters and hall theaters, far from imposing a restriction on the actors and playwrights, meant that even in scenes of pretended darkness the audience could see and respond to the visual media of the actors' craft. The largely ungovernable stage lighting of the era underscores how much we lose owing to our lack of evidence about the acting styles of the period. But it leads us strongly to believe that the staging at the indoor and outdoor playhouses may not have been so different in regard to the particular aspect of stage production that one might have thought would define the principal difference between them.

CHAPTER 32

MUSIC AND SOUND

LUCY MUNRO

In May 1607 the Florentine agent in London, Ottaviano Lotti, reported with news of a play—now lost—that 'almost caused a very grave scandal':

> several players who were acting it on the stage performed it so that when one of the characters wanted to make a serenade to a lady he went and gathered various sorts of music, and many people appeared, with viols, violins, lutes, harps, flutes and suchlike, each one of them claiming to come from one part or another of the provinces of England. They were admitted to the band, and all together they made a concord which gave delight. At length someone arrived with a bagpipe which, besides being toneless, made such a noise that it stunned and ruined all the music. Finally he averred that he was a Scotsman, and he was bundled out and told that he had very little judgement if he thought that so villainous an instrument could harmonize and unite with others so noble and so worthy. The Scots knights who were present to hear the play thought about making their resentment plain right there, but they refrained, and hoped that the king would be greatly moved to anger. But because what I may call the merciful offices of his Majesty to lead these deputies in Parliament toward the union of the two realms have little availed with them, they say that his Majesty had dismissed them all. (Orrell 1977–8: 162)

Like many commentators, Lotti refers to the spectators going to 'hear' a play: in this case 'hearing' is obviously appropriate, as the meaning and the offensiveness with which the scene was imbued were created on an aural, rather than purely visual, level. Like many texts of the period, this play associated music with symbolic order; Ulysses in Shakespeare's *Troilus and Cressida* (Chamberlain's Men, *c.*1603) draws on a long line of rhetorical associations between music and human behaviour when he declares, 'Take but Degree away, vn-tune that string, | And hearke what Discord followes' (Shakespeare 1623, ¶¶1^{v}).[1] However, through its inclusion of the bagpipe,

[1] For detailed discussion of the thematic and theoretical associations of music, see Lindley (2006: 13–49); Wilson and Calore (2005: 289–307).

which was notoriously difficult to integrate into a musical ensemble,[2] the lost play suggested that King James's own pet project, the Union between England and Scotland, would lead not to political harmony but to discord and disunity. In a piece of musical satire which may have been an addition to the play in performance, an officially sanctioned political project is transformed into carnivalesque acoustic chaos.

Lotti's description thus raises questions relating to the practical and symbolic aspects of playhouse music, areas which have been in recent years a stimulating focus of scholarly attention. A number of valuable accounts of music in the playhouse have emerged, including Linda Phyllis Austern's *Music in English Children's Drama of the Renaissance* (1992) and the important work of Julia K. Wood and Peter Holman on Jacobean and (especially) Caroline theatre music,[3] and two complementary books on music in Shakespeare's plays: Christopher R. Wilson and Michela Calore's *Music in Shakespeare: A Dictionary* (2005) and David Lindley's *Shakespeare and Music* (2006). In addition, studies such as Bruce R. Smith's *The Acoustic World of Early Modern England* (1999) and Wes Folkerth's *The Sound of Shakespeare* (2002) have looked at music in the context of the broader acoustic environment of early modern England. With these works as background, my aim in this essay is to look at music and sound from the perspective of the early modern commercial theatre.[4]

The survival of musical cues, lyrics, and settings is haphazard even in plays that have been preserved in print or manuscript; as Tiffany Stern has recently pointed out, song lyrics and settings often circulated on separate sheets, meaning that they could be easily lost, reassigned, or inserted into another play (Stern 2004: 114–18). However, although the vast majority of compositions associated with the playhouses have been lost, those that survive give a reasonably full picture of the use of music in at least some theatrical contexts, notably in early seventeenth-century plays of the children's companies and in plays performed by the Jacobean and Caroline King's Men.[5] It is perhaps no coincidence that the dramatists most noted for their innovative use of music, William Shakespeare, John Marston, John Fletcher, and Richard Brome, worked closely with these companies. Rather than focusing on individual dramatists, however, I will first explore institutional contexts—such as the acoustic environments of the early modern playhouses, the involvement of musicians with theatre companies, and their musical resources—before examining in more detail the use of sound, and especially song, on the early modern stage.

[2] In *The Telltale* (auspices uncertain, 1630s?), for instance, Garullo's pretentious language is described as 'nothing but trencher scraps & peeces of broaken discourses left in tauernes & ordinaryes as harsh and vntunable as a still lute & a loud bagpipe' (Foakes and Gibson 1960, lines 146–8).

[3] See J. Wood (1991, 1998); Holman (1992).

[4] The musical traditions of masques and academic drama constitute separate subjects in themselves. The fullest recent account of music in masques is Walls (1996); J. Wood (1991) examines the music for academic drama alongside that of the commercial theatre.

[5] For lists of extant settings, see Duckles (1968); J. Wood (1991, app. 1); Austern (1992, app. B).

Music in the Playhouse

Until 1608 two different traditions, with distinct musical practices, coexisted in London's theatrical marketplace. Large, outdoor playhouses such as the Rose, Globe, Fortune, and Red Bull were used by adult companies such as Queen Elizabeth's Men, the Admiral's Men (later Prince Henry's Men), the Chamberlain's Men (later the King's Men), and Worcester's Men (later Queen Anna's Men), in which boy actors played female and juvenile roles but all of the other parts were taken by adult men. Their plays had long been associated with martial soundscapes in which trumpets and drums were prominent. In contrast, smaller, indoor spaces—such as the tiny theatre at St Paul's Cathedral, the first and second Blackfriars theatres, and the Whitefriars theatre—were used exclusively by companies composed entirely of children. Their plays eschewed trumpets and drums, which would have overpowered small auditoriums, and often seem to have used more complex instrumentation. In addition, Bruce R. Smith has recently argued that rectilinear indoor playhouses and round amphitheatres such as the Globe would have functioned differently in acoustic terms (B. Smith 1999: 206–17), the round walls of the amphitheatre having a focusing effect, and the roof of the indoor theatre reflecting sound back downwards. The acoustics of inn-yard conversions such as the Boar's Head and the Red Bull, and square purpose-built outdoor theatres such as the first Fortune, were presumably different again.[6]

Plays frequently call attention to the contrast in pitch and timbre between adult and boy actors' voices.[7] Robert Wilson's *The Three Lords and Three Ladies of London* (Queen Elizabeth's Men, 1588), for instance, includes a sung dialogue featuring Simplicity, a ballad singer, and the page Wit, 'both to musicke if ye will' (R. Wilson 1590, C1^{r}). The lyrics are lost, but the song must have capitalized on the comic contrast between the pitches of the voices of the adult actor playing Simplicity and the boy actor playing Wit. Companies entirely composed of children had a much higher incidence of unbroken, treble voices. In the meta-dramatic induction to Ben Jonson's *Cynthia's Revels* (Chapel, 1600), a child impersonating a hostile playgoer not only insults the music at Blackfriars but also complains that his fellow players are like small, high-pitched birds: '*They doe act like so manie* Wrens, *or* Pismires' (Jonson 1601, A3^{v}). In addition, as Gina Bloom has suggested, children's company plays written around the turn of the seventeenth century, such as *Cynthia's Revels* and Marston's *Antonio and Mellida* (Paul's, 1599), are acutely aware of the aural effects of a boy's breaking voice (Bloom 1998). In the induction to the latter, for instance, the boy who is to play Antonio worries that his performance in disguise as a woman will be unconvincing because his voice is breaking—'I a voice to play a lady! I shall nere doe it'—only to be told by another actor that an amazon should have a '*virago*-like' voice

[6] On the physical characteristics of these playhouses, see Berry (2000*a*: 452–3, 564–6, 531–2); for new evidence regarding the Red Bull, see Griffith (2001).

[7] See B. Smith (1999: 222–45) for detailed discussion of the actor's voice.

(Marston 1602, A4^{r}). Two songs in plays by Jonson, 'O, That Joy So Soon Should Waste', from *Cynthia's Revels*, and 'Still To Be Neat, Still To Be Dressed', from *Epicene* (Queen's Revels, 1609–10), would have had different effects in performance: although both songs seem to be sung by prepubescent boy actors, *Cynthia's Revels* was performed in a company entirely consisting of boys, whereas the leading actors in *Epicene* were in their early twenties.[8]

Children's company performers may have had more highly trained singing voices than the adults. The Elizabethan companies and the Jacobean Children of Paul's had strong links with choir schools, and appear to have used choristers in the plays that they performed (Hillebrand 1964; Gair 1982). I am, however, reluctant to use the common label of 'choirboy theatre' to refer to the children's companies, as the other Jacobean troupes were increasingly estranged from the choir schools and probably had less access to these trained voices. Nathaniel Giles, a manager of the Children of the Chapel on their re-establishment at the second Blackfriars playhouse in 1600, was Master of the Children of the Chapel Royal and may have used his choristers at the Blackfriars. The company certainly had some competent singers, as Giles was paid for 'a showe wth musycke and speciall songes p^{r}pared for that purpose', performed at court on Twelfth Night 1602 (Cook and Wilson 1961: 32). Frederic Gerschow, a visitor to the Blackfriars in September 1602, describes a musical entertainment before the play in which 'a boy *cum voce tremula* sang so charmingly to [the accompaniment of] a bass-viol that we have not heard the like of it in the whole of our journey, unless perhaps the nuns at Milan may have excelled him'.[9]

It is not, however, certain that these singers were choristers. Giles withdrew from the Chapel company in early 1602 after he was accused of using the patent allowing him to impress (in effect, to kidnap) children for the Windsor choir to take children for the theatre company. One of the key charges levelled by Henry Clifton, the outraged father who brought the case, was that his son and the other kidnapped children were 'noe way able or fitt for singing nor by anie the sayd confederates endevo*ur*ed to be taught to singe'.[10] In February 1604 the company was granted a royal patent and renamed the Children of the Queen's Revels; in 1606 a new patent was issued to Giles in which he was forbidden to use the Chapel choristers 'as Comedians or Stage players' (Chambers 1911: 362–3). Therefore, although it is not impossible that Chapel choristers were employed in Blackfriars plays, at least in the early days, there is no concrete evidence of any sustained overlap between the choir and the theatre company. The other Jacobean children's company, the Children of the King's Revels, also had musical resources—a 1608 agreement between their shareholders and Martin Slater specified that money taken in the theatre be used to pay for 'musique' in addition to other costs (Hillebrand 1964: 224)—but there is no evidence of any connection between this company and a choir school.

Giles was one of a number of musicians involved with the children's companies as managers, investors, and composers: notable figures include Richard Edwards,

8 On the casting of *Epicene*, see Dutton (2003: 6–8).

9 I. Smith (1964: 551–2); for the original text, see von Bülow (1892: 28).

10 The National Archives, London, STAC 5 C46/39; for a transcript, see Fleay (1890: 128).

William Hunnis, and Richard Farrant, managers of the Chapel children from the 1560s to the 1590s, Edward Pearce, manager of the Children of Paul's between 1599 and 1606, Martin Peerson, a shareholder in the Chapel/Queen's Revels company *c.*1602–4, and Philip Rosseter, the leading shareholder in a revived Children of the Queen's Revels from around 1609.[11] Another composer, John Daniel, was issued a patent for a company called the Children of the Queen's Chamber of Bristol in July 1615.[12] Although evidence of the work that these composers may have done for the companies is scanty, a few settings survive: Richard Farrant's 'Ah, Alas, You Salt Sea Gods'[13] was probably performed at the first Blackfriars (Brett 1961–2: 80; Carter 1995: 178), Pearce's 'Love for Such a Cherry Lip' (Ravenscroft 1614, no. 15) features in the Paul's play *Blurt Master Constable* (*c.*1601),[14] and Giles may have composed an anonymous setting for 'O, That Joy So Soon Should Waste',[15] from the Chapel play *Cynthia's Revels* (Sabol 1960: 228).

Musicians seem to have been involved with the adult companies as hired composers rather than entrepreneurs. The King's Men, who are better documented than any other company, had long-standing relationships with three composers: Robert Johnson (from *c.*1610), John Wilson (from *c.*1615), and William Lawes (from *c.*1634). Settings by Johnson survive for plays such as Shakespeare's *The Winter's Tale* and *The Tempest* and a number by Fletcher and his collaborators.[16] Wilson also wrote settings for Fletcherian plays, and for plays by Brome and John Ford.[17] Lawes collaborated with academic and courtly dramatists such as William Berkeley, William Cartwright, William Cavendish, and John Suckling, and with more regular professionals such as James Shirley and William Davenant.[18] These composers may not have had exclusive agreements with the King's Men, since both Wilson and Lawes wrote music for other companies. A setting by Wilson for Thomas Heywood's *The Rape of Lucrece* (revived in the 1630s by Beeston's boys) survives, as do settings by Lawes for Shirley's *The Duke's Mistress*, performed by Queen Henrietta Maria's Men in 1636, and for three plays performed by Beeston's boys: Henry Glapthorne's *Argalus and Parthenia* (*c.*1637), Ford's *The Lady's Trial* (1638), and Brome's *A Jovial Crew* (1642).[19]

Instrumentation was another area of variation between adult and children's companies in the years prior to 1608. Evidence suggests that most, if not all, adult

[11] See the entries in L. Macy (ed.), *Grove Music Online*, <http://www.grovemusic.com>, accessed 15 Feb. 2007; on Giles, Peerson, and Rosseter, see also Munro (2005: 17–18, 23, 28, 31, 38).

[12] Chambers and Greg (1909: 279–80); Daniel's brother Samuel, who had briefly acted as licenser for the Children of the Queen's Revels, seems to have helped him to gain the patent.

[13] Christ Church, Oxford, MSS 984–8.

[14] Pearce may also have composed 'What Meat Eats the Spaniard?', in the same play; see Sabol (1958).

[15] Christ Church, Oxford, MS 439, pp. 38–9.

[16] For editions, see Cutts (1971); Spink (1974).

[17] For editions, see Spink (1971); John Ford, *The Lover's Melancholy* (1629), ed. R. F. Hill (Manchester: Manchester University Press, 1985), app. B; J. Wood (1991, app. 2).

[18] See J. Wood (1998, esp. app. 1). For a recent edition of Lawes's settings, see Callon (2002).

[19] See Cutts (1961*a*); J. Wood (1998, esp. app. 1; 1991, app. 2). Other composers whose extant settings may have been used in original productions include John Atkins, Charles Coleman, Antonio Ferrobosco, George Jeffreys, Henry Lawes, John Taylor, and John Withy. See Cutts (1983, 1986); Spink (1971, no. 100); J. Wood (1991, app. 2).

companies would have had access to stringed instruments such as: treble and bass viols, violins, lutes, bandores (bass instruments similar to lutes, with wire strings, played with the fingers), and citterns (also wire-strung, but played with a plectrum); brass instruments such as trumpets and sackbuts (early trombones); wind instruments such as bagpipes, fifes, pipes, horns, and perhaps hautboys (double-reed instruments comparable with the modern oboe, albeit rougher and louder, also known as shawms); and percussion instruments such as drums and tambourines.[20] The children's companies probably had greater musical resources than the adults, but play-texts associated with the Elizabethan companies are generally non-specific about the instrumentation required; more is known about the musical resources of the children's companies revived at the turn of the seventeenth century, particularly the Children of Paul's and the Chapel/Queen's Revels children.[21] Their basic instrumentation does not differ much from that of the adult companies aside from a preference for cornets and hautboys over the noisier trumpets, but their plays are much more likely to include quieter instruments such as recorders and organs, used rarely in the amphitheatres at this time.[22] These differences in instrumentation may be related to the genres of surviving plays. Adult and children's companies performed comedies and tragedies (extant children's tragedies are relatively scarce, but clusters can be found in some repertories), but the chronicle history plays popular in the adult repertories are all but non-existent in those of the children. Instead, various tragicomic styles—including John Lyly's 'gallimaufrey', Marston's mixed-mode experiments, and Fletcherian tragicomedy—seem to have predominated, requiring a more varied and subtle use of music.

Elizabethan and early Jacobean adult companies included jigs and dances at the conclusion of their plays,[23] but the turn-of-the-century children's companies used a rather different form of extra-dramatic music: instrumental and vocal interludes before and during performances. Frederic Gerschow remarks that at the second Blackfriars playhouse, 'For a whole hour before the play begins, one listens to a delightful instrumental concert played on organs, lutes, pandorins [i.e. bandores], {mandoras, fiddles}, and flutes.'[24] A play performed there, George Chapman's *May-Day* (*c.*1602), opens with the direction 'Chorus Iuuenum cantantes & saltantes' (Chapman 1611, A2R). In addition to pre-performance music, children's companies filled the breaks between the acts of their plays—during which the candles were trimmed and replaced—with instrumental music.[25] The contrast between adult and

[20] On the musical resources of the adult companies, see Lindley (2006: 93–100).

[21] For detailed summary, see Austern (1992: 61–77).

[22] Hautboys and cornets are extremely rare in adult company plays performed before 1608; recorders are mentioned only in the 1605 and 1623 texts of *Hamlet*. See Lindley (2006: 94, 97, 99–100).

[23] The standard account of jigs remains Baskervill (1929); for more recent accounts, see Gurr (1992*b*: 174–6); B. Smith (1999: 157–63).

[24] I. Smith (1964: 551–2); I have incorporated (in braces) Peter Holman's suggestions that Gershow's *Geigen* is better translated as 'fiddles' than 'violins', and that his 'Mandoren' refers to the mandora (a small, lute-like instrument) rather than the mandolin. Since mandoras may have been unknown in England at this time, Holman argues that Gershow actually saw and heard citterns. See Holman (1993: 136; 2000: 117); for the German text, see von Bülow (1892: 28).

[25] For a summary of evidence, see Taylor (1993: 8–11).

children's company practices can be illustrated by performances of Marston's *The Malcontent* (*c.*1603–4), by both the Chapel/Queen's Revels children and the King's Men. After the King's Men had appropriated the play from the boys (seemingly in revenge for the theft of one of their own plays), it was rewritten for the Globe stage by Marston and John Webster.[26] One aim of the revision was to write material to fill the gaps left by the absent inter-act music: in a new induction sequence, Richard Burbage (playing himself) claims that the 'additions' commissioned by the King's Men are 'to entertaine a little more time, and to abridge the not received custome of musicke in our Theater' (Marston 1604, A4^{r}). 'Burbage' seems to refer not to music in general—the plays performed by his company include many musical cues and songs—but to the extra-dramatic music which prefaced and intersected plays at Blackfriars and Paul's.[27]

In summer 1608 the King's Men gained possession of the second Blackfriars playhouse, which Burbage had leased to the Chapel/Queen's Revels children, and they began to perform there in late 1609 or early 1610. The King's Men's occupation of the Blackfriars, which they used in addition to the Globe, was followed in 1616 by the construction of another indoor playhouse, the Cockpit, for Queen Anna's Men. In using indoor theatres, the adult companies seem to have adopted something close to children's companies' musical practice, and the second decade of the seventeenth century saw a move towards more varied soundscapes in the amphitheatres as distinctions between how different kinds of playhouses were used gradually broke down. Other contributing factors include changes in theatrical fashion, as the adult companies began to introduce a greater number of tragicomedies into their repertories and to perform fewer chronicle history plays.

One noticeable change was in instrumentation, as adult companies begin to use quieter instruments such as recorders, cornets, and hautboys more extensively. It is not possible to say exactly when these instruments begin to move into the amphitheatres: recorders in plays such as Francis Beaumont and John Fletcher's *The Maid's Tragedy* (*c.*1610), Thomas Middleton's *The Second Maiden's Tragedy* (1611), and Shakespeare and Fletcher's *The Two Noble Kinsmen* (1613) may have been used at Blackfriars rather than the Globe, and calls for recorders in Middleton's *A Chaste Maid in Cheapside*, first performed by Lady Elizabeth's Men at the Swan in 1613, may represent later practice, since the play was not printed until 1630. But we know that the Company of the Revels, who performed at the Red Bull in 1619–21, tried to effect a decisive change in the acoustic environment of that playhouse, making prominent use of cornets, hautboys, and recorders, and eschewing loud, percussive sound

26 Three editions of *The Malcontent* were published in 1604; the third, which differs significantly from the first and second, is said on its title page to be 'Augmented by *Marston.* | With the Additions played by the Kings | Maiesties servants. | Written by *Ihon* [*sic*] *Webster*'. Charles Cathcart argues convincingly that the additional passages in the third Quarto represent revision of the play by both dramatists for performance by the King's Men (Cathcart 2006).

27 The retention of musical cues from the first and second Quartos in the third Quarto may suggest that they were within the capabilities of the King's Men. However, the retention of a reference to inter-act music at the beginning of the second act may indicate that the third Quarto does not accurately represent the Globe text in this respect.

effects.[28] They tell their audience in the Prologue to one play, J.C.'s *The Two Merry Milkmaids*:

> This Day we entreat All that are hither come,
> To expect no noyse of Guns, Trumpets, nor Drum,
> Nor Sword and Targuet; but to heare Sence and Words,
> Fitting the Matter that the Scene affords. (1620, [A]2^{v})

Perhaps as a result of this project, or of similar efforts elsewhere, Julia K. Wood sees little evidence between the instrumentation in indoor and outdoor theatres in the Caroline period (J. Wood 1991: 89–90).

Inter-act music was also gradually adopted by the adults after 1608.[29] In December 1617, when no children's companies were active in London, Orazio Busino, chaplain to the Venetian embassy in London, was taken to an unidentified playhouse. Busino's inability to speak English meant that the tragedy he saw 'moved [him] very little', but he noted that 'one may derive some little amusement from gazing on the sumptuous dresses of the actors and observing their gestures, and the various interludes of instrumental music, dancing, singing and the like' (R. Brown et al. 1864–1947: xv. 67–8). Other mentions of inter-act music are found in plays performed at Blackfriars and/or the Globe, such as Nathan Field and Philip Massinger's *The Fatal Dowry* (King's Men, 1619), and those performed at the Cockpit, such as Shirley's *The Witty Fair One* (Queen Henrietta Maria's Men, *c.*1628). The Prologue to another Cockpit play, Thomas Nabbes's *Hannibal and Scipio* (Queen Henrietta Maria's Men, 1635), remarks that the '*Scene*' will be '*translated as the musick playes | Betwixt the acts*' (Nabbes 1637, A3^{v}). Amphitheatre plays were divided into acts by 1616, if not earlier, but only one play-text securely linked with an amphitheatre, J.D.'s *The Knave in Grain* (Prince Charles [II]'s Men, 1639), 'Acted at the *Fortune* many dayes together with great *Applause*' according to its title page, contains evidence of inter-act music.[30]

The introduction of inter-act music by adult companies may have been one factor contributing to a change in their employment of musicians. Although there is no conclusive evidence that the King's Men took over the Blackfriars musicians, adult companies seem increasingly to have preferred established bands of musicians and to have relied less on actor–musicians and/or external groups of professional musicians such as city waits. By 1624, and probably earlier, the King's Men were employing a number of professional musicians, some of whom were also London waits and/or court musicians; lists also survive of musicians working at the Blackfriars and at the Cockpit in 1634 (Cutts 1966; Lefkowitz 1965). There are many references to the 'Blackfriars Music' dating to the 1630s and early 1640s (J. Wood

[28] For the use of cornets, see *The Two Merry Milkmaids* (1619), Dekker and Massinger's *The Virgin Martyr* (1620), and Gervase Markham and William Sampson's *Herod and Antipater* (1621); for hautboys and recorders, see *The Two Noble Ladies* (1621).

[29] Taylor (1993: 6–7) summarizes references to inter-act music in Jacobean and Caroline adult company plays; see pp. 30–7 for his discussion of the timing of this change in practice.

[30] The stage directions '*sound Musick*' which appear at the opening of Acts II and III (J.D. 1640, D1^{v}, F2^{r}) may be slightly misplaced calls for inter-act music; neither seems likely to be a call for a fanfare or other scene-setting music.

1991: 26–7; Holman 1992: 298–300), and Glapthorne's *The Lady Mother* (King's Revels, 1635) includes a striking meta-theatrical reference to the personnel and musical practices at Salisbury Court, where it was first performed. Encountering a group of on-stage musicians, Crackby exclaims, 'Now on my life this boy does sing as like the boy at the whitefryers as ever I heard,' and Sucket responds, 'I and the Musicks like theires' (Glapthorne 1959, lines 675–7). The boy singer is both a member of the theatre company performing at the Whitefriars playhouse, Salisbury Court, and a dramatic character who reminds his on-stage audience of that company; the musicians are simultaneously the fictional city waits and the playhouse's real-life musicians.

Music, Song, and Sound

In his voluminous anti-theatrical tract *Histriomastix*, published in 1633, William Prynne indicts the playhouses for their indecorous noise. As the 'concomitants or circumstances of Stage-playes' he lists 'Lascivious dancing. Amorous obscene songs: Effeminate lust-exciting Musicke. Profuse, inordinate lascivious laughter, and vaine theatricall applauses' (Prynne 1633: 155–6). There is 'nothing more frequent', he declares,

> then amorous Pastorals, or obscene lascivious Love-songs, most melodiously cha*n*ted out upon the Stage betweene each seueral Action; both to supply that Chasme or vacant Interim which the Tyring-house takes up, in changing the Actors robes, to fit them for some other part in the ensuing Scene:... as likewise to please the itching eares, if not to inflame the outragious lusts of lewde Spectators, who are oft-times ravished with these ribaldrous pleasing Ditties, and transported by them into a *Mahometan Paradise*, or extasie of uncleanesse. (1633: 262)

Prynne is clearly aware of the use of inter-act music and song in the Caroline theatre, and his somewhat overheated view of the ways in which music might be used to excite the playgoer is not without a shred of truth. As Julia K. Wood writes, music is often used in Caroline plays to dramatize characteristics such as madness, drunkenness, wantonness, and joviality. Lavish scene-setting music could be required for weddings, funerals, religious ritual, military scenes, and embedded masques or dumbshows, and atmospheric music was increasingly prominent, especially for scenes involving death or the supernatural. Music might also be used primarily to entertain, although sounds designed only to please what Prynne calls 'the itching eares' of spectators usually consisted of extra-dramatic compositions such as inter-act music; extraneous songs or interludes are rare within the plays themselves (J. Wood 1998: 23–38; see also J. Wood 1991).

The uses for music that Wood describes remained relatively constant through the Elizabethan, Jacobean, and Caroline periods, but the styles of individual songs were more susceptible to change. David Greer suggests, indeed, that 'the playhouse was a breeding-ground for new idioms' (Greer 1992: 166), while Peter Holman argues that the children's companies were 'early exponents of what is, in effect, continuo song', and that 'those who seek "operatic" principles in English drama should perhaps concern themselves with the choirboy theatre rather than the masque' (Holman 1992: 293, 292). The Elizabethan children's companies quickly adopted and may even have pioneered the consort song, in which a solo voice is accompanied by a group of instruments, usually viols; these songs are often laments, designed to wring pathos from moments of high dramatic tension. Richard's Farrant's 'Ah, Alas, You Salt Sea Gods', sung by Panthea on the death of Abradates and described by Philip Brett as 'One of the finest dramatic laments' (Brett 1961–2: 80), is likely to have been used in a Chapel play,[31] and a version of another lament, 'Awake, Ye Woeful Wights', sung in Richard Edwards's *Damon and Pithias* (Chapel, 1566), also survives in manuscript.[32]

Children's companies were still using consort songs around the turn of the seventeenth century, but the songs' stylistic range had increased. For instance, three contrasting consort settings associated with the Children of Paul's survive.[33] *Blurt Master Constable* includes two such songs: a witty dialogue for three singers with a light dance melody, 'What Meat Eats the Spaniard?', and the sensuous serenade 'Love for Such a Cherry Lip'. The third, 'The Scrivener's Song of Holborn' (Ravenscroft 1612, no. 12), is sung by the maidservant Audrey in Middleton's city comedy *A Trick to Catch the Old One*; the 'learning and delicacy' of the song is somewhat incongruous within the play's grimy urban milieu (Austern 1992: 254). Further experimentation can be seen in surviving settings for two polyphonic songs in the Paul's play *The Maid's Metamorphosis*, set for four high voices; Austern argues that these settings demonstrate the influence of the madrigal, which is otherwise rare in theatre music (Austern 1992: 235–42).

The children's companies were also early exponents of the lute air, in which the polyphonic accompaniment of the consort song was reduced to a single bass line, perhaps embellished with improvised chords, generally played on lute or bass viol.[34] Settings survive for 'O, That Joy So Soon Should Waste' in *Cynthia's Revels*, which the pretentious courtier Hedon apparently sings to the accompaniment of the lyra-viol, and 'The Dark Is My Delight'[35] in Marston's *The Dutch Courtesan* (Queen's Revels, 1604–5), which the courtesan Franceschina sings to the lute. Robert Jones's lute air 'Methought This Other Night' is subjected to parodic amendment and sung 'scurvily' by the Bawd in Thomas Dekker and John Webster's *Northward Ho* (Paul's, 1605).[36] The lute air was to become dominant among theatre songs, perhaps in part because it demands only one singer and one accompanist (potentially the same actor–musician) and would presumably have demanded less preparation and rehearsal.

[31] It is possible that *The Wars of Cyrus*, attributed to the Chapel children on its publication in 1594, is a heavily cut version of the play from which this song came.

[32] British Library, Add. MS 15117, fo. 3^r^; for discussion, see Sabol (1960, n. 7); J. Long (1967); Chan (1980: 16–20; including setting). On consort songs and laments, see also Chan (1980: 15–30); Carter (1995: 177–9).

[33] For discussion of these settings, at least one of which is by Edward Pearce, see Austern (1992: 242–54).

[34] On the air, see Greer (1992: 153–67).

[35] British Library, Add. MS 24665, fo. 58^{v}; MS Egerton 2971, fo. 8^{v}.

[36] For discussion of these settings, see Austern (1992: 254–66).

The Jacobean and Caroline periods saw further changes in the styles of songs and in their delivery. Composers such as Robert Johnson, John Wilson, and William Lawes adopted a declamatory style which has been noted in embryonic form in sixteenth-century consort songs; Device in Cavendish's *The Country Captain* (King's Men, 1640) seems to refer to this style when he claims, 'I can talke loud to a Theorbo too, and that's cald singing' (Cavendish 1999, lines 316–17).[37] The 1620s and 1630s also saw an increased prominence for dialogue songs, many of which were also declamatory in style. The fact that earlier songs might be seen as old-fashioned is reflected in the composition of new settings for old songs: settings by Lawes and Wilson for Beaumont and Fletcher's *Cupid's Revenge*, Fletcher's *The Faithful Shepherdess* and *The Mad Lover*, Jonson's *Epicene*, Middleton's *The Widow*, and Heywood's *The Rape of Lucrece* were almost certainly composed for Caroline revivals of plays originally performed ten or twenty years earlier (J. Wood 1998: 15–16, 43–4, 47–8, 49–50; Cutts 1961*a*).

Catches, rounds, ballads, and popular songs were used in plays throughout the period, some composed by William Lawes, who was renowned for his drinking songs (J. Wood 1998: 25–31). Popular tunes, such as 'Fortune My Foe' and 'Go from My Window', might appear in a variety of plays, sometimes performed relatively 'straight' and sometimes subjected to parody (see Duckles 1968: 123, 129). Some plays capitalize on their audience's detailed knowledge of such tunes, such as Beaumont's *The Knight of the Burning Pestle* (Queen's Revels, 1607–8), in which the dialogue of the ageing prodigal Old Merrythought is a tissue of quotations from innumerable ballads and popular songs. Songs composed for specific plays might also appear in more than one play: 'Take, O Take Those Lips Away' seems to have been incorporated into *Measure for Measure* for a 1620s revival, having been used in Fletcher's *Rollo, Duke of Normandy* (King's Men, 1619); 'Cupid Calls, Come Lovers Come' appears in Middleton's *A Chaste Maid in Cheapside* and *More Dissemblers Besides Women* (King's Men?, *c.*1614).[38]

As noted above, more music survives for plays performed by the Jacobean and Caroline King's Men than for any other company; in addition, the loss of almost all of the settings composed for the Elizabethan adult companies and for those working in the Jacobean and Caroline amphitheatres should not be overlooked.[39] Innumerable plays performed by these troupes call for songs—for which most of the settings and many lyrics are lost—and a number call for musical effects. Robert Greene's *James IV* (Queen Elizabeth's Men?, *c.*1590) and *Orlando Furioso* (Strange's Men, *c.*1591), for instance, contain a number of intriguing directions for music, but little to indicate

[37] On declamation in English song, see Spink (1957: 157–9); J. Wood (1991: 64–7); Greer (1992: 158–9, 163–72); Holman (1992: 287–8, 292).

[38] For 'Take, O Take Those Lips Away', see Cutts (1971: 85, 172). *A Chaste Maid in Cheapside* and *More Dissemblers Besides Women* were printed in 1630 and 1657 respectively, so the song may have been a later insertion in either or both. An anonymous setting survives in the New York Public Library, MS Drexel 4175, nos 24, 56.

[39] Settings for more than 100 songs (including ballads, popular songs, and specially composed songs) performed by the Chamberlain's/King's Men in their plays have so far been traced; this outnumbers the total number of settings that have been traced for all other companies combined. Less than fifteen extant settings have been associated with amphitheatres other than the Globe.

precisely how it was used. Indeed, Greene seems to have left some crucial decisions to the companies with which he worked: a direction in *James IV* reads '*After a solemne seruice, enter from the widdowes house a seruice, musical songs of marriages, or a maske, or what prettie triumph you list*' (Greene 1598*b*, H4^v). In view of these lacunae, Peter Holman is perhaps overconfident in his declaration that before 1610 'the adult companies normally performed plays in a manner that needed little or no sophisticated music' and that 'musicians and instruments were required by the companies not so much for plays as for stage jigs' (Holman 1992: 295, 296).

Despite the paucity of surviving settings, there are traces of a growing sophistication in amphitheatre music outside the Globe. A group of interrelated saints' plays performed at the Red Bull—William Rowley's *A Shoemaker a Gentleman* (Prince Charles [I]'s Men, *c.*1618), *The Two Noble Ladies* (Company of the Revels, *c.*1619–22), Henry Shirley's *The Martyred Soldier* (Revels, *c.*1619), and Dekker and Massinger's *The Virgin Martyr* (Revels, 1620)—use music and other sound effects in strikingly similar ways in their dramatization of religious conviction and conversion. In *The Martyred Soldier,* for instance, the appearance of an angel to the Vandal general Bellizarius is heralded by the sound of thunder, quickly replaced with what Bellizarius describes as 'sweet tunes' (H. Shirley 1638, C2^v). With his conversion the play establishes an intimate relationship between music and Christian salvation. Bellizarius tells two Christians whose tongues he had ordered to be cut out before his conversion, 'you'le yet be heard; | The sighes of your tun'd soules are musicall' (1638, D2^r), and the martyrdoms of Bellizarius and his wife, Victoria, are intercut throughout with songs from the angels who rise from the playhouse's trapdoor and descend from its heavens. In a rare survival, a setting for the song that accompanies Bellizarius' death has been traced; it has a bright and triumphant tone, suiting the lyric:

Victory, victory, hell is beaten downe,
The Martyr has put on a golden Crowne;
Ring Bels of Heaven, him welcome hither,
Circle him Angels round together. (1638, I3^r)[40]

It is not surprising that Abraham Wright remarked in his 1630s commonplace book that *The Martyred Soldier* was 'very good for ye presentments and songs by angel; by wch ye people were much taken' (Kirsch 1969: 259). As I noted above, the use of music and sound by the Company of the Revels, who performed *The Martyred Soldier,* seems to have been part of a wider theatrical project.

Some generalizations can be made about the use of song in the early modern playhouse. Elite male characters rarely sing or play on stage unless they are mad, drunk, foolish, or in love, states which can make them break social prohibitions dictating that making music in public was ungentlemanly.[41] The usual substitute for an elite man is a boy singer who conveys his master's ventriloquized emotions. In *The*

[40] The setting, from the Bodleian Library, MS Don.c.57, fo. 24, is printed in Cutts (1959).

[41] In *The Compleat Gentleman,* Henry Peacham is insistent that the gentleman should confine musical activity to 'his priuate recreation at leasurable houres' (Peacham 1622: 98).

Second Maiden's Tragedy, for instance, a page accompanies Govianus' mourning at the tomb of his wife and sings a song in her honour; Govianus comments,

> Thow art an honest boye, tis donne like one
> that has a feelinge of his masters passions
> and the vnmatched worth of his dead mistris.
>
> (Anon., ed. Greg 1909, lines 1910–12)

It is perhaps a mark of the social dissonance of Volpone that he sings for himself in attempting to seduce Celia; in Dekker's *Old Fortunatus* (Admiral's Men, 1599) the 'melancholike' Orleans, languishing for the love of Agripyne, takes the lute from his boy and plays it himself, only to find that 'This musicke makes me but more out of tune' (Dekker 1600, F1^{r-v}). Madmen sing in a series of Jacobean and Caroline plays: the chorus of madmen in Webster's *The Duchess of Malfi* (King's Men, 1614), with their jarring chromatic howls, composed by Robert Johnson,[42] are followed by the tunefully deranged heroes of Fletcher's *The Mad Lover* (King's Men, *c.*1616), Middleton's *The Nice Valour, or, The Passionate Madman* (auspices uncertain, *c.*1622), and Brome's *The Court Beggar* (Beeston's boys, 1640).

Among non-elite men, a workman's singing often helps to establish him on his first appearance in a play. In Wilson's *The Cobbler's Prophesy* (auspices unknown, *c.*1590), Raph Cobler enters '*with his stoole, his implements and shooes, and sitting on his stoole, falls to sing*' (Wilson 1594, A3^{v}–A4^{r}); this convention is perhaps parodied in Dekker and Middleton's *1 The Honest Whore* (Prince Henry's Men, 1604), in which Roger sets out the tools of Bellafront's trade as courtesan while '*singing with the ends of old Ballads as he does it*' (Dekker and Middleton 1604, C3^{v}). Increasingly prominent are singing rogues: Shakespeare's Autolycus in *The Winter's Tale* is succeeded by singing thieves in Middleton's *The Widow* (King's Men, *c.*1616), singing gypsies in *More Dissemblers Besides Women* and Middleton and Rowley's *The Spanish Gypsy* (Lady Elizabeth's Men, 1623), and singing beggars in Fletcher's *The Beggar's Bush* (King's Men, *c.*1618) and Brome's *A Jovial Crew*. Clowns are required to sing in adult company plays performed throughout the period: known performers of these singing roles include Robert Armin, who probably played Feste in *Twelfth Night* and the Fool in *King Lear*, Timothy Reade, required to sing as Buzzard in *The English Moor* (Queen Henrietta Maria's Men, 1637), and William Robins, who played the singing role of Carazie in Massinger's *The Renegado* (Lady Elizabeth's Men, 1624).

Female characters are, in general, more likely to sing than their male counterparts. John Thompson, who played female roles with the King's Men in the late 1620s and early 1630s, is required to sing as three elite women: Domitia in Massinger's *The Roman Actor* (1626), Honoria in Massinger's *The Picture* (1629), and Panopia in Arthur Wilson's *The Swisser* (*c.*1631). Other elite women, like elite men, have boy singers to perform for them. In Davenant's *The Fair Favourite* (King's Men, 1638), a boy sings 'that air *Renaldo* sent to *Grittiline*...a Song of Jealousie' on the request of Eumena (Davenant 1673, pt 3, 94), while in Suckling's *Aglaura* (King's Men, 1638),

[42] For settings, see Cutts (1971: 40–5).

a boy sings 'the *Prince's* Song', 'No, No, Fair Heretic', having apparently declined to sing Aglaura's own choice of song because ''twill make you melancholly' (Suckling 1638, H1^r).[43]

Indecorous female figures, such as courtesans and madwomen, are particularly likely to sing. Whores often sing to the lute: Bellafront in the first part of Dekker and Middleton's *The Honest Whore*, for instance, or Franceschina in Marston's *The Dutch Courtesan*, who sings the delicately bawdy seduction song 'The Dark Is My Delight', with its final punchline: '*I* loue to sleepe gainst prickle. | So doth the Nightingale' (Marston 1605, B2^v).[44] In Brome's *The Novella* (King's Men, 1632), Victoria's assumption of the role of a courtesan requires her to demonstrate her musical ability. She tells her servant, 'Give me my Lute; and set me for the signe | Of what I meane to be, the fam'd *Novella*,' and as she '*playes and sings above... Many Gallants passe over the stage gazing at her*' (Brome 1653, K1^r). Visual and aural performance makes Victoria into a spectacle, but it is one that she carefully stage-manages. The association of public singing with unchaste behaviour means that women who feign lasciviousness in order to deter unwanted suitors often break into song, such as Florimell in Fletcher and Rowley's *The Maid in the Mill* (King's Men, 1623), with her refrain of 'let the mill go round'.

Female madness was connected with song and with lewd speech as early as Lyly's *The Woman in the Moon* (auspices uncertain, *c.*1590?), in which the lunatic Pandora sings wildly, but certain characteristics seem to have coalesced with Shakespeare's Ophelia, in particular her singing of old ballads and the troubling suggestions of untrammelled female sexuality that surround her madness.[45] Ophelia clearly influenced the representation of other female characters that go mad, such as the Jailer's Daughter in *The Two Noble Kinsmen* and Anglitora in *Tom a Lincoln* (auspices uncertain, *c.*1610–25). In Brome's *The Northern Lass* (King's Men, 1629), the contours of female madness, and its association with music—as established in *Hamlet* and *The Two Noble Kinsmen*—are adjusted. In *The Northern Lass*, Constance has (unlike her predecessors) been established as a singer before she becomes deranged, and her songs are specially composed pieces rather than recycled popular songs. The situation is also complicated by the impersonation of the deranged Constance by the whore Constance Holdup. Like Constance, Holdup sings to a John Wilson setting and, as Julia K. Wood notes, the contrast between the two women is conveyed through the lyrics rather than the music; in terms of the latter, Holdup seems to mimic and perhaps exaggerate Constance's deranged singing style (J. Wood 1991: 151–3). The joke is therefore on the idiotic suitor Widgeon, who is fooled by the superficial similarity of the songs and does not notice the obvious innuendo in Holdup's lyrics:

> *the Snake beneath me stird;*
> *And with his sting gaue me a clap,*
> *that swole my belly not my lap.* (Brome 1632, I4^v)[46]

[43] Settings survive for the song in *Aglaura*; see J. Wood (1998: 40–1).

[44] For detailed discussion, see Sabol (1960: 230–2); Austern (1992: 260–5).

[45] For illuminating discussions, see Fox-Good (1995); Lindley (2006: 154–61).

[46] The settings are preserved in the New York Public Library, MSS Drexel 4041, nos 11, 12, 15, and 21, and 4257, nos 99, 45, and 47; three are edited in J. Wood (1991, app. 2).

The situation is made even more ironic by the fact that Widgeon presents himself as a connoisseur of ballads, claiming, 'I haue a great many Southerne songs already. But Northern ayres nips it dead' (1632, D3^{r}); yet he is nonetheless unable to tell the difference between the songs of the northern Constance (who comes from County Durham) and the southern Constance Holdup (who claims that her father 'bore the office of a Commissioner for the peace in the West countrey'; 1632, H4^{r}).[47]

As the use of indecorous songs to represent madness suggests, plays frequently blur the boundaries between music and other forms of sound. Marston's *The Malcontent*, for instance, opens with '*the vilest out of tune Musicke*' (Marston 1604, B1^{r}), in keeping with Malevole's disordered ranting, which is as harsh and dissonant as the noises that precede it. Similarly, in John Clavell's *The Soddered Citizen* (King's Men, *c.*1630), an increasingly large group led by the drunken prodigal Brainsick creates a cacophony of song and other noise; the villainous Undermine describes Brainsick as a 'roareinge . . . Sackbutt', saying that 'Billingsgate affordes softe whispers, | Compar'd with this, diversitie of Noyse' (Clavell 1936, lines 334, 434–5).

Battle scenes often employ musical signals alongside other sound effects. In Peele's *The Battle of Alcazar* (Admiral's Men, *c.*1589), a stage direction reads, '*The Trumpets sound the chambers are dischargde. Then enter the king of Portugall and the Moore, with all theyr traine*' (Peele 1594, D4^{v}). Similar effects are used in plays performed in indoor theatres—*Antonio and Mellida* includes the direction '*Exeunt all on the lower Stage: at which the Cornets sound a florish, and a peale of shot is giuen*' (Marston 1602, B4^{v})—but their aural texture would have been different. Plays use established military conventions, such as sennets, alarums, flourishes, and retreats, to signal the progress of a battle; some add military songs, such as 'Arm, Arm, the Scouts Are All Come In' in Fletcher's *The Mad Lover* and 'On Bravely, On; the Foe Is Met' in Nabbes's *Hannibal and Scipio*.[48]

Off-stage sound is used to indicate battles and other kinds of disturbance, such as the unseen sea battle in Shakespeare's *Antony and Cleopatra* (King's Men, *c.*1606). In Fletcher and Massinger's *The Spanish Curate* (King's Men, 1622), a preparatory stage direction, '*Pewter ready for noyse*', precedes '*A great noyse within*'; Diego comments on the sound of 'Ladles, dishes, kettles, how they fly all? | And how the Glasses through the Roomes' (Beaumont, Fletcher *et al.* 1647, G2$^{r–v}$). Stage directions also suggest the manipulation of sound effects, such as changes in volume and placing the sounds in different locations: Fletcher's *Bonduca* (King's, 1610), for instance, requires '*Alarms, Drums and Trumpets in severall places afar off, as at a main Battell*' (Beaumont, Fletcher, et al. 1647, 4H2^{r}). In Rowley's *A New Wonder, A Woman Never Vexed* (Prince Charles [I]'s Men, *c.*1611) the rowdy environment of the gaming house is created through sound. While Stephen, Jack, Dick, and Hugh play dice on the main stage, the Host is called away first by '*A noyse below in the bowling Alley, betting, rubbing and wrangling*' and then by '*A noyse above at Cards*' (W. Rowley 1632, C2^{v}). Many plays use off-stage sound to suggest the presence of animals. Hunting sounds are particularly

[47] I am very grateful to Julie Sanders for this suggestion.

[48] See J. Wood (1991: 94–102); Cutts (1961*b*, 1963). For individual terms, see Dessen and Thomson (1999); Wilson and Calore (2005).

prominent; less common are the sounds of individual animals, such as '*A noyse within like horses*' in Fletcher's *The Chances* (King's Men, *c.*1617) (Beaumont, Fletcher, et al. 1647, 3B3^{v}). Birdsong is used in a number of plays; some even call for specific species, such as *The Dutch Courtesan*, which specifies that '*The Nitingalls sing*' (Marston 1605, B4^{v}) in an ironic echo of Franceschina's bawdy song about the same bird. 'A hoars sownd wthin' in *Tom a Lincoln* signals the 'dismall roare' of the dragon that the Redcross Knight eventually slays (Anon. 1992, lines 1835, 1840); since the most we see of the dragon is its severed head, the sound effect is left to create something appropriately fearsome.

Representations of the supernatural combine music, sound, and visual effects in intriguing ways: Shakespeare's *The Tempest* (King's Men, 1611–12), with its opening thunder and lightning effects, its '*Solemne and strange*' instrumental music, its '*confused noyse*', and its many songs, is only one of the best-known examples (Shakespeare 1623, B1^{r}, B2^{r}).[49] A Jacobean comment on a revival of Marlowe's *Dr Faustus* (Strange's Men?, *c.*1589) is at pains to explain how some of these effects might be produced, while also indicating something of their power in performance: 'There indeede a man may behold shagg-hayr'd Deuills runne roaring ouer the Stage with Squibs in their mouthes, while Drummers make Thunder in the Tyring-house, and the twelue-penny Hirelings make artificiall Lightning in their Heauens' (Melton 1620, E4^{r}).[50]

The conclusion of another play dealing with the supernatural, Barnabe Barnes's *The Devil's Charter* (King's Men, *c.*1606), transforms language itself into sound. In a sequence obviously influenced by *Dr Faustus*, Alexander awaits the Devil, to whom he has pledged his soul, who finally appears in a welter of noise: '*The Diuill windeth his horne in his eare and there* [*three?*] *more diuills enter with a noise incompassing him.*' The panicked Alexander's dialogue at this point becomes completely unintelligible, an oddly incantatory quality created by its repetitions, alliteration, and internal rhymes:

> Holla, holla, holla, come, come, come, what, when, where when, why, deaf, strike, dead, aliue, oh alas, oh alas, alwaies burning, alwayes freezing, alwayes liuing, tormented, neuer ending, neuer, neuer, neuer mending, out, out, out, out, why, why, whether, whether, thether.

He is mockingly echoed by the devils, who chorus 'Thether, thether, thether' and '*thrust him downe*' with '*Thunder and lightning*' and '*fearefull noise*' (Barnes 1607, M2^{v}).

In *Plays Confuted in Five Actions* (1582), Stephen Gosson writes that the theatre's 'sweete numbers of *Poetrie* flowing in verse, do wonderfully tickle the hearers eares... for that which delighteth neuer troubleth our swallow' (Gosson 1582, D8^{v}). This somewhat mixed metaphor highlights the crucial role played by sound in the production of effect in the early modern playhouse. Music and sound can create or undermine realistic, fantastic, or historic milieux; they can manipulate the reactions of audiences to the events presented to them; they can create discrete moments of pleasure within a narrative or play. Individual settings also show the extent to which companies and their

[49] For a fine, detailed account of music in *The Tempest*, see Lindley (2006: 218–33).

[50] Jonson similarly comments on the 'nimble squibbe', 'roul'd bullet', and 'tempestuous drumme' in a Prologue to *Every Man in His Humour* (Chamberlain's Men, 1598). See Jonson (1616, A3^{r}).

composers were keen to exploit changes in musical fashion. Evidence in some areas is scanty—one particularly unfortunate loss is that of nearly all of the music associated with amphitheatres other than the Globe—but what survives demonstrates the ingenuity and vibrancy of the early modern theatre's use of sound and music. These are areas to which any material history of early modern drama should be alert.[51]

[51] I would like to thank Richard Dutton, David Lindley, and, especially, Julie Sanders for their thoughtful comments on drafts of this essay.

CHAPTER 33

PROPERTIES

ANDREW SOFER

> In the mean time I will draw a bill of properties, such as our play wants.
>
> Peter Quince, *A Midsummer Night's Dream* (I. ii. 105–6)[1]

Early modern properties challenge the theater historian. On the one hand, inanimate stage objects are everywhere—so basic to theatrical commerce that it is hard to know what can profitably be said about them as a group, apart from the fact that they were crucial to performance and hence a necessary expense for the professional playing companies. On the other hand, props are elusive, giving historians the slip as soon as we try to pin down their movement and significance in performance. Their material trajectories in concrete stage space and through linear stage time are as hard for the twenty-first-century theater historian to reconstruct as those of the actors who handled them. Mobile almost by definition, props may be said to have a double life: as stubborn playhouse stuff, mere things, and as evanescent stage performers, nodes in the 'networks of material relations that are the stuff of drama and society alike' (J. G. Harris and Korda 2002: 1).

To set early modern properties imaginatively in motion once more we must be willing to stray from the realm of documented fact. 'Compared to space and bodies, even compared to sound and time, movement would seem to be impossibly elusive for a theatre historian to reconstruct and communicate,' cautions Bruce Smith. 'Considering the challenges, it is not surprising that movement should be the element of performance that has been most neglected in the history of early modern theatre' (B. Smith 2004: 134). In this essay, I will argue that the stage dynamics of props can be at least partially reconstructed from a hitherto underutilized source: the

[1] All citations from Shakespeare are from Shakespeare (1997*b*). Those from *The Alchemist* are from Bevington (2002).

property-bill (or 'bill of properties', as Peter Quince calls it). What might particular property-bills reveal about the performance life of theatrical objects? What sorts of rehearsal and production demands might a typical play make on a particular company as that company migrated from venue to venue? What constraints did conventional property use place on the period's dramatists, so frequently engaged in exploiting the semiosis of spectacular, talismanic, and transgressive objects? Before examining these questions through the lens of the property list, I will very briefly review the alternative sources of evidence from which the mobile life of properties can be gleaned, together with how recent scholarship has mined that evidence in productive ways.

After costumes and playbooks, properties were a playing company's most valuable asset.[2] Yet surviving theatrical records provide only a partial glimpse of these supporting players. The 'Plott' for Peele's *The Tragicall Battell of Alcazar in Barbarie* (1588–94) lists only spectacular props, such as 'raw flesh', 'Dead mens heads & Bones', and '3 violls of blood', omitting the play's more quotidian items (Bradley 1992: 122–3). Other theatrical records are similarly spotty. Something of a *locus propicus* for theater historians, the Rose theater proprietor Philip Henslowe's 1598 inventory of 'all the properties' owned by the Lord Admiral's Men includes specialty items that would have been inconvenient or expensive for the Rose to replace, such as the cauldron in *The Jew of Malta*, as well as character-specific accessories, such as 'Kent's wooden leg' (Foakes 2002: 319–21). But Henslowe unaccountably omits mundane yet ubiquitous 'moveables' such as coins and mugs.[3]

Our main source for the variety of objects that crowded the playhouse stage is, of course, stage directions in extant plays. The index to *A Dictionary of Stage Directions in English Drama 1580–1642* lists 183 items, from 'apricock' to 'writing', under 'Properties—small/hand held' (Dessen and Thomson 1999: 263–4). But items that must have appeared onstage, like Lear's crown, sometimes slip through the textual net. Had only the Folio Shakespeare survived, we would not know that the boy actor who appeared as mad Ophelia in *Hamlet* accompanied himself on a lute (present, like the ghost's nightgown, only in a Q1 stage direction). Eyewitness accounts, another potential source of information, are tantalizingly rare. We owe to Samuel Rowlands the information that Burbage's signature stroking of his dagger as Richard III was much imitated by swaggering gallants (Gurr 1992*b*: 114). Little such anecdotal property-lore survives, although both John Manningham (who saw *Twelfth Night* at the Middle Temple in 1602) and Simon Forman (who saw *Macbeth* and *Cymbeline* at the Globe in 1611) noted memorable properties in their diaries.

[2] Andrew Gurr estimates, for instance, that, of the £1,377 annual company expenditure at the Rose playhouse between 1597 and 1599, £96 was spent on properties, as opposed to £150 each for plays and clothing (Gurr 2004*c*: 106). It has also been estimated that the accumulated stock of costumes and properties might have cost the London professional companies more than their theaters cost to build (MacIntyre and Epp 1997: 284).

[3] For speculation regarding Henslowe's elusive criteria for inclusion, see Bruster (2002) and Orlin (2002). Henslowe's inventory is reproduced as an appendix in J. G. Harris and Korda (2002).

Despite these gaps in evidence, theater historians intrigued by early modern stage properties have benefited from a scholarly shift in focus from subjects to objects. This shift has come mainly from two critical directions. Moving beyond iconographic and psychoanalytic analyses of noteworthy props, such as Yorick's skull and Desdemona's handkerchief, scholars working in a broadly semiotic tradition have parsed the symbolic language of 'speaking properties' more generally (e.g. Salomon 1972; Bosonnet 1978; Slater 1982; Bevington 1984; Teague 1991; Dessen 1995; Sofer 2003; Kinney 2004). While these studies disagree on precisely what counts as a prop, they concur that hand-held objects were potent and potentially disturbing theatrical signs. On this view, which grows out of the Prague Structuralists' approach to stage objects in the 1930s and 1940s, props are less practical tools than textual signifiers whose stage life diverges from their real-life equivalents (Elam 1980; Teague 1991). Embedded in the text by the playwright, objects come to life in the hands of the actor. And while they may be drawn into the stage action in various ways, their default function is to convey information about the play world in a kind of visual shorthand, as when boots suggest a journey (Sofer 2003: 20).

From another direction, the materialist turn in Renaissance studies has renewed interest in the circulation and exchange of 'worldly goods' such as cloth, gloves, hats, and other objects, including stage properties (see, for example, Jardine 1996; Orlin 2000; De Grazia et al. 1996; Jones and Stallybrass 2000; and J. G. Harris and Korda 2002). The rematerialization of early modern objects has gained traction in recent years; what one scholar calls 'the cultural project of things' now rivals the body as a crucial site of inquiry in Renaissance studies (Orlin 1993: 179). Materialist scholars tend to move beyond the dramatic fiction to consider the circulation of social energy between playhouse and culture, as when, for example, priestly vestments pass from the clergy to the players in 'a significant appropriation of symbolic power' (Greenblatt 1988: 113). Objects and clothing become crucial to the formation of early modern identities, onstage and off; in the symbolic economy of early modern England, 'what *one* is depends on what one *owns*' (De Grazia 1996: 34). When property precedes personhood in the cultural imagination, objects become all-important signifiers of identity and status. The crown makes the king rather than vice versa, as Shakespeare's Richard II ruefully discovers.

Thanks to recent work in Renaissance object studies, we now know considerably more about (for instance) the general usage of hand-props across the Elizabethan and Jacobean period (Bruster 2002); the relationship between Henslowe's pawnbroking and theatrical businesses (Korda 1996); and the vital role women played within the material networks surrounding stage properties (Korda 2002). And whereas we once relied on generalizations about the 'bare stage' of the Elizabethan playhouse, we now have more quantitative information about dramatists' incorporation of properties.[4] As a pendant to her landmark semiotic analysis of Shakespeare's props, Frances Teague reconstructs property lists for every Shakespeare play and suggests

[4] For a discussion of recent qualitative versus quantitative analysis of props from a materialist perspective, see J. G. Harris and Korda (2002: 16–17).

an average of thirty-four props per play (Teague 1991: 197). Combining Teague's figures with a representative sample of twenty non-Shakespearean plays, Douglas Bruster surveys property use in plays written between 1587 and 1636. He finds 'a general decline in the number of props used' by all playwrights, and attributes this decline to 'a constriction of the number of actors and roles in early modern plays' (Bruster 2002: 85).[5]

Who was put in charge of props? While it seems virtually certain that someone must have been responsible for organizing and coordinating properties backstage during any given performance, Peter Thomson reminds us that 'There is negative evidence that properties were a lower priority for the Admiral's Men than costume—whereas the company certainly had a wardrobe master (or "tireman") there is no parallel reference to a property master, nor to any equivalent of the modern stage designer' (P. Thomson 1992: 31). Thomson assumes that the players made or provided most of their own properties, with specialized items (such as descending thrones) farmed out to craftsmen. Practices were not universal, however. The Admiral's Men rented Henslowe's props and theaters, whereas the King's Men built and owned their own theaters, costumes, and props. Playhouse wills indicate that some properties, such as rings and swords, belonged to individual players and were handed on to friends or apprentices (Honigmann and Brock 1993). Others, especially expensive and bespoke items, would have belonged to a playhouse or company. Players would periodically need to replenish their stock, but would certainly have recycled items whenever possible. It seems likely that every play that entered the repertory required the fashioning or refurbishing of at least a few props.

My aim in this essay is not to rehearse the current discourse on early modern stage props.[6] Nor is it to summarize the present state of historical knowledge about them.[7] Rather, I will sketch out the property demands made on a single company, the King's Men, by two plays securely in the company's repertoire by 1611: Jonson's *The Alchemist* and Shakespeare's *The Tempest*.[8] My selection of these two plays for

[5] Other scholars disagree with Bruster's findings: 'While costume variety increased greatly between 1580 and 1642, the variety of properties did not noticeably expand, although the number used in plays increased with the years' (MacIntyre and Epp 1997: 282). Intriguingly, Bruster correlates the de-cluttering of the stage with an intensified dramatic interest in particularized objects that take on a fetishized life of their own. In the Jacobean period, stage objects come to be viewed less as markers of identity than as uncannily personified commodities (2002: 89). Bruster invokes what some critics have seen as a link between ambiguous objects and wider cultural anxieties over subjectivity. Bevington (1984) points out that early modern props and costumes at once establish and undermine the stability of social identity and status.

[6] For an overview of materialist criticism of props, see J. G. Harris and Korda (2002: 1–31). For an overview of semiotic criticism, which expresses some reservations about the materialist approach, see Sofer (2003: 1–29). The fetishization of the object in recent materialist criticism is critiqued in J. G. Harris (2001).

[7] Our knowledge about early modern theatrical properties is concisely summarized in Gurr and Ichikawa (2000: 53–65). See also Gurr (1992*b*: 187–93) and Hattaway (1982: 34–40). For their dramatic function, see Bruster (2002); MacIntyre and Epp (1997: 279–85); Sofer (2003: 20–9); and Teague (1991: 15–34).

[8] *The Alchemist* was taken on tour to Oxford in August 1610, along with *Othello*, presumably because plague had closed the London playhouses; it probably premiered earlier that summer in London. *The Tempest*'s first recorded performance was at the Banqueting House in Whitehall on 1 November 1611, with King James in attendance. Gurr concludes that *The Tempest* 'was almost certainly written while *The Alchemist* was in rehearsal' (Gurr 1996*b*: 80).

comparison is not accidental, for both happen to be in large part *about* the charm of objects, although (as we shall see) they take up differing perspectives on that charm. My focus here is less on the dramaturgical use of props, however, than on the specific demands they make in performance. The playscripts are illuminating in this regard. Jonson meticulously prescribes the flow of stage action in *The Alchemist*, while *The Tempest* includes unusually elaborate stage directions (possibly the work of the King's Men's scrivener, Ralph Crane). While such a snapshot can be neither definitive nor comprehensive, investigating the property use by a single company at the height of its powers and popularity clarifies the material demands made on player and company in performance. In turn, those demands reveal some of the dramaturgical constraints that the period's playwrights, whatever their choice of genre or subject matter, had to bear in mind while composing for the professional London companies of the time.

Property use on the London stage was governed by the need for adaptability; plays written for and produced by the King's Men resembled properties in that they themselves needed to be portable. By 1611 the King's Men were presenting their repertory in their outdoor playhouse, the Globe; in their smaller, indoor Blackfriars theater; at court, and in private houses, by invitation; and, whenever the London playhouses were closed on account of plague, on tour (Gurr 2004c: 54–69). Whether outdoors in the Globe or indoors in the candle-lit Blackfriars, larger properties, such as thrones or beds, could be thrust out onstage or revealed in the discovery space before the tiring house façade.[9]

Although neither plays nor props could afford to be site-specific, both *The Alchemist* and *The Tempest* seem conceived with the Blackfriars in mind. *The Alchemist* is clearly a Blackfriars play, set 'here in the Friars' during the plague season of 1610 (I. i. 17). Jonson's satire takes place on a single day (either 23 October or 1 November), in a private house taken over by a rapacious servant. Stage-time merges with clock-time so that play world and playhouse world become almost indistinguishable. *The Tempest*'s formalized masque, relatively large cast, and descending goddess have led some scholars to speculate that the play's origins lie beyond the playhouse (the only recorded performances are at court in 1611 and 1613, when it was played in celebration of the Princess Elizabeth's wedding to the Elector Palatine). But, like *The Alchemist*, *The Tempest* seems especially suited to the intimate Blackfriars.[10] On tour, the players would have relied on hand-properties to help conjure Jonson's grittily realistic London interior or Shakespeare's 'uninhabited island'.

[9] For performances of *The Tempest* at court, the King's Men might have appropriated the elaborate scenic properties built for *Oberon* and other court masques (Dymkowski 2000: 116). Such expensive properties would of course have been inaccessible at the Globe and the Blackfriars. Larger, fixed properties demanding special construction, such as Cleopatra's monument in *Antony and Cleopatra*, present a special case; see Gurr and Ichikawa (2000: 62–5).

[10] 'Its off-stage music, its songs, its two spectacles (a banquet visited by a harpy, and a masque), its lack of fights or fireworks, the large proportion of scenes that call for few players on stage, in later years all became standard features of the plays written for the indoor venues' (Gurr and Ichikawa 2000: 38). For the notion that much of *The Tempest*'s content is 'Shakespeare's lived history of work in the Globe and Blackfriars playhouses', see Bruster (1995).

To render property use more visible, in my Appendix I have followed Teague's practice of compiling property lists for each play under discussion.[11] The stage properties called for in *The Alchemist* are listed as property-bill A and those for *The Tempest* as property-bill B. I include only those properties necessary for the stage action. When the text implies that a player handles a group of items together, I list them as a single item, on the assumption that the player would have thought of them as a unit (for example, the four angels that pass from Dapper to Subtle in I. ii of *The Alchemist*). A prop's return appearance is listed separately in boldface. Costume items appear only when they function as hand-properties; thus, Surly's Spaniard costume is omitted, because it is worn but not handled onstage, whereas Lovewit's is included.

It should be emphasized that these property-bills are constructions after the fact and not the fact itself. Any property count is perforce imprecise, not only because of the fuzzy distinction between costume items and props, but because several properties mentioned in the dialogue are optional in performance.[12] This is truer of Jonson's dramaturgy than of Shakespeare's. For instance, 'Captain' Face instructs his gull, Drugger, to leave his almanac behind when he exits at I. iii. 100, but there is no easy way for the prop to leave the stage should it pass to the conspirators, so it may well have been a ghost prop. The conspirators' swag is the subject of a lengthy dialogue in Act V, and the following items may or may not have emerged from the scene's trunk property in full view of the audience: a paper containing a jewel (V. V. 110); a box of various items (V. V. 113); French petticoats, girdles, and hangers (V. V. 118–19); bolts of lawn (V. V. 120); and Drugger's piece of damask and tobacco pipe (V. V. 120–1). Because it would have been extra trouble for the company to procure and manage all this booty, some and perhaps all of these items could have been mimed presences, obscured by the property-trunk and invisible to the audience. On the other hand, the audience would no doubt have relished the spectacle, so it may have been worthwhile for the company to display any readily available stock items. Because Jonson enumerates the items so carefully, I list them as (potential) props. I also note one implicit prop: Lovewit's challenge to Kastril to draw his sword in V. V makes no sense unless Lovewit has unsheathed his own weapon, although there is no stage direction to this effect, and to my knowledge no editor of the play has added one.

What does the property-bill for *The Alchemist* reveal about the King's Men's handling of props? First, the large number of props the company had to keep track of in order to stage the play—forty-three, if we include several individual items treated as a group (recall Teague posits an average of thirty-four props per Shakespeare play). So not only did the actors face the challenge of holding many repertory

[11] Whereas Teague categorizes props under six classifications—light; weapon or war gear; document; riches or gift; token of a character; and other—I note (*a*) whether the prop changes hands and (*b*) its use in the action, so as to help distinguish active props from passive ones. Semioticians disagree on the extent to which inanimate objects accrue 'action force' and/or 'dislocated function' simply by appearing onstage as a theatrical sign; see Sofer (2003: 6–11).

[12] Different editions provide variant property counts. For the reader's convenience, I base my count on the two commonly used anthologies (Shakespeare 1997*b*; Bevington 2002) cited throughout this chapter. See n. 1.

parts in their head simultaneously; they would have been responsible for memorizing a vast amount of stage business in order to keep the action running smoothly. Professional players were responsible for a bewildering number of prop entrances, exchanges, and departures from the stage. In order not to take up precious rehearsal time, the players must have developed conventional ways of handling props' entrances, exchanges, and exits; that way, more time could be spent rehearsing more elaborate business, such as swordfighting. Considerate playwrights could insert verbal stage directions in order to cue the players, as well as patter intended to fill dead spots created by onstage costume changes. 'I would I were the first that had ever dissembled in such a gown,' quips *Twelfth Night*'s Feste as he dons his curate gown and beard (IV. ii. 5–6).

Secondly, although Henslowe lists the Admiral's Men's properties and apparel separately in his 1598 inventories, we should note that the distinction between costume and property breaks down in performance whenever a costume item becomes incorporated into the action as a nonce prop. Osric's hat in *Hamlet*, for instance, reminds us that a prop is something an object *becomes*, rather than something an object *is* (Sofer 2003: 12). *The Alchemist* features several transformations of this kind. Face and Doll help Subtle remove his alchemist's gown in II. iv; Subtle and Face use a fairy 'robe' and 'smock' to bind and blindfold Dapper in III. v; Doll fetches Face's Lungs costume and dresses him in III. v; Face (apparently) passes a cloak and hat for Drugger to Subtle in V. iv; Subtle exits and re-enters in order to hand Face the Spanish cloak, hat, and ruff in return; Lovewit doffs the Spanish costume, with Face's help, in V. v.

These onstage exchanges augment a dizzying number of offstage costume changes. If we examine the scenes that *lack* props, we observe a rough correlation either with costume activity (to avoid congestion?) or with a shift of theatrical focus to some new costume or spectacular effect. Of the play's twenty-seven scenes, eleven lack props altogether: I. iv; II. i; II. ii; II. v; III. i; III. iii; IV. ii; IV. iii; IV. v; IV. vi; and V. iii. Act I, scene iv, acts as a short impromptu casting meeting in which the three conspirators, Subtle, Face, and Doll, divvy up the roles necessary to gull the greedy customers who covet the philosopher's stone. Face and Doll then exit for an offstage costume change. In II. i Sir Epicure Mammon discourses with Surly the gamester onstage, allowing Face time to change offstage from the 'Captain' to Lungs, the alchemist's sooty assistant. Since no costume change needs to be effected in II. ii, this scene's lack of properties may be attributable to the shift in stage focus to the (offstage) alchemical works and to Mammon's baroque fantasy life—itself a treasury of imagined objects. Act 2, scene v, the first scene in which the comically venal Anabaptists appear, covers Face's offstage costume change from Lungs to the Captain. Act 3, scene i, is a short outdoor scene in which the Anabaptists prepare to knock on Subtle's door, allowing Subtle (who has just cozened Drugger the tobacconist by posing as a learned doctor) to don his alchemist's gear. In III. iii, another brisk scene shared by the conspirators, Face dispatches Doll to don her Queen of Fairy costume and Subtle to assume his priest of Fairy robes. Act IV, scene ii, shifts our visual focus from properties to comely Dame Pliant, whom Subtle and Face treat as a barterable sexual commodity. During the scene Face must exit as Lungs and re-enter as the Captain less than forty lines later. Surly's absurd Spaniard disguise takes the focus in IV. iii. Act 4, scene v, features Doll's tour de force 'talking fit' as well as the explosion of the offstage alchemical works, which provides the play's aural anticlimax. Act IV, scene vi, is a brief scene that features onstage violence—Surly (still in disguise) seizes Subtle while Face escapes—rendering property use challenging. Act V, scene iii, is the play's most crowded scene, as the gulls and neighbors pile onstage along with Face and Lovewit. The visual focus becomes the tiring house door (now the front door of Lovewit's house), behind which Subtle and Dapper are concealed.

A complex dance thus unfolds as costumes convert into properties and back again. The counterpoint between property use and costume exchange is not continuously maintained, however. The scene (III. v) that contains the play's most elaborate prop business—the fleecing, binding, and gagging of Dapper the clerk, in preparation for his audience with the fictional Queen of Fairy—includes an onstage costume change (Captain into Lungs) even while mobilizing nearly 20 percent of the play's props (eight out of forty-three). But in general Jonson seems attentive to the need to balance the demands on his actors, so that the stage becomes somewhat less cluttered when the actors are preoccupied with costumes on or off the stage.

Because of its dizzying traffic in things, *The Alchemist* foregrounds property *exchange* as much as property *use*. Assigning props by character reveals the following breakdown. Subtle passes ten props and receives eight; Face passes four props and receives fifteen; Doll passes two props and receives five. With the exception of the Anabaptists, who travel light, the gulls are scarcely less busy. Mammon passes five props and receives none in return (as befits his character's addiction to fantasy); Dapper passes six and receives four; Drugger passes six and receives none. Of the play's forty-three properties, only a few do not change hands: the Anabaptists' purse in III. ii (presumably taken offstage when Tribulation and Ananias exit to inventory Mammon's ironwork); Doll's cittern in III. v, which accompanies the fleecing and binding of Dapper; Face's house keys as Jeremy the butler in V. ii; the unused tools brought onstage by Neighbor 3 to break down Lovewit's door in V. ii; the items stored in the trunk in V. iv, which may or may not be visible to the audience; the officer's staff and Lovewit's sword in V. v. If 'our memories of many early modern plays involve images of characters holding things', we are nonetheless mistaken to think of hand-props necessarily attaching themselves to individual players (Bruster 2002: 67).

Along with physical exchange, Jonson's play features the repetition and recycling of props. Money accounts for at least ten of *The Alchemist*'s forty-three properties—more if we include purses, rings, and Dapper's coin bracelet. It is possible that the same coins were recycled within a given performance; however, the knaves' concern with keeping track of the exact amounts of money changing hands implies that new property-coins were required with each exchange (Face tots up the sum at III. iii. 27–31 and V. iv. 108–9). Jonson specifies the denomination of many of the coins that change hands, so at least in the small Blackfriars theater, the players must have proffered adequate facsimiles.

The Spanish property-suit offers an interesting case of recycling, as well as a wink to a cornerstone of the London repertory, Kyd's *The Spanish Tragedy* (both Burbage and Jonson played the protagonist, Hieronimo). Posing as a Spanish count, Surly wears a Spaniard costume in IV. iii, IV. iv, IV. vi, and IV. vii. After Surly is driven offstage by the roaring boy Kastril and the Anabaptists, Face tells Drugger to use his 'credit with the players' in order to borrow 'Hieronimo's old cloak, ruff, and hat' (IV. vii. 71). Face's comment is of course a meta-theatrical joke, for Drugger presumably owes his 'credit' to his alter ego as Robert Armin, the original Feste and Touchstone: 'Did you never see me play the fool?' (IV. vii. 69). Subtle hands the Spaniard costume to Face in V. iv, who in turn passes it to Lovewit, who uses it to carry off Dame Pliant in V. v. Spectators would have enjoyed seeing Hieronimo's famous costume appropriated by the knaves, and simultaneously appreciated the company's resourcefulness in recycling an old standby (the most famous example of which is Yorick's cameo appearance as Gloriana in *The Revenger's Tragedy*).

We can fill out our picture of the King's Men's typical handling of properties by comparing the properties called for in *The Tempest*, listed as property-bill B. We might expect this shorter, more poetic, and scenically suggestive play to make more sparing use of properties than *The Alchemist*—especially given that roughly half the characters are shipwrecked with little more than the clothes on their backs. However, if we conservatively assume two supernumerary courtiers in Alonso's retinue, who draw their swords in II. i and III. iii along with the named characters ('*Enter Alonso, Sebastian, Antonio, Gonzalo, Adrian, Francisco and others*', reads the stage direction at II. i. 1), together with only the seven items of 'glistering apparel' that seem indicated by verbal stage directions in IV. i, Shakespeare calls for forty-seven props as against forty-three in *The Alchemist* (again surpassing Teague's average figure of thirty-four properties per Shakespeare play).[13] What accounts for the high volume of props in *The Tempest*? The simple answer is weaponry. Fully twenty of the play's roughly forty-nine props are weapons. Even Prospero's magic staff (or stick) arguably functions as a weapon when he forces Ferdinand to disarm. We do not ordinarily think of *The Tempest* as a play about fighting; there are no swordfights onstage. But as a visual motif—both II. i and III. iii end with the court party drawing swords—property-weapons reinforce Shakespeare's central themes of violence, usurpation, and political assassination, just as *The Alchemist*'s coin-exchange motif reinforces Jonson's theme of cupidity. Weaponry helps explain why so many of *The Tempest*'s hand-props are drawn into the action rather than merely displayed, exchanged, or used as furniture (forty-five of forty-eight, or 94 percent, of Shakespeare's props are 'live' in this sense, as opposed to thirteen of forty-three, or 30 percent, of Jonson's).

The Tempest shifts our focus from property exchange back to individual actors' property use. Most characters are masters of their own props, with Ariel and Prospero handling the largest number (seven each). As in *The Alchemist*, a character is called upon to play music; did the same boy play Doll and Ariel and use the same solo instrument? Besides Prospero's ceremonial garments, interestingly, the only props that change hands involve the clowns: the 'gaberdine' obscenely shared by Caliban and Trinculo in II. ii; the bottle that circulates to blasphemously comic effect

[13] My bill of properties is indebted to, but not identical with, that of Teague (1991: 193).

in II. ii and III. ii; and the apparel hung out by Ariel in IV. i and worn by the clowns in V. i. Perhaps clowns of the period were expected to improvise physical comedy with objects that fell to hand, and playwrights indulged them as a way of limiting the ad-libs that so offend Hamlet's delicate sensibilities in his conversation with the King's Men, who have gatecrashed their own play disguised a touring company.

As in *The Alchemist*, the hand-properties called for by Shakespeare tend to be relatively straightforward and easy for the company to acquire: swords, pieces of wood, a bottle. Even the magical staff used by Prospero to charm Ferdinand and draw a magic circle is referred to as a 'stick' (I. ii. 473), so it is possible that a crude walking stick, such as Prospero might have conceivably fashioned on the island, served Burbage in performance. But unlike Jonson, Shakespeare demands two larger mobile stage devices: the banquet property, which vanishes '*with a quaint device*' (III. iii. 52 s.d.), and the peacock-driven car in which Juno descends during the betrothal masque in IV. i.[14] Such property-business would have required more elaborate preparation and rehearsal than anything in *The Alchemist*. The 'quaint device' may have been a reversible tabletop turned by a stagehand concealed by a fringed cloth, while the boy or man playing the descending goddess in IV. i would have made use of the windlass concealed in the 'heavens' at the Globe and the Blackfriars, as might Ariel as the harpy.

With the exception of weaponry, *The Tempest*'s hand-properties tend to be emblems rather than tools. This is especially true of items of costume. Prospero's ducal hat and rapier displace his magical cloak and staff in V. i, emphasizing the transformational power of costume. Alonso surely wears a crown (unnoted in the text) as an identity token. Caliban's burden of wood in II. ii visually counterpoints Ferdinand's log in III. i, for, along with his sexual continence, Ferdinand's cheerful attitude toward menial labor signals his worthiness of Miranda in contrast to her would-be rapist and unwilling slave, Caliban. Ariel's tabor and pipe, which mockingly echo the clowns' catch in III. ii, were accoutrements of the professional fool; they both recall Feste's tabor in *Twelfth Night* and complement the unnamed instrument (possibly a lute) used by Ariel to serenade Ferdinand in I. ii. Another emblematic property is the chess game revealed in the 'discovery space' in V. i. From one perspective, the unvarnished game (possibly carved or made out of shells) is a charming lagniappe, an ingenious diversion devised by Prospero in order to keep the lovers out of sexual mischief until their union can be solemnized. But, from another, Miranda's willingness to connive with Ferdinand in a game in which kingships are at stake gestures more darkly toward the play's political themes. Most iconic of all, of course, are Prospero's robe and staff, magical properties the early modern audience would associate with a Renaissance magician like Marlowe's Faustus (interestingly, Prospero's magic books are never explicitly conjured by the stage directions). Neither *The Tempest*'s visual focus on its spectacular properties (the disappearing banquet),

[14] The stage direction '*Juno descends*' appears some thirty lines before Iris's cue in the Folio. Some editors view the stage direction as misplaced, but a more likely explanation is that the goddess hung suspended in her chariot during the dialogue between Iris and Ceres before fully descending to the stage of the Globe or Blackfriars. A conventional throne property may have been thrust on for Juno during the masque.

costumes (Ariel's nymph and harpy gear), and effects (the shipwreck, music), nor the large number of properties overall, detracts from the play's exploitation of these talismanic props.

I have already noted intertextual props as a hallmark of the period; the King's Men were obviously partial to such meta-theatrical jokes as the Spanish suit 'borrowed from the players'. What of less conspicuous recycling between plays? The property-bills indicate little apparent property overlap between *The Alchemist* and *The Tempest.* As noted above, Ariel's unnamed solo instrument in I. ii, usually glossed as a lute, may be the same cittern played by Doll in *The Alchemist* (and by the same player). It is also conceivable that Subtle's alchemical robes doubled as Prospero's magic robes. Henslowe lists a 'robe for to goo invisibell' in one of his playhouse inventories (Foakes 2002: 325); might companies have kept such a garment on hand as a readily recognizable stage convention? Whatever the case, the lack of overlap suggests that any new play would for the nonce require its own properties, and that the companies accepted the necessary expense and bother this entailed.

Such a conclusion seems justified by a comparison of the property requirements for the two plays taken by the King's Men to Oxford in 1610, *The Alchemist* and *Othello.* Of *Othello*'s forty-three props, as calculated by Teague, eleven are weapons; nine are lights; nine are documents; three are coins; and eleven are miscellaneous: Brabantio's gown, table, stoup of wine, cannikins, bagpipes, Desdemona's handkerchief, another handkerchief, pins, garter, chair, bed with curtains (Teague 1991: 184). I calculate that twenty-eight of *The Alchemist*'s forty-three props could find no place in *Othello*; conversely, twenty-one of Othello's forty-three props (as listed by Teague) have no place in *The Alchemist.* Unsurprisingly, the overlap comprises weapons, money, and paper documents, all of which the King's Men would have had on hand. In addition, they would have needed to find space on their cart for such props as Doll's cittern, Subtle's vial of acid, the Spanish cloak, hat, and ruff (yet again), and Desdemona's strawberry-spotted handkerchief.

I have sought to provide a glimpse of the period's lively traffic in stage properties by comparing two distinct stage worlds, united by the fact that the same company performed them in the same playing spaces at roughly the same time. I will conclude by remarking the divergent dramaturgical implications of Jonson's and Shakespeare's treatment of properties. That these plays seem in thematic dialogue with each other as what Harry Levin terms 'Magian comedies' invites us to speculate about their authors' attitudes toward the commercial theatricalization of objects in which both playwrights, willingly or unwillingly, participate.

Jonson's *Alchemist* consistently demystifies the theatrical trade in objects, even as his characters shamelessly fetishize them. Jonson's key visual emblem is the exchange of money. But, like the audience at the playhouse, the gulls exchange gold for an illusion, and the fantasies the knaves purvey are tellingly theatrical. Dapper meets his fairy aunt in a burlesque of *A Midsummer Night's Dream.* Drugger purchases a fantasy of bourgeois prosperity. The Anabaptists dream of becoming temporal lords. Mammon, the play's most egregious self-deluder, imagines life as a Marlovian overreacher and proffers coin after coin, receiving nothing in return except for an offstage sound effect—literally a blast of gassy air (like the fart that opens the play). It is no accident that the alchemical 'works' remains an offstage fiction conjured by words alone, for the charlatan Subtle is no alchemist but a touchstone. His imaginary philosopher's stone—a metaphor for Jonson's satiric theater—ingeniously reveals the greed at the heart of each gull's individual humor. Subtle, Face, and Doll implicitly organize their 'house' as a theatrical concern in the absence of the landlord, Lovewit. Returning unexpectedly, Lovewit ends up repossessing the house along with his share of the take, and the 'sharers' disappear. Jonson's final joke is on the spectator, who, like the play's gulls, has foolishly exchanged cash for delusory identifications.

The Tempest's exploitation of the glamour of props in the service of theatrical magic seems more ambivalent. The play takes Prospero's magic seriously by dramatizing both the charm of objects and the urge to tame or destroy them. Caliban implies that Prospero's power issues precisely from magical props: 'Burn but his books' (III. ii. 95).[15] *The Tempest* contains many sensational elements designed to amaze the audience, from the hyperrealism of the shipwreck's wet mariners to the fantastical masque Prospero conjures from thin air. Even Prospero's renunciation of his art does not extend to eschewing the charm of costume; when Prospero exchanges his magic robe and staff for a ducal hat and rapier, he assumes yet another stage costume that exerts coercive power. Nevertheless, it cannot be an accident that the conspirators against Prospero are ultimately duped by glistering apparel. For what is this 'trash' if not theatrical tat, transformed by verbal spells into objects of wonder? And if the clowns' first reaction to the shabby theatrical goods is wonder, their second is identification. Like Jonson's gulls, they dress themselves in borrowed robes as a means of donning fantasy identities. Enchanting us with his stage magic, Shakespeare nonetheless cautions us not to share the clowns' misprision and take tinsel for gold.

Early modern drama at once fetishizes and demystifies objects, alternately investing them with magic and insisting that they are just dead things. Prospero's cloak and the clowns' glistering apparel occupy the same stage—they are cut from the same theatrical cloth. This ambivalence toward theatrical 'luggage' (as Caliban dismissively calls it) inscribes itself in the era's most notorious prop: *Othello*'s mysterious handkerchief. In one account of its origins, the handkerchief's pagan 'magic in the web' conjures up psychic Egyptian soothsayers, 200-year-old sibyls in the throes of prophetic ecstasy, and dye made from lovingly preserved hearts ripped from living virgin's bodies (III. iv. 55–74). But in a conflicting version, which reverses its earlier trajectory, the napkin is merely an 'antique token' given by Othello's father to his mother (V. ii. 216). When it came to the magic of objects, Shakespeare and his fellow theatrical workers could have it both ways. Expensive to acquire and troublesome to manage, props were a necessary evil, lightning-rods for the theatrical charm that lured paying audiences into the playhouses.

15 The urge to desecrate holy or magical books is a recurrent motif in early modern drama. For example, Tamburlaine burns the Koran in *2 Tamburlaine the Great* (1587–8); the clowns steal Faustus' magic book in *Dr Faustus* (*c*.1590); Alice tears the leaves of her prayer book, which she promises to burn, in *Arden of Faversham* (1588–92); Polonius uses a prayer book as a cynical prop in Hamlet, a move which at least one critic views as 'diabolical' (Kinney 2004: 66). Playwrights were undoubtedly aware that illiterate and semi-literate spectators might associate literacy with social control and political power.

Appendix

Property-bill A: *The Alchemist*

Prop	Appears	Passes from/Used by	To	Use in action
vial of acid	I. i	Subtle	Doll	D smashes
sword	I. i	Face	Doll	D snatches
coins (4 angels)	I. ii	Dapper	Subtle	exchange
coin (angel)	I. ii	Dapper	Subtle	exchange
diagram	I. iii	Drugger	Subtle	S examines
coin (portague)	I. iii	Drugger	Subtle	exchange
coins (ten pounds)	II. iii	Mammon	Face	exchange
coin	II. iii	Mammon	Face	exchange
coin	II. iii	Mammon	Face	exchange
gown	II. iv	Subtle	Face/Doll	costume change
coin	II. vi	Drugger	Face	exchange
tobacco pipe	II. vi	Drugger	Subtle	S smokes
purse	III. ii	Anabaptists		display
paper	III. ii	Subtle	Anabaptists	exchange
tobacco pipe	III. iv	Drugger	Face	exchange
coins (specified)	III. iv	Dapper	Face	exchange
fairy robe	III. v	Subtle	Dapper	S straitjackets D
fairy smock	III. v	Subtle	Dapper	S blindfolds D
contents of pockets	III. v	Dapper	Subtle/Face	exchange
cittern	III. v	Doll		D plays
paper (with coin)	III. v	Dapper	Subtle/Face	exchange
coin bracelet	III. v	Dapper	Face	exchange
Lungs' costume	III. v	Doll	Face	costume change
gingerbread	III. v	Face	Dapper	F gags D
diamond ring	IV. i	Mammon	Doll	exchange
coin	IV. i	Mammon	Face	exchange
paper horoscope	IV. iv	Subtle	Pliant?	exchange?
piece of damask	IV. vii	Drugger	Face	exchange
keys	V. ii	Face		display
tools	V. ii	Neighbor 3		display
purse on a chain	V. iv	Doll	Dapper	exchange
Drugger's suit	V. iv	Face	Subtle	exchange
Spanish cloak, hat, ruff	V. iv	Subtle	Face	exchange
trunk(s)	V. iv	Subtle	Doll/Face	display
purse	V. iv	Subtle	Face	F counts coins
paper	V. iv	in trunk		display?
box	V. iv	in trunk		display?

(continued)

cloth	V. iv	in trunk		display?
damask	V. iv	in trunk		display?
tobacco pipe	V. iv	in trunk		display?
Spanish cloak, hat, ruff	V. v	Lovewit	Face	costume change
staff	V. v	Officer		display
Lovewit's sword?	V. v	Lovewit		drawn?

Property-bill B: *The Tempest*

Prop	Appears	Passes from/Used by	To	Use in action
whistle	I. i	Master		blown offstage
cloak	I. ii	Prospero	Miranda	costume change
lute?	I. ii	Ariel		A plays
sword	I. ii	Ferdinand		F draws on P
magic staff	I. ii	Prospero		P disarms F
lute?	II. i	Ariel		A plays
dagger	II. i	Antonio		A draws
sword	II. i	Sebastian		S draws
sword	II. i	Alonso		A draws
sword	II. i	Gonzalo		G draws
sword	II. i	Adrian		A draws
sword	II. i	Francisco		F draws
sword	II. i	Courtier 1		draws
sword	II. i	Courtier 2		draws
log	II. ii	Caliban		C carries
gaberdine	II. ii	Caliban	Trinculo	tent
bottle	II. ii	Stephano	Cal., Trinc.	drink
log	III. i	Ferdinand		F carries
bottle	III. ii	Stephano	Cal., Trinc.	drink
tabor	III. ii	Ariel		A plays
pipe	III. ii	Ariel		A plays
banquet table	III. iii	strange shapes		display
harpy wings	III. iii	Ariel		A claps on table
sword	III. iii	Alonso		A draws
sword	III. iii	Sebastian		S draws
sword	III. iii	Antonio		A draws
sword	III. iii	Gonzalo		G draws
sword	III. iii	Adrian		A draws
sword	III. iii	Francisco		F draws
sword	III. iii	Courtier 1		draws
sword	III. iii	Courtier 2		draws

(continued)

(continued)

Prop	Appears	Passes from/Used by	To	Use in action
seat	IV. i	Miranda		M sits
seat	IV. i	Ferdinand		F sits
peacock car	IV. i	Juno		J descends
clothes line	IV. i	Ariel		A hangs clothes
gown	IV. i	Trinculo	Stephano	S dons
jerkin	IV. i	Stephano		S dons
garment	IV. i	Stephano	Trinculo	T dons
garment	IV. i	Stephano	Trinculo	T dons
garment	IV. i	Stephano	Caliban	S burdens C
garment	IV. i	Trinculo	Caliban	T burdens C
garment	IV. i	Stephano	Caliban	S burdens C
staff	V. i	Prospero		magic
cloak	V. i	Prospero		P discards
hat	V. i	Ariel	Prospero	P dons
rapier	V. i	Ariel	Prospero	P dons
chess	V. i	Miranda/Ferdinand		M/F play

CHAPTER 34

EYEWITNESSES TO HISTORY: VISUAL EVIDENCE FOR THEATER IN EARLY MODERN ENGLAND

THOMAS POSTLEWAIT

I

All historians, including theater historians, struggle with a basic question in research and analysis. How can visual sources—such as drawings, etchings, woodcuts, watercolors, paintings, photographs, maps, terracotta figurines, sculptures, mosaics, frescos, and tapestries—be used as historical evidence? What are the challenges and problems? What are the methods? If, as Peter Burke argues, images 'record acts of eyewitnessing' (2001: 14), should historians give visual evidence the same kind of consideration that they give to eyewitness statements in the primary records? All historians would agree with Burke that images, 'like texts and oral testimonies, are an important form of historical evidence' (2001: 14). But the key challenge, he acknowledges, is to determine 'To what extent, and in what ways... images offer reliable evidence of the past' (2001: 16). When we attempt to measure the reliability of visual sources as historical evidence, how are their representational traits and codes to be interpreted?

If, as Burke grants, there are 'degrees or modes of reliability' (2001: 184) for images as historical documents, should we decipher the historical signs and codes of images in the same ways that we apply historical criticism to textual sources (e.g. matters of authenticity and credibility, tests of possibility and probability)? Or do we need, in addition, to apply special methods of analysis, perhaps derived from art history, that reveal artistic conventions and iconological codes? Does the rhetoric of the image differ from the rhetoric of the verbal text?

In order to proceed, we need to maintain a basic distinction between an artifact and a fact. Each historical document, in the words of Marc Bloch, offers a kind of 'track' into the past. The historian must recognize, describe, and analyze the 'mark, perceptible to the senses, which some phenomenon, in itself inaccessible, has left behind' (Bloch 1953: 55). What kind of historical 'mark' (sign, icon, trace, source, image) is provided by visual sources from the past? In what ways, for example, does the drawing of the Swan theater require skills in historical analysis distinct from those used for investigating the Fortune contract? And how and why do our observations of archeological remains, such as those for the Rose theater, require interpretive skills distinct from those we apply to the Swan drawing?[1] What are the methods for determining the reliability and credibility of each type of documentary information? What kinds of fact can we derive from each type of artifact?

Obviously, visual sources are crucial for the historical study of theater (e.g. Greek vases of the BCE era, drawings and etchings of *commedia dell'arte* performers, photographs of performances). And likewise we benefit from various kinds of material objects (e.g. shadow puppets of Indonesia, carved wooden masks for dancers in Nigeria, the costume collections of national theaters). Indeed, our knowledge of many cultures and eras depends in great measure upon visual evidence, as the cultural historian Johan Huizinga insisted: 'Most educated people of today owe their conception of Egypt, Greece, or the Middle Ages, much more to the sight of their monuments, either in the original or by reproductions, than to reading' (1955: 244–5). It is true, for instance, that our understanding of the medieval era as an ecclesiastical culture derives profoundly from our observations of visual evidence: Gothic churches, religious paintings, altarpieces, tombs, tapestries, and illuminated manuscripts. And our modern age, as we all know, delivers much of its documentary record visually, ever since the arrival of photography, followed by film, television, and the rest of the electronic revolution (e.g. the distribution of images by computers and phones today). By contrast, our knowledge of the early modern age (1500 to 1700) seems less dependent upon visual sources, perhaps in part because of the ways the printing press transformed the documentary record. Although the art and architecture of this

[1] Many visual sources—drawings, photographs, tapestries—qualify as eyewitness reports, though their credibility and reliability varies, in part because of their methods of representation. But we need to distinguish these kinds of eyewitness sources in the visual record from other kinds of visual objects, such as archeological remains or a warehouse of theater costumes. They all carry some kind of historical significance, but we do not interpret them in the same ways.

era carries vital historical significance for us (and great pleasure), our scholarship on this era often reveals a definitive preference for verbal over visual evidence.

To illustrate this point, Francis Haskell, in *History and Its Images* (1993), notes that Huizinga's *The Waning of the Middle Ages* (1955 [1913]) depends crucially upon visual evidence, but Jacob Burckhardt's *The Culture of the Renaissance in Italy* (1990 [1860]) basically ignores visual evidence, despite his knowledge of the arts and architecture. 'One of the most curious features of that book', Haskell reminds us, is 'a lack of any sustained attention to the visual arts' (1993: 335). No doubt other art historians can demonstrate that Burckhardt is not typical of cultural historians of the Renaissance. But Haskell's basic point about the disregard of visual evidence can also be applied to the field of theater history, especially in the case of our scholarship of the early modern theater in London. As I wish to illustrate, written documents usually dominate our investigations and understanding. In turn, when we do use visual sources, we often apply questionable methods in our historical descriptions and analyses.

In order to examine the scholarly uses of visual sources as historical evidence on the London theater of the early modern era, I will take up four related problems: (1) the tendency of theater scholars to depend upon reproduced illustrations, rather than original visual sources; (2) the application of iconography and iconology to visual documents in theater history; (3) the seductive appeal of arguments by analogy, often put forward without supporting historical evidence; (4) the interpretive dichotomies between *a priori* and *a posteriori* arguments, which evoke, in turn, the related dichotomies between deductive and inductive analysis, rational and empirical evidence, necessary and contingent propositions. Underlying each of these problems is the basic yet difficult task of translating visual signs and codes into reliable verbal descriptions for historical study. Unfortunately, our ability to address these four problems is hindered by the pervasive disregard of visual sources by many scholars of early modern theater. Visual images are often treated as secondary or unimportant sources, to be used merely as supplemental illustrations for the study of verbal texts. This frame of mind provides a way to avoid—rather than solve—these four problems.

After a preliminary overview of these problems, I will present a survey of some of our uses and misuses of visual sources since the publication of the first issue of *Shakespeare Survey* (1948), which featured visual evidence. In turn, I will set up two cases studies that consider a few key aspects of our scholarship on the Swan theater drawing and the Longleat manuscript drawing, which apparently is based upon an eyewitness observation of a production of *Titus Andronicus*.

II

Perhaps historians of early modern theater in England have often slighted or ignored the visual evidence because of the scarcity of sources in comparison to the abundant verbal records, including the plays themselves. For example, two of the most important studies of the twentieth century, *The Elizabethan Stage* (1923) by E. K. Chambers and *The Jacobean and Caroline Stage* (1941–68) by G. E. Bentley, give only minimal attention to visual sources. Chambers's four volumes contain a total of fourteen visual documents, including the Swan drawing, a poor reproduction in black and white of the painting of the Wedding Mask of Sir Henry Unton, the design for the Cockpit theater at Whitehall, drawings of a square and an octagonal playhouse, two diagrams of the 1596 floor plans of Blackfriars, and Wenceslaus Hollar's drawing of the interior of St Paul's Cathedral (but not any of Hollar's drawings of London neighborhoods and their theaters). Chambers also reproduces the *Coliseus sive Theatrum* from the 1497 edition of Terence in Venice and five design drawings by Sebastiano Serlio (in an appendix in Italian of Serlio's *Trattato sopra le scene*). Despite chapters in volume I on pageantry, the 'mask' (or masque), and the 'actor's qualities', not one illustration appears in these sections. Carrying forward the documentary mandates of Chambers, Bentley provides a comprehensive gathering of vital information on companies, players, plays, playwrights, and theaters. Amazingly, though, the seven volumes offer only two visual pieces of evidence: two drawings by Inigo Jones of the Cockpit-in-Court theater.

Visual evidence for London theater of this era may not be plentiful, but there are dozens of sources that Chambers and Bentley ignored. And they are not alone. One of the most impressive research projects of our times, involving dozens of scholars, is Records of Early English Drama (REED), published by University of Toronto Press (1979–present) under the admirable leadership of the executive editor, Sally-Beth MacLean, and director, Alexandra F. Johnston. Dependent upon the governmental and church records in the many towns and cities outside of London, these volumes (over thirty and growing) provide a comprehensive documentary record of written sources, unpublished and published. But they reveal only the most limited research on and application of visual sources.

Even if we grant that the mission of REED is, in the main, limited to verbal documents, this disregard of visual evidence is still notable, and symptomatic of a pervasive problem. For example, the recent *English Professional Theatre, 1530–1660* (2000), edited by three highly respected theater historians—Glynne Wickham, Herbert Berry, and William Ingram—has 517 documents, but only eighteen in this valuable collection are visual.[2] These illustrations include the Swan drawing, the frontispieces and title pages for three plays,[3] images of two players, Will Kempe and Edward Alleyn, and two drawings of the remains of the Rose theater.[4] Or consider

[2] Because Glynne Wickham's several volumes of *Early English Stages, 1300 to 1660* (1959–81) are packed with visual images and historical arguments based upon such evidence, the paucity of visual documentation in *English Professional Theatre* is quite surprising.

[3] By contrast, R. A. Foakes provides over three dozen title pages, frontispieces, and related visual images from playbooks in *Illustrations of the English Stage 1580–1642* (1985).

[4] In the book's preface, Glynne Wickham gives 'grateful acknowledgement' to people and archives that provided photographs. He explains that these photographs 'appear as illustrative documents in this book' (Wickham et al. 2000, p. xliv). Such phrasing may suggest that they are supplemental to the major textual documents, the real purpose of the book. But each illustration is given a number, consistent with

A New History of Early English Drama (1997), edited by John D. Cox and David Scott Kastan. It offers twenty-five admirable essays by leading scholars on plays, playwrights, players, playhouses, physical and social space, public and court entertainment, companies and repertories, patronage, touring, costuming, censorship, manuscripts, publishing, and many other related topics, but the collection has only five illustrations, not one of which is derived from a visual document of the era.[5]

In short, as these representative cases demonstrate, visual sources are often invisible in our historical scholarship. This disregard or diminishment of visual evidence may result from the basic fact that literary study rather than theater history guides much of the scholarship. Or perhaps publishers, attempting to control costs, are dictating a policy of few illustrations. Increasingly, the costs and responsibilities for acquiring visual sources and permissions are being transferred to scholars, who are reluctant to spend the time and funds.[6] Whatever the reasons, from a documentary perspective, the written word predominates and visual evidence is at best secondary.

Judging, then, by the scarcity of visual images in key publications of the last one hundred years, we are faced with some pedagogical problems in the classroom and some historiographical questions in our research methods. We can work around the classroom problems without too much difficulty. But the absence or diminishment of visual documents in key scholarly collections may signal to us that there is a methodological lack or a critical flaw in our historical assumptions, procedures, and aims. Ironically, the scarcity of visual representations leaves the impression that some scholars today share in the attitudes of the iconoclasts of the sixteenth century—a distrust of visual representation and spectacle. It may seem inappropriate to accuse theater historians of anti-theatrical prejudice, but is it possible that some theater and literary scholars, consciously or unconsciously, carry suspicions of, if not animosity toward, the image? Do they, like some Puritans, trust the word but distrust the eye, which leads us astray?

the organizational procedure for all documents in the book. In some cases, an illustration receives careful commentary, as occurs with the Swan drawing and the interior image of the Red Bull playhouse. In other cases, though, such as the image of the Curtain theater, the image itself receives no attention, though the historical information on the theater, its owners, and its location is fulsome. The source for the image is not given; nor do the editors identify the source of the two drawings of the Rose theater's foundation. The editors also reproduce an undated drawing of Richard Tarlton, but do not provide an explanation of the drawing. They acknowledge that John Astington has demonstrated (in 1999*b*) that the image appears in earlier broadside woodcuts, so lacks credibility as an image of Tarlton. Does this acknowledgement of Astington suggest that his series of critiques (e.g. 1991*b*,*c*, 1993*a*, 1997, 1999*b*) have convinced the editors to retreat from the use of visual sources?

[5] In his essay on staging practices at Cambridge University, Alan Nelson provides three of the five visual illustrations in the book. They are modern drawings, not visual documents. The complete lack of visual documents from the era in *A New History of Early English Drama* is surprising when one considers the excellent book *The Devil and the Sacred in English Drama, 1350–1642* (2000), by John D. Cox, one of the editors. It provides vital visual images from the era of devils on the stage, including visual evidence on costuming and staging methods.

[6] As I know from my own experience for this essay and my recent book (Postlewait 2009), the costs, in time and money, are substantial, even to acquire only ten to twenty illustrations and permissions from archives, libraries, and governmental offices.

This situation is not, however, completely dire. In recent years several exhibitions, along with their catalogues, have revealed the power and importance of visual evidence for London theater of the Renaissance era. In 2006 the *Searching for Shakespeare* exhibition at the National Portrait Gallery featured close to 200 images, including engravings, paintings, sculptural busts, frontispieces, illustrated title pages, signet rings, maps, clothing, and other material objects. The display was priceless for theater historians (e.g. offering some definitive evidence on the contending portraits of Shakespeare). But after a few weeks the exhibition closed, and the various visual documents were redistributed to the dozens of separate collections, public and private. We will not likely see them all together again—except as reproductions (see Cooper 2006).

Two issues, accordingly, confront theater historians: (1) the nature and value of visual sources; (2) the nature and relative value of original versus reproduced sources. Our understanding of the issues and problems pertaining to (1) depends in part upon our experiences with (2). As all scholars know, nothing substitutes for the contact with original sources, verbal and visual. We often discover new insights when we gaze upon these documents and objects. Of course, we benefit from an exhibition's catalogue just as we benefit from the published collections of textual documents. But especially in the case of visual sources, the replications fail to deliver the kind of detailed knowledge that we may gain from direct observation of the originals. The *presentation* of an original image carries a specific quality of information that is missing in the *re-presentation.*

Ideally, all theater historians who write on the early modern theater have opportunities to see many, if not all, of the visual documents. But how many of us, for instance, have observed the original Swan drawing since it was discovered in 1888 or visited Dulwich College in south London to observe the painting of Edward Alleyn?[7] Very few of us can claim such diligence in our research methods. No doubt a substantial number of scholars have seen the engraved image of Shakespeare in one of the copies of the 1623 Folio. And an even larger number of us have observed (sometimes in disbelief or disappointment) the bust of Shakespeare in Holy Trinity Church, Stratford upon Avon. Much of the time, however, we do not take the opportunity to examine the primary visual sources. For our historical research we rely upon reproduced illustrations, even though the best reproductions lack aspects and qualities of the original, and sadly many are often cropped, washed out, and otherwise inadequately reproduced.

Of course, this reliance on reproduced images is often necessary, given the pragmatic needs of research and publishing.[8] Most of us, most of the time, get by with reproductions of visual evidence, trusting to the images provided by other scholars and their publishers. We accept our visual sources as secondary, supplemental evidence. Likewise, we depend upon the editing and commentary of editors, who

[7] In 1994 there was an exhibition at Dulwich Picture Gallery on Alleyn. See the catalogue, Reid and Maniura (1994), with valuable essays by S. P. Cerasano, Susan Foister, and J. R. Piggott.

[8] Obviously, I include myself in this description of theater historians who depend upon reproduced images. This essay is a clear example of the pattern of dependency and distance.

may or may not be reliable guides to the visual sources they have reproduced. Does this mean that we are less rigorous than art historians, who usually insist upon examining the original art works before making judgements about them? In principle, the presence of the visual object is a methodological mandate for the art historian, who serves as the primary witness. But of course the visual object is the primary concern of the art historian, whereas the theater historian usually examines visual sources as means to another end. We try to look through these sources to what they represent, and what they can tell us about the missing theater event.

In principle, then, the absence of the visual object serves as our methodological mandate because the theater historian studies visual (as well as verbal) sources in order to reconstruct past performances and conditions that no longer exist. Depending upon surrogate eyewitnesses—the documents in the archives—we work a step removed from the ontological status of the historical events. Perhaps this condition of absence, which we share with most historians, contributes to our ready acceptance of reproduced visual sources. In terms of guiding practice and methodology, we are already cut off or removed from our subject matter; so another separation is apparently not too difficult to accept. Whatever the reasons, we regularly rely upon secondary sources, including reproductions of visual evidence. In the process, however, we accept an additional displacement in our professional activities. We are separated not only from the past events, which we attempt to reconstruct, but also from the original visual documents, which we trust to be similar to the reproduced illustration. As modern Platonists, we perceive—and make judgements upon—a representation of a representation. Living dangerously, we attempt to make a virtue out of our condition of absence, separation, and even partial blindness.

III

In the case of the early modern theater in England, we usually rely upon the publication of catalogues and collections of visual evidence. For example, R. A. Foakes's valuable *Illustrations of the English Stage 1580–1642*, published in 1985, provides seventy-nine documentary illustrations, all in black and white.[9] These images range from the Swan drawing and several London perspectives of the south bank amphitheaters to a rich collection of frontispieces and title pages with illustrations. In like manner, Clifford Davidson's *Illustrations of the Stage and Acting in England to 1580* (1991) presents a rich visual record of the English theater in the early centuries. His images are also only in black and white.[10] He doubles Foakes by providing 166 images, including illustrations

[9] On his acknowledgement page Foakes identifies the archives and libraries that provided his illustrations (for example, thirty-seven photographs came from the Huntington Library).

[10] The quality of the photographs provided to Davidson is uneven, and the reproductions by the publisher are, in some cases, somewhat washed out.

of the ruins of Roman theaters in Britain, sepulchers of churches, a pageant chariot, maps of procession routes, illuminated manuscripts with theatrical scenes, etchings in printed playbooks, and many representations of minstrels, fools, jugglers, tabor players, a morris dancer, wild men, and other entertainers. Davidson's gathering of visual evidence reveals a broad definition of performance and its visual evidence.

Despite the obvious value of these two collections by Foakes and Davidson, some cautionary notes are warranted, beyond the basic fact that we are looking at reproductions. In the case of Foakes's *Illustrations*, the measured assessment comes from John Astington in a series of essays on visual evidence (1991*a*,*b*, 1993*a*,*b*, 1996, 1999*b*), including 'Rereading Illustrations of the English Stage' (1997). Astington admires Foakes's collection, which, he reports, 'turned me towards more serious thought about theater pictures from the period' (1997: 151). Yet he identifies some problems and offers several corrections.[11]

Foakes himself recognized that some of the images he reproduced may not represent what they appear to portray. For example, the two extant copies of the 1590 publication of Christopher Marlowe's *Tamburlaine, Part 2*, feature a woodcut of a male figure, representing 'Tamburlaine, the great' in body armor (Figure 34.1). The armor covers the upper body and forearms; a sash tied diagonally across the chest has a bow at the right shoulder; the hands and legs are not visible, but the head is bare, showing a bearded face. Could this be a representation of Edward Alleyn, who likely played the role of Tamburlaine? To test the hypothesis, Foakes compared this image to the Dulwich College portrait of Alleyn by an unknown painter. The painting was likely completed circa 1620 (Reid and Maniura 1994: 71). Given this date, the portrait could be a representation of Alleyn in 1616, at the age of 50, as Foakes speculates (1985: 88–90).

Like the woodcut, the portrait of Alleyn (Figure 34.2) shows a middle-aged, bearded man. The two faces—with their drooping eyelids, long noses, and full beards—seem to represent the same man. 'It is tempting', Foakes writes, 'to connect the woodcut with the [portrait].' But Foakes concludes that the resemblances are only superficial: 'it seems more likely that the woodcut represents a typical military figure, and has no immediate connection with the play' (1985: 88). Although he leaves open the possibility that the frontispiece represents the player and his stage costume, Foakes's skepticism is warranted because the image has nothing to do with Alleyn. The illustration, as Astington notes (1997: 153), was derived from a woodcut that had been used previously, in 1587, by the publisher Richard Jones.[12] Ruth Samson Luborsky and Elizabeth Morley Ingram, providing more details, have shown that Jones also used the woodcut in 1571 and 1585 (1998: i. 442–6).[13] Because printers used

[11] See his commentary on specific illustrations, including cropping issues, missing sources, and his doubts about the relevance of some illustrations to theater history.

[12] Astington points out that Fredson Bowers had reported in his edition of Marlowe's *Complete Works* (1973) that Richard Jones had used the woodcut previously, in 1587, for G. Prouninck's *A Short Admonition of Warning, Upon the Detestable Treason*. Foakes missed this source.

[13] Besides its use in 1587, the woodcut image appeared in 1571 with the publication of Thomas Hill's *The Contemplation of Mankinde*. It also appeared in George Whetstone's *The Honorable Reputation of a Souldier* (1585). For the full record of the woodcut image, see Luborsky and Ingram (1998: i. 442–6). This valuable book needs to be consulted by all theater historians who make use of sixteenth-century illustrations.

Figure 34.1 Frontispiece for *Tamburlaine the Great, The Second Part of The bloody Conquests of mighty Tamburlaine* (London, 1590).

woodcuts repeatedly, many of the illustrations in published plays have nothing to do with the particular plays, players, or productions.[14]

Caution also needs to be applied to Clifford Davidson's scholarship on visual images. In *Illustrations of the Stage and Acting in England to 1580* (1977) he is not

[14] Holmes (1950–1) made a case for another possible portrait of Alleyn in Richard Knolles's *The Generall Historie of the Turks* (1603). Foakes entertains the possibility in *Illustrations* (1985: 89–90), but Astington also disputes the claim (1993*a*).

Figure 34.2 *Portrait of Edward Alleyn, Elizabethan Actor, Jacobean Gentleman,* **1626, by an unknown English artist. Oil on canvas, 2,038 x 1,140 mm (80¼ x 44 ⅞ in.)**

always accurate in his documentation of the many gathered images. For example (1977: 82), he misidentifies the source for the etching of Richard Tarlton, reproduced as illustration no. 91.[15] Also, though Davidson has described in several valuable publications the use of visual sources as evidence, including the application of

[15] Davidson correctly identifies British Library, MS Harley 3885, fo. 19, as the source of the sketch, but he credits it to John How of Norwich, when it should be credited to John Scottowe. See Backhouse

iconography (1977, 1986–7, 2001), his emblematic interpretations do not always rest on a solid historical critique of sources. Drawing upon not only Glynne Wickham's ideas about an emblematic theater in the medieval and renaissance eras (1959–81: ii. 1) but also key studies in art history and literary study on Renaissance emblems, icons, *impresa*, personifications, tableaux, and allegories, Davidson makes a case for the possible relations between verbal and visual codes of representation.[16] But sometimes, in the process of discovering correspondences, he moves rather rapidly from the representative (iconic) and referential (indexical) features of an image to its supposed interpretive (symbolic, emblematic, allegorical) meanings.[17] Artifact becomes fact too quickly.

For instance, Davidson argues that when Othello expresses his trust in Iago (III. iii. 479), this action parallels a visual representation of the good man and the wicked man that Davidson found in Geoffrey Whitney's *A Choice of Emblems*, published in Leiden in 1586 (Davidson 1977: 126).[18] (See Figure 34.3.) Juxtaposing play and image, Davidson weaves them together by means of thematic correspondence. He does not claim that Shakespeare knew and drew upon Whitney's emblem, but he does contend that a shared cultural attitude influenced the method of representation in two distinct media. Moreover, he posits that the Jacobean players would have expressed themselves visually in an emblematic manner, and likewise the spectators would have seen and interpreted the scene emblematically. But beyond the vague possibility of these elective affinities, what is the basis for this conjecture about parallel worlds of image and word, realized in performance? Davidson offers no supporting evidence for joining Shakespeare and Whitney in an emblematic mindset; nor does he offer evidence for his reconstruction of the players' intentions, the spectators' shared understanding, and the emblematic performance method of the King's Men. Reasoning in an expanded circle from Shakespeare to Whitney, then back to the players and spectators, Davidson applies an emblematic model of cultural analysis that requires a series of correspondences. Analogical analysis, based upon a period concept which posits an idea of unified *mentalité*, does much of the work.[19]

(Scottowe 1974) and Astington (1999*b*), who also confirm this attribution to Scottowe in an email message to me (Apr. 2007).

[16] For a recent study of the visual codes of personified characters in Shakespeare's plays, see Kiefer (2003), whose approach draws upon and complements Davidson's emblematic method. Kiefer's bibliography identifies many of the literary studies on spectacle, pageantry, dumb shows, masques, processions, and progresses that depend upon emblematic readings of visual and verbal codes of representation.

[17] Davidson is aware of the critique by Daly (1984) of iconographic and emblematic analysis of Shakespeare's plays, for he quotes Daly (Davidson 1986–7: 7). But in his assessment of iconography, Davidson tends to focus primarily on matters of terminology rather than problems of historical methodology.

[18] The quotation from *Othello* is taken from Edward Pechter's Norton Critical Edition (New York: W. W. Norton, 2004). Those from *Titus Andronicus* on p. 594 are from Shakespeare (1974).

[19] For an extended critique of Davidson's application of iconographic methods to literary study and theater history, see Hunt (1989). Hunt also presents a more general critique of the uses of iconography in drama and theater studies. All too often, Hunt cautions, we are tempted to elaborate rather fanciful 'emblematic and iconographic commentaries' that 'confuse theatrical imagery and our afterconceits about them' (1989: 161).

Figure 34.3 *Amicitia sucata vitanda* ('Feigned friendship to be avoided'), from Geoffrey Whitney, *A Choice of Emblems* (Leiden, 1586); facsimile reprint (1866).

It is true, of course, as Meyer Schapiro points out in *Words and Pictures* (1973), that 'a great part of the visual art in Europe from late antiquity to the eighteenth century represents subjects taken from a written text. The painter or sculptor had the task of translating the word—religious, historical, or poetic—into a visual image' (Schapiro 1973: 9). Many visual images in paintings represent a literal and symbolic meaning, sometimes suggested by an attached title. And sequences of images, such as Hogarth's *Marriage à la Mode*, present a visual narrative. But Schapiro also reminds us that even when we know that the artist intended a verbal and visual relationship (and much of the time we have no such record of intentionality), the 'correspondence of word and picture is often problematic and may be surprisingly vague' (1973: 9). Despite the rich heritage of some images representing verbal topics and themes, historians should begin the investigation of images with measured skepticism. As I want to show, and as Peter Burke warns: 'there is a risk in iconologists discovering in images exactly what they already knew to be there, the Zeitgeist' (Burke 2001: 40). From Burke's perspective, historians need to get 'beyond iconology' (2001: 169) in their cultural analysis of visual evidence. Iconology, by tracing the history of ideas in—and across—an era, often fails to do historical justice to the complex (and often contradictory and multiple) social and material conditions of the images. Or, to be more exact, the iconological concepts serve as presuppositions—mental images of the scholar that generate the interpretive analysis of the image under question. Instead of providing the catalyst for the questioning mind, this pre-representational mindset provides the answer.

IV

Despite this widespread tendency of literary scholars and theater historians to ignore or slight visual images, the study of London theater (1560s to 1640s) has not always been blinkered. For instance, the first issue of *Shakespeare Survey* (1948), which can serve as a touchstone for the historiographical issues being considered here, featured several essays on visual evidence, including I. A. Shapiro's 'The Bankside Theatres: Early Engravings'. Shapiro's aim was 'to determine the date and authenticity of various views and maps often put forward as evidence' (1948: 25) on the Southwark amphitheaters. He clarified why most of the panorama views, including the oft-reprinted engraving by J. C. Visscher *View of London*, 1616 (Figure 34.4), are unreliable. In fact, he helped to overturn John Cranford Adams's model of the Globe theater, for Adams had used the Visscher panorama as one of his sources. Shapiro also published a copy of John Norden's *Civitas Londini* (1600), which had never before been seen or considered by theater historians.

Shapiro's valuable essay served Richard Hosley in his major assessment of the playhouses for *The Revels History of Drama in England* (Hosley 1975). And R. A. Foakes, drawing upon Shapiro in his compilation of maps and panoramas in *Illustrations of the English Stage*, acknowledged his importance (1985, p. xv). Then,

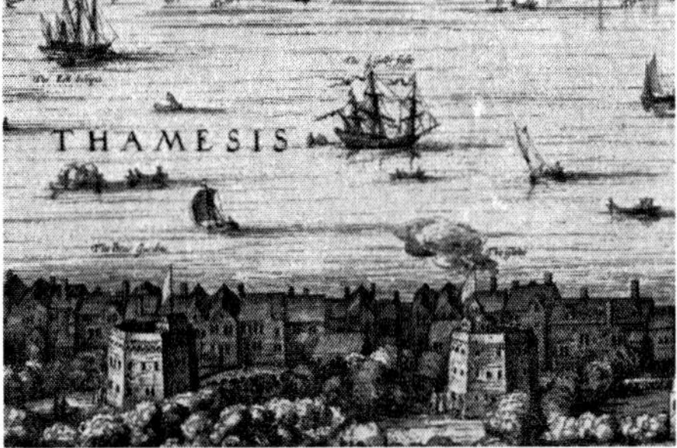

Figure 34.4 C. J. Visscher, panoramic view of London, with detail from lower right section showing south bank amphitheatres (Amsterdam, 1616), derived from J. *Norden's Civitas Londoni* (London, 1600).

just when it seemed that the assessment of these images had been basically settled, John Orrell published *The Human Stage: English Theatre Design, 1567–1642* (1988), which featured fifty-eight plates of visual documents, along with an additional fourteen drawings. Visual evidence is crucial to his study. In chapter 5 Orrell agreed with Shapiro that Visscher's panorama (1616) is unreliable, that Norden's drawing (1600) is reliable in some details, and that Wenceslaus Hollar's several drawings and etchings from the 1630s and 1640s offer the best visual evidence on the Southwark playhouses (see Figure 34.5).[20]

But in *The Human Stage* Orrell puts forward an agenda that extends beyond Shapiro's critical analysis of the separate images of Bankside theaters. Whereas Shapiro was content to determine the sources and reliability of the images, Orrell develops a comprehensive thesis about the playhouses and the visual evidence. He argues that the basic design for the London amphitheaters was derived not from the inn-yards or animal baiting arenas, as most theater historians have contended, but instead from a building tradition stretching from Vitruvius through Leon Battista Alberti and Sebastiano Serlio to the carpenter Peter Streete, who built the Fortune theater and presumably the Globe. Orrell contends that a single 'controlling idea' determined the shape of public playhouses. All of them, he proclaims, were based upon 'the coherent, integral design' (Orrell 1988: 48) provided by the *ad quadratum* geometric plans and principles, which, having been used initially for the Roman theaters, re-emerged in late medieval building designs and practices. The visual evidence, Orrell insists, supports this comprehensive thesis.

Thus, just as some art historians, schooled in the history of ideas, uncover coherent iconological patterns of classical and Christian meanings in Renaissance paintings, Orrell discovers in the visual and textual documents the abiding shape of the *homo ad circulum* and *homo ad quadratum* principles that appealed to Renaissance thinkers (see Figure 34.6). Orrell wants to demonstrate that humanism—or what he would later call 'the European Renaissance tradition' (1997*a*: 57)—unified the building practices of the era. From his perspective, European culture, both learned and popular, shared a set of humanist ideas and principles, including the principle of proportion, which resolved circles and squares into ratios of order. Fittingly, then, the round (or polygonal) Globe and the square Fortune shared the same *ad quadratum* ratio, which sanctioned the fundamental units of measurement (e.g. the statute measure of the rod at 16 feet 6 inches).

Yet, one year after Orrell proclaimed his 'controlling idea', which he applied to the reconstruction project for the new Globe theater built by Sam Wanamaker, the Rose theater foundations were unearthed. The new visual evidence in 1889, in all of its archeological credibility, made an undeniable case against coherence and proportion. Despite the evidence from the Rose, Orrell maintained his commitment to his single model, based upon his deductive principle. But he had to admit that the 'Elizabethan theater builders were a good deal more inventive in their geometry than I at least had

[20] Hollar, who lived in London between 1636 and 1642, was a careful eyewitness. From his position in the church tower of St Saviour's, Southwark, as Orrell discovered, he used a topographical device for locating and measuring the dimensions of the buildings he drew.

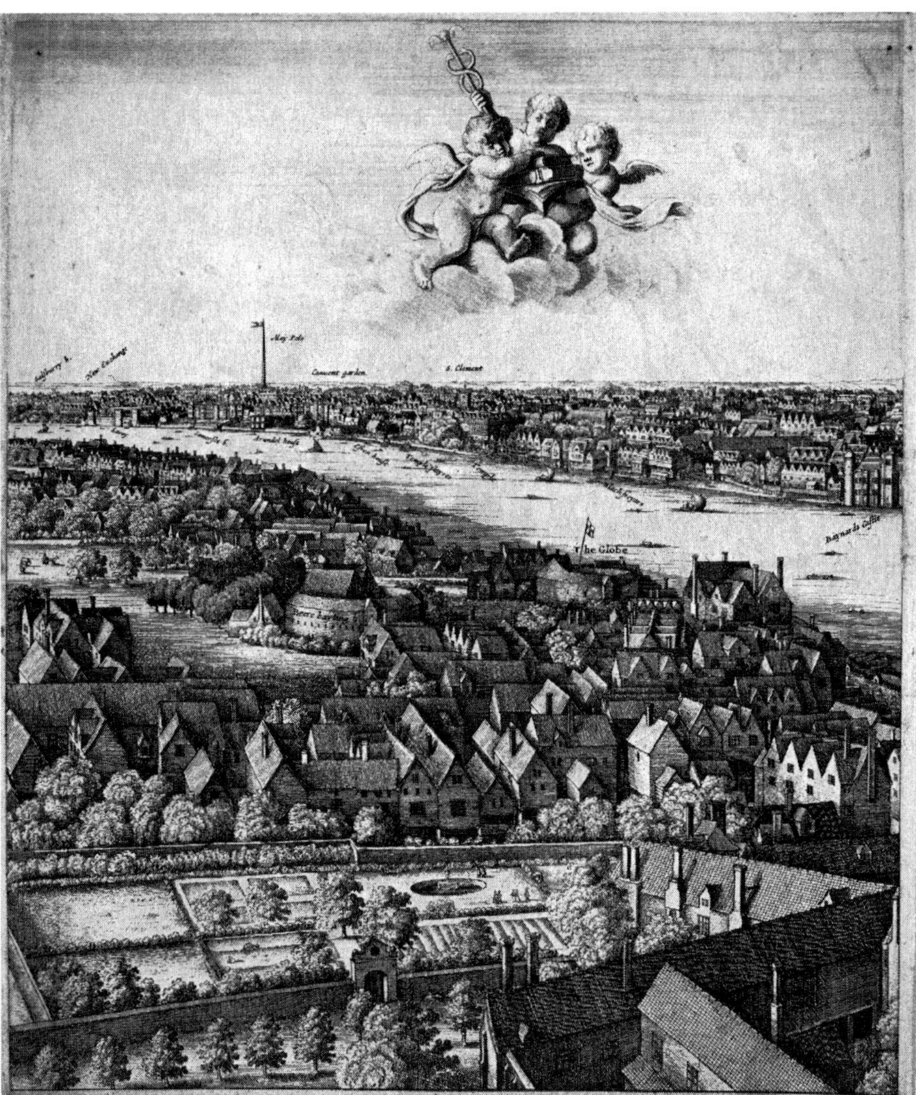

Figure 34.5 Wenceslaus Hollar, a section from his ***Long View*** of London from Southwark, 1647.

The Globe theater is mislabeled '*Beere bayting h*' and the Hope theater is mislabeled 'The Globe'.

thought likely' (Orrell 1997*a*: 59). Empirical data failed to accord with deductive and analogical reasoning. Consequently, since 1990 some scholarly advisers for the building of the new Globe have raised doubts about Orrell's propositions (see ISGC 1993).[21] Nonetheless, the construction of the Globe theater followed many of

[21] For example, in the disagreement on the size for the rebuilt Globe theater, either twenty sides and 99 feet diameter or eighteen and 90 feet, the twenty scholarly advisers invited to the deliberations voted 14 to 6 in support of Orrell's argument for the larger model (ISGC 1993: 12–13). A list of the advisers

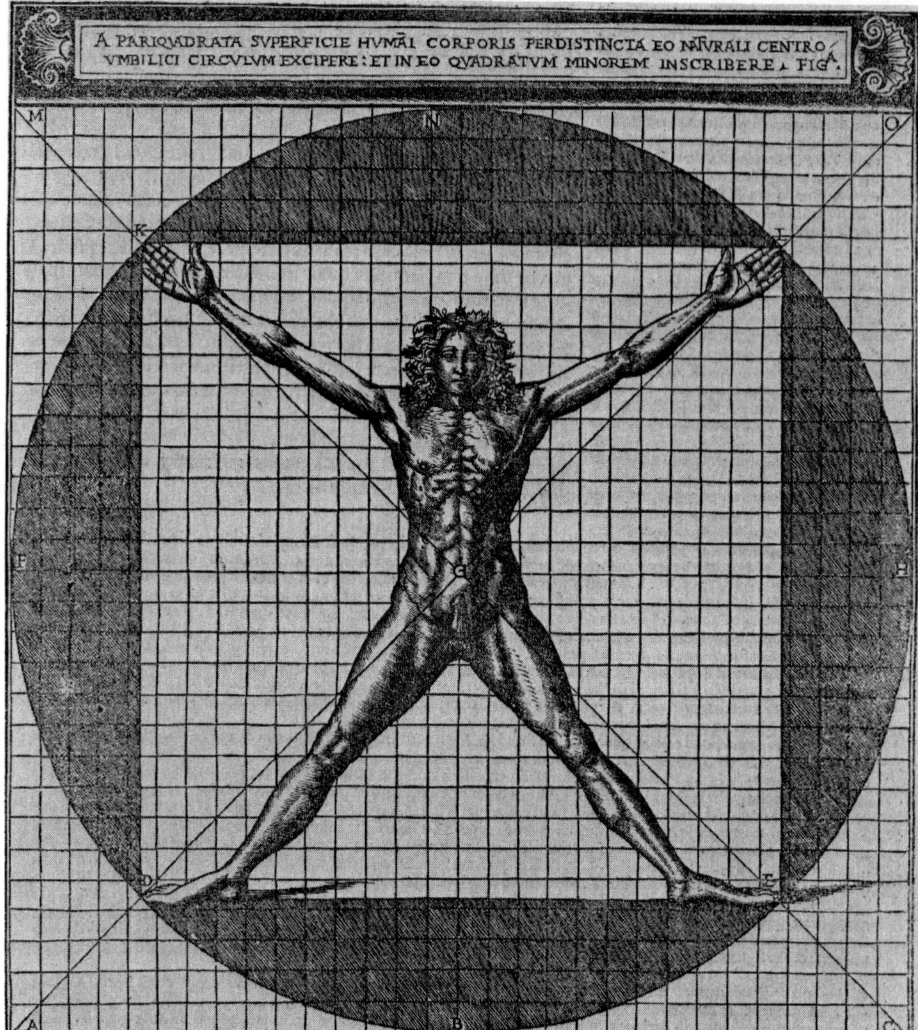
A PARIQVADRATA SVPERFICIE HVMĀI CORPORIS PERDISTINCTA EO NAVRALI CENTRO
VMBILICI CIRCVLVM EXCIPERE : ET IN EO QVADRATVM MINOREM INSCRIBERE . FIG A.
M
N
O
K
L
F
G
H
D
E
A
B
C

Figure 34.6 ***Homo ad quadratum*****, a drawing from** ***Di Lucio Vitruuio Pollione de architectura libri dece: traducti de latino in vulgare affigurati*** **(Como: Gotardo da Ponte, 1521), p. Gii.**

Orrell's ideas. The new building, which has become a visual image for us to contemplate today, is a material consequence of scholarly analysis and debates that began with Shapiro's essay and culminated in Orrell's judgements. In this way, the achieved building in the present tends to marginalize the visual evidence for the Rose theater.

appears on pp. 1–2. Also, radar surveys of the foundation for the Globe in 2003 suggest a diameter of 72 feet, not the 100 feet that Orrell derived from his calculations (Gleason 2003: 15; Foakes 2004: 31). In brief, unless we gain access to the Globe foundation, we are uncertain about its original dimensions.

Besides Shapiro's important essay, the first issue of *Shakespeare Survey* also presented evidence on the famous Swan drawing. Allardyce Nicoll, the editor, included 'A Note on the Swan Theatre Drawing', which provided information on Johannes De Witt and Aernout van Buchell, and printed the full Latin statement, *Ex Obseruationibus Londinensibus Johannis De Witt*, that van Buchell had attached to the drawing (see Figure 34.7).[22] Ever since the Swan drawing was discovered in 1888, it has been central to our understanding—or misunderstanding—of the London playhouses. To this day, in tandem with supporting evidence (e.g. stage directions in the plays, the contracts for the Hope and Fortune), the reproduced Swan drawing has guided both our descriptions and our material reconstructions of the playhouses. Among others, E. K. Chambers (1923: ii. 526–7), Glynne Wickham (1959–81: ii/1. 204), Richard Hosley (1975), and John Orrell (1983, 1988, 1997*a*) have depended upon the Swan drawing for aspects of their historical studies.

And yet major questions persist about its reliability, as Andrew Gurr insists: 'To say that a number of the features illustrated by De Witt are debatable is to put it mildly' (1992*b*: 132). The debate is front and center in two important essays on the Swan by R. A. Foakes (1993, 2004), who astutely investigates many features of the drawing. As he demonstrates, this drawing, despite 120 years of scholarly analysis, continues to generate doubtful conjectures based on questionable assumptions. Why is it so difficult to establish the value and meaning of the Swan drawing? In part, we cannot depend upon its reliability because it is a copy made by one man of a drawing by another man. Once again we face the problem of reproductions. Also, we now know that van Buchell was a less accomplished draughtsman than De Witt. We are thus back in Plato's cave, trying to determine what van Buchell's drawing, with its flaws in proportion and perspective, reveals about De Witt's original representation (see Gleason 1981; Gerritsen 1986, 1995; Foakes 1993: 2004). Nor can we determine with certainty the intentions of De Witt and van Buchell. Which aspects of the drawing reveal the understanding and aims of De Witt and which reveal those of van Buchell?

Besides these uncertainties over the drawing itself, our historical confusion also derives from lapses in our historical skills in describing and analyzing the visual evidence accurately. For instance, although we often credit the attached Latin commentary to De Witt, it is by van Buchell. It is his version of whatever De Witt originally wrote. He may have transcribed his friend's statement; he may have reworked it in key ways. We do not know.

Also, we have imposed a misunderstanding on the image because of an incorrect translation of the Latin commentary, as presented by Nicoll in *Shakespeare Survey* in 1948. Foakes points out that in van Buchell's sentence the word *forma* was miscorrected to '*forma*[*m*]', apparently by Nicoll or whoever transcribed the Latin, which

22 This reproduction, published originally by Karl Theodor Gaedertz in 1888, provides Aernout van Buchell's Latin title for his commentary, but not the text itself, which he derived from De Witt. Gaedertz removed the Latin commentary, and instead added this statement: 'Nach einer in Utrecht befindlichen Handzeichnung vom Jahre 1596' ('A hand-drawing in accord with one located in Utrecht from the year 1596'). I decided to use this 1888 reproduction because it is sharper in details and clearer in shading than the reproduction that is usually provided by the Utrecht University library (e.g. see Cooper 2006: 101).

Figure 34.7 The Swan theater, c.1596, copied by Arend [Aernout] van Buchell from a pen and ink drawing by Johannes De Witt.

Copy bound into a book entitled **Adversaria**, now located in Utrecht University Library; discovered and reproduced by Karl Theodor Gaedertz in *Zur Kenntnis der altenglischen Bühne nebst andern Beiträgen zur Shakespeare-Litteratur* (Bremen: C. Ed. Müller, 1888).

should read: '*Cuius quidem forma quod Romani operis vmbram videatur exprimere supra adpinxi*' (Foakes 2004). The error has resulted in inaccurate transcriptions of the Latin text and mistranslations in subsequent publications, including *Shakespeare's Globe Rebuilt*, edited by J. R. Mulryne and Margaret Shewring (1997). There the line is translated as 'I have drawn it above since it appears to imitate in its shape the form of a Roman structure.' Foakes comments: 'what van Buchell wrote has a significantly different meaning, roughly "I have drawn above what traces of a Roman structure it seems to express in its form." He did not draw the Swan because it was shaped like a Roman theater, but set out to sketch it in the style of a Roman theater' (2004: 30 n. 14).

Given his humanist education, De Witt was supposedly disposed to see Roman forms in the Swan theater.[23] Drawing upon the Latin transcription in *Shakespeare Survey*, John Orrell translated the line as 'its form seems to approach that of a Roman structure' (1988: 45). So understood, Orrell uses the Swan image and text as one piece of evidence to support his 'controlling idea' about the building of Elizabethan amphitheaters. For over a century, the Swan drawing has maintained its place as the primary evidence for the interior of the playhouses. As is to be expected, then, in the building of the new Globe theater, the Swan drawing rather than the Rose foundation guided the construction. The Rose, as Foakes laments, 'has been available, in plain view, as it were, yet it was pretty much ignored when the Globe reconstruction was planned, in great measure because of the difficulty in moving beyond the well-known de Witt drawing of the Swan' (2004: 16).

Consequently, the performance space and practices at the new Globe, derived in part from the Swan image, offer us a misleading idea of stage space and performance methods. Two types of eyewitness report, derived from van Buchell–De Witt and our attendance at the new Globe, create a false or inadequate idea of the early modern theaters. Our misperceptions of the visual evidence, past and present, place us in a logical hall of mirrors—a figure-of-eight sequence that loops us back and forth between the Swan drawing and the new Globe. In the process, the scholarly authorities, if not careful, serve as masters of tautology.

In order to break out of the false figuration, we need to reconsider the available evidence on the Rose in contrast to that for the Globe and the Swan. Concerning the Swan drawing, Foakes insists that we need to begin anew. He argues, for example, that the Swan theater probably had a removal stage and three doors (1993). Whether or not we agree with his reassessment, which is based upon various visual and verbal sources on architecture and performance practices from several countries, his conclusion merits our serious consideration:

> It seems to me...that we have little reason to be sanguine about the accuracy of the van Buchell/de Witt drawing, and should treat all of its features with skepticism. Moreover, whatever information can be extracted from it relates solely to the Swan, and we have less

[23] On De Witt's humanist education and his reading of Justus Lipsius' *De Amphiteatro* (1584), see Gleason (1981).

reason still to accept it as primary evidence about the theaters operated by the Admiral's and Chamberlain's Men. (Foakes 1993: 351)

Foakes's challenge is clear: instead of holding to a single model or a controlling idea for the early modern stage, we might be wiser if we entertained an idea of multiple stage spaces, in accord with a principle of historical complexity and change. The evidence resists a singular idea of the theater.

V

The 1948 issue of *Shakespeare Survey* also offered J. Dover Wilson's analysis of the image and text from the Longleat manuscript, which seems to display characters from Shakespeare's *Titus Andronicus*, arrayed in a performance scene (Figure 34.8). As usually interpreted, the image represents from left to right two Roman soldiers (perhaps sons of Titus), Titus (with staff or spear), the supplicating Tamora, two men on their knees (two of her sons), and Aaron the Moor, holding aloft a sword and gesturing with his right hand. Forty lines of verse, selected from the beginning and conclusion of the play—I. i. 104–20 and v. i. 124–44—are inscribed below the image. The continuous passage also contains a modified line, two invented lines, and a stage direction not in the play. Someone inscribed these lines, perhaps Henry Peacham (father or son?) whose name appears, with a date, on the page. Whatever the source, the text serves to explicate the image.

What, though, is the relationship between image and text? Are they provided by one or two people? And what, if anything, does the image reveal about the performance of Shakespeare's play in the 1590s? This image confronts us with two problems of representation: (1) the correspondence between image and ascribed text and (2) the correspondence between image and historical performance. Both relationships are problematic. Commentators over the years have often confused the issues that pertain to these two problems, or they have collapsed them together. But a logical contradiction confronts us, for the attempts to make the case for either one of these correspondences usually puts in doubt or disproves the other one.

The image has troubled scholars ever since E. K. Chambers discovered it in 1925. He identified the image as 'The First Illustration to Shakespeare', a title that implies a correspondence between image and performance (1925: 326). Many scholars insist that the drawing represents the play's opening scene, specifically the moment in Act I suggested by some of the appended lines from the text. But the representation of Aaron brandishing a sword does not fit this moment in the play. Nor does the image correspond to the lines and situation of Act V, when he is being hanged (without any sword). Apparently, then, the image fails to represent both the appended text and the

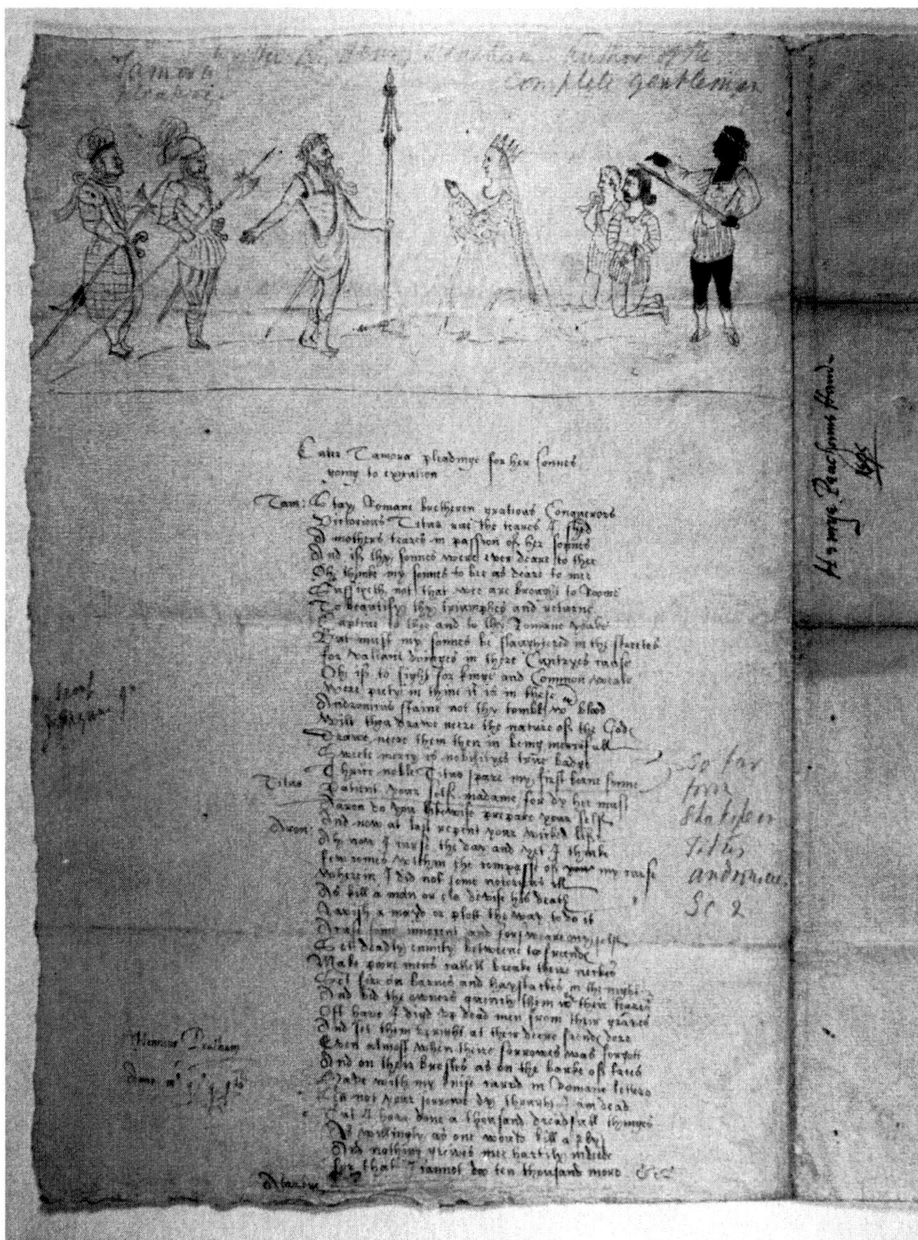

Figure 34.8 A pen and ink drawing on paper attributed to Henry Peacham (1594); paired with lines from *Shakespeare's Titus Andronicus*, I. i. 104–20 and V. i. 124–44. Folio manuscript 296 x 403 mm (11 5/8 x 15 7/8 in.) in the Longleat House library.

implied performance situation. Justifying either correspondence is thus difficult; justifying both becomes a logical challenge (if not an impossibility).

Wilson attempts to get around the difficulties of image and text by discounting their relationship. He argues that the image does not accord with the lines because the verse was added years later by someone other than the person who made the drawing. Perhaps a generation later, in a confused attempt to explicate the drawing, someone failed to understand the image. Since 1948 Wilson's supposition that the lines were added later has been accepted and repeated by several scholars, including editors of the play and R. A. Foakes, who concludes that 'the text has no direct relation to the drawing' and 'could have been added later, and by another hand' (1985: 48). Wilson's surmise lacks, however, any evidence.

The most radical challenge to the correspondence between drawing and Shakespeare's text came from June Schlueter in 1999. Accepting and quoting Foakes's statement about a lack of relationship between image and text, she goes the next step and argues that the image does not represent the bard's play. She contends that it represents a German play on the same topic, *Eine sehr klägliche Tragaedia von Tito Andronico* ('A Very Lamentable Tragedy of Titus Andronicus'), performed by the English players in Germany, and published in Leipzig in 1620. The image, she argues, represents the end of Act I of that play. She also suggests that the image corresponds to a performance in Germany. Who, then, did the drawing? Peacham is still the candidate, but key questions remain unanswered. Did he see a performance of the German play? How and when? Or did he see the lost play 'Titus and Vespasian', a precursor perhaps of Shakespeare's play that Henslowe records and credits to Lord Strange's Men? Did this lost play influence the writing of the German play? Schlueter cannot answer these questions definitively without more evidence. But if the drawing illustrates the German text, could it also represent a performance that has nothing to do with London theater or Shakespeare? If so, the scholarly suppositions about Shakespeare's play and its performance—from E. K. Chambers to recent editors of *Titus Andronicus*—are pointless as theater history. The visual evidence has not changed, but its apparent or potential meanings have been completely transformed by Schlueter's conjectures.

Countering Schlueter, Richard Levin (2002) raised questions about the appropriateness of the image for the German play. He commends her 'painstaking research', but he argues that 'there is no clear correspondence between the drawing and the Act I scene in the German play' (R. Levin 2002: 325, 326). After considering her case, including her attempt to identify the character wearing the crown in the drawing with Vespasian the emperor in *A Very Lamentable Tragedy*, Levin outlines a number of unanswered problems in Schlueter's speculations. He thus sees 'no reason to prefer the German play as the source of the drawing' (R. Levin 2002: 326). Basically, because his analysis removes any justification for supposing that the drawing might represent a performance on the Continent, Schlueter's alternative play fails to offer a convincing solution to the Longleat manuscript. Her extended argument by analogy, linking the drawing to action in the German play, is no more probable, or even possible, than

Wilson's attempted solution of separating drawing from the appended lines. The correspondence between image and text remains a conundrum.

What, then, can we assume about the correspondence between image and historical performance? Wilson insisted that the artist 'depicts, without doubt, what he actually saw at a performance of the plays' (1948: 20), but not the moment in Act I suggested by the appended verse, which can be ignored. The image, Wilson suggests, represents a later moment in the scene, after Titus has refused Tamora's supplication (after line 129). However, Foakes (along with other scholars) has dismissed this rather fanciful premise, which raises more questions than the standard yet flawed explanation. Thus, from Foakes's perspective, all of the attempts to tie the drawing to an actual performance are flawed. Among other factors, Aaron with his sword remains a problem. Foakes concludes that there is, 'in fact, no reason to suppose this drawing was made at a staging of the play' because 'the drawing does not fit any point in the action' (1985: 50).

Is it still possible, though, to use the drawing as evidence about theatrical performance in the 1590s? Reviewing the scholarship, Richard Levin maps out, in a measured analysis, the likely and unlikely possibilities (Levin 2002: 323–40). He posits that the artist who made the drawing did see a performance in 1594, the apparent date on the illustration (see Berry 1999). Levin contends that the represented costumes, rather than being based upon a reading of the play, which could not provide such details, are likely derived from what the artist witnessed on stage. This conjecture is possible, yet we must not assume that the artist attended a performance of *Titus Andronicus* (and not just because the image does not fit any moment in the play and its performance). It is also possible that the artist, having seen a number of Elizabethan performances, knew some things about costuming practices. He could have extrapolated from this knowledge to make a representation of a scene that he had read, inaccurately recalling some details (e.g. Aaron with a sword in Act I or Act V). The costumes do not prove that the artist attended a performance of *Titus*. Levin is making speculations on the basis of possibility, but not probability (and surely not certainty). What we can say, with some confidence, is that the costumes in the drawing accord with our knowledge of other historical sources on Elizabethan costumes.[24]

In considering other conjectures about what the drawing might reveal about performance, Levin shows his typical skepticism. He is unconvinced by suggestions from Stephen Orgel (1983: 37) and G. Harold Metz (1996: 244) that the line separating the image from the verse in the Longleat manuscript represents the front of 'the stage' or 'the front edge of the platform'. Levin argues that this drawing, unlike that of the Swan theater, does not reveal a stage space. Instead, he suggests that the image, similar to those of many frontispieces, represents an action occurring not in a theater but in a 'real world' setting suggested by the play (Levin 2002: 338). Levin contends

[24] Visual sources, such as the drawing of *Titus*, have provided some insights on stage costumes. But in the main scholars have depended upon clues in the play-texts. In addition, investigators have turned to art histories, social histories, and histories of costumes, clothes, and fashion for the era. See e.g. Linthicum (1936); MacIntyre (1992); Lublin (forthcoming).

that the figures 'are on gently sloping ground, which is clearly indicated beneath them' (2002: 338). The line is just a line, separating image from words. Of course, Levin's argument by analogy does not prove anything about this image, which may not follow or be derived from the artistic conventions of frontispieces. We must keep in mind that without any supporting evidence all arguments by analogy are fallacious. We need historical evidence, not just clever suppositions based upon patterns of similitude.

This disagreement between Orgel and Levin nicely illustrates the primary challenges with visual evidence. First of all, the visual representation itself needs to be accurate. As with all eyewitness reports and representations, the source must be questioned for credibility and reliability. If, as I. A. Shapiro was able to demonstrate, Visscher's drawing of the playhouses is inaccurate (because he was not in London, but instead derived his images from other sources, reproducing their inaccuracies), then a description (or model) of the Globe based upon Visscher (e.g. that of John Cranford Adams) lacks both credibility and reliability.

Even if the original source is a credible document, as is the case with the Longleat manuscript (it is not a fake; the drawing was apparently made in 1594), we still contend with problems of credibility and reliability when a scholar's verbal description of a visual image is inaccurate. All of us stumble, even the leading scholars. If, for example, Orgel and Metz describe a line as an indication of a stage but turn out to be wrong, then their analysis that depends upon this description is misguided, leading readers down the wrong path. And in turn, if Levin's suggested description of a gentle slope is misleading, then his argument by analogy has no purchase on the historical problem before us.

Accordingly, as theater historians we must recognize and distinguish between the two levels of source analysis. We must first question the accuracy of the primary source—the Swan drawing, the Visscher etching, the Longleat manuscript. Then we must also question the ways scholars have attempted to translate visual images into reliable and accurate historical descriptions. Only after we have successfully negotiated these two stages of representation are we prepared to confront the next challenge: the reliability of the analysis that is derived from (1) the primary visual source and (2) the secondary description of that visual source. Together, the accuracy of the eyewitness's representation and the accuracy of the scholar's description of that eyewitness account justify the value of the explanation.

In brief, the visual has to be transformed into the verbal. The historian needs fine descriptive skills in order to represent the visual source accurately, thereby setting the details and terms for the analysis. These steps in description and analysis may seem basic, but in the process of performing them, we need to work through the questions raised by Mieke Bal in her studies of art and literature: 'How can an image be written? And once written, how can it be read' (1997: 1)? These fundamental questions are difficult to answer, as many art historians recognize, because, in Michael Baxandall's words, 'every evolved explanation of a picture includes or implies an elaborate description of that picture' (1998: 52). Accurate description, which serves as the 'mediating object of explanation', is not easy to achieve because we have to make a series of cross-code translations from the specificity of visual images to the generalizing nature of verbal languages. In a parallel universe, as it were, we gather our proxies for the visual. We turn visual marks into remarks; we turn images into concepts. Everything is seen under a description, not simply as it is. Our descriptions are *about* the visual image, but in a quite different register, one that is often analogical. And they are about *effects* of the image upon us, effects that occur emotionally and intellectually in our minds, not in the visual source. In Baxandall's words: 'In fact, language is not very well equipped to offer a notation of a particular picture.... What a description will tend to represent best is thought after seeing a picture.... what one offers in a description is a representation of thinking about a picture more than a representation of a picture' (Baxandall 1998: 56). A pattern of displacement, condensation, and substitution occurs in the handling of all visual sources, including historical sources such as the Swan drawing, not just paintings that one can contemplate as intentional art works.

This basic problem of accurate description and representation applies to all of us who attempt to take the measure of visual sources, to use them as historical evidence. It also applies to all eyewitnesses, including those who produce visual reports. Thus, whoever drew the image in the Longleat manuscript provides us with evidence of how he thought about what he saw. The visual image, a kind of description, may suggest (but not answer) more about his thoughts than about whatever it was he was attempting to represent. The difficult relationship between the visual and the verbal thus imposes uncertainties at both the primary and secondary level of description. Here, in a muddle of transfers from the visual to the verbal, we carry out the preliminary negotiations over credible and reliable methods of representation. This hard work needs to be done before analysis can do its job.

In his assessment of the Longleat manuscript and *Titus Andronicus*, Levin is also critical of Alan Hughes's suggestion[25] that the representation of Tamora in the image reveals a boy actor because the figure is tall, the nose is large, the mouth is thin, and no breasts are visible. Reading the image as if it were a realistic representation, Hughes misapplies his modern sensibility (perhaps conditioned by photography). Bemused, Levin dismisses Hughes's ability to determine gender on the basis of the artist's rendering of noses, lips, and height. He points out that Hughes ignores the ways art conventions might contribute to the image of Tamora. In support of his argument, Levin evokes a 1992 article by June Schlueter on the representation, both visible and invisible, of female breasts on the English Renaissance stage. Also, he relies on her careful description of this image. Schlueter notes that Tamora 'wears a loose-bodied gown' and her 'extended arm obscures the view of the bodice' (Schlueter 1992: 131). We are thus unable to behold any definitive sign of breasts. Here, too, an accurate description of the visual evidence is crucial before launching into explanation.

Levin also rejects the contention of some commentators that the image of Aaron proves that the character was played by a black man. Nor can we use the image to

[25] *Titus Andronicus*, ed. Alan Hughes, New Cambridge Shakespeare (Cambridge: Cambridge University Press, 1994), 22.

prove that the player of Aaron wore black make-up, though Shakespeare describes Aaron as 'raven-colored' (II. iii. 83) and 'coal-black' (IV. ii. 99; V. i. 32). Even if scholars agreed—and we don't—that the drawing is derived from a production, the image does not justify such certainty. Nor does the image prove, as E. K. Chambers argued, that Elizabethans believed that a Moor in skin color was 'dead black' rather than 'tawny' (1925: 326). We don't know if the artist was attempting to create a 'dead black' as opposed to a tawny image in the pencil drawing. We cannot assume that the artist and Shakespeare agreed about the blackness of Aaron. And we surely cannot use this one image to generalize about the racial attitudes of all Elizabethans.

In our search for what images reveal potentially about players, productions, and theaters, we need to describe each image accurately and carefully. Details matter. Moreover, as Astington has demonstrated, we need to place these artifacts within 'a precise historical and cultural context' (1997: 151). To date, theater historians have shown limited understanding of the many factors and sources that contribute to the images we study, including the conventions of artistic representation, the drawing methods and skills of a wide range of artists, the development of the styles and careers of specific artists, the various types of publication (from frontispieces for plays to ballad and emblem books), the representative codes (iconic, referential, and symbolic), the intended audiences (both learned and unlearned), the role of patrons in commissioning and determining the images, the artisan practices of printers and printing shops, the commercial markets that guided the printers, the publishing history of various illustrations, the material on which an image was created (parchment paper, vellum, etc.), the material limitations of media (such as woodcuts), the methods of preservation across the centuries, and the changing conventions of representation throughout history. Moreover, all images have socio-economic conditions, the recovery of which may be crucial to our understanding. And some images, created in the context of politics or religion, express polemics and propaganda (e.g. the several regal images of Queen Elizabeth; the representations of the Fat Bishop and Black Knight on the title page of Thomas Middleton's *A Game at Chess*). To ignore most, if not all, of these factors is an invitation to false description, improper analysis, mistaken interpretation, and misplaced judgement.

VI

As this quick summary of recent scholarly commentary on the Longleat manuscript suggests, our historical understanding remains as confused as our comprehension of the Swan drawing. Though this image suggests some possible things about costuming practices, its historical reliability as a theatrical representation is still an issue. Perhaps this stalemate over the correspondence between image and performance explains why recent scholarship has focused mainly on the relationship between image and verse. This topic allows literary scholars to draw upon their interpretive skills, unhindered by troubling matters of historical documentation. But here too some basic problems in description and analysis emerge.

Unfortunately, when Levin shifts from historical analysis to literary interpretation, he sets aside all skepticism. In a two-part interpretive move, he posits that the Longleat manuscript page expresses not only an intentional but also a unified design. Asserting that 'the drawing and verses render a single conception of the play' (Levin 2002: 329), he then produces an analysis that fulfills this hypothesis. In the process of setting forth his thesis, he rejects or modifies the explanations of four scholars of the play and drawing: Alan Hughes, who claims that the image represents one scene that the artist drew incorrectly because of a faulty memory of a production;[26] Eugene Waith,[27] who argues for a 'comprehensive illustration' that combines two episodes from Acts I and V; G. Harold Metz (1996), who suggests that the image provides 'simultaneous representation' of events from four scenes in the play; and Jonathan Bate,[28] who claims, in accord with the tradition of iconographical and iconological readings in art history, that the image is a 'composite representation' which joins various scenes, thereby providing 'an emblematic reading of the whole play'.[29]

Intrigued by Bate's ideas and method, Levin reads the image for its simultaneous representation of literal and emblematic motifs in the play. For example, the problem of Aaron and his sword is solved by interpreting the image as 'a kind of proleptic figure warning us of the crimes to follow in Acts 2 and 3' (Levin 2002: 333). Such a reading of a scene as sequence allows Levin to transform the spatiality of imagistic representation into the temporality of theatrical representation; or, more to the point, to read the play and image as a verbal icon. Indeed, this approach combines features of the allegorical idea of representation in the iconology of Panofsky (1955, 1968) with the spatial analysis of literature that was prevalent in the New Criticism in the 1950s and 1960s.[30] Like Keats's poetic evocation of the figures on a Grecian urn, Levin's idea of narrative simultaneity unites image and text. The *Titus* image, he contends, replicates various events within the play. In order to achieve this thematic synthesis of image and play, Levin must convince himself that the sequential nature of theatrical representation, across two to three hours, is compressed into this one image. The freedom of literary interpretation offsets (and apparently nullifies) not only the temporal nature of dramatic narrative and the distinctive sequential experience of being a spectator but also the restraints of historical evidence.

Levin attempts to distinguish his 'epitomic approach' (2002: 334) from the emblematic or symbolic approach of Bate, but both scholars propose, without any supporting evidence, that the person who did the drawing was 'trying to convey

[26] Ibid. Hughes also argues that the artist cobbled together the verse lines in an attempt to justify his inaccurate drawing.

[27] William Shakespeare, *Titus Andronicus*, ed. Eugene M. Waith (Oxford: Clarendon Press, 1984).

[28] William Shakespeare, *Titus Andronicus*, ed. Jonathan Bate, The Arden Shakespeare (London: Routledge, 1995).

[29] Ibid. 41.

[30] For valuable historical critiques of Panofsky's idea of the iconological method, with its unifying concepts such as the 'Renaissance mind', see Gombrich (1968) and Summers (1987).

his reading not just of this scene but of the play as a whole' (Levin 2002: 334). In other words, just as a generation of art historians credited an iconographical or iconological design to sixteenth-century paintings, Levin and Bate assume that the person who drew this image intended and achieved a sophisticated compression of Shakespeare's play, requiring therefore a total 'reading' by an equally sophisticated literary critic. But in this mirror image, where is the origin of the intention? Whose intention unifies the Longleat manuscript? Levin's proposition is declared, and then taken as justification for analysis. Such an assessment thus allows Levin the literary critic to shunt aside Levin the theater historian.

In support of his idea of a unifying intentionality, Levin argues that the drawing reveals a 'clearly planned' design of 'two symmetrical sides', divided by the 'ceremonial staff' placed at the center. The 'stark opposition' of gestures and groups highlights certain 'features' in the drawing. But when certain other features do not fit this design (e.g. the figure of Aaron), Levin proclaims that they 'stand out as a startling violation of this symmetrical design' (2002: 332). In this manner Aaron's 'violent, defiant gesture' stands in perfect opposition to the 'passive submissiveness' of the Goths. Symmetry is total; symmetry is violated. Levin has it both ways because he assumes that all parts add up to an imaginative whole, as intended by the artist (or, in this case, by the critic).

The artistic unity of the drawing justifies Levin's 'epitomic approach'. Whereas a historian might feel compelled to accept the contradictions and inexplicable features as necessary limitations on historical research—there are always gaps in our knowledge—the literary critic achieves an interpretation that connects all of the dots. Whereas the historian would tend to work inductively, the literary critic precedes deductively, fulfilling the presupposition that the object of analysis reveals an artistic system that requires a formal analysis. The contradictions between image and text are cleverly explained away.

Despite the aesthetic mandate that guides Levin's reading of the *Titus* image, he does seek to establish a historical basis for his simultaneous method. He points out that seven frontispiece illustrations from the era, such as the frontispieces for *The Spanish Tragedy* (1615) and *Philaster* (1620), provide a composite drawing of two or three moments in a play. So, in an argument by analogy he claims that the simultaneous representation in the seven frontispieces sanctions his simultaneous reading of the *Titus* image (which, as far as we know, was not drawn as a frontispiece for a play).

Surely, a distinction needs to be made here. For example, the frontispiece for *The Spanish Tragedy* (Figure 34.9) draws together three closely related moments that occur within two scenes (II. iv and II. v). Each moment is identified in the frontispiece by the represented figures—Horatio, Hieronimo, and Balthazar and Lorenzo. Three pieces of appended dialogue further identify three of the figures, making explicit the relationship between text and image. That is, the image provides the textual terms for both a description and an explanation. Likewise, the historical details in the image complement, rather than contradict, the compressed scenic representation.[31] All scholars who have studied this image agree on its representative

[31] For example, as Foakes points out, the shoes with rosettes worn by Lorenzo 'were especially fashionable in the early years of the seventeenth century' (1985: 104).

The Spanish Tragedie:

OR,

Hieronimo is mad againe.

Containing the lamentable end of *Don Horatio*, and *Belimperia*; with the pittifull death of *Hieronimo*.

Newly corrected, amended, and enlarged with new Additions of the *Painters* part, and others, as it hath of late been diuers times acted.

LONDON,
Printed by W. White, for I. White and T. Langley,
and are to be sold at their Shop ouer against the
Sarazens head without New-gate. 1615.

Figure 34.9 Title page of Thomas Kyd's *The Spanish Tragedy* (London, 1615).

Raised dialogue is from Act II, scenes iv and v.

meaning and its derivative sources in two closely related scenes of the play, whose actions are connected.

By contrast, the image and the text for *Titus Andronicus* fail to achieve this kind of composite or compressed representation. The image provides no explicit marks or signals, such as the identifying captions of dialogue in the manner of the frontispiece for *The Spanish Tragedy.* Consequently, no scholarly consensus exists on what the image and text may mean; indeed, many commentators have concluded that image and text were produced by two different people at two different times. Because the scholars cannot agree on what they see before them, they have offered some intriguing ways to address the problem. But by arguing that the image is either a flawed or a composite drawing—derived from faulty memory, simultaneous representation, comprehensive illustration, symbolic imagining, or an epitomic perspective—Hughes, Metz, Waith, Bate, and Levin attempt to explain away rather than explain the contradictions. Absent some supporting historical evidence, Levin's intentional design of simultaneity, which requires an epitomic imagination of the artist, is actually the demonstration of the epitomic imagination of the critic. Analogical thinking, in this case, does not anchor the historical argument; it substitutes a literary understanding for historical understanding.

Of course, from a literary perspective, none of these explanations is wrong because the conclusions in each of these cases follow from the premises. The arguments may be tautological, but the deductive reasoning, when confined within each critic's own system of interpretation, is not fallacious. Still, the a priori assumptions about unified design and artistic purpose are suspect from the perspective of historical study, which must follow a posteriori models of understanding. The historical reliability and credibility of the drawing in terms of its relationship to the appended text and its correspondence to performance cannot be determined by a priori reasoning alone, which all too often transposes artifact into fact without following basic historical methods of testing sources. Historical knowledge, in these situations, cannot be merely syllogistic; it must be inductive in some primary ways. But the a priori assumptions guiding Levin and the others allow for all kinds of deductions and analogies. The propositions provide their own verification. Such assumptions allow for arguments that operate outside of the rules of empirical evidence. Their interpretations—acts of reasoning that displace the need for the presentation of supporting historical facts—separate the literary interpretation from the historical documentation. All of these 'readings', though clever, evade the historical mandate to observe basic rules for evaluating evidence. Unfortunately, no testimony is required; no supporting or external evidence is needed; no rules of credibility and reliability are followed; and no test or criticism of sources is provided.[32]

Therefore, these kinds of emblematic reading share many of the features (and problems) of iconographical methods of interpretation: a lack of control on the interpretation. Or, as Levin himself admitted: 'Once we take the high symbolic road, it is hard to know when to stop' (2002: 332). Anything goes, limited only by the

[32] For a basic guide to historical method, see Gottschalk (1969).

learning and cleverness of the scholar. In his book *Symbolic Images*, E. H. Gombrich reminds us that '*meaning* is a slippery term, especially when applied to images rather than to statements'. Our difficulties in assigning meaning to visual signs and forms occur because 'images apparently occupy a curious position somewhere between the statements of language, which are intended to convey a meaning, and the things of nature, to which we only can give a meaning' (1978: 2). When contemplating an image, it is too easy to conjure with interpretive readings that allow one to find what one seeks to find.

As many art historians know, the misuses of both iconology and iconography in twentieth-century studies, especially in the study of Renaissance art, are legend. Although Panofsky and others have discovered many fascinating meanings, classical and Christian, in the paintings of Botticelli, Raphael, and Poussin, they have also elaborated various allegorical and hieroglyphic meanings that seem to float free of both artistic intention and audience response. The most unlikely yet elaborate interpretations can be generated. As two generations of art historians have warned, the interpretive agendas of iconology and iconography have often failed to do justice not only to the likely, or even possible, motives and knowledge of the artists who created the art works but also to the cultural and social history of the era that shaped the works and their contexts.[33] Unrestrained by documentary evidence of the artist's intention and the viewer's understanding, the art historian posits a pervasive and comprehensive system of meaning shared by all knowledgeable people within a historical setting. The images, supposedly carrying Neoplatonic and Christian meanings, riddles, and enigmas, are often read as symbolic analogues of sophisticated ideas that can be discovered in literary, philosophical, and religious texts. Peter Burke warns that the method 'is too literary or logocentric, in the sense of assuming that images illustrate ideas and of privileging content over form' (2001: 41). This is the mistake that Levin makes with the *Titus* image. E. H. Gombrich sounds the general warning: 'Codes... cannot be cracked by ingenuity alone. On the contrary. It is the danger of the cipher clerk that he sees codes everywhere' (1978: 19). So, if historians, including theater historians, take up iconology and iconography in the analysis of visual evidence, they need to proceed with the greatest of care.

Interestingly, after completing his expansive literary explanation, Levin, in a measured voice, acknowledges that he cannot solve all of the problems in the Longleat manuscript. He thus concludes with questions, and a final statement: 'Unless some new evidence comes to light, these questions remain unanswerable' (Levin 2002: 340). This is the voice of the historian rather than the literary critic. Levin's essay thus breaks into two distinct parts; the careful historical scholar appears at the beginning and end of the essay, but the literary critic in the middle section. Levin,

[33] For representative critiques of and alternatives to methods of iconography and iconology, see Bal (1991); Baxandall (1972, 1979, 1985); Bryson (1981, 1983, 1992); Carrier (1987, 1991, 1993, 2003); Ginzburg (1989); Gombrich (1968, 1978, 1986); Hermerén (1969); Holly (1984, 1996); Podro (1982); Preziosi (1989, 1998); Schapiro (1973, 1985, 1994); Summers (1981, 2003). See, as well, key collections of essays on art history and its methods by leading scholars, including those edited by Bryson et al. (1991, 1994); Cheetham et al. (1998); Gee (1993); Holly and Moxey (2002); R. Nelson and Shiff (2003); Preziosi (1998).

Bate, Waith, Metz, and Hughes all feel compelled to offer up comprehensive interpretations of the Longleat document. Composite, symbolic, and emblematic readings are pervasive. An ostensive imagination takes over. But when Levin puts on the hat of the historical scholar, the need for comprehensive and total interpretation is set aside. The requirement to be true to historical possibility wins out over the desire to offer a comprehensive literary interpretation. The historian recognizes that many documents, textual and visual, are missing. Questions multiply; answers, at best, must be matters of possibility and probability, not certainty.

Consequently, sixty years after the first issue of *Shakespeare Survey*, most of the problems with visual evidence for the London theater remain with us. In 1948, when he wrote his essay on the Longleat image, J. Dover Wilson admitted that the drawing 'presents so many puzzling features difficult to interpret'. He hoped, though, that his article would 'induce others to join a symposium designed to elucidate its complex problems' (1948: 22). The symposium has invited many commentators, but no one has yet solved the puzzle. As is the case with the Swan drawing and other visual sources, we are still working out some basic historical procedures in the description and analysis of the possible evidence for the Longleat drawing.

This situation should not discourage us, however, for we are still learning our historical tasks. Though it is somewhat surprising—and disappointing—that our historical investigations of visual evidence and performance methods lag behind the challenging new work of the last few decades in the study of classical Greek and Roman theater,[34] we now have the opportunity to open up our methods of inquiry. Like the revisionist approaches to the textual editing of plays, our study of visual evidence on theaters, players, costumes, and performance invites us to begin anew. The contributions of Reg Foakes, Clifford Davidson, John Astington, and others have provided an initial historiographical foundation for the study of visual sources on early modern theater. Their investigations demonstrate that our study of visual evidence is still developing its promise of solid, careful historical inquiry.[35]

[34] On visual evidence for body language, gesture, costume, props, entrance and exit, performance methods, theater buildings and topography, and theatrical space in Greek and Roman theater, see e.g. Bergmann and Kondoleon (1999); Boardman (1989); Boegehold (1999); Bremmer (1991); Cairns (2005); Csapo and Slater (1995); Duncan (2006); Easterling (1997); Easterling and Hall (2002); Foley (2000, 2003); Goldhill and Osborne (1999); R. Green (1991, 1999, 2002); R. Green and Handley (1995); Izenour (1992, 1997*a*,*b*); Naerebout (1997); Revermann (2006); Simon (1982, 1983); Taplin (1978, 1992, 1995, 2007*a*, *b*); Wiles (1991, 1997); Winkler and Zeitlin (1990). These studies, drawing upon visual and verbal sources, are crafted and built on the foundational scholarship of Dale (1969); Pickard-Cambridge (1946, 1968); Trendall and Webster (1971); Webster (1967, 1970, 1978, 1995).

[35] I extend my gratitude to John Astington and David Wiles, who read a rough draft of this essay. Their comments helped me to develop my analysis, but of course they are not responsible for my failure to address some issues sufficiently. I also thank Richard Dutton for his encouraging commentary and guidance.

CHAPTER 35

CHRISTOPHER BEESTON: HIS PROPERTY AND PROPERTIES

EVA GRIFFITH

THIS essay, on one important level, concerns issues that confront the theatre historian when faced with the interpretation of fact. On another level it is all about a character from theatre history—namely Christopher Beeston—an actor of Shakespeare's day who once belonged to Shakespeare's company but who later both joined and, most importantly, formed and managed other companies. I use the term 'character' advisedly. For, as we shall see, with all the forms of behaviour that are given to this particular man of the stage, one could easily roam into the realm of the dramatic when discussing him. Some would argue that theatre history is forever in danger of interpreting itself into fictional form of one sort or another—a danger not helped by the field emanating out of English literature departments, fascinated with forms of the fictive anyway.

In history or in any other field, can we ever judge another human being, whether in the context of their past or our present? Personal judgement is something humanity seems to tend towards almost without realizing it is doing so, and this seems particularly so with theatre history and Christopher Beeston—actor, manager, and

I dedicate this essay to the memory of my father, the actor and documentary filmmaker Kenneth Griffith (1921–2006). Most new material given here was presented in a paper, taken from my Ph.D. thesis of 2003, at the Shakespeare Association of America (SAA) Conference, 2004.

playhouse entrepreneur. Not only did Beeston perform with, organize, and manage companies, he also leased, converted, and ran a particular theatre that these companies performed in—the Cockpit off Drury Lane—from around 1616 to his death in 1638. Bearing in mind the sweep of time and the different theatrical functions he embodies, and considering my will to interrogate theatre history's characterizations, I will be looking at two forms of 'property' that can be thought about with reference to Christopher Beeston, performer and playhouse instigator. These will include his earthbound measurable feet-and-inches kind of property and his all too human 'properties', and just in the telling I will be inviting judgement as well as interrogating the very act of judging when it comes to historical biography.

Beeston, as a character from theatre history, is an important one, in that his career spans a bridge between a late Tudor time when purpose-built theatre playing was first burgeoning, to an overconfident later period, just prior to the Civil War, when it was suppressed. Born about 1580, he was named among the annals of the Chamberlain's Men when he was listed as a performer in Jonson's *Every Man in His Humour* of 1598.[1] Christopher Beeston was a player at 18 then, and, with time, many things were bound to happen afterwards to such a young man. In the case of Christopher Beeston however, after his time with the Chamberlain's Men, he experienced marriage, the excitement of business ventures and shareholding, as well as accusations of recusancy, theft, and rape. The meat of this essay concerns these matters, the start of it coming 'in the middle of things', in 1623, and a famous court case which has given us documents about actors and their company troubles in the previous decade.[2] The company in question was the Servants of Queen Anna of Denmark, a parallel company to Shakespeare's Servants of King James, and the theatre the Queen's servants performed in was the Red Bull playhouse in Clerkenwell. Christopher Beeston took a central role in both this company and its playhouse. He was also a central concern in the court case.

The suit, known as the *Worth* v. *Baskervile* case of 1623, was one brought by the actor Ellis Worth, a member of the then Revels players, against Susan, a widow of the actor, clown, and manager of the Queen's servants' company who was called Thomas Greene. After Greene's death in 1612 the widow had remarried a James Baskervile (bigamously on the part of Baskervile, it was alleged) and had become Susan Baskervile. In 1623 'the Queen's servants' no longer existed, only the remnants of the company that had no right to the name of their patron, Queen Anna, after her death in 1619. After the death of James I's wife and queen, these remnants were known as the Revels players, still ostensibly working at the Red Bull, a converted innyard playhouse, while enduring intolerable harassment from the said Susan, who

[1] A good overview of Beeston's life is given in Gurr (2004*d*). Beeston gave his age as about 43 in a 1623 court case (the National Archives (TNA), C24/500/9). Apart from Shakespeare and Beeston, others in Jonson's *Every Man In* included Richard Burbage, Augustine Phillips, John Heminges, Henry Condell, Thomas Pope, William Sly, Will Kempe, and John Duke. See Jonson (1616); Wickham et al. (2000: 194).

[2] *In media res*—as in all epic forms such as Virgil's *Aeneid*. As an introduction to the case, see Sisson (1954). However, Sisson does not use all the deposition evidence available. See also McLuskie and Dunsworth (1997: 435–6), where at that time they did not know Susan Baskervile's share ownership of the Red Bull was pertinent to their puzzles (see also n. 12).

believed she was still owed sums from the company. The *Worth* v. *Baskervile* suit reunited a group of people—on paper at least—in an effort to set a record straight. This record concerned whomsoever had owned any portion of company shares and whomsoever had, therefore, owed money to anybody. The case principally sought to establish precedents concerning their financial arrangements because of the claims of Mrs Baskervile.

Among these one-time friends and fellows was Christopher Beeston. His Jacobean adventures with the Queen's servants found him becoming their leader and manager after the death of Thomas Greene in 1612. Into the period beyond that, he was to be in the vanguard of a new generation of theatrical entrepreneur, heading theatre and company management of his playhouse, the Cockpit. Because of the success of the King's Men and their indoor Blackfriars playhouse after the outdoor Globe, the Queen's servants, apparently through the medium of Beeston, sought and acquired this, the first theatre to be built in the Drury Lane area of London. This was in 1616. The Cockpit had been an old venue for cockfighting that was converted into an indoor arena for drama under the auspices of Beeston. With hindsight, accepted theatre history has decided that this was the way forward. With the evidence of later playhouses such as Salisbury Court and other venues, it seems there was no turning back for playhouse development from this point. The future of formal English performance was to be situated inside, out of the rain, and Beeston was part of the movement towards that future. After all the trouble that he had endured with the Queen's servants at the Red Bull, it seems he lost no time in leaving them behind, somewhat ruthlessly taking their indoor theatre with him—in 1618.

It is interesting to imagine, then, what state of mind Beeston brought to the table, as he found himself before the court secretary who was to record his depositions for the *Worth* v. *Baskervile* case of 1623.[3] Until 1618–19, when he had left the Queen's servants, he had been with that same shifting but nominally secure set of actors for nearly two decades. Since he had left, however, and with the hindsight granted to us by other records, we can see what a roller coaster ride he must have endured in terms of the perceptions and attitudes others had towards him and the reciprocal feelings he must have had for them. Over time he had been accused of many things—some of them, surely, true. Theft and rape are but two accusations levelled that will come up here—accusations that could tell us something about the supposed human properties of our subject as, at the same time, we mark out his more material ones.

The first property we might think about with regard to Christopher Beeston is, perhaps, his name. There is some sense of ambiguity concerning this subject, since he always had two. Sometimes he is down in documents as Christopher Beeston alias Hutchinson (with various spellings of both surnames) and sometimes he is Christopher Hutchinson alias Beeston. Confusing as it is, it is reassuring when we see the other name stated, as it leaves us in little doubt on these occasions that it is our Christopher we are dealing with. Unfortunately, as yet, we do not really know which name he was born with. Robert Beeston was another associate of the Queen's

[3] TNA, C24/500/9 and C24/500/103.

servants who is named among them in both the list for the 1604 coronation procession and the two licence records of *c.*1604 and 1609.[4] Although connections other than company ones can be made between the two men, there is no real evidence that they were related, so Robert Beeston's existence currently yields no help when it comes to Christopher's provenance.[5]

Apart from his motley ownership of a name, then, and his claim to a part in Jonson's *Every Man In*, what else could we say Christopher Beeston 'owned' early on in his career? It would not be too glib to say that he owned, for example, a wife. History (and literature) tells us that matrimony had everything to do with ownership and, indeed, financial matters, and we may entertain the possibility that in Beeston's case this was not different. A Christopher Hutchinson of St Botolph's without Bishopsgate married a Jane Sands of St Leonard, Shoreditch, at St Mildred Poultry on 10 September 1602.[6] In turn, this Jane Sands may have been related to James Sands who, like Beeston, is remembered in Augustine Phillips's will.[7] This was as a 'servant' in Beeston's case and as an 'apprentice' in that of Sands. With regard to Beeston's marriage, what might draw comment here is the timing of it when viewed in the context of other events in Beeston's life. If married in September 1602, it might have seemed something of an inopportune and faintly embarrassing blow when he was accused of raping a woman on 23 June that year.[8]

The documentary evidence is just that: documentary—written in black and white. But facts given by human beings have to be interpreted carefully. Our Christopher Beeston—for it was certainly he as he is specifically described as 'a plaier'—was accused by one Margaret White of having 'had the use of her bodie' at one Winter's house in Star Alley without Bishopsgate. White had been put in the Bridewell for having had a child 'in whordom' by 'Henrye Noone' of Fenchurch Street; however, this difficult situation was clearly taken as an opportunity to talk about another one. Beeston's supposed act with White was not only one of forbidden sexual sin in the eyes of the justices at the Bridewell, listening to the accusation on 27 October that year (fo. 327^{v}), but was also tantamount to modern-day rape, for White was recorded as saying that 'hee did it forciblie'. He had also apparently boasted that he had 'lyen with a hundred wenches' in his time. This was said to be reported by a 'mr Knevett', who was 'sr Henrye Billingesleys clerk' and who later came to the court on 13 November (fo. 332^{r}) denying that he had said any such thing. Earlier, on 5 November and in response to the charge, Beeston utterly denied 'the premisses' explaining that the accusation was 'done of mallice' (fo. 330^{r}). The accusation could well have been spawned of 'malice' if, perhaps, Margaret White had in some way felt aggrieved by the recent Beeston marriage to Jane

4 TNA, LC2/4/5, p. 84; SP14/2/100 (microfilm stamped no. 247); C66/1827, no. 29.

5 Other than the name and their membership of the Queen's servants, what the two have in common is the inference of a shared recusancy, although this has yet to be proved beyond doubt in Christopher's case. Robert Beeston, Robert's wife, Etheldreda or Audrey, and Christopher's wife, Jane, are all accused of not going to church, with some particular trouble for Robert in the ecclesiastical courts in 1617. See TNA, E135/12/7.

6 St Mildred's Poultry marriage registers, Guildhall Library, City of London, MS 4429/1.

7 Augustine Phillips's will, TNA, PROB 11/105, fos 241^{v}–242; Honigmann and Brock (1993: 72–5).

8 Bridewell Court Minute Books, Guildhall Library, MS 33011/4, 1597/8–1604, fos 327^{v}–332^{r}. See also Salkeld (2005: 379–85).

Sands—or wanted to take advantage of it—or simply wanted to draw attention to herself. On the other hand, the young Christopher Beeston, approximately 22 at this time, may have been a very nasty piece of work indeed.

What seems to have lent credence to White's case in the eyes of the justices was the colourful behaviour of Beeston and his friends present at the Bridewell court on 13 November. While there, 'the said Beeston and other his Confederates plaiers did verie vnreverentlie demeane themselues to certen governors and muche abused the place'. Noting reports concerning White's claims and because of the actors' seeming contempt of the court, the justices became quite severe, consent being given that 'suche a course shalbe in lawe proceeded against him as is and shalbe thought fitt for so greate a Cryme'. But it seems there is no record of actual punishment for Christopher Beeston in this instance.

The following summer—during the dreadful plague year of 1603 when Beeston's company, then the Earl of Worcester's Men, lost their clown Will Kempe—King James's official coronation could not take place for fear of the pestilence, and the procession was postponed until 1604. For that occasion Beeston was listed as one of the 'Officers to the Queen', i.e. the new Queen's servants company, along with other fellow ex-Worcester's Men including Thomas Heywood, Robert Leigh, and Robert Pallant, and the list also included their new clown and leader, Thomas Greene.[9] In that year Beeston was included in the draft patent of the company and had also acquired a son, whom he named Augustine, probably after Augustine Phillips.[10] The family were living in Halliwell in the bride's parish, St Leonard, Shoreditch, at the time. While living in Shoreditch, between 1604 and 1610, we know Beeston was possessed of three more children—Christopher, Jane, and Robert.[11] These children, it might be observed, also had the names of significant people in his life—Jane, his then wife, Robert Beeston, his name-sharer and possible relative, and, of course, himself.

Perhaps we could perceive at this point what a great deal of charm Beeston must have possessed. Somehow he had survived a rape accusation, aggravated by bad behaviour—his own as well as his friends'. What with naming a son after a master in his craft and surviving thus far in the cut-and-thrust world of the Elizabethan theatre, charm must have been a property that Christopher Beeston owned. In 1607, indeed, there was further evidence of it when he procured a share of the Red Bull from Thomas Greene. The share he obtained, according to Susan Baskervile in a suit she issued against Beeston in 1632, was an '8TH or 9TH iust p*ar*te' of Greene's half of the tiring house and yard of the Red Bull.[12] Beeston must have been charming for,

9 TNA, LC2/4/5, p. 84.

10 TNA, SP14/2/100 (microfilm stamped no. 247). Augustine Beeston was born in Halliwell, Shoreditch, and was baptized on 16 November; St Leonard, Shoreditch, parish registers, London Metropolitan Archives (LMA), X094/030.

11 LMA, X094/030, Christopher was baptized on 1 December 1605 and Robert on 2 April 1609. Jane Beeston was buried in the parish on 22 September 1607 (LMA, X094/096).

12 TNA, REQ2/709. Details of this record have been given in my SAA 2003 paper 'Sewers, Brewers, Clowns and Houses: The Worcester's Men at the Rose and the Queen's Servants at the Red Bull'; see also Griffith (2004).

as Susan Baskervile described it, he 'intreated and much importuned the saide Thomas Greene to lett him haue a share in the said Playhouse and after many parlies thereabouts at last they fell to a full conclusion concerning the same'. This took place in about August 1607.

From this year onwards, therefore, Beeston was in possession of profits from his share of the Red Bull, and this would have been so probably until Christmas 1633. This was when the original agreement made between Greene and Aaron Holland concerning Greene's half of the tiring house and yard came to an end. It would seem, however, that Beeston's property-owning ventures did not only include the Red Bull, for in 1611 he is also recorded as owning a 'parcel of pasture ground' adjacent to the Curtain theatre. Three rods and 10 perches in size, the records state that it adjoined the Curtain estate on two sides.[13] The Curtain playhouse—erected on part of this estate in 1577—was one of three theatres that the Queen's servants were allowed to use in their draft patent of 1604. In the same document of 1611, Thomas Greene is cited as holding or occupying this playhouse 'built of Timber & thatched now in decay called the Curtaine with a p*ar*cell of grounds adioyning thereto wherein they use to keepe stage playes'. Despite the decay, it is perfectly possible that performances were still given there under the auspices of the Queen's servants at this time. This is not only because of the present-tense verb 'use' employed in the manuscript but because it was still being mentioned, along with the Red Bull, in the formal licence of 1609. If it was a licensed venue in 1609, there is no reason to suspect disuse by the company two years later. Moreover, we know it was still being used as a venue in the 1620s from various Revels Office records.[14] By 1611, however, Beeston and his family had moved from Shoreditch to Clerkenwell, nearer his other property investment at the Red Bull.[15] He moved there just in time to take over Thomas Greene's management of the company in 1612, when Greene died.

With the foregoing in mind, it would seem that from 1612 onwards—with a particular hiatus at 1616–17—things became very busy for Christopher Beeston if documents about his property and characteristic 'properties' are anything to go by. Now leader of the Queen's servants' company, Beeston's leadership—on available evidence, at least—was stamped with all too human properties. Beeston was undoubtedly a sharer in company profits as well as those derived from his share of the Red Bull's tiring house and yard, and the players were seemingly under the impression that he was at the helm concerning all their monetary interests. In a case of 1619 concerning an aggrieved salesman called John Smith, the actors recorded their agreement that, for the best organization during their time together, they required 'Divers officers' among them.[16] All of the actors were expected to 'take vpon them some place and charge', but for the 'prouision of the furniture and apparrell' they

[13] TNA, C54/2075/17; Wickham et al. (2000: 405–6 n. 4).

[14] My transcription of the 1611 document queries the change to the past tense given in Wickham et al. (2000: 416) as 'use[d] to keep stage plays'. See pp. 416–18 for records concerning continued use.

[15] Anne Beeston was baptized there on 15 September 1611 and Elizabeth Morier, Beeston's servant, was buried in Clerkenwell in 1615. See Hovenden (1884–94: i. 62 and iv. 131).

[16] *Smith* v. *Beeston*, Court of Requests Proceedings, Uncalendared, James I [1619]; Wallace (1909*b*: 321).

needed 'a thriueing man & one that was of abilitie & meanes'. That man, so they thought, could be Beeston, who would 'Defaulke outt of the colleccions and gatheringes wch were made continually whensoeuer any playe was acted a certen some of money as a comon stock towardes the buyeing and Defraying of the charges of the furniture & apparrell aforesaid' (Wallace 1909*b*: 321). They were clear about the role Beeston had been assigned, describing at some length how nobody else 'should be troubled or ymployed in this busines' but him, how he should only use what was needed, '& if there did fall outt any surplusage or remainder of the Com*m*on stocke & money soe by him to be gathered, that then the said Beeston should give a true accompt vnto the company & that every one of them should haue a share & part according to there place & qualitie' (Wallace 1909*b*: 322). Beeston, however, hotly denied that he had ever accepted this role, exclaiming in reply that 'sometymes one, and sometymes another of the said Company Did provide Clothes and other necessaries for the settinge forth of the actors of that Company' (Wallace 1909*b*: 326).

This case of 1619 harked back to events that took place in June 1612. It was from the 27th of that month, according to the Fishmonger John Smith who was a supplier of goods to the company, that Christopher Beeston, Richard Perkins, Ellis Worth, and John Cumber failed to pay him for goods supplied. The value of these goods by 1619 was the princely sum of £46 5*s.* 8*d.* Beeston admitted that he had used Smith as a supplier for the needs of his children, but denied that he had ever had any dealings with him on behalf of the company. Where we have to take care when viewing the human properties of Christopher Beeston here is that in 1619 the company may well have regarded Beeston with particular disdain and therefore may have wanted to see him in a bad light. The year 1619 is too close to the time after the Cockpit disaster of 1617, which ended with Beeston leaving the company along with their supposed indoor playhouse to pursue his entrepreneurial ambitions alone. Some of the actors' views on this, as we shall see, ostensibly developed or changed over time. The events leading up to what I have marked out as a 'hiatus' around 1616–17, ending in his departure, have to be explained, and this narrative involves seeing Beeston in yet another light with regard to his property. The human properties evident here could be said to be much akin to those necessary for a man capable of outraging the court at the Bridewell. Extraordinarily 'brave' might be one of the terms we could use to describe Beeston with reference to these records; insanely 'foolhardy' might be another.

The year 1616 began well for Christopher Beeston, at least in the parochial, local sense. For—somewhat unexpectedly—he appears in parish vestry records. This was when, along with Aaron Holland, he was chosen to be a collector for the poor of the parish of St James's, Clerkenwell, at a meeting on 2 April 1616.[17] According to my research he was never noted as present either before or after this appointment—but that does not mean he was not present. In earlier 'March Anno do*m*ini 1616'

[17] St James's, Clerkenwell, Parish Vestry Minutes, 1590–1683, Islington Local History Centre, St John Street. Aaron Holland is mentioned or sets his name to the meeting thirteen times, Robert Leigh, six times, Thomas Greene, once—in a period from 1604 to 1629. Both Holland and Leigh are made collectors for the poor and churchwardens; Robert Leigh is also collector for the preacher in 1622.

i.e. March 1617—he is party to two apprenticeships with Holland named as collectors for the poor, both consenting on behalf of the parish that Alexander Jones and William Grace should be apprenticed (as a cook and cordwainer respectively).[18]

In a completely different vein, on 9 August 1616, Beeston acquired a sub-lease from John Best on the property that came to be the Cockpit playhouse, or, as described at the time, 'All that edifices or building called the Cockpitts and the Cock houses | and shedds thereunto adioyning'.[19] The lease was for thirty-one years with the rent at £45 per year, and the job of converting it must have started very soon after the paperwork had been completed. We know this because, in the first week of September, Beeston was already getting into trouble for the foundation work that had begun.[20] Records exist in the Middlesex Sessions that condemn this work because it was undertaken 'contrary to the law and his Majesty's proclamations'. Despite his parish commitment made earlier in the year, at the beginning of October he and the other Red Bull players stood accused at the Middlesex Sessions of not looking after the highways properly, thereby incurring a tax of 40*s*. a year 'by theire owne consentes'.[21] More trouble came for Beeston on 15 October when the benchers of Lincoln's Inn and other members of the Inns of Court decided to make a complaint to the Queen's Council concerning the building of the new Cockpit playhouse so close to their workplace.[22] As Herbert Berry points out, the fact that the benchers went to Queen Anna's Council instead of the Privy Council would seem to indicate that they expected the Queen's players to be performing there (Wickham et al. 2000: 627).

The Cockpit, however, was not the only property development work that Beeston was undertaking at this time. His interests were still actively exercised north of the city walls.

On 18 September 1616, the Privy Council sent a letter to the High Sheriff of Middlesex concerning the breaking of building regulations (Dasent et al. 1890–1964: xxxv. 14–15; Bentley 1941–68: ii. 366). In it Beeston is called one of 'such persons as are greate offenders in building'; however, it is not the building of the Cockpit that is alluded to with reference to Beeston but the erection of 'a base tenement, not of bricke' in Clerkenwell. Formerly, it would seem, Beeston had been forbidden to begin this work without promising to make it 'only an addition to his owne dwelling howse'. Instead of this he had 'made a tenement of it, distant from his howse, and neere to his Majesty's passage'. The note appended to this extract in the *Acts of the Privy Council* directs action, that is: 'To be pulled downe'. A month later, on 7 October, a few days after the company agreed to the 40*s*. highways fine, William and John Gore, late sheriffs, reported to the Privy Council that this building had

[18] LMA, P76/JS1/127/10 and P76/JS1/127/11. The two masters involved were John Udall, the cook, and a [?] Dawkins, cordwainer.

[19] TNA, C2/CHASI/H28/26. *Thomas Hussey* v. *Robert Rolleston, Sir Lewis Kirke and Dame Elizabeth Kirke*. See Hotson (1928: 89). The lease was to begin on 29 September that year.

[20] Le Hardy (1935–41: iii. 310–11); Bentley (1941–68: ii. 365).

[21] At a sessions heard on 3 and 4 October; le Hardy (1935–41: iv. 37).

[22] Lincoln's Inn Black Books, 6, fo. 628; Baildon (1897–2001: ii. 186).

indeed been 'for the moste parte' pulled down 'not to be inhabited' (Dasent et al. 1890–1964: xxxv. 36; Bentley 1941–68: ii. 366). However, it would seem that such Beeston behaviour, dangerous to begin with, only got much, much worse. On 29 September 1617—that is, nearly a year later—the Privy Council again wrote to the High Sheriff of Middlesex. This was to complain that the offending building that had been rightly 'pulled downe and demolished' had been 'since... buylt up agayne' and 'his Majesty of late passing that way hath taken speciall notice thereof, being highly offended with the presumption' (Dasent et al. 1890–1964: xxxv. 334; Bentley 1941–68: ii. 366–7).

Which of the King's highways that was adjacent to Clerkenwell was the one which the monarch travelled down, one wonders—somewhat incredulously—as one contemplates the gall of Christopher Beeston? And what was the purpose of the offending 'tenement' that Beeston was so desperate to build? He must have been desperate, surely, if he was prepared to go so flagrantly against previous legal orders in the teeth of the King's proclamations against the encroachment of substandard building. Or perhaps he was not desperate—perhaps despair was never one of Beeston's properties—perhaps disregard of order was his way. But his motivation must have been in some way measured as again no record exists of any punishment. We could speculate that 'his Majesty's passage' near Clerkenwell is likely to have been St John's Street, as it was the highway off which the Red Bull playhouse was located. We could further guess that the tenement could have had something to do with the playhouse (a taphouse, prop room, office—what?)—but this would all be pure speculation as yet. And, according to the aforementioned records, Beeston claimed the tenement was to be an addition to his own 'dwelling howse', not a playhouse. Of course, we will never know the full facts concerning anything about Beeston, as we will never know the full facts about anyone whose complete records and contexts are lost. However, the sheer courage of someone who is willing—on the documents we have of him—to take such risks in his business dealings can only leave us acutely aware of the kind of personality who can survive and indeed overcome obstacles at some supposed cost.

Early in 1617—during that same year when Beeston re-erected his tenement in Clerkenwell—the Queen's servants moved into the Cockpit near Drury Lane (it was off Drury Lane—between Wild Street and Drury Lane, in fact). Unfortunately, they did this only to be forced back to the Red Bull for a time because of the infamous Shrovetide riots on 4 March. Edward Sherbourne described the effect of the riots on the Cockpit in an account of 8 March. The apprentices involved

> besett the house round, broke in, wounded divers of the players, broke open their trunckes, & whatt apparell, bookes, or other things they found, they burnt & cutt in peeces; & not content herewith, gott on the top of the house, & untiled it, & had not the Justices of Peace & Sherife levied an aide & hindred their purpose, they would have laid that house likewise even with the grownd. (Bentley 1941–68: ii. 54; Gurr 1992*b*: 14)

Beeston had to find the money to rebuild the theatre, while the Queen's servants made the best of it that they could back in the Clerkenwell inn-yard playhouse.

At this time, it should be remembered, Beeston and the company owed growing sums of money to John Smith. They were also in the throes of difficulties to do with the demands of Susan and the bigamous James Baskervile, wanting their pound of flesh. And, to top it all, they were still being harassed by the Middlesex authorities for charges on highway repairs.[23] These are only three of many difficulties that faced the company while Beeston was in charge. Moreover, and to add salt to many personal wounds for this one man—on sessions held over 2 and 3 October 1617—Beeston was threatened with being outlawed (le Hardy 1935–41: iv. 273). From this published record edited by William le Hardy where the preface draws attention to a whole group of people facing this possibility at this time, the assumption is made that it is recusancy that is the cause of their difficulties.[24] We know that both Christopher's wife, Jane, Robert Beeston, and Robert Beeston's wife, Etheldreda or Audrey, all have recusancy difficulties at other times, but not Christopher in any other known record. However, this particular entry in the *Middlesex Sessions Records* is noted as 'subscribed', referring to a previous record of April 1612. This year of 1612 is understood to be one when there was a crackdown on recusants at the time when Princess Elizabeth married the Elector Palatine, so it is possible that the list of names, including Beeston's, alludes to unrepentant Catholics. However, his name does not occur on the later Process Register of Indictments book—where his wife's name does occur—so a mystery continues. Whatever the truth of the matter, we now have to try and admit the possibility—as well as everything else—that Beeston was, quite possibly, a Catholic and a somewhat recalcitrant one at that: a man of religious principle. And we also have to take it in that, historically speaking, the period around 1617 must have been an extraordinary one for him, his family, and his nominated company. The pressure on all concerned at this time—the would-be entrepreneur and his one-time friends and fellows among the Queen's servants included—must have been intolerable.

Considering all this then, perhaps it should come as no surprise when we contemplate what happened next. According to John King, a hired man with the company, the Queen's servants began to break up in about 1617, with Beeston taking their things (Wallace 1909*b*: 334; Bentley 1941–68: ii. 367). These he either used himself or 'disposed of them to other Companyes at his pleasure'. According to Beeston's evidence in the *Worth* v. *Baskervile* case, he had separated from the company by Christmas 1618. The resentment among the players is tangible in the records of the 1619 Smith case claiming that, while he had been in charge of the company, he had 'Deducted & Defaulked divers greate somes of money outt of the collecc*i*ons & gatherings... & hath w*i*th the said moneyes much enritched himself as these Defen-d*en*tes conceaue'. Considering the period with hindsight, the actors accused Beeston of embezzlement, citing an instance where he gave them what they now thought was 'a false accompte of fower hundred poundes' (Wallace 1909*b*: 322). Looking back,

[23] See e.g. Jeaffreson (1972: ii. 170), a 1620 record where reference is made to a 1617 sessions; le Hardy (1935–41: iv. 285), the sessions record of 1617.

[24] Le Hardy (1935–41, vol. iv, p. viii). The preface to this volume makes observations on a number of issues relating to Christopher Beeston.

they must have reflected on their over-trusting natures when Beeston described how all that money had been used, and their foolhardiness in not insisting on proof that what he had said was true. Moreover, although they did not state this, £400 was enough to embark upon a theatre conversion project, which was, in effect, what Beeston did. The funding of a playhouse such as the Cockpit, without the assumed need for remuneration through share division, seems as suspicious to us today as it must have seemed to Beeston's fellow actors.

Despite all this, however, and as suggested earlier, evidence exists that angry attitudes towards Beeston changed. After all, because of his continued share of the profits in the Red Bull building, it was surely in his best interests to retain an associative concern in the company's success at that venue. He was also now a major player in entrepreneurial developments in London's theatre world, which was something any actor would be forced to consider. In other words, because of his property and his remarkable human properties, he was a force to be reckoned with. And it would have been advisable for the actors to stay amicable with him.

Records after 1619 inform us of the confused feelings current among the company when it came to Christopher Beeston. In the 1623 *Worth* v. *Baskervile* case, for instance, Thomas Heywood was to depose about the company's 'Trust and Confidence in the s*ai*d Hutchinson al*ia*s Beeston, for & concerning the Managing of their Affayres, he hauing a kynde of powerfull Com*m*aunde over the now compl*ainan*tes & their s*ai*d then fellow actors'. What was deleted from his evidence concerned their continued and confirmed trust in him 'three yeares togither ^or thereabouts^ w*i*th their moneys... w*i*thout any accompt therof by him made unto the now compl*ai-nan*tes or Company to this dep*onen*tes knowledge'.[25] The reason this evidence was deleted was, perhaps, as a result of Beeston's continued power in the company and in the playhouse world at large. He had also, after all, been a trusted friend for some time. It is, moreover, interesting to note how Robert Leigh, oldest at 54 among the chiefest of them, had significantly left the company during Beeston's leadership of it. When giving evidence during the *Worth* v. *Baskervile* case, he felt no compunction about criticizing Beeston, accusing him of helping himself to the players' gallery money without accounting for it properly, and stating this without deleting a word.[26] Yet the growing tide of inter-company support for Beeston is evident from yet another case emerging in 1633 which concerned Beeston's crucial period with the company in 1617.

This case involved a haberdasher called Richard Holden, who took Beeston, Richard Perkins, and Ellis Worth to court over the sale of some hats.[27] These they promised to pay for 'by the handes of Mr Houker then paymaster under the then right honourable the then Lord Carew'—otherwise known as Sir George Carew, Baron of Clopton, Queen Anna's Vice-Chamberlain and Receiver General. He was in charge of the Queen's revenues and was therefore the person who could be a channel for company funds if the Queen's court so desired. Unfortunately, according to

[25] TNA, C24/500/9, int. 33. [26] Ibid., Leigh's answer. [27] TNA, REQ2/655, pt 2.

Holden, the money did not come, and when these and other debts could not be paid, he had the misfortune to be thrown into Ludgate Prison, where he stayed 'a long tyme'. It is from this point that Holden's fate takes on the alarming timbre of a Red Bull play as he describes it in his own words:

> p*re*sentlie after his deliuerie yo*ur* said subiect went into the parte*s* beyond the Seas hoping to recouer his owne debte*s* from such of his debtors as were fledd thither and from thence yo*ur* saide Subiect is but latelie returned, In w*hi*ch long continewance of tyme all the witnesss w*hi*ch should proue the sale of the said hatte*s* are dead and departed this life w*hi*ch the said Christopher Beeston Ellis Worth and Richard Perkins well knowing doe nowe utterlie deny and refuse to giue yo*ur* said subiect anie satisfacc*i*on for the said hatte*s* Contrary to all right Equitie and good Conscience.

The actors, in combination, were able to fudge the issue by invoking a new statute designed to make it hard for suits to be brought a long time after the event. They denied knowledge of the sale and took Holden's bill apart as a faulty piece of legal work, not specifying times and periods in the way that it should. Significantly, what the actors did not do during this suit was deny that they had been working together as a group including Beeston or deny that they had been procuring things together at the time as in the Smith case. This does not mean that Beeston, as the first person named in the suit to be seen as responsible for the payment, was not the primary player of the company who was held liable for such payments; however, it may indicate how attitudes towards Beeston could have changed in the interim since his departure.

According to Beeston, he left the company around 1618. Prior to that time, and just before the death of the company's patron, Queen Anna, in 1619, disaster seemed to befall the actors, much of it through—or allegedly through—the medium of Christopher Beeston. However, it seems—as it seems with so much else to do with this man in terms of his property and his properties—that there were many mitigating circumstances when it came to his doubtful behaviour. The rape was not a rape at all while it was only an accusation of a rape, and, as with his other misdemeanours, there is no record of real punishment for the crime if he was adjudged guilty. Did he steal from the company, keeping the money owing to suppliers as the company seemed to imply? Perhaps; and if he did, it was a dreadful thing to do. But what other options did he have in the context of massive building costs and further rebuilding outlay? If he did not steal from them, it seems he had other property to draw from—the land he leased in Shoreditch by the Curtain, for example, and the profits from his shares in the Red Bull itself—to pay for things he needed at the Cockpit.[28] Of course, he was a human being ultimately motivated only in favour of himself, and he probably benefited from his sometimes questionable ventures. But, in the case of the Cockpit, if there was no financial or legal incentive to buy actors into a theatre he was managing quite independently, then there was surely no incentive to feel guilty about not doing so.

[28] Other Middlesex records concerning people who stole from Beeston would seem to suggest that he was a 'thriving man', as the actors said. See e.g. le Hardy (1935–41: iv. 108, 306, 309).

On another level I would venture that there was much that Christopher Beeston seemed to do in the succeeding era that could be said to have assisted companies or groups of actors within companies. One way of interpreting what happened after his taking over of the Cockpit/Phoenix is that he shuffled people, moving companies and actors around the theatres to which he had some form of access. For example, tradition backed up with evidence has it that by 1619 the Prince's Men, to whom Beeston became affiliated after his association with the Queen's servants, were at the Cockpit/Phoenix after the Queen's company had been ejected back to the Red Bull. Subsequently, the Prince's Men were ejected in 1622 for the Lady Elizabeth's and so forth. But the playhouses these companies went to after leaving the Cockpit/Phoenix were always Beeston-associated playhouses, specifically the Red Bull and the Curtain.[29] According to the Master of the Revels' records of 1623 and with reference to the Red Bull, while Beeston still owned shares in the playhouse, at least three companies were performing there within a two-month period: the Prince's Men, the Lady Elizabeth's, and a company of 'Strangers' (Bawcutt 1996: 141–7). This phenomenon may have had something to do with the legal difficulties of the Revels players at war with Susan Baskervile at that time. Companies other than the original group performing at the Red Bull would not necessarily have had to pay Susan Baskervile's due. Either way, Christopher Beeston would still have been receiving something from their performances.[30]

Because of the profits we now know Beeston derived from the Red Bull, companies' movements from the Cockpit/Phoenix to Clerkenwell can no longer be interpreted as a simple demotion and/or rejection, as he clearly still hoped he would profit from them while in Clerkenwell. It no doubt was a demotion of a kind, but not of a simple kind. Moreover, there were times when the joins between and around companies in association with their playhouses seem to blur and confuse and crowd into one another in a way that may have been helpful for their survival. It is not enough to say that these companies, as entire entities, simply slotted into a playhouse vacuum as we have tried to see the situation in the past. The picture is yet more complicated. According to Thomas Basse, a Queen's servants/Revels players member, new players who had actually been drafted in as Red Bull/Revels players members since 1617 included William Rowley, John Newton, Thomas Hobbs, 'Hamlett' (probably Robert Hamlen), Mathew Smith, Anthony Smith, and Richard Baxter.[31] Five of these are from a list of actors representing a kind of cooperation or amalgamation between the Prince's and the Lady Elizabeth's Men, which G. E. Bentley wrote about in his two volumes of *The Jacobean and Caroline*

29 For this, see e.g. Wickham et al. (2000: 416–18) on the Prince's Men in particular at the 1620s Curtain, and pp. 580, 582, 584 for the Red Bull. For the Prince's Men's visit to the Red Bull during 1616–17, when the Queen's servants were at the Cockpit before the riot, Bentley suggests that Alleyn may have helped them into the Red Bull; Bentley (1941–68: i. 201–2).

30 The different monetary agreements that Susan Baskervile and her family came to with the company are many, varied, and complex. They are not covered comprehensively in Sisson (1954), nor can they be covered properly here. I give detailed accounts of these in my forthcoming book on the Queen's servants at the Red Bull.

31 TNA, C24/500/9, int. 40.

Stage (Bentley 1941–68: i. 176, 198–217; ii. 360, 459; Gurr 1992*b*: 58–60). The other two actors who were not of this grouping were Richard Baxter, who had been a hired man at the Red Bull since 1609, and Mathew Smith, about whom not much is known before this time.

In a sense, then, and in a way we should continue to contemplate, Christopher Beeston seemed to 'own' a positive share not only in the Red Bull playhouse, but in the destiny of many players who found themselves there. Speculatively speaking, we could say that, instead of seeing open-air playhouses as the blight of the past, for a time at least, Beeston may have seen them as useful spaces for company employment, development, and profit. His actions could not have been altogether as unhelpful towards the actors as has once been supposed. Feelings in 1623 must have seemed complicated towards him but, ultimately, not irredeemable, as he came forward to give his evidence in the *Worth* v. *Baskervile* suit. When Susan Baskervile took him to court in 1632 because of his non-payment of what was her due from the playhouse share her husband gave him, she observed that since 1627 he had held something against her that she could not discern. This she adjudged to be the reason for the problem. Perhaps by this time Beeston was friendly enough with the actors to see their point of view concerning Susan. Sixteen thirty-two was the year before Aaron Holland's original lease arrangement with Susan and Thomas Greene on half the tiring house and yard of the Red Bull was due to end. It therefore marked the year when Beeston's interests in the playhouse might well be affected too and could therefore further explain his indifference to paying the landlady. As a final set of thoughts, and with a flourish to yet further new material on Christopher Beeston's property and properties, we can observe that, whatever happened to his relationship with the Red Bull after 1633 when he no longer had a share in it, evidence exists that he did not give up on inn-yard ventures at this time. This evidence takes us back to Shoreditch, the area north of the city walls that had seen the first purpose-built open-air theatres (the Curtain included). With it we also return to the parish of Beeston's wife, Jane, the place where his family had first lived.

In Beeston's will, apart from his shares in the Cockpit left to his wife and something of his shares in his then company left to his wife and son, mention is also made of some property in Shoreditch that was to be left to his son William alone.[32] Of course, the assumption has been that this property should refer to his Curtain estate land which we know he held in 1611. On 7 July 1635, however, an indenture was made that was recorded in the Close Rolls of the time that described an agreement Beeston made with one Samuel Sandys concerning an inn in Shoreditch. The inn was 'knowne by the name and signe of the kinge*s* head' in St Leonard's parish and consisted of 'Two partes in three parte*s* already devided of and in one mesuage' that the King's Head represented. The two parts of three came with tenements and cottages, as well as

[32] TNA, PROB 11/178, fos 450v–451; Hotson (1928: 398–400); Honigmann and Brock (1993: 191–4).

all buildinges stables gardens yardes backsides easementes waies lightes and comodities whatsoeuer thereunto belonging or therewith all used enioyed or reputed as parcell thereof And also one ancient passage or entrie from the streete and the next Court yard with the well and the yard beyond the well called the stable yard and the Shedd of boardes in the same stable yard which last mencioned premisses are yet undevided.[33]

Perhaps we should first note the possibility that Samuel 'Sandys' who was in possession of the King's Head inn, Shoreditch, might actually have been related to Jane Beeston, neé 'Sands', of Shoreditch. This is an area that needs further investigation. Secondly, we should simply wonder at Beeston's timing and motivation; for after possibly having to relinquish his rights over the Red Bull in 1633, by 1635 he was in possession of his own inn-type property, with a 'Court yard' and a 'stable yard' included.

Perhaps, with this inn-yard property in Shoreditch, Beeston wanted to stable horses. This might have been lucrative. Perhaps he wanted to invest in housing or in a catering business. With reference to this last idea, Beeston's last wife, Elizabeth, seems to have invested in a lease of one 'George tavern' adjacent to the Cockpit. This tavern could have proved useful for pre- and post-theatre drinking, and may denote a family interest in owning catering establishments near to playhouses that they held.[34]

Or perhaps, with reference to the King's Head, Christopher Beeston wanted to build another inn-yard playhouse. This last idea, however, would counter accepted thought about privileging indoor playhouse development over outdoor at this time. That current privileging certainly does not mean we should altogether discount the possibility, however.

There is still so much more to be said about Christopher Beeston—and I know that there have been moves, suggestions, PhDs, biographies in the offing and in the past that have set out to tackle him. In this essay I have tried to produce something of a survey of the material properties of Beeston, both those honestly and those doubtfully acquired, interrogating, to some extent, how his relationship with the actors that he managed has been seen in the past. Perhaps conclusions concerning Beeston's human properties are of more interest as an exercise, however. Ruthless, charming, courageous, foolhardy, desperate, trusted, doubtful, dreadful, a possible 'man of religious principle' and—even—'a very nasty piece of work indeed' are all ways I have found to describe Christopher Beeston here. If any one of these terms were true, it must lead one to suggest that Beeston has to be—at least—one of the most fascinating people that early modern theatre history can offer.[35] Writing about him is a continual negotiation with the available data, however, and with the very temptation to characterize or judge another human being or human beings at all.

[33] TNA, C54/3060, m. 3. The King's Head property is mentioned in William Beeston's will as the estate out of which his son Sackfeild could be paid £7 per annum. Guildhall Library, MS 905/23; TNA, PROB ACL, 7 Sept. 1682; see Honigmann and Brock (1993: 219–21).

[34] TNA, C2/CHASI/H28/26.

[35] So full of life, even when, dividing his company shares in his will of 1638, Beeston wanted to live on, leaving half to the company and half to his wife so that he would be represented after he died 'as fully and amply as if I lived amongst them'.

No, you cannot assess a man by his property or his properties—certainly not those learned about from scraps of documentary evidence. Falling short of a biblical reference, judging is a very foolish thing to do, and this seems especially so with theatre history, particularly early theatre history. The data itself is all too human and frail. Mediated much of the time by early modern scribes and legal clerks under pressure to transcribe the words of other people under pressure, they can give us, at best, shadows, impressions of views once held, and emotions once felt. People in any age say and do whatever seems best for them at the time. People lie and—worse—the pages get torn and lost. Then theatre historians and biographers interpret what is left. And they are frail too. Tragic, eh?

And that is theatre history.

Bibliography

Primary Sources

Manuscripts

Bodleian Library, Oxford

Part for Secundus Miles, Bodleian Library MS, Ashmole 750.
Second Northumberland Household Book, Bodleian Library MS Eng. hist. b. 208.

Christ Church, Oxford

MSS 439, 984–8.

Corporation of London Records Office, London

(Corporation of London MSS temporarily held at the London Metropolitan Archives, London)
Journals: 8 (1470–82), COL/CC/01/01/008; 15 (1543–8), COL/CC/01/01/015; 22 (1580–5), COL/CC/01/01/022; 24 (1591–5), COL/CC/01/01/024; 26 (1602–5), COL/CC/01/01/027; 28 (1605–9), COL/CC/01/01/028.
Letter Books: H (1375–99), COL/AD/01/008; L (1461–97), COL/AD/01/011; N (1515–26), COL/AD/01/013; P (1532–40), COL/AD/01/015.
Repertories: 1 (1495–1504), COL/CA/01/01/001; 10 (1537–43), COL/CA/01/01/010.

Drapers' Hall, London

Drapers' Company Wardens' Accounts 1475–1510, MS + 403.

Dulwich College Library, London

Henslowe Papers, MS I, art. 106.
Dulwich, Mun. 58.

Goldsmiths' Hall, London

Goldsmiths' Company Wardens' Accounts and Minutes 1334–1443, MS 1518.

Houghton Library, Cambridge, Massachusetts

Book of parts belonging to Macklin, Harvard Theatre Collection MS, TS 1197 54.5.
Parts of Poore, Polypragmaticus, Amurath, Antoninus, Harvard Theatre Collection MS, Thr. 10.1.
Part for Trico, Houghton Library MS Eng. 1258 (5).

Huntington Library, San Marino, California

William Percy, *Poems*, MS HM 4.

London Metropolitan Archives, London

(*See also* Corporation of London Records Office)

J. Hancock and G. Archer (1635), Final Report of the Churchwardens and Constables of the Parish of St Saviour for the Commissioners for Buildings, P92/SAV/1327.

Mercers' Hall, London

Mercers' Company MSS Acts of Court 1 (1453–1528).

The National Archives, London

PROB 11/54/140, PROB 11/55/218, PROB 11/74/199, PROB 11/99/269, PROB 11/129/369.

Saffron Walden Town Hall

Chamberlains' Accounts.

Printed Texts

Texts of plays, poems, etc. are listed by author, not by editor. Collections of early documents, including Records of Early English Drama (REED) volumes, Malone Society Collections, Calendars of State Papers, maps, and corporation and institutional documents, are listed by editor and date. Co-authored or co-edited items are listed after items published individually by the first-named author or editor.

Anon. (1909), *The Second Maiden's Tragedy*, ed. W. W. Greg (Oxford: Malone Society).

—— (1936), *The Soddered Citizen* (*c.*1630), ed. J. H. Pafford (Oxford: Malone Society).

—— (1949), *The Three Parnassus Plays*, ed. J. B. Leishman (London: Ivor Nicholson and Watson).

—— (1959 [1958]), *The Lady Mother* [by Henry Glapthorne?] (1635), ed. Arthur Brown (Oxford: Malone Society).

—— (1960), *The Telltale* (1630s?), ed. R. A. Foakes and J. C. Gibson (Oxford: Malone Society).

—— (1990), *The Receyt of the Ladie Kateryne*, ed. G. Kipling (Oxford: Early English Text Society).

—— (1992), *Tom a Lincoln*, ed. G. R. Proudfoot (Oxford: Malone Society).

Baildon, W. P. (ed.) (1897–2001), *Records of the Honorable Society of Lincoln's Inn: The Black Books*, 6 vols (vols i–v ed. Baildon) (London: Lincoln's Inn).

Baldwin, Elizabeth, Lawrence M. Clopper, and David Mills (eds) (2007), *Records of Early English Drama: Cheshire*, 2 vols (Toronto: University of Toronto Press).

Bale, R. (1911), 'Robert Bale's Chronicle' (15th-century), in R. Flenley (ed.), *Six Town Chronicles of England* (Oxford: Clarendon Press), 114–53.

Bandello, Matteo (1890), *The Novels of Matteo Bandello Englished by John Payne*, 6 vols (London: Villon Society).

Barnes, Barnabe (1607), *The Divils Charter* (London).

—— (1913), *The Devil's Charter*, ed. John S. Farmer (Amersham: Tudor Facsimile Texts).

Bawcutt, N. W. (ed.) (1993), *Malone Society Collections*, xv (Oxford: Malone Society).

Beard, Thomas (1597), *The Theater of Gods Judgements* (London).

Beaumont, Francis, John Fletcher (1905–12), *The Works of Francis Beaumont and John Fletcher*, ed. Arnold Glover and A. R. Waller, 10 vols (Cambridge: Cambridge University Press).

—— —— et al. (1647), *Comedies and Tragedies Written by Francis Beaumont and John Fletcher Gentlemen* (London).

Bevington, David (ed.) (2002), *English Renaissance Drama: A Norton Anthology* (New York: W. W. Norton).

Birck, Sixt (1938), *Sapientia Solomonis*, ed. and trans. Elizabeth Rogers Payne (New Haven: Yale University Press).

Blount, Thomas (1656), *Glossographia* (London).

Brathwait, Richard (1634), *A Strange Metamorphosis of Man, Transformed into a Wildernesse* (London).

Brewer, J. S., J. Gairdner, and R. H. Brodie (eds) (1862–1914), *Letters and Papers, Foreign and Domestic, of the Reign of Henry VIII, 1509–47*, 21 vols in 33 (London); *Addenda*, ed. R. H. Brodie (1929–32), 1 vol. in 2 pts (London).

—— —— —— (1965), *Letters and Papers, Foreign and Domestic, of the Reign of Henry VIII*, and *Addenda*, 2nd edn, 21 vols in 37 (1920–32; London: HMSO).

Brinsley, Joseph (1612), *Ludus Literarius, or, The Grammar School* (London).

Brome, Richard (1632), *The Northern Lasse* (London).

—— (1640), *The Antipodes: A Comedy* (London).

—— (1653), *Five New Playes* (London).

—— (1873), *The Dramatic Works of Richard Brome*, ed. R. H. Shepherd, 3 vols (London).

Brown, R., et al. (eds) (1864–1947), *Calendar of State Papers and Manuscripts Relating to English Affairs, Existing in the Archives of Collections of Venice and in Other Libraries of North Italy*, 38 vols (London: Historical Manuscripts Commission).

Callon, Gordon J. (ed.) (2002), *William Lawes: Collected Vocal Music*, pt 1: *Solo Songs*, pt 2: *Dialogues, Partsongs, and Catches* (Middleton, WI: A–R Editions).

Carew, T. (1949), *The Poems of Thomas Carew with his Masque 'Coelum Britannicum'*, ed. R. Dunlap (Oxford: Clarendon Press).

Carleton, D. (1972), *Dudley Carleton to John Chamberlain 1603–1624: Jacobean Letters*, ed. M. Lee, Jr. (New Brunswick, NJ: Rutgers University Press).

Cavendish, William (1999), *The Country Captain*, ed. Anthony Johnson (Oxford: Malone Society).

Centlivre, S. (1714), *The Wonder* (London).

Chamberlain, John. *See* McClure, Norman E.

Chambers, E. K. (1907), 'The Elizabethan Lords Chamberlain', in *Malone Society Collections*, i/1. 31–42.

—— (ed.) (1911), 'Commissions for the Chapel', in *Malone Society Collections*, i/4–5. 357–63.

—— (ed.) (1931), 'Dramatic Records of the City of London: The Repertories, Journals, and Letter Books', in *Malone Society Collections*, ii/3. 285–320.

—— and W. W. Greg (1907), 'Dramatic Records of the City of London: The Remembrancia', in *Malone Society Collections*, i/1. 43–100.

—— —— (1908), 'Dramatic Records from the Lansdowne Manuscripts', in *Malone Society Collections*, i/2. 143–215.

—— —— (1909), 'Dramatic Records from the Patent Rolls: Company Licences', in *Malone Society Collections*, i/3. 260–84.

—— —— (1911), 'Dramatic Records from the Privy Council Register, 1603–1642', in *Malone Society Collections*, i/4–5. 370–95.

Chapman, George (1611), *May-Day* (London).

—— (1970), *The Plays of George Chapman: The Comedies*, ed. Allan Holaday et al. (Urbana: University of Illinois Press).

Cicero, Marcus Tullius (1948), *De Oratore*, trans. E. W. Sutton (Cambridge, MA: Harvard University Press).

Clavell, J. (1936), *The Soddered Citizen* (*c.*1630), ed. J. H. P. Pafford and W. W. Greg (Oxford: Oxford University Press).

C[leaver], R. [and J. Dod] (1598), *A Godlie Forme of Householde Gouernment for the Ordering of Priuate Families, According to the Direction of Gods Word* (London).

Colvin, H. M. (ed.) (1963–82), *The History of the King's Works*, 6 vols (London: HMSO).

Cook, David, and F. P. Wilson (eds) (1961), 'Dramatic Records in the Declared Accounts of the Treasurer of the Chamber 1558–1642', in *Malone Society Collections*, vi.

Cooke, J. (1614), *Greenes Tu Quoque, or, The Cittie Gallant* (London).

Cotgrave, Randle, and Adam Islip (1611), *A Dictionarie of the French and English Tongues* (London: Printed by Adam Islip).
Cox, J. E. (ed.) (1876), *The Annals of St. Helen's, Bishopsgate* (London: Tinsley Brothers).
Crashaw, William (1608), *The Sermon Preached at the Crosse, Feb xiiii 1607* (H.L. for Edmond Weaver).
Dasent, John R., et al. (eds) (1890–1964), *Acts of the Privy Council of England, New Series: 1542–1631*, 46 vols (London: HMSO).
Davenant, William (1630), *The Just Italian* (London).
—— (1673), *The Works of Sir William Davenant* (London).
Davies, John (of Hereford) (1611), *The Scourge of Folly* (London).
Davies, Sir John (1876), *The Complete Poems of Sir John Davies*, ed. A. B. Grosart (London).
Davis, Norman (1979), *Non-Cycle Plays and the Winchester Dialogues* (Oxford: Oxford University Press for the Early English Text Society).
Dekker, Thomas (1600), *The Pleasant Comedie of Old Fortunatus* (London).
—— (1606), *The Seven Deadlie Sinns of London* (London).
—— (1630), *The Blacke Rod, and the White Rod* (London).
—— (1884–6), *The Non-Dramatic Works*, ed. A. B. Grosart, 5 vols (New York: Russell and Russell).
—— (1953–61), *The Dramatic Works of Thomas Dekker*, ed. Fredson Bowers, 4 vols (Cambridge: Cambridge University Press).
—— (1963), *The Non-Dramatic Works*, ed. A. B. Grosart, 5 vols (1884–6; New York: Russell and Russell).
—— and Thomas Middleton (1604), *The Honest Whore* (London).
—— and John Webster (1607), *Westward Hoe!* (London).
—— —— (1911), *Westward Ho!* (1607; London: Tudor Facsimile Texts).
Douglas, Audrey, and Peter Greenfield (eds) (1986), *Records of Early English Drama: Cumberland, Westmorland, Gloucestershire* (Toronto: University of Toronto Press).
Dugdale, G. (1604), *The Time Triumphant* (London).
Earle, John (1628), *Micro-cosmographie, or, A Peece of the World Discouered in Essayes and Characters* (London).
Edwards, Richard (1980), *Damon and Pythias*, ed. D. Jerry White (New York: Garland).
Elliott, John R., and Alan H. Nelson (University); Alexandra F. Johnston and Diana Wyatt (City) (2004), *Records of Early English Drama: Oxford*, 2 vols (Toronto: University of Toronto Press).
Erler, Mary (2008), *Records of Early English Drama: Ecclesiastical London* (Toronto: University of Toronto Press).
Feuillerat, Albert (1908), *Documents Relating to the Office of the Revels in the Time of Queen Elizabeth* (Louvain: Ustpruyst).
—— (1914), *Documents Relating to the Office of the Revels at Court in the Time of King Edward VI and Queen Mary (The Loseley Manuscripts)* (Louvain: Ustpruyst).
Field, Nathan (1950), *The Plays of Nathan Field*, ed. William Peery (Austin: University of Texas Press).
Finet, John (1987), *Ceremonies of Charles I: The Notebooks of John Finet, 1628–1641*, ed. Albert J. Loomie (New York: Fordham University Press).
Firth, C. H., and R. S. Rait (1911), *Acts and Ordinances of the Interregnum, 1642–1660*, 3 vols (London: HMSO).
Fisher, John (ed.) (1981), *A Collection of Early Maps of London, 1553–1667* (Lympne Castle: Guildhall Library).

Flecknoe, Richard (1664), *Love's Kingdom... with A Short Discourse of the English Stage* (London).

—— (1674), *Short Discourse of the English Stage.*

Fletcher, John (1966–96), *The Dramatic Works in the Beaumont and Fletcher Canon*, ed. Fredson Bowers et al., 10 vols (Cambridge: Cambridge University Press).

Florio, John (1578), *First Fruites* (London).

Foakes, R. A. (1985), *Illustrations of the English Stage 1580–1642* (Stanford, CA: Stanford University Press).

—— (ed.) (2002), *Henslowe's Diary* (1961; Cambridge: Cambridge University Press).

—— and J. C. Gibson (eds) (1960), *The Telltale* (Oxford: Malone Society).

—— and R. T. Rickert (eds) (1961), *Henslowe's Diary* (Cambridge: Cambridge University Press).

Foster, Joseph (ed.) (1887), *London Marriage Licenses, 1521–1869* (London: Bernard Quaritch).

Foxe, J. (1837–41), *Acts and Monuments*, ed. S. R. Cattley and G. Townsend (London: Seeley, Burnside, and Seeley).

Fraser, Russell A., and Norman C. Rabkin (eds) (1976), *Drama of the English Renaissance*, i: *The Tudor Period* (New York: Macmillan).

Fuller, Thomas (1642), *The Holy State* (Cambridge).

Furnivall, F. J. (ed.) (1868), *Ballads from Manuscript*, i/1 (London: Ballad Society).

Gainsford, Thomas (1616), *The Rich Cabinet* (London).

Galloway, David (ed.) (1984), *Records of Early English Drama: Norwich 1540–1642* (Toronto: University of Toronto Press).

Gardiner, Samuel (1606), *A Booke of Angling, or Fishing* (London).

Gascoigne, George (1575), *Glasse of Governement* (London).

Gawdy, Philip (1906), *The Letters of Philip Gawdy*, ed. I. H. Jeayes (London).

Gayton, Edmund (1654), *Pleasant Notes upon Don Quixot* (London).

Gee, H., and W. J. Hardy (eds) (1896), *Documents Illustrative of English Church History* (New York: Macmillan).

George, David (ed.) (1991), *Records of Early English Drama: Lancashire* (Toronto: University of Toronto Press).

Gesta Grayorum (1688) (London).

Gibson, James M. (ed.) (2002), *Records of Early English Drama: Kent, Diocese of Canterbury*, 3 vols (Toronto: University of Toronto Press).

[Glapthorne, Henry?] (1959 [1958]), *The Lady Mother* (1635), ed. Arthur Brown (Oxford: Malone Society).

Gosson, Stephen (1579*a*), *The Ephemerides of Phialo* (London).

—— (1579*b*), *The Schoole of Abuse. Conteining a Plesaunt Inuectiue Against Poets, Pipers, Plaiers, Iesters and Such Like Caterpillers of a Commonwelth* (London: [Thomas Dawson] for Thomas Woodcock.

—— (1582), *Playes Confuted in Five Actions* (London).

Gower, Granville William Gresham Leveson (ed.) (1877), *A Register of all the Christninges Burialles & Weddinges within the Parish of Saint Peeters vpon Cornhill* (London).

Grafton, R. (1809), *Grafton's Chronicle* (1569), 2 vols (London: J. Johnson et al.).

Gray, William (1649), *Chorographia* (London).

Greene, Robert (1598*a*), *Menaphon* (London).

—— (1598*b*), *The Scottish Historie of James the Fourth* (London).

—— (1921), *James IV*, ed. A. E. H. Swaen (London: Malone Society Reprints).

—— (1923), *The Thirde and Last Part of Conny-Catching (1592) and A Disputation Betweene a Hee Conny-Catcher and a Shee Conny-Catcher (1592)*, ed. G. B. Harrison (London: Bodley Head Quartos).

Greene, Robert (1926), *Alphonsus of Aragon* (*c.*1587–8), ed. W. W. Greg (London: Malone Society Reprints).

Greg, W. W. (ed.) (1922), *Two Elizabethan Stage Abridgements: 'The Battle of Alcazar' and 'Orlando Furioso'* (Oxford: Malone Society).

—— (1931), *Dramatic Documents from the Elizabethan Playhouses*, 2 vols (Oxford: Clarendon Press).

Grose, F. (ed.) (1809), 'The Earl of Northumberland's Household Book', in *The Antiquarian Repertory*, iv (London: E. Jeffery).

Guilpin, Everard (1598), *Skialetheia, or, A Shadowe of Truth, in Certaine Epigrams and Satyres* (London: J. R[oberts] for N. Ling).

Hall, Edward (1809), *Hall's Chronicle: The Union of the Two Noble and Illustre Famelies of Lancastre and Yorke* (1548; London: J. Johnson et al.).

Hallen, A. W. Cornelius (transcriber) (1889), *The Registers of St. Botolph, Bishopsgate London*, 3 vols (Edinburgh: T. and A. Constable).

Hamilton, W. (ed.) (1875, 1877), *A Chronicle of England during the Reigns of the Tudors by Charles Wriothesley, Windsor Herald*, Camden Society, new ser., 11, 20.

Harbage, Alfred (1964), *Annals of English Drama 975–1700: An Analytical Record of All Plays, Extant or Lost, Chronologically Arranged and Indexed by Authors, Titles, Dramatic Companies, Etc.*, rev. S. Schoenbaum (Philadelphia: University of Pennsylvania Press).

Harvey, Gabriel (1884), *Letter-Book of Gabriel Harvey*, ed. Edward John Long Scott, Camden Society, new ser., 33.

Hayes, S., and W. Murdin (eds) (1740–59), *A Collection of State Papers . . . left by William Cecil, Lord Burghley*, 2 vols (London: HMSO).

Hays, Rosalind Conklin, and C. E. McGee/Sally L. Joyce and Evelyn S. Newlyn (eds) (1999), *Records of Early English Drama: Dorset/Cornwall* (Toronto: University of Toronto Press and Brepols).

Henslowe, Philip (1904–8), *Henslowe's Diary*, ed. W. W. Greg, 2 vols (London: A. H. Bullen).

—— (1907), *Henslowe Papers*, ed. W. W. Greg (London: A. H. Bullen).

—— (1961), *Henslowe's Diary* (*c.*1592–1604), ed. R. A. Foakes and R. T. Rickert (Cambridge: Cambridge University Press).

—— (2002), *Henslowe's Diary*, 2nd edn, ed. R. A. Foakes (Cambridge: Cambridge University Press).

Herbert, Sir Henry (1917), *The Dramatic Records of Sir Henry Herbert*, ed. Joseph Quincy Adams (New Haven: Yale University Press).

—— (1996), *The Control and Censorship of Caroline Drama: The Records of Sir Henry Herbert, Master of the Revels 1623–73*, ed. N. W. Bawcutt (Oxford: Oxford University Press).

Heywood, Thomas (1608), *The Rape of Lucrece* (London).

—— (1609), *The Rape of Lucrece* (London).

—— (1612), *An Apology for Actors* (London).

—— (1613), *The Brazen Age* (London).

—— (1631), *Fair Maid of the West* (London).

—— (1632), *The Iron Age* (London).

—— (1637), *The Royall King, and the Loyall Subject* (London).

—— (1874), *The Dramatic Works of Thomas Heywood*, ed. R. H. Shepherd, 6 vols (London).

—— (1978), *The Escapes of Jupiter* (1583), ed. Henry D. Janzen (London: Malone Society Reprints).

—— (1986), *Thomas Heywood's Pageants*, ed. D. M. Bergeron (New York: Garland).

Hill, Aaron, and William Popple (1966), *The Prompter: A Theatrical Paper (1734–6)*, ed. W. W. Appleton and K. A. Burnim (New York: Benjamin Blom).

Hill, Thomas (1581), *The Contemplation of Mankinde* (London).

Holinshed, R. (1807–8), *Holinshed's Chronicles of England, Scotland, and Ireland*, 6 vols (London: J. Johnson et al.).

Honigmann, E. A. J., and S. Brock (1993), *Playhouse Wills 1558–1642: An Edition of Wills by Shakespeare and his Contemporaries in the London Theatre* (Manchester: Manchester University Press).

Hovenden, R. (ed.) (1884–94), *A True Register of all the Christeninges, Mariages, and Burialles in the Parishe of St. James, Clerkenwell, from the Yeare of Our Lord God 1551*, 6 vols (London: Harleian Society).

Howes, Edmund (1631), *Additions to John Stow's 'Annales, or, A General Chronicle of England'* (London).

Hume, Martin Andrew Sharp (ed.) (1892–8), *Calendar of State Papers relating to English Affairs preserved principally in the Archives of Simancas*, 4 vols (London: HMSO).

Ingram, R. W. (ed.) (1981), *Records of Early English Drama: Coventry* (Toronto: University of Toronto Press).

J.C. (1620), *The Two Merry Milkemaids, or, The Best Words Weare the Garland* (London).

J.D. (1640), *The Knave in Graine* (London).

Jeaffreson, John Cordy (ed.) (1972), *Middlesex County Records (1886–92)*, old ser., 4 vols (London: Greater London Council).

Johnston, A. F., and M. Rogerson (eds) (1979), *Records of Early English Drama: York*, 2 vols (Toronto: University of Toronto Press).

Jonson, Ben (1601), *The Fountaine of Self-Love, or, Cynthias Revels* (London).

—— (1607), *Volpone* (London).

—— (1616), *The Workes of Benjamin Jonson* (London).

—— (1925–52), *Ben Jonson*, ed. C. H. Herford and Percy and Evelyn Simpson, 11 vols (Oxford: Oxford University Press).

Justices of the Peace, Quarter Sessions (1925), *Middlesex County Records: Calendar of Sessions Rolls* (1610; London: [British Library Typescript]).

Kirk, R. E. G., and E. F. Kirk (eds) (1900), *Returns of Aliens Dwelling in the City and Suburbs of London from the Reign of Henry VIII to that of James I, 1523–1571*, Publications of the Huguenot Society of London, 10/1 (Aberdeen: Aberdeen University Press).

—— —— (1907), *Returns of Aliens Dwelling in the City and Suburbs of London from the Reign of Henry VIII to that of James I, 1598–1625* (Aberdeen: Huguenot Society of London).

Kirke, J. (1638), *The Seven Champions of Christendome* (London).

Kirkman, F. (1673), *The Wits, or, Sport Upon Sport* (London).

Klausner, David N. (1990), *Records of Early English Drama: Herefordshire/Worcestershire* (Toronto: University of Toronto Press).

—— (2005), *Records of Early English Drama: Wales* (Toronto: University of Toronto Press).

Knolles, Richard (1603), *The Generall Historie of the Turks* (London).

Kyd, Thomas (1615), *The Spanish Tragedie: or, Hieronimoe is mad againe* (London).

Lambarde, William (1576), *A Perambulation of Kent* (London: [Henry Middleton] for Ralph Newbery).

le Hardy, William (ed.) (1935–41), *County of Middlesex: Calendar to the Sessions Records 1612–1618*, new ser., 4 vols (London: Guildhall).

Leishman, J. B. (ed.) (1949), *The Three Parnassus Plays* (London: Ivor Nicholson and Watson; repr. 1994).

Leland, J. (ed.) (1774), *Antiquarii de Rebus Britannicis Collectanea*, iv, ed. T. Hearne (London: Benjamin White).

Lemnius, Levinus (1576), *The Touchstone of Complexions*, trans. Thomas Newton (London).

Lemon, Robert, and Mary Anne Everett Green (eds) (1857), *Calendar of State Papers: Domestic Series of the Reigns of Edward VI, Mary, Elizabeth I, James I, preserved in the State Paper*

Department of Her Majesty's Public Record Office, 48 vols (1856–97), viii: *Reign of James I: 1603–1610* (London: HMSO).

Lenton, Francis (1629), *The Young Gallants Whirligigg, or, Youths Reakes* (London).

Lodge, Thomas (1596), *Wits Miserie, and the Worlds Madnesse* (London: Andrew Islip sold by Cuthbert Burby).

—— (1910), *The Wounds of Civil War* (1594), ed. J. Dover Wilson (London: Malone Society Reprints).

Louis, C. (ed.) (2000), *Records of Early English Drama: Sussex* (Toronto: University of Toronto Press).

Lyly, John (1902), *The Complete Works of John Lyly*, ed. R. W. Bond, 3 vols (Oxford: Clarendon Press).

McClure, Norman E. (ed.) (1939), *The Letters of John Chamberlain*, 2 vols (Philadelphia: American Philosophical Society).

Machyn, H. (1848), *The Diary of Henry Machyn, Citizen and Merchant-Taylor of London, from A.D. 1550 to A.D. 1563*, ed. J. G. Nichols, Camden Society, 42.

Madden, John (1998), *Shakespeare in Love*, motion picture (Bedford Falls, Miramax, Universal).

Madge, Sidney J. (ed.) (1901), *Abstracts of Inquisitiones Post Mortem for the City of London*, pt II: *1561–1577* (London: British Record Society).

Malone, Edmund (1790), *The Plays and Poems of William Shakespeare*, 10 vols (London).

Manningham, John (1976), *The Diary of John Manningham of the Middle Temple 1602–1603*, ed. Robert Parker Sorlien (Hanover, NH: University Press of New England).

Marlowe, Christopher (1590) *Tamburlaine the Great. The Second Part of the bloody Conquests of mighty Tamburlaine* (London).

—— (1973), *The Complete Works of Christopher Marlowe*, ed. Fredson Bowers (Cambridge: Cambridge University Press).

Marston, John (1601), *Iacke Drums Entertainment, or, The Comedie of Pasquill and Katherine* (London).

—— (1602), *The History of Antonio and Mellida* (London).

—— (1604), *The Malcontent*, 3rd edn (London).

—— (1605), *The Dutch Courtezan* (London).

—— (1934–9), *The Plays*, ed. H. Harvey Wood, 3 vols (Edinburgh: Oliver and Boyd).

Massinger, Philip (1624), *The Bond-man* (London).

—— (1976), *The Plays and Poems of Philip Massinger*, ed. Philip Edwards and Colin Gibson, 5 vols (Oxford: Oxford University Press).

Matthew, H. C. G., and B. Harrison (eds) (2004), *Oxford Dictionary of National Biography*, 61 vols (Oxford: Oxford University Press); <http//:www.oxforddnb.com>.

Melton, John (1620), *Astrologaster* (London).

Mennes, John (1817), *Facetiae*, 2 vols (London: John Camden Hotton).

Meres, Francis (1598), *Palladis Tamia* (London).

Middleton, Thomas (1953), *Honourable Entertainments* (1620–1; Oxford: Malone Society).

—— (2007), *The Collected Works*, gen. eds Gary Taylor and John Lavagnino (Oxford: Oxford University Press).

More, T. (1551), *A Fruteful and Pleasaunt Worke of the Beste State of Publyque Weale, and of the Newe Yle Called Vtopia* (London: STC 18094).

Mulcaster, R. (1999), 'The Queen's Majesty's Passage' (1559), in A. F. Kinney (ed.), *Renaissance Drama* (Oxford: Blackwell), 21–34.

Munday, A. (1580), *A Second and Third Blast of Retrait from Plaies and Theaters* (London).

—— (1985), *Pageants and Entertainments of Anthony Munday*, ed. D. Bergeron (New York: Garland).

Myers, A. R. (ed.) (1959), *The Household Book of Edward IV: The Black Book and the Ordinance of 1478* (Manchester: Manchester University Press).

Nabbes, Thomas (1637), *Hannibal and Scipio* (London).

Nashe, Thomas (1589), 'To Gentlemen Students', Epistle to Robert Greene's *Menaphon*, **1r–A3r.

—— (1958), *The Works of Thomas Nashe*, ed. R. B. McKerrow, 2nd edn, rev. F. P. Wilson, 5 vols (Oxford: Oxford University Press).

Nelson, A. H. (1980), *The Plays of Henry Medwall* (London: D. S. Brewer).

—— (ed.) (1989), *Records of Early English Drama: Cambridge* (Toronto: University of Toronto Press).

—— and John R. Elliott, Jr. (eds) (forthcoming), *Records of Early English Drama: Inns of Court*, 2 vols (Toronto: University of Toronto Press).

—— —— Alexandra F. Johnston, and Diana Wyatt (eds) (2004), *Records of Early English Drama: Oxford*, 2 vols (Toronto: University of Toronto Press).

Nichols, John (1823), *The Progresses and Public Processions of Queen Elizabeth*, 3 vols (London).

—— (1828), *The Progresses, Processions, and Magnificent Festivities, of King James the First*, 4 vols (London).

Northbrooke, John (1577), *A Treatise Wherein Dicing, Dauncing, Vaine Playes or Enterluds With Other Idle Pastimes &c. Commonly Vsed on the Sabboth Day, Are Reproued by the Authoritie of the Word of God and Auntient Writers* (London).

Olivier, Laurence (1944), *Henry V*, motion picture (Two Cities Films).

Overbury, Sir Thomas (1614), *Characters* (London).

—— et al. (1615), *New and Choice Characters* (London).

Peacham, Henry (1622), *The Compleat Gentleman* (London).

Peele, George (1594), *The Battell of Alcazar* (London).

—— (1952), *The Life and Minor Works of George Peele*, ed. D. H. Horne (New Haven: Yale University Press).

—— and John Marston (1610), *Histriomastix* (London).

Pepys, Samuel (1662), 'Saturday 27 December 1662', in *The Diary of Samuel Pepys: Daily Entries from the 17th Century London Diary*, ed. Phil Gyford, <http://www.pepysdiary.com/archive/1662/12/27>.

—— (1893), *The Diary of Samuel Pepys, M.A., F.R.S., Clerk of the Acts and Secretary to the Admiralty*, transcribed by Mynors Bright, with Lord Braybrooke's notes, ed. Henry Benjamin Wheatley (London: G. Bell and Sons).

Pilkinton, Mark C. (ed.) (1997), *Records of Early English Drama: Bristol* (Toronto: University of Toronto Press).

Platter, Thomas (1937), *Thomas Platter's Travels in England, 1599* (1599), ed. Clare Williams (London: Jonathan Cape).

Pollard, T. (ed.) (2004), *Shakespeare's Theater: A Sourcebook* (Malden, MA: Blackwell).

Prynne, William (1633), *Histrio-Mastix: The Players Scourge, or, Actors Tragædie* (London).

Puckering, Thomas (forthcoming), *The Account Book of Sir Thomas Puckering*, ed. Catherine Richardson (Stratford upon Avon: Dugdale Society).

Puttenham, George (1589), *The Arte of English Poesie* (London).

Rainolds, John, William Gager, and Alberico Gentili (1974), *Th'Overthrow of Stage Plays* (1599), introd. Arthur Freeman (New York: Garland).

Rankins, William (1587), *A Mirrour of Monsters Wherein is Plainely Described the Manifold Vices, & Spotted Enormities, That Are Caused by the Infectious Sight of Playes* (London).

Ravenscroft, Thomas (1612), *Melismata* (London).

—— (1614), *A Briefe Discourse of the True (But Neglected) Use of Charactering the Degrees* (London).

REED Patrons and Performances Web Site, <http://link.library.utoronto.ca/reed/>.

Richards, Nathanael (1641), *Poems Sacred and Satyricale* (London).

Robertson, J. (ed.) (1960 [1959]), 'A Calendar of Dramatic Records in the Books of the London Clothworkers' Company' (Addenda to *Collections III*), in *Malone Society Collections*, v (Oxford: Malone Society), 1–16.

—— and D. Gordon (eds) (1954), *A Calendar of Dramatic Records in the Books of the Livery Companies of London, Malone Society Collections*, iii (Oxford: Malone Society).

Rowley, S. (1605), *When You See Me, You Know Me* (London).

Rowley, William (1632), *A New Wonder, A Woman Never Vext* (London).

St Clare Byrne, M. (ed.) (1981), *The Lisle Letters*, 6 vols (Chicago: University of Chicago Press).

Schlueter, June (2006), 'Michael van Meer's *Album Amicorum*, with Illustrations of London, 1614–1615', *Huntington Library Quarterly*, 69: 301–13.

Scottowe, John (1974), *John Scottowe's Alphabet Books*, ed. Janet Backhouse (London: printed for the Roxburghe Club at Scolar Press).

Shakespeare, William (1598), *Loves Labors Lost* (London).

—— (1603), *The Tragicall Historie of Hamlet Prince of Denmarke* (London).

—— (1608), *M. William Shak-speare: His True Chronicle Historie of the Life and Death of King Lear and his Three Daughters* (London).

—— (1623), *Mr. William Shakespeares Comedies, Histories, & Tragedies* (London).

—— (1640), *Poems: Written by Wil. Shake-speare, Gent*, ed. Leonard Digges (London).

—— (1790), *The Plays and Poems of William Shakespeare*, ed. Edmund Malone, 10 vols (London).

—— (1968), *The First Folio of Shakespeare [1623]: The Norton Facsimile*, ed. Charles Hinman (New York: W. W. Norton).

—— (1974), *The Riverside Shakespeare*, ed. G. Blakemore Evans (Boston: Houghton Mifflin).

—— (1976), *The History of King Henry the Fourth, as revised by Sir Edward Dering*, Folger Facsimile MS, ed. G. W. Williams (Charlottesville: University Press of Virginia).

—— (1981), *Shakespeare's Plays in Quarto*, ed. Michael J. B. Allen and Kenneth Muir (Berkeley: University of California Press).

—— (1986), *William Shakespeare: The Complete Works*, The Oxford Shakespeare, gen. eds. Stanley Wells and Gary Taylor (Oxford: Clarendon Press).

—— (1994), *The Tragedy of Coriolanus*, ed. R. B. Parker (Oxford: Clarendon Press, 1994).

—— (1997*a*), *The Complete Works of Shakespeare*, ed. David Bevington (New York: Longman).

—— (1997*b*), *The Riverside Shakespeare*, ed. G. Blakemore Evans, rev. edn (Boston: Houghton Mifflin).

—— (1997*c*), *The Norton Shakespeare: Based on the Oxford Shakespeare*, gen. ed. Stephen Greenblatt (New York: W. W. Norton).

Shirley, Henry (1638), *The Martyr'd Souldier* (London).

Shirley, James (1637), *Hide Parke* (London).

—— (1833), *The Dramatic Works and Poems of James Shirley*, ed. W. Gifford and A. Dyce, 6 vols (London: Murray).

Sidney, Philip (1595), *An Apologie for Poetrie* (London).

Smith, W. (1615), *The Hector of Germanie, or, The Palsgraue, Prince Elector* (London).

Smyth, John (1883–5), *The Lives of the Berkeleys, Lords of the Honour, Castle and Manor of Berkeley in the County of Gloucester from 1066 to 1618: with a description of the Hundred of Berkeley and of its Inhabitants*, ed. Sir John MacLean, 3 vols (Gloucester: John Bellows).

Somerset, J. Alan B. (ed.) (1994*a*), *Records of Early English Drama: Shropshire*, 2 vols (Toronto: University of Toronto Press).

Southwell, Lady Anne (1984), 'Lady Southwell's Defense of Poetry', presented by Jean C. Cavanaugh, *English Literary Renaissance*, 14, n.p.

Speed, John (1611 [1612]), *The Theatre of the Empire of Great Britaine* (London: [William Hall] sold by John Sudbury and George Humble).

Stanford, Henry (1988), *Henry Stanford's Anthology: An Edition of Cambridge University Library Manuscript Dd.5.75*, ed. Stephen W. May (New York: Garland).

Statutes of the Realm (1810–28), ed. A. Luders et al., 11 vols (London: G. Eyre and A. Strahan).

—— (1993), ed. A. Luders et al. (repr., 11 vols in 12, Buffalo, NY: William S. Hein).

Stockwood, J. (1578), *A Sermon Preached at Paules Crosse* (London: Henry Bynneman for George Bishop).

Stokes, J., and R. J. Alexander (eds) (1996), *Records of Early English Drama: Somerset*, 2 vols (Toronto: University of Toronto Press).

Stow, John (1570), *A Summarye of the Chronicles of Englande* (London).

—— (1598), *The Survay of London* (London).

—— (1615), *The Annales, or, A Generall Chronicle of England*, with additions by Edmond Howes (London).

—— (1908), *A Survey of London* (1603), ed. C. L. Kingsford, 2 vols (Oxford: Clarendon Press).

Strafford, Thomas Wentworth, first Earl of (1739), *The Earl of Strafford's Letters and Dispatches*, ed. W. Knowler, 2 vols (London).

Streitberger, W. R. (1976), 'A Letter from Edmund Tilney to Sir William More', *Surrey Archaeological Collections*, 71: 225–31.

—— (ed.) (1986), *Jacobean and Caroline Revels Accounts, 1603–1642, Malone Society Collections*, xiii (Oxford: Malone Society).

Stubbs, W. (ed.) (1882), *Select Charters and Other Illustrations of English Constitutional History*, 6th edn (Oxford: Clarendon Press).

Suckling, John (1638), *Aglaura* (London).

Taylor, John (1621), *The Praise, Antiquity, and Commodity of Beggary, Beggars, and Begging* (London).

Tomkis, Thomas (1615), *Albumazar* (London).

Wasson, John M. (ed.) (1986), *Records of Early English Drama: Devon* (Toronto: University of Toronto Press).

Webster, John (1612), *The White Devil* (London).

—— (1631), *The White Devil* (London).

Whetstone, G. (1584), *A Mirour for Magestrates of Cyties* (London).

—— (1585), *The Honourable Reputation of a Souldier* (London).

—— (1910), *Promos and Cassandra*, ed. John S. Farmer (Amersham: Tudor Facsimile Texts).

White, Thomas (1578), *A Sermon Preached at Pawles Crosse on Sunday the Thirde of Nouember 1577 in the Time of the Plague* (London: [Henry Bynneman for] Francis Coldock).

Whitney, Geoffrey (1586), *A Choice of Emblems* (Leiden).

Wickham, Glynne, Herbert Berry, and William Ingram (eds) (2000), *English Professional Theatre, 1530–1660* (Cambridge: Cambridge University Press).

Wilson, F. P., and R. F. Hill (eds) (1975), *Dramatic Records in the Declared Accounts of the Office of the Works, Malone Society Collections*, x (Oxford: Malone Society).

Wilson, George (1607), *The Commendation of Cockes and Cock-Fighting* (London).

Wilson, Robert (1590), *The Pleasant and Stately Morall, of the Three Lords and Three Ladies of London* (London).

—— (1594), *The Coblers Prophesie* (London).

Wotton, Sir Henry (1624), *The Elements of Architecture* (London).

Wright, J. (1699), *Historia Histrionica* (London).

Secondary Sources

Acheson, K. O. (2001), ' "Outrage Your Face": Anti-Theatricality and Gender in Early Modern Closet Drama by Women', *Early Modern Literary Studies*, 6/3, <http://extra.shu.ac.uk/emls/06-3/06-3toc.htm>.

Adams, John Cranford (1942), *The Globe Playhouse: Its Design and Equipment* (Cambridge, MA: Harvard University Press).

Adams, Joseph Quincy, Jr. (1913), '*Every Woman in her Humour* and *The Dumb Knight*', *MLQ* 10: 413–32.

—— (1917*a*), *The Dramatic Records of Sir Henry Herbert* (New Haven: Yale University Press).

—— (1917*b*), *Shakespearean Playhouses* (Boston: Houghton Mifflin).

Adams, Simon (1995), 'The Patronage of the Crown in Elizabethan Politics', in John Guy (ed.), *The Reign of Elizabeth I: Court and Culture in the Last Decade* (Cambridge: Cambridge University Press).

—— (2002), *Leicester and the Court: Essays on Elizabethan Politics* (Manchester: Manchester University Press).

Aebischer, P. (1925), 'Fragments de moralités, farces, at mystères retrouvés à Fribourg', *Romania*, 51: 511–27.

Agnew, Jean-Christophe (1986), *Worlds Apart: The Market and the Theater in Anglo-American Thought, 1550–1750* (Cambridge: Cambridge University Press).

Anglo, Sydney (1997), *Spectacle, Pageantry, and Early Tudor Policy*, 2nd edn (1969; Oxford: Oxford University Press).

Ankersmit, Frank R. (1983), *Narrative Logic: A Semantic Analysis of the Historian's Language* (The Hague: M. Nijhoff).

—— (1994), *History and Tropology: The Rise and Fall of Metaphor* (Berkeley: University of California Press).

—— (2001), *Historical Representation* (Stanford, CA: Stanford University Press).

Arber, Edward (ed.) (1875–7), *A Transcript of the Registers of the Company of Stationers of London 1554–1640 AD*, 5 vols (London: privately printed).

Archer, Ian W. (1988), 'Hugh Alley, Law Enforcement, and Market Regulation in the Later Sixteenth Century', in I. Archer, C. Barron, and V. Harding (eds), *Hugh Alley's Caveat: The Markets of London in 1598* (London: London Topographical Society), 15–29.

—— (1991*a*), *The Pursuit of Stability: Social Relations in Elizabethan London* (Cambridge: Cambridge University Press).

—— (1991*b*), *The History of the Haberdashers' Company* (Chichester: Phillimore).

—— (2001), 'Government in Early Modern London: The Challenge of the Suburbs', in P. Clark and R. Gillespie (eds), *Two Capitals (London and Dublin, 1500–1840* (Oxford: Oxford University Press for the British Academy).

—— (2006), 'Fish, Walter (*d.* 1585)', in H. C. G. Matthew and Brian Harrison (eds), *Oxford Dictionary of National Biography*, online edn, ed. Lawrence Goldman (Oxford: Oxford University Press), <http://www.oxforddnb.com/view/article/93685>, accessed 16 June 2008.

—— Caroline Barron, and Vanessa Harding (1988), 'Introduction', in Archer, Barron, and Harding (eds), *Hugh Alley's Caveat: The Markets of London in 1598* (London: London Topographical Society), 3–15.

Arlidge, Anthony (2000), *Shakespeare and the Prince of Love: The Feast of Misrule in the Middle Temple* (London: Giles de la Mare).

Armstrong, William A. (1959), 'The Audience of the Elizabethan Private Theatres', *Review of English Studies*, new ser., 10: 234–249.

Astington, John H. (1985), 'The Red Lion Playhouse: Two Notes', *Shakespeare Quarterly*, 36: 456–7.

—— (1991*a*), 'The Messalina Stage and Salisbury Court Plays', *Theatre Journal*, 43: 141– 56.

—— (1991*b*), 'A Drawing of the Great Chamber at Whitehall in 1601', *REED Newsletter*, 16/1: 6–11.

—— (1991*c*), 'The Origins of the *Roxana* and *Messallina* Illustrations', *Shakespeare Survey*, 43: 149–69.

—— (1993*a*), 'The "Unrecorded Portrait" of Edward Alleyn', *Shakespeare Quarterly*, 44: 73–86.

—— (1993*b*), '*The Wits* Illustration 1662', *Theatre Notebook*, 47/3: 122–40.

—— (1996), 'Three Shakespearean Prints', *Shakespeare Quarterly*, 47: 178–89; repr. in Stephen Orgel and Sean Keilen (eds), *Shakespeare and the Arts* (New York: Garland, 1999), 278–89.

—— (1997), 'Rereading Illustrations of the English Stage', *Shakespeare Survey*, 50: 151–70.

—— (1999*a*), *English Court Theatre, 1558–1642* (Cambridge: Cambridge University Press).

—— (1999*b*), 'Tarlton and the Sanguine Temperament', *Theatre Notebook*, 53/1: 2–7.

—— (2003*a*), 'The Career of Andrew Cane, Citizen, Goldsmith, and Player', *Medieval and Renaissance Drama in England*, 16: 130–44.

—— (2003*b*), 'Dramatic Extracts in the Interregnum', *Review of English Studies*, 54: 601–14.

—— (2006), 'Playing the Man: Acting at the Red Bull and the Fortune', *Early Theatre*, 9/2: 130–43.

Austern, Linda Phyllis (1992), *Music in English Children's Drama of the Renaissance* (Philadelphia: Gordon and Breach).

Axton, Marie (1982), *Three Tudor Classical Interludes* (London: D. S. Brewer).

Baines, B. J. (1984), *Thomas Heywood* (Boston: Twayne).

Baker, J. (1996), 'Found: Shakespeare's Manuscript of *Henry IV*', *Elizabethan Review*, 4/1: 14–46.

Baker, J. H. (2004), 'Christmas in the Inns of Court and Chancery', in *An Inner Temple Miscellany: Papers Reprinted from the Inner Temple Yearbook* (London: Inner Temple), 41–7.

Baker, Stuart E. (1995), 'Turrets and Tiring Houses on the Elizabethan Public Stage', *Theatre Notebook*, 49: 134–51.

Bal, Mieke (1991), *Reading Rembrandt: Beyond the Word–Image Opposition* (Cambridge: Cambridge University Press).

—— (1997), *The Mottled Screen: Reading Proust Visually*, trans. Anna-Louise Milne (Stanford, CA: Stanford University Press).

Baldwin, R. C. D. (2004), 'Aldersey, Thomas (1521/2–1598)', in H. C. G. Matthew and Brian Harrison (eds), *Oxford Dictionary of National Biography* (Oxford: Oxford University Press), <http://www.oxforddnb.com/view/article/73473>, accessed 2 Dec. 2007.

Baldwin, T. W. (1927), *The Organization and Personnel of the Shakespearean Company* (Princeton: Princeton University Press).

Ball, Roma (1962), 'The Choir-Boy Actors of St. Paul's Cathedral', *Emporia State Research Studies*, 10: 5–16.

Barasch, Frances K. (2000), 'Italian Actresses in Shakespeare's World: Flaminia and Vincenza', *Shakespeare Bulletin*, 18/4: 17–21.

—— (2001), 'Italian Actresses in Shakespeare's World: Vittoria and Isabella', *Shakespeare Bulletin*, 19/3: 5–9.

Barbour, Richmond (1995), ' "When I Acted Young Antinous": Boy Actors and the Erotics of Jonsonian Theater', *PMLA* 110: 1006–22.

Barroll, J. Leeds (1975), 'The Social and Literary Context', in C. Leech and T. W. Craik (eds), *The Revels History of Drama in English*, 8 vols (London: Methuen), iii. 1–94; incl. 'Drama and the Court', 3–27.

Barroll, J. Leeds (1991), *Politics, Plague, and Shakespeare's Theater: The Stuart Years* (Ithaca, NY: Cornell University Press).

—— (2001), *Anna of Denmark, Queen of England: A Cultural Biography* (Philadelphia: University of Pennsylvania Press).

—— (2002), 'Shakespeare, Noble Patrons, and the Pleasures of "common playing" ', in Paul W. White and Suzanne R. Westfall (eds), *Shakespeare and Theatrical Patronage in Early Modern England* (Cambridge: Cambridge University Press), 90–121.

Barron, Caroline M. (2004), *London in the Later Middle Ages* (Oxford: Oxford University Press).

Baskervill, Charles Read (1929), *The Elizabethan Jig and Related Song Drama* (Chicago: University of Chicago Press).

Bawcutt, N. W. (1995), 'Sir Henry Herbert and William Sands the Puppeteer: Some Corrections', *Records of Early English Drama Newsletter*, 20/1: 17–19.

—— (1996), *The Control and Censorship of Caroline Drama: The Records of Sir Henry Herbert, Master of the Revels 1623–73* (Oxford: Clarendon Press).

—— (1997), 'Documents of the Salisbury Court Theatre in the British Library', *Medieval and Renaissance Drama in England*, 9: 179–93.

Baxandall, Michael (1972), *Painting and Experience in Fifteenth Century Italy: A Primer in the Social History of Pictorial Style* (Oxford: Oxford University Press).

—— (1979), 'The Language of Art History', *New Literary History*, 10/3: 453–65.

—— (1985), *Patterns of Intention: On the Historical Explanation of Pictures* (New Haven: Yale University Press).

—— (1998), 'Introduction', in *Patterns of Intention: On the Historical Explanation of Pictures* (New Haven: Yale University Press, 1985); repr. in Donald Preziosi, *The Art of Art History: A Critical Anthology* (Oxford: Oxford University Press), 52–69.

Bayer, Mark. (2001), 'Moving UpMarket: The Queen Anne's Men at the Cockpit in Drury Lane, 1617', *Early Theatre* 4: 138–48.

Beal, P. (1980), 'Massinger at Bay: Unpublished Verses in a War of the Theatres', *Yearbook of English Studies*, 10: 190–203.

Beckerman, Bernard (1962), *Shakespeare at the Globe, 1599–1609* (New York: Macmillan).

—— (1981), 'The Use and Management of the Elizabethan Stage', in C. W. Hodges, S. Schoenbaum, and L. Leone (eds), *The Third Globe* (Detroit: Wayne State University Press), 151–63.

Bednarz, James P. (1991), 'Representing Jonson: *Histriomastix* and the Origin of the Poets' War', *Huntington Library Quarterly*, 54: 1–30.

—— (2001), *Shakespeare and the Poets' War* (New York: Columbia University Press).

—— (2006), 'When Did Shakespeare Write the Choruses of *Henry V*?' *Notes and Queries*, new ser., 53: 486–9.

Bell, Hamilton (1913), 'Contributions to the History of the English Playhouse', *Architectural Record*, 33: 262–7.

Belling, Catherine (2004), 'Infectious Rape, Therapeutic Revenge: Bloodletting and the Health of Rome's Body', in S. Moss and K. L. Peterson (eds), *Disease, Diagnosis, and Cure on the Early Modern Stage* (Aldershot: Ashgate).

Bennett, J. M. (1988), ' "History that Stands Still": Women's Work in the European Past', *Feminist Studies*, 14/2: 269–83.

Bennett, Paul E. (1955), 'The Word "Goths" in *A Knack to Know a Knave*', *Notes and Queries*, new ser., 200: 462–63.

Bentley, Gerald Eades (1941–68), *The Jacobean and Caroline Stage*, 7 vols (Oxford: Clarendon Press).

—— (1971), *The Profession of Dramatist in Shakespeare's Time, 1590–1642* (Princeton: Princeton University Press).

—— (1977), 'The Salisbury Court Theater and its Boy Players', *Huntington Library Quarterly*, 40: 129–49.

—— (1977–8), 'The Troubles of a Caroline Acting Troupe: Prince Charles's Company', *Huntington Library Quarterly*, 41: 217–29.

—— (1984), *The Profession of Player in Shakespeare's Time, 1590–1642* (Princeton: Princeton University Press).

Bergeron, David (1971), *English Civic Pageantry 1558–1642* (London: Edward Arnold).

—— (1981), 'Women as Patrons of English Renaissance Drama', in G. Fitch Lytle and S. Orgel (eds), *Patronage in the Renaissance* (Princeton: Princeton University Press), 274–90.

—— (1985), 'Middleton's "No Wit, No Help" and Civic Pageantry', in Bergeron (ed.), *Pageantry in the Shakespearean Theater* (Athens: University of Georgia Press), 65–80.

—— (1993), 'Pageants, Politics, and Patrons', *Medieval and Renaissance Drama in England*, 6: 139–52.

—— (2000), *Practicing Renaissance Scholarship* (Pittburgh: Duquesne University Press).

—— (2003), *English Civic Pageantry 1558–1642*, 2nd edn (1971; Tempe: Arizona State University).

—— (2006), *Textual Patronage in English Drama, 1570–1640* (London: Ashgate Press).

Bergmann, Bettina, and Christine Kondoleon (eds) (1999), *The Art of Ancient Spectacle* (New Haven: Yale University Press).

Berry, Herbert (1978), 'Sebastian Westcott, the Children of St. Paul's, and Professor Lennam', *Renaissance and Reformation*, 14: 77–82.

—— (1979), 'Aspects of the Design and Use of the First Public Playhouse', in Herbert Berry (ed.), *The First Public Playhouse: The Theatre in Shoreditch 1576–1598* (Montreal: McGill-Queen's University Press), 29–45.

—— (1983), 'The Players' Apprentice', *Essays in Theatre*, 1: 73–80.

—— (1984), 'The Globe Bewitched and *El Hombre Fiel*', *Medieval and Renaissance Drama in English*, 1: 211–30.

—— (1986), *The Boar's Head Playhouse* (Washington: Folger Shakespeare Library).

—— (1987), *Shakespeare's Playhouses* (New York: AMS).

—— (1988), 'Chambers, the Bull, and the Bacons', *Essays in Theatre*, 7/1: 35–42.

—— (1989), 'The First Public Playhouses, Especially the Red Lion', *Shakespeare Quarterly*, 40: 133–48.

—— (1991), *The Noble Science* (London: Associated University Presses).

—— (1999), 'The Date on the "Peacham" Manuscript', *Shakespeare Bulletin*, 17: 5–6.

—— (2000*a*), 'Playhouses, 1560–1660', in Glynne Wickham, Herbert Berry, and William Ingram (eds), *English Professional Theatre, 1530–1660* (Cambridge: Cambridge University Press), 285–674.

—— (2000*b*), 'The Phoenix', in Glynne Wickham, Herbert Berry, and William Ingram (eds), *English Professional Theatre, 1530–1660* (Cambridge: Cambridge University Press), 623–4.

—— (2000*c*), 'The View of London from the North and the Playhouses in Holywell', *Shakespeare Survey*, 53: 196–212.

—— (2002), Playhouses', in A. F. Kinney (ed.), *A Companion to Renaissance Drama* (Oxford: Blackwell).

—— (2004), 'Brayne, John', in H. C. G. Matthew and Brian Harrison (eds), *Oxford Dictionary of National Biography* (Oxford: Oxford University Press), <http://www.oxforddnb.com/view/article/68128>, accessed 2 Sept. 2007.

Berry, Herbert (2005), 'Building Playhouses, the Accession of James I, and the Red Bull', *Medieval and Renaissance Drama in England*, 18: 61–74.

—— (2006), 'The Bell Savage Inn and Playhouse in London', *Medieval and Renaissance Drama in England*, 19: 121–43.

Bevington, David (1962), *From Mankind to Marlowe* (Cambridge, MA: Harvard University Press).

—— (1984), *Action Is Eloquence: Shakespeare's Language of Gesture* (Cambridge, MA: Harvard University Press).

—— (1996), 'Introduction', in John Lyly, *Endymion* (Manchester: Manchester University Press), 1–72.

—— and Hunter, George K. (1991), 'Introduction to *Sappho and Phao*', in John Lyly, *Campaspe; and, Sappho and Phao* (Manchester: Manchester University Press), 141–95.

Bindoff, S. T. (ed.) (1982), *The History of Parliament: The House of Commons, 1509–1558*, 3 vols (London: HMSO).

Blackstone, Mary A. (1988), 'Patrons and Elizabethan Dramatic Companies', in C. E. McGee (ed.), *The Elizabethan Theatre X* (Port Credit, Ont.: P. D. Meany), 112–32.

—— (2002), 'Theatrical Patronage and Urban Community during the Reign of Mary', in Paul Whitfield White and Suzanne R. Westfall (eds), *Shakespeare and Theatrical Patronage in Early Modern England* (Cambridge: Cambridge University Press), 176–218.

Blake, Ann (1987), ' "The Humour of Children": John Marston's Plays in the Private Theatres', *Review of English Studies*, new ser., 38: 471–82.

Blau, Herbert (2004), 'Thinking History, History Thinking', *Theatre Survey*, 45: 253–61.

Blayney, Peter W. M. (1997), 'The Publication of Playbooks', in J. D. Cox and D. S. Kastan (eds), *A New History of Early English Drama* (New York: Columbia University Press), 383–422.

Bloch, Marc (1953), *The Historian's Craft*, trans. Peter Putnam, introd. Joseph R. Strayer, note on MS by Lucien Febvre (New York: Random House).

Bloom, Gina (1998), ' "Thy Voice Squeaks": Listening for Masculinity on the Early Modern Stage', *Renaissance Drama*, new ser., 26: 39–71.

Bly, Mary (2000), *Queer Virgins and Virgin Queans on the Early Modern Stage* (Oxford: Oxford University Press).

—— (2007), 'Playing the Tourist in Early Modern London: Selling the Liberties Onstage', *PMLA* 122: 61–71.

Boardman, John (1989), *Athenian Red Figure Vases: The Classical Period* (London: Thames and Hudson).

Boas, Frederick Samuel (1914), *University Drama in the Tudor Age* (New York: Harper and Row).

Boddy, G. W. (1976), 'Players of Interludes in North Yorkshire in the Early Seventeenth Century', North Yorkshire County Record Office Publications, 10, *Journal*, 3 (Apr.), 95–130.

Boegehold, Alan L. (1999), *When a Gesture Was Expected: A Selection of Examples from Archaic and Classical Greek Literature* (Princeton: Princeton University Press).

Bosonnet, Felix (1978), *The Function of Stage Properties in Christopher Marlowe's Plays* (Bern: Francke Verlag).

Boswell, Eleanore (1932), *The Restoration Court Stage 1660–1702* (Cambridge, MA: Harvard University Press).

Boulton, James (1987), *Neighborhood and Society: A London Suburb in the Seventeenth Century* (Cambridge: Cambridge University Press).

Bourdieu, Pierre (1993), *A Theory of Cultural Production*, trans. Randal Jackson (New York: Columbia University Press).

Bowden, P. J. (1990), *Economic Change: Wages, Profits, Rents, 1500–1750* (Cambridge: Cambridge University Press).

Bowers, Roger (2000), 'The Playhouse of the Choristers of Paul's, *c*.1565–1608', *Theatre Notebook*, 54: 70–85.

—— (2004), 'Farrant, Richard (*c*.1528–1580)', in H. C. G. Matthew and Brian Harrison (eds), *Oxford Dictionary of National Biography* (Oxford: Oxford University Press), <http://www.oxforddnb.com/view/article/9186>, accessed 8 Oct. 2007.

Bowsher, J. M. C. (2006), 'Excavations at 86–90 Curtain Road, 3–15 New Inn Yard, London EC2: An Insight into Holywell Priory and the Theatre', personal communication, 20 Mar.

—— (2007), *The Rose Playhouse* (London: Museum of London Archaeological Service).

Boynton, L. (1967), *The Elizabethan Militia 1558–1638* (London: Routledge and Kegan Paul; Toronto: University of Toronto Press).

Bradbrook, M. C. (1962), *The Rise of the Common Player: A Study of Actor and Society in Shakespeare's England* (Cambridge, MA: Harvard University Press).

—— (1989), 'The Politics of Pageantry (London)', in Bradbrook, *Shakespeare in his Context: The Constellated Globe. The Collected Papers of Muriel Bradbrook*, iv (Hemel Hampstead: Harvester Wheatsheaf), 95–109.

Bradley, David (1992), *From Text to Performance in the Elizabethan Theatre* (Cambridge: Cambridge University Press).

Braunmuller, A. R. (1983), *George Peele* (Boston: Twayne).

Bray, Alan (1982), *Homosexuality in Renaissance England* (London: Gay Men's Press).

Brazell, J. H. (1968), *London Weather*, Meteorological Office Publication 783 (London).

Breight, C. (1989), 'Caressing the Great: Viscount Montague's Entertainment of Elizabeth at Cowdray, 1591', *Sussex Archaeological Collections*, 127: 147–66.

—— (1992), 'Realpolitik and Elizabethan Ceremony: The Earl of Hertford's Entertainment of Elizabeth at Elvetham, 1591', *Renaissance Quarterly*, 45/1: 20–48.

Bremmer, Jan (1991), 'Walking, Standing, and Sitting in Ancient Greek Culture', in Jan Bremmer and Herman Roodenburg (eds), *A Cultural History of Gesture* (Oxford: Polity Press), 15–35.

Brett, Philip (1961–2), 'The English Consort Song, 1570–1625', *Proceedings of the Royal Musical Association*, 88: 73–88.

Brett-James, N. (1935), *The Growth of Stuart London* (London: Unwin).

Brigden, Susan (1988), *London and the Reformation* (Oxford: Oxford University Press).

Bristol, Michael (1996), *Big-Time Shakespeare* (New York: Routledge).

Britland, Karen (2006), *Drama at the Courts of Queen Henrietta Maria* (Cambridge: Cambridge University Press).

Brodsky, Vivien (1986), 'Widows in Late Elizabethan London: Remarriage, Economic Opportunity and Family Orientations', in L. Bonfield, R. M. Smith, and K. Wrightson (eds), *The World We Have Gained: Histories of Population and Social Structure* (Oxford: Blackwell), 122–54.

Brodsky Elliott, Vivien (1981), 'Single Women in the London Marriage Market: Age, Status and Mobility, 1598–1619', in R. B. Outhwaite (ed.), *Marriage and Society: Studies in the Social History of Marriage* (New York: St Martin's Press), 81–100.

Brooks, C. W (1994), 'Apprenticeship, Social Mobility, and the Middling Sort, 1550–1800', in J. Barry and C. W. Brooks (eds), *The Middling Sort of People: Culture, Society, and Politics in England, 1550–1800* (Basingstoke: Macmillan).

Brooks, Douglas (2000), *From Playhouse to Printing House* (Cambridge: Cambridge University Press).

Brown, Pamela Allen (1999), 'The Counterfeit Innamorata, or, The Diva Vanishes', *Shakespeare Yearbook*, 10: 402–26.

Brown, Pamela Allen (2003), *Better a Shrew than a Sheep: Wichaomen, Drama, and the Culture of Jest in Early Modern England* (Ithaca, NY: Cornell University Press).

—— (2005), 'Jesting Rights: Women Players in the Manuscript Jestbook of Sir Nicholas Le Strange', in Pamela Allen Brown and Peter Parolin (eds), *Women Players in Early Modern England, 1500–1660: Beyond the All-Male Stage* (Aldershot: Ashgate), 305–14.

—— and Parolin, Peter (eds) (2005), 'Introduction', in Brown and Parolin (eds), *Women Players in Early Modern England, 1500–1660: Beyond the All-Male Stage* (Aldershot: Ashgate), 1–21.

Brown, Steve (1990), 'The Boyhood of Shakespeare's Heroines: Notes on Gender Ambiguity in the Sixteenth Century', *Studies in English Literature*, 30: 243–63.

Brownstein, Oscar Lee (1971*a*), 'The Saracen's Head, Islington: A Pre-Elizabethan Inn Playhouse', *Theatre Notebook*, 25: 68–72.

—— (1971*b*), 'A Record of London Inn-Playhouses from *c.*1565–1590', *Shakespeare Quarterly*, 22: 17–24.

—— (1979), 'Why Didn't Burbage Lease the Beargarden? A Conjecture in Comparative Architecture', in Herbert Berry (ed.), *The First Public Playhouse: The Theatre in Shoreditch 1576–1598* (Montreal: McGill-Queen's University Press), 81–96.

Bruster, Douglas (1992), *Drama and the Market in the Age of Shakespeare* (Cambridge: Cambridge University Press).

—— (1995), 'Local *Tempest*: Shakespeare and the Work of the Early Modern Playhouse', *JMRS* 25: 33–54.

—— (2002), 'The Dramatic Life of Objects in the Early Modern Theatre', in Jonathan Gil Harris and Natasha Korda (eds), *Staged Properties in Early Modern English Drama* (Cambridge: Cambridge University Press), 67–96.

Bryson, Norman (1981), *Word and Image* (Cambridge: Cambridge University Press).

—— (1983), *Vision and Painting: The Logic of the Gaze* (New Haven: Yale University Press).

—— (1992), 'Art in Context', in Ralph Cohen (ed.), *Studies in Historical Change* (Charlottesville: University Press of Virginia), 18–42.

——Michael Ann Holly, and Keith Moxey (eds) (1991), *Visual Theory: Painting and Interpretation* (New York: HarperCollins).

—— —— —— (eds) (1994), *Visual Culture: Images and Interpretations* (Hanover, NH: University Press of New England for Wesleyan University Press).

Burckhardt, Jacob (1990), *The Civilization of the Renaissance in Italy*, introd. Peter Burke, trans. S. G. C. Middlemore, with notes by Peter Murray (1860; London: Penguin).

Burke, Peter (2001), *Eyewitnessing: The Uses of Images as Historical Evidence* (Ithaca, NY: Cornell University Press).

Butler, M. (1982), 'Massinger's *The City Madam* and the Caroline Audience', *Renaissance Drama*, 13: 157–82.

—— (1984*a*), *Theatre and Crisis 1632–1642* (Cambridge: Cambridge University Press).

—— (1984*b*), 'Two Playgoers, and the Closing of the London Theatres, 1642', *Theatre Research International* 9: 93–9.

—— (2004), 'The Condition of the Theatres in 1642', in J. Milling and P. Thomson (eds), *The Cambridge History of British Theatre*, i: *Origins to 1660* (Cambridge: Cambridge University Press), 439–57.

—— (2006), 'Exeunt Fighting: Poets, Players and Impresarios at the Caroline Hall Theatres', in A. Zucker and A. B. Farmer (eds), *Localizing Caroline Drama: Politics and Economics of the Early Modern English Stage, 1625–1642* (New York: Palgrave), 97–128.

Cairns, Douglas (ed.) (2005), *Body Language in the Greek and Roman Worlds* (Swansea: Classical Press of Wales).

Callaghan, Dympna (2000), *Shakespeare without Women: Representing Gender and Race on the Renaissance Stage* (London: Routledge).

—— (2007), 'Introduction', in Callaghan (ed.), *The Impact of Feminism in English Renaissance Studies* (Houndmills: Palgrave Macmillan), 1–29.

Calthorpe, F. (1942), 'A Fair Vestal Throned by the West', *Baconiana*, 26: 171–2.

Campbell, Julie D. (2005), ' "Merry, Nimble, Stirring Spirit[s]": Academic, Salon and Commedia dell'Arte Influence on the *Innamorate* in *Love's Labour's Lost*', in Pamela Allen Brown and Peter Parolin (eds), *Women Players in Early Modern England, 1500–1660: Beyond the All-Male Stage* (Aldershot: Ashgate), 145–70.

Capp, Bernard (2003), 'Playgoers, Players and Cross-Dressing in Early Modern London: The Bridewell Evidence', *Seventeenth Century*, 18: 159–71.

Caputi, Anthony (1976), *John Marston, Satirist* (1961; New York: Octagon Books).

Carnegie, D. (1982), 'Actors' Parts and the "Play of Poore" ', *Harvard Library Bulletin*, 30: 5–24.

Carrier, David (1987), *Artwriting* (Amherst: University of Massachusetts Press).

—— (1991), *Principles of Art History Writing* (University Park: Pennsylvania State University Press).

—— (1993), *Poussin's Paintings: A Study in Art-Historical Methodology* (University Park: Pennsylvania State University Press).

—— (2003), *Writing about Visual Art* (New York: Allworth Press).

Carter, Tim (1995), 'Secular Vocal Music', in Roger Bray (ed.), *Music in Britain: The Sixteenth Century* (Oxford: Blackwell), 147–209.

Castells, Manuel, and Alejandro Portes (1989), 'World Underneath: The Origins, Dynamics, and Effects of the Informal Economy', in Alejandro Portes, Manuel Castells, and Lauren A. Benton (eds), *The Informal Economy: Studies in Advanced and Less Developed Countries* (Baltimore: Johns Hopkins University Press), 11–37.

Cathcart, Charles (2000), 'Plural Authorship, Attribution, and the Children of the King's Revels', *Renaissance Forum*, 4/2, <http://www.hull.ac.uk/renforum/v4no2/cathcart.htm>.

—— (2005), 'Authorship, Indebtedness, and the Children of the King's Revels', *Studies in English Literature, 1500–1900*, 45/2: 357–74.

—— (2006), 'John Marston, *The Malcontent* and the King's Men', *Review of English Studies*, new ser., 57: 43–63.

Cavanaugh, Jean C. (1984), 'Lady [Anne] Southwell's Defense of Poetry', *English Literary Renaissance*, 14, n.p.

Cerasano, Susan P. (1985), 'The "Business" of Shareholding, the Fortune Playhouses, and Francis Grace's Will', *Medieval and Renaissance Drama in England*, 2: 231–51.

—— (1994*a*), 'Borrowed Robes, Costume Prices, and the Drawing of *Titus Andronicus*', *Shakespeare Studies*, 22: 45–57.

—— (1994*b*), 'Edward Alleyn: 1566–1626', in Aileen Reid and Robert Maniura (eds), *Edward Alleyn: Elizabethan Actor, Jacobean Gentleman* (London: Dulwich Picture Gallery), 11–31.

—— (2004*a*), 'Alleyn, Edward', in H. C. G. Matthew and Brian Harrison (eds), *Oxford Dictionary of National Biography* (Oxford: Oxford University Press), <http://www.oxforddnb.com/view/article/398>, accessed 2 Sept. 2007.

—— (2004*b*), 'Henslowe, Philip', in H. C. G. Matthew and Brian Harrison (eds), *Oxford Dictionary of National Biography* (Oxford: Oxford University Press), <http://www.oxforddnb.com/view/article/12991>, accessed 2 Sept. 2007.

—— (2005*a*), 'Edward Alleyn, the New Model Actor, and the Rise of the Celebrity in the 1590s', *Medieval and Renaissance Drama in England*, 18: 47–58.

—— (2005*b*), 'The Geography of Henslowe's Diary', *Shakespeare Quarterly*, 56: 328–53.

Cerasano, Susan P. (2006), 'Economics', in Donna Hamilton (ed.), *A Concise Companion to English Renaissance Literature* (Oxford: Blackwell), 11–31.

—— (2007), 'Philip Henslowe and the Elizabethan Court', *Shakespeare Survey*, 60: 49–57.

—— (2008), *Relocating the Fortune Playhouse: A New History* (London: Shakespeare's Globe Publications).

—— and Marion Wynne-Davies (eds) (1996), *Renaissance Drama by Women* (London: Routledge).

—— —— (eds) (1998), *Readings in Renaissance Women's Drama: Criticism, History and Performance 1594–1998* (London: Routledge).

Chambers, E. K. (1903), *The Medieval Stage*, 2 vols (Oxford: Clarendon Press).

—— (1916), 'The Occasion of *A Midsummer Night's Dream*', in I. Gollancz (ed.), *A Book of Homage to Shakespeare* (Oxford: Oxford University Press), 154–60.

—— (1923), *The Elizabethan Stage*, 4 vols (Oxford: Clarendon Press).

—— (1925), 'The First Illustration to Shakespeare', *The Library*, 4th ser., 5: 326–30.

—— (1930), *William Shakespeare: A Study of Facts and Problems*, 2 vols (Oxford: Oxford University Press).

Chan, Mary (1980), *Music in the Theatre of Ben Jonson* (Oxford: Oxford University Press).

Charles, Lindsey, and Lorna Duffin (eds) (1985), *Women and Work in Pre-industrial England* (London: Croom Helm).

Charney, Maurice (1975), 'The Children's Plays in Performance', *Research Opportunities in Renaissance Drama*, 18: 19–23.

Cheetham, Mark A., Michael Ann Holly, and Keith Moxey (eds) (1998), *The Subjects of Art History: Historical Objects in Contemporary Perspective* (Cambridge: Cambridge University Press).

Clare, Janet (1999), *'Art Made Tongue-Tied by Authority': Elizabethan and Jacobean Dramatic Censorship*, 2nd edn (Manchester: Manchester University Press).

Clark, Alice (1919), *Working Life of Women in the Seventeenth Century* (New York: A. M. Kelley).

Clark, Sandra (2002), 'The Broadside Ballad and the Woman's Voice', in C. Malcolmson and M. Suzuki (eds), *Debating Gender in Early Modern England* (Houndmills: Palgrave Macmillan), 103–20.

Clubb, Louise George (1989), *Italian Drama in Shakespeare's Time* (New Haven: Yale University Press).

Cole, M. H. (2000), *The Portable Queen: Elizabeth I and the Politics of Ceremony* (Amherst: University of Massachusetts Press).

Cole, Maija Jansson (1981), 'A New Account of the Burning of the Globe', *Shakespeare Quarterly*, 32: 352.

Coleman, D. C., and A. H. John (eds) (1976), *Trade, Government, and Economy in Pre-industrial England: Essays Presented to F. J. Fisher* (London: Weidenfeld & Nicolson).

Collinson, Patrick (1982), *The Religion of Protestants: The Church in English Society, 1559–1625* (Oxford: Oxford University Press).

—— (1984), *Godly People: Essays on English Puritanism and Protestantism* (London: Hambledon Press).

—— (1994), 'The Monarchical Republic of Queen Elizabeth I', in Collinson (ed.), *Elizabethan Essays* (London: Hambledon Press).

Consitt, F. (1933), *The London Weaver's Company*, i: *From the Twelfth Century to the Close of the Sixteenth Century* (Oxford: Clarendon Press).

Cook, Ann Jennalie (1981), *The Privileged Playgoers of Shakespeare's London, 1576–1642* (Princeton: Princeton University Press).

Cooper, Tarnya (2006), *Searching for Shakespeare, with Essays by Marcia Pointon, James Shapiro, and Stanley Wells* (New Haven: Yale University Press).

Cope, Jackson (1974), 'Marlowe's Dido and the Titillating Children', *English Literary Review*, 4: 315–25.

Corrigan, Brian Jay (2001), 'Of Dogges and Gulls: Sharp Dealing at the Swan (1597)... and Again at St. Paul's (1606)', *Theatre Notebook*, 55: 119–129.

Cotton, Nancy (1980), *Women Playwrights in England c.1363–1750* (Lewisburg, PA: Bucknell University Press; London: Associated University Presses).

Cox, John D. (2000), *The Devil and the Sacred in English Drama, 1350–1642* (Cambridge: Cambridge University Press).

—— and D. S. Kastan (eds) (1997), *A New History of Early English Drama* (New York: Columbia University Press).

Craig, Hugh (2001), ' "An Image of the Times": Ben Jonson's Revision of *Every Man in his Humour*', *English Studies*, 82: 14–33.

Craik, T. W. (1953), 'The Interpretation of Two Tudor Interludes: *Temperance and Humility* and *Wealth and Health*', *Review of English Studies*, 4: 98–108.

—— (1958), *The Tudor Interlude: Stage, Costume, and Acting* (Leicester: Leicester University Press).

Csapo, Eric, and William J. Slater (1995), *The Context of Ancient Drama* (Ann Arbor: University of Michigan Press).

Cutts, John P. (1959), 'Henry Shirley's *The Virgin Martyr*', *Renaissance News*, 12: 251–3.

—— (1961*a*), 'Thomas Heywood's "The Gentry to the King's Head" in *The Rape of Lucrece* and John Wilson's Setting', *Notes and Queries*, new ser., 8: 384–7.

—— (1961*b*), 'Music and *The Mad Lover*', *Studies in the Renaissance*, 8: 236–48.

—— (1963), 'Thomas Nabbes' *Hannibal and Scipio*', *English Miscellany*, 14: 73–81.

—— (1966), 'New Findings with regard to the 1624 Protection List', *Shakespeare Survey*, 19: 101–7.

—— (1971), *La Musique de scène de la troupe de Shakespeare: The King's Men sous le règne de Jacques 1er*, 2nd edn (Paris: Éditions du Centre National de la Recherche Scientifique).

—— (1983), 'The Music', in R. B. Parker (ed.), *Volpone* (Manchester: Manchester University Press), app. A.

—— (1986), 'Original Music for Two Caroline Plays: Richard Brome's *The English Moor, or, The Mock-Marriage* and James Shirley's *The Gentleman of Venice*', *Notes and Queries*, new ser., 33: 21–5.

Dale, A. M. (1969), *Collected Papers*, ed. T. B. L. Webster and E. G. Turner (Cambridge: Cambridge University Press).

Daly, Peter M. (1984), 'Shakespeare and the Emblem: The Use of Evidence and Analogy in Establishing Iconographic and Emblematic Effects in the Plays', in Tibor Fabiny (ed.), *Shakespeare and the Emblem: Studies in Renaissance Iconography and Iconology* (Szegad: Department of English, József Attila University), 50–118.

Davidson, Clifford (1977), *Drama and Art: An Introduction to the Use of Evidence from the Visual Arts for the Study of Early Drama* (Kalamazoo: Medieval Institute Publications, Western Michigan University).

—— (ed.) (1984), *Word, Picture, and Spectacle* (Kalamazoo: Medieval Institute Publications, Western Michigan University).

—— (1986–7), 'Iconography and Some Problems of Terminology in the Study of the Drama and Theatre of the Renaissance', *Research Opportunities in Renaissance Drama*, 29: 7–14.

—— (1991), *Illustrations of the Stage and Acting in England to 1580* (Kalamazoo: Medieval Institute Publications, Western Michigan University).

Davidson, Clifford (2001), *Gesture in Medieval Drama and Art* (Kalamazoo: Medieval Institute Publications, Western Michigan University).

Davidson, James West (1984), 'The New Narrative History: How New? How Narrative?', *Reviews in American History*, 12: 322–334.

Davidson, Peter (2000), 'The Chamberlain's Men's Tour of 1597', in Grace Ioppolo (ed.), *Shakespeare Performed: Essays in Honour of R. A. Foakes* (Cranbury, NJ: University of Delaware Press), 56–71.

Davis, N. (1979), *Non-Cycle Plays and the Winchester Dialogues* (Oxford: Oxford University Press for the Early English Text Society).

Dawson, Anthony B., and Paul Yachnin (2001), *The Culture of Playgoing in Shakespeare's England: A Collaborative Debate* (Cambridge: Cambridge University Press).

De Grazia, Margreta (1996), 'The Ideology of Superfluous Things: *King Lear* as Period Piece', in Margreta De Grazia, Maureen Quilligan, and Peter Stallybrass (eds), *Subject and Object in Renaissance Culture* (Cambridge: Cambridge University Press), 17–42.

—— Maureen Quilligan, and Peter Stallybrass (eds) (1996), *Subject and Object in Renaissance Culture* (Cambridge: Cambridge University Press).

DeMolen, Richard (1991), *Richard Mulcaster (c.1531–1611) and Educational Reform in the Renaissance* (Nieuwkoop: De Graaf).

Derrida, Jacques (1976), *Of Grammatology*, trans. Gayatri Chakrovorty Spivak (Baltimore: Johns Hopkins University Press).

—— (1999), 'Letter to a Japanese Friend', in Julian Wolfreys (ed.), *Literary Theories: A Reader and Guide* (Edinburgh: Edinburgh University Press), 282–8.

Dessen, Alan C. (1984), *Elizabethan Stage Directions and Modern Interpreters* (Cambridge: Cambridge University Press).

—— (1995), *Recovering Shakespeare's Theatrical Vocabulary* (Cambridge: Cambridge University Press).

—— and Thomson, Leslie (1999), *A Dictionary of Stage Directions in English Drama 1580–1642* (Cambridge: Cambridge University Press).

DiGangi, Mario (1997), *The Homoerotics of Early Modern Drama* (Cambridge: Cambridge University Press).

Dillon, Janette (2000), *Theatre, Court and City, 1595–1610: Drama and Social Space in London* (Cambridge: Cambridge University Press).

—— (2002), *Performance and Spectacle in Hall's Chronicle* (London: Society for Theatre Research).

Dollimore, Jonathan (1985), 'Transgression and Surveillance in *Measure for Measure*', in Jonathan Dollimore and Alan Sinfield (eds), *Political Shakespeare: New Essays in Cultural Materialism* (Manchester: Manchester University Press), 72–87.

—— (2004), *Radical Tragedy*, 3rd edn (London: Palgrave).

Donohue, Joseph W., Jr (ed.) (1971), *The Theatrical Manager in England and America* (Princeton: Princeton University Press).

—— (1989), 'Evidence and Documentation', in Thomas Postlewait and Bruce A. McConachie (eds), *Interpreting the Theatrical Past: Essays in the Historiography of Performance* (Iowa City: University of Iowa Press), 177–197.

Doran, Susan (1996), *Monarchy and Matrimony: The Courtships of Elizabeth I* (London: Routledge).

Dovey, Z. (1996), *An Elizabethan Progress: The Queen's Journey into East Anglia, 1578* (Madison: Fairleigh Dickinson University Press).

Dowling, Margaret (1934), 'A Note on Moll Cutpurse—"The Roaring Girl" ', *Review of English Studies*, 10: 67–71.

Duckles, Vincent (1968), 'Music for the Lyrics in Early Seventeenth Century English Drama: A Bibliography of the Primary Sources', in John H. Long (ed.), *Music in English Renaissance Drama* (Lexington: University of Kentucky Press), 117–60.

Duncan, Ann (2006), *Performance and Identity in the Classical World* (Cambridge: Cambridge University Press).

Dundes, Alan (ed.) (1994), *The Cockfight: A Casebook* (Madison: University of Wisconsin Press).

Dunlop, I. (1962), *Palaces and Progresses of Elizabeth I* (London: Jonathan Cape).

Dusinberre, Juliet (2003), 'Pancakes and a Date for *As You Like It*', *Shakespeare Quarterly*, 54: 371–405.

Dutton, Richard (1989), '*Hamlet*, *An Apology for Actors*, and the Sign of the Globe', *Shakespeare Survey*, 41: 35–43.

—— (1991), *Mastering the Revels* (Iowa City: University of Iowa Press).

—— (1995), 'General Introduction', in Dutton (ed.), *Jacobean Civic Pageants* (Ryburn: Keele University Press), 7–18.

—— (1997*a*), 'The Birth of the Author', in Cedric C. Brown and Arthur F. Marotti (eds), *Texts and Cultural Change in Early Modern England* (New York: St Martin's Press).

—— (1997*b*), 'Censorship', in John D. Cox and D. S. Kastan (eds), *A New History of Early English Drama* (New York: Columbia University Press), 287–304.

—— (2000), *Licensing, Censorship and Authorship in Early Modern England* (Basingstoke: Palgrave).

—— (2002), 'The Revels Office and the Boy Companies, 1600–1613: New Perspectives', *English Literary Renaissance*, 32: 324–51.

—— (ed.) (2003), *Epicene* (Manchester: Manchester University Press).

—— (2005), '"Methinks the Truth Should Live from Age to Age": The Dating and Contexts of *Henry V*', *Huntington Library Quarterly*, 68: 173–204.

——A. Findlay, and R. Wilson (eds) (2003), *Region, Religion and Patronage: Lancastrian Shakespeare* (Manchester: Manchester University Press).

Dymkowski, Christine (2000), *Shakespeare in Production: The Tempest* (Cambridge: Cambridge University Press).

Earle, Peter (1989), 'The Female Labour Market in London in the Late Seventeenth and Early Eighteenth Centuries', *Economic History Review*, 2nd ser., 42: 328–53.

Easterling, P. E. (ed.) (1997), *The Cambridge Companion to Greek Tragedy* (Cambridge: Cambridge University Press).

—— and Edith Hall (2002), *Greek and Roman Actors: Aspects of an Ancient Profession* (Cambridge: Cambridge University Press).

Eccles, Christine (1990), *The Rose Theatre* (London: Nick Hern Books).

Eccles, Mark (1933), 'Barnabe Barnes', in C. J. Sisson (ed.), *Thomas Lodge and Other Elizabethans* (Cambridge, MA: Harvard University Press), 166–241.

—— (1958), 'Martin Peerson and the Blackfriars', *Shakespeare Survey*, 11: 100–6.

—— (1985), 'Mary Frith, the Roaring Girl', *Notes and Queries*, new ser., 32: 65–6.

—— (1991*a*), 'Elizabethan Actors I: A–D', *Notes and Queries*, 236: 38–49.

—— (1991*b*), 'Elizabethan Actors II: E–J', *Notes and Queries*, 237: 454–61.

Edmond, Mary (1974), 'Pembroke's Men', *Review of English Studies*, new ser., 25: 129–36.

—— (1993), 'Peter Street, 1553–1609: Builder of Playhouses', *Shakespeare Survey*, 45: 101–14.

—— (1996), 'Yeoman, Citizens, Gentlemen and Players: The Burbages and their Connections', in R. B. Parker and S. P. Zitner (eds), *Elizabethan Theater: Essays in Honor of S. Schoenbaum* (Newark: University of Delaware Press), 30–49.

Edmond, Mary (2004), 'James Burbage', in H. C. G. Matthew and Brian Harrison (eds), *Oxford Dictionary of National Biography* (Oxford: Oxford University Press), <http://www.oxforddnb.com/view/article/3950>, accessed 2 Sept. 2007.

Elam, Keir (1980), *The Semiotics of Theatre and Drama* (London: Routledge).

Eley, Geoff (1996), 'Is All the World a Text? From Social History to the History of Society Two Decades Later', in Terrence J. McDonald (ed.), *The Historic Turn in the Human Sciences* (Ann Arbor: University of Michigan Press), 193–243.

Eliot, T. S. (1934), *Elizabethan Essays* (London: Faber and Faber).

Elliott, John R., Jr (1993), 'Four Caroline Playgoers', *Medieval and Renaissance Drama in England*, 6: 179–96.

Ellis, H. (1798), *The History and Antiquities of the Parish of Saint Leonard Shoreditch* (London: J. Nichols).

Elton, William R. (2000), *Shakespeare's 'Troilus and Cressida', and the Inns of Court Revels* (London: Ashgate Press).

Emmison, F. G. (1964), *Tudor Food and Pastimes* (London: Ernest Benn).

Erickson, A. L. (1992), 'Introduction', in Alice Clark, *Working Life of Women in the Seventeenth Century*, 2nd edn (New York: Routledge), pp. vii–lv.

Erler, Mary C. (1991), ' "Chaste Sports, Juste Prayses, & All Softe Delight": Harefield 1602 and Ashby 1607, Two Female Entertainments', in A. L. Magnuson and C. E. McGee (eds), *The Elizabethan Theatre XIV* (Toronto: P. D. Meany), 1–25.

Erne, Lukas (2003), *Shakespeare as Literary Dramatist* (Cambridge: Cambridge University Press).

Fairholt, F. (1843–4), *Lord Mayors' Pageants*, 2 pts (London: Percy Society).

Farmer, Alan B., and Zachary Lesser (2005), 'The Popularity of Playbooks Revisited', *Shakespeare Quarterly*, 56: 1–32.

—— —— (2008), DEEP Database of Early English Playbooks, <http://deep.sas.upenn.edu>.

Ferman, Louis A., Stuart Henry, and Michele Hoyman (1987), 'Preface: The Informal Economy', *Annals of the American Academy of Political and Social Science*, 493: 10–14.

Findlay, Alison, and Richard Dutton (2003), 'Introduction', in R. Dutton, A. Findlay, and R. Wilson, *Region, Religion and Patronage: Lancastrian Shakespeare* (Manchester: Manchester University Press), 1–31.

—— and Stephanie Hodgson-Wright, with Gweno Williams (2000), *Women and Dramatic Production, 1550–1700* (Harlow: Pearson).

Finkelpearl, Philip Joseph (1969), *John Marston of the Middle Temple* (Cambridge, MA: Harvard University Press).

Fisher, Sidney (1964), *The Theatre, the Curtain, and the Globe* (Montreal: McGill University Library).

Fisher, Will (2006), *Materializing Gender in Early Modern English Literature and Culture* (Cambridge: Cambridge University Press).

Fitzmaurice, J. (2006), 'Shakespeare, Cavendish, and Reading Aloud in Seventeenth-Century England', in K. Romack and J. Fitzmaurice (eds), *Cavendish and Shakespeare: Interconnections* (London: Ashgate), 29–46.

Fleay, F. G. (1890), *A Chronicle History of the London Stage, 1559–1642* (London: Reaves and Turner).

Foakes, R. A. (1962), 'John Marston's Fantastical Plays: *Antonio and Mellida* and *Antonio's Revenge*', *Philological Quarterly*, 41: 229–39.

—— (1970), 'Tragedy at the Children's Theatres after 1600: A Challenge to the Adult Stage', in David Galloway (ed.), *The Elizabethan Theatre II* (Archon Books: New Haven), 37–59.

—— (1971), *Shakespeare: The Dark Comedies to the Last Plays: From Satire to Celebration* (London: Routledge and Kegan Paul).

—— (1985), *Illustrations of the London Stage 1580–1642* (Stanford, CA: Stanford University Press).

—— (1993), 'The Image of the Swan Theatre', in André Lascombes (ed.), *Spectacle & Image in Renaissance Europe: Selected Papers of the XXXIInd Conference at the Centre d'Études Supérieures de la Renaissance de Tours, 29 June–8 July 1989* (Leiden: E. J. Brill), 337–57.

—— (2002), *Henslowe's Diary*, 2nd edn (Cambridge: Cambridge University Press).

—— (2004), 'Henslowe's Rose/Shakespeare's Globe', in Peter Holland and Stephen Orgel (eds), *From Script to Stage in Early Modern England* (Basingstoke: Palgrave), 11–31.

—— and R. T. Rickert (eds) (1961), *Henslowe's Diary* (Cambridge: Cambridge University Press).

Foley, Helene (2000), 'The Comic Body in Greek Art and Drama', in Beth Cohen (ed.), *Not the Classical Ideal* (Boston: E. J. Brill), 275–312.

—— (2003), *Female Acts in Greek Tragedy* (Princeton: Princeton University Press).

Folkerth, Wes (2002), *The Sound of Shakespeare*, Accents on Shakespeare (London: Routledge).

Fontaine, Laurence (2001), 'Women's Economic Spheres and Credit in Pre-industrial Europe', in Beverly Lemire, Ruth Pearson, and Gail Campbell (eds), *Women and Credit: Researching the Past, Refiguring the Future* (Oxford: Berg), 15–32.

Forse, James H. (1993), *Art Imitates Business: Commercial and Political Influence in the Elizabethan Theater* (Bowling Green, OH: Bowling Green State University Popular Press).

Foucault, Michel (1979), 'What Is an Author?', in Josue V. Harari (ed.), *Textual Strategies: Perspectives in Post Structuralist Criticism* (Ithaca, NY: Cornell University Press).

Fox-Good, Jacquelyn A. (1995), 'Ophelia's Mad Songs: Music, Gender, Power', in David G. Allen and Robert A. White (eds), *Subjects on the World's Stage: Essays on British Literature of the Middle Ages and Renaissance* (London: Associated University Presses), 217–38.

Fraser, R. A., and N. Rabkin (eds) (1976), *Drama of the English Renaissance*, i: *The Tudor Period* (New York: Macmillan).

Freedman, B. (1996), 'Elizabethan Protest, Plague, and Plays: Re-reading the Documents of Control', *English Literary Renaissance*, 26: 17–45.

Froide, Amy M. (1999), 'Marital Status as a Category of Difference: Singlewomen and Widows in Early Modern England', in Judith M. Bennett and Amy M. Froide (eds), *Singlewomen in the European Past, 1250–1800* (Philadelphia: University of Pennsylvania Press), 236–69.

—— (2005), *Never Married: Singlewomen in Early Modern England* (Oxford: Oxford University Press).

Gair, Reavley (1982), *The Children of Paul's: The Story of a Theatre Company, 1553–1608* (Cambridge: Cambridge University Press).

Gaughan, Joseph P., and Louis A. Ferman (1987), 'Toward an Understanding of the Informal Economy', *Annals of the American Academy of Political and Social Science*, 493: 15–25.

Gee, Malcolm (ed.) (1993), *Art Criticism since 1900* (Manchester: Manchester University Press).

George, David (1994), 'Anti-Catholic Plays, Puppet Shows, and Horse-Racing in Reformation Lancashire', *Records of Early English Drama Newsletter*, 19: 15–22.

Gerritsen, Johan (1959), 'Stansby and Jonson Produce a Folio: A Preliminary Account', *English Studies: A Journal of English Language and Literature*, 40: 52–5.

—— (1986), 'De Witt, Van Buchell, the Swan and the Globe: Some Notes', in Peter Bilton et al. (eds), *Essays in Honour of Kristian Schmidt* (Oslo: University of Oslo, Institute of English Studies), 29–45.

—— (1995), 'The Swan Theatre Drawing: A Review', *Folio*, 2: 33–8.

Gibbons, B. (1980), *Jacobean City Comedy*, 2nd edn (London: Methuen).

Gibson, James M. (1995), 'Stuart Players in Kent: Fact or Fiction?', *Records of Early English Drama Newsletter*, 20/2: 7–8.

—— (2007), 'An Early Seventeenth-Century Playhouse in Tonbridge, Kent', *Medieval and Renaissance Drama in England*, 20: 236–55.

Gildersleeve, Virginia C. (1908), *Government Regulation of the Elizabethan Drama* (New York: Columbia University Press).

Ginzburg, Carlo (1989), 'From Aby Warburg to E. H. Gombrich: A Problem of Method', in Ginzburg, *Clues, Myths, and the Historical Method*, trans. John and Anne C. Tedeschi (Baltimore: Johns Hopkins University Press), 17–59, 170–94.

Gleason, John B. (1981), 'The De Witt Drawing of the Swan Theatre', *Shakespeare Quarterly*, 32: 324–38.

—— (2003), 'New Questions about the Globe', *Times Literary Supplement*, 26 Sept., 15.

Goldberg, Jonathan (1983), *James I and the Politics of Literature* (Baltimore: Johns Hopkins University Press).

Goldhill, Simon, and Robin Osborne (eds) (1999), *Performance Culture and Athenian Democracy* (Cambridge: Cambridge University Press).

Gombrich, E. H. (1968), *Art and Illusion: A Study in the Psychology of Pictorial Presentation* (London: Phaidon).

—— (1978), *Studies in the Art of the Renaissance*, 2 vols, i: *Norm and Form*; ii: *Symbolic Images* (Oxford: Phaidon).

—— (1986), *Aby Warburg: An Intellectual Biography, with a Memoir on the History of the Library by Fritz Saxl* (Oxford: Phaidon).

Gossett, Suzanne (1998), ' "Man-Maid, Begone!" Women in Masques', *English Literary Renaissance*, 18: 96–113.

—— (2004), 'Marston, Collaboration, and *Eastward Hoe!*', *Renaissance Drama*, 33: 181–200.

Gottschalk, Louis (1969), *Understanding History: A Primer of Historical Methods*, 2nd edn (New York: Alfred A. Knopf).

Gough, Melinda J. (2003), ' "Not as Myself": The Queen's Voice in *Tempe Restored*', *Modern Philology*, 101: 48–67.

—— (2005), 'Courtly *Comédiantes*: Henrietta Maria and Amateur Women's Stage Plays in France and England', in Pamela Allen Brown and Peter Parolin (eds), *Women Players in Early Modern England, 1500–1660: Beyond the All-Male Stage* (Aldershot: Ashgate), 193–215.

Grantley, Darryll (2000), *Wit's Pilgrimage: Drama and the Social Impact of Education in Early Modern England* (Aldershot: Ashgate).

Grassby, Richard (1995), *The Business Community of Seventeenth-Century England* (Cambridge: Cambridge University Press).

—— (2001), *Kinship and Capitalism: Marriage, Family, and Business in the English Speaking World, 1580–1740* (Cambridge: Cambridge University Press).

Graves, M. A. R. (1994), *Thomas Norton, the Parliament Man* (Oxford: Blackwell).

Graves, Robert B. (1999), *Lighting the Shakespearean Stage: 1567–1642* (Carbondale: Southern Illinois University Press).

Graves, Thornton S. (1925), 'Women on the Pre-Restoration Stage', *Studies in Philology*, 22: 184–97.

Green, Adwin Wigfall (1931), *The Inns of Court and Early English Drama* (New York: Benjamin Blom; repr. New Haven: Yale University Press, 1965).

Green, Richard (1991), 'On Seeing and Depicting the Theatre in Classical Athens', *Greek, Roman and Byzantine Studies*, 32: 15–50.

—— (1999), 'Tragedy and the Spectacle of the Mind: Messenger Speeches, Actors, Narrative, and Audience Imagination in Fourth-Century BCE Vase-Painting', in Bettina Bergmann and Christine Kondoleon (eds), *The Art of Ancient Spectacle* (New Haven: Yale University Press), 37–63.

—— (2002), 'Towards a Reconstruction of Performance Style', in P. E. Easterling and Edith Hall (eds), *Greek and Roman Actors: Aspects of an Ancient Profession* (Cambridge: Cambridge University Press), 93–126.

—— and Eric Handley (1995), *Images of the Greek Theatre* (Austin: University of Texas Press).

Greenblatt, Stephen (1980), *Renaissance Self-Fashioning: From More to Shakespeare* (Chicago: University of Chicago Press).

—— (1985), 'Invisible Bullets: Renaissance Authority and its Subversion, *Henry IV* and *Henry V*', in Jonathan Dollimore and Alan Sinfield (eds), *Political Shakespeare: New Essays in Cultural Materialism* (Ithaca, NY: Cornell University Press), 18–47.

—— (1988), *Shakespearean Negotiations: The Circulation of Social Energy in Renaissance England* (Berkeley and Los Angeles: University of California Press).

—— (2002), *Hamlet in Purgatory* (Princeton: Princeton University Press).

—— (2007), 'Shakespeare and the Uses of Power', *New York Review of Books*, 54/6: 75–7, 81–2.

Greenfield, Peter H. (1983), 'Entertainments of Henry, Lord Berkeley, 1593–4 and 1600–05', *Records of Early English Drama Newsletter*, 8/1: 12–24.

—— (1988), 'Professional Players at Gloucester: Conditions of Provincial Performing', in C. E. McGee (ed.), *Elizabethan Theatre X* (Port Credit, Ont.: P. D. Meany), 73–92.

—— (1996), 'Festive Drama at Christmas in Aristocratic Households', in M. Twycross (ed.), *Festive Drama* (Cambridge: D. S. Brewer), 34–40.

—— (1997), 'Touring', in John D. Cox and D. S. Kastan (eds), *A New History of Early English Drama* (New York: Columbia University Press), 251–68.

—— (2001), 'The Occasional Patronage of "Lord Henry the Harmless", or, A History of Lord Berkeley's Men', Shakespeare Association of America seminar paper (unpublished).

—— (2004), 'Drama outside London after 1540', in J. Milling and P. Thomson (eds), *The Cambridge History of British Theater*, i: *Origins to 1660* (Cambridge: Cambridge University Press).

Greenstreet, James (1889), 'The Whitefriars Theatre in the Time of Shakespeare', *New Shakespeare Society Transactions*, ser. 1, pt 3 (London: Kegan Paul, Trench, Trübner), 269.

Greer, David (1992), 'Vocal Music I: Up to 1660', in Ian Spink (ed.), *Music in Britain: The Seventeenth Century* (Oxford: Blackwell), 138–74.

Greg, W. W. (1904–8), *Henslowe's Diary*, 2 vols (London: A. H. Bullen).

—— (1907), *Henslowe Papers* (London: A. H. Bullen).

—— (1970), *A Bibliography of the English Printed Drama to the Restoration*, 4 vols (London: Bibliographical Society).

Griffin, A. (1972), *Pageantry on the Shakespearean Stage* (New York: AMS).

Griffith, Eva (2001), 'New Material for a Jacobean Playhouse: The Red Bull Theatre on the Seckford Estate', *Theatre Notebook*, 55: 5–23.

—— (2004), 'Baskervile, Susan (*bap.* 1573, *d.* 1649)', in H. C. G. Matthew and Brian Harrison (eds), *Oxford Dictionary of National Biography* (Oxford: Oxford University Press).

Griffiths, Paul (1993), 'The Structure of Prostitution in Elizabethan England', *Continuity and Change*, 8: 39–64.

—— (2003), 'Contesting London Bridewell, 1576–1580', *Journal of British Studies*, 42/3: 283–315.

Guillory, John (1983), *Poetic Authority: Spenser, Milton, and Literary History* (New York: Columbia University Press).

Gurr, Andrew (1987), *Playgoing in Shakespeare's London*, 1st edn (Cambridge: Cambridge University Press).

Gurr, Andrew (1988), 'Singing through the Chatter: Ford and Contemporary Theatrical Fashion', in M. Neill (ed.), *John Ford: Critical Revisions* (Cambridge: Cambridge University Press), 81–96.

—— (1989), 'The Shakespearian Stage, Forty Years On', *Shakespeare Survey*, 41: 1–12.

—— (1992*a*), 'Cultural Property and "Sufficient Interest": The Rose and the Globe Sites', *Journal of Cultural Property*, 1: 9–25.

—— (1992*b*), *The Shakespearean Stage 1574 –1642*, 3rd edn (1970; Cambridge: Cambridge University Press).

—— (1993*a*), 'The Chimera of Amalgamation', *Theatre Research International*, 18/2: 85–93.

—— (1993*b*), 'Three Reluctant Patrons and Early Shakespeare', *Shakespeare Quarterly*, 44: 159–74.

—— (1994*a*), 'Playing in Ampitheatres and Playing in Hall Theatres', in A. L. Magnusson and C. E. McGee (eds), *Elizabethan Theatre XIII* (Toronto: P. D. Meany), 47–62.

—— (1994*b*), 'The Loss of Records for the Travelling Companies in Stuart Times', *REED Newsletter*, 19/2: 2–19.

—— (1996*a*), 'Entrances and Hierarchy in the Globe Auditorium', *Shakespeare Bulletin*, 14/4: 11–13.

—— (1996*b*), *The Shakespearian Playing Companies* (Oxford: Clarendon Press).

—— (1996*c*), 'Some Reasons to Focus on the Globe and on the Fortune: Stages and Stage Directions: Controls for the Evidence', *Theatre Survey*, 37: 23–33.

—— (1999), 'Stage Doors at the Globe', *Theatre Studies*, 53: 8–18.

—— (2002), 'Privy Councilors as Theatre Patrons', in Paul Whitfield White and Suzanne R. Westfall (eds), *Shakespeare and Theatrical Patronage in Early Modern England* (Cambridge: Cambridge University Press), 221–45.

—— (2004*a*), 'A New Theatre Historicism', in Peter Holland and Stephen Orgel (eds), *From Script to Stage in Early Modern England* (Basingstoke: Palgrave), 71–88.

—— (2004*b*), *Playgoing in Shakespeare's London*, 3rd edn (1987; Cambridge: Cambridge University Press).

—— (2004*c*), *The Shakespeare Company 1594–1642* (Cambridge: Cambridge University Press).

—— (2004*d*), 'Beeston, Christopher', in H. C. G. Matthew and Brian Harrison (eds), *Oxford Dictionary of National Biography* (Oxford: Oxford University Press).

—— (2005), 'Henry Carey's Peculiar Letter', *Shakespeare Quarterly*, 57: 51–73.

—— and Mariko Ichikawa (2000), *Staging in Shakespeare's Theatres* (Oxford: Oxford University Press).

See also ISGC (1993).

Guy, John (ed.) (1995), *The Reign of Elizabeth I: Court and Culture in the Last Decade* (Cambridge: Cambridge University Press).

—— (1997), *The Tudor Monarchy* (London: Arnold).

Haaker, A. (1968), 'The Plague, the Theater, and the Poet', *Renaissance Drama*, new ser., 1: 283–306.

Hafter, Daryl M. (ed.) (1995), *European Women and Preindustrial Craft* (Bloomington, IN: Indiana University Press).

Haigh, Christopher (1998), *Elizabeth I*, 2nd edn (1988; London: Longman).

Halasz, Alexandra (1997), *The Marketplace of Print: Pamphlets and the Public Sphere in Early Modern England* (Cambridge: Cambridge University Press).

Hall, Edith (2006), *The Theatrical Cast of Athens* (Oxford: Oxford University Press).

Halpern, Richard (1991), *The Poetics of Primitive Accumulation: English Renaissance Culture and the Genealogy of Capital* (Ithaca, NY: Cornell University Press).

Halstead, W. L. (1939), 'A Note on Dekker's *Old Fortunatus*', *Modern Language Notes*, 54: 351–2.

Hammer, Paul E. J. (1995), 'Patronage at Court, Faction and the Earl of Essex', in John Guy (ed.), *The Reign of Elizabeth I: Court and Culture in the Last Decade* (Cambridge: Cambridge University Press), 65–86.

—— (1999), *The Polarisation of Elizabethan Politics: The Political Career of Robert Devereux, 2nd Earl of Essex, 1585–1597* (Cambridge: Cambridge University Press).

—— (2003), *Elizabeth's Wars: War, Government and Society in Tudor England, 1544–1604* (Basingstoke: Palgrave).

Hanawalt, Barbara A. (1993), *Growing Up in Medieval London* (Oxford: Oxford University Press).

Harbage, Alfred (1941), *Shakespeare's Audience* (New York: Columbia University Press).

—— (1952), *Shakespeare and the Rival Traditions* (New York: Macmillan).

—— (1964), *Annals of English Drama 975–1700: An Analytical Record of All Plays, Extant or Lost, Chronologically Arranged and Indexed by Authors, Titles, Dramatic Companies, &c.*, rev. S. Schoenbaum (London: Methuen).

Harris, John, and A. A. Tait (1979), *Catalogue of the Drawings by Inigo Jones, John Webb, and Isaac de Caus at Worcester College Oxford* (Oxford: Clarendon Press).

Harris, Jonathan Gil (2001), 'Shakespeare's Hair: Staging the Object of Material Culture', *Shakespeare Quarterly*, 52: 479–91.

—— and Natasha Korda (2002), 'Introduction: Towards a Materialist Account of Stage Properties', in J. G. Harris and Natasha Korda (eds), *Staged Properties in Early Modern English Drama* (Cambridge: Cambridge University Press), 1–31.

Hart, Alfred (1934), *Shakespeare and the Homilies* (Melbourne: Melbourne University Press).

Haskell, Francis (1993), *History and its Images: Art and the Interpretation of the Past* (New Haven: Yale University Press).

Hasler, P. W. (ed.) (1981), *The History of Parliament: The House of Commons, 1558–1603*, 3 vols (London: HMSO).

Hattaway, Michael (1982), *Elizabethan Popular Theatre: Plays in Performance* (London: Routledge and Kegan Paul).

Hays, Rosalind Conklin (1992), 'Dorset Church Houses and the Drama', *Research Opportunities in Renaissance Drama*, 31: 12–23.

Heal, Felicity (1990), *Hospitality in Early Modern England* (Oxford: Clarendon Press).

Heinemann, Margot (1980), *Puritanism and Theatre: Thomas Middleton and Opposition Drama under the Early Stuarts* (Cambridge: Cambridge University Press).

—— (1991), ' "God Help the Poor: The Rich Can Shift": The World Upside-Down and the Popular Tradition in the Theatre', in G. McMullan and J. Hope (eds), *The Politics of Tragicomedy: Shakespeare and After* (New York: Routledge).

Henry, Stuart (1987), 'The Political Economy of Informal Economies', *Annals of the American Academy of Political and Social Science*, 493: 137–53.

Herlihy, David (1990), *Opera Muliebria: Women and Work in Medieval Europe* (New York: McGraw-Hill).

Hermerén, Göran (1969), *Representation and Meaning in the Visual Arts: A Study in the Methodology of Iconography and Iconology* (Stockholm: Norstedt).

Hickman, D. (1999), 'Religious Belief and Pious Practice among London's Elizabethan Elite', *Historical Journal*, 42/4: 941–60.

Higgott, Gordon (2006), 'Two Theatre Designs by John Webb in 1660', for the session 'Stages for Shakespeare's Theatre', 32nd International Shakespeare Conference, Shakespeare Institute, Stratford upon Avon, 6–11 Aug. 2006.

Hildy, Franklin (1993), 'If You Build it They Will Come', in *The Design of the Globe*, app. 3 (London: International Shakespeare Globe Centre), 89–106.

Hill, Christopher (ed.) (1977), *History and Culture* (London: Mitchell Beazley).

Hill, Tracey (2004), *Anthony Munday and Civic Culture: Theatre, History, and Power in Early Modern London, 1580–1633* (Manchester: Manchester University Press).

Hillebrand, Harold Newcomb (1964), *The Child Actors* (1926; New York: Russell and Russell).

Hirschfeld, Heather (2004), *Joint Enterprises: Collaborative Drama and the Institutionalization of the English Renaissance Theater* (Amherst: University of Massachusetts Press).

Hodges, C. Walter (1953), *The Globe Restored* (rev. 1968; London: Oxford University Press).

Holderness, B. A. (1984), 'Widows in Pre-industrial Society: An Essay upon their Economic Functions', in R. M. Smith (ed.), *Land, Kinship, and Life Cycle* (Cambridge: Cambridge University Press), 423–42.

Holland, Peter (2003), 'Series Introduction: Redefining British Theater History', in W. B. Worthen, with Peter Holland, *Theorizing Practice: Redefining Theatre History* (Basingstoke: Palgrave Macmillan).

—— (2004*a*), 'Redefining British Theatre History', in Peter Holland and Stephen Orgel (eds), *From Script to Stage in Early Modern England* (Basingstoke: Palgrave), pp. xi–xiii.

—— (2004*b*), 'Theatre without Drama: Reading *REED*', in Peter Holland and Stephen Orgel (eds), *From Script to Stage in Early Modern England* (Basingstoke: Palgrave), 43–67.

—— and Stephen Orgel (eds) (2004), *From Script to Stage in Early Modern England* (Basingstoke: Palgrave).

Hollindale, Peter (1985), 'Review', *Review of English Studies*, 36: 80–1.

Holly, Michael Ann (1984), *Panofsky and the Foundations of Art History* (Ithaca, NY: Cornell University Press).

—— (1996), *Past Looking: Historical Imagination and the Rhetoric of the Image* (Ithaca, NY: Cornell University Press).

—— and Keith Moxey (eds) (2002), *Art History, Aesthetics, Visual Studies* (Williamstown, MA: Sterling and Francine Clark Art Institute).

Holman, Peter (1992), 'Music for the Stage I: Before the Civil War', in Ian Spink (ed.), *Music in Britain: The Seventeenth Century* (Oxford: Blackwell), 282–305.

—— (1993), *Four and Twenty Fiddlers: The Violin at the English Court, 1540–1690* (Oxford: Oxford University Press).

—— (2000), Review of Bruce R. Smith, *The Acoustic World of Early Modern England: Attending to the O-Factor* (Chicago: University of Chicago Press), *Journal of the Royal Musical Association*, 125: 115–18.

Holmes, Martin (1950–1), 'An Unrecorded Portrait of Edward Alleyn', *Theatre Notebook*, 5: 11–13.

—— (1978), *Shakespeare and Burbage* (London: Phillimore).

Honigmann, E. A. J. (1998), *Shakespeare: The 'Lost Years'* (1985; Manchester: Manchester University Press).

—— (1998), *Myriad-Minded Shakespeare*, 2nd edn (London: Macmillan).

Hope, Jonathan (1994), *The Authorship of Shakespeare's Plays: A Socio-linguistic Study* (Cambridge: Cambridge University Press).

Horne, D. H. (1952), 'The Life', in Horne (ed.), *The Life and Minor Works of George Peele* (New Haven: Yale University Press), 3–146.

Hosley, Richard (1957), 'The Gallery over the Stage in the Public Playhouse of Shakespeare's Time', *Shakespeare Quarterly*, 8: 15–31.

—— (1975), 'The Playhouses', in C. Leech and T. W. Craik (gen. eds), *The Revels History of Drama in English*, 8 vols (London: Methuen), iii. 119–235.

—— (1979), 'The Theatre and the Tradition of Playhouse Design', in Herbert Berry (ed.), *The First Public Playhouse: The Theatre in Shoreditch 1576–1598* (Montreal: McGill-Queen's University Press), 47–79.

Hotson, Leslie (1928), *The Commonwealth and Restoration Stage* (Cambridge, MA: Harvard University Press).

—— (1954), 'Shakespeare's Wooden O', *The Times*, 26 Mar., 7, 14.

—— (1962), *The Commonwealth and Restoration Stage* (1928; repr. New York: Russell and Russell).

Howard, Jean E. (1994), *The Stage and Social Struggle in Early Modern England* (London: Routledge).

—— (2007), *Theater of a City: The Places of London Comedy, 1598–1642* (Philadelphia: University of Pennsylvania Press).

Howard, S. (1998), 'In Praise of Margaret Brayne', paper presented at the Shakespeare Association of America conference, Cleveland, Ohio.

Hoyman, Michele (1987), 'Female Participation in the Informal Economy: A Neglected Issue', *Annals of the American Academy of Political and Social Science*, 493: 64–82.

Hufton, Olwen H. (1974), *The Poor of Eighteenth-Century France, 1750–1789* (Oxford: Clarendon Press).

Huizinga, Johan (1955), *The Waning of the Middle Ages*, trans. F. Hopman (1913; Harmondsworth: Penguin).

Hunt, John Dixon (1989), 'Pictura, Scriptura, and Theatrum: Shakespeare and the Emblem', *Poetics Today*, 10/1: 155–71; repr. in Stephen Orgel and Sean Keilen (eds), *Shakespeare and the Arts* (New York: Garland, 1999), 335–51.

Hunter, George K. (1962), *John Lyly: The Humanist as Courtier* (London: Routledge and Kegan Paul).

—— (1996), 'Theatrical Politics and Shakespeare's Comedies, 1590–1600', in R. B. Parker and S. P. Zitner (eds), *Elizabethan Theater: Essays in Honor of S. Schoenbaum* (Newark: University of Delaware Press), 241–51.

—— (1997), *English Drama, 1586–1642: The Age of Shakespeare* (Oxford: Clarendon Press).

Hyde, Ralph, John Fisher, and Roger Cline (1992), *The A to Z of Restoration London* (London: Guildhall Library.

Ill, Sarah Ann (2007), 'Visibility and Resonance: Tapestries on and around the Early Modern Stage', M.Litt. thesis (Mary Baldwin College, Staunton, VA.).

Ingram, William (1978), *A London Life in the Brazen Age: Francis Langley 1548–1602* (Cambridge, MA: Harvard University Press).

—— (1985), 'The Playhouse as an Investment, 1607–1614: Thomas Woodford and the Whitefriars', *Medieval and Renaissance Drama in England*, 2: 209–30.

—— (1988), 'The Early Career of James Burbage', in C. E. McGee (ed.), *The Elizabethan Theatre X* (Port Credit, Ont.: P. D. Meany), 18–36.

—— (1992), *The Business of Playing: The Beginnings of the Adult Professional Theater in Elizabethan London* (Ithaca, NY: Cornell University Press).

—— (1993), 'The Costs of Touring', *Medieval and Renaissance Drama in England*, 6: 57–62.

—— (2002), 'Playhouses Make Strange Bedfellows: The Case of Aaron and Martin', *Shakespeare Studies*, 30: 118–27.

—— (2004), 'Langley, Francis', in H. C. G. Matthew and Brian Harrison (eds), *Oxford Dictionary of National Biography* (Oxford: Oxford University Press), <http://www.oxforddnb.com/view/article/68131>, accessed 2 Sept. 2007.

Ioppolo, Grace (2006), *Dramatists and their Manuscripts in the Age of Shakespeare, Jonson, Middleton and Heywood: Authorship, Authority and the Playhouse* (New York: Routledge).

ISGC (Andrew Gurr, Ronnie Mulryne, and Margaret Shewring) (1993), *The Design of the Globe* (London: International Shakespeare Globe Centre).

Ives, E. W. (2004), *The Life and Death of Anne Boleyn 'The Most Happy'* (Oxford: Blackwell).

Izenour, George C. (1992), *Roofed Theatres of Classical Antiquity* (New Haven: Yale University Press).

Izenour, George C. (1997*a*), *Theater Design*, 2nd edn (New York: McGraw-Hill).

—— (1997*b*), *Theater Technology*, 2nd edn (New York: McGraw-Hill).

Jackson, Shannon (2004), 'Resist Singularity', *Theatre Survey*, 45: 241–6.

James, Mervyn (1983), 'Ritual, Drama, and Social Body in the Late Medieval English Town', *Past and Present*, 98: 3–29.

Jardine, Lisa (1996), *Worldly Goods: A New History of the Renaissance* (New York: Nan A. Talese).

Jensen, Ejner J. (1968), 'The Style of the Boy Actors', *Comparative Drama*, 2: 100–14.

—— (1975), 'The Boy Actors: Plays and Playing', *Research Opportunities in Renaissance Drama*, 18: 5–11.

—— (1984–5), 'Review', *Comparative Drama*, 18: 82–4.

Jensen, P. (2003), 'Recusancy, Festivity, and Community: The Simpsons at Gowlthwaite Hall', in R. Dutton, A. Findlay, and R. Wilson (eds), *Region, Religion and Patronage: Lancastrian Shakespeare* (Manchester: Manchester University Press), 101–20.

Johnson, David J. (1969), *Southwark and the City* (Oxford: Oxford University Press).

Johnson, Gerald D. (1988), 'The Stationers versus the Drapers: Control of the Press in the Late Sixteenth Century', *The Library*, ser. 6, 10: 1–17.

—— (1992), 'Thomas Pavier, Publisher, 1600–25', *The Library*, ser. 6, 14: 12–50.

Johnson, M. (1974), *Images of Women in the Works of Thomas Heywood*, Salzburg Studies in English Literature: Jacobean Drama Studies, 4 (Salzburg: Institut für Englische Sprache und Literatur).

Johnson, Nora (2003), *The Actor as Playwright in Early Modern* Drama (Cambridge: Cambridge University Press).

Johnston, A. (2002), 'The City as Patron: York', in Paul Whitfield White and Suzanne R. Westfall (eds), *Shakespeare and Theatrical Patronage in Early Modern England* (Cambridge: Cambridge University Press), 150–75.

Jones, Ann Rosalind, and Peter Stallybrass (2000), *Renaissance Clothing and the Materials of Memory* (Cambridge: Cambridge University Press).

Kathman, David, Biographical Index of English Drama before 1660, <http://shakespeareauthorship.com/bd>.

—— (2004*a*), 'Grocers, Goldsmiths, and Drapers: Freemen and Apprentices in the Elizabethan Theater', *Shakespeare Quarterly*, 55: 1–49.

—— (2004*b*), 'Reconsidering *The Seven Deadly Sins*', *Early Theatre*, 7/1: 13–44.

—— (2004*c*), 'Smith, William (*c*.1550–1618)', in H. C. G. Matthew and Brian Harrison (eds), *Oxford Dictionary of National Biography* (Oxford: Oxford University Press), <http://www.oxforddnb.com/view/article/25922>, accessed 2 Dec. 2007.

—— (2005*a*), 'Citizens, Innholders, and Playhouse Builders, 1543–1622', *Research Opportunities in Medieval and Renaissance Drama*, 44: 38–64.

—— (2005*b*), 'How Old Were Shakespeare's Boy Actors?', *Shakespeare Survey*, 58: 220–46.

—— (2006), 'Richard Tarlton and the Haberdashers', *Notes and Queries*, 252: 440–2.

—— (forthcoming), 'London Inns as Playing Venues for the Queen's Men', in Helen Ostovich (ed.), *Locating the Queen's Men, 1583–1603: Material Practices and Conditions of Playing* (Aldershot: Ashgate).

Katritzky, M. A. (2005), 'Reading the Actress in Commedia Imagery', in Pamela Allen Brown and Peter Parolin (eds), *Women Players in Early Modern England, 1500–1660: Beyond the All-Male Stage* (Aldershot: Ashgate), 109–43.

Keenan, Siobhan (2002), *Travelling Players in Shakespeare's England* (Basingstoke: Palgrave Macmillan).

—— and Peter Davidson (1997), 'The Iconography of the Globe', in J. R. Mulryne and M. Shewring (eds), *Shakespeare's Globe Rebuilt* (Cambridge: Cambridge University Press), 147–56.

Kellett, J. R. (1958), 'The Breakdown of Gild and Corporation Control over the Handicraft and Retail Trade in London', *Economic History Review*, 2nd ser., 10/3: 381–94.

Kellner, Hans (1989), *Language and Historical Representation: Getting the Story Crooked* (Madison: University of Wisconsin Press).

—— (1995), 'Introduction: Describing Redescriptions', in Frank Ankersmit and Hans Kellner (eds), *A New Philosophy of History* (London: Reaktion), 1–20.

Kernan, Alvin (1995), *Shakespeare the King's Playwright. Theater in the Stuart Court, 1603–1613*. New Haven: Yale University Press).

Kezar, Dennis (2001), *Guilty Creatives: Renaissance Poetry and the Ethics of Authorship* (Oxford: Oxford University Press).

Kiefer, Frederick (2003), *Shakespeare's Visual Theatre: Staging the Personified Characters* (Cambridge: Cambridge University Press).

Kilroy, G. (2005), *Edmund Campion: Memory and Transcription* (Aldershot: Ashgate).

King, Thomas J. (1963), 'Production of Plays at the Phoenix 1617–42', diss. (Columbia University).

—— (1971), *Shakespearean Staging: 1599–1642* (Cambridge, MA: Harvard University Press).

Kingsford, C. L. (1917), 'Historical Notes on Medieval London Houses', *London Topographical Record*, 11: 28–81.

Kinney, A. F. (1974), *Markets of Bawdrie: The Dramatic Criticism of Stephen Gosson* (Salzburg: Institut für Englische Sprache und Literatur).

—— (2002), *A Companion to Renaissance Drama* (Oxford: Blackwell).

—— (2004), *Shakespeare's Webs* (New York: Routledge).

Kipling, G. (1997), '"He That Saw It Would Not Believe It": Anne Boleyn's Royal Entry into London', in A. F. Johnston and W. Hüsken (eds), *Civic Ritual and Drama* (Amsterdam: Rodopi), 39–79.

—— (1998), *Enter the King: Theatre, Liturgy, and Ritual in the Medieval Civic Triumph* (Oxford: Clarendon Press).

Kirsch, Arthur C. (1969), 'A Caroline Commentary on the Drama', *Modern Philology*, 66: 256–61.

Klausner, David (1990), *Records of Early English Drama: Herefordshire/Worcestershire* (Toronto: University of Toronto Press).

Klein, David (1967), 'Time Allotted for an Elizabethan Performance', *Shakespeare Quarterly*, 18: 434–8.

Knights, L. C. (1937), *Drama and Society in the Age of Jonson* (London: Chatto and Windus).

Knowles, J. (1993), 'The Spectacle of the Realm: Civic Consciousness, Rhetoric and Ritual in Early Modern London', in J. R. Mulryne and M. Shewring (eds), *Theatre and Court under the Early Stuarts* (Cambridge: Cambridge University Press), 157–89.

—— and Heaton, G. (2003), '"Entertainment Perfect": Ben Jonson and Corporate Hospitality', *Review of English Studies*, new ser., 54: 587–600.

Knutson, Roslyn L. (1984*a*), 'Play Identifications: *The Wise Man of West Chester* and *John a Kent and John a Cumber: Longshanks* and *Edward I*', *Huntington Library Quarterly*, 47: 1–11.

—— (1984*b*), 'Henslowe's Diary and the Economics of Play Revision for Revival, 1592–1603', *Theatre Research International*, 91: 1–18.

—— (1985), 'Henslowe's Diary and the Economics of Play Revision for Revival, 1592–1603', *Theatre Research International*, 91: 1–18.

—— (1991), *The Repertory of Shakespeare's Company 1594–1613* (Fayetteville: University of Arkansas Press).

—— (1995), 'Falconer to the Little Eyases: A New Date and Commercial Agenda for the "Little Eyases" Passage in *Hamlet*', *Shakespeare Quarterly*, 46: 1–31.

Knutson, Roslyn L. (2001), *Playing Companies and Commerce in Shakespeare's Time* (Cambridge: Cambridge University Press).

—— (2002), 'Playing Companies and Repertory', in Arthur F. Kinney (ed.), *A Companion to Renaissance Drama* (Oxford: Blackwell), 180–92.

—— (2006), 'Everything's Back in Play: The Impact of REED Research on Elizabethan Theatre History', in Audrey Douglas and Sally-Beth MacLean (eds), *REED in Review: Essays in Celebration of the First Twenty-Five Years* (Toronto: University of Toronto Press), 116–30.

Korda, Natasha (1996), 'Household Property/Stage Property: Henslowe as Pawnbroker', *Theatre Journal*, 48: 185–95.

—— (2002), 'Women's Theatrical Properties', in Jonathan Gil Harris and Natasha Korda (eds), *Staged Properties in Early Modern English Drama* (Cambridge: Cambridge University Press), 202–29.

—— (2004), 'Labors Lost: Women's Work and Early Modern Theatrical Commerce', in Peter Holland and Stephen Orgel (eds) (2004), *From Script to Stage in Early Modern England* (Basingstoke: Palgrave), 195–230.

—— (2005), 'The Case of Moll Frith: Women's Work and the "All-Male Stage" ', in Pamela Allen Brown and Peter Parolin (eds), *Women Players in Early Modern England, 1500–1660: Beyond the All-Male Stage* (Aldershot: Ashgate), 71–87.

—— (2008), 'Gender at Work in the Cries of London', in Mary E. Lamb and Karen Bamford (eds), *Gender and Oral Traditions in Early Modern Literary Texts* (Aldershot: Ashgate).

Kowaleski, Maryanne (1999), 'Singlewomen in Medieval and Early Modern Europe: The Demographic Perspective', in J. M. Bennett and A. M. Froide (eds), *Singlewomen in the European Past, 1250–1800* (Philadelphia: University of Pennsylvania Press), 38–81.

Lacey, Kay E. (1985), 'Women and Work in Fourteenth and Fifteenth Century London', in Lindsay Charles and Lorna Duffin (eds), *Women and Work in Pre-industrial England* (London: Croom Helm), 24–78.

Lake, P., and M. Questier (2002), *The Antichrist's Lewd Hat: Protestants, Papists, and Players in Post-Reformation England* (New Haven: Yale University Press).

Lalou, Elisabeth E. (1991), 'Les Rolets de théâtre: Étude codicologique', in *Théâtre et spectacles hier et aujourd'hui: Moyen Âge et Renaissance*, 115e Congrès National des Sociétés Historiques et Scientifiques, Avignon, 1990 (Paris: Éditions du CTHS).

Lancashire, Anne (1992), 'St. Paul's Grammar School before 1580: Theatrical Development Suppressed?', in John Astington (ed.), *The Development of Shakespeare's Theater* (New York: AMS).

—— (2002), *London Civic Theatre: City Drama and Pageantry from Roman Times to 1558* (Cambridge: Cambridge University Press).

—— (2004), 'The Mayors and Sheriffs of London 1190–1558', in C. M. Barron, *London in the Later Middle Ages: Government and People 1200–1500* (Oxford: Oxford University Press), 308–55.

—— (forthcoming *a*), 'The Comedy of Love and the London Lord Mayor's Show', in K. Bamford and R. Knowles (eds), *Shakespeare's Comedies of Love: Essays in Honour of Alexander Leggatt* [working title] (Toronto: University of Toronto Press).

—— (forthcoming *b*), 'Dekker's Accession Pageant for James I', *Early Theatre*, 12/1.

Lancashire, I. (1976), 'The Auspices of *The World and the Child*', *Renaissance and Reformation*, 12: 96–105.

—— (1980*a*), 'Orders for Twelfth Day and Night *circa* 1515 in the Second Northumberland Household Book', *English Literary Renaissance* 10, 7–45.

—— (ed.) (1980*b*), *Two Tudor Interludes: 'The Interlude of Youth,' 'Hickscorner'* (Baltimore: Johns Hopkins University Press).

—— (1984), *Dramatic Texts and Records of Great Britain: A Chronological Topography to 1558* (Toronto: University of Toronto Press; Cambridge: Cambridge University Press).

Lawrence, W. J. (1926), 'Elizabethan Players as Tradesfolk', *Modern Language Notes*, 41: 363–4.

—— (1932), 'Dramatic Documents from the Elizabethan Playhouses', *Review of English Studies*, 8: 219–28.

—— (1935), *Those Nut-Cracking Elizabethans: Studies in the Early Theatre and Drama* (London: Argonaut).

Leech, C., and T. W. Craik (eds) (1975–83), *The Revels History of Drama in English*, 8 vols (London: Methuen).

Lefkowitz, Murray (1965), 'The Longleat Papers of Bulstrode Whitelock: New Light on Shirley's *Triumph of Peace*', *Journal of the American Musicological Society*, 18: 42–60.

Leggatt, A. (1992), *Jacobean Public Theatre* (London: Routledge).

Leinwand, Theodore B. (1982), 'London Triumphing: The Jacobean Lord Mayor's Show', *Clio*, 11/2: 137–53.

—— (1994), 'Redeeming Beggary/Buggery in *Michaelmas Term*', *English Literary History*, 61: 53–70.

—— (1999), *Theatre, Finance, and Society in Early Modern England* (Cambridge: Cambridge University Press).

Lemire, Beverly (1997), *Dress, Culture and Commerce: The English Clothing Trade before the Factory, 1600–1800* (New York: St Martin's Press).

—— (2001), 'Introduction: Women, Credit and the Creation of Opportunity: A Historical Overview', in Beverly Lemire, Ruth Pearson, and Gail Campbell (eds), *Women and Credit: Researching the Past, Refiguring the Future* (Oxford: Berg), 3–14.

—— Ruth Pearson, and Gail Campbell (eds) (2001), *Women and Credit: Researching the Past, Refiguring the Future* (Oxford: Berg).

Lennam, Trevor (1975), *Sebastian Westcott, the Children of Paul's, and 'The Marriage of Wit and Science'* (Toronto: University of Toronto Press).

Lesser, Zachary (2004), *Renaissance Drama and the Politics of Publication* (Cambridge: Cambridge University Press).

Levin, Carole (1998), '"We Princes, I Tell You, Are Set on Stages": Elizabeth I and Dramatic Self-Representation', in S. P. Cerasano and Marion Wynne-Davies (eds), *Readings in Renaissance Women's Drama: Criticism, History and Performance 1594–1998* (London: Routledge), 113–24.

Levin, Richard (1989), 'Women in the Renaissance Theater Audience', *Shakespeare Quarterly*, 40: 165–74.

—— (2002), 'The Longleat Manuscript and *Titus Andronicus*', *Shakespeare Quarterly*, 53: 323–40.

Lillywhite, Bryant (1972), *London Signs* (London: Allen and Unwin).

Lin, Shen (1991), 'How Old Were the Children of Paul's?', *Theatre Notebook*, 45: 121–31.

Lindley, David (1984), *The Court Masque* (Manchester: Manchester University Press).

—— (2006), *Shakespeare and Music* (London: Thomson Learning).

Linke, Hansjürgen (1988), 'Versuch über deutsche Handschriften mittelalterlicher Spiele', in Volker Honemann and Nigel F. Palmer (eds), *Deutsche Handschriften 1100–1400: Oxforder Kolloquium 1985* (Tübingen: Max Niemeyer Verlag).

Linthicum, M. Channing (1936), *Costume in the Drama of Shakespeare and his Contemporaries* (Oxford: Clarendon Press).

Llewellyn-Jones, Lloyd (ed.) (2001), *Women's Dress in the Ancient Greek World* (Swansea: Classical Press of Wales).

Loades, David M. (1986), *The Tudor Court* (London: Batsford).

—— (1992), *The Tudor Court*, 2nd edn (Gwynedd: Headstart History).

Lobanov-Rostrovsky, S. (1993), '"The Triumphes of Golde": Economic Authority in the Jacobean Lord Mayor's Show', *ELH* 60/4: 879–98.

Loengard, Janet S. (1983), 'An Elizabethan Lawsuit: John Brayne, his Carpenter, and the Building of the Red Lion Theatre', *Shakespeare Quarterly*, 34: 298–310.

Loewenstein, Joseph (2002), *Ben Jonson and Possessive Authorship* (Cambridge: Cambridge University Press).

Long, John H. (1967), 'Music for a Song in *Damon and Pithias*', *Music and Letters*, 48: 247–50.

Long, William B. (1985), 'Stage Directions: A Misinterpreted Factor in Determining Textual Provenance', *Text*, 2: 121–37.

Lublin, Robert (forthcoming), *Costuming the Shakespearean Stage: Visual Codes of Representation in Early Modern Theatre and Culture* (Burlington, VT: Ashgate).

Luborsky, Ruth Samson, and Elizabeth Morley Ingram (1998), *A Guide to English Illustrated Books 1536–1603*, 2 vols (Tempe, AZ: Medieval and Renaissance Texts and Studies).

Lusher, P. (1940), 'Studies in the Guild-Drama in London in the Records of the Drapers' Company (1515–1553)', doctoral thesis, 2 vols (University of London).

MacCaffrey, Wallace T. (1961), 'Place and Patronage in Elizabethan Politics', in S. T. Bindoff et al. (eds), *Elizabethan Government and Society* (London: Athlone Press), 97–126.

—— (1981), *Queen Elizabeth and the Making of Policy, 1572–1588* (Princeton: Princeton University Press).

McCarthy, Jeanne H. (2003), 'Elizabeth I's "Picture in Little": Boy Company Representations of a Queen's Authority', *Studies in Philology*, 100: 425–62.

—— (2006), 'The Queen's "Unfledged Minions": An Alternate Account of the Origins of Blackfriars and of the Boy Company Phenomenon', in Paul Menzer (ed.), *Inside Shakespeare: Essays on the Blackfriars Stage* (Selinsgrove, PA: Susquehanna University Press), 93–117.

McCurdy, Peter (1993), 'Shakespeare's Globe Theatre: The Construction of Two Experimental Bays in June 1992', in F. W. B. Charles (ed.), *The Timber Frame—from Preservation to Reconstruction: Papers Presented at the International Council on Monuments and Sites UK Timber Seminar Held at Haydock Park on 26 April 1993* (London: Icomos UK), 1–20.

—— (2007), 'Metalwork or Carpentry? The Joinery of the Theatre and the Globe', personal communication, 15 Jan.

McGee, C. E., and J. Meagher (1981–99), 'Preliminary Checklist of Tudor and Stuart Entertainments', *Research Opportunities in Renaissance Drama*, 24: 51–155 (1558–1603); 25: 31–114 (1485–1558); 27: 47–126 (1603–13); 30: 17–128 (1614–25); 36: 23–95 (1625–33); 38: 23–85 (1634–42).

McIntosh, Marjorie K. (1988), 'Money Lending on the Periphery of London', *Albion*, 20/4: 557–71.

MacIntyre, Jean (1992), *Costumes and Scripts in the Elizabethan Theatres* (Edmonton: University of Alberta Press).

—— and Garret P. J. Epp (1997), '"Cloathes worth all the rest": Costumes and Properties', in John D. Cox and David Scott Kastan (eds), *A New History of Early English Drama* (New York: Columbia University Press), 269–86.

Mackintosh, Iain, Jon Greenfield, Gordon Higgott, and Stanley Wells (2006), 'Four Shakespearean Stages', 32nd International Shakespeare Conference, Shakespeare Institute, Stratford upon Avon, 6–11 Aug.

MacLean, Sally-Beth (1993), 'Tour Routes: "Provincial Wanderings" or Traditional Circuits?', *Medieval and Renaissance Drama in England*, 6: 1–14.

—— (2002), 'Tracking Leicester's Men: The Patronage of a Performance Troupe', in Paul Whitfield White and Suzanne R. Westfall (eds), *Shakespeare and Theatrical Patronage in Early Modern England* (Cambridge: Cambridge University Press).

—— (2003), 'A Family Tradition: Dramatic Patronage by the Earls of Derby', in Richard Dutton, Alison Findlay, and Richard Wilson (eds), *Region, Religion and Patronage: Lancastrian Shakespeare* (Manchester: Manchester University Press), 205–26.

McLuskie, Kathleen (1981), 'The Plays and the Playwrights, 1613–1642', in C. Leech and T. W. Craik (eds), *The Revels History of Drama in English*, 8 vols (London: Methuen), iv. 127–258.

—— (1985), 'The Patriarchal Bard: Feminist Criticism and Shakespeare: *King Lear* and *Measure for Measure*', in Jonathan Dollimore and Alan Sinfield (eds), *Political Shakespeare: New Essays in Cultural Materialism* (Ithaca, NY: Cornell University Press), 88–108.

—— (1991), 'The Poets' Royal Exchange: Patronage and Commerce in Early Modern Drama', *Yearbook of English Studies*, 21: 53–62.

—— (1994), *Dekker and Heywood: Professional Dramatists* (London: Macmillan; New York: St Martin's Press).

—— (1996), 'The Shopping Complex: Materiality and the Renaissance Theatre', in Edward Pechter (ed.), *Textual and Theatrical Shakespeare* (Iowa City: University of Iowa Press), 141–64.

—— (2006), 'Politics and Aesthetic Pleasure in 1630s Theatre', in Adam Zucker and Alan Farmer (eds), *Localising Caroline Drama Politics and Economics of the Early Modern Stage, 1625–1642* (Basingstoke: Palgrave Macmillan), 43–68.

—— and Felicity Dunsworth (1997), 'Patronage and the Economics of Theater', in John D. Cox and D. S. Kastan (eds), *A New History of Early English Drama* (New York: Columbia University Press), 423–40.

McManus, Clare (2002), *Women on the Renaissance Stage: Anna of Denmark and Female Masquing in the Stuart Court 1590–1619* (Manchester: Manchester University Press).

McMillin, Scott (1976), 'Simon Jewell and the Queen's Men', *Review of English Studies*, new ser., 27: 174–7.

—— (1991), 'Sussex's Men in 1594: The Evidence of *Titus Andronicus* and *The Jew of Malta*', *Theatre Survey*, 32: 214–23.

—— and Sally-Beth MacLean (1998), *The Queen's Men and their Plays* (Cambridge: Cambridge University Press).

McPherson, David (1976), 'The Origins of Overdo: A Study in Jonsonian Invention', *MLQ* 37: 221–33.

Macy, L. (ed.), *Grove Music Online*, <http://www.grovemusic.com>.

Maguire, Laurie (2000), 'Shakespeare and the Death of the Author', in Andrew Murphy (ed.), *The Renaissance Text: Theory, Editing, Textuality* (Manchester: Manchester University Press).

Manley, Lawrence (1995), *Literature and Culture in Early Modern London* (Cambridge: Cambridge University Press).

—— (2001), 'Playing with Fire: Immolation in the Repertory of Strange's Men', *Early Theatre*, 4: 115–29.

—— (forthcoming), 'Why Did London Inns Function as Theaters?', in Jean Howard and Deborah Harkness (eds), *Spaces and Places of Early Modern London*, *Huntington Library Quarterly* special issue.

Manning, R. B. (1988), *Village Revolts: Social Protest and Popular Disturbances in England, 1509–1640* (Oxford: Clarendon Press).

Marcus, Leah S. (1988), *Puzzling Shakespeare: Local Reading and its Discontents* (Berkeley: University of California Press).

Marcus, Leah S. (1995), 'Of Mire and Authorship', in David L. Smith, Richard Strier, and David Bevington (eds), *The Theatrical City: Culture, Theatre and Politics in London 1576–1649* (Cambridge: Cambridge University Press), 170–81.

Marotti, Arthur (1995), *Manuscript, Print and the English Renaissance Lyric* (Ithaca, NY: Cornell University Press).

Martindale, Charles (1993), *Redeeming the Text: Latin Poetry and the Hermeneutics of Reception* (Cambridge: Cambridge University Press).

Masten, Jeffrey (1997), *Textual Intercourse: Collaboration, Authorship, and Sexualities in Renaissance Drama* (Cambridge: Cambridge University Press).

Masters, B. R. (1968), 'The Secondary (City Officers 2)', *Guildhall Miscellany*, 2/10: 425–33.

Mateer, David (2006), 'New Light on the Early History of the Theatre in Shoreditch', *English Literary Renaissance*, 36: 335–75.

Mattera, Philip (1985), *Off the Books: The Rise of the Underground Economy* (New York: St Martin's Press).

Meagher, J. C. (1973), 'The London Lord Mayor's Show of 1590', *English Literary Renaissance*, 3: 94–104.

Megill, Allan (1995), '"Grand Narrative" and the Discipline of History', in Frank Ankersmit and Hans Kellner (eds), *A New Philosophy of History* (London: Reaktion), 151–73.

Mendelson, Sara, and Patricia Crawford (1998), *Women in Early Modern England, 1550–1720* (Oxford: Clarendon Press).

Menzer, Paul (ed.) (2006*a*), *Inside Shakespeare: Essays on the Blackfriars Stage* (Selinsgrove: Susquehanna University Press).

—— (2006*b*), 'The Tragedians of the City? Q1 *Hamlet* and the Settlements of the 1590s', *Shakespeare Quarterly*, 57: 162–82.

Metz, G. Harold (1996), *Shakespeare's Earliest Tragedy: Studies in 'Titus Andronicus'* (Madison: Fairleigh Dickinson University Press).

Mirabella, Bella (2005), '"Quacking Delilahs": Female Mountebanks in Early Modern England and Italy', in Pamela Allen Brown and Peter Parolin (eds), *Women Players in Early Modern England, 1500–1660: Beyond the All-Male Stage* (Aldershot: Ashgate), 89–105.

Montrose, Louis (1996), *The Purpose of Playing: Shakespeare and the Cultural Politics of Elizabethan Theatre* (Chicago: University of Chicago Press).

Muir, Kenneth (1951), 'Introduction, *Macbeth* by William Shakespeare', in Shakespeare, *Macbeth*, ed. Kenneth Muir, The Arden Shakespeare (London: Methuen; repr. London: Routledge, 1994).

Muldrew, Craig (1998), *The Economy of Obligation: The Culture of Credit and Social Relations in Early Modern England* (New York: St Martin's Press).

Mulholland, P. A. (1977), 'The Date of *The Roaring Girl*', *Review of English Studies*, new ser., 29: 19–31.

Mullaney, S. (1988), *The Place of the Stage: License, Play and Power in Renaissance England* (Chicago: University of Chicago Press).

—— (1995), *The Place of the Stage: License, Play and Power in Renaissance England* (Ann Arbor: University of Michigan Press).

Mulryne, J. R., and M. Shewring (eds) (1993), *Theatre and Government under the Early Stuarts* (Cambridge: Cambridge University Press).

—— —— (1997), *Shakespeare's Globe Rebuilt* (Cambridge: Cambridge University Press). *See also* ISCG (1995).

Munro, L. (2005), *Children of the Queen's Revels: A Jacobean Theatre Repertory* (Cambridge: Cambridge University Press).

Naerebout, G. G. (1997), *Attractive Performance: Ancient Greek Dance: Three Preliminary Studies* (Amsterdam: J. C. Gieben).

Neale, John E. (1934), *Queen Elizabeth: A Biography* (London: Jonathan Cape; repr. Garden City, NY: Doubleday Anchor Books, 1957).

Neill, Michael (1978), '"Wit's Most Accomplished Senate": The Audience of the Caroline Private Theaters', *Studies in English Literature*, 18: 341–60.

Nelson, Alan H. (1990), 'Women in the Audience of Cambridge Plays', *Shakespeare Quarterly*, 41: 333–6.

—— (1992), 'Hall Screens and Elizabethan Playhouses: Counter-Evidence from Cambridge', in J. Astington (ed.), *The Development of Shakespeare's Theater* (New York: AMS).

—— (1994), *Early Cambridge Theatres: University, College, and Town Stages, 1464–1720* (Cambridge: Cambridge University Press).

—— (2003), *Monstrous Adversary: The Life of Edward de Vere, 17th Earl of Oxford* (Liverpool: Liverpool University Press).

Nelson, Robert S., and Richard Shiff (eds) (2003), *Critical Terms for Art History*, 2nd edn (Chicago: University of Chicago Press).

Nelson, William (ed.) (1956), *A Fifteenth-Century School Book: From a Manuscript in the British Museum (MS. Arundel 2449)* (Oxford: Clarendon Press).

Nicoll, Allardyce (1948), 'A Note on the Swan Drawing', *Shakespeare Survey*, 1: 23–4.

North, Marcy L. (2003), *The Anonymous Renaissance: Cultures of Discretion in Tudor–Stuart England* (Chicago: University of Chicago Press).

Nungezer, Edwin (1929), *A Dictionary of Actors and of Other Persons Associated with the Public Representation of Plays in England before 1642* (New Haven: Yale University Press).

O'Callaghan, M. (2004), 'Tavern Societies, the Inns of Court, and the Culture of Conviviality in Early Seventeenth Century London', in Adam Smyth (ed.), *A Pleasing Sinne: Drink and Conviviality in Seventeenth-Century England* (Cambridge: D. S. Brewer), 37–54.

O'Neill, James J. (1926), 'Elizabethan Players as Tradesmen', *Times Literary Supplement*, 8 Apr., 264.

Orgel, Stephen (1975), *The Illusion of Power: Political Theater in the English Renaissance* (Berkeley: University of California Press).

—— (1983), 'Shakespeare Imagines a Theatre', in Kenneth Muir, Jay L. Halio, and D. J. Palmer (eds), *Shakespeare, Man of the Theatre: Proceedings of the Second Congress of the International Shakespeare Association, 1981* (Newark: University of Delaware Press), 34–46.

—— (1996), *Impersonations: The Performance of Gender in Shakespeare's England* (Cambridge: Cambridge University Press).

—— (1999), '*Macbeth* and the Antic Round', *Shakespeare Survey*, 52: 143–54.

—— (2004), 'A View from the Stage', in Peter Holland and Stephen Orgel (eds), *From Script to Stage in Early Modern England* (Basingstoke: Palgrave), 1–8.

—— and Roy Strong (eds) (1973), *Inigo Jones: The Theatre of the Stuart Court*, 2 vols (London: Sotheby Parke Bernet; Berkeley: University of California Press).

Orlin, Lena Cowen (1993), 'The Performance of Things in *The Taming of the Shrew*', *Yearbook of English Studies*, 23: 167–88.

—— (ed.) (2000), *Material London, ca. 1600* (Philadelphia: University of Pennsylvania Press).

—— (2002), 'Things with Little Social Life (Henslowe's Theatrical Properties and Elizabethan Household Fittings)', in Jonathan Gil Harris and Natasha Korda (eds), *Staged Properties in Early Modern English Drama* (Cambridge: Cambridge University Press), 99–128.

—— (2007), *Locating Privacy in Tudor London* (Oxford: Oxford University Press).

Orrell, John (1977–8), 'The London Stage in the Florentine Correspondence, 1604–1618', *Theatre Research International*, 3: 157–76.

—— (1982), 'The Theatre at Christ Church, Oxford, in 1605', *Shakespeare Survey*, 35: 129– 40.

—— (1983), *The Quest for Shakespeare's Globe* (Cambridge: Cambridge University Press).

—— (1985), *The Theatres of Inigo Jones and John Webb* (Cambridge: Cambridge University Press).

Orrell, John (1988), *The Human Stage: English Theatre Design, 1567–1640* (Cambridge: Cambridge University Press).

—— (1992), 'Nutshells at the Rose', *Theatre Research International*, 17: 8–14.

—— (1997*a*), 'Designing the Globe: Reading the Documents', in J. R. Mulryne and M. Shewring (eds), *Shakespeare's Globe Rebuilt* (Cambridge: Cambridge University Press), 51–66.

—— (1997*b*), 'The Theatres', in John D. Cox and D. S. Kastan (eds), *A New History of Early English Drama* (New York: Columbia University Press), 93–112.

Osborne, Laurie E. (1999), 'Staging the Female Playgoer: Gender in Shakespeare's Onstage Audience', in Viviana Comensoli and Anne Russell (eds), *Enacting Gender on the English Renaissance Stage* (Urbana: University of Illinois Press), 201–17.

Otter, Monika (2005), 'Functions of Fiction in Historical Writing', in Nancy Partner (ed.), *Writing Medieval History* (London: Hodder), 109–30.

Palfrey, Simon, and Tiffany Stern (2007), *Shakespeare in Parts* (Oxford: Oxford University Press).

Palmer, Barbara D. (2005), 'Early Modern Mobility: Players, Payments, and Patrons', *Shakespeare Quarterly*, 56: 259–304.

—— (2006), 'Star Turns or Small Companies?', in David N. Klausner and Karen S. Marsalek (eds), *'Bring furth the Pagants': Essays in Early English Drama Presented to Alexandra F. Johnston* (Toronto: University of Toronto Press).

—— (2007), 'Provincial Players: Over the River and through the Woods?', paper presented at the Shakespeare Association of America conference, San Diego, Apr.

Panofsky, Erwin (1955), *Meaning in the Visual Arts: Papers in and on Art History* (Garden City, NY: Doubleday).

—— (1965), *Perspective as Symbolic Form*, trans. William Tallon (Chicago: University of Chicago Press).

—— (1968), *Idea: A Concept in Art Theory*, trans. Joseph J. S. Peake (Columbia: University of South Carolina Press).

Parolin, Peter (2000), '"A Strange Fury Entered My House": Italian Actresses and Female Performance in *Volpone*', *Renaissance Drama*, 29: 107–35.

Parry, Graham (1981), *The Golden Age Restor'd: The Culture of the Stuart Court 1603–1642* (Manchester: Manchester University Press).

Partner, Nancy F. (1977), *Serious Entertainments: The Writing of History in Twelfth-Century England* (Chicago: University of Chicago Press).

—— (1986), 'Making Up Lost Time: Writing on the Writing of History', *Speculum*, 61: 90–117.

—— (1995), 'Historicity in an Age of Reality-Fictions', in Frank Ankersmit and Hans Kellner (eds), *A New Philosophy of History* (London: Reaktion), 21–39.

—— (ed.) (2005), *Writing Medieval History* (London: Hodder).

Paster, Gail Kern (1995), 'The Idea of London in Masque and Pageant', in D. M. Bergeron (ed.), *Pageantry in the Shakespearean Theater* (Athens: University of Georgia Press), 48–64.

—— and Howard Skiles (eds) (1999), *A Midsummer Night's Dream: Texts and Contexts* (Boston: Bedford/St Martin's Press).

Patterson, A. (1989), *Shakespeare and the Popular Voice* (London: Blackwell).

Peacock, John (1995), *The Stage Designs of Inigo Jones* (Cambridge: Cambridge University Press).

Peck, Linda Levy (ed.) (1991), *The Mental World of the Jacobean Court* (Cambridge: Cambridge University Press).

Perkins, David (1992), *Is Literary History Possible?* (Baltimore: Johns Hopkins University Press).

Pettegree, Andrew (1986), *Foreign Protestant Communities in Sixteenth-Century London* (Oxford: Clarendon Press).

Phythian-Adams, Charles (1972), 'Ceremony and the Citizen: The Communal Year at Coventry, 1450–1550', in Peter Clark and Paul Slack (eds), *Crisis and Order in English Towns, 1500–1700: Essays in Urban History* (London: Routledge and Kegan Paul), 57–85.

Pickard-Cambridge, A. W. (1946), *The Theatre of Dionysus in Athens* (Oxford: Clarendon Press).

—— (1968), *The Dramatic Festivals of Athens*, 2nd edn, rev. John Gould and D. M. Lewis (Oxford: Clarendon Press).

Pinchbeck, Ivy (1930), *Women Workers and the Industrial Revolution, 1750–1850* (New York: A. M. Kelley).

Pincombe, Michael (1996), *The Plays of John Lyly: Eros and Eliza* (Manchester: Manchester University Press).

Pinks, William I. (1881), *The History of Clerkenwell* (London: Charles Herbert).

Plummer, Alfred (1972), *The London Weavers' Company, 1600–1970* (London: Routledge and Kegan Paul).

Podro, Michael (1982), *The Critical Historians of Art* (New Haven: Yale University Press).

Portes, Alejandro, Manuel Castells, and Lauren A. Benton (1989), 'Conclusion', in Portes, Castells, and Benton (eds), *The Informal Economy: Studies in Advanced and Less Developed Countries* (Baltimore: Johns Hopkins University Press), 298–310.

Postlewait, Thomas (2003), 'Theatricality and Antitheatricality in Renaissance London', in Tracy C. Davis and Thomas Postlewait (eds), *Theatricality* (Cambridge: Cambridge University Press), 90–127.

—— (2004), 'Theatre History and Historiography: A Disciplinary Mandate', *Theatre Survey*, 45: 181–8.

—— (2009), *The Cambridge Introduction to Theatre Historiography* (Cambridge: Cambridge University Press).

—— and Bruce A. McConachie (eds) (1989), *Interpreting the Theatrical Past: Essays in the Historiography of Performance* (Iowa City: University of Iowa Press).

Poulsen, R. (2005), 'Women Performing Homoerotic Desire in English and Italian Comedy: *La Calandria*, *Gl'Ingannati* and *Twelfth Night*', in Pamela Allen Brown and Peter Parolin (eds), *Women Players in Early Modern England, 1500–1660: Beyond the All-Male Stage* (Aldershot: Ashgate), 171–91.

Prest, Wilfrid R. (1972), *The Inns of Court under Elizabeth I and the Early Stuarts, 1590–1640* (London: Longman).

Preziosi, Donald (1989), *Rethinking Art History: Meditations on a Coy Science* (New Haven: Yale University Press).

—— (ed.) (1998), *The Art of Art History: A Critical Anthology* (Oxford: Oxford University Press).

Purdon, N. (1974), 'Myth in Action: The Substructure to *A Midsummer Night's Dream*', in Purdon, *The Words of Mercury: Shakespeare and English Mythography of the Renaissance*, Salzburg Studies in English Literature, 39, Elizabethan and Renaissance Studies (Salzburg: Institut für Englische Sprache und Literatur), 167–204.

Raber, Karen (2001), *Dramatic Difference: Gender, Class and Genre in the Early Modern Closet Drama* (Newark: University of Delaware Press).

Rackin, Phyllis (2005), *Shakespeare and Women* (Oxford: Oxford University Press).

Ramsay, G. D. (1975), *The City of London in International Politics at the Accession of Elizabeth I* (Manchester: Manchester University Press).

Ranke, Leopold (1824), *Geschichten der romanischen und germanischen Völker von 1494 bis 1514* (Leipzig: Duncker und Humblot).

Rappaport, Steve (1989), *Worlds within Worlds: Structures of Life in Sixteenth-Century London* (Cambridge: Cambridge University Press).

—— (1991), *Worlds within Worlds: Structures of Life in Sixteenth-Century London* (repr. Cambridge: Cambridge University Press).

Rastall, Richard (1985), 'Female Roles in All-Male Casts', *Medieval English Theatre*, 7: 25–50.

Rawcliffe, C. (1978), *The Staffords, Earls of Stafford and Dukes of Buckingham* (Cambridge: Cambridge University Press).

Read, Conyers (1913), 'Walsingham and Burghley in Queen Elizabeth's Privy Council', *English Historical Review*, 28: 34–58.

Reed, A. W. (1926), *Early Tudor Drama* (London: Methuen).

Reid, Aileen, and Robert Maniura (eds) (1994), *Edward Alleyn: Elizabethan Actor, Jacobean Gentleman*, with essays by S. P. Cerasano, Susan Foister, and J. R. Piggott (London: Dulwich Picture Gallery).

Revermann, Martin (2006), *Comic Business: Theatricality, Dramatic Technique, and Performance Contexts of Aristophanic Comedy* (Oxford: Oxford University Press).

Reynolds, G. F. (1940), *The Staging of Elizabethan Plays at the Red Bull Theater, 1605–1625* (New York: Modern Language Association).

Richardson, Catherine (2008), 'Material Culture in Early Modern Warwick', in Christopher Dyer and Catherine Richardson (eds), *William Dugdale, Historian, 1605–1686: His Life, his Writings and his County* (Woodbridge: Boydell and Brewer).

Rickert, E. (1923), 'Political Propaganda and Satire in *A Midsummer Night's Dream*', *Modern Philology*, 21: 53–87, 133–54.

Riddell, James A. (1997), 'Jonson and Stansby and the Revisions of *Every Man in his Humour*', *Medieval and Renaissance Drama in England*, 9: 81–91.

Riggs, David (1989), *Ben Jonson: A Life* (Cambridge, MA: Harvard University Press).

Ringler, W. (1942), *Stephen Gosson: A Biographical and Critical Study* (Princeton: Princeton University Press).

Roberts, B. (1990), 'The Informal Sector in Comparative Perspective', in E. Smith (ed.), *Perspectives on the Informal Economy* (New York: University Press of America), 23–48.

Rogers, Kenneth (1937), *Signs and Taverns round about Old London Bridge* (London: Homeland Association).

Rollins, Hyder E. (1919), 'The Black-Letter Broadside Ballad', *PMLA* 34/2: 258–339.

Ronayne, John (1987), 'Style', in J. R. Mulryne and M. Shewring (eds), *'The Shape of the Globe' and 'The Interior of the Globe': Reports on Seminars held on 29 March 1983 and 12 April 1986*, *Renaissance Drama Newsletter Supplements*, 8 (Coventry: University of Warwick Graduate School of Renaissance Studies), 25–8.

—— (1997), 'Totus Mundus Agit Histrionem [The Whole World Moves the Actor]: The Interior Decorative Scheme of the Bankside Globe', in J. R. Mulryne and M. Shewring (eds), *Shakespeare's Globe Rebuilt* (Cambridge: Cambridge University Press), 121–46.

Rowan, D. F. (1970), 'A Neglected Jones/Webb Theatre Project', *Elizabethan Theatre*, 2: 60–73.

Runnalls, Graham A. (1990), 'Towards a Typology of Medieval French Play Manuscripts', in P. E. Bennett and G. A. Runnalls (eds), *The Editor and the Text* (Edinburgh: Edinburgh University Press).

Rutter, C. C. (1984), *Documents of the Rose Playhouse* (Manchester: Manchester University Press).

Sabol, Andrew J. (1958), 'Two Songs with Accompaniment for an Elizabethan Choirboy Play', *Studies in the Renaissance*, 5: 145–59.

—— (1959), 'Ravenscroft's *Melismata* and the Children of Paul's', *Renaissance News*, 12: 3–9.

—— (1960), 'Two Unpublished Stage Songs for the "Aery of Children"', *Renaissance News*, 13: 222–32.

Sahlins, Marshall (1991), 'The Return of the Event, Again: With Reflections on the Beginnings of the Great Fijian War of 1843 to 1855 between the Kingdoms of Bau and Rewa', in Aletta Biersack (ed.), *Clio in Oceania: Toward a Historical Anthropology* (Washington: Smithsonian Institution Press), 37–100.

Sale, Carolyn (2004), 'Slanderous Aesthetics and the Woman Writer: The Case of Hole *v.* White', in Peter Holland and Stephen Orgel (eds), *From Script to Stage in Early Modern England* (Basingstoke: Palgrave), 181–94.

Salkeld, Duncan (2004), 'The Bell and the Bel Savage Inns, 1576–1577', *Notes and Queries*, 249: 242–3.

—— (2005), 'Literary Traces in Bridewell and Bethlem, 1602–1624', *Review of English Studies*, new ser., 56: 379–85.

Salomon, Brownell (1972), 'Visual and Aural Signs in the Performed English Renaissance Play', *Renaissance Drama*, new ser., 5: 143–69.

Schama, Simon (1991), *Dead Certainties: Unwarranted Speculations* (New York: Alfred A. Knopf).

Schapiro, Meyer (1973), *Words and Pictures: On the Literal and the Symbolic in the Illustration of a Text* (The Hague: Mouton).

—— (1985), 'On Some Problems in the Semiotics of Visual Art: Field and Vehicle in Image-Signs', in Robert E. Innis (ed.), *Semiotics: An Introduction* (Bloomington: Indiana University Press), 206–25.

—— (1994), *Theory and Philosophy of Art: Style, Artist, and Society* (New York: George Braziller).

Schlueter, June (1992), '"Stuffed, as they say, with honorable parts": Female Breasts on the English Renaissance Stage', *Shakespeare Yearbook*, 3: 117–42.

—— (1999), 'Rereading the Peacham Drawing', *Shakespeare Quarterly*, 50: 171–84.

—— (2006), 'Michael van Meer's *Album Amicorum*, with Illustrations of London, 1614–15', *Huntington Library Quarterly*, 69: 301–13.

Schoenbaum, Samuel (1966), *Internal Evidence and Elizabethan Dramatic Authorship* (Evanston, IL: Northwestern University Press).

—— (1975), *William Shakespeare: A Documentary Life* (Oxford: Clarendon Press).

—— (1981), *William Shakespeare: Records and Images* (London: Scholar Press).

Scott, Virginia (2004), 'Dark Thoughts about [Theatre] History', *Theatre Survey*, 45: 189–93.

Sebek, Barbara (1994), 'Cracked Commodities, Cursed Gifts: Transacting Women and Conceptualizing Exchange in Early Modern Drama', Ph.D. diss. (University of Illinois).

Sewell, William H., Jr. (1996), 'Three Temporalities: Toward an Eventful Sociology', in Terrence J. McDonald (ed.), *The Historic Turn in the Human Sciences* (Ann Arbor: University of Michigan Press), 245–80.

Shapiro, I. A. (1948), 'The Bankside Theatres: Early Engravings', *Shakespeare Survey*, 1: 25–37.

Shapiro, Michael (1977), *Children of the Revels: The Boy Companies of Shakespeare's Time and their Plays* (New York: Columbia University Press).

—— (1982), 'The Children of Paul's and their Playhouse', *Theatre Notes*, 36: 3–5.

—— (1999), 'The Introduction of Actresses in England: Delay or Defensiveness?', in Viviana Comensoli and Anne Russell (eds), *Enacting Gender on the English Renaissance Stage* (Urbana: University of Illinois Press), 177–99.

—— (2002), 'Patronage and the Companies of Boy Actors', in Paul Whitfield White and Suzanne R. Westfall (eds), *Shakespeare and Theatrical Patronage in Early Modern England* (Cambridge: Cambridge University Press), 272–94.

—— (2006), 'The Westminster Scholars' *Sapientia Solomonis* as Royal Gift Offering', in Paul Menzer (ed.), *Inside Shakespeare: Essays on the Blackfriars Stage* (Selinsgrove, PA: Susquehanna University Press), 118–22.

Sharpe, Kevin (1992), *The Personal Rule of Charles I* (New Haven: Yale University Press).

—— and Peter Lake (eds) (1994), *Culture and Politics in Early Stuart England* (Houndmills: Macmillan).

Sharpe, Pamela (1996), *Adapting to Capitalism: Working Women in the English Economy, 1700–1850* (New York: St Martin's Press; London: Macmillan).

—— (ed.) (1998), *Women's Work: The English Experience, 1650–1914* (New York: Oxford University Press; London: Arnold).

—— (1999), 'Dealing with Love: The Ambiguous Independence of the Single Woman in Early Modern England', *Gender and History*, 11: 209–32.

Sharpe, Robert Bois (1935), *The Real War of the Theaters: Shakespeare's Fellows in Rivalry with the Admiral's Men, 1594–1603* (Boston: D. C. Heath).

Shepherd, T. H. (1841), 'Middle Temple Hall', in *London Interiors: with their Costumes and Ceremonies from Drawings*, 2 vols in 1 (London: pub. for the Proprietor by J. Mead), i. 57–61.

Sherwood, Roy (1977), *The Court of Oliver Cromwell* (Totowa, NJ: Rowman and Littlefield).

Shugg, Wallace (1977), 'Prostitution in Shakespeare's London', *Shakespeare Studies*, 10: 291–313.

Simon, Erika (1982), *The Ancient Theatre*, trans. C. E. Vafopoulou-Richardson, 2nd edn (New York: Methuen).

—— (1983), *Festivals of Attica: An Archaeological Commentary* (Madison: University of Wisconsin Press).

Sisson, C. J. (1936), 'Mr. and Mrs. Browne of the Boar's Head', *Life and Letters To-Day*, 15/6: 99–107.

—— (1954), 'The Red Bull Company and the Importunate Widow', *Shakespeare Survey*, 7: 57–68.

Slater, Ann Pasternak (1982), *Shakespeare the Director* (Brighton: Harvester Press).

Smith, Bruce R. (1994), *Homosexual Desire in Shakespeare's England* (Chicago: University of Chicago Press).

—— (1999), *The Acoustic World of Early Modern England: Attending to the O-Factor* (Chicago: University of Chicago Press).

—— (2004), 'E/loco/com/motion', in Peter Holland and Stephen Orgel (eds), *From Script to Stage in Early Modern England* (Basingstoke: Palgrave), 131–50.

Smith, Colin (2002), 'The Wholesale and Retail Markets of London, 1660–1840', *Economic History Review*, 55: 31–50.

Smith, E. (2004), 'Whetstone, George (*bap.* 1550, *d.* 1587)', in H. C. G. Matthew and Brian Harrison (eds), *Oxford Dictionary of National Biography* (Oxford: Oxford University Press), <http://www.oxforddnb.com/view/article/29198>, accessed 2 Dec. 2007.

Smith, G. Gregory (1904), *Elizabethan Critical Essays*, 2 vols (Oxford: Clarendon Press).

Smith, Irwin (1952), 'Theatre into Globe', *Shakespeare Quarterly*, 3: 113–20.

—— (1964), *Shakespeare's Blackfriars Playhouse: Its History and its Design* (New York: New York University Press).

Smuts, R. M. (1989), 'Public Ceremony and Royal Charisma: The English Royal Entry in London, 1485–1642', in A. L. Beier, D. Cannadine, and J. M. Rosenheim (eds), *The First Modern Society: Essays in English History in Honour of Lawrence Stone* (Cambridge: Cambridge University Press), 65–93.

Snell, K. D. M. (1985), *Annals of the Laboring Poor: Social Change and Agrarian England: 1660–1900* (Cambridge: Cambridge University Press).

Sofer, Andrew (2003), *The Stage Life of Props* (Ann Arbor: University of Michigan Press).

Somerset, J. Alan B. (1994*b*), '"How chances it they travel?" Provincial Touring, Playing Places, and the King's Men', *Shakespeare Survey*, 47: 45–60.

—— (1999 [1998]), '"Beginning in the middle...": Warwickshire Locations and Families as Audiences for Early Modern Music and Drama', *Medieval English Theatre*, 20: 77–94.

Southern, R. (1973), *The Staging of Plays before Shakespeare* (London: Faber and Faber).

—— and C. W. Hodges (1952), 'Colour in the Elizabethan Theatre', *Theatre Notebook*, 6: 57–60.

Spicksley, Judith M. (2003), 'To Be or Not to Be Married: Single Women, Money-Lending, and the Question of Choice in Late Tudor and Stuart England', in Laurel Amtower and Dorothea Kehler (eds), *The Single Woman in Medieval and Early Modern England: Her Life and Representation* (Tempe: Arizona Center for Medieval and Renaissance Studies).

Spiegel, Gabrielle (ed.) (2005), *Practicing History: New Directions in Historical Writing after the Linguistic Turn* (New York: Routledge).

Spink, Ian (1957), 'English Seventeenth Century Dialogues', *Music and Letters*, 38: 155–63.

—— (ed.) (1971), *English Songs, 1625–1660*, Musica Britannica, 33 (London: Stainer and Bell for the Royal Musical Association).

—— (ed.) (1974), *Robert Johnson: Ayres, Songs and Dialogues*, English Lute Songs, 2nd ser., 17, 2nd rev. edn (London: Stainer and Bell).

Stallybrass, Peter (1996), 'Worn Worlds: Clothes and Identity on the Renaissance Stage', in Margreta de Grazia, Maureen Quilligan, and Peter Stallybrass (eds), *Subject and Object in Renaissance Culture* (Cambridge: Cambridge University Press), 289–320.

Starkey, David, D. A. L. Morgan, John Murphey, Pam Wright, Neil Cuddy, and Kevin Sharpe (1987), *The English Court: From the Wars of the Roses to the Civil War* (London: Longman).

States, Bert O. (1985), *Great Reckonings in Little Rooms: On the Phenomenology of Theater* (Berkeley: University of California Press).

—— (1992), *'Hamlet' and the Concept of Character* (Baltimore: Johns Hopkins University Press).

Stedman Jones, Gareth (1976), 'From Historical Sociology to Theoretical History', *British Journal of Sociology*, 27: 295–305.

—— (2005), 'The Determinist Fix: Some Obstacles to the Further Development of the Linguistic Approach to History in the 1990s', in Gabrielle Spiegel (ed.), *Practicing History: New Directions in Historical Writing after the Linguistic Turn* (New York: Routledge), 62–75.

Steele, Mary Susan (1968), *Plays and Masques at Court: 1558–1642* (1926; New York: Russell and Russell).

Stein, Robert (2005), 'Literary Criticism and the Evidence for History', in Nancy Partner (ed.), *Writing Medieval History* (London: Hodder), 67–87.

Stern, Tiffany (2000*a*), *Rehearsal from Shakespeare to Sheridan* (Oxford: Clarendon Press).

—— (2000*b*), 'You that walk i'th galleries': Standing and Walking in the Galleries of the Globe Theatre', *Shakespeare Quarterly*, 51: 211–16.

—— (2004), *Making Shakespeare: From Stage to Page* (London: Routledge).

—— (2006), 'Taking Part: Actors and Audience on the Stage at Blackfriars', in Paul Menzer (ed.), *Inside Shakespeare: Essays on the Blackfriars Stage* (Selinsgrove, PA: Susquehanna University Press), 35–53.

Stokes, James (1993), 'Women and Mimesis in Medieval and Renaissance Somerset (and Beyond)', *Comparative Drama*, 27/2: 176–96.

—— (2005), 'Women and Performance: Evidences of Universal Cultural Suffrage in Medieval and Early Modern Lincolnshire', in Pamela Allen Brown and Peter Parolin (eds), *Women Players in Early Modern England, 1500–1660: Beyond the All-Male Stage* (Aldershot: Ashgate), 25–43.

Stone, Lawrence (1965), *The Crisis of the Aristocracy 1558–1641* (Oxford: Oxford University Press).

—— (1979), 'The Revival of Narrative: Reflections on a New Old History', *Past and Present*, 85: 3–24.

Stopes, Charlotte Carmichael (1913), *Burbage and Shakespeare's Stage* (London: Alexander Moring).

Straznicky, Marta (2002), 'Closet Drama', in Arthur F. Kinney (ed.), *A Companion to Renaissance Drama* (Malden, MA: Blackwell), 416–30.

—— (2004), *Privacy, Playreading and Women's Closet Drama, 1550–1700* (Cambridge: Cambridge University Press).

—— (2006), 'The Red Bull Repertory in Print, 1605–60', *Early Theatre*, 9/2: 144–57.

Streitberger, W. R. (1976), 'A Letter from Edmund Tilney to Sir William More', *Surrey Archaeological Collections*, 71: 225–31.

—— (1978), 'On Edmond Tyllney's Biography', *Review of English Studies*, new ser., 29: 11–35.

—— (1992), 'Court Performances by the King's Players, 1510–1521', *Medieval English Theatre*, 14: 95–101.

—— (1994), *Court Revels, 1485–1559* (Toronto: University of Toronto Press).

—— (1997), 'Personnel and Professionalization', in John D. Cox and D. S. Kastan (eds), *A New History of Early English Drama* (New York: Columbia University Press), 337–55.

—— (2004), ' "Last of the Poore Flock of Hatfield": Sir Thomas Benger's Biography', *Review of English Studies*, new ser., 55: 674–81.

—— (2008), 'New Evidence for Dating the Letter from Edmund Tilney to Sir William More', *Surrey Archaeological Collections*, 94: 343–4.

Strong, Roy (1984), *Art and Power: Renaissance Festivals 1450–1650* (Woodbridge: Boydell Press).

Styan, J. L. (1967), *Shakespeare's Stagecraft* (Cambridge: Cambridge University Press).

Sugden, Edward H. (1925), *A Topographical Dictionary to the Works of Shakespeare and his Fellow Dramatists* (New York: Longmans, Green).

Summers, David (1981), *Michelangelo and the Language of Art* (Princeton: Princeton University Press).

—— (1987), *The Judgment of Sense: Renaissance Naturalism and the Rise of Aesthetics* (Cambridge: Cambridge University Press).

—— (2003), 'Representation', in Robert S. Nelson and Richard Shiff (eds), *Critical Terms for Art History*, 2nd edn (Chicago: University of Chicago Press), 3–19.

Sutton, Dana (gen. ed.), Philological Museum web site, <http://www.philological.bham.ac.uk/index.html>.

Sypher, Wylie (1955), *Four Stages of Renaissance Style* (New York: Doubleday).

Tames, Richard (1999), *Clerkenwell and Finsbury Past* (London: Historical Publications).

Taplin, Oliver (1978), *Greek Tragedy in Action* (Berkeley: University of California Press).

—— (1992), *Comic Angels and Other Approaches to Greek Drama through Vase-Paintings* (Oxford: Clarendon Press).

—— (1995), 'Opening Performance: Closing Texts?', *Essays in Criticism*, 45/2: 93–120.

—— (2007*a*), *Pots and Plays: Interactions between Tragedy and Vase-Painting of the Fourth-Century* BC (New York: Oxford University Press).

—— (2007*b*), 'A New Pair of Pairs: Tragic Witnesses in Western Greek Vase Paintings?', in Chris Kraus (ed.), *Visualizing the Tragic: Drama, Myth, and Ritual in Greek Art and Literature: Essays in Honour of Froma Zeitlin* (Oxford: Oxford University Press), 177–96.

Tawney, R. H., and Eileen Power (eds) (1924), *Tudor Economic Documents: Being Select Documents Illustrating the Economic and Social History of Tudor England*, 3 vols (London: Longman).

Taylor, Gary (1993), 'The Structure of Performance: Act-Intervals in the London Theatres, 1576–1642', in Gary Taylor and John Jowett (eds), *Shakespeare Reshaped, 1606–1623* (Oxford: Clarendon Press), 3–50.

Taylor, M. (1973), *Bottom Thou Art Translated: Political Allegory in 'A Midsummer Night's Dream' and Related Literature* (Amsterdam: Rodopi).

Teague, Frances (1991), *Shakespeare's Speaking Properties* (Lewisburg, PA: Bucknell University Press).

Thaler, Alwin (1919), 'Playwrights' Benefits, and "Interior Gathering" in the Elizabethan Theatre', *Studies in Philology*, 16: 187–96.

—— (1922), 'Minor Actors and Employees in the Elizabethan Theater', *Modern Philology*, 20: 49–60.

Thomas, Keith (1975), 'An Anthropology of Religion and Magic, II', *Journal of Interdisciplinary History*, 6: 91–109.

Thompson, Ann (1996), 'Women/"Women" and the Stage', in Helen Wilcox (ed.), *Women and Literature in Britain, 1500–1700* (Cambridge: Cambridge University Press), 100–16.

Thomson, Leslie (1996), 'A Quarto "Marked for Performance": Evidence of What?', *Medieval and Renaissance Drama in England*, 8: 176–210.

—— (2006), 'Who's In, Who's Out? The *Knight of the Burning Pestle* on the Blackfriars Stage', in Paul Menzer (ed.), *Inside Shakespeare: Essays on the Blackfriars Stage* (Selinsgrove, PA: Susquehanna University Press), 61–71.

Thomson, Peter (1992), *Shakespeare's Theatre*, 2nd edn (London: Routledge).

—— (2003), 'Conventions of Playwriting', in Stanley Wells and Lena Cowen Orlin (eds), *Shakespeare: An Oxford Guide* (Oxford: Oxford University Press), 44–54.

Thurley, Simon (1993), *The Royal Palaces of Tudor England* (New Haven: Yale University Press).

Titherley, A. W. (1952), *Shakespeare's Identity* (Winchester: Warren and Son).

Tittler, Robert (1991), *Architecture and Power: The Town Hall and the English Urban Community c.1500–1640* (Oxford: Oxford University Press).

—— (1994), 'Money-Lending in the West Midlands: The Activities of Joyce Jeffries, 1638–49', *Historical Research*, 67: 249–63.

Tomlinson, Sophie (1992), '"She that Plays the King": Henrietta Maria and the Threat of the Actress in Caroline Culture', in Gordon McMullan and Jonathan Hope (eds), *The Politics of Tragicomedy* (London: Routledge), 189–207.

—— (2003), 'Theatrical Vibrancy on the Caroline Court Stage: *Tempe Restored* and *The Shepherd's Paradise*', in Clare McManus (ed.), *Women and Culture at the Courts of the Stuart Queens 1603–42* (Houndmills: Palgrave Macmillan), 186–203.

—— (2005), *Women on Stage in Stuart Drama* (Cambridge: Cambridge University Press).

Trendall, A. D., and T. B. L. Webster (1971), *Illustrations of Greek Drama* (London: Phaidon).

Tricomi, Albert H. (1996), *Reading Tudor–Stuart Texts through Cultural Historicism* (Gainesville: University of Florida Press).

Trousdale, Marion (1982), *Shakespeare and the Rhetoricians* (Chapel Hill: University of North Carolina Press).

Twycross, M. (1983), 'Transvestism in the Mystery Plays', *Medieval English Theatre*, 5/2: 123–80.

Ungerer, Gustav (1961), 'An Unrecorded Elizabethan Performance of *Titus Andronicus*', *Shakespeare Survey*, 14: 102–9.

—— (2000), 'Mary Frith, Alias Moll Cutpurse, in Life and Literature', *Shakespeare Studies*, 28: 42–84.

—— (2003), 'Prostitution in Late Elizabethan London: The Case of Mary Newborough', *Medieval and Renaissance Drama in England*, 15: 138–223.

Unwin, George (1908), *The Gilds and Companies of London* (London: Methuen).

Van Lennep, W. (1962), 'The Death of the Red Bull', *Theatre Notebook*, 16: 126–34.

Varholy, Christine (2001), 'Representing Prostitution in Tudor and Stuart England', PhD diss. (University of Wisconsin).

Veevers, Erica (1989), *Images of Love and Religion: Queen Henrietta Maria and Court Entertainments* (Cambridge: Cambridge University Press).

Vickers, Brian (2002), *Shakespeare, Co-author: A Historical Study of Five Collaborative Plays* (Oxford: Oxford University Press).

Vince, Ronald W. (1989), 'Theatre History as an Academic Discipline', in Thomas Postlewait and Bruce A. McConachie (eds), *Interpreting the Theatrical Past: Essays in the Historiography of Performance* (Iowa City: University of Iowa Press), 1–18.

von Bülow, G. (1892), 'Diary of the Journey of Philipp Julius, Duke of Stettin-Pomerania, through England in the Year 1602', *Transactions of the Royal Historical Society*, new ser., 6: 1–67.

Walker, Garthine (1994), 'Women, Theft and the World of Stolen Goods', in Jennifer Kermode and Garthine Walker (eds), *Women, Crime, and the Courts in Early Modern England* (Chapel Hill: University of North Carolina Press), 81–105.

Wall, Wendy (1993), *The Imprint of Gender: Authorship and Publication in the English Renaissance* (Ithaca, NY: Cornell University Press).

Wallace, Charles William (1909*a*), 'Shakespeare in London: Fresh Documents on the Poet and his Theatres', *The Times*, 2 and 4 Oct.

—— (1909*b*), 'Three London Theatres of Shakespeare's Time', *Nebraska University Studies*, 9: 291–337.

—— (1912), *The Evolution of the English Drama up to Shakespeare, with a History of the First Blackfriars Theatre* (Berlin: Georg Reimer).

—— (1913), *The First London Theatre: Materials for a History* (Lincoln: University of Nebraska).

—— (1969), *The First London Theatre: Materials for a History* (1913; London: Benjamin Blom).

Walls, Peter (1996), *Music in the English Courtly Masque 1604–1640* (Oxford: Clarendon Press).

Warren, Michael J. (1998), 'Greene's *Orlando Furioso*', in Laurie E. Maguire and Thomas L. Berger (eds), *Textual Formations and Reformations* (Newark: University of Delaware Press), 67–91.

Wasson, John M. (1988), 'Elizabethan and Jacobean Touring Companies', *Theatre Notebook*, 42: 51–7.

—— (1997), 'The English Church as Theatrical Space', in John D. Cox and D. S. Kastan (eds), *A New History of Early English Drama* (New York: Columbia University Press), 25–37.

Webster, T. B. L. (1967), *Monuments Illustrating Tragedy and Satyr Play* (London: Institute of Classical Studies.

—— (1970), *Greek Theatre Production*, 2nd edn (London: Methuen).

—— (1978), *Monuments Illustrating Old and Middle Comedy*, 2nd edn, rev. and enlarged J. R. Green (London: Institute of Classical Studies).

—— (1995), *Monuments Illustrating New Comedy*, 2 vols, 3rd edn, rev. and enlarged J. R. Green and A. Seeberg (London: Institute of Classical Studies).

Weimann, Robert (1996), *Authority and Representation in Early Modern Discourse*, ed. David Hillman (Baltimore: Johns Hopkins University Press).

—— (2000), *Author's Pen and Actor's Voice: Playing and Writing in Shakespeare's Theatre* (Cambridge: Cambridge University Press).

Wells, Stanley, Gary Taylor, John Jowett, and William Montgomery (1987), *William Shakespeare: A Textual Companion* (Oxford: Oxford University Press).

Wernham, R. B. (1966), *Before the Armada: The Emergence of the English Nation: 1485–1588* (New York: Harcourt, Brace & World).

—— (1980), *The Making of Elizabethan Foreign Policy, 1558–1603* (Berkeley and Los Angeles: University of California Press).

Werstine, Paul (2006), 'Margins to the Centre: REED and Shakespeare', in Audrey Douglas and Sally-Beth MacLean (eds), *REED in Review* (Toronto: University of Toronto Press), 101–15.

Westfall, Suzanne R. (1989), '"The actors are come hither": Literary Analogues of Itinerant Player Troupe Procedures', *Theatre Survey*, May, 56–68.

—— (1990), *Patrons and Performance: Early Tudor Household Revels* (Oxford: Clarendon Press).

—— (1997), '"A Commonty a Christmas Gambold or a Tumbling Trick": Household Theater', in John D. Cox and D. S. Kastan (eds), *A New History of Early English Drama* (New York: Columbia University Press), 39–58.

White, Martin (1998), *Renaissance Drama in Action: An Introduction to Aspects of Theatre Practice and Performance* (London: Routledge).

White, Paul W. (1993), *Theatre and Reformation: Protestantism, Patronage, and Playing in Tudor England* (Cambridge: Cambridge University Press).

—— (1994), 'Patronage, Protestantism, and Stage Propaganda', *Yearbook of English Studies*, 21: 38–52.

—— (2002), 'Shakespeare, the Cobhams, and the Dynamics of Theatrical Patronage', in Paul W. White and Suzanne R. Westfall (eds), *Shakespeare and Theatrical Patronage in Early Modern England* (Cambridge: Cambridge University Press), 64–89.

—— and Suzanne R. Westfall (eds) (2002), *Shakespeare and Theatrical Patronage in Early Modern England* (Cambridge: Cambridge University Press).

Whitney, Charles (1999), '"Usually in the werking daies": Playgoing Journeymen Apprentices, and Servants in Guild Records, 1582–1592', *Shakespeare Quarterly*, 50: 433–58.

—— (2001), 'The Devil his Due: Mayor John Spencer, Elizabethan Civic Antitheatricalism, and *The Shoemaker's Holiday*', *Medieval and Renaissance Drama in England*, 14: 168–85.

Wickham, Glynne (1959–81), *Early English Stages*, 4 vols (London: Routledge).

—— (1979), '"Heavens", Machinery, and Pillars in the Theatre and Other Early Playhouses', in Herbert Berry (ed.), *The First Public Playhouse: The Theatre in Shoreditch 1576–1598* (Montreal: McGill-Queen's University Press), 1–15.

——Herbert Berry, and William Ingram (eds) (2000), *English Professional Theatre, 1530–1660* (Cambridge: Cambridge University Press).

Wiesner, Merry E. (1986), *Working Women in Renaissance Germany* (New Brunswick, NJ: Rutgers University Press).

—— (1987), 'Spinning Out Capital: Women's Work in the Early Modern Economy', in Renate Bridenthal, Claudia Koonz, and Susan Stuard (eds), *Becoming Visible: Women in European History* (Boston: Houghton Mifflin), 221–49.

Wiggins, M. J. (2005), 'Copies for Ruff and Cuff', *Around the Globe*, 30: 20–1.

Wiles, D. (1987), *Shakespeare's Clown: Actor and Text in the Elizabethan Playhouse* (Cambridge: Cambridge University Press).

—— (1991), *The Masks of Menander: Sign and Meaning in Greek and Roman Performance* (Cambridge: Cambridge University Press).

—— (1997), *Tragedy in Athens: Performing Space and Theatrical Meaning* (Cambridge: Cambridge University Press).

Williams, George Walton (1976), *The History of King Henry the Fourth, as Revised by Sir Edward Dering*, Folger Facsimile MS (Charlottesville: University Press of Virginia).

Williams, George Walton and Gwynne Blakemore (1974), *Conflation of Henry IV Parts 1 and 2* (Charlottesville: University of Virginia Press).

Williams, Gweno, Alison Findlay, and Stephanie Hodgson-Wright (2005), 'Payments, Permits and Punishments: Women Performers and the Politics of Place', in Pamela Allen Brown and Peter Parolin (eds), *Women Players in Early Modern England, 1500–1660: Beyond the All-Male Stage* (Aldershot: Ashgate), 45–67.

Williams, P. (1996), *The Late Tudors* (Oxford: Clarendon Press).

Wilson, Christopher R., and Michela Calore (2005), *Music in Shakespeare: A Dictionary* (London: Thoemmes Continuum).

Wilson, J. (1980), *Entertainments for Elizabeth* (London: D. S. Brewer).

Wilson, J. Dover (1948), '*Titus Andronicus* on the Stage in 1595', *Shakespeare Survey*, 1: 17–22.

Winkler, John J., and Froma I. Zeitlin (eds) (1990), *Nothing to Do with Dionysos? Athenian Drama in its Social Context* (Princeton: Princeton University Press).

Withington, R. (1980), *English Pageantry: An Historical Outline*, 2 vols (1918–20; New York: Arno Press).

Womack, Peter (1986), *Ben Jonson* (Oxford: Blackwell).

Wood, Julia K. (1991), 'Music in Caroline Plays', PhD thesis (University of Edinburgh).

—— (1998), 'William Lawes's Music for Plays', in Andrew Ashbee (ed.), *William Lawes (1602–1645): Essays on his Life, Times and Work* (Aldershot: Ashgate), 11–67.

Wood, Michael (2003), *In Search of Shakespeare* (London: BBC Worldwide).

Worthen, W. B., with Peter Holland (2003), *Theorizing Practice: Redefining Theatre History* (Basingstoke: Palgrave Macmillan).

Wright, Pam (1987), 'A Change in Direction: The Ramifications of a Female Household, 1558–1603', in David Starkey et al., *The English Court: From the Wars of the Roses to the Civil War* (London: Longman).

Wright, Sue (1985), ' "Churmaids, Huswyfes and Hucksters": The Employment of Women in Tudor and Stuart Salisbury', in Lindsay Charles and Lorna Duffin (eds), *Women and Work in Pre-industrial England* (London: Croom Helm), 100–21.

Wynne-Davies, Marion (1992), 'The Queen's Masque: Renaissance Women and the Seventeenth-Century Court Masque', in S. P. Cerasano and Marion Wynne-Davies (eds), *Gloriana's Face: Women, Public and Private, in the English Renaissance* (New York: Harvester Wheatsheaf), 79–104.

Yachnin, Paul (1997), *Stage-wrights: Shakespeare, Jonson, Middleton and the Making of Theatrical Value* (Philadelphia: University of Pennsylvania Press).

—— (2003), 'Reversal of Fortune: Shakespeare, Middleton, and the Puritans', *ELH* 70: 757–86.

Yeandle, Laetitia (1986), 'The Dating of Sir Edward Dering's Copy of *The History of King Henry the Fourth*', *Shakespeare Quarterly*, 37: 224–6.

Yiu, Mimi (2007), 'Sounding the Space between Men: Choric and Choral Cities in Ben Jonson's *Epicoene; or, The Silent Woman*', *PMLA* 122: 72–88.

Young, Alan (1987), *Tudor and Jacobean Tournaments* (London: George Philip).

Zammito, John H. (1998), 'Ankersmit's Postmodernist Historiography: The Hyperbole of "Opacity" ', *History and Theory*, 37: 330–46.

—— (2005), 'Ankersmit and Historical Representation', *History and Theory*, 44: 155–81.

Zucker, Adam, and Alan B. Farmer (eds.) (2006), *Localizing Caroline Drama: Politics and Economics of the Early Modern English Stage, 1625–1642* (New York: Palgrave), 97–128.

Indexes

There are two indexes, one of *Plays and Other Dramatic Writings* and one of *People and Things.*

Plays and Other Dramatic Writings
Plays, masques and other dramatic works are listed by title. This index also gives, where appropriate, names of authors and of the players for which the work was written. Non-italicised titles are not extant. Two-part plays are listed like this: *1 & 2 The Honest Whore*, alphabetically under H. Titles of plays also appear in entries for individual authors in the *People and Things* index, but without further information. Non-dramatic works are fully detailed under entries for their writers.

Plays and other dramatic texts

People and Things

Names of acting companies

The names of acting companies were extremely fluid, and this is reflected in the usage of contributors to this book. The same troupe might be referred to as the *men*, *servants*, or *players of* a patron, whose titles themselves varied over time. Charles Howard, Lord Howard of Effingham became Lord Admiral in 1585 and Earl of Nottingham in 1597–any of these titles might attach to his company. There were three Earls of Derby who were very active patrons of theatre in the period, which causes further ambiguity. Boy companies (sometimes *Children of*, sometimes merely *boys*) were equally problematic. The company which occupied the Second Blackfriars theatre from 1600 to 1608 is particularly problematic: properly the Children of the Chapel (or Chapel Royal) in 1600, they were patented as the Children of the Queen's Revels in 1604 but lost royal patronage by 1606 and become known as the Children of the Revels or Children of the Blackfriars. In 1610 a new patent is issued for the Children of the Queen's Revels, which merged some earlier players with those of the Children of the King's Revels. Understandably, it is common for all of these operations to be covered in a single title, usually Chapel boys, Blackfriars boys, or Queen's Revel boys.

In this index I have tried to disambiguate as far as possible. The leading companies are identified by the shorthand titles most commonly used modern scholars. So

Howard/Nottingham's players are listed as the Admiral's Men. The two identifiable Shakespeare companies are the Chamberlain's Men and the King's Men (treated as two units, for all their continuities). In the case of the Earls of Derby, the players of the fourth Earl are listed under the Earl himself as a patron of players (as is often done with somewhat less prominent patrons); those of the fifth Earl are listed under Strange's Men, from the courtesy title he used until he (only briefly) inherited the earldom; Derby's Men is reserved for the players of the sixth Earl. Queen's Men denotes the company set up in 1583 under the patronage of Elizabeth I. Although it could also denote the players patronised by Queen Anna and Queen Henrietta Maria (and is used in that sense in some chapters), they are listed here as Queen Anna's Men and Queen Henrietta's Men. Boy companies are listed under their briefest forms (Chapel boys, Paul's boys, Queen's Revels boys).

Aristocratic and royal titles

My normal practice has been to list peers by their most senior titles, with sufficient cross-referencing to track the more familiar names. So—again to take the most extreme case—Charles Howard appears under Nottingham. Charles Howard. first Earl of; Lord Howard of Effingham. Lord Chamberlain 1583–5. Lord Admiral 1585–1619. That is, senior title first, Christian and family name; whether first, second etc. in the line of creation; a commonly used lower title; offices held which are of note in theatre history. This is cumbersome, but avoids ambiguity. There were many other Howards in the period, several of whom were active patrons of players. There were several Lords Chamberlain, two of whom (father and son) were patrons of the *famous* troupe which we simplistically call *the* Chamberlain's Men. And one other Lord Admiral—the Earl of Lincoln—was an active patron of players.

Queen Anna, wife of James I, is listed in this, her preferred style, throughout the index, though sometimes referred to as 'Queen Anne' in chapters. The players of the future Charles I are denoted as Prince Charles [I]'s Men, to distinguish them from those of the future Charles II, which are listed as Prince Charles [II]'s Men.